Bank of Scotland

A History
1695–1995

Bank of Scotland

A History
1695–1995

Richard Saville

EDINBURGH UNIVERSITY PRESS

Edinburgh University Press Ltd
22 George Square, Edinburgh

Typeset in Goudy by Bibliocraft, Dundee
Printed and bound in Great Britain at
the University Press, Cambridge

A CIP record for this book is available
from the British Library.

ISBN 0 7486 0757 9

CONTENTS

LIST OF TABLES AND FIGURES

LIST OF PLATES

Between pages 316 and 317, and pages 636 and 637

LIST OF APPENDICES

LIST OF TABLES IN
STATISTICAL APPENDIX

FOREWORD

As the 300th anniversary of Bank of Scotland's constituting Act of Parliament was approaching, the board of the Bank felt that a new academic history should be commissioned focusing, in particular, on the contribution made by the Bank to the social and economic development of Scotland over the period since 1695. The history was also to cover the parts played by the Union Bank of Scotland and the British Linen Bank, which have become part of Bank of Scotland Group since the last history was published to celebrate Bank of Scotland's 250th anniversary.

Dr Richard Saville of the University of St Andrews was commissioned to produce the current work, and I believe that the outcome is a valuable addition to our understanding and knowledge of the period. Bank of Scotland is pleased to have been associated with this production.

Sir Bruce Pattullo
Governor and Group Chief Executive

PREFACE

Bank of Scotland is the oldest-established clearing bank in the British Isles. The three centuries of the Bank's history have been closely and intimately associated with the economic and political evolution of Scotland and with the general course of British history on both sides of the Border. The services of banking sectors have everywhere provided a necessary stimulus and encouragement to the general growth of the economy in all the countries of the industrial world. Certainly, the experience of Scottish banking was an essential constituent within the remarkable history of Scotland in the eighteenth century, with its transformation from a poor, economically backward country to the firm beginnings of an industrial society by 1800.

Those who over these three centuries have directed the management and business affairs of Bank of Scotland have generally, usually very clearly, acknowledged their role in the desired expansion of commerce and industrial growth. It was with this understanding that the present Governor, Sir Bruce Pattullo, and his senior colleagues agreed upon the publication of a volume acknowledging the Bank's tercentenary: a history that would position Bank of Scotland within the general development of Scottish society. The internal records of Bank of Scotland go back to its foundation in 1695 and for most periods are complete, or nearly so. These have been made available to me without restriction for research and publication. There is, in this respect, one qualification to be made. It was laid down in the contract between myself and Bank of Scotland that there would be no restriction upon any commentary from 1695 to 1979. It was understood that the Bank's lawyers would draw attention to statements that might lead to legal action, and it was also accepted, as with all banking histories, that customers' accounts, whether corporate or individual, would remain confidential; but otherwise the text is my responsibility, derived in the first instance from the records of the Bank.

The years from 1979 to 1995, covering the contemporary history of the Bank, were under a different agreement in respect of content and presentation. It was accepted, before research began, that certain matters of substance relating to contemporary banking matters might well have to be omitted or only partially summarised. These will remain, therefore, to be expanded further by historians in the next century, since it may be assumed that we will not have to wait another 300 years for the next academic history. It must be noted, and indeed emphasised, that in these last chapters from 1979 the discussion is straightforward, even though there are important questions that still remain to be elaborated.

It remains only for me to offer my gratitude to the Governor, to the General Manager and Secretary, Hugh K. Young, and to their colleagues, past and present, for their generous encouragement of my research and the writing of this volume. To be offered the opportunity to work over the three centuries of the banking history of this remarkable institution has been a privilege of which I have become deeply conscious; and I once again express my warm appreciation to all those, and there have been many, who have offered in different ways their encouragement and understanding.

Dr Richard Saville
University of St Andrews
15 January 1996

ACKNOWLEDGEMENTS

The research involved in the writing of a volume covering 300 years has obviously meant drawing upon many areas of specialist knowledge. I count myself fortunate in terms of the general ways in which academic historians, archivists and those involved in contemporary banking affairs have offered their knowledge and recollections. My various drafts of different aspects and periods of Bank of Scotland have been read by many, and to all I offer my thanks. I must, of course, make the usual disclaimer that, down to the end of Chapter 26, which covers events to 1979, no-one but myself is responsible, in the final analysis, for any errors of fact or interpretation.

Since October 1991, I have benefited greatly from the consistent hard work of Seonaid McDonald, who was largely responsible for the Statistical Appendix and for many of the individual tables and figures in the text. Only those who have worked on bank ledgers will understand the difficulties involved. She also catalogued many of the miscellaneous papers of the Bank, among other tasks, and I much appreciated her careful reading of every chapter. Seonaid McDonald was appointed to the permanent staff of the Bank in October 1994 with the rank of assistant manager, archives.

Professor Emeritus John Saville read every chapter to 1979, and he offered robust criticism and advice on numerous occasions. I am most grateful for being able to draw on his wide-ranging knowledge of historical matters. G. R. Smith, drawing on her experience as a civil servant, was able to provide considerable assistance, especially on administrative and research matters. Dr Nicholas Phillipson of Edinburgh University, and Dr Charles Munn, chief executive of the Chartered Institute of Bankers in Scotland, read the chapters on the eighteenth and nineteenth centuries, and I am fully appreciative of their efforts and for the many discussions that I had with them. Dr William Ferguson, formerly of Edinburgh

University, was generous with his advice on the earlier chapters. Professor Emeritus Maxwell Gaskin of Aberdeen University, whose *The Scottish Banks: A Modern Survey* has proved a most useful work of reference, kindly read several chapters and offered the benefits of his considerable understanding.

Bank of Scotland has had a continuous connection with the forerunners of Coutts & Co., and I am grateful to this important and distinguished company, and to their late archivist, Barbara Peters, and the present archivist, Tracey Earl, for access to their archives and for the comments which they made on the chapters dealing with the eighteenth century. I am similarly indebted to Vicki Wilkinson, archivist at the Royal Bank of Scotland, who granted me access to the archives and also read the chapters covering events to 1800. The archives of both banks are extraordinarily rich. Dr John Shaw and Dr David Brown of the Scottish Record Office were able to read the chapters on the eighteenth century and offered much sound advice.

I am most grateful to a wide network of academics and writers with whom I have discussed this project. Paul Auerbach of Kingston University gave me the benefit of his considerable knowledge of financial affairs. Dr Stana Nenadic of Edinburgh University was particularly helpful over the discussion of Scottish business in the nineteenth century, among other historical questions. Professor R. J. Morris of Edinburgh University offered much useful advice on many subjects. Professor Ian Blanchard and Henry Palairet, also of Edinburgh University, discussed a number of financial themes with me. I would also like to mention Professor Emeritus Peter Payne of Aberdeen University, Professor Henry Roseveare of King's College, London, and Professor Patrick O'Brien, director of the Institute of Historical Research, for various discussions in recent years on a variety of topics. From St Andrews University, I wish to thank Professor Bruce P. Lenman, Professor R. H. Houston, Dr Hamish Scott, Dr Alan Hood and C. J. Schmitz; from Glasgow University, Professor A. Slaven; and from Stirling University, Alan McKinlay. I discussed a number of questions with Professor Leslie Hannah of the London School of Economics. I am grateful for the assistance given over several months by Ann McCrum of Edinburgh University, and by Sarah Kane and Alison Nicol, for help on constructing several of the tables in the Statistical Appendix.

As I have made clear, my first, overall, debt is to the Governor and to the general manager and Secretary of the Bank, the two senior officials with whom I had most contact. I wish also to thank members of Bank of Scotland's tercentenary committee, past and present, several of whom read drafts of the text. Alan Cameron, the Bank archivist, was most helpful at numerous points, and I am grateful for the assistance provided

ACKNOWLEDGEMENTS

by him and his deputy, Helen Redmond-Cooper. They made my task easier than it might have been. Among the senior officials of the Bank with whom I had discussions on various topics, I wish to thank in particular Sir John Shaw, Deputy Governor; Peter Burt, Treasurer and chief general manager; Gavin Masterton, Deputy Treasurer; Robin Browning, general manager; Tom Abraham, chief inspector; and Fraser Campbell, Iain Scott, Alasdair Macdonald and Colin Matthew, general managers. I also wish to thank Tom Borthwick and Chris Brobbel, divisional general managers; Bill Mutch, Group compliance officer; A. L. Webster, Group chief accountant; G. E. Mitchell, general manager; D. C. Ball, Centrebank; W. M. Murray, chief manager; Iain Fiddes, chief manager; and John Hunter, who succeeds as Secretary from 1996. I had numerous discussions with officials over lunch and dinner, and many visits to various departments of the Bank, including Centrebank, Card Services, Inspectors Department and Treasury Services, and to the branches at London Chief Office, Piccadilly Circus and Dundee, and I am grateful for the help and hospitality offered.

Among those officials who have retired from the Bank, and who were generous with their time, I wish to thank A. T. Gibson, who, as a member of the tercentenary committee, read and commented on various drafts; Alan Thomson, general manager; David Jenkins, economist; John F. Wilson, general manager; and Mr and Mrs John Rankin. I also wish to mention the work of David Antonio, a past Secretary of the Bank, and Duncan Ferguson, a retired general manager, who conducted interviews with many retired members of staff. Several past directors were generous with their time, and I wish to thank, among the directors with whom I discussed the Bank, Lord Balfour of Burleigh, Sir Thomas Risk, James Gammell, Sir Alastair Blair, Sir William Lithgow and James Lumsden.

A number of persons, within and outwith the Bank, were involved in administration, typing some drafts and liaising with the tercentenary committee. These included T. Prime and S. C. Arbuckle of the Bank property department; A. Morrison, M. Purdie, A. Frain, G. Daley, R. Herriot, G. Kidd, D. Burns and P. Calder, all staff of the archives and tercentenary department; and, from outside the Bank, W. Elliott, M. Richards and D. Williamson. I am grateful to Nan Brownlie, of the Bank's executive office, for dealing with numerous inquiries throughout the project, and to others from the executive office, including A. Macrae, K. Bothwell, P. Walker, T. Bryce, P. Hunter, S. McLean, S. Hogg and D. Hunter. From the Bank reception desk, I wish to thank K. Kendall, J. Fowler, M. Craigie, R. Allan and G. Watters.

I was impressed by the remarkable growth of NWS Bank plc, and I wish to thank Sydney Jones, past chief executive, for his hospitality and discussions on the history of the company. I also thank John Mercer, chief executive, for his patience over the drafting of Chapter 28. I much enjoyed my discussions with the staff of NWS Bank plc, and I would mention in particular John Brown and Tony Williams.

A project as substantial as the history of Bank of Scotland requires recourse to many libraries and archives. Apart from those mentioned above, I am indebted to the Librarian and staff of the Institute of Historical Research, London. The facilities at the Institute and within walking distance are unrivalled, and I wish to thank the Librarian at Senate House, University of London, the Librarian of the Goldsmiths Library, Senate House, and the Librarian of the British Library. I used all these facilities extensively. I also wish to thank the Librarians of the National Library of Scotland, the London School of Economics, the Guildhall Library, St Andrews University Library, Hull University Library, Edinburgh University Library and the Central Reference Library, Edinburgh. I made much use of the Scottish Record Office, and am indebted to the Keeper, Patrick Cadell, to his officials, Alison Rosie and Peter G. Vasey, and to other staff who proved helpful on many occasions. I am grateful to the Keeper of the Public Record Office, London, and to the Archivist, Fife Regional Council and the Curator, Numismatic Collection, National Museum of Scotland. The computing services department of Edinburgh University was able to offer helpful advice on several occasions, and my thanks go to Christine Rees and Peter Burnhill. I am grateful to the Earl of Elgin and Charles, Lord Bruce, for help over the past few years.

The agreement between Bank of Scotland and the University of St Andrews enabled me to devote all my time to the Bank. I wish to record my personal thanks to Principal Struther Arnott for his consistent support for the work. I also wish to thank Professor John Guy and Professor Paul Wilkinson for their help over certain administrative problems.

Edinburgh University Press has been extremely helpful over the production of this book. I wish to record my personal appreciation of the work done by Penny Clarke, until recently the managing desk editor, who handled all matters relating to editorial procedures and much else that is not normally associated with publishing; to Ivor Normand, who single-handedly copy-edited the entire text; and to Marguerite Nesling, who was copy-editor for much of 1994. I also express my thanks to the senior staff of the Press.

Richard Saville

NOTES ON USAGE

BANK OF SCOTLAND

Bank of Scotland has enjoyed a continuous existence for 300 years. It is always referred to here without the definite article, as 'Bank of Scotland', or, where it is used, as simply 'the Bank'. The term 'the old Bank' will be found in many eighteenth-century records. Bank of Scotland is owned by its proprietors, and from the Act of Parliament of 17 July 1695 the full title has always been 'The Governor and Company of Bank of Scotland'. In the Bank's internal records, the plurals 'we', 'our' and 'us' are used to denote the Bank and its activities, a similar usage to that which has obtained in the Bank of England. The Bank board of directors was divided in 1695 into two parts: the ordinary directors, initially twelve in number, and the extraordinary directors, also twelve. The former – usually merchants, lawyers and other professional persons – were expected to attend regularly at the Bank to carry out day-to-day business, and the extraordinary directors – aristocrats, judges of the Courts of Session and Justiciary, government officials – when occasion demanded. Both groups faced annual elections, as did the Governor and Deputy Governor. As will be shown, both these groups of directors were crucial to the administration of the Bank. The number required for a quorum was laid down in 1695 as seven directors, although in practice, where this was condition was not met, decisions could be endorsed by a later, quorate, board of directors. By the twentieth century, it was found less helpful to distinguish the ordinary from the extraordinary directors, and there are now none of the latter. The Governor and the Deputy Governor were additional to the twenty-four directors. Of these two posts, the Deputy Governor was the more involved, until recent times, in everyday business. Since 1981, the post of Governor has been a full-time position. The board of directors has regularly formed subcommittees, both to manage day-to-day business and to deal with specific tasks, and in recent times the latter has included the computer committee, the investments committee and the property committee, among others. Some committees are mentioned in the Minutes, although there is sometimes little written material extant. Since 1981 there has existed a management board, meeting every fortnight, which comprises a fluctuating number of the most senior managers, and meets primarily for the purpose of discussing developments in the Bank and for recommending advances to the main board of directors. It may be helpful to think of the main board as now fulfilling the functions of the extraordinary directors, and of the management board as fulfilling the usual functions of a bank board of directors.

RANKS AND TITLES

The most senior proprietor is the Governor, and since 1696 there has always been a Governor. There has always been a Deputy Governor, and since 1977 there have been two Deputy Governors; in recent years, one has been given primary responsibility for the London operations of the Bank. The standing of the individual directors has varied, and the composition of subcommittees likewise, but no other set ranks have ever been laid down.

The relative positions of the senior management, again in continuous existence since 1696, have varied, no doubt in part due to personality and in part due to changes in functions. In the early eighteenth century, the Treasurer received instructions on lending from the directors, although the position was also advisory. As business expanded, so did the importance of the Treasurer's role, although it was not until after 1815 that it became the obvious and pre-eminent position among management. The Secretary handled all legal work, much of the correspondence and the keeping of records, including the minutes of meetings of the directors. At certain times, the Secretary has taken on other functions. The accountant, and the tellers, also have a continuous existence from 1696. The function of the chief inspector emerged in the late eighteenth century. These senior managers maintained their roles in the Victorian era, although by this time the role of the branch manager was quite crucial to the running of the Bank. In the rapid expansion of the Bank, and of Bank departments, since the 1960s, more senior officials have been required. The order of rank inside the Bank is now as follows: Governor and group chief executive, Deputy Governor, Treasurer and chief general manager, general manager and deputy Treasurer, general manager and Secretary, seven other general managers, ten divisional general managers, chief manager, twenty-six assistant general managers, senior manager, manager, assistant manager, then clerical and manual grades, including secretaries and temporary staff. To avoid confusion, the senior positions are given here by their designations of Treasurer, Secretary etc. A number of other senior posts, namely group chief accountant, chief inspector, group compliance officer and archivist, are separately named.

THE BANK'S SUBSIDIARY COMPANIES

In 1995, Bank of Scotland had six principal subsidiary companies. North West Securities, now NWS Bank plc, has been since its acquisition in 1958 the most important and most successful subsidiary. Nws Bank plc has four subsidiaries in its own right. The British Linen Bank, founded in 1974, has five subsidiaries; and other principal subsidiary companies have their own subsidiaries.

MONEY AND INTEREST

Before the 1707 Union of Parliaments, Scotland enjoyed its own currency, and the smallest Bank of Scotland banknotes were issued in this currency. The relationship of the pound Scots to the pound sterling is discussed in Appendix 3. Throughout the text, where 'pound' is used without qualification it is the pound sterling, and this follows the usage of the Bank ledgers and papers, which exhibit various abbreviations of '£-s-d' (standardised in the text as '£ s d'). Such figures are often expressed as a percentage; for example, '8s 6d per cent' means 8s 6d per £100.

The Bank has always issued its own paper currency, for larger notes even before 1707 in sterling. At 28 February 1995, the Bank had in circulation £353 million in banknotes. The rate of interest charged by the Bank in the eighteenth century was always calculated at a simple rate of interest, thus, a 5 per cent charge on a bill of exchange meant 5 per cent over a whole year, and not 5 per cent compound.

NAMES

Scottish names before the nineteenth century are often found under various spellings, reflecting uncertain views on clan and place – thus Dundas of Arnistoun, or Arniston; the Macdonalds, McDonalds or MacDonalds of Glencoe. This book follows the spellings as they appear in Bank accounts and ledgers, only standardising where there is agreement among historians on a particular version – thus Arniston, and MacDonald. Stewart, not Stuart, is used for the Jacobite royal family, as this spelling was used by Professor G. Donaldson, and by Professor B. P. Lenman, for reasons too well known to require reiteration. The Bank's second Governor (1697–1728), David Melville, third Earl of Leven, is here referred to thus, by his better-known title. Upon ennoblement, a person's title is used thereafter. For example, Henry Dundas is referred to as Viscount Melville after 1802. In the eighteenth-century ledgers of the Bank, there are sometimes recorded more than one designation for the same business connection where there is more than one account current – thus Fordyce & Co., or Fordyce & Fordyce. In such designations, some spellings of personal names also vary – thus Fairholme or Fairholm; Cumming or Cuming. I have adopted the name which appeared to be the most appropriate for the context.

DATES AND LENDING

All dates are as given in the Bank records. The figures mentioned on p. 50 referring to bills bought by the Bank were taken from the Minutes, and represent bills to which the directors had agreed. The figures in Table 3.1 were taken from the General Ledger and represent bills actually discounted in the months listed therein. The figures on lending mentioned on p. 89 refer to totals on those dates, while those in Figures 5.1 and 6.1 represent new lending for the particular month in question.

AGREEMENTS AND UNDERSTANDINGS

There is no clear date for the origin of the 'Agreements and Understandings' between Bank of Scotland and the Royal Bank of Scotland, although the benefits were obvious to both parties from the later 1730s. There does not appear, however, to have been a formal agreement, although there were informal understandings, before the Secretary of State for Scotland, the Marquis of Tweeddale, called for one in 1742. As will be shown, by the mid-Victorian years, the regular meetings of the senior general managers of the Scottish banks, in the General Managers Committee (GMC), decided a wide range of matters relating to banking practice. The GMC was not formally abolished until 1971.

IDENTIFICATION OF CUSTOMERS

Bank of Scotland rightly opposes any practice which would identify the details of customers' accounts to outside parties. Where current customers are mentioned in the text, permission has been sought and granted, however far back the connection goes. It is gratifying to notice that the

business customers mentioned here have been happy to be identified with
Bank of Scotland.

FOOTNOTES

Footnotes are given in the text where historians usually require a source
to be identified. Exceptions are for well-known political and economic
events. For the years after 1945, a number of matters have not been
sourced except in general terms, and this stricture is especially important
for the years after 1979.

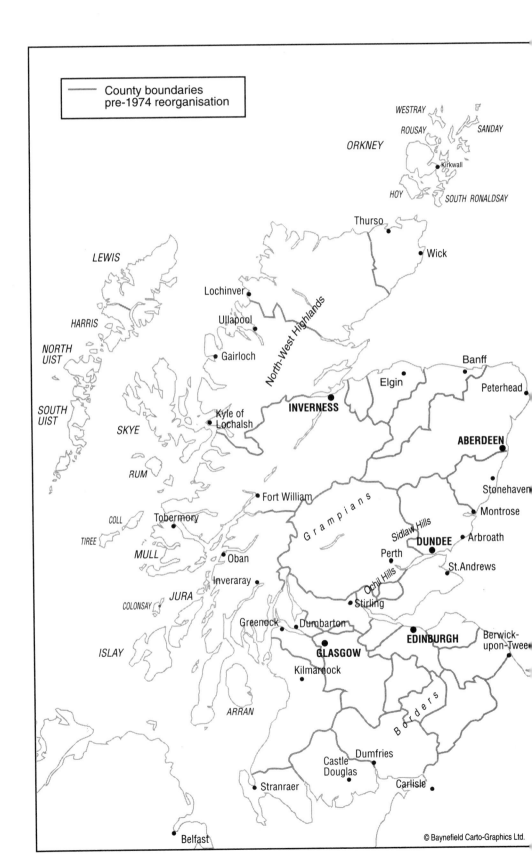

County boundaries
pre-1974 reorganisation

WESTRAY
ROUSAY
SANDAY
ORKNEY
Kirkwall
HOY
SOUTH RONALDSAY

Thurso
Wick

LEWIS

Lochinver
HARRIS
Ullapool
NORTH
UIST
Gairloch
North-West Highlands
Banff
Elgin
Peterhead
SOUTH
UIST
SKYE
Kyle of
Lochalsh
INVERNESS
ABERDEEN
RUM
Stonehaven
Fort William
Montrose
COLL
Tobermory
Grampians
Sidlaw Hills
Arbroath
TIREE
DUNDEE
MULL
Oban
Perth
St.Andrews
Inveraray
Ochil Hills
JURA
Stirling
COLONSAY
Greenock
Dumbarton
EDINBURGH
Berwick-
upon-Tweed
ISLAY
GLASGOW
Kilmarnock
Borders
ARRAN
Dumfries
Castle
Douglas
Carlisle
Stranraer

Belfast

© Baynefield Carto-Graphics Ltd.

INTRODUCTION

The foundation of Bank of Scotland in 1695 was closely associated with the political events in Scotland which followed the overthrow of James VII in the Revolution of 1688–9. The accession of William and Mary acted as a catalyst for a significant remodelling of the institutions of the country, notably within the legal system, the Kirk, the military forces and Parliament, and to a lesser extent the burghs and the universities. There was a dramatic enhancement in the position of the nobility in all walks of public life. Together these changes amounted to a more thorough and wide-ranging revolutionary transformation than occurred in England. New institutions and forms of business arose, of which Bank of Scotland was the most conspicuous example, whereas before 1688 political problems had inhibited their establishment. To understand why these changes were so comprehensive, some aspects of the political history of the Restoration need to be remarked upon.

From 1660 to 1685, Scotland was ruled by the restored king, Charles II, and after his death by his brother James VII. Both expected acquiescence in their personal rule and, as they were rarely present in Scotland, from their representatives in the Scottish Parliament and on the Scottish Privy Council. They required acknowledgement from legislators, clerics and judiciary that kingship gave unquestioned rights over public affairs and that the delegation of these rights to others was a grant to be recalled at will. Thus the Scottish Parliament which met in 1661 framed an oath acknowledging the royal prerogative and supremacy 'over all persons and in all causes' ecclesiastic as well as civil.[1] It was, in other words, an absolute rule in Scotland, and exercised with only occasional modifications under political pressures grudgingly tolerated for as short a time as possible.

1 A. Lang, *A History of Scotland from the Roman Occupation*, 2nd edn, 4 vols (Edinburgh: 1909), vol. iii, p. 294.

Charles II was more flexible than his brother – he once remarked that he had no wish to embark on his travels again – but he was more accommodating in English politics than north of the Border.

The restored Stewart dynasty was welcomed by the Scottish nobility, the lairds (the landed gentry) and the high-ranking ecclesiastics, although there was less enthusiasm among those on the lower rungs of public life. There was uncertainty about the benefits of a separate Parliament in Edinburgh and the reimposition of the old, pre-Cromwellian legal system, and about much else from the Stewart past. Nevertheless, open opposition was at first confined to religious groupings, of which the Covenanters were the most prominent, and these were gradually worn down by repression and persecution. In Parliament sat the aristocracy, the most important estate, shire commissioners representing the lairds, delegates from the royal burghs, and the archbishops and bishops, who took their seats after legislation in 1662 had re-established Episcopacy. In the first decade of the Restoration, these estates, and the members of the Scottish Privy Council, showed little more independence than was usual in the time of James VI and Charles I, and the occasional squeaks of opposition tended to be personal and swiftly dealt with. The old Stewart management of Parliament was reimposed with the election of 'Lords of the Articles' through whom all Parliamentary business was directed, and the right of members to attend these deliberations was later abolished. The reasons for this passivity were clear: in the early years, the landowners were 'haunted by fears of [popular] revolution'.[2] Sir James Stewart, a landowner and later critic of the government, was stating the views of many contemporaries when he described it as a Parliament 'of unparalleled submission and resignation'.[3] While a range of economic and local legislation was passed which was actively supported by the estates, in political and religious affairs we are left with Sir James's harsh verdict, that 'out of meer compliance with his Majesty's will our Parliament doth consent, and the people silently acquiesce to Presbyteries unexpected overthrow and Prelacies re-established ... in a word ... we could refuse nothing'. A cleverer king could have ruled easily with such an alliance. In fact, Charles II proved a poor judge of his Scottish nobility and misunderstood their earnest support for his Restoration as justification for royal and ministerial control over fiscal, monetary, clerical and other areas of patronage in public life.

2 B. P. Lenman, *The Jacobite Risings in Britain 1689–1746* (London: 1984), p. 23; G. Donaldson, *Scotland, James V to James VII*, The Edinburgh History of Scotland, vol. iii (Edinburgh: 1978), pp. 358–9; R. S. Rait, *The Parliaments of Scotland* (Glasgow: 1924), pp. 75–6; Lang, *History of Scotland*, vol. iii, pp. 293–4; for the docility of the Scottish Parliament as seen from London, see R. Hutton, *Charles the Second King of England, Scotland, and Ireland* (Oxford: 1989), pp. 268–9.
3 Sir James Stewart of Goodtrees, *An Accompt of Scotland's Grievances by Reason of the Duke of Lauderdale's Ministrie* (1671) [GL 1676].

Apart from the engrossment of office by his favourites who supported him in exile, the setting-up of the bishops, the wearing of vestments and the encouragement of those regarded as idolaters were guaranteed to arouse deep-seated fears among the Scots.

The key royal manager for two decades after 1660 was John Maitland, second Earl of Lauderdale, whom Charles first appointed as Secretary of State for Scotland, and who was described by his biographer as a man of insight into character, with 'fertility of resource, a strong will, coolness and courage, extreme selfishness, readiness to strike at the right moment, keen discernment in choosing his tools and utter unscrupulousness'.[4] Lauderdale's pre-Restoration years in politics and the Kirk, his iron will and physique, an ability to deal with an endless volume of work, and his deep knowledge of the Bible meant that he was well fitted in the context of the times to outmanoeuvre opponents. By 1667 he was in control of the Kirk, had organised the wars against the Covenanters and was the *de facto* authority for appeal from the Court of Session, and later the courts were brought more completely under the control of his party and were used for its members' personal aggrandisement and fortune.

The power of the Earl of Lauderdale grew steadily, and he rose high in the circles of Charles's government in London. He was a member of the inner group known as the Cabal (with Thomas, Lord Clifford, the Earl of Arlington, the Duke of Buckingham and Lord Ashley) and was thus a party to the discussions in 1670 over the secret treaty of Dover with France and the subsequent treaty of London, which were designed to bring the two crowns closer together as well as providing a French subsidy for Charles's Exchequer. In 1671, Lauderdale was involved with the decision to renege on the payment of interest on state debts, known as the 'Stop of the Exchequer', a decision which led to the collapse of around twenty-five London private banking houses and earned the government the undying enmity of most financiers in the City of London.[5] By this time, Lauderdale was President of the Privy Council, Scottish Secretary in London, Commissioner of the Treasury, Captain of Edinburgh Castle, Captain of the Bass Rock, court agent for the royal burghs and one of four extraordinary Lords of Session, as well as Charles's Commissioner to the Scottish Parliament. Opponents estimated his yearly income at a minimum of £16,350 sterling and that of his brother Charles Hatton at £2,000, together with the profits of the Scottish Mint.[6] Their circle dominated office: to notice two well-known figures, the Earl of Atholl

4 'Maitland, John', *Dictionary of National Biography*, 1st edn, ed. S. Lee (London: 1893), vol. 35, pp. 360–7.
5 See below, Chapter 1.
6 See below, Chapter 4.

was Lord Privy Seal, Lord Justice General, Captain of the King's Guard and a Lord of Session, while the Earl of Kincardine held the monopoly on salt and was a Commissioner of the Treasury, a Lord of Session and Vice-Admiral of Scotland. The official record is replete with such largesse as the grant in 1672 of licences for wine imports worth £3,000 per year to Lord Elphinstone, who was married to Lauderdale's niece. By that year, Lauderdale was 'at the height of insolence and power. His influence over Charles was complete. Scotland was at his feet: all places were filled by himself and his friends . . . more like the Vizier of an oriental sovereign than the servant of a constitutional king.'[7] Yet this system was unstable, as favours were granted at will; and there was a groundswell of opinion which gathered strength as the threat of the Covenanters receded, with important magnates, including the Duke of Hamilton, the Duke of Queensberry, the Earl of Dumfries and the Earl of Roxburghe, leading the voices for a broader distribution of government patronage.[8]

The aristocrats who found themselves marginalised by the government have been described as forming an opposition, and over the whole period of the Restoration this is a reasonable description. But it took many years for this to coalesce, and there were many hurdles. Their main achievement by 1673 was to upset the government sufficiently to see Parliament dissolved; but it was not until 1679, when Lauderdale was in declining health, that they were able to insist on some replacements in government offices and on the investigation of some aspects of royal power. Yet this was modest indeed, and short-lived. At the height of the hysteria of the Popish Plot in 1679–80 and again during the subsequent exclusion crisis from later in 1680 to 1682, James, Duke of York, resided in Scotland and took an active part in political management as Charles's Commissioner to Parliament. James was determined to exercise control of the northern realm, and, in July 1681, Parliament passed legislation which made the religious belief of the heir irrelevant to the inheritance of the crown. Furthermore, a test Act had imposed on holders of public office a complicated oath, and, when the ninth Earl of Argyll consented in 1681 to take it, he did so only 'insofar as it is consistent with itself, and with the Protestant faith'.[9] For this he was condemned to death, and he fled to the Netherlands. When James left Scotland, the opposition was as cowed as at the height of Lauderdale's power. In 1683, the royal grip was strengthened when the conspirators of the Rye House Plot failed to kill Charles II on his return from one of his frequent visits to the Newmarket

---

7 'Maitland, John', *DNB*, vol. 35, p. 365.
8 For these years, see G. Donaldson, *Scotland*, pp. 378–9.
9 Lang, *History of Scotland*, vol. iii, p. 368.

races; the king had left the town early on the day chosen. The government soon learned of the plot, and there were executions. More Whigs, from both sides of the Border, fled to the opposition in the Netherlands, among whom were several founders of Bank of Scotland.

The accession of James VII in 1685 saw the government administration as well entrenched in Edinburgh as in London. In the spring, potential opponents were rounded up, and the Earl of Argyll, as general of the forces invading Scotland in support of the Duke of Monmouth's claim to the throne, found a people as unwilling to rebel as the English were to help the Duke. Few lairds rose, and Argyll was captured and executed. With sound management of the sensibilities of the Scottish nobility and care towards matters of the Kirk, James might have enjoyed a long reign. Yet he soon turned most nobles and lairds against himself. James was an avowed Roman Catholic who openly practised his religion in a country with few Romanists and a vigorous Protestant belief. He defined the loyalty of his ministers more narrowly than had his brother, and predominantly by their religion; a few of his Scottish officials converted, and the Duke of Gordon, also a Romanist, was given the command of Edinburgh Castle. In the second Parliament, in 1686, James offered a number of concessions on the passage of goods across the Border to the benefit of landowners, but only if the laws against dissenters and Roman Catholics were lifted. Astute negotiation could have managed a compromise; but the king was stubborn, and, when criticism was raised, Parliament was dissolved. When in the following year a royal proclamation announced tolerance, the Presbyterians were excluded. A Catholic chapel was founded at Holyrood with a Jesuit school, and a press for printing Catholic propaganda was set up.

These moves by the king were monumental blunders: they overlaid the question of the royal prerogative and the nobility's rights of office with the greater popular force of a resurgent Presbyterianism. In the aftermath of the revocation of the Edict of Nantes in France in 1685, rumours spread of the massacres of French Protestants by Catholics. To the aristocratic opposition, the developments after the Rye House Plot and the failed invasion of 1685, together with the behaviour of James VII, were further proof, if that were needed, that the Crown would pursue the policy of the Earl of Lauderdale and Charles II. There would be little chance of internal reform, and the only meaningful alternative was rebellion. Thus the pillars of the Scottish Revolution were in place: fear of the Counter-Reformation, the isolation of the natural governing class from the government, a lengthy record of grievances, and the arrogance and obsessions of James VII, with only his armed forces and relatively few supporters to defend his rule. When William of Orange invaded England, there was little doubt which way the majority of the Scots would go.

Nevertheless, Scotland was slow to mobilise, and the Scottish Convention of the Estates in March 1689 was careful to listen to the appeals of both parties. But they soon agreed that there would be no return to an obsequious role for landowners in political life, and, as discussed below, the nobility moved to correct all manner of sufferings inflicted in the previous three decades. Furthermore, William cast a wide net, 'being resolved to put nobody in Despair, till once he know how they intended to behave for his Interest'.[10] The associations of opposition now became distinct groups associated with the greater magnates, and they waged an effective political and military defence of their new position. By the summer of 1691, the war was over in Scotland, and Scottish regiments sailed to the fighting in the Netherlands and Flanders. This political and military background is essential for understanding the foundation of Bank of Scotland. The Bank would not have been formed under the old Stewart regime; some other form of financial organisation might have evolved, but not as it did, nor with the restrictions and privileges which it enjoyed.

The financial intricacies which faced the nobility and lairds of Scotland, and which underlay the animosities about government office before and after the Revolution, were the result of a gradual monetisation of payments, a pressure common to all countries in northern Europe and Scandinavia. But this was a slow process. Scotland was operating with agricultural and trading systems of payments which were typically active four or five times a year and which included varying elements of barter. It was quite clear, even with the modest pressure of wartime taxation, that the means of payment which could easily be converted into gold and silver were inadequate. There was no problem with raising goods as such, but much Scottish production was suitable only for local consumption and for barter, and thus inappropriate for sale on the international markets for cash. Furthermore, as Scotland had no copper or tin which could have substituted for the precious metals which the country lacked, there evolved a robust but often confusing system of multiple currencies and barter, of different coinages and a mass of credit and debt sufficient to keep payments in some sort of order. The existence of repeated complaints about the level of interest rates charged for gold and silver coin, and the failure to keep the levels below the legal maximum of 6 per cent, were a testimony to this lack of coin. There was therefore little footloose credit available in Scotland at the time of the Revolution. What credit there was had to be searched for among the lawyers, goldsmiths and factors of Edinburgh, Glasgow and the Scottish connections in London, and cultivated in complicated relationships of debt and family obligations.

10 Lenman, *The Jacobite Risings*, p. 24.

Obtaining credit was thus often slow, tedious and expensive, drawing on the deep-rooted culture of hospitality between landowners and their factors and inevitably complicated by seemingly endless legal disputes.

The highest aristocrats in the land were affected. In the autumn of 1691, the Edinburgh merchant and factor George Watson, later appointed the first Accountant of Bank of Scotland, received word from the tenth Earl of Argyll that two bills of exchange drawn on his Lordship in London and payable to Watson would not now be paid.[11] The Earl of Argyll was under very considerable pressure. Upon his return to Scotland he set about raising a regiment of foot, and he was appointed to the Privy Council and the Treasury Commission. Should the Stewarts return, Argyll knew the fate in store for him: it would be exile or death. On the surface, his economic standing was considerable; the family held extensive lands, and the ultimate credit of these was sound. In spite of their political difficulties, his predecessors had expanded their rentals and made considerable efforts with livestock sales. They were involved with mineral exploitation, notably for coal, which found a ready market in the west of Scotland and was exported to Ireland.[12] Thus they possessed significant resources; but, in common with most of his fellow landlords, Argyll had insufficient credit to pay bills if they fell due before rentals and other incomes were received. Moreover, he found what every occupier of Scottish office discovered at this time, that power gave benefits but was expensive. Tax revenues were inadequate to pay the demands of office, and the army and office-holders' own estate revenues were unable to carry much of the burden.

Inevitably, the Earl of Argyll looked to his connections in Edinburgh and elsewhere; in this case, George Watson was asked to carry the bills, one of which was down to his brother, a colonel in the army, and the other to Lord Maitland, whose affairs were in some disorder. Yet, as the war in Europe progressed and the demands on the Scottish Parliament increased, Watson found himself with multiple demands on his business, as, inevitably, did many other lawyers and merchants in Edinburgh. The customary structures and relationships were pressed into service under quite exceptional pressures, in effect, to underwrite the most expensive war effort of the century. This background, the political commitment to the Revolution of 1688–9, and the demands that this made upon the taxation system in Scotland are crucial to understanding the legislation of the Scottish Parliament during the years of war after 1689. It was primarily

11 Edinburgh City Archive, Edinburgh Merchant Company MSS, Miscellaneous papers collection, no. 11, Earl of Argyll, Inveraray, to George Watson, 11 October 1691; George Watson's career is discussed below in Chapter 1.
12 SRO E 72/2/11, Exports, 1 November 1682 to 1 November 1683; SRO GD 103/2/247, Earl of Argyll at Inveraray to Dougall Campbell of Melfort, on prospecting for gold.

the question of how an economy, predominantly agricultural and faced with considerable difficulties in the export market, could support the financial demands of war. There were also pent-up pressures expressed in Parliament that the Stewart depotism had impeded the accumulation of capital and that, in particular, the possibilities for joint-stock enterprise were under-explored. These are matters central to the discussions which preceded the establishment of Bank of Scotland.

It was of considerable benefit to the Scottish people, as they embarked on the journey to a modern society, that the leading estates had some clear ideas about the sort of society and economy that they wanted, and about how best to achieve this. There was also a healthy understanding of the economic and civic shortcomings of the country. This complicated process of thought was advanced for its time. It should also be stressed that the members of the Scottish Convention which met in 1689 had a world-view and methods of thinking which brought religious and political questions into their debates on economic matters, since many of the perceived impediments to economic progress were regarded as religious or political.

When leaders are involved in religious disputes and in military conflict, they are likely to carry over the qualities needed for these spheres into more peaceful pursuits. These battles of politics and religion were intricate, made considerable intellectual demands and undoubtedly gave the leading members of Parliament a tenacity and forthrightness in debate over economic affairs. Furthermore, it is important to mention that, while the religious debates among the nobility, lairds and the professions found considerable support at lower levels of society, when it came to the economy the landowners had an agenda which was quite definitely their own. For fifty years, through the troubles of the 1640s and the Cromwellian period, and during the reigns of Charles II and James VII with their whims, favours and abuses, the aristocracy and the lairds, while important, had not been in control of the levers of power. This concentrated the minds of the nobility on what they could now achieve.

This pattern may be summarised succinctly. The landowners and their professional allies dominated the debate over economic growth, and tried to design their future by uniting individual fortune to a wide-ranging cooperation. This was seen as a long-term effort, although there were inevitably a number of short-cuts which members of Parliament hoped to take. The evidence suggests that MPs were surprisingly well informed about business organisation and were to favour what was eventually recognised as the most effective form of capitalist organisation, the joint-stock company with transferable stock. They made mistakes: in particular, there were some curious weaknesses in the information before Parliament about some foreign trades. Concerning home matters, though, there were few illusions, and the debates of these years were blunt, well informed and finely tuned to policy. Among the MPs' biggest problems was the shortage of specie and credit: there was simply not enough money. What money there was attracted high interest rates, often well above the legal maximum of 6 per cent. There were inevitable legal wrangles over even quite small sums. The existing use of bills of exchange, and the movement of funds by factors in Edinburgh and elsewhere, was simply too restricted. The central question which had to be addressed was how to increase the total pot of credit, especially long-term credit, at a rate of interest below the legal maximum. This is why Parliament discussed a bank.

While the history of Bank of Scotland is inevitably focused upon Scottish economic and political development, the country's position in a changing Britain was always of importance for banking and finance. The British context determined much of what happened to the Bank. The periodic moods of British political life, the upsets of the trade cycle and movements in the London markets were matters always carefully weighed in Edinburgh. To operate Bank of Scotland in the eighteenth century meant working in a world of uncertainty, of military and political crises, cyclical trends, climatic disasters and war. This was a harsh school, especially so for a bank reliant on low margins and high turnover; but, as will be shown, the directors were able to build a new type of financial structure of immense toughness and resilience and to utilise their very considerable political connections to defend their institution.

CHAPTER 1

THE FOUNDATION OF
THE BANK IN 1695

O N 17 JULY 1695, the Scottish Parliament passed the Act which founded Bank of Scotland.[1] The Bank was designed as a public joint stock to which all could subscribe; the nominal capital was £1,200,000 Scots, of which one-third was to be raised in London and the rest in Edinburgh.[2] The maximum permitted holding was £20,000 Scots, and fears about stockjobbing led Parliament to fix tough controls on share sales. The directors were forbidden to use the stock for dividend payments; these were only to be paid out of profits of the joint stock and with the prior concurrence of a general meeting of 'adventurers', the term used to denote subscribers. They were limited in their liability for Bank debts only up to their subscription. The company was to have a monopoly of joint-stock banking in Scotland for twenty-one years, though this was broken briefly by the Company of Scotland trading to Africa and the Indies (the Darien company) in the summer of 1696. This monopoly was not tested again before it lapsed in 1716.

The Bank was to be controlled by a court of no fewer than twenty-four directors, and in the early years the management was open to scrutiny by adventurers. The stock was only to be used for the trade of banking which the Act loosely defined, though it made specific mention of loans at interest of no more than 6 per cent (the legal maximum rate), the issue of a paper currency (in bills and 'ticquets') and the discount of bills of exchange. Trading in commodities was prohibited except in certain prescribed circumstances. The legislators were keen to allow the Bank to lend money on the security of Acts of Parliament, although such loans

1 *The Acts of the Parliaments of Scotland*, vol. 9, 1689–1695, pp. 494–7, 'Act for Erecting a Public Bank'; the Act is printed in Appendix 1 below.
2 The official rate of exchange was £12 Scots to £1 sterling, although in the summer of 1695 the market rate was close to 11 to 1.

1

were authorised only where they were attached to a specific fund, with an assurance that repayment would, if required, come from other funds. The Act banned direct loans to the Crown, however arranged. Heavy penalties were fixed on directors should these restrictions be ignored. Lastly, the legislature added automatic Scottish citizenship for anyone who subscribed. The statute did not indicate every matter of concern to the directors of the new bank, who were given rights to enact by-laws. The Bank derived a further significant legal benefit from the basis of Scots law in the European tradition of Roman law. This meant that, *ceteris paribus*, the civil courts of Scotland, headed by the Court of Session in Edinburgh, would follow the general intent of the legislators in disputes; when a sensible interpretation could be made by the Bank, the court would rule in its favour. To make certain that the message was understood, several senior judges appointed after the Revolution of 1688 were elected directors.

The Act appointed twelve persons of wealth and status to a foundation committee, five in Edinburgh and seven in London. The elegant subscription book for Scotland, weighing 15 lb and bound in red leather, was open for two months from 1 November and was kept at Patrick Steill's 'Cross-Keys' coffee house in Covenant Close near Parliament Square, Edinburgh. Steill was a long-standing opponent of the Stewarts and subscribed £3,000 Scots. Parliament appointed Alexander Campbell WS, a cousin of Archibald, tenth Earl of Argyll, as collector of subscriptions. Another book was kept in London. The first directors elected by the adventurers agreed to an initial call of £120,000 Scots (10 per cent of the capital allowable) to be paid in before the Bank opened its doors on 27 March 1696. Payments were to be in proportion to individual shareholdings. The cash called up in London, which amounted to £40,000 Scots, was to remain there and its use was to be supervised by a committee chosen by the London subscribers, chaired by James Foulis, an exchange dealer and merchant. This sum was largely used to fund a remittance trade between London and Edinburgh which the directors hoped would deliver cash in both cities below the existing charges made by exchange dealers. As a result of several early crises which afflicted operations in Scotland, the working capital was increased to 30 per cent in early August 1696. This additional sum of £240,000 Scots was similarly raised in proportion to the nominal worth of shares held and was repaid the following year when trading conditions improved. Several London adventurers objected to the call-up for political reasons, though the desperate shortage of coin in England at that time was also mentioned, perhaps unconvincingly, as a factor.[3]

3 BS 1/5, Minutes: 6-7 August 1696; the political objections are discussed below in Chapter 2.

Of the original 172 adventurers, 136 were resident in Scotland and thirty-six in London. Forty-one gave their occupations as merchants, fourteen were lawyers and judges (all in Scotland), and there were seven women. Most London adventurers were merchants, though there were several high officials of the English East India Company and a number of government office-holders, including the Secretary of State, James Johnston. In Scotland, the subscribers fell into three main groups: first, there were twenty-four nobles and thirty-nine lairds whose wealth was usually based on land and whose estates were spread widely across lowland Scotland. These formed the most significant group of subscribers. The nobility provided around £190,000 Scots and the lairds just under £200,000; thus incomes from land contributed nearly half the Scottish total of £800,000 of the capital stock.[4] The subscription lists show a marked bias towards the part of the Whig interest which later became known as the Squadrone; many of the subscribers were prominent supporters of the Revolution, and several had been in exile. Then came a group of twenty-five merchants predominantly located in Edinburgh, though Dundee, Montrose, Aberdeen and Kirkcaldy were also represented. They raised around £300,000 Scots. The third group included the lawyers and judges, often connected by business or family ties to other subscribers, though by the late seventeenth century there were many families who were first and foremost involved in legal affairs. A handful came from the medical profession, and there were a few vintners and goldsmiths.

There emerged a significant difference between Bank of Scotland and the Bank of England (founded in 1694) in respect of ownership. The latter was primarily a creation of the City of London, with management controlled by a group of powerful financiers and merchants who worked closely with the Treasury. The strengths of this financial interest were such that they had little need of government office-holders, members of the House of Lords or judges. The Bank of England was granted its royal charter by a government desperate for funds to prosecute the war with France after the projectors agreed to lend it £1,200,000. While the initial subscribers numbered 1,272 and were widely spread through the mercantile classes and the professions, few of the nobility subscribed. Those that did so 'put their names down out of patriotism or political expediency',

4 The aristocratic contribution has been taken to include immediate relatives, heirs and wives. Also included within this category are David Crawford, Secretary to Anne, Countess of Hamilton, and Alexander Ramsay, servitor to the Marquis of Tweeddale. These two subscribed £6,000. There was an overlap between the Court of Session judges and the landed gentry; the sum for the latter includes the six judges appointed in 1689. For a discussion of the contribution from the aristocracy, see Appendix 2 below.

but overall their contribution was 'negligible'.[5] Moreover, the Bank of England subscription was raised in twelve days with 60 per cent paid up, compared with two months for Bank of Scotland and a call of 30 per cent by August 1696, reduced to 10 per cent again the following year.

In Scotland, the support of the aristocracy and landed gentry was crucial for the establishment of the Bank. Political conditions for several years after 1688 were markedly unsettled even for a country inured to religious warfare, feuds and the periodic ravages of Highland clans upon lowland areas.[6] A bitter military struggle after the overthrow of James VII saw three set-piece battles, at Killiecrankie (27 July 1689 – a Jacobite victory), Dunkeld (21 August 1689 – inconclusive) and Cromdale (1 May 1690 – a victory for the government), and innumerable skirmishes thereafter. The war continued in the Highlands until early 1691, and the government nearly rekindled it with the massacre of the MacDonalds of Glencoe on 13 February 1692. The threat of internal warfare and rumours of invasion forced the government to maintain high levels of military expenditure in the mid-1690s, which put immense pressure on the tax-collection system in Scotland.

Apart from their physical survival, a central preoccupation of the landed classes who supported the Revolution – the majority – was the security of their family estates and fortunes. Parliament and the Privy Council were both, in practical terms, committees of the two senior estates of the nobility and lairds. They dominated the proceedings of the former, and few commoners counted for much on the Council. The fear of arbitrary arrest had disappeared with the flight of James VII in 1688, and these two institutions displayed an openness of debate that had not been witnessed since the civil war. Members of the landed classes who had suffered under James demanded compensation and office. The remnants of James's supporters were removed where they had not undertaken a speedy volte-face; thus the Court of Session, the Privy Council, the military organisation and all the subordinate offices of state were mostly restaffed with the kin of loyal nobles and gentry. So important were these offices thought to be for family incomes that the nobility put immense efforts into ingratiating themselves with William of Orange and organised intrigues which led to considerable infighting inside Parliament.[7] Indeed, several of

5 J. H. Clapham, *The Bank of England. A History* (2 vols, Cambridge: 1944), vol. i, *1694–1797*, pp. 273–4.
6 W. Ferguson, *Scotland: 1689 to the Present*, The Edinburgh History of Scotland, vol. iv (Edinburgh: 1968), ch. 1.
7 P. W. J. Riley, *King William and the Scottish Politicians* (Edinburgh: 1979), chs 1 and 2; W. Ferguson, *Scotland's Relations with England: A Survey to 1707* (Edinburgh: 1977), p. 175ff.; for church patronage, W. L. Mathieson, *Scotland and the Union: A History of Scotland from 1695 to 1747* (Glasgow: 1905), pp. 204–14; P. Hopkins, *Glencoe and the End of the Highland War* (Edinburgh: 1986), ch. 13.

these intrigues encouraged the formation of distinct factions among the nobility.

The insistence upon the security of their estates and the return of lands confiscated by the Stewarts was the absolute priority of the Parliamentary legislation (public and private) and the numerous orders in council of the early 1690s. All factions agreed on this. As part of this tangled legal process, Parliament provided a necessary skeleton for a new Scottish system of finance and credit which culminated in the Bank. A vindictive Act of James VII of 1685 which allowed the Crown to decide whether to grant prior claims on confiscated estates was abolished, and all legal claims to an estate were henceforth to be paid.[8]

A general 'Act of dissolution of the forefaulted lands' annexed by James, passed in 1690, made any subsequent legal challenge to any post-Revolution grant a challenge to all such grants.[9] Thus the resumption of their estates by Revolution supporters and the confiscation of some Jacobite estates did not lead directly to debt repudiation. This meant a sound legal basis for lending on landed property. To some extent, therefore, we have an answer to the question as to why the Bank was not founded earlier. The priorities of the nobility and gentry in the early sessions of Parliament from 1689 were their estates, winning the war against the Jacobites, and intrigues over office.

While they understood the financial benefits of government office, it was also necessary for the long-term development of the country and their estates that members of the Council and Parliament should emphasise the connection between the general level of economic activity and landed incomes. The legal changes for land had only provided a basis for secure accumulation of wealth – what was then required was an agenda which united individual fortune to economic progress in general. This became a matter of some urgency to the Privy Council because of difficulty with the collection of taxes to pay for the army in Scotland; the revenue-generating export economy was simply too thinly spread to counteract a chronic shortage of silver and gold. Scotland had a per capita tax base inferior to that of England, and the collection procedures were later found by Parliamentary inquiries to be inadequate and open to corruption. The consequences of these difficulties were a shortage of funds for government needs and arrears of pay. This also had the unfortunate result that the administration was unable to provide for the protection of Scottish

8 APS, vol. 9, p. 76, c. 75, 'An Act in favours of the Vassals & Creditors of Fore-faulted persones', 1689; p. 225, c. 104, 'Act for security of the Creditors, Vassalls & Heirs of entail of persons forefaulted', 1690.
9 Ibid., pp. 194–5, c. 48.

shipping against French privateers, and thus representations had to be made to the English Admiralty.[10]

The fourth and fifth sessions of Parliament (1693 and 1695) tackled economic matters in earnest.[11] A number of Acts for economic development were passed, usually involving the establishment of joint stocks; they included a new linen company (to which the Bank was to lend money), the celebrated Act for the Company of Scotland and that for Bank of Scotland. In these sessions, a working relationship between the mercantile classes and the landowning estates was developed which relied more on money than affinity and obligation. The landed classes came to see the establishment of Bank of Scotland as an important milestone in their own general interest of self-preservation. Therefore, the nobles and lairds who wholeheartedly backed the Revolution – including those like the Argyll family who had few subscribers to the Bank – had good reason to welcome a sound financial institution which could impart a rigid structure for new credit creation. Unfortunately, in this alliance of aristocrats and merchants one group was left behind: the economic legislation largely bypassed the Convention of the royal burghs. They had taken the lead for an investigation into trade conditions in 1692, but most burgh guilds were collections of petty producers, and they ignored the potential of joint stocks.[12] The narrower horizon of their small-scale industrial producers and their guilds did not fit well in the new public companies, though several burghs implored the new Bank to open branches within their boundaries.

The presence of these aristocrats and lairds as adventurers and directors of Bank of Scotland, together with the legal changes of the Revolution land settlement, gave some guarantee against arbitrary seizure of assets or repudiation of debts. This apprehension was soundly based. Few financiers had foreseen the stop of the English Exchequer in 1671 when Charles II blocked the payments of principal and interest on government debts owed to government suppliers and private bankers. The limited resumption of interest payments failed to save at least twenty-five bankers from bankruptcy by 1690 along with many government suppliers.[13] The

10 Ibid., p. 98 Appendix, 1695.
11 Before 1693 there was only one Act of Parliament for a new trade: 'Act in favours of Mr James Gordon for a gunpowder manufactory', APS, vol. 9, p. 160 and p. 42 Appendix 1, 30 June 1690. The English Privy Council frowned on artillery or gunpowder works in Scotland and Ireland, although in 1695 a powder mill was established in Scotland and continued for several years. There is a note on both projects in W. R. Scott, The Constitution and Finance of English, Scottish and Irish Joint-Stock Companies to 1720 (3 vols, Cambridge: 1912), vol. iii, division IX, section IX, p. 193.
12 'Register containeing the state and condition of every burgh within the Kingdom of Scotland in the year 1692', in J. D. Marwick (ed.), Extracts from the Records of the Convention of the Royal Burghs of Scotland 1677–1711 (Edinburgh: 1880), Appendix 3.
13 J. K. Horsefield, 'The "Stop of the Exchequer" Revisited', Economic History Review, 2nd series, 35 (1982), 511–28; for the frauds at the Scottish Mint in the reign of Charles II, see below, Chapter 4.

difficulties experienced by these unfortunates lasted well into the 1690s and were widely talked about. As the political history of Scotland was more unstable than that of England, the idea that Bank of Scotland required political protection, even from supporters of the Revolution, was wholly reasonable. Indeed, within a few months of opening for business, the directors decided that they urgently required more political support. Among the dozen new directors elected in August 1696 were David Melville, third Earl of Leven and Governor of Edinburgh Castle,[14] Basil, Lord Hamilton, and John, Lord Belhaven; places were also given to three Lords of Session. The other six were related to landed families.

The lairds made an important contribution to the raising of funds (just under £200,000); their most common holding (twenty-two out of thirty-nine) was £3,000, and the average at £4,700 was £2,000 below that of the aristocracy. The geographical spread was wide, from the Lothians, Ayrshire, Berwickshire and the Borders, Perthshire, Forfar and Fife. Some may have come in because of advice from those merchants, nobles and other lairds who were to put substantial expertise into the early management. Parliament appointed to the foundation committee the future Deputy Governor, Colonel William Erskine, along with Sir John Swinton of that Ilk and Sir Robert Dickson of Sornbeg. It would have been difficult to find three more determined opponents of the old regime. Both Dickson and Erskine were military officers, and the latter was Governor of Blackness Castle, an important fortress in central Scotland. The family of Swinton of that Ilk had been dispossessed on the restoration of Charles II in 1660 and their lands seized by the Earl of Lauderdale.[15] Until 1688, they were forced to live in the Netherlands, where they were active in trade, recovering their lands after the legislation of 1690. Swinton was to urge all manner of economic and trade proposals on Parliament. He was one of many ex-émigrés who helped to bring to the board and to adventurers' meetings of Bank of Scotland a wide experience of Dutch and European trade.

The restaffing of the Court of Session on 1 November 1689 with judges loyal to William and Mary was important for the Bank.[16] Six of these twelve men subscribed. The features common to all judges were, first and foremost, that William could depend on their support in the face of a

14 David Melville (1660–1728) was the third Earl of Leven and the second Earl of Melville: see Sidney Lee (ed.), *Dictionary of National Biography*, vol. xiii; Sir James Balfour Paul (ed.), *The Scots Peerage, founded on Wood's edition of Sir Robert Douglas's Peerage of Scotland*, vol. vi (Edinburgh: 1909), pp. 110–13.
15 *APS*, vol. 9, p. 221, c.95, 'Act Rescinding the Forfeiture of the deceist John Swintone of that Ilk', 1690; C. A. Malcolm, *The Bank of Scotland, 1695–1945* (Edinburgh: n.d. [1948]), pp. 21–3.
16 G. Brunton and D. Haig, *Account of the Senators of the College of Justice from its Institution in 1532* (London: 1832), p. 433ff.

Jacobite threat; further, they were all connected to land and subscribed to and voted for various projects for industry and trade in two sessions of Parliament in 1693 and 1695, and they also held other offices or revenue-collection positions. For example, Sir John Home of Blackadder was a Commissioner for the land taxes (known as the cess), was created a Lord of Justiciary (the senior Scottish criminal court) and was appointed to the Privy Council. Sir William Anstruther of that Ilk, who had opposed the Stewarts from 1681, was also a member of Parliament and the Privy Council, and derived income from an appointment to the Exchequer.[17] Another subscriber was James Smollett, a judge of the Commissary Court (wills and marriages), who put up £3,000; and there were six Writers to the Signet. In later years, the holdings by the legal profession grew. As with the nobility and lairds, the longer-term contribution of the legal profession was not just to be calculated in terms of money; their usually wide network of contacts and business connections, their influence on landowners and in Edinburgh politics and their role in the courts were in times of crisis to be of great benefit to Bank of Scotland.

The Edinburgh mercantile classes provided thirty-four subscribers to the Bank for a total of £221,000, an average of £6,500 each. This was a most interesting collection of merchants. Whereas most of the nobility and gentry, if not all, were by and large interested in domestic tax and industrial matters, many merchant families looked to overseas trades for their main incomes. By this period, Scottish merchant families had spread far and wide over the Baltic ports and western coasts of Scandinavia and continental Europe. There was, indeed, a flourishing group of Scottish merchants in London, many of whom invested in Bank stock and of whom more is written below. From what is known, these Scots abroad had extraordinarily diverse interests, their trading often had little direct connection with Scotland, and they were quite prepared to deal in smuggled goods and the illegal export of coin. In political terms, they were probably more sympathetic to the aims of the 1688 Revolution than to the Jacobites, though many Scots lived happily in France and collaborated with their Protestant cousins in other countries.

The merchants addressed the problem of the quality of Scottish manufactures by importing better ones. Scotland was good at producing a range of basic products cheaply – white fish, salmon, some of the finest coal in Europe, grain (in some years), cattle and sheep. In manufactured goods, however, the country was sadly lacking in range, volume and quality and had begun to import a burgeoning range of colonial produce, such

17 The other four judges who subscribed were Sir David Home of Crossrig, second son of Blackadder; Hew Dalrymple, the third son of Viscount Stair (politically the least dependable); Sir Archibald Hope of Rankeillour; and Sir John Hamilton of Halcraig. (For further details, see Appendix 2.)

as sugars, rice and tobacco; hence a deficit on the balance of payments, which was probably worse by 1700 than it had been in 1660.[18] While contemporaries were not always precise about how they expressed the problems which this caused, and they lacked accurate statistics, there was an underlying conflict between some of these merchants and domestic producers. This may have lain behind the opposition of some Edinburgh burgesses to the foundation of Bank of Scotland; perhaps they saw the Bank as providing just another source of finance for importers.

While the Scottish economy was at a primitive stage in the manufacture of commodities which required much labour to work them up for sale (precisely the question which Parliament tackled in 1693 and 1695), the international trade sector was highly sophisticated and used the very latest accounting and financial techniques. Moreover, superior merchant houses operated not only from the principal burghs, from Glasgow and Edinburgh/Leith, as we would expect, but also from Lerwick, Montrose, Aberdeen, Dundee and even Perth, and for the Irish trade from several minor ports on the west coast. The import and export figures for the smaller ports kept in the Scottish Record Office show that the European sector had some depth. In Aberdeen, for example, over thirty merchant houses were handling foreign shipments in the 1690s, as were around ten apiece from Montrose and Dundee. Not only merchants were involved in foreign trade; several aristocratic families and numerous lairds organised their own imports and exports. This ranged from the purchase of Dutch paintings and quality consumer goods for their houses and castles to the huge coal export trade run by the Wemyss family from Fife to Scandinavia and the Netherlands. The luxury and consumer imports were responsible for an increasing part of the total balance of payments deficit.

The international trade sector required the very best education. Languages were necessary; Scots had to master one or more of their own internal languages (one-third of the population spoke Gaelic), as well as French and/or Dutch and often a Scandinavian language. Their education required hard work for many years. The early career of George Watson, appointed the first Accountant of Bank of Scotland in 1696, is an example. Watson was born in Edinburgh in 1645, his mother and father were merchants and the trade connection may have gone back for several generations. When his father died, his mother Marion and his aunt, Lady Curriehill, brought him up and provided him with financial support. At the late age of 24, he was apprenticed to an Edinburgh merchant for five years, and he received tuition in the capital in 1669 and 1670 in a wide range of book-keeping techniques.[19]

18 This matter is discussed in Chapter 4 below.
19 Edinburgh City Archive, EMC MSS, George Watson papers, *Book of solved questions most fit and*

In 1673, Watson was sent to the Netherlands at a time of war with France; his exercise books, largely compiled in Dutch, show that he was taught mathematics and accounting and a range of subjects from bills of exchange to the differing legal systems of countries with which he was expected to trade. This gave Watson a first-hand acquaintance of many of the houses which he was later to deal with when he returned to Edinburgh. Numerous Scotsmen were sent to France and the Low Countries at this time; they studied medicine, the law, and Catholic or Protestant religion, as well as trade, and most probably learnt some business techniques whatever station in life they were destined for.[20] A sound political common sense was required for a Scottish merchant. The life of Watson, for example, spanned the Cromwellian occupation, three occasions when the English dragged Scotland into wars with the Dutch, an endless series of clan wars and raids, the Covenanter troubles, and after 1689 a twenty-five-year war with France. To be good at business, it was necessary to be conversant with politics, religious differences, clan disputes and party factions.

In spite of the geographical spread of the leading merchants among the Scottish ports, those who subscribed to the Bank came predominantly from Edinburgh. From Glasgow, only George Lockhart subscribed, and then just for £3,000. Quite why such an important centre was so slightly involved is unclear; the burgh already had sizeable mercantile discount houses, and perhaps tying up capital in a venture with so many government officials, judges and pro-Revolution politicians lacked appeal. Robert Whyte, a Kirkcaldy merchant whose daughter later married into the Bruce of Broomhall family, paid in £1,000;[21] John Scrymsour of Dundee bought £2,000, and several merchants with connections in other ports also subscribed. This was also modest and suggests that the trade in the smaller ports may have been already adequately supported by facilities for the discounting of bills of exchange. Caution, of course, may have played a part. Nevertheless, it is on Edinburgh merchants that we must focus.

necessary to know as the ground of . . . Italian book-keeping. The existence of these papers suggests that the size of the Edinburgh merchant groups had encouraged at least one teacher to settle in the capital. For a later period, see D. J. Withrington, 'Education and Society in the Eighteenth Century', in N. T. Phillipson and R. Mitchison (eds), *Scotland in the Age of Improvement* (Edinburgh: 1970), pp. 169–99.
20 In each year before the Revolution, there may have been over twenty Scots in the Netherlands studying accounting and trade. William Dunlop of Glasgow, who studied in Dort in 1681, had five in his class and mentioned many more at Rotterdam: T. M. Devine, 'The Merchant Class of the Larger Scottish Towns in the Later Seventeenth and Early Eighteenth Centuries', in G. Gordon and B. Dicks (eds), *Scottish Urban History* (Aberdeen: 1983), p. 96; Andrew Russell, whose career has been discussed by T. C. Smout in *Scottish Trade on the Eve of Union 1660–1707* (Edinburgh: 1963), pp. 99–115, was a sort of tutor-cum-moneylender to some of these.
21 S. G. Checkland, *The Elgins, 1766–1917: A Tale of Aristocrats, Proconsuls and Their Wives* (Aberdeen: 1988), ch. 1.

The Edinburgh of 1695 had a taxable population of just over 20,000, with around 5,611 households in the eleven parishes of Edinburgh and Leith (the nearest port on the Forth) and another 5,000 in villages within a ten-mile radius which supplied food, hay and miscellaneous building and manual labour.[22] The area was dominated by the virtually impregnable fortress of Edinburgh Castle, whose Governor, the Earl of Leven, was elected Governor of the Bank in March 1697. In 1694 and 1695, some 528 of these burgh households each had stock valued at 10,000 Scots merks or above, and 165 of these householders were listed as merchants.[23] From later records, we know that a few of this group each had stock worth more than 30,000 merks. This top group represented 30 per cent of Edinburgh merchants. To strengthen their standing, the merchants founded various societies and lobbied the Privy Council and Parliament; the royal charter of the Edinburgh Merchant Company was granted by James, Duke of York on 28 November 1681. A group of the wealthiest merchants, the importers of wine and brandy from France, also met as a society, as did the merchant retailers, although the Merchant Company became the main focus of opinion after 1700. They were distinguished in the poll-tax registers from the ordinary craftsmen who kept shops or stalls, and with whose craft companies the merchants and burgh council had frequent disputes. In general, the importers lobbied for free trade in manufactured goods whereas the craftsmen demanded protection.[24]

The Bank of Scotland Act appointed two Edinburgh merchants, George Clerk the younger and John Watson, a cousin of George Watson, to the foundation committee. Clerk imported wine and manufactured goods and was destined to play a leading role in Bank affairs before his early death in 1699. With his father, he was an investor in the New Mills Woollen Manufactory which made cloth for the army, though unlike his father he refused to invest in the Company of Scotland.[25] He initially put

22 H. M. Dingwall, *Late Seventeenth-century Edinburgh: A Demographic Study* (Aldershot: 1994), p. 26; and see idem, *The Social and Economic Structure of Edinburgh in the Late Seventeenth Century*, Ph.D. thesis (University of Edinburgh, 1989), ch. 1. Both texts discuss the 20,603 listed in the 1694 poll tax and compare this figure with the 1691 hearth tax, which gave 8,708 taxable hearths.

23 One Scots merk = 13s 4d Scots, thus 10,000 merks = £6,666 pounds Scots. At the official exchange rate of 12 to 1, these 10,000 merks were equivalent to £555 10s sterling; stock was defined as moveable assets and goods for sale. There may have been significant under-reporting.

24 EMC MSS, vol. 1, Minutes, 1681–1696, 7 June 1696, petition to Parliament for a free trade; and 24 June 1689, petition and committee to lobby for removal of prohibition of some imports; pp. 25 and 29 for details of lobbying of Parliament in 1689 and 1690; p. 69, 24 June 1695: the EMC opposed a demand from the Glovers Company for prohibition on import of foreign gloves.

25 W. R. Scott (ed.), *The Records of a Scottish Cloth Manufactory at New Mills, Haddingtonshire, 1681–1703*, Scottish History Society Publications, vol. 46 (Edinburgh: 1905); J. H. Burton (ed.), *The Darien Papers: being a Selection of Original Letters and official Documents relating to the establishment of a colony at Darien by the Company of Scotland trading to Africa and the Indies 1695–1700*, Bannatyne Club, vol. 90 (Edinburgh: 1849).

in £10,000 and Watson £6,000, and when a shortfall loomed at the end of December 1695 they added £10,000 and £4,000 respectively. Other important merchants included Robert (later Sir Robert) Blackwood, a recent dean of the Edinburgh Merchant Company (EMC), who put up £20,000 and his son £6,000, and James McLurg, also a past dean of the EMC (£8,000).[26] Alexander Brand, an international arms dealer, subscribed £10,000; he had been indicted in 1693 for offering bribes to two Treasury officials in return for favourable treatment over a cargo of Dutch arms and ammunition, but he later received a knighthood. Three members of the Marjoribanks family together subscribed £20,000, and James Marjoribanks was appointed the first Treasurer. The family was important in foreign trade, and their connection with the Bank lasted until the nineteenth century. Several other families were involved in sizeable stakes with subscriptions in Edinburgh or London. In this last category, for example, came Patrick and Thomas Coutts who subscribed £24,000, and James and David Nairn (£23,000). Of the thirty-four Edinburgh merchant contributions, two guaranteed £20,000, six were for over £10,000 and ten were for over £5,000. Apart from Clerk and John Watson, other merchants (William Elliott, Robert Watson, James Marjoribanks and Alexander Campbell) also increased their stakes at the end of December to help complete the £800,000 allocated to Edinburgh, as did Colonel William Erskine, his brother Lt-Colonel John Erskine and several government office-holders.

It might be appropriate to add that contributions came from goldsmiths: Robert Inglis subscribed £3,000, James Cockburn £20,000 and the Company of Goldsmiths together 'for common use and behoove of the Box and public stock' £10,000. The goldsmiths acted as buyers and sellers of bullion and coin, on occasion worked closely with the Scottish Mint, and were required to follow the fluctuations in the international precious metals markets. Only one other trade is mentioned, that of vintner, and in both cases the sum involved was only £3,000. One was Patrick Steill, in whose tavern the Bank founders had their initial meetings; but he was hardly a typical craft member. In fact, in terms of the expertise required to operate on the foreign exchanges and assess the creditworthiness of potential borrowers in Scotland, the Bank did not require ordinary craftsmen. What the directors needed among their number were men who knew how to run a foreign business, lend money and organise the domestic cash loans and goods on long-term credit accounts which typified the relationship that Edinburgh lawyers and factors had with their clients among the lairds and aristocracy. The Edinburgh-based subscribers provided this.

---

26 EMC MSS, vol. 1, Minutes, 1681–1696.

The Bank Act appointed seven subscribers to the London foundation committee: six Edinburgh burgesses who had settled in London (James Foulis, David Nairn, Walter Stuart, Hugh Fraser, Thomas Coutts and Thomas Deans), and John Holland, who was later appointed Governor of the Bank and stayed in Scotland for the first four months after the doors opened. They all subscribed the maximum holding of £20,000. Twenty-nine others joined, mainly merchants and office-holders; the average contribution of all London-based adventurers, at £11,100, was significantly above the level in Edinburgh.

A number of the London Scots made a living out of their connections with the military or office-holders. Foulis, Deans, Nairn and Stuart had combined in 1693 for a joint-stock wool manufactory incorporated by the Scottish Parliament, and were joined in that endeavour by William Graham, James Campbell and James Chiesly, who each subscribed £8,000 to the Bank.[27] The baize cloth was ideal for army tunics and cloaks. As it happened, three of the baize cloth directors were also agents for Scottish regiments in the 1690s: William Graham was agent for the regiment of Scots Guards, for Colonel Mackay's regiment of Foot, for Sir Charles Graham's Foot, and for that commanded by Colonel Buchan. David Nairn was agent for Colonel Maitland's regiment and Colonel Ferguson's regiment, and James Campbell for the Earl of Argyll's regiment, known as Lord Lorne's Foot in England. At least two more London subscribers were regimental agents, namely William Hamilton, a past under-secretary of state who put up £16,000, and David Campbell (£10,000).[28] George Campbell, a relative of the Earl of Argyll, earned commission on the sales of clothing and consumer goods to Scots regiments in Flanders in the 1690s.[29] George Campbell also provided facilities for remittance to and from Scotland and dealt in all manner of goods and cattle. Important though all this was, the London Scots were still relatively unimportant in the London financial world. In 1694, the foundation of the Bank of England saw few Scots subscribe, and the decision the following year by their court of directors to curtail facilities to non-subscribers, apart from a number of favoured connections, created a potential difficulty for the Scots in London.[30] Perhaps Campbell and Coutts thought that if they were to remain competitive with London merchants then they also needed the facilities of a mercantile discount house, preferably issuing its own paper.

27 APS, vol. 9, pp. 313–14, c.49, 'Act in favour of the Manufacturing of Baises and erecting them in a free incorporation', 1693.
28 David Campbell was agent for the Earl of Denbigh's Dragoons; Hamilton for Sir Thomas Levinston's Royal Regiment of Foot, Sir David Coliear's Foot, Colonel Lauder's Foot and Sir George Hamilton's Foot.
29 Coutts & Co., MSS, Letter Book of George Campbell, 1692–1694.
30 Bank of England, MSS, Ledger 'B', p. 124, 17 April 1696.

As we shall see in the next chapter, this is exactly how some of the London Scots saw the new Bank of Scotland.

Before the London subscription book for the Bank opened on 1 November 1695, questions of international politics began to crowd the stage. In the 1693 session, the Scottish Parliament passed an Act on foreign trade which gave merchants trading to and from Scotland the right to form joint stocks to trade to Africa, India and the Caribbean. This passed largely unnoticed in London, probably because a joint-stock company was not formed by the Act. A number of Scottish merchants were already keen smugglers of goods to the English colonies, so little of substance was changed. The creation of the Company of Scotland trading to Africa and the Indies in June 1695 was different. This allowed a huge joint stock to be launched, with a nominal capital of £600,000 sterling and with powers to raise in London as well as Scotland. A great deal of propaganda was then trumpeted around Scotland and among Scots abroad about how this was going to transform the country and make stockholders very rich indeed. By the late summer of 1695, it had become clear that Scottish merchants in London would be joined by disgruntled English and Dutch traders who were opposed to the English East India Company.[31] David Macpherson suggested a century later that the Scots were mere dupes; the Darien Company, 'said to have been set on and encouraged by the interlopers in the English East India trade, who, finding that both King and Parliament inclined to favour the Company, flattered themselves with hopes, that by their encouraging the Scottish design they might obtain their own particular ends'.[32] When the London subscription book opened, it quickly gained 200 subscribers and pledges of £250,000 sterling; the ingredients were thus ready for a tremendous international row, which duly occurred. On 6 December 1695, the court of the English East India Company, 'finding that reports are spread abroad that several of the [English Company] adventurers are concerned in the Scotch Act', ordered that every member of the general court 'declare on oath . . . that none of them was involved'.[33] Three days later, the court agreed to petition Parliament and lobby Westminster politicians.[34] From that time onwards, the Company of Scotland had to contend against the enormous powers of the English East India Company and the English state, and later the military strength of the Spanish empire as well. The unfortunate subscribers eventually lost their

31 For the background, see W. Foster, 'The East India Company, 1600–1740', in H. H. Dodwell (ed.), *The Cambridge History of India*, vol. v, *British India 1497–1858* (Cambridge: 1929), pp. 97–8.
32 David Macpherson, *Annals of Commerce, Manufactures, Fisheries and Navigation* (4 vols, London: 1805), vol. ii, p. 664.
33 India Office Library, MSS, East India Company, Minutes, B/41, ff. 38 and 41, 11 November and 6 December 1695.
34 IOL, MSS, East India Company, Minutes, B/41, f. 42, 9 December 1695.

entire working capital, though not just because of that opposition.[35] At no point, however, did the East India Company, or the Bank of England, oppose Bank of Scotland.

The most highly-paid official of the East India Company at the time of the declaration against the Company of Scotland was Francis Beyer, a Dutchman who held the rank of Auditor General and was paid £600 sterling per annum.[36] Beyer had been the Accountant General of the East India Company from 1675. So impressed was the Company with the way in which he tackled its accounts, which are best described as complicated and multi-layered, that by the early 1680s he was the most senior official after Robert Blackborne the secretary, and was already paid more. Beyer came in at a time of fast expansion of Company trade, when it was obvious that an overhaul of the accounting system was urgently required. The office work was reorganised, various officials were demoted, more assistants were appointed and the better ones paid higher salaries.[37] One of these new men whom Beyer brought in was John Holland, initially paid £40 in 1684, later promoted to be an accountant dealing with cotton imports and by 1692 receiving £60.[38] Beyer subscribed £5,000 to Bank of Scotland at exactly the time the East India Company were turning their attention to destroying the Company of Scotland. Another of Beyer's appointees, Edward Bannister, by 1695 the storekeeper for the island of St Helena, paid in £11,000. An official from the Admiralty Secretary's office, Phineas Bowles, also subscribed.[39]

The expertise represented by Francis Beyer and John Holland cannot be overestimated. What they succeeded in doing was to reorganise their books with suitable checks and balances and to make book-keeping central to the decision-making of the East India Company. This meant that a truer picture of the trades could be advised to the secretary and the court at a critical time in the history of the Company. Beyer continued to

35 The story is well told in G. P. Insh, *The Company of Scotland Trading to Africa and the Indies* (London: 1932); also J. Prebble, *The Darien Disaster* (London: 1968).
36 IOL, MSS, East India Company, Minutes, B/41, f. 6, 17 May 1695; Beyer was brought out of partial retirement in spring 1695, 'the Court taking into consideration the present state of the Company affairs', and appointed to examine every facet of the accounts from India and at home, and much else besides. Initially offered £500, which was twice the salary that the next highest-paid official received, he asked for £600, and received it: f. 7, 21 May 1695, f. 8, 24 May 1695.
37 Beyer's work can be followed in the Court Minutes: IOL, East India Company, Minutes, B/35, 1678–80; B/36, 1680–2; B/37, 1682–4; B/38, 1684–7; B/39, 1687–90; B/40, 1690–5; B/41, 1695–9.
38 Captain Philip Holland, his father, served in the Cromwellian navy and was deprived of his command on the Restoration. During the second Anglo-Dutch war, he joined the Dutch and was one of their pilots during the attack on the Medway in 1667 in which the English fleet was burnt at anchor. John Holland appears to have been educated in the Netherlands and returned to London by 1682; A. Cameron, *Bank of Scotland 1695–1995: A Very Singular Institution* (Edinburgh: 1995), p. 19.
39 IOL, MSS, L/Accountant general/1/19 Ledger H. Bowles purchased china and lacquered chests at Company sales.

counsel his replacement as Accountant General after May 1692 when he took a partial retirement; although when the problems of the Company deepened, Beyer returned. He was refused leave to retire a second time after sorting out the accounts and his recommendations for dismissals being accepted. Beyer re-employed John Holland after May 1695, and their achievements redounded to Holland's credit. One of George Watson's correspondents, the London firm of Kincaid and Pitcairn, praised his abilities: 'nobody knows [John Holland] better than John Pitcairn or has better reason to speak well of him as the best deserving man in a nation both of common sense, honesty and good breeding, he has been a long time truly the balance that adjusted the East India Company . . . and made them to go right'.[40]

John Holland's aptitude for commerce and accounts was only part of the story; the main reason why he was appointed as Governor of Bank of Scotland appears to have been his ability to deal with political quagmires, although the exact sequence of events which preceded his appointment is unclear. It has been suggested that he may have proposed certain of the clauses for the original Bank Act.[41] From the time he arrived in Scotland in March 1696, he took a leading role in the political fight between the East India Company and the Company of Scotland.[42] As will be shown, John Holland made quite certain that the latter received minimal support from the Bank; this created enemies in Scotland, but, as it transpired, more than probably saved the Bank from an early demise. For his payment, he suggested either 6 per cent for twenty-one years from the profits, or 10 per cent of the profits after 12 per cent had been paid to the adventurers on their paid-up capital.[43] It was this latter which was accepted.

The establishment of Bank of Scotland addressed several of the gravest weaknesses in Scottish economic life which became more prominent after 1688. The most serious concerned the availability of sufficient cash in coin or good commercial paper to use for taxes, for government payments and for internal trade. While we cannot be precise about how grave this problem was, it affected all estates of Parliament and most of those who subscribed to the Bank. The position of the tax-collection system was particularly serious by the summer of 1695, and it then deteriorated further. The rate of interest was far above the legal maximum by the date of foundation – some funds raised by the Scottish Privy Council cost 15 per cent – and the available stock of good coin in Scotland was depleted for export to England as the recoinage crisis of 1695 and 1696 worsened.

40 SRO GD 277, Box 14, Bundle 8, 18 April 1696, Kincaid and Pitcairn, London, to George Watson.
41 F. W. Ogilvie, 'Who Promoted the Bank of Scotland in 1695?', Scottish Historical Review, 23 (1926), 234–5.
42 This is discussed in Chapter 2 below.
43 Malcolm, The Bank of Scotland, p. 19.

Bank of Scotland offered a constructive way forward based upon the issue of a paper currency, denoted as 'ticquets' or 'bills' by Parliament payable in coin or other acceptable paper on demand. This was the most significant and talked-about support given by the Bank to the Scottish economy. These notes were to be given out at a lower rate of interest than the prevailing rate in Edinburgh; the Act fixed this at 6 per cent, though after his arrival in Edinburgh John Holland brought the level down to only 4 per cent. The intention was to provide support for tax-farmers, landowners in general and their factors, merchants and lawyers, but also others who could meet the required demands for adequate security on lands or by guarantees from family or associates (known as cautioners).

For the tax-farmers, the Bank came at a critical time when receipts were well short of estimates and the local areas with which they dealt were already desperately short of coin – a situation which worsened after the Bank opened its doors. Bank loans enabled the tax-farmers to pay receipts in paper and return the coin, in various ways, to the local economy. If the government and tax-farmers could maintain the fiction that bank paper was really one step away from good coin of an intrinsic worth in silver or gold equal to the face value, then the economy would benefit along with the government. This in turn required the suppliers of the government, in particular the brewers and victuallers for the army and fortresses, also to accept the paper. Finally, if the Bank was so managed that it could not pay cash in the early years, then it would suffer the same fate as a number of other experiments in paper in Europe at the close of the seventeenth century. Fortunately for Bank of Scotland, most borrowers had a real interest in the maintenance of the value of the paper; if the paper collapsed and was returned, their own loans would be recalled. Moreover, a number of loans were made to lawyers and merchants in Edinburgh who then lent on to others at a higher rate of interest. Thus a new network of credit rapidly spread out from the doors of the Bank.

Alongside the loans and paper in Scotland came the remittance trade between London and Edinburgh and between London and Amsterdam. All the subscription collected in London and probably most of that in Scotland was earmarked for use in this trade, which, as noted above, was intended to deliver cash in one or other place at below the costs charged by the private money-exchangers. The one perennial complaint of remitters of cash across the Border was about the cost involved, though at the time of foundation this had fallen somewhat following the temporary rise in value of the pound Scots.[44] It is also possible that a number of borrowers

44 For this, see below, Appendix 3.

and adventurers had in mind the raising of a bank loan which then freed their own coin reserves for export to England.

There were, it is necessary to emphasise, serious political reasons why Bank of Scotland had to succeed. The Bank derived broad support from a large number of the nobility, the landed gentry and others active in opposition to James VII, namely those who had fought to remove him in 1688. For these families, the victory of the Revolution was a matter of survival; they were used to fighting, and most possessed armouries and travelled, even in Edinburgh, with armed retainers, guns, swords and hunting dogs. Many had relatives who had been executed by the Stewart regime; they often had personal experience of exile and sequestration of estates; and they had lived in fear of death. What they lacked was not valour, but cash. This Bank would help them, and, in return, the nobility closest to the board of directors proved to be of immense benefit to the Bank for over a century, although on several occasions, as will be made clear, they were not as successful as they would have liked to be.

CHAPTER 2

THE CRISIS OF 1696–7

T HE OPTIMISTIC afterglow from the passage of the Bank of Scotland Act had faded by the time the adventurers elected the first board of directors on 14 February 1696. The economic portents were gloomy; the boom which had encouraged the economic legislation of 1693 and 1695 was over. The harvest of 1695 was seriously deficient, and the winter of 1695–6 was harsh. By the time the Bank opened its doors on 27 March, the collection of taxes was seriously in arrears[1] and, by the late spring, famine was spreading across the country. In early July, John, Lord Belhaven, and David Boyle of Kelburn (later Lord Glasgow), both directors of the Bank and tacksmen of the inland excise, warned the Privy Council that the consequences of so 'many people falling down dead' would be a further shortfall in receipts.[2] Gold and silver drained out of Scotland to pay for grain and other imports and to fuel currency speculation in London. To make matters worse, there was a deepening financial crisis in England over the deterioration of the English government finances and the effects of the English recoinage. These damaged the creditworthiness of London bankers and created difficulties for London-based Scots. In financial and economic terms, the directors could not have chosen a worse time, on both sides of the Border, to open for business.

The Bank was also faced with a potentially dangerous threat provoked by the launch of the Company of Scotland trading to Africa and the Indies (known at the time as the Africa company and to posterity as the Darien company). To deal with this, the new board required all the political expertise it could muster. In December 1695, the English Parliament

1 SRO E 7/8, Treasury Registers, p. 400, 17 March 1696; p. 411, 3 April 1696. The cess and excise taxes raised £2,727,881 Scots from 1 November 1693 to 1 November 1695, but only £1,921,911 from 1695 to 1697.
2 SRO E 7/8, Treasury Registers, p. 446, 6 July 1696.

19

arraigned the London directors of the Company of Scotland on charges of high treason for infringement of the monopoly of the East India Company. A number of London-based Bank of Scotland adventurers were involved with the trading company; if the Bank was seen to help, it might suffer as well. By the end of January 1696, the London directors of the Company had either made a grovelling apology to Parliament (which most did), or fled. This was not the end of the story, but the episode had the interesting legacy of strengthening the position of those Bank adventurers who insisted on an accommodation with London institutions. At some point around this time, the Edinburgh subscribers agreed to appoint John Holland, the ex-official of the English East India Company, as the first Governor.

Lack of adequate state political and legal protection proved an immense hindrance to the safety of goldsmiths and private banking after the repudiation of government debts in 1671 by Charles II in what became known as 'the Stop of the Exchequer'. This fear of the majority of those in court circles continued to frustrate the development of banking on both sides of the Border right up to 1688. It was no accident, therefore, that it was the city fathers who invited William of Orange to enter London. Commercial and government banking required a benign political atmosphere, and it was a widely-held opinion in the City that William would be more sympathetic to finance and banking. As we saw in Chapter 1, Bank of Scotland possessed excellent political connections, with major political and legal figures as subscribers and directors. Their men controlled several of the main fortresses of the country. The nobility and gentry among the adventurers possessed over fifty other castles, fortified houses and blockhouses; their estates amounted to hundreds of thousands of acres. They could raise numerous cavalry and foot-soldiers from among their tenants, and moved around the country with small armies of retainers; they dominated many offices of state and tax commissions. Bringing in the East India Company confirmed that they were prepared to go a long way to guarantee a political framework for the Bank. Yet mastery of the commanding heights of high politics was not enough; running a successful bank required the addition of rigorous business methods in which day-to-day business was governed by commercial criteria.

The directors launched two areas of banking operations. The debates in Parliament had outlined the benefits of credit creation, and their primary concern was to start lending to tax-collectors, landlords, merchants and others as soon as possible. The provision of a currency of banknotes, the 'ticquets' of the 1695 Bank Act, was intended as the main form that this new credit creation would take, with the gold and silver from the subscription as a reserve. They also agreed on a remittance trade across the Border to London and over to Amsterdam. The experience of the merchant subscribers gave the new board sufficient knowledge to organise this trade; it was highly technical and produced good profits for several years. The common form of accounts for lairds and aristocrats held by Edinburgh agents covered advances of cash and goods with balances settled at one or more of the four payment terms of Whitsunday, Lammas, Lady Day and Martinmas. For reasons which are unclear, but which may be because of an unsatisfactory legal position, it was decided not to compete with Edinburgh agents by instituting similar accounts. The Bank instead favoured the more formal lending by bond and by bills of exchange. Again, previous knowledge of directors was sufficient to weigh up creditworthiness, strict rules were laid down for loans, and, for example, all directors concerned with any particular loan had to vote in favour, otherwise the request was refused.[3] The difficult part was the essential core of the new banking system, the issue of banknotes in Scotland far beyond what could be immediately changed with the cash base in Edinburgh. This was to be a distinctive contribution of Scottish banking, and it was carefully watched elsewhere in Europe. As part of the discussions which followed the passage of the Act, several burghs urged that branches should be established. The directors arranged for offices at Glasgow, Montrose, Aberdeen and Dundee, although their early optimism for these was to fade in the face of the difficulties of the economic and political crisis.

European practices showed that limited banknote operations could be successful, but gave few clues as to how Bank of Scotland directors could organise the huge issue which they had in mind. Many bankers, including the London private banks, issued notes akin to 'dock warrants' against sums lodged, though their use tended to be closely tied to deposits at their London offices. None of the well-known names of northern Europe, for example, the Bank of Amsterdam or the Hamburg bank, issued banknotes payable to the bearer.[4] The former was really a storehouse of treasure which ran a simple book-keeping system by which merchants could make book transfers between each other. Probably the most sophisticated paper systems operated in Italy, but such notes as the *biglietti di cartulari* of the Bank of Genoa were also based on huge holdings of coin and goods. The Bank of Sweden, known as the Palmsbuch bank after its original projector of 1656, started an issue of banknotes in 1661, but with only a small gold and silver base. Unfortunately, the notes were soon over-issued,

---

3 For rules on lending, see below, Appendix 4.
4 A. Andreades, *History of the Bank of England* (London: 1909), ch. 3; Sir Albert Feavearyear, *The Pound Sterling: A History of English Money*, 2nd edn, revised by E. V. Morgan (Oxford: 1963), pp. 107–8; E. F. Heckscher, 'The Bank of Sweden in its Connection with the Bank of Amsterdam', in J. G. van Dillen (ed.), *History of the Principal Public Banks accompanied by Extensive Bibliographies* (The Hague: 1934), pp. 161–99; J. G. van Dillen, 'The Bank of Amsterdam', in ibid., pp. 79–124.

and in 1668 the Swedish Diet had to nationalise the bank. Sweden then returned to a coinage based on copper, of which it had considerable natural supplies. In 1695 came a short-lived attempt by the flamboyant Bergen merchant and official administrator of trade, Jørgen Thormøhlen, to issue paper, limited to the west and north of Norway. Thormøhlen's wealth came from St Thomas, the Danish colony in the West Indies, and the northern staples of coal, fish, timber and foodstuffs.[5] Along with other Bergen merchants, he had suffered losses at sea and persuaded the Danish king that a note issue, to a maximum of 100,000 rix-dollars with a royal seal affixed to each numbered note and signed by himself and two royal officials, would encourage recovery. After the issue of 21,000 rix-dollars' worth, the system collapsed and Thormøhlen spent many years trying to repay his debts.

Then came the example of the note issue from the Bank of England which began in 1695. It first issued 'sealed bills' to the value of £1,200,000, of which £480,000 was given to the government as 40 per cent of the original loan. The bills not paid over (£720,000) were then available for commercial business. Its second type, known as 'running cash' notes, became the ordinary banknote without interest; in November 1697, Parliament was informed that £694,527 4s 5d worth were at that time liabilities on the bank. There were also £68,669 6s 1d of 'specie notes', and, on two-thirds of this sum, for notes above £20, interest was payable.[6] By that date, the directors had £1,657,996 10s 6d outstanding on the three types of bills, with £17,876 owing in interest. By the time Bank of Scotland started to issue notes on Tuesday 1 April 1696, the Bank of England was the only note-issuing institution in Europe whose paper substantially exceeded the available cash base. By this time, its notes had fallen to a slight discount against their sterling face value, and this grew rapidly worse. The experience of London goldsmiths who also issued notes based on deposits may have been a model for the London directors of Bank of Scotland when they decided to issue their own in London. Perhaps £2 million sterling of goldsmiths' notes circulated in England by 1695, and their use may have increased at the time of the English currency crisis of 1695 and 1696. The exact form of the London Scottish notes is unknown, and circulation ceased by 1698.

It is reasonable to suggest that all these issues of paper may have encouraged the acceptance of a paper currency in Scotland. But this did not give

5 A. B. Fossen, *Jørgen Thormøhlen, Forretningsmann, Storreder, Finansgeni* (Bergen: 1978), ch. 4, Nedgang og Fall 1693–1708; examples of these notes survive in the Mint Cabinet, Historical Museum, Oslo; a reprint is in Fossen, p. 151; a lengthy discussion is in A. Nielson, 'De authoriserde pengsedler i det nordenfjeldske norge 1695–1696', *Bergens historiske Foreningsskrifter*, 33 (1927), 41–91.
6 J. H. Clapham, *The Bank of England. A History* (2 vols, Cambridge: 1944), vol. i, 1694–1797, pp. 43–4.

sufficient operational guidance to Scots. The late seventeenth-century pamphlet literature was sparse on the *detailed* workings of banknote operations.[7] Most of these amounted to little more than common sense; ideas on banks were similarly opaque. The proposals for a Scottish land bank of 1693 came into this category: they gave the appearance of a rational method but unfortunately left too many questions unanswered for Parliament to allow a large-scale monetary experiment.[8] There were a number of schemes in the American colonies which deserve notice, although it is doubtful whether these ventures had any influence on events in Britain. In 1685, a merchant in Quebec issued cards to stand in for eventual payment. Similar schemes followed, with government officials endorsing the cards, which circulated at par.[9] Captain John Blackwell, a financial official under Oliver Cromwell, and who later served as a Deputy Governor to William Penn of Pennsylvania, worked on a scheme for a bank of credit, but this failed to materialise, although details were printed in London in 1688.[10] In 1691, the Massachusetts Colonial Government authorised a paper circulation of £40,000, because of a shortage of coin. Both the English and Scottish Parliaments in 1694 and 1695 vetoed the suggestion that banknote issues should be legal tender; in the London case, the goldsmith bankers' complaint that it would hit their issue and the convertibility of notes appealed to parliamentarians as a control on over-issue. As it turned out, it was not always a very effective power where boom conditions relaxed vigilance.

Crucial to any banking operation of the scale envisaged for Bank of Scotland was a system of accounts which would show exactly the state of every penny of liabilities and assets. The managers needed a method of book-keeping which could incorporate several layers of accounts and

7 There were more extensive comments on coinage; Sir William Petty the political arithmetician, for instance, stated that coinages should accord with the conditions of trade and population and also the velocity of circulation, but without detailed guidance: Sir William Petty, 'A Treatise of Taxes and Contributions', repr. in C. H. Hull, *The Economic Writings of Sir William Petty* (2 vols, Cambridge: 1899), vol. i, p. 26. The British printed and manuscript collections on finance, coinage and banking are vast.

8 For land banks and lombard banks (which provided credit against goods), see J. K. Horsefield, *British Monetary Experiments, 1650–1710* (London: 1960), pp. 95–9. Hugh Chamberlain's land-bank proposals were considered in detail by the Scottish Parliament Committee of Trade, for which see below, Appendix 5; there are brief ideas on banks based on gold and silver, and goods deposited or pledged, in Sir William Petty, *Quantulumcunque concerning money, 1682*, repr. in C. H. Hull, *The Economic Writings of Sir William Petty*, vol. i, pp. 466–7; and J. K. Horsefield, 'The Duties of a Banker, I: The Eighteenth Century view', in T. S. Ashton and R. S. Sayers (eds), *Papers in English Monetary History* (Oxford: 1953), pp. 1–15.

9 A. M. Davis, *Colonial Currency Reprints 1682–1751* (Boston, MA: 1910; repr. New York: 1964), pp. 24–6.

10 'A Model for erecting a Bank of Credit with a Discourse in explanation thereof, adapted to the use of any trading country where there is a scarcity of moneys, more especially for His Majesty's Plantations in America' (London: 1688), repr. in Davis (see note 9 above).

show daily changes in cash balances, interest charges and the formal legal state of claims on assets. Once established, the core of the system was labour-intensive: all operations were entered as they happened in cash books and other draft books, and the transactions were forwarded to a summary listing in the journal books and then logged under appropriate heading in the final ledgers. This basic scheme, which became immensely complicated, was supplemented with other account books and papers, files of correspondence and letter books, bills of exchange and bonds, a mass of legal papers, a separate set of books for changes in adventurers' stockholding, and books for minutes. Within a few years, the office was 'awash with paper' and the first complaints surfaced of overwork from Bank clerks.

The Bank was fortunate in securing the services of professional accountants and auditors: George Watson operated a cohesive accounting system for his private business, and we have mentioned John Holland's contribution to the East India Company.[11] The system had to be reasonably accessible; that is to say, a check at random on any item could be followed through all the books by a director not working in the office, or for example, at the triennial balance of books. Ease of access was especially important for identification of loans which could be reclaimed speedily at time of crisis. By and large, the book-keeping methods met most criteria from their beginning.

Efficient book-keeping should indicate the changes in trend for the perennial problem for the pre-industrial bank manager: the management of the ratio of banknotes out to recallable assets (short-dated loans and bills), coin, bullion and goods. However, it could not indicate what that ratio should be. Those directors who were Edinburgh merchants brought to the board their experience of seasonal patterns, or what we would now recognise as primitive time-series studies – and, above all, the caution necessary for a banker. A thorough grounding in the Old Testament was common to seventeenth-century Scottish Episcopalian and Presbyterian education alike. It offered excellent counsel; few successive years were alike, and great disasters struck at random. The characteristics required were summed up with the Scots word 'canny', which implied far more in the late seventeenth century than it did in later devaluation by English commentators.[12] Prudence, sagacity, attention to detail, refusal

11 It should be noted that the earlier of George Watson's account books mixed up household and commercial affairs, and some items mentioned in his correspondence were not included in the accounts. There were improvements as his business expanded.
12 In the first edition of the *Oxford English Dictionary* – J. A. H. Murray (ed.), *A New English Dictionary on Historical Principles*, vol. 2 (Oxford: 1893) – 'canny' was still imbued with 'qualities considered characteristically Scottish', though English commentators had already undermined its precision south of the Border. The word was probably imported from Scandinavia by the early seventeenth century;

to be swayed against one's better judgement in order to be part of the crowd, equal treatment for all, scrupulous honesty: these were the essential characteristics which the Scottish pre-industrial ethos passed on to later generations.

The use of what may appear rather high-minded terms to describe the characteristics which bankers required extends a step further when we look at the overall management of the Bank in the early years. It was designed to operate as a team. From the arrival of John Holland in Edinburgh on 18 March 1696, the main decision-making group at the regular meetings of directors comprised William Erskine (Deputy Governor), Lord Ruthven, Sir John Swinton, Sir Robert Dickson and a group of Edinburgh merchants and lawyers, namely Robert Blackwood, John Marjoribanks, John Watson, Robert Innes ws, James Smollett and George Clerk and his son. David Spence (Secretary), James Marjoribanks (Treasurer) and George Watson (Accountant and Book-keeper) signed all the notes. This was the group charged with the launch of banknotes payable to bearer to be given to borrowers, the 'general good' of which would 'tend to the accommodation' of the areas in which the notes circulated.[13] There had to be a general consensus, and difficulties were caused when several of the group veered towards the Company of Scotland in May 1696.

This inner group kept secret the details of note issue, lending or cash; certain of the summary totals were omitted from the main double-entry account-book series except in an audited snapshot every three years. Details of the daily cash balance and notes in circulation have not survived for this period. If some part of the loans was paid in coin or foreign currency, we cannot tell from the surviving ledgers. Two types of notes were printed: the most important were those payable to bearer at the Bank of Scotland head office or branch whence they were issued; these were given to most borrowers. The second were notes intended as a payment from one town to another with Bank branches, or within Edinburgh; these 'premio' notes were similar in nature to the modern Post Office postal orders.[14] The name of the payee was inserted and a small charge was levied. The design for both notes was executed in Scotland and printed on local paper. The main series were issued to the Treasurer at the face value of £125,000 sterling and indicated that the directors expected a high paper-to-cash ratio; with a maximum coin-holding in Edinburgh of only £6,666 13s 4d, they prepared for a gearing ratio of almost 19.[15]

on the religious contribution to Scottish development, see G. Marshall, *Presbyteries and Profits: Calvinism and the Development of Capitalism in Scotland, 1560–1707* (Oxford: 1980).
13 BS 1/149/1, Letter Book, to Aberdeen trustees, 22 May 1696.
14 BS 1/149/1, Letter Book, 29 May 1696.
15 They intended to issue £100 banknotes × 400 (£40,000); £50 × 1,000 (£50,000); £20 × 600 (£12,000); £10 × 1,600 (£16,000); and £5 × 1,400 (£7,000), a total of £125,000 sterling.

Fraud was not expected to be a serious problem. Notes were numbered and signed by the Secretary, Treasurer and Book-keeper; when given out, they were cut along the left-hand margin and the matching stub and details kept by the Bank.[16] This 'check-book and record are so excellently adapted to one another . . . that no forgery or falsehood of notes can be imposed upon the Bank, for any sum of moment, before it is discovered'.[17] Scotland was too socially cohesive for passers of forged notes to escape detection; it was usually possible to trace back the holders of notes to the original source. Most convicted forgers of Scottish banknotes and their accomplices in the pre-industrial era were hanged, banished or transported to the West Indies.

The smallest circulation of Bank paper came from the 'premio' notes, and they disappeared before 1700. Second came the bearer notes circulated by the four branches: £3,000 worth, mostly in denominations of £5 and £10, were sent to Glasgow, £4,000 to Dundee, £3,000 to Aberdeen and £3,000 to Montrose. Each issue was organised by the local trustees, though how loans were made is unclear. Initial demand in these four towns was brisk, and requests were made to have the notes payable at any office. Unfortunately, the premio notes and bills of exchange in which branches dealt were in greatest demand for payments at Edinburgh. Thus, if notes payable to bearer were allowable for payment outwith the town of issue, they would have gravitated to head office and the object of increasing local circulations would have been defeated. Down to mid-July 1696, circulation posed few problems: 'the credit of the bills, as fast as they were issued out, obtained to a degree beyond expectation and the Bank had universal applause'.[18]

The most substantial part of lending came in the form of bank loans on heritable or personal bonds formally granted to individuals. Many loans were for groups of tax-collectors and to families of whom several members were involved. The Bank laid down strict regulations. Aspiring borrowers on land were obliged to give a true account of the value of the estate, prior infeftments, apprisings, adjudications, inhibitions and registrat hornings, 'at least that [the] estate is free to a third part above the sume he looks to borrow'.[19] The Bank officials then searched the

16 They were similar to Jørgen Thormøhlen's Norwegian banknotes of 1694.
17 Richard Holland, *An Historical Account of the Establishment, Progress and State of the Bank of Scotland* ([Edinburgh:] 1728), p. 7.
18 John Holland, *A Short Discourse on the Present Temper of the Nation with respect to the Indian and African Company; and of the Bank of Scotland. Also, of Mr Paterson's pretended Fund of Credit* (Edinburgh: 1696), p. 6.
19 See below, Appendix 4; BS 1/5, Minutes: General rules, 9 April 1696. Andrew Fletcher of Saltoun criticised the early lending policy of the Bank as part of the attempt to establish a rival in 1705: see NLS, MS 17498.

Register of Sasines, that wonderful Scottish record of landownership and encumbrances wherein every claim on estates had to be recorded. If they found further encumbrances, no loan was granted. Bonds were also granted on personal security (up to a maximum of £500) and against commodities such as linen and timber; these required two cautioners to guarantee the repayment. The interest charge was fixed, at the insistence of John Holland, at only 4 per cent (2 per cent below the legal maximum), although the real rate of interest in Edinburgh at times reached 15 per cent. John Holland surmised that this rate would gain the Bank support among the Scottish establishment and be viewed favourably by a Scottish Privy Council wrestling with low tax yields and high wartime costs. Failure to pay the interest (usually within thirty days of either of two law terms per year) led to a 2 per cent penalty from the date of the most recent payment or, where not applicable, from the start of the bond. On every £1,000 of banknotes lent, there would be a minimum yearly return of £40; a circulation of £50,000 would have raised £2,000 and more than paid for start-up costs and the first year's administration. There was some appreciation at this time of the connection between the provision of the paper currency and the lowering of the rate of interest:

> there can be no other way of lowering of interest of money, than by making it more plentiful and this I say is really done by the Bank, the money of the nation being artificially multiplied by bank bills and that this is not at all an imaginary but a real multiplication of money is evident, if we consider that so much of the current money of the nation, as is necessary for the making of payments between man and man, is in effect so much dead and lost stock to the place.[20]

In the four months to the end of July 1696, the Treasurer paid out £25,846 in forty-five loans, of which thirty-one were for personal bonds, totalling £9,580. The average on personal lending was thus a little over £300, whereas that on land (£16,266) averaged above £1,160.[21] One heritable bond was even on plate, for £500 to the Earl of Strathmore, recently released by the Privy Council from prison,[22] but these were usually granted only after a search of the registers. There were two ways of looking at the balance sheet of the Bank at the end of the first four months. The conventional way would balance liabilities (that which has to be paid) and

---

20 Anon., 'A Letter to a Member of Parliament concerning the Bank of Scotland and the lowering of Interest of Money' (Edinburgh: 1696); the author reiterated the point that bank money increased the velocity of circulation.
21 BS 1/94/1, General Ledger; BS 1/5, Minutes, 1696.
22 SRO PC 4/2, Privy Council Minute Book, 1696–9, order to set the Earl of Strathmore at liberty, 17 March 1696. The Earl later borrowed £80 from the Company of Scotland on the security of his subscription thereto: RBS EQ/9/1, Africa Company Minute Book, 1696–8, p. 153, 6 October 1696; he was unable to repay the Bank, and told the directors to sell the plate.

assets (on which the bank has a claim). In the event of crisis, however, some additional assessment of how quickly liabilities would be met was required.

At this date, the Bank had liabilities in notes of approximately five times the holding of coin, well under the forecast ceiling but still posing a potential problem.[23] The claim of £25,846 plus interest at 4 per cent (on the assets side of the balance) was largely illiquid, and return would require the cooperation of the borrowers. Legal distraint was politically out of the question. In an emergency, banknotes might be saleable for cash, though as James Foulis discovered in London, this would involve a discount. The experience of the Scandinavian banks and the Bank of England by June 1696 showed that, once confidence in paper had fallen, it was difficult to recover. Indeed, on 6 May 1696 the Bank of England suspended cash payments. The inescapable conclusion was that a panic return of notes would force calls on the adventurers.

As mentioned, the 1695 Bank Act forbade formal loans to the government unless underwritten by Parliament. This ensured that the relationship of the Bank to the Scottish government would be different from that of the Bank of England to the regime in London, for which the greater political uncertainty north of the Border must be held accountable.[24] Nevertheless, it was fortunate for Bank of Scotland that the loan book involved considerable support for government officials and tax-collectors, negotiated in the prescribed fashion, as personal loans on bonds and with cautioners where the loans were not on land. At least twenty borrowers and cautioners had some connection with the Exchequer tax-collection system; for example, those named as Commissioners of Supply in the 1695 six months' supply on land included Lt-Colonel John Erskine, Governor of Stirling Castle and the Commissioner for Stirling, who borrowed £2,400 on land, John Glass of Sauchie (also Stirling, £350), Sir John Gibson of Pentland (Edinburgh, £2,250), William Cochran of Kilmarnock (Ayr, £1,700) and £500 for Lord Yester, a Commissioner for Fife. Several of the tacksmen of the 1693 and 1695 poll tax, and their later fourteen co-partners, turned into direct collectors in 1695 and borrowed from the Bank, as did two of the four financiers who bought the second tack of the 1695 poll tax, Sir John Houston of that Ilk (£500) and Sir Robert Dickson of Sornbeg (£200). Patrick Murray, the collector of the cess for

---

23 BS 1/5/3, Minutes; liabilities consisted of £25,846 in loans, as above, plus approximately £3,500 in banknotes remaining out at the four Scottish branches.
24 P. G. M. Dickson, *The Financial Revolution in England: A Study in the Development of Public Credit 1688–1756* (London: 1967), chs 3 and 4, for discussion of heavy discounting of tallies and Exchequer bills and slowness of payments in general after 1689; this is confirmed by many private sources. The records of Coutts & Co. discuss the difficulties of Scottish regimental agents reliant on the London Treasury for payments.

Midlothian, borrowed £200. Several office-holders were lent to, including Viscount Tarbat (£400), who signed the Bank charter on behalf of the Crown.

At least three groups of Edinburgh merchants involved in tax-collection, or in underwriting the same, borrowed up to the maximum allowed on personal bonds. Robert Blackwood the elder first took £300, then paid it off and was advanced £500; he also acted as cautioner for James Blackwood and Company (£500). The Marjoribanks family and the associates of George Clerk the younger acted similarly as both borrowers and cautioners. Outside Edinburgh, other syndicates operated in a similar way, including that of Sir John Home of Blackadder, George Home of Kimmerghame and Sir David Home of Crossrig, who together took £500 on two loans.

In several cases, such as that of Sir John Erskine, Sir William Bennet the elder and his son Sir William Bennet of Grubbet (Commissioner for Roxburgh), the borrowers held several state offices in the army and in the fortresses; all military payments were in serious arrears by the summer of 1696. While an exact breakdown is not possible, at least half of the total lent on bond in the first ten weeks (to 12 June) went to those involved in tax-collection or state offices. Office-holders also made extensive use of the Bank for remittance of cash to and from London. Several borrowers were involved in the supply of military goods including Robert Anstruther of Wrae (granted £200) and the directors of the Edinburgh Linen manufactory, six of whom were holders of Bank stock, who received £500. A few loans were made to landowners who wished to consolidate previous loans at a lower rate of interest; into this category came John Byres of Coats (£3,166 13s 4d), who wanted to clear his estate of all encumbrances and establish the Bank as sole creditor. Three loans were made to women: Lady Hiltoun (£100), Dame Bethia Harper (£1,000) and Dame Magdalen Kinloch (£150).

The Bank lent mainly to persons who had considerable wealth in land, property, minerals and rents, but also to those for whom cash flow was a serious and worsening problem. It was not just that new opportunities were available, such as the investment in the Company of Scotland whose own subscription opened on 28 February, but also that, for various reasons, money was tighter in 1696 than it had been a year earlier. The available coinage was to be squeezed still further as agricultural conditions deteriorated in the worst dearth for fifty years. This did have one positive result for the Bank: it was in the interest of borrowers that their loans remained out, and in everyone's interest that nothing reduced the acceptability of the banknotes. In this, the original holders, as befitting their station in the Scottish establishment, appreciated that if they panicked on rumours about the Bank's liquidity they would only damage the government, themselves and their friends. Bank of Scotland directors explained at a number of meetings in August 1696 that a run on the cash reserve would force them to request repayment of loans. The use of high-value notes may have helped to stave off a run; few £50 or £100 notes came back in 1696. They were mainly used for tax payments and in the rest of the government system or for remittances to and from Edinburgh estate factors. Some stability may thus have been imparted by the restricted market for this paper.

The remittance-of-funds trade merits a brief comment. In April 1696, when congratulating George Watson on his appointment as book-keeper and accountant, John Pitcairn singled out this 'something to facilitate payments' and the proposed 'fund of credit to supply want of money' as the hallmarks of the Bank.[25] The exchange trade was high-risk, and even in quiet times it ran with high margins to cover against unexpected coinage and exchange fluctuations. Bank of Scotland directors intended to operate on low margins and a high volume. By the end of April, the court had formed a subcommittee to deal in exchange, and it later agreed a fund of £4,000 to cover bills.[26] Yet, by the spring of 1696, all sorts of problems encouraged caution: uncertainties remained about the supply of coin in London, Bank of England notes were depreciating against sterling, and ominous rumours suggested that the Company of Scotland might be interested in its own exchange and banking trade. There was also disagreement over the correct method of drawing bills, in particular how to specify the method of payment.

In November 1696, when the financial and political situation was more subdued, the trade was restarted by George Clerk supervised by a subcommittee. The Bank agreed that bills which he bought and sold through his private business were to be offered to this committee, 'at such a rate as he hath or shall negotiate ... and no ways be applicable to his or any other personal behoof until the committee refuse them'. Nor was he to buy cheaper or sell dearer on his private account, for which he was to receive a commission of ¼ per cent. The London exchange committee was to receive ½ per cent. In addition, James Foulis and James Marjoribanks were allowed to transact bill business provided that they observed a daily rate of exchange laid down by each committee.[27] Under no circumstances would the Bank grant letters of credit.

The four months to the end of July 1696 provided most of the income and the losses of the first financial year (ending 27 March 1697). On the

25 SRO GD 277, Box 14, Bundle 8, 18 April 1696, John Pitcairn to George Watson.
26 BS 1/5, Minutes: 30 April, 28 May, 12 June 1696.
27 BS 1/5, Minutes: 6 November 1696; BS 1/149/1, Letter Book, 12 December 1696.

debit (costs and losses) side of the profit and loss account, there was a loss of £83 8s incurred when the Scottish Privy Council lowered the Scots coin by 12 per cent in June 1696. Fortunately, inside information from Councillors enabled the directors to minimise the loss.[28] The Bank also lost £163 4s on the English recoinage. The costs of keeping the office, the salaries and weekly payments to directors came to £1,518 14s. On the credit (income) side came £183 6s, from shares forfaulted and resold, gains from the London exchange trade of £108 14s, and £34 8s from premio bills. By far the largest profit came from £1,025 on the interest from lending on bonds. The profit and loss account thus showed a balance of £1,765 7s, with a net loss of £346 10s, but the real situation was somewhat worse. £366 13s 4d of interest was due to the Bank but unpaid; in fact, every account was underpaid and on three bonds nothing had been received. If the Bank had followed the accounting convention apparently in use by some London private banks, and not credited unpaid interest, the loss would have been £713 18s.[29] The Bank's accounts also omitted the £1,111 2s 2½d paid to Lord Pitmedden for his stone tenement in Parliament Close wherein the offices were sited from July 1696. This turned out to be a poor investment, as fire destroyed the uninsured tenement in 1700. The Bank secured temporary offices in the High Street and then moved to Pearson's Close, Lawnmarket, where it remained for the next century.

The banknote issue by Bank of Scotland was under threat by the summer of 1696. The lesser danger was the gradual fall from par value of the notes of the Bank of England. The figures listed on Table 2.1 are, in the main, the values reported to Edinburgh at the time. The earliest falls coincided with the peak of note issue in Edinburgh and at the branches, and, by the time Bank of Scotland stopped new lending, the slippage had reached 8 per cent. The price of guineas (in sterling) was rising and the cross-border exchange was (temporarily) at par, but no-one could be certain where these three indices would go next. The deterioration in Bank of England notes sapped confidence in paper. The group of London financiers who were to control the early years at the Bank of England, which included John Houblon (the Governor in 1696) and Sir Stephen Theodore Janssen, were at first clear that a joint-stock bank not involved in commodity trade 'could hardly hope to carry on without the "custom of giving notes" payable to A.B. or bearer', as the goldsmiths' notes now

---

28 BS 1/149/1, Letter Book, letters to trustees in Dundee and Montrose, 21 May 1696; for figures, see Statistical Appendix, Table A1.
29 Provision for accruals of interest was omitted from several London bankers' accounts in the late seventeenth century: see B. S. Yamey, H. C. Edey and H. W. Thomson, *Accounting in England and Scotland: 1543–1800* (London: 1963; repr. New York: 1982), p. 193; in the disturbed conditions of this time, there was much to be said for not crediting unpaid interest.

Table 2.1 *The London exchange on Scotland, values for guineas and the discount of Bank of England notes as reported to Scottish merchants, 1695–7*

London exchange on Scotland		Values for guineas		Discount of Bank of England notes against sterling	
March 1695	3.5%	5 January 1695	22s 9d to 23s		
April 1695	4–5%	7 March 1695	24s 6d to 25s		
9 April 1695	2.5–3%	9 April 1695	25s		
22 February 1696	2–3%	1 June 1695	29s to 30s		
3 March 1696	2%	15 February 1696	27s		
28 March 1696	1.5–2%	22 February 1696	24s to 25s		
23 May 1696	par	28 March 1696	22s		
6 June 1696	par	3 March 1696	24s	20 June 1696	6–7%
13 August 1696	par	18 April 1696	21s 6d to 22s	6 June 1696	7%
3 October 1696	3%			14 July 1696	8%
				13 August 1696	11%
				20 August 1696	14%
				5 September 1696	14%
				3 October 1696	17%
				November 1696	13–16%
				4 February 1697	19%
				11 May 1697	19.5%
				10 July 1697	14.5%
				24 July 1697	11%

Source: SRO GD 277, Box 14, Bundle 8, Miscellaneous correspondence to George Watson, 1696, mainly from John Pitcairn and Michael Kincaid, London.

mostly were. Yet, a year later, Janssen was sufficiently chastened by the experience of the fall from par that he questioned the whole basis of the Bank of England note issue; the continent was right, he wrote, and London was wrong.[30]

A major political danger came from the formation of the Company of Scotland and especially from William Paterson, a leading projector therein whose influence increased over the subscribers in the course of 1696. Paterson's background included trade in the Americas and the West Indies, several brushes with the Spanish Empire and various collaborations with buccaneers preying on Spanish trade. He had tremendous energy which carried him through a succession of difficulties and the ultimate disaster of the Darien adventure. In 1694 he was among the projectors of the Bank of England, but he fell out with the main financiers and failed to be elected to their board. With other projectors, he tried to reorganise the City of London Orphans' fund (also in 1694), but ended up in bitter disputes with the City Chamberlain. Paterson was regarded by the persons in charge of these institutions as a crook, and by the time of the Company

30 Clapham, *The Bank of England. A History*, vol. i, p. 16, citing Sir Stephen Theodore Janssen, *A Discourse concerning Banks* (London: 1697) [GL 1742]; Janssen suggested that issuers of paper money would have to follow the continental experience of a close match of paper to deposits of gold and silver.

of Scotland project he and his group had made numerous enemies.[31] The basic problem with Paterson's ideas was their attempt to include in already grandiose schemes hidden agendas for schemes that would make himself and his friends wealthy. In the case of the Company of Scotland, as early as June 1695 he advised the move into banking and was furious when he heard of the foundation of Bank of Scotland. This did not stop him from persuading the London proprietors of that Company to establish a 'fund of credit' or loan facility offering loans to subscribers before the English subscription was complete.[32]

When William Paterson fled London after charges of treason were laid against him by the English Parliament, he arrived in Edinburgh in January 1696 a hero. The toast of Edinburgh society, 'whatever was offered to him' to further the aims of foreign trade 'is received with applause, without any inquiry into the truth'.[33] The grateful Company directors showered him with favours; a present of £15,000 in cash followed in May. What little influence the Bank directors had on the Company of Scotland had waned by this time; new elections for a board of twenty-five directors saw only ten with Bank shares.[34] Some of these, including Robert Blackwood, Sir Robert Dickson of Sornbeg and Sir John Swinton, began to argue that Paterson's vision of unbounded wealth was attainable and that the Bank should fund the Company. When Paterson announced his banking operation in mid-May 1696, the split with the Bank was complete and several directors ceased to attend the Bank court.[35]

John Holland's position as Governor of Bank of Scotland was undermined by persistent rumours. It was suggested that he was 'a spy from the England East India Company', which paid him a pension or fee, and that he had accepted the post of Governor of the Bank in order to thwart the Company of Scotland.[36] By early June, he had decided that the accusations had to be answered publicly. Holland was entirely open about his continuing links with the East India Company: 'from my first being here, in all companies I came into, I declared that I was sworn to the *English*

---

31 S. Bannister (ed.), *The Writings of William Paterson, Founder of the Bank of England*, 2nd edn (3 vols, London: 1859; repr. New York: 1968), contains a record of Paterson's life. None of his entourage in London was wealthy; they were among the projectors who swarmed around Whitehall and the City in the war years, and Paterson was one of the cleverest of these 'second-rank' men. One of his colleagues was Paul D'Aranda, a founder of the Royal Bank of Scotland, for whom see below, Chapter 5.
32 J. H. Burton (ed.), *The Darien Papers: being a Selection of Original Letters and official Documents relating to the establishment of a colony at Darien by the Company of Scotland trading to Africa and the Indies 1695–1700*, Bannatyne Club, vol. 90 (Edinburgh: 1849), p. 5, 15 August 1695; *House of Commons Journal*, vol. 9, p. 404, 27 November 1695.
33 John Holland, *A Short Discourse*; p. 10.
34 RBS EQ/9/1, pp. 5, 32–3: 24 March, 12 May 1696.
35 Ibid., p. 46: 18 May 1696.
36 John Holland, *A Short Discourse*.

East India Company; that so no man might talk anything before me, that he thought I would or could take an advantage of against their Indian and African company, and I have and ever will pay all manner of respect to that Society'.[37] He accused Paterson of misleading the Scots about the financial organisation of the East India Company, and of crooked intent in his relations with the Bank of England, the Orphans' fund and the London subscription of the Company of Scotland. In June, however, nothing could affect Paterson's standing, and the Company of Scotland proceeded with his banking scheme. Perhaps not surprisingly, John Holland decided to return to London.

The directors of Bank of Scotland closed at least two routes by which they might have aided Company of Scotland. By mid-May, they had scrutinised the trade connections of all loan applicants.[38] Subscribers to the Company were ruled out and existing borrowers warned that if their notes were returned by Paterson for cash they would be pressed for repayment and denied further assistance. On 18 June, a general meeting of Bank adventurers was called to ratify a stop to most new lending.[39] Faced with a deterioration in their coin stock, the directors asked James Foulis to send north his surplus from London. Unpaid bills of exchange at London were also sent back and payment demanded in Edinburgh; the first legal action followed shortly afterwards.[40]

On 26 June 1696, the first banknotes of the Company of Scotland were distributed to borrowers who applied to its Edinburgh office and at agencies in Glasgow, Aberdeen, Dundee, Montrose and Dumfries.[41] By 16 July, so many Bank of Scotland notes had been returned for cash that the sad decision was taken to order the branches to return as much cash as they could to Edinburgh. Aberdeen was told to ship £900, Montrose to send £400 to Dundee and Dundee £1,200 to Edinburgh. John Bethune, the Glasgow cashier, was asked to attend in person with £1,000 in coin.[42] Two days later, the directors wrote in some panic to John Holland that 'a great deal of noise has been made here . . . about the business of our Bank, and we understand there are formed designs to break us, and so far advanced as that emissaries are dispatched by the African company', whose job was to substitute their notes for those of Bank of Scotland which were then presented for cash in Edinburgh.[43] Rumours abounded

37 Ibid., p. 13.
38 BS 1/5, Minutes, p. 26: 21 May 1696.
39 BS 1/5, Minutes: 18 and 25 June 1696.
40 BS 1/5, Minutes: 1 July 1696; the first action was against Henry Mein, though he was able to find more security against payment: ibid., 13 August, 24 December 1696.
41 See Appendix 6 for the banking operations of the Company of Scotland.
42 BS 1/5, Minutes: 16 July 1696.
43 BS 1/149/1, Letter Book, 18 July 1696.

that 'there is a design to surprize us by calling for their money all at once'. Here, then, were the ingredients for a banking collapse: uncertainty about the stability of paper money, a tiny cash base and undisguised enmity by a well-organised enemy.

On 6 August, after a clear instruction from John Holland, the adventurers voted for a call of another 20 per cent, though they disguised this as a 'loan', after the practice of English government departments, with 6 per cent on sums outstanding at six months. Whereas the quarterly payment term of Whitsunday (15 May) had passed without difficulty, pressure built up at Lammas (1 August).[44] Several merchants at the linen cloth fair and a number of bondholders who were importing corn presented banknotes, as did William Paterson. The Edinburgh Lord Provost and his officials, who ought to have behaved more responsibly, followed suit. After this municipal example, the shopkeepers and petty traders in possession of £5 and £10 notes panicked.

The call of 20 per cent from adventurers gave 'a disappointment to all the designs formed against us'; £13,332 came into the Edinburgh office mostly in coin, and by the end of August the worst of the crisis was thought, mistakenly, to be over.[45] The call in London faced the problem of the 'public calamity of want of money' following the recoinage of the silver currency in 1696, and it took until the end of the year to collect their 20 per cent.[46] The London office also sold some of its issue of banknotes and bills of exchange, 'at as small a loss to the Company as possible', though part of this was really a loan from London adventurers.[47] Early in September, George Clerk the younger agreed to pay in £1,416 10s at Martinmas (11 November), drawing on the London office for a credit in banknotes.[48]

The crisis of July and August 1696 forced the Bank to utilise all its political connections and reorganise the board. Francis Beyer, the Auditor General of the English East India Company, was confirmed as a director in London in August (although all directors there were now called trustees). Beyer remained on the London board for the next two years. In July, at the height of the hysteria around the Company of Scotland, the Edinburgh directors of the Bank met William Paterson and others from his board.[49] The cash position of the Company was vastly superior; it had over £50,000 in its chest at that time. The Bank's delegation

44 By Acts of the Scottish Parliament, 1690 and 1693, the four quarter days for payments were fixed as 2 February (Candlemas), 15 May (Whitsunday), 1 August (Lammas) and 11 November (Martinmas).
45 BS 1/149/1, Letter Book, 4, 8 and 20 August 1696, letters to James Foulis in London.
46 BS 1/5, Minutes: 3 December 1696.
47 BS 1/5, Minutes: 20 August 1696.
48 BS 1/5, Minutes: 10 September 1696.
49 BS 1/149/1, Letter Book, 18 July 1696.

was significant, with James Smollett, the Commissary Court judge, Lords Halcraig and Rankeillor of the Court of Session, Hew Dalrymple, and Deputy Governor William Erskine. George Clerk and James Cockburn represented merchant expertise. It was a symbol of the range of powers which the Bank could muster, and 'nothing resulted' from the meeting.

Where they could, the directors played for time. Tedious negotiations opened with the Privy Council over problems with the old merk and half-merk coins, which had the effect of reminding their Lordships of the public service involved with the Bank's notes.[50] Lord Anstruther, of the Court of Session, and the later Lord Boyle were sent to 'discourse' with John, Lord Murray, eldest son of the first Duke of Atholl and one of the Secretaries of State.[51] We have already noted the addition of a dozen 'extraordinary' directors on 6 August which increased the political, military and legal strength on the board.[52] A further round of talks with the Company began on 27 August 1696.[53]

In early October, when the finances of the Bank deteriorated for a second time, London directors were sent a copy of the Edinburgh cash book to show how serious the situation was.[54] By 17 October, the Bank was 'altogether out of cash' and was only saved by 20,000 merks borrowed from Sir George Gordon of Haddo, the Earl of Aberdeen, and 6,000 more from an Edinburgh merchant.[55] Various costs were cut, including fees to directors (temporarily abolished), and two tellers were dismissed.[56] Serious though this was, by the autumn the political context had shifted in favour of the Bank. It was gradually realised by the political establishment that if William Paterson broke the Bank, it could have widespread ramifications which would include adverse effects on tax-collection. The Bank subscription would remain called up until borrowers repaid their loans. In turn, this would affect further calls for the Company of Scotland as the demands for money passed through the system. Moreover, by September it was clear that the harvests had failed more disastrously than in 1695, and great numbers of the rural poor were crowding into the towns. This meant that gold and silver would be required for grain imports. A meeting of London merchants made it plain in December to John Haldane of

50 SRO, Privy Council Register; BS 1/5, Minute Book, no. 1: 16 July 1696.

51 BS 1/5, Minutes: 13 August 1696.

52 See above, Chapter 1; see also C. A. Malcolm, *The Bank of Scotland, 1695–1945* (Edinburgh: n.d. [1948]), pp. 302–3 for a list of directors at this time.

53 RBS EQ/9/1, Africa Company Minute Book, 1696–1698, 14 September 1696; both Lord Ruthven and Hew Dalrymple represented the Company of Scotland at these talks, and both by then supported the Bank's caution.

54 BS 1/149/1, Letter Book, 3 October 1696.

55 Aberdeen had refused to take the oath of allegiance to William and was jailed for a time in Edinburgh Castle; 26,000 merks at the rate of exchange of 11:1 would have yielded £1,575 16s sterling.

56 BS 1/149/1, Letter Book, 12 November 1696.

Gleneagles, sent by the Company of Scotland, that the clash was a matter of great concern.[57] The Scottish landowners, tax-collectors and merchants, on the brink of the worst subsistence crisis for fifty years, needed Bank of Scotland.

By December 1696, the Company of Scotland was in difficulties of its own. From mid-July, its surplus cash had begun to diminish as payments exceeded income. It became clear that huge sums would be required for payments abroad for ships, guns and supplies. The issue of its own banknotes was stopped by early October and was followed by an urgent search for economies among staff, for its banknotes were returning to deplete the reserves required for trade. Thus the banking operations failed. William Paterson then had another ill-considered idea. He proposed to pay for supplies and ships purchased in the Netherlands by drawing bills of exchange on London because, he argued, the English–Dutch exchange was bound to move in favour of London. If this was organised 'in-house', it would save the commission costs. This led to a Flemish contact of his, James Smyth, receiving and embezzling £17,500, making a loss by the end of the year of nearly 20 per cent of their paid-up subscription, £8,500 of which was lost forever. Paterson's role in this business was never satisfactorily explained.[58]

These political conflicts made a deep contrast with the complexities of everyday business, which led to an inevitable separation between the titled directors and the commoners. The ordinary directors were to work on the basis of a weekly rota for daily business, whereas the extraordinary directors comprised the front line of political and legal influence. Thus there was less need for the nobility, judges and gentry to attend the board meetings when routine business was transacted, but they would be mobilised when their particular expertise was required. These important people, a number of whom made it clear by their show of power and wealth that they were indeed very important, had many other duties within the Scottish establishment. The role of coordination between the two groups fell to those ordinary directors and, as it turned out, to the Deputy Governor, who were closest in the social hierarchy to the higher estates. This was especially the case when legal disputes required adjudication by the Court of Session. The really significant political crises were of course the stuff of everyday discussion, and the directors had a wide range of these informal links to lawyers, with factors being widely used. This intelligent

---

57 NLS, MS 1914, Company of Scotland Letter Book, ff. 18–19, 2 December 1696: John Haldane was in London as the representative of the Committee of Foreign Trade of the Company.
58 The figures given for this fraud vary; those in RBS EQ/9/1, The several Journals ..., 1696–8, 22 December 1696, show total payment to Smyth of £16,997; the extent of Paterson's other financial mistakes is covered in Appendix 6.

and flexible division of the board remained a hallmark of Bank of Scotland for almost 300 years, and with only a few exceptions has served a valuable purpose in its contrasts.

By the close of 1696, it was clear that Bank of Scotland had survived, though only with guarantees and support from the government and the nobility. The directors then had some hard choices to make, and the branches were gradually wound down. Aberdeen and Montrose closed in December 1696, Glasgow the following month and Dundee in 1698. Nevertheless, this setback should not obscure the progress made. The directors had launched a note issue and a new trade of lending, and had increased their financial credibility with their refusal to fund William Paterson. 'It has been a hard beginning', noted one director; but at least their position had been publicly vindicated and they could now look forward to an undisputed role in Scottish banking.

CHAPTER 3

FROM THE DEARTH TO THE UNION, 1697–1707

BY 1697, Bank of Scotland was faced with the consequences of a second year of harvest collapse, accompanied by a sharp rise in food prices and export of coin to cover imports. In the two years from 1695, prices of grain increased by as much as 110 per cent depending on the area affected, which resulted in widespread starvation and a flood of desperate rural poor into the towns.[1] In 1697, prices moderated a little, but in 1698 and 1699 they rose to new heights.[2] Though precise figures do not exist, large numbers of the population died from starvation and disease. The dearth had serious consequences for rural incomes; many tenants failed to produce a surplus. Thus not only did Scottish burghs suffer the social problems of an influx of rural beggars, but also their tradesmen endured the effects of diminished rural purchasing power.[3] This weakened urban economy had to cope with an increase in the level of poor rates. Corn price levels remained high until 1700, and in some areas they took a year longer to settle down. This was the worst famine in Scotland since the end of the 1640s and was dubbed in Jacobite propaganda the 'seven ill years' of King William.[4]

The famine inevitably affected the Bank in ways which reinforced caution in lending. Its borrowers suffered because their expected incomes,

1 W. Ferguson, *Scotland: 1689 to the Present*, The Edinburgh History of Scotland, vol. iv (Edinburgh: 1968), pp. 78–9; T. C. Smout and A. Fenton, 'Scottish Agriculture before the Improvers – An Exploration', *Agricultural History Review*, 12 (1964), 73–93, Appendix: East Scottish Bread and Grain Prices; R. Mitchison, 'The Movements of Scottish Corn Prices in the Seventeenth and Eighteenth Centuries', *Economic History Review*, 2nd series, 18 (1965), 278–91.
2 Figures for Fife, Haddington and Aberdeen oats and Fife barley show 1698 and 1699 as worse than for the first three years of the famine: Smout and Fenton, 'Scottish Agriculture', Appendix, p. 92.
3 H. M. Dingwall, *Late Seventeenth-century Edinburgh: A Demographic Study* (Aldershot: 1994), ch. 8.
4 P. Hopkins, *Glencoe and the End of the Highland War* (Edinburgh: 1986), p. 438; T. S. Ashton, *Economic Fluctuations in England and Wales 1700–1800* (Oxford: 1959), p. 16, refers to the 'eight barren years' before 1700.

from land, taxation or from government offices, declined. It was a particularly difficult time for the army officers who had borrowed from the Bank: their falling incomes coincided with the sharply rising costs of feeding their men. The crisis began to affect companies founded in the boom years, as well as traditional burgh merchants and lowland lairds. The Edinburgh and Leith victuallers and brewers were involved as early as the autumn of 1695;[5] out of forty-seven Scottish joint-stock companies in operation or founded between 1690 and the end of 1695, only a dozen appear to have survived to 1700.[6] There was a sharp increase in the number of persons indebted to the New Mills textile company, and a mass of complicated legal proceedings enveloped Scottish trade as people desperate for money tried to extract payments from their buyers.[7] Before the end of the financial year 1696–7, the position of bank loans looked grim; the directors had failed to persuade any borrowers on bond to repay their loans whether originally made for trade, agriculture or as a support for tax-gathering. This situation continued into the subsequent financial year, with a number of tax-gatherers, including Patrick Murray, collector of the cess in Midlothian, refusing, or unable, to repay.[8]

The stop to Bank lending in July 1696 led to a power struggle within the Bank. The opposition group was led by Sir John Home of Blackadder, Sir Robert Dickson of Sornbeg and Robert Blackwood, who wished to mobilise Bank support for the Darien trading scheme. They gained some support from persons who wanted bank loans to tide them over the dearth. The cautious parties who had masterminded the policies of the first financial year were led by the Earl of Leven and George Clerk the younger and, of course (from August 1696 in London), John Holland. Both groups presumably appreciated that the consequences of the agricultural crisis were a weakened economy, a lower stock of coin and precious metals, and a tax system and government finances under strain – and this in a Scottish political context which was less favourable to William III than at any time since 1690. They knew that the potential loss on the Bank profit and loss account exceeded the stated figure. The conclusion of the cautious group was that, while becoming profitable depended in part on economic and taxation circumstances beyond their control, there was

5 Excise charges were waived for some victuals destined for the military; this alleviated one problem but reduced incomes for the collectors.
6 W. R. Scott, *The Constitution and Finance of English, Scottish and Irish Joint-Stock Companies to 1720* (3 vols, Cambridge: 1910–12), vol. i, p. 356; these included Lord Yester's paper works, the Darien Company, Bank of Scotland, four companies associated with wool, two linen companies and several joint stocks established for sugar refining, and other food processing, in Glasgow.
7 W. R. Scott (ed.), *The Records of a Scottish Cloth Manufactory at New Mills, Haddingtonshire, 1681–1703*, Scottish History Society Publications, vol. 46 (Edinburgh: 1905), p. xlvii.
8 BS 1/5, Minutes: 1 July 1697.

much that the Bank could do in the future to limit exposure to adverse forces. The Bank elections for Governor and directors in March 1697 were a decisive vindication for prudence. The Governorship went to the Earl of Leven, 'born and bred an enemy to the [Stewart] royal family and [who] . . . cheerfully embraced and significantly promoted the Hanoverian succession, the Union and everything against its interest'.[9] He defeated Lord Belhaven (closely associated with the Darien), Lord Carmichael, the Earl of Panmure and Lord Ruthven. William Erskine also stood, but was seriously ill and died within a month. Within a few years, Leven was re-elected annually by acclamation, and he kept the post for over thirty years until his death in 1728. His Governorship epitomised the Presbyterian ideal of the cautious approach to lending and discounting. He was also remembered as a kind and humane figure. As Governor of Edinburgh Castle, he was 'rather very civil to all the Cavaliers especially such as were prisoners in the castle . . . from whence he gained more of their favour, than any man in the Government'.[10] George Clerk the younger was appointed Deputy Governor, beating off challenges from his father (another Darien supporter) and James Smollett; Home of Blackadder and Robert Blackwood polled three votes and one vote respectively.[11] Why they managed quite such low figures is unclear, though it may denote a concerted attempt by the opposition to elect George Clerk the elder. The extraordinary directorships went to the aristocracy, military officers, the gentry and the Lords of Session, the class of office-holders and men of high status who would be needed in a crisis, with the ordinary posts going in the main to Edinburgh merchants.[12] All the aristocrats defeated for the Governorship were elected directors. The importance accorded to the participation of the judges cannot be underestimated, and within a few years directors' meetings were fixed for three o'clock after the Court of Session closed.[13] It may be appropriate to note that Sir William Binning, the Governor of the Edinburgh Linen Company, was soundly defeated for the post of Deputy Governor, though not because of any Darien

9 George Lockhart of Carnwath, *Memoirs concerning the Affairs of Scotland from Queen Anne's succession to the throne to the commencement of the Union of the two kingdoms of Scotland and England in May 1707*, St Andrews University archives, ms DA. 805 M2 (old ref. BN. 3.77), p. 48, from an original of 17 August 1714, and later translated from the French mss in 1810. The attribution to Lockhart is given by J. Kennedy, W. A. Smith and A. F. Johnson, *Dictionary of Anonymous and Pseudonymous English Literature*, vol. iv (London: 1928), p. 47; the Memoir was certainly written by a supporter of the exiled Stewarts.
10 George Lockhart of Carnwath, *Memoirs concerning the Affairs of Scotland*, p. 48.
11 The figures were, for Governor, Earl of Leven 460, Lord Belhaven 175, Earl of Panmure 81, Lord Ruthven 24, Lord Carmichael 21, William Erskine 18; for Deputy Governor, George Clerk Jr 531, his father 156, James Smollett 64, William Erskine 24, William Binning 17, Home of Blackadder 3, Robert Blackwood 1: BS 1/149/1, Letter Book, 3 March 1697.
12 BS 1/5, Minutes: 18 March 1697.
13 BS 1/5, Minutes: 4 July 1700.

association; with several Edinburgh merchants and customs officers, he had been involved in defrauding the government over the import of Dutch arms in 1694.[14] Instead of keeping quiet, he named his associates, and was told by the Privy Council that the severity of their fine (£300 sterling) was a warning not to bring public officers into disrepute in like cases.[15] There were parallel elections in London for thirteen trustees; those re-elected included Francis Beyer and John Holland.

Although the adventurers voted to endorse caution in March 1697, the Governor and his supporters had to justify their approach, in particular the burden of the extra 20 per cent subscription. To provide for profits, the directors inevitably had to lend and discount well above their meagre holdings of cash. The profit and loss account for 1696 showed that remittance of money to and from London, along with the Scottish premio bills to and from branches, and a small foreign and Scottish bill of exchange account had yielded a profit for the Bank which was both 'real', in the sense that coin and notes were lodged in the Bank chest, and a quick return for the investment which could be calculated in advance. Premio bills turned over within a few days, remittance on London usually within ten days and most bills within two months. The premio bills were, however, reduced with the closure of the branches, and disappeared in the course of the financial year 1697–8. The new board was thus left with two avenues for new earnings: the *remittance of money* by means of foreign bills of exchange between Edinburgh, London and Amsterdam, and lending against *inland bills of exchange*. Both had good potential for growth, and would alleviate the immediate cash-flow problem for the Bank while the directors coordinated a longer-term lending policy. These were to prove significant sources of profit in the first few years of bank operations until longer-run lending on bonds at low rates of interest could be restored.

In 1696 and 1697, the Bank tried to pay bills of exchange in London using Bank of Scotland banknotes. Once the Bank of England notes returned to par, in 1697, few in London wanted Scottish notes. James Foulis then returned ten books of £10 notes and ten of £5 to Edinburgh, and later the plates, presses and stamps used for Bank of Scotland notes in London.[16] Thus ended note issue in London, though Scottish notes continued to be accepted in payments by Scottish merchants and bankers in England. This forced Foulis back on the traditional task of the exchange dealer, weighing up the intrinsic values of coin, working out the market

---

14 For details, see above, Chapter 2.
15 SRO E 7/8, Treasury Registers, p. 510, 23 April 1697; Sir Thomas Kennedy was fined £800 st. and Baillie Brand £500 st. They were convicted on Binning's evidence, though other conspirators appear to have avoided fines. Binning received seventeen votes.
16 BS 1/5, Minutes: 1 September and 6 October 1698, 2 February 1699.

value of paper offered, and hoping that receipts would cover all the costs of payment in Edinburgh and make a profit.

The Bank accounts show an early (net) profit to 1697 on the exchange trade of £106; encouraged by this, the directors on both sides of the Border agreed to employ an agent in Amsterdam, Adam Cossiga, to conduct transactions there.[17] This gave Bank of Scotland a strong position in one of the main markets where Scottish merchants traded. The next results (1697–8) were also positive, as profits rose in the London office to £219 and reached £128 on the Amsterdam exchange; in 1698–9, income was somewhat down to £105 in Amsterdam and £142 in London, but in 1700–1 the Edinburgh–London account alone made £342. These positive results concealed a serious problem. The London money market was swollen with numerous entrants who had made money in the war years, a number of whom now provided competition on the English–Scottish exchanges. In a desperate search for turnover, they cut margins to the bone. In November 1700, the Bank committee decided that Amsterdam exchange dealings should be shut down while those for London and Edinburgh should continue but 'with all imaginable prudence and caution for the Company's [the Bank's] safety'. Unfortunately, James Foulis then made heavy losses on his own account, so that by the end of the financial year 1700–1 bankruptcy proceedings were concluded against him in London and his sixteen Bank shares were sold to pay debts owing to the Bank.[18] The directors decided by 1701 that this trade was the 'most dangerous' of all banking trades, to quote Theodore Janssen, and best left to money-changers with low overheads and a high tolerance for personal stress.[19] The Bank still had to follow the exchanges and to remit money, but did not actively seek out the exchange business.

The second source of new earnings in the dearth came from a modified bill-of-exchange trade. The directors were advised by the lawyers and judges on the board that, provided that loans were organised with the usual form of the foreign bill of exchange, then a higher annual charge could be made than the legal maximum of 6 per cent under the Scots usury laws. International merchant law would be given precedence in the Court of Session, they advised, when the recognised form of the bill of exchange was instituted for the loan. It was regarded as Emption and Vendition of goods, and not Mutuum, the borrowing and lending of money. It thus

17 For the profit and loss account, see Statistical Appendix, Table A1.
18 BS 1/5, Minutes: 1 May and 11 June 1701.
19 Sir Stephen Theodore Janssen, *A Discourse concerning Banks* (London: 1697). H. Hamilton, *An Economic History of Scotland in the Eighteenth Century* (Oxford: 1963), p. 295, notes that the directors found dealing in bills of exchange 'very troublesome, unsafe and improper'; he is perhaps confusing remittance of money across the Border with bills of exchange.

required 'a sufficient drawer and two acceptors [who would include the true borrowers] to be bound conjunctly and severally', and the person to whom the bill was payable (who had paid the drawer the value) would endorse it over to the Treasurer of the Bank, who would pay the value less the interest and charges and claim the full face value at expiry. The only problem arose where advances remained unpaid at expiry (the Bank decided on sixty-day bills); in this case, further charges could only be made at the legal maximum for the country, namely 6 per cent. If the directors were unhappy with the extension of a bill, they had the option of summary process against the guarantors.

This new bill trade became most important for the finances of the Bank and for the financial markets in Edinburgh. In the financial year 1697–8, there was a small beginning at £4,752 sterling, and in the following year the volume rose to £17,170, then later to an annual average of around £35,000 down to the summer of 1704; figures of this magnitude yielded a yearly income from £600 to £800.[20] The rapid increase in this trade, not necessarily based on goods, filled a gap in short-term provision in the Edinburgh financial market, and rapidly developed as the burgh emerged from the subsistence crisis. The rates charged somewhat undercut the cost of short-term borrowing in the Edinburgh market and probably encouraged private dealers to reduce their charges. Occasional bills were negotiated at the Bank for 15 per cent, though by October 1698 the usual rate was 12 per cent for bills below £50 and 8 per cent for those above. For the first year (from November 1697), the Bank preferred bills of above £100 presumably because they were more secure, and for a few years thereafter the Bank insisted on prompt payment, although it rarely enforced summary proceedings. After 1699, with the economy recovering, the directors passed many more bills for under £100 and allowed an increasing proportion of bills to lie unpaid, with the Bank crediting itself with the interest charge of 6 per cent per annum.

While the lending on short-term bills of exchange was an important addition to that envisaged in 1695, and these could be renewed as often as required by borrowers provided that interest was settled, the fact remained that only long-term lending of large sums on bond would yield profits sufficient to justify the adventurers' investment. Throughout 1697, it was clear that many of these borrowers were in difficulty, especially tax-collectors like Patrick Murray or men in the position of Lt-Colonel John Erskine who had not received payments due for the armed forces.[21] When in April the Bank tried to reduce the total lent by £6,752, its efforts were

20 BS 1/5, Minutes, p. 109, 18 August 1698; BS 1/94/1–2, General Ledgers, inland bill figures.
21 BS 1/5, Minutes: 5 August 1697.

unavailing, and successive deadlines to Candlemas 1698 produced only minor repayments.[22] The subsistence crisis led to such a scarcity of money that although 'the debitors security be good and undoubted' it was difficult to raise 'any considerable sum of money'.[23] To complicate matters, there was uncertainty about the right of the Bank to the penalty of 2 per cent extra annualrent where the interest charge of 4 per cent remained unpaid thirty days after the term fixed for payment. In 1696, following previous practice, the eighteen-month cess upon the land rent had allowed 'every debitor owing money within the kingdom at 6 per cent of interest . . . in the payment of his arents' for the term of the tax to have it reduced to 5 per cent, provided that the same was paid towards taxes.[24] As hundreds of pounds were at stake, the Bank presented a bill to the Court of Session in June 1697 craving their opinion whether the Bank Act and later rules would allow annualrent of 6 per cent, 'notwithstanding the burden of retention imposed . . . by [these] subsequent Acts'.[25] The Bank pleaded that it was a society founded by law, with the privilege of making by-laws, and the 2 per cent was 'but like a penalty or termly failing in a bond' and could not be accounted usury. For the debtors, Patrick Murray disputed his 2 per cent on £200, arguing that 'private pactions cannot derogate from the public law' and therefore he was liable for only 5 per cent as per the statutes; otherwise there was nothing to stop the Bank, or any other, from charging 7 or 8 per cent.[26] Their Lordships were divided on this point, and a majority found that the whole six was due, 'not as annualrent but as damages liquidated betwixt the parties'.

The depressing response to the recall of old loans and the continued economic crisis held up new initiatives. Apart from a loan of £2,300 to the poll-tax collectors in April 1697, it was more than a year before a resumption was made in July 1698 to advances on bonds, which, incidentally, coincided with the first Darien expedition.[27] New, tighter rules were imposed for lending on personal bond: the loan spread was fixed at £300 sterling to £500, annualrent payment terms were to start at six months from the date of the loan, with a basic rate 25 per cent above the 1696 rate, at 5 per cent, and a full 6 per cent would be payable if payments were thirty

---

22 BS 1/5, Minutes: 22 April and 18 November 1697.
23 BS 1/5, Minutes, p. 127, 30 March 1699.
24 'Act anent the supply of 18 months cess upon the land rent', *The Acts of the Parliaments of Scotland*, vol. 10, p. 25, c.1; this policy had long existed under Scots law and was confirmed after the Revolution (APS, vol. 9, p. 236b); tax statutes of 1698 and 1700 also allowed a one-sixth or one-twelfth abatement.
25 BS 1/5, Minutes: 17 June 1697.
26 William Maxwell Morison (ed.), *The Decisions of the Court of Session*, vol. xxxviii (Edinburgh: 1801 edn), p. 16,419, 'Usury' case no. 23, 23 July 1697.
27 BS 1/5, Minutes: on 13 August 1697 the Bank agreed in principle to lend £500 to any three tacksmen of the customs not already bound to the Bank.

days overdue after the term. Instead of one principal and two cautioners, there now had to be three co-principals, an easier position from which to demand repayment.[28] In November 1698, the Bank converted all 1696 loans to 5 per cent, with a 1 per cent penalty unless they were returned by Candlemas 1699, and restricted heritable lending to sums under £2,000.[29] The inland bill-of-exchange trade and the new start to lending on bond were altogether easier to organise than the remittance trade or the foreign bill trade. It also meant that most of the business and the attention of directors was now focused on Scotland. Perhaps because of these changes, the number of London resident proprietors declined.

This appraisal by the Bank directors of the stresses involved in lending coincided with a reassessment by members of Parliament and the Privy Council of the boom of the years 1693–5. The crisis had revealed serious weaknesses in the conditions which affected the accumulation of wealth and the level of activity in trade and industry. A smaller number in Parliament and on the Privy Council went further and came to the conclusion that the surface problems were manifestations of serious structural shortcomings in the lowland economy which specifically Scottish remedies would be unlikely to solve; their conclusion to this was the necessity of a complete economic union with England.

The Parliament session which opened on 21 May 1700 allowed both 'schools' to voice a platform through petitions signed by considerable numbers of local lairds, burgh merchants and, to a lesser extent, the nobility. Their common threads were 'the sensible decay of trade both at home and abroad' and foreign prohibitions which hindered the passage of Scottish linen and wool cloth (the French were singled out as particularly unhelpful over cloth, coal, salmon and herring). Scots coin was 'carried out by the importation of commodities from places where ours are prohibited', and Scotland was isolated over the settlement at Caledonia (on the Darien peninsula), which 'may now too probably a second time fall'.[30] Several lowland burghs mentioned the continuing crisis in agriculture and the dislocation caused by the multitude of destitute poor, and a few, including Stirling and Perth, complained of the depredations from marauding Highland bands. In general, more support was demanded of the government, both in positive measures for manufactures and by prohibitions on imports. The underlying economic problems were raised in Parliament again during short-lived negotiations in 1702 on a treaty of union with England and again after the financial crisis of December 1704.[31]

28 BS 1/5, Minutes, pp. 106–7, 27 June 1698.
29 BS 1/5, Minutes, p. 127, 30 March 1699.
30 APS, vol. 10, Appendix p. 36, 27 May 1700; and see later petitions to this session.
31 Ferguson, Scotland: 1689 to the Present, pp. 37–8.

These 'whither Scotland' debates were fraught with grave implications for the Bank. As was to happen at regular intervals in Scottish financial history over the next 150 years, the expression of economic and industrial problems led to schemes designed to expand the medium of exchange and the level of credit. The legacy of the subsistence crisis meant tight credit and shortage of coin, and from several areas the tax-collectors reported an extension of barter. A comprehensive scheme for a new paper currency was championed in Parliament in 1700, the basis of which would have been notes to the value of £300,000 sterling, in units from one shilling to £100, in part acceptable for tax purposes. This 'state' paper would be distributed among the royal burghs in proportion to their tax liabilities; burgh taxpayers would receive and pay in these notes, though exactly how this would affect their debtors in turn was uncertain, and one-tenth of burgh obligations to government could be paid thus. As the notes returned to the Exchequer were to be destroyed, it was unclear how the government would benefit.[32] It was a familiar scheme for easing debt, with many precursors and the temptation of non-cancellation and over-issue. Also in 1700 came another version of Hugh Chamberlain's land bank; its obvious attraction for penurious lairds at a time when news of the first Darien disaster reached Scotland ensured that it would be taken seriously. The land-bank ideas surfaced a third time via his Scottish partner James Armour in 1702.

The Bank answered these threats on two fronts. In response to the coin shortage, it was dec' ' ' that the issue of small notes of various denominations below £5 could be 'a great advantage to the Bank' and 'convenient for the nation'; the Bank would conserve the stock of coin and avoid arguments at the counter about intrinsic values.[33] John Holland suggested brass coins (not a new idea), presumably in the nature of tokens, and wooden tallies; but both suggestions were dropped because of fears of counterfeiting. This was not an idle worry; counterfeiting of coins remained widespread in Europe, and at this date the Bank had its first case of altered notes which forced it to reissue the entire stock with separate designs for each denomination. The Earl of Leven organised an effective obstruction to Hugh Chamberlain's proposed land bank in the Parliament of 1700, by pointing to the depreciation of the paper which might follow on from any difficulty with convertibility and ridiculing the high fees which he demanded.[34] However, with the gradual recovery of trade and an increase in lending, the demands for new paper credit subsided.

32 Scott, *Constitution and Finance*, vol. iii, p. 260, citing SRO PA 7/17/1, Supplementary Parliamentary Papers, 'Proposal for advancing Trade' (1699).
33 BS 1/5, Minutes: 9 January 1700.
34 *APS*, vol. 10, p. 53, 21 November 1700. The directors minuted their thanks to Leven: BS 1/5, Minutes: 13 March 1701.

The directors of Bank of Scotland also moderated their rules on lending. Moreover, the Bank adopted a relaxed policy to non-payment at the end of the sixty-day period, and by 1702 it was usual for the Bank to carry over a fluctuating, though growing, volume of bills beyond their expiry date. These reached over £6,000 by March 1703. The monthly average for new discounts in 1703 and 1704 was slightly below £3,000, with November and December 1703 averaging £3,941, and in the following August a level of £5,134 was reached. The upturn in lending on personal and heritable bonds was also sustained; new loans granted after 1698 and still outstanding by the end of the financial year in March 1703 amounted to over £10,000 on heritable loans, with another £22,569 of personal loans. With those outstanding from 1696, the total of all loans on bonds exceeded £40,000.[35] The Bank started the issue of £1 notes in April 1704, initially printing £9,000 worth, though it is unknown how many of these were actually issued. By this latter date, it was clear that Bank of Scotland was regarded as the provider of a widely-circulating banknote issue that was an important factor in the commercial life of the nation as well as in the finances of the government.

The increase in economic activity in Scotland from the end of the subsistence crisis to 1704 may only have restored the country to the levels seen a decade earlier. It was basically a period of recovery, but even the modest upturn exposed the serious imbalance between exports and imports in the balance of payments.[36] The outflow of coin from Scotland encouraged rumours in the summer of 1703 that the pound Scots was to be devalued against sterling, which would have had the supposed advantage of increasing exports and making imports dearer. Patrick Campbell pointed out to his Edinburgh relatives that, as such information would be well worth knowing before the public announcement, they should ask their kinsman the Duke of Argyll, who was privy to such state secrets, to give them advance warning.[37] Economic and political events south of the Border also developed a momentum which had adverse consequences for Scotland. From 1697, England experienced a sharp increase in foreign trade, and after 1700 there was a sustained building boom in London and the south. The downturn came after the autumn of 1703, when a colossal storm on 28–29 November ravaged the south coast, sank large numbers of Dutch and English ships and caused considerable inland destruction on both sides of the Channel as it progressed northwards. While the damage appears to have temporarily strengthened the demand

---

35 BS 1/94/1, General Ledger, advances on bond, March 1703.
36 This matter is considered in Chapter 4 below.
37 Coutts & Co., Letter Book no. 2, f. 11, 24 June 1703: John Campbell to Alexander Campbell and Robert Bruce.

for building materials already associated with the construction boom, the losses reinforced the impact of the war with France declared in 1702.[38] By early 1704, several Bank correspondents had noticed an increase in the cost of buying coin on both sides of the Border caused by the export of precious metals for the war effort on the continent. The continued pressure of imports for the building trades, augmented by demands from merchant and naval shipbuilding which also saw peaks in 1704 and 1705 following the storm, demanded increased facilities for credit, much of which was at rising rates of interest. For the first time in several years, in the summer of 1704, John Campbell complained to Alexander Campbell ws and Robert Bruce in Edinburgh that money was so scarce despite the droving sales that they should cease paying out cash wherever possible.[39] There were also indications that more plate and bullion than usual was substituted for coin in some payments abroad.[40] At the end of October, news arrived in London of French political and military success in Spain and of a French invasion of Germany as well as Catholic successes elsewhere in Europe. All the main London stocks – the Bank of England, the East India Company, the Royal Africa Company and the Million bank – fell 'to their lowest quotations of the year', alongside substantial demands for cash from bankers and merchants.[41] A major crisis was averted by a rise in the long-term interest rate for London bonds and by the issue of several substantial loans by the government and the East India Company which attracted back some of this cash.

In Scotland, with smaller financial markets and far less coin, the situation in the autumn of 1704 spiralled out of control. John Campbell summed up the problems as 'scarcity of money, the bad payments and the apparent [political] troubles' that threatened Scotland.[42] The difficulties with the remittance of coin from the sales of cattle and the difficulties of persuading drawers and cautioners to repay loans and bills due were evident from August. The Bank found a disturbing increase in the number of bills staying out after their repayment date, which was well above previous seasonal fluctuations. Nevertheless, the directors ignored the path of caution and proceeded to discount bills right through the autumn;

38 J. P. Lewis, *Building Cycles and Britain's Growth* (London: 1965), p. 14. There is a mild reservation as to whether 1704 and 1705 represented a real peak, or a plateau from which activity fell, though 'we can be certain that the years around this date saw a great deal of activity'.
39 Coutts & Co., Letter Book no. 2, f. 107v, 26 August 1704.
40 John Law, *The Circumstances of Scotland considered with respect to the present scarcity of money, together with some proposals for supplying the defect thereof and rectifying the balance of trade* (Edinburgh: 1705), p. 4.
41 Scott, *Constitution and Finance*, vol. iii, pp. 220–1; Ashton, *Economic Fluctuations in England and Wales*, p. 13.
42 Coutts & Co., Letter Book no. 2, f. 128, 5 December 1704, John Campbell to Campbell and Bruce in Edinburgh. Ferguson, *Scotland: 1689 to the Present*, pp. 43–4.

Table 3.1 *Bank of Scotland inland bill account, 1704–7*

Month	Total bills discounted	Month	Total bills discounted	Month	Total bills discounted
Jan 1704	2,568	May 1705	0	Sep 1706	1,245
Feb 1704	2,940	Jun 1705	0	Oct 1706	1,587
Mar 1704	3,190	Jul 1705	0	Nov 1706	1,525
Apr 1704	2,880	Aug 1705	25	Dec 1706	2,082
May 1704	2,694	Sep 1705	365	Jan 1707	1,658
Jun 1704	2,833	Oct 1705	740	Feb 1707	1,839
Jul 1704	2,542	Nov 1705	1,775	Mar 1707	1,224
Aug 1704	5,102	Dec 1705	1,409	Apr 1707	1,495
Sep 1704	2,374	Jan 1706	2,061	May 1707	2,165
Oct 1704	2,255	Feb 1706	3,265	Jun 1707	1,975
Nov 1704	2,750	Mar 1706	1,354	Jul 1707	1,932
Dec 1704	1,745	Apr 1706	2,925	Aug 1707	2,254
Jan 1705	0	May 1706	2,754	Sep 1707	926
Feb 1705	0	Jun 1706	2,146	Oct 1707	425
Mar 1705	0	Jul 1706	2,364	Nov 1707	410
Apr 1705	0	Aug 1706	1,923	Dec 1707	435

Note: Figures above show transactions, while the Minutes list authorisations, which usually differ.

Source: BS 1/94, General Ledgers.

in October they authorised the purchase of £2,321 and in November £3,297, the highest November figure to that date. Long-term lending continued, including £400 granted to the Musselburgh woollen manufactory. Whereas in 1703 a rumour had been spread that the pound Scots was to be devalued (to be worth less against sterling coin) to encourage exports, it was now rumoured that the opposite was about to happen and that the Privy Council was contemplating a revaluation of the coinage (a Scots coin would then be worth more against sterling).[43] From late November, an increasing number of the smaller notes were presented by Edinburgh merchants and shopkeepers gambling on a rise. Then rumours circulated to the effect that the Bank was unable to pay its notes. The Bank was slow to put pressure on bill repayments in the autumn; in September and October these were slightly below the level of new discounts, and in November only £2,860 was paid back, over £430 below new authorisations. Only in the first half of December did the directors heed the warning signs, as repayments of bills reached £2,161 from the 1st to the 15th. Bond repayments in the nine months before the crisis showed even slacker efforts to recover debt, with under £3,000 redeemed. Too late, on 12 December 1704, did the directors impose much tougher demands for repayments; but six days later they were forced to stop cash payments and

43 John Law, *Money and Trade Considered; with a proposal for supplying the nation with money* (Glasgow: 1750), p. 39, suggests that the rumour 'only occasioned a demand from the people of Edinburgh'.

Table 3.2 *Balance sheet of Bank of Scotland at 18 December 1704*

		£	s	d
Debit				
To Bank Bills charged upon the Treasurer p. accop. in Ledger d. fol.3	146735			
Deduct for so much thereof in the Treasurer's hands this day	95888			
Remains nett of Bills running throughout this kingdom		50847		
Ballance due to the Adventurers		12352	0	$8\frac{1}{6}$
Summa		63199	0	$8\frac{1}{6}$
Credit				
By cash in the Treasurer's hands, remaining in old Merks		1600		
By debts due upon Heritable Bond, per particular a/c, besides interest thereon		21968	6	8
By debts due upon movl. Bond, p. particulars, besides running interest as above		27682	8	$5\frac{1}{2}$
By Inland Bills, due per particular list, besides running interest		11253	16	8
By the Bank office, for the first cost of their house besides all reparations		694	0	$10\frac{2}{3}$
Summa		63199	0	$8\frac{1}{6}$

Source: Privy Council Paper, 1704.

all lending and discounting.[44] The stop on payments lasted for five months and that on discounting bills for eight months (see Table 3.1).

For the bankers, it was a salutary lesson on the limitations of paper in a financial market which, despite its sophistication, was still heavily reliant on the goodwill of a much poorer trading world than that of London or the Netherlands and far more reliant on the support of the legal profession and politicians who had other financial interests to protect. The Bank thus faced a situation which required firm government intervention. The Governor went to the Privy Council, chaired by his friend the Marquis of Tweeddale and packed by men with Bank interests, and it was agreed to issue a reassurance based on a balance sheet (see Table 3.2). The statement confirmed that in theory the Bank was able to pay all £50,847 worth of notes with the public, plus the capital and yearly profits due to the adventurers, from a credit side with over £60,000 owing from bills and bonds, and £1,600 remaining in cash. The directors called up another 10 per cent from adventurers, at 5 per cent interest, and issued a demand for repayment of all loans on both bond and bill. Holders of banknotes were to receive 6 per cent until they could be paid off.[45] Letters of reassurance were sent to correspondents within and outwith Scotland, stating that proof had been given to the Privy Council that the Bank had 'effects sufficient to pay all their bills and £12,000 over' but had been unlucky because of rumours of revaluation.[46] A meeting was held at Lancaster between John Holland and directors from Edinburgh, although it is unclear what was said.

44 BS 1/5, Minutes: 12, 15 and 18 December 1704.
45 BS 1/5, Minutes: 18 December 1704.
46 Coutts & Co., Letter Book no. 2, f. 133v, 26 December 1704.

After the stop, bill repayments rose to £3,519 by the end of December but thereafter faltered, and by the close of the financial year on 27 March bills and interest outstanding were still one-third of that owing on 18 December, which confirmed how illiquid bills could be in a crisis with no re-discount market.[47] Strenuous efforts were made thereafter to secure repayments of bonds, although this proved more difficult than for bills; of the £40,000 of post-1698 loans still outstanding at the end of March 1703, only £10,170, or slightly over 25 per cent, was repaid in the six months before the end of May 1704. The stop encouraged 'at least some' of the directors to try to 'procure ane act of Parliament appointing their notes to be taken in all payments' (as legal tender).[48] Plans were drawn up to focus a greater proportion of bank loans on the army and office-holders, moving away from 'trade and manufactures' and shopkeepers prone to panic. As it would have been difficult to stop notes moving from 'statesmen, pensioners and army' towards shopkeepers and merchants, this idea was not followed up. The notion of the Bank as a paymaster of the armed forces was also floated but not put into practice.

The difficult financial situation faced by the Bank had widespread repercussions on Scottish credit. From 18 December 1704 until the end of August 1705, the Bank bought no bills at all, and lending on bonds ceased until December 1706. Though not impossible to use for payments, banknotes proved difficult to pass in the immediate aftermath of the stop among shopkeepers and burgesses; before payments resumed on 18 April 1705, this caused serious disruption because of their previous widespread use.[49] In spite of a clear statement from the Privy Council that revaluation of the pound Scots was not under consideration, this was not apparently believed, and much of the remaining silver and gold coin disappeared from circulation. The news of the stop was received with consternation in London among those who had bills due for payment in Edinburgh or whose connections included those affected by the stop. John Campbell and Patrick Campbell used all their skills of persuasion to stop those who held bills drawn on Edinburgh from protesting about non-payment. Alexander Campbell, a bank director in private business with Robert Bruce, told their London correspondents 'not to draw any bills on them'. As the sluggish payments for the Scottish regiments by the English Treasury were partly to blame, efforts were redoubled in Whitehall.[50] Patrick Campbell was particularly concerned about the health of the Queen, whose personal order had been required for a number of Scottish payments which might

47 BS 1/94/1, General Ledger, bills of exchange, September 1704 to March 1705.
48 NLS, MS 17498, Fletcher of Saltoun Papers.
49 John Law, *The Circumstances of Scotland considered*, p. 5.
50 Coutts & Co., Letter Book no. 2, f. 144, 23 January 1704/5.

fall if she died. For several months, the crisis made 'terrible confusion and stops all business' in Edinburgh, while the cost of the cross-border remittances in January rose to 16 and 17 per cent.[51] John Campbell expressed the view to the Glasgow merchant James Walkinshaw that not only was he sorry for the 'misfortune of your Bank' but he wished that 'it had been the fate of ours' (i.e. the Bank of England), a sentiment which expressed the concern of London Scots that the Bank of England was too restrictive in its dealings.[52] As with every crisis, some benefited, including money-changers in Edinburgh and 'some people on the exchange'.

The occasion of the stop brought out very sharp criticism of Bank of Scotland. It was alleged that the directors had exported bullion on their own account; moreover, that 'being entrusted with the nation's money' they had for 'love of gain' lent it out 'never concerning themselves whether it was to stay in the kingdom or not', and so much had gone that it had 'in a manner left us beggars'.[53] Accusations were made in Parliament about the internal Bank proposals for future lending; in particular, attention was drawn to the suggestion of a closer relationship with the government, although these links were already close.[54] A host of schemes were expounded for the extension of credit. For the fourth time in a dozen years, Hugh Chamberlain, with his associate Patrick Armour, put forward a scheme for a land bank, this time suitably revised and with a timespan for redemption of only twenty-five years. Parliament was persuaded to order its printing, though it was rejected at the end of July. This was not quite the end of the proposal, as several of the committee of trade were still inclined 'to think favourably' of it, but it disappeared from view in August.[55] Another, quite different type of scheme put to the Parliament committee of trade would have involved Bank of Scotland in an issue of debased coins minted from £50,000 of plate deposited with the Bank, with a face value of £75,000. The depositors of plate would receive £50,000 of the debased coin; Bank of Scotland would retain £25,000 and on this erect £100,000 of credit. With an interest charge of 4 per cent and £1,000 going to expenses, some £3,000 could then be added to the original stock at the end of year one. After six years of compound growth, the 'cash' would be equal to £51,931 and the credit multiple £207,724.[56] This scheme,

---

51 Ibid., letters anent Scotland, f. 135v ff.
52 Ibid., f. 135, 28 December 1704.
53 NLS, pamphlets 1.349 (16), *An Essay for promoting of Trade, and increasing the Coin of the Nation* (1705).
54 NLS, MS 17698, Fletcher of Saltoun, Parliament committee of trade papers.
55 APS, vol. 11, 12 July, p. 218, 28 July 1705, Appendix p. 77, 8 August 1705; BS 1/5, Minutes, 26 June 1705; Scott, *Constitution and Finance*, vol. iii, pp. 264–5.
56 This scheme is discussed in Scott, *Constitution and Finance*, vol. iii, pp. 266–7, wherein the table of compound growth is printed.

which had the touching faith of the political arithmetic projections of the previous century, does not appear to have made allowance for the acceptance of debased coin, whether it would be inflationary, how the plate would be extracted from owners, or how it would affect the existing circulation of good coin.

Apart from Chamberlain's scheme, which may have come close to adoption, the plan which stood out in 1705 was penned by John Law of Lauriston (1671–1729), a close associate of the Duke of Argyll, appointed Commissioner to Parliament in April 1705. This was the John Law who was to become notorious as the originator of the French Mississippi speculation in 1719 and 1720. The son of an Edinburgh goldsmith, Law inherited a small estate, most of which he squandered after the Revolution in gambling in the social world of London. In 1694, he fled to the Netherlands after a duel in which he killed his adversary. While there, he studied banking, and by the time he returned to Scotland he was probably fluent in Dutch and French. In 1701, he wrote the influential *Reasons for constituting a Council of Trade*. Though it is unclear when or why he signed up with Argyll, it was probably because he was a mathematical genius, 'who has a head for calculations of all kinds to an extent beyond anybody'.[57] Other reasons attributed to George Lockhart of Carnwath, who was a Bank adventurer and the only Jacobite to sit on the 1706 negotiations for the Union, suggested that since Law inherited his estate he had

> lived by gaming and sharping and being a cunning fellow . . . found a way quickly to get into my Lord Duke of Argyll's favour and in confidence of his and the Squadrone . . . presented a very plausible scheme all the Court and the Squadrone (except some that were monied men) espoused the same because it was so found that in process of time it brought all the estates of the Kingdom to depend on the Government.[58]

John Law was able to correct the erroneous impression that banking had been invented by Catholics: 'Sweden, not Italy invented banks', and in two published criticisms of Bank of Scotland he was careful not to offend the generality of Bank adventurers; indeed, the Bank was 'a very good thing'. But he went on to argue that Scotland had insufficient money as, he asserted, only one-sixth of the £2.2 million coined in Scotland since

---

57 *Dictionary of National Biography*, vol. 11, 'Law, John (1671–1729)', p. 672, citing the Earl of Stair, who met Law in Brussels in 1715.
58 George Lockhart of Carnwath, *Memoirs concerning the Affairs of Scotland*; Lockhart was misleading about the Squadrone, who were opposed to Argyll by this time. The Squadrone Volante (Flying Squadron) was the nickname its opponents gave to the New Party, which took office in 1704: see W. Ferguson, *Scotland's Relations with England: A Survey to 1707* (Edinburgh: 1977), p. 229.

the recoinage of 1686 remained in circulation; the primary causes of this loss were the Darien adventure, the poor quality of manufactures which had damaged exports, and imports of luxuries.[59] Moreover, the Bank had encouraged coin export:

> Our Bank . . . undoubtedly gave great occasion to the export of coin for our imaginations were so blinded with the notion of there being grat sums of species in the Bank that we thought the national stock of money secure and satisfied ourselves with pieces of paper which either were readily exchanged for species or circulated amongst us upon the credit of the managers. In the meantime the exporters of money took occasion to send away whatever came to their hands.

Law added that none of his criticism was designed to discredit the Bank, though the 20-shilling sterling notes had taken away 'almost all use for money; which had then emigrated. Bank of Scotland should have kept to large notes.[60] His recommendations to Parliament were clear-cut: the Bank should be taken over by Parliament, presumably on the Swedish model of 1668, and incorporated into a new National Bank, or the Bank should be reconstructed, which would also have required a confiscatory statute. What lent his proposals authority was the power of his patron. Either would have given Argyll and his supporters considerable powers over the supply of Scottish credit. It was this fear which led to a resolution of August 1705 that 'the forcing of any paper credit [or similar] by act of Parliament was unfit for the nation'.[61] The fraught nature of relations between members of Parliament at this time was shown by an argument between Andrew Fletcher of Saltoun (who supported Argyll) and the Duke of Roxburghe (who backed the Bank). They decamped to Leith sands to fight a duel, and were about to shoot it out when dragoons, sent from the castle, arrested them.

These schemes spoke for a deep-rooted and widespread fear about credit and finance, summed up in one letter to Parliament that 'the state of this country is worse than 'tis generally thought [and though] the imaginery specie the bank furnishes us with is of great help it made the Scots less sensible how little coin was left'.[62] Most factions among the nobility and lairds in the session of 1705 had a short-term interest in Bank of Scotland

59 John Law, The Circumstances of Scotland considered; idem, Money and Trade Considered; he may have penned or advised on other tracts including NLS, pamphlets 1.349 (15), Two Overtures Humbly offered to his Grace John Duke of Argyll, Her Majestie's High Commission and the right Honourable Estates of Parliament (1705).
60 John Law, The Circumstances of Scotland considered.
61 APS, vol. 11, p. 218; Lockhart of Carnwath, Memoirs concerning the Affairs of Scotland; Ferguson, Scotland: 1689 to the Present, pp. 38–48; W. L. Mathieson, Scotland and the Union: A History of Scotland from 1695 to 1747 (Glasgow: 1905), p. 94ff.; B. P. Lenman, An Economic History of Modern Scotland 1660–1976 (London: 1977), pp. 53–6.
62 NLS, pamphlets 1.349 (11), A Letter to a Member of Parliament, concerning manufacture and trade (1704).

reopening. This was why Tweeddale, the Lord Chancellor, leader of the 'new' party and a Bank adventurer, had been quick to orchestrate support after 18 December 1704. Unfortunately for the Bank, the Argyll interest was one of the strongest in Scotland, and was growing more powerful as time passed. Within two years, Parliament had passed the treaty for the Union of Scotland with England, and in so doing ultimately enabled the Argyll interest, increasingly after 1707 in the hands of the second Duke's brother, the Earl of Ilay, to mount further pressure on Bank of Scotland.

The Bank was also caught up with the political uncertainties of Scotland's deteriorating political relations with England. William died on 8 March 1702 after a fall from his horse. By an Act of 1696, the Scottish Parliament was to meet within twenty days of the sovereign's death. Yet the Scottish Privy Council ignored this, 'most likely' to permit a declaration of war with France on 30 May 1702 which the Scottish Parliament might not have supported.[63] When Parliament convened, the Commissioner, the Duke of Queensberry, persuaded members to approve negotiations for a full union; but the English side were reticent, especially over demands for compensation for the investors in the Darien company. Although on 3 February they ended the discussion, there had been a lengthy debate on the issues involved. The most important constitutional question was the need to secure a line of succession to Queen Anne, as both her husband and last surviving child were dead. In England, Parliament passed the Act of Settlement in 1701 which recognised the right of the House of Hanover to succeed Anne.[64] In France in September 1701, James VII died and Louis XIV proclaimed James VIII as the rightful king. The Scottish Parliament refused to acknowledge either, and by the Act of Security of 13 August 1703 left the matter to a review of the general constitutional position. There were further conflicts: in September 1703, Parliament decided that if Anne died without heirs, only they could make treaties of peace or declare war, though they did agree that whoever was on the throne could order the suppression of invasions and rebellions, 'according of former laws'.[65] They also refused to raise any more taxes. As supply for the army was essential, the English ministers agreed that a modified Act of Security could pass; and it went through Parliament with few changes.[66] The English Whigs were furious and compelled Lord Treasurer Godolphin to agree to the 'Aliens' Act which passed the Commons on 1 February 1705 and the Lords on the 5th.[67] It was to run from Christmas

63 Ferguson, Scotland: 1689 to the Present, p. 37.
64 Ibid., pp. 40, 41.
65 APS, vol. 11, p. 107, c.6, 'Act anent peace and war', September 1703.
66 Ibid., p. 136, 5 August 1704.
67 Statutes of the Realm (1821), vol. 8, pp. 349–50, 3 & 4 Anne c.6: 'An Act for the effectual securing

1705 until 'the successors to the Crown of Scotland be declared and settled by Act of Parliament in Scotland'. Four crucial Scottish products, namely black cattle, sheep, coal and linen, would have been banned from England. No other product was thought important enough to prohibit.[68]

If the prohibitions had been imposed and been effective, then Bank of Scotland would have suffered by the reduction of its bill-of-exchange business, though less so for the personal remittances to and from London. The Bank might have expected a fall in income of perhaps only £200 or £300. Lending by bond would have become less attractive in the short term, as many of the lairds who took up these loans would have been hard hit by a border closure. A number of loans out would probably not have been repaid.[69]

The Scottish Parliament renewed discussion on a treaty in the summer of 1705, and negotiations were agreed on 1 September. It was left to the Queen to decide who would represent Scotland, and formal negotiations opened on 16 April 1706. These need not detain us. The financial inducements agreed at the negotiation gave clear advantages to the Bank borrowers and subscribers.[70] There was to be freedom of trade within the new kingdom, open access to the English colonies and a financial clause (number XV) which laid out the compensation to be paid by the English government to Scotland of £398,085 10s. The Scottish customs and excise taxes would rise to English levels, and receipts above pre-Union levels would go to pay other Scottish debts – this was the 'arising equivalent' which would follow the 'encrease of trade and people (which will be the happy consequence of the Union)'. This 'whole encrease of the revenues of Customs . . . and excises in Scotland over and above the annual produce shall go and be applied (to other Scots debts) for the term of seven years' and would be reconsidered for a further extension.[71] The £398,085 10s was to be applied in strict order, first to the losses which 'private' persons may sustain from reducing the coin of Scotland to the standard and value of the coin of England, then to pay off the capital stock and interest at 5 per cent

the Kingdom of England from the apparent dangers that may arise from several Acts lately passed in the Parliament of Scotland', to come into force on 25 December 1705.
68 The export of arms and horses from England and Ireland was banned, although this would have been difficult to enforce and they were easily obtainable from Scandinavia or Europe. By 3 & 4 Anne c.7, Scottish linen was banned from Ireland. There is some ambiguity in the text of the first Act as to whether cattle and sheep products (leather, skins, beef, tallow and even wool) were included.
69 For the background to these discussions, see Lenman, *An Economic History of Modern Scotland 1660–1976*, p. 55; Ferguson, *Scotland: 1689 to the Present*, p. 47; P. W. J. Riley, *The Union of England and Scotland* (Manchester: 1978), ch. 5; J. Mackinnon, *The Union of England and Scotland: A Study of International History* (London: 1896); W. Ferguson, 'The Making of the Treaty of Union of 1707', *Scottish Historical Review*, 43 (1964), 89–110.
70 5 Anne c.8, 'An Act for an Union for the Two Kingdoms of England and Scotland'.
71 S. R. Lambert (ed.), *House of Commons Sessional Papers of the Eighteenth Century*, vol. 2, *George I, Scotland, 1717–1725*, pp. 79–82.

of the Darien Company, with the remainder to go to all other public debts, such as the arrears of office-holders, pensions and the pay due to the armed forces, as determined by Parliament. The arising equivalent would also go to these ends. When payment of the Darien debts was completed, the Company was to be wound up. In the summer and autumn of 1706, there followed the 'greatest political job of the eighteenth century', with lavish inducements held out to those who agreed to vote in favour. David Boyle, Earl of Glasgow, a Bank director and member of the Queensberry interest, covertly laid out £20,000 sterling given to him by Sidney Godolphin, Lord Treasurer. Arrears of pay to any particular member were made conditional on his vote being cast for the treaty.[72]

By the summer of 1707, the Bank had been trading for eleven years. In that time, the proprietors had seen a serious attempt to establish the Company of Scotland as a rival and on two further occasions had fought off attempts to break the monopoly of banking allowed by the 1695 Act. The first five years had witnessed an economic background as severe as any in seventeenth-century Scotland, although recovery from 1700 was swift. The director who commented in 1697 that the Bank had had a hard introduction to the business could hardly have envisaged that the next decade was to throw up worse. Nevertheless, huge strides had been made. The Bank was now a national institution, with lending spread across Scotland from Inverness to the Borders. The Bank directors could be excused for thinking that the Union agreements would have worked to increase trade and circulation, which in turn would justify an increase in lending and discounting. Thus this political process was seen as contributing in tangible ways to an increase in profits. Bank of Scotland stood to benefit from the Union arrangements and from the arising equivalent. Unfortunately for the Bank, as we shall see, events proved more complicated.

72 Ferguson, 'The Making of the Treaty of Union of 1707', p. 107.

CHAPTER 4

THE BANK AND THE ECONOMY OF SCOTLAND TO THE UNION OF 1707

THE DEBATES IN the Scottish Parliament from 1689 to the Union of 1707 came back repeatedly to a basic problem: Scots made fewer goods by value for overseas markets compared with those that they imported.[1] It appeared to contemporaries that their strong export earners could not keep pace with the proliferation of household and consumer imports which had shown such a marked increase in the later seventeenth century. This in turn led to the oft-made comment that the 'luxury' of the rich drained the country of gold and silver coin for which the paper money of Bank of Scotland had in part compensated. To complicate matters, some in the Parliamentary debates of 1705 even tried to blame the Bank for the shortage, rather as John Law blamed the lack of small silver on the new £1 notes. Inevitably, therefore, the Bank was drawn into national economic and financial debates, although at least such controversy recognised the importance of the Bank and banking facilities in the period before the Union.

How accurately could contemporaries assess the real state of the balance of payments, seasonal movements of goods and periodic changes in the supply of coin? Good statistical evidence was scarce. Perhaps the import and export trades were best catered for; there had been investigations into trade in the seventeenth century, but, as the country lacked an efficient customs and excise organisation, the data collected were of varying usefulness. Nevertheless, in 1704 and 1705 Parliament tried again and examined the commercial statistics for imports and exports by product, value and their revenue-generating potential, and listed these by the port

---

1 The basic text for trade remains T. C. Smout, *Scottish Trade on the Eve of Union 1660–1707* (Edinburgh: 1963); there is also much useful material in G. P. Insh, *Scottish Colonial Schemes, 1620–1686* (Glasgow: 1922) and idem, *The Company of Scotland Trading to Africa and the Indies* (London: 1932).

Table 4.1 *Scottish exports and imports by value, 1704 estimate*

Exports	£ Sterling	£ Scots	Percentage of total
Linen	40000	480000	21.7
Linen yarn	5000	60000	2.7
Wool, sheepskins	25000	300000	13.6
Plaid, serges	12500	150000	6.8
Stockings	16000	192000	8.7
Black cattle	20000	240000	10.9
Herrings	25000	300000	13.6
Salmon	8000	96000	4.3
Salt, dry cod	1000	12000	0.5
Lead, lead ore	8000	96000	4.3
Coal	10000	120000	5.4
Salt	6000	72000	3.3
Pork, beef and hides	3000	36000	1.6
Other skins	4000	48000	2.2
Eggs	—	10000	0.4
Total value	184300	2212000	

Imports	£ Sterling	£ Scots	Percentage of total
Linens, muslins, cottons	50000	600000	14.0
Leather	40000	480000	11.2
Furniture, mirrors, clocks	30000	360000	8.4
Tobacco	25000	300000	7.0
Wines	16667	200000	4.7
Brandy, spirits	10000	120000	2.8
Coaches, saddles	10000	120000	2.8
Wool, silk, stockings	10000	120000	2.8
Pitch and tar	10000	120000	2.8
Iron, copper, steel	20000	240000	5.6
Flax, hemp	18333	220000	5.1
Diverse stuffs	10000	120000	2.8
Spices	6000	72000	1.7
Sugars	10000	120000	2.8
Confections	1000	12000	0.3
Neeps and onions	1500	18000	0.4
Lint seed	6000	72000	1.7
Seeds	1000	12000	0.3
Soap, oil	5000	60000	1.4
Silk and hair	10000	120000	2.8
Pots and pans	5000	60000	1.4
Drugs	5000	60000	1.4
Glassware, earthenware	2000	24000	0.6
Porcelain, tea, coffee, chocolate	2000	24000	0.6
Pewter, tin	2000	24000	0.6
Arms, ammunition	5000	60000	1.4
Ships, stores	10000	120000	2.8
Paper and box	6667	80000	1.9
Knives, tools	2000	24000	0.6
Iron and brass	1667	20000	0.5
Combs, boxes	1667	20000	0.5
Horses	2000	24000	0.6
Liquorice	833	10000	0.2
Mum, beer	1000	12000	0.3
Prunes, dates, raisins, figs and currants	3333	40000	0.9
Musical instruments	1000	12000	0.3
Foreign salt	5000	60000	1.4
Russia leathers, black beer	1000	12000	0.3
Olives, capers, anchovies, pickles	833	10000	0.2
Florance oil, perfume oil	1000	12000	0.3
Olive oil	4000	48000	1.1
Wigs, fans	2500	30000	0.7
Total value	356000	4272000	
Surplus of imports over exports	£171,700	£2,060,000	

Source: NLS, MS 17498, f. 76, Fletcher of Saltoun Papers, 1704.

of entry and exit. Although the resulting lists were for different periods (March 1703 to March 1704, and the calendar year 1704) and there were wide differences between some values, the relative ranking of commodities was similar (see Tables 4.1 and 4.2).[2]

The most important export trades were, first and foremost, the textile industries of linen goods and yarn, wool, stockings, serges and plaiding; second came live cattle and the sheep trade with leather and skins; third, white fish, herring and salmon; and lastly, at this date some way behind the others in value, coal and lead ore. These figures confirmed what contemporaries had gradually realised over the previous half-century – that there was a slow but sure increase in the foreign and colonial markets for textiles (especially linens), expansion in the European markets for coal, textiles, animal products and fish and in England for coal and linens, and an apparently insatiable demand for cattle and sheep.[3] The English Whigs who drafted the Aliens Act clearly understood this basic trade pattern.

All these products required varying degrees of skilled and semi-skilled labour, especially the production of textiles and leather products and the digging of coal. For many decades, the royal burghs, the Privy Council and the Scottish Parliament had passed statutes and by-laws designed to improve their quality and the supply of labour, and although the decade before the Union was particularly difficult for exporters, the efforts of legislators had seen some positive results. The exports of linen goods from Glasgow to Ireland and the English colonies were particularly encouraging. Furthermore, these efforts emphasised that outputs and sales in the textile and leather trades required cooperation between landowners and merchants – an important social interaction for the future economic progress of the country. Yet the need for the by-laws and other legislation also underscored what pamphleteers pointed out repeatedly: international competition and protectionism was on the increase, and if Scots wanted to sell more overseas then better quality had to be strived for. This meant a long-term perspective for investment, stricter discipline of labour, a better education and training (for all involved), improved business organisation and, of course, a focus on a sound coinage, on long-run cash flow, on banking facilities and a cheapening of the costs of borrowing. This broader appreciation of the conditions of progress was a part of the gradual

2 The figures reprinted here are from Goldsmiths Library, MS 81; NLS, MS 17498, f. 70ff., Fletcher of Saltoun Papers.
3 Smout, *Scottish Trade on the Eve of Union*, chs 10 and 11; see also the discussion in T. M. Devine, 'The Union of 1707 and Scottish Development', *Scottish Economic and Social History Review*, 5 (1985), 23–40; and T. C. Smout, 'The Anglo-Scottish Union of 1707, I: The Economic Background', *Economic History Review*, 2nd series, 16 (1963–4), 455–67.

Table 4.2 Scottish exports by value, November 1703 to November 1704

Type of goods	Value (£ Scots)
Linen goods[1]	896320
Cattle	156948
Woollen cloth[2]	116332
Skins	71357
Stockings	58104
Coal	31045
Wool	30534
White leather	21291
Sheep	16850
Tallow	10503
Victual (pork, beef)	7698
Salt	6480
Total (top 12 categories)	1423462
All others[3]	60964
Total Scottish exports[4]	1484426

Table 4.2.1 Scottish linen and woollen cloth exports broken down by burgh, 1703–4

Burgh	Linen Volume (ells)	Linen Est value (£ Scots)	Woollen cloth Volume (ells)	Woollen cloth Est value (£ Scots)
Leith	16750	8375	9900	4950
Edinburgh	8330	4165	890	445
Prestonpans	760	380	3334	1667
Kirkcaldy	132790	66395	7050	3525
Bo'ness	1240	620	43420	21710
Dundee	294314	147157	4400	2200
Montrose	182135	91068		
Aberdeen	22040	11020	138926	69463
Perth	271140	135570	1200	600
Glasgow	755715	377858	2950	1475
New Port Glasgow	620	310	550	275
Ayr	1200	600	300	150
Irvine	14047	7024		
Dumfries	65130	32565	60	30
Alisonbank	5050	2525	350	175
Jedburgh	1040	520		
Kelso	4270	2135		
Aiton	16070	8035		
Inverness			19835	9918
Total	1792641	896320	233165	116582

Notes:
1 See Table 4.2.1 for breakdown by burgh.
2 See Table 4.2.1 for breakdown by burgh.
3 The minor products included in this category were linen gloves, hats, linen yarn, eggs, linseed, horns, bark, horse, salted hides, oysters, feathers, whale oil, timber and books.
4 The important categories of fish, salmon and herrings, barrels, stone and invisible earnings are excluded. Both the sets of figures in Table 4.1 (from the Fletcher of Saltoun papers) and this table confirm that the Aliens Act had the potential to affect adversely around 90 per cent (by value) of Scottish exports.

Source: Goldsmiths Library, MS 81, 'Report off the state of the Trade of the Nation so farr as can be gathered from the Custom House books, and that from November 1703 to November 1704, taken conforme to order and appointment of the Rt Honourable the Councill of Trade'.

transition of the attitudes of landowners in the lowlands of Scotland in the pre-industrial period. The economic legislation of the 1693 and 1695 sessions of Parliament was perhaps a hot-house attempt to speed up this process. It was unfortunate that the new joint stocks of linen, wool and food processing had no sooner established themselves than they ran into the subsistence crisis after 1695 and most then disappeared.

In one important respect, the activity of legislators and burgh councils was a complete failure: apart from the cases cited here, the country produced few handicrafts and manufactured goods of a standard acceptable in foreign markets and even, in some products, nothing at all. This record may be illustrated in various ways. Virtually no ocean-going shipping was built in Scotland; only small fishing smacks and rowing boats. Attempts to encourage shipbuilders to settle, for example in 1681 by the abolition of dues on all shipbuilding imports, came to nought.[4] Competition from Dutch and English shipyards, a want of good workmen and lack of sustained government support meant that there was no progress by the Union. When the Company of Scotland decided to buy ships, it went to Hamburg and Rotterdam and also went abroad for the sails, the cordage, most of the ironwork, even the lead for the bread ovens. Perhaps most disheartening for such a martial nation, the Company found that Scotland made no cannon and produced no small arms and ammunition of acceptable quality; even the gunpowder came from the Netherlands. This cost the Company over £25,000 sterling; perhaps its banking operations might have been turned to advantage had it been able to buy these supplies at home. The Privy Council had a similar experience; when it needed frigates to defend Scottish traders in 1693 and 1703, it was to the Thames that it went.

Ships, guns, explosives and their accessories were all in the vanguard of European industry in 1700. Yet the picture was similar for consumer manufactures and household goods. Thus there were only a handful of glassmakers, and all the better-quality glassware was imported. So too were most iron goods, copper pots and pans, and all the pewter and tin goods; even earthenware came in large quantities from England. There were no serious scientific instrument makers; the leading Scottish mathematicians had to ask London makers for even the simplest of devices. The statistics for imports reprinted here show a sorry tale where most of the new consumer demands of the later seventeenth century were supplied from outwith Scotland. Even in household furniture (such things as mirrors, clocks, watches and cabinets), the total of imports was £360,000 Scots.

---

4 P. Hume Brown (ed.), *The Register of the Privy Council of Scotland*, 3rd series, vol. vii, *1681–1682* (Edinburgh: 1915), pp. 97ff., 103, 168, 671.

The two major investigations of the late seventeenth century, in 1681 and 1692, were also pessimistic, and the report by the royal burghs particularly so.[5] What few manufactures were exported were usually re-exports.

There were some areas with potential for expansion. The leading edge of technical progress was probably organised by the coal-mining landowners and covered such matters as drainage, haulage and surveying. Coal was an industry with considerable scope and already had strong export markets in Europe, Ireland and England. In the Glasgow area, the processing of colonial products, notably sugar and to a lesser extent tobacco, made rapid strides after 1660. The figures for imports of these products before 1707 do not quite show the potential of later decades, but a solid basis for colonial trade existed, and there was a wide network of Scottish merchants straddling many countries. Facilitating legislation was passed by Parliament under the umbrella of protection, notably for pottery, brewing, textiles, coach-making and barrel-making, though many found life after the Union harsh.[6] In other words, overall, the main export earners remained few, the newer industries were irrelevant to the scale of the balance-of-payments problem, and the country was several decades away from the first main stage of industrialisation.

When the English Parliament decided to aim a sledgehammer at Scottish trade in the 'Aliens' Act (effective from 25 December 1705), it only needed to single out the four top trades, namely the cross-border cattle and sheep trades, seaborne coal, and the products of the linen industry. The Scottish nobility and lairds were thus presented with an ultimatum which would have cut their incomes sharply just at the time when the diversified options of joint stocks and the Company of Scotland legislated for in the sessions of 1693 and 1695 had failed. The possible adverse effects on the Bank's profits have been estimated above at several hundred pounds and perhaps more if loan repayments from landowners had been held up.

The figures from 1703 and 1704 covered what we now call 'visible' trade, yet Scots earned far more overseas and in England than foreigners did in Scotland; these extra earnings were divided between 'invisibles' and incomes from smuggling and illegal trades. It should be emphasised that before the Union the view of Bank of Scotland directors was that the Bank should encourage Scottish traders and military men in a broad sense, hence the third of the capital earmarked for London (plus the note issue there) and the efforts made to organise the remittance among

5 Ibid., introduction and p. 651ff.; this was a survey of the conditions of trade in the major ports and burghs and covered manufactures. A survey by the royal burghs in 1692 was a flimsier exercise but drew similar conclusions.
6 Smout, *Scottish Trade on the Eve of Union*, chs 11 and 12.

the Netherlands, England and Scotland from 1696 to 1701. Remitting military and civil government funds from any part of the English dominions to Scotland was legal, and many Scots in London sent varying sums north on behalf of army officers and office-holders; in this way the martial expertise of the Scots was a benefit to the balance of payments as well as to numerous persons with whom Bank of Scotland conducted business.

It was a different story for those Scots involved in colonial trade. The Restoration of Charles II had broken up the Cromwellian customs union of Scotland with England. Under the terms of the English Navigation Acts of 1660 and 1663, no goods were to be imported into, or exported from, any of the King's colonies in Asia, Africa or America in any other than English, Irish or plantation-built ships, 'whereof the master and at least three fourths of the mariners shall be Englishmen'. Further, no goods were to be imported into England of the growth of Asia, Africa or America but in English-owned ships, navigated as before.[7] Of particular importance, Scots were absolutely barred from the lucrative 'triangular' slave trade (England–Africa–Caribbean and its connections to Spanish and other American colonies) by the controls and licence system exercised by the Royal Africa Company. In fact, Scots often ignored these English laws and continued to freight ships after 1660 just as they had done under Cromwell. They sent all manner of goods to the English colonies and returned a rising volume of sugar, dyestuffs, timber and tobacco. The forty years after the Restoration were a lawless time in the Caribbean: minor wars between islands, sporadic conquests and Indian wars in the North American colonies engendered a feeling of distance from Europe. The controls over the slave trade by the Royal Adventurers' monopoly in the 1660s and those of the Royal Africa Company from 1672 were especially irksome to planters. There was also inconsistency in London policy; in time of war (1664–7, 1672–4 and 1678), the bans were suspended, and on two occasions royal licences were granted to Scots to trade.[8] By the time the Bank was founded, this illegal (in English law) trading was widespread and well organised from numerous ports. Although a great deal of literary, legal and business correspondence survives to attest to its importance, the scale of its contribution to visibles or invisibles in the Scottish balance of payments is not possible to ascertain.

Examples from the career of George Watson, the first Accountant of Bank of Scotland, illustrate one aspect of foreign earnings. In November 1695, he entered into an agreement with the London Scottish firm of Michael Kincaid and James Pitcairn for an illegal African venture ('we are in a plot', noted Kincaid).[9] Their associates were James Foulis, the manager of the London end of Bank of Scotland, Alexander Lorimer (involved in London–Dutch trade), William Gordon (another London Scot) and Robert McKerrall, who worked from Dublin. By June 1696, they had paid for the fitting-out of a slave 'runner' of 120 tons, two decks and twelve guns, built to look like a frigate and 'fit to carry Negro's and elephants teeth'; they were hard negotiators and cut the original estimate of £1,200 for a purpose-built model to only £420 for a second-hand ship. They estimated that the cargo for the purchase of the slaves would cost £900 and the cargo for the gold and ivory about the same, and a slave price of £25 each in Barbados would yield a total profit of 50 per cent remitted from the island by bill of exchange on London.[10] They kept the trade a secret as they were breaking two sets of English laws, and people who 'make a grat noise of everything they doe' were not approached for supplies. The contrast with the Company of Scotland, launched at the same time in Edinburgh, could not have been sharper, and Watson later worked on similar trading schemes.

Watson was also involved in the contribution to 'invisible' earnings through the illegal export of Scots coin. Fluctuations in intrinsic values between countries meant periodic profits for coin exporters. After 1686, the intrinsic value of the Scots silver coins was devalued 8.5 per cent below the par of 12:1 to around 13:1, although the real rate until the early 1690s fluctuated even lower, from 10 to 15 per cent below par. However, by 1694 the deterioration in the English currency through clipping meant that the silver coinage was worth, one bag of coins with another, far less than its face value. Therefore, unclipped coins were at a premium. In 1695 and 1696, gold guineas rose well above their face value of 21 shillings in sterling to reach almost 30 shillings. Scots coin thus rose above the par to reach 11:1. The export of these sound Scots coins enabled enterprising Scots to buy up underweight English coin 'to catch the time to get a good pennyworth' by awaiting the English silver recoinage of 1696.[11] They then cashed in the underweight coins, received full-weight new coins from Isaac Newton's mint and sent these back to Scotland or lodged them in London accounts.

It is not possible to gauge how far these foreign, invisible and smuggling trades altered the Scottish balance of payments. The general drift of policy

9 SRO GD 277, Box 8, Bundle 1; Box 14, Bundle 8, letters from Kincaid and Pitcairn to Watson.
10 The actual profits would probably have been below this; the death rate among slaves reached 10 per cent, and £25 was around the top end of the range for fit male adults.
11 SRO GD 277, Box 8, Bundle 1, 7 December 1695. Michael Kincaid reminded George Watson to keep quiet about this; for the recoinage, see J. H. Clapham, *The Bank of England. A History* (2 vols, Cambridge: 1944), vol. i, *1694–1797*, pp. 34–6; for the cross-border remittance, see below, Appendix 3.

and comment suggests that the payments position was worse by the time of the Union than it had been in the 1680s. As for the shortage of silver coin, much of the comment we have came from parties interested in abolishing the monopoly of the Bank, and in any case Bank of Scotland notes – up to around £70,000 worth in the autumn of 1704 – were a more accurate medium of exchange. But the position was difficult, and it was not in the interest of Bank of Scotland, as a profit-making institution, or most of the Bank's merchant correspondents, to see a worsening of economic relations with England.

Apart from the real and potential political problems of foreign and cross-border trade, the Bank was also affected by the internal fractures of the Highland–Lowland divide. For numerous Bank correspondents, the products of the Highlands and the accounts which they held for clan chieftains were part of their bread and butter. The area was much more important, economically as well as politically, in the pre-industrial period than in the nineteenth century. Around 30 per cent of the Scottish population of 1.2 million in the early eighteenth century lived there, and most spoke Gaelic, a language which the Privy Council and Parliament had tried to curtail.[12] The Gaelic speakers lacked even a translation of the Bible, and the first non-English translation to be distributed, in the 1690s, was in Irish.[13] To most outsiders, the Highlands were an alien land, marked out by the use of pagan incantation and magic, Catholicism and high church ritual, and ruled by barbaric chiefs who reigned with the full force of primitive feudal laws which had long since been replaced elsewhere in the British Isles.[14] Alex Mudie's *Scotiae Indiculum* designed for a London audience was plain; the clan people were 'hardy and cunning, inclinable to war' and much given to private feuds, and their usual weapons were swords, bows and arrows.[15] To William of Orange and many non-Highlanders, they were 'savages', and the MacDonalds of Glencoe deserved to be massacred (13 February 1692).[16]

12 There are no precise figures before 1831. The main account, by Alexander Webster in his *Account of the Number of People in Scotland* in 1755, suggested that out of 1,265,380 for the whole country perhaps 30 per cent lived in the Highlands and Islands; J. G. Kyd (ed.), *Scottish Population Statistics: including Webster's Analysis of Population, 1755*, Scottish History Society, 3rd series, vol. 43 (Edinburgh: 1952). See also W. Ferguson, *Scotland: 1689 to the Present*, The Edinburgh History of Scotland, vol. iv (Edinburgh: 1968), p. 175; R. Mitchison, *A History of Scotland* (London: 1970), p. 348; T. C. Smout, *A History of the Scottish People 1560–1830* (London: 1969), ch. 11.
13 R. Mitchison, *Lordship to Patronage, Scotland 1603–1745* (Edinburgh: 1983), pp. 91, 195; G. Donaldson (ed.), *Scottish Historical Documents* (Edinburgh: 1970), pp. 171, 178; idem, *Scotland, James V to James VII*, The Edinburgh History of Scotland, vol. iii (Edinburgh: 1965), pp. 258–9; Ferguson, *Scotland: 1689 to the Present*, p. 175.
14 Only a few pockets remained outside Scotland; the last feudal powers of any significance, on the Isle of Man, were bought by the British state from the Duke of Atholl in 1763.
15 A. M. Philopatris, *Scotiae Indiculum, or the Present State of Scotland* (London: 1681).
16 Ferguson, *Scotland: 1689 to the Present*, pp. 22–3; William signed the warrant for the extermination

The Highlands were important to the Bank because of the huge revenues which their cattle exports generated south of the Border.[17] Every summer and autumn, the Bank discounted numerous drovers' bills and lent long and short on personal bonds to cover purchases at the Scottish cattle and sheep fairs. The products were a sound investment for the Bank. Any animal which could survive a Highland winter out of doors could walk 400 miles to provide effective competition to English cattle. Indeed, for a short time in 1663, the English Parliament banned the trade. This hostility was noticed a century later by Sir Walter Scott in his *The Two Drovers*, which ended with the vindictive hanging of an innocent drover. Adam Smith was right to assign to cattle their place as the main generator of income for the Highlands and islands, though his claim that their rise in price after 1707 was perhaps the greatest benefit to Scotland of the Union was exaggerated.[18]

The trade in cattle and to a lesser extent in sheep enabled the drovers to generate large cash balances at fairs in the fattening areas in East Anglia and around London. These were a magnet for Scottish bankers in England who needed cash and who could also provide goods for delivery in Scotland and cash from accounts held by associates. Thus, for many years, John Campbell travelled to the fairs in East Anglia, buying up the cash by bills of exchange payable at London and Edinburgh and then arranging for goods to be carried north.[19] The advantage of the cattle trade for Bank of Scotland was its fast turnaround; the Bank lent from April to August and the returns came back from June to November. After 1700, the amount of lending on bills to interests associated with droving rose sharply, and the income compensated for the loss of the ordinary exchange trade; it also gave many landlords and their Edinburgh factors an interest in the solvency of the Bank.

The choice of Glasgow, Aberdeen, Dundee and Montrose as the burghs wherein to site the first branches of Bank of Scotland may be largely inferred by the importance of those towns in the trade statistics from 1703 to 1704 which, by and large, confirm the pattern of the surviving customs records of the pre-Revolution years. The irregular pattern of Scottish

---

of the MacDonalds of Glencoe. There was widespread outrage at the breach of hospitality involved in the massacre.

17 Figures for cattle and sheep exports before 1691 have survived in SRO GD but probably understate the true figures. See R. B. S. Haldane, *The Drove Roads of Scotland*, 2nd edn (Edinburgh: 1973); Smout, *Scottish Trade on the Eve of Union*, p. 214; for the sheep, see R. A. Dodgshon, 'Agricultural Change and its Social Consequences in the Southern Uplands of Scotland 1600–1780', in T. M. Devine and D. Dickson (eds), *Ireland and Scotland 1600–1850: Parallels and Contrasts in Economic and Social Development* (Edinburgh: 1983), pp. 46–59.

18 Adam Smith, *An Inquiry into the Nature and Causes of the Wealth of Nations* (1776), ed. E. Cannan (2 vols, London: 1904; repr. 1961), vol. i, pp. 244, 246–7.

19 Coutts & Co., Letter Book, no. 2, f. 107v.

topography and the appalling state of the roads, especially in winter, ensured that every area had a self-contained supply system served by a seaport. All the towns included in this category – Inverness, Kirkcaldy, Perth, Dunbar, Dumfries, Ayr and Bo'ness – and many smaller ones had merchants who traded overseas to continental Europe, Scandinavia, Ireland (if in the west) and in several cases to the Caribbean and America. The larger trading burghs were probably chosen for branches for the simple reason that they were bigger, with more trade, than the others; each chosen had a strong contingent of merchants and some diversity in local industry.

The northernmost branch was at Aberdeen, a burgh of 8,000–10,000 inhabitants with a relevant hinterland which stretched up the rivers Don and Dee far into the eastern Highlands. The burgh was a notable Episcopalian centre, and the traders had the distinction of being among the most multilingual of all merchant groups, with Doric (the dialect of the northeast) spoken in a wide area in and around the town, Gaelic inland, and of course English, Norwegian and a smattering of other languages needed for foreign trade. The arable countryside which stretched north of Aberdeen and twenty miles to the west was dotted with villages and hamlets, and the climate was mild enough for the cultivation of flax and bleaching of linen. Aberdeen had a long history of foreign trade, from northern Norway to the Mediterranean and across the Atlantic to the colonies.[20] When Scotland was expelled from the Navigation system, Aberdeen merchants continued to trade with the plantations. The customs figures for the 1680s show a large export of woollen goods, plaiding, serges, stockings and some quaint mixtures of Doric and Flemish; fingrams, grograms and flemmings.[21] There is some evidence that increased competition by 1688 made the export of woollen and linen goods harder.[22] Certainly, the figures from 1703 to 1704 show high levels of imports for foreign linen, cotton and silk goods. The fish trade probably suffered less than any other in the Aberdeen area, and prices rose at the end of the seventeenth century. By 1704, the total export may have reached 14,500 barrels, with perhaps another 1,400 barrels of salmon (each of 250 lb) from the Don and Dee.[23]

Trades of the diversity and size listed in Table 4.2 meant a sound business base for a bank branch. At the time of the 1688 Revolution, the customs records indicated that around fifty merchants ran the foreign

20 B. P. Lenman, *From Esk to Tweed: Harbours, Ships and Men of the East Coast of Scotland* (Glasgow: 1975).
21 SRO E 72/1/18–20, Aberdeen exports and imports, 1 November 1689 to 1 November 1691.
22 Smout, *Scottish Trade on the Eve of Union*, p. 142; T. Keith, *Commercial Relations of England and Scotland, 1603–1707* (Cambridge: 1910), p. 45.
23 Goldsmiths Library, MS 81; V. Clark, *The Port of Aberdeen: A History of its Trade and Shipping from the 12th Century to the Present Day* (Aberdeen: 1921), p. 37.

trades; some of these could manage shipments of up to 2,000 double ells of plaid, 4,000 leather skins, or 400–500 dozen stockings.[24] In return they brought in a lengthening list of consumer and industrial goods, including Swedish iron, Bergen timber, madder, copperas, alum, hemp and hops as well as lead shot, soap, prunes, raisins, figs, aniseed, ginger, cinnamon, rice, pepper, coriander, almonds, coffee, tobacco, wines and growing amounts of sugar. From their shops on Aberdeen's high street, the seventeenth-century consumer revolution reached out to even the remotest parts of the Highlands. A number of the merchants, John and Alexander Forbes, James Gordon, William Soupar and Messrs Ragg, Mitchell, Orem and Ramsay (all called Alexander), made multiple shipments and formed part of the richest group of Aberdeen merchants who were valued in the 1694 poll tax as worth over 10,000 Scottish merks.[25] The problem for Bank of Scotland was that premio bills and other paper payments were very popular with Aberdonians wishing to pay debts in Edinburgh, yet there were few demands for payment in Aberdeen. It should be noted here that the merchants and landowners of the Aberdeen area remained loyal to the Bank during the political difficulties of the first half-century of business.

To a lesser extent, what was true of Aberdeen was the case with Montrose and Dundee, the other two, smaller, eastern seaports where the Bank opened branches, though they too were unable to support a balance in the early banking trade with the capital. The trading figures of Glasgow marked the burgh out as the dominant western port for the Atlantic and Irish trades. Yet the merchants of the burgh were reluctant to take up the banknotes offered by the branch, and it was not until the end of the famine period that banknotes circulated more freely in the west and many loans were made to the area. By the 1740s, the value and volume through the Glasgow ports began to surpass that of Leith, and by then Bank of Scotland had excellent relations with a number of Glasgow traders. Looking at the figures for 1703 and 1704, it is perhaps surprising that Bo'ness was not considered for a branch, though in fact the burgh was rarely mentioned in the Bank minutes in the first half of the eighteenth century. Part of the answer lies in the nature of the trades: Bo'ness (which included a number of smaller ports) was used as a distribution centre by merchants from Edinburgh and elsewhere, as it was cheaper to ship goods up the Forth than to move them overland. The burgh's great coal-export trade was largely in the hands of the landowners and mine operators. They dealt direct with markets overseas and negotiated their own bills of exchange.

24 SRO E 72/1/18–20, Aberdeen exports and imports, 1 November 1689 to 1 November 1691.
25 T. M. Devine, 'The Merchant Class of the Larger Scottish Towns in the Later Seventeenth and Early Eighteenth Centuries', in G. Gordon and B. Dicks (eds), Scottish Urban History (Aberdeen: 1983), 92–111.

Bo'ness was thus an important port but different in nature from the three eastern burghs where the Bank set up branches.

Finally, why did the Scottish economy apparently take so readily to Bank of Scotland notes; why did the Scottish government in the 1690s not simply increase the output of the Scottish Mint by the purchase of bullion overseas and fix the exchange so as to keep it within the country? There are two main parts to the answer. The most important was a striking historical legacy of the rule of Charles II. At the Restoration, Charles confirmed that the prerogative would once again include the coinage of Scotland. As noted before, John Maitland, second Earl of Lauderdale, was appointed Secretary of State, from which office he built up his personal rule. His younger brother, Charles Maitland, Lord Hatton, was appointed as Master General of the Scottish coinage in 1661.[26] Hatton then proceeded to organise three large-scale coinage frauds: a secret debasement of the silver coin, the production of foreign counterfeit coin and a huge over-issue of debased copper coinage, all for circulation in Scotland. These operations ran with little hindrance under the protective umbrella of Lauderdale and the court nominees to the Court of Session. There was some opposition, but none was effective until Lauderdale lay dying in 1681 and Charles was under political threat from the Whigs. Representations made at that time to the Scottish Privy Council stated that the ducatoon, especially the Spanish, 'is the coyne amongst us of the best intrinsick value'.[27] It was not until 1682 that the Scottish nobility felt confident enough to settle their scores with Hatton and won the backing of a judicial inquiry which found that his gains from the copper frauds alone had reached £673,400 Scots. The failure of the Ryehouse Plot delayed reform of the Mint until 1686. It was no wonder, then, that an entrenched attitude developed for merchant transactions in favour of sterling or foreign coin, or that such institutions as the Aberdeen masonic lodge and the Edinburgh Merchant Company fixed their fines in rix-dollars.

The legacy of Stewart rule proved the point that trust about coinage may take decades to build up but be easily lost. Coin was not difficult to debase, and though the Mint after 1686 was run properly and the coins were of the value stated, this distrust lingered, hence the popularity of a promise to pay in sterling. The second reason for the spread of banknotes was that even with sound coins the fluctuations of the exchanges led to

26 For the details of this extraordinary story, see R. W. Cochran-Patrick, *Records of the Coinage of Scotland* (2 vols, Edinburgh: 1876); Sir George Mackenzie of Rosehaugh, *Memoirs of the Affairs of Scotland* (Edinburgh: 1821); Sir James Stewart of Goodtrees, *An Accompt of Scotland's Grievances by Reason of the Duke of Lauderdale's Ministrie* (1671); G. M. Hutton, 'Stair's Public Career', in D. M. Walker (ed.), *Stair Tercentenary Studies*, Stair Society Publications, 33 (Edinburgh: 1981), pp. 1–68.
27 P. Hume Brown (ed.), *The Register of the Privy Council of Scotland*, p. 660.

temporary shortages. Banknotes stayed within the country and kept their nominal value, and fraud was difficult to perpetrate. By the Union of 1707, both sides of the Border were well down the road of a paper currency for large and small sums, of little silver coinage and a basis of gold, slightly overvalued against silver, for international payments.

By way of summary, we might well reflect on the paradox presented by the Scottish economy, broadly interpreted, in the years just before the Union. The country had a very long way to go to match the more advanced areas of Europe in the production of manufactures. Indeed, a wider gap probably existed by 1707 than, say, before 1688. The apparent degree of success for foreign textiles was particularly worrying. Nevertheless, all the Scottish manufactures sold abroad had potential for growth. Demand for the natural product of the nation and its seas remained buoyant. Only political difficulties, such as the Aliens Act, or protectionism could damage their prospects. However, growth was not seen by contemporaries as likely to be spectacular, and indeed the Parliamentary debates voiced many concerns about even the best-placed exports, such as salmon and herrings. Thus, prospects were difficult although not dire.

Early eighteenth-century Scotland was developing some very positive economic traits. It had a most advanced paper currency, built up on little support from gold and silver and with an adverse international payments position. There were numerous sophisticated merchant houses in the main burghs and seaports. The leading political estates, the aristocracy and gentry, were seriously interested in economic and financial concerns and provided a great deal of support to trade and industry. Although the political society was fractured among many competing interests, and the problems of the Jacobites remained for another half-century, business benefited from an honest and disciplined religious culture. These benefits were all powerful contributions to the extraordinary economic expansion of Scotland in the eighteenth century.

From the vantage point of 1707, several significant conclusions may be drawn from the early years of Bank of Scotland. The most important in respect of politics was the involvement of the nobility, the legal profession and the merchant classes, who wanted the Bank to survive and gave their active support. The history of these years confirmed that a paper currency, far outstripping its cash reserve, could succeed provided that during crises enough cash could be raised and enough political support generated. In respect of internal management, the Bank had learned by 1697 how to divide the responsibilities of directors and managers between everyday work and the political and strategic questions which were the preserve of the nobles and judges among the extraordinary directors. Furthermore, the mixture of caution, political understanding and gradual increase in lending pursed under the Governorship of the Earl of Leven was sufficient to establish the Bank as a major national institution by 1707.

There were occasions when political difficulties almost overwhelmed the directors. In the case of the company of Scotland, the survival of the Bank was secured after the failure of the schemes of William Paterson, although political support remained vital. The currency schemes mooted after 1700 were defeated because of the manoeuvres in Parliament. The most difficult hurdle to overcome, that of the assault by John Law and the Duke of Argyll, eventually petered out after vigorous discussion and the threats of violence between members of Parliament. None of the Currency-scheme projectors, Hugh Chamberlain, James Armour, John Law or William Paterson, contributed anything positive to the state of Scottish credit and finance before the Union, except to underline, in contrast to their failings, the achievement of the Bank.

CHAPTER 5

FROM THE UNION OF 1707 TO THE FOUNDATION OF THE ROYAL BANK

O N THE COMPLETION of the Treaty of Union, the Bank of England endeavoured to extract full financial advantage in respect of how the compensation under the terms of the Act (the Equivalent) would be paid. Its court issued secret instructions to the four Bank of England commissioners specified in the Act, and to the several bank officials who were to travel to Edinburgh with them, to insist that Exchequer bills were a suitable means of payment for £298,000 and that only £100,085 would be sent in gold.[1] Opposition from the Scottish commissioners was expected, but they were not 'in any wise to admit of such refusal'.[2] 'We should be very glad', the instructions added, 'if you and the rest of the commissioners might find means to make your payments in the said Exchequer bills which we think not be difficult and would tend to the more general circulation of them'.

Exchequer bills were first issued in 1696 to extend the credit available to the government and by so doing ease the shortage of cash in the economy. By the Act of the English Parliament which first gave them currency (7 & 8 William III c.31), they could pass in payment 'to any person or persons that shall be willing to accept and take the same' and were issued in notes of £5 and £10 to facilitate acceptance. From 1697, they were allowable 'in all payments to receivers of collectors of supplys' with one exception, and by the reign of Anne were accepted for all 'Aids, Taxes, Loans and

---

1 Bank of England, MSS, Court Minutes, vol. E, G4/6, p. 155, 8 May 1707; the instructions were cleared with the Lord Treasurer, Sidney Godolphin.
2 Ibid., draft of instructions to the English commissioners, p. 164ff.

payments whatsover to Her Majesty'. They bore interest at 2d per cent per day.[3] By the Act of 6 Anne c.21, the Bank of England agreed to take £1.5 million of the Exchequer bills at $4\frac{1}{2}$ per cent, and as long as these remained current the bank charter was to remain in force; thus there was every incentive to encourage their circulation. They were only payable in cash at the Bank of England.

Some of the Scottish debts required payment in London, so officials of the Bank of England thought that they would have an opportunity to organise the remittance. They were given instructions to draw upon the cashier in London at sight or any short time, for 'such sums of money as may be offered you in exchange, paying the same to the commissioners and taking the value in Exchequer bills'. On receipt, these were to be cancelled and sent back to London. If the circulation of Exchequer bills and the remittance of funds on this paper had worked, then the English bank would perhaps have achieved a permanent presence in Scotland. We can only guess at the extent of its plans, as the court kept its intentions secret, although the Duke of Queensberry and the Secretaries of State, the Earls of Loudoun and Mar, may have known something more.[4]

The proposed Exchequer bill circulation was seen as a challenge to Bank of Scotland notes, and the attempt to run a cross-border exchange threatened the livelihoods of the Edinburgh exchangers. Both schemes failed. There were lengthy delays to the convoy from London, which arrived on 5 August, and there was rioting when the contents were known. Many creditors of the Company of Scotland refused the bills and demanded bills of exchange on London or gold.[5] The Scottish commissioners insisted that more gold be despatched, and £50,000 duly arrived in half the time it took the earlier convoy to make the journey. Few, if any, of the Exchequer bills remained in circulation by Christmas 1707. The attempt to return the bills by exchange, with the usual charges, was also a failure; at the end of October, the Bank of England, after discussion with the Treasury, empowered the Scottish commissioners to draw bills from Edinburgh, 'by exchange without loss payable at three or four days sight any sums for the service of the Equivalent'.[6] Had the Court of the Bank of England drawn their plans in concert with the directors

3 J. H. Clapham, *The Bank of England. A History* (2 vols, Cambridge: 1944), vol. i, 1697–1797, pp. 38–9.

4 The Bank of England held discussions with the Duke of Queensberry and the Earls of Loudoun and Mar, although exactly what was disclosed is unclear. For the formal bond between the Bank of England and these ministers, see Bank of England, MSS, Court Minutes, vol. E, G4/6, p. 161, 10 July 1707.

5 W. M. Acres, *The Bank of England from Within: 1694–1900* (2 vols, London: 1931), p. 99; Daniel Defoe, *The History of the Union between England and Scotland* (n.d.; repr. London: 1786), pp. 590–1, mentions the resentment expressed on payment by Exchequer bills.

6 Bank of England, MSS, Court Minutes, vol. E, G4/6, p. 178, 30 October 1707.

of Bank of Scotland, then this circulation might have survived, although the circumstances of its operation in London were not present in Scotland and shortly thereafter the directors of the English bank lost interest in a Scottish circulation. The occasion of their new charter in 1707 and a subsequent amendment provided the opportunity for renewal of the arrangements for Exchequer bills. A subsequent Act, 9 Anne c.7, specified payment to the Bank of England, from the Exchequer, of £45,000, and by 12 Anne c.11 a further £8,000 was added as a fee for circulation. Known as the 'Subscription of the Circulation', it was underwritten by subscribers from among the Bank's 'inner circle' and remained a lucrative source of income until November 1760. The bills, which could be cashed at the Bank of England, usually circulated without the need for funds from subscribers. The rare occasions, in 1714, 1715, 1719 and 1745, when such funds were required were, it may be inferred, the result of financial panic caused by Jacobite activity.[7]

Bank of Scotland derived considerable short-term benefits from the Union. While the directors were concerned in August at the use of Exchequer bills, the priority of the board was advances. Unprecedented numbers of banknotes were printed and passed out from mid-August in exchange for coin and Exchequer bills and against a sustained increase in bonds and bills of exchange. From a monthly average of £2,850 from August to December 1705, and inconsequential sums for the same period of 1706, the Cashier was credited with £157,000 for these months in 1707. The monthly average of £31,400 was a higher figure than for any year since 1696. This optimism was well placed, as most of the £232,840 debt owing to the subscribers of the Company of Scotland was paid off by Christmas 1707. From 5 September to 1 January 1708, seven deposits, to a total of £23,755, ranging in size from £550 to £10,000, were made at the Bank by lawyers and factors acting for Darien subscribers. Thereafter, smaller sums came and went, usually from private customers for a few hundred pounds although occasional deposits exceeded this, and the directors decided to write out rules for deposits and repayments.[8] This taking-in of deposits gave the Bank another of the functions of the continental banks, although they made no charge and paid no interest.[9] A further change from this time came with the funds lodged by government officers and revenue-collectors. These could be considerable and included £3,200 for Her

7 For a description of the Subscription, see Clapham, *The Bank of England*, vol. i, pp. 65–72.
8 BS 1/5, Minutes: 2 April 1708. £500 was to be the minimum deposit and £100 the minimum repayment. These limits were ignored by the Treasurer to avoid inconvenience to depositors.
9 J. G. van Dillen, 'The Bank of Amsterdam', and H. Sieveking, 'Die Hamburger Bank', in J. G. van Dillen (ed.), *History of the Principal Public Banks accompanied by Extensive Bibliographies of the History of Banking and Credit in Eleven European Countries* (The Hague: 1934), pp. 79–124, 125–60.

Majesty's Troop of Guards after the invasion scare of February and March 1708, and in August 1711 Robert Sinclair of Quandell, Cashier of the Excise, lodged £17,500.[10] The deposits supported a doubling of advances in the four years from 1710.[11]

The Bank was awarded a pivotal role in the administration of the Scottish recoinage. All the coin circulating in Scotland was reduced to the London Mint par for sterling and, in the case of worn English and all Scots coin, was recast at the Scots Mint. The new coin was handed out to the original owners at the face value of the old; existing English silver coin was cried down to the standard and the loss made up with new coin or notes from the Bank. To minimise smuggling into Scotland of defective English coin, the Privy Council appointed burgh magistrates in Edinburgh, Glasgow and Aberdeen to collect the English coin on one day only, 14 April 1708.[12] Thereafter, all such coin was to be charged as bullion. For the old Scots coin, the Bank was granted the collection and issue to the Mint and was authorised by the Privy Council, upon receipt, to issue its banknotes or coin 'in the option of the demander'. It was tedious work for the Bank tellers; all coin had to be weighed and assessed, and the impending abolition of the old Scots Mint in the Cowgate soured relations with their officers. When the recoinage books were closed in 1709, coin to a worth of £411,000 sterling had been despatched from the Bank: £142,180 of pre-1673 Scots 'hammered' silver coin, £96,856 of post-1673 silver, £132,080 of foreign coin and about £40,000 of English and £30,000 of gold coin. Some coins went back as far as the fifteenth century.[13] Although most worn and debased coin probably came in, there was under-recording of more modern Scots coin; George Watson was still dispensing advice on these in later years.[14]

There was an unfortunate sequel. Although the Scottish Privy Council Proclamation for the Recoinage stated that the Bank would be paid a fee of ½ per cent in sterling value of all coin received, it offered no formal contract. On 1 May 1708, the Privy Council was abolished after manoeuvres, designed by the Squadrone and supported by the English Whigs, to restrict the influence of ministers of the Crown in Scottish elections. This terminated the only executive power in Scotland which could order payment. In January 1709, the Earls of Leven, Seafield and Glasgow petitioned in London for the £2,056 owing on the last six

10 BS 1/5, Minutes: 11 March 1708, recorded a 'very extraordinary demand on the Bank occasioned by the news and report of an invasion from France'.
11 BS 1/94, General Ledgers, 1710, 1713.
12 'A proclamation concerning English coin', repr. in Daniel Defoe, *History of the Union*, pp. 699–700; the Council oversaw the collection by magistrates in Edinburgh.
13 N. Munro, *The History of the Royal Bank of Scotland 1727–1927* (Edinburgh: 1928), pp. 25–6.
14 Edinburgh City Archive, EMC MSS, Letter book no. 44, J. Anderson to George Watson [1713].

certificates signed by the Mint officers. There followed other delegations to anyone who might have influence: the Duke of Queensberry, the Earls of Loudoun and Mar, the Earl of Oxford (the Lord Treasurer) and even the Queen. When Anne died in 1714, the Bank gave up its attempts.[15]

The dispersal of the new coin led to an easing of the cost of exchange to and from London by October. In spite of a short-term rise caused by the Jacobite invasion scare of 1708, the tendency of the London–Edinburgh exchange thereafter was a move towards par.[16] There was also a gradual easing of interest rates, and this process was influenced by the Bank in September 1709 when the rate for bills of exchange was cut to 6 per cent for the first sixty days. In 1714, when the legal maximum for British interest rates was reduced to 5 per cent, the Bank of Scotland rate for bills went to 4½ per cent on loans given 'punctual payment' and 5 per cent where the thirty-day grace period had expired.[17] Although the Union may have speeded up these changes in Scotland, it was unlikely to have been the sole cause. By the close of the war in 1714, the European financial markets were under less pressure for funds, and thus a longer-term movement towards lower interest rates and exchange costs set in; but this would have happened even if the old constitutional status of Scotland had persisted. It may be noted that while interest rates fell, they rarely converged on those in London; for most of the eighteenth century, they remained from ½–1 per cent higher in Scotland. With the increase in coin and the improvement in payments, a run on the Bank was unlikely, although fears were raised that this might happen.[18] There was some concern that the reduction in value of coin might be prejudicial to 'noblemen, gentlemen and others who have vast sums of money to pay per bond' denominated in sterling, but this worry also faded.

After 1707, the great Scottish magnates fought their disputes at Westminster, and as a consequence there was, for a few years, less political interest in Bank of Scotland. Being left in relative peace, more merchants

15 BS 1/5, Minutes: 18 January 1709; 5 May 1709, letters to Queensberry, Loudoun and Mar; 13 December 1709, reminder to Leven, Seafield and Glasgow; 6 July 1710, delegation to Seafield; 23 July 1711; 3 January 1712, the Bank court decided against direct petition to Queen Anne; 6 November 1712; 5 November, discussion with Mar; 3 December 1713, Mar promised to see the Queen; January 1714, letters to Barons of the Exchequer and Lord High Treasurer.
16 Daniel Defoe, *History of the Union*, p. 446, exaggerated this effect: 'in one day all the English money (viz. all the silver money) in the kingdom was reduced to the English value and went after that as in England and for no more; and as the rate of exchange always attends the intrinsic value of the species so the exchange, which before ran at eleven or twelve per cent to the disadvantage of Scotland, immediately came to a par, and money ran between London and Edinburgh at a half per cent, or at most one per cent sometimes this way sometimes that way as the demand of remitters and drawers happened to alter the case'. At the time of the Union, Defoe was in the pay of the English government.
17 BS 1/5, Minutes: 15 September 1714, order for reduction of rate for inland bills to 5 per cent.
18 Anon., 'A Letter to a Member of Parliament anent the Application of the £309,885–10sh Equivalent with Consideration of reducing the coin to the value and standard of England' [GL 1706].

and lawyers were attracted to Bank affairs and there was a shift among the directors towards these professions.[19] Apart from the Governor, the Earl of Leven, by 1711 the highest-ranking members of the extraordinary board were the legal luminaries Sir James McKenzie the Lord Clerk Register and Sir Hew Dalrymple, along with Sir James Elphinstone of Logie. Otherwise the board was left to merchants, lawyers and lairds. The Deputy Governor was almost always an Edinburgh merchant or lawyer, usually elected for a two-year term of office, a tradition which lasted for almost fifty years.[20]

The leaders of the Squadrone and their allies maintained close links and guaranteed loans, such as £400 underwritten by the Earl of Seafield (later Findlater) for John Philp, the Auditor of the Revenue in the Exchequer, and several advances were made to the Duke of Montrose for £2,000 and above.[21] Moreover, the pattern of lending shifted towards Edinburgh merchants and lawyers for personal bonds, and their usually meticulous preparation lifted some pressure from the Bank staff over, for example, searches of the Register of Sasines for heritable bonds. Apart from the endless requests from writers and merchants in Edinburgh for bills and bonds for their clients in the country, lending to groups of merchants from several burghs became a commonplace. Money also went to the Deans of Guild, to burgh officials in Falkirk and Dundee and to the New Mills Company, although that was now in difficulties because of competition from England. The board was more open to arrangements for lending; advances by bill of exchange came to be treated in a similar way to the later cash account in credit, allowing frequent payments and withdrawals. In July 1709, the directors raised the ceiling for individual advances on heritable bonds to £2,000 and the total to £20,000; by the close of 1710 another £28,683 was lent out on bonds, followed by £22,908 in 1711.[22] Business now approached that of the best times before the stop of 1704–5. Whereas the balance of March 1706 showed total lending of £24,118 and a dismal £6,052 in notes out, four years later lending was £45,513 and circulation £28,221. In fact, March was usually a low point

19 For a discussion of the political vacuum in Scotland after 1707 and the place of the legal profession in the leadership of society, see N. T. Phillipson, 'Lawyers, Landowners and the Civic Leadership of Post Union Scotland: An Essay on the Social Role of the Faculty of Advocates 1661–1830 in 18th Century Scottish Society', *Juridical Review*, 21 (1976), 97–120.
20 C. A. Malcolm, *Bank of Scotland, 1695–1945* (Edinburgh: n.d. [1948]), p. 236. Five directors, namely James and Andrew Marjoribanks, John Jamieson of Balmure, Alexander Arbuthnot and John Forrest, each served for more than one term as Deputy Governor.
21 For lending, see below, Chapter 12; more members of the Squadrone, in proportion to their number, borrowed from Bank of Scotland and/or held Bank stock than among the members of the three rival political groups. For lists of the factions in 1710, see D. Szechi, *Jacobitism and Tory Politics 1710–14* (Edinburgh: 1984), Appendix 2, 'Computation of peers 30 August 1710 by Mr Thomas Bruce son to the Earl of Kincardine', pp. 204–5.
22 BS 1/5, Minutes: 21 March 1710.

in the financial year and at Lammas and Martinmas totals were higher, often considerably so.[23] As noted above, advances soared in the four years to 1713 to reach £91,000 and a circulation of almost £40,000. These years were among the most profitable in the eighteenth century. In the nine years from 1699 to 1707, an annual average of 14 per cent was paid in dividends, and from 1708 to 1715 this rose to an average of 22.25 per cent, with 1713, 1714 and 1715 being 30 per cent. Quotations for stock prices showed a rise in eight years after the Union of 27.5 per cent to 227⅔.[24]

The rules for recoveries were variously refined and there were, for example, frequent difficulties in extracting annualrents on time, but in the aftermath of the Union there appeared less need to pursue borrowers. There were occasional worries; so tangled were the lists of cautioners by June 1711 that the directors ordered an alphabetical list to be drawn up, 'to see who stood bound as debtors'.[25] The accounting system remained tightly controlled; George Watson, for example, remained a member of the auditing committee which reported to the adventurers each year, and John Holland was regularly in touch. The directors paid him £60 for his expenses in visiting the Bank in September 1709.

The sharp rise in bank lending in the five years from 1709 were indicative of an agricultural economy which benefited from the active links with English markets. There was a vigorous if not always widespread interest in 'improvement' in lowland Scotland at this time, and the good prices realised for cattle, and buoyant conditions in general, encouraged lairds to borrow a few hundred pounds for various arable, pasture and food-processing ventures.[26] Nevertheless, the Bank had to be careful. The three years 1708–10 saw sharp increases in grain prices, although not as prolonged as those which ended the seventeenth century.[27] Of course, the economic prospects of the agrarian sector were only part of the story, for, in the view of the board, there was the presence of adverse political factors which threatened to upset the potential for secure advances. Underlying the treaty of Union was widespread bribery and corruption of members of Parliament, and this venal attitude to public affairs carried over to the

23 For seasonal peaks and troughs, see below, Chapter 12; for balances, see BS 1/94/2, General Ledger.
24 See Statistical Appendix, Table A2; W. R. Scott, *The Constitution and Finance of English, Scottish and Irish Joint-Stock Companies to 1720* (3 vols, Cambridge: 1910–12), vol. iii, division X, section III, p. 268.
25 BS 1/5, Minutes: 7 June 1711.
26 T. C. Smout and A. Fenton, 'Scottish Agriculture before the Improvers – An Exploration', *Agricultural History Review*, 12 (1964), 73–93; R. Mitchison, 'The Movements of Scottish Corn Prices in the Seventeenth and Eighteenth Centuries', *Economic History Review*, 2nd series, 18 (1965), 278–91.
27 A. J. S. Gibson and T. C. Smout, *Prices, Food and Wages in Scotland 1550–1780* (Cambridge: 1995), pp. 86–8, Table 3.3: a comparison of fourteen sets of fiars' oat prices for 1708–10 compared to those of 1707 shows an increase of 22–23 per cent for three prices, 41–48 per cent for five, one each for 56, 66, 69 and 81 per cent, and three for over 100 per cent.

forty-five Scots in the Commons and the sixteen representative peers. All factions sought the incomes of government office and pensions from the secret service funds. In return for these payments, members concerned gave regular attendance and supported the government, whether Whig or Tory. Thus, by the accession of George I, Parliamentary politics in Scotland had degenerated into a 'spoils system', with the election of peers 'pure farce'.[28] It was even suggested on good authority that a typical Scottish MP could be bought by the government for ten guineas a week. But this approach to public office was inherently unstable, and factions could be swayed to change voting intentions when they felt aggrieved. There was an underlying tone of unease, shared by all factions, which wondered whether the Union would live up to expectations. In 1708, for example, the leading members of the Squadrone were quite ready to form an alliance with the Jacobites.[29] The Scots found that the Irish linen producers were already well organised, and attempts in Parliament to raise bounties for Scottish coarse linens floundered.[30] The loss of the Privy Council on 1 May 1708 had left a void in economic planning, and it seemed to legislators that Westminster was an inadequate substitute for the clamours of Scottish industry and trade. To this feeling, the Earl of Oxford, the Lord Treasurer, offered a partial solution in November 1711 with a commission of chamberlainry and trade, formed to discuss economic matters and disburse funds for coarse wool nominally available under article XV of the treaty. After a desultory existence, it folded when the board of trade claimed that this usurped their functions. There was the vexed question of taxation, as the hopes of the legislators for a rising level were not borne out. Article IX of the treaty fixed the cess (land tax) at a net £48,000 after all charges, collected by the Receiver General, Archibald Douglas of Cavers, hereditary sheriff of Roxburgh.[31] It was a sensitive post, as Douglas was required to pay pensions to Jacobites and government informers, and there were a series of disputes over assessments. Although only the land tax produced a significant surplus for the Exchequer before 1725, the modest changes made to the linen and salt taxes and a proposal in 1713 for a malt tax encouraged additional criticism of the Union. In May 1713, all the Scottish magnates agreed to present the Queen with a proposal for dissolution of the Union, and on 2 June this was moved in the Lords by the Earl of Findlater; the administrative

28 W. Ferguson, Scotland: 1689 to the Present, The Edinburgh History of Scotland, vol. iv (Edinburgh: 1968), p. 137.
29 Ibid., pp. 56–7.
30 C. Gill, The Rise of the Irish Linen Industry (Oxford: 1925), ch. 4.
31 W. R. Ward, 'The Land Tax in Scotland, 1707–98', Bulletin of the John Rylands Library (1953–4), 288–308; R. H. Campbell, 'The Anglo-Scottish Union of 1707, II: The Economic Consequences', Economic History Review, 2nd series, 16 (1963–4), 468–77.

and political consequences of Union had weakened aristocratic power, significantly added to the burdens of taxation and led to 'the ruin of our trade and manufactorys'.[32] There was some substance to the charge that the finer end of industrial production for earthenware, glass, iron and copper utensils and general household goods and textiles had been unable to compete with English imports, but the main concern of legislators was expressed over the need for higher bounties for linen and other potential exports. The motion was defeated by only four votes.

The political debates took place in a climate of intrigue and active military preparation by the Jacobites. At the death of Queen Anne, they proved characteristically indecisive, and the Whigs secured the reins of power before George I arrived for his coronation.[33] Moreover, in the early months of the reign, the leading Scottish magnates all sought office and discouraged opposition. The elections of February 1715 resulted in a Parliament loyal to the Hanoverians, and subsequent aggressive moves by ministers persuaded many Tories and the Jacobites that they could expect little from the new regime. They might have been easily placated, but George I was a haughty and arrogant monarch who looked on even his most loyal ministers with contempt and was vindictive towards any who advanced the status of his son, the future George II. On 6 September, the Earl of Mar raised the Stewart flag at Braemar. There were soon 10,000 men in arms, and had Mar acted swiftly he could have expected to take Edinburgh. But the Earl was a poor strategist, and on 13 November he was defeated at the battle of Sheriffmuir by the Duke of Argyll and the rebellion petered out. The government found that virtually every estate seized was encumbered with debt, and the legislation of 1690 had ensured that debtors had a prior claim before the government; the Bank, for instance, lodged claims against the estate of the Earl of Southesk and James Stirling of Keir for advances.[34] The Earl of Panmure was the only adventurer whose shares were forfeited.

The political uncertainty and subsequent fighting seriously affected the work of the Bank. Advances on bond ceased in January 1714, although some advances by bill continued until September 1715. The speculation about Jacobite intent caused 'extraordinary demands' on the Bank's cash reserves in August, and on 19 September the directors halted payments

32 There was some justification for the view that manufactures were adversely affected by English imports: Ferguson, *Scotland: 1689 to the Present*, p. 61; for taxation, Campbell, 'The Anglo-Scottish Union of 1707', pp. 470, 473; for the political crisis, G. Holmes, 'The Hamilton Affair of 1711–1712: A Crisis in Anglo-Scottish Relations', in C. Jones and D. L. Jones (eds), *Peers, Politics and Power: The House of Lords, 1603–1911* (London: 1986), pp. 151–76.
33 Ferguson, *Scotland: 1689 to the Present*, pp. 63–4.
34 BS 1/5, Minutes: 28 November 1716, 7 February 1717, 7 August 1718; Ferguson, *Scotland: 1689 to the Present*, p. 139.

and issued a notice that all banknotes would henceforth carry 5 per cent annualrent. All holders of past-due bills were asked to repay by 1 November, although many did not. During the ensuing twelve months there were no advances, and no dividend was declared in March 1716. At this time, £65,070 of notes were 'standing out and not yet cancelled', with around £80,000 in assets as bills and bonds. Little business was transacted before February 1717, and for the rest of the year only £6,400 was lent by bond. Bill discounting increased after the summer of 1717 but also remained subdued.

The inadequate provision for Scottish debts in the Treaty of Union eventually enabled the second Duke of Argyll to lay siege to the Bank and, in 1727, to help found the Royal Bank. This proved the most intractable political problem which the Bank of Scotland directors faced in the first half of the eighteenth century. The basic difficulty was the insufficiency of the Equivalent funds to pay the pre-1707 creditors of the government and the lengthy attempts after the Union to solve this problem. In the first instance, against a background of a chorus of protest from persons owed money, the Treaty commissioners and the Barons of the Exchequer in Scotland secured additional powers to decide who was, or was not, a creditor.[35] These granted an issue of debentures at 5 per cent, signed by the Lords of Session, and by 1713 £138,201 7s worth had been issued. But these were not convertible to other government stock, were not redeemable, and lacked an adequate fund to pay the interest. By article XV of the treaty, it was assumed that the customs would increase above £30,000 and excise above £35,000, and this 'arising equivalent' was to be applied to the national debts and the coarse wool trade. But, for the six years to 1713, the customs fell short of expectations, and although the excise produced a profit the collectors avoided payments of interest on the debentures. They thus fell to a fraction of their face value. The Duke of Atholl, for example, was informed that his debentures, granted in lieu of payment for regimental clothing, were 'worth very little money'.[36] Patrick Campbell of Monzie, later Lord Monzie, was offered some salvage from the Darien Company, 'old sails, cordage, muskets, nails, candlesticks and other junk'. William Paterson was offered £3,000 for the £18,000 worth of debentures he held. By 1713, 'several hundreds' of the debenture holders had formed a committee, on which sat the Governor of Bank of Scotland, and they met regularly in Edinburgh.[37] The committee managed

---

35 *Statutes of the Realm* (1821), vol. 8, p. 776, 6 Anne c.51, 'An Act for the further directing of the Equivalent money'.
36 Munro, *The History of the Royal Bank of Scotland*, pp. 28–9.
37 P. W. J. Riley, *The English Ministers and Scotland 1707–1727*, Institute of Historical Research Publications, no. 15 (London: 1964), ch. 14; BS 1/5, Minutes 1713 and 1714, for mention of this committee.

one success. Payments from the 'arising Equivalent' were due to terminate after seven years, but in the Parliament of 1714 this was extended and additional claims were allowed, namely £10,992 in fees and perquisites due to the Barons of the Exchequer, £14,000 for coarse wool manufactories (but never paid), £15,129 for the salaries of Commissioners and £44,758 for interest. This gave a new total of £230,308 issued in new debentures, again with 5 per cent interest but with no source of redemption other than the revenues listed in the treaty.[38] However, as this coincided with a resurgence of the Jacobite threat and the end of the European war, the holders were given hope when a payment of one year's interest of £15,828 was authorised by Parliament.[39] The invasion of 1715 and its aftermath was sufficient pressure on the Treasury to recommend a further two years' payment, both for the original £230,308 and £18,242 compensation for William Paterson.[40]

The leading Scots among the holders of the debt after the rebellion were the second Duke of Argyll and his younger brother the Earl of Ilay, later the third Duke, Colonel John Campbell of Mamore, later the fourth Duke, Patrick Campbell of Monzie, John, third Lord Belhaven, a gentleman of the bedchamber to the Prince of Wales, and others including George Middleton, the London banker, and William Paterson. They were part of what was soon to be the most powerful political interest in Scotland. In 1719, the second Duke was appointed Lord Steward of the Household and created Duke of Greenwich, and when Robert Walpole became Lord Treasurer in 1721 various members of the Argyll interest were promoted to government office.[41] Government endorsement was sought for a refunding by which the debentures would receive a fixed annual sum and the holders a charter of incorporation. The first end was secured in June 1719 (by 5 George I c.20) when funds of £10,000 for interest were settled for the £248,550 of debentures, and £2,000 for the woollen manufacture, both from the Scottish customs and excise. Should a deficiency arise, it was to be made good out of other Scottish revenues. Payments were free of taxes and fees, and the Scottish courts, which were not part of the Argyll interest, were prohibited from interfering. The Act also included a clause whereby the king, if so advised, could incorporate the proprietors of the debentures as a corporation with perpetual succession, with all

---

38 *Statutes of the Realm*, vol. 9, p. 924, 13 Anne c.12 (1713), 'An Act to discharge and acquit the Commissioners of the Equivalent . . .'; figures from *House of Lords Journal*, vol. 19, 7 July 1714.
39 1 George I c.27, 'An Act for taking and stating the debts due and growing due to Scotland by way of Equivalent in the term of the Union and for relief of the creditors of the public in Scotland and the Commissioners of the Equivalent'; Munro, *The History of the Royal Bank of Scotland*, p. 29.
40 3 & 4 George I c.14, 'An Act to continue an Act', and 1 George I c.9, private acts, 'An Act for relieving William Paterson out of the equivalent money for what is due to him'.
41 Riley, *English Ministers and Scotland*, ch. 16.

the legal security of such bodies, with the additional but vague phrase that they could have 'such other powers to do and perform such other matters and things appertaining to them to do or perform touching or concerning the said capital'.[42] The projectors then tried to obtain such a charter. Adopting a proposal from William Paterson, a majority of the holders signed an indenture styling themselves the *Society of the Subscribed Equivalent Debt* to claim borrowing and issuing rights, to deal in mortgages, pledges, purchases of goods and lands and the bill-of-exchange trade. They agreed to restrict note issue to paper payable at six months from the time of borrowing and ruled out notes payable on demand while the Bank of England existed. One-tenth of the profits was to go to Paterson for twenty-one years. Their request for a charter was one of numerous projects floated during the financial boom of this time.

In early August 1719, the Bank of England objected that any such charter should confine the proposed Company to the receipt and distribution of the £10,000 interest with £600 for administration. The Bank of England lawyers advised that what was proposed would constitute the proprietors a corporation of an unlimited nature with the same powers and privileges as the Bank of England but with the addition of trading rights from which the Bank itself was restrained.[43] The projectors argued that the vague phrases of the 1719 statute did indeed imply the rights listed in their indenture, and when rebuffed by the Attorney General they suggested a clause virtually identical to that obtained by the South Sea Company in 9 Anne c.22 which had prohibited them from acting as a bank.[44] This put the Attorney General in some difficulty; the restriction in the South Sea Act had not stopped the South Sea Company from conducting banking operations. In November, he advised that the clause 'offered by the proprietors of the Equivalent is a proper and reasonable security to the bank of England, the same being framed in the words and according to the tenor of the clauses which the parliament hath thought fit to enact on other occasions'.[45] This infuriated the court of the Bank of England.[46] Bank of Scotland's directors did not help matters by informing the Attorney General that they found the limiting clause proposed by the debenture holders acceptable.[47] The collapse of the South Sea stock

42 5 George I c.20, 'An Act for settling certain yearly funds payable out of the revenues of Scotland'.
43 Bank of England, MSS, Court Minutes, vol. H, G4/11, pp. 79, 82: 6 and 27 August 1719.
44 PRO, T 1/223/no. 8, 27 November 1719, Attorney General Lechmere to the Lords of the Treasury.
45 Ibid.
46 Bank of England, MSS, Court Minutes, vol. H, G4/11, p. 82: 27 August, 24 December 1719.
47 PRO, T 1/223/no. 8, 27 November 1719, Attorney General Lechmere to Lords of the Treasury; it is entirely consistent with the contemporaneous activities of George Middleton, Patrick Campbell of Monzie and the Duke of Argyll and the other leading financiers of the Equivalent that, if granted a charter, they would have launched a 'stockjobbing' exercise to raise the share price, borrow money

after 24 June 1720 brought their efforts to an end.[48] From July 1720 to September 1722, the Attorney and Solicitor General's offices refused comment on the application while they unravelled the traumas of the stockmarket crash.

Having failed in their scheme, the debenture-holders made three attempts in 1720–1 to force an amalgamation with Bank of Scotland. In the first, they proposed that those among the Equivalent debenture-holders who supported the scheme would make over their part of the £10,600 income from government and in return would receive Bank of Scotland notes to the value of 90 per cent of each subscriber's debt. The remaining 10 per cent of their debt would be 'joined' with the 10 per cent of paid-up capital of the Bank subscription. They suggested to the Bank directors that 'many advantages to the Bank may be obtained from the Government, such as the £2,000 yearly allowed for all pretensions of growing equivalents due to Scotland, and the disposal of the £14,000 for wool'.[49] The proposal was rejected.

The holders then established an Edinburgh Society for insuring houses against loss by fire.[50] It had nothing to do with its title and was timeously perceived as a cover for another assault on the Bank. When their advances for amalgamation were also rebuffed, they presented £8,400 in notes and demanded cash but failed to persuade the commissioners of the customs, the excise, and the Receiver General of taxes to remove their balances from the Bank. The Bank called up another £10,000 in capital, to make £20,000, and restricted discounts for bills of exchange. There was a short-lived run, but this petered out by early June 1720. Lastly, the Edinburgh Society proposed an amalgamation which would have involved a transfer of 600 Bank of Scotland shares for which they would receive £200 Scots per share (the sum of £10,000 sterling for the whole) – a value on the shares of £16 13s 4d sterling (at 12:1).[51]

There was also a proposal at this time from the Royal Exchange Assurance, forwarded by James Armour ws, the old collaborator of Hugh

---

and issue notes for other speculative purposes in London and Paris. As they would have launched their scheme towards the height of the London boom, this might have sunk the Argyll interest.
48 For the collapse of the South Sea stock after 24 June 1720, when it reached 1,000, see Scott, *Constitution and Finance*, vol. iii, pp. 409–11; a further effort by the debenture-holders is recorded in PRO, T 1/223/no. 17, 22 December 1719; for the course of the Bubble, P. G. M. Dickson, *The Financial Revolution in England: A Study in the Development of Public Credit 1688–1756* (London: 1967), chs 5 and 6; for Scottish participation in the speculation, see pp. 152–3.
49 Richard Holland, *An Historical Account of the Establishment, Progress and State of the Bank of Scotland* ([Edinburgh:] 1728).
50 The four managers of the Edinburgh Society were Baillie Robert Wightman, George Drummond, Mungo Grahame of Guthrie and Sir Robert Sinclair, the Cashier of the Excise. The last three named were all active in the formation of the Royal Bank; BS 1/5, Minutes: 21 April, 5 May, 17 May 1720. The Society closed after the passage of the Bubble Act, 6 George I c.18, 11 June 1720.
51 Richard Holland, *An Historical Account*, pp. 19–20.

Figure 5.1 Monthly lending on bills and bonds, November 1697 to December 1730

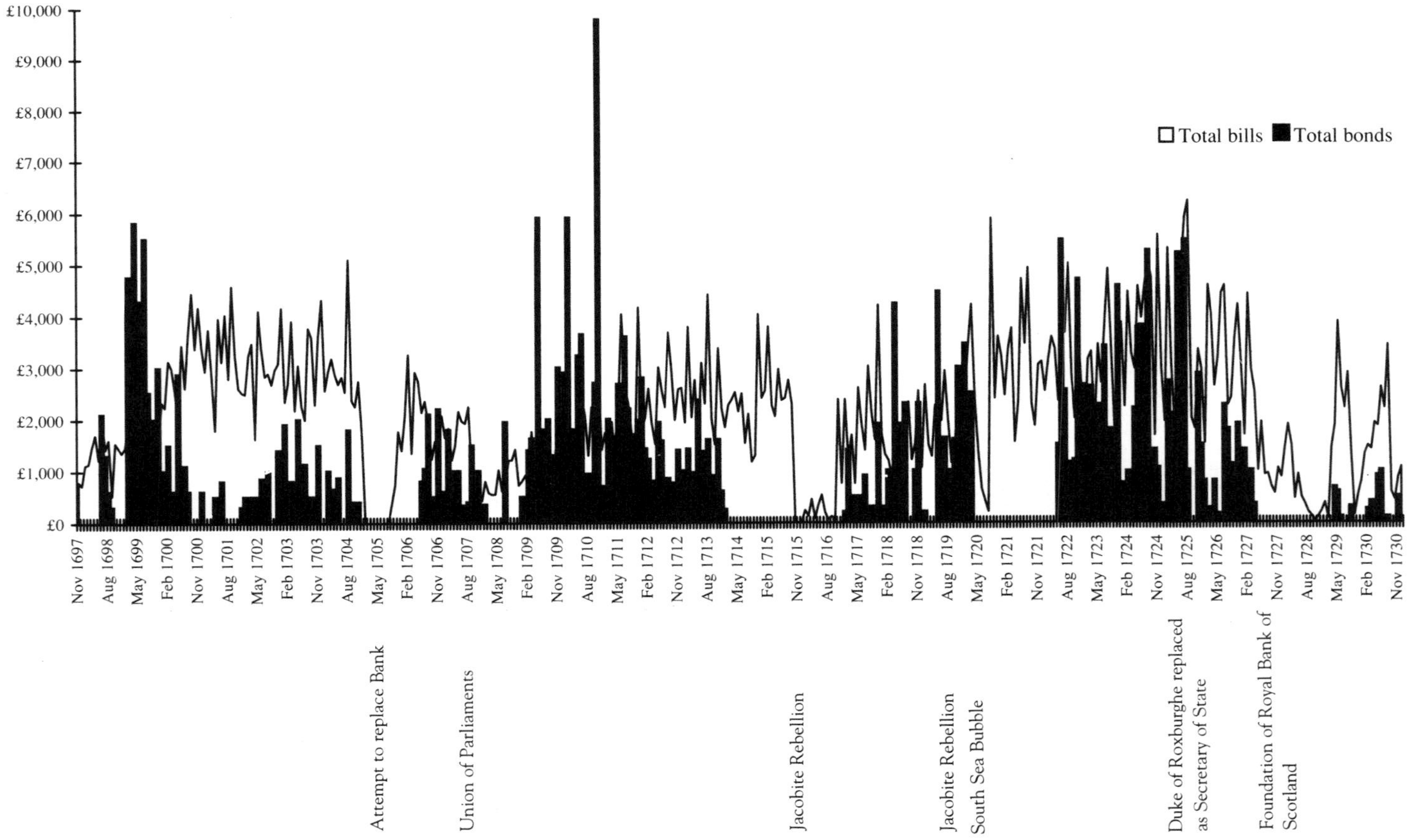

Chamberlain. It proposed to lend Bank of Scotland £20,000 in sterling, and in return asked for half the Bank profits, after £2,500 was reserved for the adventurers. The Royal Exchange share price had collapsed in the autumn of 1720 and the company was later forced to recapitalise its business, so it was not in a strong negotiating position.[52] Richard Holland suggested that the Royal Exchange expected a return of at least 11 per cent but would have avoided any liability beyond its loan. While it was in the interest of Bank of Scotland to stabilise seasonal fluctuations in the London–Edinburgh exchange perhaps in conjunction with a reputable London company, there were too many suspicions in these years for this to come to anything. By 1725, the Royal Exchange was well on the way to a recovery from its earlier misfortunes, and the matter disappeared from view.

As mentioned before, Bank of Scotland made a slow recovery from the Jacobite-inspired troubles of 1715. The Bank was able to pay the interest on its banknotes and reorganised lending; by 27 March 1719, circulation totalled £31,400, bonds stood at £52,685 and bills at £10,000. In the first three months of 1720, £8,350 was lent by bond, but in April the directors were so concerned over the drain of coin to fuel speculation in London that further advances by bond were stopped. On 5 May, a fourth part of all debts was recalled and nothing more was lent on bond until May 1722. Advances by bill were less severely curtailed; they declined for four months from August 1720 and then recovered. In fact, by March 1722, lending exceeded that before the crisis known as the South Sea Bubble. By March 1725, banknotes in circulation totalled £46,625, bonds stood at £87,783 and bills at £31,727. Deposits were especially strong at almost £50,000; one from Andrew Fletcher, cashier of the excise, totalled £28,500, and other government departments accounted for the bulk of the rest. A total of £95,243 was lent on bond in the five years to 1726, and the figures for bills were always more than double the level of the previous annual peaks in 1710–13 (see Figure 5.1). It was an optimistic time for the landed classes. June 1723 saw the launch in Edinburgh of the *Society of Improvers in the Knowledge of Agriculture*, and dozens of advances were made to lawyers and merchants involved with landed projects.

By 1725, there were indications of economic difficulty south of the Border. Urban development proceeded apace in the first wave of Georgian rebuilding of English cities which commenced in 1713, and by 1725 this showed signs of strain. T. S. Ashton and J. P. Lewis agree with Sir John Summerson that the second half of 1726 saw a downturn in the building

---

52 Scott, *Constitution and Finance*, vol. iii, pp. 397–410; Richard Holland, *An Historical Account*, pp. 21–4.

cycle, although this varied from town to town, and the outbreak of war with Spain in 1727, which pushed up interest rates, was likely to have been the actual turning point.[53] Some of the advances of Bank of Scotland were associated with buoyant trading conditions across the Border. Moreover, Scottish trade and agriculture saw a number of speculative investments, and the Bank directors restricted heritable bonds in July 1725 'as the extent is too great, until a part is paid back'.[54] While thirty-four bonds were granted, of an average of £719 in 1725, in the following year the average of thirty-three fell to only £316, and none exceeded £500.

In 1724, an Act of Parliament incorporated the holders of the Equivalent debts, with their capital of £248,550, into the *Society of the Equivalent Company*.[55] It had thirteen directors including Sir Hew Dalrymple, the Lord President of Session, Patrick Campbell of Monzie, and Patrick Crauford, and a number of the old associates of William Paterson in London financial circles.[56] As 210 out of 238 shares in the company were held by London residents, their new office was fixed there although they maintained a branch in Edinburgh. Its functions were limited to the collection and dispersal of the £10,600 from the government, and they still required a charter which would convert all, or part, of the Company capital to a proposed bank along with the payments from the government.[57]

In this aim, the Society was immeasurably helped by the growth in strength of the political position of the Duke of Argyll and the Earl of Ilay and their allies. Conversely, the Squadrone, who remained the political allies of Bank of Scotland, were in decline.[58] They were loyal Hanoverians after the rebellion of 1715, though rather more monarchical in their views than most Whigs, and for this reason the Duke of Roxburghe, appointed the third Secretary of State in 1716, remained in office until 1725. His fall from power was orchestrated by Robert Walpole, who, from April 1721, secured the position of First Lord of the Treasury and Chancellor of the Exchequer and an alliance with the Newcastle-Pelham families

53 T. S. Ashton, *Economic Fluctuations in England and Wales 1700–1800* (Oxford: 1959), pp. 91–2; J. P. Lewis, *Building Cycles and Britain's Growth* (London: 1965), p. 16; Sir John Summerson, *Georgian London* (London: 1945), p. 111; for the high levels of bankruptcies in 1726 south of the Border, see J. Hoppit, *Risk and Failure in English Business, 1700–1800* (Cambridge: 1987), Appendix 1.
54 BS 1/5, Minutes: July 1725.
55 Munro, *The History of the Royal Bank of Scotland*, pp. 32–3.
56 PRO, T 1/243/no. 64, 14 June 1723; T 1/248/no. 3, 3 July 1724, report of the meetings of the Equivalent proprietors in London.
57 Bank of England, MSS, Court Minutes, vol. K, G4/13, p. 253, 16 March 1726–27, p. 258, 30 March 1727, at which time they warned that they would oppose any scheme if they felt it necessary; Richard Holland, *An Historical Account*, p. 26.
58 See the discussion in J. S. Shaw, *The Management of Scottish Society 1707–1764* (Edinburgh: 1983), pp. 48–9; also W. L. Mathieson, *Scotland and the Union: A History of Scotland from 1695 to 1747* (Glasgow: 1905), pp. 321–7.

which kept him as undisputed leader of Parliamentary politics for over twenty years.[59] Robert Walpole realised that the Argyll interest had more influence than the Squadrone; in 1725 the Duke of Roxburghe was blamed for his inept handling of the imposition of a new malt tax which led to rioting in Glasgow, and was removed from office in August. All Scottish business was henceforth arranged by the two English Secretaries of State, with the Earl of Ilay as effective controller of Scottish politics.[60]

After the fall of the Duke of Roxburghe, the Duke of Argyll insisted that the Equivalent Society be granted the right to organise banking, and at this time Robert Walpole was less concerned with the protests from the Bank of England than he was in later years. Nevertheless, in eighteenth-century politics, nothing could be taken for granted, and as late as February 1727, George Middleton advised caution over the purchase of Equivalent Society stock, 'a fund no ways saleable like others', as there was no certainty that a charter would be granted and, even if it were, it might not include the right to organise a bank. Middleton also realised that the start-up of a bank could be painful; the stock might not rise 'to such a vast degree' as some hoped, though his own holding of £9,611 worth gave him an interest in any growth.[61]

Furthermore, the Equivalent Society sought to capitalise on the political strength of the Argyll interest. Rumours circulated in Edinburgh and London to the effect that Bank of Scotland was disaffected; that it had refused to lend the government money in 1715 and at other times had refused to take Exchequer bills. There were even suggestions that Bank of Scotland supported the Jacobites, a line reiterated by some historians: 'After the Treaty of Union there survived for many years a governmental suspicion of the Old Bank's political integrity; its Tory directors had objected to the Treaty; its Treasurer was a Jacobite . . .'.[62] David Drummond, Treasurer of the Bank from 1700 to 1741, 'was indeed a staunch supporter of the Stuart cause [and] he acted as Treasurer of a fund for the defence of the prisoners tried after 1715'. This was correct, although it was not difficult to link public figures with the Jacobite cause, including members of the Court of Session, representative peers, Barons of the Exchequer and the Faculty of Advocates. Moreover, the post of

59 J. H. Plumb, *The Growth of Political Stability in England 1675–1725* (London: 1967), ch. 6; T. J. McCann, *The Correspondence of the Dukes of Richmond and Newcastle 1724–1750* Sussex Record Society, vol. 73 (1982–3); J. H. Plumb, *Sir Robert Walpole: The King's Minister* (London: 1960).
60 Shaw, *The Management of Scottish Society*, pp. 43–8; Ferguson, *Scotland: 1689 to the Present*, p. 141.
61 Coutts & Co., Letter Book, vol. 16, p. 479: 18 May 1727, George Middleton to Robert Campbell in Edinburgh.
62 Munro, *The History of the Royal Bank of Scotland*, pp. 52–3; and see S. G. Checkland, *Scottish Banking: A History, 1695–1973* (Glasgow: 1975), pp. 48, 58, 72, 74; Malcolm, *Bank of Scotland*, pp. 52–3.

Treasurer lacked the stature it was to have in the nineteenth century; the directors meeting several times a week decided on advances, while the Treasurer and Accountant managed the cash and kept the books. For much of the eighteenth century, the Secretary was a more important figure, dealing as he did with political matters in a turbulent society. Whatever the personal views of directors and managers, the power of the Duke of Argyll ensured his success; on 31 May 1727, a charter was obtained under the Great Seal of Scotland which provided the right to organise banking in Scotland using that part of the stock of the Equivalent Society subscribed for the purpose. Once the new Bank was established, the stage was set for a determined assault on Bank of Scotland.

In the fourteen years which followed the Union, the Bank was subjected to disturbances resulting from Jacobite invasions and the intrigues of domestic financiers which forced periodic stops to payments and lending; in 1715 this damage lasted for seven months. In 1719 and 1720, the speculation was fuelled by the manias in Paris and London, though good management in the timely contraction of credit insulated the Scottish economy from the worst excesses despite lending by bond being stopped again, this time for over two years. Each of these threats had repercussions for the extent of the facilities available for trade and business, and inevitably there was an adverse effect on profits and reserves. From these events, the management of the Bank emerges with some credit. The directors had learned a lesson about the need for caution after the stop of 1704–5 and were unimpressed by the schemes of 1719 and 1720. They were to show how their cautious approach, within a relatively benign political framework, could provide substantial expansion of facilities to business and trade. Perhaps the more important of the lessons of the post-Union period for banking practices was the growth of the deposit system and within that the placing at the Bank of the tax receipts. The continued acceptance of Bank of Scotland notes was obviously important. Deposits meant that the Bank could increase advances, the directors worried less about runs on their cash, and, of course, a request for an increase in capital beyond that of 1720 did not seem an urgent matter. These lessons of banking appear to have been understood by the organisers of the Royal Bank, and most of the basic organisational structures of Bank of Scotland were adopted by the new rival. Where Bank of Scotland was less successful was in the maintenance of political support when the Squadrone system began to lose its influence in Parliament. For several years after 1728, there were adverse consequences as the Argyll interest used the new Royal Bank as part of their political schemes, and this had inevitable repercussions for Bank of Scotland.

CHAPTER 6

POLITICAL AND BUSINESS HISTORY, 1727–44

THE GRANT OF THE royal charter to the Equivalent Company on 31 May 1727 created a powerful financial and political power base for the Argyll–Ilay interest. Alongside and in close association with the new Royal Bank came the Commissioners and Trustees for improving fisheries and manufactures in Scotland, established in the same year by the Treasury Lords and firmly under the Earl of Ilay's control. A majority of the trustees were holders of the Equivalent Company stock. The Treasury, with Robert Walpole as First Lord, provided the trustees with £20,000 in cash ostensibly to support their role as the statutory authority regulating the output of the Scottish linen trade. While their work has rightly been seen as a spearhead for a renewed government commitment to the trade, this sum and an additional Treasury grant of £2,000 per year were to benefit, in a number of ways, many in Ilay's political circle. The older connections between the financiers in the Equivalent Company, which remained in being, were also brought into the support of the new financial nexus. Thus Edward Harrison, Governor of the Bank of England and a director of the Equivalent Company, arranged a £30,000 credit from Threadneedle Street in March 1728 against which bills could be discounted in London.[1] Other facilities followed later. The Treasury agreed that after the charter was granted the Royal Bank would receive the yearly perpetual interest of £5,010 from the government on the £111,347 of Equivalent stock subscribed for the Royal Bank and would arrange for its distribution. The Treasury also arranged for government revenues and the funds for the army to be channelled through the new bank. Moreover, the

---

1 The Earl of Ilay and five directors of the Royal Bank signed a bond guaranteeing repayment of the £30,000 to the Bank of England: Bank of England, mss, Law papers, M5/551, pp. 350–3, 17 February, 26 March 1728. For details of the account, see 'The Bank of England – Agent of the Royal Bank of Scotland', *The Three Banks Review*, 39 (September 1958), 33–49.

political patronage of the Argyll–Ilay network had numerous connections within the tax system, notably in the excise and the land tax, and these placemen now channelled funds from deposits at Bank of Scotland towards the Royal Bank. All these financial benefits followed from the political power of this interest and were to extend strength to the cash flow of the new bank and reduce the call on shareholders. Events were to show, however, that the survival of the Royal Bank required more than government favour and public funds.

The directors of the Royal Bank had considerable experience of political office and the taxation system, and all but one were appointed to the board because of their connections with the Argyll–Ilay interest. It was therefore most fortunate that the long-standing London banker of the Argyll family, George Middleton in the Strand, was ready with advice and assistance. Middleton dealt with financial matters for several regiments under the command of the second Duke of Argyll. For several years in the aftermath of John Law's Mississippi scheme, Middleton faced bankruptcy, and the income from the army was probably a decisive factor in his survival.[2] He was also closely involved in helping to minimise losses of members of the Argyll–Ilay interest contracted during the French financial disasters. In addition, Middleton was the London conduit for credit paid to John Law, a resident in Venice in the years after his flight from France.[3] Using his knowledge of how to run a bank, Middleton recommended persons as tellers, organised the etching of the plates for the notes and insisted, for example, that Patrick Crauford the elder became a director with 'others of equal probity and sense', as 'so much depends on your first setting out'. Conversely, he opposed Crauford the younger because of inexperience. Middleton pressed for strong legal and political representation on the board, following the precedent of Bank of Scotland with its membership from the Court of Session, government and trade, as well as the division between the extraordinary directors and the ordinary, the latter managing the daily affairs of business. The advice, which doubtless came from several quarters, was followed. Among those on the first extraordinary board were James Nimmo, originally an Edinburgh merchant and from 1726 cashier of the excise; his main role in the early years was to deposit his cash with the Royal Bank and provide as many Bank of Scotland notes for conversion as he could find.

---

2 George Middleton dealt with General Charles Ross, the Earl of Stair, Colonels Harrison and Whitworth, Major Peter Naison, Captains Farrer, Abercrombie, Tracey and Dalrymple, and a number of regimental factors.
3 E. Healey, *Coutts & Co. 1692–1992: The Portrait of a Private Bank* (London: 1992), p. 56; John Law remained a close associate of the second Duke and forwarded information on various matters from Venice. For Law's bills on London, see Coutts & Co., Minutes, vol. 16, p. 386, 6 January 1727.

Charles Cathcart was the Receiver General of the land tax, George Ross was a Commissioner of the Excise, there were several persons from the legal field, Mathew Lant was Chief Baron of the Court of Exchequer in Scotland, Sir John Clerk was another Baron, James Erskine and Hew Dalrymple were Senators of the College of Justice, and Charles Areskine was Solicitor General for Scotland.

Unfortunately, George Middleton was busy enough in his shop in the Strand, and the most important person available for the direction of the Royal Bank in Edinburgh in its first year was Patrick Campbell of Monzie, a Lord of Session; he had been involved with numerous financial calamities, including the Darien Company, several schemes at the time of the South Sea Bubble, the Mississippi disaster and the Equivalent Company, and was appointed to the Trustees in 1727. After the Bubble, he saw himself as the leading financial expert of the Argyll–Ilay interest.[4] At first the Edinburgh directors deferred to Lord Monzie. Within a few years, however, his amateurish management, which is discussed below, began to tell, and the leading role fell to Lord Milton, Ilay's 'leading henchman' in Scotland.[5] The Earl of Ilay and Lord Milton kept up a frequent correspondence on the progress of the Royal Bank and the work of the board of trustees, on which Milton also sat. He was the spymaster for the Royal Bank board; at least one servant of a Bank of Scotland director was paid to pass on information, and evidence suggests that there may have been others.[6] Daily business was in the hands of the ordinary board. Apart from Lord Monzie and Lord Milton, there sat Richard Dowdeswell, Secretary of the Excise Board since 1707, who had been taken up by Ilay in 1726 and was made a Commissioner in 1730. Another from the tax system was John Philp of Greenlaw, appointed Deputy Auditor of the Exchequer in 1727 following support for Ilay in Kirk politics. George Drummond was Lord Provost of Edinburgh and a business partner of James Nimmo; Hew Somerville ws 'veered towards the right persuasion', and George Irving, town clerk of Edinburgh, was one of Ilay's 'truest agents'.[7] James Paterson of Kirkton, one of the Commissaries of Edinburgh, was probably picked for his financial role on the burgh council, though he was only a director of the Royal Bank for a year. The other key figure in Edinburgh was Allan Whiteoord, Receiver General of the land tax from 1729, who was made Cashier of the new bank; apparently he kept his tax

---

4 After the debacle of the Mississippi scheme, Lord Monzie tended to rely for advice on George Middleton, who was himself in serious difficulties. Perhaps because of his need for income from the Argyll–Ilay interest, he was prepared to humour Monzie.
5 J. S. Shaw, *The Management of Scottish Society 1707–1764* (Edinburgh: 1983), p. 147.
6 NLS, MS 16538, Fletcher of Saltoun Papers, f. 48.
7 Shaw, *The Management of Scottish Society*, p. 120.

income in a chest in the bank vault.[8] The only 'independent' was Sir Hew Dalrymple, Lord President of the Court of Session, who was made Deputy Governor; his presence was some safeguard in the event of legal action, though, as events were to show, not enough. In London sat the directors of the Equivalent Company, who had converted part or all of their stock to the new bank; most of the well-known names from the 1720 project were there – Edward Harrison, Benjamin Longuet, Jacob Mendes da Costa and Paul D'Aranda, and they led the London interests who dominated the share lists of the new bank in the 1730s.[9] They were an essential group in the financial operations who were to keep the Royal Bank going in the early years and expected a return for their investment. As we shall see, there was something of a marriage of convenience about the relationship between the London financiers and the Ilay interest, and conflicts soon developed.

Whereas the board of Bank of Scotland had developed as an instrument for the conduct of banking, the Royal Bank board was organised for fighting a bank war on behalf of a political interest, and Lord Monzie, and later Lord Milton, were clearly in charge. This made for fast decision-making, but the broadly-based and more experienced directorate of the older bank also had considerable advantages in adverse circumstances. Bank of Scotland always enjoyed good relations with the Edinburgh legal fraternity; apart from the several advocates and writers to the signet, directors included Sir James Mackenzie, Lord Royston, a Lord of Justiciary, and Robert Dundas of Arniston, Dean of the Faculty of Advocates. Dundas was an ideal lawyer for a political struggle; he was Solicitor General in 1717, appointed Lord Advocate 1720 and elected Dean of the Faculty of Advocates in 1721, and sat in Parliament for Edinburgh county in 1722. In that station he supported the Squadrone, and when the Duke of Roxburghe fell in 1725 he was removed as Lord Advocate. Dundas had a fast mind, was a brilliant speaker and was well versed in the complexities of Scots law. In 1734, he orchestrated the defeat of Walpole and Ilay over the Scottish elections bill. Elevated to the bench in 1737, succeeding Sir Walter Pringle, in 1748 he was made Lord President. His family maintained a long association with the Bank which brought important financial and political benefits later in the century. Other directors with extensive political connections included Sir John Anstruther, Sir John Elphinstone and Alexander, the Earl of Marchmont, who was appointed

8 RBS RB/12/1, Minute Book of the Court of Directors, p. 49, 12 January 1728; W. A. S. Hewins, *The Whitefoord Papers* (Oxford: 1898), p. xv.
9 RBS, General Journal of the Accounts of the Commissioners of the Equivalent, vol. 3, 1717–21; RBS, Ledger A, commencing 1 January 1728; most Equivalent stockholders converted only part of their holdings. For the 1720 project, see above, Chapter 5.

Governor in 1728. Ordinary directors also came from some of the strong-est merchant houses in Edinburgh, including three directors from the Marjoribanks family. There was a wide network of Squadrone and other opposition families – the Duke of Roxburghe, the Earls of Haddington, Aberdeen, Montrose, Tweeddale, Rothes and Findlater, and numerous lairds. These represented huge tracts of territory and thus the political, legal and military influence which came with their heritable jurisdictions. The Bank had also acquired a professional staff over the three decades; its Treasurer David Spence was in continuous service from 1696, and together with the tellers and accountants the management developed an expertise in creditworthiness and seasonal fluctuations and a sense of how to accommodate themselves with customers, which took years to refine. They had over thirty years of close association with government and tax-collection and links with hundreds of private merchant and legal houses in Edinburgh, Glasgow, Dundee, Aberdeen and the lesser burghs.

The foundation of the Royal Bank came at a difficult time in the lend-ing cycle of Bank of Scotland. As noted above, from 1722 to December 1726 lending had rapidly increased, although by 1725 the directors had noticed signs of difficulty and, when the intentions of the Argyll–Ilay interest were known, steps were taken to curtail lending. In the first four months of 1727, new advances totalled only £3,400, and there was nothing thereafter for over two years. Their caution was well founded. The summer of 1727 saw not only the foundation of their opponents but also a deterioration in the harvest; fiars' prices for 1728 rose sharply in most areas, and especially so in Aberdeen, Edinburgh and the east and central areas of Scotland.[10] This was enough to cause a 'great scarcity of money' and derangement in local settlements; 'even good and responsal persons' found difficulties in timely repayments of rents and bills of exchange. The pattern was not dissimilar to the harvest crises of 1708–10, 1713–14 and 1722–3 to which the response of the Bank directors had been to increase lending on bills and bonds and then to allow debtors to extend their period of credit where they so wished. This is precisely what the directors decided to do, in principle, in the summer and autumn of 1727, and many loans passed the dates when interest or repayment was due.[11] Yet this positive reaction was only plausible if the Royal Bank was also serious about its stated intention of support for the economy, the main indicator of which would be respect for the integrity of the Bank of Scotland note issue. Unfortunately, this was not to be.

---

10 A. J. S. Gibson and T. C. Smout, *Prices, Food and Wages in Scotland 1550–1780* (Cambridge: 1995), pp. 89–93, Table 3.4: for eighteen county fiars for oats in 1728 compared with 1727, eight rose over 19 per cent, another five over 9 per cent.
11 BS 1/5, Minutes: 9 October 1727.

Indications of how serious the coming storm would be came when James Nimmo and Allan Whitefoord ran down their deposits with Bank of Scotland.[12] Further, there was the £20,000 available for the Trustees for Manufactures intended to support trade and industry. Their response to the shortage of credit should have been to lodge part of this with Bank of Scotland. The money would have provided an additional basis for maintaining bills beyond their end dates and allowed the Bank to discount new bills. It would also have given a strong indication that payments would be supported by the whole financial and political establishment, a response analogous to previous harvest crises. The trustees could not have dispersed the money themselves, as at this point they lacked a network in Scotland. On 8 December 1727, when it was clear that the November payments situation was disastrous and further difficulties loomed for payments due at Christmas, Bank of Scotland proposed borrowing £10,000 or half the stock of the trustees, at 5 per cent. The trustees refused, so the directors offered to take all £20,000, 'to lend it out for accommodating the country in the present straits by scarcity of money'.[13] They refused this as well. By the New Year, reports were coming in that the Royal Bank was buying up Bank of Scotland notes and substituting its own.

The problems for Bank of Scotland were clear enough. By far the most serious was the challenge to the note issue, as £80,000 in notes were in circulation while the actual cash in the reserve was only a few thousand pounds. There was a growing scarcity of coin in Scotland caused by the need to import grain, and Lord Monzie thus hoped to spark off a general return of Bank of Scotland notes. On 4 January, Bank of Scotland directors moved to protect 'against all attempts that may be made by the Royal bank for bringing their Company under any difficulties and inconveniences'.[14] The loan and bill registers were searched, and many of those deemed to be able to be repaid by Candlemas (2 February) were recalled, as were those deficient on interest payments and where co-obligants were dead. This came to around £30,000. It was hard on the traders and landlords involved, but the actions of the Royal Bank and the refusal of the Trustees for Manufactures to help left little room for manoeuvre. There is some evidence that while in public Bank of Scotland talked of equal misery, in practice it followed a discretionary policy; borrowers connected to the Argyll–Ilay network were vigorously pursued while some sympathetic to the old Bank were left alone. In turn, a small army of merchants, lairds and

---

12 BS 1/94, General Ledger, 1727, 1728.
13 BS 1/5, Minutes: 8 December 1727, 2 January 1728; this would have involved no profit for the Bank as the money would cost 5 per cent, and bills then paid the same.
14 BS 1/5, Minutes: 4 January 1728.

lawyers pressurised their debtors and tenants for coin or notes due in the summer and autumn of 1727 to pay debts to the Bank. Initially, pressure on proprietors was modest; they were suffering already from curtailment of advances. Another 10 per cent of the original subscription was called up to make 30 per cent paid; 40 per cent of this sum of £10,000 came from a stop to the 4 per cent dividend due to be paid after 27 March 1728, leaving £6,000 due from proprietors, most of which came in as banknotes. It may be thought an inadequate reaction to the crisis, but the directors probably judged it expedient to be sensitive to their proprietors at an early stage of what they judged would be a long struggle.

There was no general disquiet with Bank of Scotland facilities, note provision or any fear of ultimate failure among the general trading public. For the first three months of the war with the Royal Bank, notes still circulated much as they always had. In all the main towns of Scotland and in numerous smaller settlements, the Bank had developed long and constructive relationships. The case of Glasgow is particularly interesting. The merchant house of Robert and James Robertson energetically passed Bank of Scotland notes within the burgh, 'the country thereabout and the places where they have correspondence'.[15] Along with other Glasgow merchants, they ensured that Patrick Cochrane, a supporter of the Royal Bank, found his note issue difficult. In some counties, namely Roxburghshire, Aberdeenshire, Forfarshire and Banffshire, the Royal Bank made no headway at all. Indeed, the fact that the crisis was engineered by one political interest appears to have caused great annoyance among landed and burgh creditors alike in what might be loosely termed the political and economic establishments of lowland Scotland. Within Edinburgh, some institutions, including the Edinburgh town council, backed the Royal Bank, but the Faculty of Advocates, the Court of Session and the Edinburgh Merchants Company remained loyal to Bank of Scotland, as did numerous lawyers and merchants who lent small sums on deposit while the stop was on.

At the start of the banking war, the Royal Bank cash base involved only £10,000 from the first call on subscribers. In January, £20,000 was added by the trustees, in addition to £9,000 from James Nimmo, £700 from James Corrie, Provost of Dumfries, and £541 from Hew Somerville ws, and some land-tax receipts. Not all of this was in coin; the trustees' money came partly in government bonds, and the excise and land-tax receipts included Bank of Scotland notes. Moreover, the trustees' money was lodged at 5 per cent, to match the interest offered by Bank of Scotland,

15 See below, Table 7.3, for the cash account of Robert and James Robertson for November 1731 to December 1741.

and interest was payable on the Dumfries loan. The income from the tax-collectors could be held for many months, but eventually Royal Bank notes would have to be paid out to the government. This income, 'being deemed sufficient for carrying on their business of banking', enabled a much lower reliance on paid-up capital than would otherwise have been the case.[16] Lord Monzie may have thought he needed to act quickly to unsettle the old Bank, and though he substituted some notes in the course of trade, he relied more upon those deposited from the tax-collection system. This meant that Lord Monzie accumulated a great deal of Bank of Scotland paper but faced only a moderate risk in return as fewer Royal Bank notes circulated. Indeed, he ridiculed the idea of an early start to an extensive lending for this reason.

This was a serious miscalculation. Bank of Scotland's reaction to Monzie meant demands for repayment on an increasingly wider circle in Scotland and thus considerable anger at its cause. Yet Monzie refused to relieve those distressed by replacing their loans. He then panicked, and made the serious mistake of writing to his associates in the Equivalent Company and to the Earl of Ilay for large loans. 'Like a man a litle haired', he demanded in a 'sudden peremptory manner' funds for up to £60,000 by the end of January.[17] His description of the recall of loans by Bank of Scotland as a 'distress' caused some of these London financiers to question whether he understood how banks responded to adversity. It also focused attention on what Lord Monzie had initially proposed to do. George Middleton and George Campbell put the evidence succinctly: the reserve of £10,000 was entirely inadequate; on the basis of their political power, credits had been raised from the Bank of England and the trustees on which interest at 4 and 5 per cent was liable, yet income from lending would only be 5 per cent at best, and some time in arriving, and carried risks. The proposal to borrow £60,000 was Monzie's attempt to solve the inadequate reserve, but thanks to his letters this could now only be raised at 5 per cent. Surely, wrote George Middleton, 'in their infancy they'll not be so mad as to lend money upon the prospect of these credits that must soon blow them up'.[18] Yet this was exactly what Monzie, backed by Milton, tried to do: borrow huge sums now, replace Bank of Scotland lending, and hope that Bank of Scotland liability to pay notes to bearer would blow them up sooner, leaving the Royal Bank with a clear field for lending. The overall effect was to damage the credit of the Royal Bank and to undermine, for several years, confidence in the Edinburgh board.

16 This point was noticed by William Maitland, *The History of Edinburgh from its Foundation to the Present Time* (Edinburgh: 1753), p. 352.
17 NLS, MS 16538, Fletcher of Saltoun Papers, f. 30: Lord Ilay to Lord Milton, 20 January 1728.
18 Coutts & Co., Letter Book, vol. 17, George Middleton to Patrick Crauford of Auchenames, 30 January 1727/28, and other letters for January and February.

Lord Monzie also managed to create further rifts. The first occasion concerned a tentative agreement reached by Paul D'Aranda, one of the Equivalent directors, whereby Monzie proposed him for the London agency of the Royal Bank at £200 a year, in preference to George Middleton, who offered to conduct the correspondence with Scotland more cheaply, on the basis of the ordinary merchant rate. When the Earl of Ilay heard of this, he threatened to resign as Governor; if the new bank 'at its first setting out dipped into jobs for private views I would have no more to do with them'.[19] Ilay also threatened to resign a second time after the Edinburgh directors arranged to sell some Equivalent stock at a loss, the benefit to go to one of their number; this was not banking, exclaimed Ilay, but 'stockjobbing' – 'if they don't alter their measures I shall be forced to drop them'.[20] By November, Ilay was incensed about schemes from D'Aranda to 'turn our bank into a bubble for him to stockjob in'.[21]

The supporters of Bank of Scotland correctly identified the weak credit position of the Royal Bank and swiftly exploited the rifts that followed. They conducted this in terms of the damage caused to Scotland, a relatively easy matter to convey, and then exploited the shadowy and ambiguous discussions begun in Edinburgh between several Bank of Scotland directors and Lord Monzie. Towards the end of January 1728, rumours spread in London of an impending, though somewhat vague, agreement (or agreements) between the old Bank and the new which would isolate the English shareholders of the Royal Bank. The report suggested that the banks would amalgamate on the basis of paid-up share values and profits from lending; the beneficiaries, it was implied, would not be the Equivalent men. Members of the Squadrone also pointed out that it was common knowledge that a large number of Bank of Scotland notes to the credit of James Nimmo were in the Royal Bank but had not been exchanged, thus an impending agreement would render such exchange unnecessary as the Royal Bank's holdings would then support the credit of Bank of Scotland. It did indeed appear rather odd in London that the Royal Bank management in Edinburgh was claiming in early February 1728 that Bank of Scotland was about to stop payment yet kept significant quantities of the old banknotes, a position which Ilay found incomprehensible.[22] Within the world of London financiers, these

---

19 NLS, MS 16538, Fletcher of Saltoun Papers, f. 30: Lord Ilay to Lord Milton, 20 January 1728. This was a point made to at least one other director.
20 Ibid., 6 August 1728.
21 Ibid., 23 November 1728, Lord Ilay to Lord Milton.
22 Ibid., 11 February 1728, Lord Ilay to Lord Milton. This was correct; the Royal Bank held around £5,000 in Bank of Scotland notes by the end of January. There are three possible explanations for this: (1) Lord Monzie was in secret discussions with Bank of Scotland; (2) whether these were serious or not, he thought a stop by the old Bank on a general return preferable to the Royal Bank enforcing a stop, perhaps for political reasons; (3) he was himself in no position to start lending, or did not want

assiduously-cultivated rumours did immense damage to the credit of the Royal Bank. The result was explained by a rattled Ilay to Milton at the end of the month:

> the notion they [the Equivalent men] had here [in London] that our folks [the Edinburgh board] under a private desire of making an agreement with the old bank would either do nothing or enter into some foolish disadvantagious scheme made them very cautious of entering into methods to countenance us, it would have in a little time made them quite indifferent what had become of us.

More to the point, borrowing would be at the legal limit of 5 per cent. The Squadrone also tried to undermine the support given by the Treasury; at one point it was being rumoured that the Earl of Ilay and Robert Walpole were about to break with each other.[23]

Rumours apart, Bank of Scotland management were able to focus closely upon all the routes by which credit, cash or their own notes could arrive at the Royal Bank. We have noted that many connected with the new bank had their credits recalled in January. In February, Bank of Scotland directors turned towards the droving trade. Their target was to block the cash from the sales of Scottish cattle south of the Border going to the Bank of England or to correspondents of the Royal Bank in London. If they achieved this and the cash was returned directly or through non-Royal Bank agents, then considerable upset would be caused to the new bank's London operations. This became more urgent when news of the Bank of England's cash credit for £30,000 was announced at the end of March, as any run-down on this credit by bill discounts could be replenished from these sales. Secret discussions were held with drovers and a number of cattle owners in the Dumfries and Galloway area. The result was to deny at least a part of the drovers' cash to traditional buyers; George Middleton, for example, lost a part of his income that summer. Robert Maxwell of Arkland in Galloway arranged for the proceeds from his sales to be remitted to avoid the Royal Bank; some drovers whom Middleton had long dealt with simply ignored him. When this happened, his zeal for the new bank rather waned. 'I wish', he wrote to William Stewart of Dumfries in reply to bad news about the drovers, that 'your banks would come to some settlement for the sake of the country'.[24] Other

to lend yet, and therefore was biding his time. It should also be remembered that once notes were returned to Bank of Scotland it was an easy matter to identify their origin and take action to recall the credits of those concerned.

23 NLS, MS 16538, Fletcher of Saltoun Papers, f. 36, 30 January 1728; there may have been some truth in this. Ilay had only been in power for three years and members of the Squadrone were viable alternatives for public office. This may explain the extraordinary tone of Ilay's letters in the first nine months of 1728.

24 Coutts & Co., archives, Letter Book no. 17, 20 July 1728.

pressures were exerted upon Middleton by members of the Squadrone who had accounts with his shop (these included the indefatigable Lady Grizzell Baillie, who requested cash from Middleton in London, on long-dated bills), and by the Earl of Marchmont's sons who asked for cash at Middleton's Strand office, with which Middleton had to comply, as a refusal would have been out of the question.[25] The Royal Bank's tardiness in the payment of its midsummer dividend caused further annoyance.[26] Moreover, its directors were told by the Bank of England that they were to sign their bills as the 'Royal Bank of Scotland' and not to pretend that they were *the* Royal Bank. George Middleton urged Lord Monzie to make more calls, even 20 per cent, rather than force his London financiers to extend further credits. Scottish stockholder Patrick Crauford was bluntly warned by Middleton, who held Crauford's stock as security, to sell rather than demand extra credit, as 'you know how far we have already gone to accommodate you'.[27]

Seen in this context, the inevitable cessation of cash payments by Bank of Scotland was only one event in a long-drawn-out bank war and by no means the most important, not least because it was expected. Lord Monzie chose the morning of the annual general meeting of Bank of Scotland on 27 March 1728, and, to avoid the opprobrium which would result, asked Andrew Cochrane, one of the agents of the Royal Bank and Lord Provost of Glasgow, to present banknotes worth £900. 'This day', recorded the Minutes, 'payments being stopt at the office . . . arising from causes and means well known both in city and county'.[28] The Earl of Leven announced that they would fight on. Notes of £5–£100 with a date after 1716, virtually all those out, were to carry 5 per cent interest, and most 20-shilling notes were listed likewise. As the note liability was £71,188 sterling, this entailed a hefty commitment to interest accruals.[29] The Bank started to issue new 'cash notes' to favoured customers soon afterwards. Richard Holland, the son of John Holland, recommended the adoption of the optional clause in December 1729, to pay cash to bearer or at six months with 5 per cent interest in the option of the Bank.[30] Milton's spy informed him that the Bank had kept some cash in reserve for its own customers, to which Milton's characteristic response was: 'we should now fall on methods to keep them ever opening again'. Creditors of the old Bank were urged to take out diligences and embargoes

25 Ibid., 13 July 1728.
26 Ibid.
27 Ibid., p. 143/4, 28 March 1728, to Patrick Crauford.
28 BS 1/5, Minutes: 27 March 1728.
29 There are slight differences in the figures for banknotes in circulation at the end of March; that for the balance on 27 March gave £70,603.
30 C. A. Malcolm, *The Bank of Scotland, 1695–1945* (Edinburgh: n.d. [1948]), pp. 48–50.

on proprietors' effects by arrestment and inhibition.[31] There were a series of meetings in May and June 1728 between the two banks, although nothing came of them. The strain proved too much for the Earl of Leven. After his death, the adventurers unanimously elected Alexander, Earl of Marchmont, as Governor.

It is doubtful whether an Edinburgh merchant or lawyer would have risked such legal action against the Bank, which action was now raised by Patrick Cochrane before the Court of Session. There was considerable prevarication by their Lordships. Not until 1 June 1728 was the judgement issued; summary diligence by horning was ruled not competent upon the notes of the Bank. Allan Whitefoord, this time directly on behalf of the Royal Bank, then petitioned for letters of inhibition and arrestment on a dependence upon Bank of Scotland notes. What followed was a testimony to the close connections between the Bank and the Court of Session. A majority of the judges, who included Lord Kimmerghame, the Earl of Marchmont's brother, affirmed that the old Bank, 'being by the narrative of their Act designed for the service of the country, and having proved so, it was unreasonable to grant any diligence against them which might harrass [sic]' the Company as a whole or individual proprietors. Another Lord ruled that he had 'never heard of any diligence sought on a bank note and he was not for novelties'.[32] Whitefoord was a poor plaintiff, and he so upset the court that they denounced him for his 'indecent and disrespectful manner'. Lord Milton was furious: 'the Session seem to me to be stark mad'; and, worse than madness, their actions were an alliance between Jacobites and the Squadrone. Indeed, in some drafts he even suggested that the Bank itself was actually in the hands of the Jacobites.[33] Not a man to be outmanoeuvred, Milton persuaded Walpole to rule against Bank of Scotland notes as legal tender, though orders were not finally issued until January 1729, and then only to the customs and excise.[34] Naturally, the Bank tried to lobby for reversal. Thomas Pringle ws was despatched to London in March 1729 with £500; he stayed three months, realised it was a hopeless case and spent only half his budget. The directors awarded him 130 guineas.[35] Unfortunately, the Royal Bank decided to take the Court of Session case to the House of Lords, which, being an English-dominated

---

31 NLS, MS 16538, Fletcher of Saltoun Papers, f. 48 [by inference 28 March 1728]. The proprietors were liable up to the nominal worth of their stock, but no further.

32 Ibid., f. 63, July 1728, Lord Milton to Lord Ilay.

33 Ibid.: letter and drafts.

34 PRO, T 1/266/no. 7, f. 29: John Campbell, John Drummond and James Campbell, Customs, Edinburgh, to Treasury Board, London, 15 August 1728; J. Reddington (ed.), Calendar of Treasury Papers, 1720–28 (London: 1889), pp. 523–4: 23 October, 31 December 1728; W. A. Shaw (ed.), Calendar of Treasury Books and Papers, 1729–30 (London: 1897), p. 3: 2 January 1729, John Scrope to Commissioners of the Excise in Scotland.

35 BS 1/5, Minutes: 13 March and 4 July 1729.

court and close to the government, reversed the decision in June 1729; but by this time Bank of Scotland was in a much firmer position.

The negotiations between Lord Monzie and Bank of Scotland had petered out in August 1728. We cannot be certain of what passed in the earlier discussions beyond the rumours spread by members of the Squadrone, though details of the later round have survived, albeit from the viewpoint of Ilay and Milton. The proposals put by the Royal Bank again concerned amalgamation and involved, first, a halt by Bank of Scotland on calls on borrowers: an absurd suggestion which would have led to further note-picking by the Royal Bank. There would then be a vague general valuation of their respective stocks, counting the whole equivalent contribution for the Royal Bank as paid up. The amalgamation would thus have been a takeover. Bank of Scotland directors, on the other hand, were well aware that their overriding need was to reduce liabilities, a slow process. They delayed until after the first Court of Session decision and replied that a proper valuation required an exchange of information on the paid-up contribution of proprietors, an account of money lent out and borrowed, whether long or short, on bills or bonds, and the state of any interest account owing for sums deposited and the conditions thereon. This was the only serious way to measure the true worth of a banking company. The negotiations floundered after the August payments season. It was, the directors announced, 'well known from what spring the distress lately brought upon them did flow and that they have hitherto used their debtors with all their moderation and tenderness which the circumstances they have been brought into by the present distress could admit of'.

The support of the Court of Session enabled the Bank to organise a general appeal for deposits of £100 and above from six months to a year. Various sums were deposited, including £8,000 from Sir Alexander Ramsay of Balmain and David Ochterlony of Tullifriskie and £900 from Sir James Raehead. The state of borrowers' accounts also improved, and from 27 June £6,000 of 20-shilling notes were called for repayment, followed by the £900 held by Cochrane. By August, the Bank liability in notes was fast falling; indeed, demands on borrowers had the effect of gradually increasing the pressure on Royal Bank notes swiftly returned by Edinburgh merchants looking for cash or Bank of Scotland notes which could be paid to the Bank against clients' debts. On 21 August, authorisation was given by the directors to repay all £50 notes, a month later £20 notes and from 13 November the £10 notes. The Royal Bank was asked for its holdings, but refused, whereupon it was informed that its hoard would not accrue more interest. By 7 March 1729, all debts against banknotes had been repaid, although this was far from the close of the bank war.

With all notes paid off with interest, and new issues arranged, a modest restart to lending by bond was made by Bank of Scotland in March 1729. This vindicated those who had held faith in the management. As so often when fierce struggles are won, or in this case fought to a draw, the process strengthened the determination of the proprietors to remain independent. At the general meeting of 13 March 1729, when Robert Marjoribanks stood down as Deputy Governor he was replaced by James Gordon of Ellon, a well-known Aberdeenshire Jacobite who was reported to have been active in 1715.[36] Already a director, he orchestrated support from the Aberdeen area and the Gordon interest. The echoes lasted: twenty years later, the Royal Bank admitted that it had not a single cash account in Aberdeen, and Bank of Scotland was to remain the stronger of the two banks in the north-east down to the present day.

There remains the question of Royal Bank lending in the first fifteen months; how large it was, in what form it was made, and whether it represented a real increase in facilities within Scotland over and above borrowings. The initial conclusion from the financial evidence confirms the impression given by Lords Monzie and Milton; in the fifteen months from 1 January 1728, Royal Bank facilities were only sluggishly extended to Scotland's trade and agriculture. The lending by means of the (usually sixty-day) bill of exchange, a straight copy of that pioneered by Bank of Scotland, managed to reach only £8,921 by 29 August 1728, with much of this paid off. Thereafter it grew to £21,548 by the end of March 1729. Lending on bonds started on 6 March 1729, and managed under £15,000 for the next year. The much-vaunted cash account was a straight 'cash only' version of the ancient style of 'cash and goods' accounts kept by innumerable Scottish merchants and lawyers for out-of-town customers among the landed classes and small burgh merchants.[37] The rules for this were not drawn up by the Royal Bank until 31 May 1728, and the total credit extended by March 1729 was under £12,000. When a cash account went into overdraft, two guarantors were required, exactly as with the bill system. The cash account was a useful device for supporting circulation and collecting notes; seen in this light, the development had political overtones. The biggest trade in the first fifteen months was £54,937 for remittance to and from London, with around £10,744 standing out unsettled. This was not new credit; the facilities were readily available within Edinburgh legal and merchant circles, and much was conducted

36 A. and H. Tayler, *Jacobites of Aberdeenshire and Banffshire in the Rising of 1715* (Edinburgh: 1934), p. 108.
37 RBS RB/12/1, Minute Book of the Court of Directors, first mentions 'cash accounts' in November 1727, but in the context of the deposit of money, not in the terms in which it came to be understood as a lending and deposit facility.

for the Argyll–Ilay interest and the government. Some historians have noted the Royal Bank's willingness to exchange Bank of Scotland notes after the stop of 27 March 1728 and in particular to extend a helping hand to drovers and merchants in difficulty. In fact, the Royal Bank board remained ultra-cautious. The note exchange was given an absolute ceiling of £2,000; it was only to be for 'the poor' to a maximum of 'three or four' 20-shilling notes at any one time; and the same person did 'not come too often'.[38] As for help to merchants and drovers, the Royal Bank was only prepared to take Bank of Scotland notes as security, and solely for lending on a sixty-day bill of exchange which had to be paid off at the end of that period. So what was on offer was a loan by bill. Surprisingly, only a handful of merchants and a lone drover, Malcolm McLaren who wanted to go to Skye, took advantage of this generous offer.[39]

By the end of August 1728, the total lending by the Royal Bank had reached £40,000. A further 10 per cent call on the £106,748 of the Equivalent subscription incorporated into the capital of the Royal Bank raised another £10,670 and was used to support the exchange operation in London. This limited extension of credit should be weighed against the £20,000 initially denied to Scottish trade by the trustees, the withdrawal of the balances of the excise and the land tax from Bank of Scotland, and the behaviour of the Royal Bank board in starting a note war. All these actions meant that the economy had less credit available than if the Royal Bank had not been established. Thereafter, lending by the Royal Bank expanded, although, as mentioned before, it was a slow business. To the end of 1730, 112 cash accounts were opened, although many were second facilities with different guarantors, and 250 advances against bills were made. When put against the effect on Bank of Scotland lending in 1728 and 1729, we can conclude that the net effect on Scotland's bank credit of the arrival of the Royal Bank was negative and most of the profit went to persons living in London.

Thus closed the most dangerous phase of an exhaustive bank war. In spite of all the patronage, arm-twisting, government subsidies and help from the Bank of England, the Argyll–Ilay interest suffered a significant setback; they had their new financial platform but a much weaker one than they had hoped for. A very large number of the wealthy and influential in Scotland remained independent of the government interest in financial matters. The old Bank retained their loyalty because for over thirty years it had strengthened the effectiveness of borrowers who required accommodation at payment times or for longer-term projects.

38 Ibid., p. 94, 27 March 1728.
39 Ibid., March 1728 and thereafter.

Numerous lawyers and merchants' houses were better able to deal with their clients in the country because of these facilities, and everybody benefited from the notes out, which at peak seasons in the 1720s had reached close on £100,000. All this was jeopardised by the aggressive behaviour of the new bank and its supporters and appointees on the board of trustees and in the revenue services.[40]

In the early 1730s, Lord Milton and his board continued to draw up schemes to strengthen their position in Scottish finance and weaken the standing of Bank of Scotland.[41] The most visionary of these was advanced in the spring of 1732 as a step beyond the remittance trade to and from London. At certain times of the year, when Parliament met and in the spring and early summer, more bills required to be paid in London than in Edinburgh. Therefore, at these times, the demand in London exceeded that in Edinburgh and the exchange cost would rise, sometimes by as much as 2 or 3 per cent. At other times, for example when the drovers' funds were paid in at London, the exchange was at or near par and bills could be sent south more cheaply. The Royal Bank correctly assumed that if it could remit money on bills of exchange at the lowest rates for the whole year, it would considerably extend its existing business. More important, there was a real chance of finishing off Bank of Scotland: 'if we once had the command of the exchange and consequently of the cash of the country (considering we had already the revenue) the old Bank must accept of our terms'.[42] To operate this trade, it was proposed to buy East India Company bonds, which would pay interest, and to lodge these in the Bank of England. Other funds from the Treasury, notably for the army, which already came to the Royal Bank, would be lodged likewise. This London fund, managed by the Equivalent directors in London, would be augmented by the purchase of money as and when required. Thus, at all times of the year, when money was required in London and remitted by bill from Edinburgh it could be paid in Bank of England notes or gold in London at only a modest charge. And vice versa, though in Scotland the exchange would continue to be paid in Royal Bank notes. It was an inspired idea; £6,700 of East India bonds were bought and some start was made to the operation. Yet, in practice, the Royal Bank found that the total demands on London from Scotland were always greater than the

40 As late as 1889, George Chalmers, *Caledonia or a Historical and Typographical Account of North Britain*, new edn (Paisley: 1889), vol. 4, p. 743, declared that the Royal Bank was established 'with an invidious eye to the Bank of Scotland . . . the contest and competition which ensued between these rival banks brought forth an impeded circulation, one of the greatest evils which can afflict an industrious nation'.
41 NLS, MS 17591, Fletcher of Saltoun Papers, 14 April 1732: Patrick Crauford of Auchenames, paper for Royal Bank board on operations against Bank of Scotland.
42 Ibid. f. 71v, paper from London to Royal Bank board.

reverse flow, and its funds were insufficient to engross the whole of this trade. In a limited area, for its own customers, it helped to reduce the costs of exchange in the 1730s.

The Royal Bank board continued with its plots and intrigues for several years because its senior directors, the Earl of Ilay, Lord Milton and Lord Monzie, were first and foremost politicians. Ilay drew ever closer to the two great schemers of government politics, the Duke of Newcastle and Sir Robert Walpole, and Lord Milton who was based in Scotland looked after their concerns at home. Thus both Ilay and Milton strengthened their interests because they understood how far they could go in their respective positions in this grand English–Scottish alliance with Newcastle and Walpole. Ilay established a political position which, with a modest interruption from 1742–6, gave him a senior office of state from 1726 until his death in 1761. The public bodies that Ilay packed with his nominees and the movement of public funds across the Border and within Scotland continued to benefit the Royal Bank.[43] All this was bad news for Bank of Scotland as much as for the political careers of members of the Squadrone.

Viewed from the boardroom of Bank of Scotland, the political and banking realities in the first half of the 1730s could only result in caution in lending, regardless of the state of agriculture and trade. There was more room for manoeuvre once the Royal Bank extended its circulation after 1730 and the pressures on note returns became more equal, though the long-term outlook remained gloomy. How did the Bank conduct itself? The wide geographical coverage of Bank of Scotland advances has been mentioned, and the support for this came from the connections between, on the one side, Edinburgh lawyers, merchants and the Bank's own directors and staff, and on the other the recipients whose creditworthiness and wealth were known. There was another factor which emerged in the recent history of Bank of Scotland, namely the reliance upon merchants and lairds who lived outwith Edinburgh and their agents in Edinburgh for information about local conditions and the supply of funds to several who lent on to others in their vicinity. This partial decentralisation of lending had allowed a wider circulation and thus a larger profit. This was the backcloth to several experiments launched in July 1731. The first was to formalise an agency system. Many merchant houses in the main trading towns used their regular connection with the Bank to work on their side in the bank war. In Glasgow, Messrs James and Robert Robertson and their nephew James, who were involved in the Virginia tobacco trade, proved so effective that they were paid eighty guineas for their support

43 Shaw, *Management of Scottish Society*, ch. 3, interests; ch. 4, agents.

of note circulation.[44] In July 1731, this role was formalised when Robert Robertson was settled as Bank correspondent in the greater Glasgow area, with an annual fee of £25 and £300 in banknotes as a fund for buying and selling notes. The Robertsons kept up this connection. Apart from the notes, of their total debt of £4,536 by 1740, £500 (11 per cent) was from the Bank, in addition to their cash account.[45] Three more merchants were appointed with the same remit: Benjamin Grieve at Berwick, on a salary of £20 and a fund of £200, George Dempster the Dundee linen merchant, and John Burnet at Aberdeen, both on £15 with funds of £200 apiece. They were to organise the note circulation in tandem with Alexander Arbuthnot of Knox, a Bank director and associate of the Squadrone.[46] The sums may seem small, but the key was a fast delivery service of Royal Bank notes to and from Edinburgh in exchange for Bank of Scotland notes. The correspondents were also given powers to arrange small loans in the name of the Bank and some latitude as to how these were managed.

The operation lasted for two years and strengthened the Bank in the areas concerned, though it was probably unnecessary in Aberdeen. In these two years, bond lending recovered somewhat and, of course, there was a sharp rise in cash account facilities, although lending by bill remained subdued. In the summer of 1733, lending was generally low for several months and the Bank directors decided to stop the fees to correspondents. In the cases of George Dempster of Dundee, his partner the 1745 Jacobite Henry Pattullo and the Robertsons in Glasgow, the exercise proved useful as a training in banking techniques which they put to use in their own businesses.[47] It is clear that by this time facilities were granted for bill discounts and credit by numerous houses associated with Bank of Scotland. Some of these became well known; the Whyte family in Kirkcaldy (linen) came into this bracket, the Maxwells in Galloway (cattle) and the Ochterlonys in Montrose (linen). There were several dozen with the knowledge and resources to engage in most banking functions, and, as we shall see, some were later to support the early provincial joint-stock banks. It seems therefore that a case could be made that the bank war enabled merchants in outlying burghs to acquire new expertise.

A number of changes were made in lending policy, the end result of which was to enable Bank of Scotland to face the more competitive situation after 1728 and ultimately the challenge of the provincial banks.

---

44 BS 1/5, Minutes, p. 124, 25 February 1731.
45 T. M. Devine, *The Tobacco Lords: A Study of the Tobacco Merchants of Glasgow and their Trading Activities c. 1740–1790* (Edinburgh: 1990), p. 95.
46 BS 1/5, Minutes, p. 141, 14 July 1731. In the early 1740s, Knox was the sole supporter of the Marquis of Tweeddale on the Board of Customs; see Shaw, *Management of Scottish Society*, p. 65.
47 BS 1/5, Minutes: 10 July, 1 November 1733.

In July 1731, it was agreed to encourage deposits from private individuals, for which 4 per cent would be paid if these were left over twelve months and 3 per cent from six to twelve, a facility taken up by a wide range of individuals and institutions, including George Watson's Hospital, Edinburgh. The directors also extended their previous practices on the partial repayments of bills and bonds which, as noted before, had begun to look rather like the operation of cash accounts by 1710. In 1729, formal cash accounts were opened alongside the conversion of bonds and bills to cash accounts, and vice versa, and, as before, partial payments on a bill could be connected to a new bill for a greater sum than the original.[48] In 1735, the directors agreed to lend on pledges, known as 'pledge and impignorate' accounts, whereby sums were placed in the Bank at 4 per cent and an account opened with a charge of 5 per cent for sums lent out.[49] By this time, the directors were prepared to consider any serious suggestion for short-term loans against appropriate security.[50] Regular use of the Bank as a safe deposit for papers and valuables came in by 1739, and management expertise was called upon for some trustee cases from this time.[51] Indeed, by the middle years of the eighteenth century, the Bank appears to have developed a reputation for a professional approach to advising on heritable and personal wealth in the event of the demise of borrowers. These initiatives helped the directors to cope with the aftermath of the foundation of the Royal Bank and the disturbed decade which followed. Fear of Lord Ilay and the power of his government network must have been a strong thread in their discussions.

In fact, the simple lines drawn in the bank war began to blur soon after it commenced. As early as the summer of 1728, after suffering from Bank of Scotland countermeasures, George Middleton expressed his hope that some agreement could be reached. Edward Harrison, Governor of the Bank of England, had reached a similar opinion by 1732, even suggesting that he would sell out his stock unless the Royal Bank 'had a near view of agreeing with the old bank'.[52] Morale was, at times, low among the Royal Bank staff; an internal assessment correctly identified several of their shortcomings, that Bank of Scotland proprietors mostly lived in Scotland and lent their support, whereas Royal Bank proprietors lived mainly in London and the profits therefore left Scotland, which was unpopular. Furthermore, attempts to broaden the shareholding of the Royal Bank led to bitter recriminations and accusations of stockjobbing.[53] When the

48 BS 1/5, Minutes: 22 February, 15 March 1739.
49 BS 1/5, Minutes: 1735 and thereafter.
50 BS 1/5, Minutes: 1 May 1735, advance of £1,764 to Archibald Tod.
51 BS 1/5, Minutes: 22 July 1739, Earl of Mortoun.
52 NLS, MS 17591, Fletcher of Saltoun Papers, f. 71v.
53 NLS, MS 16540, Fletcher of Saltoun Papers, f. 69; the paper was probably written in 1729.

exchange equalisation programme failed to achieve its aim of engrossing the Scottish financial system, even Lord Milton must have wondered whether he would have to coexist with the old Bank, however unpalatable a conclusion that was for such a skilled and determined politician.

The financial records of Bank of Scotland suggest that the total of the Bank's liabilities fell by over one-third for the six years from 1728 compared to the six years before. The sums lent by the Bank on bond after 1728 did not exceed £8,000 per year before 1739, when £10,470 was advanced. Discounts of bills of exchange were also subdued, although the movement of cash accounts showed a more positive pattern. Down to the end of 1732, advances by cash account reached only a little above £10,000. As confidence grew, the figures rose to £14,000 in the financial year 1732–3 and to a yearly average of £19,151 for 1735 and 1736. A year later, the credit balance rose to £28,143 and, in 1739, £34,956. The growth in 1740 and 1741 was sustained, and passed £50,000 (see Figures 6.1 and 6.2, and Statistical Appendix, Table A17). These figures suggest that the directors of Bank of Scotland grew in their confidence that there would not be another run. Lending was much more open by 1738; the Bank, for example, lent £1,500 on bond to a group of agents supplying the North British Dragoons, and in March 1739 it was agreed that directors no longer needed to co-authorise payments on cash accounts.

By the close of 1739, reports had come in from all over Scotland to the effect that the harvests had failed, and they failed again the following year.[54] Requests for new cash accounts were few; in December 1740 the Bank granted only two, for £200 and £300, both for the linen trade, and only one in January 1741, to an Edinburgh lawyer. Nothing followed until April and only eleven for the rest of the year. Requests for advances by bond virtually ceased from July 1740 to April 1741. There appears to have been an understanding between the two banks to alleviate conditions by an expansion of credit; the Bank lent £5,000 to Edinburgh council at nil interest to buy meal, £550 to Dunfermline and £400 to Perth, and payments were made to several landowners to alleviate distress. Advances by the Royal Bank included £2,500 to Edinburgh and £4,000 for Glasgow.[55] Apart from this humanitarian effort, the key to support for the economy in this crisis was the rise in cash account balances from 1739.

After 1736, Bank of Scotland directors also found that political events were moving in their favour. The most important of these was the gradual estrangement between the second Duke of Argyll on the one side and the

54 Gibson and Smout, *Prices, Food and Wages in Scotland*, pp. 89–93, Table 3.4: of the seventeen county fiars for oats listed in 1740, compared with 1739, twelve saw an increase in price of 50 per cent or more, four of 30–49 per cent.
55 Munro, *The History of the Royal Bank of Scotland*, p. 86.

Figure 6.1 *Monthly lending on bills and bonds, January 1725 to December 1742*

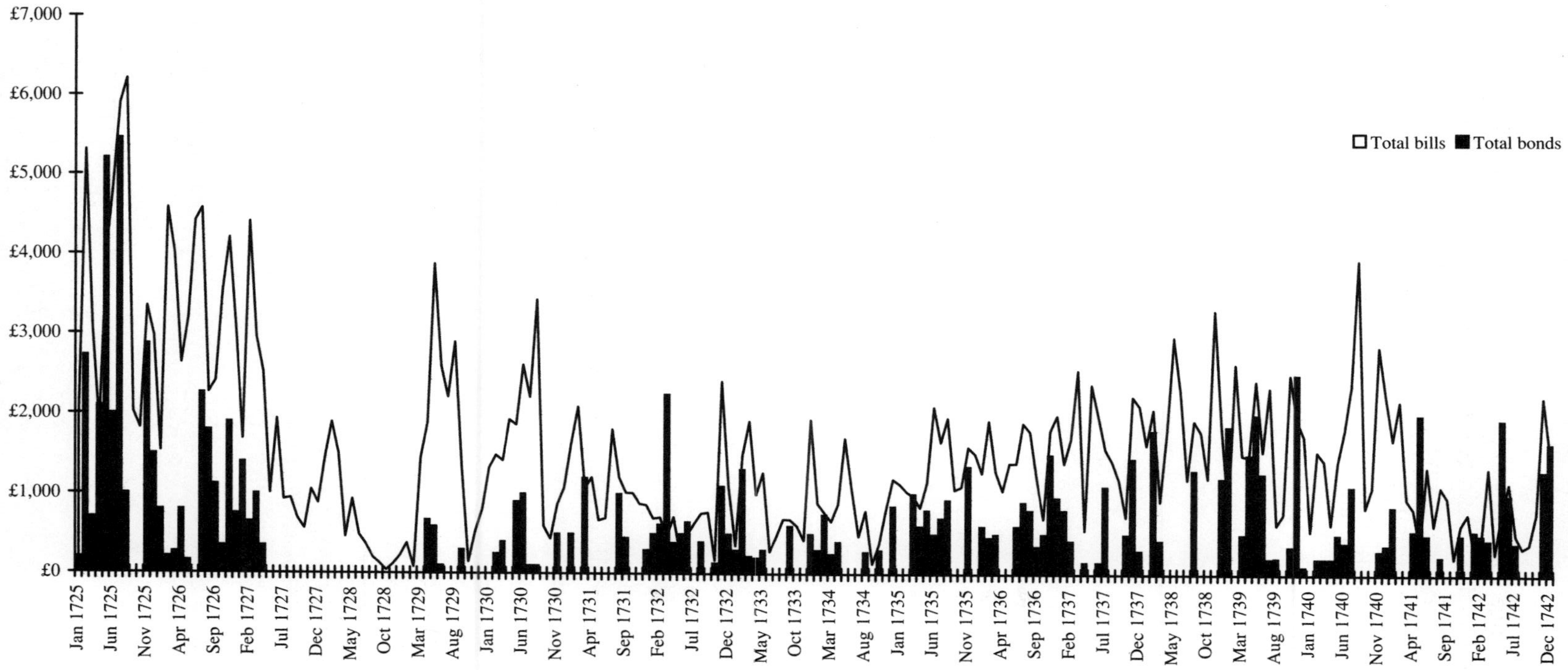
£7,000
£6,000
£5,000
£4,000
£3,000
£2,000
£1,000
£0
Total bills
Total bonds
Jan 1725
Jun 1725
Nov 1725
Apr 1726
Sep 1726
Feb 1727
Jul 1727
Dec 1727
May 1728
Oct 1728
Mar 1729
Aug 1729
Jan 1730
Jun 1730
Nov 1730
Apr 1731
Sep 1731
Feb 1732
Jul 1732
Dec 1732
May 1733
Oct 1733
Mar 1734
Aug 1734
Jan 1735
Jun 1735
Nov 1735
Apr 1736
Sep 1736
Feb 1737
Jul 1737
Dec 1737
May 1738
Oct 1738
Mar 1739
Aug 1739
Jan 1740
Jun 1740
Nov 1740
Apr 1741
Sep 1741
Feb 1742
Jul 1742
Dec 1742

Sources: BS 1/94, General Ledger (Account of inland bills); BS 1/5, Minutes.

Figure 6.2 Total sum of outstanding end-of-month balances on all cash accounts, November 1729 to December 1742

Earl of Ilay, with his English allies, on the other. Argyll was a military man, with a long career in the service of the Hanoverians. In his own right, as William Ferguson has reminded us, he was 'too much the monarch in the west Highlands', victorious from clan wars and Jacobite invasions and ill at ease in the world of London politics and the bowing and scraping of court life.[56] He was a considerable force in Scottish politics, with great personal strength and reserves of energy, and by 1736 felt he was being deliberately slighted in London court circles. His main love was the army, and he saw Treasury-inspired reductions in military expenditure in peacetime after 1730 as a plot which would leave the country open to invasion. In September 1736, there occurred a relatively minor scuffle following an execution of a condemned smuggler in Edinburgh. Smuggling was as popular in Scotland as in England, and the Edinburgh mob attacked the guard after the hanging. Its captain, John 'Black Jock' Porteous, ordered the soldiers to fire, and several in the crowd were killed and many wounded. The city fathers arrested Porteous and found him guilty, but while awaiting the inevitable royal reprieve the mob stormed the Tolbooth and carried out the execution.

The Duke of Argyll had cultivated the city fathers for over two decades, and retribution from the government would have affected his standing. When Robert Walpole decided that Edinburgh was to be punished, and brought in a tough bill, Argyll organised a strenuous opposition in 1737 to tone down the penalties.[57] It did nothing to dampen his paranoia about how he was viewed by the government interest. When war on Spain was declared in 1739, commonly known as the war of Jenkins' ear, he spoke out against the unpreparedness of the armed forces; this further estranged him from the court party and George II, and he was duly dismissed from office. His revenge came in the elections of 1741. Argyll used his influence to defeat government candidates, and, in conjunction with the Squadrone, twenty-six Squadrone, Argyll or independent members were returned compared with only nineteen for the Earl of Ilay. In February 1742, Walpole fell from office as First Secretary of the Treasury, and John, fourth Marquis of Tweeddale, was appointed Secretary of State, a position which he held until 1746. For the first time since 1725, Bank of Scotland now had friends in high office.

Bank of Scotland directors recommended the Marquis of Tweeddale as their Governor when news of his appointment arrived in Edinburgh. This greatly pleased the Marquis, who was speedily rebuilding his interest. It

---

56 Ferguson, *Scotland: 1689 to the Present*, pp. 144–6.
57 P. Dickson, *Red John of the Battles* (London: 1973), pp. 220–1. In the event, the Lord Provost was disqualified from office and a fine was imposed on the burgh: Ferguson, *Scotland: 1689 to the Present*, p. 145.

was made clear in his public correspondence that he would support the Bank: 'As I am fully convinced of the good intentions of the directors in pursuing such measures as may be of general benefit to the country, I shall not be wanting in my part to contribute as far as lys in my power to render such measures successful'.[58] Tweeddale also made it clear that, amid the many demands on his time, 'it occurs to me that if a proper agreement could be brought about betwixt the two Banks it might be greatly for the advantage of both as well as a convenience to the Public'.[59] In any event, Bank of Scotland would enjoy his continued 'protection'. Whether a formal agreement was signed at this time, or left unwritten, is unclear. What is clear is that commercial pressures encouraged such. Profits in banking were proportional to lending, and the interest came from this and from the time that notes were out and not required for exchange into cash or others' notes. The bank war had put restrictions on the volume of notes that could be out, and thus on lending, and forced both banks to hold reserves which in the absence of politically-inspired obstacles could now be used to increase lending and note circulation.

After the autumn of 1742, new cash account facilities agreed for Bank of Scotland customers reached a record level, and over £20,000 worth were arranged in 1743. Actual lending confirmed that a marked upturn had begun in late 1742 in the end-of-month balances as well. Bond lending followed a similar pattern, although more hesitant, with nearly £10,000 in 1744 and £15,140 in the eight months to August 1745. Overall, the balances of the Bank showed an increase of around 20 per cent in notes out in the three years after 1742. There was little effort made to recall loans or enforce bill payments where interest was unpaid. Some bill debts were converted to bonds, and the burgh loans were left to run, in the case of Edinburgh until February 1744.[60] Of course, ordinary commercial rivalry continued. In Glasgow, for example, the Royal Bank collected around twenty cash accounts and probably had a larger note circulation. The Court of Session stayed with Bank of Scotland and deposited £13,000 in July 1744, and the directors were careful to give their Lordships 5 per cent interest, above the level normally given for deposits. In competition for the complicated trusteeship of the estate of Merchiston, Blair and Lethern in 1745, Bank of Scotland won against the Royal Bank. But the banking war was now in the past, and the actions of both managements allowed lending to increase with demand.

58 NLS, MS 14427: John Hay, fourth Marquis of Tweeddale, to Alexander Arbuthnot, 4 May 1742.
59 NLS, MS 14427: John Hay, fourth Marquis of Tweeddale, to Thomas Hay, 9 March 1742, 8 March 1744, 13 March 1744.
60 BS 1/5, Minutes: 2 February 1744; for the detail of lending, see below, Chapter 12. For balances, see BS 1/94/9, General Ledger.

By the eve of the 1745 rebellion, Scotland possessed banking facilities and a note issue which were endorsed by the two main political establishments of the Earl of Ilay (after 1743 the third Duke of Argyll) and the Squadrone led by Secretary of State Tweeddale, by the Court of Session and Justiciary and the wider legal system. The fierce antagonism of the bank war had died away and in its place was a legacy predominantly professional, articulate and adaptive to the needs of the economy. The attitudes of the directors and managers of Bank of Scotland may be summed up as a general responsibility for the financial strength and stability of the country. This perspective the Royal Bank was willing to adopt, albeit belatedly, with the onset of famine and the defection of the second Duke of Argyll. The extraordinary experiences of wars, the periodic threats of invasion, the dearths and harvest crises, the deliberate attempts by this or that faction and latterly by the Argyll–Ilay interest had been a hard tutor. To use the word 'cautious' to sum up the directors' approach to banking would tend to trivialise the enormous difficulties which Bank of Scotland faced year on year and the flexible methods of lending which they developed. Prior to 1727, over two-thirds of their lending was in adaptable, often very long-term, heritable and personal bonds with the remainder in the form of shorter-term bills, all of which could be renegotiated. Bank directors were usually prepared to allow any form of lending to stand out for years at a stretch. In agricultural crises, borrowers were rarely expected to keep up their interest payments. All the lending after 1710 was at some of the lowest rates of interest in Europe. The insistence upon good security, usually in the form of two or three guarantors, unencumbered land or urban property, forced borrowers to put together the nearest thing Scotland had in the early eighteenth century to business plans. In this respect, Bank of Scotland was in advance of the practice of the merchants and lawyers of Edinburgh who before 1696 often had little alternative than to extend credit to their clients, for whatever scheme, and the lack of proper controls had enabled many a Scottish estate to rack itself with debt. Perhaps this was one of the most important attributes of this banking system, namely to stop at least some people with wealth from losing it through ill-considered projects.

Apart from some areas of the Highlands and the Borders, where barter remained the predominant form of exchange and whose position was relatively barren and isolated, the banking system by 1745 was comprehensive, with two sets of note issue coexisting. Yet, even in the wilderness of the Grampians and on the remote islands, the chiefs bought and sold cattle with the drovers using banknotes. The organisation of accounts and lending enabled merchants and lairds to spread payments over a longer timespan than the traditional payment times, and in bad seasons to extend their credit. At this stage of development, merchants and lawyers were extensively used as factors in Edinburgh, with authority to supervise accounts for their correspondents. This was an intermediate stage on the road to a branch network, and attempts to establish one from 1728 to 1733 were inappropriate. There were obvious benefits to the political interests involved in banking; indeed, the establishment of the Royal Bank was seen from all sides as a means to reinforce the political powers of the Argyll–Ilay interests through financial strength. After the famine of 1740–1, political interest remained very important, but in different ways that were sometimes more complicated than in the first fifty years of Bank of Scotland. In respect of the economic integration of the country, the importance of banking cannot be underestimated, and this forms part of the underlying theme for the history of the Bank for the remainder of the eighteenth century.

CHAPTER 7

BANK OF SCOTLAND, 1745–65

THERE WAS A MARKED improvement in the political and the financial position of Bank of Scotland in the four years from the end of the famine of 1739–41 to the Jacobite rebellion of 1745–46. Monthly cash account balances exceeded £75,000 by 1744, almost 50 per cent in advance of those in 1740; while £8,900 worth of new cash accounts were authorised in 1742, £19,000 the following year, £20,900 in 1744 and £16,700 worth before a halt to new lending was ordered on 22 August 1745. There was a steady increase in the number of bills discounted from a low level in 1741, but the bill as a means of long-term lending was now used less frequently by borrowers, and this change was encouraged by the board of directors. New advances by bonds reached almost £10,000 in 1744 and £15,140 in the first eight months of 1745. In March 1744, the proprietors agreed that this increase in the scale of the Bank's commitment required an increase in the paid-up capital to 50 per cent, and £10,000 was transferred from the surplus in the profit and loss account to the adventurers' stock. There were few political problems in these years before the rebellion, and this increase was carried through for commercial safety. To celebrate their improved finances, the directors ordered a renovation of the boardroom and two dozen new chairs, 'with two elbow chairs' for the Governor and Deputy Governor.

While the political situation was much calmer, there was to be a further, and ultimately successful, attempt by Lord Milton to safeguard the institutional base of his political interest. The opportunity for this lay with the constitution and finances of the Board of Manufactures, which his interest controlled, and the progress made by the linen trade. By 1733, the Board had stamped over 4.5 million pieces of cloth, and the annual value of this cloth rose from £132,600 in the five years to 1732 to nearly

£200,000 by 1739.[1] The Board was interested in the entire range of linen manufacture from flax cultivation to the colonial market. In its annual reports, forwarded to the Treasury and the board of trade, it was made clear that faster progress could be made if its funds were enlarged and more artisans enticed from Europe to work in Scotland. Nevertheless, there was progress in the quality of the coarse linen trade, and at the Picardy works, in the village of Broughton near Edinburgh, the board employed French cambric weavers to manufacture the finer qualities.[2] When war was declared in 1739, substantial orders were placed for linen cloth by the armed forces. Although the British government had to balance the needs of consumers against producers, ministers listened to demands for protection when the quality of home products was satisfactory. The new Secretary of State in 1742, the Marquis of Tweeddale, endorsed legislation for a bounty on the export of linens in that year, and, when it was found inadequate in its level of financial support, this was reinforced by higher bounties in 1745.[3]

When the second Duke of Argyll began his opposition to Robert Walpole's punitive measures against Edinburgh following the Porteous riots, Lord Milton tried to persuade his fellow board members to transfer the business at Picardy to a private company managed by William Dalrymple of Cranston. As the political threat was unclear and several of the trustees were loyal to Argyll, he was turned down, though Dalrymple may not have had sufficient capital. In January 1739, Milton formed the Edinburgh Linen Company, a co-partnership managed by Dalrymple, supported by a £3,000 subscription, with a cash account at the Royal Bank. It specialised in the import of linen from Campvere in Holland, bleached near Edinburgh and then re-exported via London.[4] Initially it suffered from the dreadful weather of 1739 to 1741, aggravated by trading difficulties, the higher costs of freight and insurance caused by the war, and inexperienced management. However, the defeat of Walpole and Ilay in the elections of 1741 spurred Milton to make his second, and this time successful, attempt to take the Picardy works into private hands. On his appointment to state office, the Marquis of Tweeddale made it clear that, as the board of trustees was dominated by his political opponents, it was

1 A. J. Warden, *The Linen Trade, Ancient and Modern* (London: 1864); A. Durie, *The Scottish Linen Industry in the Eighteenth Century* (Edinburgh: 1979), p. 23; R. H. Campbell (ed.), *States of the Progress of the Linen Manufacture in Scotland 1727–1754* (Edinburgh: 1973), p. 141, Abstract; there was a modest fall in output during 1739–41 but recovery thereafter, which was partly due to an improvement in the weather.
2 Durie, *Scottish Linen Industry*, pp. 48–9; C. A. Malcolm, *The History of the British Linen Bank* (Edinburgh: 1950), p. 4.
3 Durie, *Scottish Linen Industry*, p. 52; the 1742 Act, 15 George II c.29, was operational from 25 March 1743, and 18 George II c.25, which strengthened the former, from 24 June 1745.
4 J. S. Shaw, *The Management of Scottish Society 1707–1764* (Edinburgh: 1983), p. 155.

in need of reform. Before he could replace them, Lord Milton persuaded the trustees to transfer the Picardy works to the Linen Company.[5] It was a remarkable coup; a business established and supported with public funds was transferred to a political interest worsted in the recent elections.

Lord Milton's next step was to broaden the political connections of the Edinburgh Linen Company and to increase its capital. His vision this time was even grander – a 'Grand Manufactory', as he put it – and he raised £16,750 of which one-fifth was paid up and supported by another cash account from the Royal Bank.[6] Raising such a sum on a co-partnership involved a large number of persons who would be distant from the management. To provide some reassurance to proprietors, Milton brought onto the board two Lords of Session, Strichen and Tinwald, as well as William Grant the Lord Advocate, William Kirkpatrick the Clerk of Session, and several other lawyers. He enjoyed the cooperation of John Coutts, the Edinburgh merchant who was Lord Provost in 1742, and Archibald Stewart, the Lord Provost of 1744. Milton's main legal problems were solved by these appointments. The co-partnership also included Patrick Crauford of Auchenames, MP, Lt-General St Clair, whose family had linen interests near Kirkcaldy, and a group of merchants and lairds involved in the linen trade.[7] Among the London subscribers were William, Earl of Panmure, Lord Somerville and George Middleton, the banker, as well as several wealthy linen drapers. The managers were two linen merchants, Ebenezer McCulloch and William Tod, who had their own accounts with the Royal Bank and were required to subscribe £2,000 in the venture.

With the foundation of this new Edinburgh Linen Co-partnery, Lord Milton set in train an application for a royal charter. This would limit the adventurers' liability for losses to the extent of the nominal capital investment in the business, and thus exclude debts incurred by any partners in the course of the trade, 'which, it seems, the law of England might subject them to'.[8] Lord Milton looked for a conversion of the existing co-partnership to the incorporated company with the additional right to issue paper credits and to raise up to £100,000 from proprietors.

5 Shaw, *Management of Scottish Society*, pp. 158–60.
6 Ibid., p. 156; Malcolm, *The British Linen Bank*, p. 6.
7 Malcolm, *The British Linen Bank*, pp. 5–7, relates the early history of the co-partnership and its membership. The other Scots included Thomas Allan and Alexander Sharp, merchant councillors in Edinburgh; several linen manufacturers and traders and their legal representatives, George Buchan of Kelso, Andrew Wright of Ormiston, Alexander Monteith of Kinross, George Ochterlony of Montrose, Walter Riddell and George Gordon of Dumfries, David Kinloch, James Armour ws, Thomas Gibson and Gabriel Napier. Coutts and Stewart were later to play a part in helping the Jacobite army to enter Edinburgh, for which Stewart was jailed. See R. Sedgwick (ed.), *The History of Parliament: The House of Commons 1715–1754*, vol. i (London: 1970), pp. 592–3.
8 Malcolm, *The British Linen Bank*, p. 8.

For this extension of the business, more political support was thought desirable; James, Earl of Lauderdale, George, Earl of Kinnoull, Lord Viscount Dupplin and William Beckford of Fonthill, the richest West Indian planter in Europe, agreed to join the company. The petition to the government duly went forward in June, with the projectors showing supreme confidence that it would be granted.[9] Lord Milton naturally had the support of the Earl of Ilay who was biding his time before a return to office, and the scheme was seriously considered by the Treasury.

The War of the Austrian Succession encouraged widespread dissatisfaction with the Hanoverian regime. The French had reason enough to provide encouragement, but only in Scotland was it likely to lead to open rebellion.[10] In early 1744, a substantial French force designed to land in Scotland put to sea but was forced to return due to bad weather. There were further setbacks which delayed promised support from the French, the consequence of which was that Prince Charles Edward settled for a much smaller endeavour. He landed at Eriskay in the Outer Hebrides with a handful of companions and on 19 August 1745 raised the Stewart standard at Glenfinnan in Inverness-shire. A cautious campaign by the Hanoverian commander-in-chief Sir John Cope failed to stop Charles's growing army, and on 17 September the Jacobites entered Edinburgh, to general rejoicing. Four days later, Cope was routed at Prestonpans with 400 dead and 1,200 wounded. The news was received with grave concern in London. After Prestonpans, Andrew Stone, under-secretary of state to the Duke of Richmond, suggested that the Jacobites would 'soon be able to reduce the Castle and consequently be masters of all the Arms and all the wealth of that country'.[11] In fact, Charles lacked the wherewithal to besiege the Castle. He languished in Edinburgh for over a month, and on 31 October, as autumn turned towards winter, he left with 5,500 soldiers and marched into England, never to return to his capital. The Jacobites reached Derby, and though it has been a matter of contention whether they could have overthrown George II, the clan

9 R. B. Sheridan, 'Planter and Historian. The Career of William Beckford of Jamaica and England, 1744–1799', *Jamaica Historical Review*, 4 (1964), 36–58; Malcolm, *The British Linen Bank*, p. 8, petition reprinted in Appendix One, pp. 231–3. The other signatories were Charles Erskine, Lord Tinwald; John Maule of Kellie, a neighbour of Panmure; James Abercromby; Patrick Crauford; John Mackye; William Douglass; James Gordon of Dumfries; Samuel Martin; John Yeamans; Mathew Mills; George Middleton; Galfridus Mann; John Goodchild the linen draper; Samuel Bethel; and William Tod, one of the managers of the co-partnership.
10 W. Ferguson, *Scotland: 1689 to the Present*, The Edinburgh History of Scotland, vol. iv (Edinburgh: 1968), pp. 148–52; there was an attempt to stage a revolt in 1743, but without French aid the clans refused to rise.
11 T. J. McCann, *The Correspondence of the Dukes of Richmond and Newcastle 1724–1750*, Sussex Record Society, vol. 73 (1982–3), p. 173, 23 August 1745.

chiefs insisted on a withdrawal, and on 6 December started the long trek back into Scotland. On 17 January they defeated Cope's successor at Falkirk, but this was rather a false dawn as with winter came supply difficulties, munitions were low and the artillery was inadequate. Those in Charles's army who argued for intermittent skirmishes and a wearing-down of the foe were overruled. On 16 April 1746 on Culloden moor, the Duke of Cumberland had the chance to use his overwhelming superiority in artillery, one-third of the Jacobite force was dead or wounded before they charged, and by nightfall Cumberland's soldiers were butchering the wounded and prisoners; it was 'slaughter rather than a battle'.[12]

The effect of this last Jacobite insurrection on Bank of Scotland was short-lived and it suffered less than the Royal Bank, whose directors were associated with everything anathema to the Jacobite cause and had to pay £3,076 to Charles.[13] The Bank ceased lending on 22 August 1745. On 6 September, General Preston, Governor of Edinburgh Castle, was asked for a room in which to deposit the Bank's books, papers, cash and notes. Although the Bank was formally closed, many transactions proceeded, with duplicates sent to the Castle. The main precaution was the destruction of £82,775 of banknotes. The Jacobite forces were ill-provided with gold, and it was thus in their interests to encourage the circulation of paper. Charles Edward issued a proclamation at Holyrood Palace on 25 September which acknowledged the upset that his arrival had caused and the 'great distress and many inconveniences [which] have attended the removal of the two Banks into the Castle and that the credit of the said banks have suffered much from an opinion industriously spread that we intended to seize on money wherever it was to be found, to the detriment of our Father's subjects'.[14] He offered a reassurance that the banks

> shall be intirely sure under our protection and free from all contribution to be exacted by us in any time coming so that the proprietors may return with safety to their former business of banking under this special protection and we ourselves shall contribute so far in the re-establishment of public credit as to receive bank notes in payment made to us, of public or other monies and shall issue the same in payments to be made by us, so that our arrival in this kingdom, shall in no wise hurt or influence the credit formerly established.[15]

---

12 Ferguson, *Scotland: 1689 to the Present*, pp. 152–3.
13 S. G. Checkland, *Scottish Banking: A History, 1695–1973* (Glasgow: 1975), p. 73; Malcolm, *Bank of Scotland*, p. 53, states that the sum paid by the Royal Bank was £6,100.
14 The evidence suggests that payments were held up and banknotes refused from some time after the landing of Charles Edward until the retreat into the Highlands after the battle of Falkirk. The extent of the difficulties is unknown. For a report from Glasgow, see NLS, MS 14422, Yester Papers, f. 73: William Anderson, Glasgow, to Marquis of Tweeddale, 23 October 1745.
15 Proclamation cited in William Maitland, *The History of Edinburgh from its Foundation to the Present Time* (Edinburgh: 1753), pp. 129–30.

Business at Bank of Scotland restarted by 16 November, although lending was kept to modest sums on cash accounts and bills. The main exception was an advance for £10,000 in January 1746 to General Husk for soldiers' wages.[16] The Bank's accounts and coin remained in the Castle until 1 May 1746. There were a few legal consequences; the Edinburgh writer William Robertson requested interest on both Bank and Royal Bank notes during the enforced suspension and was refused. A number were torn up by soldiers, and, as nothing survived, repayment was also turned down.[17] The Royal Bank was worried – for a time – that the Bank of Scotland directors might be tempted by the invasion to renew the bank war. In fact, by this time the two banks were closely intertwined: note-picking was in the past, and they held each other's notes as part of their reserve and by these understandings afforded a more extensive circulation. The managers of the two banks met during the emergency to exchange their notes. By comparison with 1715, the troubles after 1728 and more recently the dearth of 1739–41, the Forty-five was a minor interruption. There was soon a huge increase in activity and the circulation of notes, and more formal agreements to support each other were negotiated.

The rebellion marked the end for the Marquis of Tweeddale; he was dislodged from office in January 1746. The position of Secretary of State then lapsed. London ministers expressed robust views about the country, the Jacobites and the failures of Tweeddale. The Duke of Richmond, shortly after the battle of Falkirk, referred to Scotland as the 'sinke of the earth', and after Culloden he informed the Duke of Newcastle that 'nothing but force will ever keep that stinking corner of the kingdom quiet'.[18] Nonetheless, Scotland was part of Britain and had to be managed somehow, so Newcastle and Richmond turned to the Argyll interest. Lord Milton had sent to English ministers detailed information collected by his spy system throughout the emergency and, together with other services from the Argyll interest, this assured their associates a paramount place at Westminster. Inevitably, Lord Milton's petition for a royal charter for the British Linen Company was endorsed by the senior law officers of Scotland – on 17 March 1746 – and it received the royal seal on 5 July. The directors of the old co-partnership, now 'by the name and stile of the British Linen Company', appointed the third Duke of Argyll as Governor, with Lord Milton as Deputy Governor. On the board sat John Coutts, the banker, William Beckford and sundry Edinburgh merchants; Allan Whitefoord, Cashier of the Royal Bank, joined in 1748. The charter granted the right

---

16 BS 1/5, Minutes: 10 January 1746.
17 BS 1/5, Minutes: 18 November 1745, 6 February and 10 December 1746.
18 McCann, *Correspondence*, pp. 24, 224: 6 February and 4 June 1746.

to raise a capital of £100,000, and it was agreed to raise, in the first instance, half this figure as a fund for the expansion of the production and sale of linen cloth and yarn. Of the £70,600 subscribed, £32,650 was from London. The lists included many Scottish aristocrats and lairds associated with the Argyll interest and also included Edinburgh judges, lawyers, tax-collectors and merchants involved in linen manufacture and exports to the colonies.[19] As was only to be expected, there was an overlap of subscribers with proprietors of the Royal Bank, of which institution Lord Milton remained Deputy Governor. All of these changes implied possible difficulties for Bank of Scotland. The government granted additional protection to the cambric trade in 1747.

Bank of Scotland directors took full note of the founding of the British Linen Company. The overlap in subscriptions, the history of the linen co-partnership, the involvement of the Royal Bank and the new alignment at Westminster meant that the Bank had no choice but to accept the new situation. Lord Milton's banking scheme involved the issue of banknotes of £100 to carry interest after three months, and ordinary notes for £20, £10 and £5 with no interest. These were initially in the form of promissory notes given out by the Company for linen cloth, though they were changed in 1750 to bearer notes to encourage wider circulation. The paid-up capital of £46,882 made the Company the third largest joint stock in Scotland. The Royal Bank provided its reserve to pay demands on British Linen banknotes through a cash account for £10,000; experience was to indicate that cover of 10–15 per cent was ample for the circulation.[20]

The British Linen Company bestowed a number of benefits on the linen industry, particularly on the production and quality of linens for export. The output of linen cloth fluctuated between 1734 and 1742 around 4.4 to 4.9 million pieces. Only after 1746 was an upward trend discernable, and by 1750 output had reached 7.5 million pieces. By then the Company had made advances equal to around 10 per cent of the final value of Scottish linen production, and five years later it was around 15 per cent. Banknotes allowed borrowers to finance production and the Company to buy their flax and cloth. The historian William Maitland noted in 1753 that by the advance of money the linen manufacturers were able to return their money 'in half the time they normally did'.[21] The certainty of payment also helped the Company to discriminate in purchases.

The British Linen Company was a pioneer in the organisation of weaving sheds, or factories, which proved that tighter supervision could

19 BS(BL), Stock Ledgers; Malcolm, *The British Linen Bank*, Appendix 2, for the original fifty-eight subscribers.
20 Durie, *Scottish Linen Industry*, p. 119, Table 7.2.
21 Maitland, *History of Edinburgh*, p. 325.

produce products better adapted to market needs. The technology of weaving had improved in the first half of the eighteenth century, the quality of cloth was more uniform, productivity was much higher and unit costs were well down. Within the limits of the hand-operated loom and lint mill, the linen industry made remarkable strides with machinery, with the organisation of labour, management and cost accounting.[22] Yet the technology remained within the grasp of the master weaver working from home, and by the Seven Years' War the Company was losing its cost advantage. In 1758 the directors decided to run down the factories, though they continued with the putting-out of yarn to home-based weavers.[23] Their share of the total purchase of Scottish linen fell from 8.98 per cent in 1751 to half that a decade later, by which time the directors had moved towards joint ventures with other manufacturers and merchants and the marketing of linens. Thus the longer-term effect of Lord Milton's design was to force the Scottish hand-loom weavers to think in terms of the marketplace and concentrate on quality and uniformity of output. The British Linen Company was one of the most conspicuous fruits of the early British Empire, being an association of landowners and traders on both sides of the Atlantic supported by the leading officers of state, enjoying legislative protection against European linen suppliers, securing sales from the expansion of the North American and Caribbean slave plantations and colonists and periodic purchases from the British armed forces.

Yet it proved difficult to make profits even with the support of bounties. In 1752, 'the necessity of reserving a fund for losses appeared in so strong a light' that the dividend was cut from 5 to 4 per cent. It was, however, the withdrawal of the bounties in 1754 which caused the most damage. The Company was to recall that

> for the manufacturers or weavers, who had sett up looms, hired servants and got credit from the Company and others for flax and yarn to carry on their trade with, finding a certain charge unavoidably growing upon them, for living, and wages to their servants but no sale for their work, became bankrupt and fled the country, whereby it was justly computed that full 2000 looms were thrown idle in Scotland, and by these manufacturers becoming bankrupt the Company lost considerably.[24]

The withdrawal uncovered the fundamental weakness of the Scottish linen trade. It could survive in a limited way against continental and Irish competition, and the evidence suggests that its products improved

22 Warden, *The Linen Cloth Trade*, p. 421ff.
23 Durie, *Scottish Linen Industry*, pp. 134–5.
24 BS(BL) 6/5/1, Minutes of the meetings of proprietors of the British Linen Company 1749–1803, pp. 94–106.

in quality. But success in export markets in mid-century required political support, and it was fortunate for the Company that the government agreed to restore the bounties, although this was not carried out until the eve of the Seven Years' War.[25] Had the war not intervened to encourage renewal and purchases for the army and navy, it is doubtful whether such a large joint stock could have survived.

Lord Milton's original plan was an inspired attempt to strengthen links between the linen industry and his political interests. Yet he soon found practical problems over dividends. The British Linen board later noted

> with concern ... the impatience of the proprietors to have dividends annually ... while the company was in its infancy, struggling with all the ... difficulties in establishing their trade, and before any fund was earned and laid up to answer losses, and their continuing to make such dividends even after the withdrawing the bounty had greatly hurt the linen trade ... is another great cause [of later difficulties].[26]

Nevertheless, advantages accrued from this dividend policy: 'it is to [the] good opinion which mankind have formed of [the British Linen] that their notes have obtained a pretty extensive circulation, and that the credit of them has been supported ... when they seemed under a cloud'.

Profits during the war proved more buoyant.[27] Nevertheless, the directors realised that with the 'expectations of peace' the demand for their linens had slackened, 'and this together with the great demand for money has sunk the value of goods from 10 per cent to 20 per cent'. With peace would come a drastic fall in government purchases and a renewal of foreign competition. There was a fall in the banknotes in circulation: from over £50,000 in 1757–9, by May 1760 they were down to £39,373 and in 1762–3 to under £20,000. This contraction coincided with the resignation of the Company's long-standing Scottish manager, Ebenezer McCulloch, who formed a company supported by William and Robert Alexander, an Edinburgh banking firm, in 1763. After his departure, the directors discovered a list of bad debts which totalled £8,609 and a list of possible debts of £31,000. Conditions appeared so difficult that one director even suggested 'the best and justest thing we can do is to wind up'.[28] The directors agreed to give up, albeit gradually, direct involvement in linen production and sale and to concentrate on banking.

The new plans were endorsed by the British Linen board in 1764. The central feature was the 'issuing of cash-credits to such persons concerned

25 29 George II c.15; BS(BL) 6/5/1, Minutes of the meetings of proprietors, 5 July 1762.
26 BS(BL) 6/5/1, Minutes of the meetings of proprietors, pp. 94–106.
27 Figures from BS(BL) 6/5/1; but see below, Statistical Appendix, Table A20.
28 Malcolm, *The British Linen Bank*, p. 50.

in the linen trade' and the discounting of bills of exchange payable in Scotland and England, with the intention of keeping the circulation of banknotes around £80,000. The directors were now less reliant on the Royal Bank; by May 1764 the credit on the cash account was down to just £549.[29] Lord Milton, who was not wholeheartedly in support of these changes, and was in any case more obstinate than in earlier days, resigned as Deputy Governor in 1764 and died two years later. He was succeeded by Sir David Kinloch of Gilmerton, who later became Governor.[30] In 1766, James Guthrie, an Edinburgh private banker, was appointed to the board, and the following year the facilities for accounts and bills were extended to those outwith the linen trade. The extensive network of agents was now gradually converted to work for the banking operations, and these were to form the first permanent network of branches in Scottish banking.

The role of the British Linen Company in the provision of credit for linen manufacture should not be exaggerated. The Royal Bank and Bank of Scotland had extended their advances to the trade as it grew in the 1730s. Even prominent British Linen proprietors, including George, Earl of Kinnoull and Walter Riddell of Riddell, borrowed from the Bank, for £3,000 and £4,000 respectively. Nevertheless, the British Linen, through its network of agents, was able to advance credit to manufacturers with only one or two looms, and to encourage spinning and dressing in remote areas, while also financing the Picardy works and the bleachfield at Saltoun. For this work, it has been described as Scotland's first industrial bank. As its board included some very influential persons, it was able to exert pressure on government policy; lesser groups of Scottish merchants might have been less successful. Bank of Scotland was not reconciled to the British Linen for many years, although the wishes of the Royal Bank that it be treated more favourably than other banking companies were accepted as part of the early Agreements and Understandings between the two banks.

After the defeat of the Jacobites, lending by Bank of Scotland resumed an upward curve. For the five years 1746–50, the directors agreed to 246 new cash accounts – an average of £25,433 for each year – and the March 1744 balance of £108,000 had grown to £160,000 by 1750. The figures for bills followed the subdued pattern which the directors preferred, and for a few years after 1745 the average for bonds was below £10,000. There were occasional substantial loans, such as £5,000 to Archibald Scott of Rosie, the £4,000 aforementioned for Walter Riddell of Riddell, and £5,000

29 Durie, *Scottish Linen Industry*, p. 119, Table 7.2.
30 Archibald, third Duke of Argyll, died in 1761 and was succeeded as Governor by Charles Douglas, third Duke of Queensberry and second Duke of Dover: Malcolm, *The British Linen Bank*, pp. 200–1.

to Sir William Nairn of Dunsinnan, but these were exceptional. The years around the mid-century saw an increase in cash account advances to industrial enterprises, especially those concerned with brewing in the Edinburgh area, metalworking and the linen trade. While part of the increase can be explained by the understandings with the Royal Bank, there was an autonomous increase in demand. There was considerable optimism north of the Border about prospects for trade before the peace of Aix-la-Chapelle (1748) towards the end of the War of the Austrian Succession; the growth in lending was marked from June 1746 to May 1747 and a renewed surge from October until the summer of 1751, resumed again in the autumn of 1752. In England, there were indications of growth in the building trades and Bank of England discounts grew fast, but overall the conditions of credit remained tighter until the war had ended.[31] The optimism in Scotland encouraged laxness in management of advances, and the directors occasionally asked for more care over security and the payments of annualrents.[32]

There were substantial payments from London after the defeat of the Jacobites. Henry Pelham and the Duke of Newcastle persuaded Parliament to pass the Heritable Jurisdictions (Scotland) Act (1747), which agreed that compensation would be awarded by the Court of Session. In 1748, £164,233 was duly granted to the aristocracy and lairds whose legal rights were eliminated.[33] Claims from the creditors of estates forfeited because their owners were active Jacobites were also settled by compensation, and over £200,000 was paid out over the next ten years. The increase in the land market gave further encouragement to the banks. There was also the general monetary context; the government engineered a reduction in the rate of interest payable on the national debt. The total nominal worth of the 4 per cent Funds at the close of the war in 1747 was £58,703,405; by a skilful alliance with City financiers, Henry Pelham and his landed supporters in Parliament were able to convert this obligation to 3.5 per cent, to run from December 1750 to December 1757, and thereafter to 3 per cent. It was a testimony to the wealth of the country that the conversion was accepted by the City for all but £3 million, which was paid

31 D. M. Joslin, 'London Bankers in Wartime 1739–84', in L. S. Pressnell (ed.), *Studies in the Industrial Revolution* (London: 1960), pp. 156–77 (162–4); T. S. Ashton, *Economic Fluctuations in England and Wales 1700–1800* (Oxford: 1959), pp. 147–8; J. P. Lewis, *Building Cycles and Britain's Growth* (London: 1965), p. 19. For lending, see Statistical Appendix, Table A17.
32 BS 1/30/3, Agents' Letter Book, Secretary to John McKye of Palgowan, 'The annual rents on your and your brothers bond to the Bank for £250 . . . are resting since 9 December 1745 and I am ordered by the directors of the Bank to acquaint you that it is against the rule of the Company to allow annual rents to lie so long over'.
33 G. Menarty, *Life and Letters of Duncan Forbes of Culloden* (London: 1936), ch. 18; A. J. Youngson, *After the Forty-Five: The Economic Impact on the Scottish Highlands* (Edinburgh: 1973), pp. 25–6; H. Hamilton, *An Economic History of Scotland in the Eighteenth Century* (Oxford: 1963), p. 307.

off.[34] This inaugurated six years of cheap money, and the cost of borrowing on both sides of the Border was never lower in the eighteenth century.[35] The progress of the economy undoubtedly helped, and the cross-border costs of exchange remained around 1 per cent. Such a rate suggested an inflow of gold from England to take advantage of the higher rates of interest, typically 3½ to 4 per cent, available north of the Border.

By 1745, the main gap in the business operations of many merchant houses in respect of their banking side was the issue of banknotes payable to bearer. They remitted funds, lent on accounts and took in deposits, as well as dealing in goods, much as merchant houses did in most centres in Britain and Europe. An issue of notes would not benefit from the limited liability of the three chartered banks and perhaps not the support of local magnates, but as the economy was obviously growing such concerns seemed of lesser weight. Bank of Scotland granted cash accounts to several of these houses and acted as a reserve at times of need, utilising their services for foreign transactions and for the buying-in of coin. In February 1742, for example, when the Bank found that 'specie does not increase at the office' as it would usually do in winter, Adam and Thomas Fairholme (or Fairholm) were asked for £5,000 in coin.[36] A few of the private bankers sat on the ordinary board, and in 1748 Thomas Fairholme was elected Deputy Governor.

After the British Linen Company, the first provincial co-partnership bank was formed in Aberdeen. Bank of Scotland had long had close links with Aberdeenshire with advances on bills and bonds, but the distance between Edinburgh and Aberdeen encouraged few merchants to open cash accounts, although a number had joint accounts with Edinburgh merchants. In the summer of 1747, for reasons which remain obscure, a co-partnery of Aberdeen merchants led by William Mowat, William Brebner, John Dingwall, Alexander Livingstone, James Legerwood and Alexander Osborn registered their intention to form a banking company.[37] In November, two months after the British Linen had first issued promissory notes, they opened an office and started to circulate banknotes from £50 to 10 shillings sterling. Bank of Scotland underwrote the venture with cash accounts up to £1,000 for several of the partners. The full sums were rarely

34 L. S. Sutherland, 'Samson Gideon and the Reduction of Interest, 1749–50', *Economic History Review*, 1st series, 16 (1946), 15–29; idem, 'Samson Gideon: Eighteenth Century Jewish Financier', *Transactions of the Jewish Historical Society of England*, 17 (1951–2), 79–90; G. Yogev, *Diamonds and Coral: Anglo-Dutch and Eighteenth-Century Trade* (Leicester: 1978), p. 52.

35 L. S. Pressnell, 'The Rate of Interest in the Eighteenth Century', in idem (ed.), *Studies in the Industrial Revolution* (London: 1960) pp. 178–214 (p. 179); these observations are confirmed by the rates charged north of the Border.

36 BS 1/5, Minutes: 3 February 1743.

37 NLS, MS 17591, Fletcher of Saltoun Papers, ff. 131a–133; this registration was a requirement of the Scots law for co-partneries. Books were open to public examination.

Table 7.1 *Outstanding end-of-month balances on cash account of Robert Dunlop and Allan Dreghorn*
(Ship bank)

Date		Balance	Date		Balance
Nov	1749	−2,000	Jan	1751	−2,600
Dec	1749	−3,260	Feb	1751	−900
Jan	1750	4,855	Mar	1751	−5,900
Feb	1750	−3,125	Apr	1751	−7,650
Mar	1750	−3,115	May	1751	−9,150
Apr	1750	−3,295	Jun	1751	−10,000
May	1750	−2,545	Jul	1751	−10,000
Jun	1750	−3,245	Aug	1751	−6,900
Jul	1750	−4,145	Sep	1751	−5,340
Aug	1750	−1,715	Oct	1751	−1,880
Sep	1750	0	Nov	1751	−3,102
Oct	1750	−410	Dec	1751	−2,602
Nov	1750	−1,200	Jan	1752	0
Dec	1750	−1,400			

Note: The cash account was opened in the names of Robert Dunlop and Allan Dreghorn, merchants in Glasgow. The cautioners (guarantors) were Andrew Buchanan, Colin Dunlop and Alexander Houston (merchants in Glasgow) and William Macdouall of Castle Semple.

Source: BS 1/106/11–12, Cash account progressive ledger.

required; the fact that the notes were underwritten by Bank of Scotland was apparently sufficient to secure their circulation. Moreover, the Bank itself increased support for the neighbourhood and granted over £6,000 of new cash accounts in the four years from March 1747, and, among several bonds, granted £2,000 to the Dowager Duchess of Gordon.

The next issue of banknotes by a co-partnership was also endorsed by Bank of Scotland, this time in Glasgow in the autumn of 1749. Frequent criticisms had been raised in the west of the stringency of Edinburgh banks' lending conditions and their limitations on total lending. Rightly or wrongly, they were reproached for an alleged failure to recognise that the Glasgow trades required both more credit and greater flexibility in the settlement of accounts 'such as a delay in the sale' of tobacco.[38] The absence of Edinburgh branches in the greater Glasgow area and the requirement for Glasgow firms to negotiate through private banks and merchants in Edinburgh for some of their business proved expensive in time and money. The new company was known as Dunlop, Houston & Co., and more commonly as the Ship bank, a name taken from the picture printed on its banknotes. The partners were later described before the Court of Session as 'men of property', namely John Grahame of Dougalstoun, a landowner, and five wealthy merchants with landed connections, Andrew Buchanan, Allan Dreghorn, Alexander Houston

---

38 NLS, MS 17592, Fletcher of Saltoun Papers, ff. 29–30v, memorandum from Lord Milton, 2 October 1756.

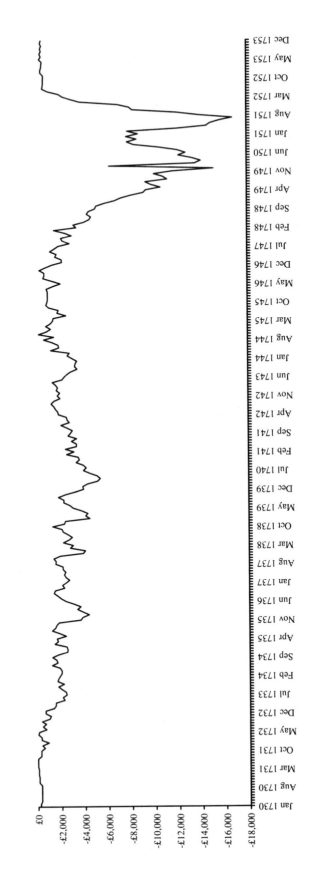

Figure 7.2 Total end-of-month balances on all Glasgow cash accounts, 1730–53

Source: BS/106/1–12, Cash account progressive ledgers.

and Robert and Colin Dunlop. Their paid-up capital was £15,000. They had made extensive gains from the American tobacco trades and from the export of coal, linen and other manufactures, and drew on their expertise in the handling of commercial bills of exchange and banknotes on both sides of the Atlantic.[39] Several had links with Bank of Scotland, and the directors extended to the new enterprise the largest cash account to that date, £10,000, first drawn on in November 1749 (see Table 7.1). There was an understanding that Bank of Scotland notes would be circulated by the Ship bank. During the next two years, the cash account only came close to the limit in the spring and summer of 1751. Furthermore, the overall figures for advances to Glasgow from Bank of Scotland on cash accounts show a huge rise from 1746 to 1752 (see Figure 7.2 and Table 7.3).

The reaction of the board of the Royal Bank to the Aberdeen company was confined to questioning its legal status and that of its notes.[40] The argument was based on an interpretation of two Acts of Anne (3 & 4 Anne c.9, made perpetual by 7 Anne c.25) which gave to promissory notes the same privileges in England possessed by the holders of bills of exchange, whereas in Scotland a holder of a promissory note could not demand summary execution and if it was not holograph could not 'even be the ground for [a legal action] above £8-6sh-8d'. To avoid these potential legal obstacles, the Aberdeen partners subscribed in the Burgh Court books an additional obligation to pay their notes. In autumn 1749, after discussions with Bank of Scotland, the Royal Bank directors agreed not to pursue legal moves. They later decided, in the summer of 1750, to support thirty-one Glasgow merchants in the new Glasgow Arms bank.[41] The circulation of Royal Bank notes was well established in Glasgow: they earned interest on twenty-seven cash accounts with a maximum advance of £16,700 and conducted a remittance trade on behalf of some Glasgow merchants.[42] The Royal Bank extended a cash account facility for £6,000 in November 1750, and it was agreed that the Arms bank would help circulate their notes. The new endeavour secured credit in London from Campbell & Bruce, forerunners of Coutts & Co., for £5,000, against which bills of £100 at thirty days' date could be drawn, the interest to be 5 per cent and settlement every six months.[43] The Glasgow

39 Grahame was replaced in November 1749 by William Macdouall of Castle Semple, another landowner; see Checkland, Scottish Banking, p. 97; C. W. Munn, The Scottish Provincial Banking Companies, 1747–1864 (Edinburgh: 1981), p. 11.
40 NLS, MS 17591, Fletcher of Saltoun Papers, ff. 131a–133; ibid., Attorney General and Solicitor General, report on the bank at Aberdeen, 14 July 1748.
41 Munn, The Scottish Provincial Banking Companies, p. 11; Checkland, Scottish Banking, p. 99.
42 NLS, MS 17591, Fletcher of Saltoun Papers, ff. 139–143: Royal Bank cash accounts at Glasgow in 1749 and 1751.
43 Coutts & Co., archives, Letter Book no. 3, 23 April 1751.

Table 7.3 Examples of three Glasgow cash accounts, 1731–51.

Outstanding end-of-month balances on the accounts of Robert and James Robertson,[1] George Bogle junior of Daldowie[2] and Andrew Buchanan,[3] merchants in Glasgow

Balance at end of:	January			February			March			April			May			June		
	R	GB	AB	R	GB	AB	R	GB	AB	R	GB	AB	R	GB	AB	R	GB	AB
1731	-470																	
1732	0			0			0			0								
1733	-700		515	0			0			0			-400			-400		
1734	-800		-210	-290		-254	-370		-321	-600		-321	-450		-200	-300		-200
1735			-462	-110		-126	-300		-241	-200		-72	-600		-160	-250		-20
1736	-620	-420	-175	-560	-420	-379	-300	-420	-384	-576	-420	-384	-900	-400	-247	-400	-350	-197
1737	110	-320	-278	-570	-420	-195	-160	-500	-195	-230	-500	-145	-400	-500	-396	-300	-500	-396
1738	-450	-500	-330	355	-500	-173	-95	-500	-173	-195	-500	-173	-660	-500	-207	-430	-500	-207
1739	-282	-500	-185	-150	-500	-350	-300	-500	-405	-150	-500	-280	-995	-500	-273	-935	-350	-418
1740	-500	-500	-255	-450	-500	-165	-540	-500	-140	-720	-500	-465	-720	-400	-200	-720	-500	-85
1741	-330	-500	-305	-330	-500	-405	-330	-500	-305	-330	-500	-140	-330	-300	-395	-330	-240	-195
1742		-400	-120		-400	-305		-360	-170		-500	-305		-270	-250		-300	-405
1743		-185			-415	-170		-400			-300	0		-500	-305		-270	-305
1744		-500			-400			-320			-320			-420			-500	
1745		-380			-320			-60			0			0			-420	
1746		-60			-60			-10			0			0			0	
1747		-40			-160			0			0			-100			0	
1748		0			0			-50			-50			-50			-100	
1749		-200			-50			-180			-120			-120			-260	
1750		-180			-180												-120	
1751		-40			0													

Balance at end of:	July			August			September			October			November			December		
	R	GB	AB	R	GB	AB	R	GB	AB	R	GB	AB	R	GB	AB	R	GB	AB
1731	-100			-400			0			-300			-200			-200		
1732	-500			-500			-150			-600			0			0		
1733	-800		-244	-650		-184	-400		-64	-450		0	-100		-40	-100		10
1734	-200		0	0		-200	-100		-147	-800		-147	-800		-147	-800		-247
1735			-80			-119			-209	0		-311		-200	-391		-420	-441
1736	-130	-300	-396	100	-250	-196	35	-250	75	0	-250	0	0	-200	-175	0	-120	-175
1737	-630	-500	-207	-199	-150	-113	-109	-150	-175	-439	-150	-66	-675	-150	-20	-675	-500	-88
1738	-795	-400	-458	-565	-400	-325	-415	-400	-350	-420	-400	-345	-70	-400	-435	-70	-500	-420
1739	0	-350	-165	-265	-350	0	0	-350	40	-200	-350	65	-760	-500	-45	-760	-500	-175
1740	-500	-500	-445	-500	-300	-285	-500	-300	-285	-500	-500	-305	-330	-500	-305	-330	-485	-235
1741	-330	-485	-525	-330	-485	-525	-330	-485	-525	-330	-485	-525	0	-485	-335	0	30	-305
1742		-300	-305		-500	-305		-500	-305		-500	-280		0	-260		-500	-210
1743		-385			-275			-335			-280			-410			-380	
1744		-350			-50			-190			-190			-380			-60	
1745		-420			-60			-60			-60			-60			-40	
1746		0			0			0			0			-40			0	
1747		0			-100			0			0			0			-200	
1748		-200			-200			-300			-300			-200			0	
1749		-260			-260			-260			-260			0			-40	
1750		-40			-40			-40			-40			-40				
1751																		

Notes:

1. The account of Robert Robertson and his nephew James Robertson was opened in November 1731 with a credit limit of £1,000. Robert Robertson was a tobacco merchant and the two were private bankers in Glasgow for a time in the late 1720s and early 1730s. The cautioners (guarantors) on the account were James Smith and James Rae, merchants, Glasgow, Robert Robertson, maltster, Glasgow and John Robertson, writer, Glasgow.

2. The Bogles were one of the old Glasgow merchant families which had gained control of the bulk of the tobacco trade by the 1740s. George attended Glasgow University and completed his education with a 'Grand Tour' in the 1720s, when he travelled through some of the German states, the Netherlands, France and Flanders acting as a travelling agent for his family's business. His business activities, in addition to the tobacco trade, included partnerships in the Easter Sugar House, Glasgow Cudbear Works and Smithfield Iron Co., as well as lending money on bond to hard-up local landowners. The account was opened in November 1735 with a credit limit of £500, the cautioners being Matthew Bogle and Laurence Scott, merchants, Glasgow and George Sinclair, advocate (his brother-in-law?). He was a cautioner on six other Glasgow cash accounts operating between 1733 and 1752, and his account was one of the many Glasgow accounts closed in 1751–2 as a result of the public banks' action against the Glasgow banks. Bogle was registered as a burgess of Glasgow in 1752 and was Lord Rector of Glasgow University in 1737, 1743, 1747 and 1757.

3. The cautioners of Andrew Buchanan were George Buchanan, Archibald Buchanan, James Montgomerie (all Glasgow merchants) and Pat Montgomerie, merchant in Edinburgh. The credit limit was £500, although this was restricted to £250 between March 1740 and January 1741.

Sources: RB 1/106/1–23, Cash account progressive ledgers; Checkland, *Scottish Banking*; T. M. Devine, *The Tobacco Lords* (Edinburgh: 1990).

company originally asked for an account free of any charges, but this was refused.

By the summer of 1751, both Bank of Scotland and the Royal Bank had changed their attitudes to the Glasgow ventures. There were various reasons, the most important being the situation on the exchanges. The relationship between Edinburgh and London and the level of price movements in Scotland tended to give Bank of Scotland and Royal Bank managers prior warning of the dangers of over-extension before this was apparent in the City of London. The Bank experienced this as an increase in the demand for gold, a deterioration on the exchange as coin was exported to fuel activity in London, and usually, though not always, a rise in prices of imported goods; at this, the Bank curtailed advances to reduce pressure for coin. It also became clear by 1750 that the operation of the Glasgow banks made it more difficult for cash account holders in the west to obtain regular bills on Edinburgh 'for cash' to remit to their accounts. This raised the possibility of losing cash accounts to Glasgow banks.[44]

The break between Edinburgh and Glasgow occurred remarkably quickly. On 19 July 1751, two directors of Bank of Scotland met Lord Milton and two directors from the Royal Bank to discuss what was thought to be a crisis 'with regard to the great circulation of paper credit occasioned by private persons erecting themselves into Banking companies'.[45] In a series of agreements thrashed out over four days, they agreed to close their cash accounts for both Glasgow banks, the Aberdeen bank and the accounts of merchants who were partners or whose credit was thought to support these banks. Bank of Scotland and the Royal Bank would accept only each other's banknotes and those of the British Linen Company. Any person or house circulating Glasgow notes in Edinburgh would have their accounts stopped, and both public banks compiled a list of errant accounts.[46] They would operate against coin exporters and close down accounts to block credit where necessary and support each other's credit and note issue. The note exchange was regularised with appropriate rules. Bank of Scotland despatched a letter to eighteen Glasgow merchants and two in Paisley noting that the directors, under consideration of the circumstances of the country, 'think it their duty to abridge the number' of accounts. Withdrawals were to cease and the balance was to be paid up.[47] Bank of Scotland cut the overdraft to the Ship bank from £10,000 in

---

44 BS, Uncatalogued, Miscellaneous Letter Book (Secretary's), c.1707–1790s: David Nisbet, Glasgow, to James Spence, Secretary Bank of Scotland, 19 February 1750.
45 BS 20/2/1, Miscellaneous papers.
46 BS 1/5, Minutes: 'Articles of 14 August 1751', 2 January 1752; BS 20/2/1, Miscellaneous papers.
47 BS 1/30/3, Agents' Letter Book, to sundry merchants in Glasgow and Paisley, 31 August 1751.

June 1751 to £3,540 in October, and it was finally cleared on 11 January 1752. Most of the cash accounts in both burghs were closed by March. The Royal Bank put a stop to twenty-two cash accounts worth £12,300 from August 1751, and its loan to the Arms bank was recalled.[48] In 1752, Bank of Scotland directors closed the Aberdeen bank account and those of nine local merchants.[49] When Bank of Scotland later presented £1,400 for cash, the Aberdeen bank directors gave up their attempt at note issue.[50]

The reduction in credit for the Ship and the Arms banks was confounded by economic and financial trends. In the aftermath of the war, the profits of the Glasgow trades soared. Huge increases in imports and exports greatly strengthened merchant houses, and the boom showed few signs of waning. The gloomy predictions of Bank of Scotland of a drain on the currency were not borne out. On the two occasions when the Bank imported gold and silver, in November 1752 and again for a few months in 1754, the full cost (purchase of coin, commission, insurance and freight) varied between 1.23 and 1.72 per cent, and imports were slight – a combined total of below £21,000. The reasons were to be found in the abundant credit conditions at low rates of interest in London; Government 3½ per cent stocks remained obstinately at par. From 1752, Bank of Scotland also increased advances, from a balance at March 1747 of £120,000, to £160,000 by 1750 and £197,000 in 1756. This meant a more complicated and diversified portfolio with a responsibility for the credit of hundreds of merchants and lawyers and their borrowers, plus an increasing number of industrial co-partnerships. The directors also gave strong support for new building work in Edinburgh: for example, they lent £5,000 in 1753 on the 'Act for erecting several public buildings', the scheme of municipal building launched by William Alexander, Lord Provost; and extensive credits were granted to builders in other burghs.[51] In March 1753, the directors placed £10,000 from undivided profits to the adventurers' paid-up stock, which then stood at 60 per cent.

By the autumn of 1755, Bank of Scotland directors were again preoccupied with the possibility of financial crisis. War with France was anticipated, and the directors were concerned that this would lead to a rise in London interest rates and thus a withdrawal of funds from Scotland. The control of speculation and note issue was thought to be a key to managing this, though the directors could neither estimate a 'correct' level nor control the note issue of the Glasgow banks. The competition

48 NLS, MS 17591, Fletcher of Saltoun Papers, f. 143, 30 August 1751.
49 Ibid., letters to Aberdeen, 29 February 1752.
50 Munn, *The Scottish Provincial Banking Companies*, p. 14.
51 BS 1/5, Minutes: 1 February 1753; A. J. Youngson, *The Making of Classical Edinburgh 1750–1840* (Edinburgh: 1966), p. 55.

from the Ship and the Arms banks was felt by their circulation; they were very successful, and by 1756 this had reached £130,000. There was also a plethora of smaller houses issuing notes, some for as low as a few shillings sterling, and offering to pay in cash or goods.[52] And there was a legal complication. In June 1756, the Court of Session confirmed the legal standing of co-partnerships which offered banking facilities.[53] The Glasgow companies used thirty-day bills on London to evade payment in Glasgow, and substituted Glasgow notes for those of the Royal Bank and Bank of Scotland, for which their agents in Edinburgh demanded coin. A premium emerged for Edinburgh banknotes, and different prices were charged for goods depending on the medium of payment. In May 1756, the Bank and the Royal Bank wrote to fifty-seven account holders and asked them to close all dealings with the Glasgow banks or their notes.[54] Those who refused included the private banks of William Cumming, Thomas and Adam Fairholme and George Chalmers.[55] The Glasgow banks later admitted that this was a vulnerable time, as the tobacco trade required longer credits and the war had increased freight and insurance rates. For a time, they were concerned to secure an amicable settlement.[56] They considered a restriction in their note issue 'to the immediate support of their trade and manufactures in the City of Glasgow and neighbourhood', which Lord Milton later stated as no greater an area than Glasgow, Paisley, Port Glasgow and Greenock.[57] In return, the Edinburgh banks would increase their facilities in Glasgow and open a joint office there. Yet the Glasgow banks, led by Lord Provost Murdoch, insisted that the shires of Lanark, Ayr, Dumbarton and Argyll be included with a note issue of £120,000. Lord Milton regarded this as 'no limitation at all' and demanded that, with the extra facilities from Edinburgh, the Glasgow banks should limit their issue to £50,000 or £60,000 and confine advances to the tobacco trades and other local mainstays.[58] The Glasgow banks' final offer was £100,000 with little concession on lending. The negotiations ceased in February 1757 without result.[59]

---

52 J. H. Clapham, *The Bank of England. A History* (2 vols, Cambridge 1944), vol. i, 1694–1797, p. 241; Checkland, *Scottish Banking*, pp. 104–6.

53 *Scots Magazine*, June 1756, pp. 303–7.

54 BS 1/5, Minutes: 1 and 21 July 1756; BS 20/2/1, Miscellaneous papers, 27 May 1756, warning to Fairholme, Chalmers and Cumming.

55 BS 20/2/1, Miscellaneous papers.

56 NLS, MS 17592, Fletcher of Saltoun Papers, f. 50.

57 Ibid., ff. 29–30v, 2 October 1756.

58 Modifications in the offers were made by both sides; NLS, MS 17592, Fletcher of Saltoun Papers; Checkland, *Scottish Banking*, pp. 101–2.

59 NLS, MS 17592, Fletcher of Saltoun Papers, f. 59; BS 20/2/1, Miscellaneous papers. There was a short-lived disagreement between the Royal Bank and the Bank in June 1757 over credit to persons in Edinburgh who had circulated Glasgow notes. This was dealt with amicably: BS, Minutes of conferences between the Royal and the Bank, 25 May, 7 and 17 June 1757.

Bank of Scotland and the Royal Bank then joined forces for the most controversial part of their assault on the Glasgow banks. Archibald Trotter, a former partner in the private Edinburgh bank of John Coutts & Co., opened an office in Glasgow to substitute Edinburgh notes for Glasgow ones and present the latter for cash payment. Trotter was granted £2,000 free of interest, 'to enable him to furnish Edinburgh notes to such people in the west country as choose to circulate them rather than Glasgow notes whereby he will increase our circulation and consequently enlarge our business'.[60] His work confirmed a strong preference for Edinburgh notes among the Glasgow business community. This substitution may have had the effect of a reduction in the Glasgow banknote issues, although Trotter found great difficulties in exchanging these. A mixture of feigned incompetence, long-dated bills on London and payments in small coin held up his demands, and in January 1759 he took out a lawsuit to force payment.[61]

Bank of Scotland surmised that the eventual outcome of a boom fuelled by excess paper credit and an irresponsible attitude from the Arms and the Ship banks would be a deterioration of the exchanges and an outflow of coin. Nevertheless, in the first three years of the war, the cross-border exchanges remained at 1–1.5 per cent below par and there was little pressure to purchase coin for import. Government $3\frac{1}{2}$ per cent consolidated stock fell in 1755 from just above par by 12 per cent. It then stabilised around 86–91 in early 1758 when the price rose around 5 per cent, but from early 1759 it fell again and by 1762 was 30 per cent below par.[62] Investors withdrew funds from Scotland to invest in consols on the assumption that they would rise after the war.[63] London private bankers saw deposits fall sharply, so they called in loans where they could; the overall effect was 'comparative stagnation' in their lending activity from 1759 to 1764.[64]

The pattern of lending activity by Bank of Scotland was more positive. There were sixty-six new cash accounts opened in 1755, including eleven in Aberdeen, to a total of £57,400; by 1756, signs of decline were worrying the Bank, so borrowing was temporarily restricted. In 1757, figures again rose sharply, and the pattern of advances for cash accounts shows further

---

60 BS 20/2/1, Miscellaneous papers, 1757.
61 Ibid., instructions to tellers when exchanging notes, 1766; BS 20/9/18, Miscellaneous papers, History of circulation, 28 May 1844; Munn, *The Scottish Provincial Banking Companies*, pp. 15–16; Checkland, *Scottish Banking*, describes Trotter's work as 'sordid', pp. 102–3.
62 Sir John Sinclair, *The History of the Public Revenue of the British Empire*, 3rd edn (3 vols, London: 1803), vol. ii, Appendix II.
63 Pressnell, 'The Rate of Interest in the Eighteenth Century', p. 213; there was little stagnation in the construction trade, although there was a decline from the levels seen before the war. Lewis, *Building Cycles*, p. 20; Ashton, *Economic Fluctuations*, pp. 96–7.
64 Joslin, 'London Bankers in Wartime 1739–84', pp. 167–72.

strong activity to 1761. The overall credit advances between 1756 and 1759 remained stable at under £200,000, although there was upward pressure at payment terms. Thereafter, demand by customers soared, and in March 1762 the balance exceeded £271,000 (including £17,000 of Royal Bank notes, £19,000 from other banks and £37,000 of miscellaneous paper). Two years later, it reached £352,000 with unprecedented increases in cash account overdrafts.

This buoyant trend ran up against difficulties by 1761, which were characterised by some contemporary writers as an exchange and balance-of-payments crisis. It showed itself in a deterioration from the par on remittances from Edinburgh to London in the autumn payments season of 1761 and demands on the three chartered banks for gold and silver which was then exported. In 1760, the premium on London bills bought in Edinburgh was only ½ per cent; there was a modest rise to ½–1½ per cent the following year, but by 1762 the range was 2¼–4½ per cent, and it remained as high as 3–3½ per cent in 1763 and 1764.[65] This was a complicated problem for the banks, as it was unclear whether there were longer-term distortions in the price levels of the Scottish economy which had been aggravated by an excess of paper credit by the Glasgow banks. This was made worse by the aforementioned investment opportunities in London and the remittance of funds by bill. It was also argued that the deterioration was fuelled by changes in the structure of social life which encouraged an increase in the imports of luxury goods. This had led to an 'imbalance' in the payments with England which would be unlikely to be corrected except by the course of economic progress, necessarily a long-term process. Neither contemporaries nor subsequent writers have found it possible to construct more than partial evidence on these longer-term trends in cross-border payments, although it does appear that there was a change in the movements of funds by 1760 which lasted for several years. An assessment by the board of the Royal Bank concluded that Parliament

in order to raise the subsidies necessary for carrying on the war for 1761 were under the necessity of borrowing a very large sum of money, at a higher rate of interest than usual. At this period there were many considerable sums lent out by Englishmen upon heritable security in Scotland because the interest given was higher than in England ... opinion was that public funds would rise when peace came, so many took money out of Scotland and put it into the funds ... Scotland became much more indebted to England than usual, the natural effect was that the exchange or premium paid for bills on London rose considerably and to save this high premium many chused to make their remittances in specie

65 'The Royal Bank and the London–Edinburgh Exchange Rate in the Eighteenth Century', *The Three Banks Review*, 38 (June 1958), 27–36 (p. 31).

and therefore the demand increased upon Edinburgh banks.[66] This explanation was repeated in a variety of writings. It was also suggested that the wealthy landowners remitted £100,000 a year in rents to support their estates in England.[67] The eminent writer Sir James Steuart thought that a large part of an estimated £500,000 invested by English residents was withdrawn at this time for speculation in London, although this has been questioned.[68] There were complaints about tax remittances and withdrawal of soldiers. On the larger canvas of Great Britain, Sir John Clapham thought that the speculative movements from Scotland could not 'have gone very far to meet the final needs of London and the Bank [of England]. And it cannot be followed in the Bank records where, if it entered them, it would have left only a very faint trace.'[69]

The autumn of 1761 was regarded by directors of all three chartered banks as a turning point in demands for specie, and this dominated the regular meetings between Bank of Scotland and the Royal Bank. Before this time, with an exchange at par, £100 sent to or from London would buy £100 less charges, and thus there was little incentive to use gold in Scotland. When the exchange on London deteriorated, then £100 sent to Scotland would buy more than £100. Conversely, the remittance of £100 by bill from Scotland would realise less in London with the exchange below par, therefore 'many of those who had remittances to make to London, chose rather to run the risque of transporting specie, than submit to the high exchange'.[70] Further, 'several merchants in Scotland in order to profit by the high exchange, set on foot a new trade of picking up species in the country and from the Bank, which they sent by the Common wagon to London, as funds to enable them to draw and receive the high premium of exchange'. Even if this comment was exaggerated, and the banks had methods of dealing with such merchants, it would be good business practice for sellers of goods in Scotland, who wished to send their funds to England, to request gold and not bills on London. There were additional problems with the payments for the armed forces in Scotland. On Treasury instructions, a contract signed in 1750 between William Pitt, then Paymaster General of the Forces, and the Royal Bank, agreed that officers in Scotland were required to take funds from the Royal Bank, 'and them only' upon bills to be granted by the said officers upon their agents at London payable to the Cashier of the Royal Bank. When the exchange deteriorated, the officers in Scotland approached the private bankers for

66 NLS, MS 17592, Fletcher of Saltoun Papers, f. 38, 29 March 1762; MS 17593, ff. 195–6.
67 Anon., 'Considerations on the Present Scarcity of Gold and Silver Coin in Scotland' [GL 1763].
68 Sir James Steuart, An Inquiry into the Principles of Political Economy (2 vols, London: 1767), ed. A. Skinner (Edinburgh: 1966), vol. ii, p. 188.
69 Clapham, The Bank of England, vol. i, p. 242.
70 NLS, MS 17593, Fletcher of Saltoun Papers, ff. 195–6.

cheaper rates, or conducted the supply of funds directly in a similar manner to private traders.[71]

When Bank of Scotland and the Royal Bank thought that demands for gold were for speculative purposes, account holders were reminded that those whom the directors 'accommodate with credit . . . will not use it to the Company's detriment by drawing away specie of which there is a penury in the country'.[72] From late April, dormant accounts or those whose users were suspected of sending gold south were closed; thirty-three were dealt with in May, including that for Henry Home (Lord Kames, the jurist), who had borrowed £600. In 1761, the number of new accounts granted was only twenty-five, under half the usual annual level. In this year, the Glasgow Thistle bank was founded, and not one cash account was granted by Bank of Scotland to a western merchant for the next twelve months. The gold drain now became serious. For summer payments, the Royal Bank imported 6,470 half-guineas and 3,530 guineas, but this was not thought exceptional. The autumn payments were much more difficult, and by 11 November imports had risen to 19,480 guineas and 8,870 half-guineas.

At the regular monthly meeting of the two banks in January 1762, it was agreed to institute a new rule whereby a holder of a cash account could not draw for and pay in money on the same day, and after customer complaints the banks agreed to have alternate days of paying and receiving and to make these the same at both banks.[73] It was also agreed that, as the price of exchange and the demand for cash were expected to deteriorate, neither bank would advance funds for new bonds or cash accounts, and another cull was taken of cash accounts. Three of the Edinburgh private banks, William Alexander & Sons, Adam & Thomas Fairholme and William Cumming & Sons (also known as William Cuming & Son), were told 'to give up being agents or factors for the Glasgow banking company, and their practice of supplying them with Edinburgh notes or picking up specie' or they would find their cash accounts closed.[74] The following month, eight merchants and banking houses were given verbal warnings.[75] When Adam and Thomas Fairholme later inquired about reopening their account at the Royal Bank, the matter was placed before the joint committee of directors.[76] In March, a subcommittee met leading

---

71 NLS, MS 17592, Fletcher of Saltoun Papers, ff. 126–7, 24 April 1761, memorial to Lord Milton; ibid., ff. 152–3, to Lord Milton.
72 BS 1/30/3, Agents' Letter Book, to Archibald Johnson, merchant at Kelso, 15 April 1761.
73 BS 20/2/1, Miscellaneous papers, Meetings of Committee of directors of both banks, 1762.
74 BS 1/5, Minutes: 10 February 1762.
75 These were Mansfield & Hunter, William Hog & Sons, Fordyce & Malcolm, Arbuthnot & Guthrie, Bertrams & Williamson, George Chalmers, William Alexander, Coutts Bros & Co.
76 BS 20/2/1, Miscellaneous papers.

private bankers and merchants to explain that further measures to restrict credit would follow unless there was an immediate halt to conversion. A notice was sent to all bank customers:

> The Directors order the Secretary to intimate to all such as have credits . . . that if they are found directly or indirectly drawing specie from the Company or shall either themselves or by others for their behoof purchase bills from persons residing in England and for which specie must of consequence be drawn from the Bank the credit afforded to such persons will be stopt and the balance due upon their accounts called for.

The banks approached the Bank of England through the London agent of the Royal Bank, James Mathias, and inquired whether they could draw for £100,000 to try and stabilise the exchanges, but were declined. The directors could not have known the concern of the Treasury committee of the Bank of England about the fall in the stocks of gold in their own vaults. The joint committee inquired of arrangements by which payments could be agreed 'without the need for specie' and turned to the example of the Bank of Amsterdam, which operated a book-keeping system which credited the accounts of their customers without the need for cash. As conditions did not improve, in early May 1762 the banks agreed to contract all credit by one-quarter, moved gold between each other's offices, jointly ordered supplies from Newcastle and London and fixed deposit rates at 5 per cent for six months or longer, and 4 per cent on cash account deposits. The committee of directors of both banks agreed on 3 May that, as these higher rates would attract more deposits, they could direct funds to support the landed interest at the ensuing payment term: 'each bank should lend as they see occasion to the extent of £20,000 upon bonds, heritable or personal, bills at sixty days or on discounted bills, but not upon cash accounts'.[77] The British Linen Company also faced a serious run on its notes, in part because landowners supported moves to protect Bank of Scotland and the Royal Bank.[78]

On 1 April 1762, after lengthy discussions, the two banks agreed to operate the optional clause for their notes and five days later announced that no further specie payments would be made above £50, for whatever reason, and that the accountants were to mark the banknotes if the presenter insisted. The next day, the maximum was cut to £20. These severe measures had their intended effect and enjoyed widespread support from the landed community. By mid-May, the exchange was falling back and a start was made to lending on bonds. Joint discussions were held over

77 RBS RB/12/8, Minutes, 7 May 1762.
78 Malcolm, *The British Linen Bank*, pp. 50–1.

the next several months about how far credit could be restored.[79] The topics raised at their monthly meeting of July 1763, in preparation for the payments season, are instructive. They included the rate of interest on cash accounts, the details of individual accounts, an investigation of the sums owing on cash accounts 'for carrying on the improvements about the town of Edinburgh', and a discussion of a letter from Lord Forbes to Lord Strichen advising 'that the gentlemen of the county of Aberdeen had resolved not to accept of Glasgow Bank notes in payments after the first of November'. The committee considered, in the light of this development, whether to send all their Glasgow notes to Archibald Trotter 'to be presented for immediate payment'.[80] The support from the aristocracy and the legal profession was acknowledged at the elections for extraordinary directors of Bank of Scotland in March 1763. Robert Dundas (the Lord President), Sir Lawrence Dundas, the Earl of Elgin, the Earl of Hopetoun, the Earl of Leven and James Smollett were among those appointed. Bank of Scotland was keen to foster good relations with London bankers: the Earl of Marchmont talked to several Bank of England directors 'and would continue with all my acquaintance in the Bank of England to wipe off any unjust impressions they may have received of Bank of Scotland'.[81] But it was an uphill task, and the Bank had more success with long-established London Scots.

Mention is appropriate of the Agreements and Understandings between the Bank and the Royal Bank on the holding of each other's banknotes. From 1740, these developed into arrangements whereby the holdings were regarded as part of the reserve, with regular notification of the balances. There was not, in these early years, a frequent note exchange with settlement by gold or bill. It was appreciated that the pattern of demand by customers varied between the banks; at one time one bank would hold a balance, but this could be reversed. Notification had several purposes. It signalled the rate of interest to be paid on balances, usually 2 or 3 per cent. Thus in 1765 the committee of both banks agreed, in reflecting on the operation of their comprehensive agreement reached in 1752, 'that for further keeping up and cementing that mutual harmony the rate of 3 per cent per annum interest on the weekly balances shall be due by the one bank to the other', and confirmed 'that at settling the interest accompt annually the Secretarys of both banks as authorised by their respective Courts shall sign mutual declarations that no undue

79 BS 20/2/1, Minutes of the Committee of the Royal Bank and Bank of Scotland.
80 BS 20/2/1, Minutes of meeting of directors of Bank of Scotland and Royal Bank of Scotland, 5 July 1763.
81 BS, Uncatalogued, Miscellaneous Letter Book (Secretary's), c.1707–1790s: Earl of Marchmont, 24 April 1760.

means have been used by their respective Courts to possess themselves of the notes of the other bank'.[82] They also confirmed that 'no specie shall be demanded for the balances during the subsistence of this contract but the friendly borrowing of specie in the former agreement to be part of this and enlarged to £20,000'. While the arrangements were designed to minimise administration, notification enabled each bank to increase or decrease notes out on cash accounts and to regard the note balance as a deposit at interest. Further, notification enabled each bank to increase credit in regular stages roughly in step with the other, and the pattern of advances from 1740 indicates that it worked well. Notifications were straightforward: thus in May 1760 the Royal Bank handed over £25,000 of Bank of Scotland notes and in return received £21,000 of its own notes, 'which with former receipts makes the Bank of Scotland indebted' to the Royal Bank for £22,000.[83] In proportion to capital, these balances could be very high: in the summer of 1765, for example, the balance in favour of the Royal Bank reached £44,000, although the usual sums were below this and fluctuations could be extensive (see Table 7.4).

Bank of Scotland and the Royal Bank pursued a range of policies in respect of the exchanges with England from the close of the Seven Years' War. They persisted with regular checks on those who requested specie in London, and curtailed balances and closed accounts where this seemed the only way to curtail speculation. The banks revived their plan, originally put to the Bank of England, for a fund in London against which periodic surges of demand for accommodation could be drawn, and which would enable the banks to offer a rate which would bring 'the exchange so low that it shall be no man's interest to send or carry specie out of the country'. Various versions were placed before the respective boards, the core features of which depended on a reserve in London, at several of the private banks, of £100,000 or even £150,000. Bank of Scotland and the Royal Bank 'should draw to every person who asks it at a flat price and date. This will . . . bring the exchange to that rate, or rather below it, for it is not to be supposed that private banks will give the same price as those drawn by the Bank.'[84] In 1764, the banks appointed an agent in London to whom bills were to be remitted, to be turned into cash to be sent to Scotland as a joint stock 'and used by both banks according to their exigencies'.[85] These proposals would have required a fund to be invested in London, and preliminary moves were made over the next few years. By March 1768, for example, the Royal Bank had drawing rights of

82 RBS RB/12/9, Minutes, Friendly Agreement of 19 November 1765.
83 RBS RB/12/8, Minutes, 26 May 1760.
84 BS 20/2/1, letters to Andrew Drummond & Co., 1763; BS 1/5, Minutes: 23 January 1764.
85 BS 20/2/1, papers for 1764.

Table 7.4 *Bank of Scotland, Royal Bank of Scotland: balance of banknotes, 1768–71*

	Balance in favour of	£
1768		
14 March	Royal Bank	21,000
20 June	Royal Bank	28,000
27 June	Royal Bank	25,600
11 July	Royal Bank	31,100
12 September	Royal Bank	6,300
19 September	Royal Bank	17,100
28 November	Royal Bank	1,500
12 December	Royal Bank	200
19 December	Royal Bank	5,200
1769		
21 March	Bank of Scotland	12,800
24 April	Bank of Scotland	5,900
12 June	Bank of Scotland	8,700
27 November	Bank of Scotland	17,600
1770		
29 January	Bank of Scotland	20,300
5 February	Bank of Scotland	26,300
12 February	Bank of Scotland	17,700
26 February	Bank of Scotland	12,400
5 March	Bank of Scotland	8,900
30 April	Bank of Scotland	12,400
19 November	Royal Bank	13,200
26 November	Royal Bank	3,500
1771		
5 March	Bank of Scotland	10,700
8 May	Bank of Scotland	5,700
5 June	Bank of Scotland	6,300
10 July	Bank of Scotland	4,200
3 September	Bank of Scotland	14,200
6 November	Bank of Scotland	27,500
26 November	Bank of Scotland	21,400
26 December	Bank of Scotland	26,000

Source: RBS RB/12/10, Minutes, 1767–71.

£30,000 with Coutts and £80,000 with the Bank of England, and Bank of Scotland had drawing rights with Andrew Drummond & Co. for £50,000. When over £10,000 in debit, the Bank would remit bills at three or four months, on a ½ per cent commission. It also negotiated a facility with Roger Hog and Kinloch for £20,000. Unfortunately, in the decade after the Seven Years' War it was not possible to operate these as effectively as the banks would have wished.

Bank of Scotland and the Royal Bank took advantage of a growing concern in government that, with the war over, attention should be paid to the proliferation of paper credits and currencies in Great Britain and the North American colonies which had depreciated against their stated worth in gold. In 1763, as part of a major investigation by the British

Treasury into colonial administration, legislation was drafted to curb the more serious abuses. The Act is relevant to the debate in Scotland: 'Whereas great quantities of paper bills of credit have been created and issued . . . by virtue of Acts, orders, resolutions or votes of assembly, making and declaring such bills of credit to be legal tender . . . and whereas such . . . have greatly depreciated in their value, by means whereof debts have been discharged with a much less value than was contracted for', all such acts were now void and the paper was to be called in.[86]

Before the close of the war, Bank of Scotland and the Royal Bank had intimated that they might raise a process of declarator against all banking companies not legally established to have them declared 'public nuisances', although this was not proceeded with because of the difficulty which such an action would create for the Scots law of co-partnership. There were further legal problems with the private banks of Edinburgh, several of which now issued their own notes, and the Royal Bank insisted that the British Linen Company was to be left in possession of 'whatever right their charter gives them'.[87] In December 1762, the two senior banks sent Commissioners to London to request legislation to stop the overproduction of paper money, but neither the Bank of England nor the Treasury was prepared to countenance an outright ban. Not only were there the legal obstacles with co-partnerships, but also a ban would have implications for all merchant activity which overlapped with banking, including the use of the bill of exchange as a negotiable instrument, which bills, suitably endorsed, were in widespread use as a means of payment. The Treasury offered the abolition of the optional clause and a ban on all notes under £5 sterling. On 13 March 1764, the joint committee of Bank of Scotland and the Royal Bank agreed to these proposals (although it later requested that the minimum be reduced to £1 sterling) and that a clause be included to allow summary execution upon all notes after a refusal to pay, in the same manner as the Bank Act of 1695 had prescribed for bills of exchange.[88] Frequent public meetings calling for abolition of the optional clause were held in Scotland at this time, and by the summer the Treasury had made it clear that it would recommend legislation. The Bank and the Royal Bank agreed to enforce new regulations after this became law. If a customer held an account with both banks, one would be closed. No new credits were to be granted by one board without consultation. Restrictions

---

86 4 George III c.34, 'An Act to prevent paper bills of credit'; H. Roseveare, *The Treasury: The Evolution of a British Institution* (London: 1969), pp. 97–8; for the difficulties of enforcing the British mandate in the colonies, see D. M. Clark, *The Rise of the British Treasury: Colonial Administration in the Eighteenth Century* (New Haven: 1960), ch. 4; J. J. McCusker, *Money and Exchange in Europe and America 1600–1775* (London: 1978), pp. 126–31.
87 RBS RB/12/9, Minutes, 6 January 1764.
88 BS 20/2/1, Minutes of Committee, 13 March 1764.

on cash account limits were to come in at £2,000 along with an agreement on 4 per cent deposit interest on monies placed for over twelve months, and 3 per cent when left for six to twelve months. Archibald Trotter would be sent £5,000 worth of Glasgow notes each week for cash. The Bank Secretary, James Spence, arranged with his opposite number the wording of a printed letter to go to all customers. Further to this, the directors of both banks agreed to draft the bill and 'procure some friends in Parliament' to promote it, although they insisted on restrictions in addition to the abolition of the optional clause. There was opposition from the Arms, Ship and Thistle banks, but they lacked influence at Westminster and their representations were passed over by the Privy Council and the Treasury.[89] The Act of 1765 laid down that all notes under 20 shillings were to be abolished from 1 June 1765 and that no notes were to be issued in Scotland except those payable on demand in 'lawful money of Great Britain' after 5 May 1766.[90] Every offence would incur the penalty of £500 and all costs and interest, 'which complaint the said Court of Session is hereby authorised and required summarily to determine'. Post bills payable at seven days were exempt. The importance of this Act cannot be underestimated. The issue of notes now entailed a severe and summary liability, and many issues disappeared. The provincial banking companies, with their modest capitals, were forced to follow a sound attitude to lending, or suffer the consequences.

89 The Glasgow position is discussed in W. Mure (ed.), *Selections from the Family Papers Preserved at Caldwell*, Part 2, 1765–1821, Proceedings of the Maitland Club, 71 (Glasgow: 1854).
90 5 George III c.49, 'An Act to prevent the inconveniences arising from the present method of issuing notes and bills by the banks, banking companies and bankers . . . in Scotland'.

CHAPTER 8

FROM 1765 TO THE AFTERMATH OF THE CRISIS OF 1772

AFTER THE PASSAGE of the 1765 Scottish Bank Act (5 George III c.49) and with a satisfactory body of agreements and under-standings between them, neither the Royal Bank nor Bank of Scotland had a financial or managerial interest in fundamental changes to their joint operations. They continued to impose sanctions on merchants and private bankers who exported gold for speculative purposes, although there were fewer references to these problems immediately after the Act.[1] Both banks recognised the pressure for increased accommodation, and in 1765 responded positively to the heritors of Banff and Aberdeenshire when they asked for more facilities. In the case of Aberdeen, Bank of Scotland appointed George Garioch, a merchant of that burgh, as their agent, and the Royal Bank agreed 'to go hand-in-hand with the Bank of Scotland in the measure', with the expense to be shared.[2] The death of Lord Milton gave the directors of Bank of Scotland an opportunity to suggest to the board of the Royal Bank that support for the British Linen Company should be withdrawn, now that the Company had announced its intention to expand banking operations. The Company had been active in note substitution, and, according to an assessment by managers of Bank of Scotland, had one-quarter of the Scottish circulation. George Garioch presented evidence in February and March 1767 that the British Linen agent had picked up Bank of Scotland notes and, further, that merchants were now to consider the formation of a banking company.

---

1 There was a notable case in 1766 where gold was exported for speculative purposes: 'Any merchants who are customers of Bank of Scotland or Royal Bank of Scotland who are found dealing with, or accommodating, Johnstone & Smith, merchants, will have their cash accounts stopped, the credits withdrawn and balances due called for'; BS 20/2/1, Minutes of Committee, Meeting of Committees of Directors, 1 July 1766; also meeting of 13 December 1765, Agreements of 1752 confirmed and updated in respect of the Glasgow banks.
2 BS 20/2/1, negotiations with Banff and Aberdeen agents, 1765 and 1766.

The Royal Bank was much less sympathetic to the British Linen than in the days of Lord Milton; Sir Lawrence Dundas of Kerse was Governor from 1764, and the new Deputy Governor in 1766 was Andrew Pringle, Lord Alemoor of the Court of Session. They agreed to close the account for the British Linen if its activities did not cease. Yet both the senior banks agreed to support the new Aberdeen Banking Company, founded in 1767, with a supply of Edinburgh notes. It was a substantial co-partnership (originally 109 partners) with the support of many landowners in the north-east, and the new bank was pleased to hold the notes of both Bank of Scotland and the Royal Bank as part of its reserve. The arrangements with George Garioch were closed down. By this date, as well as the Aberdeen Banking Company there were two banking co-partnerships in Perth, one each in Dundee, Ayr and Dumfries and the three aforementioned in Glasgow.[3]

By late 1767, the pace of economic and speculative activity was again to exercise the directors of both senior banks. It was found expedient to warn nine Edinburgh private banks and twenty-nine merchants and 'grocers' against dealings with English exporters who demanded gold in place of notes, and who regularly refused bills drawn at par on London. In January 1768, after discussions with the Edinburgh agents of the leading provincial banks, the Royal Bank and Bank of Scotland jointly proposed an agreement on gold:

> The Bank of Scotland and the Royal Bank being informed by your Agent here that your Company was willing to agree to any reasonable scheme that should be proposed to lessen the great demand for specie that is at present made upon the banking companies in Scotland, are of opinion that if these different companies firmly concur in the following resolutions it would tend greatly to remedy the evil complained of:
>
> 1. That they shall agree to bring all the specie they shall have occasion for directly from London and shall upon no pretence whatever pay any premium for specie picked up in Scotland or the north of England, nor advance notes free of interest for any period to any person for that purpose.
> 2. That they shall draw bills on their respective correspondents in London, at their different offices to all persons desiring the same at a rate of exchange to be fixed on by the two established banks here ... and that this rate of exchange shall from time to time be altered according to circumstances and the different banking companies to be advised duly of such alterations and that on Monday 8 February [1768] next they shall begin to draw in the manner above mentioned at 60 days par upon which day the Bank of Scotland and the Royal Bank begin to draw at that rate.[4]

3 C. W. Munn, *The Scottish Provincial Banking Companies, 1747–1864* (Edinburgh: 1981), p. 16, Table 1.
4 BS 1/30/3, Agents' Letter Books, Secretary, Bank of Scotland, to the Thistle, Arms, and Ship banks

These arrangements failed to materialise, although there were informal agreements to the effect that provincial banks would cease searches for specie, fix agreed rates for bills, draw only on London and not on Edinburgh, and stop the credits for local merchants who dealt with English note-exchangers. These efforts were undermined by the private bankers and merchant houses in Edinburgh and the main burghs which possessed insufficient cash resources to meet the opportunities offered by the economy. These houses rapidly developed the bill of exchange on Edinburgh and London as a source of credit. They usually gave a better rate of return (allowing for commission, remittance charges and interest) and a potentially far more extensive trade than ordinary lending by credit accounts or bonds. Many of these houses joined the ranks of note-issuers and, while printing none under £1, very considerably added to the volume of paper in circulation.[5] The interest of borrowers on bills, many tied up with accommodation bills, often using several private banks to take these, coincided with the need for as large a trade as possible to keep profits up for the smaller bankers.

The increase in the use of banknotes and bills of exchange involved the two senior banks in an assessment of creditworthiness; the cash base for these varied from strong, as in the case of the Aberdeen Banking Company, to uncertain or dubious. If Bank of Scotland and the Royal Bank had accepted notes and a wider range of bills, they would have conferred respectability and substantial benefits upon private bankers and merchant houses. It was in the latter's interest to switch the facilities offered by the chartered banks towards bills, either as a re-discount operation, or as direct loans to finance private operations on bills. There were, however, potential implications for the senior banks. When a bill fell due, the temptation in a boom and when money was in short supply was to re-discount the bill and pay the interest or, if on London, draw another bill in place of the one paid off.[6] The money eventually due to be settled depended on the maintenance of buoyant conditions in foreign trade and rising asset and property values. Yet, by comparison with the lending by bill pioneered by Bank of Scotland in 1698, it proved more time-consuming for a Scottish banker by the mid-eighteenth century to ascertain the extent of a customer's bill operations. It was easier with the increase in the number of private bankers for a borrower to keep a set of

in Glasgow; the Aberdeen Banking Company, the Dumfries Bank, Douglas, Heron & Co. at Ayr, the United Banking Company at Perth, and George Dempster & Co., bankers in Dundee, 25 January 1768.
5 Munn, *The Scottish Provincial Banking Companies*, p. 23, estimated a circulation of perhaps £713,000 from eleven provincial companies by 1769.
6 See below, Appendix 3; Adam Smith noticed the drawing and redrawing of bills on London, in *An Inquiry into the Nature and Causes of the Wealth of Nations* (1776), ed. E. Cannan (2 vols, London: 1904; repr. 1961), vol. i, book 2, ch. 2, pp. 328–33.

transactions from the view of bankers dealing with another. Worse, it was difficult to know how many bills were drawn on a particular consignment of goods as it passed from producer to customer, or even to assess whether there were any goods at all. The system unfortunately lacked an equivalent of the Register of Sasines.

These matters were appreciated at the time. The problems with bills led several houses, including Coutts & Co. and Andrew Drummond & Co., to block speculative and accommodation bills where they could. The 'first resolution' taken by the young William Forbes and James Hunter in 1761, 'on finding ourselves practically the sole conductors of [Coutts Bros], was to wind up the corn-speculations then existing, and to relinquish that trade entirely, so as in future to confine the house to its proper and natural business of exchange and banking, by which prudent resolution, and by unremitting assiduity and attention, we were enabled to go on without any apparent diminution of business'.[7] The eventual outcome of the 1772 crisis was an enhanced position for Coutts & Co. and Andrew Drummond & Co. They both worked closely to the views outlined by Forbes and survived all trade and speculative crises thereafter. Sir William Forbes, who was one of the few private bankers in Edinburgh to come through the crisis of 1772, suggested that the absence of major failures in the previous decade later encouraged the belief that banking and trade could be linked. It was perhaps unfortunate that there were not more early examples of collapse such as that of Adam Fairholme of Edinburgh, a long-standing customer and proprietor of Bank of Scotland. He had made a fortune in London, perhaps as much as £70,000 by 1763, by using balances from Scotland. Thereafter, he lost heavily and in 1764 was declared a bankrupt. Fleeing aboard a ship for France, 'a Bow Street officer came alongside in search of a culprit who had made his escape from justice, and Mr Fairholme, having unhappily conceived the idea that the officer was in search of him, threw himself overboard and was drowned'.[8] His family in Edinburgh survived into the next decade and even retained a seat on the board of Bank of Scotland until 1770, but failed to recover their former standing.[9]

After 1765 there was a gradual extension of the influence of the private bankers on the board. A straight takeover would have been difficult, as an individual's shareholding was restricted to a maximum of £20,000 Scots; but in the atmosphere of optimism which pervaded Scottish business circles, the board in January 1767 was persuaded to extend its purchase

7 Sir William Forbes, *Memoirs of a Banking House* (Edinburgh: 1860), p. 15.
8 Ibid., p. 20.
9 For Adam and Thomas Fairholme, see below, Table 9.1, note 6.

of bills on London and to increase the level of discounts.[10] The new policy had a marked effect on the profit and loss account; the credit from London bills and bill discounts in the year to March 1768 rose to £1,585 from an annual average in 1762–7 of only £380. To support the increased trade and to help keep the exchange on London close to par, the board negotiated drawing rights of £50,000 on Andrew Drummond & Co. in March 1768 followed by rights of £20,000 on Roger Hog and Kinloch, one of the Edinburgh private banks which had offices in both London and Edinburgh.[11] Special accounts were granted by Bank of Scotland to the private banking companies of Mansfield, Hunter & Co. (£10,000), William Cuming & Son (£10,000) and Andrew St Clair & Co. (£5,000); they could lodge up to these sums with freedom to draw and pay on the same day and still receive 3 per cent interest at close of business for their balance.[12] To help support this shift to bills, the Bank and the Royal Bank agreed to limit their ordinary cash accounts to a maximum of £1,000, although they noted that a desire to restrict coin exports was a factor.[13]

In March 1769, at the annual general meeting of Bank of Scotland, the private bankers secured the removal of the Earl of Elgin from the board of directors. Elgin, the Grand Master of the Masonic Order, was also a pioneer of several industrial enterprises.[14] For him, as for many other landowners, the cash account with the Bank was a convenient way of managing bills payable in Edinburgh. With him ousted, the way was clear for decisive changes on the cash account facility and the old-style advances of money on bills. The latter were virtually abolished and the cash accounts for personal and industrial customers cut to a maximum of £500 in May 1769. The sole reason given was that 'it would be more for the interest of the bank to promote the practice of discounting bills' on London and Edinburgh, which, of course, was a pretext to enable the private men to discount more bills at the Bank. Thus the private houses arranged the bill, lent the cash, earned commission, and recovered their loan by discounting the bill with Bank of Scotland, which then had to wait for payment from the acceptor. Whereas there had been good reason to curtail credit by cash accounts down to 1768 where clients were suspected

10 BS 1/5, Minutes: 7 January 1767. A committee was established chaired by John Forrest, Deputy Governor (1753–7 and 1757–71), a man very much in the cautious tradition. At first, the members had to be unanimous on each bill. The other members were John Inglis, Andrew St Clair and James Seton; St Clair was declared bankrupt in the 1772 crisis.
11 BS 1/5, Minutes: 2 March and 27 August 1768.
12 BS 1/5, Minutes: 24 August 1768; following the usual practice of bankers, these second accounts were given different names in the ledgers, viz. accounts for Mansfield & Co., William and Thomas Cumming, Andrew St Clair & Son.
13 RBS RB 12/10, Minutes, 2 December 1768; BS 1/5, Minutes: 14 December 1768.
14 For the industrial development of the Elgin estates, see S. G. Checkland, The Elgins, 1766–1917: A Tale of Aristocrats, Proconsuls and Their Wives (Aberdeen: 1988), pp. 2–4.

of involvement in the export of coin, the new arrangements hurt many involved in industrial production and foreign trade. The Earl of Elgin, for instance, was hit very harshly in respect of credit for his extensive works at Limekilns on the Forth. A modest request for an exemption from the order was refused, and he was told to curtail his account by 1 December 1769.[15] With his industrial works only half completed and 'far from producing a profitable return', Elgin struggled on until 14 May 1771 when he 'suddenly' died at the age of only 39, leaving a wife and four children. The estate was put into trusteeship.[16] The treatment of Elgin, and other landowners involved in trade and manufactures, contrasted with the liberal facilities given to the private bankers to whom restrictions on cash accounts did not apply. Ebenezer McCulloch & Co., for example, was granted a cash account for bills up to £6,000, and Bertram, Williamson was granted a £2,000 facility, with the right to pay and draw on their cash account the same day.[17]

At the annual general meeting in March 1770, the Edinburgh private bankers secured their position: John Forrest, the Deputy Governor in office almost continuously since 1753, and no fewer than thirteen directors were removed from office. On the ordinary side of the board, from whose numbers came the management and bill committees, nine out of twelve came from private banking houses.[18] The elections for extraordinary directors were somewhat mixed; alongside Colonel James St Clair and Sir Hew Crawford, associates of the Solicitor General, Henry Dundas, there were five new aristocratic directors, the Earls of Leven, Glasgow, Hopetoun, Lauderdale and Panmure.[19] It was particularly unfortunate that long-standing associations with the Edinburgh legal profession were curtailed. Henceforth, although for only a short period, all bank policy focused on the needs of bill-discounters and private houses.

The March 1770 meeting also overturned the recommendation of a 4 per cent dividend and voted for 4.5 per cent. The proposal of the outgoing board to call up the remaining £30,000 (three-tenths) allowable by the Bank Act of 1695 was vetoed. Instead, £10,000 (one-tenth) was paid from reserves to the adventurers' stock. The new directors changed the

15 BS 1/30/3, Agents' Letter Book, 22 June 1769; the Earl was also given a hard time over a bill for £215 drawn on and accepted by Adam Bogle, a Limekilns shipmaster, which the Bank discounted but which was delayed in payment: ibid., 5 July 1770.
16 Checkland, The Elgins, 1766–1917, p. 3; BS 1/30/4, Letter Book, 13 June 1771. The Bank was quick to harass his surviving relatives, Christian and Sarah Bruce, who had drawn bills in respect of his industrial projects, and the board demanded that the estate trustees repay the Earl's cash account.
17 BS 1/5, Minutes: 5 May 1769, 5 September 1770, 3 April 1771.
18 These were Thomas Cumming, Roger and Thomas Hog, Alexander Keith, Robert Williamson, Patrick Miller, Alexander Tait, James Seton and James Stuart.
19 BS 1/5, Minutes: March 1770; the challenge appears to have been rather hastily organised, as two private bankers initially elected, George Chalmers and Andrew Crosbie, were ineligible for office.

rules to benefit private bankers. They constituted a committee for bank by-laws, dominated by private men; it voted later to abolish itself and virtually all controls on how the directors' committees managed affairs. An ambiguous resolution which had been passed to stop directors of 'other' banking companies from sitting on the board was ignored (most bankers were noted as 'merchants' in the records) and was overturned the following year. Three unused accounts held from earlier in the century by William, Earl of Kilmarnock (1713), Charles, Earl of Erroll (1717) and Colonel William Ker (1720) were abolished and the sums credited to reserves.

The new board of 1770 searched every aspect of the Bank administration for savings. The staff were instructed to tighten up the management of cash accounts and to demand timely payment of interest. The fractions of pennies lost on cash account transactions were now stored until each complete penny could be charged for. Thirty-six accounts were closed and sixty-six hereditary and personal bonds recalled. Edinburgh lawyers were especially affected by these cutbacks.[20] The politeness in correspondence which had been the hallmark of Bank of Scotland went into abeyance. Cash-account holders were told that the 'directors of Bank of Scotland finding that your cash account is of no use to the bank and having occasion for the money . . . inform you that at the term of Lammas first [1 August] they want payment of the balance, principal and interest'.[21] In the spring of 1771 it was recommended that 'all heritable debts' to gentry, nobility and judges be recalled, even where the interest had actually been paid. With letters like these and abrupt closures of long-standing relationships, the new directors ensured that when the crisis finally came they would receive little sympathy.[22] Such measures contained the advance of lending long-term on cash accounts and bonds; earnings on these were steady from March 1769 to March 1771 and rose slightly in the year to March 1772, but then fell sharply. By contrast, the board used its increased resources to take up bills. The restrictions of the 1767 committee were scrapped; the bill committee comprised private bankers and operated on an ad hoc basis. Only two board members were required for bills under £300, three for bills under £500 and four for those to £1,000; as this later proved inconvenient, it was agreed that just three private bankers could decide on higher-value bills.[23] Income from bills rose from £1,611 for the

20 BS 1/30/3, Agents' Letter Book, August and September 1770.
21 BS 1/30/4, Letter Book, 9 May 1771; Thomas Craig of Riccarton was offered a lump sum on personal bond instead of his cash account, a less convenient and more expensive way of borrowing; he later borrowed £300 from the Royal Bank.
22 It was fortunate for the Solicitor General, Henry Dundas, aged 31 in 1771, that he was at the start of his political career.
23 BS 1/5, Minutes: 3 April 1771.

year to March 1769 to £2,130 the following year, and reached £2,955 in the year to March 1772.

The full extent of the adverse impact on the direction of the Bank became clearer in relation to the liberal policy extended towards the banking company of Douglas, Heron & Co. which opened for business on 6 November 1769. Known to posterity as the Ayr bank, it became synonymous with the crisis of 1772. Its ostensible aim was the support of the rapid expansion of commerce, trade and agricultural investment. The leading proprietors included the young Duke of Buccleuch who returned from his grand tour with Adam Smith in 1768, the Duke of Queensberry (Governor of the British Linen Company), Archibald Douglas (the Earl of Dumfries) and Patrick Heron of that Ilk. In the speculative conditions of 1768 and 1769, there was some feeling that the two senior banks were unwilling to extend advances, and many of the landowners of the counties of Dumfries, Ayr, Galloway and Kirkcudbright subscribed to the first capital of £160,000, divided into £500 shares to a maximum of four for each subscriber, of which £96,000 was paid up by November 1769.[24] Offices were established at Ayr, Dumfries and Edinburgh, each run by a committee of nine proprietors, and a tough set of rules was laid down for management of lending and the taking of security.[25] Agencies were opened at Glasgow, Inveraray (the seat of the Argyll family), Kelso, Montrose and Campbeltown. There was a sense of tremendous optimism, which may have encouraged landowners to disregard the fact that their liability was unlimited, an error which was to cost many their estates.

Unfortunately for the proprietors, the direction of the bank in Ayr and Edinburgh attracted persons primarily interested in speculation and bill discounts. At Ayr, much of the early lending went to a number of companies engaged in the American, Irish and West Indian trades with an especial interest in tobacco, sugar and the export trade. These firms, among which were Oliphant & Co., Whiteside & Co., Maclure & MacCree, Campbell & Co., Montgomery & Co. and Campbell, Crawford & Co., had expanded as rivals to other west of Scotland merchants. The later investigation into the collapse of the bank was quite specific:

24 Munn, *The Scottish Provincial Banking Companies*, pp. 29–36; H. Hamilton, 'The Failure of the Ayr Bank, 1772', *Economic History Review*, 2nd series, 8 (1956), 405–17; F. Brady, 'So Fast to Ruin: The Ayr Bank Crash', *Collections of the Ayrshire Archaeological and Natural History Society*, 11 (1973), 27–44.

25 *Report of the Committee of Inquiry appointed by a general meeting of the partners of Messrs Douglas, Heron & Co., late bankers in Air held at Edinburgh*, in *The Precipitation and Fall of Messrs Douglas, Heron & Company, Late bankers in Air with the causes of their distress and ruin investigated and considered by a committee appointed by the Proprietors* (Edinburgh: 1778). The rules included a ban on employees giving surety for cash accounts, only one member of any trading company could be a director at any of the three offices, there was an injunction to discount only good bills at three months, and there were restrictions on directors discussing discounts affecting their own companies.

'a variety of enterprising companies ... closely connected and linked together ... in different kinds of foreign and domestic trade' placed their members as partners of the bank. The Cashier and 'four or five' of the Ayr directors were 'deeply connected to one or more of these companies and proceeded to grant each other cash accounts acting as cautioners to each other, and organising a bill trade. The common desire and necessity of promoting mutual credit could not fail to unite this confederacy in the closest manner.' The Edinburgh branch of the Ayr bank linked up with 'circulation-houses who dealt in fictitious bills of exchange ... opening cash accounts under the pretence of 4% accounts and allowing them to overdraw those accounts and to become the debtors instead of the creditors'.[26] It may have been a suspicion about the direction of the Ayr bank which led the directors of Bank of Scotland, in November 1769, to refuse an initial request by the Earl of Dumfries for an exchange of banknotes. The impending collapse of Ebenezer McCulloch & Co. (December 1769) wherein the Earl was a cautioner and called on to pay for serious losses may also have been a factor.[27]

This hesitation was dropped after the March 1770 Bank of Scotland election, and bills of exchange were bought from the Ayr bank as part of the new liberal policy. After fifteen months, the directors of Bank of Scotland announced that they would accept the banknotes of Douglas, Heron & Co.[28] The benefit offered was remarkably generous. The new bank would be allowed to accumulate a credit of up to £10,000 in its notes held by Bank of Scotland; only the overplus had to be paid immediately, in cash, Bank of Scotland or Royal Bank notes (which accounted for only small sums) or in bills drawn on London at fifty days payable to Bank of Scotland agents (Andrew Drummond & Co. or Hog and Kinloch). The outstanding balance against Douglas, Heron & Co. was to be settled weekly at 5 per cent interest and the account cleared (i.e. paid off and restarted) every three months. By 31 May, Bank of Scotland was inundated with notes.[29] It was perhaps typical of the times that acceptance began before the Secretary of Bank of Scotland had received the contract from the Ayr directors. When their version arrived, it was found that they had tried to include 'an article or two which might imply that the partners of Douglas, Heron are answerable for the amount of their shares and to the extent of their stock [£160,000] only and that they are not bound conjunctly

26 *Precipitation and Fall*, Appendix 4, 11 January, 13 and 17 April 1770 cites a short-lived opposition to the volume of notes passed out by the Ayr branch in the autumn and winter of 1769–70 by the managers of the Edinburgh branch.
27 BS 1/30/3, Agents' Letter Book, 18 November, 14 and 26 December 1769.
28 BS 1/30/4, Letter Book, p. 11: 15 and 23 May 1771; BS 1/5, Minutes: 15 May 1771.
29 The first bills on the excess were drawn on the Ayr bank agents in London: Mayne and Needham (for £2,100) and Dimsdale, Archer and Byde (for £2,000) at the end of the month.

& severally' for all debts.[30] Whether the lesson in the Scots law of co-partnership sent in reply was sufficient to correct this misunderstanding remained to be seen.

Bank of Scotland directors pressed on with their support for the private houses. In mid-June 1771, they agreed to receive the notes of Johnston, Lawson & Co. of Dumfries (the Dumfries bank) and granted them a credit balance of £5,000 on similar terms to Douglas, Heron & Co. On 10 July, they announced acceptance of the notes of the three largest Glasgow banks, the Ship, the Arms and the Thistle. After a 'trial' which lasted exactly one week, they then agreed to take all provincial notes. Only the Aberdeen Banking Company, which was in a note war with Douglas, Heron & Co., refused to cooperate.[31] In general, though, Edinburgh private bankers could now transact a wider range of business and could credit their accounts with the two senior banks in whatever paper they chose. Thus the terms of the facilities which they had recently gained from the Royal Bank and Bank of Scotland were made even more generous.

In theory, a note exchange (which contemporaries called a 'circle') was expected to operate as an automatic control over the over-issue of notes, with the debtor paying interest charges and the costs of specie used in settlement. The short-lived Scottish note exchange of 1771–2 was more complicated. The understandings between the Royal Bank and Bank of Scotland reached after the 1739–41 famine, and encouraged by the Secretary of State, the Marquis of Tweeddale, provided for substantial holdings of the other's banknotes. The reluctance to accept newcomers' notes was brought about by the difficulties over conversion to cash and the problems of dealing with Glasgow bankers. Bringing most note-issuers into an exchange would only work if the paper concerned was instantly convertible. Anything less would damage the worth of Royal Bank and Bank of Scotland notes and would create a new chain of bills on London. As we have seen, the enthusiasm with which some Scottish banks had printed paper over the previous decade had heightened the cost of the exchange on London and also lowered the value of much of that paper against sterling, a point which underlay the suspicions about Scottish paper that was held by the Bank of England after the Seven Years' War. Yet the agreements arranged by the private bankers on the board of Bank of Scotland in effect led to these note-exchange debts being normally recycled through London without recourse to specie payments at Edinburgh.

30 BS 1/30/4, Letter Book, 12 June 1771.
31 BS 1/30/4, Letter Book, 19 June, 3 and 10 July 1771; there were also difficulties with the Merchant Company of Glasgow and delays with the Perth United Banking Company and George Dempster, bankers in Dundee.

In summer 1771, there were thus two aspects to this note exchange. The private banks (although not the provincial note-issuers themselves) could use virtually *any* notes to pay their obligations to the chartered banks. Further, the new facilities for credit and exchange were only sound on the assumption that the bills on London would be paid. In the event of a crisis, the capital involved would be tied up until a tedious legal process was completed; thus *some* losses could be expected. Bank of Scotland was obliged to provide facilities for the exchanges in the financial year 1771–2 of over £40,000 at any one time – and the Royal Bank a similar figure. The scale of the eventual disaster owed as much to these arrangements as to the failings of the management of Douglas, Heron & Co. It is instructive to read what the proprietors of that company thought as they faced financial ruin:

> The general error seems to have been . . . overtrading and endeavouring to force a circulation of the Company's paper beyond the natural limits which must ever regulate and confine operations . . . The extent of the circulation of any country must ever be regulated by the extent of its trade and industry. It can only employ in circulation a certain quantity either of money or of paper . . . But this position, however obvious, was not attended to by the managers of the company. In consequence of credits given out in various forms too profusely and too rapidly a much greater quantity of the Company's paper was . . . thrown into the circle than could be employed in it.

The excess was allowed to pile up in Bank of Scotland, the Royal Bank and in other banks, and Douglas, Heron & Co. had to 'perpetually [contract] debt somewhere' to pay this off, namely in London by bills on London houses. The volume soon became 'formidable and enormous' as the debts with London houses had to be serviced by yet more drafts.[32] Their directors were 'flattered and deluded by speculative notions' because of the ease with which they could obtain new credits in London and Edinburgh. They may have aimed at a monopoly of banking services in the south-west of Scotland by the purchase in late 1771 of the Ayr bank (John McAdam & Co.) for £18,000 and the Dumfries bank (Johnston, Lawson & Co.) for £7,350.[33] The handling of the finances became so complicated that it proved impossible a few years later to reconstruct the exact pattern between the private bankers and Douglas, Heron & Co.'s operations.

In these final months, it had been obvious to many in Edinburgh that the collapse of Douglas, Heron & Co., and its mountain of credit, was

---

32 *Precipitation and Fall*, pp. 18–19.
33 Munn, *The Scottish Provincial Banking Companies*, pp. 32–3; the Ayr bank purchase was at twelve years, and there may have been serious mismanagement in the Dumfries bank; the takeover of the Ayr bank alone resulted in absorption of £60,000 of cash accounts by Douglas, Heron & Co.

only a matter of time. In August 1771, the Company was rebuked by the Royal Bank and Bank of Scotland after it was stated that the Ayr bank would give country banknotes in its note exchange (instead of Bank of Scotland and Royal Bank notes). By the end of October, the Edinburgh branch had been warned to stop manoeuvres designed to force surplus notes onto the chartered banks.[34] Unease was expressed at the proprietors' meetings of Douglas, Heron & Co. in May and November, and new rules were laid down for cash accounts, but these were largely ignored. A further sign of concern came in December when they were asked to reduce the credit that they had been granted at the note exchange for £10,000, 'altogether a dead loan', to £5,000.[35] By January 1772, the basis for the note exchange had become even more fragile when it was clear not only that the volume of Dumfries banknotes was not 'much reduced yet' but also that Douglas, Heron & Co. (the new owners) refused to exchange them unless the old £5,000 facility for the Dumfries bank was maintained. This broke an undertaking from Douglas, Heron & Co. to retire the Dumfries notes on their takeover of that bank, and at the end of the month Bank of Scotland directors were 'greatly surprised to learn lately that these notes are still issued currently in Glasgow'.[36] Worse still, it transpired that the Dumfries notes would only be retired in Dumfries on sixty-day bills payable in London.

Early in 1772, the Bank of England, worried by a deterioration in the internal payments situation, curtailed discounts on Scottish paper and refused entirely some Scottish houses which dealt with the Netherlands.[37] Given this lead, a robust approach by the chartered banks – to refuse all discounts for Douglas, Heron & Co. and to break up the note exchange by insistence on convertibility in coin – would have stopped the crisis from reaching the proportions which it eventually did. But it would have resulted in losses, and perhaps by the late winter it was already too late for some private bankers. At times like this, men tend to put off the inevitable; thus it was not surprising that the Royal Bank and Bank of Scotland did the exact opposite and raised their level of support for the

34 BS 1/30/4, Letter Book, 22 August, 28/29 October 1771.
35 Ibid., 5 December 1771.
36 Ibid., 3, 22, 28 and 29 January 1772.
37 J. H. Clapham, *The Bank of England. A History* (2 vols, Cambridge: 1944), vol. i, 1694–1797, p. 245, notes that the political situation was the main factor for the Netherlands; Adam Smith has been cited in support of the view that Douglas, Heron & Co. intended to 'supplant all the other Scottish banks'; in fact the word 'supplant' appears in a passage which stressed the general contribution of Douglas, Heron & Co. to the relief of the country, and the use of this word should not be used to confirm the overall policy of the directors, which required liberal facilities from other banks: *Wealth of Nations*, vol. i, p. 335. As Charles Munn has suggested, it is more proper to confine the suggestion of monopoly to the south-west of Scotland after the purchase of the Dumfries and Ayr banks. See also T. S. Ashton, *Economic Fluctuations in England and Wales 1700–1800* (Oxford: 1959), pp. 156–7.

Ayr bank.[38] Bank of Scotland even lent Douglas, Heron & Co. £15,000 in gold. In further moves to benefit private bankers, the directors suddenly informed the Court of Session that their Lordships' deposit account was now to receive only 4 per cent, and if they objected they were requested to remove their account by Martinmas. Moreover, 'seeing that' Roger Hog and Kinloch the Edinburgh/London bankers 'are very great proprietors' with two directors on the board of Bank of Scotland, they were now granted half the remittance business previously in the hands of Andrew Drummond & Co. Drummond promptly refused to cooperate with this and closed the Bank of Scotland account.[39] From April 1772, while Douglas, Heron & Co. were plunging deeper into debt and offering generous facilities to London houses which would help them, the board of Bank of Scotland ordered the discount of unprecedented volumes of bills, both for private bankers and for Douglas, Heron & Co. On the account of the note exchange, the average bill drafts came to £1,333 in the first two months of 1772, then rose to £8,000 by March, £23,100 for May and £25,900 to 23 June. The only sensible moves which the directors made were to recommend a 10 per cent increase of capital, from reserves, and to give a shorter time for bills on London, which slightly increased the income of bill transactions.

The crisis finally broke on 10 June 1772 when Neale, James, Fordyce and Downe, the London branch of Fordyce, Grant & Co., were unable to continue with bill transactions.[40] Alexander Fordyce, 'an attractive and plausible Aberdonian' hosier who married into the aristocracy, was their leading partner. He was responsible for stock-exchange and bill debts of at least £243,000. To avoid arrest, he fled to France. The common story is that a rider brought the news north in forty-three hours; certainly, Bank of Scotland received late on 11 June a letter from Hog and Kinloch about 'several' failures. There was an immediate crisis. All the Edinburgh and Glasgow banks came under pressure for coin. Douglas, Heron & Co. offered £100 reward on conviction of anyone passing on rumours about their condition, and when that failed they asked Bank of Scotland and the Royal Bank for £20,000 each and later in June for £50,000. The coin crisis made compliance impossible, although the exchange of notes was kept up

38 The more honourable course would have been to cease discounts and work with the Bank of England; yet if this was considered, there is no trace in the records of Bank of Scotland.
39 RBS, Drummond & Co., General Ledger Books, 1772. The letter sent to Drummonds barely mentioned the help extended by the London house, which had been considerable in the previous decade. Perhaps Andrew Drummond was worried that the board of Bank of Scotland would hide some part of its transactions. The account was closed and balanced by 10 June.
40 Fordyce, Grant & Co., and Neale, James, Fordyce and Downe are recorded under a variety of names in banking records: in Clapham, Bank of England, vol. i, p. 247 as Neale, James, Fordyce & Co.; for details of the house, see NLS, MS 1801(ii), List of Scottish Banks, 1695–1848, compiled by John Buchanan, Glasgow, 1862, from an original made up by Bank of Scotland officials in January 1848.

and even more bills on London were discounted; Bank of Scotland alone took £16,500 in the ten days to 22 June. By then, the standard pattern of a trade collapse had set in; private bankers and merchant houses tried to call in debts but held up payments. Edinburgh lawyers were especially hard-hit because of their relationship with country estates that could not possibly repay debts at short notice. William Alexander the banking and tobacco house stopped in mid-June, and Arbuthnot and Guthrie, the private bankers associated with the Duke of Queensberry and the British Linen Company, failed on 24 June, quickly followed by several others including Andrew St Clair & Co. on 6 July and Alexander Kincaid the week after. The philosopher, David Hume, wrote to Adam Smith from Edinburgh on 27 June 1772:

> We are here in a very melancholy situation: continual bankruptcies, universal loss of credit and endless suspicions. There are but two standing houses in this place, Mansfield's and the Couttses: for I comprehend not [William Cuming] whose dealings were always very narrow. Mansfield has paid away 40,000 pounds in a few days but it is apprehended that neither he nor any of them can hold out till the end of next week, if not alternative happen. The case is little better in London. It is thought Sir George Colebrook must soon stop; and even the Bank of England is not entirely free from suspicion. Those of Newcastle, Norwich and Bristol are said to be stopped. The Thistle Bank has been reported to be in the same condition. The Carron company is reeling which is one of the greatest calamities of the whole; as they gave employment to near 10,000 people.[41]

Over the next few months, fifteen Edinburgh private bankers went bankrupt. The crisis completely destroyed the credibility and social standing of these private bankers.

Douglas, Heron & Co. closed their Edinburgh branch on 25 June with an announcement that they would reopen in three months. In desperate straits, and unable to gauge the extent of the crisis, the Dukes of Queensberry and Buccleuch and the Earls of Douglas and Heron were despatched to the Bank of England. The latter already held £150,000 of Ayr bank paper and offered to take £150,000 more on condition that these four aristocrats supported it by bonds on English lands with a rental of at least £10,000 a year plus deposits of government securities.[42] In the circumstances, this was generous; land prices fell 20 per cent in 1772 and the scale of the known debts of Douglas, Heron & Co. expanded day by day. Perhaps under pressure from members of their families concerned at

---

41 E. C. Mossner and I. S. Ross, *The Correspondence of Adam Smith* (Oxford: 1977), pp. 161–3; for the panic in London, see Clapham, *Bank of England*, vol. i, pp. 246–8.
42 Bank of England, MSS, Court Minutes, G4/21, 2 July 1772.

the implications of such a deal, or from Adam Smith, who was closely attached to the Buccleuch interest and advised His Grace in the aftermath of the collapse, it was decided not to proceed.[43] The plan would have made the aristocrats absolutely responsible for the eventual settlement of £300,000 in addition to their obligations as co-partners. It gradually emerged that in the twelve days after 11 June, before the closure of the Edinburgh office of Douglas, Heron & Co., some of their managers had shifted their private obligations on bills to the company; in one case, David Campbell moved £12,000 to Douglas, Heron & Co. bills payable in London, £8,000 of which were dishonoured.[44] Directors and managers tried to escape personal liability by claiming that the losses were in the normal run of business; in any case, it was impossible to prove otherwise.

The subsequent report was one of the most important documents in eighteenth-century European literature on how to mismanage a bank; it performed a similar function for the early industrial period to the investigations into the collapse of the Western Bank (1857) and of the City of Glasgow Bank (1878) for the Victorian years. Yet unlike these, which reaffirmed the principles of Scottish banking, the report on the Ayr bank helped to mould opinion as to a suitable regulatory framework. It showed how regulations and rules were flouted, it discussed a pattern of irregular loans and explained how bills of exchange transactions supported property, West Indies and stock-exchange speculation and 'every kind of social pretension'.[45] It carried the message that, on a personal level, bankers and lawyers should live within their normal incomes. A disdain for conspicuous consumption has remained within Scottish banking ever since.

After eventual settlements from cash-account holders and other persons to whom money had been lent, each nominal share of £500 was liable for another £2,200 to make up the debt of £663,397 (see Table 8.1).[46] Some of the debts proved impossible to collect. By the summer of 1775, a contemporary suggested that there had been 114 bankruptcies or near-failures among the 226 proprietors. A figure of £750,000 has since been advanced for the value of lands which eventually changed hands, although this probably included the extensive sales and distraint which attached to

43 Adam Smith, *Wealth of Nations*, vol. i, p. 333, note 1. Unfortunately, Smith supervised the destruction of most of his personal papers before he died. When David Hume heard that the Duke of Queensberry had signed the bonds alone, he noted the 'madness' of such a commitment, calling it 'not very wise in him and them in any case': Mossner and Ross, *Correspondence of Adam Smith*, p. 165, David Hume to Adam Smith, October 1772.

44 *Precipitation and Fall*, discussion of bill discounts, p. 63.

45 Munn, *The Scottish Provincial Banking Companies*, p. 31, notes that there was exaggeration in the report over the flouting of regulations.

46 Ibid., p. 34.

Table 8.1 *Balance sheet of Douglas, Heron & Co.*

Liabilities at 23 June 1772		
Deposits		300000
Note circulation		220000
Drafts on London correspondents outstanding		600000
		1120000
Capital called up	130000	
Arrears of capital	25587	
		104413
Assets		
Cash (no record found)		
Debts at Edinburgh, Dumfries and Ayr		694175
of which partners themselves	400000	
Debts at several agencies (Inveraray, Campbeltown, Montrose etc)		133788
Bills of exchange		409079
of which became dishonoured	180000	
		1237042
Sums raised after stoppage upon redeemable annuities		457570
Number of partners	226	
Called up from partners and paid into stock account, 31 March 1804		248141
Received from partners as 'contribution'		419867
		668008
Assets then recoverable estimated at	8940	
Debts still due by bank	4329	
		4611
Leaving a loss to the partners of		663397

Source: NLS, MS 1801(ii), List of Scottish Banks, 1695–1848, compiled by John Buchanan, Glasgow, 1862.

the estates of partners of the Edinburgh private bankers. Litigation lasted for almost half a century.[47]

The management of Bank of Scotland, the Royal Bank and the British Linen Company showed considerable maturity in handling the monetary and credit situation. Much building work in all Scottish towns and south of the Border ceased for the summer of 1772, which made this time one of the most depressed points in the eighteenth-century building cycle. Work on both the Monkland and the Forth and Clyde canals stopped.[48] The Carron company found itself unable to pay wages and debts and was saved only when Bank of Scotland agreed to re-discount three-month bills for £250 per week drawn by the company.[49] At the end of June 1772, the Royal Bank and Bank of Scotland arranged for a delegation from the Ship,

47 Hamilton, 'The Failure of the Ayr Bank, 1772', p. 415.
48 H. Hamilton, *An Economic History of Scotland in the Eighteenth Century* (Oxford: 1963), pp. 324–5; A. Slaven, *The Development of the West of Scotland 1750–1960* (London: 1975), p. 33; Ashton, *Economic Fluctuations*, p. 99.
49 BS 1/30/4, Letter Book, 23 July 1772. The Bank discounted ninety-day bills for £253 4s 6d each week, drawn by Charles Gascoigne on behalf of the Carron Company and accepted by John Clark, merchant in Edinburgh. The Bank insisted on all Carron co-partners subscribing to this arrangement.

Arms and Thistle banks to carry back to Glasgow £9,000 (£6,000 in notes and £3,000 in specie). There was a rapid expansion of cash accounts both in number and limits from Bank of Scotland and the Royal Bank, and their managers and directors met almost daily to discuss the creditworthiness of the ultimate recipients of these funds. The shortage of credit, against the demand for it, lasted into 1774.[50]

The most intractable problem was the sum of 'about two hundred thousand pounds in bank notes' in circulation.[51] Public announcements by the Duke of Argyll, the Faculty of Advocates and numerous burghs that they would continue to take these in payments provided time to raise other money. However, there was such confusion within Douglas, Heron & Co. that it was not until July 1773 that Bank of Scotland and the Royal Bank felt confident enough to treat these notes as part of their reserve. By November 1773 the holdings by Bank of Scotland had grown to £45,150 and in April 1774 to £62,750.[52] The plan to underpin the continued acceptance of Douglas, Heron & Co.'s notes came in two parts and was accepted by the proprietors on 2 November 1772. The first was an agreement by the proprietors to approve a sale of redeemable annuities. Unfortunately, these annuities, which raised £450,000, redeemable at par plus a half-year's annuity, were raised at a discount equivalent to interest of nearly 15 per cent, and some of the money was channelled towards a few proprietors, whereupon £6,000 disappeared without trace.[53] The next move was more considered. With the support of the British Treasury Lords and the Bank of England, Parliament agreed to replace the annuities with bonds bearing 5 per cent, 'rendered to all intents and purposes negotiable and vendible, like East India bonds, Navy and Exchequer bills'. Introduced by Henry Dundas, the Solicitor General, it allowed a committee which included the Dukes of Queensberry and Buccleuch to raise up to £500,000.[54] This provided the cash to retire much of the outstanding debt.

The aftermath of the 1772 crisis marked a turning point in the history of Bank of Scotland and the rest of the banking system. It provided an opportunity for the managers of the two senior chartered banks to

---

50 Mossner and Ross, *Correspondence of Adam Smith*, David Hume to Adam Smith, 10 April 1773; Adam Ferguson to Adam Smith, 23 January 1774.

51 Adam Smith, *Wealth of Nations*, vol. i, p. 334.

52 BS 1/30/4, Letter Book, 22 February, 4 and 21 April; BS 1/5, Minutes: December 1772, agreement with the Royal Bank to take the notes of Douglas, Heron & Co. but not put into effect until 12 July 1773; prior to this, the banks took some Ayr notes but bound those paying in as liable for ultimate payment.

53 Munn, *The Scottish Provincial Banking Companies*, p. 35.

54 14 George III c.21; 5 per cent interest was estimated to require £24,000 a year, and the Act provided for specific estates in land unentailed in Scotland to the clear amount of rent of £32,000 or upwards, to be subjected by mortgage to a corroborative security for discharge of principal and interest of bonds.

reassert their authority. By mid-October, the four Glasgow banks had agreed that the widespread employment of country agents, part of whose income was derived from substitution of their notes for Edinburgh ones, was responsible for much instability. Bank of Scotland argued for the complete suppression of the agents and that local banks should provide for local conditions; when pressure was exceptional, recourse could be had to Edinburgh. The underlying insistence on caution and limits to lending returned to dominate Scottish banking.[55] For the remainder of the century and well into the next, the leading members of the government, the legal profession and the nobility took a direct interest in the organisation of the chartered banks and through these the management of the system as a whole. They could not afford the recurrence of a crisis of this magnitude in such a tightly-knit country. The board of Bank of Scotland was reorganised. The Deputy Governor was replaced in 1773 by the Earl of Leven, who was succeeded in March 1775 by Henry Dundas, created the Lord Advocate the following May. Dundas was later elected Governor and remained in the post until his death in 1811. More lawyers returned to the board, and the strong representation of the nobility was retained: thus the board went back to its pre-1770 pattern. Several of the private bankers associated with now bankrupt houses were replaced by more cautious hands; and, among others, onto the board came Edward Marjoribanks and George Ramsay, of Ramsay, Bonar & Co. In September 1773, the remaining two-tenths of the original capital were called up from proprietors and arrangements were made to double the capital to £200,000. The petition to Parliament, presented by Henry Dundas, emphasised the national role of the Bank and was fully supported by the Treasury and the government party.[56] By March 1774, arrangements had been completed to use Bank of England post bills for some cross-border payments.[57] In the same month, it was agreed to restart the note exchange on the express understanding that no party would flout the rules in the manner of Douglas, Heron & Co. and that the arbiters in the case of a dispute would be Bank of Scotland and the Royal Bank. By and large, this arrangement worked. To underline their status, the Treasury used the two senior banks for the collection of old coin and distribution of the new British coinage in 1774.

Bank of Scotland directors considered several ways in which their enlarged capital and superior standing could be used to support Scottish industry and trade. The £500 limit on cash accounts for industrial and personal customers was abolished. The Bank took a firm line with

55 For an exception to this, the case of the Glasgow Arms bank, see Chapter 9.
56 BS 1/5, Minutes: 9 February 1774; the subscription book was open from 18 May to 18 November 1774.
57 BS 1/5, Minutes: 9 March 1774.

cash-account holders who resided in country areas and drew orders on their accounts via agents of other banking companies, 'by which means a circulation . . . of the notes of Bank of Scotland, a material consideration in granting the credits is . . . entirely frustrated'.[58] In future, cash accounts were to be drawn by the holders or their servants and the notes carried back to the country. From autumn 1773, significant loans – of £1,000 and above – were made on heritable and personal bonds. In the year before the rebellion in the American colonies, some huge loans – £4,000 and above – were made to military officers, and several to tax-collectors, and for estate and mining development the Bank directors were prepared to advance over £10,000 apiece; the largest loan which the Bank granted was £22,000. The directors also decided, against the wishes of several private bankers, to open agencies after the model of the British Linen Company in the south of Scotland at Dumfries and Kelso.[59] Of course, an agent was unlikely to succeed without local influence and connection and a positive response from landowners. Their early operations were tightly controlled; requests for cash accounts had to be approved by the board in Edinburgh and were limited to between £100 and £300. Bills on Edinburgh and London could be bought, but the agents' securities were liable in case of any loss or refusal. This virtually guaranteed that only 'real' bills or those where the acceptor agreed to pay would be bought.[60] The early success of these two branches encouraged the directors to open agencies in Kilmarnock and Inverness (May and June 1775), at Ayr (November) and in April 1776 in Stirling. The branches proved to be important earners and greatly contributed to the circulation of Bank of Scotland notes.

The longer-term consequences of the crisis were soon established. In the early stages of industrialisation, the centre of the Scottish banking system revolved around Edinburgh and the two senior chartered banks. The attempts by the trade-cum-banking partnerships in Glasgow to develop a rival system succeeded only for their locality and required facilities in Edinburgh to support them from time to time. Their co-partnerships' capitals were too small; the Merchant bank closed during the crisis, the Ship closed in 1775 and was later reorganised, and problems with the Arms bank exercised Edinburgh bankers for many years before it closed in

---

58 BS 1/30/4, Letter Book, p. 126, 16 November 1772; the tone of these letters was more polite than under the rule of the private bankers, and apologetic handwritten notes were sent to the nobility.
59 While Bank of Scotland wanted the connection, there was also interest from aristocrats associated with Henry Dundas; three out of four of the staff at Dumfries and Kelso were attached to nobles involved in Douglas, Heron & Co.; at Dumfries, Robert Riddick of Corbieton became agent and David Staig accountant; at Kelso the ex-chamberlain to the Duke of Buccleuch was appointed agent, but the accountant, John Curll, was previously the cash account keeper at the Carron Company.
60 BS 1/5, Minutes: 27 July and 26 September 1774.

1793. The twenty-fifth anniversary of the first Glasgow bank was hardly a time for celebration, and from 1776 the war with the American colonies put further strains on their resources because of the disruption of the tobacco trades.

Bank of Scotland and the Royal Bank had re-emerged by 1772 as the dominant banks at which all others had to have facilities; they controlled the note exchanges and credit limits within that system for each of the provincial banks. Relations were particularly effective with those banking companies, notably the Aberdeen Banking Company and the British Linen Company, which had sufficient reserves and connections with London to weather the 1772 crisis. There were fewer complaints of incompetent behaviour in respect of provincial banks for the remainder of the eighteenth century. For the next twenty years, the two senior banks also developed something of a demarcation in their supervisory role. The Royal Bank looked to strong relations with the provincial banks; Bank of Scotland developed a branch network. They continued their regular meetings on controls over cash accounts and the pattern of bill discounting, and, as indicated below, Bank of Scotland took the premier position over the general strategy for Scottish banking before 1800.

The crisis of 1772 made it abundantly clear that whenever a bank touched bills of exchange, whether on Edinburgh or London, that bank became involved in an international trade network. The need for agents in the two capitals ensured that there were houses directly concerned in whether a business was properly conducted, and it was especially fortunate that the London banking houses of Coutts & Co. and Drummond's were run on strictly cautious lines. The substantial quality of Scottish banking in the early Industrial Revolution, compared with that in England, also owed much to the renewed involvement of the leading politicians and aristocrats after 1772 and to a sound relationship with the government parties at Westminster. For forty years after 1772, the linchpin of this political system was the network led by Henry Dundas, who was usually involved in all major, and many minor, difficulties in respect of Scottish banking until his death. The period was one in which politics thus resumed its central character for Scottish bankers, and this remained the case long into the nineteenth century.

CHAPTER 9

FROM THE AMERICAN WAR OF INDEPENDENCE TO THE CRISIS OF 1793

T HE HISTORY OF Bank of Scotland from the Ayr bank crisis to 1815 was closely connected to changes in the management of Scottish politics. There was a recognition by the governing elite that they had a pivotal role to play in the stability of the banking system which required a different approach from that of the few years before 1772. They became involved in every major change to the structure and direction of the Bank and the Royal Bank, in appointments to head office and branches and even in matters of banking detail. There would be no repetition of the events which had led to the 1772 crisis, and it was accepted that the provision of a sound and stable monetary base and an adequate supply of finance for capital projects required a strong 'first tier' – the Royal Bank and Bank of Scotland – in the banking system. Further, the business of Scottish banking was greatly affected by the American War of Independence (1775–83) and the wars against France (1793–1802 and 1803–15), which placed very large demands on Scottish military contractors; together with the speed of the industrialisation process, these years proved to be among the most momentous in the history of the Bank.

The degree of cooperation between the Royal Bank and Bank of Scotland after the 1772 crisis was determined by the significant political changes of that decade. The key to these was the role of a number of noble and laird families, with extensive estates and wide connections in the law and in trade, who benefited from the economic progress of the middle decades of the century. Among those who sat on the board of Bank of Scotland were Henry Dundas, later first Viscount Melville (Deputy Governor, 1775–7 and 1779–90, and Governor, 1790–1811), the Earl of Marchmont (Governor, 1763–90), the Earls of Lauderdale, Leven (Deputy Governor, 1773–5 and 1777–9), Panmure, Glasgow, Dalhousie and Hopetoun, Patrick Miller of Dalswinton (Deputy Governor, 1790–1815) and Sir John Sinclair of Ulbster, all of whom supported the post-1772 changes; at the Royal Bank, senior ranks included the Duke of Montrose, the Duke of Montague, the Duke of Buccleuch (Governor, 1777–1812), Lord Alva, Campbell of Monzie, Ilay Campbell and Sir Archibald Hope of Craighall. The common factor in all these appointments was wealth in land coupled with an interest in local Scottish politics, although several of these lairds and aristocrats, including the Earl of Marchmont, lived most of the year in London. Many were active in discussions about economic progress – Sir John Sinclair and the Earl of Lauderdale were notable in this respect – and they were all, with one important exception (the Earl of Lauderdale), supporters of the government party in Scotland managed by Henry Dundas from the time of Lord North to William Pitt.[1] There was also a close association among the Bank, the Royal Bank and the leading private bankers of Edinburgh who had survived 1772, namely Coutts of Edinburgh (better known as Sir William Forbes, James Hunter & Co.), William Cuming, and Mansfield, Ramsay & Co., on all banking matters of mutual interest.

The British Linen Company was on the fringe of this story. Its Governor at the time of the Ayr crisis was the unfortunate third Duke of Queensberry, who was himself so much involved; he resigned from the British Linen in 1776 and died in 1778. Thereafter the Company tended to attract persons to senior positions who were more important to social and cultural life than to high politics, a policy which was not to its advantage. Sir David Kinloch of Gilmerton (Governor, 1776–94), appointed for no better reason than his tenure of the Deputy Governorship (1766–76), was an affable and popular laird who had been a close friend of Lord Milton but was outside the real circle of political power by the 1770s.[2] Neither George Mure ws (Deputy Governor, 1776–83) nor Richard Oswald of Auchencruive (Deputy Governor, 1783–4) had significant political influence. An improvement was made in 1784 when William Macdouall of Garthland, the politician, succeeded as Deputy Governor and in 1795 as Governor. By the 1790s, he was an important part of the Dundas–Pitt interest, and it was unfortunate that he resigned in 1800. His successor, William, the seventh Earl of Northesk, played little role in the affairs of the British Linen; an important naval commander who served at the Battle of Trafalgar in 1805, he also spent the last ten years of his Governorship as commander-in-chief, Plymouth. The British Linen, in contrast to the two senior banks, was controlled and directed by

1 R. Mitchison, *Agricultural Sir John: The Life of Sir John Sinclair of Ulbster 1754–1835* (London: 1962); 'Sir J. Sinclair', *DNB*, vol. 52, pp. 301–5; 'James Maitland, eighth Earl of Lauderdale', *DNB*, vol. 35, pp. 799–801.
2 Sir David Kinloch was a director of the Royal Bank from 1762–77.

professional managers and a small number of directors. It should be noted that its return on capital was higher than for the Royal Bank or the Bank, and proprietors may have been concerned that a substantial increase in capital would have affected the rate of return; this was a question raised on several occasions by proprietors in the case of both senior banks.

The aftermath of 1772 coincided with, and undoubtedly aided, the rise to power of Henry Dundas of Arniston, first Viscount Melville (1742–1811).[3] Dundas managed to disseminate a remarkable purpose and direction among the Scottish nobility (and numerous lairds) about their role in civic and political life. The fourth son of Lord President Dundas of Arniston, he came from a long line of Edinburgh lawyers. Admitted to the Faculty of Advocates in 1763, Henry was hard-working, with some brilliance as a debater; at the age of 24, in 1766, he became Solicitor General of Scotland, an appointment he owed to family connections with the Rockingham Whigs. Dundas was early associated with the young Duke of Buccleuch; indeed, it was suggested in 1777 by Hugo Arnot, the contemporary historian, that Dundas had pushed a hapless and confused Duke, recently returned from a tour of the continent with Adam Smith, deep into the Douglas, Heron & Co. affair: 'could the frenzy of a hundred Quixottes equal the mischief you did your country and in particular . . . the Duke in your last banking adventure?'[4] Nevertheless, Henry Dundas and the Duke of Buccleuch became close associates, even friends, and in 1774 Dundas was selected as MP for Midlothian, a seat in the gift of Buccleuch. From this point, the Duke, unbowed by the Douglas, Heron affair, saw himself as a 'prime minister' of Scotland with the organisational ability of Dundas behind him. In May 1775, Dundas was appointed Lord Advocate and thus virtually all Scottish Parliamentary business came through his hands; in that capacity, for example, he steered through the conversion of the Douglas, Heron debts in the face of opposition from the East India Company and the Bank of England.[5] In 1777 he was made joint keeper of the Scotch Signet, and in 1782 Lord Shelburne appointed him Treasurer of the Navy, with sole control of the Signet, and in effect bestowed on him all Scottish patronage. When Shelburne fell, Dundas was removed as Lord Advocate, but only for a few months, and on the accession of Pitt

---

3 J. Dwyer and A. Murdoch, 'Paradigms and Politics: Manners, Morals and the Rise of Henry Dundas, 1770–1784', in J. Dwyer, R. Mason and A. Murdoch (eds), *New Perspectives on the Politics and Culture of Early Modern Scotland* (Edinburgh: 1981), pp. 210–48. For the career of Henry Dundas, see C. Matheson, *The Life of Henry Dundas, First Viscount Melville* (London: 1933).
4 Hugo Arnot, *A Letter to the Lord Advocate of Scotland* (Edinburgh: 18 November 1777): 'when I look on the Duke of Buccleuch I hold even your [Dundas's] friendship fatal. Indeed my Lord it is truly lamentable that a person of his illustrious birth and amiable deportment should be made the dupe of a shopkeeper in Edinburgh and a cadet of the family of Arnistoun.'
5 See above, Chapter 8.

(December 1783) he was restored to office. In addition, he was appointed to the Privy Council committee on trade and foreign plantations and took charge of the new India Board of Control established by Pitt's India Act of 1784. This gave Dundas enormous scope for appointments to offices in India and London which he liberally used to enhance his interest. Moreover, the position, strengthened in 1793 when he was made President of the Board, ensured that neither the East India Company nor the Bank of England – or any other City of London interests – opposed any Scottish financial legislation while he was alive, a most important consideration for the Bank and the Royal Bank, which meant that their boards of directors could increase their capitals without opposition. In 1791, Dundas was made Home Secretary. As Treasurer of the Navy, his office oversaw the expenditure of millions of pounds for payment for supplies. In 1785, as part of the reforms of the early years of Pitt's regime, legislation was passed to stop the private appropriation of these naval funds. Henry Dundas proceeded to circumvent this Act, in part because of poor drafting of proposed controls.[6] Funds were paid out to advance his political interest, and a subsequent Parliamentary investigation, undertaken while Dundas was (temporarily) out of office, even queried the role in this of Coutts & Co., the Royal Bank and the Bank of Scotland agency managed by David Staig at Dumfries.[7]

In the last twenty years of the eighteenth century, Henry Dundas bestrode Scotland's political life 'like a colossus', an 'uncrowned king . . . of the Scottish electors and their hangers-on'.[8] It was a tiny electorate; in 1788, for example, there were only 2,662 male voters for all forty-one constituencies. His network could count on around twenty-five seats by this time, and few of the rest returned opposition candidates. Dundas possessed the perfect blend of tactical shrewdness, tolerance of personal foibles and deference which enabled him to bring together for their common good aristocrats and lairds who, all too often, hated each other. Dundas was thus very important to the government. On the personal side, he had a robust constitution and was able to cope with the gargantuan feasting, endless soirees and journeying from one castle to another.

The system which Dundas built was designed to buttress both the political and the economic power of the aristocracy and should be understood as an attempt to reinforce the authority of 'old' wealth under challenge in

---

6 25 George III c.31, 'An Act for better regulating the office of the Treasurer of His Majesty's Navy'. For a discussion of the background to reform, see H. Roseveare, *The Treasury: 1660–1870* (London: 1973), p. 151; idem, *The Treasury: The Evolution of a British Institution* (London: 1969), ch. 5.
7 See below, Chapter 10.
8 W. Ferguson, *Scotland: 1689 to the Present*, The Edinburgh History of Scotland, vol. iv (Edinburgh: 1968), p. 237; *DNB*, vol. 6, pp. 186–91.

the early Industrial Revolution. It was his especial intention to buttress those families who lived and worked in Scotland, and he encouraged them to appreciate that 'improvement' had a bearing on their political influence. Nobles should live on their estates and cultivate the local lairds, who would then be inclined to vote for their candidates. Scottish-based national institutions, and local cultural and social life, should be supported. Dundas even tried to stop the aristocracy from splitting their landed seniorities to create extra 'client' votes; this device upset lairds and led to bitter antagonisms.[9]

The target of these policies was 'new' wealth, the nouveaux riches who purchased estates and competed for political influence with the old nobility. They included followers of Clive of India and other East India Company men who had taken advantage of the small electorates to bolster their numbers in Parliament. There was a painful struggle, for example, with Sir Lawrence Dundas of Kerse, a government contractor made wealthy by the Forty-five and the Seven Years' War, who had gained considerable influence in the 1760s and whose nominees controlled both Edinburgh and Stirling burghs.[10] Sir Lawrence was also the Governor of the Royal Bank from 1764, and, with his supporters on the board, influenced lending policy in favour of his interest; it was thus inevitable that the banking system would be involved in the power struggles of the 1770s.

Henry Dundas went through two phases in his approach to banks; the first, simplistic, ended with the catastrophe of the Ayr crisis. Early in his rise, he supported changes on the board of Bank of Scotland, and in 1770 together with five noble allies was elected an extraordinary director. As the Duke of Buccleuch was pushed further into the Douglas, Heron & Co. affair by Dundas, neither paid much attention to the detail of the banking side. The most generous interpretation of Henry Dundas's role would be that he was inexperienced in financial matters and had drawn the wrong lessons from the ups and downs of Scottish financial history. Quite rightly, Dundas stood down (he had little choice) from the board of Bank of Scotland in 1772. When he came back, as Deputy Governor, in 1775, the Bank had completed the return to pre-1769 financial and lending policies. The lairds who had lost their accounts had been invited back, the emphasis had switched to loans on bond and cash accounts, bills were discounted where it suited account holders but were not pushed, and the new policies which were to provide the framework for how the board approached their role had been largely worked out.[11] Thus, in the

9   J. Dwyer and A. Murdoch, 'Paradigms and Politics', p. 216.
10 For the struggle for Edinburgh council, see Hugo Arnot, *History of Edinburgh* (Edinburgh: 1777); J. Dwyer and A. Murdoch, 'Paradigms and Politics', p. 216.
11 See below, Chapter 12.

second phase of Dundas's role in Scottish banking, he listened to what he was told by the old-style directors; as this involved the role of the Royal Bank, the opportunity arose to damage the power of Sir Lawrence Dundas of Kerse.

By late 1774, Henry Dundas, in association with several members of the board of Bank of Scotland, had begun a complicated operation to buy up shares in the Royal Bank. Over-extension in bill purchases in 1771 and 1772 had led to losses at the Royal Bank, and its shares had fallen by one-third by 1774. Share transfers were facilitated by the absence of any limit on individual holdings or on voting rights such as existed, by contrast, at Bank of Scotland until 1784. The pattern of dealing in Royal Bank shares saw considerable activity before and just after Sir Lawrence was appointed Governor in 1764, but the most notable development of the decade before 1772 was the large purchases (and sales) made by the Edinburgh private bankers who used the shares as a way of holding funds. After the bankruptcy proceedings subsequent to the Ayr crisis, the main houses left in Edinburgh, namely Mansfield, Ramsay & Co.; Sir William Forbes, James Hunter & Co.; William Cuming; and Thomas Kinnear were all, without exception, close to Dundas and Bank of Scotland. Mansfield's, the more important, had bought eighteen blocks of Royal Bank shares in late 1774, just prior to Dundas's appointment as Deputy Governor of the Bank. Several of his associates on the board and among the proprietors bought up Royal Bank shares, the more notable being Patrick Miller of Dalswinton; James Stirling; Alexander Mackenzie ws; Sir Hew Crawford; the Earl of Lauderdale; Hugh Warrender ws; John Wordie; the Duke of Montague; and Oliver Coult. Around 40 per cent of the Royal Bank shares changed hands in 1775 and 1776. By 1777 this group held a majority of shares, and, realising that defeat was inevitable, Sir Lawrence stood down as Governor at the elections of 1778, to be replaced by the Duke of Buccleuch. Lord Alemoor, the Deputy Governor, was replaced by James Veitch, Lord Elliock, a Court of Session judge and associate of Dundas; six directors were replaced, among whom were David Kinloch of Gilmerton, Governor of the British Linen Company (1776–94).

We have seen that, ever since c. 1742, the two banks had been working in general agreement; but the significance of these share purchases was immense. First, it became public knowledge in 1776 that Dundas intended the banks to function as part of the government (and his own) interest. The affiliation of the two banks meant that, broadly speaking, the Tory interest of Scotland controlled the largest potential credit for party political purposes of any group in eighteenth-century Britain. Second, this remodelling had further implications for the financial system. Among their statements to the Royal Bank proprietors at the 1778 elections, the

Dundas side stated that it was 'for the substantial good of both banks [that they should] co-operate on a larger scale but not . . . [formally] unite'.[12] Thus their lending and monetary policies henceforth marched in step with each other, with different spheres of activity clearly delineated between them, and all matters pertaining to their respective businesses considered at regular meetings. The rates of interest on bills of exchange, cash accounts and bonds; the balances each would carry of the other's notes, 'their mutual credit arrangements'; the level of security and notes they would hold from the country banks to whom they granted facilities; the passing of information to stop the exchange of their notes for gold by 'riders' working for English firms – all this, as well as mundane information on fraud and commercially sensitive data, passed between the banks as it had done (in varying degrees) since c. 1742. But now there was a crucial difference: Bank of Scotland could enforce its wishes, and the power of Dundas was behind it in case of difficulty. In 1774 and 1775, Dundas defeated the East India Company and the Bank of England in Parliament when they opposed the financial reconstruction of the debts of Douglas, Heron & Co., and every increase in the Bank and Royal Bank capitals was passed through Westminster under his management.[13] To underline the permanent nature of the affiliation, Mansfield, Ramsay & Co. kept control of around one-sixth of Royal Bank shares throughout the 1780s, and sizeable holdings remained with Bank of Scotland directors. The Royal Bank shares rose 20 per cent by 1782, and those of the Bank another £15 to £140. For Henry Dundas and his interest, the affiliation between the Royal Bank and the Bank and the support of the private banks in Edinburgh was a lasting monument to their political expertise; it marked a decisive defeat for the nouveaux riches, confirmed that the Glasgow banks would be second-tier banks and, let it not be underestimated, gave the government the power in Scotland of a united, well-organised banking system when it was under the greatest pressure in the aftermath of the French Revolution. These events also sent a clear signal to London that Scottish politicians were supported by a banking network, the framework for which was decided in Scotland, and that there was only a limited role for the Bank of England.

The facilities provided by Bank of Scotland for the Scottish economy saw an unprecedented expansion in the last quarter of the eighteenth century; the basic support for this was a sharp increase in capital. In September 1773, the final two-tenths of the original £100,000 capital

12 Anon., 'Bank Disputes or credit without above, submitted to the considerate observation of stock holders in the Chartered Banks of Scotland' (Edinburgh: 1778) [GL 1778]; Anon., 'A letter to the proprietors of the Bank of Scotland and the Royal Bank' [GL 1778].
13 The role of Henry Dundas in the crises of 1793 and 1797 is discussed below, Chapter 10.

granted by the Act of 1695 was called up.[14] A month later, Parliament was asked for permission to increase capital to £200,000, and both the petition to London and the Parliamentary speeches of Henry Dundas stressed the urgent and 'national' necessity for more capital in the aftermath of the crisis.[15] In 1782 there was a 'great deficiency' in the arable crops, and the Bank provided aid to Edinburgh 'and all burghs wherein the Bank has branches' at 3 per cent, totalling £14,800 and later followed by another £4,000 for Edinburgh and £1,000 for the Charity Workhouse. The crisis worsened: 'the directors having taken into consideration the calamitous state of this country occasioned by the failure of the last years' crop, [and] the difficulties that must thence arise to manufactures, farmers and others', agreed in March 1783 to discount four-month bills on seed imported from England at 3 and 4 per cent for immediate consumption, and to go as low as £10: 'as it is thought many persons of moderate circumstances are well disposed to assist their poorer neighbours'.[16] By the spring, there was a huge increase in bills down to Bank of Scotland with Hog and Kinloch, from £119,000 to £260,708, and cash account overdrafts also rose sharply. By June, the support given by Bank of Scotland was so extensive that the directors, in commenting on a proposed stamp duty on one-guinea notes, stated bluntly: 'this Bank is in respect to Scotland what the Bank of England is in respect to England'.[17] The activity required an adjustment of the capital–advances ratio, and the directors requested another £100,000 to bring the capital to £300,000.[18] In the aftermath of the French Revolution, the government placed significant military contracts in Scotland; Dundas then piloted through another increase in capital, of £300,000, in December 1791. By the time the capital was fully called (November 1793), it had been shown by the commercial crisis that even greater sums were required; Parliament thereupon authorised a further £400,000. Thus,

14 These were the funds requested by John Forrest, Deputy Governor in 1769, but turned down by the private bankers who were in a majority on the board of directors.
15 BS 1/5, Minutes: 3 November 1773, 9 February 1774; the petition to Parliament included the phrase 'that the said bank has proved a great national advantage and it would be highly beneficial for the commerce and interest of that part of Great Britain called Scotland if the capital stock of the bank was increased but which cannot be done without the authority of Parliament'. At this time, Henry Dundas was granted a cash account, together with Laurence Dundas, son of George Dundas.
16 BS 1/5, Minutes: 31 December 1782, 19 March 1783.
17 BS 1/5, Minutes: 11 June 1783; for bankruptcy figures in England and Wales at this time, see Sir John Sinclair, *The History of the Public Revenue of the British Empire*, 3rd edn (3 vols, London: 1803), vol. ii, Appendix.
18 The 1774 Act allowed existing proprietors to subscribe for one new share for every old one they held; the books were open from 18 May to 18 November 1774 and only ninety-nine shares were not taken up out of the 1,200 issued. These were sold by roup at a premium of over 50 per cent above the reserve price of £1,000 Scots (£83 6s 8d sterling). The 1784 Act (presented on 31 May, royal assent 16 July) also granted the right to subscribe for shares in proportion to existing holdings although, in a significant move, the limit on the number of shares held (1695–1774 £20,000 Scots, 1774–84 £40,000 Scots) was abolished.

by the time this was paid up in autumn 1796, the capital of the Bank stood at £1 million.

The Royal Bank was slow to follow the lead of Bank of Scotland; the original capital of £111,347, with a power to increase this by £40,000, stood until the aftermath of the 1782–3 crisis, when £38,653 was added from undivided profits. In 1784, a fourth royal charter was granted to the Royal Bank which secured a rise of £150,000, again paid from reserves.[19] The upsurge in commerce persuaded the board to ask Dundas for a fifth, and an increase to £600,000 was authorised in June 1788, one-third of which came from reserves and the remainder from the proprietors. The subsequent addition of another £400,000, paid up by 1796, followed intensive negotiations involving the Royal Bank, Bank of Scotland, Thomas Coutts & Co. in London, Henry Dundas and the Treasury. It was realised that the scale of the war effort required unprecedented mobilisation of financial resources which had to include, inter alia, enlarged banking facilities and, where required, direct government support for commercial transactions. In 1804, a further increase in the capital of the two senior banks, to £1.5 million each, was agreed after similar discussions.

The directors of Bank of Scotland and the Royal Bank asked Dundas to obstruct requests from the British Linen Company to increase its capital. The British Linen had been tardier in understanding the relationship of capital to lending; in any case, the expansion of its agency network in the 1760s had not put a strain on its resources, as these were ready-made connections from the old linen agency network. It even had unutilised funds in the aftermath of the collapse of Douglas, Heron & Co. which may have lulled its directors into a false sense of security; as late as 1774, its listed capital was only £23,721,[20] and in this year the company forwarded a petition to Tod & Co., its London agent, which asked that the government issue a charter to confirm the British Linen as a permanent bank and thus bring it into line with the Royal Bank and the Bank. This was dropped, probably because such a charter only made sense if the capital was to be increased.[21] In 1781, the directors realised that this was essential; yet Kinloch and his board lacked the political power that Lord Milton

19 N. Munro, *The History of the Royal Bank of Scotland 1727–1927* (Edinburgh: 1928), pp. 149–50, 155–6.

20 This was not directly comparable to the stock of the Royal Bank and Bank of Scotland. The British Linen revalued its capital each year according to results.

21 The royal charter of 1746 imposed no limit on the life of the British Linen, although the Crown legal officers in 1746 recommended that if the Company engaged in banking it should be closed. As a check on this, they suggested that the charter run for only thirty years, after which Parliament should reconsider the case. It would have been inconceivable for the Commons to revoke a charter where general principles of property rights would have been affected. C. A. Malcolm, *The History of the British Linen Bank* (Edinburgh: 1950), pp. 74–5; S. G. Checkland, *Scottish Banking: A History, 1695–1973* (Glasgow: 1975), pp. 150–5.

had wielded. Their senior brethren viewed the British Linen Company as a second-tier bank not entitled to favours from government. After this failure, the British Linen settled back and concentrated on steady improvements to its business; in fact, the authorised capital of £100,000 was not fully paid up until 1801. The directors tried again in 1805 when the attention of Dundas was focused on his threatened impeachment for large-scale corruption and fraud. The following year, in conditions of considerable secrecy, the directors managed to persuade the Treasury to authorise a new charter with a right to double their capital. In 1810, they failed to secure an increase to £500,000 when Bank of Scotland intervened with the politicians to block the request. This was the last occasion when the Bank intervened to stop an increase in the capital of another bank.

The increases in capital ensured that the two senior chartered banks dominated the banking system of Scotland in the last quarter of the century and into the first decade of the nineteenth. Their importance in the system was underlined when, in 1797, the Privy Council proclamation which authorised the suspension of cash payments by the Bank of England, and the two Acts of Parliament which confirmed the order, specifically recognised their status.[22] The chartered joint stock, with its liability limited to the extent of the capital reinforced by successive royal charters and Bank Acts, supervised by boards of directors among whom were some of the highest officers of state, was an attractive investment. The 1784, 1791 and 1793–6 increases in capital for Bank of Scotland proved highly popular; shares remained well above the nominal worth, as dividends were above the 5 per cent interest allowable by statute. These were among the largest banks in the world after the collapse of the Bank of Amsterdam in 1797. They remained the largest British banks, apart from the Bank of England, until the 1826 Bank Act authorised the establishment of joint-stock banks in provincial England and, by a subsequent Act in 1833, within London.

The increase and direction of business of Bank of Scotland can be clearly seen. The influence of the regime of the private bankers in 1770–2 was short-lived; by 1775, the old style of support for industry, trade and agriculture was once again given pride of place in board decisions on lending. There was a sharp increase in loans on bonds and cash accounts from head office to support all manner of trades and industries during the American wars. Although by 1780 there was a gradual and tightly-controlled increase in bill discounts via branches, the decision to discount a bill was based on a request from customers; the Bank did not force customers to take bills by refusing to increase lending by cash accounts. By

22 See below, Chapter 10.

1793, the total credit from bills to the profit and loss account was between four and five times greater than twenty years earlier, although this in no way affected the availability of the other channels of credit. Adjustments for inflation underestimate the scale of the increase of this facility for the economy; margins on bills fell, shorter dates became more common, and borrowers tended to be swifter in crediting cash accounts. The total volume of Bank of Scotland notes out continued to see seasonal and trade fluctuations, but they rose from an annual average of over £100,000 in 1772 to £480,000 in 1794 and £670,000 in 1800.[23]

The power and effectiveness of Bank of Scotland, the Royal Bank and the British Linen were enhanced by the spread of their networks of branches and agencies. The choice of agents was primarily a political matter at Bank of Scotland, for they were usually connected to the Dundas interest, although the Bank was also naturally interested in their financial expertise and personal probity. Several were local politicians of note: David Ferguson in Ayr, David Staig at Dumfries, John Mackintosh in Inverness and Robert Banks at Stirling. David Staig was involved in the remittance of public funds by Henry Dundas on the latter's private account, a matter which came before the Lords in 1805 at the trial of Melville but was not explained in the detail that some of his accusers wished for. Bank of Scotland was concerned that agents should have local connections and the social standing essential for the development of business. By 1780, Bank of Scotland had twelve of these agencies in addition to the head office in Edinburgh, and by June 1785 another six were added; a decade later, this total was twenty-four, of which only two, at Paisley and Greenock, were closed because of the competition from local banking companies (see Table 9.1 and Appendix 8). The agents were not usually formal employees of the Bank, although they swore an oath of allegiance to the Bank, their contract specified an annual fee plus a commission, they were liable for all of their losses on bills of exchange, and they were given lists of instructions which gradually grew more comprehensive as time passed. Agents were usually assisted by an accountant who was in the employ of the Bank. Tellers and messengers, where required, were usually employed by the agent. In virtually every case, agents were involved in trade or a legal practice; there was therefore a potential conflict of interest. The controls could not stop agents from transferring funds to their own businesses or those of their acquaintances. But this was inevitable given the involved nature of Scottish burgh politics, although the Bank enforced some discipline through its refusal to allow any losses by agents on bills of exchange and a rigorous pursuit of cautioners for cash accounts. From this

---

23 BS 1/70/11, Figures for annual average of notes in circulation.

Table 9.1 Scottish banks established before 1780

Name	Place	Established	Retired/stopped (if prior to 1780)	Comments
Public banks				
Bank of Scotland	Edinburgh	1695	?	by Act of Scottish Parliament
Royal Bank of Scotland	Edinburgh	1727		by royal charter
British Linen Company	Edinburgh	1746		by royal charter (for banking 1763)
Private banks				
Coutts, Patrick	Edinburgh	?pre-1696	?	retired
Clerk, George	Edinburgh	c. 1700		gone by 1720
Coutts, John & Co.	Edinburgh	1704	?	retired
Robertson, Robert & James	Glasgow	c. 1727		not known to have been in business after 1735
Blair, James	Glasgow	c. 1730		disappeared by 1740
Alexander, William & Sons	Edinburgh	c. 1730s	1776	failed – not known if creditors paid in full; had stopped temporarily 1772
Coutts, John & Co.	Edinburgh	c. 1730s		known also as Coutts Brothers & Co., c. 1750, and as Sir William Forbes, James Hunter & Co. from 1773
Glasgow Tanwork Co.	Glasgow	c. 1736		disappeared by 1760
Mansfield, Hunter & Co.	Edinburgh	1738		later Mansfield, Ramsay & Co., then Mansfield, Bonar & Co., and from 1807 Ramsay, Bonar & Co.
Ramsay, Bonar & Co. – see Mansfield, Hunter & Co.				
Fairholme, Adam & Thomas	Edinburgh	c. 1740s	1764	failed
Kinnear, Thomas & Sons	Edinburgh	1748		never issued notes
Arbuthnot & Guthrie	Edinburgh	?	1772	failed
Berry and Baillie	Edinburgh	?	1772	failed
Bertram, Williamson	Edinburgh	?	1772	failed
Chalmers, George & Co.	Edinburgh	?	1772	failed
Cumming, William & Sons	Edinburgh	?		
Fordyce Grant & Co.	Edinburgh	?	1772	failed – 6s 6d per £ paid; not known if issued notes
Fordyce, Malcolm & Co.	Edinburgh	?	1772	failed

No.	Name	Place			Notes
	Gibson and Balfour	Edinburgh	?	1772	failed
	Gibson and Hogg	Edinburgh	pre-1772	?	mentioned by Forbes – also corn merchants
	Hogg, William & Sons	Edinburgh	?	1769	failed
	Hogg, William Jr	Edinburgh	?	1772	failed
	Miller, Patrick	Edinburgh	?	1772	failed
	St Clair, Andrew	Edinburgh	?	1772	failed
	Wardrop, John & Co.	Edinburgh	?		
	Waugh, John	Edinburgh	?	1772	failed
	Craig, John & Smith, David	Glasgow	?		disappeared by 1772
	Campbell, Thomson & Co.	Stirling	?	1798	retired
12	Seton, Houston & Co.		pre-1754		became Seton, Wallace & Co., 1791
	Seton, Wallace & Co. – see Seton, Houston & Co.				
	Foggo, Samuel	Edinburgh	c. 1760	1772	failed
	Fyffe, John & Co.	Edinburgh	c. 1760	1772	failed
13	Johnston, Smith & Co.	Edinburgh	c. 1760	1772	failed – 15s per £ paid
	Scott Moncreiffe & Ferguson	Edinburgh	c. 1760	1772	failed
	Sinclair, William & Co.	Edinburgh	c. 1760	1772	failed
	Watson, David	Glasgow	c. 1763		became J. & R. Watson c. 1793
	Watson, James & Robert – see Watson, David				
14	Smith, Donald & Co.	Edinburgh	1773		never issued notes
15	Bertram, Gairdner & Co.	Edinburgh	1776		never issued notes
	Allan, Alexander & Co.		c. 1776		never issued notes
	Fyffe, John & Co. (2)		1778	1790	retired
16	Wardie (or Wordie?), John	Edinburgh	c. 1778	c. 1781/87?	failed
	Johnston, Robert	Edinburgh	1779		
	Provincial banking companies				
17	Banking Company of Aberdeen	Aberdeen	1747	1753	co-partnery dissolved
18	Dunlop, Houston & Co. (Ship bank)	Glasgow	1749		stopped 1772; reorganised 1775–6 (became Moores, Carrick & Co.); from 1783 Carrick, Brown & Co.
19	Cochrane, Murdoch & Co. (Arms bank)	Glasgow	1750		required support 1772; from 1763 to c. 1782 Speirs, Murdoch & Co., then Murdoch, Robertson & Co.
20	Maxwell, Ritchie & Co. (Thistle bank)	Glasgow	1761		
21	Dundee Banking Co. (Geo. Dempster & Co.)	Dundee	1763		
22	MacAdam, John & Co.	Ayr	1763	1771	joined Douglas, Heron & Co.

Table 9.1 *continued*

Name	Place	Established	Retired/ stopped (if prior to 1780)	Comments
Perth United Banking Co.	23 Perth	1763		junction of five quasi-banks: re-formed in 1787 as Perth Banking Co.
Johnston, Lawson & Co.	24 Dumfries	1766	1771	joined Douglas, Heron & Co.
Aberdeen Banking Co.	25 Aberdeen	1767		
General Bank of Perth	26 Perth	1767	1772	failed – creditors paid in full
Douglas, Heron & Co. (the Ayr bank)	27 Ayr	1769	1772	closed temporarily 1772
Glasgow Merchant Banking Co.	28 Glasgow	1769		
Hunters & Co.	29 Ayr	1773		
Stirling Banking Co.	30 Stirling	1777		
Private banks which issued notes for under £1 during scarcity of specie[31]				
Tannery Co. (Stewart, Richardson & Co.)	Perth	c. 1763	1765	
Craigie Co. (John Ramsay & Co.)	Perth	c. 1763	1765	
Stewart, John & Co.	Perth	c. 1763	1765	
Blacklaws, Wedderspoon & Co.	Perth	c. 1763	1765	
MacKeith, Rintoull & Co.	Perth	c. 1763	1765	
Scrimgeour, James & Son	Bo'ness	c. 1763	1765	
Fleming, Alexander & Co.	Kirkliston	c. 1763	1765	
Keller, George & Co.	Glasgow	c. 1763	1765	absconded December 1764
Yeaman, William & Co.	Dundee	c. 1763	1765	

Notes:

1 George Clerk was one of the first directors of Bank of Scotland appointed by the Scottish Parliament.
2 Robert Robertson was a tobacco merchant. They had a Bank of Scotland cash account between 1731 and 1741, with a credit limit of £1,000.
3 Director of Bank of Scotland from 1728.
4 According to Forbes, their main business was purchasing tobacco for the farmers general of France, although they were also considerable money-dealers. They failed in June 1772 but resumed business in July 1772 with a credit from the Bank of England on security of the value of their real estates in Grenada. These were sold for £100,000 in 1790, against an advance of £160,000 (Checkland, p. 157).
5 James Mansfield began as a small draper who dealt in bills of exchange and had a cash account with Bank of Scotland from April 1737. James Hunter died in January 1765, after which

James Stirling (who had made his money in the West Indies) was made a partner. In 1773 he was elected a director of Bank of Scotland; he later became Sir James Stirling of Larbert. He was Lord Provost of Edinburgh in 1792. Other partners were William Ramsay of Barnton (a Royal Bank director), James Mansfield and Patrick Miller of Dalswinton (directors of Bank of Scotland). Ramsay, Bonar & Co. was wound up by Bank of Scotland, and Peter Ramsay, the surviving partner, became the Edinburgh agent of Western Bank until his death in 1855.

6 Large dealers in corn. The Fairholmes, along with Alexander Arbuthnot, had two Bank of Scotland cash accounts, which were often in credit to fairly large sums, opened in 1735 and 1741 respectively. Arbuthnot was a director of Bank of Scotland from 1729 and Deputy Governor on three occasions (1733–5, 1737–9 and 1742–5). Thomas Fairholme was a director from 1732 and Deputy Governor 1748–50, and Adam a director from 1748.

7 Thomas Kinnear was originally an insurance broker.

8 Also large dealers in corn.

9 Dealt mainly in corn. He became a director of Bank of Scotland in 1760.

10 Inherited his father's (Patrick Cumming's) cloth shop in Parliament Close and turned it into a banking house. Left a large fortune on his death.

11 The company was largely indebted to Douglas, Heron & Co. The partners were Alexander Fordyce of London (originally a hosier in Aberdeen), John Fordyce, Receiver General of Customs and Andrew Grant of Torerie, brother of Baron Grant. They also had a banking house in London (Neale, James, Fordyce & Downe) which failed at the same time, owing £32,003 of public monies to the Crown. Alexander Fordyce ruined the companies through stockjobbing and absconded in June 1772.

12 Originally woollen merchants.

13 One of the partners was Donald Smith, who later went on to form Donald Smith & Co. in 1773. The other was Robert Johnston (see note 16).

14 Donald Smith was the grandfather of the Donald Smith who became manager of the Western Bank. He was originally a partner in the private bank, Johnston, Smith & Co. (failed 1772). His new venture was financed by money gained through marriage. He became a director of Bank of Scotland in 1807 and Lord Provost of Edinburgh in the same year.

15 Partners at sequestration were John Gairdner, Adam Keir and Robert Forrester, who were also partners of the London banking firm Baillie, Pocock & Co. which failed at the same time. The liabilities were £14,5000 of which £127,000 was liquidated.

16 Robert Johnston was originally a partner (with Donald Smith) of Johnston, Smith & Co, which failed in 1772. He resumed as a private banker, but his main line of business was as a toy, hardware and grocery merchant.

17 Partners were Alexander Livingstone, William Mowat, William Bremner and John Dingwall.

18 6 partners at date of founding.

19 31 partners at date of founding.

20 6 partners at date of founding.

21 36 partners at date of founding.

22 15 partners at date of founding.

23 87 partners at date of founding.

24 19 partners at date of founding.

25 109 partners at date of founding.

26 43 partners at date of founding.

27 136 partners at date of founding.

28 48 partners at date of founding. At the stoppage of 1772 there had been seventy partners. A new partnership contract was formed in 1776. The main cause of failure was the abscondment of the cashier to America with a large sum of the company's money. The loss ultimately fell on the only two solvent partners, Robert McLintock of Thornbank and Robert Thomson of Camphill.

29 4 partners at date of founding.

30 8 partners at date of founding.

31 The notes of these quasi-bankers were usually retired in Edinburgh by various private bankers, with whom they had an agreement. They were prevented by the 1765 Act from continuing to issue notes for under £1.

Sources: BS 20/2/7, Papers re history of Scottish banks; BS 1/70/9, An account of the constitution, objects and practice of the Bank of Scotland (1841), appendix G; NLS, MS 1801(ii), List of Scottish Banks, 1695–1848, compiled by John Buchanan, Glasgow, 1862; S. G. Checkland, *Scottish Banking: A History, 1695–1973* (Glasgow: 1975); C. W Munn, *The Scottish Provincial Banking Companies, 1747–1864* (Edinburgh: 1981).

the directors only relented in exceptional circumstances, the first recorded occasion being after the 1793 crisis. Six agents were allowed an abatement after consideration of the overall benefit derived from the agency and with cuts to their fees. The regular inspection of agencies started after the crisis of 1782–3. This involved periodic visits by directors and full-time officers from head office, and henceforth all agencies were checked at least once every eighteen months.[24] The total number of agents, accountants, tellers and head-office staff by the close of the first century of the Bank was around 175. The general success of the agencies in the early years probably derived from the insistence that trade bills of exchange be based on real transactions which actually involved trading, and from the requirement to send a weekly list of the state of bills and balances to Edinburgh (see Table 9.2). The 1772 collapse continued to cast a dark shadow on Scottish life: the legal cases dragged on into the nineteenth century, and the 1778 report on Douglas, Heron & Co. was widely circulated. This, without doubt, influenced the conduct of banking personnel.

Bank of Scotland had a good sense for an impending crisis, with few exceptions, notably in 1704 and 1772. The agency network enabled the committees of ordinary directors to be made aware of irregular patterns of activity by provincial banks and merchants, difficulties with bills being an especially good predictor of crises. The Bank had early warning of the crises of 1782–3, 1788 and 1793 and exchanged information with the Royal Bank and, to a lesser extent, with the British Linen Company. The spread of the influence of the chartered banks and their wide connections to London and abroad gave them an advantage over the provincial companies with their more limited connections. Thus, in 1782, Bank of Scotland curtailed new credit on bills from the early summer once it was clear that the crisis would be a national one. The relative sophistication of its system was appreciated by Thomas Coutts, of Coutts & Co., who suggested to the Bank of England in 1793 that it would be better able to discharge its obligations to England if it adopted a branch system on the lines of the 'Scots National Bank', a proposal which annoyed Threadneedle Street.[25] Thomas Coutts meant this both in the sense of the superior information which it would give the bank and, perhaps as important, because of the standing in the local bill market that such branches would have. Already

24 Inspections concentrated on four main checks: that (1) the cash equalled the balance in the books, (2) the bills were all properly listed, were all in course of payment and had interest properly paid when overdue, (3) private trade accounts of agents were not mixed up with work for the Bank, (4) cash accounts were properly listed and interest paid. It was virtually impossible to stop a determined fraud and difficult to work out which bills were accommodation bills without detailed local knowledge.

25 Coutts & Co., archives, Special Letter Book, 16 March 1793: 'I understand it is in contemplation for the Bank [of England] to issue £5 notes and I suggested today to some gentlemen who met upon the public loan that it might be worth their while for the Bank to consider of making country branches as the Scots' National Bank do'.

Table 9.2 Bill discounts and sums credited to profit and loss account at Bank of Scotland branches, 1783–6

Branch	Agents	1783–4		1784–5		1785–6	
		Bills	Credit	Bills	Credit	Bills	Credit
Dumfries	David Staig	310066	1319	356126	1749	304553	1851
Banff	George Robinson & Co.	44414	169	38035	104	34867	289
Aberdeen	Leys & Smith	224538	1316	223335	1075	234726	1276
Stirling	R. Banks	242796	1955	239527	2042	188532	1994
Inverness	J. Mackintosh	110593	730	109519	692	106783	612
Elgin	J. Forsyth	37211	142	47566	169	53859	404
Glasgow	G. Hamilton	n/a	n/a	n/a	n/a	63482	n/a
Ayr	David Ferguson	97312	794	104174	831	101019	823
Huntly	G. Davidson	16640	130	28799	161	30087	349
Kilmarnock	D. Parker	212897	1191	247556	1387	222648	2016
Perth	G. Blaikie	—	—	112288	289	266345	2009
Kirkcaldy	Fergus & Sons	—	—	—		90470	151
Cupar	Robert Geddie	—	—	—		80095	213
Haddington	R. Wilkie	67396	—	97964	222	116489	657
Montrose	J. Brand	—	—	43200	—	194231	858
Kelso	Robert Scott	173852	866	194460	992	180214	1380
Dunfermline	J. Dickie	157542	1083	261196	1602	250172	1893

Source: BS 1/94/24–5, General Ledgers.

by this time, a refusal by the Bank of Scotland agent to endorse a bill (they were always marked as such), or for that matter by the Royal Bank agency in Glasgow, was enough to stop further circulation. The branch network also allowed Bank of Scotland to try some rather advanced experiments on note issue. In 1791, it marked all the notes sent to Kelso to check on the length of time that they remained in circulation and to assess the degree of substitution by other banking companies; the less this happened, the greater the worth of a bill or cash account beyond the more easily-measured interest and fee charges.[26] Perhaps the most useful function of the branches for small traders and shopkeepers was their supply of banknotes in which customers could have confidence.

Before 1784, the Royal Bank largely eschewed an agency network, although from time to time agents were appointed, as in 1763 at Dumfries.[27] It also set up an agency in Banff in 1765 and joined with Bank of Scotland for the Aberdeen agency in 1766. At the time of the Ayr crisis, the greatest contribution to the profits of the Royal Bank came from the receipt of deposits from the customs and excise, the Commission for forfeited estates, the army and remittance across the Border. The Royal Bank derived a modest profit from credits to several provincial banking companies, and with the demise of most of the private bankers in Edinburgh this facility was greatly increased: by 1778, £10,000 was available to the Aberdeen Banking Company and £5,000 each to the Perth banking company and the Merchant Company of Glasgow and, in 1783, £5,000 to the Paisley banking company. These were more than just credits: they offered a considerable public guarantee with an implicit suggestion that additional help would be available in time of trouble, which was indeed the case. Smaller sums and miscellaneous transactions were negotiated for other provincial companies. The repercussions of the crisis of 1782–3 in the west of Scotland persuaded the Royal Bank to move directly into Glasgow; its bill discounts for the western trades and those of the Bank of Scotland agencies at Paisley and Greenock indicated that Glasgow houses were unable to supply sufficient accommodation. The situation there was serious. The Merchant Company was kept solvent by the Royal Bank and William Cuming, the Edinburgh private banker, and Coutts & Co. staved off a collapse at the Arms bank. With this background, the Royal Bank opened an agency in 1783 run jointly by David Dale (1739–1806), the linen and cotton manufacturer, and Robert Scott Moncreiffe (1748–1814), a man with considerable knowledge of Edinburgh banking affairs.[28] Within a

26 BS 1/5, Minutes: 7 November 1791.
27 RBS RB/12/8, Minutes, 1 July 1763: Hugh Lawson, later partner in Johnston, Lawson & Co., bankers, Dumfries 1766, incorporated by Douglas, Heron & Co., 1771; C. W. Munn, *The Scottish Provincial Banking Companies, 1747–1864* (Edinburgh: 1981), pp. 29, 32.
28 Checkland, *Scottish Banking*, pp. 145–7.

decade, they were discounting around £400,000 worth of bills annually, a figure which rose to over £636,000 in 1807 and £700,000 by 1810. This was a most important support for industry in the west. In 1787, Bank of Scotland appointed Gilbert Hamilton, merchant in Glasgow and agent for the Carron Company, as the Bank's correspondent for securing payment on bills sent from Edinburgh. From 1795 he received £150, and in April 1802, together with his son, he negotiated a 'caution and security unprecedented in the Bank', by which the Bank took half the risk on the bills which the Hamiltons accepted.[29] At this time, the Royal Bank and the Bank agreed to proceed with their request for a 50 per cent increase in capitals, most of which was destined for the support of the western men. The Bank quickly became the second largest discounter in the west of Scotland after the Royal Bank.[30] Aside from the political impact of the network of these agencies, Thomas Coutts thought that the competition which they provided with the provincial banking companies 'would in time extinguish the private circulation of notes'. To Coutts, who devoted much of his working life of over sixty years to the search for stability and arrangements to mitigate crises, this would have represented a great step forward.[31] The Glasgow banks lacked sufficient expertise and capital to cope with the demands of the first stage of industrial capitalism, and it was a tribute to the senior Scottish banks that they were able to provide permanent support.

The success of the new Scottish financial system after the Ayr crisis required strong connections with London bankers. Almost without exception these were Scots; many had been born and educated in Scotland, had family ties there, travelled back frequently and entertained their Scottish cousins and politicians on their journeying south. Their ledgers were full of Scottish accounts, personal, business and political, and they were often asked for all manner of services; for example, the Coutts' partners received a stream of letters seeking the employment of various kith and kin. A number of the Scottish houses, possibly a majority, were asked to handle political matters; Kinloch & Hog and Coutts & Co., for instance, were sufficiently close to Henry Dundas and the Duke of Buccleuch to manage secret transactions. For these houses, the term 'correspondent' does not convey adequately the closeness of the banking arrangement.

The Scottish banking houses in London were called upon to expand their business in line with the growth of the system in Scotland. Indeed,

29 BS 1/146/1, Private Letter Book, pp. 491, 497, 506.
30 Checkland, Scottish Banking, p. 229, Tables 5 and 6.
31 Coutts & Co., archives, Special Letter Book: 3 April 1786, to William Ramsay, Royal Bank. In fact, the public had nothing to fear from well-run provincial banks, and the last such note-issuer, the Dundee Banking Company, was absorbed by the Royal Bank in 1864.

on the banking side, the London houses remained as much a part of the northern system as they had been earlier in the century. But the volume of transactions now forced the London houses to increase their staff in considerable numbers. In the aftermath of the Ayr crisis, Bank of Scotland kept two London correspondents, Kinloch & Hog and Coutts & Co., although its business gradually shifted towards Coutts and in 1793 the account with Kinloch & Hog was closed.[32] These London Scots worked together as the occasion required, over banking crises, for example, and in the sale of government stock and the transferable bonds for Douglas, Heron & Co., so as not to weaken prices.[33]

The most prominent and time-consuming transactions between London and Bank of Scotland in Edinburgh in the last quarter of the century were those for bills of exchange. Simply stated, the Bank dealt in two broad categories of bill (although each of a bewildering variety), the first being those which it asked Coutts or Kinloch to demand payment of, on presentation, to the drawee (usually a London bank or merchant). These bills had been purchased by Bank of Scotland in Edinburgh, or by its agents, from persons who wanted cash, and they normally ran from the date of purchase for a number of days (sixty days was common in this period) laid down in the meetings between the Bank and the Royal Bank. The price paid for the bill involved a discount against the face value at a rate of interest, again agreed between the two banks and rigidly adhered to. It was usually below the legal maximum of 5 per cent, and in peacetime 2½ to 3½ per cent was usual. On receipt in London, a (junior) member of staff sought the drawee's endorsement for later payment. When that day arrived, the staff collected banknotes or a note against an account at Coutts (or Kinloch); but, as there were numerous bills to be collected, many of them in the City and south of the river, the returns were rarely completed before the afternoon. The second category of bill was that bought by persons in Scotland, making a payment to the Bank or its agents, due for payment at an agreed number of days, and which were sent to London for settlement. The same procedure then applied in reverse: the recipient in London sent the bill to Coutts (or Kinloch) for endorsement (the Bank had usually notified them of the bill's details), and on the agreed day it was presented for banknotes or gold, or against an account. Yet, as Coutts occasionally reminded the Bank, payments out were usually in the morning, thus Coutts faced a deficit which often rose above £100,000 for a few hours before the returns came in. Coutts & Co. thus had to ensure

32 Coutts & Co., archives, Miscellaneous papers. It was suggested as early as 1785 that the Bank should retain Coutts as its sole London house. The Bank came to appreciate the quality of advice from Coutts, and this undoubtedly had a bearing on the final decision.
33 BS 1/5, Minutes: 15 March 1780.

that it held enough gold and notes to cover all the demands made against the Bank and its other clients, among whom were the Royal Bank, the Aberdeen Banking Company and several English provincial companies.

As the bill business expanded at a phenomenal pace in the decade before the French Revolution, there were times when the Bank overstepped agreed credit limits with Coutts (£15,000 in 1777, £20,000 by 1779, £25,000 in 1785 and raised to £50,000 in 1793).[34] Politicians and other important people would present for payment bills on Bank of Scotland at sight when they arrived in London, and Coutts had little choice but to cash these. Moreover, Coutts noticed that there was a gradual tendency, usually coincident with the payment terms in Scotland, for Bank of Scotland to draw 'at short dates' but remit at long so that 'our advance of money may [temporarily] far exceed [the agreed] £50,000 [of 1793] though the general balance might be greatly within that sum'.[35] Thus more gold and banknotes were tied up in Coutts' vaults overnight, there being no 'overnight' deposits for cash balances. Even with the provincial companies, it proved difficult to curtail unagreed balances; the Aberdeen Banking Company admitted that it might draw for '£1,000 or £2,000 more than they have remitted', and a reminder that it was contrary to Coutts' rules 'in the common tract of our business to accept any bill but when the money is actually lodged before such acceptance' proved impossible to enforce. Winter played havoc with the post, and there were especial difficulties in times of crisis.[36]

The huge increase in business meant that Coutts & Co. asked the Bank, the Royal Bank, Mansfield, Ramsay & Co. and even the Aberdeen Banking Company to make over suitable reserves in London in convertible funds over which Coutts had first call. The matter was pressed after the 1782–3 crisis, not from a worry that banks as sound as Bank of Scotland might crash, but from more complex reasoning. In that crisis, as in 1772, Coutts found that it was faced with huge demands for payment and discounts originating in Scotland which far exceeded cash paid in on Scottish accounts. Thus, in the later crisis, the Aberdeen Banking Company deficit ran to £72,000 and that for the Bank to over £100,000, although a steady flow of cash continued in both cases. It would help, Coutts reasoned, for the public to know that such a reserve existed, listed in the registers of companies and government. Then the payments to and from Scotland could proceed more smoothly than if only the word of Coutts (and other hard-pressed London houses) was on offer as a guarantee:

34 Coutts & Co., archives, Special Letter Book: 11 September 1777 to Patrick Miller, 30 October 1777 to Thomas Steuart, 8 February 1779 to Patrick Miller.
35 Coutts & Co., archives, Miscellaneous papers: 18 March 1793 to James Fraser at Bank of Scotland.
36 Coutts & Co., archives, Special Letter Book: to Alexander Simpson, 14 May and 11 July 1782.

> it would be for the advantage of all great banks in the long run to carry on matters so as not to depend on anything but their own funds and as the Bank of Scotland may occasionally want money in London I submit it to you whether it would not be better ... to keep an adequate part of their capital there, as a fund of credit and a necessary operation of their business.[37]

Coutts would be unlikely to sell these in a crisis when funds were down, but it would ensure a greater readiness to advance payments and enhance general confidence. A solution was on hand. In the discussions at the close of the Seven Years' War, various proposals for holding reserves in London were discussed, but in the event the Royal Bank and Bank of Scotland negotiated satisfactory arrangements with their agents. Part of the £100,000 raised in new capital in 1774 was placed in Douglas, Heron & Co. transferable 5 per cent bonds and in Navy and Victualling bills, but these were sold by January 1777. In 1779, more Navy and Victualling bills were bought and some Bank of England stock, and by March 1780 the total book value was a little over £100,000. By 1782, the Bank had bought £140,000 worth of 3 per cent consolidated stock at a cost of £81,142. From this time, Bank of Scotland always held a mixture of London stocks: 3 per cent consols, Exchequer bills, Bank of England stock, Navy and Victualling bills, and its own stock. The market value of these fluctuated for the rest of the decade between £100,000 and £150,000.[38]

The period from 1772 was marked by a considerable upturn in the profile of the London Scots' banking houses, which in general pursued stable and severe financial regimes. Both Coutts and Kinloch & Hog refused to engage in trade. Thomas Coutts noted that they engaged in no trade after 1760; it was 'incompatible with the trust reposed in a banker by his customers for him to run risks or be concerned in commerce or any kind of separate business'.[39] Further, neither Kinloch nor Coutts paid interest on balances in credit: 'I believe no banker here who acts on these principles [refusal to take risks] will allow interest or can afford to do it'; 'My shop is of too long a standing and too well established to require such sort of arts [paying interest] and if it were otherwise such a proceeding by no means accords with my temper and habits, which has ever been to prefer reality to appearances'.[40]

The rewards of such prudence were long-term survival and a privileged position in London banking. The market for existing stocks was conducted by numerous houses, but for new government issues a smaller number of

---

37 Coutts & Co., archives, Special Letter Book: to Patrick Miller, 8 April 1785.
38 BS 1/94/21–6, General Ledgers.
39 Coutts & Co., archives, Special Letter Book: to Alexander Simpson, 23 December 1784.
40 Coutts & Co., Special Letter Book: to Alexander Simpson, 23 December 1784; to Samuel Henrick, Bewdley, 25 January 1783.

the private banks acted as intermediaries between the Treasury and buyers and underwrote an issue. After Samson Gideon's successful cooperation with the government in 1752, this group of banks remained few in number, although the Treasury made occasional efforts to widen the net.[41] Lord North, for example, in 1780 wanted 'all the world to write for sums'.[42] They did, but included speculators who bought for a quick sale, which served to depress the prices of further issues. The Treasury then abandoned any pretence at an open market. Certain of the top private bankers, including Coutts, Drummond, Child, Thornton and Payne, were used for all government borrowing by the close of the American war. Loyal bankers in Scotland and the provinces who wished to secure government stocks had to convince their London correspondents that they and their clients were interested in the long term and would not sell for short-term profits. It did not work as well as the Treasury had hoped, but even in the hectic conditions of the early years of the French wars they operated with their favoured London bankers to curtail speculation. In this respect, with tighter prices and open market operations by the Commissioners for the Reduction of the National Debts, which 'tend very much to keep up the prices of the Funds', the emphasis was on long-term investment or as a reserve in London for bill transactions, with provincial men advised by their London houses.[43] There was, it must be emphasised, a fundamental difference between the American and the French wars. The Revolution threatened the British upper classes with the same fate as their cousins in France, and this fear dominated high finance after 1789. The Scottish banks, like all others, were expected to lend to the government and not to engage in speculation. The symbiosis of public and private interests within a political context and the threat from the personal consequences of invasion very much served to encourage the growth of these London reserves.

Thomas Coutts was importuned by customers about appointments in his office. After long experience, he came to realise that the higher the social class, the less fitted the offspring; the business would never 'thrive but in the management of those who have been in the early and long habits and who have by that means become fond of regularity and application'.[44] On occasion he took into his office the sons of peers, but they usually had too many distractions: 'young men so taken up may

41 For Samson Gideon's role, see above, Chapter 7.

42 The profits from these loans, offered only to a privileged few, were in the range of 7–11 per cent: Roseveare, *The Treasury: The Evolution of a British Institution*, p. 113.

43 Coutts & Co., archives, Special Letter Book: 21 October 1794, 5 October 1795.

44 Coutts & Co., archives, Special Letter Book: Thomas Coutts to Hon. Lord Ankerville, 19 June 1779, 10 May 1780.

attend a counting house at working hours and do the work that is then required but their hearts are absent'. To become a partner was 'a sort of drudgery' which only some young men disciplined from their early years took to. Indeed, in the nineteenth century, Coutts & Co. made a point of preferring the sons of the clergy, who knew about unremitting toil and were usually honest.

The London Scots' banking houses were an important part of the system of physical control within Scottish finance. They could exercise this by the amount that they were prepared to advance in normal times and, in times of crisis, by the sums advanced without collateral security. Coutts & Co. saved the Aberdeen Banking Company in 1782 by advancing £72,000 (uncovered by London funds), and in the early stages of the 1793 crisis they advanced an extra £30,000 to the Royal Bank, £50,000 to Bank of Scotland, and to Mansfield, Ramsay & Co. £80,000 over and above their agreed credit limits. Obviously, the earmarked funds held in London had a bearing on these sums, as did the larger reserves, and in this sense their existence was an acknowledgement that the system worked, being publicly-acknowledged funds to support bills of exchange with other reserves in London stocks. The effectiveness of a system can also be judged by how far discipline can be taken. The case of the Glasgow Arms bank (Murdoch and Robertson) indicated some of these limits and how far cooperation could go between the Royal Bank, the Bank, Coutts and the Edinburgh private bankers.

Coutts & Co. opened an account for the Glasgow Arms bank in 1752 and supported it by bill operations throughout the early years of difficulty. It was an open credit which, on occasion, saw a deficit of over £20,000 without the backing of London funds. It was, Thomas Coutts recalled, the only account that he allowed of this nature, in part because in the early years of the Arms bank the wealth of the partners in land, tobacco and sugar far exceeded liabilities. After two decades, Coutts even appeared nostalgic over the connection. In the aftermath of the Ayr crisis, his attitude slowly began to change. There appeared to be a problem in the institutional arrangements made for the provision of liquid funds by the Glasgow co-partnerships, all of which were in difficulties after June 1772. The Merchant bank temporarily stopped, and the Arms, the Ship and the Thistle requested loans from the Royal Bank and the Bank. Both the Merchant and the Ship were restructured with more partners in 1776 but remained minor trade banks for the rest of the century. The potential problem for these co-partnerships had always been the 'double' use of their capital, for trade as well as banking. In 1776, the American war raised further questions about the strength of their security. The Arms was the weakest bank and by 1784 was down to just two partners, Peter Murdoch and John Robertson; it was of concern to Thomas Coutts that the Arms relied on an assumption that others would take its bills of exchange and accept its banknotes in the belief (wrongly) that there were sufficient liquid assets to cover liabilities.

From 1772, the condition of the Arms bank was regularly monitored by Coutts, and in 1784, when its deficit reached £21,000 (£15,000 over its limit), Thomas Coutts insisted that another partner 'of known fortune' be brought in.[45] The Arms traded on the goodwill of the rest of the Scottish banks and the fear of repercussions should it have its bills refused. So low was its credit that attempts to find another London banker by the Arms' partners failed. At the occasion of the crisis of 1788, Coutts decided to close the account, as the Arms was around £14,000 in deficit: 'I have long expressed my dissatisfaction with your transactions and false delicacy has till now induced me to continue an account which is the only one in my books that makes me weary and is out of the road of my business'. It had a 'great many' bills due and, unless very careful, faced being protested.

> I am persuaded if you lay your affairs before the Royal Bank and can show them a solid fund they will not refuse you their support. Mr Ramsay is a friend of mine and is a man of a very liberal mind, write to him. I must be free to tell you that in my opinion your company is upon too small a scale for a bank and I must add that I think no private bankers should be allowed to circulate their notes especially it seems improper when the partners are at the same time concerned in trade or manufactures of any sort. If you should come to the determination of quitting the banking business I think you would find the greater disposition in those gentlemen to assist you.[46]

Coutts wrote the same day to inform William Cuming, the Royal Bank and Bank of Scotland. In the event, apart from protestation, there was no legal mechanism to enforce closure. However, the Arms found that its bills would only be paid if funds were already available, and it finally collapsed in the crisis of 1793.[47]

By the French Revolution of 1789, Scotland possessed the most advanced banking system in Europe outside London. It also proved a most stable platform for weathering the convulsions that followed the outbreak of war. At the apex of this system were Bank of Scotland and its allies among the political elite. Their 'takeover' of the Royal Bank in 1778 gave the country a strong first tier of public banks able to provide a substantial part of the credit needs of Scotland directly or indirectly

45 Coutts & Co., archives, Miscellaneous papers, 3 April 1784, Thomas Coutts to John Robertson; the Bank, the Royal Bank and William Cuming made the same point to the Arms Bank partners.
46 Coutts & Co., archives, Special Letter Book, 6 May 1788.
47 Munn, *The Scottish Provincial Banking Companies*, p. 49; the partners were able to pay all their liabilities.

through support for the provincial banks. The close connection of finance and high politics enabled the boards of Bank of Scotland and the Royal Bank to determine the structural arrangements which they felt most convenient whether by legislation at Westminster or by local agreements and understandings. Bank of Scotland also drew renewed benefits from its long-standing association with London Scottish houses. The advice given by Coutts directors, over many years, proved an invaluable second sight for the board in Edinburgh. Further, the overall Scottish system enabled the Scottish aristocracy and lairds to face the French Revolution and domestic unrest with one of the most effective parts of a rapidly-growing economy, namely long-term credit and a sound issue of banknotes backed, where required, by government.

CHAPTER 10

BANK OF SCOTLAND, 1793–1815

THE FRENCH REPUBLIC declared war on Great Britain on 1 February 1793. For the next nine years, until the peace of Amiens was signed on 15 March 1802, Britain was faced with unprecedented military expenditure. At first the war went well. William Pitt and Henry Dundas orchestrated a vast European reaction of monarch and noble against the Revolution. By August 1793, material and financial support was agreed by the government for Tsarist Russia, to the Prussian aristocracy, to the Spanish crown and to Austria, Sardinia and Hesse-Cassel, and troops were despatched to the Netherlands. It was a huge effort which meant soaring incomes for Scottish agriculture and manufactures whose products went to the armed forces of this alliance. By 1797, the first stage of the long struggle had largely failed. The British were routed in the Netherlands in 1794, Prussia sued for peace in 1795, French diplomacy persuaded the Spanish to declare war on the British on 8 October 1796, encouraged by fears of British colonial policy towards Latin America, and at Campo Formio (1797) the Austrian army was destroyed and its government forced out of the war. In April 1797, that part of the Royal Navy based at Spithead was convulsed by a mutiny whose demands the government met, followed by the mutiny of the Nore which was suppressed. Only in some colonial fighting and in Egypt were the British more successful, although at great cost in soldiers. On 2 April 1801, the British fleet attacked the Danes at anchor in Copenhagen harbour and sank seventeen ships, a carnage which humiliated the Danish government and ensured that the Danes remained pro-French for the rest of the war.

Throughout these war years, Henry Dundas was at the zenith of his political power. In 1794 he was appointed Secretary of War; he already had his India office and the Treasurership of the navy, and in 1800 he was made Keeper of the Privy Seal of Scotland. In the elections of 1796, his interest won thirty-six of Scotland's forty-five seats, the highest figure ever for Dundas, who was supported by all but a few of the sixteen representative peers.[1] He was Governor of Bank of Scotland, and his associate, the Duke of Buccleuch, was Governor at the Royal Bank. Shortly after the outbreak of war, both boards of directors were given a written guarantee, from himself, that if times proved hard the government would provide whatever support was required to underpin credit. No-one, he was fond of telling Scottish bankers, had done more for the banking interest and would do so for the future. There was considerable truth in this: indeed, so important did he regard the London Scottish banking companies that in the years after the French Revolution, Alexander Trotter of Dreghorn, Paymaster of the Navy, and George Swaffield and James Slade, Cashiers of the Navy Pay Office, maintained substantial balances of navy funds, drawn from the Bank of England, with Coutts & Co. Nevertheless, this power, which was exercised in the best interests of Scottish manufactures and commerce, coexisted with a rise in sustained political criticism by many in the middle classes. Dundas ruled on the basis of a tiny electorate; in 1790 this comprised only 2,665 voters, 1,318 of whom were non-resident appointees of the greater landowners who owned the superiorities. In twenty-nine seats there was no contest.[2] This electorate was strongly biased towards landed wealth and was unrepresentative not just of the professions and mercantile wealth, as it had always been, but also of the mass of new middle-class incomes and industrial concerns. The French Revolution encouraged considerable pressures for change in Scotland, not just for Parliamentary elections but also for burgh reform, for amendment of the system of appointments to government offices, for education and even, on the fringes, for land reform. Ultimately, after the peace of Amiens, Whig businessmen and lawyers began to think about the establishment of a bank unconnected with Henry Dundas and the Duke of Buccleuch.

Until 1794, the Whig and radical proponents of reform had made considerable inroads into public support: the academic community, the Faculty of Advocates and the middle classes of the burghs remained impressed by the swift removal of feudal institutions in France and the creation of more widely representative institutions than Scotland enjoyed. They were supported by some of the aristocracy, among whom was James, Earl of Lauderdale (representative peer from 1790 and director of Bank of Scotland), who challenged the Duke of Richmond to a duel, settled

---

1 H. Furber, *Henry Dundas, First Viscount Melville 1742–1811* (Oxford: 1931), Appendix A.
2 H. Meikle, *Scotland and the French Revolution* (Glasgow: 1912), p. 10; W. Ferguson, *Scotland: 1689 to the Present*, The Edinburgh History of Scotland, vol. iv (Edinburgh: 1968), p. 247.

by negotiation, over the royal proclamation on seditious writing, and who later fought General Benedict Arnold (pistols were fired though both missed).[3] Lauderdale further incensed his fellow Scottish aristocrats by endorsing the Revolution on a visit to Paris in August 1792. Dugald Stewart, Professor John Millar and other writers wrote and lectured on the general benefits of this new stage of society. Robert Burns supported the Revolution in verse, even sending three carronades to France in February 1792. Thomas Paine's *Rights of Man* had sold perhaps 200,000 copies in Britain by the time war was declared, and may have been translated into Gaelic.[4] It had an effective message: war was to be opposed, taxation should be voted through by taxpayers, public monies should go for beneficial ends, and there was to be an end to the 'old corruption' of appointments so skilfully used by Henry Dundas and his interest.

In spite of an increasingly violent Tory response, greatly encouraged by the arguments of Edmund Burke in *Reflections on the Revolution in France* (1790), Dundas was losing the argument within the middle and labouring classes before the war began. On George III's birthday, 4 June 1792, mobs smashed the windows of Tory supporters in Edinburgh, Glasgow, Dundee and Aberdeen and burnt Dundas in effigy.[5] The exceptional growth in the press, from eight newspapers in 1782 to over thirty by 1792, and the regular meetings and dinners to present demands for reform and to drink disloyal toasts were symptomatic of government weakness. In January 1793, Dundas tackled seditious publication and secured the outlawry of a minor publisher. Numerous prosecutions followed the outbreak of war, and in August Thomas Muir, a young advocate, was sentenced to fourteen years' transportation.[6] From this time, the tide of middle-class opinion turned in favour of the government, loyal addresses flooded in, and in August 1794 convictions in the case of the 'Pike Plot' secured a huge political benefit.[7]

From 1785 to early 1788 there had been a considerable increase in economic activity on both sides of the Border, and, although there was then a modest fall, the onward march of industry and trade was resumed in the summer of 1789 with unprecedented energy. The buoyancy of the economy was strengthened by activity in the financial markets, as gold and

3 *DNB*, vol. 12, pp. 799–800.
4 Ferguson, *Scotland: 1689 to the Present*, pp. 249–51.
5 Meikle, *Scotland and the French Revolution*, p. 81; Furber, *Henry Dundas*, ch. 3, 'The attack on Jacobinism, 1791–94'.
6 Meikle, *Scotland and the French Revolution*, ch. 6; H. Cockburn, *Examination of the Trials for Sedition in Scotland* (2 vols, Edinburgh: 1888, repr. in 1 vol., New York: 1970), ch. 7. There were other prosecutions, including those of Thomas Fyche Palmer and William Skirving, Maurice Margarot and Joseph Herald, which also ended in transportation; in 1845 an obelisk was raised in their memory in the Old Calton burying-ground.
7 Ferguson, *Scotland: 1689 to the Present*, pp. 259–60.

silver were smuggled out of France; huge increases in foreign and domestic trade brought extra income to shipping firms, and speculators crowded around Parliament with bills for new port, canal, turnpike and enclosure schemes.[8] The demand for increased banking facilities which was met in Scotland by the Bank and the Royal Bank, and to a lesser extent by the British Linen and the second-tier banks, was characterised in the south by a further spread of under-capitalised country banks with their inevitable over-issue of paper and discounts.[9] The Commissioners of the National Debt retired £9.4 million of the government-consolidated stocks in the six years to 1792, and the price of 3 per cent consols rose by 20 per cent in the two years to August 1792, with India stock up 25 per cent in the same time.[10] There was also a modest rise in government expenditure on the navy and on the ordnance in the four years before the war was declared.

Agricultural prices fell after the 1791 harvest, and within a year the expansion in the foreign trades had faltered.[11] It would have been most unlikely that the pace of growth could have continued in any event, but by October the political situation had worsened and belligerent speeches from the government party had led to a general erosion of confidence; consols and stock prices slipped, credit became more difficult to obtain, new schemes were shelved and the seasonal rise in bankruptcies was even more pronounced. The senior men at the Bank were fully aware of the harmful direction which this could take, and at the end of November the Secretary, James Fraser, penned a blunt warning to Henry Dundas. The historical record offered a repetition of the crises of 1772, 1782–3 and 1788: although 'it is easy weather at present, . . . such tempests as these or greater' could be close. 'In such situations, the present Inundation of paper money, issued from uncertain Capitals, would be dangerous in extreme. We have already seen great private Banking Companies, one in Scotland, and another in England, breaking, and leaving scarcely a Wreck behind them.'[12] The declaration of war on 11 February 1793 was the trigger: bills were returned unpaid, the Bank of England looked to its reserve and

8 D. S. Landes, *The Unbound Prometheus: Technological Change and Industrial Development in Western Europe from 1750 to the Present* (Cambridge: 1970), ch. 2.

9 For Bank of England circulation, bullion reserves and private securities, see A. D. Gayer, W. W. Rostow and A. J. Schwartz, *The Growth and Fluctuation of the British Economy 1790–1850* (2 vols, Oxford: 1953), vol. i, pp. 20–2; for discussion of the weak reserve position of English country banks, see L. S. Pressnell, *Country Banking in the Industrial Revolution* (Oxford: 1956), pp. 229–34.

10 Gayer, Rostow and Schwartz, *Growth and Fluctuation*, vol. i, pp. 22–3; while the impact is uncertain, some contemporaries thought that it contributed to speculation.

11 G. Hueckel, 'Agriculture during Industrialisation', in R. Floud and D. McCloskey (eds), *The Economic History of Britain since 1700*, 2 vols, vol. i, 1700–1860 (Cambridge: 1981), pp. 182–203.

12 BS 20/32/58, Melville Papers, 30 November 1792: James Fraser to Henry Dundas. Fraser was appointed Treasurer in June 1792, remained to oversee the Secretary's office, in 1802 stepped down as Treasurer (aged 76), and continued as Principal Secretary until his death in November 1808 (aged 82).

curtailed credit, stocks were held in warehouses and not forwarded to manufacturers, and domestic orders were cancelled. The early casualties were houses which had negotiated speculative bills for the foreign trades, and the banks with little capital and few reserves to pay bills in London. Dundas received numerous warnings from the Bank and the Royal Bank:

> the credit of the kingdom hangs at present by a very slender thread, owing in some degree no doubt to that unlimited dangerous nay pernicious extension of paper circulation . . . by private societies and which is now from an uncommon demand for London's money since the late and continued depression of the public funds, so severely felt by each [the Bank and the Royal], that they have been obliged for some time past to refuse to discount almost to any, even their best customers.[13]

The two boards met every weekday. They monitored the crisis, rearranged debts, and on 15 April agreed a joint loan of £20,000 to Stirling, Hunters & Co., a leading London export house, later increased to £25,000.[14] But the scale of the debts in Glasgow threatened to overwhelm the Royal Bank itself: the agency run by Scott Moncreiffe and David Dale at this time was the largest provider of credit in the west, and in spite of £150,000 provided by Bank of Scotland towards the end of April the Royal Bank faced closure. This was soon extended to £186,500. When James Fraser warned Dundas that 'To you Sir, the Directors look; to you the whole of this part of the United Kingdom looks, for exerting the powers and influence which providence has for such momentous occasions as the present, put into your hands', he meant exactly that. The crisis could only be solved at Westminster.

Dundas was presented with a scheme for Exchequer bills whereby a few senior banks would pay these over to lesser houses on the security of goods already in warehouses but held because of the inability of the purchaser to pay.[15] These Exchequer bills would thus pay off the bills of exchange, which would enable the banks to extend new credit and manufacturers to restart work. There would still be an obligation to pay the Exchequer bills, but that would be in the future, once trade had recovered. The key assumption was that the February crisis was a temporary interruption to

---

13 BS 20/32/60, Melville Papers: James Stirling to Henry Dundas, 25 February 1793.
14 BS 1/5, Minutes: 15 April and 24 August 1793.
15 R. Mitchison, *Agricultural Sir John: The Life of Sir John Sinclair of Ulbster 1754–1835* (London: 1962), pp. 137–8, points to Sir John's role as the originator of the scheme; the question is considered by J. H. Clapham, *The Bank of England. A History* (2 vols, Cambridge: 1944), vol i, 1694–1797, p. 264 note 4, who mentions the role of the City committees active during this period and whose members gave evidence to the Select Committee on 27 April. If Sinclair was the first to persuade Pitt of the scheme, and there is no evidence to the contrary, then the idea was quickly taken up. See also F. W. Fetter, *The Development of British Monetary Orthodoxy 1797–1875* (Cambridge, MA: 1965), p. 12ff.

trade, and thus the government would not be burdened with a long-term commitment to bankrupt manufacturers and banks; of this view Pitt and Dundas were probably convinced by Sir John Sinclair before the Parliamentary Select Committee was convened on 27 April. Nevertheless, to make quite certain that the case was properly made out, the Bank and the Royal Bank despatched James Mansfield and Innes of Stowe to appear before the Select Committee, and several of Dundas's interest from Glasgow also attended.

The relatively narrow scope required of government support for the west of Scotland and its likely effect on the crisis was summarised by William Macdouall, MP for Glasgow burghs:

> The present distress does not appear . . . to arise from a want of property or funds, but from the stop which has been lately been put to discounting bills at any of the Glasgow, Paisley or Greenock banks, who have not for some time past discounted to any extent, from their notes being poured in upon them for gold and from the alarm which the present situation of credit in London has occasioned . . . The manufacturers have plenty of goods on hand in London and in Glasgow which they cannot sell but at so reduced a price, as renders it perfectly absurd for them to think of disposing of their goods in order to obtain immediate relief.[16]

Innes of Stowe, for the Royal Bank, pointed to the likely scale of the crisis if aid was not forthcoming, and reiterated the Exchequer bill plan, that paper issued on government security and advanced on the deposit of goods 'or other unquestionable private security' would be suitable relief. The Select Committee needed little convincing, and the House endorsed the proposals for Exchequer bills on 29 April, with royal assent granted on 9 May.

Sir John Sinclair and the Scottish view were proved correct as a guide to the nature of the crisis. Application was made for £3,856,000 of the bills, yet only £2,202,000 (£400,000 in Scotland) was actually called, and this balm restored the workings of domestic trade. Over the next year, twenty-six English country banks closed, the Glasgow Arms bank and Andrew and George Thomson (a Glasgow private bank) also failed, and the Glasgow Merchant bank and the Edinburgh private bank of Bertram, Gardner & Co. were closed for a time.[17] But most companies

16 *First report from the Select Committee appointed to take into Consideration the present state of Commercial credit*, 29 April 1793, p. 9; repr. in S. R. Lambert (ed.), *House of Commons Sessional Papers of the Eighteenth Century*, vol. 88, *George III: Finance and Fees, 1792–93* (Wilmington: 1975), p. 59. William Macdouall of Castle Semple was a staunch supporter of William Pitt and Henry Dundas. He inherited estates in the West Indies and had excellent connections in the Glasgow trades; see R. G. Thorne (ed.), *The History of Parliament: The House of Commons 1790–1820* (London: 1986), vol. iv, *Members G–P*, pp. 491–3.

17 S. G. Checkland, *Scottish Banking: A History, 1695–1973* (Glasgow: 1975), pp. 218–20; C. W. Munn, *The Scottish Provincial Banking Companies, 1747–1864* (Edinburgh: 1981), pp. 49–51.

were able to resume normal working by the summer of 1793, helped by the increased flow of government funds for war materials as well as by the Exchequer bills. The crisis showed that the British banks supplied a crucial, if unquantifiable, volume of paper credit, and thus a collapse was to be feared because of their pivotal role in the industrial system.[18] This was the really important lesson for the Dundas interest at the pinnacle of its British influence.

The crisis forced the boards of the second-tier Scottish banks to be more cautious, as for several of their number the mixture of trade and banking had proved very nearly as fatal as it was for the Arms bank and the Thomson bank. It was also an object lesson to the Royal Bank and the Bank about the necessity for tight controls over their lending to the provincial banks. The Greenock Banking Company was one such case. It had four partners: James Dunlop of Garnkirk, a Glasgow merchant; Andrew Houston of Jordanhill; James Gammill, a Greenock merchant; and James Macdowall of Glasgow, who traded together under the name of Dunlop, Houston, Gammill & Co., bankers in Greenock.[19] The Royal Bank agency in Glasgow accepted their notes, as did Sir William Forbes in Edinburgh. The arrangements at Glasgow involved a charge of 5 per cent when Dunlop, Houston were in debit to the Royal Bank and 4 per cent when in credit. The important point was that Dunlop ran the Glasgow part of Dunlop, Houston and he also ran his own business; their overall circulation is unknown and was estimated at the time as between £100,000 and £200,000.

Dunlop stopped payment on his own account on 21 March 1793, at which time there was a balance of 'upwards' of £9,100 due to a cash account which he held with the Royal Bank. On 22 March, the day before he was told to close it, the Greenock bank was informed that it was liable. The legal case hinged on this: could Dunlop's actions in discounting bills bind his co-partnership? Under Scots law, Lord Kames had ruled on 22 January 1766 that such matters depended on the wording of the co-partnership and the transaction in question. English law tended to favour the other partners where they did not have prior knowledge, whatever the agreement. Thus Lord Mansfield ruled in December 1774 in the case of Alexander Fordyce that a guarantee of the house by a partner, even in his own writing and signature, to Hope & Co. (of Amsterdam) was not valid: 'any trick or connivance between the partners and the person with whom he deals to cheat the house by drawing them into a guarantee

18 On British banking at this time, see Fetter, *British Monetary Orthodoxy*, p. 24.
19 British Library, 1245 (h5) 1–8, 'Information for the Governor and Company of the Royal Bank of Scotland and William Simpson their Cashier . . .', 13 May 1794; the case is considered in Munn, *The Scottish Provincial Banking Companies*, p. 50.

clandestinely should make the guarantee void'. On that precedent, the House of Lords ruled that the claim by the Royal Bank lay only with Dunlop and could not be spread to the three other co-partners of the Greenock bank. Their bank remained open and eventually retired in 1813 with a part of their business transferred to Bank of Scotland.[20]

The crisis had another positive result in respect of the remittance of government funds in which Bank of Scotland had no share. As James Fraser, Secretary, Bank of Scotland, put it: 'It is a wrong Expression of the thing meant, to say, The Benefite of *Remitting* the public Money. The Benefite arises from *Keeping* it', adding: 'It is delicate to speak the Truth here'. The explanation was straightforward. Revenue was forwarded each quarter, from the collector to his banker, and was sent by bill drawn on London. The banker enjoyed the use of the funds before remittance, less interest paid to the collector and the use for the twenty days over par before the bill fell due.[21] It was later recorded by Bank of Scotland that, as it had to buy bills of any date falling due prior to their twenty-day draft, a part of the money was ready well before the time due. Profits after fees could thus be minimal.[22]

Government contracts were important sources of income for the three banks, and in 1789 a rise in the excise taxes gave Sir William Forbes a further advantage. Their banking reserve had hitherto consisted of Royal Bank and Bank of Scotland notes, but in the 1780s they started to issue their own and return the senior notes for a bill on London when the time came to remit. Thus the senior banks had their own circulation curtailed and they had to keep extra funds in London to pay these demands, funds that 'would otherways be employed in supporting and promoting the useful industry of Scotland'.[23] Sir William Forbes negotiated an agreement in 1790 to keep £50,000 at 3 per cent interest with Bank of Scotland and draw on a cash account for this sum. For several years the private firm was able to buy considerable holdings of Bank of Scotland stock, but never enough to exercise a decisive influence on the board.[24] Moreover, William Ramsay of Mansfield, Ramsay & Co., a leading director of the Royal Bank whose private banking house had some influence on the board, led a fierce campaign to have the excise transferred to the two senior banks. But problems emerged. First, William Pitt refused to condone any 'violent and partial step taken by Government to deprive some individuals of a benefit they possess in consequence of a connexion with Government which

20 BS 1/5, Minutes: 12 April 1813.
21 BS 20/32/50, Melville Papers, 30 November 1792, James Fraser to Henry Dundas.
22 BS 1/31/20, Letter book to agents: to Coutts & Co., 23 October 1809.
23 BS 20/32/10, Melville Papers, 25 February 1790, James Stirling to Henry Dundas.
24 BS 20/26/1, Agreements between the Royal Bank, Bank of Scotland and Sir William Forbes & Co., 21 January and 10 February 1790, 8, 11 and 14 May 1792, 5 May 1794; BS 1/5, Minutes: 8 February 1790.

Table 10.1 *Distribution of remittance of government funds business, 1793*

Bank	Description	Amount
Sir William Forbes, James Hunter & Co.	Excise	£250,000
Royal Bank of Scotland	Customs	£50,000
Royal Bank of Scotland	Land taxes, window taxes, house taxes and carriage taxes	£63,000
Royal Bank of Scotland	Stamp taxes	£58,500
Mansfield, Ramsay & Co.	Post Office	£32,000

they have done nothing by their own misconduct to forfeit'.[25] Second, in spite of the support given by Sir William Forbes to Sir Lawrence Dundas of Kerse in the struggle over control of the Royal Bank, Henry Dundas was unwilling to regard this, by itself, as sufficient. A successful political interest required accommodation with new parties and people. Dundas, who was on good terms with Sir William, stated that there had to be a compelling reason for the government to reconsider the remittance. The 1793 crisis provided the reason. Henceforth, it was one of Dundas's objectives to divide the public revenues into four parts, one each for the four banks of his interest, being the two private houses (Mansfield, Ramsay & Co.; Sir William Forbes, James Hunter & Co.) as well as the Bank and the Royal Bank. The British Linen was excluded (see Table 10.1).

In 1794, the board of Bank of Scotland considered proposals to supplant the provincial banks by a new-style branch system.[26] The Bank had few proprietors in the burghs wherein lay its agencies; the price of Bank stock was high and sales were rare. The board agreed to double the capital available to each branch by sales of stock to local residents at par, with half the profits to go to these proprietors. Local committees would help supervision, although they would not control staffing, policy and use of their money. The idea proceeded as far as the 1794 bill to increase capital and was kept distinct in the clauses from the main purpose of raising another £400,000. Yet Dundas was wary of the political problems that might result, and the proposals were dropped. The Royal Bank and the Bank also jointly canvassed a new joint-stock bank in Glasgow. The local burghers had failed to develop their own banking beyond the small capitals more typical of concerns south of the Border. But few Glaswegians came forward, and this project was also abandoned. With their increase in capital, both the Royal Bank and the Bank were enabled to increase their funds for the west.

From the summer of 1793, business made a swift recovery. The scale of government purchases continued upward in 1794 and 1795 and most,

25 BS 20/32/4, Melville Papers, 20 June 1789, Henry Dundas to William Ramsay.
26 BS 20/32/68, Melville Papers, James Fraser to Henry Dundas, 7 February 1794.

including the subsidies to allies, was actually spent in Britain. There was a sound position on the exchanges: gold continued to flow into the Bank of England in both years, the counterpart of the disappearance from everyday life of coin in France at the height of the inflation of their paper bonds, known as assignats.[27] Yet by the spring of 1795 the French government had begun to limit its issue of paper, and, with the gradual restoration of a gold coinage, considerable profits accrued to those able to smuggle gold into France.[28] The Bank of England 'wisely' limited its discounts and hence note issue as the reserve fell in 1796. The basic strength of the contemporary Scottish banking framework was undeniable; for nearly four years after the crisis of 1793, the position of the Bank and the Royal Bank was fortified from the spending on war supplies, from the commitment by Dundas to the balances at Coutts & Co. on which bills could be discounted, and by the controls on the issue of notes by the provincial banks. But this position was vulnerable to a short-term run on gold, and in the longer view the Bank and the Royal Bank required to think about extra reserves in London.

On 23 February 1797, a French squadron landed a small party at Fishguard on the Pembrokeshire coast. There was panic as the news spread. Gold was withdrawn from circulation, bills were stopped, and farmers in the coastal areas of Midlothian were ordered to drive cattle inland.[29] The board of Bank of Scotland and its astute official, James Fraser, came up with various ideas and sent these down to Dundas.[30] As gold drained from the circulation, the private bankers insisted on action, and on 26 February the Privy Council issued an order, commonly known as the Bank Restriction or the Suspension of Cash Payments, which represented one of the most important events in British financial history. By this and the terms of the two Parliamentary statutes of 13 May and 22 June 1797, which confirmed the Council ruling, it was agreed:

1. 'it shall not be lawful for the Governor and Company of the Bank of England to issue any cash in payment of any debt or demand whatsoever.' Gold and silver deposited with the bank could be paid out again to three-quarters of the face value and the remainder in notes.
2. The Bank of England, at the discretion of the Governor and Company, 'may advance for the accommodation of the persons dealing as bankers in London, Westminster and Southwark in cash any sums of money not exceeding £100,000 in the whole'.

---

27 By 32 George III c.61, Parliament banned the circulation of assignats within Great Britain.
28 Clapham, Bank of England, vol. i, pp. 268–9.
29 Checkland, Scottish Banking, p. 220.
30 BS 20/32/74, Melville Papers, 25 February 1797.

3. For Scotland, 'it shall and may be lawful to and for the said Governor and Company of the Bank of England upon application being made to them by and on the behalf of the Treasurer of the Bank called The Bank of Scotland or by and on the behalf of The Royal Bank of Scotland to issue and pay . . . for the sole use of the said banks such sum or sums of money in gold and silver as may be required not exceeding the sum of £25,000 for each of the said banks'.[31]

When the terms of the Privy Council order were known in Scotland, the bankers decided to follow the suspension. For this they required the concurrence of the Judges of the Court of Session, and on 1 March 1797 a number of their Lordships passed a resolution to this effect. Meetings in Edinburgh and Glasgow added further to the sense that the Scottish paper system would be maintained and, in effect, only small sums of gold and silver would be passed over the counter.[32] After 1797, small imports of coin from the Mint sufficed for everyday business. These years also saw relatively good relations with the provincial banks and the Edinburgh private banks. The system was sufficiently disciplined to halt any tendency to issue banknotes to the point where the exchanges would have been adversely affected. The Bank and the Royal Bank emphasised their dominance by their rescue of Alexander Houston & Co. in September 1798 when both agreed to extend £16,280 each for bills on Boyd, Benfield & Co.

The period from the winter of 1791–2 to the peace of Amiens saw the fastest rate of business growth in the history of Bank of Scotland since its foundation, supported by the expansion of capital and deposits. The total credit to the profit and loss account of £31,013 in the former year rose to an average of £89,200 in the three years ending March 1802. In this decade, bills on London expanded fourfold and inland bills within Scotland sixfold, and income from branches (mainly cash accounts and bills) went from £19,580 to £68,215 by 1800–1. By 1804, Bank of Scotland was the most important discounter of bills in the west of Scotland, their value exceeding even that of the Royal Bank. The two banks had been severely tested by the two serious banking crises, first in 1793 and again in 1797 on the occasion of the suspension of cash payments. Both crises involved timely action by leading politicians, including Henry Dundas working in conjunction with the Scottish bankers, the Bank of England and the leading Scottish private bankers in London. The increase in Bank of Scotland capital encouraged an increased purchase of London stocks.

---

31 Coutts & Co., archives, Miscellaneous papers; the terms of the Privy Council order, 26 February 1797, were reiterated by 37 George III c.45 (3 May 1797) and by 37 George III c.91 (22 June 1797).
32 BS 20/32/74, Melville Papers, 4 March 1797; Sir William Forbes, *Memoirs of a Banking House* (Edinburgh: 1860), pp. 83–4.

From this decade emerged the view that in uncertain trading conditions, where large numbers of bills required re-discounting, the London money markets would be reassured by the knowledge that Bank of Scotland had significant holdings. By March 1796, the book value of Navy and Victualling bills was £376,376; Exchequer bills £81,830; Bank of England stock £144,000 (market value £249,500); 5 per cent annuities £85,000; Bank of Scotland stock £21,883 (market value £30,188) and East India stock £5,000. The market value of all the Bank's holdings at this time was £844,155. Coutts & Co., as noted above, extended varying credit to Bank of Scotland with the right to sell stock if the Bank's debit become too onerous.

The results of the first nine years of war for Scottish banking were generally positive; there was sustained support for domestic industry and commerce and some colonial success which helped foreign markets. But the almost total failure in Europe meant that the insistence by William Pitt and Henry Dundas on total victory was unsustainable; in 1801 they bowed to the inevitable, and negotiations followed. This was a political defeat which had serious consequences for Bank of Scotland and the Royal Bank. Pitt and Dundas were replaced by Henry Addington, who became first Lord of the Treasury, in February 1801.[33] Addington had made his name as a reactionary Speaker of the House of Commons committed to the war and repression, but one who believed from 1799 that a stalemate had been reached and that further fighting between an immovable land power and the might of the British navy was unlikely to bring about a decisive outcome. Thus, to save unnecessary expense, peace should be negotiated. Addington was alive to the costs to the taxpayer of the foreign subsidies abroad, the costs of grain imports and the temporary depreciation of the pound sterling on foreign exchanges in 1799. He was a good listener to complaints of distress from shire members, and with the treaty of Amiens he gave the tired and war-weary the promise of lower taxes, abolition of the income tax, an expansion of trade and drastic reductions in the costs of the armed forces.[34] The main army was reduced to 95,000 and the navy from 130,000 to 70,000, and in 1802 Addington saved £25 million. Important accounting reforms were brought into the Treasury, and naturally Addington won the election of 1802. By contrast, there was a decline in the position of Henry Dundas: he was down to thirty-one MPs out of forty-five, and five of the sixteen representative peers were his opponents.[35] Pitt and Dundas supported Addington in public;

33 Henry Addington, first Viscount Sidmouth, better known to history as the initiator of repression in later years.
34 J. S. Watson, *The Reign of George III 1760–1815* (Oxford: 1960), p. 402ff.
35 B. P. Lenman, *Integration, Enlightenment and Industrialisation, Scotland, 1746–1832* (London: 1981), p. 107.

they appreciated the mood of the country and wished to avoid offence to George III, who favoured Addington. The king continued his drift into nervous and psychological disorder, and his grip on political reality was slowly ebbing.

In the short-lived interval between the peace of Amiens and the British declaration on 17 May 1803 of war on France, loans and discounts by Bank of Scotland sharply increased, and in that year total credits to profit and loss rose a further 12 per cent. The fears of renewed warfare and the agricultural crisis of 1803 resulted in a number of bankruptcies. The directors appreciated the dangers as early as January 1803. Agents were ordered to curtail credit and follow their strict rules on loans and discounts except *in extremis*, and in particular to prefer only 'the steady friends of the Bank'. Yet all the evidence of the weekly returns confirmed that some agents ignored this advice: the Perth branch busily funded the changeover from the linen to the cotton trade which marked the business life of the burgh at this time by bills of exchange repeatedly renewed. The Haddington agent funded his own business activities and that of his friends; the west-coast agencies of Greenock and Glasgow 'pay no attention to [our] instructions'. The St Andrews agent was simply rolling over £5,000 of bills on speculation in commodities. It was difficult for the directors not to be caught up with the euphoria of the export boom to continental markets. The directors admitted that their hopes for peace had encouraged some laxness in lending, but with the renewal of hostilities they ordered a retrenchment to a ceiling of £4.2 million a year (£83,600 a week) for agencies plus an unspecified sum to be allowed to be lent at head office. Specific orders for weekly maxima were issued to all agents.[36] The directors hoped for peace because their investments in the government funds used to support their credit at Coutts had fallen as a result of the war and could not be sold, except at a loss.

By July 1803, the situation of the banking system on both sides of the Border was critical. The Royal Bank advised an immediate joint application to government for an issue of Exchequer bills, on similar lines to those for the crisis of 1793. As ever, Coutts & Co. sat in the middle, between their near-hysterical correspondents in Scotland and the government of Henry Addington. On 15 July, Coutts was informed by directors of Bank of Scotland that 'they see the continuing encrease of bankruptcies in this part [of the UK] and credit and confidence everyday growing worse. The two banks established here by law have endeavoured to give aid as far as they can but it is not sufficient to stem the present tide.' The problems were explained at length by the four main banks (the Bank; the Royal

36 BS 1/21/1, Private Letter Book, 25 May 1803.

Bank; Coutts; Smith, Payne & Smith). The Royal Bank and the Bank had lent much more – almost 20 per cent – in 1802–3 than in 1801–2; government cutbacks in expenditure on the supply of stores had forced a number of merchants and manufacturers to re-discount bills, and the banks – all the Scottish banks – had little choice but to accept these or precipitate a crisis. Further, six new provincial banks were launched in 1802 and 1803, all eager to expand credit.[37] Manufacturers in difficulties offered only long-dated securities, but these could not be realised in the crisis except at a severe discount. There was also a severe problem within Coutts & Co. because of the withdrawal of the balances deposited by Alexander Trotter of Dreghorn. Extra credits in London at Coutts, at Smith, Payne & Smith and at the Bank of England would require funds from Scotland for their support. The occasion demanded some government paper, the ideal being Exchequer bills.

Coutts was asked to address 'yourselves to such persons as you think most proper for producing the desired effect', and forwarded detailed reports of the collapse of financial and merchant houses to ministers.[38] Addington was quite unable to appreciate the extent of the industrial and commercial crisis which his retrenchment had done so much to encourage. All his prejudices were those of the extreme Tory and country party. Aware of how the Scottish banks provided sustenance to the Melville interest, he exaggerated their influence; the small size of the electorate was more important. He recommended Dundas for a peerage and thereby succeeded in damaging Dundas's relations with William Pitt. There was, further, some general antipathy among English shire MPs for any aid to Scotland.

In support of Addington, there sat as joint-secretary at the Treasury Nicholas Vansittart, later Baron Bexley. Vansittart was a skilled diplomat who had been sent to Denmark in February 1801 to detach their court from the French. To his surprise, the Danes rejected his overtures. He proved as keen as Addington on retrenchment, and together they rejected the pleas of Coutts & Co. and Scottish banks, and of other private banks in London. Instead, they offered their good offices to the Bank of England and suggested an increased credit for the re-discount of good bills.[39] This, of course, was a direct rebuff to the Scottish banks. Vansittart acknowledged that the Royal Bank and the Bank were also the proper vehicles for these credits, but, as to Exchequer bills, he termed these 'legislative interference' and was certainly not about to transfer any more public funds

---

37 Munn, *The Scottish Provincial Banking Companies*, p. 58.
38 Coutts & Co., Special Letter Book, 24 May 1803; BS 1/21/1, Private Letter Book, 15 July 1803.
39 BS 1/21/1, Private Letter Book, to the Lord Chief Baron, 30 July 1803.

to Coutts.[40] An exasperated Thomas Coutts wrote on 8 August 1803 to Bank of Scotland that Coutts had forwarded the replies to Vansittart's refusal from the two Scottish banks to Vansittart and the Lord Chief Baron, but had experienced unusual difficulty in securing an audience: 'we entirely agree in sentiment with you both as to the inefficiency of the move proposed by Mr Vansittart and that the only practicable way [of solving the crisis] being that of the issue of Exchequer bills'.[41]

The refusal to grant relief had entirely expected results. By the end of the first week of August 1803, there was a sharp rise in demand for cash; the Royal Bank panicked and insisted that 'protection against payments in specie similar to what the banks of England and Ireland possess' was essential. The only legislative protection then in place was the original clause of 1797 for drawing rights of £25,000, already exhausted. Henry Dundas, now the first Viscount Melville, could do little; his past assurances were now worthless, and his only influence was as a member of the Privy Council and the peerage. In public, the Royal Bank and the Bank tried to pretend that nothing was amiss (which few believed) and that their own gold reserves were substantial (which was untrue), and they kept bags of gold in view of customers who entered their head offices. The crisis of 1803 in Scotland lasted well into 1804 and caused a wave of unnecessary bankruptcies which might have been staved off by government credit. It confirmed the urgent need to remove Vansittart and Addington from office, and ensured rock-like support for Melville from all Parliamentary Scots, Whig or Tory, when the time came.

The refusal to issue bills meant that the proprietors of Bank of Scotland had to carry a financial burden in the shape of more bad debts, even when their customers were not the original defaulters. The ramifications of retrenchment were thus widespread. A £6,000 internal fund for answering losses, established in 1803, proved inadequate, and profits paid to the profit and loss account fell by 7 per cent in 1803–4. Both the refusal of bills and the fears of a run on cash forced the directors of both senior banks to order a further curtailment of credits, at the end of 1803, at precisely the time when the opposite was required. By October 1803, when all political avenues were exhausted and Addington was still firmly in office, the two

---

40 Checkland, *Scottish Banking*, pp. 274–5; Glasgow Chamber of Commerce passed resolutions requesting the issue of Exchequer bills to support trade in 1793, 1803, 1810 and 1826.

41 Coutts & Co., archives, Special Letter Book, 8 August 1803 to James Fraser, Bank of Scotland; Coutts failed again later that year to interest Addington in their request for the government to intervene with the French in 1803 over the detention of the Earl of Elgin in Paris: 'Lord Elgin's case seems so particularly cruel and distressing in every circumstance and at the same time so extremely unjust and unmerited'. Elgin was on his way back from Greece, and the French were annoyed that he, not they, had saved the famous Parthenon marbles for posterity (21 December 1803); S. G. Checkland, *The Elgins, 1766–1917: A Tale of Aristocrats, Proconsuls and Their Wives* (Aberdeen: 1988), ch. 7.

banks decided to appeal to Parliament to double their funds from £1 million to £2 million each, to come in the first instance from existing shareholders, though the banks later dropped this to £1.5 million each.

Increases in capital for Bank of Scotland and the Royal Bank in the eighteenth century had proved complicated, as there was potential opposition from a number of vested interests, notably the East India Company and the Bank of England. The presence of Henry Dundas (as he then was) ensured success; but with him (now Melville) on the sidelines and uncertainty about the reaction of the government party, little could now be taken for granted. From early November, representatives of both banks spoke to every important person in the Scottish interest. They were assured of support in the Lords, but the Vansittart–Addington interest could muster over sixty members in the Commons, and a clash had to be avoided if the bills were to succeed. The joint instructions to Alexander Fraser, Bank of Scotland solicitor in London, on 2 February 1804 were blunt. The aid of Sir William Pulteney, 'one of the richest commoners of the Empire', was to be enlisted in moving and carrying the bills. Pulteney, originally from Westerhall, Dumfries, and latterly of the Castle, Shrewsbury, represented the latter town, and was a strong supporter of Addington's policy of retrenchment. An opponent of Pitt, he was an excellent choice.[42] Nevertheless, a solicitor was too junior for this task; Pulteney would be approached by James Mansfield, the Edinburgh private banker, and the Lord Advocate. If, however, Fraser thought it was a mere matter of form (which it was not), 'you may get any respectable member a friend of the present administration to present it. *But you must on no account take any person inimical or even dubious with regard to the Minister* [Vansittart] because the bill proceeds upon the idea of its being agreeable to administration.'[43] The main 'idea' expected to calm government fears was the intention to raise money only from existing proprietors, and, although this merely followed previous practice, the precedent was not mentioned.[44] The bill also included tougher penalties for forgers of banknotes. Parliamentary agents for Sir William Forbes & Co., and for several provincial banks, objected to the wording of this last clause, 'though they were sensible enough not to antagonise Pulteney'.[45]

By the time the Act, 44 George III c.23 (1804), had passed the Commons, Addington was in difficulty. He lost two crucial motions, on 23 and

42 Thorne (ed.), *The History of Parliament*, pp. 902–4.
43 BS 1/21/1, Private Letter Book, to Alexander Fraser, 11 February 1804.
44 BS 20/4/1, 'A bill for further increasing the capital stock of the Governor and Company of the Bank of Scotland', 1804.
45 BS 20/4/1, 13/14 March 1804, Alexander Mundell to Sir Wm Forbes, James Hunter & Co.; 17 March 1804.

25 April 1804, and Pitt, the only serious choice and successor, returned to power on 7 May after tedious negotiations with a distraught king. Nicholas Vansittart was dismissed in June, but before he departed he had a last foray against the Scottish banks. Vansittart was influenced by the strange notion that if a bank took back its own banknotes and then reissued them, it constituted an 'extra' issue of paper instead of maintaining the same level. He was determined to curtail Scottish banknotes and force the destruction of old stamped paper. No notes over 10 guineas were to be reissued at all, and all smaller notes were to be valid for only one year after the stamped date. As large notes (£100, £50, 10 guineas) were regularly taken in and reissued in Scotland, sometimes several times a day in the course of ordinary bank transactions, the proposal would have levied a tax on business and damaged the efficiency of the system. Scottish MPs and peers were deluged with complaints, and the proposals were defeated. In deference to George III, William Pitt consoled Vansittart with the Secretaryship for Ireland, from which office he proceeded to harass the Bank of Ireland. Nicholas Vansittart represented the extreme party, although his views were to cast long shadows into the future.[46]

Unfortunately for Bank of Scotland and the Royal Bank, the welcome return of William Pitt and Viscount Melville marked only a short interlude before the enemies of Melville orchestrated his second downfall. While in office, Addington had established a Commission of Naval Enquiry to investigate the extent to which Melville, when Treasurer, and Alexander Trotter of Dreghorn his paymaster, had kept naval funds in bank accounts other than those with the Bank of England. Under Acts sponsored by, among others, Edmund Burke in 1780 and thereafter, Parliamentary and Treasury scrutiny of public accounts and the dispersal of public monies was made more penetrating than previously; for instance, the paymasters of the forces and the Treasurer of the navy were to keep their public funds at the Bank of England and not, as so often was the practice, with their private bankers.[47] Alexander Trotter and the navy pay office cashiers had indeed kept their accounts thus, but withdrew funds for current use, which they were legally entitled to do, and placed these at Coutts & Co., where they duly accumulated along with other funds. As noted above, this had the effect of supporting the huge increase in the London–Scottish bill trade. The hectic situation of the anti-Jacobin war and the need for speed in payments required Dundas (as he then was) to use both the Bank of England and Coutts to manage the enormous

46 This episode was a much more serious threat to the Scottish banks than the later attempt to abolish the £1 note; see below, Chapters 13 and 15.
47 These Acts were part of a process of administrative reform which Henry Dundas opposed; H. Roseveare, *The Treasury: The Evolution of a British Institution* (London: 1969).

increase in naval expenditure. That was acceptable, and the Commons endorsed specific government support for Boyd, Benfield & Co., but the more general support for trade seemed less defensible to a hostile audience. The Lords' investigation for the impeachment even went so far as to order Coutts to supply the complete accounts of its dealings with Melville, although fortunately for Melville, Coutts, which took its Scottish responsibilities seriously, was able to provide sufficient information to Parliament without going so far as to compromise the relationship with its client. It was a political investigation, and the conclusions reached by the committee were entirely to be expected.

Melville was charged with corrupt practices. In the Commons the vote was tied, with 216 each for and against, and the Speaker voted against Melville and for criminal proceedings. Melville was on the defensive; Pitt was forced to say that he would no longer support him for office; it was a bitter personal blow which, of course, did serious damage to the Scottish interest. Melville's friends feared that a criminal case in the courts could be worse than an impeachment before his peers.[48] The trial opened in 1806 before one of the largest attendances the Lords had seen. The more serious charges were: (1) that after 10 January 1786 Melville 'allowed' Alexander Trotter of Dreghorn to place sums withdrawn from the Bank of England into new accounts at Coutts; (2) that some of these funds then went to non-naval purposes; and (3) that in 1803 Melville and Trotter (and unnamed associates) destroyed as much evidence as they could. The prosecution, led by the Solicitor General and Samuel Whitbread, the brewer, made a most effective case. The various routes and personages by which funds had been sent to and from Scotland were analysed. The names of Coutts & Co., Smith, Payne & Smith, Mansfield, Ramsay & Co. and Sir William Forbes, Sir James Hunter & Co. were brought up, as were a number of agents in Scotland and London, including David Staig, the Bank of Scotland agent at Dumfries. By the close of the prosecution and interrogation of witnesses, including Trotter, one of whose payment books was reprinted by the prosecution, a case against Melville had been established; indeed, on two clauses (including that of destroying evidence) the votes were reasonably close (83 to 52 and 88 to 47), although the margin was wider on the remainder. Most of the Scots voted ten to nil in Melville's favour, as did the majority of Tories, the royal princes and the heir to the throne. Lauderdale gave Melville seven guilty votes and only three in support.[49] Weakened by 1802, his interest was even more damaged thereafter. In the general election of 1807, only twenty-four out

48 Watson, *The Reign of George III*, pp. 419–20.
49 House of Lords, *The trial of Henry, Lord Viscount Melville* (London: 1806).

of forty-five MPs were identified with Melville's interest together with fifteen of the peers, led by Buccleuch and Robert Dundas, Melville's son.[50]

Although Melville was acquitted, the result was of immense significance for Scottish banking. Henceforth, there was a perceptible decline in the regulatory role and prestige of Bank of Scotland and the Royal Bank. The first important change went through while Melville still faced his prosecutors. Entirely in secret, the British Linen, with all correspondence handled by its general manager, persuaded the Crown to grant a new charter which authorised an increase in capital from £100,000 to £200,000. The boards of the Royal Bank and the Bank first heard of this when the grant of the charter was announced.[51] The British Linen had thus broken out of its straitjacket of almost four decades. Further, there were stirrings among the proprietors of the senior banks. Neither board felt able to call up any of the new stock taken up by proprietors. The two boards felt susceptible to stockholder criticism of favouritism towards the private banking companies. In August 1805, the Bank and the Royal Bank began discussions on the cessation of interest payments to Sir William Forbes & Co., 'the main reason being that Forbes will naturally draw out their money when scarce in the country and load the Banks with it when [plentiful]'.[52] But the tide was turning in public life, and criticisms in March 1807 resulted in replacement of half the ordinary directors of Bank of Scotland and a change in the rules so that three were retired each year. In 1807 and 1808, determined efforts were made by a minority of Bank of Scotland proprietors to remove representatives of private and provincial banks from the board; they failed, but the Bank's position was weakened.[53] Sir William Forbes died in 1806 and William Ramsay in 1807. There was no-one with their authority to succeed them.[54]

In 1810, the British Linen board decided that its new capital of £200,000 was insufficient and should be raised to £500,000. This required a third charter. Spencer Perceval was now First Lord of the Treasury and Chancellor of the Exchequer. Intensely interested in economic matters, he headed a strong Tory government supported by the Melville–Buccleuch interest and their allies, so it was inevitable that British Linen would be opposed. The application ran into the Byzantine intrigue surrounding the Regency Bill. In November 1810, the king's favourite (and youngest)

50 Lenman, *Integration, Enlightenment and Industrialisation*, pp. 107–9; Watson, *The Reign of George III*, pp. 418–20.
51 BS(BL) 6/6, Minutes: 10 February and 21 July 1806; British Linen Company, Charter, 1806; 'Proceedings in and on the 5 June 1806. Application at the Treasury for an increase of capital by the British Linen Company' (London: 1813).
52 BS 20/26/1, Draft agreement of the Royal Bank and Bank of Scotland not to pay interest to Sir William Forbes & Co. on deposit accounts after 1 January 1806, 12 December 1805.
53 BS 1/5, Minutes: 27 March 1807.
54 Checkland, *Scottish Banking*, pp. 166–8.

daughter, Princess Amelia, died of smallpox, which triggered a further bout of his melancholy. Perceval brought in a Regency Bill which was finally signed by a dubious 'commission' standing in for royal assent on 5 February 1811. The Prince Regent was delighted. In 1806 he had voted for the first Viscount Melville at the impeachment, and now he helped the second Viscount by blocking the charter application.

The arguments used by the Bank and the Royal Bank in 1810–11, and again in 1813 when the British Linen reapplied, were archaic and legalistic. It was, they insisted, important that the British Linen be kept to its original charter aim of support for the linen trade, and they supported this by quotations from Judge Blackstone and English lawyers on the limitation of a corporation's powers. There was no need of another public bank – the two senior banks were sufficient. If the British Linen was allowed to raise its capital, it would over-issue; the government intended an adequate return for the proprietors of the senior banks, and the British Linen would threaten this.[55] Whereas there were sound monetary arguments against an increase in paper in 1810 and 1811, this was less important by 1813; grain prices had fallen, the exchanges had settled down and the economy was in an upward phase.[56] Unfortunately for the Bank and the Royal Bank, in 1813 the Earl of Liverpool was First Lord of the Treasury and Nicholas Vansittart was now Chancellor, with Addington, now Lord Sidmouth, as Home Secretary. Their antipathy to paper money combined with their even stronger antipathy to the Melville–Buccleuch interest, and they recommended the British Linen charter to the Prince Regent.

The Bank had suffered an erosion of income after the 1803–4 crisis, which continued to be aggravated by the competition from the provincial banks. The provincials had long tried to encourage deposits by paying a higher rate. The chief difficulty for all three chartered banks this time was the growing success of the provincials' lending and the fact that more burghs were covered: several paid 3½ and even 4 per cent on six-month deposits.[57] Bank of Scotland was forced to follow suit or face the erosion of its deposits. The directors of Bank of Scotland had other reasons for concern, namely the evident weakness of their political interest and the realisation in 1801 that their bank agent at Haddington had lost over £120,000, mostly unsecured, which, of course, was kept secret from proprietors.[58] Strict new measures of control over agents were imposed. On 27

55 Coutts & Co., archives, Miscellaneous papers: 'Memorial of the Governor, deputy-Governor and directors of Bank of Scotland & the Governor, deputy-Governor and directors of the Royal Bank of Scotland. To his Royal Highness the Prince Regent' (1811); BS 1/5, Minutes: 15 October 1810; BS 20/20/2–3, British Linen Company papers.
56 Gayer, Rostow and Schwartz, Growth and Fluctuation, vol. ii, Tables on prices.
57 Munn, The Scottish Provincial Banking Companies, ch. 3, section 2, for expansion after 1800.
58 See below, Appendix 7, and Statistical Appendix, Table A1.

June 1801, accountants were ordered to attend the agents for working out the weekly states. Controls from head office over agents were tightened. From August, regular unannounced inspections were brought in. More rigorous assessment of branch profitability led to closures at Paisley and Greenock. An increase was agreed from £30,000 to £50,000 in the mutual credit arrangements between the Bank and the Royal Bank, more funds were lodged with Coutts in London, and in April 1809, a full year before the commercial crisis of 1810, Bank of Scotland agreed to curtail discounts and cash accounts. From a nadir of 1803–4, trade recovered by 1809 to just above its best previous levels, and at a lower price level; only in the boom year of 1809–10 did profits show a marked rise, to £108,940, up 7–8 per cent on 1798 and 1799.

The decline in the power of Henry Dundas did not immediately affect attempts to control the activity of the provincial companies. Three in particular, the Falkirk Union Banking Company (founded in 1803 with fourteen partners), the Falkirk Banking Company (1787) and the Galloway Banking Company of Castle Douglas (1806) gave cause for concern in 1809 and 1810. A committee of the Royal Bank and the Bank of December and January 1808–9 found that their own notes had been withdrawn by the two Falkirk companies. Retaliation for this note-picking was swift. On Monday 23 January, the Falkirk Union was presented with a demand for £3,228 (for Bank of Scotland, Royal Bank or Bank of England notes, or cash) and the older company for £11,426. Both refused at first but paid the following day.[59] Bank of Scotland demanded its full legal costs and publicly announced its refusal to accept the Falkirk notes. It was a clear response to the iron traders, although not sufficient to persuade the Falkirk companies to modify their lending policy. Both were in severe difficulty in 1810.

An interesting case of regulation occurred over the Galloway Banking Company, founded in 1806 as a trade, agricultural and industrial bank for Kirkcudbrightshire and Wigtownshire in the south-west of Scotland.[60] The principal partner was Sir William Douglas of Castle Douglas, an industrialist with a long commitment to local trade and industry, whose intention it was to provide more support than that available from the local branches of Bank of Scotland and the British Linen Company. Initial assurances were given by the partners that they would confine their activity to an office covering the immediate area around Castle Douglas 'on which assurances the Bank of Scotland . . . agreed to take their notes at . . . Dumfries, Kirkcudbright and Wigton'.[61] The Galloway company opened

59 BS 1/5, Minutes: 25 and 30 January 1809.
60 Munn, *The Scottish Provincial Banking Companies*, pp. 60–1.
61 BS 1/5, Minutes: 27 February 1809.

offices in Kirkcudbright and Dumfries, and, in the time-honoured manner pushed its own notes in circulation against those of other banks: 'persons on the part of the [GBC] go through the shops and public houses in Dumfries and the adjacent country asking for notes of Bank of Scotland . . . [they] have even come into the Bank of Scotland office and solicited such an exchange'.[62] Offers were made of bills on London at thirty days at par instead of the usual twenty days. George Sandy, Secretary of Bank of Scotland, collected £28,189 of the GBC notes and on 20 February went to Castle Douglas to demand payment for £4,000. The GBC refused anything but a bill on Edinburgh, and in the ensuing argument issued an instrument for legal action against Bank of Scotland for £50,000 in damages. On 1 March, the GBC agents in Edinburgh paid up plus four days' interest. The Company continued until 1821 when it faced losses on bills for the cattle trade of £55,000 and withdrew from business.[63] The post-war depression from 1815 was to provide a severe lesson to the smaller banking companies over the dangers of enthusiastic banknote issue and over-indulgent bill discounting. When partners understood the basic rules and refrained from note-picking, then relations with the senior banks in Edinburgh were generally amicable. Occasionally, temporary rules were imposed, such as on the Dundee Union bank, founded in 1809 with eighty-five partners. The Bank agreed to take its notes, but only at the branch in Dundee.

After the second British Linen charter of 1806, the most serious breach in the dominance of the Royal Bank and the Bank came from the Whig political interest in Edinburgh. At the close of 1810, numerous Whigs signed a co-partnership agreement for a joint-stock bank, to be called the Commercial Bank of Scotland, with a nominal capital of £3 million. Their only legal requirement was to register with the burgh council, and by December 1815 673 shareholders had paid the first call of 20 per cent, by which time the shares stood at a premium of 50 per cent.[64] The Commercial Bank thus had more shareholders than the three chartered banks put together. The Whigs first asked Lord Moira to act as Governor, and when he refused they asked the Earl of Lauderdale, a strong symbol of Whig politics although in later years more of a cross-party elder statesman.[65] The Commercial board subscribed to a visionary image of its role:

> the previously formed establishments have long acted solely on a policy
> of security rather than of subserviency to the advancement of the trading,

62 Ibid., 10 April 1809.
63 Munn, *The Scottish Provincial Banking Companies*, p. 73.
64 'Abstract of the Articles of Co-partnery of the Commercial Banking Company of Scotland' [GL 1810]; the co-partnership was fixed at forty-five years from 25 March 1810, with shares of £500. See J. Anderson, *The Story of the Commercial Bank of Scotland Limited during its Hundred Years from 1810 to 1910* (Edinburgh: 1910).
65 Checkland, *Scottish Banking*, pp. 284–94, for the early years of the Commercial Bank.

manufacturing and agricultural interests of the country, a great proportion of their capital being permanently invested in the Government funds, so that in truth a very great proportion of the banking business of the country came to be done by and the circulating medium to consist of the notes and obligations of one two or more individuals associated together in the different districts and private companies.[66]

This view was reiterated by the Whig press. Henry Cockburn, the Whig advocate who sat on the board, later underlined this view in a strict but not wholly unfriendly appreciation of the Edinburgh banks of 1810:

> The rise of the Commercial bank marks the growth of the public mind . . . the principle on which [it] was erected must be understood. No men were more devoid of public spirit and even the proper spirit of their trade than our old Edinburgh bankers. Respectable men they were but without talent, general knowledge or any liberal objects they were conspicuous sycophants of existing power. What else could they have been? All the Whig business of the country would not have kept them going for a week, and the Government dealt out its patronage in the reception and transmission of the public money only to its own friends. So they all combined banking with politics. Not that they would discount a bad bill to a Tory, or refuse to discount a good one to a Whig; but their favours and graciousness were all reserved for the right side. A demand for a bank founded on more liberal principles was the natural result of this state of things . . . hence the origin of the Commercial, professing to be the bank of the Citizens.[67]

Cockburn went on to deny that the Commercial acted as a political engine and that its main effort 'deeply and silently improved the condition of our middle classes', a view echoed by several historians. In the sense that more facilities for banking meant more opportunities, Cockburn's general thesis may be agreed with; in the crisis of 1810, for example, Bank of Scotland was perhaps too cautious in advances on cash accounts. Many of the early staff came from the old banks: Edward Robertson, the first Secretary of the Commercial, came from Bank of Scotland; Alexander Shiells, the first teller, was also a Bank man, and recommended by Alexander Young ws, an official of the Bank. The three chartered banks and the private banks took its notes on a normal exchange basis; Lord Elphinstone even ordered an armed guard for them. As regards differences between the Commercial's lending pattern and that of the two senior banks, the Commercial was exceptionally careful in the early stages of its business, and as its directors concentrated on persons whom they knew in the Whig

---

66 RBS CS/13/1, Commercial Bank, Minutes, 17 December 1811.
67 H. Cockburn, *Memorials of His Time* (Edinburgh: 1856), new edn (Edinburgh: 1910), pp. 238–40; J. Simpson, *Scottish Banking: A Historical Sketch* (Edinburgh: 1877), p. 34.

business community in and around Edinburgh, it made few losses and even managed a profit of £5 12s 5¼d in the first year.[68] The Commercial lent, like all other banks, to its shareholders, which meant that much of its early lending was to persons of substance. It insisted on proper security. There is some evidence that it was prepared to be more adventurous for the Edinburgh hosiery and linen trade, which had numerous women and girls as owners as well as workers. But these were small matters compared with the large industrial loans of Bank of Scotland, the Royal Bank and the British Linen, and it was some years before the Commercial felt confident enough to develop a more adventurous loan book. As to its efficiency in managing a bank, the Whig board had mixed results. It appointed as its first Treasurer John Pollock ws, an unstable neurotic who argued with other staff or refused to acknowledge them, ignored instructions and was involved in an attempted fraudulent conversion of shares to his own name. He was dismissed in July 1812 and handed over the keys to his office only after the Sheriff of Midlothian was asked to intervene.[69]

For Bank of Scotland, the Napoleonic Wars were divided into two phases. In the first, it enjoyed full political support from the powers at Westminster and the active cooperation of the Bank of England. Unfortunately for the Bank, the war went on too long. When Addington came in, he started a political process which undermined the old relationships of Scottish banking and political power; the next few years showed that much damage could be done to a banking system when political conditions changed. In the crisis of 1803-4, hundreds of Scottish companies were in trouble, the Bank lost over £20,000 in bad debts and income was depressed for several years. But the main consequence of the decline of Dundas's interest was greater space for the British Linen Company and then for the Whig party to expand their own bank capitals. Bank of Scotland, the Royal Bank and the private bankers took this very hard. By 1815, the regular Edinburgh meetings involving the banks were broadened to include the Commercial Bank, and the British Linen Company was now more influential in its counsels than it had been. This was all positive and a good basis for lending in the second, and more difficult, phase of industrialisation.

The negative side was, first, that the Scottish system had a weaker grip on Westminster politics; and second, while the ideas which pushed the system forwards in the later eighteenth century came from Bank of Scotland and its associated lawyers and politicians, after 1801 the Whigs began to break out of this system. They came late to banking,

---

68 RBS CS/13/1, Commercial Bank, Minutes, 17 December 1811.
69 Ibid., July 1812.

and the attitudes shown by Cockburn and the Commercial were to carry over into the 1820s and 1830s and encourage others, usually Whigs, to establish big joint-stock banks. These were run on inferior lines to the Edinburgh banks, without the overriding concern for security, solvency and political common sense which had stood the Scottish system in good stead. Furthermore, the ideas and banking practices of the banking system in Scotland were to come under increasing challenge from monetary theorists and politicians after the end of the wars. Of particular note, the Whigs suggested that Bank of Scotland and the Royal Bank had large funds tied up, unnecessarily, in London stocks. It was some years before they were to realise that this was quite essential if they were to act in difficult times for the benefit of their customers.

CHAPTER 11

THE MIND OF THE SCOTTISH BANKERS

THE SCOTTISH Enlightenment of the eighteenth century can be set alongside the French Enlightenment of the same century as among the most interesting and intellectually exciting times in modern European history. The methodologies used in different disciplines, and the subjects discussed, were extraordinarily diverse. Among the more significant theorists were sociologists Adam Ferguson and John Millar; the linguist Lord Monboddo; a group of distinguished jurists including Lord Kames; and, in philosophy and political economy, Sir James Steuart, David Hume and Adam Smith. Although precursors can be found in Scotland before 1700, especially in legal studies, David Hume's *A Treatise of Human Nature* (1739) may be taken as the outstanding introduction to the stimulating decades which followed. These writers are often regarded as a 'school' in that they shared methods of approach and criticism, were influenced by the great thinkers of eighteenth-century France and, above all, had a clear view of their role in the vanguard of philosophical inquiry, although naturally they differed on numerous matters of interpretation. They were at their most comprehensive and incisive about matters economic and the relationships between politics, institutions, law and commerce. They brought to their inquiries ways of thinking about change which were refreshingly free from religious and political dogma and which allowed them to conceptualise development of society in a far more sophisticated way than most of their European contemporaries. Because of this they were translated and widely read in western Europe, but their direct historical importance lay in their influence upon the Scottish aristocracy, the lairds of the lowlands and the middle classes and the ways in which these classes saw their respective roles in the early period of industrialisation. The Scottish writers were very much a part of a society in transition, and socially were well connected: several sat on the Court of Session and on the boards of Bank of Scotland, the British Linen Company and the Royal Bank; their ideas were taught in the universities and reviewed in the press, and they were discussed in the social clubs, freemasons' lodges and salons of polite society. Their presence in Scotland lent a distinctive pattern to literary and philosophical culture that marked out the Scottish middle and upper classes as more critical and incisive on economic matters than the English. David Hume was to discover that the English thinkers had only a superficial appreciation of the historical conditions under which their commerce, culture and the great changes of their politics had emerged, and for this the feebleness of their universities and the limitations of polite society were to blame.[1]

The writers widened the understanding of national needs; in particular, they were concerned that the settlement of 1707 had not been turned to as much advantage as it might have been by the roughly-hewn groups of lairds and aristocrats to whom fighting and a parochial outlook were commonplace. For this to succeed, they emphasised the needs of civil society and civic virtues, and the need for tolerance of others' views. To their students they taught of an urban and rural life based on mutual bonds, undogmatic and open to new ideas. It was a view of an establishment at ease with itself, which took pride in its ability to discuss matters as equals and who considered differences in a civilised manner. This was much easier after 1745. Thus they sought to elaborate schemes of development and ground rules for behaviour which were broad in their appeal; it meant patterns of thought which Tory and Whig alike could share, and transcended clan and religious boundaries. It was through intellectual questions, put to generations of the young middle and landed classes about the conditions for progress, that unity and sympathy could blossom even between the numerous landowners who harboured old and often vicious enmities. Within a few generations, the Scottish Enlightenment had moulded a very effective and self-confident establishment and hierarchy. Even John Millar, who supported the French Revolution and civic democracy, continued to attract huge classes at Glasgow during the 1790s and be recommended by his opponents for the brilliance of his lectures.

By the close of the eighteenth century, there was a rich legacy of theory on economic growth, capital accumulation and the relationship

1 N. T. Phillipson, *David Hume* (London: 1989), p. 17. For the discussion of the intellectual divide which opened up after 1707, see idem, 'The Scottish Enlightenment', in R. Porter and M. Teich (eds), *The Enlightenment in National Context* (Cambridge: 1981), pp. 19–40, and Phillipson, 'Politics, Politeness and the Anglicisation of Early Eighteenth-century Scottish Culture', in R. A. Mason (ed.), *Scotland and England 1286–1815* (Edinburgh: 1987), pp. 226–46. There is a substantial literature on the dynamism of the Scottish universities by the mid-eighteenth century: see P. Jones, 'The Scottish Professoriate and the Polite Academy, 1720–46', in I. Hont and M. Ignatieff (eds), *Wealth and Virtue: The Shaping of Political Economy in the Scottish Enlightenment* (Cambridge: 1985), pp. 89–117.

of banking to national development. This included the historical record of Bank of Scotland and how, since 1695, the Bank had supported the advancement of commerce. In keeping with the unity forged between the Royal Bank and the Bank after 1740, submissions to politicians focused on the benefits of their joint endeavours, were often written together, and *always* passed over the difficulties of 1727 to 1739. Out of this unity on general policy, and the agreements and understandings reached over such matters of interest rates and bill rates on London, there emerged before 1770, and again shortly after the Ayr bank crisis, a remarkably accomplished political performance. While this in general worked smoothly, many financial questions were unresolved. Scottish writers after 1795, among whom were Sir John Sinclair of Ulbster (President of the Board of Agriculture, statistician and a director of Bank of Scotland) and the eighth Earl of Lauderdale (also a director of Bank of Scotland), tended to focus on narrower economic questions, the gold and paper exchanges, the sources of capital and the organisation of credit, and, for example, the role of information and statistics. As will become clear, the extraordinary achievement of the eighteenth century was, in part, to encourage bankers to reflect upon their role in society, as well as on the political success which they had enjoyed. But this began to crumble somewhat after 1815 as economic progress and political change raised new problems, practical and theoretical, and the three decades in the aftermath of war were not easy.

A feature common to the Scottish writers was the conceptualisation of the move from a primitive stage of society through a succession of more advanced stages which required new types of growth and methods of organisation and institutions. The form that each stage of society took was determined, by and large, by the type and scale of trade and commerce, and these productive forces attracted political forms which best accorded with their progress. The usual scheme ended in a modern commercial society after the political and economic elites had rejected 'le système féodal pour embrasser le commercial'.[2] The more advanced schemes involved a three- or four-stage progression from a rude state, akin to primitive communism 'where the means of subsistence are procured with difficulty' largely by hunting and fishing, to a pastoral society with sheep and cattle. The next step, which combined pastoralism with tillage in a developed agricultural society, with private property side by side with communal lands, encouraged manufactures and exchange of goods. Finally, mankind developed commercial society with advanced

2 E. Hobsbawm, 'Capitalisme et agriculture: les réformateurs écossais au XVIII siècle', *Annales: économies, sociétés, civilisations*, 33:3 (May–June 1978), 580–601; R. Pascal, 'Property and Society: The Scottish Historical School of the Eighteenth Century', *The Modern Quarterly*, 1:2 (March 1938), 167–79.

agriculture, manufactures and foreign trade. One of the most lively aspects of these writers' discussions was the diversity of their explanations and the occasional denial, exemplified by Adam Ferguson, that a more modern stage improved the moral standing of man.[3] There was also a pessimistic vein which held that progress was not irreversible and that the fate of the Roman Empire could befall the modern world. The sense of unease about the forces of barbarism and savagery gave a sharpness to discussions about the Highlands long after the Jacobite Rebellion of 1745.

The explanation for the move from one society to another was material-istic, rooted in the economic fault lines that crossed the commercial world and the development of trade, but writers discussed changes in ways which owed much to psychology, language and education. They were usually at pains to extol the virtues of the more advanced stage; John Millar in his *Origin of the Distinction of Ranks*, for instance, explained that the position of women would only improve with economic change. In their descriptions of the modern commercial system, the writers highlighted the benefits and diversification of middle-class life, the availability of goods and leisure – and certain advantages, virtues and attitudes which would only develop when man was freed from the shackles of feudalism and poverty. Writers often stated how change should take place or implied such, as in the case of Adam Smith's vivid descriptions of the inhumanity and backwardness of the Highland feudal system in which he linked economic conditions with political life. There was thus a coherence in their deductions about society which forced readers to think in terms of how change could contribute to society. The attraction of this for the Scottish middle and upper classes was underlined by the enthusiasic re-ception given to their writings and lectures and the harmonious relations enjoyed with the most important men in Scottish government and law. Few schools of thought have held a similar position in modern society.

The school provided a number of theories about growth which were of relevance to Scotland. In the work of Adam Smith (and to a lesser extent that of Sir John Sinclair), the concern for economic growth was their main focus of attention, in particular how the relatively small number of Scottish landowners with a surplus and who employed labourers could become wealthier and thus employ more labour, given a development context which included civic humanism. In 1776, Adam Smith offered a comprehensive growth theory which required the active involvement of lairds. The differing proportion of investment as between productive and

---

3 Adam Ferguson, *An Essay on the History of Civil Society* (Edinburgh: 1767), ed. D. Forbes (Edinburgh: 1966), pp. 92–3.

unproductive labour was the basic determinant of whether there would be more surplus or less:

> though the whole annual produce of the land and labour of every country is no doubt ultimately destined for supplying the consumption of its inhabitants and for procuring a revenue to them yet when it finally comes either from the ground, or from the hands of the productive labourers, it naturally divides itself into two parts. One of them and frequently the largest is, in the first place, destined for replacing a capital or for renewing the provisions, materials and finished work which had been withdrawn from a capital; the other for constituting a revenue either to the owner of this capital, as the profit of his stock, or . . . as the rent of his land.[4]

That part of the 'annual produce of the land and labour of every country' which replaced a capital went only to productive hands, but that which constituted a revenue 'either as profit or rent may maintain indifferently either productive or unproductive hands'. Unproductive labour which 'does not fix or realise itself in any permanent subject, or vendible commodity' produced nothing for which an equal service could afterwards be procured. In this unproductive category, Smith included the entire defence forces and some of the 'gravest and most important', 'churchmen, lawyers, physicians, men of letters of all kinds', as well as some of the most 'frivolous' professions, 'players, buffoons, musicians, opera-singers, opera-dancers'.[5]

The proportion of total produce which went to productive and unproductive labour determined 'the general character of the inhabitants as to industry or idleness'.[6] With this as their guide, the employers of labour and the lairds could move on to consider the other elements in Smith's theory, in particular banks and credit (of which more below), and the role of the division of labour, foreign trade, markets and urbanisation. The moral importance of this for the Scottish lairds as to the connection of economic to political duty could not be clearer. Every landlord could become an agent of progress by a reduction in current unproductive consumption. It is little wonder that Henry Dundas commended the Wealth of Nations and in 1778 rewarded Smith with a Commissionership in the Scottish customs.[7]

4 Adam Smith, An Inquiry into the Nature and Causes of the Wealth of Nations (1776), ed. E. Cannan (2 vols, London: 1904; repr. 1961), vol. i, p. 353, citing book 2, ch. 3: 'of the accumulation of capital and of productive and unproductive labour'.
5 Ibid., book 2, ch. 3, pp. 352–3.
6 Ibid., p. 356. Smith built on a long tradition of Scottish criticism of unproductive and luxury expenditure, and several writers of the Scottish school linked this to the fortunes of individual families. David Hume noted that landlords and moneylenders, 'living idly, squander above their income and the former daily contract debt, and the latter encroach on their stock till its final extinction': 'Of Interest', in E. Rotwein (ed.), David Hume: Writings on Economics (Edinburgh: 1955), pp. 47–59 (p. 58).
7 J. Dwyer and A. Murdoch, 'Paradigms and Politics: Manners, Morals and the Rise of Henry Dundas, 1770–1784', in J. Dwyer, R. Mason and A. Murdoch (eds), New Perspectives on the Politics and Culture

It was an advantage, at this stage of society where collective work in so many walks of life was crucial to progress, that the Scottish writers, by and large, suppressed individual achievement and dismissed the role of 'great men' in history. Francis Jeffrey, for example, the editor of the *Edinburgh Review*, in his summary of John Millar's writings in 1803 concentrated on the main themes without qualification. Little was owed to 'arbitrary or accidental causes', the 'character or exertions of an individual' or the policy and whims of legislators. For great changes – and Millar pushed his theory to include every facet of law, morals, government, science and the role of women – 'everything . . . arose spontaneously from the situation of society, and was suggested or imposed irresistibly by the opportunities or necessities of their condition'.[8] In practice, this materialism was sufficiently moderated by most writers, including Smith, to allow for the remarkable breakthroughs and codifications which post-medieval thought had witnessed and for the background of polite and sympathetic discourse as part of the tradition of civic humanism. There was obviously a role for advanced thinkers and institutions as a witness, or pointer, to the direction in which the society should move. Here was a sufficiently lucid historical learning with which property-owners, Tory and Whig alike, could identify and provide their families with a clear perspective.

The relationship of banks to economic growth was discussed by Scottish writers, although in a fast-changing environment it was perhaps inevitable that this would remain unsatisfactory and unfinished by the close of the eighteenth century. There were two main aspects of debate: the overall role of bank credit in the economy and the function of paper credit and coin. The board of Bank of Scotland held the view that significant extensions of paper credit were beneficial to Scotland. This was achievable before 1727 because of general support from property owners. The actions of the Royal Bank from 1727 down to the famine of 1739 forced a period of retrenchment, lower profits and higher capital–earnings ratios. This was a decade of tighter money, *low* interest rates, a lower level of circulation and endless political meetings. From this era, the lesson was learned and argued for by the political allies of Bank of Scotland (and accepted around 1740 by the Royal Bank) that only cooperation would see an extended paper circulation (and increased profits) which could be easily defended by both banks and their respective economic and political

of Early Modern Scotland (Edinburgh: 1981), pp. 210–48. For a rigorous interpretation of the *Wealth of Nations*, see Hobsbawm, 'Capitalisme et agriculture'; see also P. Deane, *The Evolution of Economic Ideas* (Cambridge: 1978), ch. 3.

8 Francis Jeffrey, *Edinburgh Review*, vol. 3, no. 5 (October 1803), 154–81 (p. 157), discussed in W. C. Lehmann, 'John Millar, Historical Sociologist: Some Remarkable Anticipations of Modern Sociology', *British Journal of Sociology*, 3:1 (March 1952), 30–46.

interests.[9] This was now a point of principle in Scottish banking; each could increase advances and note circulation provided that the notes out remained roughly in step with each other, then balances could be settled amicably and measures adopted to stop demands for gold and silver. The exchanges on London were not adversely affected in the 1740s, which suggested that the volume of banknotes was not excessive and thus there was space for more. This was an understanding which fitted with the development of civic society in Edinburgh and the comprehension of mutual interest.[10]

By the start of the Seven Years' War there were two camps in Scottish banking, although they should be understood as only partially opposed to each other. The more prominent comprised Bank of Scotland and the Royal Bank, which wished to limit the issue of paper to support the exchanges and which tried, and failed, by negotiation and legal action to bring the Glasgow bankers into an agreement on the volume of paper. These latter ignored convertibility by a variety of subterfuges, and their paper fell between 5 and 10 per cent below the value of Edinburgh paper and the value of full-weight coin. Each group argued that its position was best for economic well-being, and inevitably each side attracted intense support; it was one of the first serious conflicts between the burghs of Glasgow and Edinburgh which has marked the modern history of Scotland. It should be emphasised that the conflict was not one of geography but was due to the differing patterns of wealth creation and how banking funds contributed to this.

Into this argument on the role of banks came the greatest thinkers of the day. It was inevitable that the banks would be incorporated into general views of how civic society should operate and how economic progress could go forward in harmony with social ends. As has been shown, there were enormous benefits for landed proprietors and commerce from these agreements and understandings, underlined, for example, at the time of the Jacobite Rebellion of 1745–6 when both the Bank and the Royal Bank held sizeable holdings of each other's notes during the crisis, and by the subsequent collaboration of which the agreement of 1752 was one. This is important for the understanding of how Bank paper could help an underdeveloped economy. Indeed, throughout the whole period from 1707 to the foundation of the Glasgow banks, Scotland was pre-eminent

9 See above, Chapter 6, for the role of the Marquis of Tweeddale in 1742 when Secretary of State for Scotland.
10 It should be noted that the understandings which emerged after the famine of 1739–41 did not hinder Lord Milton from pressing on with the foundation of the British Linen Company (1746), nor support by Bank of Scotland in 1747 for the Aberdeen Banking Company and the Glasgow Ship Bank in 1748; see above, Chapter 7.

in Europe as a model of how paper issues could far exceed the monetary base of banks and contribute to the long-run accumulation of capital. In the first half of the century, the board of the Bank discussed its work in terms of the 'public and national' role laid down in the Bank Act of 1695, and this discussion emphasised how fragile the extension of note issue could be. In the second half of the century, the model, or view, that large extensions of paper could be managed over many years, without a crisis, came under periodic criticism. A rival, effective banking system was in France, and was based on gold and silver, with bankers' notes a lesser form of credit and closely tied to the stock of precious metals held by private bankers. The most advanced of French thought came from Richard Cantillon, a banker who made enormous sums by his insight into market movements during the Mississippi scheme, which he prudently moved to Amsterdam and London before the crash of 1722. While in London, he continued to trade as a banker dealing in foreign exchange, and from 1730 to 1734 he wrote the *Essai sur la nature du commerce en général*. Cantillon was murdered by his cook in 1734 and the text remained unpublished, though it may well have been circulated, until its appearance in a French edition in 1755, published in London.

Cantillon recognised an infrequent case where a banker, catering for a stable and rich clientele, could maintain a cash reserve of only one-tenth of his deposits. But this was exceptional, and most bankers had to keep a reserve of one-half to two-thirds of their deposits. For those who dealt with 'entrepreneurs and merchants who pay in large sums daily and soon after draw them out it will often happen that if the Banker divert more than one third of his cash he will find himself in difficulty to meet the demands'.[11] The overall contribution of banks to the economy was limited: 'that all the advantage of Banks, public or private in a City, is to accelerate the circulation of money and to prevent so much of it from being hoarded'.[12] Richard Cantillon dismissed the role of paper money in credit, as, for instance, it existed in Scotland:

> An abundance of fictitious and imaginary money causes the same disadvantages as an increase of real money in circulation, by raising the price of land and labour, or by making works and manufactures more expensive at the risk of subsequent loss. But this furtive abundance vanishes at the first gust of discredit and precipitates disorder.[13]

Following on from a discussion of the importance of the crisis of 1720, he added:

11 Richard Cantillon, *Essai sur la nature du commerce en général* (London: 1755), ed. H. Higgs (London: 1931), p. 303.
12 Ibid., p. 305.
13 Ibid., p. 311.

This example shows that the paper and credit of public and private banks may cause surprising results in everything which does not concern ordinary expenditure for drink and food, clothing and other family requirements, but that in the regular course of the circulation the help of banks and credit of this kind is much smaller and less solid than is generally supposed. Silver alone is the true sinews of circulation.[14]

This was the basic argument used by foreign exchange dealers and other commentators to criticise the development of paper credits, rather than addressing the more substantial question of what may be an optimal level for paper for an economic system in which the two main inputs are land and labour, and both were known to be under-utilised.

A variant of this European position on money was expounded by David Hume in 1752 in his *Political Discourses*, a view, it should be stated, which attracted few if any followers among the Scottish bankers. According to David Hume, coin and bullion were natural and beneficial, 'in every kingdom into which money [coin] begins to flow in greater abundance than formerly, everything takes a new face: labour and industry gain life; the merchant becomes more enterprising, the manufacturer more diligent and skilful and even the farmer follows his plough with greater alacrity'. Only in foreign trade is it 'rather disadvantageous by raising the price of every kind of labour'. By contrast, paper currency and other substitutes for coin lacked virtually any redeeming features.[15] His position followed from the adverse consequences of a rise in the price of labour which followed an inflow of gold and silver; this was unavoidable 'and the effect of that public wealth and prosperity which are the end of all our wishes'. But, he went on,

> there appears no reason for encreasing that inconvenience by a counterfeit money, which foreigners will not accept of in any payment and which any great disorder in the state will reduce to nothing . . . to endeavour artificially to increase such a credit can never be the interest of any trading nation, but must lay them under disadvantages by encreasing money beyond its natural proportion to labour and commodities and thereby heightening their price to the merchant and manufacturer. And in this view it must be allowed that no bank could be more advantageous than such a one as locked up all the money it received and never augmented the circulating coin . . . the natural advantage, resulting from the low price of labour and the destruction of paper credit would be a sufficient compensation.[16]

David Hume's *Essay on the Balance of Trade* was adamant on this general principle:

14 Ibid., p. 319.
15 David Hume, 'Of Money', in E. Rotwein (ed.), *David Hume: Writings on Economics*, pp. 33–46 (35–7).
16 Ibid. pp. 35–6.

I scarcely know any method of sinking money below its level, but those of institutions of banks, funds and paper credit which we are in this kingdom (Scotland) so much infatuated. These render paper equivalent to money, circulate it throughout the whole state, make it supply the place of gold and silver, raise proportionately the price of labour and commodities and by that means either banish a great part of those precious metals, or prevent their further increase.[17]

Hume cited France when he wanted an example of best practice:

It is not to be doubted but the great plenty of bullion in France is, in great measure, owing to the want of paper credit. The French have no banks: merchant bills do not there circulate as with us: Usury or lending on interest is not directly permitted; so that many have large sums in their coffers: Great quantities of plate are used in private houses; and all the churches are full of it. By this means, provisions and labour still remain cheaper among them, than in nations that are not half so rich in gold and silver. The advantages of this situation, in point of trade as well as in great public emergencies, are too evident to be disputed.[18]

For the worst practice, he looked to the British colonies: when paper money was introduced there, 'the least inconveniency that has followed is the total banishment of the precious metals'.[19]

In the early editions of Hume's *Essays* (1752, 1753–4, 1758, 1760), there were no qualifications to this thesis; thus he was completely at variance with the position of the Glasgow banks and, to a lesser extent, the Edinburgh banks.[20] It was an exposition repeated in the *Scots Magazine* and other journals of polite society, and it drew numerous comments during the years of the remittance crisis.[21] The bankers relied heavily on the experience of the country, which confirmed, contrary to David Hume, that paper money and credit were essential to stimulate trade. But at this point they parted company, in a more intense discussion than that

17 David Hume, 'Of the Balance of Trade', in Rotwein (ed.), *David Hume: Writings on Economics*, pp. 60–77 (p. 68).
18 Ibid., p. 69.
19 For the position in the colonies, see J. J. McCusker, *Money and Exchange in Europe and America 1600–1775* (London: 1978), pp. 125–31; and also above, Chapter 7.
20 In 1755, there appeared in London a curious pamphlet after Hume's style which endorsed his position and included quotations from his original text: Anon., *Essay on Paper Money, Banking etc.* (London: 1755). Patrick Elibank, Lord Elibank of the Court of Session, was later accused of authorship, which he denied; and indeed the styles of the two were quite different. Elibank was harder to follow, and legalistic; he supported a limited paper currency in his *Thoughts on Money, Circulating & Paper Currency* [written 1753 or 1754, published 1758]. The Court of Session judges always supported the issue of paper money.
21 'From Mr Hume's Political Discourses', *The Scots Magazine*, 24 (1762), 33–9; Scotus, 'The Baneful Influence of Paper Credit', *SM*, 24 (1762), 129–30; for an article critical of Bank of Scotland, *SM*, 24 (1762), 89–94, and reply pp. 130–3.

over the propositions from David Hume. The Glasgow banks, for their part, argued that the facilities offered by Bank of Scotland and the Royal Bank in the west of Scotland were inadequate before the Ship and the Arms were founded, and, further, that the profits of banking should not be limited to Edinburgh. In 1750, someone in Glasgow, it is unclear who, was sufficiently impressed by the brilliance of John Law's career to pay for a splendidly-bound reprint of *Money and Trade Considered* which, as we have noticed, contained enough arguments for a huge extension of paper as anyone could wish for.[22] It is not known which side was intended to benefit from publication. Another tract suggested that Presbyterianism was at the root of banknotes whereas Episcopacy stood for gold and silver, but which city stood for which money was unclear.[23] The Edinburgh banks were not averse to an extension of their note issue, although the details of the offer in 1755, put by Lord Milton, were insufficient and the talks collapsed.[24] The argument was overshadowed by the government's need for supplies and finance in the Seven Years' War (1756–63) and by the 'remittance' crisis attributed to the adverse exchange on London after 1760, which lasted after the war was over, and later still by the policy of the Ayr bank before its collapse in June 1772. The extent of the fall from par of the exchange on London, the damage to the credit of the public banks and even the influence of the paper on the rise in the price of labour against gold and silver thus remained unresolved to that date, at least in the popular sense that two camps coexisted. In fact, from the viewpoint of the Edinburgh banks, they were intellectually more isolated than the banks in Glasgow.

In 1764, in his fifth edition of *Political Discourses*, Hume qualified his earlier stance. He 'confessed' (sic) that:

> as all these questions of trade and money are extremely complicated there are certain lights in which this subject may be placed, so as to represent the advantages of paper credit and banks to be superior to their disadvantages. That they banish specie and bullion from a state is undoubtedly true; and whoever looks no farther than this circumstance does well to condemn them; but specie and bullion are not of so great consequence as not to admit of a compensation and even an overbalance from the encrease of industry and of credit which may be promoted by the right use of paper money.[25]

To the economist, this might seem a move towards the position of the Edinburgh banks. Yet the context of economic progress, recognised by

22 John Law, *Money and Trade Considered, with a proposal for supplying the nation with money* (Glasgow: 1750).
23 Anon., 'A letter from a Gentleman in Glasgow to his friend in Edinburgh concerning bank-notes and paper credit' [GL 1752].
24 See above, Chapter 7.
25 David Hume, 'Of the Balance of Trade', in Rotwein (ed.), *Writings on Economics*, p. 70.

David Hume, could be interpreted as more sympathetic to the increase of banking facilities. The war years had encouraged companies to issue paper notes using the optional clause, as well as to increase the bill trade. And as there was no legal prohibition in Scotland, this was the ground over which the Edinburgh banks had to contend and where for several years they were rather isolated.

In this situation, the episode of the 1765 Act of 5 George III c.49 was significant. It followed the general Currency Act of 1764, applicable to the North American colonies, which subjected all colonial paper money to commercial law; thus colonial paper could not be imposed as legal tender for debts.[26] It was a guarantee to merchants that they would receive full value for their goods, either in bills on London or coin, and was an important signal that the British legislature would not tolerate fraudulent intent by the colonists. The Act of 5 George III c.49 was drafted, at the behest of the Edinburgh banks, to stop the deferment of payment by any optional clause whatsoever, and was thus also a guarantee of payment in bills on London, or Scottish banknotes, or other acceptable paper, or sovereigns. The Act was one of those defining moments in British financial history designed to maintain the value of the pound sterling and the integrity of commerce. The Privy Council and the Treasury approached this question with a variety of financial concerns, and these included the problem which the government had experienced, in the Seven Years' War, of raising money and extending credit. This required a range of London-based banks, but by this time the Treasury had begun to appreciate the ways in which provincial and Scottish banking facilities had a bearing upon the operations of the City of London. The abolition of the optional clause and the draconian penalties for non-payment of paper ensured that new Scottish banking companies would have proper reserves. This removed the fraudulent and the smaller companies, which faced the immediate return of their notes for cash. Yet, as the economy grew and more provincial companies and private bankers opened their doors, the Royal Bank and Bank of Scotland became relatively less important. As these adverse circumstances moved to their climax with the attempt by the Edinburgh private bankers to change the policy of the public banks, there was published the soundest exposition of the older-style, patrician view of the role of the Bank and the Royal Bank in Sir James Steuart's *Principles of Political Economy*.[27]

26 4 George III c.34; for this question, see above, Chapter 7.
27 Sir James Steuart, *An Inquiry into the Principles of Political Economy being an Essay on the Science of Domestic Policy in Free Nations* (2 vols, London: 1767), ed. A. Skinner (Edinburgh: 1966). The first edition has been used for those chapters on banks omitted in the reprint.

Sir James Steuart (1713–80) was a European scholar of great distinction. His family came from the middle ranks of Scottish landowners and had supported, although not too enthusiastically, the overthrow of James VII. His grandfather was Lord Advocate in 1693, in which role 'he wrought havoc amongst witches'; his mother, Ann, was the eldest daughter of Lord President Dalrymple and one of the cleverest women of her generation, and his father was Solicitor General from 1709 to 1717.[28] By all accounts, the young Sir James inherited the brains of his mother; at Edinburgh University his close associates included later professors, and he passed the Scottish bar examinations in 1735. Then he went abroad on a tour which lasted until 1740, during which time he learned Dutch, French, Italian and Spanish. But he also met James VIII, and by his return to Scotland he was a convinced Jacobite. In 1743, Sir James married Lady Frances Wemyss, one of the more intelligent decisions of his life, as by that time he was closely involved in political intrigues on behalf of the Jacobites. After Charles's army was victorious at Prestonpans (21 September 1745), Steuart worked hard for the Jacobites and in late October was despatched to France to encourage a French invasion. He thus missed Culloden, and, although not attainted for treason, was regarded as a serious enemy of the state and remained in exile. His first request for a pardon was rejected in 1749, although his wife organised subsequent attempts to pave the way for his eventual return at the end of the Seven Years' War. Steuart had a modest income which allowed him to travel around European courts and academic circles.

Steuart's return thus coincided with the intense debates on monetary matters, and much of his time was occupied with his analysis of this for the *Principles*. The long sojourn in Europe had impressed him with the need for a government committed to alleviating the dire conditions of the lower classes of society. His first chapter was in the European tradition of strong civic government; man was a social animal and all societies agreed to a voluntary subordination to authority, 'with a view to promote the general good'.[29] 'Constant and uninterrupted experience has proved to man that virtue and justice in those who govern are sufficient to render the society happy, under any form of Government. Virtue and justice when applied to Government, mean no more than a tender affection for the whole society and an exact and impartial regard for the interest of every class.' It was the duty of the statesman, on certain principles, to attend to the exact 'sketch of that plan of Government which experience has proved to be best adapted to the spirit of the people', and Steuart often laid out what

---

28 Ibid. (1966 edn), vol. i, p. xxi ff.
29 Ibid., ch. 1, pp. 20–1.

legislators should do on banking, exchange and interest rates.[30] Banks and credit, he argued, were central to the economic system and were thus a proper role for the legislator.

His model approximated to the position which the public banks would have preferred; there should be a national bank (or banks) at the top (the first tier), a group of provincial ('subaltern') banks which also issued notes (the second tier) and a group of exchangers and discounters of bills as a third tier. These subaltern banks and exchangers would look to the national bank for coin and bill discounts as they required: 'it was in the interest of the country to have a sufficient quantity of bank notes which would all pass everywhere'. The problem was how to stop the private, short-term greed of the exchangers and provincial banks from damaging the system (and thus trade and industry) and to ensure that subaltern notes were not restricted in exchange: 'while no public regulation is made with regard to banking everyone will carry on the trade according to his views of profit and private animosities between different companies will only tend to distress the nation'.[31] If provincial banks were to be on a 'good understanding' with each other, they needed firm principles for their issue of paper backed by solid security. For the national bank(s), these were:

1. a large stock of property in pledge to support the banknotes;

2. this security should be easily saleable and cover all interest;

3. debts should not be recalled as long as interest was paid;

4. proprietors of the bank could call on it for credit;

5. securities which the bank pledged for loans should be held by government;

6. government should support the national banks where required;

7. there would be no optional clauses, and the holder of banknotes could choose repayment in coin or inland bills or hold an interest-bearing deposit in the bank.[32]

30 In the two volumes of the 1767 edition, 160 pages were devoted to population and agriculture, 360 to trade and industry, 220 to money and coin, 40 to interest, 220 to banks, exchange and the balance of payments, and 280 pages to public credit and taxes.
31 Sir James Steuart, *Principles of Political Economy* (1767 edn), book 4, part 2, ch. 15: 'of subaltern banks of circulation and of their competition with one another'. It was unclear whether this would lead to too much or too little paper.
32 In a comment to Provost Ingram of Glasgow, Sir James Steuart endorsed the view that the optional clause should be abolished: 'Memorial on Scottish banks', 2 January 1764, in W. Mure (ed.), *Selections from the Family Papers Preserved at Caldwell*, Part 2, 1765–1821, Proceedings of the Maitland Club, 71 (Glasgow: 1854), p. 217 note 9.

Steuart also argued that if the national banks had branches they would render subaltern banks unnecessary. If there were no national banks, then any note-issuer should be obliged 'to keep open books to be inspected regularly by some authority or other in order to see upon what security that paper stands'.[33] Otherwise secrecy would only lead, by knavery, misconduct or misfortune, to the collapse of a particular bank, which 'would cast a general discredit upon all paper and be a means of bringing on those calamitites which we have so often monitored'. It was wrong that the law should favour counterfeit or speculative paper – every man had the right to detect false coin, and all should be given the right to find out the extent of a particular note issue and the extent of securities behind it. If Steuart's policy had been followed whether a national bank existed or not, some speculation before 1772 would have been avoided.[34] Steuart was rather before his time in 1767, although, as noted elsewhere, many of these ideas were favoured by the Edinburgh banks and were in operation within a few years of the Ayr bank crisis.

Both Hume and Steuart were widely read, and for sheer intellectual power the range of Hume's thought was astonishing; but the influence of Adam Smith was more significant. Part of Smith's theory of growth in the *Wealth of Nations* (1776) included the 'judicious operations of banking'.[35] These could not augment the capital of a country by themselves, but would enable unutilised stock and capital in land to be converted into active and productive stock, such as pastures and cornfields. Likewise the gold and silver money, which 'is a very valuable part of the capital of the country' but produces nothing, could now by the substitution of paper enable the country to convert 'a great part of their dead stock into active and reproductive stock'. This was largely an automatic process, and the gold and silver would go abroad for the purchase of foreign goods. Following a similar vein to the case of productive/unproductive investment, it could be used to buy 'such goods as are likely to be consumed by idle people who produce nothing, such as foreign wines, foreign silks etc.', or it could purchase materials and tools to be worked on by industrious people at home, 'who reproduce with a profit the value of their annual consumption'. In fact, the greater part of the coin would be employed on the latter, not for the maintenance of idleness. Thus the substitution of paper for gold and silver made a significant addition to the annual value of land and labour. While the conduct of all those different companies had sometimes been found wanting

33 Sir James Steuart, *Principles of Political Economy* (1767 edn), ch. 17: 'When and in what case banks should be obliged to keep open books'.
34 Open books would have given the proprietors of banks a chance of spotting disparities, although fraud in accounts is more difficult to find than false statements over security.
35 Adam Smith, *Wealth of Nations*, book 2, ch. 2: quotations here are taken from this chapter.

and has accordingly required an Act of Parliament to regulate it [5 George III c.49] the country, notwithstanding had evidently derived great benefit from their trade. I have heard it asserted that the trade of the city of Glasgow doubled in about fifteen years after the first erection of the banks there and that the trade of Scotland had more than quadrupled since the first erection of the two public banks at Edinburgh . . . Whether the trade, either of Scotland in general, or of the city of Glasgow in particular has really increased in so great a proportion, during so short a period I do not pretend to know. If either of them has increased in this proportion it seems to be an effect too great to be accounted for by the sole operation of this cause. That the trade and industry of Scotland, however, have increased very considerably during this period and that the banks have contributed a good deal to this increase cannot be doubted.

This part of Smith's argument was unexceptional by 1776.

Smith also discussed ideas which were still very much in debate. He argued that in the normal course of trade there was no possibility of banks forcing too much paper on the country; what was above requirements would return for coin:

> Let us suppose that all the paper of a particular bank which the circulation of the country can easily absorb and employ, amounts exactly to forty thousand pounds, and that for answering occasional demands, this bank is obliged to keep at all times in its coffers ten thousand pounds in gold and silver. Should this bank attempt to circulate forty-four thousand pounds the four thousand pounds which are over and above what the circulation can easily absorb and employ will return upon it almost as fast as they are issued. For answering occasional demands therefore this bank ought to keep at all times in its coffers not eleven thousand pounds only, but fourteen thousand pounds. It will thus gain nothing by the interest of the four thousand excessive circulation and it will lose the whole expence of continually collecting four thousand pounds in gold and silver which will be continually going out of its coffers as fast as they are brought into them.

Smith mentioned the cash account system and the circulation of accommodation bills by drawing and redrawing and the rise of this method of finance since the 1750s. The implication of most of what he wrote was to condemn any but real bills, although he was to modify this somewhat when he came to sketch the background to the foundation of Douglas, Heron & Co. in which his patron the Duke of Buccleuch was so heavily involved. Smith was opposed to notes under £5 and to any optional clause. The damage to trade done by 'beggarly bankers' (he cited Yorkshire in this instance) who produced notes as low as 6d or 1 shilling and by those who refused payment in coin was not to be confused with 'natural liberty'.

Yet Smith realised that not every banking company had understood how the issue of excess paper affected its business, and thus Scottish banks had to buy bullion and coin in London at a premium of $2\frac{1}{4}$ to $2\frac{3}{4}$ per cent. For this they had only themselves to blame. Smith offered advice as to how they should operate. Banks should not advance the whole 'or even the greater part' of the working capital of a trader.

> Still less could a bank afford to advance him any considerable part of his fixed capital; of the capital which the undertaker of an iron forge, for example, employs in erecting his forge and smelting house, his work-houses and warehouses, the dwelling houses of his workmen etc, of the capital which the undertaker of a mine employs in sinking his shafts, in erecting engines for drawing out the water, in making roads and waggon-ways etc; of the capital which the person who undertakes to improve land employs in clearing, draining, enclosing, manuring and ploughing waste and uncultivated fields . . . The returns of the fixed capital [are] a period by far too distant to suit the conveniency of a bank.

The basic scheme of banking outlined by Smith was thus far removed from the reality of the Scotland of his day. This was an ideal sketch of a minimalist banking system where no distinctions were drawn between the banks, where each was careful to control the issue of paper, where geographical and other impedients to paper conversion were non-existent, where little or nothing was advanced for fixed capital, circulation bills or long-run overdrafts on cash accounts and where gold was available when asked for. The theory described a static world free of business and climatic cycles or geographical distance, with the banks uninvolved in any assessment of the long term or in the major investment decisions of a capitalist economy. In building this rarified model, with great skill it must be added, he did less than justice to the complexity of Scottish banking or the growing needs of the industrial and landed sector.

In respect of possible damage done to exchange rates by an over-issue of paper, Smith acknowledged that in the case of the American plantations such a depreciation of money against gold had indeed happened. Where the domestic currency had been thus depreciated, 'no law could be more equitable than the Act of Parliament so unjustly complained of in the colonies, which declared that no paper currency to be emitted there in time coming should be a legal tender of payment'.[36] But this came as a qualification to his previous argument that damage could not accrue from the normal course of a paper currency; he also failed to confront the various subterfuges and time-lags exploited by Scottish provincial banks to avoid payment in cash which continued in spite of the 1765 Act. The self-adjusting mechanism (cited above) missed the point that the creation of paper allowed an increase in the circulation of bills and only a part

36 Ibid., p. 348; the Act in question was the Currency Act of 1764, 4 George III c.34.

of this could be retired by the settlement date. In a boom, a bank would find itself tied up with a continuation of paper; experience had provided a wealth of reasons for this from client and proprietor pressure to fear of collapse.

Smith was inaccurate and partial on the Douglas, Heron & Co. crisis. Following his notes about drawing and redrawing bills, he suggested that the more prudent Scottish banks had reduced their support for discounts, the date for which is not given, 'by refusing ... to give more credit to those to whom they had already given a great deal too much, took the only method by which it was not possible to save either their own credit or the public credit of the country'.[37] 'In the midst of this clamour and distress a new bank was established in Scotland for the express purpose of relieving the distress of the country. The design was generous but the execution imprudent and the nature and causes of the distress which it meant to relieve were not perhaps well understood. This bank was more liberal than any other had ever been.' Smith suggested that some traders who would otherwise have folded had continued for about two years by borrowing from Douglas, Heron & Co. Yet he failed to come to terms with the extent of new speculation and avoided an opportunity to question the role of his patron and his fellow aristocrats in their miserable failure to supervise the Ayr or Edinburgh offices. Where he may have been right (the evidence is inconclusive) is in whether or not the operations of Douglas, Heron & Co. had taken over from 'those rivals whom it meant to supplant' and enabled the latter to avoid collapse. As it stands, Smith's account suggested that the Ayr bank was a natural and generous response to a crisis, and this, on a benevolent interpretation, is both misleading and too charitable by far to the leading proprietors who failed in their duty of supervision.[38]

The common strength of most of the pre-industrial writings was their attempt to find and explain immutable patterns of economic activity in a context of a unified civic society. This gave the common writings of the Scots a sound base for exploring the coexistence (or otherwise) of different types of economic system with societies fractured by religious and political dogma. But they also led to an assumption that there might be a normal pattern of banking activity. Thus the earlier writers (with the partial exception of Steuart) missed the need to have ideas about disequilibrium caused by trade, climate and war built into these general views. They

---

37 Adam Smith, ibid., p. 333; in the years from 1765 to the foundation of the Douglas, Heron company, there is no evidence of this in the archives of either the Royal Bank or Bank of Scotland.
38 Edwin Cannan is incorrect (*Wealth of Nations*, p. 333 note) in his claim that Smith's account of the Ayr Bank proceedings was 'extremely accurate'; the investigation carried out by the shareholders, *The Precipitation and Fall of Messrs Douglas, Heron & Company* ... (Edinburgh: 1778), cited by Cannan, differs in many points from that of Smith.

recognised periodic crises but not as a fundamental part of the economic condition. In Smith's case, there was little association of periodic crises and of the geographical impediments to banknote conversion, and he failed to acknowledge the first and second tiers of banks shown so vividly in 1772. If he had done so, it would have begged the question of how the first tier should behave towards the second and what sort of regulations should be adopted, both by government and by the banks. On the structure of Scottish banking, it was Steuart who described it most accurately, although he had to wait some years after 1767 before it became evident that he was right. But by then his writings had faded from public view, outshone by the greater attraction of the *Wealth of Nations*.

Moreover, Hume and Smith completely omitted the political dimension to Scottish banks. Enough evidence is available from the history of Bank of Scotland, the Royal Bank and the British Linen Company to indicate that all three banks were close to the heart of British political power before the close of the Seven Years' War, and they retained some influence before the reorganisation of Scottish politics after the crisis of 1772 which led to the hegemony of the two senior banks. Where Steuart remained valid as a guide, and where Smith was not, was in the resumption of a vigorous connection between the Bank and the Royal Bank for the half-century after the Ayr crisis. It would be wrong to tax Smith with missing the reconstruction of Scottish banking after 1772, but it meant that by the date of his first edition, Smith was unhelpful as a guide to Scottish finance or for guiding the reader on the importance of politics in the everyday life of Edinburgh bankers.

Hume and Smith provided hints of joint activity, which they implied was collusion, between the Bank and the Royal Bank. In this they were more correct than they realised. Neither they, nor other critics such as the writers of the *Scots Magazine*, grasped the extent and detail of the meetings between the Bank and the Royal Bank. It was from this coming-together, a regular feature from 1740, and monthly meetings from 1752, that a set of views emerged about how first-tier banks should operate in respect of second-tier banks. The aftermath of 1772 provided a powerful impetus for a further set of agreements and understandings and in particular a clearer consensus about the role of paid-up bank capital, liquid and not-so-liquid reserves, the relationship of reserves in London and Scotland and what the obligations of Officers of State were towards the banks. Together with this, there emerged theorists among the leading bankers although, because of the need for secrecy, their audiences were few in number. Some hints occasionally filtered down from directors; Sir John Sinclair and the Earl of Lauderdale published ideas, although they kept silent on much of the system.

The aftermath of 1772 involved the reassertion of the financial power of Bank of Scotland and the Royal Bank over the second-tier banks and a renewed responsibility for the system as a whole, although it was not until 1778 that the position of the two senior banks was firmly in place. As already noted, the Deputy Governor of Bank of Scotland, John Forrest, had been involved in the monetary controversy of 1762 and was sacked in 1768 shortly after he proposed an increase in the paid-up capital. At an early point after the June 1772 collapse, which led to the bankruptcy of fifteen Edinburgh private bankers (we cannot be precise, but not later than October), the directors accepted the need to raise more capital. A doubling of paid-up capital followed in 1774, and by 1797 it had reached £1 million. By 1774, with the removal of the speculators from the board of the Bank, a clear line of thought had emerged. In this we find one of those groups which from time to time seem to appear within the secret world of the Edinburgh banks. This was an association of Bank of Scotland and the Royal Bank directors active by 1776 in the removal the following year of Sir Lawrence Dundas of Kerse from the Governorship of the Royal Bank.[39] They were led initially by 'M', whose identity is unclear. Their intentions were (a) to follow the lead of Bank of Scotland and increase the capital of the Royal Bank, (b) to reorganise the Royal Bank to form a counterpart for Bank of Scotland branches, particularly in the Glasgow area, and (c) to form a more extensive connection between the two banks on a regular basis and arrange for an increase in note issue. Crucial to the implementation of their plans was the political power of Henry Dundas, Deputy Governor of Bank of Scotland, and his associate the Duke of Buccleuch who replaced Dundas of Kerse as Governor of the Royal Bank in 1777. The 'M' group explained in September 1777 to Henry Dundas, through George Home of Branxton ws (a Royal Bank proprietor and holder of the stock of Douglas, Heron & Co.) exactly what he was expected to do and what was the banking theory which underlay their proposals.[40] Virtually all that Home put to Dundas was enacted.

George Home ws presented the paper after Dundas of Kerse had conceded defeat in 1777.[41] There were thirteen summary principles preceded by an explanation of the monetary theory to which the group subscribed, the structures which they sought and an acknowledgement of the measures enacted by Bank of Scotland (branches and increased capital). Dundas was urged to recognise the ideas behind the Bank of Scotland move which the Royal Bank should imitate: the capitals of the two chartered banks were known and their constitutions 'such that no sudden

---

39 See above, Chapter 9.
40 BS 20/32/1, Melville Papers, George Home ws, 'Observations on a late conversation'.
41 RBS RB/494, Share Transfer Books, 2 April 1777: 2,000 shares sold by Sir Lawrence Dundas.

danger was to be apprehended from their management'. By contrast, the public 'was and must necessarily continue in the dark' as to the capitals of the provincial banks and the 'propriety of their management', and 'for many and obvious reasons' they were more 'liable to be deeply affected by any sudden check given to credit'. When this happened, George Home argued, industry and employment were adversely affected; people would be rendered 'desperate by their wants' or obliged to emigrate. Thus it should be an object of policy to address the financial management of the country.

The most important conclusions outlined the need to increase the paid-up capitals of Bank of Scotland and the Royal Bank. The banknote circulation of Scotland was estimated at £900,000, supported by capitals of £400,000 (Royal Bank and Bank of Scotland) and about £200,000 (nine provincial banks and the British Linen). This two-thirds proportion for the leading banks was insufficient in times of crisis to cope with demands and this too required to be increased, though to what extent was not indicated. This would be done by royal charter for the Royal Bank and by Act of Parliament for the Bank. They both required further support from Henry Dundas already given for the Act of 1774 and the Act of 1776 for the reconstruction of the Ayr bank. The existing proprietors of the banks would not receive lower dividends; profits were already higher than commonly thought in Edinburgh business circles (8–10 per cent was mentioned by Home).

A circulation of one-fifth above paid-up capital would return 6 per cent gross, and 'a much greater circulation might be attempted with safety under good management'. Even if this lower figure were adhered to, the value of a 6 per cent return compared with the normal annuity rate of 4 per cent would give bank shares a 50 per cent premium. This was the key point for proprietors: a sharp increase in capital, a banknote circulation at least 20 per cent above this and a return of 6 per cent or above.

Would this huge increase in paper from the two banks damage the value of money vis-à-vis gold and silver? George Home dismissed the views of David Hume:

> speculative men of the first eminence have indeed endeavoured to demonstrate that the substituting of paper for gold and silver will in the end ruin our trade and manufactures, by heightening the price of provisions and labour and their reasonings on this head are almost universally adopted. It might therefore seem rash and presumptuous to suppose that they are founded upon erroneous principles.

Yet 'the experience of near a century in Scotland has not discovered any inconvenience to over balance the establishment' of banks and paper credit.

Unlike David Hume and Adam Smith, the group around George Home was not primarily concerned to elaborate a theoretical system. Its audience was a practical lawyer and his entourage who wielded immense power and functioned as the organiser of patronage, complicated networks of relationships and the staffing of institutions as diverse as the Court of Session and the East India Company. Henry Dundas was apparently unimpressed with sophistry: 'even the philosophical enquiries . . . of the Scottish Enlightenment, posed no problems to his closed mind'; and though George Home implied a more rigorous refutation of David Hume, he passed swiftly on to practical matters.[42] It was the case, he pointed out, that the managers of the two senior banks: 'are tied down by fixed and determined rules', were accountable to 'zealous proprietors . . . [and] have it not in their power to conceal their transactions, and lye under no temptation to engage in hazardous enterprises from a prospect of extraordinary profit'.[43] 'As a guardian in some measure of the public credit of Scotland', the public banks took the longest time horizon and had a culture which emphasised stability and 'prudence'. George Home and his associates thus spoke to Henry Dundas as potential allies, and thereafter, in his thirty years in power, he usually aided the Bank and the Royal Bank when asked.

George Home also spoke for men who saw that the changes in the Scottish economy called for a sound financial platform. They were unimpressed with the petty country banks which abounded in England and which collapsed with monotonous regularity at every crisis. Within a few years – by 1781 at the latest – Coutts & Co. felt able to discuss with the Edinburgh banks general matters of stability and credit, reserve policy, the negotiation of bills from Scotland and how, for example, the Edinburgh banks should act to retire the Glasgow Arms bank from trading. The importance of the London Scots in riveting the Edinburgh–London exchanges along cautious lines was of inestimable value given the central position of the bill on London in internal trade. It was very much a two-way process. In March 1793, an exasperated Thomas Coutts cited the structures presided over by Bank of Scotland and the Royal Bank as the best practice then in existence in the British Isles for coping with a financial crisis and which should be adopted by the Bank of England. There were also other financial and political services which this network performed. To the mind of the bankers at the Royal Bank and Bank of Scotland, they had created the institutional structures which the

---

42 W. Ferguson, *Scotland: 1689 to the Present*, The Edinburgh History of Scotland, vol. iv (Edinburgh: 1968), pp. 236–7.
43 BS 20/32/1, Melville Papers, George Home ws, 'Observations on a late conversation'.

economic changes demanded, and they had created these with a conscious vision. It is impossible to tell which were the greater influences on them while they did this; the ideas and concerns of philosophical inquiry and their thought on economic change were probably somewhere to the fore, if only as a rigorous training in how to think about change. There was also an important practical reason why Henry Dundas would accept the argument from George Home. The Ayr crisis threatened to destroy the fortunes of several hundred shareholders, many of whom were landed proprietors in the south-west of Scotland. The increase in general credit offered by the two senior banks would be of considerable assistance to Henry Dundas as he grappled with the political results of the crisis. Following agreement in August 1773 to wind up the affairs of Douglas, Heron & Co., a committee of twelve, including the Duke of Buccleuch and the Duke of Queensberry, took over this task and appointed George Home as their factor. For twenty years he carried out this task, and it was not until 1793 that he felt able voluntarily to relinquish his salary.[44]

Apart from the political and regulatory system based on large capitals for first-tier banks, developed through experience and found to be of immense utility to economic development in Scotland, the Edinburgh bankers developed justifications for not linking the banknote issue directly to the behaviour of the exchanges but to a broader range of considerations. In the remittance crisis at the close of the Seven Years' War, the detailed memoranda prepared by the Edinburgh banks outlined a 'real bills' doctrine. The first consideration was that banks should only lend to those who were sound, and these customers would not borrow more than they could make a profit on as they faced interest charges on their debts. The banks would identify and stop chains of accommodation bills; local agents were governed by regulations and had an interest in minimising mistakes, liable as they usually were for a proportion of losses. The huge capitals of the banks could carry a proportion of past-due bills to enable customers to survive periodic crises. The problem for this Scottish bankers' view was that this could not guarantee an exact par for sterling on the foreign exchanges, only an intuitive understanding of an average balance of note issue and return over the long run. An average around par might be thought a useful rule for a national banking system; unfortunately the exchange dealers in London were to insist on something less problematic and, to their view, less open to speculative endeavour.[45]

---

44 NLS, MS 1801(ii).
45 The 'real bills' doctrine was one of the central issues of the monetary controversies from 1797 to 1845; for a guide, see F. W. Fetter, *The Development of British Monetary Orthodoxy 1797–1875* (Cambridge, MA: 1965), pp. 9–10, 39–43; also R. Green, 'Real Bills Doctrine', in J. Eatwell, M. Milgate and P. Newman (eds), *The New Palgrave* (London: 1989), pp. 310–13.

Before 1810, there was little demand for an automatic connection between the supply of banknotes and the par value of sterling against gold. For twenty-five years after the recoinage of 1774, the price of an ounce of gold bullion on the international market hovered around £3 17s 7¾d sterling, against a Mint price of £3 17s 10½d per ounce. In 1797 and 1798, the Bank of England continued to buy gold at the Mint price. The very poor harvests of 1799 and 1800 resulted in high imports of grain, and the Bank of England and the Scottish banks, with their duty to the nation at war, increased their discounts; by the autumn of 1800 the discount for sterling at Hamburg was almost 10 per cent, and sovereigns passed for 22s and 22s 6d. In 1801, nature was kind to the pound sterling, the price of grain fell, and peace in 1802, though short-lived, righted the exchanges. From 1803 to 1808, the price of bullion fluctuated around £4 an ounce, a modest premium for a country to pay under unprecedented wartime pressure. Nevertheless, the short-lived debate at the turn of the century led to theoretical discussions about the behaviour of the international exchanges which would be used against the Scottish position.[46]

Gold reached £4 10s 0d in 1809, and on 29 August the economist and stockjobber, David Ricardo, published the first of three letters in the *Morning Chronicle* on the need for a strict control over the issue of paper.[47] Following the ideas of Henry Thornton in his *Enquiry into the Nature and Effects of the Paper Credit of Great Britain*, Ricardo pointed out that before 1797 the Bank of England had tended to contract its note issue when the exchanges were adverse. But the suspension had enabled the Bank of England 'to increase or decrease at pleasure the quantity and amount of their notes'. The bank was no longer bound by fears for its own safety 'to limit the quantity of their notes to that sum which shall keep them of the same value as the coin which they represent. Accordingly we find that gold bullion has risen from from £3-17-3¾d, the average price previous to 1797, to £4-10sh-0d, and has been lately as high as £4-13-0d per ounce.' Ricardo then proceeded to elaborate one of his famous principles:

> When the motive for exporting gold occurs, while the Bank do not pay in specie, and gold cannot therefore be obtained at its Mint price, the small

---

46 For a discussion of these issues, see Deane, *The Evolution of Economic Ideas*, ch. 4; Henry Thornton MP, *Enquiry into the Nature and Effects of the Paper Credit of Great Britain* (London: 1802). Thornton was in favour of government loans and paper credits, although he outlined how an increase in paper circulation would tend to push up prices and raise the sterling price of gold. In the House of Commons, he denied that paper had increased the price of foodstuffs and blamed the harvests: R. G. Thorne (ed.), *The History of Parliament: The House of Commons 1790–1820* (London: 1986), vol. v, *Members Q-Y*, pp. 370–3; for the view from the Bank of England, see J. H. Clapham, *The Bank of England: A History* (2 vols, Cambridge: 1944), vol. ii, *1797–1914*, pp. 18–19.
47 David Ricardo, 'The High Price of Bullion, a Proof of the Depreciation of Bank Notes', repr. and ed. P. Sraffa and M. H. Dobb, *The Works and Correspondence of David Ricardo* (11 vols, Cambridge: 1951), vol. iii, *Pamphlets and Papers 1809–1811*, pp. 47–99, and 'Appendix', pp. 99–127.

quantity that can be procured will be collected for exportation and bank notes will be sold at a discount for gold *in proportion to their excess*. In saying, however, that gold is at a high price, we are mistaken, it is not gold, it is paper which has changed its value. Compare an ounce of gold or £3-17-10½d to commodities, it bears the same proportion to them which it has before done and if it do not it is referrible to increased taxation or to some of those causes which are so constantly operating on its value. But if we compare the substitute of an ounce of gold, £3-17-10½d in bank notes, with commodities, we shall then discover the depreciation of the bank notes. In every market of the world I am obliged to part with £4-10sh-0d in bank notes to purchase the same quantity of commodities which I can obtain for the gold, that is in £3-17-10½d of coin.[48]

If the Bank of England had kept to its pre-suspension principle for the note issue, then 'we should not have been now exposed to all the evils of a depreciated, and perpetually varying, currency'.[49] The core of David Ricardo's thesis followed Henry Thornton's analysis of a self-equilibriating exchange mechanism, but shorn of qualification and economic circumstance, entirely oblivious to the perilous military situation and presented with a remorseless logic as an eternal truth. David Ricardo was the most influential economist of the first half of the nineteenth century, and his support for a strict gold standard was cited long after his death.

On 1 February 1810, David Ricardo's friend, Francis Horner MP (1778–1817), with the enthusiastic support of the discount houses, moved for a Select Committee on the high price of gold bullion. Francis Horner was the right member for a task of interrogation of the Bank of England. A devout Scottish lawyer, he had moved to the Chancery bar in 1802, and in 1806 entered Parliament on his first of three rotten borough seats; it was said of him that 'the commandments were written in his face: no judge or jury who saw him would give the smallest degree of credit to any evidence against him'.[50] A founder of the Whig *Edinburgh Review*, he enjoyed several careers, the Carnatic Commission, the Chancery bar, Parliamentary politics and 'a very numerous and select acquaintance'.

Francis Horner was careful to appear balanced in his views before the committee sat; while paper money was the most likely cause of the depreciation of sterling, consideration should be extended to the unfavourable balance of trade caused by the influx of naval stores and grain, a view endorsed, among others, by Francis Baring. Overall, however, the evidence taken from 22 February to 25 May 1810 was doggedly against the Bank of England, whose directors 'as economists [came] less well out of the debate'.[51] They had not been consulted about the composition of

48 Ibid., p. 80.
49 Ibid., p. 95.
50 Thorne, *The History of Parliament*, vol. iv, pp. 237–47.
51 Clapham, *The Bank of England*, vol. ii, p. 26.

the committee. The arguments of the directors tended to mix dogmatism, the real-bills doctrine and outrage, and their denials that discounts and banknotes had anything to do with depreciation read unconvincingly. They received little support from the Scottish senior banks. Ebenezer Gilchrist, the general manager of the British Linen Company, made a most cautious and stilted witness on 19 March, failing to realise why a defence of the flexible issue of banknotes was required.[52] The Select Committee came to a simple conclusion: the policy of the Bank of England following suspension had involved 'great practical errors', and they looked for some stronger control than an assessment of what were good and bad bills, and thus emphatically rejected the real-bills doctrine.

The importance of their conclusions was soon realised by the Scottish bankers; Sir John Sinclair, for example, later replied, in defence of paper money, in September 1810 with his *Observations on the Report of the Bullion Committee*.[53] It was May 1811 before Parliament debated the report, and by then the worst of the commercial crisis had lifted, although Napoleon was still the dominant force in Europe. Francis Horner moved sixteen resolutions, and these formed the centrepiece of Parliamentary debate on currency reform for the next thirty-five years; indeed, Sir Robert Peel cited both the arguments used in the debate and the Bullion report in 1844 and 1845 when debating the proposed changes in banking legislation.[54] Francis Horner recognised that although some impact on the foreign exchanges was attributable to military expenditure and grain imports, the 'extraordinary' degree to which they were depressed was the result of depreciation of paper in Great Britain compared to the money of other countries (resolution no. 13). The Bank of England was to advert to the state of the foreign exchanges and the price of bullion in respect of its issues (no. 14). The suspension was to end six months from the ratification of a peace treaty but no longer, in any event, than two years (i.e. 6 May 1813) (no. 16).[55]

This was an impossible position for any responsible government to adopt. Spencer Perceval ridiculed it as 'a parliamentary declaration that

52 T. C. Hansard, *Parliamentary Debates*, 19 March 1810; *Report, Together with Minutes of Evidence and Accounts, from the Select Committee on the High Price of Gold Bullion* (House of Commons, 8 June 1810), repr. in Irish University Press Series of British Parliamentary Papers, vol. i, *Monetary Policy General* (Dublin: 1969).
53 Sir John Sinclair, *Observations on the Report of the Bullion Committee*, 10 September 1810; R. Mitchison, *Agricultural Sir John: The Life of Sir John Sinclair of Ulbster 1754–1835* (London: 1962), p. 240.
54 *Hansard*, 6 May 1844: 'In 1810 men of sagacity observed that the exchanges had been for a considerable period unfavourable to this country, more unfavourable than could be accounted for by the balance of trade or the monetary transations of this country'.
55 *Hansard*, 6 May 1811.

we must submit to any terms of peace rather than continue the war'.[56] Nicholas Vansittart led for the Tories with seventeen resolutions, all adopted by the government, and was, of course, strongly supported by the Scots. The key platform was that Napoleon's continental blockade mounted in 1806–7 and 'enforced with a degree of violence and rigour never before attempted' had increased costs and cut exports, while war expenditure and grain imports were the predominant cause of the depreciation on the exchanges (nos 4 and 13). Thus the suspension or the issue of notes had not caused the exchange problem or high price of bullion (no. 6). There was no concern in the country over Bank of England notes, which were acceptable as legal tender (no. 3). All the government resolutions were passed. Sir John Sinclair attempted to grapple with the theory involved. He repudiated a tract penned in 1797 wherein he had called for an end to restriction. The new paper system had answered the public well. The case of China showed that coining precious metal was not 'indispensably necessary' for a populous, civilised and commercial nation. Sinclair outlined six principles for a monetary system: (1) that it be provided with little trouble and superseded the necessity to export goods and property 'to the extent of many millions merely to obtain a circulation'; (2) that it could be increased when required by business; (3) a country should export metals for war and grain; (4) paper was an important addition to government revenues and created a saving of coinage; (5) it made a nation independent; and (6) that 'it [paper] possesses a *species of magical influence* on the internal prosperity of a nation'. Further, low interest and plentiful credit were the key factors that a banking system could provide to encourage economic growth.

Sir John Sinclair was important for the part which he played in bringing to the attention of the Edinburgh establishment the underlying significance for economic growth of their management of banking in the period of the suspension. Both he and the Earl of Lauderdale expressed views fully in keeping with the tradition established by George Home ws and the 'M' group in the aftermath of the Ayr crisis. Yet, by 1810, their type of reasoning over banknotes and credit was less acceptable than it had been when the political system was presided over by Henry Dundas and William Pitt. The London discount houses were growing in importance with the growth of international trade and so was their influence on the board of the Bank of England. The precision of Ricardian thought, combined with the needs of the discount houses, created a powerful view which linked the value of the pound sterling to successful economic

56 Clapham, *The Bank of England*, vol. ii, p. 29, citing John Wilson Croker, *Correspondence and Diaries*, vol. 1, p. 35.

progress. The vagaries of the Scottish real-bills doctrine and its reliance on the common sense of boards of directors to manage a banking system had less and less appeal. After 1810, high politics was more fragmented and the rise of the Whigs and the reforming Tory administrations marginalised appeals to precedent, sympathetic discourse and polite society.

CHAPTER 12

BANK LENDING AND ECONOMIC AND SOCIAL CHANGE IN THE EIGHTEENTH CENTURY

'SCOTLAND IS A country the most barren of any Nation in these Parts of Europe, they have nothing of their own growth to export, except corn, coals, cattle and some wool; nor nothing to form any manufacturers but what they receive from their neighbours. There is nothing hinders Scotland from being a Trading Nation but the want of goods to export.'[1] These words from a petition to Parliament about the year 1720 did not exaggerate the poverty of Scotland. There had been some expansion in the second half of the seventeenth century, and the economic legislation of Parliament in 1693 and 1695 encouraged certain, albeit limited, developments. The gap in productive capacity and in national income per head between Scotland and England remained obvious to contemporaries; with a population of one-fifth that of England, the land tax in 1707, for example, gave Scotland an assessment of only one-fortieth of the English level. The acceptance of Union in 1707 was in large part the decision of various political and religious interests, but there was also a clear recognition of the economic benefits that could be expected by the settlement. Several clauses in the Act of Union were directly concerned with economic problems, and as a result of the Union Scotland became part of the largest free-trade area in Europe – a junction with a society in which the indices of growth were beginning to exhibit cumulative change within an increasing sophistication of institutional structure. And, not least for Scotland's development in the eighteenth

---

1 H. Hamilton, *An Economic History of Scotland in the Eighteenth Century* (Oxford: 1963), quoted on p. xiii; B. P. Lenman, *An Economic History of Modern Scotland 1660–1976* (London: 1977), chs 2 and 3.

century, there was a closer association than previously with a colonial empire whose populations (especially in North America) were to grow fast throughout the decades that followed, and which produced cheap raw materials, notably tobacco, timber, sugar and cotton. Glasgow was as well placed for trade with the tobacco-producing colonies as the large English ports concerned with the North Atlantic trades, and the import and re-export of tobacco was the first large-scale trading result of the new integration into the British Empire.[2] Within a few decades of the Union with England, Scottish society was moving steadily towards the transition to the modern industrial state. There had long been close connections between the aristocratic families on both sides of the Border, and between Edinburgh and London; but now the incorporation of the Scottish economy with the greatly advanced society of England was without a doubt a major factor in the transformation that was to take place. There were certain particular characteristics within Scotland that require emphasis in this context.

England was the first society to make the transition to an advanced capitalist system. Inevitably, it was a slow, uneven and uncoordinated evolution which in time was spread over more than three centuries before 1800. In Scotland, the change from the traditional order was accomplished within little more than half this time, although, like all developing societies, much that was customary remained or was modified only in part. In Scotland as in England, the radical core of change was the commercialisation of the agrarian structure, the Highlands and Islands remaining somewhat apart. The critical relationships between agrarian change and commercial and industrial growth have been much commented upon, and it is only necessary here to remark upon the role of the landed proprietors in Scotland in the improvement of their estates.[3] The legal basis for the shift to a capitalist agrarian sector was clearly defined in Scotland, as the Parliament before 1707 had been prepared to pass general, as well as specific, measures of support for agricultural change and property rights. As Sir John Sinclair wrote in 1814: 'In no country in Europe are the rights of proprietors so well defined, and so carefully protected', and when he wrote this he could look back to legislation and legal enactments from the seventeenth century.

The sources of capital accumulation necessary for the development and emergence of an industrial society naturally differ between societies.

---

2 Lenman, *An Economic History of Modern Scotland*, p. 91.
3 The lengthy background of agricultural change in England is now generally accepted as part of a 'conjoined' development of agrarian and industrial change: 'Introduction: Modern Conceptions of the Industrial Revolution', in P. O'Brien and R. Quinault (eds), *The Industrial Revolution and British Society* (Cambridge: 1993), p. 22; see also T. S. Ashton and C. H. E. Philpin (eds), *The Brenner Debate, Agrarian Class Structure and Economic Development in Pre-Industrial Europe* (Cambridge: 1987).

Profits from the agrarian sector – which in both England and Scotland included incomes from mining – have always been important. Scotland was a poor country, and both the sources of capital and their rate of growth through time were naturally limited. What emerged during the eighteenth century was a financial infrastructure that was admirably adapted to the requirements of economic growth, a generalisation that must include recognition of the inevitability of crises, including the paramount importance of the fluctuations in harvests, and speculation. What was required for growth in such a society as eighteenth-century Scotland were institutional structures that were able to move through crises without serious or disastrous consequences to their general viability, and it was to this model that the banking system of Scotland contributed as the eighteenth century progressed. The system established by the Bank of Scotland Act of 1695 provided mechanisms for building a substantial basis of credit on a relatively small capital by the issue of paper money. This advance was buttressed by the institutions of society, politics and the legal system and, although it encountered many difficulties, was able to develop into one of the most important parts of the credit available to agriculture, industry and commerce. The two senior banks of Edinburgh were at times criticised by contemporaries, and by some later historians, for caution in their lending policies. Yet in the context of the eighteenth century, with the upheavals caused by successive Jacobite rebellions, the frequent political uncertainties, such as the bitter assault on Bank of Scotland by the Duke of Argyll's interest after 1727, occasional speculation in paper credits, and the intellectual and commercial doubts as to what constituted an effective, safe and efficient banking system, their business conservatism and general vigilance were prudent and sensible. Overall, it is necessary to recognise that the banking system, looked at for the eighteenth century as a whole, was an important and stimulating factor in economic growth, and its role within the successful story of development must not be underplayed.[4]

There were other factors in the Scotland of the eighteenth century that were different from those which obtained in England. It would be a difficult exercise in historical terms to compare the role and place in economic growth of the landed aristocracies of the two countries. Both had improvers in agricultural change, and many on both sides of the Border engaged in entrepreneurial roles in respect of mining, building and textiles. The aristocracy in Scotland were conscious of the backwardness of their economy, and certainly there was no parallel in England with the

---

4 For essays on the role of finance in the transition to a modern economy which are relevant to the Scottish case, see A. Gerschenkron, *Economic Backwardness in Historical Perspective* (London: 1965), chs 1–3; J. G. Gurley and E. S. Shaw, *Money in a Theory of Finance* (Washington, DC: 1960).

involvement of the aristocracy in Scotland with banks and banking. There was in Scotland an awareness of the problems of economic progress that does not seem to exhibit itself to anything like the same extent among the landed classes in England, and this can be easily appreciated given the material comparison between the two countries. In several important respects, the beliefs of society were different in Scotland; for example the recognition of the place and role of education, which in the middling ranks of society had no parallel in England, even with recognition of the part which academies established by dissenters enjoyed. The position of the Kirk contributed to a more cohesive society. The conflicts over the Highlands and the gradual erosion of Gaelic were other sources shaping the focus of Scottish thinkers. The intellectual brilliance and the relevance to economic concerns of the Scottish Enlightenment and its diffusion through the upper ranks of society at the four universities and the clubs and salons of polite society again had little counterpart south of the Border.

It was made clear in the preamble to the original Bank of Scotland Act of 1695 that the Bank was established as 'a Publick Bank' for national purposes 'according to the Custom of other Kingdoms and States'. The Act went on in some detail as to how the business dealings of the Bank were to be regulated and supported by the structure of ownership, and with such rules that the Bank could not be easily damaged by speculators, or by the government. The primary concern of the legislators was over the evident failings in the fractured and expensive framework for the provision of credit for agriculture and trade, and this new endeavour, which so closely related to national achievement, was not to be diverted by the speculative activity which had been evident in both Scotland and England for a few years prior to 1695. The formation of policy was left to the adventurers, 'endowed with these Powers, and Authorities, and Liberties, necessary and usual in such Cases'.[5] The 'public and national' ethos was repeated again and again in the unstable political world of the early industrial period; before the Court of Session, the Bank always started its pleas with a short historical appreciation of its role, although with so many judges interested as proprietors and directors this took on rather a symbolic meaning. In the British Parliament after 1707, whose English members could not be expected to be as knowledgeable, it was a different matter. Henry Dundas, when he was Lord Advocate, moved all the Bank of Scotland bills with a discourse on the history of Scottish banking. After drafting a number of such statements in the course of a long and distinguished career as Bank Secretary, George Sandy ws argued in his *Observations on the Acts of the*

5 See below, Appendix 1.

Bank of Scotland that the bank was established 'for national objects, for the Legislature does not make Public Statutes for objects of private interest. The Intendment of National benefit is repeated in all the succeeding statutes, which bear testimony to the justness of these expectations – e.g., in that of 14 Geo III c.32 $.2 (1774)', and he then regaled his distinguished readership with the preamble of that Act.[6] George Sandy also went a little further and suggested that the joint stock was a public fund, 'subject only to the operation of the Statute'. The incorporating enactment, while it communicated to the proprietors a capacity of holding property, did not vest this in the corporation. Even the clause for the naturalisation of foreigners was brought into view; it was designed to draw capital to the country, without distinction of religion, vocation, residence, etc. His case could have been further strengthened by drawing attention to the blatant discrimination against the diminutive British Linen Company in 1784 by Henry Dundas, Governor of Bank of Scotland, as part of the grand design to keep the Royal Bank and the Bank at the apex of financial power. But in George Sandy's time, political power was more widely diffused and the Bank and the British Linen were good friends. Thus all those interested in the well-being of the commercial and landed interests could not fail to hear the message that the responsibility of Bank of Scotland at times of crisis was 'national and public', proved by its attention to the flow of credit, through bills, overdrafts on cash accounts and bonds; and, when in difficulty after 1772, the board would draw the attention of the political magnates and Parliament 'to the great national advantage' of the Bank over its many decades of work. This was the overriding view among the senior levels of the Bank through which every Bank official and director interpreted his role, which encouraged a long-term view on lending. Bank officials even collected together historical details to support their case. Although to political factions opposed to the Bank these statements of public intent read as merely the pleading of a special interest, in every major crisis of the early industrial period the Bank alone, or in combination with the Royal Bank, tried to provide a stable national framework which involved financial obligations to civil society in addition to funds for Scottish provincial bankers and the Edinburgh private banks.

The social and political context after 1689 was favourable to a national Bank sanctioned by Parliament. After three decades of subservience to

---

6 George Sandy ws was Secretary of Bank of Scotland from 1810 to 1837 and was thus in a good position to comment on several crises; see below, Chapter 14. The *Observations on the Acts of the Bank of Scotland* (undated) exist in manuscript in the Bank archives; they were printed for a wider audience. C. W. Boase thought these of sufficient merit to offer a précis in *A Century of Banking in Dundee; being the Annual Balance Sheets of the Dundee Banking Company from 1764 to 1864*, 2nd edn (Edinburgh: 1867), pp. 15–16. Sandy also penned a *Diary*.

the Crown, the landed proprietors were the most important part of the body politic; it was in their direct political and economic interest that the Bank Act was passed. Before the overthrow of James VII, decisions on the coinage and currency were decided by the Crown. The supply of money had been undermined by counterfeit and foreign coins to the point where proprietors required the services of the goldsmith and exchanger side by side with their lawyer and the estate factor. There were numerous exchange rates, which brought all the costs and drawbacks common to multiple-currency systems. Further, the country was obviously short of capital, and the devaluation of the pound Scots in 1686 was clearly insufficient for the encouragement of enterprise.[7] The intention of the legislature was to establish a unified currency, and a measure of the value of coin, organised under an acceptable umbrella which could not easily be taken over by the Crown and subverted as the Mint had been; it is in this sense that the grant of the monopoly for twenty-one years should be understood. This was quite a different meaning from the common idea that those who engaged in an enterprise should have a protection for their investment. Beyond this, the Bank could have gone in various directions because the Act was quite vague; if George Sandy ws was right and the 'reference to other banks in the preamble . . . was to the national banks of Venice, Genoa and Amsterdam: not to the Bank of England', then the intent might well have been to bring together, in the new bank, the foreign bill trade of the nation, or for it to act as a store of treasure and plate on which notes were based. In all three of the continental banks, it was the urban and merchant elites which dominated the formation of policy and took trade to be synonymous with national interest. Obviously, if Bank of Scotland was to be a 'public and national' bank, and if the concerns of the legislators were to be addressed, something more would be needed, some broader dimension for lending and borrowing. George Sandy ws may or may not have been right as to the influence of foreign banks on the original vision, but the early history of lending showed that the founders had home-grown ideas of what the Bank should do which arose out of their existing civil society, and landed wealth came at the top of the list. In one important sense, Bank of Scotland required no break with the past; it was established with a legal framework which was remarkably adaptable to the needs of commercial bank lending. The laws on wadsets and debts, codified by Sir James Dalrymple of Stair in *The Institutions of the Law of Scotland*, were sufficient protection, in theory, to enable recovery

7 When Hugh Chamberlain came forward with his scheme for creation of paper money against land valuations, it was rejected because it would have created another currency, which ran the risk of falling to a discount on its face value and would be uncertain as to its negotiability. Scotland needed a clearer sense of plain dealing if paper credit was to be acceptable.

of advances against land or persons.[8] Only one modification was needed in the original Bank Act: casting inland bills into the same legal basket as foreign bills. Advances on bonds were catered for by the feudal and other land laws, and the early enactments on property of the Scottish Parliament under William and Mary provided additional guarantees.

There were significant issues at stake in the attitudes to banking and credit in early eighteenth-century Scotland. They fall within that general category which historians call 'social attitudes' of civil society. The leading representatives of society grappled with what all too often appeared as intractable, even insoluble, problems of poverty, unemployment, faction and party. At times their perspectives were clouded by an overwhelming sense of despair, even desperation in the aftermath of the great famine of 1695–1700, and a few years later when the trades supported by the Scottish Parliament wilted under English imports it was often quite impossible to discern whether the economy was moving for better or worse. Indeed, as late as the mid-eighteenth century, some writers remained distinctly pessimistic about the chance of closing the gap in standards and behaviour between Scotland and England. Yet, in spite of very real drawbacks, it is evident that the Scots had developed ways of looking at economic matters which, although often crude and mechanistic, addressed the problems of capital accumulation and progress and discussed, often quite accurately, which policies and interventions worked and which had not. One great advantage which they had was the experience of the two senior banks. Their reflections may have lacked theoretical sophistication, but to the writers of the Scottish Enlightenment the early thinkers bequeathed a legacy from which the complexity of economic progress could be viewed, and in particular the conditions under which capital accumulation in Scotland was likely to succeed.

The social group with the greatest liquid resources and the most significant claims to unutilised assets were the landed proprietors, whose stake in Bank of Scotland has been documented.[9] Thus, any consideration on the development of capital accumulation and business enterprise, as well as the direction of bank lending, has to address how Bank of Scotland, and later the other banks, related to this social elite. First, it must be emphasised that for the entire eighteenth century landownership was concentrated in only a few hands. The exhaustive examination of landownership by Loretta Timperley showed that in the 817 parishes and other parochial areas, there were in 1770 10,210 property valuations held

---

8 Sir James Dalrymple of Stair, *The Institutions of the Law of Scotland*, ed. D. M. Walker (Edinburgh and Glasgow: 1981), book 2, for the complexities of Scottish land law.
9 See above, Chapter 1.

by only 7,838 proprietors or owner-occupiers in a population of between 1.3 and 1.4 million. They ranged in size from the 'bonnet lairds', with lands but little income, to the immense tracts owned by the leading nobility whose families criss-crossed the history of eighteenth-century Scotland, some of whom, such as the Earls of Aberdeen and Panmure and the Dukes of Argyll and Buccleuch, were important players in British political life. Together these were the heritors (landowners and owner-occupiers) who paid taxes listed in the valuation rolls and formed at most 2.5 per cent of the adult population.[10] The rest of the agricultural population were tenants (often called farmers and cottagers and possessors of houses), but, however defined, they were not owners of the land they tilled and lived on. This was a remarkably concentrated pattern of ownership compared, say, with Sweden, where around 20 per cent of males over 15 owned land in 1805, or the United States, where 50 per cent owned landed property in 1798. Sir John Sinclair noted that although about one-third of the land of Scotland was strictly entailed, Scots land law greatly helped the agrarian improvers. An Act of 1770 'To encourage the improvement of lands . . . in Scotland held under settlements of strict entail' permitted proprietors of entailed estates to become creditors of their heirs for three-fourths of the money expended on enclosing, planting, drainage and general improvement.[11] With proprietorship went the control of local government and justice, as justices of the peace and commissioners of supply (for taxes); to be appointed to the former office one needed lands yielding £200 per year, for the latter £100. These proprietors were the main decision-makers on every local issue, on the supply of labour for the roads, on the interpretation of the laws on serfdom and servants; and in their hands was the choice of those to be called out to oppose the Jacobite forces in 1715 and 1745.[12] The relatively narrow base for Scottish landownership enabled advances from Bank of Scotland to be larger and of often lengthier duration than they would have been in an egalitarian

10 Owner-occupiers received only 4 per cent of total annual rents: L. R. Timperley, 'Landownership in Scotland in the Eighteenth Century', Ph.D. thesis (University of Edinburgh, 1977); idem (ed.), A Directory of Landownership in Scotland c. 1770, Scottish Record Office, new series, no. 5 (Edinburgh: 1976); idem, 'The Pattern of Landholding in Eighteenth Century Scotland', in M. L. Parry and T. R. Slater (eds), The Making of the Scottish Countryside (London: 1980), pp. 137–54. There is a summary of the material in L. Soltow, 'Inequality of Wealth in Land in Scotland in the Eighteenth Century', Scottish Economic and Social History, 10 (1990), 38–60. There were two other categories of landownership: that owned by institutions and by persons together, and land owned by a wadsetter until the debts on that land were paid. This may have increased the total number of owners to 8,500. There was also land tilled by a tacksman and clansmen for a Highland chief, but this gave no title in law.

11 10 George III c.51; for discussion of this and long leases, see Hamilton, An Economic History of Scotland, p. 71.

12 For a discussion of the legal and taxation role of the landowners, see A. E. Whetstone, Scottish County Government in the Eighteenth and Nineteenth Centuries (Edinburgh: 1981).

system. Further, it gave this bedrock of lending a measure of security; even where estates were sequestrated for political reasons, advances by the Bank ranked high in the list of creditors and were always repaid by the government.

The lending figures for Bank of Scotland from 1697 to 1705 show the importance of long-term advances on heritable and personal bonds, the majority of which were to landowners, drawn by themselves or in conjunction with writers and factors in Edinburgh. Advances were usually on their lands, named in the bonds, or by their personal guarantee, and occasionally by pledge of Exchequer bills or plate. By these methods, from £2,500 to £5,000 a month was lent by the Bank to a cross-section of the landed of lowland and southern Scotland. There was an inevitable decline after 1707 as the Equivalent monies were distributed, but from 1709 the figures climbed swiftly again. Single loans to the aristocracy could reach £2,000; the Duke of Montrose, the Earl of Hyndford, the Marquis of Tweeddale and Sir Hew Dalrymple took sums this large, and before the election of 1710 the Duke of Roxburghe and retainers of his family, and the Duke of Montrose, borrowed sums over £5,000. The aristocracy went to war with monies from Bank of Scotland. In the eighteenth century, the aristocracy raised their own regiments and were paid later, often much later, by the government – hence the need for bank funds. The Earl of Stair, for instance, was the lead borrower in four bonds for £500 apiece in 1710; thus we meet the Earl together with William and George Dalrymple, George, Lord Forester, and Captain Cornelius Kennedy in Brigadier Douglas's regiment and Lieutenant James Gardiner in the Earl of Stair's own regiment. At this time and later, they raised further loans in combination with other soldiers. The most common bond for landed proprietors by 1710 was for £500, often with an Edinburgh lawyer or agent in tow; such were the cases of Sir Robert Anstruther of Balcaskie, and Sir James Campbell of Aberuchil; sometimes landowners worked together, as in the case of Sir James Roehead of Innerleith and Sir Francis Kinloch of Gilmerton. Over 100 landed proprietors, singly or in association, borrowed £500 apiece from the Bank from the Act of Union to the Jacobite invasion of 1715, and more than this number took smaller sums or were associated together with a group of borrowers. John Stewart of Garntullie, for example, who held lands north of Perth, borrowed £300 in 1709, and John Forbes of Culloden, in association with Archibald Dunbar of Thundertoun and Thomas Calder of Muirtoun, who took £200. Narrow expectations of what could be achieved in estate improvement and fear of falling further into debt were a constant worry for landowners in the early eighteenth century. Many, as we know, were slow to improve and waited until foodstuff prices rose later in the century. But, for those prepared to borrow, Bank of Scotland offered innumerable combinations of lending by bond, at the legal rate of interest, with the knowledge that the money would not be demanded back until the proprietor was able to pay, and the arrangements for repayment testify to a willingness to accept part-payment or conversion into bills of exchange, or incorporation into another and larger advance.

There were occasional advances of £1,000 to merchants, as in 1711 to a joint enterprise of merchants in Glasgow and Edinburgh, but the maximum sum was usually £500 taken, for example, by the New Mills cloth manufactory in the same year and guaranteed by Sir Robert Sinclair, together with a merchant, several goldsmiths, two tailors and the master of the New Mills. Merchants usually asked for less before 1720: for example, £250 for printing some books, £200 for an Edinburgh brewery, £100 for an apothecary. There were exceptional applications: in July 1725, £3,000 was paid out on six bonds to a group of eleven merchants, acting with two coppersmiths, a goldsmith, two maltsters, two wrights, a hammerman and two tailors, all from Glasgow. But this was at the height of the boom, and the court of directors of the Bank soon decreed a stop to further heritable lending, 'as the extent is too great, until part is paid back'.

The peaks for lending by bond were higher and the troughs lower than for those by bill of exchange. There were three important phases in the first three decades; pre-1704, from 1709–14 and from May 1722 to March 1727. In this last period, just under six years, some £98,593 was lent out on bonds, and much stayed out for years to come. In between came fallow times, usually caused by political or military trouble such as the stop of 1704–5, caused by the intrigues within Parliament; there were the invasion crises of 1708–9 and 1714–16 and later the fears engendered by the boom which led to the collapse of the South Sea Bubble and the Mississippi scheme in France. The short-lived halt in 1725 was due to a genuine trade boom, but the crisis of 1727 was caused by politics again. It was a hard school for learning: in thirty-two years there were no fewer than three attempts to break the Bank, three invasions and military crises, two serious trade crises and numerous minor scares for everything from politics to climate. But harsh environments bring their rewards: in the crisis of 1727, landowners, judges of the Court of Session, merchants and even bankers in London showed their appreciation of the Bank by their support.[13] After 1727, the bond languished as a method of advancing money until a modest revival after 1742, but by then the cash account was the premier method of borrowing. There is some indication that Bank of Scotland performed an important service in reducing the

---

13 See above, Chapter 6.

rate of interest, although the evidence is inconclusive. Prior to 1689, the real rate of interest exceeded the legal maximum of 6 per cent. During the subsequent war, the rate rose and 15 per cent was quite common for bills discounted in Edinburgh; John Holland also suggested that lawyers and agents borrowed from the Bank to lend on at higher rates. The Bank charged rates of 8 and 12 per cent for bills of exchange in the early years, but bonds were always fixed at 5 per cent. After the Union of 1707, the general level of interest in Europe was falling, and by 1714 the Bank of Scotland rates for all bills of exchange had fallen to 5 per cent. Thereafter it should be stressed that several rates of interest coexisted in Scotland. Bank of Scotland interest on shorter-term deposits, six months or less, was usually 1 or ½ per cent below that for longer-term deposits. There were exceptions, such as the higher rates paid to the Court of Session for their funds. In general, peacetime saw deposit rates of 3–4 per cent, except at times of stress, such as 1727 and after the Seven Years' War.

By the 1760s, Scotland had moved to the forefront of the British Industrial Revolution, and landed proprietors became central to the process. The main focus of economic change lay in the most stable part of the country, the central lowlands – the lands south and east of the Highlands and north of the Borders. Widely dispersed across this area lay extensive coal seams which ensured that many landed families would remain a part of the industrial fabric of Scotland well into the twentieth century. Many estates benefited from iron and lead deposits and limestone, and in fact coal was often found with iron or with limestone, or together with good-quality clays for bricks, and stone quarries. A laird was unfortunate indeed not to have some useful mineral on his land. With rising prices for agricultural products after 1740, landed proprietors found themselves in a peculiarly strong position, from which a range of new avenues in business was explored, and which, as W. H. Marwick observed many years ago while discussing the links between the cotton trade and landed proprietors, required 'a close co-operation between the landed and industrial interests'.[14] Further, the scale of resources and incomes enabled some aristocrats to proceed alone, at least with some of their endeavours, from the building of planned villages like the Earl of Elgin's model settlement at Charlestown, to the £125,000 advanced by Bank of Scotland to James Alexander Stewart Mackenzie, the Earl of Seaforth, in June 1825 'on his heritable bond and disposition under reversion of the lands and kelp shores of Lewis, Uist and Barra', a brave attempt to sustain

14 W. H. Marwick, 'The Cotton Industry and the Industrial Revolution in Scotland', *Scottish Historical Review*, 21 (1924), 207–18; and see T. C. Smout, 'Where Had the Scottish Economy Got to by the Third Quarter of the Eighteenth Century?', in I. Hont and M. Ignatieff (eds), *Wealth and Virtue: The Shaping of Political Economy in the Scottish Enlightenment* (Cambridge: 1985), pp. 45–72.

the population before newer manufacturing processes superseded the primitive kelp trade.[15] Of course, it need hardly be mentioned that much of this enterprise enabled other businesses to open; for instance, Henry Scotland was granted a £1,000 cash account to supply the Elgin estate. There were very few general difficulties with bank advances to landed estates in the early phase of the Industrial Revolution. Problems began to appear after the Napoleonic Wars for all the Edinburgh banks, as some estate investment undertaken prior to 1815 was unable to generate good cash flows due to the general fall in prices for agricultural commodities.

Port and harbour developments were widespread. Like the construction of markets and manufacturing villages, landowners and trustees of estates which bordered waterways built wharves, basins, harbours and lighthouses and joined in the subscriptions for ports and road links. There was usually a clear economic reason, as in the case of the Earl of Elgin's docks at Limekilns on the Forth, or the Duke of Argyll's wharves at Inveraray, and innumerable jetties mushroomed on most navigable waterways to carry agricultural produce and minerals and act as terminals for ferry services. The Bank provided cash accounts of varying sizes; some were specific, for example, that for a new ferry service from Kinghorn to Kirkcaldy, but many were developments paid for by funds borrowed from the Bank for unspecified improvements. Landed proprietors and burgh authorities were also at the centre of turnpikes and road improvement trusts. From 1750 to 1844, 350 private Acts created road trusts in Scotland, with the greatest push in the 1780s, during the Napoleonic Wars, and occasional bursts such as that which contributed to the boom of 1825. At first, landlords tended to concentrate on local roads to waterways and grouped together to fund improvements to old drove routes and inter-burghal ways. As the projects grew in size and the new methods of John Loudan McAdam made possible all-weather highways, bank funds became increasingly important. In the summer of 1793, for example, the Bank lent by cash account to committees of road trustees in Fife (£700), Tranent (£2,000), Corstorphine (£700), Dalkeith (£1,800) and Dunkeld (£300). Where the main landowner was very wealthy, the advances could be much higher, thus £6,000 went to the Duke of Atholl for the road from Perth to

---

15 T. C. Smout, 'The Landowner and the Planned Village in Scotland, 1730–1830', in N. T. Phillipson and R. Mitchison (eds), *Scotland in the Age of Improvement* (Edinburgh: 1970), pp. 73–102; kelp is a seaweed from which an alkaline ash used in soap and glass was extracted. Prices rose by 1800 to around £10 a ton and by 1810 to £20. Thereafter they fell to £7 by 1825 and a few years later to £3 and £4 a ton. This was serious for estates such as that of Seaforth, which a little later produced 900 tons a year: M. Gray, 'The Kelp Industry in the Highlands and Islands', *Economic History Review*, 2nd series, 4 (1951–2), 197–209 (p. 198); advance confirmed, BS 1/5, Minutes: 20 June 1825. In 1809 the Bank provided the trustees of the Clanranald estate with a £6,000 cash account for further investment in kelp. The Bank also provided finance for the developing chemical industry.

Dunkeld. In some cases, the Bank opened more than one account: three, for example, were opened for the Kilpallet Burn Road in 1801. In 1823, the Bank lent £10,000 for the Gorbals and Kilbride road on the guarantee of George, Earl of Glasgow, Sir John Maxwell of Pollock and Colonel William Mure of Caldwell, £5,000 for the Paisley and Lochwinnoch road and £3,000 for a Corstorphine road.[16] Roads were a safe investment for the banks; security was usually provided by local heritors who tended to take a proprietorial interest in the quality of construction. In return for the investment, usually by way of a cash account, banks benefited because the building of a section of road increased the circulation of banknotes and led to frequent deposits of cash. In several cases, such as the new bridge at Montrose, the Bank even joined the subscription. Overall, the pattern of road-toll receipts showed a satisfactory rise to 1815, but thereafter they stagnated and later fell with competition from canals and railways, although some roads serving industrial areas continued to do well.

The building of canals in Scotland does not appear to have received much support from the banks in the early years.[17] Landowners preferred the building of wharves and jetties and their piecemeal road schemes; doubtless they were easier and more convenient for their farm labourers.[18] Yet Scots had long dreamed of various improvements to the coastal routes, and, for example, a connection between the Forth and the Clyde was often mooted by early improvers. After years of public discussion, Parliament authorised a company promoted by the Duke of Queensberry in March 1768 with a capital of £150,000 in £100 shares. Construction started in the summer of that year at the Forth end and by 1773 had reached Kirkintilloch, nine miles north-east of Glasgow; but by then it was £40,000 over budget and the share price had fallen to £56. A number of promoters were badly affected by the crisis over Douglas, Heron & Co. (including the Duke of Queensberry), and, as they were unable to raise more funds, canal construction halted in July 1775 just three miles short of Glasgow. Almost a decade passed before Henry Dundas, the Lord Advocate, secured legislative support in 1784 to finish the work with £50,000 from the reserves of the Commission for Forfeited Estates. By

16 Hamilton, *An Economic History of Scotland*, pp. 222–34; in several cases, trusts applied to Parliament for additional funds. The 100-mile Glasgow to Dumfries route, for example, was completed after 1816 with £50,000 from the government. Sir John Sinclair suggested in 1819 that over 3,000 miles of new roads had been built by road trusts, three-quarters since 1790. Total investment lay between £2 million and £3 million by 1814, although Sir John implied that all 'internal communications' were covered by this figure. See also *The New Statistical Account of Scotland*, vol. vi, *Lanark* (Edinburgh: 1845).
17 For bank finance of canal development in England, see L. S. Pressnell, *Country Banking in the Industrial Revolution* (Oxford: 1956), pp. 389–400.
18 H. Hamilton, *The Industrial Revolution in Scotland* (Edinburgh: 1932), p. 235, suggests that the first canal to be finished in Scotland was that from the Stevenston collieries to Saltcoats in 1772.

1789 it was reported that the cost of moving bulk goods from the two cities was under 10 per cent of the old cost over land. The Monkland coal and iron canal, started in the same boom conditions, was also halted after the 1772 crisis, again for ten years, and was not finished until 1792. There were problems with most canals in Scotland; neither the landed proprietors nor the banks felt confident enough to advance sufficient funds to guarantee continuous construction work. Yet, after the capital of the Bank had reached £1 million in 1796, the board was open to suggestions for large-scale aid. The Crinan Canal project was granted a £5,000 cash account in 1804, although the Bank could hardly refuse, as the cautioners were the Duke of Argyll, the Earl of Breadalbane and Lord Frederick Campbell, Clerk Register for Scotland. A similar sum was made over to the Aberdeen harbour trustees in 1812. In 1818, the Forth and Clyde navigation wished to extend their works and borrowed £30,000.

Long before the foundation of Bank of Scotland, the bill of exchange was used for the foreign trades of Scotland, and in 1682 the full legal protection of merchant law was extended to foreign bills payable within the kingdom. The Bank Act of 1695 extended these legal norms to inland bills, and on this basis the Bank offered a valuable service to traders and agents using the form of the foreign bill for advances due to be paid in Scotland. These bills, usually sixty days in duration, ranged upwards from £20, and occasionally reached £350, although this was exceptional. In the two years after 20 November 1697, over 600 bills were drawn at the Bank, by 263 persons; the most common were for £25 and £50, although around 20 per cent (in number) were for over £100.[19] The pattern was unmistakable. These bills were frequently treated as advances renegotiated every two months, and a borrower was able to act as a guarantor for other borrowers. Sir William Binning the arms dealer, for instance, in conjunction with William Baird and the Viscount of Tarbit, as he was described in the ledgers, ran bills for many months and put their names down as guarantors for others. The Earl of Buchan kept a bill on Sir William Benholm for over a year, rediscounting every sixty days with a one-third reduction when it suited him. Some bills were transferred between parties. The average drawn was for £142, with Sir James St Clair at the top for £1,000; the Earl of Leven reached £350 during his time as Governor of Edinburgh Castle. Even Patrick Steill, the Whig plotter and tavernkeeper, borrowed a modest £20, although he quickly repaid it. While many of the borrowers were not identified as to profession, certain patterns emerge. The majority of bills bought by the Bank were drawn in favour of merchants, writers and agents with an

19 BS 1/94/1, General Ledgers, Account of inland bills, 20 November 1697 to 17 November 1699.

admixture of lairds, army officers and government personnel. This was thus a facility whose recipients were much broader in social class than for bonds. Whereas in the first two years of use from 1697 the sums advanced remained below £2,000 a month, as the economy recovered and the Bank gained in confidence the figure commonly reached £2,500 to £3,000, and, in eight different months before November 1705, £4,000 was drawn or redrawn. The crisis of that month stopped the trade, although many bills were repaid only slowly, and the effect of the Union, as with bonds, was further to discourage borrowing.[20] As the years passed, the directors could see a seasonal pattern: bills fluctuated on a month-to-month basis more sharply than bonds, and appeared to follow the times for agricultural payments. The general pattern was for higher discounts in May, August and November, while February, April and September were usually much quieter, with peak to trough ranging from 1:3 or even 1:4 over a year. They were also used in such a flexible way by 1710 that borrowers could receive and pay even on the same day and charge sums to their debit as they required. In spite of the later popularity of the cash account, the inland bill of exchange remained an important lending device for those looking for short-term accommodation – under a year – who required advances but who did not wish to make regular repayments or need cash facilities in Edinburgh.

Something has been said of the larger cash accounts made out to landed proprietors, and public bodies, for road construction and canals from the later eighteenth century. This was a development which came with the Industrial Revolution. The earlier cash accounts were for smaller sums, particularly useful for traders and shopkeepers. Bank of Scotland opened the first 'current account of credit' on 24 November 1729 for Dame Magdalene Scott and Hugh Clerk ws, and the first transaction was for Alexander Blackwood a few days later. By April 1730 there were over eighty such accounts, and the total debit at the end of each month had passed £5,000. By August, with balances out nearing £9,000, the directors reluctantly cut back; Lord Monzie was picking up more notes and demanding gold. As the year drew to a close, on the advice of Richard Holland, the board took the unwelcome decision to bring in an optional clause, that addition to the writing on the banknotes which announced that the Treasurer would pay the bearer the face value or 'in the option of the directors' the value plus interest at 5 per cent in six months 'after the day of the demand'.[21] At first, the clause was only on £5 notes, so as not to inconvenience the traders of modest means, but later all notes were

---

20 See above, Chapter 5.
21 See above, Chapter 6.

covered, after the Royal Bank had presented £1 notes in large numbers. The Bank always made it clear that loyal customers would receive coin for business transactions, and those journeying to London received bills on London houses for cash there. It was not until November 1731 that the directors were confident enough to allow the cash accounts to exceed £10,000 (see Figure 6.2); yet, as confidence grew over the next few years, they became more sanguine over extensions of credit. By 1736 the limit had passed £17,000, and in November 1739, £35,558. There was a fall in the early months of 1740, although balances then rose swiftly and passed £50,000 in May 1741. During these harsh times, average balances rose 25 per cent to over £270 and the numbers opened reached almost 200.[22]

Who opened the new accounts? The Bank listed the occupation of all the holders and the guarantors. In the years 1729 to 1763, 38 per cent were opened by merchants and shopkeepers and another 7 per cent by persons in trade and manufacture who might be expected to make regular use of accounts (see Figure 12.1). This 'regular use' was very important in the response to the Royal Bank. Under the lending regime of bills and bonds it was common for the notes to be paid out, but little might be received until the bill was renegotiated or paid off. The new cash accounts encouraged holders to minimise their credit by daily paying in their cash and notes – a relatively easy matter, as most of these accounts were for businesses in Edinburgh and Leith. And of course they ensured a steady supply of other banknotes; the cash account was rarely used as a dead loan. Another 16 per cent were kept by writers and members of the legal profession connected to landed proprietors and others sympathetic to the Bank.

In the first half of the eighteenth century, the population of Scotland stagnated around, or just above, 1 million. It perhaps rose a little in the early 1710s and 1730s and fell in the famine years of 1726–7 and 1740–1.[23] By mid-century it was rising, and the first, although amateur, census put the number of Scots at 1,265,000 in 1755; by the time of the 1801 census, there were 1,599,068.[24] The proportion living in urban areas was also on the increase. From the 5.3 per cent of Scots who lived in burghs with over 10,000 (Glasgow and Edinburgh), there were 9.2 per cent in 1750 (now with Aberdeen and Dundee) and 17.3 per cent in 1801, by which time perhaps twenty burghs could be described as recognisable urban areas with a growing range of services associated with town life. The growth of urban centres and their associated consumer-oriented trades and services were of singular importance to the development of the banking network. When

22 BS 1/106/1–6, Cash account progressive ledgers, 1729–1742.
23 R. Mitchison, 'Scotland 1750–1850', in F. M. L. Thompson (ed.), *The Cambridge Social History of Britain 1750–1950* (2 vols, Cambridge: 1990), vol. i, *Regions and Communities*, pp. 155–207 (p. 157).
24 Hamilton, *An Economic History of Scotland*, p. 4.

Figure 12.1 *Occupational spread of a sample of cash-account holders, November 1729 to December 1763*

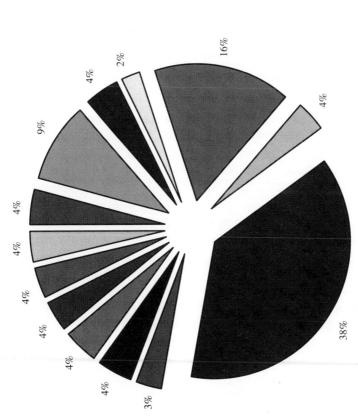

■ Peers/gentry
■ Estate owners
■ Tenants
□ City councils
■ Legal profession
■ Government appointments
■ Merchants
■ Manufacturers
■ Trades
■ Medics
■ Women
■ Unknown
■ Miscellaneous

Note: Sample represents 10 per cent of all cash-account holders listed in indices to ledgers 1–23.

Source: BS 1/106/1–23, Cash account progressive ledgers.

the scope is widened to include the scattered industrial hamlets in the coal and iron areas and the growth of smaller burghs, then the proportion of the population in urban areas was even greater. The densities of Renfrew, emerging as the leading industrial county, grew from 113.9 per square mile in 1755 to 333.6 by 1801, and in Fife from 162.2 to 186.4 compared with the older textile and agricultural counties such as Forfar (111.5 in 1801) or Ayrshire (82.9).[25] There was a considerable demand for means of payment from these industrial areas. Yet, the experience of Bank of Scotland had shown, in 1696–8 and in the war with the Royal Bank from 1727, that branches could be expensive unless they had clearly-defined roles. What could these be?

By the close of the Seven Years' War, the board of Bank of Scotland had a clearer idea of how branches might develop into sound and profitable opportunities which could broaden the base of the Bank. The longer the banknotes remained in circulation, the more the Bank earned. The Bank and the Royal Bank had long relied on their networks of directors and political supporters when inquiries were made over opening a cash account; the logical next step was to use a local agent to garner business. Both senior banks had used agents before, but the first extensive record of such instructions came from the British Linen Company from 1759. Agents were to 'open accounts with such friends as could be depended on', with an interest charge of 3 per cent on advances and discounts of bills.[26] The Company preferred to choose agents from among the more important local merchants, lawyers and landowners; thus Gilbert Gordon of Halleoths was chosen for the Dumfries agency in 1766, at Forres in 1771 Provost Alexander Forsyth was appointed, and John Auldjo, a prominent wine merchant, was appointed at Aberdeen in 1760. But it soon found that important agents were very busy and their attendance on Company business irregular, and they had an annoying tendency to mix up personal and Company accounts. Only later, after the 1772 crisis had removed several banking companies, did the profession of bank agent become sufficiently lucrative to overcome this. The Aberdeen Banking Company, established in 1767, was the first provincial company to open branches with salaried officials, and by 1770 it had offices in seven burghs along the north-east coast from Inverness to Montrose.[27] Then came Douglas,

---

25 Hamilton, *An Economic History of Scotland*, p. 18; T. M. Devine, 'Urbanisation', in T. M. Devine and R. Mitchison (eds), *People and Society in Scotland*, vol. i, *1760–1830* (Edinburgh: 1988), p. 28; A. Dickson (ed.), *Scottish Capitalism, Class, State, and Nation from before the Union to the Present* (London: 1980), ch. 4. The rate of population increase was faster after 1801; it was 1,806,000 by 1811 (an increase of 1.2 per cent per year) and 2,092,000 in 1821 (1.6 per cent per year): Lenman, *An Economic History of Modern Scotland*, pp. 44–5.
26 C. A. Malcolm, *The History of the British Linen Bank* (Edinburgh: 1950), pp. 173, 177–85.
27 C. W. Munn, *The Scottish Provincial Banking Companies, 1747–1864* (Edinburgh: 1981), p. 173.

Heron & Co. with a series of offices in the west from Dumfries to Inveraray and in Edinburgh, but after June 1772 these were all closed.

The reasons why Bank of Scotland opened its first agencies in 1774 have not been recorded; the decision probably owed something to the politics of the south-west after the collapse of Douglas, Heron & Co., and the first two commenced at Kelso and Dumfries in July.[28] The instructions to the agents have survived, and, as would be expected, covered advances on bills and cash accounts. Nonetheless, more attention was paid than in the case of the British Linen. At Kelso, Robert Riddick of Corbieton had to find security of £10,000; he could discount bills payable at Dumfries or Edinburgh and purchase bills on London, but was strictly limited in his ceilings which were initially at £2,000. For cash accounts, he could only recommend to the board, and the sums were kept to under £300. There was a similar exactitude for Dumfries and later branches. The taking of security was a serious obligation. Most cautioners lived in Scotland but some in England; in 1809, Archibald Hamilton, the proposed Glasgow agent, offered as his cautioners Gilbert Watson, the Glasgow private banker, and James Watt, of the engineering company of Boulton & Watt, Soho, Birmingham.[29] To appreciate the significance of these facilities for local conditions, it is necessary to say something about the growing diversity of the 'middling sorts' in these and other burghs. First, there were the owners of property who employed labour, the businessmen, merchants, makers of goods, shopkeepers and the upper ranges of craftsmen. These were crucial to the circulation of banknotes and bills of exchange. Second, the Bank ledgers confirmed that the professionals from the law, church, medicine and the universities, and schoolmasters, tended to keep positive balances. Third, there were the salaried employees in the customs and excise, clerks of companies, servants and 'secretaries' to well-off families and accountants. A fourth category, already important for deposits, were the rentiers: independent people of 'leisure', widows, and beneficiaries of family trusts.[30] The middle classes may have taken occasional bonds and discounted bills; more likely they kept their cash, like Samuel Pepys, in a large iron-bound chest with locks. They might lend their surplus to a writer, or to the Kirk, or invest in property. The cash account offered an opportunity to change this, and from this time such chests began to be used for decorative purposes in middle-class homes. In 1763, when Bank

---

28 See Appendix 8 for branches of Bank of Scotland.
29 BS 1/5, Minutes: 13 March 1809.
30 This follows the division of the middle classes set out by Stana Nenadic in 'The Rise of the Urban Middle Class', in T. M. Devine and R. Mitchison (eds), *People and Society in Scotland*, vol. i, *1760–1830* (Edinburgh: 1988), pp. 111–12; for the growth of the education sector, see D. J. Withrington, 'Schooling, Literacy and Society', in ibid., pp. 163–87.

of Scotland raised the interest on deposits to 5 per cent and advertised for deposits, it was inundated by middle-class depositors, a majority of whom were women. By 1800 there was still some way to go before all middle-class families held a bank account, although it is clear from the records that the middle class and banking were by then inextricably linked. Without these groups, especially the categories of depositors, branch banking would not have taken the form it did, if it had developed at all.

The straightforward nature of the early agency could accommodate itself to any secure lending proposition, from whatever trade. They were soon an important source of profit to the Bank, and between 1800 and 1815 almost half the yearly profits were attributable to branches. For the development of small merchant and shopkeeping business, the cash account proved immensely important. The lending figures show that accounts for £200 and £300 and later for £500 and more were opened at all branches; year on year, new business came in representing every line of business and civil society including medicine and education. Only two or three guarantors were needed, and these needed only to be of modest means. Thus for William Finnie, ironmonger at Kilmarnock, they were the quartermaster of the Queen's Dragoons and a local glazier. The rector of the old grammar school of St Andrews, William Dick, was supported by a friend back from India and a local surgeon. They could be work associates; for a £300 cash account, John Campbell of Melford, the Lt-Governor of Fort St George, was joined by three fellow officers. Small accounts proved attractive to shopkeepers, farmers, tacksmen and tenants of various descriptions; in the southern burghs, applications began to come in from the north of England. In 1809, Ann Potts, a farmer of Meldrum in Northumberland, was granted a £400 cash account at Kelso. (Indexes of early cash-account holders are given in Appendices 14 and 15.)

By 1800 it was apparent that a greater proportion of account holders and depositors were women than in the mid-eighteenth century. The records of the cash accounts for both the Bank and the British Linen show a number of women managing cash accounts and bill transactions for their own businesses, apart from their husband's work, as widows or as single women, often in conjunction with another woman. The typical format for the single female cash account at Bank of Scotland was a joint account between two women operating a retail and small manufacturing business guaranteed by relatives, lawyers or local merchants, sometimes their suppliers. Thus Mary and Janet McDonald, milliners in Edinburgh, were granted a £200 account in 1815, supported by two merchants. There was the case of Miss Helen Hunter, a straw-hat manufacturer in Aberdeen, whose £150 account was guaranteed by two farmers. Another industrial connection was a yarn spinner who acted as one of three guarantors for

Miss Catherine Thomson, a milliner at St Andrews in 1818. There was the growth of that subgroup of the genteel on low incomes, usually from better-off families who had failed to follow in their parents' footsteps: landscape and portrait painters, journalists and other writers, governesses for children. The grant of cash accounts at branches before 1790 confirms active interest; but only at Edinburgh and Aberdeen, and occasionally elsewhere, did the number of new authorisations exceed a dozen a year. Sums were usually at or below £300, the most common figure; in 1787, for example, only twenty-one of 159 grants were for £400 and above, and the following year, in spite of the lingering trade depression, thirty-four out of 158. In the first fifteen years of the new branch network, demand in Edinburgh exceeded that in all other places, although this included cash accounts for residents of burghs elsewhere. There had, as noticed before, always been account holders in Glasgow, often with account limits of £1,000 and occasional overdrafts much above this. The importance of Edinburgh grew in the early years of the Napoleonic Wars, as industrial companies with government contracts sought facilities and opened offices. Aberdeen, Perth and Dumfries attracted large numbers of accounts and most branches drew in customers from many miles around, with market days seeing increased activity. The end of the 1780s marked a divide, and thereafter there were fewer limits on industrial and trade cash accounts. From this time, cash accounts for several thousand pounds in textile production, paper-making, brewing, glassworks, iron and shipowning became common. In 1792, eight new accounts exceeded £1,000, and in 1793 there were twenty-one such, of which one was for £11,000 and that for the Carron Iron Company was £12,000. Overdrafts regularly exceeded these limits, often by a considerable margin. Discounts of bills could also rise far higher than these figures, as they were conducted on the basis of the worth of the parties involved and whether their London agent would be likely to pay. So complicated and extensive did the transactions for the Carron become that separate bill books were kept for it. The pattern of cash accounts for the British Linen Company from 1765 to 1797 show regular grants up to £1,000, the most common before 1790 being £300 to £500. Although £2,000 to £3,000 was granted by its board, and occasional larger sums for groups of linen merchants and for infrastructure projects, its most common advance by cash account was lower than for either the Royal Bank or Bank of Scotland. Its smaller capital was undoubtedly a factor in this, yet the more conservative approach was maintained into the nineteenth century when limitations on capital were no longer an obstacle.

Before the development of the branch system, the heaviest demands came in clear seasonal patterns wherein limits were often exceeded for shorter or longer periods. This caused problems, and from an early date the board of Bank of Scotland was concerned by the attitudes of some customers. Demands were made for overdrafts at the payment terms, especially those in August and November, although later in the century as demand for bank credit grew the peaks were more widely spread. It became common for customers to ignore their limits and demand new levels of credit unrelated to the payment terms. The directors recognised this as a symptom of the changing nature and complexity of the economy, but their response in the development of branches and the increases in capital led to some Bank agents ignoring cash limits and guidelines for bills if it was thought advantageous for the support of local business.

The trade figures indicate the pressures that the Bank and its agents were under (see Figure 12.2). The linen output grew from 13.4 million yards in 1780 to 20 million by 1789.[31] The tonnage for coastal and foreign shipping went from 54,407 tons in 1759 to 109,895 in 1771. Timber imports, one of the most useful barometers we possess of general building activity, show a sustained rise from 1755. From 1785, the first record of the brick excise, there was a sharp rise in output to a peak in 1787–8, then a fall the following year before a rise to a new peak in 1792–3. The coal output had reached perhaps 1.3 million tons by the time of the Ayr bank crisis, and another million tons was added by 1800.[32] Only the tobacco trade required smaller facilities. From a maximum of 44.8 million lb imported in 1771–5, it collapsed following the outbreak of the American war of independence.[33] The rapid growth of miscellaneous services and manufacturing trades encouraged the plethora of note issues before the Currency Act of 1765. It was this industrial and service activity that the branch networks of Bank of Scotland and the British Linen began to address. But their directors came up against new types of demands which forced a reconsideration of the whole question of bill and cash account limits.

The new cotton industry was one catalyst. A sustained rise of the industry with imports from the West Indies began in 1777 (256,650 lb) and reached 1,364,193 lb in 1787. By 1792, imports were above 3

31 A. J. Warden, *The Linen Trade, Ancient and Modern* (London: 1864), p. 480; Hamilton, *An Economic History of Scotland*, Appendix 4; idem, 'The Failure of the Ayr Bank, 1772', *Economic History Review*, 2nd series, 8 (1956), 405–17; A. Thomson, 'The Scottish Timber Trade, 1680 to 1800', Ph.D. thesis (University of St Andrews, 1991); A. K. Cairncross and B. Weber, 'Fluctuations in Building in Great Britain 1785–1849', *Economic History Review*, 2nd series, 9 (1956–7), 282–97.
32 Baron Frederick Duckham, *A History of the Scottish Coal Industry*, vol. i, *1700–1815* (Newton Abbot: 1970), pp. 28–9; S. Pollard, 'A New Estimate of British Coal Production 1750–1850', *Economic History Review*, 2nd series, 33 (1980), Table 14, p. 229.
33 Hamilton, *An Economic History of Scotland*, Appendix 9; J. M. Price, 'The Rise of Glasgow in the Chesapeake Tobacco Trade, 1707–1775', *William and Mary Quarterly*, 3rd series, 11 (April 1954), 179–99; A. Slaven, *The Development of the West of Scotland, 1750–1960* (London: 1975), pp. 20–6.

Figure 12.2 *Indices of economic activity, 1755–1800 (1755=100)*

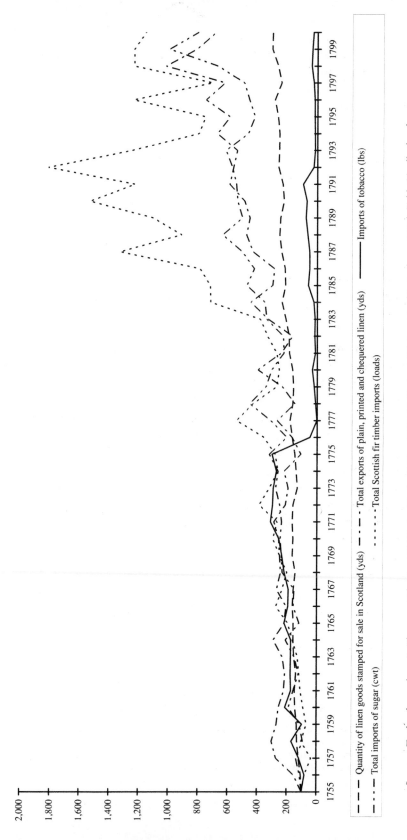

2,000
1,800
1,600
1,400
1,200
1,000
800
600
400
200
0

1755 1757 1759 1761 1763 1765 1767 1769 1771 1773 1775 1777 1779 1781 1783 1785 1787 1789 1791 1793 1795 1797 1799

‒ ‒ Quantity of linen goods stamped for sale in Scotland (yds)   ‒ ‒ ‒ Total exports of plain, printed and chequered linen (yds)   ——— Imports of tobacco (lbs)

‒·‒· Total imports of sugar (cwt)   ······· Total Scottish fir timber imports (loads)

Sources: Timber figures from A. Thomson, 'The Scottish Timber Trade, 1680 to 1800', Ph.D. thesis (University of St Andrews, 1991), Table 23; all other figures from H. Hamilton, *An Economic History of Scotland in the Eighteenth Century* (Oxford: 1963), Appendices 4, 6, 9 and 11.

million lb and, after a trough from 1794–7, recovered to 7.5 million lb in 1801.[34] The first mill opened at Rothesay in 1779, followed by Neilston (Renfrew) in 1782 and Johnstone (Renfrew) and East Kilbride (Lanark) in 1783, and Deanston in 1785. The famous mills of New Lanark were opened in 1786 by David Dale and Richard Arkwright and bought by Robert Owen in 1797; Catrine was opened in 1787, as were the Stanley Mills on north Tayside, built by George Dempster, the Dundee banker. In several cases, such as the Ballindalloch cotton works in Stirlingshire and at Kirkcudbright in 1795, landowners took the initiative, rather as Queensberry, Milton and Argyll had done in their support of the linen industry in a previous era.[35] By 1797, cotton had overtaken linen in value, with £462,904 spent on raw cotton, and £490,200 invested in plant with a total employment of 181,753 people 'in all the various branches' of the trade, although this was an optimistic statement; Sir John Sinclair estimated 151,300 in 1812, mainly homeworkers. By then there were 120 spinning mills, representing capital of £1.4 million and £490,200 invested in the mills.[36]

This volume of production made great demands on the banks both by cash accounts for wages and for bills to purchase raw cotton; this business, for example, formed a cornerstone of David Dale's Royal Bank agency in Glasgow. Some accounts were modest, such as £200 for Elizabeth Brown & Co., cotton spinners; but typical grants to companies with mills were £1,000, with the understanding that they might overdraw by agreement and that discounts would be much over this sum. Thus the Rothesay Spinning Company had £1,000 at Greenock in 1799, and Crombie and Carnegie, cotton spinners at Glasgow, a similar sum in 1812, both with higher periodic bill discounts. There are occasional references which suggest that bank monies enabled a company to set up a new concern; Fraser, McPherson, Cobban & Co. received £600 for a proposed woollen manufactory at Inverness, later raised to £800.

Both the cotton and linen trades encouraged investment in chemicals and bleaching processes.[37] In 1749, John Roebuck, a chemist, and Samuel Garbett, a metals manufacturer from Birmingham, started at Prestonpans

---

34 Hamilton, *An Economic History of Scotland*, Appendix 7, citing PRO, Customs, 14, Imports to Scotland.
35 Hamilton, *Industrial Revolution*, p. 127.
36 Ibid., p. 132; and see also Marwick, 'The Cotton Industry', pp. 207–18; J. Butt, 'The Scottish Cotton Industry during the Industrial Revolution 1780–1840', in L. M. Cullen and T. C. Smout (eds), *Comparative Aspects of Scottish and Irish Economic History 1600–1900* (Edinburgh: 1977), pp. 116–28 (p. 117); T. M. Devine, 'Colonial Commerce and the Scottish Economy', in ibid., pp. 177–90.
37 S. Fairlie, 'Dyestuffs in the Eighteenth Century', *Economic History Review*, 2nd series, 17 (1965), 488–510; A. Clow and N. L. Clow, *The Chemical Revolution* (Oxford: 1952); for a discussion of scientific achievements, see A. L. Donovan, *Philosophical Chemistry in the Scottish Enlightenment: The Doctrines and Discoveries of William Cullen and Joseph Black* (Edinburgh: 1975).

that long and successful development which led to a modern bleaching industry. Charles Macintosh is perhaps best remembered for his invention of waterproofed clothing for the British army, using a solution of rubber pressed between two layers of linen.[38] In 1783, Macintosh opened his first chemical works at Barrowfield in Glasgow to manufacture sugar of lead for calico printing and the turkey red dyes, then in 1793 another, for dyeing muslin, at Pollokshaws. But it was his chemical experiments which were more important for the banks; he opened a plant in Renfrew for making alum in 1795, and in 1798 in association with Charles Tennant at St Rollox, Springburn, Macintosh made chloride of lime, a bleaching powder. By 1834 it was the largest such plant in Europe, supported by a £33,000 cash account from Bank of Scotland and arrangements for bill discounts that reached £70,000 and £80,000.

In 1758, the first successful endeavour to smelt ores with coal in Scotland began on the Carron river near Falkirk.[39] There were three initial partners: William Cadell, a merchant from Cockenzie, near Edinburgh, John Roebuck, who managed the Prestonpans sulphuric acid works, and his partner Samuel Garbett. There were several factors in their eventual success. They were efficient administrators with proven success in chemicals and iron. Cadell and Roebuck had cash accounts with several banks, including the Royal Bank and Bank of Scotland, and excellent connections with the bill of exchange market in Edinburgh. They planned on a grand scale: four blast furnaces, four reverbatory (air) furnaces, a boring mill for cannon and cylinders, forges for wrought-iron goods; and in 1759 they bought a small rolling mill at Cramond near Edinburgh. Using a core of English workmen and specialist casters, they soon dominated the Scottish market for industrial, domestic and agricultural castings – everything from cast-iron skillets to garden rollers.

The Carron Company became world-famous for the manufacture of the short-barrelled cannon known as the 'carronade', perhaps invented by Patrick Miller of Dalswinton.[40] One of the main armaments of the Royal Navy in the Napoleonic Wars, its design allowed for a faster reloading in action than the typical long-barrelled naval cannon. Its eventual adoption, after a number of false dawns and obstruction by influential English politicians and conservative naval officers, confirmed the

---

38 *The New Statistical Account of Scotland*, vol. vi, *Lanark* (Edinburgh: 1845).
39 H. Hamilton, 'The Founding of Carron Ironworks', *Scottish Historical Review*, 25 (1928), 185–93; R. H. Campbell, *Carron Company* (Edinburgh: 1961).
40 There has been some controversy as to who invented it. The accepted view is that this accolade should go to General Melville. C. Carswell, in *The Life of Robert Burns* (London: 1930), gave the credit to Miller, later Deputy Governor of Bank of Scotland. The issue is noted in Hamilton, *Industrial Revolution*, pp. 159–60; Burns sent three carronades to the French Assembly as a present after the French Revolution.

close-quarters school of naval warfare. By the mid-eighteenth century, the thick wooden sides of the larger naval ships could withstand enormous punishment from long-range bombardment. The more successful naval officers (on both sides of the Channel) thus favoured shooting the rigging and masts off enemy ships and then boarding to fight it out in savage hand-to-hand combat. The Carron cannon was unsuitable for accurate long-range shooting but had a greater cumulative effect at close range; when loaded with grapeshot at short ranges, it had an action akin to that of a sawn-off shotgun.

How important were the banks for the survival of the company? The original capital of 1759 was £12,000 from the three partners and their families.[41] To support their wage bills and supplies of materials, they borrowed from the Royal Bank £3,000 on a cash account by 1761, and £8,000 from Adam and Thomas Fairholme, the Edinburgh private bankers, increased in 1762 to £17,000.[42] The latter company went bankrupt in 1763, and Mansfield, Hunter & Co. took over the account the following year. The capital position of Carron by 1769 indicates the scale of its reliance on bankers: £28,255 in direct support from banks, £21,768 in drafts on London, plus £13,571 sundry debts and royalties, and another £12,959 in loans. In 1769 and 1770, Mansfield, Hunter & Co. extended their advances to £15,000, the Thistle bank lent £200 a week on London bills with 120 days for each bill (a total of £3,400), and the British Linen lent £100 a week for twenty-eight weeks. Douglas, Heron & Co. extended a £5,000 cash account at Edinburgh, with £300 on weekly bills each to run for six months. There was a very complicated financing of bills on London. In the 1772 crisis, five of the Carron partners failed and their London agents, Adam and Wiggins, fell along with the Ayr bank. Carron was in deep trouble, aggravated by a poor record of gun proofs in London.

The Carron Company would have failed in 1772 had it not been for the enlightened attitude of the chartered banks. The Royal Bank agreed to discount weekly bills of £250 at three months, later increased to £500 over six months. In December it granted a cash account for £12,500, although not all was called. In 1773, Bank of Scotland paid off the Royal Bank and advanced another £7,500. The British Linen Company also advanced funds. The position was not saved until a decade later, by which time the carronade was selling in large numbers to the Royal Navy. To support the Carron Company in the Napoleonic Wars, Bank of

41 Details are taken from R. H. Campbell, 'The Financing of Carron Company', *Business History*, 1 (1958), 21–34.
42 The Carron Company was asked to reduce its cash account at the Royal Bank in 1762, in line with the agreement with Bank of Scotland designed to reduce speculative activity. Lord Milton, the Deputy Governor of the Royal Bank, made a personal loan to cover the reduction.

Scotland advanced varying sums on weekly bills and in 1793 agreed a cash account for £12,000.[43] Facilities were granted to other iron companies; for example, Napier & Co. received an account for £1,000 in 1800, and the Dalnotter ironworks and the Glasgow Phoenix Foundry each received a similar sum in 1804. In April 1805, members of the Cadell family joined in an application for a cash account and bill facilities for the Clyde Iron Company, and were also granted £1,000, raised in 1819 to £5,000 after many years of overdrafts. For the building trades, the Bank granted several cash accounts around £1,000 and £2,000; in 1811, £6,000 was granted for one Edinburgh firm, and two years later £10,000 for the construction of the Greenlaw prisoner-of-war camp. In 1816 the directors supported development at the Leith docks with a £10,000 cash account, matched by a similar sum from the Royal Bank and £5,000 from Sir William Forbes. In 1817 a consortium was given £10,000 for middle-class housing in Edinburgh. These sums were now more common for large industrial firms; in 1818 Leys, Masson & Co., flax manufacturers in Aberdeen, received £10,000, and from this time there were similar advances to the new gas and water utilities, the largest of the early grants being the £100,000 for the West India docks in London. The advances to the Tennant company for the St Rollox works have been mentioned, and by the second phase of the Industrial Revolution such grants were regularly considered.

There is no convenient summary of lending trends which would encapsulate all the oddities and apparent bypassing of cash limits. Agents would allow cash accounts to exceed levels laid down by the head office and what directors would regard as prudent for discounts, often done because of the family and business links of the agent. Thus it was inevitable that difficulties arose which might have brought down banks with lesser resources. Yet, as with the case of the Carron Company, there were often sound reasons for long-term debts, although this involved a risk for the Bank and, inevitably, some turned sour. These problems were aggravated by the changing nature of the trade cycle. For a decade after the Ayr bank crisis, the directors of Bank of Scotland were extremely careful to watch advances, and kept a close eye on what the new agencies were about. They could not insulate themselves, however, and there were commercial and agricultural crises in 1782–3, 1787, 1793 and 1797. Betweentimes, the Bank watched the dramatic increases in demand by domestic and agricultural processing trades, and from shopkeeping and the building trades, alongside the minor crafts associated with burghs in a growing economy. The important consideration for the bankers was not to become involved in speculation, or, where that proved impossible, to be sufficiently careful

---

43 BS 20/11/3, Miscellaneous papers on Carron Company.

over guarantees to cover a market collapse. An example of such a serious mistake occurred with the whisky and grain trades. The legal whisky industry did particularly well in the mid-1780s but, in tandem with many manufacturing enterprises and the cotton trade of Glasgow, was hit hard in 1787. Sir William Forbes and Allan Stewart & Co. were over-extended on grain bills; but for the intervention of the Royal Bank and Bank of Scotland, they might have folded.[44] The rules on cash accounts were relaxed in February 1787 when the scale of the whisky crisis was known, and proprietors were allowed to open accounts on their own security (and that of their stock) alone and a second account at their local branch. Bank of Scotland also made considerable extra advances through its branch network to support burgh life, and from July 1787 to November 1788 the directors sent no funds to London other than those required for settlement of bills. These actions were similar to the rescue operations carried out by Bank of Scotland and the Royal Bank after the Ayr bank crisis and were precursors to their extraordinary interventions in 1793 and 1797.[45]

The crises of the later eighteenth century and the speedy recovery from each proved beyond doubt that the political and financial system constructed by Bank of Scotland could manage serious crisis, by extension of discounts and past-due bills with support from the government where required. Many of its borrowers benefited from the inflation after the mid-century and their greater attention to estate costs and earnings. Many more benefited from the huge increase in government expenditure in wartime; the figures for the increase in real output in the 1790s confirm that government and defence were the fastest-growing sectors of the economy.[46] There was almost no difficulty with any landed account in the records of Bank of Scotland or the British Linen in the last twenty years of the century. By 1800, the boards of both banks saw no reason to curtail lending in anticipation of a crisis, although they would issue instructions for a detailed attention to individual accounts. Lending always went up, not down, in crisis years.

The changes in the social and economic fabric of Scotland between 1740 and the early nineteenth century shifted the industrial and economic balance (and wealth) towards Glasgow and the manufacturing burghs of the central lowlands. A number of industries grew from virtually nothing to employ unprecedented numbers and generate a host of middle-class incomes and salaries. These developments entangled the Scottish economy

---

44 J. P. Lewis, *Building Cycles and Britain's Growth* (London: 1965), pp. 22–3; S. G. Checkland, *Scottish Banking: A History, 1695–1973* (Glasgow: 1975), pp. 217–18; Sir William Forbes, *Memoirs of a Banking House* (Edinburgh: 1860), p. 79.
45 See below, Chapter 13.
46 P. Deane and W. A. Cole, *British Economic Growth 1688–1959* (Cambridge: 1962), p. 78, Table 19: index of eighteenth-century real output.

in a pattern of financial and trade fluctuations far more complex than that earlier in the eighteenth century. Bank of Scotland and the British Linen Company tended to focus on a broadly-based deposit and lending business which meant a move into general burgh banking and further development of their long-established rural and Edinburgh connections. To the extent that the provincial banks were insulated from the American trades and adapted their lending pattern to fit the broad expansion of middle-class incomes, they also thrived. The Royal Bank, after the takeover by associates of Bank of Scotland in 1778, focused its attention on Glasgow. Although the Royal Bank too had extensive connections in Edinburgh and with landed wealth, it was rather over-extended from time to time and in 1797, for example, required to borrow short-term nearly £200,000 from Bank of Scotland. By contrast to the well-developed network in Edinburgh, the Glasgow banks were narrowly based, with inadequate capital, and unable to meet the challenges of the crisis of 1772 or the American war. Until after 1830, it was thus the Edinburgh banks and their agencies in Glasgow which provided the greater part of the banking facilities for industrial companies in the west of Scotland. The measure of a sound banking business over the long term is the ability to develop new structures for the organisation which better accord with economic conditions, and to be able to move funds to the sectors of the economy with the greatest potential. In the later eighteenth century, this meant building branch structures and strengthening the relations with London bankers. This required a much stronger capital structure than the one established in the pre-industrial era and a significant move into large holdings of London stocks. An ability to take measured risks with some industrial lending, such as that for the Carron Company, was obviously an aspect which Bank of Scotland appears to have handled well.

CHAPTER 13

FROM THE CLOSE OF THE NAPOLEONIC WARS TO THE REFORM ACT (SCOTLAND) 1832

For Bank of Scotland, the close of the Napoleonic Wars marked the end of an era. The regulation of banking practices through agreements and understandings was now shared with the Commercial Bank and the British Linen Company and after 1825 with the National Bank of Scotland, founded in that year in Edinburgh. The transition to peace also saw changes in Bank of Scotland business. While lending on cash accounts, bills and bonds had risen every year from 1804 (when £1.8 million was lent), a peak was reached at over £2.6 million for the two years 1812–14. Decline then set in, and in the next nine years the average was a little over £2 million. Lending rose in the years leading up to the boom of 1825 and much was carried over for several years, but, by the Reform Act (Scotland) 1832, lending was well down again. By contrast, deposits from business and the general public steadily increased. Whereas in 1804 funds on deposit were only half the sums lent, in 1815, for the first time in the Bank's history, they were roughly equal with lending at £2.2 million. From 1823, deposits exceeded lending, and in 1832, at £3.2 million, were well above advances.

The increase in deposits changed the nature of the balance sheet; there were now insufficient lending opportunities in Scotland, and the most suitable alternatives were investments in London and government stocks. Dividends on stock thus grew as a proportion of total income. Prior to 1814, dividends had raised 33 per cent of total bank income; by 1819, when lending to trade and industry was depressed, the figure was 55 per cent. The growth of investments in London stocks rose above £1 million after 1800 and in 1813 reached £1,256,700 (at book value).[1] The slack demand for loans coupled with the rise in deposits pushed investments by 1819 to £1,646,384. From this time onwards, the Bank always kept three lists for its investments: the nominal, face value of the stocks, commonly called the book value; the historic cost, or what the Bank had paid for the stocks; and the current market value. By March 1819, for example, this market price was £1,918,351, a 'profit' of £285,509 over the historic cost. From this time, the movements of these prices of London stocks became a fundamental part of the internal assessment undertaken by the management of the financial state of the Bank. This was the second substantial connection with the state of the London market, the first being the long-established connection with Coutts & Co. for bill discounts. It also meant that the directors and management of Bank of Scotland, and their counterparts in the British Linen and the Royal Bank who were in a similar financial position, were bound closely to London political and financial affairs. In fact, the rise in the proportion of London stocks on the asset side of the balance sheet was to have a major influence on Scottish bankers' practice for over 150 years, and this was to have a conservative influence on how they viewed the proper role of government. As will be seen in later chapters, this was often to the benefit of the Scottish banks, but on occasion the dependence on London stocks had serious adverse consequences.

The profits of the Bank supported a rising dividend payment; the normal payment after the Napoleonic Wars was around 8 and 9 per cent, and in 1818 £200,000 was distributed from reserves, with a positive effect on the stock price, and another £200,000 paid out in 1825 (see Figure 13.1).[2] The good years did not last; there was a sharp turn for the worse as a result of the financial crisis which began in December 1825, profits plunged with a decline in incomes from all parts of the business, and there were unprecedented losses on bills.

In several quite fundamental ways, the Scottish economy was changing. The transition from the early Industrial Revolution to a more mature and broadly-based industrial economy was, however, a fraught process which caused immense difficulties for the banks. The exceptional profits available to enterprises in the cotton, iron, brick, coal and food-processing industries, much encouraged by wartime expenditure, were now largely in the past. In the favourable market situation of the late eighteenth century, capital investment in fixed plant had, typically, been paid off from income in a few years. A rate of profit of 15 or

1 BS 1/70/11.
2 See also Statistical Appendix, Table A2.

Figure 13.1 Selling price in market of Bank of Scotland stock, 1800–41

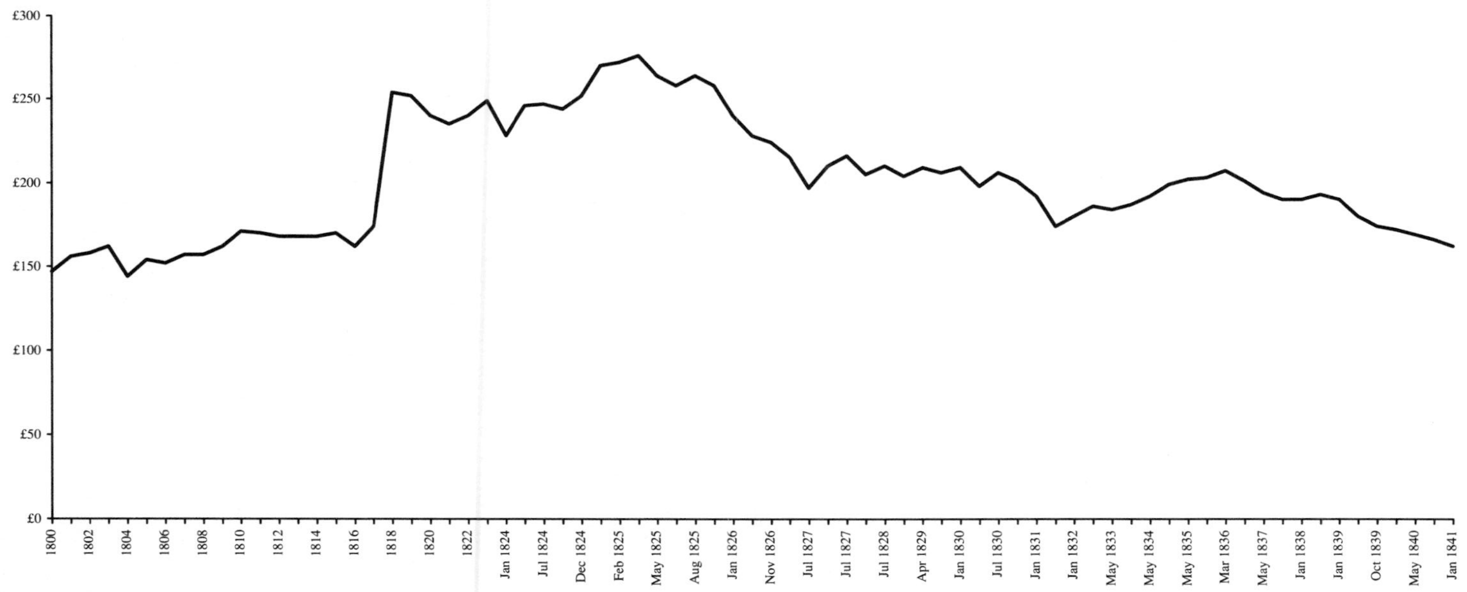

Source: BS 1/70/9, An account of the constitution, objects and practice of the Bank of Scotland (1841), appendix C.

20 per cent was not uncommon among large companies and public utilities.[3]

High earnings were derived from rapidly-expanding markets in which profits involved an element of monopoly.[4] Firms were also helped by the gradual rise in the price level before 1790 and the legal ceiling on interest rates which made the use of capital relatively cheap.[5] This was the case north and south of the Border, whether the instrument used was a circulation bill, cash account or mortgage, all often available for under 5 per cent. There were thus cheap ways of building up a business and financing stocks. The Napoleonic Wars reinforced the gradual inflation of the later eighteenth century with the flow of a sustained demand for war materials. When the war ended, a number of iron and engineering firms, including the Carron Company, and numerous textile firms, were adversely affected and business activity declined. Further, the expansion of industry and the growth of competition led to a long-term decline in profits as a proportion of capital.

After 1815, the general movement of prices was downward; thus borrowing became relatively expensive and companies paid more attention to the reduction of cash account overdrafts and the substitution of cheaper credit where it could be found. This was achieved by several means. Some firms in the west of Scotland moved accounts to the old Glasgow bank, and after 1830 to the new joint-stock banks of Glasgow. There is evidence that businessmen were ready to use the personal wealth locked up in their family savings and those of friends and professional contacts. The Scottish legal network was one such source. As seen by Bank of Scotland, the post-war years raised issues which the banks had to adjust to, yet they also raised quite crucial longer-term questions which the banks were less well equipped to understand. The turning point which brought all the problems together was the commercial crisis which broke in December 1825, which observers soon realised was of a different nature to earlier trade crises, and more serious than any before.

The economic situation in the two decades after the war was thus notably more unstable, and more complicated, than in the previous twenty-five years. By 1813, the continued rise of Scottish agricultural prices was past; henceforth, high prices brought in imports and, apart from occasional peaks, the price of oats and barley began a long post-war

3 F. Crouzet, 'Capital Formation in Great Britain during the Industrial Revolution', in idem (ed.), Capital Formation in the Industrial Revolution (London: 1972), pp. 162–222; W. G. Rimmer, Marshalls of Leeds, Flax Spinners, 1788–1886 (London: 1960); R. H. Campbell, Carron Company (Edinburgh: 1961), Statistical Appendix.
4 S. Pollard, The Genesis of Modern Management (London: 1967), pp. 285–6.
5 The long-run terms of trade between industry and agriculture moved in favour of agriculture from 1740 to 1815, but this rarely influenced investment decisions except in occasional years.

fall, buoyed up somewhat by the protectionist Corn Laws, but uncertain enough to discourage new investment.[6] Cattle and sheep prices also fell, although by less; and those excellent sources of information, the weekly returns from branches, showed the downturn in prices and the difficulties with bills. The Bank inevitably began to be more cautious in respect of advances to agriculture.[7] There are indications that a number of sales of Bank stock were made because proprietors who were over-extended needed cash: the Duke of Montrose raised £5,832 in this way in 1817, and Sir John Sinclair was forced to dispose of shares to pay off an overdraft on his cash account. This agricultural slide fell hard on the prestigious Edinburgh private banks, which were heavily involved in agricultural finance. Their decline has been meticulously recorded in the stock registers of the senior banks; Ramsays, Bonar & Co.'s holdings of Bank of Scotland stock fell below £100,000 in 1815 and by October were down to £50,021. Their holdings in the stock of the Royal Bank also fell. These sales inevitably reduced the influence of the private banks; within another generation, with their reserves gone, either they were absorbed – Ramsays, Bonar & Co. by Bank of Scotland in 1837 and Sir William Forbes by the Union Bank of Glasgow (from 1838) – or they went bankrupt or otherwise retired from business.

With the colder post-war environment, Coutts & Co. encouraged Bank of Scotland to make over more London funds to cover bill discounts. The Bank continued to rely on Coutts & Co. to carry the periodic extensions of bills; thus Bank of Scotland's account there reached *minus* £68,700 by 19 August 1815, at a time, the Bank was reminded, when 'the pressure for money is so great that 7 or 8 percent is given in the City' for extension of bills, and, because of the state of Bank of Scotland's account, 'when we [Coutts] are applied to with great earnestness for assistance by our private friends, a great portion . . . we are unable to accommodate'.[8] As in the eighteenth century, the difference in hours between demands on Coutts to pay for Bank of Scotland bills (usually a.m.) and the returns on Bank of Scotland accounts (usually p.m.) resulted in a temporary deficit at Coutts which often rose above £100,000. But these bankers had much experience among them and regarded most of the accounts which they dealt with as sound. The bankers at Coutts showed exceptional abilities to look underneath the surface phenomena of the London markets, and, as

6 B. R. Mitchell and P. Deane, *Abstract of British Historical Statistics* (Cambridge: 1962), section 16, p. 465; P. Mathias, *The First Industrial Nation*, 2nd edn (London: 1983), p. 441.
7 BS 1/5, Minutes, for decisions on lending; A. D. Gayer, W. W. Rostow and A. J. Schwartz, *The Growth and Fluctuation of the British Economy 1790–1850* (2 vols, Oxford: 1953), vol. 1, part 1, ch. 3, 1812–21; Sir William Beveridge, 'The Trade Cycle in Britain before 1850', *Oxford Economic Papers* (1940), 74–109.
8 Coutts & Co., archives, Special Letter book, 19 August 1815.

a precaution, they told the Bank of Scotland directors in 1815 that they would have to pay a higher charge for Coutts' services and accept that, henceforth, when their overdraft reached £50,000, Coutts would have the right to sell British government securities held in the Bank's name. From the Bank point of view, a prudent course was then to increase the reserve in London against further fluctuations; as noted above, the ordinary run of the business in Scotland was pushing in this direction. There were indications that the opening of the Commercial Bank in 1810, the greater activity of the Glasgow bank and the increase in the capital of the British Linen were taking trade from Bank of Scotland. Extension of new cash accounts at Bank of Scotland was well down after the war; in April and May 1815, thirty-five were opened, but from June to October the average was only six a month. Recovery in 1816 and 1817 was slow.

The perceptiveness of the board of Bank of Scotland must not be exaggerated; in several respects the directors proved unequal to the magnitude and variety of the problems which surfaced. The early years after the war were not thought to require especial caution, and in the crises of 1815–16 and 1819 the board extended existing facilities in the expectation that sooner or later a recovery of trade would clear the majority of debts. In 1818, when £31,784 was set aside for non-recoverable debts, it represented only 15 per cent of that year's profit. Of course, these must have seemed minor matters when in this year the board decided to distribute £200,000 from its reserve. In 1820, the directors thought, when faced with a bad debt total of £24,595, that it was 'not necessary at present to make further provision'. In the later months of 1821 and into 1822, information on bills and cash account debts from agencies indicated that the Scottish economy was indeed improving and customers were repaying debts. The undivided profits grew from £147,482 in 1819 to £211,609 in 1823, although, because of the improvement in business conditions at this time, there was a fall in income which was reflected in a cut in the dividend to 8 per cent for two years from the autumn of 1823.

Changes in management were on traditional lines. Attention was paid to the agreements and understandings with the Edinburgh banks on such things as London bill charges and deposit interest rates and opening hours. There were scattered references in correspondence after 1815 in respect of the paucity of borrowers compared with the size of deposits; Coutts & Co. mentioned this when occasionally asked for a cash account on the Scottish model, and always refused.[9] Bank of Scotland also started to pay attention to the difficulty which some branches had in attracting new

9 Ibid., 3 December 1818: 'I have been informed the public banks as well as bankers in Scotland have had so much money lodged in their hands by individuals that they have found difficulty in employing it'.

borrowers, and a few branches were closed for this reason. There were successes: the Bank was awarded the administration of the recoinage of 1817, and in 1819 attempts by Nicholas Vansittart to abolish the £1 and £2 notes were defeated. The board complained, but not very publicly, about the foundation of the National Bank in 1825. In general though, none of the Royal Bank, the British Linen or the Bank, or for that matter Coutts & Co., had reason to suspect that the Scottish banks would be unable to cope with a major crisis. The time of the extraordinary directors of the Bank was taken up with their pressing political and legal matters, as well as their active social life. Board elections attracted little attention, and a group of Tory lawyers remained in a majority on the ordinary side.[10] Indeed, it was the obvious satisfaction with their stewardship that made them elect one of their own, William Cadell of Tranent, as Treasurer in 1824 with enlarged powers as 'general' manager. In March 1825, proprietors 'unanimously' agreed to a proposal from their directors that virtually the whole of the undivided profits in reserves be given out as a 20 per cent dividend. This was apparently popular, and there was little change on the board for several years.[11] It was, however, a disastrous error.

There were serious underlying problems in these post-war years. In the twenty-five years of war, the bill advances had become an enormous managerial task which grew more complicated the greater the volume at branches. The self-interest that agents and accountants had in increasing their cash flow had to be countered from head office by stricter and more precise controls. Yet these were very often too late, and proved difficult to enforce. It was also hard for occasional inspections from head office to distinguish genuine transactions and sensible credits from bill discounts and increases in cash account limits. These showed apparent profits but in times of crisis brought losses.[12] Down to the close of the war, the directors were relatively secure in the knowledge that their tighter controls on advances limited the potential for damage, and gave every incentive to agents to refuse suspect bills. Losses through evasion of rules and ordinary commercial difficulties rarely exceeded 10 per cent of branch profits, and were often less. To this extent the system worked.

In December 1825, the Scottish banks were caught up in what was probably the most serious commercial and financial crisis of the nineteenth century, with a prolonged slump in industry and commerce which

10 BS 20/3/4, *Address by Sir F. W. Drummond and George Mercer of Gorthy to the proprietors of the Bank of Scotland* (1830).
11 There were suggestions that the Royal Bank should dispose of some of its capital as a dividend after the war because of the difficulty of attracting sound borrowers. This was not done; the Royal Bank had higher losses after 1815, and it would have benefited the private banks which were ousted from their special arrangements after 1816.
12 The rise of an efficient inspectorate and stricter office procedures are discussed below, Chapter 14.

brought to light the underlying defects of management. It began with a spectacular English banking and commercial crisis. Thomas Joplin, the Northumberland banker and a great advocate of the reform in English banking, calculated that on average thirteen banks a year went down in the twenty years prior to 1818. In 1824, eighteen failed. By the autumn of 1824, there were signs that the price rises of the preceding two years had reached their peak, and there was a gradual fall in stocks and shares as 1825 progressed.[13] Pressure developed upon the banking network for bills to pay calls on shares bought at the peak in one or other of numerous speculative schemes. In the first ten months of 1825, nine houses folded, as did three more in London. On 12 December, the Northampton firm of Osborn, George & Co. closed its doors, and by the New Year another thirty country banks and five London houses had collapsed. An avalanche of famous names went under: Sykes & Wilkinson; Sir Walter Stirling; Smith, Wyne & Co.; Wentworths of York; and Smith, Moger & Evans, a firm known to wealthy visitors to Bath. Even Pole, Thornton & Co., London bankers to the Royal Bank, who were given a Bank of England guarantee for £400,000 on 9 December, were eventually closed by the one partner who remained sane.[14] The crisis brought down another twenty-six banks in January and February 1826; and for the two years 1825 and 1826, no fewer than eighty went bankrupt, with ten more in London, plus dozens of trading houses which mixed commerce and bill discounting. Houses which escaped at first went down later; Lasman and Mugridge of Brighton, the favourite spa of the Prince Regent, closed its doors in 1829. As Sir John Clapham put it, 'All current criticism of English banking law and practice seemed justified'.[15] In a well-known if rather dense passage, the economist Thomas Tooke outlined events in a classic statement of the working of the trade cycle: in the early part of 1825 there was

> a rapid decline [in stock exchange prices] . . . The process by which the fall took place is simple and obvious:- As regarded the schemes, a more accurate appreciation of a greater outlay, and of smaller returns, than had been before anticipated; and a limitation of the demand for investment in them, to such persons only as could afford to depend upon remote contingencies for an income, where any income was to be expected; above all, a general deficiency of means among the subscribers to pay up the succeeding instalments, as they

13 Gayer, Rostow and Schwartz, *The Growth and Fluctuation of the British Economy*; part 2, ch. 2, 'Cyclical and secular changes in share prices'.
14 This story was told by the sister of Henry Thornton, the young partner concerned: 'Letters from a Young Lady' [Miss Marianne Thornton to Mrs Hannah More], *The Three Banks Review*, 6 (June 1950), 29–46. The figure of £400,000 is listed in the Coutts archives; J. H. Clapham, *The Bank of England*, mentions only £300,000.
15 J. H. Clapham, *An Economic History of Modern Britain: The Early Railway Age, 1820–1850* (Cambridge: 1967), p. 273.

had relied for the most part upon a continued rise, to enable them to realise a profit before another instalment should be called for, or upon the same facility as had before existed, or raising money for the purpose at a low rate of interest;- and as applied to foreign loans, the absence of security for some of them, and the rise of the state of interest in this country, which had the same depressing effect upon all of them. It is to be considered that the greater part of the transfers of the original shares in the foreign loans, and in the new schemes, while the payments on them were light ... were carried on by a medium engendered in a great degree by those very transactions; and that the profits realised or anticipated by the successive shareholders, afforded a fund of additional credit, as well as of nominal capital, with which they might and did appear as purchasers of other objects of exchange. But as new loans and schemes were successively brought forward on grounds more or less specious, all tending to the additional absorption of capital, while the increasing calls, with the high premium payable on the former loans and schemes, were beginning to press upon the shareholders, the weakest, in the first instance, would endeavour to realise without any longer finding ready buyers.[16]

Tooke deserves notice, apart from his intellectual industry, because of his connections with Scottish bankers, including Alexander Blair, joint general manager of the British Linen, who was appointed Treasurer of Bank of Scotland in 1832. It was at Blair's library at Drylaw that Tooke put together part of his great work on early nineteenth-century crises. Tooke's explanations, although not always easy to follow, were widely quoted in the nineteenth century to bankers as the warning signs to be looked for in a stock-exchange and commodity price boom, the usual pattern of which, feeding on earlier capital exports, would lead within eighteen months or two years to extensive distress. The 1825 collapse was relatively worse in England than Scotland, although, as Alexander Blair, whose careful husbanding of the resources of the British Linen protected it from speculative demands before the crisis broke, explained before Parliament in March 1826, the increase in trading speculators in Scotland 'had the effect of increasing demands on the banks from sound customers, which resulted in an increased circulation'.[17]

Although the onset of the crisis and the speculative background were correctly and carefully recorded by Tooke and other contemporaries, there were in most manufacturing areas certain longer-term obstacles to the necessary growth in capital stock which was required by the second phase of industrialisation. It was right that contemporaries should be concerned about the phenomena of speculative crises because of the damage that

16 Thomas Tooke, *A History of Prices and the State of Circulation from 1793* (6 vols, London: 1838–57), vol. ii, pp. 158–9.
17 House of Commons, *Report from the Select Committee on the Circulation of Promissory Notes under the Value of £5 in Scotland and Ireland*, 26 May 1826, (402) vol. iii.

these events did, and to search out solutions, for example, to the regulation of the labour market and the problems of the English banking system. But it was also significant that the board of Bank of Scotland had some understanding of the changes needed in the accumulation of capital for Scottish industry and trade. The bankers at head office on the Mound may not have articulated this effectively in 1825; they may have been more influenced in their more adventurous lending by past experience and the continued influx of deposits. But the fact remains that their policy was in the long-term interest of Scottish commerce and industry, whereas the small capitals of the English country banks were insufficient for manufacturing needs and clearly unable to stand up to economic convulsions. While the Scottish banks were appropriate for the needs of modern factory industry, the English country bank was more suitable for shopkeeping and small-scale business. Coutts Trotter noted that Peter Free at Pole, Thornton & Co. 'had been inexcusably imprudent in not keeping more cash in the House, but relying on that credit in them which never had been shaken and which would enable them to borrow whenever they pleased'. In this, the larger scenario of the problem of English versus Scottish banking, the resolution of the 'crisis' problem was not a simple matter of an issue of Exchequer bills and accommodation at the Bank of England. When in early 1826 Lord Liverpool and Sir Robert Peel focused on the problems of an enigma that they did not fully understand and which undoubtedly required structural reforms to tackle the restrictive six-partner rule, the tiny capitals and the small sums in hand easily overwhelmed when bills were returned unpaid, they inevitably looked north to the banking system which had largely withstood the collapses which had affected England.

On appointment as Treasurer in 1824, William Cadell was given additional powers in respect of loans and was instructed to seek new ways of extending the Bank's advances in line with the increase in deposits, apart from investments in London and government stocks.[18] Renewed efforts were made on circulation and loans in the Glasgow area. Advances on cash accounts and bonds to west-of-Scotland textile companies commonly reached £5,000–£6,000 with discount facilities on London and Edinburgh as high as £50,000 or even £60,000. Among bank customers were some of the great names of nineteenth-century Scottish industry: firms in the cotton trade included John and James White; Bogle, Ferguson & Co.; and Locke & Dunlop. There were the engineers and ironfounders, Hugh and Robert Baird at Canal Basin, Glasgow; William Dixon ironfounders, Glasgow; Tod and Paterson, distillers; and several shipping companies, including the pioneering Clydesdale Steam Boat Co. The Bank held the

18 BS 1/5, Minutes: Court instructions to William Cadell, 11 October 1824.

accounts of other important ironfounders, including the famous Shotts Company (a £10,000 cash account), and the Carron Company was given another cash account for £10,000 in May 1827. Stewart, Turnbull, Arthurs & Co., bleachers and chemists in Dunbartonshire, received a cash account for £4,000. This period saw the start of a lengthy rela-tionship with the great name in chemicals, Charles Tennant & Co. of St Rollox, Glasgow, first with a £10,000 cash account in March 1828, which increased to £35,000 in 1834 and associated with facilities for bill discounting which often exceeded £70,000 and £80,000. Bank of Scotland thus extended its already sustained involvement with the fortunes of the new era of chemicals, iron and engineering which were to dominate the Scottish industrial economy in the second and third quarters of the century. The social development of the new industrial areas was not forgotten: a £1,500 cash account went to the Police Establishment of the Barony of Gorbals in 1827, and funds were advanced for this work regularly thereafter. The branches of the Bank continued to open cash accounts for such small businesses as Miss Martha Dunlop, millinery and dressmaking (Glasgow, £300, 1827), Miss Mary Ann Maiben in Perth (£200, 1828) and numerous others, just as they had always done. The really important change, however, was the way in which William Cadell directed resources of the Bank into the second phase of industrialisation and did so with a determined long-term view. In this view, Cadell's tenure of office was a positive one for Scottish development.

The crisis which broke in December 1825 did not, at first, have the impact north of the Border that it did in the south, and none but the Fife Banking Company failed. But in England it was different: 'We have had a very anxious time', Coutts Trotter wrote to William Cadell. 'The scarcity of money had been very great and the difficulties of banking houses in various parts of the country have excited considerable alarm for their correspondents in London.' A number of London Scottish correspondents soon collapsed as they were involved in credits on their own accounts which could not be recalled.[19] Bank of Scotland, the Royal Bank and the Edinburgh private banks soon realised that the severity of the crisis might impede the usual extension of bills on London. The Scottish banking system weathered the storm, in part because the leading banks had significant funds in London and government stocks, against the security of which they could increase bill discounts and borrow cash. The two senior partners of Ramsays, Bonar & Co. arrived in London on 14 December and asked Coutts & Co. to support their application to

19 Clapham, *The Bank of England*, vol. ii, p. 99; 'Letters from a Young Lady' [Miss Marianne Thornton to Mrs Hannah More], *The Three Banks Review*, 6 (June 1950), 29–46.

the Bank of England for credit.[20] They had £340,000 worth of 3½ per cent consols besides £20,000 of bank stock 'and other large funds', and required a loan from Threadneedle Street of £100,000. On the same day, William Cadell's son was given an introduction by Coutts & Co. with the same intent: 'to carry funds to Scotland as a protection against the alarm prevailing there and which recent events here will greatly increase'. The powers held by Coutts over £110,000 of reduced 3½ per cent consols were offered as security 'for an intermediate advance' of £70,000–£80,000. He was given £81,000. On 17 December, Coutts were given extra power of attorney over £200,000 3½ per cent consols for bill transactions. It was, stated Coutts, 'much to be regretted that there is not a confidential understanding between [Bank of Scotland] and the Royal', although the 'wise' course of raising interest rates was noted.[21] In fact, all five public banks provided relief in the form of discounts and re-discounts on Edinburgh, which involved an increase in circulation; they also extended cash accounts to their own customers, and Bank of Scotland provided a special credit of £20,000 to the Paisley Banking Co. at the end of February 1826.

This positive view must be tempered with an understanding of the scale of the losses at Bank of Scotland. The size of the Bank's resources enabled it to provide cover for several years, but eventually losses had to be written off. In 1827, the directors of Bank of Scotland cut the half-year dividend to £30,000. The actual profits were now down to as low as £30,000, and some directors suggested that the cut should therefore have been greater to bring home the seriousness of the crisis which had reduced profits by over half. A minority group on the board reported in March 1827 that the 'permanent diminution of future profit from our bad debts can hardly be doubted'; these had reached £120,000 and would erode profits by £5,000–£6,000 per year for the foreseeable future.[22] 'Funded property wherein the London reserves were kept had fallen' to the point where the Bank's assets were actually 'below the price they were rated at' in the accounts; the 'rate of deposit interest had risen', and the circulation of notes and transactions in Scotland had 'greatly diminished'. The distribution of the £200,000 bonus in 1825 was singled out for especial

20 Coutts & Co., archives, Miscellaneous papers, 1825.
21 Coutts & Co., archives, Special Letter Book: Letter to Gilbert Innes of Stow, Deputy Governor of Royal [and others], 8/9 December 1825; the Bank and the Royal Bank maintained their agreement over support for each other, although that was primarily intended for temporary runs on one or other bank. It is unclear what further understanding Thomas Coutts was looking for, although this may refer to a need to increase funds, secured to Coutts & Co.
22 BS 20/9/5; the report is discussed in 'Memorandum regarding the Bank of Scotland states', 22 March 1827; and in 'Memorandum on the Bank of Scotland's proposed reduction of dividend and on Mr Scott's notes'.

criticism, and the Bank was urged by a number of proprietors to build up a fund to meet losses by cutting dividends and interest. It was little consolation to know that all the Scottish banks were affected, although the British Linen Company was in a relatively strong position.

William Cadell, whose judgement was now to be proved increasingly faulty, argued that this was too pessimistic. The causes of the decline in profits were temporary, not permanent, and a distinction should be made between the post-crisis increase in the rate of interest on deposits (the more important) and the 'increase of obligations on which interest is not regularly received' (bad debts), both of which were 'a matter of management at all times within the control of the directors and office bearers'. Whatever the effect on the profits of the 1825 crisis, neither 'need have any effect in future'. Cadell noted that although the more important result hoped for was a reduction in the rate of interest paid out, it required the cooperation of all the banks, which he fully anticipated. He dismissed the view that the payment of the bonus in 1825 had reduced the profit potential and increased costs; profits rose in the year to March 1826, and the rise in costs was a consequence of a rise in business. The proprietors were entitled to expect that the reserves ('the surplus profit') be used in difficult times to maintain the dividend, a steady level of which would reduce speculation in Bank stock. Political consequences might result from a reduction, especially, Cadell noted, as this was the aftermath of the attempt by the Bank's enemies in England to remove the £1 note.[23] With a decrease in interest, the dividend could remain at 8 per cent, with the rest to come from reserves for the present emergency. For the future, 'we are not surely to continue losing at the same rate by bad debts'; indications from past crises suggested that the Bank could look forward to a rise. In respect of the fall in the price of British government securities, past rises had not been accounted as profit, so why should falls now be accounted as losses?[24] There was little to be concerned about: 'the present defalcation arises entirely from temporary causes', and thus there was no need to reduce the dividend. The Edinburgh banks agreed to cut deposit interest rates to 3 per cent on 27 May 1827, on 19 May 1828 to 2½ per cent, and from 25 May 1829 to 2 per cent for sums above £500.

How did the banking crisis of 1825 really affect the balance sheet? In every year from 1827 to 1831, Bank of Scotland made an *apparent* profit, on average £65,000, about enough to cover a 6 per cent dividend. Cadell contained costs but failed to reduce losses or increase reserves. Moreover,

23 For this, see the discussion later in this chapter and in Chapter 15.
24 The seventh point is: 'I am also aware . . . [and] the accounting procedure meant that losses or gains on any London investments would not be listed on the balance sheet, only the original cost of the stock given . . .'.

the provision made for losses from 1826–9 was not conservative enough. Every month, the directors considered lists of 'offers of composition' from manufacturers and merchants who were bankrupt or nearly so. The span was wide and ran from as high as eighteen shillings in the pound down to as low as one or two shillings. There were numerous cases where borrowers made detailed arrangements to pay off their debts by remaining in business, and the Scottish legal system was especially supportive of such cases. The directors were reduced at one point to hawking a distrained linen factory. By December 1828, as the debts piled up, the board appointed the agent in Leith as an assistant to William Cadell; however, Cadell refused to cooperate.[25] By the autumn of 1829, it was clear that the situation of the desperate and irretrievable debts, and past-due bills, was not properly catered for. By March 1829, two directors had calculated that bad debts amounted to £193,293, with a lengthy list of bills which extended back seven years.[26] Aghast that 'some of [these] were unprecedented in the money and mercantile world', silence was implored outside the boardroom. The directors now agreed that the bonus of 1825 was a mistake, for the figures before them indicated 'that almost no profits were made from 1825 to 1829', and that the provision stated to proprietors was misleading. A further pessimistic view included account losses on cash accounts at £50,000 per year from 1824 to 1830. This excluded the problem of British government securities where both yields and price had not recovered.[27] The directors had few ideas as to how to handle this situation, and the general state of the Scottish economy provided little comfort.

In the summer of 1829, a committee of five directors toiled over the accounts and administration. Their report indicated that the financial situation was serious, although it could be stated differently depending on the view taken of past-due bills, gilts and cash account debts. Further, 'the expectations formed at the time of the Treasurer's appointment have not been realised and . . . the duties which were exacted of him, perhaps from their extensive and complicated variety have not been fulfilled'.[28] The majority view that Cadell should be given another chance was endorsed by the board on 11 January 1830. Yet the state of the Bank's debts continued to be aggravated by further poor judgement in the following year. Although it is unclear how much of this was known to the public, there was an opposition list at the board elections in March and some directors were replaced. The election of Thomas Mansfield, the private

25 BS 20/3/4, criticism of William Cadell by senior officers, June 1831.
26 BS 20/18/7, View of bad debts and of the fund applicable thereto, March 1829.
27 For the price of consols and fall in interest paid, see below, Chapter 14.
28 BS 20/3/4, *Address by Sir F. W. Drummond*, p. 7.

banker, caused some comment. He possessed no stock, so a majority of the directors voted to transfer some of the Bank's own holdings to Mansfield and, to enable him to pay for this, granted him a cash account to the sum required. In July, political events in Belgium and France caused political uncertainties which in turn led to difficulties for Coutts & Co. and other Scottish correspondents in London.[29]

The situation by April 1830 was clearly beyond the abilities of the ordinary board. From this time, the second Viscount Melville and Sir Robert Dundas of Beechwood began to attend on a regular basis. At first they struggled with the immensity of the situation, making firm decisions on simple matters; thus in August a request for head-office pay rises was turned down, the agents at Stirling and Leith were refused allowances for losses on bills and other agents were told to carry a part of their losses. By the late summer, however, Melville had realised that total losses threatened to swamp the Bank. A sudden demand for cash, perhaps from a French invasion, or more likely rumours about the true state of the accounts, was uppermost in his mind. Negotiations were opened with the Bank of England for a credit of £200,000 for discounts of bills on the security of £50,000 of Bank of England shares and £200,000 of 3½ per cent government new annuities.[30] It was no consolation that the Royal Bank appeared also to be in serious difficulties, although it was more forthcoming with its proprietors. In 1828, the Royal Bank had announced debts on bills of £105,000 in Edinburgh and another £117,000 in Glasgow, in addition to cash account losses elsewhere. John Thomson, the Cashier, asked Coutts & Co. to open negotiations with the Treasury in May 1829.[31] In tripartite talks involving Coutts & Co., the Royal Bank and the Treasury, it was agreed that the Royal Bank needed £500,000 added to its capital (£1.5 million to £2 million), covered in the meantime by an equivalent facility at the Bank of England.[32] The Treasury supported the modification to the Royal Bank charter, although it insisted that the capital be fully called up. Neither the Royal Bank nor the Bank was in a position to oppose charter applications from the National Bank and the Commercial Bank, both awarded in 1831.[33]

At the annual meeting of Bank of Scotland in March 1831, there was fierce criticism of the management. Before the proprietors was the worst

---

29 Coutts Trotter pointed out in December 1830 that the situation in Belgium was affecting the price of British government securities, and the worry lasted until the summer of 1831.
30 BS 1/5, Minutes: 27 December 1830. The Bank initially thought that it would be 3½ per cent consolidated stocks, but Coutts decided to use the 3½ per cent annuities: Coutts & Co., archives, Special Letter Book, 11 January 1831.
31 Coutts & Co., archives, Special Letter Book, 30 May 1829.
32 S. G. Checkland, *Scottish Banking: A History, 1695–1973* (Glasgow: 1975), pp. 351–6.
33 Ibid., pp. 440–2.

set of figures for nearly a century. The level of 'profits derived from current business' remained subdued at £65,324, and, after current bad debts, the board wrote off £30,000. The meeting agreed to apply for a new Act to extend business in England and double the stock qualifications for directors, and, in a move to limit the nepotism shown by the appointment of William Cadell, it was agreed that no past director (going back five years) was to be eligible for any office in the Bank. A proposal to limit representation on the board from any one profession to one-third was passed, with the exception of the law officers of the Bank. A time limit of six years for directors was fixed, with one year out before they were eligible for re-election.

In 1832, Viscount Melville again reported heavy losses. This finished William Cadell's career, and he resigned on 5 July 1832. The board deferred consideration of his £400 pension for a whole year, and the annual meeting almost blocked it. The proprietors defeated Melville over representation on the board by private bankers, who were henceforth debarred. The tenure of office by William Cadell must be judged the most disastrous in the history of Bank management, worse even than the years around the Ayr bank crisis. It was a bad time for Viscount Melville in other ways, as the Tories lost most of their representation in the reformed Parliament.[34] The events at the Bank add credence to the view that 1832 was more than just a political watershed in Scottish history. No longer could the Tory interest claim to be the guardian of sound banking, and this had severe repercussions for the reputation of the Scottish system within the upper echelons of the Bank of England.

This view of Scottish bankers from 1824–32 was, by and large, kept entirely secret from the outside world. In fact, the crisis of 1825 marked the high point of influence with British public opinion on the merits of the Scottish over the English banking system: the one large-scale and with numerous branches, the other tied to six partners, with few branches and prone to bankruptcies. It is from this decade that the old caricature of the disloyal Scot vanishes from the repertoire of the English satirist. The dominant Victorian image was of the hard-working, God-fearing, intellectual Scot; the Kirk minister, the accountant, the banker, the lawyer: such contrasts made excellent copy. In February 1822, Thomas Joplin the Newcastle banker published a seminal pamphlet, *On the General Principles and Present Practice of Banking in England and Scotland*. Entirely favourable to the Scottish system, it went through five editions by 1826 and was widely quoted from in the provincial press.[35] It was discussed

34 W. Ferguson, 'The Reform Act (Scotland) of 1832: Intention and Effect', *Scottish Historical Review*, 45 (1966), 105–14.
35 C. W. Munn, *The Scottish Provincial Banking Companies, 1747–1864* (Edinburgh: 1981), pp. 81, 85.

at public meetings of businessmen in his native Northumberland and in Manchester and Liverpool, and in May 1822 was even reviewed in *The Times*.[36] In June 1824, Joplin helped the launch of the Irish Provincial Banking Company, whose prospectus emphasised that it was organised on Scottish lines.

Joplin based his case on the historical evidence, the success of Scottish banks; compared to the English, they 'rarely if ever failed or lost money'.[37] The true cause of the difference 'is to be found in the nature of their respective banking establishments: the Scotch banks being joint-stock companies, while the English banks are private companies'. This institutional difference made for a clear divide in their approach to investment. The Scottish banks, with large capitals, organised a money market between their shareholders', depositors' and borrowers' funds and reserves. They were enabled to transact business greater in size and for much longer periods, whether based on mortgages and other long-term assets, cash accounts or roll-over bills of exchange. English country banks were too small to trade in money and arrange long-term loans, and even the London private banks were too strict over mortgages. The typical country bank dealt in short-term loans, usually the buying and selling of short-term bills on London. Further, the Scottish banks pioneered professional management, accounting and controls, their agents and managers were required to offer security and were paid reasonable salaries, and they carried part of the losses. The widespread location of branches ensured that a national stability for note issue was guaranteed. Their success meant that their stock was a sound investment: in the case of the British Linen, with £500,000 capital and £300,000 reserves, it stood at a premium of 200 per cent.

The resumption of cash payments, finally agreed in 1819, had already begun a considerable discussion which involved analysis of the country banks and their note issues. Thomas Joplin's writings were only part – an important part – of the general debate. The crisis of 1825 resolved a number of questions. Lord Liverpool's ministry was determined to reform the system after the very large number of failures, and by the time Parliament reassembled in February 1826 the government had decided to act on banking reform. The small notes of the country banks were to be forbidden and joint-stock banks allowed to be established. The Bank of England was to be encouraged to set up branches outside London.

36 It was not only about the Scottish system, as the subtitle suggested, 'with observations on the Justice and Policy of an Immediate Alteration in the Charter of the Bank of England' [GL 1822]; *The Times*, 23 and 25 May 1822.
37 Joplin noticed only three Scottish bank failures, with 'few' partners: Grace's Bank of Dumfries, the Merchant Company of Stirling, and the Falkirk Union Bank.

On 13 February 1826, Robert Peel made a definitive statement of the government's case for change. He emphasised the problem of the issue of small notes being put into circulation by 'no less than 800' country banks. The central theme of Peel's argument was the inevitable consequences of the unrestricted issue of notes, and especially of small notes. It was not the fault, he went on to argue, of any one bank, but was inherent in the system. The increase in notes would always follow the increase in prices, and similarly note circulation would decrease as rapidly as prices, 'so that the tendency always existed in the system, to aggravate the evils of the country'. Further, while he did not wish to 'overstate' the evil, there was no doubt that the circulation of the £1 and £2 notes increased the tendency to speculation.

Peel then continued with a remarkable encomium of the Scottish system: 'He could not help thinking that if, in the year 1783, a set of banks had been established in this country, on the system of the Scotch banks, it would have escaped the danger in which it was then involved'. Peel then quoted figures of the failures of country bankers in 1793 – 'not less than 100' – and went on to list the bankruptcy figures for 1810–16 and 1825:

> Let the House now look at what had been the case, under a different system, in Scotland. It would be seen, by the evidence taken before the committee in 1819, that a Mr Gilchrist, who had been a manager [of the British Linen Company] there for many years, was asked how many banks had failed in Scotland within his memory. His reply was, that there had only been one; that the creditors were immediately paid fourteen shillings in the pound as a dividend, and, upon the winding up of the concern, the whole of their demands.

Peel ended this section of his speech by agreeing that the Scottish system might not be 'quite perfect', but it was certainly preferable 'to that under which we [in England] had been so long acting'.[38]

During this period of debate in the House of Commons, there had been set up two committees, one in the Commons and the other in the Lords, to inquire into the issue of small notes in Scotland and Ireland.[39] The Commons Committee opened with the evidence of Alexander Blair, joint general manager of the British Linen Company. Robert Peel himself took the chair on this first day. Alexander Blair was followed by

38 *Hansard*, new series, vol. 14, cols 289–92, 13 February 1826: 'Debate on Bank Charter and Promissory Notes Acts'.
39 *Report from the Select Committee on the Circulation of Promissory Notes under the Value of £5 in Scotland and Ireland*, 26 May 1826, (402) vol. iii; *Report from the Lords' Committee on the Circulation of Promissory Notes under the Value of £5 in Scotland and Ireland*, 6 April 1827, (245) vol. vi.

Kirkman Finlay, a Glasgow merchant and a director of the Royal Bank, and other Scottish witnesses included Robert Paul (Commercial Bank of Scotland), John Thomson (Cashier of the Royal Bank), and Thomas Kinnear (an Edinburgh private banker and a director of Bank of Scotland). The last named underlined a century of development in Scotland, the ways in which a historically evolved system had focused on the accumulation of capital and the importance of a surplus of production over consumption: 'I say we have become a rich nation . . . because our accumulation has been rapid, our consumption not nearly equal to it, and our national losses have been comparatively trifling'. Scotland was still poorer than England. 'Providence has not been so bountiful to us as it has been to England: it is very well known that the power of accumulation in the Highlands or the Islands, a poor and extended country, is by nature very slow', and though easier in the rest of Scotland was still more difficult than south of the Border. As the metallic currency had been sparse, Scotland had resorted to a paper circulation, a mixture of notes and innovative forms of bank accounts and, later, the branch system. Other parts of Great Britain were not injured by these developments, but Scotland would be by the replacement of paper by gold. The Scottish witnesses were wholly united against the suppression of the small note issue. It was explained by several witnesses that the branch system was efficacious in encouraging investment and saving and that the note-exchange system provided controls against the over-issue of notes. In this, the crucial role of summary protest for banknotes was realised.

The Lords and the Commons reached similar conclusions, accepting the arguments about economic growth and accumulation. They might not be entirely convinced of the importance of £1 notes for cash accounts and local branch profits, but they agreed that uniformity between the parts of Great Britain was not essential: 'it is also proved by the evidence and by the documents that the banks of Scotland whether chartered or joint-stock companies or private establishments, have for more than a century exhibited a stability which the Committee believe to be unexampled in the history of banking'. Therefore, unless stronger evidence could be exhibited to the contrary, the 'Scotch system' should remain untouched. England, by contrast, had reached an impasse. While the structure and decision-making of Bank of Scotland, the Royal Bank and the British Linen were prepared for the industrial era, England remained bound by an institutional framework suitable for the small country town and the personal business of the wealthy in London.

The Act limiting the issue of new notes under £5, or, after April 1829, to deny any reissue of notes under £5, was passed in Parliament on 26 March 1826 (7 George IV c.6) but applied only to England

and Wales. Before the Act was finally passed, however, Lord Liverpool had announced that it was intended to introduce a similar measure for Scotland and Ireland. It was this which occasioned the most vigorous opposition against the proposal. It included the famous letters published by Sir Walter Scott in defence of the Scottish £1 note. As Sir John Clapham wrote, 'Scotland ... rose solid against the encroaching and treacherous Southron, Sir Walter blowing the pibroch dressed as Malachi Malagrowther'.[40] Certainly the matter became one of national concern, and it aroused strong national feeling, but it is incorrect to argue that this was 'primarily a problem of Scottish Home Rule, not of economic analysis'.[41] Apart from the strong economic reasons why the Scottish banking system should remain untouched, the Scottish writers had pointed out that much of the cause of speculation came from the use of the larger notes and bills in trade, which in the English provincial system of small country banks went on with less effective regulation than with the two tiers of the banking system in Scotland. Ireland also retained its small note issue. There was another Scottish banking Act in 1826 which allowed the unincorporated banks, on certain easily-fulfilled conditions, to obtain the power to sue and be sued – an important matter in legal identity.[42] There was a further Act in 1828 (9 George IV c.65) which prohibited the circulation of Scottish notes in the north of England. The circulation of Scottish notes in Cumbria, Northumberland and Durham was quite common, and, in spite of this Act, their circulation in regions contiguous with Scotland still continued.

Political activity around matters such as Catholic emancipation and the Reform agitation now dominated Parliamentary life, although public debate over monetary issues outside Westminster continued unabated.[43] It was in these years that the ideas which came later to be known as the currency principle – that the note circulation should be related to the

40 Clapham, *An Economic History of Modern Britain*, vol. i, p. 274; A. Cameron, *Bank of Scotland 1695–1995: A Very Singular Institution* (Edinburgh: 1995), pp. 9, 113; Sir Walter Scott (Malachi Malagrowther), *Thoughts on the proposed change of currency and other later alterations as they affect, or are intended to affect, the Kingdom of Scotland* (Edinburgh: 1826).

41 This was F. W. Fetter's comment: *The Development of British Monetary Orthodoxy 1797–1875* (Cambridge, MA: 1965), p. 122 – somewhat unexpected, since later on the same page he notes the main differences between Scottish and English banking and in particular the importance of the small note issue and the practice of the credit system. There is, of course, no doubt that the proposed action of the Liverpool government was seen as an affront to Scotland, and the nationalist reaction could be expected; but there were sound economic reasons for the protests.

42 7 George IV c.47; A. W. Kerr, *History of Banking in Scotland*, 4th edn (London: 1926), p. 192.

43 Fetter, *Monetary Orthodoxy*, pp. 126–43, analysis of sixteen pamphlets on banking issues published in the single year 1830, of which eleven were hostile to the Act of 1819 which re-established the gold standard. Fetter also noted the establishment in 1827 of the Committee of Country Bankers which through the next two decades published in the columns of its *Circular to Bankers* a permanent opposition to the Bank of England and the 1819 Act.

holding of gold in the Bank of England – began to come together as a coherent theory; and it was above all this question of the note issue, and Scotland's particular place in the system, that was to occupy increasing attention in the years that led to the Bank Charter Act of 1844 and the Scottish Banking Act of the following year.

CHAPTER 14

BANK OF SCOTLAND, 1832–49

ALEXANDER BLAIR was appointed Treasurer of Bank of Scotland in June 1832 at a salary of £1,200. By then he had served over twenty years in business and banking, first in Liverpool and from 1812 with the British Linen Company, where he was appointed joint general manager with Thomas Corrie in 1828. It was agreed by the board of Bank of Scotland that his service with the British Linen would count towards his pension. The British Linen was the most profitable of the chartered banks; it had emerged from the 1825 crisis with the strongest reserves, the smallest ratio of bad debts to capital and the highest-priced stock. Alexander Blair was thus established as a successful manager at a time when this was sorely needed at the Mound. After his move, he quickly made his mark as an effective banker, at once energetic and disciplined with an ability for work on accounts, the auditing and control of branches and the huge volume of administrative work required of a Bank Treasurer; he also kept up his wide-ranging correspondence far beyond the remit of his office. In the Parliamentary inquiry of 1826, he had shown himself to be a skilled advocate of Scottish principles and methods, and the search for theoretical and empirical justification for his views led to contact with several of the advanced thinkers of the time. This diplomatic ability was demonstrated in negotiations with the Bank of England and the Treasury down to the passage of the Scottish Bank Act of 1845. Alexander Blair was highly regarded among bankers in Scotland and came to epitomise the Victorian ideal of the austere general manager, a man of good connections, rather aloof from junior staff, yet totally committed to the ethics and honesty of Scottish banking. He was keenly aware of the need to adapt Scottish principles to the increasing complexity of the British economy in a rapidly-changing world, and from his friend Thomas Tooke he paid close attention to price movements and cyclical change;

yet he failed to present a theoretical position before the 1844 and 1845 Bank Acts strong enough to counter the ideas and influence of the Bank of England and the London discount market. This failure to maintain the pre-eminence of Scottish banking ideas rather clouded his judgement in later years and induced a reluctance to take part in national debate, although in purely banking terms he was well able to deal with the periodic crises of the banking system. Thomas Corrie stayed as general manager of the British Linen after 1832 and died in office in 1859 within a month of Alexander Blair. They had worked together for almost fifty years.

The appointment of Alexander Blair signified a shift in the balance of power at the Mound. Henceforth the deliberations of the board were anchored around lending, the distribution of assets and the general policy on reserves and investments. The directors had now to learn to be com-plementary to the senior management, as their Treasurer was determined to lay down the main guidelines of how the Bank should proceed. Indeed, his appointment was made on the understanding that the faults of the management under William Cadell would be corrected. The days were over when the ratio of reserves and investments to capital would be cut in order to boost the stock price and dividends. No longer would directors be allowed to dominate appointments to the agencies and to head office. While Blair could not ignore kinship networks, his rule was epitomised by a managerial concern that the pressures of politics and family should be balanced by the long-term needs for efficiency and profitability. The changes at board level in the years 1830–2 which removed several associates of William Cadell, together with the realisation of the serious state of the asset side of the balance sheet, undoubtedly helped. With a few close associates in the management, and the benign support of Viscount Melville, Alexander Blair came to dominate the direction of the Bank more forcefully than had his predecessors. His tenure of office marked a divide with the past, not just for the introduction of managerial reforms and the adoption of greater professionalism, but also in the more limited role given to the directors and leading politicians on the board. Indeed, within twenty years there was even a proposal, taken quite seriously, that the Treasurer be considered for the post of Deputy Governor.

Alexander Blair inherited a system with detailed checks, balances and controls; there was little wrong with this basic administration and inspection machinery which, in normal times, worked satisfactorily. As this system dominated the working day at the Mound and occupied a great deal of management time, an analysis is required to understand the magnitude and complexity of the task which Blair faced and why this inheritance was flawed. The information on Bank activity was compiled in several ways; the figures available to measure the Bank performance, one week with another, were breviates which showed the composition and distribution of the trading capital. These were accounting statements which simplified branch and head-office advances and deposits but could prove a useful guide to where problems might lie, which could then be followed up in more detail. Only a few directors and managers had regular access to these figures. Yet, as had become clear before his appointment, these balances were unreliable as a guide to the state of the assets, as even a few 'hidden' debts could substantially reduce the level of profits. Bank of Scotland's practice of granting long-term advances by bill and cash account made it difficult for head office to assess the true state of its assets and the creditworthiness of its customers. This much was conceded by 1832, and the problem was to take up much of the Treasurer's time in his first few years with the Bank.

The simplest breviate was the states of advances, deposits and investments updated on a weekly basis.[1] When Alexander Blair took over in 1832, the figures showed almost £5 million on the liabilities side of the balance, for £1,788,600 of which the Bank 'pays nothing' (capital, reserves, fund for losses and circulation), and £3,191,000 on which interest was paid, in the main on depositors' funds. There were four significant divisions of these assets. Just over £2 million was invested in British government securities and Scottish stocks, with £1,393,000 used for current discounts and past-due bills, £1,013,000 for cash accounts and £334,000 for permanent interest-bearing bonds. Each of these categories posed problems, but the most time-consuming were the £2.4 million of assets in bills of exchange and cash accounts which formed the main advances to industry, commerce and private individuals. They were split between the eighteen branches of 1832, and business was negotiated at the Mound, with 25–35 per cent of the value of bills in Edinburgh and 50 per cent of cash accounts. From this £2.4 million came a gross yield of around 4–5 per cent. There was a turnover in bills of over £8 million in 1832 and the accounts were updated on an early but nonetheless complicated form of spreadsheet at least every week, and from the larger agencies daily reports were forwarded. It was to cover the losses in this business that £152,272 was held in the Fund for Losses account to which £51,453 was added at that angry meeting of proprietors in March 1832, bringing the total credit in the account to £203,725. But the true irrecoverable loss to March 1832, in what was called the 'old' account, was later ascertained at £300,314; thus another £96,589 had to be removed from the profit and loss account and cancelled before these pre-1832 accounts were closed in 1839. The potential bad debts were higher still, as another £206,000 was uncovered

1 BS 1/70/12, Appendix 1; BS 1/70/2, States of the Bank of Scotland.

by 1835 alone – close to a staggering three years of profits – although £117,751 was later recovered by legal action. Alexander Blair was careful to write all recoveries to the Fund for Losses account, not to profit and loss, until he was quite sure that all losses had been accounted for.[2]

In recognition that the supervisory role had been insufficiently rigorous, the senior Secretary, George Sandy ws, stood down from this role and was appointed the Law Officer of the Bank in charge of diligence cases, with a general supervision of his work by the law committee of the board of directors. The external Law Agent, Harry Davidson ws, a past director of the Bank, and his accountant Thomas Syme ws, were given the portfolio of general legal work through the Scottish and English courts.[3] Alexander Brodie ws, the new Joint Secretary, was given charge of bills to be discounted, overdue bills, the occasional inspection of branches and the examination of states from the agents; but when legal action was decided upon it was left to Davidson & Syme. Alexander Blair encouraged several career bankers: Charles Campbell, the Bank Inspector since 1817, took charge of the Glasgow agency; William Simson, who progressed from being an apprentice and teller at the Dunfermline branch to a position at Glasgow, was brought to Edinburgh in 1833 as assistant accountant, and in 1839 he was appointed Inspector.[4] With this stronger legal and inspection system, the Bank was better placed to tackle the multiplicity of claims arising from past-due bills, unpaid cash accounts and the chain of bankruptcies and liquidations from 1825. It was tedious work but essential. In September 1837, George Sandy ws retired after thirty-three years in the service of the Bank and was awarded a pension of £400 a year.[5] The board then decided that he need not be replaced and his work, too, was devolved to Thomas Syme ws, who remained a partner in Davidson & Syme although he was required to swear the Bank oath of allegiance and keep clerks at the Mound. Scottish bankers have always emphasised the critical role of legal work, as the slightest error in drafting or protesting, or even in timing, could lose an asset should it become a matter of dispute. Thomas Syme's contract, for example, enjoined the 'instant despatch' of legal business, the noting and protesting of bills, preparation of bonds for cash accounts and personal bonds, all legal correspondence of the Bank and the preparation of all deeds and documents, the handling of all Life and Fire policies and payments of premiums, the transfer of stocks and then

---

2 BS 1/70/12, pp. 19–20, and Appendix 15, 'Fund for Losses account'.
3 A. Blair, *Davidson & Syme, ws: Two Centuries of Law* (private publication, [Edinburgh:] 1980), pp. 8–10.
4 BS 20/10/3, Miscellaneous papers. William Simson was appointed Cashier in 1846, and later rose to be Assistant Secretary, Joint Secretary and then Secretary.
5 BS 1/5 Minutes: 18 September 1837.

the minute examination of warrants and decrees of the Court of Session as they affected Bank business. Further, he was to examine all 'opinions in cases of emergency and upon ordinary banking and commercial questions in order that no points of law may be left as the foundation for law suits or disputes with the Bank's connections'. There was a mass of work related to land and feudal tenures, insolvency, bankruptcy and conveyance.[6] To keep up with this and handle the various court appearances and bad debts meant that he required exceptional stamina. Thomas Syme never married and held the post for over thirty years to his death in 1868. Through his guidance, the weekly states of the Bank assets began to resemble a more accurate picture of debts and recoveries than at any time since 1824, a very important guide for Alexander Blair as to the real state of Bank of Scotland.

A significant group of debts on cash accounts and past-due bills were due to the profligate lending policy of the branch network as well as insufficient rigour in their control. Yet Blair and Simson had to be careful. The agents in 1832, as with their predecessors of 1774, were 'almost all persons belonging to their respective districts', and most were associated with the Melville and Tory interest. Although Alexander Blair inherited a hierarchy at the Mound, which he proceeded to strengthen, the old political role of local agents made it more difficult to enforce the regulations at branch level. Indeed, some agents in this system would hardly accept a professional banker as their social superior. Nonetheless, some of the financial and inspection arrangements were strengthened. The most important control on the agents and their cautioners was the security which they gave for the discharge of their obligations to the Bank and the fact that they were bound for a proportion of their losses. It was expected that this would curtail facilities for customers who overtraded and would encourage 'diligence and enquiry of the state of the[ir] accounts'. In the aftermath of the loss at the Haddington agency discovered in 1801, which cost the Bank £41,855, improvements had been made in reporting procedures to the Mound and more frequent visits made by directors to inquire into agents' affairs. Printed spreadsheets were provided and a weekly state and abstract of all transactions recorded thereon, while the accountant certified the balance of cash and notes. By 1810, a few of the larger branches were sending in an abstract and commentary on a daily basis. All bills past due and the total obligations of each party to all bills where drafts, endorsements and acceptances amounted to £500 or more were listed on these sheets and notes attached where the agent wished to bring attention to a particular account. The Bank Inspector – a formal

---

6 Blair, *Davidson & Syme*, p. 10.

appointment from 1817 – and the Secretary's department could check, for example, whether guarantors and borrowers, through family or business connections, were drawing from more than one branch.[7] All the details were entered into the head-office journals and ledgers, and the earnings and obligations to depositors at each branch calculated. The business of several branches was placed before the board each week. This system was acceptable when the level of concealed debts was low, but was insufficiently rigorous for the multiplicity of debts, bankruptcies, concealment of losses, strings of accommodation bills and fraudulent transactions after 1825 by which businessmen on both sides of the Border tried to maintain their credit. Further, a new and ominous development surfaced after 1825 when some London bankers forwarded bills drawn on apparently sound houses for re-discount in Scotland at a time when some of these firms were already failing.

Alexander Blair insisted on changes to strengthen the system. Agents were regularly invited to head office to meet officials and directors. For customers who wanted a facility to discount £500 or more, the agents were required to recommend a maximum to be allowed which, when approved by head office, was not to be exceeded. It was hoped that this would stop excessive discounts.[8] Further, each bill was to be properly examined in its relation to the drawee's business, although in practice this was necessarily perfunctory, and cash accounts were to be cleared before renewal to reduce uncertainty about how 'real' a year's accounts of a customer were. The branch at Glasgow, which transacted 15 per cent of the total bill business in 1832 and whose agent had been responsible to a local board for his actions, was placed under Charles Campbell, the Bank Inspector, who was required to visit Edinburgh once a month. But at most branches it was still thought important to have respected agents well acquainted with local conditions.[9] There was only a slow move in favour of professional staff: a sub-manager was appointed at Glasgow in 1833 and at Dundee in 1836, and after the crisis in the west of Scotland in 1841 the Mound appointed sub-managers at Paisley and Greenock. A number of the accountants in the branches came from the Mound, and after 1841 Alexander Blair began to insist on some salaried appointments at all agencies. But the most important change after 1832 was in the rigour with which the rules were

---

7 It was more difficult to check on the total obligations of a customer, although agents were expected to have a detailed knowledge of local business networks.

8 BS 1/70/12, p. 10.

9 BS 20/10/3, Miscellaneous papers, W. J. Duncan to Alexander Blair, 26 April 1837, wherein the importance of local connections was described as a rule of the Bank. The guide to the local managers' life in later Victorian years is George Rae, *The Country Banker* (London: 1917 edn), though this was written for an English audience; north of the Border, more emphasis was placed on religious life and Sunday observance.

enforced and the agreement by the directors that local political advantage was no longer a prime consideration in dealing with agents. In this, the collapse of the old municipal interest in Scotland after the burgh reform Act of 1833 was an undoubted factor. 'The mass of the new middle-class electors were anti-Tory', and the cliques which ran the Scottish burghs gave way to a broadly-based political control which was usually Whig.[10]

By 1835, Alexander Blair had made it clear in a number of legal actions against agents and debtors that overdrawn cash accounts and long-dated past-due bills must be settled. But this was time-consuming, especially for the lawyers. The case of William Haig of Seggie, the distiller, whose account was with the Bank agent at St Andrews, illustrated the laxity of the old system. Haig operated a distillery and earthenware business at Guardbridge on the River Eden, five miles from St Andrews.[11] By dealing in grain on a rising market from 1829–31, using bills drawn on Bank of Scotland and the British Linen Company, he was caught when prices subsided with the excellent harvests thereafter.[12] Unable to retire his bills, he opted for a string of redrawals and overdrew his cash account by £1,388. Both practices were familiar, and Blair was determined to stop them. In April 1835, supported by the board, he overruled the agent and Haig was told to pay or face legal action. William Haig threatened his own legal action for damages but thought better of it and offered to pay £500 to the cash account if the Bank agreed to pay £9,000 of his bills on London! Harry Davidson ws then secured a diligence by poinding the assets and books. The Bank, however, was only one of the creditors; the British Linen Company, for example, held a lien over the Seggie farm estate. With so many cases at this time, it became common for all the banks to agree on settling debts as in this case; there were frequent references in the Bank minutes to recoveries of only a few shillings in the pound.

As early as 1833, Alexander Blair felt confident enough to discipline agents who openly espoused political interests. John MacKenzie, the Provost and agent at Inverness, was criticised in the press and was told either to desist or to retire from service. He was a relatively successful agent: by 1843 his losses on bills averaged only 8s 6d per cent (see Table 14.1).[13]

10 W. Ferguson, Scotland: 1689 to the Present, The Edinburgh History of Scotland, vol. iv (Edinburgh: 1968), p. 303; 3 & 4 William IV c.76, 'An Act to alter and amend the Laws for the Election of the Magistrates and Councils of the Royal Burghs in Scotland' (28 August 1833), and also 3 & 4 William IV c.77, 'An Act to provide for the Appointment and Election of Magistrates and Councillors for the several Burghs and Towns of Scotland which now return or contribute to return [sic] Members to Parliament and are not Royal Burghs' (28 August 1833).
11 BS 1/5, Minutes: 28 April; 4, 15, 18, 20 and 25 May 1835.
12 J. H. Clapham, An Economic History of Modern Britain: The Early Railway Age, 1820–1850 (Cambridge: 1967), pp. 171–2, 239.
13 BS 20/12/5, Miscellaneous papers. The Tories recovered Inverness-shire in 1835, but the Whigs held Inverness Burghs: Ferguson, Scotland: 1689 to the Present, p. 306.

Table 14.1 *Losses on bills at branches of Bank of Scotland as at 31 December 1843, sorted by percentage average loss per annum*

Branch	Loss on bills (£)	Average lent on bills (£)	Period From	Period To	No. of years	Average loss per annum (£)	Average loss per annum (%)	Agent
Airdrie	5000	20050	1836	1842	6	833.33	4.156	Mack, A. A.
Paisley	32224	127550	1835	1843	8	4028.00	3.158	Findlay, James
Castle Douglas	243	3030	1840	1843	3	81.00	2.673	Ireland, William
Greenock	7572	39450	1836	1843	8	946.50	2.399	Baine, Robert
Whithorn	157	1320	1838	1843	5	31.40	2.379	Dinwoodie, J. C. and McHaffie, J.
Strathaven	559	12050	1837	1838	2	279.50	2.320	Cross, John
Dundee	30950	148327	1833	1843	11	2813.64	1.897	Sturrock, John
Dundee	30950	148327	1833	1843	11	2813.64	1.897	Sturrock, John
Glasgow	34448	150000	1818	1833	15	2296.53	1.531	Aitken, Robert
Fraserburgh	534	4681	1835	1843	8	66.75	1.426	Chalmers, Lewis
Leith	564		1825	1828				Brodie, A.
Leith (contd)	3663	25850	1828	1843	8	457.88	1.771	Jones, Thomas
Dumfries	3005	32470	1837	1843	7	429.29	1.322	Threshie and Crichton
Falkirk	1392	27150	1826	1830	4	348.00	1.282	Ramsay, A. and son
Blairgowrie	1015	18920	1839	1843	5	203.00	1.073	Robertson, R. and A.
Ayr	5377	23213	1815	1843	28	192.04	0.827	McClelland, Thomas
Lauder	189	2120	1833	1843	11	17.18	0.810	Romanes, John
Kilmarnock	535	13920	1838	1843	5	107.00	0.769	Cowie, Adam
Dunfermline	5105	75000	1822	1831	9	567.22	0.756	Beveridge, W.
Stirling	826	10954	1832	1843	11	75.09	0.686	Brodie, Alexander
Glasgow	10388	158000	1833	1843	11	944.36	0.598	Campbell, Charles
Stirling	8190	57126	1809	1832	24	341.25	0.597	McMillan, John
Kirkcudbright	1630	19180	1828	1843	15	108.67	0.567	McLellan, W. H.
Strathaven	250	10080	1838	1843	5	50.00	0.496	Tennant, Thomas and John
Dunfermline	4727	74130	1831	1843	13	363.62	0.491	Ronaldson, James S.
Cumnock	303	10650	1839	1843	6	50.50	0.474	McKerrow, Matthew
Haddington	4577	38570	1817	1843	27	169.52	0.440	Todrick, Archibald and Thomas
Inverness	4909	63890	1825	1843	18	272.72	0.427	McKenzie, John
Dumfries	5899	78000	1818	1837	18	327.72	0.420	Barker, John

Table 14.1 *continued*

Branch	Loss on bills (£)	Average lent on bills (£)	Period From	Period To	No. of years	Average loss per annum (£)	Average loss per annum (%)	Agent
Perth	4673	44830	1813	1843	30	155.77	0.347	Stewart, P. G.
Aberdeen	7967	126835	1816	1836	20	398.35	0.314	Duguid, Peter
Montrose	1131	45100	1835	1843	8	141.38	0.313	Barclay, John
Falkirk	1729	42900	1830	1843	13	133.00	0.310	MacFarlane, Alexander
Kirkcaldy	2376	32450	1818	1843	26	91.38	0.282	Morgan, D. and A. G.
Duns	265	9842	1833	1843	11	24.09	0.245	Purves, A. and William
St Andrews	836	26930	1829	1843	15	55.73	0.207	Bain, John
Kelso	1448	23483	1809	1843	34	42.59	0.181	Darling, James, Robert and Peter
Stonehaven	538	21896	1825	1843	19	28.32	0.129	Stewart, William
Ardrossan	30	7100	1839	1843	5	6.00	0.085	Mack, D. J.
Aberdeen	0	80253	1836	1843	7	0.00	0.000	Thomson, Arthur
Banchory	0	4050	1838	1843	6	0.00	0.000	Ogg, John
Castle Douglas	0	500	1843	1843	1	0.00	0.000	Brown, Thomas
Montrose			1843	1843				Hunter, Robert J.

Table 14.1 continued

Branch	Loss borne by Bank (£)	Loss borne by Bank (%)	Agent's liability	Security	Remarks
Airdrie	5000	4.156			Under interim management since resignation of Mack in March 1842. Few bills discounted.
Paisley			1/4th	5000	No settlement yet – liability not to exceed retained salary fund.
Castle Douglas			1/4th	2500	Ireland died January 1843 – no settlement yet with sureties.
Greenock	6372	2.019	1/4th	3000	£800 not settled for – agent's liability not to exceed retained salary fund.
Whithorn	118	1.788	1/4th	2000	McHaffie resigned November 1841 – Dinwoodie now sole agent.
Strathaven	311	1.29			Cross resigned October 1838.
Dundee	29500	1.808	1/4th	5000	Sturrock's liability not to exceed his salary in any one year. Liability settled for therefore £200.
Dundee	29500	1.808	1/4th	2000	Andrew Neilson appointed assistant manager in June 1838 – liability 1/4th, security £2,000.
Glasgow	32074	1.426			Agent died 1833.
Fraserburgh	401	1.071	1/4th	5000	
Leith					
Leith (contd)	3663	1.771	none		Bills approved by Bank before discount – agent not liable.
Dumfries	2867	1.261	1/3d	8000	
Falkirk	696	0.641	1/4th	2500–3000	Ramsays resigned in July 1830. Agent also paid about £100 in law expenses.
Blairgowrie	3745	0.576	1/2th	6000	No settlement yet.
Ayr			1/4th	3000	
Lauder			1/4th	4000	No settlement.
Kilmarnock					No settlement.
Dunfermline	4378	0.649	1/4th	3000	Beveridge resigned in 1831.
Stirling	695	0.577			£131 not settled for.
Glasgow	9300	0.535			
Stirling	4540	0.331			McMillan resigned in 1832.
Kirkcudbright	1402	0.487	1/4th	3000	
Strathaven			1/4th	4000	No settlement yet.
Dunfermline	3971	0.412	1/2th	5000	Agent had settled for £400 – £356 remained not settled for.
Cumnock			1/2th	4000	Settled for £196.

Table 14.1 *continued*

Branch	Loss borne by Bank (£)	Loss borne by Bank (%)	Agent's liability	Security	Remarks
Haddington	2748	0.264	1/3d	6000	£535 not settled for – Thomas Todrick became joint agent in 1835.
Inverness	3413	0.297	1/2th	10000	£732 not settled for.
Dumfries	5399	0.385			Barker died in April 1837.
Perth	3694	0.275	1/4th	3500	£15 not settled for.
Aberdeen	5469	0.216			
Montrose	1131	0.313			Barclay resigned in October 1843.
Falkirk	493	0.088	1/4th	3000	£1,236 not settled for.
Kirkcaldy	1830	0.217	1/2th	7400	£158 not settled for – A. J. Morgan joined in agency in May 1841.
Duns			1/4th	3000	No settlement yet.
St Andrews	106	0.026	1/2th	6000	£730 not settled for.
Kelso	566	0.071	whole	8000	£882 not settled for – Robert and Peter Darling joined in agency in November 1826.
Stonehaven	538	0.129	whole	6000	
Ardrossan			1/4th	2500	No settlement yet.
Aberdeen	0	0	1/8th	8000	£2,500 of security special for bills.
Banchory			1/2th	4000	
Castle Douglas			1/4th	2000	At liberty not to discount.
Montrose			1/4th	3000	Liability not to exceed £75 in any one year.

Source: BS 1/70/3, Private Reports and Statements, p. 278.

Criticisms were voiced over the reliance by agents on local cautioners who might, and often did, borrow from the agent.[14] This sort of robust action encouraged the professional bankers to think and communicate in terms of the primary position of the Bank's depositors and proprietors as above party and sectional interests. Accounts were now discussed more in terms of their effect on the financial health of the Bank. This was important given the decision, again on the advice of Blair, that the Bank should follow the practice of the British Linen Company and the Commercial Bank and open more branches. While several of the smaller agencies were closed, sixteen new offices were opened by 1840. Each was allocated at least one official as the accountant who had served in head office or at Glasgow. Several of the new branches, of which Airdrie, Kilmarnock, Paisley, Montrose, Dundee, Duns and Greenock were the more notable, became important sources of deposits (see Table 14.2).[15] Apart from the more extensive employment opportunities for staff, the board raised salaries, by 10 per cent in August 1832 and another 15–20 per cent eighteen months later. The new English and Glasgow joint-stock banks were keen to recruit Scots, and a number of staff from agencies with excellent records left the employment of the Edinburgh banks. This loss of talent had an adverse effect on decision making by mid-century.

How successful was Blair with his new branch policy? At the sixteen old branches open in 1832, the average loss on bills to 1841 was reduced to 5s 6d per cent of total advances, compared with an average loss for the fifteen years prior to 1832 of 13s 7d per cent. Thus Blair's rule saw good results here. Yet at the sixteen new branches the average loss reached £1 17s 6d per cent. The problem was complex. There was the old problem of new agents keen to expand business who accepted accounts on terms which agents of longer standing might have refused (see Table 14.3). Advice would be given to head office which was insufficiently supported by local conditions, and discounts and cash-account levels were set above a prudent level. In normal years, this would not be a problem and could be managed by stricter controls. But in the first decade of Blair's tenure there were two serious crises, with the worst results at Dundee in 1836 and Paisley in 1841.

The intelligence system at the Mound worked rather well for general economic and financial conditions. Regular reports monitored grain prices

---

14 BS 20/10/3, Miscellaneous papers, Charles Campbell, to Alexander Blair, 29 August 1833.
15 Bank of Scotland opened branches in 1833 at Dundee, Duns and Lauder, in 1835 at Fraserburgh and Montrose, in 1838 at Greenock, Paisley, Airdrie and Strathaven, in 1838 at Cumnock, Banchory, Kilmarnock and Whithorn, in 1839 at Ardrossan and Blairgowrie, and in 1840 at Castle Douglas: BS 1/70/12, p. 4. Alexander Blair criticised former closures at Dundee, Greenock, Montrose and Kilmarnock.

and the expansion of industrial demand, in Europe and the Americas, as well as at home. Officials plotted the expansion of bank credit in France, Belgium and Germany as western Europe recovered from the political upheavals of 1830. Concern was expressed about the policy of the US President, Andrew Jackson, who paid off his country's national debt in 1835. His policy, implemented from 1833, was to distribute budget revenues to the state banks and reduce the influence of the Bank of the United States; its charter lapsed in 1836. The state banks, flush with government funds, extended their facilities, and, in the boom which followed, around 200 new banks were established.[16] As prices rose, the US and Canadian merchants and bankers borrowed cheap money in Britain and Europe to fund their purchases of commodities, certain that prices and demand would continue to rise. Money was lent on all manner of sound and dubious, but usually vague, US land companies, railways, port schemes and municipal and state buildings.[17] In England, no fewer than twenty-six joint-stock banks were added in 1835 to the thirty-four erected since the Act of 1826, and in 1836, mostly in the early months of the year, another forty-two were projected. Alexander Blair watched these developments with mounting concern; Charles Campbell, a cautious banker, warned from Glasgow of a speculative boom fuelled by accommodation bills in the west of Scotland. From 1832 to 1835, severe reductions had been imposed on bills and cash accounts, and in 1836 advances, at £358,893, were little above the level of 1833.[18]

The situation of the Glasgow branch, staffed with professional bankers, may be contrasted with the new Dundee agency, opened in 1833. Dundee already had five banks: the Dundee bank and the Dundee New bank, which later united; the Dundee Union, the British Linen branch, and the Dundee Commercial. In the course of 1833, the National Bank also opened an agency.[19] The population of the burgh grew from 30,575 in 1821 to 45,355 in 1831 and over 60,000 a decade later.[20] The sprawl of the linen and wool textile industries, with rising imports of flax from the Baltic countries, encouraged numerous small-scale spinners and weavers 'without credit' to borrow from the Dundee banks on local and inland bills of exchange. These were then re-discounted in successive waves to pay for more imports.[21] From 1815–19, an annual average of 2,577 tons of Baltic

16 Clapham, *An Economic History of Modern Britain*, pp. 513–14.
17 L. H. Jenks, *The Migration of British Capital to 1875* (London: 1927), p. 92ff.
18 BS 1/70/12, Appendix no. 3, 'Business transactions at each office'.
19 E. Gauldie (ed.), *The Dundee Textile Industry 1790–1885, From the Papers of Peter Carmichael of Arthurstone*, Scottish History Society, 4th series, vol. 6 (Edinburgh: 1969), p. 56; C. W. Munn, *The Scottish Provincial Banking Companies, 1747–1864* (Edinburgh: 1981), pp. 91–2.
20 B. P. Lenman, C. Lythe and E. Gauldie, *Dundee and its Textile Industry 1850–1914*, Abertay Historical Society, no. 14 (Dundee: 1969), p. 10.
21 BS 20/18/10, Miscellaneous papers, A. Neilson, assistant manager, Dundee, 18 December 1839.

Table 14.2 Average lent at interest and average deposited at each branch of Bank of Scotland, 1832–41

	1832		1833		1834		1835		1836	
	Lent	Deposited	Lent	Deposited	Lent	Deposited	Lent	Deposited	Lent	Deposited
Edinburgh	727100	1244700	660500	1226900	639372	1376000	656929	1705000	564450	1766300
Aberdeen	119500	127363	101000	128100	108142	134506	112807	137223	134561	133123
Airdrie									9470	5752
Ayr	10500	98000	9500	104000	8868	107019	7840	111555	9608	112204
Ardrossan										
Banchory										
Blairgowrie										
Castle Douglas										
Cumnock										
Dumfries	80000	187470	71500	176800	70000	174653	63000	183474	48727	186201
Dundee					45357	12796	136197	16315	217377	23467
Dunfermline	78000	74100	73000	72000	81736	75062	83950	74350	86659	74168
Duns					6023	15397	9793	16807	11344	25272
Falkirk	40000	60500	36000	56000	35495	58828	41203	66930	46782	69659
Fraserburgh									8150	5216
Glasgow	466000	179000	330000	168000	295500	176154	334821	175381	358893	220253
Greenock									8380	21302
Haddington	51000	133400	45500	135000	36478	131630	35372	129766	32593	142380
Inverness	72000	96100	71500	104500	72480	110838	65759	117863	65999	107443
Kelso	51800	174200	51000	156400	53000	157437	45714	172270	41442	187513
Kirkcaldy	41600	84000	47600	82800	44000	82294	46207	75580	47619	76298
Kirkcudbright	33000	94300	29000	100700	26500	110599	23455	116640	18996	110719
Kilmarnock										
Lauder					1472	10955	2080	29660	2825	39946
Leith	38000	60300	38000	61500	42886	63199	49410	70367	48266	52277
Montrose									17168	9721
Paisley									42408	7141
Perth	58000	107800	47500	107000	41853	106369	33011	107176	27763	106702
St Andrews	55500	142500	56000	140500	59384	135561	45180	142970	3954	145065
Stirling	49000	269500	32000	259200	26674	268944	23761	265371	22538	259347
Stonehaven	36000	24388	30500	26504	26177	27437	25995	33390	27819	40867
Strathaven										
Whithorn										
Total	2007000	3155621	1730100	3105904	1721397	3335678	1842484	3748088	1932791	3928336

	1837		1838		1839		1840		1841	
	Lent	Deposited	Lent	Deposited	Lent	Deposited	Lent	Deposited	Lent	Deposited
Edinburgh	686800	1818000	634207	1948107	632440	1792600	702855	1612340	884000	1627000
Aberdeen	120519	116571	108843	110263	132778	108884	132282	103321	159542	107289
Airdrie	24263	19433	21000	23680	27983	20045	27178	22061	27000	26624
Ayr	9700	100920	10350	98909	10233	103487	6951	104953	5341	107609
Ardrossan					2712	2034	7248	12920	8900	14311
Banchory			707	979	10841	5923	4744	8963	6376	10891
Blairgowrie							31508	11042	28500	12700
Castle Douglas							410	966	3550	7886
Cumnock			6360	4638	12613	16033	12618	19557	14345	21451
Dumfries	50540	191255	57720	189468	69238	175540	60594	181824	57000	191097
Dundee	259186	31071	264144	32540	266961	32674	207986	40252	194000	37529
Dunfermline	96768	71939	95312	78363	101260	79843	120950	73740	123500	72861
Duns	14012	34138	16178	40802	18522	44364	20112	49224	20800	52146
Falkirk	68528	72401	64714	75819	75884	80572	78443	85364	73000	87522
Fraserburgh	3919	12347	6090	14325	6923	10624	5000	13440	5676	17208
Glasgow	531754	320180	545777	390187	740296	437374	922144	439379	1111500	434064
Greenock	21238	41565	21758	62351	41558	72519	80155	84155	86600	89589
Haddington	31160	135350	32740	131976	33717	139546	36220	144683	36600	141510
Inverness	73267	102876	72307	109133	68787	104673	81276	103943	91500	105355
Kelso	39806	218970	43224	221652	56686	237386	57195	234022	57200	238075
Kirkcaldy	45184	90155	43188	107433	59106	117329	55479	108662	51000	103788
Kirkcudbright	21275	112877	20029	109438	24235	110804	24961	113424	25000	116146
Kilmarnock					13546	8643	18189	15834	18500	19618
Lauder	3773	48139	4687	48019	3273	46902	3317	48546	2400	51803
Leith	52975	51055	41454	62207	44126	69780	37689	69278	45000	67217
Montrose	40621	20479	51211	25687	67038	28605	65871	33856	65000	40755
Paisley	99182	19761	123677	35035	203289	44224	229645	47115	238400	50286
Perth	31827	100959	40456	98387	50966	92005	43864	87870	37000	85315
St Andrews	35746	155836	33633	158763	31680	153215	31889	150831	34700	158200
Stirling	21885	258160	24964	253160	27035	237035	26274	231374	28000	237702
Stonehaven	32057	47986	33473	51247	35922	44397	41441	43380	42000	45322
Strathaven	8622	1451	17532	4205	13089	6815	12760	12457	14400	12841
Whithorn					1678	5452	1282	8225	1250	12185
Total	2424607	4193874	2435735	4486613	2886787	4434476	3189120	4317001	3596980	4403895

Source: BS 1/70/12, Treasurer's (Blair's) Report to the directors on the affairs of Bank of Scotland, 1832–42, appendix 3 (24 March 1842).

Table 14.3 Number of bills discounted per annum at each branch of Bank of Scotland, 1832–41

	1832			1833			1834			1835			1836		
	Local	Inland	London	Local	Inland	London	Local	Inland	London	Local	Inland	London	Local	Inland	London
Aberdeen	1379	199	562	1248	438	449	1614	376	563	1466	336	529	1552	497	499
Airdrie													723	89	6
Ardrossan															
Ayr	424	63	159	350	78	63	366	86	54	295	68	38	281	71	39
Banchory															
Blairgowrie															
Castle Douglas															
Cumnock															
Dumfries	2096	155	379	1701	228	277	1999	296	601	1870	320	406	1507	281	276
Dundee				321	50	811	963	213	135	2455	418	349	3303	549	444
Dunfermline	1467	656	916	1224	745	784	1575	886	1006	1495	865	1029	1372	856	1017
Duns				170	71	20	358	104	45	507	152	64	575	171	68
Falkirk	1277	492	245	830	702	222	877	893	205	892	994	150	935	1070	222
Fraserburgh													370	76	15
Glasgow	1861	1154	970	675	1680	620	1433	2451	828	1853	2679	866	1944	3267	1074
Greenock													250	175	80
Haddington	1012	445	176	725	628	110	612	665	158	537	772	146	482	850	114
Inverness	1859	1448	330	1905	394	313	1943	1447	299	1902	398	267	2373	402	298
Kelso	661	128	321	512	249	214	578	279	221	577	318	200	528	341	206
Kirkcaldy	468	288	28	417	540	274	440	566	315	451	560	315	463	533	260
Kirkcudbright	1504	126	236	1083	169	189	1071	186	272	950	202	271	754	179	331
Kilmarnock															
Lauder				70	14	15	212	58	40	227	51	34	257	93	36
Leith	223	186	239	171	446	150	205	588	140	218	674	237	214	665	330
Montrose													400	308	77
Paisley													543	445	436
Perth	1161	250	417	736	409	333	794	481	411	675	518	408	664	911	425
St Andrews	1594	290	287	1312	441	304	1495	566	243	1520	547	275	1544	573	240
Stirling	681	336	259	310	431	221	270	455	172	217	445	228	278	377	192
Stonehaven	1640	111	82	1246	773	80	1414	154	67	1330	224	87	1331	164	79
Strathaven															
Whithorn															
Total	19307	6327	5606	15006	8486	5449	18219	10750	5775	19437	10541	5899	22643	12943	6764
Total (all bills)	31240			28941			34744			35877			42350		

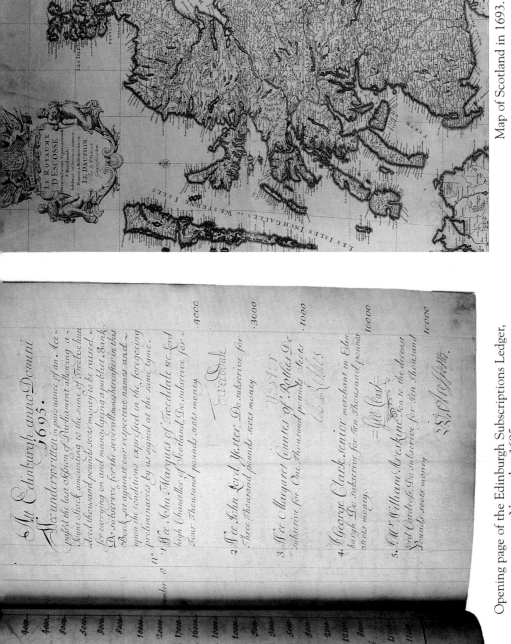

Map of Scotland in 1693.

Opening page of the Edinburgh Subscriptions Ledger, November 1695.

No 34512 Edinburgh June 24. 1723.

The Governour & Company of ye Bank of SCOTLAND constituted by Act of Parliament, do hereby oblige themselves to pay to David Spence or the Bearer Twelve pounds Scots on Demand

By order of ye Court of Directors

EDINBURGH, 7. February, 1712.

YOU have inclosed a complete List of the Adventurers in the Bank of Scotland at this Day, out of which are to be chosen a Governour, Deputy-Governour, and 24 Directors of the Scots Adventurers, for managing the Affairs of the COMPANY the ensuing Year.

You'll be pleased therefore to give in your Votes for Governour and Deputy-Governour, upon the first Wednesday of March ensuing, a general Meeting being appointed on Thursday in the Week thereafter for declaring the Choice. Likeways on the third Wednesday of the said Month, you are to give in your Votes for 24 Directors, dividing the List in two Columns, the one of 12. Entituled Ordinary Directors, and the other also of 12. marked Extraordinary Directors, A general Meeting being appointed on Friday in the Week thereafter, for declaring the Choice: You need not give in any List for Trustees in England, the Adventurers there being within the Number of 13.

By the inclosed List, you will distinguish the English Adventurers by the Letter E prefixt to their Names: As also by the Stars, who are qualified to be Governour, Deputy-Governour or Directors. You are intreated to make the Lists of your Votes Alphabetically, to prevent Trouble and Confusion in the Scrutiny; and on the Foot, as also on the out Side thereof when folded up, you are to mark the Number of your Votes in Figures, and if you cannot be personably present to give them in, you may inclose your Lists in a signed Letter, addressed to the Directors of the BANK, who will attend the two Days above, as the Bank-Office on the South Side of the Land-market, from 9 to 12 a Clock in the Forenoon, and from 3 to 6 in the Afternoon, after these peremptor Hours, no Votes are to be taken in, This by Order of the Court of Directors, is signified by

Your most Humble Servant

DA. SPENCE Secretary.

The general Meetings are at three aClock in the Afternoon at the BANK-OFFICE.

Instructions of David Spence, Secretary of Bank of

The Porteous Riot of 1736, as imagined by the artist James Drummond (1855). (National Gallery of Scotland)

The Falls of Clyde, by Jacob More (detail). The power of the falls was harnessed for David Dale's cotton-spinning mills at New Lanark. (National Gallery of Scotland)

The Trongate, Glasgow, in 1761.

Opening page of the report on the trial of Henry, Lord Melville.

VISCOUNT MELVILLE.

THE

TRIAL,

BY IMPEACHMENT,

OF

HENRY LORD VISCOUNT

MELVILLE,

FOR HIGH CRIMES AND MISDEMEANORS,

BEFORE

THE HOUSE OF PEERS,

IN

WESTMINSTER HALL,

Between the 29th of April and the 17th of May 1806.

THE IMPARTIAL EDITION.

EDINBURGH:

Printed for and by J. ROBERTSON, OLIVER & Co. and J. TURNBULL,
and Sold by JAMES ROBERTSON, No 15, *Nicolson Street*;
W. REID, *Leith*; A. DUNCAN & Co. and
BRASH & REID, *Glasgow*.

1806.

The Old Town of Edinburgh from Calton Hill, c.1822,
by Patrick and Alexander Nasmyth.

A view of Glasgow from the south in the early eighteenth century.

Castle Street, Aberdeen, in the 1820s.

Paisley in the 1820s, by John Clark.

Edinburgh from the west with the Castle and Leadhills Stage Coach, c.1821,
by Alexander Nasmyth.

The Bank House on the Mound from (the present-day) Mound Place, 1830.

Princes Street with the commencement of the building of the Royal Institution, Edinburgh, by Alexander Nasmyth. (National Gallery of Scotland)

Notice to customers about changes to deposit interest, announced by all the Scottish banks, 1882.

DEPOSIT INTEREST.

The undersigned **BANKS** hereby intimate that, from and after this date, and until further notice, the Rates of Interest to be allowed by them on Money Lodged at their **HEAD-OFFICES** and **BRANCHES** will be as follows, viz.:—

On DEPOSIT RECEIPTS, - - - 3 per cent.
No Interest to be allowed unless the Money has been lodged a month.

On CURRENT ACCOUNTS, calculated on the } $1\frac{1}{2}$ "
Minimum Monthly Balances,

On Do., calculated on the } 1 "
Daily Balances, - -

For THE BANK OF SCOTLAND,
    JAMES A. WENLEY, Treasurer.

For THE ROYAL BANK OF SCOTLAND,
    J. S. FLEMING, Cashier.

For THE BRITISH LINEN COMPANY BANK,
    JAMES SYME, Manager.

For THE COMMERCIAL BANK OF SCOTLAND, LIMITED,
    R. L. PEPLOE, Manager.

For THE NATIONAL BANK OF SCOTLAND, LIMITED,
    T. H. SMITH, Manager.

For THE UNION BANK OF SCOTLAND, LIMITED,
    CHARLES GAIRDNER, General Manager.

For THE CLYDESDALE BANK, LIMITED,
    J. M. CUNNINGHAM, General Manager.

For the TOWN AND COUNTY BANK, LIMITED,
    G. L. RORIE, Manager.

For the NORTH OF SCOTLAND BANK, LIMITED,
    ROBT. LUMSDEN, Manager.

For the CALEDONIAN BANKING COMPANY, LIMITED,
    E. H. MACMILLAN, Manager.

17th August 1882.

	1837			1838			1839			1840			1841		
	Local	Inland	London	Local	Inland	London	Local	Inland	London	Local	Inland	London	Local	Inland	London
Aberdeen	1157	467	495	1231	465	484	1234	600	466	1003	825	483	995	758	495
Airdrie	1079	169	14	1098	86	12	1239	127	14	1178	102	4	1063	52	
Ardrossan							183	63	8	396	180	21	536	189	22
Ayr	251	91	43	242	81	46	266	156	106	217	317	115	186	293	68
Banchory				179	26	25	378	11	7	487	38	16	546	130	19
Blairgowrie							595	80	24	841	187	48	803	506	37
Castle Douglas										58	141	4	300	76	17
Cumnock				610	38	10	801	45	17	748	72	30	783	26	26
Dumfries	1684	369	290	1897	398	240	2158	377	233	1560	500	238	1248	493	285
Dundee	3307	522	584	2579	594	539	2394	663	636	1785	676	686	1724	665	555
Dunfermline	1590	955	1062	2579	915	1171	1773	939	1077	2126	1064	958	2000	1023	895
Duns	544	193	60	1566	185	80	483	194	106	467	263	133	527	327	117
Falkirk	1179	1296	228	1178	1213	240	1210	1207	211	1214	1254	134	1141	1299	121
Fraserburgh	564	48	23	630	47	15	541	38	14	252	76	12	218	75	13
Glasgow	2255	3950	1318	2180	3908	1196	2715	4627	1601	3087	4677	1606	3340	4787	2109
Greenock	400	243	104	444	290	116	564	356	167	648	483	230	602	555	281
Haddington	609	830	120	644	865	115	755	805	123	769	888	126	738	782	105
Inverness	2610	416	327	2661	477	343	2278	367	257	2420	423	313	2950	432	264
Kelso	525	296	197	492	280	175	543	349	103	577	383	218	546	226	400
Kirkcaldy	435	600	245	503	703	320	578	809	332	663	887	296	440	966	326
Kirkcudbright	728	244	242	745	176	243	720	201	219	764	322	208	653	781	272
Kilmarnock				38	7	2	512	187	83	467	275	120	431	274	120
Lauder	335	73	35	333	72	34	250	81	31	221	164	26	174	216	39
Leith	230	722	400	259	522	299	248	676	291	157	373	323	174	487	331
Montrose	562	312	108	650	344	137	661	431	187	629	450	146	751	404	180
Paisley	947	785	730	1024	640	638	1745	988	842	2031	1171	892	1801	1477	784
Perth	741	625	380	956	691	370	1019	685	382	880	723	382	686	678	381
St Andrew	1676	628	223	1426	544	190	1260	656	176	1202	731	206	1095	739	186
Stirling	410	434	254	500	551	255	500	612	203	464	616	177	491	630	202
Stonehaven	1442	160	61	940	165	65	844	152	52	760	140	47	822	144	48
Strathaven	696	34		1040	14	8	863	27	9	955	36	15	888	68	13
Whithorn				2	1	1	68	42	73	78	76	57	102	98	46
Total	25956	14462	7543	26540	14298	7369	29378	16551	8050	29104	18513	8270	28754	19698	8757
Total (all bills)	47961			48207			53979			55887			57209		

Source: BS 1/70/12, Treasurer's (Blair's) Report to the directors on the affairs of Bank of Scotland, 1832–42, appendix 8 (24 March 1842).

flax had been unloaded at Dundee docks; by 1836 this had reached 41,305 tons.[22] Coastal tonnage inward doubled to 200,000 tons in the seven years to 1836. It was inevitable, therefore, that Alexander Blair would think of Dundee as a suitable burgh for a branch. Although the board recognised the 'risk attendant upon the creation of business in a district where the bank had to contend with the influence and capital of the local establishments', this was not insurmountable if the local economy was sound.[23] The directors then proceeded to make a cardinal error. Their choice for agent, John Sturrock, the convenor of the finance committee of the harbour trustees, was an advocate of rapid burgh expansion, and, in a departure from normal practice, the letters of appointment bound him for only £200 of losses in any one financial year.[24] There was to be no faster expansion in discounts and cash accounts at any other branch of Bank of Scotland. In 1836, discounts totalled 3,303 local bills and 993 inland and London bills; advances rose from £45,357 in March 1834 to £259,186 four years later. It was the extent of local bills which was at fault, as Dundee businessmen borrowed from all the banks and, in turn, guaranteed advances to their friends.

Problems with bad debts surfaced in the London markets by the spring of 1836 as a number of English joint-stock banks discounted blocks of paper drawn by speculative firms. By June, the Bank of England faced a drain on bullion and had also discovered that it held acceptances from seven firms associated with the Atlantic trades and the financing of US loans which, it was thought, might result in difficulty.[25] Baring's were annoyed at inclusion on this list, and returned 'much and rather patronising advice'. They understood the US business and told the Bank of England that the word of Baring's was enough; they knew a good from a bad bill. They were right. Others were to survive, but three firms, widely known as the three 'W's', were in difficulty. The Bank of England had discounted bills worth almost £1 million, and bank rate went to 4½ per cent in July 1836: 'by general consent of well-informed critics then and since', this was overdue.[26] In August, the rate was 5 per cent and all bills were refused from note-issuing English joint-stock banks, and, although Sir John Clapham was to consider that there was some justification for

22 G. Jackson, with K. Kinnear, *The Trade and Shipping of Dundee 1780–1850*, Abertay Historical Society, no. 31 (Dundee: 1991), pp. 7–8.

23 BS 1/21/7, Private Letter Book, Blair to John Sturrock, Agent at Dundee, 6 January 1837.

24 John Sturrock, 'An Account of the Trade of the Port of Dundee during the Three Years Ended 31 May 1838', *Journal of the Statistical Society of London*, vol. 1 (London: 1839), 522–9; BS 1/70/3, Private Reports and Statements.

25 Clapham, *An Economic History of Modern Britain*, p. 515; idem, *The Bank of England. A History* (2 vols, Cambridge: 1944), vol. ii, *1797–1914*, pp. 151–2.

26 Ibid., pp. 152–3.

this, a blanket 'seemed vindictive'. But the Bank of England was right to stop further accumulations of unsound paper; had it not done so, the subsequent crisis would have been worse.

As the summer of 1836 turned into autumn, the 'season of suicides' took an unusually heavy toll. Harvests were poor over much of western Europe. In November, the Irish Agricultural and Commercial bank failed and the Bank of Ireland brought gold from London to support the Irish system. At the end of that month, the Northern and Central Bank of England, a note-issuer with thirty-nine branches centred in Manchester, was at the door of the Bank of England pleading for help. Threadneedle Street exacted stiff terms and by Christmas took entire control, 'under warrant of attorney signed at the pistol's point'. The shareholders of the Manchester bank were the main losers when, by order of the Bank of England, it was closed.[27] All this news, together with the reports on prices and market conditions, were reviewed, rather nervously, at the Mound. Glasgow was firm, as advances had risen by 48 per cent – £172,861 – to £531,754, but this was only 12 per cent above the level of 1832. Business at the Mound went up by £122,350, or 22 per cent, to £686,800, but again this was little above recent years, and 1835–6 was quiet. Branches which existed prior to 1832 did little to excite concern, and most of the newer ones observed their regulations.

The exception to this careful testimony of Scottish banking was in Dundee. In the early months of 1836, John Sturrock's attention was drawn to the rise in price of Russian flax and Bengal indigo and to the dangers of over-capacity inherent in the rush to build new spinning mills. He was warned to decline accommodation above agreed limits and given an absolute ceiling of £200,000, and told to curtail discounts to various business groups. The proportion of past-due bills in all categories – London as well as inland and local – reached 60 per cent by August. Remonstrances were sent from the Mound and ignored. Alexander Blair discussed the general problems posed by Dundee with Thomas Corrie and John Thomson, but for some months none of the Edinburgh banks was prepared to act decisively. By late November, the Irish and us crises had affected trade and payments; new credit was unobtainable from any bank in Dundee. Alexander Blair now felt that he could take action. William Simson was sent 'to remain there until recalled'. Everything connected with the bills and cash accounts was to be examined, new office arrangements for recovery of overdue bills installed and more detail on businesses in Dundee to be forwarded. He was asked to call on all the other bankers in the burgh and convene agreements between them on

27 Ibid., pp. 155–6.

interest rates and charges. It was rather late to bring to John Sturrock's notice that 'we expect our connections to have capital, a character for prudence, and to be engaged in a trade yielding a fair profit', and even then to be very careful.[28] William Simson remained for nearly two years trying to sort out losses and put in place businesslike arrangements. In that time, the directors of the Dundee Commercial Bank discovered that their capital of £50,000 and 'about half as much more' was lost in the crisis.[29] Fearful that this might become public knowledge, an orderly transfer of the business was made in 1838 to the Eastern Bank of Scotland, founded by several partners of the Dundee Commercial. For some months, the new bank issued Bank of Scotland notes to reassure the public of its probity. The Royal Bank, too, had severe losses in Dundee and closed its agency. John Sturrock admitted in 1838 that the importation of flax was excessive, although the blame lay with lack of demand in foreign markets.[30] Henceforth, he was controlled more closely from head office. The eventual losses were £25,255 on bills, which wiped out all the nominal profits made in Dundee in the first decade of its reopening. This would undoubtedly 'have been very considerably more' had head office not cut activity. There were further, although smaller, losses in other manufacturing districts.

A second group of serious debts was incurred at Paisley in 1841. The branch was opened in December 1835 with James Findlay, a local merchant, as agent, and by the following year 947 local bills were discounted, a figure which rose to 2,031 in 1840. Nominal profits soared to £3,921. This was achieved through a strong demand for Paisley textiles, including the famous shawls and patterned cottons and linens. In 1841, the cessation of demand for these goods in England, 'owing to the bad harvests and the distressed state of trade', cut orders for Paisley goods sharply, but Alexander Blair recorded that the disaster which overwhelmed the burgh 'must also be attributed in a great measure to the folly of the Paisley manufacturers who continued to manufacture in the face of an absence of demand and to force sales at great sacrifices'.[31] Once again, the agent had exceeded his powers and been carried away on a tide of local optimism. The slowness of recovery and changes in fashion made it difficult for firms to recover their losses. Bank of Scotland later wrote off £24,224. In an assessment for the board, Alexander Blair placed part of the responsibility for agents' mistakes on competition: 'The numerous banking offices in manufacturing places now enable a trader to go on with the ruinous system

28 BS 1/21/7, Instructions to William Simson, 26 November 1836.
29 C. W. Boase, *A Century of Banking in Dundee; being the Annual Balance Sheets of the Dundee Banking Company from 1764 to 1864*, 2nd edn (Edinburgh: 1867), pp. 403–4.
30 John Sturrock, 'An Account of the Trade of the Port of Dundee', p. 527.
31 BS 1/70/12, p. 9; BS 1/70/3, Treasurer's reports.

Table 14.4 Profits/losses at head office and branches of Bank of Scotland, 1832–41

	1832	1833	1834	1835	1836	1837	1838	1839	1840	1841
Head office	25222	24323	27099	27673	30946	23574	29406	26040	20182	18904
Branches										
Aberdeen	1840	1812	1920	1922	2224	2273	1736	2331	2319	2318
Airdrie					-159	177	202	275	174	145
Ayr	966	1009	311	277	642	223	399	-37	-430	32
Ardrossan								-98	-36	11
Banchory							-209	-126	-71	-68
Blairgowrie								-51	427	269
Castle Douglas									-207	-228
Cumnock							-202	-54	-20	55
Dumfries	2663	2471	2152	2100	2338	1227	2007	1176	157	678
Dundee			311	1102	2419	4210	2807	3346	2797	2071
Dunfermline	1178	1107	1221	1205	1367	1512	1242	1450	1861	1397
Duns			51	85	228	192	380	299	293	220
Falkirk	742	633	653	781	1012	1166	1116	1157	882	808
Fraserburgh					-241	-109	1	-19	-29	-41
Glasgow	4726	4147	4742	4342	5075	10858	8241	11083	17492	15150
Greenock					-176	251	400	349	1020	1066
Haddington	1808	1798	1472	1398	1830	845	1344	986	721	396
Inverness	1065	1257	1322	1329	1238	911	972	780	843	795
Kelso	2366	2088	1880	1803	2303	1235	2262	1885	1259	1078
Kirkcaldy	1070	1082	821	755	907	690	971	1264	836	481
Kirkcudbright	1067	1107	971	1023	1092	389	750	508	223	111
Kilmarnock							-331	-393	-274	-257
Lauder			5	187	392	149	367	187	24	12
Leith	824	924	775	912	760	846	700	906	803	682
Montrose					-226	594	536	920	1113	724
Paisley					-83	1258	1072	2422	3921	2371
Perth	1466	1420	1103	1042	1259	670	925	830	678	350
St Andrews	2010	1957	1734	1597	1755	910	1668	897	32	306
Stirling	3370	2965	2343	2154	2644	653	1863	518	-899	84
Stonehaven	378	353	353	370	559	486	675	533	580	469
Strathaven						-43	-43	-71	-79	-65
Whithorn								-236	-206	-209
Total (branches)	27539	26130	24140	24384	29159	31573	31851	33017	36204	31211
Total (Ho and branches)	52761	50453	51239	52057	60105	55147	61257	59057	56386	50115

Note: Head-office profits before deduction of charges.
Source: BS 1/70/12, Treasurer's (Blair's) Report to the directors on the affairs of Bank of Scotland, 1832–42, appendix 9 (24 March 1842).

to a great extent unchecked'.[32] By contrast, the records of the Glasgow branch showed that good controls and a broadly-based management could make sustained profits. Although affected by both the crises of 1836 and 1841, the management proved much more adept: in the six years to 1841, a loss of £8,443 was offset by profits of over £65,000, which made it the most profitable of the Bank of Scotland branches (see Table 14.4).

The outstanding difficulty identified by Alexander Blair in negotiations with the British Linen and the Royal Bank was the emergence of a more competitive environment in Scotland which squeezed interest income and commission. This had been largely caused by the establishment of joint-stock banking companies in Glasgow, whose banking policies Blair hoped he could influence. The Glasgow Union Banking Company opened its doors in 1830 with an initial nominal capital of £2 million, and was followed in 1832 by the Western Bank of Scotland, with a nominal capital of £4 million. Together they attracted over 1,000 founding shareholders and in their early years benefited from the extensive range of their businesses, the aggressive Whig and even radical politics of the greater Glasgow area and a sense of local nationalism that banking profits made in the west should accrue to the west. They followed an energetic note and discount policy and opened numerous branches to push their banknotes. In 1838, the Clydesdale was established by business interests among whom were Whigs active in Glasgow municipal politics, and by 1841 they had a paid-up capital of £500,000. The City of Glasgow was launched in 1839 and it, too, had no difficulty in reaching an initial call-up of £656,250 from 779 subscribers. With these new companies, the paid-up capital employed in Scottish banking rose from £4.9 million in 1825 to £9 million in 1840.

The main motivation for these four new banks was the need for greater accommodation by the huge growth of Glasgow business, although expansion was not limited to the western region. Alexander Blair noticed several other attempts to establish banks in the 1830s, and all four of the new joint stocks raised capital from Edinburgh. Further, there was a difficulty with the policy of low interest rates for depositors which the seven Edinburgh banks achieved between 1828 and 1836 when the deposit rate stayed at 2 per cent.[33] This, with the fall in share prices and yields, encouraged investors to advance funds to public utilities and to the new joint stocks: 'hence the anomaly that at a period when the business of banking is less remunerative than formerly the public have shewn a great disposition to engage in undertakings of this description'.[34] As this pushed

32 BS 1/70/12, p. 9.
33 BS(BL), Miscellaneous papers, Tables of interest rates.
34 BS 20/1/11 (Miscellaneous papers), Alexander Blair, report to board, 1840.

banking facilities beyond the volume of business activity, the profits for all banks fell.

Throughout the 1830s, the Edinburgh banks subscribed to the view that while a number of banks catering for different trades and areas were beneficial to society at large, unrestricted competition and note issue through reckless discounting was a recipe for low profits and would, ultimately, lead to crisis: 'the public and private calamities of society caused by loss of property have arisen not from want of credit, but from the abuse of it'.[35] In their support, the Edinburgh banks cited the periodic crises in England, the issue of assignats by the revolutionary government in France, and the vicissitudes of monetary policy in the USA of 1814 and 1835–6 whereby the over-issue of paper money and subsequent collapse proceeded to ruin large numbers of depositors and bank partners. They specifically dismissed as unstable an open or free banking system such as that imposed in the USA in 1836. The contrary position was in keeping with the tradition of the regulated and disciplined civic capitalism inherited from the eighteenth century, an altogether more stable system of capital accumulation than that of the episodic crises which ruined depositors and shareholders in England and America. The Edinburgh banks thus advanced two basic policies: the one 'endeavoured to keep the rate of interest low' and thus 'carry on the business of the community upon the most economical principles as regards circulation and capital', the other desired by regulation to halt the over-production of credit before it led to the unfortunate consequences of 1825.[36] To do this, they tried 'to preserve the few general rules which would insure uniformity of practice'. Thus a proportion of funds should be invested in British government securities and the stock of long-established institutions such as the Bank of England, and this investment should be well above the sums required to support their bill operations on London. In 1841, Alexander Blair reiterated his conviction that the reserve in Bank of Scotland against deposits should not be less than the whole paid-up capital, and this should continue in the public stocks 'unconnected with trade and not likely to be influenced by the same causes which produce a demand for deposits'. Further, he kept in his office a list of Bank assets in point of convertibility and the categories of those 'to be immediately available' – gold and silver, Bank of England notes, Exchequer bills and government stocks, and these totalled 28 per cent. Blair calculated that the yield on British government stocks fell around 20s per cent from 1815 to 1840, which reduced income by £10,000 per £1 million invested. Although there were many fluctuations, by

35 BS 20/2/14 (Miscellaneous papers), memorandum by Alexander Blair.
36 Ibid., p. 17.

1841 the return on these assets held by Bank of Scotland had slipped to £3 4s 1d per cent. The policy of the Edinburgh banks, as noticed before, was to hold the rates paid to depositors down, which enabled a gap of around 2 per cent to be kept between these payments and the rates for cash accounts and bills, which could be held close to 4 per cent. It was, as they described it, a cheap money policy, but one regulated by their views on the creditworthiness of customers and not just by demand.

All four of the new Glasgow banks adopted a different structure for their asset base. Why, they asked, should they invest their capital and part of their depositors' funds in London stocks which had the consequence of depressing interest paid for deposits, reducing the funds available for industrial advances, and lowering dividends for shareholders? Why should money which could earn 4 per cent and from the autumn of 1836 as much as 5½ to 6 per cent in Scotland be sent to London to earn less on stocks there or the Exchequer bill rate? The Glasgow view was that public confidence did not require large sums in London, as joint-stock banks with large capitals and funds advancing to broadly-based foreign trade would survive the periodic trade crises. Further, Glasgow believed that while the Edinburgh banks could normally hold down bad debts by a cautious approach, this was not in fact a true 'real bill' doctrine, which should sanction advances against all trade bills, long- and short-term, and the banks should be prepared to carry over past-due bills and cash account overdrafts which their large trading capitals allowed. If banks lent widely to industry and trade, then occasional losses would be unlikely to affect their overall strength.

Before 1836, the business conducted by the Glasgow Union Banking Company and the Western bank did not disturb the discount policy of the Edinburgh banks. By the autumn, events had combined to undermine this. In 1833, a clause in the Act renewing the charter of the Bank of England enacted that henceforth bills of exchange and promissory notes made payable at or within three months would not be subject to any penalties under the usury laws.[37] This would, in times of crisis, tend to allow the cost of money to rise above 5 per cent. In August 1836, the Bank of England minimum discount rate was set at 5½ per cent, and the two Glasgow banks followed suit. The protestations made by Alexander Blair, Thomas Corrie and John Thomson to the Bank of England were dismissed by Horsley Palmer, the Governor of the Bank of England, in terms that were familiar: policy was designed to squeeze inflationary pressure and adjust the foreign exchanges to raise the value of the pound sterling.[38] The Scottish bankers

37 4 & 5 William IV c.98, clause 7, 'An Act for Giving to the Corporation of the Governor and Company of the Bank of England certain privileges'.
38 Checkland, *Scottish Banking*, ch. 11, section 9.

should modify their lending to support these national concerns, and, if they were affected by a rise in discount rates, they should not look to the Bank of England for help.

This rise in the discount rate in 1836 and another the following year, coupled with the growth of the Glasgow business, brought out a significant difference in the structure of liabilities within Scottish banking which had passed unremarked hitherto, and ensured that for several years a uniform discount rate and interest-rate policy could not be enforced. The corollary of the old view that a proportion of assets should be held in government stock and Exchequer bills, with their low interest rates, was the payment of low interest rates to depositors – hence the importance of the agreements negotiated by William Cadell in 1827 and 1828.[39] The British Linen, Bank of Scotland and the Commercial Bank all had a deposit-gathering network, and when deposit interest was low and bad debts minimal they made adequate profits. Deposits and reserves exceeded capital by a substantial margin, and the 2 per cent gap between the bill rate and the deposit rate, effective from 1828 to 1836, yielded a higher rate of return than a narrower gap. But this policy was not in the interest of banks whose deposits were more nearly equal to capital. Bank of Scotland appreciated that the main difficulty with enforcement of its preferred interest-rate policy lay with this contrasting distribution of liabilities as between the Royal Bank and the Glasgow banks on the one side and those of Bank of Scotland, the British Linen Company and the Commercial Bank on the other. The losses at the Royal Bank after 1825 which forced an increase in its capital of £500,000 in 1830 meant that for some years it was closer to the new joint stocks in its structure of liabilities. The remaining Edinburgh banks, with their large branch networks in agricultural areas, always found that deposits exceeded advances.[40]

Banks with deposits equal or close to capital, argued Blair, received little or no benefit when they moved from 4–5 per cent to a 2–4 per cent gap. Moreover, when this happened, the Glasgow banks suffered as deposits tended to gravitate to the older banks. It will be observed, wrote a Bank of Scotland commentator, 'that the peculiarity of the position of these banks consists in the proportion of capital to deposits and that any other

---

39 For this, see above, Chapter 13.
40 Bank of Scotland illustrated this: 'let [it] be supposed that a bank has a capital of £1,000,000 and deposits to the extent of £1,000,000 forming its trading means lent out at 5%. Let it also be supposed that the interest paid upon its deposits be 4%. It is evident that such an establishment must necessarily wish to keep the value of money high because at a difference of 1% between discount and deposit interest it loses by every successive fall in the rate of interest a portion of its profits. This is supposed to be the case of the new joint stock banks with the superadded necessity of providing in many cases for the wants of a needy proprietary, of acquiring business and of guarding against discredit and difficulties arising from the practice of expedients, such as high dividends and sale of their own stock at a premium' (paper, 13 June 1842, pp. 6–7, in BS 20/1/11, Miscellaneous papers).

change short of a difference beyond 2% in the proportion of their rates of interest deposit and discount would not increase their profits', although a 2 per cent gap by 'depriving them of their power of competition would leave them no chance of acquiring business except by the legitimate means of time and industry'. A number of variants on this theme were discussed among the British Linen Company, Bank of Scotland and the Commercial Bank as it became clear that the Royal Bank had no immediate interest in the 2–4 per cent ratio, and in 1839 Thomson came close to a break with his colleagues in Edinburgh. The Royal Bank had no branches outwith Glasgow and Edinburgh in 1830, and found that developing a branch network was hard work.

Advances by the Glasgow banks reduced the income from banknotes for the Edinburgh banks. From 1834 to 1839, the average weekly circulation in Scotland rose only from £3,111,348 to £3,247,535. It was inevitable, therefore, that the increase in branches of the joint-stock banks would act against the circulation of existing banks. The true worth of banknote circulation was calculated by the interest earned on the net circulation less clerical and printing costs. Agents were urged to attract accounts to which frequent payments were made (usually sovereigns, silver and the notes of other banks) and through which banknotes were distributed. Calculations of the length of time that a batch of notes remained out were regularly carried out, and thus the total income from notes was known (see Table 14.5). In 1835, for example, the issue of Bank of Scotland notes totalled £9,412,617 which produced an average circulation of £390,386 bearing interest; in other words, it took payments of £24 in notes to keep £1 out. Yet by 1841, an increase in issue to £12,325,702 had led to a circulation bearing interest of £379,785, thus it required £32 in payments to keep £1 out.[41] The smaller £1 and £2 notes remained in circulation longer; it took £8 of these to keep out £1 in circulation in 1835 and £12 in 1841. But business pushed the larger notes, £5 and above, back to the banks much faster: a ratio of 52:1 in 1835 went to 74:1 by 1841. Indeed, the larger notes were often returned several times a day. A greater keenness on deposit income by business explained part of the difficulty, but Alexander Blair concluded that competition by Glasgow banks was the more serious threat.

Alongside the slide in income from note circulation, the board of Bank of Scotland was concerned with a fall in the income from stocks. This was a long-term movement in prices and yields in the aftermath of the Napoleonic Wars which received legislative encouragement, notably in 1822 when annuities paying £5 per cent at par were converted to £4 per

41 BS 1/70/12, Appendix 6.

Table 14.5 *Statement of the amount of notes issued per annum at the branches of Bank of Scotland, the circulation and the proportion which they bear to it, 1835–41*

		Issues	Circulation	Notes issued to keep one in circulation
1835	Large	7350791	140190	52
	Small	2061826	250196	8
	Total	9412617	390386	24
1836	Large	8066410	152794	53
	Small	2352460	258222	9
	Total	10418870	411016	25
1837	Large	8543200	148364	58
	Small	2560896	259961	10
	Total	11104096	408325	27
1838	Large	9314270	150458	62
	Small	2752891	265457	10
	Total	12067161	415915	29
1839	Large	10304090	147528	70
	Small	2936858	266767	11
	Total	13240948	414295	32
1840	Large	9186560	135801	68
	Small	2927773	259086	11
	Total	12114333	394887	31
1841	Large	9397720	126602	74
	Small	2927982	253183	12
	Total	12325702	379785	32

Source: BS 1/70/12, Treasurer's (Blair's) Report to the directors on the affairs of Bank of Scotland, 1832–42, appendix 6 (24 March 1842).

cent at £105, and in 1824 when they were converted to £3 10s 0d per cent.[42] This was tolerable when the relevant gap in Scottish discount and interest income was between 2 and 4 per cent for advances, but when the discount rates in London rose in 1836–7 and again from 1839, on both occasions to over 5 per cent, the income accruing to Bank of Scotland from government and London stocks moved little from the 3.292 per cent received in 1832–3. The board agreed in 1840 to hold fewer London stocks, and the holdings were reduced from an average of £2.35 million in the years from 1832–9 to £1,802,300 by 1842; the surplus money was moved to bill discounts and cash accounts. The reduction of the par exchange on London for the remittance of the public revenues now cost the Scottish banks somewhat more by the end of the decade. The usual

42 3 George IV c.9, 'An Act for transferring several annuities'; 5 George IV c.2, 'An Act for raising . . .'; 5 George IV c.11, 'An Act for transferring . . .'. Annuitants who did not accept these terms were paid off at par.

commission charged on inter-bank transactions had fallen to only $\frac{1}{8}$ per cent by 1830, and attempts to raise it in 1836 and 1838 proved difficult to enforce. The profit margins were thus becoming somewhat narrower in a number of different financial areas.

As early as the autumn of 1834, there was a clash between Bank of Scotland and the Western Bank. The initial cause lay with the collapse of the Edinburgh private bank of Kinnear, Smith & Co.[43] In 1831 it had amalgamated with Donald Smith & Co., a small private bank, which held irrecoverable debts of £6,347 15s 10d to which, in the following year, were added £4,435 11s 1d of unpaid bills due from the Glasgow private bank, Robert Watson & Co. Debts, dating from 1825, on public utilities and bills had brought its trading losses to £35,502 12s 7d. Part of Kinnear, Smith's assets were held in British Linen and Bank of Scotland shares, but the latter had fallen 30 per cent in the nine years to 1834, and subsequently, after all available funds were added together, it was found that liquid assets of £186,331 16s 1d faced liabilities of £295,628 16s 0d. This alarming situation was clear to the directors of Kinnear, Smith by the spring, although it was completely unknown outside their board. Kinnear, Smith acted as agents for several Scottish provincial banks, and, after the usual note exchanges in Edinburgh on 18 and 21 July, they wrote two drafts in favour of the Western Bank, for £2,700 and £6,300, drawn on their London agents. The Western, in lieu of note-exchange debts to Bank of Scotland, endorsed these over to the Bank, which retained both until 22 July, instead of forwarding them to Coutts & Co. and Smith, Payne & Smith for payment. On that day, the £6,300 draft was endorsed to the Royal Bank, which sent it to London in the 9:40 a.m. post on 23 July. Between 6 and 7 a.m. on 23 July, two partners of Kinnear, Smith called on Blair to inform him of imminent closure. Someone at Bank of Scotland then sent the remaining draft, for £2,700, to London by the ordinary post. Alexander Blair, however, also sent an express to warn George Smith of Smith, Payne & Smith, who in turn warned George Carr to stop payment on both drafts. On arrival, both bills were protested and returned for non-payment. As the matter stood, the Western still owed £2,700 to Bank of Scotland and £6,300 to the Royal Bank. The funds everywhere in the banking system due to Kinnear, Smith were frozen and were henceforth available to all creditors of the failed bank, not just to the Western, which would take its share but without precedence. It was furious and issued instructions to its lawyers on the grounds that, had the drafts been forwarded immediately, it would have been paid by Kinnear,

43 This case is collected in papers at BS 20/30/9; Thomas Kinnear was founded as a private bank in 1748, Donald Smith in 1773.

Smith's agents, the two London firms of Smith, Payne & Smith and Carr, Glyn & Co.

This accusation found Alexander Blair wrestling with his conscience. Yet the delay in forwarding the drafts was a common business practice designed to find, where possible, other uses for a draft and thus avoid unnecessary stamp taxes. By a happy coincidence, George Smith of Smith, Payne & Smith was Blair's brother-in-law, and reassured him that although the sequence of events on 22 and 23 July 'was not a probable circumstance', it was 'a positive one and if you could save your friends from loss by acting as you did, I do not see any blame could attach to you . . . it is all very well for those who may have lost by it to complain'. Thomas Syme ws also provided reassurance; the endorser of a bill was bound to give true information to any party, and forwarding by express the details of the failure protected Bank of Scotland from a demand from Smith, Payne & Smith or the Royal Bank from Carr, Glyn & Co. The Court of Session later ruled in favour of the Mound. The settlement secured for the Western, alongside other creditors, was 11 shillings in the pound. At least two former members of the staff of Kinnear, Smith were taken on by Bank of Scotland.[44]

These events weakened the liquid part of the Western Bank's assets. In early October 1834, Jones, Loyd & Co., the London agents for the Western Bank, stopped payment of its drafts.[45] All seven Edinburgh banks then refused Western banknotes and insisted on cash at the exchanges. The Western was forced to offer assurances to Jones, Loyd & Co. that its reserves position would be addressed, and that sufficient funds were guaranteed by certain shareholders. It also negotiated a credit with Bank of Scotland for £30,000. Jones, Loyd & Co. agreed on 10 October to restore the confidence of the London market.[46] Dark rumours of an Edinburgh plot circulated in Glasgow: 'an idea is afloat and no doubt has been industriously circulated by those interested, that the Chartered banks of old standing are inimical to the local establishments, that they were endeavouring to crush the Western and that if they succeed . . . a similar attempt may be made against the Glasgow Union'.[47]

The response of the Edinburgh banks to the view that the Western could not avoid addressing the problem of inadequate London reserves was sharp but reasonable as to the time required. They would 'not take

44 BS 20/10/4, Miscellaneous papers, Kinnear, Smith to Bank of Scotland.
45 BS 20/10/51, Miscellaneous papers, Charles Campbell to Alexander Blair; the British Linen and the Royal Bank were informed by Richard Duncan, the manager of the Thistle bank.
46 BS 20/9/14, Miscellaneous papers, 10 and 11 October 1834; some concern was expressed by several bankers about the resumption of exchanges for Western banknotes.
47 BS 20/9/14, Miscellaneous papers, Charles Campbell to Alexander Blair, 17 October 1834.

the notes of any bank conducting their business without resources to meet contingencies, or even those demands upon them which may be a little out of the ordinary course of business'. As the Edinburgh banks invested 'a sum equal to their whole circulation and one-third of their deposits' in securities which could be swiftly converted to cash, 'it does not appear . . . that any good reason exists why the same rule which is universally allowed to be necessary and reasonable in the administration of the affairs of the most respectable chartered and private banks should not be equally applicable to the management of a joint-stock banking company'.[48] After 14 October, none of the Glasgow banks was prepared to advance credit for the Western; Richard Duncan, the manager of the Thistle bank, strongly supported Edinburgh. The Western reserve fund was inadequate; it was a business 'so scantily supplied with deposit money' that it was forced to use virtually all its shareholders' funds for its bill business, which earned a little over 4 per cent. But unless 'a great increase soon takes place', the Western could not afford a dividend to its proprietors: 'How the last one of 6% was made up is not very evident'.[49] John Miller, the general manager of the Western, agreed 'without delay, to make myself acquainted with the principles generally acted on by our national banking establishments', although 'as a solvent establishment' he insisted that it would not be dictated to.[50] However, he was informed that if the Western desired help, it should modify the structure of its balance sheet, and on receipt of its assurance the three senior banks advanced £100,000 on 30 October to cover bill operations in London by the purchase of government securities.[51] Towards the end of November, the Secretary of the Western opened accounts with Bank of Scotland, the Royal Bank and the British Linen in Glasgow, to deposit their bills of exchange as security against the exchanges.[52] In March 1835, all the Edinburgh banks agreed to admit the Western to a new general agreement for settling the balances of banknotes.[53] As the Western Bank continued to struggle to collect deposits, its board continued to maintain a balance of government securities, mostly Exchequer bills, which Jones, Loyd & Co. and the Edinburgh banks still thought insufficient.[54] Nonetheless, by

48 BS 20/30/9, Miscellaneous papers, Alexander Blair to the General Manager, Western Bank, 23 October 1834; part of the correspondence was later published as a pamphlet by Bank of Scotland, and is reprinted as James Simpson Fleming, *Scottish Banking: A Historical Sketch with Notes and an Appendix*, 3rd edn (Edinburgh: 1877), Appendix E.
49 BS 20/10/14, Miscellaneous papers, Richard Duncan to Alexander Blair, 28 October 1834.
50 BS 20/9/14, Miscellaneous papers, John Miller to Alexander Blair, 25 October 1834.
51 BS 1/5, Minutes: 3 November 1833.
52 BS 20/9/14, Miscellaneous papers, Secretary of Western Bank to Bank of Scotland.
53 BS 20/9/14, Miscellaneous papers, copy of letter to the Western from Bank of Scotland on behalf of the Royal Bank, the British Linen, Sir William Forbes, Commercial Bank and National Bank, 20 March 1835.
54 Fleming, *Scottish Banking*, Appendix E.

1837 the paid-up capital of the Western had reached £600,000, it had seventeen branches and it was able to place more funds in London when pressed by the Edinburgh banks. In this boom year of 1837, however, the Western Bank again broke its 1834 agreement, and the Edinburgh banks threatened from 21 July 1837 to refuse to accept Western notes; once again, the Western had to give way.[55]

It proved difficult throughout these years to maintain a consistent policy on interest rates and charges among all the Scottish banks, although before 1837 Edinburgh had a uniform practice. In the country as a whole, there was a 'constant tendency from competition, to break through the agreement'. The Dundee Banking Company, for example, reduced its deposit rate in 1828 from 4 to 3 per cent, still above the Edinburgh rate, and kept this until May 1834, when a further ½ per cent was taken off.[56] The Glasgow joint-stock banks were always seeking additional deposits by offering ½ and sometimes 1 per cent above the Edinburgh banks. Likewise, commission and charges varied. In December 1836, during the pressures of a trade crisis, a uniform schedule of charges was again agreed by the Edinburgh banks and circulated to all the Scottish banks.[57] The response was uneven.

The tendency in the years 1836–42 was for the smaller partnership and provincial banks to retire or amalgamate.[58] There were twenty-two provincial companies active in 1826; fifteen were taken over, or merged, retired or failed from 1836 to 1842. In 1838, three new joint stocks were formed, the Caledonian, the Southern and the Clydesdale, and it was in this year that even the venerable firm of Sir William Forbes & Co. felt compelled to join the Glasgow Union Banking Company. Other large new banks followed: the City of Glasgow in 1839, and the Glasgow Joint Stock in 1840. Again, the severe warnings of 1836–7 and 1841–2 should have encouraged cooperation, but the differing structure of assets between the two main groups of banks was enough to impede progress. The new joint stocks all started life with that optimism which only bad debt and hardship could temper. It was thus to be expected that there would remain sufficient diversity in interest rates and charges to encourage frequent negotiations, and hardly a week passed without some communication between the various bankers.

Before 1838, the Edinburgh banks had moved together to maintain the gap of 2 per cent, at least in and around Edinburgh. Thus from 1 December

55 Checkland, *Scottish Banking*, p. 335; Fleming, *Scottish Banking*, p. 62.
56 Boase, *A Century of Banking in Dundee*, banking memoranda, 1827 to 1837.
57 BS 20/9/17, Miscellaneous papers, uniform rate agreement, 30 December 1836; agreement on distribution, January 1837.
58 Munn, *The Scottish Provincial Banking Companies*, p. 87, Table 10.

1836, with the deposit rate at 3 per cent, they charged 5 per cent and ⅛ per cent commission on all bills.[59] Yet in Glasgow and some other branches, the gap was below 2 per cent. From February to June 1838, the Edinburgh banks felt secure enough to cut the deposit rate to 2½ per cent (3 per cent in Glasgow) and their three-month bill rate to 4 per cent, followed on 11 June by a firm 2–4 per cent gap. The driving force for the 2 per cent gap and agreed charges by the Glasgow and the Edinburgh banks, and the associated adoption by the former of Edinburgh principles on assets, remained Alexander Blair: 'If you succeed you will deserve to have one statue voted to you by the Banks and another by the people of Scotland'. Thomas Corrie tempered this thought with pessimism: 'all the existing arrangements on principles of long standing are crumbling to pieces'.[60] Within a year, the British Linen faced a severe drain in Dumfries and Galloway as the new branches of the Glasgow banks, the Commercial and the National, offered better rates. It was always the problem with rural areas: they were excellent for gathering deposits but low on lending potential, and local money followed the highest rates. Earnings in the burghs and advances to business everywhere led to more stable relation-ships between bank and customer, the latter more cautious about moving between banks in case of future trading difficulties. Charles Campbell reported no drain on deposits even with lower rates, as trade was buoyant, but he did complain of some lost business, and it was impossible to keep the Glasgow bankers to agreements for a few years after 1838. There was even disagreement in Glasgow with the British Linen; when Campbell convened the Glasgow men in October 1838, neither the British Linen nor the Royal Bank attended.[61] So agreements were partial and temporary; when complaints from the public 'became loud against any particular charge some expedient is likely to be fallen upon whereby the charge is eluded'. Indeed, the exchange on provincial burghs was mostly ignored. The public was also a nuisance, going from one bank to another requesting better treatment and threatening to close accounts. The Eastern Bank, whose directors had suffered from the losses of the Dundee Commercial, could not be brought into the fold.[62]

By March 1840, Alexander Blair had reluctantly admitted that on all important matters the attempt at agreements had 'utterly failed'. Offers of generous bill rates in Glasgow had not affected the business of the Glasgow banks. The attempt to persuade them to buy more London securities was ignored. By January 1841, two Glasgow banks were paying 4 per cent

59 BS 1/70/9, Appendix D; BS 1/518/1, Private Letter Book.
60 BS 20/9/3, Miscellaneous papers, Thomas Corrie to Alexander Blair, 2 July 1839.
61 BS 20/9/8, Miscellaneous papers, Charles Campbell to Alexander Blair, 10 October 1838.
62 BS 20/9/3, Miscellaneous papers, August 1839.

on deposits, and all Glasgow banks refused to consider 3 per cent. John Thomson offered to accept 3½ per cent, but only if every other bank did likewise; 'but if this is not agreed to within fourteen days the bank will act for itself'. In the same round, the Glasgow and Ship opposed any new charges and inquired into the reason for the Edinburgh banks offering 4 per cent in Kirkcaldy. There was localised progress over the following year. The Glasgow banks conformed to Edinburgh rates in Edinburgh, and in some burghs the agents tired of cuts and agreed to impose uniform scales.[63]

The negotiations over the agreements and understandings and the harsher atmosphere at the Parliamentary hearings in 1841 weakened Alexander Blair's resolve that the Edinburgh banks could grow in their existing institutional setting. The public debate before the Bank Charter Act, 1844, and the Scottish Bank Act, 1845, did little to revive optimism that Parliament would assist, and thereafter representations in London were left to other general managers. Competition for deposits from non-banking sources was another problem. The Scottish life assurance societies proved attractive to savers in regular employment. By the close of the Napoleonic Wars, the life assurance business in England was regulated with such mathematical accuracy 'and the probable duration of human life ascertained with so much certainty, by the test of actual experience, as to enable an office to determine the exact amount of premium which with the accumulation of interest will produce at the end of the period assigned to the life a fund' which would pay the sum assured, all costs and add to reserves of the life office.[64] Although the legal framework in Scotland was more favourable to life assurance societies than in England, the first life company on mutual principles, Scottish Widows, did not commence until 1815, to be followed by Scottish Amicable (1826) and Scottish Equitable (1831). The first proprietary assurance company, the Edinburgh, commenced in 1823, followed by, among other famous names, Standard Life in 1825.[65] The secret of their success was low-cost networks of agents and solicitors whose regular collections proved popular with savers, while next of kin were guaranteed a payment, often with a bonus, on the policy-holder's death. The life assurance movement, like the savings

---

63 BS 20/9/5 (Miscellaneous papers), 20/1/11 and 20/1/15: reports and papers.
64 Frederick Blayney, A Practical Treatise on Life Assurance (London: 1826), p. xi; the English courts in the later eighteenth century ruled that assurance societies lay outwith the remit of 6 George I c.18 (commonly called the Bubble Act). The provisions of the Act were abolished by 6 George IV c.91.
65 H. Maxwell, Annals of the Scottish Widows Fund Life Assurance Society 1815–1914 (Edinburgh: 1914), p. 131; Anon., A History of the Scottish Amicable Life Assurance Society 1826–1976 (Glasgow: 1976); Checkland, Scottish Banking, p. 368; W. T. Thomson, The Present Position of the Life Assurance Interests of Great Britain (Edinburgh: 1852); British Library, 713, Tracts relating to Scottish Life Assurance Offices.

banks, was supported by members of the aristocracy, and there were soon connections with the banks at board level. Arguments over the suitability of life policies as security for advances continued for many years.[66]

There was a threat to bank deposits from the stockmarkets.[67] In the boom of 1825, shares in over fifty companies were traded in Edinburgh. Although activity fell in the crisis, the public had learned of the potential of stocks offering higher yields than bank deposits. By 1832, the interest shown in Glasgow bank shares had begun to concern the Edinburgh bankers and they were mentioned by Alexander Blair for their effect on deposits. Stocks with plant and equipment behind them, such as the new gas and water utilities, the railways and steamship companies, proved attractive, although by 1840 69 per cent of the £18.6 million of Scottish stocks was still represented by banking, insurance and investment companies. It was, above all, English railway shares that dominated the markets from 1844 to 1847, with bank deposits moved to London for purchases of shares, again a matter of regret to the Scottish bankers.[68]

The uncertainties and disturbances in the financial world after 1845 continued to prey on Alexander Blair.[69] He was highly sceptical of the bank charter legislation, and remained deeply concerned with what he considered to be the dubious reserve policies of the joint-stock banks of the western region. Blair's solution was to propose a centralisation of power and put forward a detailed scheme for the merger of the three senior banks; and, in the aftermath of the 1842 crisis and the political arguments of 1844–5, their senior officers initially showed some sympathy to the idea of a united system.[70] The scheme was based on the old ideas that profits would only grow in a regulated system and the assumption that placing the three chartered banks under one roof would enable enforcement to be carried out.

There were political attractions for the Governor of Bank of Scotland, Viscount Melville, whose Tory interest was unable to compete effectively at this time with the Whigs.[71] Alexander Blair's scheme seemed, at first, to offer a powerful financial institution, second only to the Bank of England,

---

66 Rae, *The Country Banker*, Letter XVI, 'Securities which are not Security', rejected these for advances.

67 R. C. Michie, *Money, Mania and Markets. Investment, Company Formation and the Stock Exchange in Nineteenth-Century Scotland* (Edinburgh: 1981), pp. 45, 52.

68 For a brief account of the relations between the Scottish banks and the early railway age, see below, Chapter 15.

69 This section draws on BS 20/32/192–202, Melville Papers.

70 The dismissal of John Thomson in 1842 from his position of Cashier of the Royal Bank may have helped this feeling of unity; for a discussion of the circumstances, see Boase, *A Century of Banking in Dundee*, pp. 432–3. Thomson was the agent of Bank of Scotland in Aberdeen from 1806–17.

71 I. G. C. Hutchinson, *A Political History of Scotland, 1832–1924* (Edinburgh: 1986), pp. 23–5; Ferguson, *Scotland: 1689 to the Present*, pp. 302–3.

and in the hands of supporters of the Tory interest. This could then act to control the speculators and Whig financiers of the west. When Melville advocated the scheme to Sir Charles Wood, Chancellor of the Exchequer, in October 1846, he passed by the technical side, 'the practical details', and reiterated that it was not because of the interest of Bank of Scotland that he was writing:

> the proposed union involves other and more important considerations, and while on the one hand it would invest the united establishment with a greater degree of influence over the banking concerns and circulation of Scotland, it would, on the other, give a degree of fixed solidity to that influence which would form a most useful check to our attempts at speculative banking without adequate capital. Any endeavour to establish such checks by legislative enactments is very difficult . . . but the influence of the Bank of England, acting as is generally the case with the knowledge of the Government and in concert with it, is of a very different character, and the proposed new establishment in Scotland would naturally proceed on the same principle and very much in concert with the Bank of England; such at least would be my own speculation.[72]

By 1847, Viscount Melville had moved from his overriding concern that the Glasgow joint stocks or the railway exchange companies might destabilise the system. More concerned with the position of Bank of Scotland as the embodiment of sound finance, his attention moved to the maintenance of the status quo. If the financial world was to be a harsh place, then Bank of Scotland had to stand for sound banking. He opposed a proposal to fund a national investment trust based in London, in association with the Royal Bank, as inconsistent with the duty of Bank of Scotland conferred in the original Act of Parliament. When in early 1847 Sir Alexander Charles Gibson Maitland, the Deputy Governor of Bank of Scotland, died, Melville argued for Sir George Clerk as the replacement; the directors should be encouraged in their role at the 'head of the banking establishments of Scotland, and in connection with the executive Government in like manner as the latter is in the habit of doing with the Bank of England'. Thus the new Deputy Governor should be accustomed to public business. The board voted Sir George the necessary stock from reserves. By 1847, with competitive pressures weaker, neither the Royal Bank nor the British Linen felt a necessity for the national investment trust.[73] There was the chance of public criticism and loss of accounts from those who wished to hide the true extent of assets spread

---

72 The text cited here is the final draft of his letter: BS 20/32/193, Melville Papers, 30 October 1846, Viscount Melville to Charles Wood; he added that he was unsure how far his friend Alexander Blair would go along with this principle.
73 Checkland, *Scottish Banking*, p. 370.

among the chartered banks. Closures of branches would lose agents, who might move to other banks. This was the last attempt by Alexander Blair to reinterpret the system of regulation which he could remember from his younger days. A marked hesitation to involve himself in discussions at the Parliamentary level set in after 1841; in reply to a request from Viscount Melville in 1848, he felt 'considerable reluctance to engage with the Currency Committees . . . I doubt very much if their committees as they are conducted do not serve quite as much to propagate error as to discover truth, particularly when clever witnesses are called who have a tendency to paradox'.[74] It was not until the crisis of 1857, which brought down the Western Bank and the Edinburgh and Glasgow Bank, that an agreement could be held in place between the Scottish banks implementing the views put forward by Alexander Blair.

74 BS 20/32/202, Melville Papers, 23 February 1848.

CHAPTER 15

THE SCOTTISH BANKS IN VICTORIAN BRITAIN

THE ROLE OF Bank of Scotland, the Royal Bank and the British Linen Company in the extension of facilities for trade and industry was a notable feature of the early phases of industrialisation. Individual cash accounts and bill discounts for many thousands of pounds were negotiated, and by 1800 the tendency was for facilities to become more extensive, often rising to tens of thousands of pounds. Indeed, the encouragement given to new industries was one of the significant contributions of the Scottish banking system to enlargement of industry north of the Border, and the structure of the system was sufficiently stable to be accepted as the model for reform of English banking in 1826. There were losses associated with industrial advances after 1815 for all the Scottish banks; nevertheless, the size and direction of the chartered and joint-stock banks enabled expansion of business to proceed in the two decades after 1825, when there emerged the central components of Scottish industrialisation during the nineteenth century. The 'sudden and gigantic' expansion of the iron industry marked the character of the industrial economy of the next half-century.[1] At the beginning of the 1830s, there were twenty-seven blast furnaces in Scotland with an output of 37,500 tons of pig iron, a small fraction of British production; by 1838 the total was 147,000 tons, yet in 1847 the eighty-nine Scottish furnaces were producing 540,000 tons out of a total British output of 2 million tons. This rapid expansion utilised the blackband ironstone discovered in the western region by the metallurgist David Mushet in 1801.[2] Until the

---

1 J. H. Clapham, *An Economic History of Modern Britain: The Early Railway Age, 1820–1850* (Cambridge: 1967), p. 425; and for the eighteenth-century development of the linen and other textile industries, A. Slaven, *The Development of the West of Scotland, 1750–1960* (London: 1975), ch. 4.
2 Slaven, *Development of the West of Scotland*, p. 116ff.; B. P. Lenman, *An Economic History of Modern Scotland 1660–1976* (London: 1977), pp. 129–34.

early 1830s, this blackband ironstone, a ferrous ore mixed with a hard, low-sulphur coal, had produced a much inferior iron. The crucial change came with the invention by James Beaumont Neilson, manager of the Glasgow Gas Company from 1817–47, of the hot blast in 1828, which by 1834, after a number of improvements to furnaces, had reduced the consumption of coal required for one ton of cold blast iron from eight tons to just under three tons when the hot blast was used. Until further technical improvements were made, Scottish iron did not match the best quality produced in Staffordshire or South Wales, but from about 1836 quality levels converged. A high proportion of Scottish pig iron in these early days was exported.

Scotland possessed a huge range of high-quality coals, from semi-anthracites and coking coals to steam-raising and household coals, which gave industrial users one of the finest ranges of cheap coals in nineteenth-century Europe.[3] By the early 1860s, production had reached 12 million tons, rising to 18.5 million tons a decade later; under the impetus of foreign demand, 30 million tons were being mined by 1900 and 42.5 million in 1913. The number of coal mines went from 413 in 1870 to 542 by the First World War. Total mining employment (including casual workers) soared from over 30,000 in the later 1840s to 108,000 in 1901 and 147,500 in 1913.[4] Cheap supplies of coal supplied to urban areas, rapid innovation in chemicals based on swift development of scientific knowledge of coal chemistry, as well as gas production, pig-iron smelting and the increasing use of coal in general industry assured the fortunes of landowners and colliery operators across much of lowland Scotland.

Bank of Scotland, in common with the other Edinburgh banks, attracted numerous colliery accounts, of which several, including the Shotts Iron Company and the Glasgow Iron Works, owned assets in both the iron and coal industries. From quite early in the nineteenth century, the Edinburgh banks received regular comments on coal prices, and the long-term viability of the industry and its wide range of markets gave little cause for concern. In fact, apart from railways, the cash accounts for coal companies after 1850 gave rise to less comment in Bank of Scotland papers and minutes than for general industrial and iron companies. The

3 The average Scottish steam coal contained under half the sulphur content of English coal, with many seams down to a sulphur content of only 0.2 per cent.
4 Slaven, *Development of the West of Scotland*, pp. 123, 167; C. H. Lee, *British Regional Employment Statistics 1841–1971* (Cambridge: 1979). The figures for employment are complicated by seasonal factors and differences in collection criteria before 1872; the official figures given in the census data and Returns of Inspectors of Mines may understate employment by up to 50 per cent: 12,400 in 1821, 13,600 in 1831, 32,969 in 1854 and 50,600 in 1870. The revised figures show 76,100 by 1874: B. R. Mitchell and P. Deane, *Abstract of British Historical Statistics* (Cambridge: 1962), 'Fuel and Energy', Table 5, Parts A and B, p. 253.

only exceptions were from 1875–80 and 1884–6, which saw stagnation and falling prices. There were close connections between coal and iron: the manufacture of pig iron took 20 per cent of coal output in the 1860s, although this weakened thereafter, and by 1913 only 6 per cent of Scottish coal was going to the blast furnaces. Exports more than compensated by this later date, when 38 per cent of all coal output was for foreign markets and coastal shipments. There was particularly vigorous growth in the Lothian, Central and Fife coalfields for the export trade. By 1900, the larger coal companies were being run by professional managers, with marketing and accounts departments and strong use of engineers and electrical experts. By this time, Scotland was ahead of the rest of the UK in the use of mechanical and hydraulic equipment, lighting and conveyors, and this technical lead gave Scottish mines the highest productivity in Britain.[5]

In the early Victorian years, the development of international trade provided the background for the emergence of Clydeside as a major centre of world shipbuilding and associated engineering. Vessels using steam engines had begun to be built on the Clyde from 1800, and after the Napoleonic Wars the greater Glasgow area developed a technological base which became an important part of the second wave of industrialisation. By 1830, some two-thirds of a still small industry of British steam tonnage was being built on the Clyde, and the region continued to remain important for its technical innovations; David Napier, for example, was one of the outstanding innovators in marine engineering for twenty years after 1814. The screw propeller began to be widely accepted from about 1840, and the first effective marine compound engine was in use in 1853. Iron began to be substituted for wood more frequently from the mid-1830s, yet as late as 1850 93.2 per cent of the British-owned merchant fleet consisted of sailing vessels. This dominance was down to 70 per cent by 1870 and 30 per cent a decade later. One of the last institutions to overcome its prejudice against iron and steam was the Admiralty, which fought the Crimean War (1854–6) with sail and wood; fortunately, the Russians were even more backward.

The early start, rapid innovation and enthusiastic support from the Edinburgh and Glasgow banks ensured that the Clyde was the dominant wrought- and cast-iron and marine-engineering region of the world in the mid-Victorian years. The lead was extended with a move to steel plates, initially more expensive than iron, but stronger and by the 1880s lighter

5 R. A. Church, *The History of the British Coal Industry*, vol. iii, *1830–1913: Victorian Pre-eminence* (Oxford: 1986), pp. 470–96; N. K. Buxton, *The Economic Development of the British Coal Industry* (London: 1978); P. L. Payne, *Growth & Contraction Scottish Industry c. 1860–1990* (Glasgow: 1992), pp. 17–19.

and cheaper as well. On this basis there developed a massive increase in the launchings along the Clyde, and already in 1870 some 50 per cent of all British tonnage came from the western region, a dominance that continued until the First World War. There were, in addition, numerous general engineering companies which supplied a rapidly-increasing variety of iron products, and the demand for banking facilities from these also grew apace from around 1830. The growth of the chemicals industry has been mentioned above, and it was the interaction of all these trades and the social consequences of their growth which so impressed contemporary writers.

While the heavy industries of coal, iron, steel, shipbuilding and mechanical engineering were the most significant part of the Scottish economy and their performance was closely watched by the banks, there was considerable interest in a much wider group of industries, notably the textile trades. The strong performance of many Scottish cotton textile firms merited long-lasting support. There were still 163 cotton-spinning mills in 1861 and numerous smaller weaving establishments with well-developed and diversified high-quality cottons. Nevertheless, by the 1870s it had become much harder to sell traditional lines in foreign and Empire markets. It was soon apparent that only a few of the cotton firms, predominantly owned by individual families and small partnerships, could develop adequate market-oriented responses.[6] While it was inevitable that foreign competition would erode markets, some firms managed robust responses. The Clyde Spinning Co. and the Glasgow Spinning Co. were particularly successful, as was J. & P. Coats, the sewing-thread combine, which through a series of amalgamations and successful management emerged in 1896 with a capital of nearly £8 million.[7] The mid-nineteenth century saw spectacular growth in the bleaching, printing and dyeing trades: the Thornliebank Company built the largest cotton-printing works in the world in the 1860s. It was after Queen Victoria's death that international competition made its greatest inroads into the Scottish cotton trades, and by 1910 only nine companies remained.

The older flax-spinning and linen industries found their markets eroded by the greater attractions of cotton, although many firms moved into specialist textiles with a higher value-added content, and in the Forfar and Dundee area there was the notable transition to the manufacture of jute. Profits and growth were strong until the 1870s, by which time Dundee had gained a reputation as the jute capital of the British Empire.

6 Payne, *Growth and Contraction*, pp. 9–17.
7 A. K. Cairncross and J. B. K. Hunter, 'The Early Growth of Messrs J. & P. Coats, 1830–83', *Business History*, 29 (1987), pp. 157–77.

The carpet trades saw significant growth, and at Kirkcaldy the linoleum and jute manufacturers, Nairn's, were able to build up a thriving business which took them into overseas manufacturing.[8] From the mid-Victorian years, smaller markets in specialised products offered opportunities to many family firms. Some grew out of the small-scale firms in the domestic woollen trades; Robert Pringle & Son, for example, catered for the growing demand for woollen knitted goods, with a high proportion of sales in England and abroad. The extraordinary range and extent of the banking and industrial connections were of major significance for the rapid growth of the economy in Victorian Scotland.[9] The relatively smooth absorption of the provincial banks and the private banks, mostly completed by 1850, indicated that the growing needs of the economy were appreciated earlier than they were in England. Large-scale firms apart, the question of encouragement for small and medium-sized firms requires some comment, if only to reassure the reader that the Scottish banks' long involvement in branch banking and the active competition for accounts ensured that local business had several opportunities for banking facilities. The figures for new openings of smaller-sized cash accounts at Bank of Scotland branches confirmed a very active policy of soliciting for new small business accounts. It was, of course, a matter of good banking practice to encourage the circulation of banknotes by purchase of bills as well as cash account operations, and large numbers of small, regularly-used accounts was one method of encouraging this.

We know that, well before the Victorian years, middle-class family ideas in Britain were 'set according to the morality of religious ideals'.[10] The Scottish banks were pillars of respectable society and set high ethical standards for their dealings with customers, expecting, in turn, plain dealing in the handling of accounts. Tight control of lending decisions and the keeping of local information on creditworthiness reinforced these ethical standards. Of course, under pressure from competitive environments, businessmen were forced to take difficult decisions and, in particular, often treated their workforces badly. But, within the limitations of their ethical framework, the entrepreneurs nonetheless saw wider social obligations as

8 R. J. Morris, 'Urbanisation and Scotland', in W. H. Fraser and R. J. Morris (eds), *People and Society in Scotland*, vol. ii, *1830–1914* (Edinburgh: 1990), pp. 73–102.
9 For a discussion of finance for British industry in the Victorian era, see P. L. Cottrell, *Industrial Finance, 1830–1914: The Finance and Organisation of English Manufacturing Industry* (London: 1980); M. Collins, *Banks and Industrial Finance in Britain 1800–1939* (London: 1991).
10 S. Nenadic, 'The Small Family Firm in Victorian Britain', *Business History*, 35 (1993), 86–114 (p. 89); and see R. Rodger, 'Concentration and Fragmentation: Capital, Labour, and the Structure of the Mid-Victorian Scottish Economy', *Journal of Urban History*, 14 (1988), 178–213; C. W. Munn, 'Aspects of Bank Finance for Industry: Scotland 1845–1914', in R. Mitchison and P. Roebuck (eds), *Economy and Society in Scotland and Ireland 1500–1939* (Edinburgh: 1988), pp. 233–41 (p. 235).

a strong motive, which contributed to a marked paternalism among some family firms and no doubt facilitated good relationships between small businesses and Scottish banks. Through long experience, the Scottish banks realised that social respectability and paternalism were usually safe guides to how an entrepreneur would behave in business and towards his obligations when in receipt of credit.

Whether a company was short-lived was thus not a problem for banks; many business people moved in and out of firms and into new business opportunities as the environment altered, and the facilities granted by the banks could be swiftly altered. Thus Scottish bank practices, based on regular reviews of the cash accounts and careful vetting of bills offered for discount, were admirably suited to nineteenth-century business conditions and were geared to speedy distribution of assets in the event of illness or death. The volatility of the business and commercial world and the unpredictable nature of service and production incomes over the economic cycle placed a premium on speed of access to finance and speed of repayment. It is not surprising that, trained in such an environment and putting great emphasis on respectability, Scottish bankers were in such demand in English and colonial banks.

These industrial and commercial developments naturally effected major changes in the economic and social structure of Scotland and accelerated changes in the nature of banking. The populations of most rural counties reached their peak between 1830 and 1861, but large-scale internal migration steadily increased the degree of urbanisation.[11] Scotland remained more rural than England, but by 1911 around 50 per cent of the population lived in towns and cities of more than 20,000 inhabitants. The population of Scotland grew from 1,625,000 at the first census of 1801 to 2,888,742 in 1851 and 4,472,103 in 1911. For the Scottish banks it was the growth and well-being of the middle classes that drew their particular attention, for it was from this fraction of the population that the bulk of deposits were derived. It was a commonplace in much of the evidence of Scottish bankers to the many governmental inquiries of the nineteenth century that 'everybody who has any money at all has a bank account', although for many banks the sum of £10 was the minimum deposit, and friendly societies and savings banks were well supported by working people.[12] Thus 'everybody' reached quite low down in the social hierarchy, and the thriftiness of the Scottish people was an indisputable fact.

11 Despite the Highland clearances, the population of the Highlands increased until at least the census of 1831. For a brief account of the rural experience in the nineteenth century, see R. H. Campbell and T. M. Devine, 'The Rural Experience', in Fraser and Morris (eds), *People and Society in Scotland*, vol. ii, pp. 46–72.
12 This was a comment from James Anderson of the Union Bank of Scotland before the House of Lords Committee on Commercial Distress, 1857, Q. 3,578.

There has always been some uncertainty about the precise numbers of the middle classes in early industrial society in Britain, and in the 1831 census they were defined as 'capitalists, bankers, professional and other educated men'. Even this restricted definition covered 5.3 per cent of the Scottish male population in 1831, with Edinburgh registering some 20.4 per cent, Glasgow 5.9 and Paisley 2.7 per cent.[13] From mid-century, the census data provide useful indications of the growth of the middle classes, although there are still allowances to be made because of imperfections in definitions. In 1871, the greater Glasgow region returned about 10 per cent of its occupied workforce as middle-class, while in the Lothian area (which included Edinburgh) the figure was 15 per cent; by the end of the century the broad census groupings showed some 18 per cent in the Strathclyde area and 25 per cent in Lothian.[14] The decennial census returns confirmed the increase in middle-class numbers within a commercially and industrially maturing economy, and they also showed what again would be expected, that the larger the burgh the greater the concentration of middle-class and rentier incomes.[15] Further, as the Victorian years progressed, even the smaller burghs saw the growth of local engineering works, public utilities for gas and water and diversification in the service trades. Thus the trends in a changing social structure began to shift the attention of branch managers and agents in even the most rural of the provincial burghs away from the traditional gentry and the farming community towards those whose incomes were derived from trade, commerce and industry. The growing number of rentiers, middle-class widows and retired military men were also important for their potential as depositors. The process of growth was clearly discernable to the banks through the volume of transactions (lending and deposits) and the number of accounts in branches.[16] The detail of this information enabled the banks to assess the movements of money from branches with a surplus of deposits to areas where it could be lent with considerable accuracy on a week-by-week basis. It was evident that many burghs which had been important in the eighteenth century – Montrose, Cupar, St Andrews, Ayr, Dumfries, Thurso, Wick and Haddington, for example, although the list of market towns which served an agricultural hinterland is much longer – became relatively less important as the nineteenth century progressed. A few faded into the countryside; Portpatrick, a minor instance, struggled to reach

13 N. Morgan and R. Trainor, 'The Dominant Classes', in Fraser and Morris (eds), *People and Society in Scotland*, vol. ii, pp. 103–37 (p. 106).

14 Lee, *British Regional Employment Statistics*, Tables for Scotland; see also Morgan and Trainor, 'The Dominant Classes', pp. 106–7.

15 C. Atherton, 'The Development of the Middle Class Suburb: The West End of Glasgow', *Scottish Economic and Social History Review*, 11 (1991), 19–35.

16 For the expansion of Bank of Scotland's branch network in the Victorian period, see Appendix 8.

2,239 inhabitants in 1831, but railway developments removed what brief locational advantages it had enjoyed, and the population fell from 2,156 in 1861 to only 1,285 by 1881.[17] The volume of deposits rose at virtually every branch, but the opportunities for lending in market towns declined relative to the industrial burghs of central and western Scotland.[18]

Between 1830 and 1850, there took place a clear change in the pattern of Scottish banking, in particular with the establishment of well-funded joint-stock banks serving Glasgow and the western region. In 1830, there were thirty-five banks in Scotland: the three senior banks, two large joint-stock banks in Edinburgh (the National and the Commercial) and one in Glasgow (the Glasgow Union Banking Company), eight private banks and twenty-one provincial banks. By 1850, as a result of new starts, amalgamations and a few failures, all private banks had disappeared and only seventeen banks continued in business, mainly the large-scale chartered and joint-stock banks. Four of the old-style provincial banks remained, and the important new factor within the banking community was the presence of the substantial Glasgow joint-stock banks, of which the Glasgow Union Banking Company (1830), the Western Bank of Scotland (1832), the Clydesdale Bank (1838) and the City of Glasgow Bank (1839) were the most important. In Edinburgh, the Commercial Bank (1810) and the National Bank (1825) expanded their branch systems and rapidly overhauled the provincial banks (see Table 15.1).[19] Many of the provincial banks, concerned about a repetition of the crisis of 1825 and now faced with greater demands for accommodation, joined up with the joint-stock and chartered banks. By mid-century, there was also more competition for deposits from the Scottish life assurance mutual societies. In the uncertain conditions of Victorian Scotland, taking out life policies was widely encouraged; indeed, many bank managers were enrolled as agents of the various companies.[20] By 1860, the Standard Life Assurance Company had the largest portfolio and current income of any equivalent company in the UK, and a spread of agents and officials in Britain and Ireland. There was in addition, during the 1840s, the formation of 'exchange banks' connected with railway development, but none remained after the early 1850s; their history is briefly considered below.

---

17 N. L. Tranter, 'The Demographic Impact of Economic Growth and Decline: Portpatrick 1820–1891', *Scottish Historical Review*, 57 (1978), 87–105.
18 The difference between Bank of Scotland branches which had a surplus of deposits and those with a balance of advances at the start of the Victorian period is shown above, Table 14.1.
19 See S. G. Checkland, *Scottish Banking: A History, 1695–1973* (Glasgow: 1975), Table 11, pp. 372–3.
20 J. H. Treble, 'The Performance of the Standard Life Assurance Company in the Ordinary Market for Life Assurance 1825–50', *Scottish Economic and Social History Review*, 5 (1985), 57–77.

When the Stockton and Darlington railway opened in 1825, Scotland possessed a widespread network of horse-drawn lines, mainly for coal but also for some other goods and for passengers. Most were only a few miles in length and irregular in operation. One of the earliest known examples of steam traction came in 1817, when the Duke of Portland spent £38,167 on nine miles of the Kilmarnock and Troon railway and employed a (stationary) steam engine which was still in use in 1848. After the opening of the Liverpool and Manchester railway in 1830, usually taken as the beginning of the railway age, the Scots were slow to build railways in their own country, and until 1836 more Scottish money was invested in English development. Scottish railway lines built before 1839 were mainly for coal and minerals, with a low level of passenger traffic, although the Dundee lines along the coast to Arbroath and north to Strathmore had more broadly-based custom. As in England, coal carriage by rail sharply reduced the price per ton to the consumer. In the greater Glasgow area, domestic coal fell from twelve shillings a ton to six, and the St Rollox chemical works, which used 30,000 tons a year and was located next to the railway terminus, was able to negotiate prices of four and five shillings a ton.[21]

The spread of the railway network, which grew much faster after 1840, had profitable consequences for several of the important business and landed groups which had always been important for the Scottish banks. The new railways opened up areas for sustained mineral exploitation which, because of distance, the earlier canal network had left largely untouched. The income of many from the landowning classes of the central lowlands was thus transformed. Hitherto low rents from not always very good arable land now produced high incomes from coal and iron, reversing the decline in rentable income which had lasted for some two decades after the Napoleonic Wars. The railway in general helped to bind the Scottish economy into a more interconnected whole, with increased urbanisation as one of the inevitable results; that also meant increased incomes for landowners from land sales, feu duties and higher rents.

The financing of the early lines relied upon local sources of wealth: mine owners, landowners, the mercantile groups and lawyers. The first significant batch of Parliamentary railway bills came during the boom years of 1835–6, and the Scottish rail network had reached 282 miles by 1844, 872 in 1847 and 1,062 by 1854. Total paid-up capital was £1.96 million in 1838 and £3.84 million by 1844. The majority of lines continued to have local backing for their share capital; bank overdrafts

---

21 Slaven, *Development of the West of Scotland*, pp. 41–8; Lenman, *Economic History of Modern Scotland*, pp. 153–5; for a list of railway construction in Scotland, L. Popplewell, *A Gazetteer of the Railway Contractors and Engineers of Scotland 1831–1914*, vol. i, *1831–1870* (Bournemouth: 1989).

Table 15.1 *Scottish banks established 1780–1845*

Name	Place	Established	Retired/failed (if prior to 1845)	Comments
Public banks				
Bank of Scotland	Edinburgh	1695		by Act of Scottish Parliament
Royal Bank of Scotland	Edinburgh	1727		by royal charter
British Linen Company	Edinburgh	1746		by royal charter (for banking 1763)
Private banks				
Sir William Forbes, James Hunter & Co.	Edinburgh	c. 1730s	1838	formerly John Coutts & Co., then Coutts Brothers & Co.; taken over by Glasgow Union Banking Co.
Ramsay, Bonar & Co.	1 Edinburgh	1738	1837	previously Mansfield, Hunter & Co./Mansfield, Ramsay & Co./Mansfield, Bonar & Co. and from 1807 Ramsay, Bonar & Co.; wound up by Bank of Scotland
Kinnear, Thomas & Sons	2 Edinburgh	1748	1831	never issued notes; amalgamated with Donald Smith & Co., Edinburgh to form Kinnear, Smiths & Co.
Seton, Wallace & Co.	3	pre-1754	1806	previously Seton, Houston & Co.; not known if issued notes; retired
Watson, James & Robert	4 Glasgow	c. 1763	1832	never issued notes; previously known as David Watson; failed and paid 4s 9d per £
Cumming, William & Sons	5 Edinburgh	?	1788	not known if issued notes; retired
Smith, Donald & Co.	6 Edinburgh	1773	1831	never issued notes; amalgamated with Thomas Kinnear & Sons, Edinburgh to form Kinnear, Smiths & Co.
Bertram, Gairdner & Co.	7 Edinburgh	1776	1793	never issued notes; failed and paid 17s 6d per £
Allan and Stewart	Edinburgh	1776	1810	failed
Allan, Alexander & Co.	c. 1776			never issued notes; still existing in 1848
Fyfe, John & Co. (2)	8 Edinburgh	1778	1790	failed – not known if paid in full
Wardie (or Wordie?), John	Edinburgh	c. 1778	c. 1781/87?	failed – not known if paid in full
Johnstone, Robert	9 Edinburgh	1779	1797	died
Allan, Robert J. & Son	10 Edinburgh	1781	1834	never issued notes; sequestrated; 4s per £ paid

Scott, Smith, Stein & Co.	11	Edinburgh	1781?	1812	never issued notes; known as William Scott/Leslie & Scott until c. 1794; sequestrated; 12s per £ paid
Thomson, Andrew, George & Andrew	12	Glasgow	1785	1793	stopped – paid in full
Campbell, Thomson & Co.		Stirling	1787	1798	retired
Jamieson, Henry		Edinburgh	1788	1798	ended
Lothian, William		Edinburgh	c. 1788	by 1810	ended
Keir, Adam	13	Edinburgh	c. 1789	by 1810	ended
Sterling, James		Edinburgh	c. 1789	by 1810	ended
Leslie & Scott – see Scott, Smith, Stein & Co.		Edinburgh			
Thomson, Messrs		Edinburgh	c. 1793	by 1810	ended
Hamilton, Gilbert & Son		Glasgow	c. 1795	1802	became Glasgow agents of Bank of Scotland
Wardrop, John & Co.	14	Edinburgh	c. 1802?	1823	never issued notes; retired
Paterson, David (of Costerton)		Edinburgh	1803	1813	sequestrated; 14s per £ paid
Inglis, James & Co.	15	Edinburgh	1805	1834	known as Inglis, Borthwick (Gilchrist) & Co. until 1816; failed – 10s per £ paid
Thomson & Co.		Edinburgh	1812	1814	failed – not known if paid in full
Kinnear, Smiths & Co.	16	Edinburgh	1831	1834	an amalgamation of Thomas Kinnear & Son and Donald Smith & Co.; failed and paid 11s per £
Provincial banking companies					
Dunlop, Houston & Co. (Ship Bank)		Glasgow	1749	1836	stopped 1772; reorganised 1775–6 (became Moores, Carrick & Co.); from 1783 Carrick, Brown & Co.; amalgamated with Glasgow Banking Co. to form Glasgow & Ship Banking Co.
Cochrane, Murdoch & Co. (Arms Bank)	17	Glasgow	1750	1793	required support 1772; from 1763 to c. 1782 Speirs, Murdoch & Co., then Murdoch, Robertson & Co.; failed, but paid in full
Maxwell, Ritchie & Co. (Thistle Bank)		Glasgow	1761	1836	taken over by Glasgow Union Banking Co. (Union Bank of Scotland)
Dundee Banking Co. (Geo. Dempster & Co.)		Dundee	1763		
Perth United Banking Co.		Perth	1763		junction of five quasi-banks: in 1787 re-formed as Perth Banking Co.
Aberdeen Banking Co.	18	Aberdeen	1767		
Glasgow Merchant Banking Co.		Glasgow	1769	1798	closed temporarily 1772; retired
Hunters & Co.		Ayr	1773	1843	taken over by Union Bank of Scotland
Stirling Banking Co.	19	Stirling	1777	1826	failed, but paid in full

Table 15.1 *continued*

Name	Place	Established	Retired/failed (if prior to 1845)	Comments
Paisley Banking Co.	Paisley	1783	1837	taken over by British Linen Bank
Merchant Bank of Stirling	20 Stirling	1784	1804	failed; 14s 9d per £ paid
Greenock Banking Co.	Greenock	1785	1843	also known as Dunlop, Houston, Gammell & Co.; taken over by Western Bank of Scotland
Falkirk Bank	Falkirk	1787	1826	retired
Perth Banking Co. – see Perth United Banking Co.	Perth	1787		
Commercial Bank of Aberdeen	Aberdeen	1788	1833	taken over by National Bank of Scotland
Paisley Union Banking Co.	Paisley	1788	1838	Joined Union Bank of Scotland
Leith Bank	21 Leith	1792	1842	failed – paid 12s 11d per £
Dundee Commercial Banking Co.	Dundee	1792	1802	reformed as Dundee New Bank
Cupar Bank	Cupar	1802	1811	retired
Fife Bank	22 Cupar	1802	1825	failed – creditors paid in full
Dundee New Bank	23 Dundee	1802	1838	previously Dundee Commercial Banking Co.; taken over by Dundee Banking Co.
Renfrewshire Banking Co.	24 Greenock	1802	1842	failed – between 7s 6d and 9s 2d per £ paid
Kilmarnock Banking Co.	Kilmarnock	1802	1821	joined Hunters & Co., Ayr
Falkirk Union Bank	25 Falkirk	1803	1816	failed – 9s 6d per £ paid
Dumfries Commercial Bank (Grace & Co.)	Dumfries	1804	1808	failed – did not pay in full
Galloway Banking Co. (Douglas, Napier & Co.)	26 Castle Douglas	1806	1821	retired
Berwick and Kelso Banking Co. (Tweed Bank)		c. 1808	1810	ended
Dundee Union Bank	Dundee	1809	1844	taken over by Western Bank of Scotland
Glasgow Bank	Glasgow	1809	1843	taken over by Union Bank of Scotland; had been renamed Glasgow & Ship Bank in 1836
Kilmarnock Bank	Kilmarnock	1810	1821	joined with Hunters & Co., Ayr
East Lothian Bank	27 Dunbar	1810	1822	failed, but paid in full
Perth Union Bank	Perth	1810	1836	taken over by National Bank of Scotland
Caithness Bank	Wick	1812	1825	taken over by Commercial Bank of Scotland
Montrose Bank	28 Montrose	1814	1829	taken over by National Bank of Scotland
Maberley John & Co. (Exchange and Deposit Bank)	29 Aberdeen	1818	1832	failed – 4s 5d per £ paid

Bank	Location	Founded		Notes
Shetland Bank (Hay & Ogilvie)	30 Lerwick	1821	1842	failed – 5s per £ paid
Dundee Commercial Bank	Dundee	1825	1838	taken over by Eastern Bank of Scotland
Arbroath Bank	31 Arbroath	1825	1844	taken over by Commercial Bank of Scotland
Joint-stock banking companies				
Commercial Bank of Scotland	Edinburgh	1810		royal charter granted 1831
National Bank of Scotland	Edinburgh	1825		royal charter granted 1831
Aberdeen Town & County Bank	Aberdeen	1825		
Glasgow Union Banking Co.	Glasgow	1830		became Union Bank of Scotland, 1843
Ayrshire Bank		1830	1845	taken over by Western Bank of Scotland
Western Bank of Scotland	Glasgow	1832		
Central Bank of Scotland	Perth	1834		
North of Scotland Bank	Aberdeen	1836		
Clydesdale Bank	Glasgow	1838		
Eastern Bank of Scotland	Dundee	1838		
Caledonian Bank	Inverness	1838		
Edinburgh and Leith Bank	Edinburgh	1838		became Edinburgh and Glasgow Bank in 1844
Southern Bank of Scotland	32 Dumfries	1838	1842	taken over by Edinburgh and Leith Bank
City of Glasgow Bank	Glasgow	1839		
Paisley Commercial Bank	33 Paisley	1839	1844	taken over by Western Bank of Scotland
Glasgow Joint Stock Banking Co.	34 Glasgow	1840	1844	amalgamated with Edinburgh and Leith Bank, which became Edinburgh and Glasgow Bank
Greenock Union Bank	Greenock	1840	1843	taken over by Clydesdale
Glasgow Bank	Glasgow	1843	1844	taken over by Western Bank of Scotland
Exchange banks (prohibited from issuing notes)				
North British Bank	Glasgow	1844		
Glasgow (Commercial) Exchange Co.	Glasgow	1845		
National Exchange Co.	Glasgow	1845		
Union Exchange Co.	Glasgow	1845		
West of Scotland Exchange Investment Co.	Glasgow	1845		
Exchange Bank of Scotland	Edinburgh	1845		
Northern Investment Co.	Aberdeen	1845		
North British Exchange and Reversionary and Guarantee Co.	Aberdeen	1845		

Notes:

1 Peter Ramsay, the surviving partner, became Edinburgh agent of the Western Bank of Scotland until his death in 1855.

2 Thomas Kinnear was originally an insurance broker.

3 The original partners were woollen merchants.

4 Liabilities at failure were £79500 of which £19000 was liquidated. The Trustee was Alexander Gray, accountant, Glasgow.

5 Inherited his father's (Patrick Cumming's) cloth shop in Parliament Close and turned it into a banking house. Left a large fortune on his death.

6 Donald Smith was the grandfather of the Donald Smith who became manager of the Western Bank. He was originally a partner in the private bank, Johnston, Smith & Co. (failed 1772). His new venture was financed by money gained through marriage. He became a director of Bank of Scotland in 1807 and Lord Provost of Edinburgh in the same year.

7 Partners at sequestration were John Gairdner, Adam Keir and Robert Forrester who were also partners of the London banking firm Baillie, Pocock & Co. which failed at the same time. The liabilities were £145000 of which £127000 was liquidated.

8 Had failed in 1772. His son James Fyfe became a merchant in Glasgow and was British Linen Bank agent there c. 1797.

9 Robert Johnston was originally a partner (with Donald Smith) of Johnston, Smith & Co. which failed in 1772. He resumed as a private banker, but his main line of business was as a toy, hardware and grocery merchant.

10 Liabilities at failure were £108800 of which £22000 was liquidated. The Trustee was Robert Christie, accountant, Edinburgh.

11 The original firm of Leslie & Scott (partners George Leslie and William Scott WS, Banker, Edinburgh) was dissolved on 9 July 1793. That firm was also insurance brokers and Lottery Office keepers (*Glasgow Mercury*, 23 July 1793).

12 Partners were Andrew Thomson of Faskin, near Airdrie, and his two sons. Trustee was John McCaul, merchant, Glasgow.

13 Adam Keir had been a partner in the firms of Bertram, Gairdner & Co., Edinburgh and Baillie, Pocock & Co., London (see note 7).

14 Liabilities at failure were £118047, assets £90000.

15 Liabilities at failure were £23007, including £18808 for which other parties were primarily liable. Assets were £3000.

16 Liabilities at failure were £320000, of which about £175000 was liquidated. The Trustee was James Brown, accountant, Edinburgh. The partners at date of failure were George, John G. and Alex Kinnear and Donald, William, George and Robert Smith. The main cause of failure was heavy losses due to the misconduct of James Smith, London stockbroker, an uncle of the four Smith partners, who was employed to draw dividends on stocks belonging to the bank's customers. He used his power of attorney to sell stocks belonging to the bank's customers, and with the proceeds speculated in French Rentes on his own account. His ruin was also the bank's downfall. The main customer involved was Mr Trotter of Mortonhall. George Kinnear went on to be manager of one of the early Sydney banks, the Huddersfield Bank, and founder of the Commercial Exchange Co. Donald Smith became Manager of (and helped to ruin) the Western Bank.

17 Liabilities at failure were £183000, of which was realised £113000. The Trustee was Walter Ewing MacLae, merchant, Glasgow.

18 At the stoppage of 1772 there had been seventy partners. A new partnership contract was formed in 1776. The main cause of failure was the abscondment of the cashier to America with a large sum of the company's money. The loss ultimately fell on the only two solvent partners, Robert McLintock of Thornbank and Robert Thomson of Camphill.

19 The Trustee was Alex Smith of Glassingal.

20 The funds were £59000 and the liabilities were £50140, of which £34500 was liquidated. Andrew Belch, one of the partners, was indicted before the High Court of Justiciary, Edinburgh, on 23 December 1806, at the instance of the Trustees for forging endorsements on several bills. He was acquitted on a legal objection to the relevancy, but was recommitted on a charge of fraudulent bankruptcy. The partners originally numbered six, but had been reduced to two by the time of the stoppage. The Trustee was James Dundas, accountant, Edinburgh.

21 Liabilities at stoppage were £130000, of which £84000 was liquidated. The partners originally numbered eighteen, but had been reduced to nine by the time of the stoppage. The Trustee was James Brown, accountant, Edinburgh.

22 The capital was £30000 in sixty shares of £500 each. The loss latterly fell on only fourteen solvent partners (out of thirty-nine), who had to pay calls at the rate of £5500 per share.

23 The five partners at the date of dissolution were Lord Kinnaird, C. W. Boase, George C. Boase, Francis Molison and William Hutcheson.

24 At the failure on 1 April 1842, the capital was £35000, deposits were £300000, of which £225000 was ranked (i.e. claimed), and the note circulation was £24000, of which £17000 was ranked. The Trustee was John Ker, merchant, Greenock.

25 The original capital was £12000 and the number of partners fourteen. Liabilities at stoppage were £60000, of which £51999 was ranked and £24700 liquidated, leaving a shortfall of £27298. Six partners were sequestrated. The Trustee was James Russell, writer, Falkirk.

26 The partners were Sir William Douglas of Castle Douglas, James Hannay of Blairinnie, William Douglas of Almorness, advocate, and John Napier of Mollance, Manager.

27 Wound up voluntarily under William Paul, accountant, and a committee of partners. Liabilities were £129192, assets £63185. The call of £250 per share fell on the few partners remaining solvent.

28 The nominal capital was £100000 in 250 shares of £400 each, on which £100 per share was paid up. The capital was all lost, as well as £227 per share. The Manager, David Hill, became Montrose agent for the National Bank after the dissolution.

29 Wound up under English Fiat of Bankruptcy. The debts proved were £149082, of which was realised £76669, including the linen as well as the bank business. Official assignee was H. H. Stansfield, London.

30 The debts were £140000, of which £35000 was liquidated. They issued their own notes until 1827. The Trustee was Archibald Home, accountant, Edinburgh.

31 The managers were David Lowson, Town Clerk of Arbroath, and William Johnston. The latter was appointed Montrose agent for the Commercial Bank after the dissolution.

32 Became the Dumfries branch of the Edinburgh and Leith Bank after the amalgamation under the same Manager (Robert Laing) who had previously been a Teller at the Royal Bank, Edinburgh.

33 The Manager, Thomas Risk, had originally been accountant of the Paisley Union Bank.

34 The Manager John Robertson, had formerly been the produce broker and agent for the Greenock Bank at Glasgow.

Source: BS 20/2/7, Papers re history of Scottish banks; BS 1/70/9, An account of the constitution, objects and practice of the Bank of Scotland (1841), appendix G; NLS MS 1801(ii) List of Scottish Banks, 1695–1848, compiled by John Buchanan, Glasgow, 1862; S. G. Checkland, *Scottish Banking: A History, 1695–1973* (Glasgow: 1975); C. W. Munn, *The Scottish Provincial Banking Companies, 1747–1864* (Edinburgh: 1981).

could be significant, especially so for wages. Charles Tennant, supported by William Dixon of Govan, obtained a £10,000 cash account for the Monkland and Kirkintilloch railway from Bank of Scotland. The Royal Bank granted a cash account for £75,000 to the Glasgow, Paisley and Greenock, and £50,000 to the Glasgow, Paisley, Kilmarnock and Ayr. In the railway projection mania of 1844–7, huge sums were also subscribed from south of the Border, and by 1849 paid-up capital in Scottish railway companies had reached £19.2 million. Several lines drew more of their finance from outwith Scotland. In 1848, over 90 per cent of Caledonian Railway stock was held in England; but, for individual subscriptions of more than £2,000 for railways built by 1850, English capital accounted for less than half of Scottish capital. At this time, around half of the Scottish railway share capital came from bank loans secured on the heritable property of railway directors.[22]

In common with Victorian England, there was extensive promotion of public utilities such as cemeteries, water companies and gas works as well as industrial firms, services and life assurance societies in the boom years of 1843–7. But it was railway promotion that really caught the public imagination, and the opening of the first stage of the Glasgow to Edinburgh line in 1842 was regarded as a landmark. The spirit of this particular age was remarkable for the hazardous developments within the financial world that were promoted, or at least seriously considered. In the early spring of 1847, for example, when the absence of caution with regard to railway promotion was already becoming abundantly evident, Alexander Blair took legal advice as to whether Bank of Scotland could invest directly in railway construction. There was at this time a scheme – considered for about a month – whereby five Scottish banks, including Bank of Scotland and the Royal Bank, were to come together to facilitate loans to support railway-building using railway company stock as collateral.[23] This idea was not proceeded with. Alexander Blair had always urged caution in anticipating revenues from incomplete projects, and in this case went further: 'the charge against the exchange banks is that they are assisting the railway adventurers in an excessive anticipation of the yearly revenue of the country'.[24] Yet this was precisely one of the most interesting

22 'Early Scottish Railways', *The Three Banks Review*, 74 (June 1967), 29–39; W. Vamplew, 'Sources of Scottish Railway Share Capital before 1860', *Scottish Journal of Political Economy*, 17 (1970), 425–40; T. R. Gourvish and M. C. Reed, 'The Financing of Scottish Railways before 1860 – A Comment', *Scottish Journal of Political Economy*, 18 (1971), 209–20, Table 2, p. 215; Checkland, *Scottish Banking*, pp. 420–3.

23 See BS 20/12/17 (Miscellaneous papers) for discussion by Alexander Blair on whether Bank of Scotland was legally entitled to invest in railways. See also N. Tamaki, *The Life Cycle of the Union Bank of Scotland 1830–1854* (Aberdeen: 1983), p. 50.

24 BS 20/12/17 (Miscellaneous papers), Alexander Blair, paper on the British Trust Company, April 1847.

tributary developments during these years. There were nine exchange banks established after the first had begun business in 1845, four of them in Glasgow. Some styled themselves 'banks'; but, with the passage of the Acts of 1844 and 1845, they were prohibited from issuing banknotes, and most used the term 'exchange companies'. Their operations were those of banking practice but with fewer of the safeguards of the established banks. Deposits were encouraged by means of higher interest rates than the banks were offering, and advances were lent at rates between 5½ and 8 per cent. As long as railway share prices continued to rise, the profits earned were considerable. One of the early historians of Scottish banking suggested that the theory upon which these exchange companies were based was not necessarily an unsound one, as the Scottish banks later accepted railway stocks as security for advances. While this may have been more acceptable for the stable conditions of the mid-Victorian years, it was a highly debatable argument for earlier.[25] Certainly, the ways in which these exchange companies were managed encouraged reckless competition and unsound practices, and by 1850 most had disappeared. But the speculative ferment had not left the established banks unaffected. The joint attempt by the five banks noted above was one example; Bank of Scotland was behind the formation in 1847 of the British Exchange Company, wound up a year later in April 1848 with a payment of 3s 2½d for each five-shilling deposit; and the Union Bank had connections with the Glasgow Commercial Exchange Company, which it took over in June 1848 only to run the business down. The most bizarre event was probably the granting of a royal charter to the Exchange Bank of Scotland, founded in Edinburgh in 1845 and wound up in 1852, while both the Union Bank and the Western Bank had been refused charters a few years earlier.[26]

By 1854, the railway map of Scotland linked most industrial burghs in the coalmining and iron regions; only a few centres remained to be connected, such as Dumbarton in 1856 and Inverness by 1858. Most new lines from these years crossed agricultural areas and linked up small burghs to the main system, such as Perth to Dunkeld (1856), Huntly to Keith (1856) and the Moray Firth coast line (1859). Even Portpatrick was linked in 1859 by the British and Irish Grand Junction railway to

---

25 A. W. Kerr, *History of Banking in Scotland*, 4th edn (London: 1926), p. 217. George Kinnear, the private banker of Kinnear, Smith & Co. which failed in 1834, was prominent in exchange-company promotion; he published two controversial tracts, *Banks and Exchange Companies* (Glasgow: 1847) and *A History of the Rise of Exchange Companies in Scotland, and a Defence of their Proper Business* (Glasgow: 1848).
26 The charter of incorporation was granted to the Exchange Bank of Scotland in 1846 (8 & 9 Victoria c. 75). There was considerable indignation in Scottish banking circles: Checkland, *Scottish Banking*, pp. 342–5; and see R. C. Michie, *Money, Mania and Markets. Investment, Company Formation and the Stock Exchange in Nineteenth-Century Scotland* (Edinburgh: 1981), chs 7 and 8.

Stranraer; however, the Portpatrick branch line made a loss and was closed in 1874. Some of these later lines were sound propositions for local traffic; the Border railway, for example (1862), covered ninety-nine miles from Edinburgh to Carlisle via Hawick. Commonly known as the 'Waverley' route after the Sir Walter Scott memorial opened in 1846, and used as the company trademark, it gave the Border textile manufacturers easier access to export markets. The Tay was first spanned in 1878, but the bridge collapsed in 1879 and a sounder structure was opened in 1887; the massive Forth railway bridge was opened in 1890. Some new lines always ran at a loss; the West Highland line received a government guarantee, for reasons of state, of around £4,000 a year before 1914.[27]

Within a few years of 1847–8, the railways over most of Britain began to show steady profitability, and railway stock became a recognised safe investment. Aside from the economic effects of the railway network upon Scottish society, which in the medium and long term were wide-ranging, there were certain immediate benefits for the Scottish banks. This impact can be measured in several ways, from the purchases of supplies and the support for movement of goods, to increases in employment. The banks had an interest because of the sustained cash flows from ticket sales and freight income. The railway companies showed improved profits by the later 1850s, and these climbed as the economy expanded; but profitability fell somewhat after 1872, before tariff agreements encouraged by the railway and canal commission brought a rise in profits after 1899.[28] The impact on bank incomes was more marked in the central lowlands and the north-east of Scotland than in the Highlands, where the economic difficulties were only partially alleviated by the arrival of the railway. For the bank inspectors, the railway changed their working lives, and the construction of the electric telegraph in the 1850s continued the process of a more complete integration of communication within any one bank.[29] From this time, Bank of Scotland used a series of secret codes for telegraphic messages to protect customer confidentiality.

The accelerated growth of the Scottish industrial economy in the second quarter of the century inevitably involved the banking community in new demands as well as generally increased business activity. Between

27 Lenman, *Economic History of Modern Scotland*, pp. 171–2.
28 R. J. Irving, 'The Profitability and Performance of British Railways, 1870–1914', *Economic History Review*, 2nd series, 31 (1978), 46–66. Freight receipts rose (in pence per mile) from 70 or below from 1884–99 to reach 92.8 in 1909 and 101.1 in 1912; for a discussion of the wider benefits of railways in England and Wales, see G. R. Hawke, *Railways and Economic Growth in England and Wales 1840–1870* (Oxford: 1990).
29 The Electric Telegraph Co. was formed in 1845: L. Levi, *History of British Commerce* (London: 1872), pp. 214–15. An interesting contemporary account is in D. Lardner, *The Electric Telegraph Popularised* (London: 1855).

1825 and 1850, total deposits in all Scottish banks grew from £4,569,000 to £35,042,000, and total advances increased from £17.6 million to £36.5 million. The number of offices, including head offices, rose from 173 to 407.[30] This rapid development had to be accompanied by a reorganisation of internal structures to take into account the greater variety of customer requirements. The improvement in the efficiency of the inspectorate was one of the more important achievements in the third quarter of the century. While these changes were taking place, there was a re-examination of the theory and practice of Scottish banking and its place in Victorian Britain. As noted before, there had been throughout the later years of the Napoleonic Wars a debate concerning the restriction of payments in specie in exchange for banknotes imposed by the Act of 1797.[31] The so-called Bullion controversy – which ranged more widely than the title suggests – concentrated especially upon the relations between money, prices and exchange rates.[32] Public debate was by no means ended with the resumption Act of 1819 – 'Peel's Act' – (59 George III c.49), which ordered the Bank of England to exchange notes for bullion from 1 May 1821 at the mint price of gold per ounce, which, as before 1797, was £3 17s 10½d. In the early years, there was vociferous criticism from agricultural interests whose investment in improvement bore a heavier weight on farmers' incomes with deflation, with a consequent pressure on banks, especially the Edinburgh private banks and the provincial banking companies, which tended to have a higher proportion of farming accounts than the joint-stock and chartered banks.[33] The debates merged with broader monetary questions in the aftermath of the crisis of 1825. It was after the Bullion report of 1810 that the advocates of the currency school began to develop their ideas following the lead of David Ricardo, and the Bank of England board came to accept the gold standard as a necessary part of the monetary structure.[34] There continued to be dissidents, of whom

---

30 Checkland, *Scottish Banking*, pp. 424 and 426, Tables 14 and 15.

31 See above, Chapters 13 and 14; J. H. Clapham, *The Bank of England. A History* (Cambridge: 1944), vol. ii, *1797–1914*, ch. 1.

32 Among the specialist articles are R. S. Sayers, 'Ricardo's Views of Monetary Questions', *Quarterly Journal of Economics*, 67 (1953), 30–49; and W. E. Mason, 'Ricardo's Transfer-Mechanism Theory', *Quarterly Journal of Economics*, 71 (1957), 107–15. There is a full discussion of the controversies during the Restriction period of 1797–1815 in F. W. Fetter, *The Development of British Monetary Orthodoxy 1797–1875* (Cambridge, MA: 1965), ch. 2; and ch. 3 continues with a survey of the debates around the resumption of payments, 1816–19.

33 *Report from the Select Committee on Petitions complaining of Agricultural Distress*, 8 July 1820, (255) vol. ii. For a general survey, see A. W. Acworth, *Financial Reconstruction in England 1815–1822* (London: 1925).

34 J. R. McCulloch, probably the greatest populariser of orthodox political economy in the second quarter of the century, was as firm in his view of the desirability of the gold standard as his acknowledged master, David Ricardo; both father and son – James Mill and John Stuart Mill – were forceful in their support.

Thomas Attwood was probably the best-known in the 1830s, and there were others, including Thomas Tooke, Robert Torrens and Alexander Blair of Bank of Scotland.[35]

In 1832, the Whig government of Lord Grey committed Parliament to a major examination of the principles and practices of the banking system. The privileges of the Bank of England, last extended by an Act of 1800 (39 & 40 George III c.28), were due to expire on 1 August 1833. This was seen as a suitable occasion to consider all relevant matters and was announced to Parliament on 22 May 1832 when it was clear that the Reform bill would pass the House of Lords.[36] The 'Secret Committee on the Bank Charter, 1832', as it was known, laboured for many months; and, though no report was laid before Parliament, it was sufficiently wide-ranging in its minutes of evidence, which were made available, to be regarded as an authoritative addition to the hearings of 1826. In the new political conditions of the reformed Parliament, it was widely expected that members would be more sympathetic to the discordant voices in provincial banking, many of whose partnerships were still dealing with the results of the 1825 crisis. The Committee of Country Bankers was hopeful that its rather narrow concerns would be considered sympathetically, especially the right to issue banknotes and to judge for themselves how credit should be managed in accord with local needs.

The Secret Committee's terms of reference, set out in the introduction to the minutes of evidence, focused upon the desirability of one bank of issue for the whole of Great Britain, and whether that bank should be the Bank of England. The committee further examined the desirability of the conditions on which joint-stock banks of issue should be established and whether in general all banks of issue should be required to publish their accounts, and in what detail. The evidence was taken at length and followed by legislation (4 & 5 William IV c.98).[37] The charter of the Bank of England was renewed with certain modifications: its notes were made legal tender and it was allowed to issue bills under three months at above 5 per cent, although the usury laws remained in place. The decision to allow joint-stock banks to establish within a sixty-five-mile radius of London, which had been strongly proposed by Scots in Parliament, aroused most opposition. The Bank of England board tried everything in its power to have the offending clause withdrawn, and when it became law the

35 Fetter, *Monetary Orthodoxy*, p. 159ff.
36 *Hansard*, vol. 12, col. 1,358, 22 May 1832. The formal passing of the Reform Bill was on 4 June, when the third reading of the Bill was accepted by the House of Lords by 122 votes to 22.
37 There was no Report. Fetter, *Monetary Orthodoxy*, ch. 5; Clapham, *Bank of England*, vol. ii, pp. 121–30; Clapham, *An Economic History of Modern Britain: The Early Railway Age, 1820–1850* (Cambridge: 1967), pp. 508–11; T. E. Gregory, *The Westminster Bank Through a Century*, 2 vols (London: 1936), vol. i, chs 1 and 2.

board was obstructive. All banks were required to make returns of their banknote issues to the Commissioners of Stamps and Taxes, including the Scottish banks, but Bank of Scotland and the British Linen Company were successful in their claim to be exempt. The relation between the issue of banknotes by the country banks and the foreign exchange, which came up in the questioning on many occasions, was to remain unresolved until the legislation of 1844 and 1845. The bank that became known as the London and Westminster Bank was the first to open, with J. W. Gilbart as manager, and a less competent personality might well have met with failure.[38] T. E. Gregory, the historian for the first century of the Westminster Bank, was emphatic that William Douglas of the Scottish merchant house of Douglas, Anderson & Co., acting on the legal advice of Messrs Blunt, Roy, Blunt & Duncan, was the 'true founder' of this, the first London joint-stock bank.[39]

The Bank Charter Act of 1833 was of concern to Scottish bankers, as it was clear that the Bank of England directors favoured stricter regulation of note issue; and this was raised in earnest at the Select Committees on Banks of Issue in 1840 and 1841.[40] The committees inquired, following contemporary business and banking interest, into the alleged problems of the note issue and its relation both to the Bank of England and its policies, and the ways in which the note issue affected prices, foreign exchanges and the state of trade. In a number of respects, the Scottish banks were not really central to the discussions. Scottish banking at this time continued to be regarded, on all sides, as well organised in structure and efficient in operation. Nevertheless, three Scottish bankers gave evidence, and their answers provided accounts both of their theoretical understanding and of their daily banking practice.

Alexander Blair, the Treasurer of Bank of Scotland, was the first to be interviewed. He explained that the majority of the chartered banks of Edinburgh – the Royal Bank, the Commercial Bank of Scotland and the British Linen Company – were broadly in agreement with what he was going to say, the exception being the National Bank of Scotland which had expressly declined any agreement. Blair provided the committee with a written statement concerning their note issues, but in the questioning he declined to state the exact proportion that the circulation of notes had

---

38 Clapham, *Bank of England*, vol. ii, p. 134; Gregory, *Westminster Bank*, vol. i, ch. 3.
39 Gregory, *Westminster Bank*, vol. i, p. 67.
40 *Report from the Select Committee on Banks of Issue, with the Minutes of Evidence, Appendix and Index*, 7 August 1840, (602) vol. iv; *First Report from Select Committee on Banks of Issue*, 4 June 1841, (366) vol. v; *Second Report from Select Committee on Banks of Issue, with the Minutes of Evidence, Appendix and Index*, 15 June 1841, (410) vol. v.

in relation to deposits. Other information of interest to the committee was provided, including details of the note exchanges and how balances were settled between London and Scotland. The proportion of Bank of England notes and gold to the total circulation of banknotes he put at around a quarter; a third of the notes of other banks in Bank of Scotland tills were included, but this was an exaggeration. Blair again refused to be specific about the rate of circulation of their notes although, as noticed above, the Mound collected very precise information on this. Nevertheless, his answer to the question 'To what do you attribute this rapid return of notes?' provided an interesting summary of the place of the banks in Scottish business and why legislative control over note issue was unnecessary:[41]

> The notes are not held by the public, but are paid into their accounts: in consequence of the rate of interest allowed by the banks, no one in Scotland has any inducement to keep bank notes in his pocket, and the general practice of the country is to keep the circulation at as low a rate as possible: then the numerous branches which are situated up and down the country are the means of taking the notes of their neighbours out of the circle as speedily as possible, and they are transmitted, of course, without delay to Edinburgh, to be exchanged, and in this way it is not possible for the circulation to be more than what is really absolutely necessary for the transactions of the country; in fact it is at a minimum.

Alexander Blair also agreed that the practice of keeping a banking account was general in Scotland; that all cash accounts in credit were paid interest; and that, while there was no positive rule laid down, £10 was around the lowest amount accepted for an account to be opened. He reiterated the distinction between deposit receipts, which were expected to lie for some period in the bank, and deposit accounts – similar to what in England were called 'drawing accounts' – which were normally used for daily business. The interest was the same, and it was paid from the day of deposit. Blair stated that cash accounts were offered for balances between £200 and £1,000, that they were of the greatest benefit to the small trader and that it was obvious that no great commercial transactions could be carried out on such relatively small amounts. In fact, as the detailed evidence from Bank of Scotland ledgers has underlined, he was not providing the committee with accurate information. Cash accounts were often far in excess of the figures he was prepared to give in public. But his statement, together with his answer on the limited circulation of

---

41 Ibid., Q. 1,727. This was an accurate answer for the larger-value notes but, as the internal figures showed, not quite so for the £1 and one-guinea banknotes.

notes, countered suggestions that banknotes were available in other than the tightest conditions.

On the second day of his interview – 27 April 1841 – those attending included Sir Francis Baring (the Chancellor of the Exchequer), Sir Robert Peel and Henry Goulburn, who was to be Chancellor in the Peel government of September 1841. The matters mainly discussed were of a more theoretical kind relating to the changes that were to come about in the Bank Charter Acts of 1844 and 1845. Blair's position may be summarised thus: notes which were convertible could not affect prices, although gold would. In the case of metallic currency, prices were affected by the volume in circulation; but, as paper currency was convertible, prices were not affected, because if the paper was in excess it would be immediately converted into gold. The gold being part of the capital of the country might affect prices, but the paper certainly would not. Blair was cross-examined at length on this question; but he was adamant that he could not 'conceive paper being in excess so long as it is convertible', and for the next thirty questions he maintained this position – a similar tenor to the long-held views of Scottish bankers on real bills.[42] The cross-examination then turned to the ways in which the volumes of loans and discounts were regulated, and here Blair made a sharp distinction between the circulation of the note issue and the total of loans and discounts which, he insisted, 'should be regulated with reference to the foreign exchanges, in order that the conventional mode in which the Bank of England settle the exchanges might be assisted by the operations of the different banks throughout the country'. By 'the conventional mode', he referred to the Bank of England's general rule of maintaining a reserve of bullion in proportion to its liabilities. After many questions on this particular matter of policy, Blair continued to insist that whatever the circumstances which followed action on the minimum discount rate by the Bank of England, Bank of Scotland 'invariably' followed this changing position while at the same time avoiding precipitate action in respect of those to whom advances had been made. Thus Bank of Scotland's position at this time was to follow the rate of interest laid down by Threadneedle Street, but not to contract or expand advances on this basis.

The questioning then moved on to link the matter of note issue to the discussion of the relationships between the currency and the foreign exchanges. The chairman, Charles Wood,[43] inquired whether, if the committee were ultimately of the opinion that the circulation of Scottish

---

42 Ibid., Q. 1,841.
43 Charles Wood (1800–85) was Chancellor of the Exchequer in Lord John Russell's government, July 1846, and was created Viscount Halifax in 1866: *DNB*, vol. 62 (1900), pp. 353–4.

banks should be regulated with reference to the foreign exchanges, Blair could suggest any mode in which that necessity could be enforced upon them. The reply came:

> No, I cannot; I may say, that in as much as in the Report of the Committee that sat upon small promissory notes in Scotland in 1826, it was stated that it was not the opinion of the Committee that any change whatever should take place in the circulation of Scotland; and as nothing has occurred since that period to show that the circulation of Scotland is carried on otherwise than upon a sound principle, and as the evidence taken before that Committee proved the beneficial effect of the circulation of Scotland upon the transactions of the whole kingdom, and the great importance it was to the whole country; . . . I should presume that there can be no intention to interfere in any way with the currency of Scotland at this moment; and as regards England, I cannot offer an opinion with respect to English practice; but I think it hard that a Liverpool merchant, trading to India with distant returns, should be exposed to have his credit suddenly recalled, and his affairs thrown into confusion by the operations, and probably mistaken operations, of the corn merchants of Middlesex.[44]

Joseph Hume, the radical politician, asked around a dozen questions about the collaboration between the banks in Scotland in the matter of interest rates and the rates of discount. Blair was again cautious and merely confirmed that some agreements had existed since he joined Bank of Scotland in 1832. As with other Scottish bankers on subsequent occasions, he denied that they interfered with competition in the money market. The questioning never approached the complexity of the Agreements and Understandings.

The last main matter examined was the composition of the reserves held against liabilities, about which, as noticed, there was disagreement among the Scottish bankers.[45] Blair argued that reserves should be unconnected with the general business, and that convertible securities, regardless of their lower interest rates, were always to be preferred to commercial bills. When asked whether a bank holding a portion of its funds with the great discount brokers would be as secure and satisfactory as one keeping such in government securities, he replied:

> I do not think that the state of the bank would be equally secure, provided that the practice was to be general, and was to obtain with all banks, because under

---

44 *Second Report from Select Committee on Banks of Issue*, 15 June 1841, (410) vol. v, Q. 1,909. There were two Committees in 1826 to whose recommendations Blair was referring: *Report from the Select Committee on the Circulation of Promissory Notes under the Value of £5 in Scotland and Ireland*, 26 May 1826, (402) vol. iii; *Report from the Lords Committee on the Circulation of Promissory Notes under the value of £5 in Scotland and Ireland*, 6 April 1827, (245) vol. vi.
45 See above, Chapter 14.

such circumstances, if there were to be a pressure for money in the country, it is quite clear that the amount advanced upon discounts throughout the kingdom would necessarily be lessened, and banks, if they had demands made upon them from their depositors, must pay them by allowing such reserves to run off, which would occasion a pressure upon trade and manufacture, and, in point of fact, it would be directly the reverse of what was stated a short time ago, when it was said that the necessary consequence of any restriction or pressure upon the money market was, that an increased application for discounts was made and acceded to by the banks; in that view of the case the banks, instead of depending at such times upon bills, should rather expect to have increased application for discounts. Therefore, I consider that bills are not a fit reserve; they are, perhaps, safe to a certain extent, but they are only safe because it is not the general practice throughout the whole kingdom for banks to hold such securities as reserves, and I think it very probable, . . . that one cause of the increased application for discounts to the Bank of England, and other great banks of the country, at a time of pressure, may arise from bills held as reserve by many of the country banks being allowed so to run off for the purpose of meeting demands made upon them.

It was the state which would act as the final reserve of Scottish banks, not the general condition of the bill market. This involved a necessary sacrifice of income in the general interests of stability.

Alexander Blair was followed, three days later, by Primrose Kennedy, manager of the Ayrshire Bank, who explained that he had been chosen, along with James Anderson of the Glasgow Union Banking Company, to represent the Scottish joint-stock banks.[46] Kennedy was a landed proprietor as well as a banker; in evidence, he said that he had 'a much deeper interest as a landed proprietor in the prosperity of the country than as a banker'. The questions asked of Kennedy and Blair were broadly similar, and in some matters their answers were identical. Like all Scottish bankers, Kennedy willingly agreed that Scottish banking was both cheap to its customers and efficiently run. He was adamantly opposed, as were all north of the Border, to legislative action on the establishment of a single bank of issue. He showed the usual objections to the introduction of limited liability: 'unlimited responsibility is a check upon imprudent action'. With his defence of the Scottish issue as an integral part of the effectiveness of the Scottish banking system, he offered some figures on the profitability of the note issue, although these were of a more general kind than the figures collected as a matter of course within each bank. About a third of the aggregate profit of his own bank derived from the circulation of notes, but he added that in the larger banks the profit from circulation in relation to total profit was 'much smaller' than in banks

46 James Anderson's evidence before this Select Committee is discussed below, Chapter 18.

such as the Ayrshire. The profit in his own case was between 3½ and 4 per cent after deducting the total cost of his bank's circulation at about 1 per cent, which was rather a high figure. The profit from note issue was a major contributor towards his bank's ability to offer interest on deposits, and if deprived of it the bank would be obliged to hold much more gold or many more Bank of England notes than it did at present.

There were other incidental facts worth noting. The Ayrshire Bank had nine branches, all except one in agricultural districts; and over the previous three months, when Kennedy had been monitoring the circulation, he had found that the average rate of return of notes was between two and three weeks – a more sluggish circulation than it would be in the urban areas. On interest rates, whereas James Anderson of the Glasgow Union Banking Company reported being influenced, at least in the first instance, by what was being done in Edinburgh, Kennedy emphasised that there was no special relationship with Edinburgh rates, although he recognised that everyone would watch the operations of the Bank of England. His own bank worked within stable bands of interest rates: they had never discounted below 4 per cent or above 5 per cent. As with the other two Scottish witnesses, he underlined the virtues of the Scottish system, and on being asked whether he himself, with a long banking experience, had ever had to deal with a panic, he replied 'Never', which was a surprising answer for someone conversant with the results of 1825. He confirmed other witnesses who noted that, during May 1832, when the tactic of 'going for gold' was under way during the Reform Bill agitation, the Scottish banks were largely immune from the alarm south of the Border.[47] The debate concerning the note issue of the Scots was to surface through the rest of the century at irregular intervals and to continue through the twentieth century.[48]

The commercial crisis of 1836–7 and the debates around the evidence presented to the Select Committees on the Banks of Issue of 1840 and 1841 focused political opinion upon the desirability of some kind of control. Sir Robert Peel and his colleagues favoured the general ideas of the currency school, and there is no doubt that Peel would have preferred a single bank of issue. But, as he said in the debate in early June 1845:

> If, indeed, I had to deal with the question as a *res integra*, I might establish a single bank of issue; but I know too well the difficulties in the way. I have had

---

47 For the 'go for gold' agitation, see J. R. M. Butler, *The Passing of the Great Reform Bill* (London: 1914), ch. 9, 'The Days of May'.
48 For the twentieth-century discussion, see M. Gaskin, 'The Note Issue in Modern Scottish Banking', *Scottish Journal of Political Economy*, 1 (1954), 154–73; idem, 'The Profitability of the Scottish Note Issues', *Scottish Journal of Political Economy*, 3 (1956), 188–204; and idem, *The Scottish Banks: A Modern Survey* (London: 1965), pp. 99–103.

too many interviews with Scotch gentlemen not to be aware of the fact, that they would offer their most rigorous and determined opposition to a single bank of issue.[49]

The Bank Charter Act of 1844 (7 & 8 Victoria c.32) applied to the whole of the UK a clause which prohibited the establishment of any new bank of issue after 6 May 1844. In other currency matters it dealt with England and Wales, leaving the note issues of Scotland and Ireland for later legislation. There were provisions for submission of bank accounts to the Commissioners of Stamps and Taxes, who were given the right to inspect bank records. Where the partners of an existing note-issuer did not exceed six, they would cease to issue notes should the number rise above six. If two private banks came together, provided that the membership of the new partnership did not exceed six in number, they could retain the aggregate of their note issues and, again, would lose it if the number rose above six. Where the number of partners exceeded six and a joint-stock-issuing bank absorbed a private bank of issue, or if two joint-stock banks amalgamated, the new note issue was limited to that already enjoyed by the absorbing bank. Furthermore, should any joint-stock bank of issue amalgamate with a bank which had an office within sixty-five miles of central London, or move there, its right of issue would be forfeit, as it had been in 1833. The objective of these provisions was to establish the Bank of England's legal tender of £5 notes and above in as strong a position as possible, leading in the end to a position of monopoly.[50]

The Bank Charter Act was followed in the same year by an Act 'to regulate the Joint Stock Banks of England' (7 & 8 Victoria c.113). The Act laid down a requirement that letters patent were required for new joint-stock banks, which should have a paid-up capital of £100,000, the main consequence of these clauses being to discourage the establishment of new banks. In the next decade only three were launched, and more open regulations were enacted in 1857.[51] Of much greater importance to Scotland was the Act of 1845 'to regulate the Issue of Bank Notes in Scotland' (8 & 9 Victoria c.38). It had never been Sir Robert Peel's intention to alter the note issue of Scotland, but there were deputations and memorials, although nothing that was comparable to 1826. Peel's speech introducing the measure to the House of Commons covered both Ireland and Scotland, although he was always careful to distinguish their

49 *Hansard*, vol. 81, col. 144, 5 June 1845.
50 It took longer than expected; the last issuing bank in England was absorbed by Lloyds Bank in 1921.
51 'An Act to amend the Law relating to Banking Companies' (20 & 21 Victoria c.49), 17 August 1857. For the background to the legislation, see W. F. Crick and J. E. Wadsworth, *A Hundred Years of Joint Stock Banking* (London: 1936), pp. 25–8.

banking systems where they differed. He settled the worries concerning the issue of notes below £5, about which he did not propose to legislate:

> I say nothing, however, as to the future . . . The discretion of Parliament must be left unfettered in respect to them. If the continuance of the privilege affects no interests, if it has no injurious effect upon the circulation either of Scotland or of other parts of the Empire, there is no doubt whatever that a future Parliament will entertain the same forbearance, and will not disturb the settled habits of business of a whole country, or run counter to its feelings, for the mere purpose of carrying out some theoretical principle. I do not propose any vexatious interference with that system, which at present exists in both countries. I do not propose to establish any proportion between notes below £5 and notes above £5 . . . The banks of Scotland and Ireland will thus have two advantages – they will have first the advantage of being protected from competition; and they will also retain a privilege which the banks of this country have been compelled to relinquish for nearly twenty years – namely, that of issuing notes under £5.[52]

The reference that Peel made to protection from competition on the part of the Scottish banks came out of the prohibition under the 1844 Act of new banks of issue. The nineteen Scottish banks which existed at the time of the Act were therefore effectively protected from any increase in the number of banks, since no Scottish bank without the power to issue its own notes could be expected to succeed.[53] There were other differences with England; for example, the Act of 1844 had calculated the note issue allowed to country banks or joint-stock banks on the average for the twelve weeks preceding 27 April 1844. In the 'Act to regulate the Issue of Bank Notes in Scotland' (8 & 9 Victoria c.38), the average was derived from a period of thirteen lunar months prior to the same date. The variation of circulation, Peel noted in a Commons speech, was 'very great' in Scotland: 'In May and in November the amount of the issues exceeds the amount of the issues at other times'.[54] Scotland was additionally favoured by the permission to increase its note issue beyond that already agreed provided that it was covered by specie; and banks which amalgamated were allowed to issue their combined total as the fiduciary issue for the new bank. The level of banknote issue would be regulated by the Commissioners of Stamps and Taxes, who could inspect bank records. All banks except Bank of Scotland, the Royal Bank and the British Linen now had to return the name, residence and occupation of their shareholders.

---

52 *Hansard*, vol. 79, cols 1,332–3, 25 April 1845.
53 Crick and Wadsworth, *A Hundred Years of Joint Stock Banking*, pp. 385–6, offer a short account of the unsuccessful attempt to establish the Bank of Glasgow, whose prospectus as a non-issuing bank was published in October 1844; the project was absorbed by the Clydesdale Bank. See also C. W. Munn, *Clydesdale Bank: The First One Hundred and Fifty Years* (Glasgow: 1988), p. 20.
54 *Hansard*, vol. 79, col. 1,335.

Sir Robert Peel met most of the concerns of the Scottish banks that came within his general understanding of what the banking system of a country ought to conform to, but there were Scots who could not accept the principle of a connection between Bank of England notes and the state of the foreign exchanges, or his failure to legislate over the disposition of bank reserves to cover liabilities. Alexander Blair remained unconvinced for many years about the usefulness of the banking legislation of 1844 and 1845, in particular with this refusal to recognise the crucial importance of a reserve that was not connected with the business activities of the bank in question.

In the debates of these years, there emerged a better understanding of the short-run difficulties which aggravated mercantile and banking crises. This made a most important contribution to the acceptance of the joint-stock banking system, recognised a greater role for the Bank of England, acknowledged that the absorption of the provincial banks made for better stability, and also acknowledged the importance of retaining on bank balance sheets securities, saleable in crises, of which government stocks were the most important. In particular, the Edinburgh bankers insisted on having the dates of the liabilities on the balance sheets matched by the assets. This tended to put land mortgages and long-dated securities under scrutiny. Alongside this improvement in the public understanding of the relationship of crises to the composition of assets and liabilities went a continued acknowledgement of the strength of the Scottish banks. This extended to varying degrees of interest in multiple banks of issue and the relationship between gold reserves and the foreign exchanges.

In several respects, the 1845 Act was severely criticised. Before the Act, gold had been kept in Scotland for local demands; for the wider needs of trade, a bill on London was all that was required and was covered, in the settlement of accounts, by the public stocks held by the respective correspondents. But, after the Act's passage, more gold was required to cover the fluctuations of circulation. *The Economist* explained that since the Act had come into force there was a 'large' sum of gold

> uniformly locked up in Scotland and another considerable sum constantly travelling back and forward . . . If a period arrives when a Scotch bank expects an increased demand for its notes, a box of gold is brought down from London; when this period is past, the same box, generally unopened, is sent back to London.[55]

More gold tended to be kept in Scotland than was necessary, thus depriving the Bank of England of bullion; and this position continued for the remainder of the Victorian period and down to 1914.

55 'The Scotch Bank Bill – 1845', *The Economist*, 23 October 1847, pp. 1,214–15.

By this time, the Scottish banks were of the view that extensive business connections of Scottish trade and industry made it vital that Scottish banks should open offices in London. London was not dominant in the commerce and industry of the UK; there were many rapidly-growing provincial and Scottish centres, but the importance of Empire trade and the bill on London encouraged reference by the banks to London money markets. Thus on 6 February 1863 the general managers of the Scottish banks decided that henceforth their branches would automatically follow changes in the Bank of England's minimum discount rate without reference to their head offices. Furthermore, Scottish businessmen argued that facilities in London would help their companies. In 1864 the National Bank opened a London office, and in the next year there was an attempt to launch a new London bank. Four of the Scottish banks – Bank of Scotland, the British Linen, the Clydesdale Bank and the Union Bank – went into two years of negotiations with Glyn, Mills, Currie & Co. The proposal was to take over Glyns – although in most of the correspondence the name was not mentioned – and operate the new bank under the Companies Act of 1862. Discussions were ended in 1867 after the failure of Overend, Gurney & Co.[56] In that year, Bank of Scotland opened its own London office, a right which the legal officers of the Bank argued it possessed from the original 1695 Act of Parliament. The Royal Bank, however, met with considerable obstruction in its attempt. The charter of 1727 was deemed legally insufficient to allow it to promote a position in London, the government of the day was positively unhelpful, and only after much effort did the Royal Bank obtain an Act of Parliament which permitted it to open a London office in 1874.

The legislation of 1844 and 1845 marked a stage in the hostility towards the Scottish banking system from the English country banks and the City of London, and there were several examples of obstruction in the mid-Victorian years. After the collapse of the Western Bank in 1857, the liquidators endeavoured to save the Western note issue, which at £337,938 was 10.9 per cent of the authorised Scottish issue.[57] As early as April 1858, an application had been made to Benjamin Disraeli, Chancellor of the Exchequer, to provide legislative sanction by which the note-issue total could be sold by the shareholders of the Western Bank on the grounds that this 'property' was guaranteed by the 1845 Act, and Bank of Scotland pressed for the division of the issue among the Scottish banks.[58] There were further attempts over the next decade

---

56 See below, Chapter 16.
57 For the fate of the Western Bank, see below, Chapter 16.
58 C. A. Malcolm, *The Bank of Scotland 1695–1945* (Edinburgh: n.d. [1948]), p. 122; BS 1/21/10, Private and Confidential Letter Book.

– one when W. E. Gladstone was Chancellor – and all were refused.[59] Gladstone always took a hard line in respect of the Bank Charter Act of 1844 and was convinced that Sir Robert Peel preferred a single bank of note issue.[60] Gladstone supported a bill of 1869 'for restraining with a view to ultimately abolishing the circulation of the notes of private banks . . . [but] recognised that the Scotch and Irish notes would be hard to deal with until the English case is disposed of '.[61]

There was further criticism after the establishment by the Clydesdale Bank of branches at Workington, Carlisle and Whitehaven in 1874, with widely-rumoured reports that it was intending to move into London. George Joachim Goschen, who had been President of the Poor Law Board and then First Lord of the Admiralty in Gladstone's first administration (succeeded by Disraeli's government in February 1874), introduced the Bankers' Act Amendment Bill into the Commons in March 1875.[62] Sir Stafford Northcote was Chancellor and had already asked Sir Henry Thring, head of the office of Parliamentary counsel, for a view of the legality or otherwise of 'Scotch joint-stock company banks of issue' opening branches in England.[63] Thring had an exceptional technical and legal mind: he 'knew by instinct whether suggestions presented to him were capable of legislative expression'. But he was also capable of bias and omission, and displayed both in his memorandum to Northcote; Scottish joint-stock banks were banned from within sixty-five miles of London by the Act of 1826 and by general prohibitions of 1697, 1708 and 1800 which he claimed were still in force, although the Royal Bank was allowed to enter London by its private Act. Thring was later to admit that clause three of the 1833 Act might indeed allow Scottish banks into London, a matter he had overlooked. Parliamentary pressure on the Scots also came from MPs in Cumberland and Westmorland; and Goschen, MP for the City, was supported by Thomas Matthias Weguelin, MP for Wolverhampton and ex-Governor of the Bank of England, and Thomas Charles Baring, MP for South Essex. Goschen's speech in moving the second reading of the bill was prefaced by a statement that the subject would be referred to a Select Committee. It did not, however, inhibit Goschen from engaging

---

59 Kerr, *History of Banking in Scotland*, pp. 236–7.
60 Gladstone repeated this view during his speech in the Commons debate inaugurated by George Goschen in March 1875.
61 J. Morley, *The Life of William Ewart Gladstone*, 3 vols (London: 1903), vol. ii, pp. 650–1.
62 G. J. Goschen (1831–1907), son of a German merchant in London, became a Liberal Unionist in the 1880s and occupied the position of Chancellor of the Exchequer, 1887–92. He was recognised as an outstanding financial politician and was created the first Viscount Goschen of Hawkhurst, Kent, in 1901: *DNB*, 2nd supplement, vol. 2, pp. 134–40.
63 Sir Henry Thring, memorandum to Sir Stafford Northcote, 25 May 1874, reprinted in *Report from the Select Committee on Banks of Issue, together with the Proceedings of the Committee, Minutes of Evidence, Appendix and Index*, 22 July 1875, (351) vol. ix.

in a vigorous attack upon the Scottish banks; they enjoyed privileges which were not accorded to English banks. When Scottish note-issuing banks opened offices in London, they could do so without losing their right to issue notes, yet when the National Provincial Bank began banking business within the sixty-five-mile limit it surrendered a note issue of nearly £500,000.[64] Moreover, the Scottish banks paid no tax on their £1 notes. The central question which Goschen emphasised was

> whether you ought to allow a privileged system of issues to go on and increase in value day by day. I think it is perfectly fair to take the course proposed in the Bill, and to say to the Scottish Bankers – 'If you drop your issues, you can come to England, and to London like any other bank; but as long as you enjoy the practical subsidy and those privileges which were granted to you thirty years ago, and which have never been interfered with, so long we think your wings ought to be clipped, and you ought to be confined to your own preserves'.

He further supported the issuing banks established in the north of England: 'the present state of things is intolerable to them, because it is perfectly clear that they cannot compete with the Scotch banks'.[65]

Gladstone congratulated the House on the widespread view that this was not a party matter, and he was unequivocal in his support for Goschen, although he asked that the position of the Irish banks also be reviewed. Gladstone was the only member now in the House who had been a member of Peel's Cabinet in 1844–5, and he himself saw no reason for the inquiry which the government was proposing, since he thought the question 'quite clear and simple'; a statement he later amplified:

> I am one of those disposed to adhere firmly to the principle of the Act of 1844, and I am disposed to adhere firmly to the principle laid down by the Chancellor of the Exchequer – namely that all issue is the privilege and prerogative of the State, and that nothing can be more fallacious and mischievous than confounding the privilege of banking with the privilege of issue. Nothing could be more strictly accurate, and, at the same time, more felicitous, than the expression of my right hon. Friend (Mr Goschen) when he spoke of the issue banks being subsidized by the State. They are so subsidized in the strictest sense, because they have in their own hands, in their notes, a power which, if exercised by the State, would be directly productive of considerable funds available for the relief of the taxpayer.[66]

George Goschen and Stafford Northcote prepared their case for the Select Committee with meticulous care; both understood the London bill

---

64 Crick and Wadsworth, *A Hundred Years of Joint Stock Banking*, p. 309, n. 2, note that this office was purely administrative in function until 1866.
65 *Hansard*, vol. 222, cols 1,971–2, 1,975, 17 March 1875.
66 Ibid., col. 1,988, 17 March 1875.

market, and it is not an exaggeration to state that the former knew as much as anyone in public life about banking. In questioning, it was established that Scottish banknotes circulated in London and the north of England, that a loophole in the 1845 Act allowed the Scots to issue their notes unconstrained by a ceiling, only by an average taken every four weeks, and that in 1857 the Western had exceeded its average of £440,000 and by the time it closed its doors enjoyed a circulation of £720,000. Further, the Scots 'borrow, owe and take-up money in England', which evaded the clear intent of the 1826 Act to ban note-issuers from within sixty-five miles of London; they eluded competition by a cartel in order to raise their charges, and their public accounts failed to list their true profitability.

The legal right to remain in London was central to the argument. J. S. Fleming of the Royal Bank, who gave evidence on behalf of the Scottish banks, accepted that the Act of 1826 excluded Scottish banks from London but insisted that clause three of the 1833 Act only did so if they issued banknotes in London. Fleming realised that he faced politicians for whom no argument would suffice, and that he thus had to present a robust case. When Sir John Lubbock, MP for Orpington and Maidstone, inquired how 'An Act for the better regulating co-partnerships of certain bankers in England' (the 1826 Act) 'relieves the Scotch banks from their disabilities under a previous Act of Parliament' and how they could now enter England outside their sixty-five-mile radius, Fleming replied: 'I do not think that the title of an Act has much to do with its enacting parts; for example, the Bank of England was established under an Act imposing, according to its title, duties upon beer'. When Lubbock contended that the 1833 Act was only a qualifying Act and that privileges 'clearly not given' by the Act of 1826 could not be given by the later Act, Fleming retorted:

> that by no means follows ... because it was the very object of the Act of 1833 to permit what the Act of 1826 expressly prohibited. The Act of 1826 prohibited any joint-stock banks coming to London or within 65 miles of it, whereas the Act of 1833 was expressly and avowedly for the purpose of allowing the formation of joint-stock banks within the 65 miles circle.[67]

The Select Committee on Banks of Issue of 1875 provided detailed information as to banking practices but added nothing of significance to the theory of banking, and the committee could not agree on a report, so the matter was dropped from the legislative agenda. Too many vested interests were involved, and any change in the existing banking

67 *Report from the Select Committee on Banks of Issue, together with the Proceedings of the Committee, Minutes of Evidence, Appendix and Index*, 22 July 1875, (351) vol. ix; evidence, 22 April 1875, especially questions 86, 87, 91, 99 and 105.

structure would have brought out manifold opposition from very mixed groups on both sides of the Commons.[68] The hostility towards the Scots remained, although three more London offices – those of the British Linen Company, the Union Bank and the Clydesdale Bank – were opened in 1877. After the collapse of the City of Glasgow Bank in 1878, the government introduced a bill to allow banks to incorporate the principle of limited liability. The central idea came from George Rae, a Scotsman and the author of *The Country Banker*, who suggested the new formula of 'reserved liability' which provided that the unpaid portion of bank shares could be divided into two parts: one to be called at the discretion of the directors, and the other only in the event of the winding-up of the company.[69] Clause eight of the original bill excluded any bank of issue which had offices in a country of the UK apart from where the head office was located – a qualification that was obviously directed at the Scottish and Irish banks. After a great deal of opposition from Irish and Scottish MPs, the clause was deleted and the Act applied without discrimination throughout the UK. The five Scottish chartered banks were reluctant to add the word 'limited' to their title – they already possessed the principle of limited liability – and they collectively promoted three Parliamentary bills to permit them to adopt the new principle of 'reserved liability'. Gladstone's Liberal government was unwilling to grant the points as proposed, and indeed tried to begin discussions again about the whole question of note issue; the three banks then abandoned their attempt to obtain these new powers. Thereafter, the question of the Scottish note issue, while certainly not forgotten by the government and the Bank of England, did not become a matter of public debate and discussion before the outbreak of the First World War in August 1914.[70]

The explanation of why the hostility subsided lies partly with the success of the City of London and the growth of the English joint-stock banks in the last quarter of the century. These joint-stock banks found many ways of developing their businesses faster than the Scottish banks: for example, they absorbed English country banks and opened new branches to tap deposits. Financial services for the Empire generated

68 The English country bankers were responsible for beginning the agitation against the Scottish banks, although they were by no means united in their approach. It was, moreover, a matter on which all the Irish and Scottish MPs would have voted en bloc against any government attempting to restrict the existing powers of their banks, and this was a political confrontation which Disraeli was not prepared to enter upon: M. Gaskin, 'Anglo-Scottish Banking Conflicts, 1874–1881', *Economic History Review*, 2nd series, 12 (1960), 445–55.

69 For George Rae (1817–1902), see Crick and Wadsworth, *A Hundred Years of Joint Stock Banking*, pp. 425–35; and A. R. Holmes and E. Green, *Midland: 150 Years of Banking Business* (London: 1986), p. 62.

70 The hostility did not go away: see below, Chapter 17, for the letter from the Bank of England to the London manager of Bank of Scotland at the time of the Baring crisis of 1890.

higher and faster revenues for financiers than in the earlier years of the century. The figures for the growth of total assets and liabilities show that 1880s marked a watershed. Whereas in 1880 the ten Scottish banks had held 35.5 per cent of the sums of the English and Welsh joint-stock banks, by 1900 this was down to 22.8 per cent. In 1880, the two systems were more nearly equal in their branches – Scotland had 65 per cent of the English total – but by 1900 the English had made rapid advances with the number of branches (see Table 15.2). In resources, Scotland's £133.9 million was only 19.7 per cent of the English £677.3 million, and there was a further relative decline by 1914 to 16.4 per cent. There were no more telling indicators of the long-term results of exclusion from the English provinces. As will be shown, the Scottish banks made serious efforts with their London business and pushed both deposits and advances. But, without the deposit-gathering networks and branches in the major centres of lending which helped the English banks, it was inevitable that the gap would grow wider.

The asset, liability and profit figures of the Scottish banks are of considerable interest. There were eleven Scottish banks in 1879 and eight in 1914, and the business of the City of Glasgow Bank was divided up among all the banks. Bank of Scotland absorbed the ailing Caledonian Bank in 1907, and in the following year two other Aberdonian banks – the North of Scotland Bank Ltd and the Town and County Bank Ltd – amalgamated to form what ultimately became known as the North of Scotland Bank. Within the Scottish banking economy, Bank of Scotland remained a leading institution, helped by an increase of thirty-two branches from the absorption of the Caledonian in a part of the country in which the Bank had hitherto had little representation. The Caledonian's authorised note issue was £53,434, and Bank of Scotland took over total deposits of around £1,250,000. The Caledonian's shareholders received £1 5s of Bank of Scotland stock for each Caledonian share of £2, or they could take an optional cash payment of £5. The directors of the Caledonian continued to act as an advisory board for a period of ten years. On the basis of comparison of the published figures, Bank of Scotland and the Royal Bank struggled in the depression, and in various years to the end of the century were required to make substantial provision for bad and doubtful debts. All the other banks had exceptional difficulties to contend with, and this made them move more of their resources towards London and colonial investments in the search for a higher yield. The British Linen Company, after a fluctuating performance in the 1880s, achieved sound success in the next decade relative to all the other banks, largely because of a low rate of loss from bad and doubtful debts and by caution on advances. By 1900, Bank of Scotland and the Royal Bank were to recover

Table 15.2 *Comparison of joint-stock banks of Scotland to those of England and Wales, 1880–1932*

Year ending (varying dates for each bank)	Scotland			England and Wales		
	Number of banks	Number of branches	Total assets or liabilities (£ millions)	Number of banks	Number of branches	Total assets or liabilities (£ millions)
1880	10	877	98.7	89	1335	278.2
1881	10	883	99.8	93	1369	296.0
1882	10	884	102.0	100	1487	315.7
1883	10	893	105.2	104	1553	331.0
1884	10	931	105.4	107	1542	348.9
1885	10	935	103.5	110	1498	359.8
1886	10	949	101.8	109	1546	364.1
1887	10	950	104.0	109	1655	373.0
1888	10	963	106.1	111	1710	400.5
1889	10	964	110.6	103	1918	420.2
1890	10	975	114.2	104	2203	441.4
1891	10	986	115.1	106	2244	470.0
1892	10	995	115.3	102	2326	475.1
1893	10	1002	115.9	99	2515	471.4
1894	10	1007	117.0	99	2624	496.8
1895	10	1013	119.2	99	2695	535.0
1896	10	1016	120.7	94	3051	577.7
1897	10	1147	122.4	90	3454	609.8
1898	11	1178	124.5	87	3577	633.4
1899	11	1071	129.3	83	3826	652.1
1900	10	1075	133.9	77	3757	677.3
1901	10	1080	134.4	74	3935	674.2
1902	11	1115	134.8	68	4146	692.7
1903	11	1132	131.6	65	4334	680.5
1904	11	1145	129.1	61	4415	693.7
1905	11	1159	128.7	59	4558	719.5
1906	11	1176	133.0	55	4722	740.7
1907	10	1155	136.5	52	4822	738.8
1908	10	1178	133.3	50	4963	764.5
1909	9	1185	134.3	46	5022	774.5
1910	9	1221	134.3	45	5202	809.8
1911	9	1225	140.2	44	5410	836.3
1912	9	1225	147.5	44	5577	864.6
1913	9	1240	154.3	43	5797	901.4
1914	9	1253	162.3	38	5869	987.1
1915	9	1251	173.0	37	6027	1084.3
1916	8	1243	201.5	35	5993	1247.5
1917	8	1242	236.1	34	6004	1462.8
1918	8	1249	269.6	26	6501	1683.8
1919	8	1264	312.0	21	7195	1986.8
1920	8	1283	333.6	20	7612	2097.4
1921	8	1308	341.1	20	7963	2111.2
1922	8	1352	316.8	20	8235	1970.5
1923	8	1417	295.1	19	8491	1958.3
1924	8	1468	293.1	18	8676	1952.7
1925	8	1536	291.7	18	8873	1948.8
1926	8	1565	288.9	18	9105	1994.0
1927	8	1589	293.4	17	9381	2039.2
1928	8	1614	301.0	16	9595	2100.1
1929	8	1633	304.9	16	9815	2059.6
1930	8	1659	312.7	16	10082	2127.7
1931	8	1718	299.6	16	10178	1961.8
1932	8	1663	332.5	16	10066	2205.6

Source: D. K. Sheppard, *The Growth and Role of UK Financial Institutions 1880–1962* (London: 1971).

their earlier position, and after 1910 Bank of Scotland was first in the league table for profits (see Table 15.3). Yet, as will be seen in Chapter 17, this concealed a range of growing problems on the asset side of the balance sheet which grew steadily worse as the First World War approached.

Paid-up capital and published reserves increased at a very moderate rate, from £14 million to £16.7 million for all Scottish banks, from 1900 to 1914. From the time of the City of Glasgow catastrophe, dividends had remained on a national average of about 12 per cent through the 1880s and 1890s before improving steadily during the early twentieth century. On the eve of the First World War they were around 16 per cent, with almost all banks paying their dividends free of tax. There were some interesting changes in trend during these last three or four decades, with the City of Glasgow debacle providing something of a line of divide, although deeper movements within the economy were of a greater long-term influence. The shift of Scottish money to London in the twenty years before 1900 was a reflection of the difficulty in the relatively depressed conditions of finding profitable outlets for advances in Scotland, while, by contrast, more profitable opportunities emerged within England as a result of the development of world trade and the successful Empire, with the City of London its financial heart. There were enormous opportunities to be grasped. For instance, when Benjamin Disraeli was offered the opportunity to purchase 44 per cent of the Suez Canal company's shares and wanted £4 million immediately, he turned to Baron de Rothschild who at once agreed to advance the total amount, from which a profit of almost £100,000 was made.[71] Only the revival of trade, prices and profits in the last decade of Victoria's reign, encouraged by the naval re-armament, helped to offset the financial opportunities within the City of London.

In the Victorian era, there was a strengthening of the connections between Scottish financial institutions and the upper reaches of society. The board of Bank of Scotland had always benefited in varying ways from such connections.[72] Unfortunately, in the last years of Victoria's reign, when there was perceived to be a growing threat from France and Germany, this close identification of the Scottish aristocracy with the British state worked against the needs of the banks because the leading nobility invariably projected their role as statesmen, yet on financial matters the banks needed closer attention to how public policy affected

---

71 D. Kynaston, *The City of London*, vol. i, *A World of Its Own, 1815–1890* (London: 1994), pp. 335–6.
72 There are guides to the boards of directors, Governors and Deputy Governors in the two works by C. A. Malcolm, *The History of the British Linen Bank* (Edinburgh: 1950), ch. 19; and *Bank of Scotland*, ch. 12, Appendix D.

Table 15.3 Scottish banks' published net profits,[1] 1878–1914

	Bank of Scotland	Royal Bank of Scotland	British Linen Bank[2]	Commercial Bank	National Bank[3]	Union Bank	Clydesdale Bank[4]	Aberdeen Town & County Bank[5]	North of Scotland Bank[6]	North of Scotland and Town & County Bank[7]	Caledonian Bank[8]	All Scottish banks' total	BS as percentage of total
1878	183000	197000	160000	143000	159000	146000	123000	37000	54000		9	1202000	15.22
1879	177000	197000	144000	112000	132000	131000	109000	33000	52000		9	1087000	16.28
1880	169000	198000	146000	151000	155000	128000	130000	34000	52000		6000	1169000	14.46
1881	177000	200000	173000	146000	180000	133000	136000	34000	52000		10000	1241000	14.26
1882	178000	211000	154000	147000	175000	136000	147000	34000	51000		13000	1246000	14.29
1883	183000	216000	154000	151000	175000	148000	127000	34000	50000		13000	1251000	14.63
1884	187000	196000	154000	148000	162000	140000	117000	31000	53000		14000	1202000	15.56
1885	177000	184000	147000	148000	155000	121000	131000	32000	53000		13000	1161000	15.25
1886	182000	185000	158000	147000	155000	131000	125000	32000	55000		13000	1183000	15.38
1887	174000	185000	151000	146000	153000	129000	116000	32000	51000		12000	1149000	15.14
1888	169000	187000	153000	152000	156000	136000	110000	33000	41000		11000	1148000	14.72
1889	162000	188000	158000	158000	171000	137000	122000	33000	36000		12000	1177000	13.76
1890	165000	192000	164000	168000	177000	136000	133000	34000	36000		14000	1219000	13.54
1891	172000	200000	174000	175000	173000	132000	134000	34000	37000		14000	1245000	13.82
1892	180000	184000	185000	165000	161000	134000	128000	35000	37000		17000	1226000	14.68
1893	170000	189000	194000	181000	171000	134000	133000	36000	37000		17000	1262000	13.47
1894	173000	107000	210000	166000	157000	138000	118000	35000	39000		16000	1159000	14.93
1895	157000	164000	202000	176000	159000	119000	125000	37000	40000		14000	1193000	13.16
1896	161000	168000	283000	193000	178000	141000	135000	36000	43000		15000	1353000	11.90
1897	172000	177000	335000	203000	193000	149000	144000	37000	45000		13000	1468000	11.72
1898	175000	190000	252000	221000	302000	151000	152000	38000	46000		15000	1542000	11.35
1899	161000	201000	275000	237000	241000	159000	155000	37000	47000		16000	1529000	10.53
1900	181000	226000	249000	248000	249000	165000	170000	37000	46000		14000	1585000	11.42
1901	202000	235000	274000	226000	255000	174000	171000	37000	48000		14000	1636000	12.35
1902	212000	245000	277000	246000	258000	180000	181000	38000	48000		15000	1700000	12.47
1903	223000	251000	289000	232000	233000	189000	184000	38000	49000		14000	1702000	13.10
1904	202000	241000	273000	228000	230000	185000	181000	38000	53000		13000	1644000	12.29

Year												
1905	224000	240000	299000	244000	221000	188000	172000	38000	60000		15000	1701000	13.17
1906	232000	243000	275000	240000	220000	193000	179000	37000	61000		12000	1692000	13.71
1907	237000	254000	263000	233000	222000	190000	183000	38000	62000			1682000	14.09
1908	273000	240000	265000	240000	231000	193000	192000			76000		1710000	15.96
1909	282000	230000	287000	233000	221000	200000	204000			103000		1760000	16.02
1910	288000	238000	277000	227000	223000	205000	213000			106000		1777000	16.21
1911	293000	247000	269000	230000	228000	201000	217000			107000		1792000	16.35
1912	306000	268000	268000	239000	231000	203000	230000			109000		1854000	16.50
1913	319000	276000	258000	241000	232000	207000	237000			109000		1879000	16.98
1914	321000	266000	266000	250000	237000	209000	251000			116000		1916000	16.75

Notes:
1 To nearest £1,000.
2 Became a subsidiary of Barclays in 1919.
3 Became a subsidiary of Lloyds in 1918.
4 Became a subsidiary of Midland in 1919.
5 Merged with the North of Scotland Bank in 1907–8.
6 Merged with the Aberdeen Town & County Bank in 1907–8.
7 Became a subsidiary of Midland in 1923.
8 Taken over by Bank of Scotland in 1907.
9 Closed for eight months as a result of the City of Glasgow Bank failure.

Source: BS 1/70/14, Analysis of the resources of Bank of Scotland.

their interests. This is not to be confused with the development of state-funded business; in fact, the benefits of militarisation and naval rebuilding were of great moment to Scottish banks. The problem lay in government financial policy. After George Goschen's conversion of 1884, there was always the chance that British government consolidated stocks would decline in value. The movement was not a sudden one, but the 2¾ per cent consols stood at 111½ in 1899, and the final stage of the conversion brought them down to only 86⅞ in 1903, falling to 75 by 1912.[73] This meant pressure on the banks' internal reserves and encouraged secrecy where robust demands on government were required. Several banks, of which the British Linen was one, were led by these difficulties to be very cautious on lending. Thus the decline in consols wiped out the addition to the British Linen reserve funds (£500,000) made in 1892, and after the South African war the company reduced the level of credit offered to account holders; in 1900 it had advances and bills for £6,580,000 and in 1912 £5,367,158. The decline in the value of these consols was the main factor in the British Linen's caution. This matter is considered below, in Chapter 17, in respect of Bank of Scotland in more detail.

After the City of Glasgow failure, which affected the thinking of a whole generation of Scottish bankers, the connections with the British state were reassuring, although there were no overt crises of any major kind which required immediate political intervention. The banks' main response to the events in 1878 was to organise themselves on very efficient lines, not least with the very careful detail exercised by the inspectorate. There was much soul-searching, and every bank, in various ways, refined its managerial techniques. In the case of the British Linen, this task fell to Hamilton Hotson, general manager from 1886. Originally trained at Bank of Scotland, he rose to be assistant manager in the London office and was subsequently sub-manager of the Bank of Liverpool. Hotson decreed that merit should be the determining reason for advancement; agents and managers were to discuss records of progress, and staff were more frequently transferred. As C. A. Malcolm put it – somewhat delicately – in his 1950 history of the British Linen, the new methods 'cannot have proved popular with the staff of that time'.[74] The General Managers Committee continued with the Treasurer of Bank of Scotland, as the most senior banker, in the chair. But the world continued to change, and the tendency to complacency and conservatism in the Scottish banking world began to show itself in a number of ways. It was inevitable that, once the

---

73 Malcolm, *The British Linen Bank*, pp. 141–2. See also Statistical Appendix, Table A20, notes 31 and 39.
74 Ibid., p. 138; he was recalling events within the memory of retired staff at the time he wrote.

English banks began their large-scale amalgamations, they would soon outgrow the Scottish banks; and the emergence of new kinds of financial intermediaries – insurance and property investment companies as well as the success of the Scottish savings banks – offered a competitive intensity which the banks, for the most part, failed to confront with innovative ideas.[75] The unofficial proposal for a merger of the Commercial and the National in 1910 was developed in a memorandum remarkable for its positive ideas – which regrettably fell upon stony ground.[76]

The young men of the middle classes began to be attracted to employment in the banks in increasing numbers during the third quarter of the nineteenth century. By 1880, there were some 6,000 employees, of whom five-sixths were clerks. It was becoming the practice for the banks to take on a good many more apprentices than they would need once the three-year apprenticeship was completed, but this seems to have come to be accepted. Emigration was increasing quite rapidly, and there seems to have been a relatively easy entrance for young men trained within the Scottish banking system. It was estimated that, on the eve of the First World War, two-thirds of the whole of the banking staff in Canada was of Scottish origins.[77] The internal organisation of the Scottish banks was steadily refined during these years. In June 1865, the senior managers of several Scottish banks discussed a proposal to establish a Faculty of Bankers similar to the Faculty of Actuaries, established in 1856.[78] The managers looked at examination papers and manuals, and, though their proposals were shelved, the main ideas formed the basis for the Institute of Bankers in Scotland, the world's first such institute, founded in 1875. The round of discussions was renewed with an article in the *Money Market Review* of

---

75 Considerable sums of Scottish capital found their way into both the formal and informal Empires. C. J. Schmitz, 'Patterns of Scottish Portfolio Foreign Investment 1860–1914', unpublished report (St Andrews: 1991), p. 27, gives an estimate for the holdings in ventures abroad, in 1914, by Scottish-registered limited-liability companies of £254–330 million. This figure may exceed £500 million when the life assurance companies and Scottish banks are included. In Australia, which in the late 1870s and throughout the 1880s was taking a high proportion of British overseas investment, it has been estimated that Scottish solicitors, on behalf of their clients, placed between £1 and £2 million sterling in the late 1880s at a time when Australian pastoral borrowing reached a peak of around £5 million per annum: J. D. Bailey, 'Australian Borrowing in Scotland in the Nineteenth Century', *Economic History Review*, 2nd series, 12 (1959–60), 268–79. During the 1870s, four investment trusts were established in Edinburgh and four also in Dundee, and by 1880 these companies had placed £4.2 million in the USA. For a general and account, see W. T. Jackson, *The Enterprising Scot: Investors in the American West after 1873* (Edinburgh: 1968).
76 Checkland, *Scottish Banking*, p. 513, provides a summary of these proposals.
77 The *Scottish Bankers Magazine* guessed this figure in 1912 (vol. 4, p. 36). Net immigration into Canada between 1901 and 1911 was at least a million, accompanied by a massive inflow of capital: A. K. Cairncross, 'Investment in Canada, 1900–1913', in A. R. Hall (ed.), *The Export of Capital from Britain, 1870–1914* (London: 1968), pp. 153–86. For an interesting specialist piece, see B. P. Lenman and K. Donaldson, 'Partners' Incomes, Investment and Diversification in the Scottish Linen Area, 1850–1921', *Business History*, 13 (1971), 1–18.
78 BS 20/12/17 (Miscellaneous papers), Proposal to establish a Faculty of Bankers, June 1865.

2 May 1874 by A. W. Kerr, whose later *History of Banking in Scotland* was an early survey which went into its fourth, and last, edition in 1926. Kerr's 1874 article suggested the need for a professional education for young entrants to the banking community, and the idea was well received by a number of personalities prominent in the banking world: John Gifford, Cashier of the National Bank, Hamilton Hotson, and above all James Adams Wenley, who at the time was the Glasgow manager of Bank of Scotland. In the immediate and longer term, Wenley was probably the most influential. He was to become Treasurer of Bank of Scotland in 1879 and to enjoy a notably successful career of office. The Institute of Bankers was inaugurated on 6 July 1875, and within three years its membership was just under 1,000. Entrance to the Institute was by examination from 1878, and once within the Institute there were examinations with appropriate certificates for the different levels of achievement. The Institute certainly encouraged what Kerr called 'the spirit of self-improvement', although its grades of merit were probably more helpful, in the earlier years at any rate, to young bankers who emigrated to the colonies than in Scotland itself, where promotion by seniority was mostly, although not invariably, the rule; in this regard, change came slowly.[79] There were a number of connections with the universities; in 1905, for example, the Charles Bruce lectureship in banking was endowed at Edinburgh University.

Bankers have always been conscious of their physical surroundings and of the need, no doubt, to encourage worthy thoughts of probity and assurance in their customers. They have always, too, been mindful of the security of the realm. In 1803, at the time of widespread alarm about the expected invasion of Britain by Napoleon's troops, Bank of Scotland offered to equip fifty of its staff for the Royal Edinburgh Volunteer Regiment. The collection of flintlock muskets and pistols at head office remained for many decades. At the time of Peterloo, the Commercial Bank made payments to the staff who enrolled in the Volunteers, but after 1819 there do not seem to be records of further military involvement until the great movement of 1859–60, the third nationwide panic of the mid-nineteenth century, when it was widely believed, through all ranks of society, that the French were once again on the point of attempting an invasion of Britain. Within the cabinet during late 1859 and early 1860, the discussions over the nature and character of the Budget focused upon Palmerston's insistence that the defences of Britain required urgent renewal and extension. He was supported by hysterical public opinion. There was, indeed, no evidence for alarm at this time or on the previous occasions of 1848 and 1853–4, for which Richard Cobden in one of the

---

79 Kerr, *History of Banking in Scotland*, p. 242.

great polemical pamphlets of the nineteenth century – *The Three Panics* (1862) – provided abundant documentation; but, for Victorian people at this time, sober facts were not easily assimilated.[80] Regiments of men and of youths from the age of 18 were formed all over the country, and Edinburgh made a full contribution from the professional classes in particular. The staffs of the six public banks applied to form a Bankers' Company of the Edinburgh Volunteer Regiment, and, as a Company was limited to 100 members, only twenty-one from the Bank of Scotland were enrolled, the remainder in each bank being placed on a list of 'Effective Supernumeraries'. It was organised as a Masonic Lodge. The first in office was Samuel Hay, manager of the Union Bank; George Tytler of Bank of Scotland was his lieutenant, and James Reid, Secretary of the Commercial Bank, the second lieutenant.

The Bankers' Company existed from around this time and at a later date merged into the Territorial Army, becoming No. 7 Company of the 1st Battalion of the Queen's Edinburgh Rifles. Within Bank of Scotland, a group of clerks in 1882 petitioned the directors to provide a guard for the Bank against Irish 'dynamiters' whose activities were being widely reported in Glasgow and Edinburgh, although the amount of damage was limited. The directors agreed to the purchase of twenty-one Martini-Henry rifles, and the 'Bank Guard' continued to master rifle-shooting; at Queen Victoria's Diamond Jubilee of 1897, each member was given a £2 gold piece. It is this military tradition that would account for the large call-up of Bank employees at the beginning of the First World War, in addition to those who volunteered.[81] The *Scottish Bankers Magazine*, whose first issue appeared in 1908, carried many articles on military matters in the early years of publication.

In one important respect, the chartered banks encouraged thrift among the lower classes. In May 1810, the Rev. Henry Duncan, supported by his patron the Earl of Mansfield, opened a savings bank at Ruthwell in Dumfriesshire. Both the British Linen Company and Bank of Scotland had branches in Dumfries in 1810, and it was with the British Linen that the Rev. Duncan deposited the first funds and gained a rate allowing payment to the savings-bank depositors of 4 per cent. Shortly afterwards, the directors of Bank of Scotland agreed to accept a wide range of officially-sanctioned funds, whether by Parliament, the Court of Session or the

---

80 *The Three Panics*, first published in 1862, went through six editions. It was reprinted in [Richard Cobden,] *The Political Writings of Richard Cobden* (notes by F. W. Chesson), 4th edn (London: 1903), vol. ii, pp. 537–710. For the Budget discussions and Gladstone's general attitude, see Morley, *The Life of William Ewart Gladstone*, vol. ii, chs 2 and 3.
81 Much of the detail concerning the Bank Volunteers has been taken from Malcolm, *The Bank of Scotland*, especially p. 258ff.

order of a Justice or arbiter, 'and also on money deposited by or on account of any trustees' with the proviso that they be lodged for a minimum of six months. Bank of Scotland was to attract numerous savings-bank accounts, and gave advice on ledger procedures where required. By the end of the Napoleonic Wars, there were forty such schemes in Scotland.[82] In 1817, Parliament passed an Act which set out that savings-bank funds in England and Wales were to be channelled via the Bank of England to the Commissioners of the National Debt. The government was generous and legislated for a return which would give 4 per cent to depositors. However, Scottish politicians managed to persuade Parliament that savings banks north of the Border should continue to deposit their funds as the trustees wished, which usually meant with the Scottish banks, which at that time paid slightly above the guaranteed government rate. As a result, these savings banks were omitted from the Act. In 1819, Parliament passed a diluted Act for Scotland, which enjoined trustees of savings banks to register with the Justices of the Quarter Sessions. They were exempt from stamp duty and received powers to distribute deposits to heirs in accordance with Scots law. This Act did not legislate against savings-bank funds being deposited with the Scottish banks. From this time, deposit rates fell; and, after the Agreements and Understandings of May 1827, rates remained below 3 per cent for most of the next decade. Even with the premium of $\frac{1}{2}$ to 1 per cent granted by the Scottish banks, savings societies could now pay less to their savers than their counterparts in England and Wales. By 1835, Scottish savers received only 2.1 per cent compared with 3.85 per cent in England.[83] After the Reform Act, the Whigs passed legislation in 1835 which allowed savings banks, as in England, to register with the Commissioners of the National Debt.

By the second half of the nineteenth century, the Scottish savings banks had established firm roots in the industrial towns and in numerous rural centres. They attracted the better-off artisan and working-class saver both for their accessibility and for the slight advantage in deposit rate. Moreover, the savings-bank movement developed certain images of sobriety from the 'habits of wise and prudent economy' which put it close to the temperance movement and the radical wing of the Liberal Party. By 1890, some 372,920 persons held an average balance of £25 12s 5d, yet their £9,533,000 in aggregate was 10 per cent of the deposits of the Scottish banks.[84] Limits on the level of deposits were gradually raised, and the growth in professional management and auditing meant that the

82 For the background history, see M. Moss and A. Slaven, *From Ledger Book to Laser Beam. A History of the TSB in Scotland from 1810 to 1990* (Edinburgh: n.d. [1992]).
83 Ibid., p. 24.
84 Ibid.; contains a wealth of useful statistics.

early supervisory role of the main Scottish banks soon faded. Indeed, with William Meikle the actuary in the Glasgow Savings Bank from 1840 to 1903, the savings banks had the longest-serving senior manager of any nineteenth-century Scottish bank. By 1870, the Savings Bank of Glasgow was the largest in the UK. The legislation of the later nineteenth century, by increasing the total amount allowed to be deposited, began to alter the social character of the depositors in that the lower middle classes now began to use the savings banks, thereby increasing the competition for deposits for the issuing banks.[85] By 1900, deposits had reached £16,442,000 with 496,000 members (average £33 2s 6d), and by 1905 they were £18,200,000, or 18 per cent of the level of the main banks. Little of this money went to the chartered or joint-stock banks; the usual investment was in government consolidated stocks. The general importance of the movement was indicated in 1910 when, on the centenary of Duncan's bank in Ruthwell, over 300 delegates attended the celebrations, including visitors from Australia and North America.

85 Kerr, *History of Banking in Scotland*, p. 143.

CHAPTER 16

THE SENIOR BANK IN SCOTLAND, 1850–80

T HE YEARS BETWEEN 1848 and 1854 have been described as 'quiet and rather lean' for the Bank of England, and this is also a suitable view for Bank of Scotland and the Scottish system as a whole.[1] The political threat to the constitution associated with the great Chartist demonstration in April 1848, which had so worried Scottish bankers, now faded. Indeed, the movement disappeared on both sides of the Border. Even in Paisley and the radical textile burghs of the west of Scotland, the early 1850s were more stable than for many decades. The quiescence of the social situation was reinforced by the removal of the speculators of the railway exchange companies, which disappeared under a tide of recrimination and bankruptcy.[2] Bank of Scotland wound up its own ill-judged foray into this business, the British Exchange Company, in 1849. Alexander Blair and the directors remained chastened by the losses; the market price of the railway shares which they held remained below the purchase price until 1853. The tenor of the reports on trade conditions received by Blair emphasised the mood of hesitancy, and his reports to the board remained pessimistic. Although the general economic situation improved, reports of losses and bankruptcies and falls in applications for new discounts came in from many areas of the east coast; at Montrose, for example, new loans fell for several years after 1852 to levels unseen since the mid-1830s. Profits here slumped from around £1,200 per year in 1848–50 to barely enough to cover expenses.[3] The poor outcomes were the result of the phenomenon whereby some firms which managed to survive the worst of a crisis would be kept going by partners' and bank funds, only to succumb a year or two later.

1 J. H. Clapham, *The Bank of England. A History*, 2 vols (Cambridge: 1944), vol. ii, 1797–1914, p. 219.
2 S. G. Checkland, *Scottish Banking: A History, 1695–1973* (Glasgow: 1975), p. 344.
3 BS 20/2/5 (Miscellaneous papers), report on Montrose.

Not until March 1854 did a general feeling of confidence return to the board of Bank of Scotland, as Britain and France announced that they would support the ailing Ottoman Empire and duly invaded the Crimea.[4] This provided a huge demand for war materials from the industrial burghs of Scotland. For the first time in many years, the Scottish banks could confidently discount and negotiate bills on London for textiles and arma-ments. The effects on bank profits were striking. The 'sound and cautious' Dundee Banking Company, where every potential loss or expense was deducted before net profit was listed, saw the advantages of the wartime rise in linen and jute sales, with an average net profit of £11,858 in the four years before the war rising to £14,615 in 1854–5, a dip to £13,768 in the following year and a further rise to £15,764 as the last war bills were settled in 1856–7, giving a 20 per cent rise in profits.[5] Bank of Scotland saw profits pass £100,000 (after all provisions) in 1856–7 for the first time in over thirty years. The British Linen Company, the Union Bank, the Royal Bank and most other Scottish banks also saw good results. The Russian Empire had yet to build railways from its industrial and administrative centres at St Petersburg and Moscow to the Crimea. If these had existed, the war might have lasted longer and British government expenditure might have exceeded the £90 million laid out on wages and materials.

The optimistic tone to board deliberations at Bank of Scotland after 1854 was encouraged by the phenomenal expansion of the British economy and overseas trade. Exports of manufactures between the years 1844–6 and 1854–6 increased from £51.4 million to £83.1 million and total exports from £58.4 million to £102.5 million.[6] There was marked growth in France, Germany, the northern USA and in trade with Australia, Canada, India and China. A welcome new impetus to the growth of world trade came from the increase in the production of gold in California and Australia. Whereas in 1800 world output of gold had been around £4 million and probably only £1 million more by 1840, in 1848 it was £7 million and by 1855 £33 million (see Table 16.1). In 1851, Australia produced £990,000 worth of gold, itself a cause for comment, but in 1852 it despatched £10.7 million to London and in 1856 £14 million.[7] The Bank of England estimated that the gold coin which circulated in the UK soared to almost £50 million in the six years after 1851 – a rise of perhaps 30 per cent, although no-one was quite sure, as flows in and out were

4 *The Annual Register* (London: 1855), ch. 2, pp. 53–108.
5 C. W. Boase, *A Century of Banking in Dundee; being the Annual Balance Sheets of the Dundee Banking Company from 1764 to 1864*, 2nd edn (Edinburgh: 1867), balance sheets, 1850–7.
6 R. Davis, *The Industrial Revolution and British Overseas Trade* (Leicester: 1979), Table 38, pp. 88–9. There is a discussion of invisibles in A. H. Imlah, 'British Balance of Payments and Exports of Capital, 1816–1913', *Economic History Review*, 2nd series, 5 (1952–3), 208–39.
7 Boase, *A Century of Banking in Dundee*, p. 453.

Table 16.1 *World gold production (£), 1800–58*

Year	World gold production	New South Wales, Australia (gold)	World silver
1800	4000000		6000000
1830	3000000		6750000
1840	5000000		6750000
1846	6000000		6750000
1848	7000000		6750000
1849	8000000		7750000
1850	11000000		8500000
1851	14000000	990000	8500000
1852	22000000	10700000	8500000
1853	35000000	11480000	8500000
1854	34000000	9930000	8500000
1855	33000000	12660000	8500000
1856	34000000	14010000	8500000
1857	35000000	15000000	8500000
1858	34000000	14000000	8500000

Source: C. W. Boase, *A Century of Banking in Dundee*, 2nd edn (Edinburgh: 1867), p. 453.

unrecorded.[8] Demands for trade accommodation intensified, especially from the USA and Europe. One London house with a capital of only £10,000 had created by the autumn of 1857 £900,000 of credit; thirty London houses mentioned to Parliament the following year with assets together of under £3 million were liable for over £9 million.[9]

At times, more went out than came in; Britain could only absorb so much gold, and it was in the interests of trade that much should be exported again. The directors of Bank of Scotland were initially uncertain as to the consequences of this inflow, and as late as 1856 they had formed only general ideas of the effects of the increase on commodity prices, mostly culled from articles in the financial and learned press.[10] They were concerned about the likely reduction in the value of bank capital and the benefits to debtors of the depreciation of the currency.[11] There was also a difficulty in attracting new deposits; the level increased by under 10 per cent from the £4.8–£5.0 million of 1843–6 to reach only £5.16–£5.46 million a decade later (see Table 16.2). The directors remained cautious about advances, which grew by 14.5 per cent in the years 1853–6, concerned as they were that the trade cycle might be near its height and that the war might end. Yet there was unease on the board as the

8 Clapham, *Bank of England*, vol. ii, p. 225.
9 Boase, *A Century of Banking in Dundee*, p. 481.
10 BS 20/9/20 (Miscellaneous papers), (Alexander Blair,) 'On the probable effects of the discovery of the Californian and Australian gold mines', September 1856.
11 BS 20/9/12 (Miscellaneous papers), papers on gold and gold discoveries, 1850–2.

Table 16.2 Loans (on discounts and current accounts) and deposits, 1853–63, with the rates of interest received and paid thereon

	1853	1854	1855	1856	1857	1858	1859	1860	1861	1862	1863
Loans on discounts	1933000	2188000	2073000	2223000	2701000	2834000	2628000	2994000	2955000	2752000	3089000
Loans on current accounts	1469000	1545000	1588000	1693000	1787000	1783000	1675000	1655000	1826000	1739000	1640000
Total loans	3402000	3733000	3661000	3916000	4488000	4617000	4303000	4649000	4781000	4491000	4729000
Total deposits	5165000	5137000	5311000	5461000	5496000	6527000	6312000	6002000	5893000	5969000	5822000
Interest received (£)	137912	187882	181543	213072	277629	225386	182597	213008	267346	191710	218763
Interest received (%)	£4 1s 1d	£5 0s 8d	£4 19s 2d	£5 8s 9d	£6 3s 8d	£4 17s 8d	£4 4s 10d	£4 11s 8d	£5 11s 8d	£4 5s 4d	£4 12s 6d
Interest paid (£)	112115	144295	144093	176176	210209	138899	129379	132582	162564	125583	136753
Interest paid (%)	£2 3s 5d	£2 16s 2d	£2 14s 3d	£3 4s 6d	£3 16s 6d	£2 2s 6d	£2 0s 11d	£2 4s 2d	£2 15s 2d	£2 2s 0d	£2 6s 11d
Difference between interest received and paid	£1 17s 8d	£2 4s 6d	£2 4s 11d	£2 4s 3d	£2 7s 2d	£2 15s 2d	£2 3s 9d	£2 7s 6d	£2 16s 6d	£2 3s 4d	£2 5s 7d

Source: BS 20/4/12, Treasurer's reports, 'General View of Assets and Liabilities on Deposits, Loans and Cash Accounts', 1863.

new English joint-stock banks attracted business faster than the Scottish banks. In 1855, the directors began to think of a strategy to expand the business.

By this date, the hitherto very firm views about the dangers of extension of credit which had been central to the board's thinking did not look as relevant in the context of changed conditions in economic progress and overseas markets: 'the effects of the gold discoveries' were 'so likely to be permanent'.[12] A more adventurous lending and investment policy could be justified both as safe and as leading to a better return than that obtained from London and government stocks. Even the austere Alexander Blair was sufficiently impressed with the possibilities of progress, and he presented the board with ambitious plans. The underlying assumption was that the gap between the interest paid to depositors and that earned on investment and discounts would tend to remain around £1 17s per cent. This was below the basic target for the bankers' gap, which Blair had usually put at around 2 per cent between interest paid and received; this had dominated the discussions between Glasgow and Edinburgh banks in the 1830s and always proved hard to achieve. It was now considered that conditions were right to adopt a relatively adventurous course and place some of the Bank investments in Indian and railway stocks and, following the lead of the Glasgow banks, devote a higher proportion of funds to bills on London. Both would give a wider margin between the interest on deposits and income received; Blair thought that around 1 per cent was attainable. To illustrate the point, he cited an (unnamed) Scottish bank which earned £130,000 on a similar capital to Bank of Scotland compared with its own latest profits of £94,094 4s 8d; the difference, 'roughly stated', arose from the employment of £1 million of additional deposits for a 'comparatively large discount of commercial bills which when safely conducted is the most profitable investment for a Scottish bank'. The board noticed that the Glasgow banks had the advantage of boards comprising local merchants and industrialists assisted by many 'large and influential' proprietors. It was apparent from the prices of stock that 'public opinion has hitherto considered that the facility of making profit does more than compensate for the risk'. Blair and his directors agreed on £805,000 as the increase to which they could safely go for new discounts.[13] This required £500,000 in extra deposits, and with existing resources would allow another £3,505,000 to be lent on the security of bills of exchange offered in Glasgow. Should they have a separate Glasgow

---

12 BS 20/2/5 (Miscellaneous papers), papers on gold, 1855.
13 This decision is mentioned by C. W. Munn, 'Aspects of Bank Finance for Industry: Scotland 1845–1914', in R. Mitchison and P. Roebuck (eds), *Economy and Society in Scotland and Ireland 1500–1939* (Edinburgh: 1988), pp. 233–41 (p. 237).

board with an Edinburgh director as an inspector? Were assessors the best way to run this adventure, reporting direct to Edinburgh? Could they safely leave it to the Glasgow manager assisted by an inspector?

A Glasgow board was ruled out, and as an interim position the Bank confirmed the opening of three new branches in Glasgow, with the new loans negotiated by the Glasgow chief office manager and the agent at Glasgow Laurieston, both of whom would continue to report in the usual way to Edinburgh and be subject to regular inspections. For eighteen months from the summer of 1855 the Bank increased all forms of lending by nearly £800,000, in particular the buying of bills from the west of Scotland and north of England manufacturers and traders. Bills were also re-discounted from a number of English banks, and by 1857 Bank of Scotland held substantial amounts from the Liverpool Borough Bank, the Leeds Bank and the Northumberland and Durham Bank. There were also increasing numbers of bills from merchant houses in Manchester and the north of England. The board noted that the business required good training in Bank of Scotland procedures, 'an obliging turn, energy and sound judgement'; and, as this was a straightforward marketplace, 'local influence . . . may be left out of view altogether'. To support this, lending instructions were issued to managers to increase deposits by canvassing account holders at branches and also to ten new small burgh branches where agents who knew local conditions were employed to seek out money.[14] This overall policy, which was similar to that pursued by several Scottish banks, was to have some unfortunate consequences.

The change in Bank policy attracted more firms active in the American markets. In former years, American buyers had usually provided for their purchases with endorsed bills upon the UK or by credits upon one of the leading houses in London or Liverpool. But business was showing a tendency to increase the volume of acceptances of houses in North America payable in Britain where 'such houses [have] no property or resident partner at this side'. Thus the new practice 'bases each transaction upon the credit of the American house without any provision of means' in Britain. As William Simson (Bank Secretary, 1847–58) put it to Andrew Neilson, manager of Glasgow chief office, in a classic statement of banking practice:

> The character of the acceptor is a test of the prudence of the drawer, and the acceptor of a bill is the person to whom we must look mainly for payment as he has got the value out of which it should be retired. In the ordinary course his acceptances are seen by bankers in his own district or country. There must

14 BS 20/2/5 (Miscellaneous papers), papers on lending in Glasgow.

always be difficulty in getting reliable opinions of a person resident abroad, and the difficulty is increased if the person inquired about has transactions which begin and end in a distant country beyond the observation of the correspondent applied to. It is evident in such circumstances that the banking risk to be taken up on the responsibility of the indorsers must be increased considerably beyond that which ordinarily obtains; and we wish you to consider the whole matter, and say how you proposed to meet the difficulties of the case, so as to bring the practice within ordinary banking risk.[15]

Yet it was impossible to do this unless the Bank was granted security in the old manner. Some firms promised initially to deal on Scottish acceptances or short-dated London paper but instead supplied American acceptances. A. S. Henry & Co., a Manchester house involved in the US cotton trade, opened a Bank of Scotland account in 1855 on the understanding that they would offer Glasgow bills and acceptances arising from the trade between Glasgow and Manchester with occasional drafts on London. Yet, half the bills were American acceptances of nearly four months. Furthermore, 'our experience of the account amounts ... to this, that the operations are dormant when [the Bank of England rate of] interest is low and active when the rate advances', which practice adversely affected Bank of Scotland reserves in London, as their capital value invariably slipped with the advance of interest rates. Moreover, William Simson was concerned not to undercut the Bank of England rate, as this would interfere with the action of Threadneedle Street at a time 'when all banking establishments should be responding to the Bank of England, both on public and private grounds, in its attempts to maintain its reserves and so the full circulation'.[16]

There were worrying signs of over-expansion on both sides of the Atlantic. In France, the launch in 1852 of the Crédit Mobilier, the brainchild of Isaac and Émile Péreire who followed the ideas of Saint-Simon (1760–1825), a founder of French utopian socialism, provided huge amounts of credit for public concerns, industry, art and culture.[17] Its success encouraged numerous imitations across Europe, and even within the Ottoman Empire the Péreires managed to float a bank. For British industry, the advantage of war and new credit was plain: buyers went for British goods, in particular railways, engines, track, gas installations and iron plant, and of course British management, entrepreneurs and workmen. In this era, the reputation of the British and the Irish navvy for sustained hard work spread across the globe.[18]

15 BS, Uncatalogued, Branch Letter Book, 1856, pp. 122–3, W. Simson, Secretary, to Andrew Neilson, Glasgow, 4 January 1856.
16 Ibid., p. 156, 22 October 1856.
17 M. Marion, *Histoire financière de la France depuis 1715*, vol. v, 1819–1875 (Paris: 1928), pp. 342–9.
18 L. H. Jenks, *The Migration of British Capital to 1875* (New York: 1927), especially ch. 6.

The modifications to lending policy in the Glasgow area may be seen from the Quarterly List of Glasgow bill accounts, where the average limits exceeded £2,000, thirty-one in number. In the year from April 1855, Bank of Scotland increased its limits on these accounts from £605,000 to £806,000. Including bills, acceptances, cash accounts and miscellaneous credits, the actual level on these accounts exceeded £1 million. For the first four months of 1857, Bank of Scotland continued its usual policies of granting new discount facilities to suitable applicants, and allowed average advances on all facilities to exceed £100,000 for long-established customers. One account held in this way was that of Charles Tennant & Co., to whom advances rose to £123,053 in April 1857. The books also show several refusals, yet the general pattern of accommodation did not indicate anything more than the usual concern for security and proper references. About one-third was business from the north of England and the Midlands, and the rest came from mixed industry and merchant business in Scotland, overwhelmingly the Glasgow area.[19] The Glasgow chief office was granted another clerk on 23 March. The board was more cautious from early May, and advances were reduced somewhat in Glasgow and to English interests. The total lending for July 1857 was down to £974,780 for these thirty-one large accounts.[20] There had been a small rush of minor failures in America in the spring of 1857, and by mid-June news of the Indian Mutiny had reached London. By July the prices of commodities had begun to decline, especially those awaiting shipment to America, and later those for Europe. It was not however until 'about the 10th October' – the words are those of the Chancellor of the Exchequer in the House of Commons – that symptoms of the impending crisis began to appear. 'From that day a perceptible deterioration began',[21] and the country was on the threshold of a financial and economic crisis comparable with that of 1847. On 27 August the 'disgraceful failure' of the Ohio Life & Trust Co. had shown liabilities of $7 million, and during the next month there were numerous bank closures along the eastern and south-eastern coasts of the USA.[22] Some £80 million of American securities were estimated to be held by British investors, and in the previous year, 1856, between a quarter and a fifth of all British exports had gone to the USA.

19 There were a number of large cash account and bill facilities; for example, on 27 January 1857, Peter McIntosh, the Glasgow tanners, received a facility whose 'average' was set at £16,000; Thomas Corbett, a Glasgow merchant, £25,000; A. D. McLaurin of Bradford, £7,000, W. & A. McUrie, Glasgow engineers, a cash account for £5,000; W. Thomason & Co. of Glasgow, £10,000; Anderson & Co., Glasgow warehousemen, a bill limit of £30,000; and J. & R. Cogans, cotton spinners and power loom manufacturers of Glasgow, an increase in their maximum average bill limit to £80,000.
20 For examples of these accounts, see Statistical Appendix, Table A19.
21 *Hansard*, 3rd series, vol. 148, col. 146, 4 December 1857.
22 W. T. C. King, *History of the London Discount Market* (London: 1936), p. 197; for a chronological account of the crisis as seen from London, see Clapham, *Bank of England*, vol. ii, pp. 226–34.

The outflow of bullion from the Bank of England between 10 October and 18 November reduced the total held there from £10,110,000 to £6,484,000, while the reserve of notes declined from about £4,500,000 to £1,400,000. On 8 October, the Bank of England had raised its discount rate to 6 per cent, to 7 per cent four days later, and at the end of the next week to 8 per cent. Alexander Blair, not unnaturally, had become increasingly worried about the general situation, and on 13 October he presented to the board of Bank of Scotland a 3,500-word report.[23] His memorandum was the presentation of a highly competent and conscientious senior banking official, although there was no appreciation of the seriousness of the situation in the west of Scotland and in Liverpool, the two areas most clearly affected by the American news that was coming across the Atlantic, and the economic intelligence available to him seems to have been somewhat parochial. After a perfunctory reference to the critical state of affairs in general, Blair then moved straight into the negative influences on the Bank, these being certain of the highly competitive practices of the joint-stock banks, the overbanking in Scotland with the proliferation of branches, and the general unpredictability of interest rates.[24] He reminded the board, referring to the financial crises of November 1840 and October 1847, that 'the principle of one-third Reserve was laid down as a rule in the conduct of the Bank's affairs', and his main concern was to alert the directors to the various possibilities that might occasion an excessive demand upon the Bank's resources. In eight months, deposits at Bank of Scotland had fallen £323,000 although advances were up £458,000; this caused a decrease in reserve of £756,000, 'or about £100,000 a month' largely for loans through Glasgow. Another £594,775 remained undrawn on credits agreed; and since, in every crisis, depositors withdrew funds, 'such a demand might reach £500,000 to £800,000'. Yet there were only reserves of £1,530,536 in convertible stocks and £610,000 inconvertible. Blair reminded the board that the Bank of England would not favour 'any operation on our permanent credit with them, unless they suit their convenience at the time they are required'. The main resolution underwrote the cautiousness with which Blair was proposing to operate in the current situation:

> It is now proposed that the Directors admit the principle of a simultaneous reduction in the investments of the Bank whether Government Securities or Scottish investments in the manner and on the occasions indicated so far as regards Discounts, and for the future until the order be rescinded no Cash Credit be granted for a larger sum than £10,000 – any further advance being optional

23 See Appendix 9a.
24 For the growth of Bank of Scotland's branch network, see Appendix 8.

to the Bank, whatever the nominal credit may be – or that the money be lent absolutely without option on sufficient security. Also that a general limit be placed to advances of this description. The loss on Cash Accounts is small, but there is no reason why this advantage should not be enjoyed without the present concomitant disadvantage.

Blair then remarked that the Bank's practice in the matter of credits would obviously be introduced gradually, and he ended his report with a brief analysis of the relations with London, which were profitable if sensibly conducted; but English bills outside London, or the acceptances of American houses, would not be countenanced.

As the Chancellor of the Exchequer insisted in the later House of Commons debate, the crisis of 1857 was not connected with matters internal to the UK, but 'the almost exclusive cause of the commercial distress was the derangement of the American trade'.[25] It was not the whole picture, although the first main indicator of the crisis in Britain was the failure of the Liverpool Borough Bank on 27 October. The previous day, the Bank of England, which knew what was likely to happen, had offered £1,500,000 with the proviso that the bank should 'cease to transact new business and liquidate its affairs'.[26] Several mercantile houses in Glasgow had already failed, of which Macdonald & Co., Monteith & Co. and Wallace & Co. were the most important, all deeply indebted to the Western Bank. On 7 November, the large firm of Dennistoun & Co. stopped payment. It had offices in London, Liverpool, Glasgow, New York and New Orleans, and there were debts of nearly £2 million owing from American firms which it was impossible at this time to recover. Dennistoun's had also lost £300,000 by the failure of the Liverpool Borough Bank. The firm's commercial and financial basis was sound in the medium term, and as expected it paid all its liabilities in full, with interest. The Union Bank of Scotland was closely involved with Dennistoun's, and its temporary stoppage considerably increased the anxieties within Glasgow.

The reserve position of the Western Bank had long given a valid cause for concern. In the crisis of October 1847, it was unable to gather sufficient funds from the exchange in London to support demands there, and the Bank of England granted a temporary facility for bills to a maximum of £300,000.[27] In fact, in early November 1847, William Cotton, Governor of the Bank of England, suggested that this was an opportune time for Bank of Scotland, together with the Royal Bank and the British Linen,

25 *Hansard*, 3rd series, vol. 148, col. 152, 4 December 1857.
26 Clapham, *Bank of England*, vol. ii, p. 228.
27 A. W. Kerr, *History of Banking in Scotland*, 4th edn (1926), p. 220 and ch. 21; Clapham, *Bank of England*, vol. ii, p. 191, for contemporary criticism of Bank of England policy.

to organise a takeover of the Western.[28] In the event, the negotiations involving the three Edinburgh banks turned towards their own merger. In any case, on the board of the Western Bank and among the proprietors were many successful industrial entrepreneurs from the west of Scotland, and they were hostile to any such proposal.

From the crisis of 1847, the Western carried over from year to year a growing volume of bad and doubtful debt, a position concealed from its proprietors, although Donald Smith, the general manager, appears to have contained the potential damage. In October 1852, the directors appointed John Taylor as manager. Unfortunately, his main policy was to advance funds of the bank 'in the most reckless manner' to a group of companies associated with the American and Australian trades.[29] By July 1857, the Western directors were faced, on Taylor's admission, with 'hopelessly' bad debts of £452,000 in addition to a list of doubtful debts on the USA held by four Glasgow firms whose bills the Western had discounted.

John Taylor was dismissed on 15 October 1857. Western Bank credit dried up, and on 19 October the board asked Bank of Scotland for up to £300,000 on the security of commercial bills and a similar sum from the Royal Bank and the British Linen. The Glasgow office of Bank of Scotland estimated the Western need at £1.2 million, half of which was to cover 'very imprudent advances' to America. Indeed, it had been admitted by the Western directors, wrote Blair, 'that their system of business has been more like that of a pawnbroker than of a banker'. Bank of Scotland arranged with the Union, the Royal Bank, the Commercial and the National for an initial safety net of £600,000 on 29 October on condition that the Western be wound up.[30] But, on the same day, an irresponsible article appeared in *The Times* to the effect that the Western was to be wound up, and from the following day there was an inevitable drain of deposits. The Bank of England was asked by the Western Bank for support on 26 October, but this was refused. From earlier in the month, the Bank of England had been pressed for gold from the north of England, Scotland and Ireland, and, although it was apparent that a part of this went to support credit in England, it refused, as its support would have involved more gold; should these depositors 'in a moment of distress . . . take their all out of the bank [they] would retain it in Scotland and it would not re-circulate and find its level in the general circulation of England'. In the event, the bank sent £2 million by 12 November, £1 million alone

28 BS 20/2/10, William Cotton to Alexander Blair, 23 November 1847.
29 For details of the Western Bank collapse from a contemporary view, see Boase, *A Century of Banking in Dundee*, pp. 493–9; the Bank of England was aware of some aspects of the problem. *The Times* of 11 November 1857 carried sharp criticisms of the management of the Western Bank.
30 BS 1/21/10, Private and Confidential Letter Book, 1857.

to Scotland in the previous week. The adverse consequences, in times of crisis, of the panic caused by small savers withdrawing their funds was a point of criticism made much of by the London press.[31]

The Bank of England minimum discount rate had risen steadily from 6 per cent in October to 8 per cent a fortnight later and 9 per cent on 5 November, an action which brought a petition of disapproval from the Glasgow Chamber of Commerce. On Monday 9 November, the bank rate went to 10 per cent, and at 2 p.m. the Western Bank closed its doors, as did the City of Glasgow Bank the following day, although it was to reopen five weeks later. Led by Alexander Blair, the Edinburgh banks and the Union Bank implored the Chancellor, Sir George Cornewall Lewis, to suspend the Bank Charter Act of 1844 and allow Bank of England notes to be used as legal tender in Scotland, to obviate the need to send more gold north.[32] The clamour at the Glasgow bank offices raised the question of public order, and on 11 November seven officers and 220 men of the Rifle Brigade were despatched from Edinburgh Castle to Glasgow and a detachment of Lancers based at Piershill barracks sent to Hamilton.

The appeal to the Chancellor made little impression. After a discussion with Sheffield Neave, Governor of the Bank of England, Bonamy Dobree his deputy, Thomas Weguelin the immediate past Governor and James Wilson, editor of *The Economist* and financial secretary to the Treasury, Sir George Cornewall Lewis rejected the request to make Bank of England notes legal tender. On 12 November, the bank came to the view that a letter authorising a temporary suspension was required, if it was thought appropriate, and Lord Palmerston (the Prime Minister) and the Chancellor signed the authorisation later that day.[33] There was a tacit agreement by the Chancellor that Bank of Scotland could organise an extra issue of notes up to the limit of that of the suspended banks (the Western and the City of Glasgow) against a deposit of government securities with the Bank of England, although the cabinet deferred a formal endorsement of this.

The Glasgow magistrates issued a proclamation urging their citizens not to press the banks for payment and to take the notes of all banks; and on Wednesday 11 November they distributed an order to their rate-collectors

---

31 Ibid.; *The Times*, 28 and 29 October and 12 November 1857; *Report from the Select Committee appointed to inquire into the Operation of the Bank Act of 1844 and of the Bank Acts for Ireland and Scotland of 1845 . . . together with the Proceedings of the Committee, Minutes of Evidence, Appendix and Index*, 1 July 1858, (381) vol. v: evidence of the Bank of England, p. 4, §27.
32 BS 1/21/10, Private and Confidential Letter Book, Memorial to Chancellor of the Exchequer, 11 November 1857.
33 Clapham, *Bank of England*, vol. ii, pp. 230–2; BS 20/10/57 (Miscellaneous papers), Secretary's Private Letters, Sir George Clerk to Alexander Blair on Cabinet discussions; BS 20/2/11, Papers on Banking Topics, Memorial to Chancellor of the Exchequer, 11 November 1857. The letter is reprinted in *Report . . . into the Operation of the Bank Acts*, 1 July 1858, (381) vol. v, p. x, §24; see also *The Economist*, 14 November 1857.

that they should accept all notes offered to them. On this and the following day, large remittances of gold arrived from London, taken to the banks in wagons accompanied by strong police escorts. James Robertson, the manager of the Union Bank of Scotland, told the Select Committee on the Bank Acts that while the notes of the Western Bank had been refused by some banks on the Tuesday, in the course of Wednesday they had begun once again to be accepted, and that in his opinion the panic had come to an end by 2 p.m. on Wednesday afternoon. This was the day before the government had authorised the Bank of England to suspend the Bank Charter Act of 1844 and thereby exceed its statutory fiduciary limit on note issues.[34] Pressure to do this had been very strong in London, as it was difficult to discount a bill except at the Bank of England.[35] The monetary phase of the crisis was over by the end of the month, by which time none of the extra notes which the Bank of England had issued were in circulation. 'There never was a more severe crisis', *The Economist* wrote on 5 January 1858, 'nor a more rapid recovery'.[36] It was a banking crisis for which the Report of the Select Committee of 1858 blamed the Liverpool Borough Bank, the Northumberland and Durham Bank, the Western Bank and two City of London discount houses. Each had suspended payments in 1847 and recovered because of the assistance from the Bank of England; in 1857 their inherent unsoundness was 'the natural, the inevitable result of their own misconduct'.[37]

The misconduct to which the report referred included the creation of fictitious credits by means of accommodation bills and re-discounting with the brokers on the London market without reference to the quality of the bills involved. The report discussed in detail the malpractices of the three banks named, and the elaboration of the internal history of the Western Bank was widely publicised in England, where the antipathy among many banking groups, including the Bank of England, to the practices of

34 *Report . . . into the Operation of the Bank Acts*, 1 July 1858, (381) vol. v, p. xiii. James Robertson, general manager of the Union Bank of Glasgow, gave evidence to the Committee (paragraphs 4,376 to 4,873) on the day-to-day situation in Glasgow; *The Economist*, 14 November 1857.
35 The Chancellor of the Exchequer made much of this cessation of discounting in the City of London, except by the Bank of England, in his speech in the House of Commons on the Bill indemnifying the setting-aside of the 1844 Act: *Hansard*, 3rd series, vol. 148, col. 155, 4 December 1857; Clapham, *Bank of England*, vol. ii, pp. 226–35.
36 Quoted in Clapham, *Bank of England*, vol. ii, p. 238; the opinion of *The Economist* was echoed by Friedrich Engels, who worked in the family cotton firm in Manchester: 'I must say . . . that the way the mass of overproduction which brought about the crisis has been absorbed is by no means clear to me; such a rapid ebb after such a violent flood tide has never occurred before': K. Marx and F. Engels, *Correspondence, 1846–1895. A Selection with Commentary and Notes* (London: 1934), p. 116. In fact, the trade depression lasted a good deal longer than the financial crisis: J. H. Clapham, *An Economic History of Modern Britain* [vol. ii], *Free Trade and Steel, 1850–1886* (Cambridge: 1932), p. 372.
37 *Report . . . into the Operation of the Bank Acts*, 1 July 1858, (381) vol. v, p. xxi, §§52–3; there is a summary of the report in T. E. Gregory (ed.), *Select Statutes, Documents and Reports Relating to British Banking, 1832–1928*, vol. ii, 1847–1928 (Oxford: 1929), pp. 107–23.

Scottish banking was very strongly felt and much commented upon. J. S. Fleming, who replaced John Taylor at the Western Bank on 15 October, had found large-scale debts that had been passed off in the published balance sheets as good assets. The Select Committee Report noted:

> The modes in which this kind of disguise can be accomplished will perhaps be best understood by stating the manner in which a debt called Scarth's debt . . . was disposed of. That debt amounted to £120,000 and it ought to have appeared among the protested bills. It was, however, divided into four or five open credit accounts, bearing the names of the acceptors of Scarth's bills. These accounts were debited with the amounts of their respective acceptances, and insurances were effected on the lives of the debtors to the extent of £75,000. On these assurances £33,000 have since been paid as premiums by the bank itself. These all now stand as assets in the books. Though this substitution took place in 1848, yet down to the time when Mr Fleming's examinations began to bring to light the true state of affairs, the six directors appear to have regarded these sums as part of the available property of the shareholders. This being the actual state of the accounts, the dividend was raised in 1854 from seven to eight per cent, and in 1856 to 9. Nine per cent was the dividend in June 1857, at which date a very slight acquaintance with the books must have led to the strongest suspicion, not to say to the clear conviction, that for some time a considerable portion of the capital had been lost.[38]

Deception was not limited to the Western Bank. One of the leading mercantile companies with which it dealt – Macdonald & Co. of London and Glasgow – began life as a muslin manufacturer supplying the British and American markets, but at some point in its history started to draw fictitious bills and represent them as 'genuine business transactions'. The firm employed people, on commission, 'to put their names to fictitious bills which were then discounted', mostly in Glasgow. When the company failed in October 1857, it was indebted to the Western Bank for £422,000.[39]

All these matters have a direct relevance to the motives of Bank of Scotland at this time and how the Bank has been seen by historians. The collapse of the Western Bank provoked bitter recriminations against the Edinburgh banking establishment from various groups and newspapers in Glasgow. There had always been rivalry between the two cities, and most historians of Scottish banking who have commented on the banking crisis of 1857 have suggested, in varying degrees of criticism, that the Edinburgh banks could have done more to succour the Western Bank. One historian has felt able to suggest that 'the Edinburgh banks took the opportunity

---

38 *Report . . . into the Operation of the Bank Acts*, 1 July 1858, (381) vol. v, p. xviii, §48.
39 Ibid., p. xii, §30.

to eliminate the risky as well as formidable Western Bank', and singled out Alexander Blair as playing a central part in the elimination.[40] The sequence of events was described by J. S. Fleming, who was appointed a liquidator of the Western and in 1871 was selected as general manager of the Royal Bank, in his evidence before the 1857 Select Committee and in the correspondence between the Western Bank and the Edinburgh banks.[41] There are certain differences regarding the chronology, and the various offers made to the Western, in Bank of Scotland papers, but general concord on the salient points.

The Western Bank made its first approach to Alexander Blair on 17 October and a second, more urgent, four days later.[42] Fleming asked that the Scottish banks refrain from encouraging the withdrawal of deposits from the Western Bank. Blair suggested that the correct course was an appeal to the Bank of England; and, on its refusal to offer assistance, the Edinburgh banks on Monday 26 October offered the Western Bank £500,000 in consols on condition that the Western Bank 'shall dissolve and wind up the concern'. The Western Bank refused this condition, among other reasons because the directors lacked authority in the matter, and the Clydesdale and City of Glasgow banks appealed to Edinburgh to withdraw this particular condition, which was done. On 29 October the initial safety net for £600,000 was in place, but at the end of the month a further loan requested by Fleming was refused, as the scale of the debts was now much clearer. The Clydesdale Bank had already provided a further £100,000 on its own account. The situation in Glasgow and the surrounding region was made much worse by the article in *The Times* (29 October) stating that the advances given by the Edinburgh banks were linked with the condition that the Western Bank was to be wound up; and, although a denial was later made, a great deal of further uncertainty had been engendered. There were also tentative discussions about a merger between the Western and the Clydesdale which very quickly came to nothing. The stoppage of payments by Dennistoun & Co. on 7 November inevitably increased the

40 The quotation is from N. Tamaki, *The Life Cycle of the Union Bank of Scotland 1830–1954* (Aberdeen: 1983), p. 69. His estimation of Alexander Blair and the role of Bank of Scotland was drawn, in part, from R. H. Campbell, 'Edinburgh Bankers and the Western Bank of Scotland', *Scottish Journal of Political Economy*, 2 (1955), 133–48, wherein the analysis emphasised the historical importance of the liberal lending policy of the Western Bank to meet the expanding needs of industry and trade. Checkland, *Scottish Banking*, pp. 466–9, recognised the problems involved with the lending policy of the Western Bank, but still suggested that 'it has been implied' that the Glasgow banks 'gave much more support to the regional economy' (p. 469). Tamaki, whose book has a foreword by Checkland, was more severe in his estimate of the Edinburgh banks.
41 *Report . . . into the Operation of the Bank Acts*, 1 July 1858, (381) vol. v: evidence, paragraphs 5,343–571, 8 June 1858; Kerr, *History of Banking in Scotland*, p. 228.
42 This may be the reference in Bank of Scotland papers to the approach on 19 October, or it may be another approach, not mentioned by J. S. Fleming; BS 1/517/6, Transactions with other Scottish banks (1857 Crisis).

fears of other commercial failures, and on the same day Fleming wrote to Lawrence Robertson of the Royal Bank informing him that the Western Bank was likely to close on Monday 9 November in the absence of any further help. For the first two days after closure, until about lunchtime on Wednesday, the notes of the Western Bank were refused. Tuesday was the day of widespread and general panic, but by the Wednesday after-noon it was beginning to subside. Fleming, in his evidence to the Select Committee, emphasised the refusal to accept the Western Bank's notes as a factor which 'greatly aggravated' the crisis of confidence, and he repeated this conclusion in his historical sketch of Scottish banking published in 1877.[43] It is a reasonable argument, but so is the contrary. Many banks closed their doors and then reopened: the City of Glasgow Bank, which had suspended payments on 10 November, reopened on 14 December. This for the Western was not seriously considered, as it was the desperate condition of its internal accounts that made a recovery impossible.

The Report of the Select Committee set down the details of the malpractices in clear and incontrovertible fashion; in any case, the evidence of J. S. Fleming is devastating in its fundamental criticisms of his predecessor's banking practices. So was the report of a committee of shareholders, reprinted by the Select Committee. Almost at the beginning of its analysis, the report stated in categoric terms that 'the Committee came to the resolution that a successful resuscitation of the affairs of the Bank was at present impossible'; and, since its work would therefore be confined to 'mercantile details', the committee, composed of businessmen, did not consider it necessary to call for additional professional assistance. Its general conclusion was that if the policies of Donald Smith, who retired in October 1852, had been continued, the affairs of the bank might have shown gradual improvement; but the appointment of John Taylor as general manager had been disastrous. His management was considered dangerous and reckless, and his judgement of creditworthiness faulty; and when he left the bank, its whole financial condition was in a disorganised state. The committee's opinion was that the directors of the bank had been much to blame in negligently trusting, without sufficient inquiry or examination, the statements of the managers.[44]

The committee exonerated Fleming, who had only just taken over the management a month before the bank closed, and thanked him for his full cooperation. The report was signed by the eight Glasgow businessmen appointed by the shareholders, and dated 17 December

43 *Report . . . into the Operation of the Bank Acts*, 1 July 1858, (381) vol. v: evidence, paragraph 3,598; J. S. Fleming, *Scottish Banking: A Historical Sketch with Notes and an Appendix*, 3rd edn (Edinburgh: 1877), p. 39.
44 See Appendix 9b.

1857; and it remains a further testimony which explains the hesitations of the Edinburgh bankers during the days of the Western Bank's crisis and downfall. Alexander Blair was clearly aware of the malpractices of the Taylor administration, and it explains his reference, cited above, to the Western Bank's system of business as 'more like that of a pawnbroker than of a banker'.[45] Once the liquidators began their toils, it gradually became apparent that the position of the Western Bank was actually much worse and understated by the shareholders' report.[46] The refusal of the Edinburgh banks – with Alexander Blair obviously a major influence – to accept the notes of the Western Bank for two days after its closure may still be a debatable question, but it must be reiterated that the financial crisis in Glasgow was over by Wednesday 11 November, following the large-scale movements of gold into the city and the acceptance of all notes by the banks and the municipality.[47]

Beyond the information available to the shareholders' committee and to the liquidators, the banking crisis in Scotland was far worse than was realised by the public at this time, or by these two groups of investigators, or by most of the financial circles in London. By mid-December 1857, reserves at Bank of Scotland had dwindled close to the point where the Bank of England would have to be asked to cover for payments and for bad debts in London. The costs of support by Bank of Scotland for the Western Bank totalled £413,500 (mostly as £85,000 cash and £307,000 placed as deposits), and for the City of Glasgow the Bank held £20,000 worth of drafts, £75,000 of notes not exchanged, and £127,000 of deposits. To the Edinburgh and Glasgow Bank, which would have closed its doors without support, Bank of Scotland granted £72,500 in cash, and to the Union Bank the board gave £175,000 of securities immediately convertible in London against which bills could be retired. Thus the total granted by Bank of Scotland came to £883,000 by the first week in December. In addition, Bank of Scotland, in conjunction with the British Linen and the Commercial Bank, held £400,000 of Union Bank bills of exchange for presentation in London to Glyn, Mills, Currie & Co., but refrained from so doing. Glyns also provided an additional credit of £200,000 in London.[48]

Bank of Scotland was affected by its own losses as well. The crisis of 1857 led to debts on past-due bills on which nothing could be secured, and gold imported from London cost £858,000 of its London reserves. There

---

45 BS 1/21/10, Private and Confidential Letter Book, 20 October 1857.
46 See Appendix 9c, John Gifford, *How to Mismanage a Bank*, which compares the House of Commons Select Committee report, the Committee of Shareholders' report and the liquidators' report.
47 *The Economist*, 14 November 1857, found this the only serious criticism to level at the Scottish bankers.
48 These figures are based on BS 20/1/19 (Miscellaneous papers), 'Report on the Western Bank crisis and its results for Bank of Scotland', 10 September 1858.

was £246,000 of debts owing from the Northumberland and Durham Bank (mainly for industrial companies in north-east England) and also a loss of £130,000 on stock values in the remaining London reserves.[49] In total, by the close of 1857, Bank of Scotland had paid out £2,173,000 from its reserves; if new cash and note deposits and gold paid in by customers of £500,000 had not been forthcoming in November and December, most of which went to shore up the London reserves, then the total reserves of the Bank would have been only £300,000 by the start of 1858. It was thus evident that a reserve equal to half the liabilities of Bank of Scotland's balance sheet at the start of 1857 was barely sufficient. Both the British Linen and the Royal Bank also suffered sharp reductions in their reserves after loans to the Glasgow joint-stock banks and by losses on ordinary business.

The eventual losses carried by the shareholders of the Western encompassed the whole of their subscribed paid-up capital of £1,500,000, all their reserves and cash and another £1,089,577 called to pay uncovered liabilities. A popular version of their findings, by John Gifford, later Chief Cashier of the National Bank of Scotland, was published in 1859. There can have been few interested parties who, after reading this, would have thought that the Western Bank could have been rescued. The City of Glasgow Bank reopened on 14 December after Bank of Scotland and the Royal Bank had agreed to hold its notes until informed that an exchange would be convenient. In 1860, the City of Glasgow Bank wrote down its paid-up capital by £74,541 to £670,869. Both the Union Bank and the Edinburgh and Glasgow would also have closed their doors had the Edinburgh banks not provided support; and the latter was eventually wound up. The influence of Sir Adam Hay of Forbes & Co., an original member of the Edinburgh board of the Union Bank, and the long-standing cooperation between Forbes & Co. and the other Edinburgh banks, undoubtedly helped the latter in their decision to support the Union Bank, heavily involved as it was with the Dennistoun companies. The Union Bank directors adopted a more severe approach to new business after the crisis.[50]

Bank of Scotland's response to trade and industry during the crisis was to increase its monthly discounts of bills from the usual £1.8–£2 million,

49 BS 20/12/13 (Miscellaneous papers); advances via the Northumberland and Durham Bank included £10,000 to the Wallsend Iron Co. (never recovered), £10,000 to Sir W. G. Armstrong and Partners (paid in 1862), and £25,000 to the Liverpool Borough Bank (paid in 1861).
50 See below, Chapter 18; Tamaki, *Life Cycle of the Union Bank*, pp. 69–74, 76–9. The liquidators of the Western Bank first appointed were Robert Lumsden, inspector, Bank of Scotland; James Simpson Fleming, secretary's clerk, later the Bank's law accountant, then a writer in Glasgow; Samuel Raleigh, accountant in Edinburgh, by 1862 the manager at Scottish Widows Fund; and Charles Gairdner, accountant in Glasgow, by 1862 the manager of the Union Bank.

typical from 1854 to early 1857, to figures in excess of £2.5 million by the end of September and to £3.25 million by November (see Figure 16.3). The carry-over of past-due bills represented a peak on an otherwise flat landscape: the typical monthly pattern barely reached £80,000 for 1851–7 (see Figure 16.4). There was a huge rise in December 1857, and from May to September 1858 it went above £300,000. Overdrafts on cash accounts showed a subdued movement for several years before the crisis, typically between £1.4 and £1.75 million, but in late November 1857 they climbed above £2 million and went to £2.5 million the following month (see Figure 16.5). The division of the Western Bank's branch network among the other banks guaranteed the funds of its depositors and involved Bank of Scotland staff in a huge amount of extra work as they sifted the sound from the speculative. They even worked on Sundays. Although there were delays in the discounting of bills and provision of cash accounts while security was arranged and risks assessed, by January 1858 no business which was still open and which had been with the Western was denied accommodation. The liability on these accounts owing from the Western was slowly paid off as calls were made on its shareholders and bills fell due.

The crisis at the Western Bank came in the midst of the Parliamentary Select Committee on the working of the Bank Acts, which opened in the summer of 1857 and resumed after the Western Bank failure. At the earlier hearings, the views of the Edinburgh bankers, represented by Alexander Blair, had had a marginal influence on members. By contrast, there was a coherence to the evidence given by the directors of the Bank of England that in their view the 1844 and 1845 Acts had 'acted for the public', and where modification was suggested it was towards tighter controls; Sheffield Neave even asked that the total issue of country banks be covered by gold.[51] The former were the first to give evidence, and supplied the most significant and well-argued appendices to the final report. As Neave explained, the 1844 Bank Charter Act

> has been productive of great advantages and has fully answered the main purposes for which it was devised, *viz*, the securing the convertibility of the note circulation generally, the fixing certain impassable limits to all issues whereby insolvency has been so much less frequent; the following out of the only true principle, that the fluctuations of the currency should correspond with and be to the like amount that they would have been had it been purely metallic.

The 1845 Scottish and Irish Acts were dismissed; 'doubtless they are defective and wanting in assimilation with that for England in respect to notes

---

51 *Report from the Select Committee on the Bank Acts, together with the Proceedings of the Committee, Minutes of Evidence, Appendix and Index*, Part I, *Report and Evidence*, 30 July 1857, (220) session 2, vol. x: evidence of Weguelin and Sheffield Neave, sections 160, 170, 177, 214, 215.

Figure 16.3 *Monthly state of bills discounted, January 1851 to December 1860*

Source: BS 1/71, State of deposits, loans, investments and circulation.

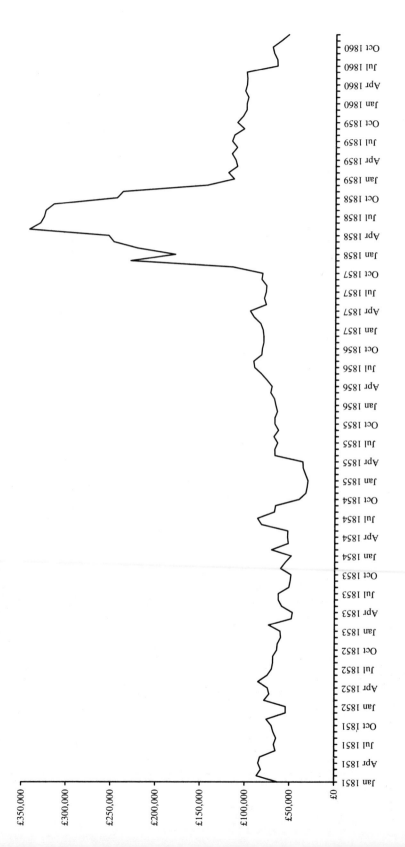

Figure 16.4 Monthly state of bills past due, January 1851 to December 1860

Source: BS 1/71, State of deposits, loans, investments and circulation.

Figure 16.5 *Monthly state of loans on current accounts, January 1851 to December 1860*

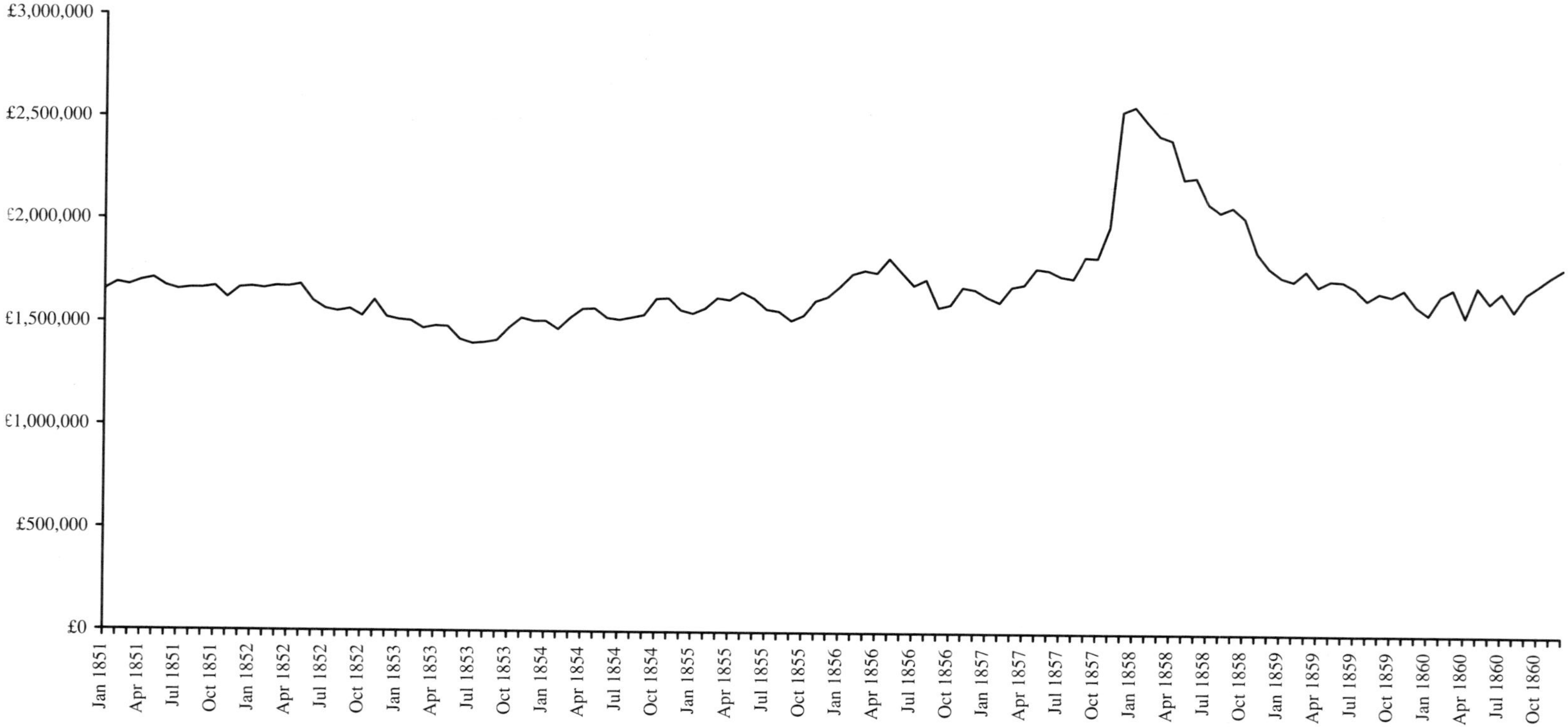

Source: BS 1/71, State of deposits, loans, investments and circulation.

under £5', for which gold was demanded in the event of discredit, which experience had shown occurred 'at the most inconvenient moments'. The Scottish paper caused a not insignificant drain and was to be suppressed altogether, with Bank of England notes provided as legal tender.[52] Some directors criticised the introduction into London joint-stock banking of the Scottish practice of interest on deposits at call and short notice, 'as depositors in the event of a monetary crisis will demand payment when they would not sell their own securities'.[53]

By contrast, the evidence of the Scottish banks was muted. The British Linen and the Royal Bank confined their written evidence to complete support for the 1845 Act. Even Alexander Blair came close to grudging recognition of its worth; while he would not support the currency-school theory, it had proved useful by 'enforcing self-reliance and the mainte-nance of reserves upon bankers and merchants'. He briefly advanced his theory that, as the total capital and deposits of the Scottish system were around £63 million and the gross circulation was not above £4 million,

> such a circulation so managed as to be a sufficient medium for the operations connected with the large trading means of the Scottish banks, proves that the regulation of the advances of capital, not of the circulation, is the correct rule for the purpose of avoiding violent fluctuations.[54]

The Clydesdale and the Western both requested an increase in their authorised circulation, and all five unincorporated banks asked for char-ters. The Union Bank expected no less: its board had recently discovered that the foundation of the private bank of Sir William Forbes could be traced as far back as 1695, a find of which they were suitably proud. The Bank of England ignored the evidence from the Scottish bankers.

By the time the Select Committee resumed deliberations on 15 Feb-ruary 1858, there was little support among English MPs, the government benches and London banking circles for an extension of banknote issue not tied to gold, or indeed for any other Scottish idea about how to run a banking system. The Scots had proved unreliable in a crisis. The drain of gold was particularly irksome, and Gladstone had already summed up the widespread view on 4 December 1857:

> That £2,000,000 of gold should have been sent to Scotland to enable people in that country to go on with a system of investing their capital in securities, instead of employing gold which would not be profitable to them, was indeed

---

52 Ibid., part 2, Appendix and Index.
53 Ibid., p. 8. Few sold securities at times of crisis because of the fall in market quotations.
54 Ibid., part 2, Appendix and Index, written evidence from Blair, Appendix 41.

a singular state of things. It was, no doubt, extremely satisfactory to them, but I hope the intellect of England is not so entirely in the background, but that they understand at whose expense this has been done. As an explanation of the present state of things I may say that no doubt the system that exists in Scotland is an extremely cheap and easy system of living for a private individual who can prevail on his friends in that way to pay his debts.[55]

The Times excelled itself in response to the petition for an increase in banknotes not covered by gold:

An attack upon our currency system from the representatives of a concern which with eight millions of British capital entrusted to its care has brought itself to bankruptcy by fostering a set of fraudulent traders to the damage of all legitimate merchants is scarcely an event to injure that system in the eyes of the public.[56]

In 1864, Charles Boase listed no fewer than thirty-four separate points of criticism raised by English commentators from the crisis.[57] It did not matter that the Scottish banks had investments in London against just such a crisis. There were more measured tones. *The Economist* reported a plan, 'which we have reason to believe was well considered', for the issue of £1 and £2 notes, 'inasmuch as notes of a lower denomination would have answered all the purposes of gold coins both in England and Scotland'. How well considered is immaterial, as the plates were not ready, and with the letter authorising suspension a similar result was achieved.[58] Further, the 1844 Bank Charter Act enabled the Bank of England to make up a lapsed note issue 'by an additional issue upon Government securities', and in the 1845 Irish Act the Bank of Ireland was enabled to do the same. The failure to legislate for this in the 1845 Scottish Act was, noted *The Economist*, a *casus omissus*, and it suggested reform on similar lines to those suggested by the Scottish bankers.

The effect of the crisis and the report and evidence from the Select Committee on the Bank Acts had a long-lasting effect on morale at Bank of Scotland. Alexander Blair was thoroughly depressed by the criticism made before the Select Committee about the Scottish system. He felt that the support given by Bank of Scotland in the winter of 1857–8 to the

---

55 *Hansard*, 3rd series, col. 178, 4 December 1857; report in *The Times*, 5 December 1857. C. W. Boase, *A Century of Banking in Dundee*, p. 492, also singled out Gladstone's theory and noted his famous retort, misquoting it as: 'The intellect of England is in abeyance if it does not see at whose expense this is done'.

56 *The Times*, 12 November 1857; The Scottish legal system was noted as another impediment to sound finance.

57 Boase, *Banking in Dundee*, pp. 501–3. *The Economist* was more sympathetic to the Scottish banks, as were Glyn, Mills, Currie & Co., and Coutts & Co.

58 *The Economist*, 14 November 1857.

system as a whole had not been appreciated; if the board had followed the principle of selfishness and self-reliance enshrined in the Bank Charter Act, the narrow interests of Bank of Scotland proprietors would have been better served.[59] Moreover, there was 'no valid reason for the assumption that in the course of a few years a similar crisis will not again produce similar effects in Scotland'. Confidence in the Scottish banks had been shaken, their system of auditing and accounting was found wanting, and shareholders were now fearful over their legal liabilities. The conclusion drawn from the experience of the last twenty years was that the system did not seem equal 'to the risk of these recurring emergencies'. His remedy was a national establishment, as suggested in September 1846, with a merger of the three senior banks to form a Bank of England in Scotland; but nothing resulted.[60]

In April 1858, Benjamin Disraeli, then Chancellor of the Exchequer, was asked to consider the transfer by the liquidators of the Western Bank of their note issue, but he refused and insisted that it should lapse. Gladstone ruled likewise in 1864.[61] In 1861, the Treasury decided to cut the number of days allowed for the remittance of tax money from the six Scottish banks which carried the London trade from seventeen with three days' grace to ten days. In vain did the banks plead that they saved the government the expense of direct collection and paid interest on credit balances. The Treasury knew that the cash flow was a significant benefit to the Scots and that cutting the time for remittance would not stop their receipt of the collections.[62]

By September 1858, the directors of Bank of Scotland could draw some consolation from the fact that as 'far as the business of the Bank is concerned' the results of the crisis were 'attended with considerable benefit'.[63] Deposits had risen by nearly 20 per cent from £5.5 million in 1856–7 to £6.5 million the following year.[64] Alexander Blair described the increase in advances and notes from November 1857 as having 'no necessary connection with the ordinary business' of the Bank, but the demands of trade pushed hard on the Bank, and profits from bills and cash accounts continued to rise. After the closure of the Western, Alexander

59 BS 1/21/10, Private and Confidential Letter Book, Alexander Blair to Deputy Governor, Bank of Scotland, Sir George Clerk, 31 December 1857.
60 BS 20/1/19 (Miscellaneous papers), paper on the 1857 crisis and reprint of September 1846 paper, 'Remarks on the expediency of increasing the capital of Bank of Scotland', 1858.
61 Kerr, History of Banking in Scotland, p. 237.
62 BS 20/13/6 (Miscellaneous papers). In addition to Bank of Scotland, the other banks affected were the Royal Bank, the British Linen, the Commercial, the National and the Union Bank.
63 BS 20/1/19 (Miscellaneous papers), 'Report on the Western Bank crisis and its results for Bank of Scotland', 10 September 1858.
64 BS 20/4/12, Treasurer's reports, 'General View of Assets and Liabilities on Deposits, Loans and Cash Accounts', 1863.

Blair and Thomas Corrie secured a permanent agreement to widen the gap between the interest charged on cash accounts and bills and that paid out on deposits. From 1853 to 1856, this gap for Bank of Scotland averaged £2 2s 9d per cent; from 1858 to 1861 the average rose to £2 10s 8d. Bank of Scotland gained £86,487 in 1858 compared with £67,420 the year before; by 1861 it even managed the sum of £104,782 (see Table 16.2).[65] The agreements between the Scottish banks remained in force thereafter, although for nearly two years the Clydesdale Bank paid ½ per cent more than the agreed rate for deposits at one month's notice. It was later persuaded to conform to the agreement.[66] Blair and Corrie also agreed in 1858 that the connections of the Scottish system with the Bank of England had to be stronger. In future, Bank of Scotland and the British Linen would conform precisely to changes in the Bank of England rates when crises occurred, and a general agreement was signed by all the Scottish banks on 6 February 1863 to follow changes in the Bank of England minimum rate of discount.[67]

The aftermath of 1857 convinced senior managers in Scottish banks that recourse to 'ruinous' competition was to be deplored. There was such an expansion of general trade and the position of the remaining banks was sufficiently secure to allow for carefully thought-out strategies; and, though these took different forms, the division between branches which had a surplus of deposits and those with more lending was common to all banks. Alexander Blair expressed this in a candid manner to Thomas Ogilvy of Corriemony, a landed proprietor in Inverness and director of Bank of Scotland:

> You know that in consequence of late events in banking, and of the extended commercial relations of Scotland, we can lend as much money as we please at Glasgow, Greenock and Dundee, that is to say that its division should be confined within a limited range and that at such a station as Inverness we should rather select our business than compete for it, and [I intend] to view it as a deposit branch, after making such advances as the district may fairly require from us. With regard to the state of credit in Inverness, I am not sure that it is particularly good among the traders you refer to and if we are to take the experience of this Bank, and my experience at a former period, the result would be very unfavourable to a Highland gentleman exercised in transactions with proprietors, sheep-farmers and family connections.[68]

65 BS 20/9/5 (Miscellaneous papers), Agreements between banks on deposit interest, 1857.
66 C. W. Munn, Clydesdale Bank: The First One Hundred and Fifty Years (Glasgow: 1988), pp. 53–4; BS 20/9/11 (Miscellaneous papers), paper on Clydesdale Bank, February 1859; ibid., 'Deposit interest' for main heads of agreement, January 1858.
67 BS 1/21/10, Private and Confidential Letter Book, 1858; Kerr, History of Banking in Scotland, p. 236. In 1833, by contrast, Alexander Blair argued that the Scottish banks should decide their own, Scottish, course for the agreed interest rates.
68 BS 1/21/10, Private and Confidential Letter Book.

On 10 June 1851, the Governor of Bank of Scotland, Robert Dundas, second Viscount Melville, died, and with him died the direct and often beneficial link between his family and the Bank which stretched back for seventy-five years. For his successor, the board chose James Andrew Broun Ramsay (1812–60), tenth Earl and first Marquis of Dalhousie.[69] Elected as a Tory for Haddingtonshire in 1837, he entered the Lords the following year. There he came to the notice of Sir Robert Peel, who appointed him vice-president of the Board of Trade in 1843 and two years later to the presidency. Dalhousie showed tremendous energy as he grappled with the effects of the railway mania; his views on the virtues of state regulation where it would benefit trade were widely canvassed. Both Peel and Russell agreed that he was the right man to reform the administration of India, and, on 12 January 1848 at the age of 36, Dalhousie was sworn in at Calcutta as Governor-General.

The historical significance of his rule lay in the firm extension of the territorial powers of the East India Company wherever it was thought that the Asiatic feudalism of the Indian states threatened to impede the modernisation of the country. This meant huge benefits for Scottish industry. In March 1849, after the second Sikh war, the Punjab was annexed. Lower Burma was conquered in 1852 after affronts to British residents, part of Hyderabad was taken for tax purposes, the smaller states of Satara, Nagpur and Thansi were annexed, and Dalhousie's final act was to confirm the seizure and disarming of Oudh in 1856.[70] The postal system was reorganised on British lines, a telegraph system set up and monies provided for education, and above all Dalhousie tried to make a reality of the commitment of the British government to open up India to imports. His grand design was a huge railway system whose progress would be unencumbered by considerations of landownership and share speculations. It was a 'remarkable' programme whereby bond- and share-holders of the railway companies 'directly but not vexatiously controlled by the Government' would receive a guaranteed interest at a rate above that of British government stocks in return for instructions as to routes and standards of engineering. Thus speculation was banished and quality assured.[71] With the threat from Russia by way of Afghanistan unresolved by the Crimean War, the development of railways was a political as well as

69 *DNB*, vol. 16; C. A. Malcolm, *The Bank of Scotland, 1695–1945* (Edinburgh: n.d. [1948]), pp. 232–4.
70 C. E. Luard, 'The Indian States 1818–57', in H. H. Dodwell (ed.), *The Cambridge History of India*, vol. v, *British India 1497–1858* (Cambridge: 1929), pp. 570–88 (p. 583).
71 The first railway line to open in India was from Bombay to Thana on 16 April 1853; Calcutta saw its first line in 1854 and Madras in 1856: D. Kumar and T. Raychaudhuri (eds), with the assistance of M. Desai, *The Cambridge Economic History of India*, vol. ii, *c. 1757 to c. 1970* (Cambridge: 1983), pp. 340, 739; W. J. Macpherson, 'Investment in Indian Railways, 1845–1875', *Economic History Review*, 2nd series, 8 (1955–6), 177–86.

an economic question. By the time Dalhousie left India in March 1856 his health was broken, and he died in December 1860 at Dalhousie Castle.[72] The 1850s were only the second time in the history of the Bank when the position of Governor was largely symbolic, although a proposal to indicate this in a formal way and elevate the Treasurer to rank of Deputy Governor was quietly dropped.[73]

Dalhousie urged the Bank to reappraise the value of foreign and Empire correspondents for the Bank and to consider investment in Indian stocks. Bank of Scotland was at 'a great disadvantage' as compared with other Scottish banks, with no direct foreign banking contacts, as the work of remittance of bills and letters of credit went via Coutts & Co. and Smith, Payne & Smith, who took the major share of the profits. In 1851, Coutts & Co. suggested that to speed up contacts between Scotland and Canada a facility should be agreed with the Bank of British North America.[74] It was a serious omission not to have foreign correspondents in India, the USA, Australia and Canada: 'the direct profit might not be so much considered, as the indirect advantages' afforded to customers by transactions of their foreign affairs 'as will prevent them being led away to other banks'. Unfortunately, Alexander Blair remained sceptical and advised against arrangements with the English, Scottish and Australian Chartered Bank in 1853, the Union Bank of Australia in 1857 and the Oriental Bank Corporation with offices in India, China and Singapore also in 1857.[75]

Alexander Blair died in 1859. His replacement, John Mackenzie, was manager of the Scottish Widows Fund and a director of the Union Bank, but for much of his time at Bank of Scotland he suffered from illness. After his retirement in 1863 he was succeeded by David Davidson, a former manager of the Bank of Montreal. Davidson was to be important in the Bank's history. Arrangements were made with the Bank of New Zealand in 1865, followed by a joint agency with the Royal Bank for the Chartered Mercantile Bank of India, Australia and China, and one with the British Linen for the Otago Bank, the Oriental Bank and the London Colonial Bank. For Canada, Davidson chose arrangements with the Bank of Montreal and the Bank of British North America for the provinces of Nova Scotia, New Brunswick and British Columbia.[76] Earnings from fees and commissions on foreign trade grew faster in the 1870s than income from any other source.

72 Malcolm, *Bank of Scotland*, pp. 232–4; Dalhousie's eldest daughter took over the management of his estate.
73 BS 20/2/5 (Miscellaneous papers).
74 BS 20/4/14, Reports and letters re correspondents and other banks; Alexander Blair to directors, March 1857.
75 Ibid.
76 BS 1/5, Minutes, 1865, 1866; Malcolm, *Bank of Scotland*, p. 127.

The advice given to the Bank by Dalhousie persuaded the directors to shift part of their London reserves to Indian stock. They examined all the interest rates and stock valuations for Indian railways and government funds. After the assumption of power in India by the Crown in 1858, the way was clear for a huge rise in railway and government loans. In 1857, the total debts of India were £59.5 million (558 million rupees), while by 1861 they had reached £101.9 million (1,014 million rupees), of which £30 million was owed in England.[77] The first loan for which Bank of Scotland tendered was the British India debentures in April 1859, paying 4 per cent half-yearly; and, as the India office could not afford the loan to fail ('their credit in India would suffer irretrievably'), information from Coutts & Co., James Capel and Smith, Payne & Smith suggested that the equivalent price of £97 at 4 per cent for existing stocks was too high. The Bank successfully bid £95 1s for £150,000 worth and maintained a diversified portfolio thereafter.[78]

Bank of Scotland found difficulty in 1858 in placing the increased deposits in first-class bills. There were too few in Scotland and the north of England. The problem persisted for several years, and as the preferred alternative was government consolidated stock there was a slight narrowing in the overall interest gap between deposits and loans. With a low level of bad debts, Bank of Scotland profits remained satisfactory, but the outbreak of the American Civil War was soon felt in 1861 by the cotton manufacturers in Glasgow and Lancashire. Profits at the Bank fell from £143,852 in 1862 to little above £117,000 the following year, and were down to £100,000 by 1864.[79]

The Bank's response was that, in June 1859, Mackenzie looked at the cost in fees to the Bank of arrangements for payments and receipts of bills and drafts in London through the Bank of England (then costing £873), through Smith, Payne & Smith (£1,118) and through Coutts (£1,000). The board was informed that in 1858–9 the weekly average balance of cash in London with these three correspondents, not earning interest, was £75,000. Applying a notional rate of interest of 3 per cent gave a further 'loss' of £2,265, which together with the fees implied a total of £5,256.[80]

---

77 R. Dutt, *The Economic History of India in the Victorian Age*, 2nd edn (London: 1906), p. 374; Kumar and Raychaudhuri (eds) with Desai, *Cambridge Economic History of India*, vol. ii, ch. 12, pp. 939–40; S. Bhattacharya, *Financial Foundations of the British Raj* (Simla: 1971), pp. 99, 131. After the war, money was cheaper in London than in India, and the debt due in Britain grew from £15,090,000 in 1859 to £35,100,000 in 1862: Bhattacharya, Table 18, p. 318.

78 BS 20/12/13 (Miscellaneous papers), India loans. James Capel and Coutts both advised a bid of £95 10s; Smith, Payne & Smith suggested that London bankers had agreed on £95, and thus a bid by Bank of Scotland of £95 1s would succeed.

79 See Statistical Appendix, Table A3.

80 BS 20/4/14, Reports and letters re correspondents and other banks, report on arrangements with Coutts & Co., 23 June 1859.

There was little point in asking the Bank of England for a reduction, and both private banks refused to offer interest. In 1863, Davidson tried again, but at first made little progress. Coutts & Co. reminded him that, because of the huge increase in business since 1839 when current arrangements were agreed, their commission had fallen from 1s 1d per cent to 8¼d per cent. Furthermore, the average daily balance of the current account on which Davidson wanted interest was not, in fact, equal to the daily amount of outstanding drafts, and, on numerous occasions from a few hours to a few days, the account fell into debit. The total number of receipts and payments at Coutts & Co. in 1858 was 33,000 from forty-two Bank of Scotland branches, and several clerks were employed solely on Bank business (see Table 16.6). This necessitated a huge accounting system. Coutts & Co. also took responsibility for references for bills, and 'recourse was had to our numerous correspondents for confidential information'. Their letters on Bank of Scotland business exhibited some of the finest business prose of the Victorian age.

Yet all the Scottish banks were pressing their London agents; and, perhaps sensing a new determination because of the alarming decline in profits, Coutts & Co. agreed, in September 1863, that the Bank would pay 9d per cent on the total value of all bill payments settled by Coutts & Co., who would pay interest when the account was in credit of 1 per cent under the minimum discount rate of the Bank of England, not exceeding 5 per cent. Should Bank of Scotland require credit, this would be charged at the Bank of England rate but with no pre-agreed ceiling.[81] In April 1864, Coutts agreed to pay the Commercial Bank for the £20,000 which it had deposited as security when its account was transferred from Jones, Loyd & Co. on the latter's closure.[82]

The fall in profits common to the Scottish banks focused attention on more significant changes in business practices. Apart from the London bill market, for many years all Scottish banks had advanced long-term loans to English companies. The next step was to open offices in London and to canvass for advances on bills directly, as well as saving the costs of London correspondents. There were numerous Scottish companies with offices in London, and there were many Scottish managers and accountants with British companies. The Bank had taken advice on the legality of such a move in 1855, but the lawyers were unsure, and as Alexander Blair was undecided the matter was shelved. There the matter rested until the National Bank opened an office in 1864; its legal advice was favourable.[83]

81 Coutts & Co., archives, Special Letter Books, 28 August and 9 September 1863.
82 Ibid., 11 April 1864.
83 BS 20/2/8, Legal opinion on a Branch in London, and on the National Bank branch, 1865.

In 1865, the good relations which existed between the senior management of Bank of Scotland, the British Linen, the Clydesdale and the Union led to discussions for a joint ownership of a new London bank, together with the London private bank of Glyn, Mills, Currie & Co.[84] The proposals set out a framework by which each of the five banks would maintain its identity, although Glyns expected to merge their business with the new entity, initially called the 'London and Scottish Banking Association' and the 'Associated Scotch Bank of London'. They even found a suitable office. The subscribed capital was agreed at 'not less' than £2.5 million with £500,000 paid up and stock to be held in equal shares and for a minimum of five years. This later rose to £3 million with £800,000 paid, but the negotiations stumbled in the early stages over the problem of limited liability which the Scottish banks insisted on but Glyns opposed.[85] If well managed, the new bank would have the transactions of all five banks and the possibility of a very considerable increase in advances. Unfortunately, the failure of Overend, Gurney & Co. on 10 May 1866 came at a critical time in the discussions; there was too much uncertainty about potential losses both in London and in Scotland, and the office was disposed of the following year.

As well as the attempted opening of the branch in London, the board considered two other routes for improved earnings. In a survey presented to the directors of Bank of Scotland for the year to February 1866, David Davidson pointed to a decline of 2 per cent in the capital value of consols; the Bank held £1,587,875 and this decline could not be easily absorbed. There was an improvement in the year's profits to £126,927, but the result on consols was ominous: the

> chief causes of the decline were the high cost of money [and] the creation of competitive investments offering in some cases equal security together with higher rates of interest and the comparatively high rates of interest obtainable on loans of money and on deposits with banks and discount houses which have paid on the average as high a rate as consols, while the principal has been guaranteed and a loss in market value saved.[86]

Railway debentures, British colonial and foreign fixed-interest stocks all offered a higher return than consols. But the board was cautious, and an

---

84 Munn, *Clydesdale Bank*, p. 73; J. M. Reid, *The History of the Clydesdale Bank, 1838–1938* (Glasgow: 1938), pp. 160–4; BS 1/70/4, Special Reports, Proposed acquisition of one or more London private banks, 9 January 1866; BS 1/6, Minutes, 3 January 1866, superseded by order of 7 March 1866; BS 20/2/14 (Miscellaneous papers), proposals and correspondence, 1865–6. There was intense secrecy around the proposals, and Glyn, Mills, Currie & Co. were not actually named in most of these papers.
85 BS 20/2/14, ibid.
86 BS 1/70/4, Special Reports, Report to board of directors, February 1866.

Table 16.6 Transactions of Bank of Scotland with Coutts & Co., 1839–62

	Debit				Credit			
Year	No. of branches	Bank of Scotland drafts	Foreign bills acceptances	Total debit	Bills remitted for collection	Sundry cash received for branches	Total credit	Average balance
1839	31	1246900	556600	1803500	754000	1067800	1821800	14200
1840	32	1026900	674800	1701700	810000	903800	1713800	14800
1841	33	1064900	488500	1553400	680000	886800	1566800	17700
1860	42	1838000	888700	2726700	1987400	753700	2741100	15300
1861	44	1910400	969800	2880200	2311500	603850	2915350	19500
1862	44	1729400	1166300	2895700	2465800	456000	2921800	23100

Source: Coutts & Co., Secret Letterbook series, 28 August 1861.

Bank of Scotland: Total Transactions, 1856–8

	Coutts & Co. (security with Coutts £25000)	
Year	Receipts	Payments
1856	2152000	2149000
1857	2303000	2300000
1858	2354000	2362000

Bank of England (credit of £30000 on £15000 Bank Stock and £100000 consols held by Bank)

Year	Receipts	Payments	Revenue Drafts and Bills
1856	2687000	2668000	1617000
1857	2317000	2361000	1110000
1858	3391000	3496000	2115000

	Smith, Payne & Smith (security with Smith, Payne & Smith £25000)	
Year	Receipts	Payments
1856	4082000	4064000
1857	4856000	4844000
1858	5418000	5314000

Sources: Coutts & Co., Secret Letterbook series, 1858; BS 20/4/14, Reports and letters re correspondents and other banks.

agreement to move from consols was given, but only in principle. This left the discount market. Over the financial years 1863 to 1866, the average current bill discounts grew from £3 million to £4.3 million, much of this placed through Glasgow by re-discounting bills offered by London houses, including Overend, Gurney & Co. This was to lead to some of the more serious mistakes which David Davidson made and which were to occupy, over many years, a disproportionate amount of management time.

A number of Glasgow firms with connections and investments in Australia, New Zealand and India discounted bills through Overend, Gurney & Co. and other London houses as well as Scottish banks. Much of this was for raw materials supplied to European industry, and inevitably investment in cotton was a priority. There were also glowing reports of the profits to be made on land developments. One such firm was James Morton & Co., which had extensive credits with Overend, Gurney & Co. and was able to secure, in 1865, an agreed six-year programme for credit. 'Feeling every confidence' in the arrangements, Morton & Co., together with other Glasgow houses, entered into numerous new business connections in these countries. As these increased, the Glasgow chief office of Bank of Scotland, in agreement with David Davidson, increased credit to Morton & Co. and to the firm's connections. Other banks did likewise, notably the City of Glasgow and the Union Bank. At first, much of this paper came under the guarantee of Overend, Gurney & Co.; but later, as trade increased, 'the bills of the same parties who were considered to be responsible were taken without [this] guarantee'. They did come, though, with promises that 'first-class securities were deposited with Overend, Gurney & Co.'.

The problems at the Scottish banks were exposed when Overend, Gurney & Co. failed on Thursday 10 May 1866 owing a total of £5 million: 'panic, true panic, came with unexpected speed and violence' the following day.[87] The house had been in a doubtful condition for some months, and the final collapse came as little surprise to the directors of Bank of England, Walter Bagehot and probably much of the City, as rumours had been seeping out over several months about the volume of low-quality bills on speculative and high-priced ventures in which Overend, Gurney & Co. dealt; and Walter Bagehot captured the mood in *Lombard Street* (1873).[88] The Bank of England lent over £4 million on the Friday 'upon the security of Government stock and bills of exchange'. Gladstone, the Chancellor, was besieged by bankers and MPs linked to the City, and, with the Prime Minister, Lord John Russell, he signed that evening the

87 Clapham, *Bank of England*, vol. ii, p. 263.
88 Walter Bagehot: *DNB*, vol. 2 (London: 1885).

by now familiar letter which authorised the Bank of England to extend its note issue.[89] The news reached the Mound by telegram on the Thursday afternoon. Although there was considerable pressure on all the Scottish banks for discounts, the suspension of the Bank Charter Act had eased the pressure in London by Monday, helped by a new bill rate of 10 per cent following the lead given by the Bank of England. Deposits remained safe and there was little panic among the general public in Scotland, although businessmen were annoyed as the 10 per cent discount rate remained in place for three months.

Bank of Scotland was owed £329,880. Only a part of this, under £200,000, came with the guarantee of Overend, Gurney & Co. It transpired that the 'first-class securities' were not actually in the hands of the company.

> It now appears that they had been content to trust very much to obligation to transfer to them the properties purchased with their credits. No actual transfer has been made of any property, although the purchase can be connected, with the credits granted for that purpose.[90]

The three Scottish banks insisted that the liquidators accept the liability whereby the bills were covered by the Australian and New Zealand securities of Morton & Co. For their part, the liquidators required the Scottish banks to continue the agreement not to call for payment in respect of the liability, and the date for eventual repayments was extended, in a subsequent legal action, to 1 April 1872.[91] In theory, the debts owed to the Scottish banks were more than covered by the book value of £1,635,251 in securities and assets of James Morton & Co., and the market value was believed to be higher; but realisation of these would take time. The Scottish banks agreed to extend bills accepted by several Glasgow firms for £370,000, the transactions based on the purchase of property in Australia and New Zealand. The whole debts of James Morton & Co. were reported by September 1867 as 'amply covered by the value of the properties'.[92] The Glasgow office of Bank of Scotland, later managed by James Adams Wenley, continued to have regular meetings with James Morton about his business affairs. It is clear from the correspondence that Bank officials believed James Morton to be honest, creditworthy and ultimately able to repay his debts. The support given by Bank of Scotland to the company

---

89 Clapham, *Bank of England*, vol. ii, pp. 261–8; the correspondence between the Bank of England and the government is reprinted in Gregory, *Select Statutes*, vol. ii, p. 124ff.; the quotation is from a letter from the Bank of England to the government, 11 May 1866, p. 124.
90 BS 1/70/4, Special Reports, Reports on James Morton & Co.
91 BS 20/30/13, Overend, Gurney & Co., Miscellaneous and legal papers.
92 BS 1/70/4, Special Reports, Reports on James Morton & Co., 17 September 1867.

continued until 1878, although with a gradual reduction in debt, when it was revealed that the City of Glasgow Bank had taken the opposite course and increased its exposure. It was noteworthy that Bank of Scotland was especially vigilant over any business connections which involved the City of Glasgow for several years before 1878.

As the negotiations over a new London Scottish bank faltered, Bank of Scotland directors, encouraged by David Davidson, agreed to proceed with their own London office. The intake of deposits had risen to £6.7 million in 1866, and the considerable improvement in economic fortunes after 1862 promised a good income. Premises were secured on a twenty-one-year lease at Old Broad Street, and the office opened for business in August 1867 apparently without complaint from the Bank's English neighbours. The office made modest progress with short-dated discounts and also, rather to the surprise of the board in Edinburgh, found a growing volume of deposits, which by the end of February 1869 had reached £422,542 and within two years had passed £900,000 (over 10 per cent of total deposits). The potential for loans among Scots in London was huge; by February 1869 they had passed £1 million (15 per cent of the total), using funds from Scotland to add to London deposits. Net profits were made in the first year and reached £3,494 in the year to 1870. The Bank sought membership of the clearing house for cheques and bills operated by the London banks, but was refused.

In other respects, the 1866 crisis was unremarkable. Deposits at Bank of Scotland rose by £403,638 in the year following; advances rose from £4.3 million in April 1866 to over £5 million from July to December. There was a modest increase in past-due bills to just over £100,000 after August, but the pattern was similar to rises in 1862 and 1865 and caused little concern at the Mound. Circulation rose in May but was below that of May 1865, and there were fewer banknotes out in the summer before the usual November surge. By February 1866 it was clear that income from bills was very much higher, up almost one-third to £304,206, and interest on cash accounts up £16,000 to £120,933; at £191,644, net profits were well above recent years. Of this, £30,000 was written to the Fund for Losses, £15,000 the next year and £28,500 in 1869. It is clear that the discounting of bills was the major factor in holding up profits in the few years after the Overend, Gurney & Co. crisis.

In 1868, agreement was reached for Bank of Scotland to purchase the Central Bank of Scotland, founded in 1833 with a capital of £100,000.[93] The negotiating team for the Central Bank was led by John Pullar, Lord

93 BS 20/2/4, Prospectus for the Central Banking Company of Perth, 1833; BS 1/70/4, Special Reports, Reports on negotiations between Bank of Scotland and Central Bank of Scotland.

Provost of Perth, Andrew Davidson, solicitor, the bank general manager Archibald Burns, and William Guild of Lindores, Newburgh. The business was based in the Perth and Kinross area, with seven branches and a surplus of deposits over local investment opportunities. This led the directors to advance £60,000 to Sir Alexander Anderson, an advocate in Aberdeen, £14,096 to Taunton & Co., sharebrokers in Liverpool, and £103,000 to railway contractors, mostly on the security of Welsh railway stocks. Funds also went to the Cambrian Railway Company of Wales. By 1868, these advances were in difficulty. The agreement with Bank of Scotland valued these advances at only £75,000, assumed recoverable over time, but there was a proviso as to the continuing liability of the stockholders of the Central Bank if these were not realised at or above this figure. The privilege of the authorised issue of banknotes was transferred to Bank of Scotland. The stockholders received £80,000 of nominal Bank of Scotland stock and £50,000 in cash. Several stockholders refused to sign over their rights and were later bought out.

In 1872, David Davidson recommended to the board that Bank of Scotland increase the nominal capital from £1.5 million (£1 million paid), granted in 1804, to £4.5 million. The resulting Act, in 1873, was important not least because of a clause which provided that the unissued stock should, when issued, bear the same relative proportions (two-thirds paid and one-third unpaid) as the previously-issued stock existing at the time.[94] It was not the intention that £3 million of new stock should be created but that the Bank should be in a position, by the creation of some additional stock, to give additional security for an increase in liabilities. In 1876, with the capital still at £1.5 million (£1 million paid), a further £375,000 was issued, on which £250,000 was called, and the proportion of two-thirds to one-third was thus maintained. David Davidson later wished to change these proportions by the issue of stock but not calling for any to be paid, a principle adopted by several English joint-stock banks to strengthen public confidence. This could have been incorporated into the 1873 Act by careful drafting, but was overlooked. The Bank was thus in the position of asking for a new private Act in November 1880, which would have modified this clause, and of arguing at the same time that there was no need to call up any part of the remaining £2,625,000 of authorised but unissued stock.[95]

Economic fluctuations in Britain as a whole were more marked than usual during the 1870s. The boom of 1871–3 affected almost all sectors of

94 'An Act to authorise the increase of the capital stock of the Bank of Scotland; and for other purposes', 36 & 37 Victoria c.99, 7 July 1873; BS 20/4/8, Miscellaneous legal papers, 1873.
95 BS 20/4/7, George Tytler, Secretary, to Proprietors. The Act was subsequently abandoned in April 1881, as the Bank refused to acquiesce in the government's wish to adopt the term 'limited' in the Bank's title.

the economy. The building of over 6,000 miles of railway in America in 1872 alone, for example, was a major stimulus to the British iron industry, for the USA was still buying most of its railway equipment from the UK; and the west of Scotland benefited accordingly, although the peak production of pig iron (1.2 million tons) came as early as 1870. Shipbuilding along the Clyde flourished, and between 1870 and 1874 average yearly launchings were 250,000 tons.[96] The boom for most industrial centres came to an end in the summer and autumn of 1873, first in central Europe and then from late September in New York.[97] There were two days of acute financial worries in London on 6 and 7 November, but the catastrophes of New York, Vienna and Berlin were not reproduced in London or in Scotland. Although the Bank of England's rate touched 9 per cent on 7 November, within a few weeks it was down to below 5 per cent. These buoyant years saw a notable increase in total deposits, advances and profits, both distributed and retained.[98]

The fall in prices which began in late 1873 was understood by contemporaries as a normal shake-out from the previous years of boom, and in part that was true. It was, however, also the start of a long-term trend in a general decline of prices that reached bottom in the mid-1890s, and was to explain Alfred Marshall's description of these twenty years as a 'depression of prices, a depression of interest, and a depression of profits'.[99] More immediately, the main concern of the Scottish banks was the agitation concerning the principles of Scottish banking which followed the return of the Tories to government after the general election of 1874. The new Chancellor of the Exchequer, Sir Stafford Northcote, thought long and hard over how Scottish banks could be removed from England, and the question became entangled in the already much-discussed question of the Scottish note issue.[100] The Select Committee on Banks of Issue in 1875 considered once again the arguments at length, and fortunately the Committee did not finalise a report. For this, the foreign and domestic difficulties of the Disraeli government were responsible, and the Scottish banks could perhaps be thankful that the inquiry took place before 1878.

---

96 A. Slaven, *The Development of the West of Scotland, 1750–1960* (London: 1975), p. 178ff.
97 Clapham, *Free Trade and Steel*, pp. 378–83. A. R. Holmes and E. Green, *Midland: 150 Years of Banking Business* (London: 1986), p. 59, make the point that unlike most regions, the investment boom in Birmingham and region went beyond the 1871–3 years.
98 See Statistical Appendix, Table A4.
99 Alfred Marshall before the Commission on Gold and Silver (1887–8), Q. 9,824, quoted in Clapham, *Free Trade and Steel*, p. 385; J. Saville, 'Some Retarding Factors in the British Economy before 1914', *Yorkshire Bulletin of Economic and Social Research*, 13 (1961), 51–60.
100 A. Lang, *Life, Letters and Diaries of Sir Stafford Northcote, First Earl of Iddesleigh*, 2nd edn (Edinburgh: 1891), ch. 13; F. W. Fetter, *The Development of British Monetary Orthodoxy 1797–1875* (Cambridge, MA: 1965), pp. 221–4.

The crisis of 1857 despatched the Western and the Edinburgh and Glasgow banks, and severely affected the Union Bank and the City of Glasgow. The Union Bank recovered, but the losses for the City of Glasgow were probably above £700,000; the figure is quite staggering, and in the light of what transpired it was unfortunate that it did not go out of business at that time.[101] Before 1878, it was the general belief among the public that bank profits were rising and that no bank was in trouble. To the public, the City of Glasgow was in a strong position; the number of its branch offices rose from eighty-eight in 1857 to 133 twenty years later, it held £8 million of deposits, and the published balance sheets indicated an active bill and loan business. It was even thought of as dynamic: Andrew Kerr, the banking historian who followed the subsequent crisis at first hand, commented that the bank's customers and shareholders would sometimes taunt officials of the older banks 'with being "old-wifish" and slow of movement'.[102] In many quarters, it was 'regarded as the most active and prospectively prosperous bank in Scotland'.

Not everyone believed this, however, as for years the inner banking world had regarded the City of Glasgow with suspicion and doubt. The reality, by 1878, was a series of intractable difficulties over loans which went back twenty years, had been exacerbated by the crisis of 1866 and were coupled to basic failings of the management. The directors rarely fulfilled their proper purpose of overseeing the work of the large loans and overall direction, the inspectors for the bank concentrated on branches, and the real decision-making powers lay with an inner circle of directors and managers. Occasional attempts by other directors to find out more about company affairs were rebuffed. In 1870, the Secretary since formation in 1839 was forced to retire because of his probing into the post-1866 financial position, with his pension payable 'at the discretion of the board'. C. S. Leresche, the replacement, had been a partner in a Calcutta firm which went bankrupt in 1866 and was told, as a condition of appointment, to leave all financial matters to Alexander Stronach, the general manager, whose private clerk was responsible for the key correspondence.[103] The board also had a resident bully, Lewis Potter, described as a 'snarling and garrulous old man', a director since 1858 and the effective agent of James Morton, who later emerged as the greatest debtor. The centre of the fraud was a huge bill-discount and loan operation. Six companies owed the City of Glasgow for bills and loans which totalled £4,084,140 in 1874, and four years later (along with two lesser companies) the exposure had reached

---

101 R. E. Tyson, 'The Failure of the City of Glasgow Bank and the Rise of Independent Auditing', *The Accountant's Magazine*, 78 (April 1974), 126–31 (p. 126).
102 Kerr, *History of Banking in Scotland*, p. 256; the author was a bank official in 1878.
103 Tyson, 'City of Glasgow', p. 128.

£6,090,800. Much of this was irrecoverable and non-performing. There was also an intractable debt in railway and dock investment in the USA which dated from 1856 and had grown to over £1 million by 1878.[104] False statements of the assets and liabilities in the annual balances had been given to shareholders since 1864.

For most of 1878, there was little to comment on except the continuation of commercial and industrial depression. The Scottish banks found, as was often the case in periods of bad trade, money accumulating for which they could not find satisfactory investment; but there were no obvious signs of any impending disaster. Then, towards the end of September 1878, worrying rumours circulated in London and in Scotland that one of the Scottish banks was in difficulty. On 30 September, the general managers of the Scottish banks meeting in Edinburgh under the chairmanship of the Treasurer of Bank of Scotland considered a memorandum from the directors of the City of Glasgow Bank.[105] The directors admitted that in the annual report of July 1878 they had substantially understated their total of acceptances by bill of exchange, and they now disclosed very heavy losses. The General Managers Committee despatched G. A. Jamieson CA to examine the large loan and discount accounts of the City of Glasgow, and on 1 October he informed the managers that on his very hasty examination the losses would approach £3 million (which he soon revised to £6 million). Upon this report, the general managers refused any financial help. The City of Glasgow then gave notice that the bank would not open on 2 October, and the general managers agreed to limit the crisis as far as possible and accept City of Glasgow banknotes for exchange or for credit of customers' accounts.

The City of Glasgow closed its doors on the evening of 1 October 1878 with total liabilities of £12,723,822.[106] Two official examiners, Dr M'Grigor and Mr Anderson, reported on 5 October that the sensible course would be liquidation, and a meeting of the shareholders was arranged for the 22nd. The report of the investigators was published on the evening of 18 October, and its content stunned the public. The bank had discounted heavily in overseas business paper in India, America, Australia and New Zealand, and much was speculative. As with the Western Bank, the City of Glasgow had allowed a small number of large firms to increase

---

104 R. E. Tyson, 'Scottish Investment in American Railways: The Case of the City of Glasgow Bank 1856–1881', in P. L. Payne (ed.), *Studies in Scottish Business History* (London: 1967), pp. 387–416.
105 The chronology for these few days is in R. S. Rait, *The History of the Union Bank of Scotland* (Glasgow: 1930), pp. 310–12. This differs in some respects from that in Bank of Scotland papers, and it should be stressed that members of the General Managers Committee had differing perspectives as the crisis unravelled.
106 There is a detailed discussion in Kerr, *History of Banking in Scotland*, ch. 25, and in Checkland, *Scottish Banking*, pp. 469–77.

their borrowing until a very high proportion of the bank's total debt was concentrated in these few firms. By 1878, three of these firms owed the bank £5,379,000 out of total advances of around £12 million. As the City of Glasgow's situation worsened, so the bank's directors and senior officials resorted to deception to maintain their public image. They bought their own shares in order to keep up the market price; they falsely stated the amount of gold in the bank; and it was announced that the balance sheets had been falsified for several years. The eventual loss after realisation of assets, to be met by shareholders, was £5,190,983. They had to find £4.4 million and take a loss of the £1 million of their paid-up capital. There were 1,819 of these shareholders (of whom 484 were trustees), and many decided to test their liability before the Court of Session, but they were largely unsuccessful. Two calls were made; the first for £500 on each £100 City of Glasgow share, the second for £2,250. At the conclusion of this process, only 129 shareholders and 125 trustees remained solvent. The crisis had a devastating effect on Glasgow society and on the standing of the banks. The combined Scottish banks' share valuation of £27,255,732 in 1875 fell to £21,666,000 in November 1878. There was little sympathy towards several directors of the City of Glasgow, including Lewis Potter, who were leading members of the Free Church of Scotland. Potter and Alexander Stronach received prison sentences of eighteen months and the six other directors eight months apiece. The crisis had a marked effect on the banking system on both sides of the Border.[107]

One unfortunate victim was the Caledonian Banking Company, which had taken four nominal £100 City of Glasgow shares as security for an advance. Such was the fear of loss that a great many Caledonian shares were sold under their real value, and the more impressionable depositors withdrew funds. On 5 December, the directors closed the bank and applied for an orderly liquidation. When the final demand from the liquidators of the City of Glasgow Bank was for £11,000 and no more, it was clear that the Caledonian could reopen. The other Scottish banks continued to circulate Caledonian notes and temporarily took over their branches; Bank of Scotland, for example, took those at Dingwall, Grantown, Kingussie and Nairn. A guarantee fund of £150,000 was raised from local well-wishers and business to cover the loss, and the Caledonian reopened in August 1879.[108] It enjoyed a modest revival thereafter, although profits fell by one-third in the 1880s and it was absorbed by Bank of Scotland in 1907. The number of bankruptcies directly attributable to the City of Glasgow liquidation was over 500, and it was this that made the crisis the

---

107 M. Collins, 'The Banking Crisis of 1878', *Economic History Review*, 2nd series, 42 (1989), 504–27.
108 The episode confirmed the fierce local pride taken in the three north of Scotland banks.

worst financial and business disaster in the second half of Victoria's reign north of the Border. It was referred to for decades thereafter in the press and in banking and business circles; details of the trial were published, and the lessons about balance-sheet management were taught in classes for the Institute of Bankers. The collapse reinforced the mood of depression which settled over the west of Scotland in the 1880s.

The absence of limited liability – a principle strongly insisted upon not only by Scottish joint-stock bankers – meant that shareholders of the City of Glasgow were called upon to meet every £100 share with £2,750, an outcome of failure which sent shock waves round Britain. In Glasgow a relief fund raised £400,000, nearly all from Scotland, but the principle inevitably came into serious question. The Parliamentary acts relating to companies had allowed the limitation of liability, but non-acceptance by banks would mean that shareholders would bear any loss beyond the original capital, as the City of Glasgow so disastrously demonstrated. After much discussion, the Companies Act of 1879 introduced the principle of 'reserve liability' whereby the banks could acquire additional capital which could only be called upon if the bank in question went into liquidation. The seven unlimited banks in Scotland decided, after much debate, to accept 'Limited' at the end of their titles; but the three chartered banks, working together, sponsored a different scheme for their 'reserve'. They already had limited liability under their Acts and charters, but were unwilling to accept any change in their constitutions that did not come directly, by private bill, through Parliament. Together they sponsored three identical private bills which would have given them the right to raise 'reserve capital'. The Treasury in London strongly resisted, and the bills were withdrawn for fear of arousing further discussion of the general status and position of the Scottish banks in the British economy.[109]

Among the banking questions that arose out of the City of Glasgow failure was the appropriateness of banks buying or selling their own shares. Banks in trouble had in the past, as was the case with the City of Glasgow, bought their own shares in the open market in order to maintain their price and thereby deflect opinion as to the true state of their affairs. There was now a great deal of public and private discussion, and the banking system in general accepted the impropriety of this practice, which was then discarded, or mostly discarded. Some Scottish banks, including Bank of Scotland, still held their own shares, but with no active trading. Similarly, while independent audits had been increasingly used before 1878, after that date they now became universally adopted.

109 BS 1/70/4, Special Reports, Reports on bank legislation.

The liquidation process of the City of Glasgow took time. Bank of Scotland, together with other banks, had £1,120,000 owing from the City of Glasgow, and the liquidators conceded a partial advance of £320,000.[110] For the rest, the banks had to wait until all other creditors were paid. This failure of the City of Glasgow and the many other bankruptcies profoundly affected the attitudes and business consciousness of the Scottish banking community; no-one who lived through the crisis ever seems to have forgotten what happened. In the short and medium term, it meant increased caution in the matter of advances and the consolidation of the general dominance of the Edinburgh banks within Scotland and of the leading position of Bank of Scotland and the Royal Bank until the First World War.

110 For the history and analysis of the City of Glasgow catastrophe, Gregory, Select Statutes, vol. ii, pp. 288–300, reprints three important articles from The Economist: those of 5 October 1878, 30 August 1879 and 25 October 1879. See also Kerr, History of Banking in Scotland, ch. 25; Rait, History of the Union Bank, p. 311ff.; Checkland, Scottish Banking, pp. 469–78; Clapham, Bank of England, vol. ii, pp. 309–12. It was 'perhaps the most discreditable British banking catastrophe of the century' (Clapham, ibid., p. 309). The English banks were not seriously shaken, and there was no public inquiry. For the effect on the Clydesdale Bank, see Munn, Clydesdale Bank, pp. 90–2.

CHAPTER 17

THE AGE OF GENTLEMANLY BANKING, 1880–1914

T HE STRAIN OF dealing with the problems which followed the City of Glasgow Bank's failure led to the retirement of David Davidson in 1879 from the Treasurer's position at Bank of Scotland. Davidson, who had had a mixed career, was succeeded by James Adams Wenley, whose term of office lasted until 1898. Wenley had been in the service of the Bank since 1855, having been successively agent in Dundee, manager in the Glasgow chief office and assistant secretary at the Mound. The failure of the City of Glasgow and the continued depression of prices and profits inevitably required the Scottish banking community to demonstrate its continued viability both within its own institutions and to the general public. There were variations in public perception, and the Edinburgh banks did not suffer as sharp a fall in share prices as did the remaining Glasgow banks. Inevitably, Bank of Scotland inquired into its own affairs in detail. There had been annual reports from the Treasurer to the board and numerous internal reports from the earliest times; and at various points, for instance with the appointment of Alexander Blair in 1832, these became more systematic and wide-ranging. The information on advances and from branches was in any case available to the board throughout the year. Nevertheless, after the crisis of 1878, Wenley was required to give especial attention to keeping the board conversant with the true position. On 18 March 1879, he provided a more comprehensive analysis than usual of the whole of the operations for the financial year 1878–9, taking the analysis back to 1872.[1] As the Scottish bankers regarded the situation as one of continued crisis, it is directly relevant

---

1 BS 1/70/6, Annual Reports of the Treasurer; these reports were based on the half-yearly reports of the Treasurer for his own use, which gave the true internal position and much relevant information on the progress of advances, interest-rate margins and market comparisons. Unless otherwise indicated, quotes from Wenley in this chapter are from BS 1/70/6.

to appreciate the very considerable pains taken by Wenley to provide up-to-date information to the directors.

The report opened in a pessimistic tone:

> The year which has passed has been an eventful one in the history of Banking in Scotland. It has seen a continuation of the dull trade and Commercial depression which have existed since 1873, an extension of these evils to the agricultural classes – before happily free from them – a great fall in the value of commodities, houses and even land, low wages, want of employment and consequent distress of working men and their families, and a very large number of failures all over the country. This unfortunate condition of affairs has been much aggravated by the failure of the City of Glasgow Bank, the most disastrous event of the kind ever experienced in Scotland. It caused the suspension of the Caledonian Bank and brought great though most unmerited discredit on the Union Bank and Clydesdale Bank, from the circumstances of their being, like the 'City', banks having their headquarters in Glasgow.

The Treasurer proceeded to emphasise the 'unbounded confidence' in Bank of Scotland, evidenced by the large increase in deposits and in the general daily business of the Bank. Yet he also acknowledged that the crisis had raised 'a spirit of enquiry among Bank shareholders' and others as to the composition of bank advances. Indeed, the potential losses for Bank of Scotland as a result of the Glasgow bank's failure were serious. The most worrying case was that of the merchant house of James Morton & Co., which had obligations to the City of Glasgow Bank 'to the almost inconceivable sum of £2,300,000' and additional debits due to Bank of Scotland of 'about £340,000'. The origin of these last went back to before 1866, and they were nominally covered by the debentures and shares of the Australian and New Zealand Land Co., which James Morton & Co. had promoted; but they were quite impossible to realise at this sum, and not at all at the present time 'to any material extent'. It was a debt which was to appear in the reports of the Treasurer for many years, although of course its full extent was not declared to proprietors. An agreement was made with the trustees of the City of Glasgow Bank (and it also applied to other Scottish banks) whereby the securities involved became Bank of Scotland's absolute property. A large sum would be required to meet losses arising from both the dullness of trade and the fall-outs from the City of Glasgow Bank failure. There was some good news, however: the General Managers Committee had recently succeeded in widening the gap of the Scottish banks' lending and deposit ratio in Scotland by 3s 4d and in London by 7s 1d (see Table 17.1), and this would realise better results in the financial year 1879–80.

By March 1879, Bank of Scotland's resources comprised capital and reserve (£2,000,000), circulation of notes (£674,000), deposits

Table 17.1 *Gap between lending and deposits: year average, 1878–82*

	1878			1879			1880			1881			1882		
	£	s	d	£	s	d	£	s	d	£	s	d	£	s	d
Scottish lending rate	4	7	6	4	19	3	4	10	1	4	5	11	2	7	9
Scottish deposit rate	2	2	4	2	10	9	1	17	0	1	16	9			
Scottish 'gap'	2	5	2	2	8	6	2	13	1	2	9	2			
London deposit rate				2	5	0	0	18	6	1	9	1	1	16	6
London 'gap'				1	13	4	1	4	10	1	10	3	1	19	5
London short loan rate				3	18	4	2	3	4	2	19	4	3	15	11
London local bill rate				3	19	9	2	1	11	2	17	8	3	14	9
Average							2	4	5	2	19	11	3	16	9

Table 17.2 *Derivation of net profit of Bank of Scotland for the year ending 28 February 1879*

Resources of the Bank		Employment of resources	
Capital and reserve	2000000	Scotland	9373000
Circulation	674000	London	2230000
Deposits	10326000	Government and other stocks	1305000
		Gold and silver coin and balances with Bank of	
Sundry accounts	782000	England and other bankers	874000
Total resources	13782000	Total resources employed	13782000

Result in profit		
Gross interest received	565697	
Gross interest paid out	265511	
Net interest		300186
Commissions	39122	
Rents	4390	
Subtotal		343698
Less charges	130985	
Leaving net profit		£212713

Source: BS 1/70/6, Annual Reports of the Treasurer, 1866–98.

(£10,326,000) and sundry accounts (£782,000), all totalling £13,782,000; the disposition of this was £9,373,000 in Scotland, £2,230,000 in London, £1,305,000 in government and other stocks, and £874,000 in gold and silver coin, balances at the Bank of England and other London bankers. The net profit account for 1878–9 was £212,713 (see Table 17.2).[2] The report then summarised all the different activities of the Bank, for each of which details were provided in a series of attached papers which itemised, down to each branch, the categories of profits, lending, bad debts, the different rates of interest received and charged and the Bank's internal costs. The Treasurer noted that the profit for 1879 was £9,386 higher than the previous year, 'a result which seems disappointing because the margin of profit was greater than in the previous year'. But, he continued:

> it must be borne in mind . . . that the average sum lent over the year was much the same as in the previous year, the increase in the Bank's resources having only recently taken place, while in the early months of the year there was on the contrary a considerable decrease.

Also, the unproductive balance at the Bank of England, on the average £190,000 higher than that of the previous year, was run up for a time to

2 See Statistical Appendix, Table A4.

nearly £1,000,000, and costs had increased by £11,723. In fact, the position was more serious. Irretrievable losses in Scotland were £27,600, and old debts required another £5,400 (there was a trifling £800 in London). The question of the size of the debts associated with James Morton & Co. was 'to be left for the future'; nevertheless, £42,000 was put aside for this. This all totalled £75,800. To pay for this, the whole of the existing Fund for Losses (£58,000) was taken and £36,000 from the profits of the current year, which left £18,200 in the Fund. The Bank's holding of its own stock, valued in the books at £314 11s 9d but with the market price at £270, was written down to £250, although there was a mark-up of British government consolidated stocks. The appropriation from current profits left £176,700 for distribution to proprietors. In view of the exceptional circumstances following the City of Glasgow collapse and the possibilities of additional commercial failures together with the continued depression of the agricultural sector, it was 'deemed prudent' to reduce the rate of dividend to 13 per cent. With the balance carried over from the previous year, the sum of £20,000 represented the undivided profits available for the coming year.

The board was provided with a complete list of all the larger current account and bill advances, the type of security and a list of the advances which were not covered by heritable property. At March 1879, there were thirty-eight businesses of which twelve were in London, holding advances between £50,000 and £100,000; these included F. S. Sandeman's of Dundee (£52,535), J. & P. Coats of Paisley (£90,655) and the Glebe Sugar Refinery Co. of Greenock (£83,409) (see Table 17.3). The total sums advanced in this category amounted to £2,730,000, of which £256,208 was uncovered. In addition came five accounts in Glasgow and five in the London office with advances above £100,000; a total of £3,245,636. The rise of loans to foreign banks, stockbrokers and bill brokers was a noteworthy feature of this category, which also claimed £412,521 of debts due from James Morton & Co. and another, separate debt of £286,589 from the Australian and New Zealand Land Co. The borrowings of merchants and manufacturers were covered by personal security, stocks and shares and only to a lesser extent by their heritable property, often factory buildings (see Tables 17.4a and 17.4b). Country gentlemen continued to provide most cover by heritable property, just as they had in the eighteenth century, but their proportion of total borrowing in Scotland was now under 4 per cent.

The lending figures for the Scottish branches show a divergence between bills and cash accounts. Borrowings on the long-established cash account and overdraft were spread widely across the branch networks (see Table 17.5). The percentage of advances was always highest at Glasgow,

Table 17.3 *Bank of Scotland advances over £50,000 at March 1879*

Branch	Name	Bills	Current or loan accounts	London obligations	Total	Uncovered
Dundee	George Gilroy		15387	47764	63151	41237
Dundee	Kinmond, Luke & Co.	39493	4500	50219	94212	7154
Dundee	Edward Parker & Co.	910	58913		59823	17499
Dundee	James Paterson		82427		82427	
Dundee	F. S. Sandeman	3810	48725		52535	
Galashiels	Sanderson & Murray	53986	45911		99897	20911
Glasgow	Arthur & Co. Ltd	97993			97993	
Glasgow	J. & W. Campbell & Co.	55868	4320		60188	
Glasgow	Clark, Wilson & Co.	34138		21264	55402	18732
Glasgow	J. R. Cochrane & Co.	54624			54624	
Glasgow	Debts formerly due by Buchanan, Wilson & Co.		54605		54605	
Glasgow	C. Dunlop & Co.		72573		72573	12573
Glasgow	James Dunlop & Co.		90575		90575	
Glasgow	John Hendrie	3100	56180		59280	21180
Glasgow	Robert Kettle & Co.	62806			62806	
Glasgow	Matheson & Alston	6994	66172		73166	
Glasgow	McIntyre, Hogg & Co.	57518	1762		59280	
Glasgow	Okell & Co.	28696	23179		51875	15179
Glasgow	Summerlee Iron Co.	2155	48090		50245	28090
Glasgow	Thomson & Gray and others	28640	54053		82693	
Greenock	Glebe Sugar Refinery Co.	23333	60076		83409	
Greenock	John Kerr & Co.	14179	55518		69697	
Greenock	Abram Lyle & Sons	2549	54595		57144	
Leith	Berry Barclay & Co.	58010	2134		60144	1124
Paisley	J. & P. Coats	38181	52474		90655	52474
Perth	John Shields & Co.	24850	64957		89807	20055
London	Adamson Gilfillan & Co.	40975	21955	8715	71645	
London	H. D. Anderson & Co.	50000	35000		85000	
London	Brown, Gurney & Baker	53276	10000		63276	
London	Edgar Corry & Co.	19752	45000		64752	
London	Grigg & Co.		65000		65000	
London	Harwood Knight & Allen	50000	50000		100000	
London	National Mortgage & Agency Co.		65500		65500	
London	National Discount Co.		100000		100000	
London	Pixley & Abell		100000		100000	
London	Sanderson Murray & Co.		75850		75850	
London	Vivian & Sons		51774		51774	
London	Speyer Brothers	59000			59000	
	Total loans £50,000–£100,000	964836	1637205	127962	2730003	256208
Glasgow	Debts formerly due by J. Morton & Co.	87799	324722		412521	
Glasgow	Martin Turner & Co.	94911	30087	157694	282692	4687
Glasgow	New Zealand & Australian Land Co.		249589	37000	286589	5000
Glasgow	Steel Company of Scotland	7926	95446		103372	20446
Glasgow	Gregor Turnbull & Co.	4934	107302		112236	75002
London	Thomas Corbett	44645	76227		120872	
London	Reeves Whitburn & Co.		220000		220000	
London	Sheppard Pelly & Co.		270000		270000	
London	Canadian Bank of Commerce		96836	468623	565459	
London	Oriental Bank Corporation			871895	871895	
	Total loans over £100,000	240215	1470209	1535212	3245636	105135
	Total loans over £50,000	1205051	3107414	1663174	5975639	361343

Source: BS 1/70/6, Annual Reports of the Treasurer, 1866–98.

Table 17.4a *Bank of Scotland advances at 28 February 1879, secured or partly secured on works*

Name of party	Branch	Total advances secured on works	Total advances partly secured on works
C. & J. Oswald	Denny	3000	
Anderson & Murray	Galashiels		25000
W. Muir & Sons	Glasgow Laurieston	5000	
McGregor, Adam & Co.	Glasgow Cross	500	
Rennie & Wilson	Glasgow Whitevale	745	
Smith & Davidson	Greenock	1578	
Taylor & Henderson	Hamilton	2000	
W. & M. Thomson	Kilmarnock		5000
J. Carlisle, Sons & Co.	Paisley	5000	
McDonald & Fraser	Perth	8000	
John Shields & Co.	Perth	20000	
J. Bradford	Dundee		2000
Gordon & Campbell	Dundee		5000
J. Laing & Sons	Dundee	10000	
J. Mitchell	Dundee	7000	
C. Norrie	Dundee	3000	
H. Samson & Sons	Dundee		2000
F. S. Sandeman	Dundee	25000	
Thomson, Shepherd & Co.	Dundee	18898	
J. Templeton & Co.	Glasgow	3000	
J. Dunlop & Co.	Glasgow		100000
John Spencer	Glasgow		3000
Dunlop & Twaddell	Glasgow		10000
McLure, Phillips & Co.	Glasgow	3000	
Colin Dunlop & Co.	Glasgow		60000
Watson, Gow & Co.	Glasgow	20000	
T. R. Johnstone	Glasgow	5000	
J. H. Young & Co.	Glasgow	10000	
G. Eadie & Sons	Glasgow	8000	
Gibson Brothers & Co.	Glasgow		4000
Total		158721	216000

Source: BS 1/70/6, Annual Reports of the Treasurer, 1866–98.

Table 17.4b *Summary of advances in Scotland at 28 February 1879 and 1880*

Category	1879		1880	
	Bills	Current accounts	Bills	Current accounts
Merchants and manufacturers	3526501	3046097	2986775	2284790
Country gentlemen	10521	244419	13445	278471
Farmers and country tradesmen	280003	622994	242951	509856
Miscellaneous	300151	602893	189016	453395
Total	4117176	4516403	3432187	3526512

Source: BS 1/70/6, Annual Reports of the Treasurer, 1866–98.

Table 17.5 *Bank of Scotland lending on current accounts at selected branches as percentage of total average lent, 1872–1919*

As percentage of total	1872	1873	1874	1875	1876	1877	1878	1879	1880	1881	1882	1883
Dundee	6.50	8.08	10.81	12.52	14.66	14.75	15.41	14.36	13.40	14.87	15.75	15.27
Greenock	4.35	6.63	6.49	4.77	5.72	6.30	7.09	6.07	5.15	4.34	3.48	5.27
Paisley	5.08	4.58	5.19	3.48	2.61	2.94	2.33	1.86	1.29	0.39	0.38	0.52
Kirkcaldy	0.56	0.44	0.38	0.34	0.18	0.44	0.69	0.91	0.85	0.89	1.27	1.73
Leith	0.77	1.44	1.80	1.57	1.30	1.28	1.08	1.07	0.90	1.16	1.39	1.29
Perth	3.14	3.01	3.33	3.01	2.89	3.11	3.20	3.00	3.30	3.69	3.89	3.21
Glasgow	28.80	29.94	37.87	40.29	37.42	35.39	33.05	36.70	39.95	32.78	32.60	34.24
Head office	23.20	17.98	5.49	5.74	6.42	6.38	5.58	5.23	8.50	6.93	6.14	5.90
Total (%)	72.40	72.10	71.36	71.72	71.20	70.59	68.43	69.20	73.34	65.05	64.90	67.43

As percentage of total	1884	1885	1886	1887	1888	1889	1890	1891	1892	1893	1894	1895
Dundee	14.48	13.25	10.97	10.82	10.32	10.18	9.59	9.41	8.79	9.37	7.97	8.53
Greenock	7.01	7.09	7.25	7.92	7.96	7.14	6.68	6.13	6.46	7.92	8.00	8.08
Paisley	0.58	0.61	2.43	1.35	1.40	2.73	2.64	4.01	4.24	3.71	1.35	0.60
Kirkcaldy	2.02	1.80	1.69	2.03	3.00	3.55	3.26	1.72	1.71	1.53	1.30	1.20
Leith	1.28	0.86	1.36	1.30	1.45	1.88	1.92	1.87	1.84	1.43	1.10	1.03
Perth	2.96	3.13	2.93	3.24	3.04	2.82	2.77	2.57	2.61	2.62	2.76	2.37
Glasgow	35.16	36.72	35.45	35.12	35.00	35.55	36.79	36.98	36.49	36.52	40.45	42.64
Head office	5.11	5.00	4.89	5.05	6.13	5.31	5.80	7.40	8.09	7.84	7.36	6.47
Total (%)	68.60	68.46	66.97	66.83	68.30	69.16	69.45	70.09	70.23	70.94	70.29	70.92

As percentage of total	1896	1897	1898	1899	1900	1901	1902	1903	1904	1905	1906	1907
Dundee	8.66	9.31	9.62	9.16	8.56	6.49	6.20	6.20	6.05	6.81	6.77	7.68
Greenock	8.84	8.75	7.64	7.15	5.49	4.46	4.47	3.87	3.24	3.09	3.64	3.02
Paisley	0.38	0.75	0.86	1.02	1.09	1.42	1.29	1.36	1.38	1.67	1.65	1.45
Kirkcaldy	1.13	1.41	1.63	1.93	2.47	3.96	5.47	5.43	5.22	4.80	4.10	2.75
Leith	1.01	1.14	0.99	1.43	1.74	2.18	2.56	2.63	2.38	2.44	2.54	2.34
Perth	2.72	3.10	3.11	3.46	3.73	3.99	4.12	4.09	3.71	3.54	3.79	3.40
Glasgow	43.88	41.10	40.96	37.49	36.25	32.61	27.21	30.97	32.96	29.80	30.27	34.53
Head office	2.64	2.16	2.34	2.95	2.95	3.13	5.23	5.17	4.75	4.94	5.99	7.20
Total (%)	69.26	67.72	67.15	64.59	62.28	58.24	56.55	59.72	59.69	57.09	58.75	62.37

As percentage of total	1908	1909	1910	1911	1912	1913	1914	1915	1916	1917	1918	1919
Dundee	8.20	7.54	8.67	9.36	8.42	8.27	8.73	9.67	6.80	6.04	4.93	4.87
Greenock	3.09	2.85	2.70	2.69	2.74	1.84	2.81	2.81	2.54	0.73	0.65	0.88
Paisley	1.31	1.30	1.54	1.85	2.15	2.24	2.27	2.61	2.75	2.87	1.90	2.03
Kirkcaldy	3.39	3.35	2.89	3.02	2.72	2.64	2.60	2.63	2.81	3.42	3.58	2.41
Leith	2.29	2.04	2.13	2.30	2.31	2.27	2.13	2.36	2.32	1.55	1.15	1.28
Perth	2.59	2.21	2.24	2.12	2.18	2.62	3.22	3.63	3.39	4.71	3.85	2.90
Glasgow	33.51	32.24	30.64	26.08	25.35	25.10	26.47	25.58	26.90	26.52	31.97	35.03
Head office	6.33	5.66	5.41	5.62	5.91	6.86	6.64	6.06	5.46	5.33	7.76	5.66
Total (%)	60.71	57.19	56.22	53.04	51.78	51.84	54.87	55.35	52.97	51.17	55.79	55.06

Source: BS 1/70/14, Analysis of the resources of Bank of Scotland.

although rarely above 40 per cent and often much below, and the seven leading branches, together with the Mound, showed a decline from over 70 per cent of advances in the 1870s to little above 50 per cent by 1914. Lending by bills remained concentrated at Dundee, Greenock, Paisley and Glasgow as well as head office, and never fell below 86 per cent. The importance of the Glasgow bill trade was striking (see Table 17.6).

James Adams Wenley always enumerated the bad and doubtful debts for the whole country, with every item named for the particular firm and the Bank of Scotland branch responsible. The largest were the aforementioned debts and securities of James Morton & Co. and the two other serious debtors connected to Morton's, namely Buchanan, Wilson & Co. and Kames Gunpowder & Co., which owed a total of £55,410 in 1879. The entire bad and doubtful debts were tabulated by firm, amount and branch under various section headings: debts for which provision was being made for the first time; debts previously provided for but become worse; debts previously provided for but become better; debts previously provided for and remaining unchanged. The summing-up recorded the debts considered 'wholly or partially bad' at £524,274, of which £412,521 was represented by the amount debited to James Morton & Co. The overall total, including this first item of debts wholly or partially bad, was £660,286, and the Treasurer calculated the total provision required during 1879–80 at £145,516. There could be no doubt as to the true position of the Bank with these papers which Wenley placed before the directors. The only criticism which might be made would be that the state of the accounts implied that less should be paid out to proprietors and extra provision made over to the Fund for Losses.

Wenley's reports to the directors for the next twenty years began with a brief summary of business conditions in Scotland and then continued with a view of the Bank's resources, their employment, the position of bad and doubtful debts, and the final net profit for the year. A series of papers was attached which provided details of various items mentioned in the main report. He would at times place the current figures in historical context while emphasising for any year the most important matters for comment. Throughout, there is a clear understanding of the relationship between the state of trade – the phrase the 'trade cycle' was not used at this time – and the general conditions within which the Bank earned its profits. In 1880, he noticed a shift in the proportion of lending between London and Scotland which was, in fact, to prove a long-term move. It was the falling-off by more than £1 million in Scottish lending, 'always the most remunerative' of all monies loaned, which was of especial concern. The surplus funds sent to London obtained for many months in 1879–80 only nominal returns. While over £8,500,000 was employed in Scotland,

Table 17.6 *Bank of Scotland lending on bills current at selected branches as percentage of total average lent, 1872–1919*

As percentage of total	1872	1873	1874	1875	1876	1877	1878	1879	1880	1881	1882	1883
Dundee	8.91	9.37	9.23	11.64	13.28	13.28	10.94	9.35	9.00	7.10	6.17	5.64
Greenock	4.60	6.46	5.55	6.02	6.42	5.62	3.74	4.55	5.19	5.02	5.21	5.13
Paisley	5.64	5.72	5.44	5.43	3.55	3.70	3.13	2.72	2.40	1.37	1.29	1.27
Glasgow (including loan accounts)	63.68	62.17	64.33	60.62	60.66	60.62	60.33	62.52	57.92	64.25	62.55	64.67
Head office	1.14	1.00	0.99	1.00	1.04	1.67	2.27	2.42	2.46	1.96	1.95	1.55
Remaining branches	8.11	7.17	6.14	8.31	7.81	7.01	11.42	8.97	12.74	11.18	13.62	13.08
Total (%)	92.08	91.89	91.68	93.02	92.76	91.90	91.83	90.53	89.71	90.88	90.79	91.34

As percentage of total	1884	1885	1886	1887	1888	1889	1890	1891	1892	1893	1894	1895
Dundee	5.15	5.61	5.47	5.62	5.35	5.13	5.62	5.01	6.89	7.05	5.50	4.13
Greenock	4.56	2.75	5.15	4.33	2.25	1.76	0.84	0.72	0.77	1.21	1.15	0.80
Paisley	1.44	1.56	1.19	0.89	1.05	1.55	0.94	1.06	0.63	0.82	0.56	0.32
Glasgow (including loan accounts)	66.87	64.41	61.58	63.08	65.97	67.42	67.97	68.60	65.95	65.17	66.42	71.25
Head office	1.10	1.60	2.35	2.25	1.91	1.72	2.44	2.95	3.24	3.10	2.49	2.76
Remaining branches	12.44	14.36	14.91	14.54	14.46	13.20	9.63	9.20	9.60	10.15	10.52	9.49
Total (%)	91.56	90.29	90.65	90.71	90.99	90.78	87.44	87.54	87.08	87.50	86.64	88.75

As percentage of total	1896	1897	1898	1899	1900	1901	1902	1903	1904	1905	1906	1907
Dundee	3.27	2.73	3.27	4.33	3.93	4.38	4.19	3.60	3.99	4.72	4.12	3.50
Greenock	0.75	0.79	0.62	0.38	0.30	0.19	0.23	0.21	0.30	0.36	0.36	0.40
Paisley	0.13	0.23	0.23	0.10	0.07	0.19	0.12	0.10	0.08	0.04	0.07	0.07
Glasgow (including loan accounts)	74.19	74.69	69.86	71.56	71.65	70.89	69.60	72.18	71.86	71.31	74.93	75.70
Head office	1.23	1.03	1.56	1.96	2.25	2.21	2.40	2.21	2.15	2.10	1.95	1.95
Remaining branches	9.50	9.63	10.95	10.51	11.08	11.39	11.24	10.38	10.77	10.61	9.87	9.14
Total (%)	89.07	89.10	86.49	88.84	89.28	89.25	87.78	88.68	89.15	89.14	91.30	90.76

As percentage of total	1908	1909	1910	1911	1912	1913	1914	1915	1916	1917	1918	1919
Dundee	4.16	3.75	2.72	2.61	2.35	2.08	2.83	4.16	3.13	1.56	1.83	2.19
Greenock	0.43	0.48	0.39	0.24	0.11	0.16	0.13	0.10	0.00	0.00	0.00	0.00
Paisley	0.08	0.04	0.04	0.03	0.04	0.39	0.04	0.05	0.14	0.17	0.10	0.00
Glasgow (including loan accounts)	71.62	66.83	69.08	72.53	72.34	70.44	68.03	64.37	66.41	74.72	76.97	80.90
Head office	1.80	1.49	1.21	0.90	1.45	1.37	1.44	1.52	2.42	1.04	0.96	0.73
Remaining branches	12.03	14.73	14.86	13.70	13.77	14.57	15.02	16.40	16.51	13.85	11.46	10.71
Total (%)	90.12	87.32	88.30	90.01	90.06	89.01	87.49	86.60	88.61	91.34	91.32	94.53

Source: BS 1/70/14, Analysis of the resources of Bank of Scotland.

the figure rose above £4 million in London – a significant increase in the London–Scotland ratio compared with before 1878 (see Figure 17.7).[3]

The trade patterns of the 1880s as described by Wenley follow the well-known cyclical movements long accepted by economic historians. From the later months of 1880, trade generally moved on an upward but somewhat irregular trend, and economic improvement was reflected in the accounts of Bank of Scotland. The Treasurer even wrote of the 'partial prosperity' of 1881, but this also reflected a marked increase in the 'demand in London for stock-exchange purposes'. Deposits in this year continued to show substantial increases, and the resources of the Bank in these years were larger than ever. Farming continued in a 'very unsatisfactory state'. The beginning of the break in the upward movement of trade – these years, as J. H. Clapham noted, were the last when British railway materials were exported to the USA[4] – was noted by the Treasurer in his report for 1883–4, and in the following year he registered a depression in all sectors of industry and emphasised the remarkable fall in commodity prices with the accompanying rise in the number of failures and the growth of bad debts. Profits, which had increased to 1884, when they reached £237,467, fell in 1885 to £185,255, lower than any year since 1877.[5] Writing off bad debts was the main cause. All the main problems of the Scottish banks were discussed at the regular quarterly meetings of the General Managers Committee; and, as the depression continued, concern was expressed that the very detailed cooperation to widen the interest-rate margins could only stem the deterioration, not reverse it. By 1884, the figures for profits as a percentage of deposits were giving cause for alarm (see Table 17.8).

The report for 1885–6 continued the gloomy picture for industry and trade in general. Under these circumstances, Bank business was to be conducted with anxiety. The dullness of trade in Scotland 'restricted the demand for money for local discounts and advances, so that [a] large proportion of our resources has been unavoidably employed in London at low rates'. Losses from bad debts were considerable. Looking to the future, Wenley suggested that 'there seems to be ground for much apprehension, for it is difficult to see how, in the present state of trade and agriculture, failures can be prevented'. The next year's report was more optimistic about the 'unmistakeable signs' that trade and business were improving. The jute and coal industries were especially remarked upon as showing

3 See Statistical Appendix, Table A18.
4 J. H. Clapham, An Economic History of Modern Britain [vol. ii], Free Trade and Steel, 1850–1886 (Cambridge: 1932), p. 227. In 1881, the USA imported 294,000 tons of British railway materials; in 1884 the total was 18,000 tons.
5 See Statistical Appendix, Table A4.

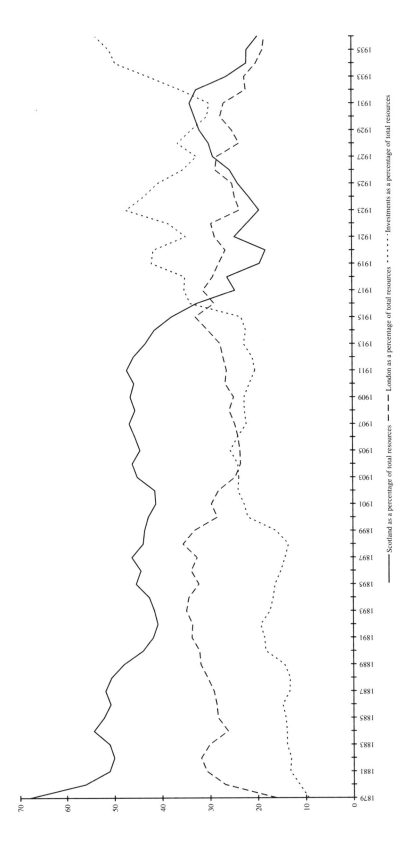

Figure 17.7 Employment of Bank's resources in Scotland and London, and investments, as a percentage of total resources, 1879–1936

——— Scotland as a percentage of total resources · · · · · London as a percentage of total resources · · · · · · · · · · Investments as a percentage of total resources

Source: BS 1/70/14, Analysis of the resources of Bank of Scotland.

Table 17.8 *Falling-off in the percentage of Scottish banks' profits from deposits since 1869*

		Paid-up capital and reserves*	Deposits*	Declared profits*	Deduct 4 per cent on paid-up capital and reserves	Amount of profit from deposits	Profit on deposits as a percentage of deposits
Bank of Scotland	1865–9	1275000	7317000	136777	51000	85777	1.17
	1870–4	1317000	8930000	142170	52680	89490	1.00
	1875–9	1759000	10708000	175253	70360	104893	0.98
	1880–4	2015000	12725000	178553	80600	97953	0.77
Royal Bank of Scotland	1865–9	2368000	8464000	186678	94720	91958	1.09
	1870–4	2420000	9042000	181065	96800	84265	0.93
	1875–9	2542000	10383000	199605	101680	97925	0.94
	1880–4	2739000	12169000	204512	109560	94952	0.78
British Linen Bank	1865–9	1308000	7155000	143357	52320	91037	1.27
	1870–4	1348000	7432000	142929	53920	89009	1.20
	1875–9	1392000	7872000	154678	55680	98998	1.26
	1880–4	1650000	9555000	156395	66000	90395	0.95
Commercial Bank of Scotland	1865–9	1281000	7505000	148185	51240	96945	1.29
	1870–4	1372000	8255000	155308	54880	100428	1.22
	1875–9	1418000	9342000	157048	56720	100328	1.07
	1880–4	1494000	9397000	141578	59760	81818	0.87
National Bank of Scotland	1865–9	1276000	7740000	135565	51040	84525	1.09
	1870–4	1341000	9081000	159985	53640	106345	1.17
	1875–9	1447000	10964000	171665	57880	113785	1.04
	1880–4	1572000	12163000	163474	62880	100594	0.83
Union Bank of Scotland	1865–9	1231000	8195000	139760	49240	90520	1.10
	1870–4	1316000	8685000	146216	52640	93576	1.08
	1875–9	1342000	9288000	148141	53680	94461	1.02
	1880–4	1344000	10425000	137118	53760	83358	0.80
Clydesdale Bank	1865–9	1137000	4754000	109524	45480	64044	1.35
	1870–4	1186000	5798000	129679	47440	82239	1.42
	1875–9	1500000	6575000	139216	60000	79216	1.20
	1880–4	1522000	7426000	129963	60880	69083	0.93
Town & County Bank	1865–9	210000	1423000	27446	8400	19046	1.34
	1870–4	271000	1544000	23723	10840	12883	0.83
	1875–9	373000	1875000	36046	14920	21126	1.13
	1880–4	378000	1946000	33156	15120	18036	0.93
North of Scotland Bank	1865–9	362000	1749000	35555	14480	21075	1.20
	1870–4	378000	1983000	36752	15120	21632	1.09
	1875–9	554000	2589000	51418	22160	29258	1.13
	1880–4	606000	2847000	51490	24240	27250	0.96
Caledonian Bank	1865–9	160000	691000	18105	6400	11705	1.69
	1870–4	179000	821000	19116	7160	11956	1.46
	1875–9	217000	1113000	22289	8680	13609	1.22
	1880–4	160000	624000	8218	6400	1818	0.29
All banks (averages)	1865–9	10608000	54993000	1080952	424320	656632	1.19
	1870–4	11128000	61571000	1136943	445120	691823	1.12
	1875–9	12544000	70709000	1255359	501760	753599	1.07
	1880–4	13480000	79277000	1204457	539200	665257	0.84

*Averages of five years.

Source: BS 20/4/17, Scotch Banks: Falling off in the percentage of profits from deposits since 1869.

improvement. Farming was the exception, the previous year having been one of the worst in the general depression so far. From the point of view of the Bank's business, however, the cumulative effects of the economic stagnation of recent years meant that the volume of bad debts was higher than for several years, increased unexpectedly by a loss of £24,000 in the London office.

In respect of Bank advances, the most significant change during this period, as already noticed, was the relative weakness of industrial and commercial investment within Scotland and the more buoyant outlets for Scottish money in London, although these were usually placed at lower rates of return. *The Economist's* banking supplement of May 1878 pointed out that there was 'a close connection between the opening of the London office of a Scottish bank and the increase of its mercantile acceptances'. In fact, in 1876–7 those acceptances of Bank of Scotland and the National Bank in London were equal to nearly a quarter of the 'total acceptances of all the London joint stock banks together'.[6] At the London office of Bank of Scotland, the managers were in no doubt as to the business potential. The patterns of world trade were altering from the 1870s with the expansion of multilateralism to cover mercantile relations involving the industrial nations with the primary producers. London became the financial centre of a global system of payments, to which the Indian Empire was quite crucial, with sterling virtually the equivalent of gold.[7] By 1870 there were around 120 banks in the City of London, and these included some forty overseas companies, many from the Dominions and colonies. Twenty years later, there were 128 major banks in addition to a large number of foreign banks represented often by a single office.[8] The combination of trade depression in Scotland and the growing financial enlargement of London's operations explains the shift in resources in the 1880s to the London offices of the Scottish banks.

From 1878 to 1880, overall deposits at Bank of Scotland rose by almost £1.8 million, and this provided the funds for the redeployment of resources. While advances declined in Scotland from 1880 and remained below this level until 1908, advances through the London office rose from around £1.1 million in February 1878 to £4.1 million two years later and

6 *The Economist*, 11 May 1878.
7 An early, succinct statement is in League of Nations, *The Network of World Trade: A Companion Volume to 'Europe's Trade'* (Geneva: 1942), pp. 73–97; a more detailed and somewhat controversial account is in C. K. Harley and D. McCloskey, 'Foreign Trade: Competition and the Expanding International Economy', in R. Floud and D. McCloskey (eds), *The Economic History of Britain since 1700*, vol. ii, *1860 to the 1970s* (Cambridge: 1981), pp. 50–69. There is a more elementary but acceptable survey in A. G. Kenwood and A. L. Lougheed, *The Growth of the International Economy 1820–1990: An Introductory Text*, 3rd edn (London: 1992), ch. 6.
8 J. H. Clapham, *Bank of England*, vol. ii, p. 350. There were nearly 100 in what Clapham calls the 'second list'.

remained at around one-third of Bank resources to the end of the century (see Figure 17.7). There were other reasons for this shift; a number of Scottish firms moved to London in the depression, and there was a relatively slower growth of new industries in Scotland compared with England. The board was concerned in the aftermath of the City of Glasgow disaster that the much-increased loans made in London should be properly covered by adequate securities, and in November 1880 a committee of directors investigated the arrangements in the London office. For loans to bill brokers, it was not the practice to require a margin of security: 'where an acceptor of a bill failed the rule was to call on the borrower [the broker] at once to take it away and lodge a good bill in its place'.[9] For advances to stockbrokers against stocks and bonds, a margin of 1 per cent was required, with railway securities and foreign bonds attracting the highest margin, at 10 per cent. It was understandable that the London office was prepared to make huge advances for short periods, given that the securities offered were tradeable and their prices well known. Nevertheless, the committee was dissatisfied with the size of some loans, and recommended a limit of £500,000 and the opening of more brokers' accounts 'for the purpose of spreading the risks'. The directors were also concerned about the 'convertibility of certain foreign securities of apparently little value in themselves', but received assurances from a leading broker that even in the worst of times such securities were readily saleable. In general, the London office remained tightly run and was subject to regular inspections, and while Wenley remained Treasurer the directors, many of whom were fully conversant with London markets, kept an active control over business at the London office.

The shift in use of overall resources to London, and the growing familiarity with the London bill trade and stockmarkets, encouraged further moves by Bank of Scotland in the direction of the stock and bond markets directly utilising its own resources.[10] In 1879, the Bank investments comprised £957,500 of 3 per cent consols, £105,600 of Canadian government 4 per cent bonds, five UK railway stocks and £85,742 of Bank of Scotland stock, which, together with smaller individual holdings of colonial and UK investments, came to £1,319,564. Over the next year the Bank bought another fifteen US, colonial and railway stocks, including debentures of six Indian railways, and together these had a market price of £2,154,475. Investments never fell below 13 per cent of resources in the next decade. Thus one of the consequences of the crisis of 1879 was to press the board to find higher rates of return in London and abroad and to ensure that,

9 BS 1/70/4, Special Reports; BS 1/6, Minutes, 23 November 1880.
10 For the rise in London business, see Statistical Appendix, Table A18.

on balance, Bank of Scotland provided a permanent source of funds for these investments.

The export of British capital was rising, somewhat irregularly but substantially, throughout the 1880s, and the Bank of England by the end of the decade was watching the exchanges closely.[11] The bank rate had been 6 per cent at the end of 1889, and only in April and May 1890 did it fall below 4 per cent. On 7 November 1890, the bank rate was raised again to 6 per cent, and this was a prelude to what became known as the Baring Crisis. It was common knowledge in the City that Barings were in difficulties, and as early as July 1890 Wenley had been advised of the problem.[12] The House of Baring, merchant bankers, were specialists in Latin American affairs. The City, in the later 1880s, was flooded with prospectuses of all manner of Latin American enterprises, all promising a high return. A number of these projects were associated with politicians and businessmen who mixed their serious investment with fraud and speculation. As *The Economist* later wrote, 'the temptation to add riches to riches is hard to resist'. Barings faced liabilities of almost £21 million and had no choice but to approach William Lidderdale, Governor of the Bank of England, who in turn talked with the Chancellor of the Exchequer, George Goschen. The government was not willing to intervene at this stage, and Goschen told Lidderdale that 'the great houses must get together and give the necessary guarantee'.[13] The sequence of events has been told by the historian of the Bank of England. William Lidderdale refused the suggestion of a temporary suspension of the 1844 Bank Charter Act and set about raising a guarantor fund. The bank itself put in £1 million; the London private bankers made large contributions followed by the five principal joint-stock banks, which contributed as much as the Bank of England and the private banks together – a measure of the commanding place which they were beginning to occupy in British finance. By the end of the first week of negotiating, Lidderdale was able to tell the Chancellor that the fund would now exceed £17 million, as a result, wrote J. H. Clapham, of the 'Scottish, provincial and colonial and foreign banks' having come in with their contributions together with other discount houses, finance houses, private banks and mercantile firms.[14] What Clapham omitted was the story of how some of these additional guarantors 'came in'; and the story of Bank of Scotland and other Scottish banks in this affair is unlikely to be unique.

---

11 There is a considerable discussion of the consequences of the export of capital in A. R. Hall (ed.), *The Export of Capital from Britain, 1870–1914* (London: 1968).
12 BS 20/3/9, K. Gibson to J. A. Wenley, 19 July 1890.
13 Clapham, *Bank of England*, vol. ii, p. 329.
14 Ibid., p. 335.

It was either late on Friday 14 November or early on the Saturday morning that William Lidderdale and the Deputy Governor, David Powell, met Robert Davidson, London office manager of Bank of Scotland, for a serious discussion on the amount of financial assistance that could be forthcoming. Davidson then sent a coded telegram to Wenley in Edinburgh which provided a summary of the discussions but without putting a figure to the total of money demanded. At 11:37 a.m., a further telegram, in plain English, was sent to Wenley asking him to call a meeting of all Scottish managers on the following Monday. Davidson had a further, difficult meeting at the Bank about the sums involved, and arranged to go to Edinburgh to report in person. On Monday, the deputy manager of the London office confirmed to Edinburgh that the fund stood at £10 million, and at the general managers' meeting Bank of Scotland, the Royal Bank and the British Linen each offered £250,000. Nothing was promised from the other Scottish banks, and there was some opposition to a guarantee without security.

Robert Davidson returned to London, and on Tuesday 18 November he was told that the sums offered were quite unacceptable. It was pointed out that the London and County had the same paid-up capital as the Royal Bank but had come forward with an offer of £750,000, and that Bank of Scotland and the British Linen together had a capital equal to the London and Westminster, which had also offered £750,000. Lidderdale then sent a note to Davidson later on 18 November which encapsulated certain deep-rooted prejudices of the City of London:

> I am ashamed of my countrymen. £250,000 each from the three most important Scotch Banks as a contribution towards an effort to avert a national disaster! You Scots Bankers are dependent upon the Bank of England for the prompt return of the large sums employed in this Market and for the safety of a considerable part of the security you hold against that money. If the Bank of England had failed to save Barings, not a bill you hold would have been beyond question. Are you wise to be so shabby? The presence of your Agencies in London is not favourably regarded in England and next time your privileges are considered in connection with the general question of Note issues will it help you to have it on record that the Scotch Banks did so little in Nov. '90 for the common welfare?[15]

There were other threats. The manager of one joint-stock bank which had called in bills to brokers was sent for and informed that if the guarantee agreement was not upheld the Bank of England would close its account

15 BS 20/2/23, Bank of Scotland correspondence on Barings, William Lidderdale to Robert Davidson, 18 November 1890.

and place an announcement to that effect in the London press.[16] By this day, the seven largest Scottish banks had already agreed on £250,000 each, but Lidderdale continued to insist on £2 million. Wenley then offered by telegram to Davidson another £100,000 with the hint that the Royal Bank and the National would follow suit. By that afternoon, Wenley seems to have realised their mistake over the politics involved, and he left for London by the overnight train. There he saw Bertram Currie of Glyn, Mills, Currie & Co., who was a friend of the Baring family and 'admittedly the first authority in the City on banking questions'.[17] Later, Wenley talked with Lord Rothschild. They both assured him that Barings was ultimately sound. By 12:30 he was at Threadneedle Street, but the Governor was engaged and Wenley conveyed his message through David Powell. The Scottish banks, Wenley insisted, had misunderstood the view of the Bank of England, and in turn the Governor accepted the £2 million. 'The fact is', Wenley wrote later to the Royal Bank, 'that the Governor is making the matter of Barings a personal affair, and it is highly expedient in our own interest to humour him'.[18] Lidderdale also gave Charles Gairdner of the Union Bank 'a good jagging', although the precise form that this took has not been recorded.

Wenley was right to fear further moves against the Scottish banks. The following Saturday, *The Times* noted that 'it is thought probable in well-informed quarters that the supply of gold from abroad would require a Royal Commission to look at the Bank Charter Act of 1844'. Further, 'it has been known for some time past' that George Goschen wished to make 'changes in the law affecting bank-note issues'.[19] These 'well-informed quarters' were none other than Lidderdale and Goschen, who were considering once again an independent Bank of England with the sole right of note issue for the United Kingdom.

The total guarantee raised for Barings was £17 million against liabilities of around £21 million. The wording of the guarantee agreement, to which all guarantors subscribed, was reprinted in *The Economist* of 22 November 1890.[20] All subscribers were committed to make good to the Bank of England 'any loss which may appear whenever the Bank of England shall determine that the final liquidation of Messrs Baring Brothers and Co. has been completed'. Liquidation was to be on a pro-rata basis and completed within three years. Barings was restructured as a limited company, and by

16 E. T. Powell, *The Evolution of the Money Market* (London: 1915), p. 527; quoted in R. C. K. Ensor, *England 1870–1914* (Oxford: 1936), p. 283, note 1.
17 Clapham, *Bank of England*, vol. ii, p. 331.
18 BS 20/2/3, Bank of Scotland correspondence on Barings.
19 *The Times*, 24 November 1890, reprinted in T. E. Gregory (ed.), *Select Statutes, Documents and Reports Relating to British Banking, 1832–1928*, vol. ii, *1847–1928* (Oxford: 1929), pp. 193–4.
20 Ibid., pp. 199–200.

mid-January 1895 – fourteen months after the expiry date of the original agreement – settlement was complete.

Not all public sentiment in England was sympathetic to the initiatives taken by the Bank of England, and, while a collapse would have precipitated serious consequences, the Scottish banks were uneasy with the exclusive concern shown towards Barings by the Bank of England.[21] But Wenley told the General Managers Committee that when the interests of the City 'clash with those of outsiders' the former would be given preferential treatment by the Bank. In March 1892, the General Managers Committee insisted that the position of guarantors ought to be more distinctly defined, and that they should sit alongside the Bank of England as liquidators. As to the extension of the liquidation agreement beyond three years, either the guarantors had to be 'absolutely released' or they had to have sole and ultimate control of the securities. Wenley wanted Bank of Scotland to take the initiative

> in making it known that we are not to be coerced by appeals to a generosity in which we are not called on to indulge, to fall in with any project for the benefits of debtors for whom the City of London may have sympathy from a keen appreciation of past favours or future benefits.[22]

At the time of the negotiations for an extension to the period of liquidation, several London banks were in opposition, but Davidson advised the Mound not to take the initiative in raising the issue; and, as already noted, the guarantee was extended for a further year and finally wound up in January 1895. It had been a great success for the Bank of England.[23]

The crisis at Barings had little discernable effect on the state of the British economy, although bankers had to think about whether they ought to make provision for their guarantees. There was a short-lived boom over 1890 and into 1891, but pessimism returned by the close of the year. Bank of Scotland at this time had 114 offices on a full-time basis, with five sub-offices open less frequently. The distribution of resources between London and Scotland showed a very considerable increase of nearly £750,000 for London during the year, so that the total employed in London was only £1.5 million less than in the whole of Scotland (see Figure 17.7). In the

21 *The Economist*, 22 November 1890, thought the guarantee 'rather too far-reaching'. For accounts of the Baring crisis, see W. T. C. King, *History of the London Discount Market* (London: 1936), p. 301ff.; G. Ingham, *Capitalism Divided? The City and Industry in British Social Development* (London: 1984), pp. 164–7; D. Kynaston, *The City of London*, vol i, *A World of Its Own, 1815–1890* (London: 1994), ch. 21.
22 BS 20/2/3, Bank of Scotland correspondence on Barings, J. A. Wenley to General Managers Committee, and to Robert Dundas, 23 March 1892.
23 Clapham, *Bank of England*, vol. ii, pp. 338–9.

following year, Wenley expressed the hope that the flow of money to London had been checked in that there was almost no difference in the totals of 1891 and 1892. 'As far as good mercantile bills are concerned there is now no inducement to discount there, the special rates charged in Scotland being the same as in London'; but what determined the lending for one region as against another was the general state of trade, as the later results were to show. As already noticed, throughout the 1880s and early 1890s there was a slow but fairly steady growth in the total invested in stocks and bonds, and even some effort at trading. The latter phenomenon began in a more systematic way in the mid-1880s, both to improve profits in any one year and to move into higher interest-bearing investments. For example, in 1895–6 the Bank made a profit of £20,000 on the sale of colonial and South American securities as well as £18,000 on the sale of £150,000 worth of consols.

The period 1892–3 was dismal throughout the UK. Many of the London clearing banks reduced their dividends; but, although net profits for Bank of Scotland were some £30,000 less than the previous year, the dividend was maintained. The Bank began to collate a yearly profit forecast, updated each week as the financial year progressed, to highlight areas which needed attention. This was a most interesting use of financial data. The year began with a net profit at the rate of £210,000 per annum for the first week, rising in six weeks to £247,000. But in the seventh week, because of losses, the rate fell to £191,000. The profit forecast went on declining week by week until the twenty-second week, when it reached the low point of £136,000. From weeks 23–33 it rose from £139,000 to £149,000, then from weeks 34–47 from £177,000 to £208,000, followed in the forty-eighth week by a decline to £182,000. This last figure was slightly improved during the concluding four weeks of the year, ending at £195,000. As a Bank of Scotland dividend and bonus of 13 per cent amounted to £162,000, the long continuance of so low a rate of profit naturally gave rise to great disappointment. Yet this pessimistic feeling was common to the Scottish banks, and in September 1892 the General Managers Committee agreed to discontinue interest on cash accounts. In this 1892–3 report, Wenley complained about the balances at the Bank of England and with other London clearing banks, most of which were 'unproductive', and about the gold held at the Mound against the banknote circulation (£974,000).

> To the extent to which the circulation is fiduciary, there is of course a profit; but to the extent to which it is not, there is not only a loss of interest in respect of the gold held against it but also the loss represented by the cost of supplying the notes. On the other hand it must be borne in mind that the indirect advantage of the note circulation is very great.

The year 1893, in Scotland as elsewhere in the UK, continued the improvement on previous years with an enhanced profit on ordinary business for the Bank, largely due to the rise in London interest rates. Bank of England rates rose to counter an outflow of bullion at various stages of the year, and Scottish rates automatically followed. But the year which followed, already showing itself in the closing months of 1893, was much worse, and 1894 was by far the worst that the Bank had experienced since 1872. It was also 'exceptionally unfortunate in point of losses from bad debts' in Dundee and London. In Dundee, it was the failure of three old-established jute firms brought down as a result of speculative activity. In the London office, losses had to be paid, after six years of negotiations, concerning cheques forged by one of Bank of Scotland's clerks. The differential rates for discounts and advances in Scotland compared with London emerged as a concern to the Scottish business community during the depression years. In 1882, the Glasgow Chamber of Commerce proposed to lobby Westminster to restrict or abolish Scottish banking privileges and encourage English banks to establish themselves in Scotland. After lengthy consultations at the General Managers Committee, it was agreed in January 1884 that the differential rate between London and Scotland for sums under £600 should be abolished, but Scottish firms were aware that further pressure could not usefully be exerted, given their dependency upon their local banking institutions. Differences in the lending rates between London and Scotland remained, in part because, as Wenley noted to his board in 1890, 'it must be borne in mind that many of the London discounts and loans are of the choicest kind as regards safety, and therefore of necessity command the lowest rates'.

At the bicentenary celebrations of 1895, it may be noticed in passing, the board had intended to raise the dividend and distribute a bonus to staff; but because of the very poor trading figures and an increase in bad debts, the dividend was reduced to 12 per cent with nothing for staff, and it was to remain at this level until 1902 when it was increased to 13 per cent and to 14 per cent in 1903. The upturn in banking profits for the year ending February 1896 was mainly the result of the agreed reduction by the General Managers Committee in the Scottish deposit rate to 1 per cent just over a year earlier. The Bank of England rate had remained at 2 per cent, and the return on Bank of Scotland's employment of funds in London was 'necessarily very small'. It should be noticed that the branch results were often excellent; in 1896, for example, at ninety of the Bank's branches no losses at all were recorded.

In the closing months of 1895, there began a sustained revival in the fortunes of the Scottish banks. The foreign trade figures were improving and the home trade was showing quite striking gains: 'Scotch whisky, which has of late years risen to such importance as an article of commerce, appears to be in greater demand than ever before all over the world . . . and the Bank's connections with the trade have shared in the general prosperity'. Shipbuilding and housebuilding were especially buoyant, and the latter was to provide a major component of the domestic boom of these years. The census count of houses is only an approximation to the extent of the expansion of housebuilding – in most parts of Britain largely concentrated in the development of urban suburbs – but in the decade to 1901 it showed a 15 per cent increase in the number of houses in England and Wales and 13 per cent in Scotland.[24] The improvement in the economy had meant a greater demand for Scottish funds – around 45 per cent of the Bank's total resources in advances were employed in London. In both 1897 and 1898, satisfactory results from the business activities of Bank of Scotland were due 'not so much to the higher rates of interest received on the advances as to the lower rates paid on the Deposits. In point of fact the lending rates produced very little more than those of the preceding year, but the deposit rates have effected a saving of over £24,000.'

During the last years of Wenley's Treasurership, there were serious problems with several Glasgow accounts, including that of Gregor Turnbull & Co., sugar plantation owners of Trinidad, who owed £330,397.[25] The advances negotiated by the Glasgow office and the difficulties that might befall the long-term connections were well illustrated. The fall in sugar prices on the world market had begun to be felt by producers from about the mid-1880s. In 1871, the average export value of a ton of cane sugar was just over £16; in 1891 it was £14 12s, and in 1901–2 it was down to £10. The Bank had made the advances when sugar prices were good, and it was decided to send out an employee to report on a deteriorating situation. James Bain, sub-manager of the Bank in Glasgow, reached Trinidad on 8 May 1894. He divided his survey into four parts: sugar estates under cultivation; abandoned sugar estates; cocoa estates; and coconut estates. It was the sugar estates under cultivation that mainly concerned him, and he provided a context of the local economy, a survey of each estate which included the organisation of the labour force, much of it 'indentured', salaries of the managers and payment of 'free labourers', and estimates of current and future profits. His summary conclusions made specific

24 B. R. Mitchell and P. Deane, *Abstract of British Historical Statistics* (Cambridge: 1962), Table 3, p. 239. The domestic boom in Britain after 1894 coincided with a vigorous building boom: housebuilding expanded after 1895, reached a peak in 1898 and continued at a somewhat lower but still significant level until 1903, after which building slumped until 1914 and after.
25 The details which follow in this section are taken from a series of Special Reports: BS 1/70/5. The report on Trinidad quoted in the text comprises a number of separate documents written within the Bank.

recommendations. Against the advance of £330,797, the gross receipts for 1894 were estimated at £122,000 and the net income from all the estates was put at £21,000 before the expenses of the Glasgow office of Gregor Turnbull had been deducted. James Bain's main conclusions were to close down three of the estates surveyed, to put another up for sale and if it was not sold then to crop for one more year after which it should be abandoned, and that only two estates should be continued under new management. Bain concluded:

> I would urge the Bank not to allow the supervision of the business to go out of their hands. Some one directly in the bank's service, and loyal to their interests, should look closely after it. The plan I have suggested for the future working, if carried out vigorously under such supervision, will, I think, in time clear off the advances. If allowed to go into the hands of Trustees . . . the possible loss might be great.'

The report by James Bain was considered by a special committee of directors appointed on 31 July. They held four meetings, two of which were attended by Bain and the Glasgow manager, Robert Gourlay. The committee began by asking the central question, namely, whether it would be in the interest of the Bank to place the firm into bankruptcy or to allow it to continue under new management 'for some time longer'. Bain had, of course, recommended the latter course, and the committee concurred with his judgement, partly because of the hoped-for improvement in profitability following the suggestions made, partly on the possibility of a sale 'within two or three years, of the Estates and business to an American company, for cash'. James Bain had estimated that, of the various debts outstanding, some £25,000 was irrecoverable.

The committee agreed that he should go out again within a year to see whether his proposed improvements in management had been carried through, and that at a later date another of the Bank's officials should also visit the estates and report back. The report, and the views by the special committee of directors, were submitted to outside accountants. Their conclusions were that the capital account – amounting to £225,000 – should now be closed and that revenue being generated should be allocated first to reduce this capital account, the assumption being that an estimate of £10,000 annual profit would be met each year; and that any revenue should be paid at 4 per cent interest upon the account. Further, in order to reduce the debt stated in the Bank balance sheet, 5 per cent of the indebtedness should be provided for during each of the next five years.

James Bain paid a second visit to Trinidad during the early summer of 1895, and his report was considered again by the special committee of directors in July 1895. Organisation and methods on the sugar estates had been improved, the unproductive estates were now all abandoned, and only the exceptionally low price of sugar prevented a considerable profit from being made. Nevertheless, the estates would pay their way and leave a small margin over for interest payments. In general, it was a carefully optimistic report compared with the conditions of the previous year. Two years later, R. L. McGlashen, who had been the Bank's Inspector in Edinburgh and who was now sub-manager of the Glasgow branch, visited the sugar estates and wrote a report for the committee of directors. His main conclusion was that the continuation of the business and the repayment of the Bank's debt would depend to a great extent upon the recommendations of the Royal Commission on the West Indies whose report was about to be submitted to Parliament. If the Royal Commission was unable to offer support to sugar prices, the Bank would suffer a very large loss on the account. The committee's report ended with the conclusion that 'the proper course for the Bank, as soon as a purchaser can be found, [is] to dispose of the Estates and wind up the business'. In the present state of the cane sugar industry, given the countervailing bounties on beet sugar, there was no chance of sale. It was fully appreciated that the economies introduced by the Bank were working satisfactorily, but the final paragraph summed up the committee's recommendations:

> It cannot be reasonably expected that a sale will be effected, even within a moderate period, excepting at great sacrifice. The Committee therefore recommend that in addition to the sum of £75,000 already provided, the Bank Fund for Losses should now be credited with a similar sum, making £150,000 in all, [and that] in the very exceptional circumstances of the case, the present additional provision be drawn from the surplus arising on the Bank's Stock Investments.

After many years of discussion, the British government intervened in 1903–4 in an endeavour to curtail bounties on beet sugar; but the Trinidad export value in 1906–7 was no higher than that of 1901. Bank of Scotland had been reasonable in terms of the self-interest of proprietors, and the reorganisation which James Bain had initiated had been effective in bringing down costs of production. It was the global factors involved in the world prices of cane sugar that impeded the Bank's serious efforts to assist the producers.[26]

The Scottish pig-iron industry was seriously affected by the depression. In the years 1863–5, output averaged 1,161,000 tons per year and, after

26 B. Porter, *The Lion's Share. A Short History of British Imperialism 1850–1883*, 2nd edn (London: 1984), pp. 190–226, 144–5; M. D. Ramesar, 'Indentured Labour in Trinidad 1880–1917', in K. Saunders (ed.), *Indentured Labour in the British Empire, 1834–1920* (London: 1984), pp. 57–77.

a decline, climbed a little to 1,175,000 tons per year from 1869 to 1871.[27] By 1891, Scottish output was only 674,000 tons. Prices also fell: in the four years to 1871, a ton of finished pig fluctuated around 54 to 56 shillings, then rose to 115s in 1873 and then collapsed. In spite of agreements between producers and smelters, prices for most of the 1880s stayed between 38 and 48 shillings. It was only to be expected that a number of long-standing Bank of Scotland connections would be nursed through these times. The oldest account in this category, on the Bank's books at Glasgow, was Colin Dunlop & Co., coalmasters and ironsmelters. The account had been opened on 3 March 1824 and was kept in the same name until, by 1895, Colin John Dunlop was the fourth generation to have banked with the Glasgow branch. Originally, they were ironmasters at the Clyde Iron Works, near Glasgow, and subsequently also at Quarter, Lanarkshire, where they also worked coal mines leased from the Duke of Hamilton. In 1855, James Dunlop and his brother Colin R. Dunlop separated their interests, the former taking the Clyde Iron Works and the latter those at Quarter. Messrs Colin Dunlop & Co. continued with their iron and coal interests until 1886 when, owing to losses 'sustained by them and most of the other iron manufacturers in Scotland they, at the request of the Bank [of Scotland]' gave up the iron works and confined themselves to coal. At that date, they owed the Bank £120,000. It was a very active account, as these coal and iron firms regularly paid out banknotes for wages and local supplies and were active buyers of inland bills. With economies at the works, and without the loss-making iron interests, by the close of the financial year 1892 the account stood in debit by £76,000. This figure then began to rise: at the close of 1893 it was –£93,000, the following year –£113,000, in 1895 –£125,000 and by the close of 1897 –£138,000. The details of the expenditures on coal and iron from 1883 are shown on Table 17.9.

The collieries and workings had some value, but only if maintained as operating units. The situation was examined in detail by Andrew McCleland CA of Glasgow, who undertook a number of investigations for the Bank in these years. The conclusions were positive. The consumption of coal was rapidly increasing, owing to the increase in manufacturing and shipping and also to household consumption: 'it is only reasonable to expect that coal will gradually rise in price, and at no very distant date this rise may be sufficiently marked to make the coal trade more remunerative than it has been during the past three or four years'.[28] It was thought that an output of 500,000 tons per year was feasible, that

27 Mitchell and Deane, *Historical Statistics*, Metals, Table 2; Slaven, *West of Scotland*, pp. 169–73.
28 BS 1/70/5, Special Reports, Colin Dunlop & Co.

Table 17.9 *Cash account balance of Colin Dunlop & Co., iron and coal masters, 1883–97*

31 December 1883   Cash account balance: Dr £ 87,622
'In the end of 1882, the new Ironstone field at Crossbasket was opened up and cost about £10,000. This Ironstone was very cheaply worked and was intended to be used for making iron mixed with cinders from the Malleable works, and was highly successful.'

31 December 1884   Cash account balance: Dr £ 95,420
'During this year the price of Pig Iron fell to 38/- per ton, and it was found impossible to make iron at a profit, and accordingly arrangements were made to use up all the stocks of ironstone and as soon as possible to discontinue making Pig Iron at Quarter.'

31 December 1885   Cash account balance: Dr £104,467
'The process of winding up the Pig Iron Works was continued and the liabilities in connection therewith began to be discharged . . .'

31 December 1886   Cash account balance: Dr £121,516
'The Pig Iron Works were . . . closed this year and a commencement made towards developing the coal trade. A considerable sum of cash was now outstanding for coal accounts.'

31 December 1887   Cash account balance: Dr £105,792
. . .

31 December 1888   Cash account balance: Dr £104,338
'The price of coal in 88 was low and so also were wages but the output was not high. But sufficient was made to prevent an increase in the account.'

31 December 1889   Cash account balance: Dr £108,148
'During this year [and the following] the coal trade was extended and the output considerably increased . . .'

31 December 1890   Cash account balance: Dr £107,140
. . .

31 December 1891   Cash account balance: Dr £ 89,423
'This was an excellent year, the profit being 2/- per ton on the output.'

31 December 1892   Cash account balance: Dr £ 76,328
'In August of this year No. 8 Pit was commenced . . . and £15,000 was received from the Caledonian Railway Co., being the price of the railways at Quarter.'

31 December 1893   Cash account balance: Dr £ 90,775
'During this year No. 8 Pit was being sunk and fitted but was not completed.'

31 December 1894   Cash account balance: Dr £113,073
'No. 8 Pit was completed and the coal cutting machines were purchased at a cost of £1,600. But the year was disastrous on account of the Colliers' strike.'

31 December 1895   Cash account balance: Dr £125,395
'Trade was exceptionally bad . . . and great difficulty was experienced in selling the large output of coal – No. 8 having been started and a large stock accumulated in bings of coal and dross, some 40,000 tons at 4/- per ton.'

31 December 1896   Cash account balance: Dr £133,510
'This year saw no improvement until November and December, on the previous one. Repairs about the Collieries, to keep them in a thoroughly efficient state, were rather heavier than usual and the stocks of coal increased by 9,000 tons, say, at 4/- per ton.'

31 December 1897   Cash account balance: Dr £138,494
'During this year a small profit has all along been shewn and, towards the close, better results and a larger output. It is in every respect a better one than either 94, 95 or 96.'

Source: BS 1/70/6, Annual Reports of the Treasurer, 1866–98.

the coal would continue to be of a high quality and that Colin Dunlop & Co. would thus reduce their indebtedness. The Bank received detailed reports on physical assets, and as the firm's banker it had a clear view of finances. There was also a difficulty with the other main branch of the family, James Dunlop & Co., Tollcross, which had inherited the Clyde Iron Works.[29] In the prosperous days of Scottish ironsmelting, the account 'was always on the right side and it has only been since the decadence of that trade' that James Dunlop had been borrowers from Bank of Scotland, a debt which by 1897 had reached £131,000. The ironworks were sold in 1886 for £50,000 and the company was left with the adjoining Tollcross estate, by then an eastern suburb of Glasgow. The Corporation of Glasgow bought part for a public park, and it was hoped that the sale of the rest for housebuilding would cover the remainder of the debt. Bank of Scotland had many similar accounts as a result of the changed conditions brought on by the depression.

There were underlying difficulties facing banking in Glasgow. The good years were remembered, in an oversimplified manner, by Robert Gourlay, the Glasgow manager, in 1894:

> During seven to eight years after 1869 there was great prosperity, prices became inflated in property, in coal and iron etc., but all this came to an end with the failure of the City of Glasgow bank, and the effects of its collapse have been felt more or less ever since.[30]

Over these years, there were fewer inland bills as business turned to the use of cheques and cash and the best bills went to London. Most houses 'of any standing' had a London account through which they passed their provincial cheques and retired their acceptances, 'depriving us at this end of valuable commission'. Nevertheless, there was some good news. In 1869, Glasgow chief office deposits had provided only 30 per cent of cover for loans, but by 1894 this figure was 50 per cent; and, if the Glasgow branches were included together, almost all advances were covered. Bank of Scotland was not alone in facing large losses. The British Linen lost over £160,000 from Peter Lawson & Son, the National Bank £30,000 from Ferguson, Davidson & Co. of Leith and three accounts of £40,000 apiece in Glasgow, the Union Bank £120,000 from Alexander Collie, and the Clydesdale Bank over £200,000 from two sugar accounts.[31] The North of Scotland Bank lost £233,000 through ill-advised loans to fish-curing firms

29 P. L. Payne, *Colvilles and the Scottish Steel Industry* (Oxford: 1979), pp. 47–54.
30 BS 20/18/12, Memorandum from Glasgow Chief Office, February 1894.
31 Ibid.

in Aberdeen in the crisis of 1888, the second occasion that its reserves had been wiped out.[32] The directors at the Mound, looking intently at the stronger performance in London, were apt to forget that the business at Glasgow was broader and more complicated; as Robert Gourlay noted, the advances at London were largely to

> Corporations, public bodies such as Parochial Boards, bankers on bills, bill brokers on the finest paper and stockbrokers. The private customers are to a considerable extent Scotch firms of high standing who give to London the best of their bills. The deposits are made by provincial banks and other [banks] and the business of a general kind from the public – from whom in Glasgow it is entirely drawn – is not in London a large one.[33]

In one respect, Glasgow moved closer to London. Prior to 1869, Bank of Scotland had refused to advance to stockbrokers and private parties in Glasgow against railway securities and other stocks for the purposes of speculation on the Glasgow stock exchange. Other Scottish banks did advance thus, and the experience of the London office encouraged the directors to change their minds. By 1894, this was 'no inconsiderable part of our lending business' and was carefully controlled.[34] In January 1896, when reports suggested that war was imminent between France and England over the Sudan, Gourlay was instructed to call in funds from stockbrokers on the next account day, 16 January:[35]

> we must hold our hands from lending any money in Scotland except in the ordinary way of advances for current mercantile purposes. On no account should we make loans for speculative purposes – e.g., to buy stocks at the depressed prices which may be looked for – even to our best customers. Rich men like the Coatses and the Bells, should be shown that it is their duty . . . to strengthen credit and to abstain from speculations outside of their own business . . . unless they can enter upon them with their own money . . . Don't say much about our policy, but quietly act on it.

This was typical of J. A. Wenley: cautious, above all else, aware of what rumour could do to damage credit. But it was always difficult for Robert Gourlay, on his own, to curtail a valued customer such as Archibald Coats, who merely complained to higher authority. In 1896, for example, when the Coats family was busy amalgamating four thread-making companies into the new empire of J. & P. Coats, there was considerable buying of

32 S. G. Checkland, *Scottish Banking: A History, 1695–1973* (Glasgow: 1975), p. 502.
33 BS 20/18/12, Memorandum from Glasgow Chief Office, February 1894, p. 7.
34 Ibid., p. 2.
35 BS 1/21/26, Treasurer's private letters to Glasgow, 8 January 1896.

Coats's shares, and Bank of Scotland directors ruled that no new advance was to be made to Messrs Coats or to those associated with them in the company.[36] But Messrs J. & P. Coats were also active in the bill market: in the autumn of 1896 they effected a reduction in Bank of Scotland funds in London of nearly £1 million through operations on account of the newly-formed combine. This amount may not have seemed much to a family whose firm now embraced a capital of £8 million, but at the Mound it was too large an exposure. In December 1896, Robert Gourlay was given the unenviable task of explaining policy to Archibald Coats. Wenley stressed that at the meeting Gourlay was to take the blame for not having told Archibald Coats about the decision to curtail stock speculation, but to be careful: 'very naturally [Archibald Coats] may take exception to what he may regard as a sudden and recent change of view on the part of the Bank'.[37] The Fashoda incident of November 1898 caused another round of cautionary letters from Wenley. There were other periodic warnings over combinations from coal to whisky; almost at the end of his tenure, Wenley would write that the long-standing whisky broker combination had endorsed bills for enormous amounts with all the Edinburgh banks: 'sooner or later it is certain to end in a collapse'.[38]

There were two other procedures of note associated with the last years of Wenley's Treasurership. When he came to office in 1879, the paid-up capital had stood at £1,250,000 and the published reserve fund at £750,000; there was no increase in the former during his tenure and only a modest rise in the reserve to £825,000 by 1897. The significant change occurred with the internal reserve, known as the Fund for Losses. By 1884 the fund stood at £163,255; it grew somewhat from 1889, and significant sums were written to the fund from the profit and loss account from 1897 (see Table 17.10). From this time, the board of directors decided to prepare for a really substantial loss, which they presumed would come from London or Glasgow, and which none could predict with any precision but all knew could happen with the growth of share and company speculation among customers. These funds were gradually increased to enable the internal position to carry over from one year to another and ensure that should a crisis occur a smooth path could still be declared for net profits and published reserves. The second change associated with Wenley was to put much of the increased deposits into Indian government and other foreign stocks and investments; they only fell below £1 million from 1889 to 1894, and in 1898 and 1899 he bought heavily into these, usually

---

36 BS 1/6, Minutes, 15 September 1896.
37 BS 1/21/26, Treasurer's private letters to Glasgow, 23 December 1897.
38 Ibid., 15 June 1898.

Table 17.10 *Build-up of inner reserves, 1884–1918*

Year ending 28 February	Balance at Fund for losses	Contingent account
1884	163255	
1885	156214	
1886	134236	
1887	140188	
1888	160377	
1889	191586	
1890	225358	
1891	221687	
1892	235860	
1893	238553	
1894	208567	
1895	201187	
1896	232867	
1897	290840	
1898	422542 [1]	
1899	348867 [2]	
1900	394972	
1901	430518 [3]	
1902	482178 [4]	
1903	448135 [5]	100000 [6]
1904	574147 [7]	100000
1905	449563 [8]	150000
1906	477211	200000
1907	470893 [9]	260000
1908	555770 [10]	300000
1909	616658 [11]	325000
1910	696274 [12]	375000
1911	723094 [13]	415000
1912	772956 [14]	465000
1913	854535 [15]	465000
1914	934284 [16]	500000
1915	1462089 [17]	370000
1916	1307100 [18]	370000
1917	2087731 [19]	370000
1918	2106551 [20]	0

Notes:

1 £58000 transferred from profit and loss, £60000 from consols written up and £125000 from reserve fund.

2 Losses £109589; £33000 transfer from profit and loss.

3 Losses £74769; transfers of £50000 to reserve fund, £83000 to Fund for losses and £5000 to heritable property suspense account were made from profit and loss.

4 Losses £10363; transfers of £50000 to reserve fund and £61327 to Fund for losses were made from profit and loss.

5 Nothing transferred (losses £34213).

6 £18684 from Fund for losses, £81316 from profit and loss.

7 Losses £6385; transfer from profit and loss £100000.

8 Losses £268629, of which £250961 for Gregor, Turnbull & Co. and £7500 Trinidad Estates.

9 Losses £30940.

10 Losses £4647; £89500 was transferred from profit and loss.

11 Losses £4442; £65250 was transferred from profit and loss.

12 Losses £14363; £85000 was transferred from profit and loss.

13 Losses £6586; £33177 was transferred from profit and loss.

14 Losses £12935; £62500 was transferred from profit and loss.

15 Total losses £103527, including Argyll Motors debts £29723 and Buchanan and French debts £50073; £180117 was transferred from profit and loss.

16 Losses £13528; £92929 was transferred from profit and loss.

17 Losses £2419; £188500 was transferred from profit and loss, £200000 from reserve fund and £130000 from Contingent Account.

18 Losses £483342, of which £43381 required for conversion of £1335350 2.5 per cent consols to £890233 4.5 per cent war loan; £150000 was transferred from reserve, £178000 from profit and loss account. In 1915–16, a loss of £44435 was made on large sales of thirty-two USA stocks; surplus on sale of twenty-five USA stocks £9206 (i.e overall loss of £33329).

19 Losses £61142; all of Contingent account transferred to Fund for losses; £300000 transferred from reserve and £157500 from profit and loss.

20 Losses £149691, of which £100000 required to write down cost of 3.5 per cent war loan in books; £158627 was transferred from profit and loss.

fixed-interest, securities. Overall, the financial position of Bank of Scotland was very well handled by Wenley, and his work after the crisis of 1878 was as important in its different way as that carried out by Alexander Blair. They both took over the affairs of the Bank at particularly difficult times and avoided flamboyant gestures. While they might be criticised for caution, Alexander Blair for not expanding earlier in Glasgow and for his hesitancy over opening a London office, both left the Bank more secure than when they joined and with an enlarged business. Both men took the directors into their confidence and relied on their collective wisdom; compared to their respective successors, they were outstandingly successful.

George Anderson, general manager of the North of Scotland Bank in Aberdeen, took up his post as Treasurer of Bank of Scotland on 9 December 1898, when economic conditions were moving in the Bank's favour. The large-scale export of capital from the UK, the growth of world trade and the domination of the Clyde region in world shipbuilding provided the conditions for the general increase in economic activity in the western region of Scotland. The decision by the government to embark on a naval rearmament programme was a major factor in the general buoyancy of the Scottish economy in the two decades before 1914. The expansion of the Clyde shipyards, for merchant as well as naval building, was the most important factor in the economy of the western region.[39] There were some significant advances: Fairfields Shipbuilding & Engineering Co. regularly extended its permanent overdraft to £250,000, as did John Elder & Co. up to £150,000. Yet overall advances from Bank of Scotland grew only slowly before 1907. Deposits expanded a little in 1901–2 and then fell for the next four years. The most time-consuming problem which faced the Bank was the use of funds for share speculation:

> I should think there was no lack of good arguments in present times to convince people of the danger of 'investing'. Almost everybody who has tried this of recent years would be richer today had they been content instead with the moderate interest obtained from banks.[40]

Nevertheless, the income from loans to stockbrokers was too good a source of income, and by these years the Bank had advanced £500,000 to Glasgow and over £1.5 million to London for share purchases for each of the stock exchanges' accounting periods. But demand in London for

39 A. Slaven, *The Development of the West of Scotland, 1750–1960* (London: 1975), pp. 178–82. For the importance of employment in the coal mines, mechanical engineering, shipyards and associated companies, see C. Lee, *British Regional Employment Statistics 1841–1971* (Cambridge: 1979); J. H. Treble, 'The Occupied Male Labour Force', in W. H. Fraser and R. J. Morris (eds), *People and Society in Scotland*, vol. ii, *1830–1914* (Edinburgh: 1990), pp. 167–93.
40 BS 1/21/25, Treasurer's private letter book, 27 January 1904, Anderson to Gourlay.

speculative funds was always high, and before the rise in deposits from 1907 Sir George Anderson (he was knighted in 1905) spent long hours holding back advances in London and elsewhere to fund Glasgow ship-building. On occasion, these demands could be sudden: on 20 November 1905, for example, Fairfields drew for £275,000 with little warning. The overall profit figures (called 'net' in Bank books) were improving and by 1903 had risen above £300,000 for the first time in the Bank's history.[41] A second inner reserve, the Contingent Account, was established with £100,000 in 1903, and by 1912 this contained £465,000. There was little real growth in the Fund for Losses for the first decade of Anderson's Treasurership, and not many write-offs, although £250,961 was written off in 1905 for Gregor Turnbull & Co. From 1908, the fund was sharply increased, and by 1913 it had reached £772,956.

Anderson continued his predecessor's policy of keeping a close watch on firms believed to be in difficulty while supporting those with good prospects. One of these was the Argyll Motor Vehicle Co.[42] The founder, Alexander Govan, envisaged a mass market, and at Alexandria the firm built an integrated production facility which was among the most modern in Europe. Unfortunately, the company was under-capitalised and relied on bank loans and long lines of trade credit. In the depression of 1907, Bank of Scotland directors, with interests in the engineering trades, instructed Anderson to reduce the advance: car sales were well below production, the position at Argyll was deteriorating and the company was placed in receivership later in the year. Argyll was reorganised and more capital was raised, but the market was oversupplied and the company never realised its potential before closure in 1914. The directors criticised Anderson for extending bill discounts in 1907 when it was known that Argyll was in trouble.

The price of British government stock was of concern to all Scottish banks[43] which held sizeable holdings, as did many customers. At the turn of the century, there were five London stock-exchange quotations for government stock: £32 million of $2\frac{1}{2}$ per cent annuities; £5 million of $2\frac{3}{4}$ per cent annuities; £50 million of $2\frac{3}{4}$ per cent consolidated stock; £32 million of $2\frac{3}{4}$ per cent national war loan; and £43 million of 3 per cent local loan stock issued to the savings banks under the National Debt and Local Loans Act, 1887. George Goschen, Chancellor of the Exchequer

---

41 See Statistical Appendix, Table A4.

42 G. T. Bloomfield, 'New Integrated Motor Works in Scotland 1899–1914', *Industrial Archaeology Review*, 5 (1981), 127–41; S. McKinstry, 'The Albion Motor Car Company: Growth and Specialisation, 1899–1918', *Scottish Economic and Social History Review*, 11 (1991), 36–51.

43 The basic statistics cited here are in Pember and Boyle, *British Government Securities in the Twentieth Century: The First Fifty Years*, 2nd edn (private circulation, London: 1950); there is a useful commentary in R. G. Hawtrey, *A Century of Bank Rate* (London: 1938).

1887–92, was determined to reduce the level of interest on the national debt, and in 1884 holders of the then 3 per cent stocks were offered conversion into 2 per cent annuities. The relatively minor conversion of £4.6 million of 3 per cent stock to 2¾ per cent annuities also went through at this time. By the National Debt Conversion Act, 1888, holders of the old 3 per cent 'consols' were offered a reduced stock, 2¾ per cent until 5 April 1903, and after this date 2½ per cent. The offer was £100 new for each £100 old, with 5 shillings per cent offered to the oldest category of 3 per cent. Agreement was secured for all but £19 million, which was paid off in cash. At par on conversion in 1888, consols steadily fell to 93½ by November 1890. From 1891 there was an irregular climb to 99 by February 1894, and with the Bank of England rate at 2 per cent for two-and-a-half years coupled to the depression of trade and prices, consols reached 112⁹⁄₁₆ in September 1896. They were still 111 in March 1899, but the outbreak of the war in South Africa pushed them below par. Then began a decline – which contemporaries assumed would not be prolonged – but which continued steadily after 1902.

The mistake made by Scottish bankers, trustees and investors everywhere was to assume that because these securities were at par in 1888, and for several years of cheap money in 1894–8 were at a premium of 10 per cent, at some time in the future they would return to these high prices. But they never returned to these levels, except briefly, in another episode of cheap money, nearly fifty years later. Economic and financial conditions after the South African war favoured higher interest rates; there were more equities on the stock market, and more foreign companies offering higher interest stocks and bonds. So consols fell; year-end prices were 88–89 in 1903–5, 82 by 1909 and only 75 by 1913. There were fluctuations, and the astute trader could make money from these, but the trend was ineluctably downward. Even with the fall in price and thus a rise in yield, the highest gross yield prior to 1914 was £3 9s 8d, in 1913. There was considerable understanding of how these prices and yields interacted with the Bank of England minimum discount rate and with equities and general conditions. Nevertheless, Bank of Scotland, the Union Bank, the British Linen Company and most of the other Scottish banks kept their substantial holding in consols, lamenting in annual reports and in numerous letters their continued decline.

When George Anderson took over from J. A. Wenley, the Bank had benefited from the several years when the price of 2¾ per cent consols was above par, and the price paid (listed in the Bank books) for their £1,350,000 worth, and the market value of all other stocks held, was also above par in the Bank books (see Table 17.11). For three years after the conversion of the 3 per cent consols to 2¾ per cent, the Bank's

Table 17.11 Bank of Scotland holdings of British government and other stocks, 1865–1915

	Consols [1]				Other British government stock [2]				Other British government stock [3]				All stocks (including British government)			
	Amount of stock (nominal value)	Price in books [4]	Proceeds at market value	Balance [5]	Amount of stock (nominal value)	Price in books	Proceeds at market value	Balance	Amount of stock (nominal value)	Price in books	Proceeds at market value	Balance	Price in books	Proceeds at market value	Balance
1865	792636	727738	699503	-28235	669638	610008	585096	-24912	125601	114416	109744	-4672	1839928	1785507	-54421
1866	892636	814465	773245	-41220	569638	522658	489176	-33482	125601	114416	107859	-6557	1745769	1663453	-82316
1867	892636	814082	807836	-6246	569638	523498	508402	-15096	125601	114416	112099	-2317	1750550	1739472	-11078
1868	892636	814082	825688	11606	569638	523498	525965	2467	125601	114416	115866	1450	1785120	1821475	36355
1869	1000000	914933	925000	10067	469638	430280	435589	5309	20000	17329	18600	1271	1500587	1518800	18213
1870	1000000	914933	920000	5067	319638	293012	292468	-544	20000	17329	18300	971	1557339	1562274	4935
1871	1000000	914933	911250	-3683	319638	292999	290071	-2928	20000	17329	18200	871	1491004	1479011	-11993
1872	1000000	915994	918750	2756									1032909	1034829	1920
1873	1000000	915994	921250	5256									1049611	1054256	4645
1874	1000000	915994	916250	256									1133384	1135507	2123
1875	1000000	915995	925000	9005									1176589	1191495	14906
1876	1000000	915995	938750	22755									1114801	1144275	29474
1877	1000000	915995	957500	41505									1797849	1861888	64039 [6]
1878	1000000	925995	946250	20255									1322882	1349041	26159 [7]
1879	1000000	946995	957500	10505									1303519	1319564	16045 [7]
1880	1000000	946995	973750	26755									2105448 [8]	2154475	49027 [9]
1881	1000000	946995	987500	40505									2188385 [8]	2247390	59005 [10]
1882	1000000	946899	995000	48101									2059718 [8]	2130342	70624 [10]
1883	1000000	946899	1015000	68101									2513638 [8]	2616134	102496 [10]
1884	1000000	946914	1012500	65586									2219122 [8]	2320433	101311 [10]
1885	1200000	1146569	1172400	25831	100000	99895	98000	-1895					2578935 [8]	2643981	65046 [10]
1886	1200000	1146569	1209000	62431	100000	99895	100750	855					2312753	2404802	92049 [10]
1887	950000	897250	952375	55125	100000	99895	100250	355					2261447	2333451	72004 [11]
1888	750000	693875	763125	69250	100000	99895	101250	1355					2018377	2130609	112232 [12]
1889	1200000	1142587	1180500	37913	126800	10000	10000	0					2869020	2955915	86895 [13]
1890	1200000	1142587	1165100	22513	276800	284448	284250	-198					3272587	3349585	76998 [14]
1891	1350000	1285149	1301400	16251	276800	283756	285242	1486					3619305	3665700	46395
1892	1350000	1285149	1290937	5788	276800	283064	284066	1002					3476126	3479078	2952
1893	1350000	1280149	1336375	46226									3115814	3170469	54655
1894	1350000	1280149	1346625	66476									3140720	3236469	95749
1895	1350000	1280149	1407375	127226									2727388	2885206	157818

	(1)	(2)	(3)	(4)	(5)	(6)	(7)	(8)	(9)	(10)	(11)	(12)	(13)	(14)	(15)
1896	1200000	1137539	1312000	174461			27300						2707714	2937578	229864
1897	950000	876310	1066375	190065			27300						2296754	2507101	210347
1898	950000	876310	1065583	189273			28140						2694600	2912689	218089
1899	1150000	1156434	1272667	116233									3929559	4055747	126188
1900	1200000	1208121	1208121	0	27300	27300	25116	0					4338472	4270312	−68160 [15]
1901	1200000	1208121	1165200	−42921	47300	45715	42806	−2184	199700 [16]	157162	160302	3140	4557586	4393819	−163767 [17]
1902	1200000	1208121	1130700	−77421	47300	45715	43043	−2909	199700 [18]	195754	199301	3547	4497590	4747282	−190308
1903	1200000	1208121	1108000	−100121	47300	45715	43280	−2672	21000 [19]	20582	20627	45	4578315	4354135	−224180 [20]
1904	1200000	1208121	1034250	−173871	47300	45715	41624	−2435	100000 [21]	98224	98063	−161	4715935	4343226	−372709 [22]
1905	1200000	1208121	1092000	−116121	27300	28140	24297	−4091	120000 [23]	116407	118493	2086	4626793	4378072	−248721 [24]
1906	1200000	1208121	1081200	−126921				−3843					4338022	4075596	−262426 [25]
1907	1200000	1208121	1039650	−168471									4216835	3858102	−358733
1908	1335350	1325876	1166762	−159114	27700	27423	25450	−1973					5009254	4608719	−400535
1909	1335350	1325876	1123920	−201956	27700	27423	23684	−3739					4777860	4366052	−411808
1910	1335350	1325876	1088310	−237566	27700	27423	22870	−4553					4813360	4357317	−456043
1911	1335350	1325876	1077961	−247915	27700	27423	23285	−4138					4384393	3930011	−454382
1912	1335350	1325876	1043576	−282300	27700	27423	22104	−5319					5138130	4630148	−507982
1913	1335350	1325876	992388	−333488	27700	27423	21000	−6423					5353464	4697020	−656444
1914	1335350	1325876	1010749	−315127	27700	27423	21329	−6094					5568837	4854139	−714698
1915	1335350	1325876	910709	−415167	27700	27423	19598	−7825					7233734	6253739	−979995
									1978600	1879670	1879670	0			

Notes:

1 From 1865–88 these were 3 per cents, from 1889–1903 2.75 per cents and from 1904–15 2.5 per cents.

2 These were New 3 Per Cents for the years 1865–71 and 1885–8, Local Loans Stock 3 per cent for the years 1889–92, Greek Government Guaranteed 2.5 per cent Gold Bonds for the years 1899–1905 and India 3 per cent Stock from 1908.

3 These were Reduced 3 Per Cents for the years 1865–71, National War Loan 2.75 per cent, Exchequer Bonds 3 per cent, Transvaal Government 3 per cent Guaranteed Stock and Irish Land 2.75 per cent Guaranteed Stock for the years 1901–5 (see notes 16, 18–19, 21 and 23) and War Loan 3.5 per cent Stock for the year 1915.

4 Price in books was price paid when purchased by the Bank.

5 Balance = market value less price in books.

6 The total number of holdings ranged between eight and thirteen in the years 1865–77, but increased to twenty-one in 1878.

7 The total number of holdings was twelve.

8 The largest holding (other than consols) for the years 1880–2 was £229287 (nominal) 4 per cent preference stock of Australian and New Zealand Land Co. This was reduced to £233243, £189313 and £129563 in successive years to 1885, when it was no longer the largest holding.

9 The total number of holdings was twenty-nine.

10 The total number of holdings in 1881 was forty-seven, of which thirteen were Australian and New Zealand Land Co. investments. This was reduced to twelve holdings of ANZL Co. investments out of fifty-three (total), then 10/57, 4/32, 3/28 and 2/23 in successive years.

11 The total number of holdings was twenty-nine.

12 The total number of holdings was thirty-five.

13 The total number of holdings was fifty-two.

Table 17.11 *continued*

14 The total number of holdings was sixty-two.
15 Reduced to £57576 by surplus of £10584 on sale of stocks.
16 Consisted of £21000 (nominal) N.W.L. 2.75 per cent and £178700 (nominal) Exchequer Bonds 3 per cent with prices in books of £20582 and £136580 and market values of £20496 and £139806 respectively.
17 Reduced to £146508 by surplus of £17259 on sale of stocks.
18 Consisted of £21000 (nominal) N.W.L. 2.75 per cent and £178700 (nominal) Exchequer Bonds 3 per cent with prices in books of £20582 and £175172 and market values of £20601 and £178700 respectively.
19 National War Loan 2.75 per cent only.
20 Reduced to £218178 by surplus of £5982 on sale of stocks.
21 Consisted of £50000 (nominal) N.W.L. 2.75 per cent and £50000 (nominal) Transvaal Government 3 per cent Stock with prices in books of £48774 and £49450 and market values of £50000 and £48063 respectively.
22 Reduced to £366271 by surplus of £6438 on sale of stocks.
23 Consisted of £50000 (nominal) N.W.L. 2.75 per cent, £50000 (nominal) Transvaal Government 3 per cent Stock and £20000 (nominal) Irish Land 2.75 per cent Guaranteed Stock with prices in books of £48899, £49450 and £18058 and market values of £50000, £49781 and £18712 respectively.
24 Reduced to £240921 by surplus of £7800 on sale of stocks.
25 Reduced to £260376 by net surplus of £2050 on sale of stocks (i.e. £11592 surplus, less £9542 deficit on sales).

Sources: BS 1/70A/1–4, Treasurer's Half-Yearly Statements, View of Government and other stocks held by the Bank, 1880–1908; BS, Uncatalogued, Views of Stocks, 1865–79, 1909–15.

holding remained close to the book price and then rose in the years of cheap money; some of these profits, £39,000, were realised in December 1896, when the holding was brought down to £950,000.[44] The fall in the market value of consols set in from 1898, in which year George Anderson purchased another £200,000 worth. The onset of the South African war in October 1899 saw the Bank of England minimum discount rate rise to 4 per cent and for a short time to 6 per cent. In 1900, the Bank holdings in consols, by now a nominal £1,200,000, were rated with no loss or gain in the books, and thereafter fell to –£77,421 by February 1902; and the 1903 conversion to 2½ per cent – the last stage of George Goschen's scheme – aggravated the position, now down to –£173,871. There was a modest recovery to –£116,121 in 1905, the best result of the next decade, and the board even increased its holding of the now 2½ per cent consols to £1,335,000 in 1910. By balance day in February 1913, when the 2½ per cent consols stood at 75, they were written as a loss of –£340,000 against the book value.[45] The information available to the Bank – indeed to all banks – on interest rates and stock prices was exceptionally good, and the board had the services of numerous managers and stockbrokers. The main reason why consols appear to have been kept was because of their instant convertibility into cash, even in times of crisis. The consequences of inaction meant that provision had to be made for interest to cover against possible loss, in case it proved a permanent decline, as indeed it did.

The losses on the 2½ per cent consols were one of several serious troubles which had beset the Bank by the outbreak of the First World War. Although government stocks were a matter in which the board of directors took a particular interest, the role of the Treasurer was central to every adverse position. The gradual move by Bank of Scotland into foreign and colonial stocks, British, Indian, American and other railway bonds has been remarked upon as a significant feature of the tenure of David Davidson, whose policy was maintained by J. A. Wenley. The figures show that in every year from 1880 the overall market value of the holdings of fixed-interest foreign bonds (called 'stocks' in the Bank books) of all kinds ran above the purchase price. There were some difficult cases, notably the debentures for the Australian and New Zealand Land Co., but such isolated cases were set against the overall good result (see Table 17.11). Wenley was sufficiently confident about the prospects of foreign stocks to increase the holdings by nearly 50 per cent to a book value of £2,869,000 by 1889 and to over £3,272,587 by 1890. From 1894, increased demand for foreign stocks saw the margin between market and book value fluctuate

44 BS 1/94/107, General Ledger; Hawtrey, *Century of Bank Rate*, pp. 111–2.
45 Pember and Boyle, *British Government Securities*, p. 145, 2½ per cent consolidated stock.

between 5 and 10 per cent. Prices of foreign stocks began to fall by 1899, and the final year of the South African war saw the last of these surpluses.

George Anderson invested heavily in foreign and domestic fixed-interest stocks. In his first three years of office to February 1902, he brought the total to almost £5 million, with an overall loss on market value of £190,308. These stocks gave a somewhat higher rate of return than on consols – 4 per cent was the most usual – and there was an especial focus on railway stocks from the USA, the UK and Canada. The income from all holdings in 1901–2 was £151,325, of which the non-government stocks yielded £117,748.[46] The management of these funds was shared from this time by George Anderson with Thomas Aitken, the manager of the London office of Bank of Scotland, and purchases were usually made through London brokers. Few holdings exceeded £50,000, and the most common were in the range £10,000–£30,000. The London office was, relatively speaking, of immense importance to the Bank, lending short- and medium-term to numerous bill brokers, stockbrokers, foreign banks and companies, and taking in often very large deposits. In February 1902, for example, the branch held deposits of £1,299,000 including several from other banks. For a concern the size of Bank of Scotland – and all the larger Scottish banks were in a similar position – the management of the internal money market within the Bank was a vital matter, and the London and Glasgow offices, as the largest sources of deposits, were crucial to this. Where funds were needed for payments, the gaining of deposits or a reduction in balances with stockbrokers was often a more cost-effective means of raising cash than selling investments whose market value fluctuated. These questions were regularly noted in the correspondence with the Mound, and an agile and flexible group of managers with good connections in the City and with local business in these two offices was essential. It should be stressed that demands for cash from trade and industry could not be forecast accurately, although every effort was made to anticipate the more substantial demands by regular contact with the larger account holders.

Unfortunately, the views of George Anderson and Thomas Aitken began to diverge from those of several directors who expressed concern that the rapid development of Scottish trade and industry should remain the prime responsibility of the Bank. As the investments position deteriorated by the end of the South African war, they raised their fears with the board and asked for stronger controls. There was also particular unease about the agreement signed on 11 November 1898 between the Bank and the Canadian Bank of Commerce, which with later extensions

46 BS 1/70/6, Annual Reports of the Treasurer: Treasurer's half-yearly balances, February 1902.

gave the Toronto-based bank access to credits of £1.39 million, on bills of exchange, backed by various securities deposited in London as cover.[47] To Thomas Aitken there was little to be concerned about; the securities were regularly checked, the rules on replacing bills likely to be dishonoured were adhered to, and the cash advance yielded a rate usually above the average for foreign bonds. It was support for trade and British exports and not for share speculation.

Nevertheless, such considerable activity and the difficulties of balancing the advances and deposits led Anderson and Aitken to ignore the periodic warnings of some directors about the advance to the Canadian Bank and other considerable exposures. The advantages in income terms were acknowledged, but a turning point in relations with the board arrived in the financial crisis of 1907, 'the worst between 1890 and 1914'.[48] The Bank of England and the London money markets had faced difficulty from the spring of 1906, and on 19 October the bank rate went to 6 per cent and was not reduced to 5 per cent until 17 January 1907. The Canadian Bank of Commerce increased its demands on the London bill market, and by March 1907 Thomas Aitken held over £1.5 million of its paper; this was the month when the crisis started in New York, but the Bank of England, in conjunction with the City, managed the situation, and the bank rate was maintained at 4½ per cent. But this was the eye of the storm. From July the crisis began to crawl back, though it took time, as few banks had an interest in speeding its return. Bank of Scotland directors, for example, endorsed the £1.5 million credit for the Canadian Bank, although they distinctly understood this as an 'extreme figure and covered all acceptances except special credits'.[49] Foreign stocks, especially those in the USA, were marked down, borrowers put pressure on Bank of Scotland, and correspondence with the Mound was more pessimistic. By the end of October when the crisis was at its height, the Bank of England intimated to Thomas Aitken its concern at the holding of so large a volume of Canadian acceptances. The Canadian Bank's bill circulation in London reached £2.5 million, and for a few days there was such difficulty with discounting these that its management even asked Bank of Scotland to sell its own consols to support the bills. Anderson was worried:

> I am strongly hopeful that our friends will get their bills discounted and that no emergency such as we dread may arise. But it should be understood that

47 From November 1872, the position of the Canadian Bank of Commerce in London was stated separately in the aggregate accounts. From this date to February 1877, the CBC took 87 per cent of total current account loans, but this declined to an average of 34 per cent for the ensuing three years. Thereafter, Wenley was determined to reduce the exposure, and the agreement of 1898 was thus negotiated after many years of quiet trading.
48 R. S. Sayers, *The Bank of England 1891–1944* (Cambridge: 1986), p. 58.
49 BS 1/21/25, Treasurer's private letters to London.

if the trouble does come we shall look to them and to their securities for the necessary relief.[50]

By 1 November, the branch held £1,650,000 of the Canadian Bank's bills. Aitken was prohibited from going beyond these figures, and for the first time Anderson offered some mild criticism of his London office for 'accepting drafts against remitted bills without asking the authority of the head office', adding that if he had had any idea of the scale of the Canadian Bank's London bill trade he would have reined in the limits: 'such excessive figures were bound to attract the attention of the Bank of England and of other banks and firms and were seen to be detrimental to us'. Nonetheless, he too felt little alternative but to increase the temporary limits to £1.75 million. It was December before the bank rate fell to 7 per cent and another month before the crisis was really felt to have passed.

In the aftermath of the crisis, several directors took a firm position on holding agreed limits.[51] Their strictures were of some effect and certainly well intentioned, but it remained the case that Aitken and Anderson regarded very large loans to some London stockbrokers and banks and investment in foreign stocks as productive of higher net incomes than investment in a wider range of British trade bills, industrial loans and British bonds. While the Bank 'never' bought the ordinary share stocks of home concerns, the London office was prepared to grant loans against these and foreign shares. This became more important as the 1907 crisis faded[52] and all Scottish banks found margins contracting. In May 1909, for example, Glasgow Corporation three-month bills were offered at only 1 5/16 per cent per year: 'pitiful enough', as Anderson recorded.[53] 'Groaning under the miserable rates we are receiving for such a lot of money just now', the correspondence between London and the Mound was peppered with lamentations about tight margins eroding profits and how the very sharp competition between banks made it difficult to hold deposits. Thus, the needs of the yearly profit position pushed the London office, and the Glasgow office as well, into more high-interest stockbroking and foreign connections. Further, there was the public's perception of the Bank – indeed of all banks – that after the crisis of 1907 they needed to present a strong public face at the annual balance dates. Yet, as deposits were often withdrawn suddenly, it became an annual worry to ensure that each yearly balance should show deposits at least close to, and preferably above, the previous year's position. Sharp temporary dips in deposits might give rise

50 BS 1/21/25, George Anderson to Thomas Aitken, 1 November 1907.
51 BS 1/21/25, George Anderson to Thomas Aitken, 3 and 25 January 1908.
52 BS 1/21/25, 6 February 1908.
53 BS 1/21/25, 12 May 1909.

to the wrong impression. But of course, high-interest advances helped the deposit position, as managers could offer more to customers. A brief mention should be made of the fact that, in common with other banks, Bank of Scotland sought temporary funds against a sudden withdrawal around balance days. This became known at a later date as 'window dressing', but there was nothing irrational about a practice designed to obviate misunderstandings on the part of those who did not appreciate the ebb and flow of deposits on a day-to-day basis.[54]

The good results from the London office obscured a gradual deterioration in the market value of foreign assets. There were two problems of note. Over the first few years of George Anderson's tenure, the favourable balance between purchase and market prices deteriorated to a negative one. By 1904, with £4,715,935 held, the balance against the Bank was £372,709. There was an improvement in the buoyant financial conditions of 1905 and for two years thereafter, but by February 1907 the market values were deteriorating again, and by the following year, on a holding of £5 million, the loss had reached £400,535. Over the next two years the directors insisted on some sales, but by 1912 the Bank still held £3,791,999 at a market value of –£222,000, and this rapidly worsened as the First World War approached. To make matters worse, the Bank held over £200,000 of Mexican railway bonds and another £310,000 of Brazilian and Argentinian fixed-interest debts. By autumn 1913, civil war had broken out in Mexico and all bonds were marked down; in January 1914 the National Railways of Mexico stopped payment, and a further fall in values proceeded.[55] By December 1913, even Anderson was worried: 'prices on the stock exchange are too dreadful for words', and he went on: 'I am greatly concerned over the continued heavy fall in Brazil railway stocks, and its connections. I trust it does not portend serious trouble.' At the annual balance, Anderson exhibited that confusion between good current income and underlying asset values which had marked the recent years of his Treasurership:

> We shall again have excellent profits but we have a good deal to meet, apart from our investments which have of course materially improved of recent weeks. The fearful loss in the [bonds] of the unfortunate Mexican North Western Railway we have to face as sundry other matters.[56]

The material improvement was short-lived, and the true position on the eve of the First World War was very much worse. Aitken, supported by

---

54 In this respect, see BS 1/21/25, 25 January and 16 February 1911.
55 R. Roberts, *Schroders: Merchants and Bankers* (London: 1992), p. 144.
56 BS 1/21/25, George Anderson to W. Smiles, London office manager, 28 February 1914.

Anderson and several directors, had made over £2 million in large loans to several groups of financiers, company promoters and railway developers, the securities for which were, in the main, Latin American stocks.

The agreement signed in 1898 between Bank of Scotland and the Canadian Bank of Commerce was the culmination of a thirty-five-year direct connection with Canadian banking institutions. Economic progress was marked in Canada in the second half of the nineteenth century by very considerable demands for capital and labour, and the innumerable trade connections invariably required facilities. Thus, well before the close of the Victorian period, the London and Glasgow offices were involved in the discounting of Canadian bills and other facilities for contractors and financiers of varied descriptions. Apart from the crisis of 1907, relations were usually straightforward, and the facilities provided made a substantial contribution to the London office income. Yet, by 1910, Thomas Aitken was being drawn in rather too closely, as it transpired, to the world of these Canadian businessmen.

There was the imposing figure of Sir William Mackenzie, international contractor and financier, and President of the Canadian Northern Railway, to whom Bank of Scotland lent various sums for a variety of enterprises including Canadian nickel mining, of which £460,000 was outstanding by 1914.[57] Then came James Hamet Dunn, joint partner with Charles Louis Fischer in the City of London merchant house of Dunn & Fischer Co. Ltd, founded in 1905.[58] Dunn was born in Canada in 1874, studied law for a career, and, as with so many lawyers before and since, found this a convenient training for company promotion. His firm's speciality was to link Canadian and other contractors with European finance. The companies so formed concentrated on utilities, railways and ports, mostly in Latin America and the Caribbean. Dunn & Fischer were none too cautious about the claims which they made for their endeavours, and regularly engaged in practices designed to limit the supply of stocks and bonds and maintain their market values. Some of the information supplied was false, but there was always sufficient hard evidence of investment to maintain the interest of the investing public. In this sense, they were not simply fictitious but exaggerated. In addition to the issue of stocks and bonds, Dunn persuaded Aitken, among several London bankers, to advance funds for construction and for the payment of interest due to stockholders, giving as collateral the bonds of the said companies. By 1914, Aitken had advanced £260,000 to the Brazilian Traction, Light and Power Co. Ltd, incorporated in Canada and founded

---

57 Sir William Mackenzie: *DNB* (1922–30), pp. 544–5.
58 'Dunn, Sir James Hamet', in D. J. Jeremy (ed.), *Dictionary of Business Biography* (London: 1984), pp. 210–12.

by Dunn & Fischer in 1912. Aitken also advanced, on a variety of other Latin American securities (often unquoted) to Dunn & Fischer and their associates, another £485,000 by 1914, partly under the guarantee of Sir William Mackenzie. Other companies to which Aitken lent money were the Port of Pará (Brazil) scheme, for £275,000: the Pará Construction Co., for £100,000; the São Paulo (Brazilian) Railway Co., for £300,000; the Mexico Tramways Co., for £30,000; and the Madeira Mamore Railway Co., for £100,000. When the value of the stocks and bonds held by the Bank against these advances began to fall quite sharply from the autumn of 1912, Aitken advised holding the collateral. By October 1913, as the political situation in Latin America deteriorated, Aitken estimated that, of these '£1.5 millions of securities which we hold, not more than £200,000 could be turned into cash in an emergency'.[59] Matters were not helped when Fischer disappeared that year leaving considerable unpaid debts. By August 1914, the situation was very serious for Dunn, his remaining associates, the Canadian Bank of Commerce, Bank of Scotland and numerous other connections and private investors.

Why had this position been allowed to develop? When the Bank decided to move funds to London after the City of Glasgow collapse, it became just too convenient to curtail the good earnings on these advances and from the connections brought in train from the Canadian Bank of Commerce and the various financiers and company promoters. It appeared that the London office was well managed, the securities were apparently saleable, and there was only one big crisis, in 1907, which was overcome, though with some misgivings. Furthermore, many of the larger Scottish companies were doing more business in London as their activities expanded, and these wanted advances through London and their bills discounted there as well. There were also connections between several directors and overseas company promotion; some board meetings tended to send mixed signals to Aitken and Anderson about the preferred policy. But not all directors, fortunately, agreed with what was happening: 'several were much opposed' and made their position clear, especially so after 1907. Yet in these varied circumstances, with some support on the board, Anderson and Aitken found it convenient to ignore limits on large loans and sometimes instructions on investments as well. While the directors made it quite clear, in 1911 and not for the first time, that £100,000 should be the maximum for a single large loan transaction in London, this was regularly disregarded before 1914.

Aitken also acted entirely on his own. In July 1910, when the board authorised the sale of £250,000 of investments, Aitken promptly sold

<hr />

59 BS 1/21/25, Treasurer's Private Letter Book, Sir G. Anderson to Thomas Aitken, 25 October 1913.

£300,000. He continued to take large blocks of unquoted stocks from London brokers, including Kitcat and Aitken, although the board had expressly instructed against the practice.[60] He was reprimanded over misleading and exaggerated statements on foreign stocks, and his wish to accept a directorship of the Pennsylvania railway was vetoed, as the board did not wish to see the London office manager closely associated with one enterprise whose bonds were used as collateral for loans. In 1913, Aitken was asked by J. H. Dunn to be the main financial advisor to the Mexican North Western railway, and was offered a trip to Mexico to see conditions at first hand.[61] In November 1911, when Aitken wished to advance £300,000 to the Mexican Securities Corporation, Anderson replied: 'I would not be averse to the proposed increase. But the views of our friends upstairs must be respected and I am certain that the tack of £300,000 to this one company on nothing but its own bond would lead to protest.'[62] In April 1912, Aitken put forward another suggested £300,000 advance, with collateral as unlisted South American stocks; in the autumn, the board was persuaded to take up a loan to a Brazilian enterprise of £160,000, on soon to be near-worthless stock, and Aitken immediately came back with a request for another £400,000, also for Brazil.[63] Even while stocks in Brazil and elsewhere in Latin America were falling, and the fall was noteworthy in 1912 as the continent lurched into one of its periodic political convulsions, the London office continued to cultivate contacts and to extend and renew advances. It was quite clear that Thomas Aitken was conducting important business on behalf of the Bank for which tighter control would have been appropriate. The desperate nature of the situation was to become apparent after 1914.

60 BS 1/21/25, 9 August 1910.
61 Ibid., 1 April 1913.
62 Ibid., 16 November 1911.
63 Ibid., 18 December 1913.

CHAPTER 18

THE UNION BANK OF SCOTLAND, 1830–1914

ETWEEN 1830 AND 1845, the capital subscribed for banking in Glasgow, the ownership of these banks and the control and level of profits were transformed. Prior to this time, banking facilities had been offered by branches of nine banks (Bank of Scotland, the Royal Bank, the Commercial Bank, the British Linen Company, the Greenock Banking Company, the Paisley Union, the Paisley Banking Company, the Renfrewshire Banking Company and the Leith Banking Company) and by four companies registered in the burgh (the Ship, the Thistle, the Glasgow Bank and James & Robert Watson, a private bank). By then, the Ship and the Thistle were a shadow of their former glory. Neither had found a solution to the damage caused by the periodic trade crises and both were seriously affected by the 1825 crisis. Only the Glasgow, founded in 1806 with strong connections in Dundee and Kirkcaldy, carried on an extensive trade; it amalgamated with the Ship in 1836. Watson's was declared bankrupt in June 1832.[1] The branches of the Royal Bank and Bank of Scotland were of immense benefit to Glasgow trade, as each discounted more bills than all the other banks together. Both were deeply involved in industrial, commercial and property investment in Glasgow, with an emphasis by 1815 on the Clyde frontage, around the St Rollox chemical works and to the west of the old merchants' quarter. In the aftermath of 1825, the Edinburgh banks granted extensive facilities to private developers in support of burgh initiatives; in 1827, for example, Bank of Scotland offered to lend funds to the burgh for a new Post Office and even suggested a joint venture for such.[2] The buoyancy of the west

1 In 1826, Kirkman Finlay, in evidence to the Select Committee on Promissory Notes in Scotland and Ireland, House of Commons, (402) vol. iii, Appendix 17, p. 58, 22 March 1826, mentioned that most of the provincial banks had agencies in Glasgow.
2 R. Renwick (ed.), *Extracts from the Records of the Burgh of Glasgow*, Scottish Burgh Records Society, vol. xi, 1823–1833 (Glasgow: 1916), p. 270, 16 October 1827.

of Scotland economy encouraged the British Linen to open its branch in 1829.

By 1829, the opportunities offered by trade in the west had encouraged Glasgow and Edinburgh merchants and Glasgow burgh councillors, both Whig and Tory, to avail themselves of 7 George IV c.67 (1826) for the encouragement of co-partnerships in Scottish banking.[3] The Act extended to all banks of issue in Scotland the legal right to sue (and be sued) under their corporate identity; only a 'manager, cashier or other principal officer' needed to be listed in the legal paperwork. They were required to lodge with the Commissioners of Stamps and Taxes the name of every partner, in order to identify those liable for the debts of a bank on failure.[4]

The prospectus for the Glasgow Union Banking Company was published on 1 January 1830:

> Seventy years have elapsed since a Native Bank was first established in this City, and during the long interval between 1760 and 1829, the population of Glasgow has increased from 25,000 to 200,000 souls; whilst its Manufactures, Shipping, and General Trade have increased in a much higher ratio. Accordingly, the three local Banking Establishments of this City, (which have in all not more than thirty partners) have proved so inadequate to answer the demand for Bank accommodation, that, no fewer than nine Branches of Banks, not indigenous to Glasgow, have been introduced to supply the deficiency, and are now in such active operation, as to engross a very large proportion of her Banking business. Thus have *others* been allowed to reap those profits, which, had her own citizens been more active, and more alive to their own interests, would have been realised by themselves.[5]

Glasgow had been slow to develop other financial services as well; in 1816 there were no fire insurance offices owned in the burgh, while twenty-two branches of English firms conducted this business. Scotland's slowness to develop life insurance companies before 1815 has already been noted,

---

3 7 George IV c.67 (26 May 1826), 'An Act to regulate the mode in which societies or co-partnerships for banking in Scotland may sue or be sued'. The Act regulated the issue of licences and the reissue of notes by the Stamp Office in Edinburgh; a bank with branches had to take three licences to cover principal offices and one other licence for all other branches.
4 Bank of Scotland, the British Linen Company and the Royal Bank were exempt from this provision.
5 The prospectus is reprinted in full in R. S. Rait, *The History of the Union Bank of Scotland* (Glasgow: 1930), pp. 214–20; and see below, Appendix 10. The original printed copy is at BS(U), Uncatalogued, GUBC Minutes, 1, insert, and pp. 1–5, 1 January 1830. There is a copy in the Goldsmiths Library, University of London. At the time it was being discussed, there were a few changes made in the final resolution adopted at meetings of 15 January and 2 February 1830. Rait points out that there were two minor errors in the first paragraph: it was eighty years, not seventy, since the establishment of the Ship Bank; and the partners of the latter in 1830 did in fact number more than thirty persons in all. See BS(U), Uncatalogued, GUBC Minutes, 1, 1 February 1830 for subscribers and occupations, from a wide cross-section of Glasgow business, retail, wholesale and manufacturing.

and when they started they opened first in Edinburgh.[6] The prospectus followed with a critical comment on the geographical location of the existing banks in the western end of Glasgow to the neglect of the eastern and central part of the city. It went on to emphasise that private banks could seldom command sufficient capital for extensive business, and it underlined the 'Peculiar facilities, also, afforded to such a company (as was being proposed) by the liberal policy of the Legislature in conferring by the recent Act 7, Geo. IV, c.67, corporate powers upon such associations as the present'. There were seventeen Glasgow names at the end of the pro-spectus making up the interim committee along with William Mitchell, designated interim manager, and one person apiece from ten other burghs.[7] The only Edinburgh representative was Roderick Mackenzie ws who drew up the contract of co-partnership, revised subsequently by two counsel.[8] There was disagreement among both the members of the interim committee and the partners, caused by their differing perceptions of the role of the proposed bank.[9] From the close of the Napoleonic Wars, it had been evident that business and the middle classes were moving to the centre and west of Glasgow, away from the eastern side. The burgh council had facilitated development to the east and north of the Trongate and built there a courthouse, a new jail and the slaughterhouses, rebuilt the cattle markets and enclosed and improved Glasgow Green next to the Clyde. In 1829, the property developers and landlords in the east of Glasgow demanded that the burgh move all public buildings to the Cross, and in the following year they opposed the extension of the burgh to include Blythswood.[10] This group included many wealthy industrialists and traders, and it was inevitable that they would seek to influence the prospectus and the composition of the board. In the first they succeeded, but they failed to dictate the board. Subsequent elections by subscribers saw a mixed response; a speculative builder was voted chairman, but a 'sound banking' group led by John Leadbetter, a Tory, won most of the

6 J. H. Clapham, *An Economic History of Modern Britain: The Early Railway Age, 1820–1850* (Cambridge: 1967), p. 287.

7 These were Greenock, Stirling, Perth, Ayr, Lanark, Haddington, Dunbar, Dunblane, Paisley and Hamilton. There were no aristocrats or army officers on the board. In the Glasgow list, only three had status as lairds: David McHaffie of Overton (who took the chair), Joseph Bain of Morriston and William Dick of Wester Lumloch. John Wilkie ws (not on the list) was chosen as acting secretary.

8 Roderick Mackenzie was a leading member of a group of Edinburgh lawyers and merchants who had launched a prospectus in 1829 for a Caledonian Bank of Glasgow. It failed to attract interest in Glasgow, but a group of Glasgow merchants led by Robert Stewart, wine dealer, held discussions with Mackenzie which brought about the establishment of the Glasgow Union Banking Company. For the Caledonian project, see Goldsmiths Library, mss 579, John Wilkie mss.

9 Rait, *Union Bank*, pp. 220–33, provides an account of the complicated discussions which preceded the adoption of the final resolution. See bs(u), Uncatalogued, gubc Minutes, 1, February 1830; there is more detail in Goldsmiths Library, mss 579.

10 Renwick (ed.), *Extracts from the Records of the Burgh of Glasgow*, vol. xi, pp. 325, 349, 359, 360–1.

seats. At a general meeting on 2 February, the developers resigned and sent 'a grossly inaccurate account' to the *Glasgow Chronicle* in which it was suggested that the meeting had been split among three factions.[11] Several from the defeated group later schemed for the Western Bank, founded in 1832, and were involved in the launch of the Clydesdale Bank in 1838.

On 16 February 1830, the contract of co-partnery was adopted by a general meeting of no fewer than 425 subscribers.[12] The constitution had been agreed at the first general meeting of 2 February, and it defined its business as 'banking in all its branches' and for no other purposes of trade or merchandise. The Company was to operate in Glasgow and other towns in Scotland. Nominal capital was fixed at £2 million sterling, divided into 8,000 shares of £250 each, and powers were taken for an increase of capital in the future. Twenty per cent on each share was to be called up, and it was in the power of future general meetings to increase this instalment, although in fact no further call was made. Subscribers would have the right to a cash account up to half their paid-up capital. There would be a board of ten ordinary directors who would be elected at the annual general meeting, and, after the first two years, two of the directors would retire annually and not be eligible for re-election until after the lapse of a year. The ordinary directors were obliged to have at least twenty shares each and to live within ten miles of Glasgow. It was their responsibility to elect ten extraordinary directors. None of the directors could be a partner in any other Scottish bank apart from a joint-stock company with more than fifty partners, and private-bank directors and any other bank agents were also excluded. The board was presided over by a chairman or deputy chairman, but neither could be part of the 'Management or Ordinary Direction', and this also applied to the extraordinary directors. The financial year was to end on 1 May and the annual general meeting was to be held on the second Thursday of the month. All disputes in respect of the co-partnership were to be referred for arbitration in the Glasgow tradition: in order, to the first Assessor of the City of Glasgow, then to the Professor of Scots Law at the University of Glasgow, and lastly to the Dean of the Faculty of Advocates.

Voting powers were weighted towards the small shareholders. One share entitled the owner to one vote; three shares to five; four to ten; five to fifteen; six to twenty, and there was to be one vote for every twenty additional shares. It was a skilful contract, and the support shown by such a broad section of Glasgow wealth greatly helped to establish confidence

11 Rait, *Union Bank*, pp. 226–7; Goldsmiths Library, MSS 579, p. 84: votes recorded for directors on 16 February 1830 were Robert Stewart (1,189 votes), James Browne (1,134), Walter Ferguson (1,101), Alexander Drysdale (1,070), Alexander McEwan (1,001), John Miller (998), Robert Kerr (965), John Leadbetter (962), James Roberton (899), Elias Gibb (881). See also BS(U), Uncatalogued, GUBC Minutes, 8 February 1830.
12 BS(U), Uncatalogued, GUBC Minutes, 1, lists of partners, 16 February 1830.

in the new bank. There was still a fear that Glasgow was a place of 'speculators', and there were also political differences between the Tory bankers of Edinburgh and the more Whiggish supporters of the new bank, although there were Tories among the proprietors, including John Leadbetter. The majority of Glasgow merchants supported Parliamentary reform and attended banquets in support of the moderate Glasgow Political Union, but none of the early board of the Glasgow Union Banking Company was among the political leadership of the agitation.[13] One of the first decisions of the new board was to appoint a Glasgow merchant, James A. Anderson, as manager, over the head of William Mitchell, the choice of the interim committee.[14] Mitchell was demoted to deputy cashier, but soon delved into the scheme for the Western Bank, and he left early in 1832. It was a happy release.[15] James Anderson had no direct previous experience of banking, yet he proved to be efficient and remained in the post until 1852. His salary was fixed at £700 with three increments of £100 in the succeeding years. London and Edinburgh correspondents were appointed, and the first joint-stock bank in Glasgow opened for business at 10 a.m. on 13 May 1830. The new board was in no hurry to elect the 'honorary offices' of chairman, deputy and extraordinary directors, the first of whom came in October 1831. The specific posts went to Glasgow merchants, five more also came from commerce, and there were two military men: Colonel Sir Neil Douglas KCB (79th regiment), and Captain Francis Hay from Ayr.[16] All the directors swore an oath of secrecy, as did their opposite numbers on the Edinburgh local board.[17]

The new board reassessed whether the lease of premises at 114 Trongate was the most suitable place for a head office. In January 1832, James &

13 F. A. Montgomery, 'Glasgow and the Struggle for Parliamentary Reform, 1830–1832', *Scottish Historical Review*, 61 (1982), 130–45. The Reform Act still left urban areas under-represented (Edinburgh three seats, Glasgow two): M. Dyer, '"Mere Detail and Machinery": The Great Reform Act and the Effects of Redistribution on Scottish Representation, 1832–1868', *Scottish Historical Review*, 62 (1983), 17–34, Table 1; D. A. Teviotdale, 'Glasgow Parliamentary Constituencies 1832–1846', B. Litt. dissertation (University of Glasgow, 1963); W. Ferguson, 'The Reform Act (Scotland) of 1832: Intention and Effect', *Scottish Historical Review*, 45 (1966), 105–14; F. A. Montgomery, 'Glasgow and the Movement for Corn Law Repeal', *History*, 64 (1979), 363–79.
14 Security required in 1830 was £10,000 for the manager (reduced to £8,000 in 1836), £8,000 (£6,000) for the cashier, £1,000 (£1,000) for the Accountant, £3,000 (£2,000) for each teller, and £3,000 (£2,000) for the secretary.
15 William Mitchell's subsequent career showed him to be unbalanced and vindictive. On leaving the Union, he refused to complete the legal paperwork for his successor. When the Western was launched, he was appointed general manager, but he resigned in 1835 and again refused to complete the paperwork. While there, he tried to sue Bank of Scotland in the aftermath of the collapse of Kinnear, Smith & Co. He was appointed as the manager of the Agricultural and Commercial Bank of Ireland, but may not have taken up position, and by the later 1830s he was a burgh constable in Dumfries. He emigrated to Australia and became a preacher in Melbourne, where he died in 1866; see Rait, *Union Bank*, p. 241; and BS 20/30/9, Miscellaneous papers.
16 Rait, *Union Bank*, p. 240.
17 BS 20/29/9, GUBC Edinburgh branch, Bond of secrecy, December 1830.

Robert Watson's private bank was robbed of a substantial sum; only part was recovered, and Bank of Scotland suggested that the Union move closer to the main banking centre. In June, the purpose-built office of J. & R. Watson's at the foot of Virginia Street was bought for £4,000 when the bank was declared bankrupt.[18] In 1838, the Union board decided to erect a new head office on the site of the Thistle bank five minutes' walk up Virginia Street, and the Union moved there in 1840.[19] In 1844, the Union moved into the spacious premises of the Glasgow and Ship Bank (another five minutes up Virginia Street) following their amalgamation. The Union was now only a couple of minutes from Bank of Scotland and close to the other banks.

The first year was one of cautious advance and consolidation as the directors tried to evolve a distinctive pattern for advances. It was not until August 1830 that the Union Bank invested in British government securities; only three branches were established although ten were considered; the bank's notes began to cross the Border at Carlisle, and a note exchange within Glasgow was arranged with the Royal Bank in January 1831. By the time the first balance sheet was made up, on 30 April 1831, the number of shareholders had increased to 608, the profit on the first year's business was £8,880, and the Union Bank had become accepted as part of the financial network of this rapidly-expanding city.[20] The annual general meeting on 12 May was attended by 279 partners.

At the time of foundation, great efforts had been made to secure the support of Edinburgh money, and a promise was given to open an office there. At first the board agreed that Robert Allan & Co., a private banking company, would act as its agents, and such accounts as were opened were handled there. This infuriated a number of Edinburgh subscribers, and in September 1830 it was insisted that the directors convene a board of six subscribers to supervise an office. The new branch was opened at 67 North Bridge Street, with the agent paid on a sliding scale designed to encourage caution and the search for good cash account and bill opportunities.[21] Instructions were given to the Edinburgh committee on calling regular meetings, on the establishment of a subcommittee to attend daily at the office and on some basic rules on lending, and to Robert Burns, agent, to the tellers and to the accountant. These included instructions to open

18 Rait, *Union Bank*, p. 242; the main difficulty for J. & R. Watson's was losses on past-due bills.
19 Ibid., p. 265.
20 The first balance sheet, of 30 April 1831 (BS(U), Uncatalogued, GUBC Minutes, 2), was exhibited to the general meeting on 12 May 1831; repr. in N. Tamaki, *The Life Cycle of the Union Bank of Scotland 1830–1954* (Aberdeen: 1983), Appendix A. See below, Statistical Appendix, Table A22, for annual balance figures.
21 Rait, *Union Bank*, p. 237. The agent, Robert Burns, was paid £250, and on all net profits up to £5,000 he was to receive 10 per cent and for losses a deduction of 10 per cent to a maximum of £1,000.

a book into which 'every customer of the Bank and such as may be customers be entered a designation of a scale: 16 (meaning very bad), 16c17 (bad), 17 (fair), 17c18 (very fair), 18 (good), 18c19 (very good) and 19 (undoubted)'.[22]

There were numerous problems with the Edinburgh branch. The winter of 1830–1 was a difficult time for Scottish business; the existing banks had the best business, and there was fierce competition for good bills. There was also a clash of personalities, and the manager was twice called to Glasgow and instructed to be more cooperative with the local board and to give its members access to the accounts and record of discounts: 'without knowing the amount of the bills current the local board will just be making a leap in the dark'.[23] The branch was unable to gain much first-class business. It needed accounts such as those of William Mair, an Edinburgh wine and spirit dealer with a 'rather extensive and profitable business besides being a steady and respectable man and possessed of property', and of Messrs Morrison & Wilson, ironmongers, 'industrious, sober and attentive'.[24] There were several active accounts opened by pawnbrokers, but overall it was a disappointing start in Edinburgh. Instead, requests were all too frequent from the class of ex-bankrupt traders and shopkeepers: for instance, William and Jane Whyte, tobacconists in Leith, once significant importers but who 'have failed more than once and are now in a limited trade. They are industrious but poor'; or John Cameron of Falkirk, a commercial agent who had broken in 1826 and had been turned down at other banks.[25] The branch also gained few good industrial accounts. In August 1831, the Prestonpans pottery opened an account, but the next important one was not opened before July 1832 when the Alloa Glass Company asked for a £5,000 cash account. After the collapse of Kinnear, Smith & Co. in that year, a number of middle-class accounts were opened. The board discovered another problem: a review of cash accounts granted for houses in Leith found none to be operative, and the accounts were treated as loans, so the notes were returned by other banks for exchange and the Union Bank had little of the benefit of an active account. With this situation, the Edinburgh committee was forced into discounting; but this was hard work. After a modest profit of £276 in the financial year 1830–1, the branch lost £138 the following year; in 1832–3 losses rose to £1,000, and in spite of buoyant trade the branch still managed a loss

22 BS(U), Uncatalogued, GUBC Minutes, 1, copy of instructions to the local committee of the Edinburgh branch, 30 December 1830; see also BS 18/1/1, UBS Local Edinburgh Board Minutes, 15 November 1830.
23 BS(U), Uncatalogued, GUBC Minutes, 2, 6 December 1830; BS 18/1/1, UBS Local Edinburgh Board Minutes, 6 and 8 December 1830, 1 August 1831.
24 BS 18/1/1, UBS Local Edinburgh Board Minutes, 15 December 1831, 16 May 1833.
25 Ibid., 8 December 1831.

over the next two years. This was a deplorable record. Of the gross losses of the Union from all branches, £4,347 recorded in the years 1832–6 and covering the first six years of business, Edinburgh succeeded in losing one-third.[26] In 1838, the agency was closed and the staff dismissed on the occasion of the junction with Sir William Forbes, James Hunter & Co., whose directors insisted that for the six years before their complete amalgamation the appointment of office staff was entirely a matter for them and not for the committee of Edinburgh shareholders, which body then lapsed.

Apart from Edinburgh, the Glasgow board opened only two branches in the first year, at Greenock and Bathgate. The basic financial regime for branches involved the discounting of bills and the opening of cash account facilities; loans were at 4 per cent while deposits were paid at $2\frac{1}{2}$ per cent, the gap of $1\frac{1}{2}$ per cent determining the calculation of profits, half of which were credited to the branch and half to the head office. In practice, to attract business, agents paid higher rates for some deposits. Furthermore, agents discounted bills turned down by the Edinburgh banks, though a higher rate was generally levied. This has been interpreted as a more liberal policy for the Glasgow banks compared with Edinburgh, but requires some qualification in view of the subsequent history of losses and bad debts. The gains from branches were £732 in 1831–2; there followed a slight loss, but profits rose to over £2,013 in 1835–6. Of the gross profits of £7,916 for branches to 1836, Greenock managed £5,799. With trade in such difficulties, the Union looked for gaps in the coverage of the existing banks. The openings of 1831–2 came on the River Forth at Alloa, and at Ayr to take advantage of the Irish trade. There were frequent applications from commercial travellers and shopkeepers for agencies at the more isolated burghs. The nearest banks to Anstruther, for example, were at Cupar and St Andrews, yet the opportunities offered by the locality and the fishing trade suggested a profitable circulation where notes would stay out. For the Alloa branch, an interesting assessment has survived:

> there is but one branch vizt the Commercial Bank and besides it is a shipping port and various extensive works in the town and neighbourhood abounding with coal and other minerals – it is also in the heart of a rich agricultural country and not distant from Kincardine where a great trade in shipbuilding is carried

26 BS(U), Uncatalogued, GUBC Minutes, 2, accounts 1 May 1832, general meeting 10 May 1832; Minutes, 3, accounts 1 May 1833, general meeting 9 May 1833 (102 attended); accounts 19 April 1834, general meeting 8 May 1834 (98 attended); accounts 20 April 1835, general meeting 14 May 1835 (66 attended); Minutes, 3 and 4, accounts 20 April 1836, general meeting 12 May 1836 (79 attended).

on besides distilleries and at Limekilns where the Earl of Elgin's coalfields are situated and Clackmannan, Dunfermline, etc., where part of the banking business is carried to Falkirk, besides Alloa is a resting point with commercial travellers and it is said the agent for the Commercial Bank is not popular and Stirling is only distant seven miles and as the projected bank appears to have failed.[27]

The Union continued to target market towns and ferry terminals where the bill business was considerable and where notes would circulate through local shopkeepers.

When the Glasgow office opened for business on 13 May 1830, the nominal capital was £2 million although a part of this was held by the bank for later sale at a premium.[28] In the early 1830s, the Union eschewed significant purchases of London stocks, and by August 1830 only £25,000 in British government securities had been bought and placed with Jones, Loyd & Co., its London agents, as a guarantee against bad debts. The investment in government stocks was affected by political events: £20,000 was invested in 2½ per cent annuities bought at 99, and by May 1831 these stood at 87, which the general manager calculated involved a loss of £2,517 10s. In the first annual report for the shareholders' meeting of 12 May 1831, it was noted that no

> prudently conducted banking business can dispense with having a sum of money in London so invested as to be at all times available to meet exigencies and the directors have invested the smallest sum which they considered a concern of this magnitude required to have so invested. When they inform the meeting that the whole amount of the investments referred to is under £25,000 the partners will not feel much alarm for the loss which may possibly accrue should the bank be obliged to sell at any unfavourable period.[29]

This report of May 1831 from the directors signified to the shareholders serious difficulties. They admitted that 'a newly established bank is peculiarly liable to loss, as well from inexperience and natural over-anxiety to extend the business and employ the capital as from the attempts that never fail to be made upon it by persons unworthy of credit whom other banks take such an opportunity to shake off'.[30] The directors went on to say 'that the losses hitherto sustained have not been considerable either in number, or amount, and they have reason to hope that the bills, now

---

27 BS 18/1/1, UBS Local Edinburgh Board Minutes, 19 January and 7 March 1832.
28 Prospectus of the Glasgow Union Banking Company: see Appendix 10.
29 BS(U), Uncatalogued, GUBC Minutes, annual meeting, 12 May 1831; also cited in Rait, *Union Bank*, p. 239. The sum was indeed small and may have reflected the need of Jones, Loyd & Co. for business. They collapsed in 1835.
30 BS(U), Uncatalogued, GUBC Minutes, annual meeting, 12 May 1831.

current, are at least not of a worse description than those already off the circle'. The Union was already deep into one of the most serious mistakes a banker could make, loans to grain merchants which relied on rising or stable prices and thus no significant improvement in weather conditions or increases in imports. In April 1832, the Glasgow grain trade collapsed. The losses were too close in time to the annual balance to allow of a precise sum in provision, and they later proved more extensive, with claims to merchants' security, buildings and grain shared with other creditors. The directors admitted in May 1833 that the grant of a dividend the previous year had been mistaken.[31] Later in the year, they agreed that the Stranraer branch would be unlikely to make a profit in the foreseeable future, and it was closed. The dividend for 1832, 1833 and 1834 was only 2½ per cent per year on paid-up capital. In 1834, the board was forced to acknowledge at the annual meeting that a shareholders' committee of inspection could view the accounts, as provided for in the original contract.

After four years of business, the fund of goodwill from stockholders dried up. A few branches were in profit, many customers were high-risk and the board had proved unable to surmount the difficult trading conditions. Dividends averaged under 2 per cent a year. The board noted the 'excessive extension of banking operations' and made the unsurprising announcement that this required more caution 'in the erection of new branches as well as increased vigilance' for the existing openings.[32] Did the Union have a future? Three directors thought not, and sold their shares.[33] There was a steady sale of shares for some time. The dividend was pushed to 4 per cent in April 1835 and 5 per cent the following year, but this was only managed by raiding reserves, and the Union entered the financial year from April 1836 with a much-depleted balance in the profit and loss account, although thereafter the figures began to improve.[34] An application for a royal charter in 1834 was refused, in part because of objections raised by the three senior Edinburgh banks.

From the beginning of its banking business, the Glasgow Union Banking Company's most important source of advances was the discounting of bills. In the first year, over 90 per cent of all advances negotiated at the Glasgow office were discounts, with the rest on cash accounts; and, although the proportion declined somewhat over the next six years, the discounting of bills was still over 85 per cent of all advances in the financial year 1835–6. There were two further outlets for funds. The first was publicly-quoted stocks: British government securities, Bank of

31 BS(U), Uncatalogued, GUBC Minutes, 2, 10 May 1832, 9 May 1833.
32 BS(U), Uncatalogued, GUBC Minutes, 3, annual meeting, 8 May 1834, 14 May 1835.
33 BS(U), Uncatalogued, GUBC Minutes, 3, 20 May 1834, 14 May 1835.
34 See Statistical Appendix, Table A23.

England stock and Exchequer bills. Although purchase (and disposal) was effected mainly through their correspondents in London, the directors, gaining confidence in their own financial discretion, steadily increased their advice and instructions. The second outlet for funds was inter-bank loans, mainly to the English and Irish banks, and an important correspondent in this respect was the Provincial Bank of Ireland.[35]

In these early years, the Union found it difficult to attract sufficient long-term, established business accounts, or new accounts with reputable borrowers who would circulate their banknotes. The most common cash accounts were for sums under £1,000, made to shopkeepers, commodity dealers and importers and small-scale manufacturers, as well as to some who had been refused accommodation elsewhere. Yet the economy of the west of Scotland was growing fast. The great cotton and linen textile industries of the west were at the beginning of some serious problems, but the iron industry was on the threshold of its great expansion, and with iron went coal. The Clyde in the 1830s was already asserting its predominance in the construction of steam tonnage, and in general this second quarter of the century would witness the western region of Scotland becoming one of the great expanding centres of heavy industry. James A. Anderson, in evidence before the Select Committee on the issue of banknotes in 1841, cited mining and agriculture as in a 'state of extraordinary prosperity in the west of Scotland', and shipbuilding and steam-engine-making were described as 'prosperous'.[36] The size of industrial units was increasing, and the small capitals of the provincial and Glasgow banks made it difficult to provide the lending which the new and expanding companies required. The answer, so the Union Bank's experience was to exhibit, was amalgamation with these older and more experienced banks, a number of which were in financial trouble from the crises of 1825 and 1835–6. Yet they had mature staff and good connections. Earnings on commission and on bills of exchange and fees were in decline; the par of exchange on London had been progressively reduced in the 1820s from the forty and fifty days typical at the close of the Napoleonic Wars to five to ten days.[37] The circulation of banknotes tended to decline as a proportion of lending because of faster settlement of accounts and the use of cheques, and this reduced profitability.

The years between 1836 and 1843 saw five amalgamations of banking companies with the Glasgow Union Banking Company which

---

35 For the Irish banks, see G. L. Barrow, *The Emergence of the Irish Banking System 1820–45* (Dublin: 1974); P. Ollerenshaw, *Banking in Nineteenth Century Ireland: The Belfast Banks, 1825–1914* (Manchester: 1987).

36 *Second Report from Select Committee on Banks of Issue*, 15 June 1841, (410) vol. v, Q. 2,466.

37 C. W. Munn, *The Scottish Provincial Banking Companies, 1747–1864* (Edinburgh: 1981), p. 93.

transformed it into a national institution in which the total liabilities of the bank increased from £1.65 million in 1837 to over £6.29 million in 1844. The surplus rose from £19,742 (plus £18,000 in dividends) to £46,481 in 1838 (plus £20,940 in dividends). The dividend in 1836 and 1837 was 6 per cent, with 7 per cent in 1839 and 8 per cent in 1841. The report of the directors on 9 May 1839 asked the proprietors to note that the rate of 7 per cent was 'above the rate generally paid by the Scotch banks'. The difficult years of 1835–7 were absorbed without serious problems, but by that time the first amalgamation had been effected.

The Thistle bank was founded in 1761 and pursued an adventurous banking policy. Its notes became accepted all over Scotland. By the end of the eighteenth century it was regarded as a prosperous co-partnership, but like many small banks it fell upon difficult times during the second quarter of the nineteenth century. In early June 1836, the directors of the Thistle bank approached Elias Gibb and James Browne of the Union with a view to the sale of the older bank.[38] The Thistle board provided a detailed account of its financial situation: assets included a surplus of £8,632 in reserves and property; circulation was a little over £30,500 and deposits £450,000, with a strong list of customers and sound local roots. Here was an opportunity for the Union to grow without pain. The board made a conservative assumption that if £300,000 of the deposits remained, and most of the circulation, there would be a gross yield of £5,350. On that basis, the two boards agreed compensation and incidental charges of £6,500 payable to co-partners. Virtually all the old customers stayed with the Union, and the price of bank stock rose in the autumn.[39]

The conduct of James Anderson during the difficult years of 1835–6 and his determination to strengthen reserves in London had been thoroughly approved by Alexander Blair of Bank of Scotland and by other Edinburgh bankers. James Anderson also supported the Edinburgh banks in their disputes over the reckless bill discounting of the Western Bank in 1834, and so had Richard Duncan, manager of the Thistle bank.[40] In early 1838, the directors of Sir William Forbes, James Hunter & Co. proposed an agreement with the Union Bank that was to be legally described as a 'junction' rather than an amalgamation. Sir William Forbes was the most important addition to the resources of the Union Bank during this first main period of amalgamations. It provided a base in Edinburgh which the Union Bank could not possibly have achieved through its own endeavours. Forbes had excellent political contacts in Edinburgh, London

---

38 There is an entertaining chapter on the early years of the Thistle bank in Rait, *Union Bank*, ch. 5.
39 Ibid., pp. 248–50; BS(U), Uncatalogued, GUBC Minutes, 4, 21 June 1836.
40 BS 20/10/4 (Miscellaneous papers), Richard Duncan to Alexander Blair, 28 October 1834; see above, Chapter 14.

and abroad, and conducted business on behalf of many wealthy Scots. It was also a core member of the Edinburgh banking circle, and thus held similar views about the conduct of banks, and reserves in London, to those of Alexander Blair at Bank of Scotland. It was a Tory bank, in the Edinburgh tradition, and thus an interesting partner with the Whiggish businessmen in Glasgow. The agreement arrived at was announced in the report submitted to the proprietors on 10 May 1838:

> A junction has been negotiated and concluded, upon terms of mutual advantage, between this company and that of Sir William Forbes, James Hunter & Co., Edinburgh – a firm oldest in point of date and first in character and connections among the private banking companies in Scotland, with a business about equal to our own, and with gentlemen of perfect honour and distinguished talents in its management. All the members of that company now become partners of this, and the two concerns will henceforth be carried on as one.

The Agreement explained that it would not be possible 'nor proper' to expound the detailed arrangements, a sentiment fully appreciated by the shareholders, who supported unanimously a resolution which expressed 'full confidence in the prudence and discretion of the Directors'. Sir William Forbes was a profitable concern with assets of £1,580,000 and a net profit in 1836 of £16,000. In fact, the new agreement gave the Forbes partners a cash income of two-thirds of the £16,000 to be met by, first, the issue of 1,000 Union Bank shares whose nominal value was £250,000 and whose assumed income was £3,000, and, second, cash annuities to four of the Forbes partners. These partners were to remain for a minimum of six years as the management of the bank in Edinburgh, with Charles Forbes, one of the four, to work in the head office in Glasgow. Outstanding debts which dated from before 1 January 1830 were to remain the property of the Forbes partners. At the 1838 annual general meeting, the directors were authorised to issue 1,000 shares of the capital to meet these terms, and they gave notice of a motion to increase the bank's capital to £2,500,000 by the issue of 2,000 additional shares of £250 each; and this was adopted at the meeting of the following year.[41] In later years, Edinburgh customers continued to refer to their bank as Forbes, and Coutts & Co. used this designation in correspondence and accounts with Edinburgh for over two decades.[42]

---

41 For the announcement to shareholders and details of the working arrangements of 1838, see Rait, *Union Bank*, pp. 252–5; and see BS(U), Uncatalogued, GUBC Minutes, 4, 'Heads of agreement between Sir William Forbes, James Hunter & Co. and the Glasgow Union Banking Company', 24 April 1835.
42 Coutts & Co., archives, Ledgers, 1850–1860. In the first years of the 'junction', the bad-debts position of Forbes was worse than had been originally appreciated, and the four partners agreed to an abatement of the agreement on annuities.

The success of the junction was soon evident. In terms of management, the Glasgow directors could leave the Edinburgh business to the Forbes partners and concentrate upon the western region and its branches. In 1838–9, with a year behind them and a write-off of Edinburgh bad debts and the costs of the 'junction', the new group had a reserve of £55,501 after a dividend of 7 per cent (£27,930) on a paid-up capital of £399,000.[43] By April 1840, the reserves had reached £108,226, partly funded by the sale of stock, and the capital was now £478,800. Thus the new joint bank was already stronger than its original two groups as separate institutions. In August 1845, the four Forbes directors asked for the appointment of an Edinburgh manager who would work with them until their retirement, and in January and March 1846 a manager and a secretary were appointed, whereupon the amalgamation proper now came into being. By this date, the profit from the Edinburgh branch, including payments on the annuities, was £15,353, a rise of about 10 per cent in three years.[44]

The Paisley Union Bank had been established in early September 1788. Ten co-partners subscribed £500 each in cash with a promissory note for a similar sum on demand. There were two local lairds, and the remainder were merchants and manufacturers from Paisley and Glasgow. Forbes & Co. acted as their agents in Edinburgh and extended a £5,000 facility should this be required; this was a standard arrangement for a new provincial bank, and it would enable the Paisley Union to offer a known reference to London discount offices.[45] Paisley had long been a centre for the production of textiles with a marked degree of specialisation on high-quality and luxury goods. Silk gauze weaving was introduced in the 1750s and reached the peak of its output and prosperity by the close of the American war, with the value of its output in 1784 estimated at £350,000 per annum and employment given to at least 5,000 weavers in Paisley and the surrounding districts, with probably about the same number engaged in ancillary occupations. By the end of the decade, the silk gauze industry was already in decline, and this epitomised the fluctuating problems of Paisley's economy through the first half of the nineteenth century. After 1800, cotton became the most important sector in the town and region, based upon small-scale manufacturing units and vulnerable as before to rapid changes in demand. The post-Napoleonic depression lasted in the local trades until 1822, and there were further heavy losses in 1825, 1829, 1831 and 1837. The leading partners of the Paisley Union Bank decided

---

43 See Statistical Appendix, Table A23.
44 BS(U), Uncatalogued, Glasgow Committee minutes, Edinburgh profit and loss accounts, 1843–6.
45 Rait, *Union Bank*, ch. 9; C. F. Freebairn, 'An Old Banking Institution: The Paisley Union Bank', *Scottish Bankers Magazine*, 16 (1924), 110–20. Eight provincial banks were founded in 1783–8: Munn, *Scottish Provincial Banking Companies*, p. 41, Table 3.

to retire, and, declining possible arrangements with the Western Bank and the newly-founded Clydesdale Bank, approached James Anderson, who then consulted the committee which had been established to conduct the negotiations with Forbes. It found that, while the business in Paisley had been running down, the bank was profitable in good years, but the running total of bad debts on bills had continued throughout the dozen years to 1838 at around £18,000–£20,000. The purchase price for the co-partnership – there were only two partners in 1838 – was fixed at £20,000 payable in annuities of £2,500 for each of ten years and 100 shares of the Union. Property valuations on banking premises in Glasgow and Paisley were agreed, the cashier of the Paisley Union became the agent, and the bank became absorbed by the Union on 30 June 1838.

The purchase of the Paisley Union was the most serious financial error made by the board in this first decade of its business life. The Glasgow Union Banking Company management in Glasgow failed to impose a realistic diagnosis on the over-trading and speculation in Paisley which preceded the crisis of 1841 and 1842.[46] The directors noticed that many borrowers in the west were in difficulty in 1840, but they actually raised the dividend in 1841 by 1 per cent to 8 per cent. Towards the end of May 1841, the directors decided that the worsening situation in Paisley, and in the west generally, nevertheless required a detailed statement to their agents:

> The directors upon examining the transactions of the last year and on a general review of the business since the establishment of the Bank have concurred in an opinion which they are anxious to impress strongly upon the managers and agents of the company that a general error prevailing throughout the concern has been an undue anxiety to extend discounts and a want of sufficient caution and circumspection in the selection of customers and that a decided improvement in these respects is greatly to be desired and ought forthwith to be attempted.
>
> It is not for the purpose of finding fault with what is past that the directors call attention to the subject. They are sensible that a number of causes arising from the circumstances of our situation have co-operated in producing the error which they think has been committed: The zeal of gentlemen entering upon a newly established concern, their anxiety to form connections and to extend transactions in competition with rival banks, their general want of previous experience in banking and of the circumstances and characters of parties offering business, together with the natural tendency to form their practice upon that of their previous mercantile pursuits where larger profits justified

---

46 For a more extended account of the background of the times, see T. Clarke and T. Dickson, 'Class and Class Consciousness in Early Industrial Capitalism, Paisley 1770–1850', in T. Dickson (ed.), *Capital and Class in Scotland* (Edinburgh: 1982), pp. 8–60.

and compensated for greater risks ... But the duration of the Bank and the large business which it has acquired have now taken away the temptation and excuse for such extraordinary risks whilst the competition of additional rivals has reduced and will probably still further reduce the profits so as to leave no sufficient allowance to compensate for bad debts.[47]

The board impressed upon the officers and agents the need to take only good bills and to 'exclude every transaction which has the appearance of risk and to restrict themselves as far as they possibly can to paper of the first order alone', leaving it to the directors to consider lowering the terms of discount. They also issued instructions that agents, prior to opening a new discount account, should find out why the customer wished to change banker, and, when bills were offered for discount out of their home district, why this was. They were to look at all offers, unless convinced by good reason, with distrust and suspicion. The directors reiterated that the benefit of a cash account was to circulate banknotes and not to supply the capital necessary for carrying on a business.

By the autumn of 1841, serious losses were reported from a number of areas; it was later described as a 'more calamitous condition of the general commerce of the country than has occurred since the memorable period' of 1825 and 1826 and was marked by sharp falls in commodity prices, lack of demand, insolvency and ruin for a number of bank customers.[48] Paisley was the worst-affected burgh: markets for burgh products melted away, sixty-seven of the 112 manufacturers were declared bankrupt, the burgh council used up all its funds, and 25 per cent of the population were directly in receipt of poor relief. The government of Sir Robert Peel intervened with state aid.[49] Whereas the Paisley branch of the Union had recorded profits of £12,975 in the five years from purchase, it now recorded losses of £16,292 for 1842 and another £2,900 in the following year, almost half of the total Union Bank losses for these two years.[50] The crisis drove home the impracticality in modern conditions of small, narrowly-based banks where the fortunes of the local middle class, the lairds and the workforce were bound up with one industry, and underlined the shrewdness of the partners of the Paisley Union Bank in their decision to sell.

There were two other amalgamations before the Union Bank of Scotland came into formal existence. The first was with Hunters & Co. of Ayr, established in 1773. Its history was typical of the provincial banks

47 BS(U), Uncatalogued, GUBC Minutes, circular letter, 25 May 1841.
48 Rait, *Union Bank*, p. 265; BS(U), Uncatalogued, GUBC Minutes, 12 May 1842.
49 T. C. Smout, 'The Strange Case of Edward Twistleton: Paisley in Depression, 1841–3', in idem (ed.), *The Search for Wealth and Stability: Essays in Economic and Social History presented to M. W. Flinn* (London: 1979), pp. 218–42; for the effect of the crisis on Bank of Scotland, see above, Chapter 14.
50 BS(U), Uncatalogued, GUBC Minutes, 5, profit and loss account, 20 April 1842, 20 April 1843.

486

of Scotland in this period. It carried on an extensive trade in discounting bills to and from Ireland, and had large agricultural, coal and iron interests on its books. Hunters took over the Kilmarnock Bank in 1821 and had seven branches by the early 1840s. It had been troubled in the aftermath of the Napoleonic Wars, by the crisis of 1825 and by increasing problems in the seriously depressed years of 1841–3. The directors began to consider their takeover by a larger bank, a story which was told by C. D. Gairdner in his *Autobiography*, eventually published in 1902. Gairdner had been chosen to undertake negotiations with both the British Linen Company and the Union Bank. Hunters had enjoyed a long relationship with Sir William Forbes & Co., and this may well have been one of the deciding factors in the agreement and terms offered by the Union Bank. The five remaining partners of Hunters & Co. were paid £25,000, and £500,000 in deposits and seven branches were transferred to the Union Bank in 1843.

In November 1843 came amalgamation with the Glasgow and Ship Bank. The Glasgow Bank started out based on merchants and lairds in the linen trade in Dundee, merchants of Kirkcaldy and their connections in London. In 1792, these formed the Dundee Commercial Banking Co., reconstructed in 1802 as the Dundee New Bank. This new concern derived part of its capital from George, seventh Lord Kinnaird, and William Morland, partners in Ransom, Morland & Co., the London private bankers. In 1805, a further reorganisation brought in William Roberts, a clerk from the London house, as the new manager, and Henry Boase, another banker, as additional partners.[51] They were evidently successful through discounts for army clothing contractors, and in 1809 the partners invited merchants from Kirkcaldy and Glasgow to join a new co-partnership for a bank to be based in Glasgow with a branch in Kirkcaldy and agents in Edinburgh, in addition to the connections with Dundee which would become a separate concern. The Glasgow Bank Company was established with a nominal capital of £200,000 in forty shares of £5,000 apiece, 50 per cent paid.[52] It attracted the prominent Whig businessman James Dennistoun, who took ten shares, Charles, eighth Lord Kinnaird, who took four, and John Tennant, the brewer, two shares; subscriptions came from Liverpool and Bury in addition to London, Dundee and Kirkcaldy. James Dennistoun was appointed manager and remained in office for twenty years; on retirement he was given one of those enormous banquets for which nineteenth-century Glasgow was renowned.

51 C. W. Boase, A Century of Banking in Dundee; being the Annual Balance Sheets of the Dundee Banking Company from 1764 to 1864, 2nd edn (Edinburgh: 1867), pp. 222–7; Rait, Union Bank, ch. 10; the 1802 bank included John Baxter of the Dundee linen family.
52 Boase, Century of Banking, p. 262, suggests that it was £100,000 in forty shares of £2,500, all paid; 5 per cent was added to paid-up capital each year from profits. Boase lists basic balance-sheet data for later years.

In June 1830, the co-partnership was renewed with Alexander and John Dennistoun and their associates predominant. Six per cent was to be paid on the capital, and further profits placed to reserve. In the crisis of 1836, the four remaining partners of the old Ship bank (formally Carrick, Brown & Co.) asked to be absorbed by the Glasgow Bank, and this was agreed. The partners of the Glasgow decided in 1835 that, in principle, they would consider a change in their form of co-partnership from 'a private firm of the old type' into a 'public and open bank'.[53] They were not obviously under worse pressure than other banks; in the nine years 1834–43 they made an average yearly profit of £55,000 and from 1836 paid out £40,000 a year in dividends (8 per cent) and added £118,000 to the reserve fund. Deposits were £1.5 million in 1843. So confident were the directors in 1840 that they commenced work on a prestigious new Glasgow head office inspired by classical architecture and fronted by statues representing Glasgow, Industry, Wealth, Justice, Peace and Empire, each resembling one of the original Greek statues rescued for posterity by the eighth Earl of Elgin. The crisis which commenced in 1841 may have been the precipitating factor whereby, in conditions of great secrecy, the Glasgow and Ship signed an amalgamation with the Union Bank which was confirmed by a Union general meeting on 8 November 1843.

The assumptions upon which the two banks were joined were set down in a memorandum of October 1843:

> The general grounds upon which it has been proposed to unite the Glasgow and Ship Bank and the Union Bank are, that the Union Bank from its various junctions with, and assumptions of, the business of other banks, has acquired a larger disposable amount of funds than it can readily employ with profit and safety, whilst the Glasgow and Ship Bank, from its long established business connections has the means of employing this surplus to advantage; and therefore a coalition (by which a large part of the present annual expense would be saved) would be equally for the advantage of both.[54]

Before the agreement was reached, the Union Bank carried through some significant changes in its organisation. A special meeting of shareholders in May 1843 confirmed a change of name to 'The Union Bank of Scotland'. The original capital stock in 1830 had been £2,000,000 divided into 8,000 shares of £250 of which £50 had been paid up. In 1839, a further 2,000 shares of the same value had been issued, increasing the nominal capital to £2,500,000 and the paid-up portion to £500,000. Now, in May 1843, the directors recommended that the nominal capital be reduced

---

53 Rait, *Union Bank*, pp. 210–11.
54 Ibid., p. 259. Rait has anecdotal accounts of both banks, in chs 2 and 10.

to £1,000,000 divided into 10,000 shares of £100 each, with the paid-up portion being unchanged at £50. It is reasonable to conclude that ideas of the future amalgamation with the Glasgow and Ship Bank were already being considered, since the paid-up capital of the latter was also £500,000. The reserves of the Union Bank had suffered seriously from the losses incurred by the Paisley branch and by 1843 were £54,216, although the dividend paid in 1842 and 1843 was still 7 per cent, only 1 per cent down on that of 1841.

The Glasgow and Ship Bank had a reserve in 1843 of £130,000. It was agreed, as part of the amalgamation conditions, that a sum of £84,000 should be taken out of the reserve and distributed among its partners, leaving £46,000 to be added to the reserve of the Union Bank, giving a total of £100,000 for the new amalgamation and an increase in the nominal capital of the whole to £2,000,000, with a paid-up capital of £1,000,000. The manager of the Glasgow and Ship Bank was retired with compensation, and James Anderson became the general manager. The head office of the Union Bank of Scotland was immediately removed to the newly-built Glasgow and Ship building, at the top of Virginia Street and in the area where the Glasgow banking centre was now firmly established.

Towards the end of this first period of amalgamations, James Anderson gave evidence to the Select Committee on Banks of Issue.[55] It was only recently – from 1833 – that joint-stock banks had been allowed to enter London, and only a few years before then that they had been allowed elsewhere in England. The committee was interested in how the Glasgow Union Banking Company, then of ten years' standing, organised its business and banknote issue, and how, in these matters, it differed from the chartered banks of Edinburgh. Anderson's evidence came on 4 May 1841 and immediately followed the testimony given by Alexander Blair and Primrose Kennedy. The committee examining James Anderson included Henry Goulburn, a future Chancellor of the Exchequer, Sir Robert Peel, Sir James Graham, who was sympathetic to the Scottish bankers, and Charles Wood and George Grote, who were mostly not so. Indeed, it should be stressed that several committee members had not been persuaded by the testimony from Blair and Kennedy on important matters relating to banknotes and circulation. At the time of Anderson's interview, the Glasgow Union Banking Company, as it was still called, had ten principal branches and a dozen sub-agents, 'besides',

---

55 *Second Report from Select Committee on Banks of Issue*, 15 June 1841, (410) vol. v. See, in particular, F. W. Fetter, *The Development of British Monetary Orthodoxy 1797–1875* (Cambridge, MA: 1965), especially chs 4 and 5. For an account of the other Scottish evidence, see above, Chapter 15.

said Anderson, 'the establishment in Edinburgh, which is not a branch, of the bank of Sir William Forbes and Company, which forms one with us by a coalition three years ago'.[56] It was a long cross-examination with some 308 questions, and inquiry ranged widely over matters of circulation theory and advances, the degree of reliance on the Bank of England and some description of operational practice. We have therefore a statement of the degree to which James Anderson was willing to discuss, in public, the ways in which the bank at that time was being directed and organised.

The prime task that fell to James Anderson was to convince the committee that, as the Scottish banks gave interest for monies, on deposit and on current account, 'for small and large sums', this held out an 'inducement to everybody to bring whatever spare money they have to the bank; and the number of banks through the country affords facilities for this purpose'.[57] Banknotes did not remain out beyond the immediate needs of customers, and the exchanges of notes, on Tuesday and Friday, swiftly returned notes to the issuer. On these important matters, James Anderson reiterated the points made by Alexander Blair. Yet, for question after question, Charles Wood and George Grote pressed on with the suggestion that when demands were made in Scotland these were answered by an increase of paper. Anderson pointed out that it followed from his position that such rises were not circulation but capital, as the notes returned swiftly. George Grote extended the discussion and argued that when customers of the Glasgow Union increased demands for payments in England, then the bank was, in various ways, using funds available from English sources and not its own. James Anderson vigorously contested this interpretation: 'it is our capital; it is capital which we have collected in Scotland and placed in London for this purpose; it is not London currency lent to Scotland'. George Grote, in contrast, held to his view that such payments merely disposed of a part of the circulation of the Bank of England and that the Scottish discounts were thus ultimately underwritten by Threadneedle Street. As a response to the questions from the committee, Anderson's answers lacked theoretical precision, and his arguments over the needs of trade and industry were brushed aside. Indeed, the angle of questioning forced Anderson to minimise the importance of the cash accounts: 'a great deal smaller than is generally supposed'. When asked whether the circulation of notes was regulated by the state of the foreign exchanges, Anderson replied: 'Not the circulation; we regulate our business by the state of the foreign exchanges, but we consider that the circulation does

---

56 *Second Report from Select Committee on Banks of Issue*, 15 June 1841, (410) vol. v, Q. 2,305.
57 Ibid., James Anderson's evidence, pp. 207–23, evidence discussed here from pp. 208–10; and see Qs 2,320, 2,323, 2,408.

not require any regulation; our advances and loans we regulate, but not the circulation of our notes'.

By 1841, the lengthy disagreements among the Scottish banks over interest rates were evident but more subdued after the losses of the previous decade. Indeed, James Anderson even recognised that while the Glasgow banks thought a 1½ per cent margin between deposits and discounts sufficient, in Edinburgh, 'where they have had longer experience, they think it would require two per cent to give a remunerating profit to the banks'.[58] The sense of uncertainty over the Glasgow position as to which view was more suitable was underlined by his view that competition among banks harmed banking because it reduced profits. To the question as to how much notice they took of Bank of England rates, he preferred to answer that the Glasgow banks looked first to the old chartered banks. As would be expected, he confirmed that the Union was often readier to raise rates before Edinburgh or the Bank of England wished to do so.

On one important question, he disagreed with the Edinburgh chartered banks' insistence on the importance of government securities as the ultimate safeguard for any bank.

> We hold reserves of available securities of different kinds, and we look to the general amount of the whole . . . gold, Bank of England notes or Exchequer bills; then drawing accounts in London and Manchester and Liverpool . . . money in bill brokers' hands, secured by bills or otherwise; and our own bills of exchange coming due, of course, we would, in a great emergency, look to as a reserve; but as a reserve in ordinary times, we should hold bills of exchange not belonging to our own business; and we do.[59]

The committee pursued this matter, and Anderson was always firm in his statements that while his bank operated with adequate reserves he did not accept that such reserves should rely mainly or wholly on government securities. 'You think that bills of exchange may safely be relied upon at all times?' Anderson replied: 'We have Mr Gurney's authority for saying so'. It was not the only occasion during the hearings of this Select Committee when Mr Gurney's name (of Overend, Gurney & Co.) was invoked as adequate testimony for this area of policy. Anderson showed a sound grasp of the recent shifts in the price and yield of British government securities. He noticed that 5 per cent was a normal yield during the Napoleonic Wars, and, as prices were then below par, there was every reason to expect a gain on capital in the future. But the subsequent fall in interest rates and the rise in price of these securities made them now a less certain

58 Ibid., evidence discussed here from Qs 2,447, 2,438, 2,331, 2,332.
59 Ibid., evidence discussed here from Qs 2,411, 2,421, 2,455.

investment: 3⅓ per cent with a chance of a loss on capital, which would not be the case with Exchequer bills. Anderson was adamant on the necessity of unlimited liability in order to ensure the trust of the public in the bank's operations. It may finally be remarked that, in his testimony and in those of others, the failure of the Ayr Bank in 1772 was referred to on more than one occasion as an example, still remembered, by Scottish bankers.

The Union Bank of Scotland, which emerged after the five amalgamations, began the next stage of its career with twenty-nine branches and total liabilities of £6.3 million. At the fusion with Sir William Forbes, it was agreed that a committee would remain in Edinburgh, responsible for the business formerly conducted by the Edinburgh concern. The Edinburgh business was of a different order, less speculative and more personal in tone than that of Glasgow and the western region, and so the outlook of the Edinburgh committee deriving largely from the Forbes tradition was also different. This the Glasgow board recognised, although the Glasgow manager was assumed to be the senior. Over the years, the policy differences, while sometimes difficult, did not lead to internal strains that became intolerable. Edinburgh was prepared to take an independent line, and the committee was critical of what it at times considered a lack of caution in the matter of advances, insisting upon an adequate policy of reserve funds that was to prove important during the financial crises that lay ahead. The volume of business that went through the Edinburgh office was now a much larger proportion of the total, averaging in the decade after 1843 around 25 per cent of the total business. Edinburgh also became the holder of the principal stock of gold and silver that was required by the Act of 1845 to cover the circulation of notes in excess of their fiduciary issue.

There were interesting developments in banking procedures and practices in the decade or so after the Union Bank was formally established. Advances on cash account became more important than they had been at the onset of the Glasgow Union Banking Company; in 1842, 35 per cent of all advances were in this form and in 1843 40 per cent. Deposits in 1844, the year after the fusion with Sir William Forbes, were £5,112,158, and by the middle of the 1850s were over £7 million.[60] Total liabilities of £6,294,782 in 1844 expanded to over £8 million and often nearer £9 million for all but two years in the 1850s. This was a somewhat better result than at Bank of Scotland and owed much to the benefits of a strong presence in the west of Scotland. Nevertheless, in common with the other Scottish banks, the crisis of 1847 required judicious management and

60 See Statistical Appendix, Table A22.

led, for a time, to a stronger influence from the Edinburgh committee. By the winter of 1845–6, the directors were fully aware of the adverse consequences for banks of the speculative activity associated with the cotton and iron industries and notably with the formation of the railway companies. Based on their appreciation of trade fluctuations and their certainty about the failure of the two Bank Acts passed by Sir Robert Peel, they predicted the impending disaster, took some corrective action by early 1846 and duly informed the wider public at the annual meeting in May.[61] The year past

> had been distinguished by one of those periods of wild speculation which seem destined to be of inevitable recurrence in this country and for the prevention and control of which the vaunted legislative devices for the regulation of the currency have proved to be utterly impotent and fallacious.

Such crises were always attended with 'difficulty and anxiety in matters connected with the distribution of capital', and the present situation was felt 'in the diversion of capital from commerce and manufactures to shares and scrip certificates and in making the ordinary instruments of mercantile credit clandestinely subservient to the purposes of gambling speculation'. The directors admitted that they had been misled by deceit and the bank had suffered losses as a result. They acknowledged the utility of the Scottish Bank Act of 1845 in one respect only, namely the prohibition on new banks of issue to which the excitement of the boom would probably have led.

The board kept business in 1846 at a similar level to the previous year. In spite of their accurate assessment of the state of the economy, the directors made a mistake in increasing the dividend – for the second time – to 8 per cent in May 1847. Losses in the crisis were worse than expected and extended over several years as firms which initially survived succumbed later. Whereas the average net profit of the four years 1843–7 was £84,580 per year, in the year 1847–8 it fell to only £48,000; and, to meet the 8 per cent dividend, reserves were cut by £31,780.[62] There were severe losses on trade bills on London and abroad; many of these were the result of poor controls over branch discounting where agents had disregarded information about the condition of a firm. During the developing crisis, the directors examined the accounts of borrowers who might be expected to be at risk, and in May 1847 they had a list of fourteen firms whose total advances came to £163,810, of which J. & A.

---

61 BS(U), Uncatalogued, UBS Minutes, 14 May 1846. In writing the centenary history of the Union Bank, published in 1930, Principal R. S. Rait compared conditions in 1846 to the speculation of 1928.
62 See Statistical Appendix, Tables A22 and A23.

Denny, a firm in the grain trade, owed £75,640.[63] Furthermore, the cash account of Dunlop, Rowand & Co. was extended by £30,000 before they stopped payment on 2 August 1848.[64] J. & A. Dennistoun & Co. asked for special help amounting to £86,000, and there was a third, complicated, case involving Lord Belhaven, whose story is told below. The 1847 crisis affected Liverpool more than any other town, and brought about the first suspension of the 1844 Act.[65] By 1848, eight more firms whose bills the Union had discounted for commodity transactions had failed for £80,000, although these losses were shared by several banks.[66] In 1848–9, the bank failed again to earn enough to pay the 8 per cent dividend, and cut reserves by £7,473.[67] The eventual losses to the Union Bank written off from the crisis of 1846–7, on which no recovery could be made, reduced the profit by between £80,000 and £100,000 over the four years to 1850. The responsibility for most of these losses lay with the Glasgow directors who, although they anticipated the crisis, failed to appreciate the scale of railway and grain speculation. By contrast, the directors in Edinburgh warned of the size of individual credits and continued these warnings until vindicated by events. The Union Bank was also badly mauled by commodity speculation in 1851, and the collapse of Alexander Russell, ironfounders of Kirkcaldy, cost another £23,000. Losses of over £40,000 in this year resulted in another call on reserves of £14,595 in order to pay the 8 per cent dividend.[68] These crises confirmed the wisdom of Sir William Forbes & Co. on the importance of a large London reserve, which, though it earned less than on bills in good times, was a clear earner in bad times.

After 1836, there was a noticeable increase in lending to industry and trade, and it was with some pride that the directors announced their help to west of Scotland manufacturers at their annual meetings. The figures show a huge increase in advances by bill and cash accounts with, as noticed above, a marked shift towards the latter. To achieve this, the Union began to provide firms and landowners in textiles, iron, coal, shipbuilding and general utilities with much larger cash accounts, over £10,000 and even £20,000, and advances for capital investment.[69] In 1837, £20,000

63 Tamaki, *Life Cycle*, pp. 68–9, Table 20.
64 BS(U), Uncatalogued, Glasgow Committee minutes, guarantees by Michael Rowand, 2 August 1848.
65 W. T. C. King, *History of the London Discount Market* (London: 1936), ch. 5; J. H. Clapham, *The Bank of England. A History*, vol. ii, 1797–1914 (Cambridge: 1944), ch. 4.
66 Tamaki, *Life Cycle*, pp. 68–9, Table 20; the losses by J. & A. Denny and Dunlop, Rowand & Co. were properly secured. Boase, *Century of Banking*, pp. 448–9, estimated that the failures in London by grain traders in 1847 and 1848 amounted to £1,789,698 out of a total foreign trade loss of £25 million.
67 See Statistical Appendix, Table A23.
68 Ibid.
69 For a discussion of these advances, see Tamaki, *Life Cycle*, pp. 23–5.

was granted to a group of textile companies and, in August 1838, Napier & Co., the marine engine manufacturers, received £3,000 for new plant, doubled a decade later. From this time, considerable loans were made to railway companies, and by the time of the 1847 crisis several exceeded £50,000. This new policy brought the Union into line with the size of individual loans from the Edinburgh chartered banks, although the overall quality of the Glasgow book was poorer and in the case of Paisley and several other textile centres was an almost unmitigated disaster. By the 1850s, the Union was prepared to advance on discounts and cash accounts sums in the range of £50,000 to £100,000. The advantages of such large accounts for the circulation of notes encouraged the directors to canvass for business with offers of special terms and extra credits. Moreover, in the advantageous situation of the Scottish iron trade, the Union was even prepared to advance funds for takeovers and the speculative investment in iron goods for export.[70]

The growth of a lending policy towards heavy industry began to involve the Union Bank with the classic dilemmas of the industrial bankers. At times of stress, the duration of which could never be estimated, firms often required large sums beyond their notional credit limits. It was appreciated that investments in land, or the extraction of minerals, or iron production, might collapse, and the difficulties of the banks in recouping their funds without loss could become very difficult, if not impossible, except where a long-term approach was adopted. Loans for minerals and coal mines always presented problems because of the length of time before sufficient income was generated in order to repay capital. The case of Lord Belhaven illustrates some of these problems, and provided an example of the ways in which the board approached cases of this kind with sympathetic understanding.

Belhaven was descended from John, Lord Belhaven, the fierce opponent of the 1707 Union of Parliaments who was imprisoned in Edinburgh Castle for Jacobite activity. His family seat was at Wishaw on the River Calder and had long been at the centre of the family interest in agricultural improvement and industry. In the eighteenth century, the family was active in coalmining, turnpike roads and (later) railways in the parishes of Old and New Monkland and Cambusnethan (Lanarkshire) and built a model industrial village to serve the Omoa ironworks at Shotts. Of Cambusnethan, it was said that 'nearly the whole of the parish is full of coal', most of which was within 130 feet of the surface. Several seams were of the blackband ironstone, and after the invention of the hot blast furnace the landowners could hardly fail to make fortunes once an

---

70 Ibid., p. 48, for the case of Dunlop & Co.

adequate transport network was in place. Within a decade, the parish was transformed from the rural idyll described in *The New Statistical Account* into a treeless industrial sprawl of waste-bings and foul burns, criss-crossed by temporary railways and roads and flooded by cheap labour.[71] Lord Belhaven rapidly expanded his coal mines and opened an extensive spirit and whisky distillery at Wishawtown drawing water from the Calder and using his own coal. In 1845, together with several coalowners and ironmasters from his district, Belhaven embarked on a new enterprise, the West of Scotland Malleable Iron Company, which he envisaged as a supplier of iron for the new Scottish railways. He borrowed heavily from the Union Bank and the Western Bank, and by September 1848 owed £63,467 to the Western on his cash account and £39,828 on bills.[72] Unfortunately, during the crisis of 1846–7, Belhaven's other businesses fell into disarray and, faced with the need to pay his workforce and finance supplies, he extended his credit by £10,000 without warning. The Union honoured this, and by 1847 his unauthorised credit had risen to £80,200.[73] On 13 September 1848, the West of Scotland Malleable Iron Company reached agreement for the payment of debts by an advance of another £60,000 from the Union, although, as it turned out, this refinancing only delayed a sale.[74] In 1850, the ironworks were put on the market. The overall debts to the Western Bank and other creditors required a further call of £100 per share from the shareholders. In the summer of 1847, Belhaven asked that his other debts to the Union be converted to a long-term loan; this was refused, and the bank began the tedious process of an agreed liquidation of assets. The story has a satisfactory ending as the estates were worth sufficient in later years to repay the debts, and by 1883 his successor, a cousin, enjoyed £5,033 from rents and £19,621 in income and royalties from minerals.

The Monkland Iron Company was a straightforward case of a company with initially sound management which gradually degenerated through poor handling of outputs and inopportune investment. Again, the Union Bank was faced with the dilemma of a large borrower which might survive and repay advances if a formula could be arranged which would include a reduction in the exposure of the bank. The main part of the company was based at two sites, around five miles north of Belhaven's Wishaw House.

71 Sir John Sinclair (ed.), *The First Statistical Account of Scotland*, vol. xii, 'Cambushnethan' (Edinburgh: 1794); *The New Statistical Account of Scotland*, vol. vii, 'Cambusnethan' (Edinburgh: 1845), p. 610.
72 The depressing story of the company is told by R. H. Campbell, 'Early Malleable Iron Production in Scotland', *Business History*, 4 (1961), 22–33.
73 Tamaki, *Life Cycle*, p. 23.
74 For the offer by West of Scotland to the Union, see BS(U), Uncatalogued, Glasgow Committee minutes, 27 September 1848.

The first works to be erected was at Calderbank near to a foundry and forge established in 1794 and taken over in 1805 by the Monkland Steel Company.[75] The firm made steel in crucibles, nail rods, a variety of forged products and iron plates for ships. From 1826 to 1831 it erected three blast furnaces near Chapelhall to smelt blackband ironstone, and from 1836 to 1840 six more at Calderbank. The company abandoned its small-scale steel production and focused on iron; with the furnaces completed at Calderbank, it made around 11,000 tons of the Scottish output of around 40,000 tons per year. To help develop its works and cover sales, William Murray, a leading director of the now renamed Monkland Iron Company, negotiated a cash account and bill facility for £55,000 with the Glasgow and Ship Bank, building on a connection which went back nearly two decades. Something of a paternalistic employer in the tradition of Robert Owen at New Lanark, by 1850 the company had opened seven schools for the sons and one for the daughters of their employees, paid for by deductions from wages. In 1845, the company embarked on a large, integrated ironworks at Calderbank, with four blast furnaces to supply no fewer than forty-two puddling furnaces, the noise from which 'beggared description'. By concentrating on ships' plates, it was able to weather the vicissitudes of the 1840s. Nevertheless, by 1851 the first signs of difficulty were reported to the Union board. The company survived the next few years with rising demand for malleable iron, but the depressed state of demand from 1857 affected earnings. When William Murray died the following year, the Union called in McClelland, Mackinnon & Blyth, the Glasgow firm of chartered accountants, but the position was thought to be the temporary result of trade depression and it was not until July 1861 that the bank called a halt to further credits. The subsequent report valued the works at £95,098 'as a going concern' but only at £22,307 if broken up and sold. McClelland, Mackinnon & Blyth were appointed trustees to manage the estate; they concentrated output at Chapelhall and Calderbank, and by the boom of the later 1860s some 2,000 were employed. The firm was floated for £400,000 as the Monkland Iron and Coal Company in 1871; the Union and other creditors received full payment of the principal debt and 4 per cent for each year outstanding. This was a shrewd move by the chartered accountants. By 1874, with the onset of the depression, the firm was again trading at a loss. The circumstances of Lord Belhaven, the West of Scotland Malleable Iron Company and the Monkland Iron and Steel Company were similar to other industrial accounts which the Union Bank

75 G. Thomson, 'Calderbank', in idem (ed.), The County of Lanark, The Third Statistical Account of Scotland (Glasgow: 1960), pp. 222–36 (222–4); idem, 'The Iron Industry of the Monklands: The Individual Ironworks', Scottish Industrial History, 6 (1983), 10–29; I. F. Gibson, 'The Economic History of the Scottish Iron and Steel Industry, 1830–1880', Ph.D. thesis (University of London, 1955).

– and other Scottish banks – had to manage during the second half of the nineteenth century. When there were visible assets – coal mines, iron-ore sites, railways and stocks of goods – against which debts could be set, the chances of reconstruction were usually good.[76]

The non-chartered banks suffered from a legal handicap. Parliament had directed that investment of trust funds should be solely through accounts with the chartered banks. Both the Union and the Western had tried to obtain charters and failed, and the Bank Acts of 1844 and 1845 also left them without the opportunities to manage estates in trust. It was seen as more of a nuisance in the early years of the new Glasgow joint-stock era; James Anderson, reflecting on the importance of a charter for the Glasgow Union Banking Company in 1841, before the Select Committee on the Banks of Issue, noted: 'I should think a charter not of much importance to us, there are certain privileges which chartered banks have of holding monies under litigation, in trust, and that kind of thing, but those are the only advantages'.[77] It subsequently became more significant and was resolved in 1856 (19 & 20 Victoria c.79) whereby Scottish joint-stock banks of issue were allowed the right to accept deposits by trustees and accountants in bankruptcy, providing that the trustees had secured the 'highest rate of interest'.[78] There was another legal problem that required Parliamentary rectification, this time in respect of the bank's right over the shares of a partner in the event of a bankruptcy, should a charter be granted. This was legislated for with the passing of 17 & 18 Victoria c.73, 1854. The wording was clear: any Scottish joint-stock bank which later received a charter would retain unimpaired 'the right of retention or lien which in virtue of the common law of Scotland such company has or may be entitled to exercise over the shares of its partners, or in respect of any debt or liability incurred or obligation undertaken by them to the Company'.[79] The next crucial Act was the Companies Act of 1862 which provided for incorporation. This procedure allowed nearly all the benefits of a charter, so that, after 1862, the Union Bank was granted perpetual succession, as under a charter, and was permitted to hold heritable rights and securities in its corporate name. The board agreed that the shareholders would remain subject to unlimited liability.[80]

76 C. W. Munn, *Clydesdale Bank: The First One Hundred and Fifty Years* (Glasgow: 1988), pp. 55–9; S. G. Checkland, *Scottish Banking: A History, 1695–1973* (Glasgow: 1975), pp. 418–20.
77 *Second Report from Select Committee on Banks of Issue*, 15 June 1841, (410) vol. v, Q. 2,505.
78 19 & 20 Victoria c.79, 'An Act to consolidate and amend the laws relating to Bankruptcy in Scotland', 29 July 1856.
79 17 & 18 Victoria c.73, 'An Act to amend the Acts for the Regulation of Joint Stock Banks in Scotland', 31 July 1854. A Court of Session case in 1840 had established this right in case law: *Encyclopaedia of the Laws of Scotland*, vol. ii (Edinburgh: 1927), p. 83.
80 25 & 26 Victoria c.89, §182, 'An Act for the Incorporation, Regulation and Winding-up of Trading Companies and other Associations', 7 August 1862. See Rait, *Union Bank*, pp. 280–1; for

There occurred two further amalgamations. In May 1849, the board of the Union Bank appointed a committee of three to begin arrangements for taking over the Aberdeen Banking Company which was on the point of collapse. The extent of the financial weaknesses of the Aberdeen bank was not revealed at the time. There were so many uncertain assets that the negotiations took over four months. The Aberdeen partners received £2 4s for each of the 35,000 shares, a payment well down on the market value during the boom of 1845–6. The difficult debts were transferred to a separate account in the Union books, and, by holding back from immediate action, the account was eventually brought to a satisfactory condition. R. S. Rait was particularly impressed by the longer-term perspective taken by the directors which avoided any damage to the credit of the Aberdeen partners and local business which might have resulted from closure.[81] It was a very reasonable settlement for the Aberdeen shareholders, and for the Union Bank it meant entry into a region in which hitherto it had had little place. Including the head office, seventeen branches were added, making a total in 1849 of forty-eight.[82]

The Union Bank took over the Dunblane Savings Bank in February 1857 and made several offers to other banks, but the only other successful takeover, and the more important, was the Perth Banking Company in 1857. The Union made an approach in 1849, but its offer was rejected and the Perth bank continued confidently through the next decade.[83] The expansion of the joint-stock banks was, however, steadily increasing competitive pressures, and it appears that the Perth directors may have anticipated the disaster of 1857. Thus the Perth bank, with the market price of its £10 paid share standing at £200, sold out to the Union Bank for £100,050, and the last but one of the Scottish provincial banks thereby disappeared. This added twelve branches to the Union Bank, which in 1857 now headed the Scottish banks with ninety-six branches, followed by the City of Glasgow with ninety-two and the Commercial Bank with sixty-four. The note circulation after the absorption of the Perth bank reached £454,346, also the highest total of all the Scottish banks. The directors decided to make some changes in the Contract of Co-partnery, in anticipation of the passage of the 1862 Companies Act, and this was done at a general meeting in May 1862. The bank's capital was reduced from £2 million to the £1 million paid up at this date; the bank stock was

general background, see H. A. Shannon, 'The Coming of General Limited Liability', *Economic History*, 2 (1931), 267–91; J. Saville, 'Sleeping Partnership and Limited Liability, 1850–1856', *Economic History Review*, 2nd series, 8 (1954), 418–33.

81 Rait, *Union Bank*, pp. 263–4.
82 Tamaki, *Life Cycle*, p. 58, Table 16, lists the number of branches for the 1840s and 1850s.
83 There is a discussion of the Perth Banking Company in Rait, *Union Bank*, p. 142ff.; also Tamaki, *Life Cycle*, p. 65.

replaced by transferable stock, and voting rights were altered. Each partner having £100 of stock was entitled to one vote, with £500 giving two votes and £1,000 three votes. For each additional £1,000 of stock over the first £1,000, the allocation was one vote.

The 1850s, while witnessing considerable growth in industrial production and mercantile trade, nevertheless had an air of speculation and financial uncertainty, much encouraged by the discovery of gold in California and Australia. The sustained speculative activities of the middle years of the decade were marked by high interest rates and not infrequent moments of crisis. News of the Indian Mutiny reached London in June 1857, there was a drain of bullion to the east, and European discount rates began to rise. What precipitated a general crisis was the news from America of the failure in late August of the Ohio Life and Trust Company for $7 million; and in the next few weeks the news became catastrophic. In New York, sixty-two out of sixty-three banks stopped payment, and discount rates moved up to between 18 and 24 per cent. There was panic in Liverpool and Glasgow, both cities being intimately involved in the American trade. The Western story, and its ultimate collapse, is told elsewhere, but the Union Bank had such serious problems that, without the massive support it received from the Edinburgh banks, it too would probably have failed.[84]

The Union Bank first felt the crisis in September 1857 when several of its borrowers were involved in difficulties with discounts in London, and this was followed quickly by a series of failures which left a trail of potential bad debts. The Liverpool Borough Bank closed its doors on 27 October, and this involved Dennistoun & Co., who themselves were closely tied in with the Union Bank. The Whig family of Dennistoun had long connections with the Union Bank and its Glasgow predecessor. John Dennistoun of Golfhill was one of the MPs for Glasgow, 1837–47, and his brother Alexander was MP for Dumbarton. The brothers owned 1,400 shares in the Glasgow and Ship Bank in 1836. Their firm was registered under several designations with offices in Glasgow, London and Liverpool, and they traded extensively between Britain, America and Australia. Alexander Dennistoun was a director of the Union Bank, and his personal borrowings and those of his companies were always large. By 1853, his total credits were over £400,000, and he continued to extend his drawings during the increasingly speculative conditions of 1857.[85] On 7 November the firm closed its doors, although only temporarily, in order

84 BS 1/517/6, Transactions with other Scottish Banks (1857 Crisis); see above, Chapter 16, for discussion of this.
85 For a detailed discussion of the effects of the crisis on the Union Bank, see Tamaki, *Life Cycle*, pp. 70–3; and there is an important discussion in Boase, *Century of Banking in Dundee*, p. 480 ff.

to secure payment of debts owed as a result of the financial collapse in America. The liabilities amounted to £2,142,701 but realisable assets were proved at £2,935,992, and the surplus of £793,291 enabled a satisfactory settlement to be made. The family still owned 5,500 Union Bank shares in 1880.

Two days after the firm of Dennistoun temporarily stopped payment, the Western Bank closed its doors and went out of Scottish banking. This encouraged public pressure on the Union Bank, which on the day of the Western failure experienced a run on its resources from depositors and borrowers, and this continued in the days that followed, particularly in Glasgow and the surrounding region. The Glasgow directors asked their Edinburgh board to raise £2 million on local bills, which the Edinburgh directors refused on the grounds that such a large operation would put the bank at even greater risk. A delegation of Sir Adam Hay, John Fergus – both Edinburgh directors – and G. Somervell, a Glasgow director, went to London to explain their problems to the Bank of England.[86] Glyn, Mills, Currie & Co., with whom the Union Bank did so much of its London business, proved important in the role of intermediary with Threadneedle Street. The latter agreed to discount bills to the total of £2 million, and in addition Glyn, Mills, Currie & Co. provided £200,000 from their own resources. As noticed before, in Scotland the Union Bank was strongly supported from Edinburgh by Bank of Scotland, the British Linen Company and the Commercial Bank and in Glasgow by the Clydesdale Bank and indirectly by the Royal Bank. The position in the short term was thus secured, but the pressures against the Union continued into 1858. Between November 1857 and February 1858, more than 1,400 of its shares were offered for sale and the market price dropped by about one-third – the largest fall of all the remaining Scottish banks. The net profits fell by one-third in the year to April 1858. What saved the Union Bank was a combination of factors. Another bank failure would have been a very serious matter for Scottish banking and for Glasgow banking in particular, and no-one would have benefited. This certainly explains the willingness of the Scottish banks to help. The requests of the Union Bank's Edinburgh board, coming as they did from the much-respected Edinburgh committee, were an important factor in obtaining support; the standing of Sir Adam Hay in the Edinburgh banking community was certainly influential both in Edinburgh and in the negotiations with the Bank of England. Furthermore, the previous year the Union had increased the balance of the reserve fund by £40,000 to £200,000, a prudent move

---

86 Part of the correspondence, which gives a clear sense of the crisis, is reprinted in Tamaki, *Life Cycle*, pp. 71–2.

which can only have strengthened its standing.[87] In sum, while the Union Bank certainly experienced serious problems during the latter part of 1857, there were no fundamental reasons why outside assistance should not have been offered since the bank was viable, as indeed it was to prove itself in the coming decade.

The collapse of the Western Bank and the other business failures in the city had a notable effect upon banking in Glasgow, and Edinburgh's domination in the world of Scottish banking was again to reassert itself. The Union Bank was shaken by the events of 1857, and it carried over a volume of bad debts that required both caution and a new look at its managerial controls. The annual dividend remained at 9 per cent until 1862, but the bank was subject to fierce English press criticism and the share price remained 20 per cent below the 1857 level in the following year. Some of this criticism was valid. In 1859, Blaikie & Co. of Aberdeen, an account inherited from the Aberdeen Banking Company, was reported to be in difficulty, and when it failed in 1860 the potential loss to the bank was £60,000; though recoveries halved this, it was a severe blow. The temporary closure of the Monkland Iron Company in July 1861 and the problems with the Dennistoun group confirmed the view among directors, and especially by the committee in Edinburgh, that the management in Glasgow was unable to cope with the problems posed by potential large bad debts. The health of the general manager, James Robertson, gave way under this stress.[88] The board now brought in Charles Gairdner, aged 37, who had helped to unravel the affairs of the Western Bank, first as assistant liquidator and latterly as the principal.[89] His father Charles had been a director of Hunters & Co. at the time of that company's merger with the Union, and he arranged for the younger Charles to be apprenticed to McClelland, Mackinnon & Blyth, the Union Bank accountants. On expiry of his term in 1843, he went as a clerk to Peter White, accountant and stockbroker, which firm became White and Gairdner in the following year. Gairdner was one of the founding members of the Institute of Accountants and Actuaries in Glasgow in 1853. It was while he was sifting through the affairs of the Western Bank that the Union board approached him over the state of its own books. Thoroughly conversant with banking accounts and having noticed an overlap between the two banks, he was able to present the directors with an interim potential loss of £140,000. There was also a worrying decline in deposits of £518,083 (6.5 per cent)

87 See Statistical Appendix, Table A23.
88 Rait, *Union Bank*, pp. 293–4.
89 Ibid., pp. 181–4 for the career of his father; see C. W. Munn and N. Tamaki, 'Charles Gairdner', in A. Slaven and S. G. Checkland (eds), *Dictionary of Scottish Business Biography, 1860–1960*, vol. ii, *Processing, Distribution, Services* (Aberdeen: 1990), pp. 403–6.

in the two years to 1862, and while profits recovered in 1861 they fell sharply in each of the two subsequent years.[90]

In April 1862, Gairdner was appointed as joint general manager with a remit to continue his investigation. On his recommendation, £140,000 was moved from the reserve to a special guarantee account against losses, of which the Monkland debt formed the greater part.[91] By April 1863, Gairdner had cut overdrafts and bills to £6.1 million (down from nearly £7 million in 1860 and 1861), instituted tight controls over lending and written off more bad debts, though this reduced profits in his first year to £95,292, barely cover for the dividend which was reduced to 8 per cent. From the summer of 1862, for a year, he traversed the branch network, finding a number of serious irregularities with the branch inspection system. In November 1863, the inspector's function was reorganised and subsequent administrative controls maintained a strict supervision from the centre. This development was much to be commended in its early years, but became notably bureaucratic in the last thirty years of the century, thereby reinforcing the conservatism of banking practice that became the mark of Gairdner's long tenure of office. Gairdner intended that his new system would highlight all bad and doubtful debts and put a stop to speculative accounts. It was a hard year, living for a few days in a burgh, grappling with the accounts, writing interim reports and then proceeding to the next branch. He was, of course, greatly assisted by the spread of the railway network and the superior quality of the new hotels which sprang up in railway towns and which were already transforming the Scottish tourist trade. The dividend remained at 8 per cent for three years and the branch network did not expand between 1858 and 1865.

During the 1860s, and in broad terms thereafter, there developed within the national organisation of the Union Bank of Scotland some important differences between the regional groupings of the bank in the relationship between advances and deposits. This, in the main, was a straightforward reflection of the different types of economy in various parts of Scotland. There were four main divisions of the Union Bank: Glasgow and the western region (with fifty-seven branches), Edinburgh (with four branches including Kirkcaldy), Perth (with eleven) and Aberdeen (with twenty-two).[92] As we would expect from the experience of the Edinburgh banks, there were marked differences between branches, some remaining as largely deposit-taking branches, including most of those in agricultural areas, while others, somewhat fewer in number, had a stronger loan book.

---

90 See Statistical Appendix, Tables A22 and A23.
91 See Statistical Appendix, Table A23, note 24.
92 Tamaki, *Life Cycle*, pp. 88–91 analyses in some detail the money flows within the bank during the first half of the 1860s.

All three areas outside Glasgow and the western region showed more or less static deposits and a declining, or stable, level of advances. In the Glasgow industrial region, by contrast, advances increased greatly, and, on average in these years the Glasgow head office and its associated branches made about three-quarters of the total advances of the whole bank.

Under Charles Gairdner, the Union looked seriously at its London investments. In 1859–60, it sold £300,000 of consols to provide for bad debts and extend some past-due bills, which brought the total holding down to £776,207. Thereafter, more were purchased, and by 1863 the Union held £1,570,289. Charles Gairdner always made it clear that he wished to increase these holdings, and in 1868 he brought the total to over £2.1 million. The bank's search for outlets in gilts led to a change in 1874 whereby the bank extended its existing powers of investment to include public funds of all kinds, such as Indian government stock, British Colonial issues and those of the USA; it took further powers at this time to invest in and dispose of real estate in any part of the United Kingdom. At this period, the yield in US bonds was above the level of British government securities, and the bank's investment increased accordingly. In June 1874, US bonds to the value of £205,434 were added to the bank's portfolio, and this figure had increased to £884,042 by April 1877. The increased volume of investment in foreign bonds was directed through London, and the need for a London office became increasingly urgent. There had already been the failed attempt of the four Scottish banks, including the Union Bank, to establish a Scottish bank in London in 1864, and the Scottish–English conflict of the 1870s provided a further delay.[93] But Charles Gairdner was cautious, and it was not until March 1878 that the London office was opened, with a staff of twelve and a manager from the Bank of England.[94] Until this branch opened, the Union Bank had operated through twenty-five London correspondents: twelve of the joint-stock banks and thirteen private banks. Charles Gairdner proved successful in the first fifteen years of his management in strengthening the overall finances of the Union Bank and expanding the business. The reserve fund at £380,000 by 1875 was up, the credit at profit and loss was strong enough to meet periodic losses, and net profits grew well, to an average of £161,000 per annum in the three years to 1875.

But there were some lapses, of which the most notable came with the failure of Alexander Collie & Co., a firm with strong connections to the East India and China trades and with large loans outstanding from the Union Bank. And here we have an interesting insight into Gairdner as banker. Soon after he became joint manager – in name, but sole manager

93 See above, Chapter 15; Checkland, *Scottish Banking*, pp. 481–6.
94 Tamaki, *Life Cycle*, p. 110, Table 41.

in fact – Gairdner strengthened the system of 'opinion books' in which were recorded the details of the creditworthiness of the bank's borrowers. He also, like many other bankers, kept a confidential notebook for his own information. In the case of Alexander Collie, however, Gairdner took him on trust. A director of the bank had introduced him in 1872, and Gairdner appears to have made no independent enquiries. Large sums began to be lent, and within three years difficulties began. Collie's specialism was in the fraudulent use which he made of bills of exchange. His firm affiliated to a large group of houses upon which it drew bills which were then presented as trade bills to discount brokers, who in turn deposited them as security for advances, mainly with joint-stock banks.[95] News of the collapse of Alexander Collie & Co. reached the Union Bank on 16 June 1875. The firm's liabilities were estimated at £3 million. Dozens of merchant houses, discount brokers and certain joint-stock banks were directly involved. The board of the Union had no evidence upon which Collie & Co. might be taken to court: 'it is not expedient that the Bank should proceed criminally'. The London and Westminster, which held about £1 million of Collie's drafts, did take legal action, but to no avail. Alexander Collie disappeared and died in New York twenty years later. The losses to the Union Bank were £150,000, and to meet them the bank reduced the reserve fund to £300,000 and cut the credit at the profit and loss account, which, with cuts in the declared profits, allowed the absorption of the loss over two years.[96]

The most serious banking crisis in Scotland during the second half of the nineteenth century was the City of Glasgow default at the end of September 1878. The boom of the early 1870s had raised Scottish bank shares to a peak in 1875: at one time, the Union £100 shares reached £278. The collapse of the City of Glasgow brought all bank shares down, with the Union Bank being the worst-affected, its shares dropping to only £170 by mid-December 1878. As one of only two surviving banks in Glasgow, the Union Bank was the centre of much rumour-mongering (as it had been in 1857). Both the Edinburgh office and the Glasgow head office did all in their power to reassure the public and the business community. Edinburgh sent out a private letter to the bank's agents, and on 16 December the Glasgow board put out a public statement to the proprietors – a Special Report, as it was termed,[97]

> on the extent to which their interests have been affected by the suspension of the City of Glasgow Bank and subsequent failures, and this more particularly as

95 Ibid., p. 95.
96 See Statistical Appendix, Table A23.
97 This is quoted in Tamaki, *Life Cycle*, pp. 120–1, and in large part also in Rait, *Union Bank*, pp. 312–13.

four months must elapse before the Annual Meeting is held. The amount due to the Bank by the City of Glasgow Bank, exclusive of the Notes retired in the public interest, is only £4,000. These claims, it is believed will be paid in full; and the Directors have the satisfaction of informing the Proprietors that, on a careful estimate of all other bad and doubtful debts, the provision required from the profits of the current year is under £3,700.

The Directors believe it will also be satisfactory to the Proprietors to receive at this time an explicit assurance that the Accounts of the Bank are closely and constantly scrutinised by them; that the Advances are safe and well distributed; that losses are invariably provided for as they arise; that the Securities and Investments are of greater value than they stand at in the Books; and that the Bank's Capital of £1,000,000 and Rest of £330,000 are intact.

The Proprietors will have observed that an unusual fall has recently taken place in the market price of the Bank's stock. In connection with this, it is right to mention that a considerable amount of the Stock offered for sale belongs to Proprietors who, unhappily for themselves, are involved as Shareholders in the City of Glasgow Bank. The Bank sustains no loss from this circumstance; and as sales are effected, this depressing influence will, no doubt, pass away.

The Directors have delayed issuing this Report until the effects of the commercial and financial disorder of October have been so far developed as to admit of the Board reporting with confidence on their bearing on the Bank.

What was the result of the crisis for the Union Bank? In February 1878, eight months before the crash, the capital stood at £1 million and reserves at £315,000, and there was £155,975 at the credit of the profit and loss account. The bank also held £2,649,337 of consols and other British government securities.[98] This total of £4,120,312 was a sound position which covered almost half of depositors' funds. At the May annual meeting the following year, Charles Gairdner presented the board with a similar strong position, but advised a 1 per cent reduction in the dividend to 12 per cent and warned that the provision for loss in the Glasgow area would reduce profits for several years. Over £1.2 million of British government securities were later sold, though much of this was reinvested in foreign stocks. The Union Bank thus weathered the City of Glasgow crisis with little long-term damage to its internal position, and by 1881 the stock price had recovered. There were some obvious reforms which the debacle made necessary. One was an external audit, and two persons of repute, one from McClelland, Mackinnon & Blyth of Glasgow and a partner from Lindsay, Jamieson & Haldane, the Edinburgh firm, undertook this task. These were two well-known firms of chartered accountants, and their acceptance was announced in the spring of 1879 and was followed by a rise in the market price of Union Bank shares. A second change was the

98 See Statistical Appendix, Table A22.

acceptance of limited liability in July 1881, a change in the legal position of the Union Bank – and agreed at this time with the other Scottish joint-stock banks which had unlimited liability – made possible by the relevant clauses of the 1879 Companies Act.[99] The Act confirmed that limited liability did not extend to banknotes and that the appointment of auditors was to be compulsory.[100]

The Union Bank, situated as it was in Glasgow, was at the centre of the remarkable expansion of the industrial region of the Glasgow conurbation. Between 1870 and 1913, the Clyde region launched one-third of total British shipping tonnage. Clyde tonnage completed each year in the boom period of the early 1870s averaged 250,000 tons, and the shipyards led the way in the growth of the regional economy, being especially important in the encouragement of heavy engineering and the finishing trades. The most dramatic innovation of the 1870s and 1880s was the substitution of steel for iron in ship construction, and there was significant growth in the coal and metalworking industries. While the fall in industrial and commodity prices lasted for twenty years, technological change and volume increases in trade and production continued, and the demand for credit flows increased steadily. The Union Bank met this developing industrial situation with a steady increase in advances towards shipbuilding and engineering, with the traditional sectors of trade and railways also high on the list. The remarkable story of the Union Bank's close relations with the shipbuilding firm of J. and G. Thomson & Co. suggests that Charles Gairdner and his colleagues were able to recognise certain of the leading trends in the industrial economy, and the newly-built Clyde shipyards of the Thomson enterprise were a tribute to the foresight of those directing the bank. It was a not unusual example of the willingness of a Scottish bank to take a long view of industrial prospects and an acceptance for a certain period of a direct involvement in managerial decisions.[101] The Union also found, along with the other Scottish banks, an accretion of the new service and retail trades and accounts in the lighter industrial sectors.

One consequence of the years of depression was pressure from a variety of interests, political and industrial, requesting government funds for a new programme of naval shipbuilding. The first serious result was the Naval Defence Act, 1889, which brought in a five-year programme; expenditure on naval vessels rose in 1890 from £3.5 million to £5.65 million in 1892. Government support then gradually rose to £7.5 million

99 This is discussed in Checkland, *Scottish Banking*, pp. 480–1.
100 42 & 43 Victoria c.76, 'An Act to amend the law with respect to the liability of members of Banking and other Joint Stock Companies and for other purposes', 15 August 1879.
101 This most interesting case-study of bank–industry relations has been examined by Tamaki, *Life Cycle*, pp. 179–80, 188.

in 1897, £9 million in 1901 and £11.65 million in 1905. Significant contracts came to Scotland as arms manufacturers, steel companies and shipbuilders pressed for a share of these funds, and there was a decrease in the relative proportion of expenditure which went to government-owned royal dockyards and arsenals on the Thames and the south coast of England. In the five years after the 1889 Act, 53,611 tons of naval shipping were launched on the Clyde, and in the years 1895–9 another 151,635 tons.[102] The advantages of naval contracts, with their high value per ton and their complicated engineering and specialist steels, were a most useful addition to the skills base of the Clyde. It was estimated at the time that the building of one battleship involved as many man-hours as that needed for twenty cargo vessels.[103] In the naval race which preceded the First World War, Clyde yards received seventy-seven Admiralty orders of a total of 331,604 tons, and on the outbreak of war 104,018 tons were on the stocks with another 63,268 tons fitting out.[104]

While there were problems later with this emphasis on the steel, shipping and engineering industries, in the twenty-five years before 1914 the Scottish banks greatly benefited. The yards usually made substantial profits from these orders, and their owners became rich: for instance, Charles Connel died worth £264,635, Sir Peter Denny £190,979, and James Gilchrist £148,480. Several were granted baronetcies, and a few, like Sir William Burrell, built up considerable collections of art. Perhaps the most significant business development was the integrated armaments companies: John Brown of Sheffield merged with Clydebank in 1899, and William Beardmore purchased Robert Napier's yard in 1900 and proceeded to build Dalmuir, which by 1907 had cost almost £1 million, the largest naval yard in the world. Unfortunately, it later proved difficult to redirect these companies for the very different world which emerged after the First World War. The consensus among historians is that Gairdner, whose tenure lasted from 1865 to 1895, came in under the most trying circumstances, handled the affairs of the bank judiciously and correctly, and made a number of important long-term decisions to support shipbuilding and engineering, but was rather too cautious in respect of the London office and perhaps too slow in attracting new deposits. Gairdner also made a modest contribution to banking thought in the later nineteenth century.[105]

---

102 H. B. Peebles, *Warshipbuilding on the Clyde: Naval Orders and the Prosperity of the Clyde Shipbuilding Industry, 1889–1939* (Edinburgh: 1987), Appendix.
103 A. Marder, *British Naval Policy 1880–1905* (London: 1940), p. 30. The advantages of the Clyde were confirmed when Alfred Yarrow moved to Scotstoun in 1906; see S. Pollard, 'The Decline of Shipbuilding on the Thames', *Economic History Review*, 2nd series, 3 (1950–1), 72–89.
104 Peebles, *Warshipbuilding*, pp. 69, 74.
105 Checkland, *Scottish Banking*, pp. 543–50.

The profitability of the Union Bank improved after 1900 under the management of Robert Blyth. The net profits, shown as a percentage of paid-up capital, of deposits and of total public liabilities, indicated a sharp improvement in performance. Deposits had been growing from the mid-1880s, and there was quite a substantial increase in the years immediately preceding the First World War.[106] Dividends increased to 15 per cent for the years 1912–14. The flow of increased profits encouraged larger appropriations to the reserves. The London end of the Union's business had become steadily more important and the number of accounts credited to foreign customers also showed a steady increase, and the investment portfolio followed the same pattern.[107] Already by the late 1880s, Australasia, India and Egypt, in that order, were represented by substantial investments, and foreign investments in general continued to be important until 1914, rising from £1.5 million to pass £2 million by 1908. In this, the Union shared ground with Bank of Scotland, although the mix of investments was better managed and there was no such problem in the London office of the Union akin to that of the London branch of Bank of Scotland. Holdings in British government stocks increased to £1.35 million at the close of the South African war in 1902 and were reduced in 1904 and again after 1911; by the First World War, the Union Bank held £854,207 worth. In the centenary history of the Union Bank, published in 1930, R. S. Rait offered a reasonably open account of the position of the Union Bank's holding of these securities.[108] He went on to acknowledge that the Union strengthened the investments account by appropriations from profits, 'thus increasing what are sometimes called the hidden reserves of the Bank' as well as increasing the published reserve. In fact, the latter rose from £595,000 in 1899 to £1 million a decade later. In the decade after 1904, £245,000 was written to the investments account, and the credit at the profit and loss account was kept to a respectable figure, never below £150,000 after 1896. The next-largest internal reserve, which within a few years was to become the main internal account, the Guarantee Account, was actually rather small, at £81,745 at the end of the war in South Africa. It reached £223,296 in 1908, but with the decline in the value of investments it was run down to £23,502 by 1914 (see Table 21.2 in Chapter 21).

In 1910, Arthur C. D. Gairdner, a grandson of C. D. and nephew of Charles Gairdner, became general manager, promoted from the London office. He entered office at a time of growing profitability but also

106 See Statistical Appendix, Tables A22 and A23.
107 Tamaki, *Life Cycle*, p. 187.
108 Rait, *Union Bank*, pp. 327–9.

when there was increasing political turbulence which included large-scale industrial militancy. In 1911, the sum of £10,000 was provided from profits for the beginning of a Pensions and Allowance Fund, with a further £10,000 in 1912 and £25,000 in 1914. On this financial basis, a superannuation scheme was introduced in 1913, with contributions from individual members of staff and the bank. Gairdner remained general manager throughout the war years, being succeeded by George J. Scott in 1919 upon becoming chairman of the new British Overseas Bank. Scott lasted only one year with the Union Bank before accepting the Treasurer's position at Bank of Scotland. He was succeeded by Norman L. Hird, the dominant personality within the Union Bank for the whole of the inter-war period.

CHAPTER 19

THE SCOTTISH BANKS AND THE ECONOMY, 1914–39

THE FIRST WORLD War brought about a huge increase in public expenditure on the industrial products of Scotland. Companies involved in the iron and steel trades, metalworking, mechanical engineering, shipbuilding, chemicals, linen, jute and clothing did especially well, although the benefits of wartime spending were widely dispersed, regionally as well as across industrial sectors. There were few cases of bankruptcy involving industrial firms, and none of any consequence to the war effort. Employment rose fast in late 1914 and throughout 1915 to the point where serious shortages of skilled labour developed in all the heavy trades, and large numbers of women were drafted into industrial work that hitherto had been barred to them. In the decade to 1921, employment in seven heavy engineering and industrial sectors increased from 18.3 per cent of the productive workforce to 25.6 per cent, ahead of the equivalent proportion for the UK as a whole (20 per cent).[1] The average earnings of Scottish industrial workers, skilled and unskilled, tended to improve compared with their counterparts in England, and in some categories the pre-war gap between average incomes narrowed or disappeared. Wartime agricultural policies lifted the incomes of both farmers and their landlords; arable acreage, for example, increased by just over 20 per cent to 1.5 million acres by 1918.[2]

---

1 The figures are from C. H. Lee, *British Regional Employment Statistics 1841–1971* (Cambridge: 1979), tables for 1911, 1921.
2 'Board of Agriculture for Scotland. Proposed Credit to Farmers against Government Guarantee', *Scottish Bankers Magazine*, 9 (1917), 275; J. A. Symon, *Scottish Farming Past and Present* (Edinburgh: 1959), p. 219. For an important appraisal of the inter-war Scottish economy, see N. K. Buxton, 'Economic Growth in Scotland between the Wars: The Role of Production, Structure and Rationalisation', *Economic History Review*, 2nd series, 33 (1980), 538–55. For a detailed discussion of the heavy industries of the west of Scotland, see A. Slaven, *The Development of the West of Scotland 1750–1960* (London: 1975), ch. 7; for a guide to the arguments and literature, see P. L. Payne, *Growth*

The war-related industrial economy of Scotland clustered, in the main, around the burghs of the greater Glasgow area, which shared with the Ruhr and northern France the industrial characteristics required for the production of weapons of modern warfare. There was coal in abundance, a long tradition of engineering work of all kinds, an excellent rail network and a plentiful supply of general labour. The Clyde area possessed the largest and most concentrated network of naval and civil shipbuilding yards in the world. The controlling families numbered around twenty, the most famous names, the Tennants, Weirs, Beardmores, Lithgows and Colvilles, all closely connected through marriage, general business relations, politics and social affairs. Below them came several dozen more families – the tacksmen of the industrial system – dependent upon the largest firms for contracts yet crucial to the general working of the system. Scotland's economic expansion before 1914 owed much to a multiplier effect based upon the key sectors of shipbuilding and armaments. These were the consumers of a large proportion of the total output of the iron and steel industries and marine and general engineering, and employed a growing number of skilled and unskilled workers. For every man employed in shipbuilding, there were another two in the many trades that provided its materials. Warfare accentuated these connections and benefits for the workforce; as Sir James Bell, chairman of the Clydesdale Bank, noted in 1916, unemployment 'is almost unknown. Wages were never so high and in many industries quite extraordinary sums can be earned.'[3]

The high levels of output from the Clyde shipyards before 1914 concealed what historians have appreciated were growing problems within the industry. The Clyde had been dominant in world shipbuilding in 1870 and it maintained this position down to 1914, building some 18 per cent of world output in 1913. It had achieved this position and sustained it through the pre-war decades by the acceptance of continuous technical innovation. The early substitutions of steel for iron and the steady improvements in marine steam technology were most important for the Clyde Valley economy, and it was only in the years after 1900 that the first signs of technical lag began to show themselves. In 1901, the first ship with a direct-action turbine was launched on the Clyde, but it was built on licence from Charles Parsons, and it was in 1910 that the first sea-going diesel-driven ships were launched in the Netherlands and Italy.[4] The structure of the shipbuilding and engineering supply industry

& Contraction Scottish Industry c. 1860–1990 (Glasgow: 1992); for the steel industry, see P. L. Payne, Colvilles and the Scottish Steel Industry (Oxford: 1979), p. 136, Table 6.2.
3 'The Chairman of the Clydesdale Bank on the Problems of the War Crisis', Scottish Bankers Magazine, 8 (1916), 30–4 (p. 31).
4 Slaven, Development of the West of Scotland, p. 181.

Table 19.1 *Indices of business activity in Scotland and Great Britain in selected years, 1924–37*

	(1924 = 100)	
	Scotland	Great Britain
1924	100.0	100.0
1927	103.0	108.5
1929	104.0	112.0
1930	97.0	106.5
1931	85.5	98.5
1932	81.0	96.0
1933	83.5	101.0
1934	91.0	109.5
1935	94.5	113.5
1936	102.0	120.0
1937	109.5	126.0

Source: Clydesdale and North of Scotland Bank, 'Revised index number of business activity in Scotland' (unpublished, 1938).

Reprinted from N. K. Buxton, 'Economic Growth in Scotland between the Wars: The Role of Production, Structure and Rationalisation', *Economic History Review*, 2nd series, 33 (1980), 538–55.

before 1914 was still of highly competitive medium and small firms, and these were not as effective in their technology as the more competitive post-war situation was to require. There were, too, the wider economic and financial problems which the war brought about and which have been much discussed.[5] After the short post-war boom to mid-1921, the world situation changed in ways that were severely detrimental to the structures of British industry inherited from the buoyant development of the nineteenth century. The great staple industries were now confronted with new kinds of competition and were to enter upon a protracted decline interspersed with occasional more encouraging demand. Coal and shipbuilding never again achieved their pre-war output. For the UK as a whole, unemployment after 1921 never fell below one million even in the most favourable years, but during most of the inter-war years both business activity and unemployment in Scotland were less favourable than for the rest of the UK. The Scottish rate of industrial growth was slow compared with south of the Border in the 1920s and the recovery in England during the 1930s – until the very last years of the decade – was stronger than in Scotland. The indices in Table 19.1 illustrate the relative deterioration in the Scottish economic position between the wars.[6]

5 The literature is extensive: D. H. Aldcroft and H. W. Richardson, *The British Economy 1870–1939* (London: 1969), especially section B, chs 5 and 6 for an early appraisal; I. Drummond, 'Britain and the World Economy, 1900–45', in R. Floud and D. McCloskey (eds), *The Economic History of Britain since 1700*, vol. ii, *1860 to the 1970s* (Cambridge: 1981), pp. 286–307; R. H. Campbell, *The Rise and Fall of Scottish Industry 1707–1939* (Edinburgh: 1980), ch. 6.
6 Buxton, 'Economic Growth in Scotland', p. 541.

There was an additional factor within the unemployment figures which accounted for the slow recovery of Scotland from the slump of the early 1930s. There had been net emigration from Scotland for many decades, and during the 1920s the net loss of population amounted to 403,000; but the worldwide character of the economic crisis and slump in the years from 1930 reduced sharply the possibilities of work outside the boundaries of Scotland, and the net loss during this decade before the Second World War was only 73,000.[7] The wider causes for Scottish decline compared with many parts of Britain have been a matter of much debate among economists and historians, but there are certain factors which are indisputable. The relatively greater size of shipbuilding within the Scottish economy meant that its decline inevitably had a notably depressing effect upon economic growth; and there is general agreement that the overall industrial structure, with its concentration upon heavy industries, was not well able to develop the range and volume of newer industries which emerged in the south and Midlands of England. For a variety of reasons, Scotland had a poor record in its development of the 'new' industries of the first half of the twentieth century, such as electrical engineering, vehicles, man-made fibres and the many areas of chemical engineering. In terms of geographical spread, the inability to develop new industries was unfortunately extensive. In Dundee, for example, in spite of early invention and innovation in electrical engineering, employment in the sector was recorded as only 400 by 1914, while the town's economy remained dominated by jute and the textile trades after the war.[8] The range of consumer goods and services for the home market was already expanding rapidly in England. During the inter-war years, and particularly in the 1930s, there was especially fast growth in incomes among the middle classes. Scotland, however, never experienced the scale of the housing boom, and suburban growth, which was such a striking feature of the English economy after 1932. There was an increase in the number of white-collar workers and of the middle class in general, but this was not in any way comparable with the social changes in the English Midlands and the south-eastern region including the greater London area.

In 1912, there had been appointed a Royal Commission to inquire into the housing problem in Scotland, and it eventually reported in

7 Ibid., p. 542. The yearly data are in the published Annual Reports of the Registrar General for Scotland.
8 B. P. Lenman and E. E. Gauldie, 'The Industrial History of the Dundee Region from the Eighteenth to the Early Twentieth Century', in S. J. Jones (ed.), *Dundee and District* (Dundee: 1968), pp. 162–73. For Dundee in wartime, see B. P. Lenman, *An Economic History of Modern Scotland 1660–1976* (London: 1977), p. 212; J. C. Logan, 'Electricity Supply, Electrical Engineering and the Scottish Economy in the Inter-war Years', in A. J. G. Cummings and T. M. Devine (eds), *Industry, Business and Society in Scotland since 1700: Essays presented to Professor John Butt* (Edinburgh: 1994), pp. 101–24.

1917.[9] The report described at length the appalling housing conditions in Scotland and emphasised that on all counts standards were lower than those south of the Border. The contrasts with England and Wales were indeed striking. In 1911, 73 per cent of the population in Scotland lived in houses with three rooms or less. Using the English census standard of more than two persons per room, just over 45 per cent of people in Scotland lived in overcrowded accommodation, and general amenities were often intolerable. The legislation coming from Westminster that was intended to encourage working-class housing took no account of the social and physical differences north and south of the Border. In Scotland, the crucial requirement was organised slum clearance and the alleviation of overcrowding, and that involved recognition of the different housing legislation that Scotland needed. That was never offered. This absence, and the weakness of demand for houses in growing middle-class suburbs that provided the dynamic of the housing boom in England, had enormous consequences. In England and Wales by 1939, the total number of new houses built was 52 per cent of the housing stock of 1911; in Scotland the comparable figure was 28 per cent. Naturally, the scale of employment in building was proportionally smaller than in England because of the lower levels of activity, and demand for the wide variety of consumer goods and fittings in new housing was thus much reduced. Economic recovery in Scotland began from 1935–6. There was some improvement in export markets and a revival in the agricultural sector, but the main stimulus came from rearmament and its effects upon the heavy industries of the west of the country. These years were the only period between the wars when the Scottish economy grew at a faster rate than the rest of the UK.

The British government declared war on Germany at 11 p.m. on Tuesday 4 August 1914. Although there were still different opinions concerning the degree of British involvement, the foreign market had ceased to operate in any meaningful way for several days beforehand. The stock exchange was closed – and remained so until 4 January 1915 – yet there was still a considerable degree of panic throughout the City. This was the first experience of an all-embracing European war for almost a century, and the government was wise to impose a moratorium on debt payments on 6 August to give a breathing space before more considered decisions. There were especial difficulties for the discount houses. The military events had been anticipated by the Scottish banks in common

9 Report of the Royal Commission on the Housing of the Industrial Population of Scotland, Urban and Rural, Cd 8731 (1917); for an excellent, brief account of the Scottish housing problem between the wars, see M. Bowley, Housing and the State 1919–1944 (London: 1945), Appendix 1. The question of Scottish housing is discussed in A. Gibb, Glasgow: The Making of a City (London: 1983); and T. C. Smout, A Century of the Scottish People 1830–1950 (London: 1986), ch. 2.

with the rest of the financial world. The bank rate had gone from 3 to 4 per cent on the previous Thursday, 30 July, and after exceptional demands from the discount market it had risen to 8 per cent on the day following, almost certainly in expectation of a general suspension of payments in gold which duly followed on Saturday, as Germany declared war on France and Russia, with the bank rate at 10 per cent.[10] There was some panic hoarding of sovereigns in England and queues in Threadneedle Street. Scottish bank rates followed the Bank of England with immediate effect, branches being instructed to raise rates without waiting for confirmation from head office. The weekend of 1 and 2 August and the annual holiday on 3 August was extended by three more days to provide a period during which central policies would exercise a calming effect. The imposition of the moratorium added to the sense of reassurance within Scotland, and there were few reports of difficulty.[11]

The government had already announced the suspension of the Bank Acts on 2 August, and it was recognised on all sides that an issue of extra banknotes would be required. The Bank of England assumed that its notes alone would be sufficient and that other banks should pay bank rate for the privilege. There was considerable opposition from the English clearing banks, and it was wholly unacceptable to the Scottish banks. The Governor of Bank of Scotland, Lord Balfour of Burleigh, and the Governor of the British Linen Bank, the fifth Earl of Rosebery, made it clear to H. H. Asquith, Prime Minister, and David Lloyd George, Chancellor of the Exchequer, that the proposals must include the right of the Scottish banks to issue extra banknotes. Bank of England notes, even in the more convenient denominations of £1 and 10s, would not be acceptable in Scotland, and this was agreed. On Thursday 6 August, the Currency and Bank Note Act (4 & 5 George V c.14) was passed. Among its provisions, the Treasury was allowed to issue small-denomination currency notes, for £1 and 10s, as legal tender. The Bank of England, the Scottish and the Irish banks were granted the right to issue notes above their authorised limits without backing these by gold, and the notes were now legal tender.[12] There was no obligation to exchange for gold, except at their head offices, where they could choose to pay in Treasury currency notes. The board of Bank of Scotland decided that some degree of control over the note issue was essential, and in meetings during August between

---

10 The most detailed account of the early days of the war is in R. S. Sayers, *The Bank of England 1891–1944* (Cambridge: 1986), ch. 5; and see Sir John Clapham's account of August 1914 in ibid., Appendix 3, pp. 31–45; also E. V. Morgan, *Studies in British Financial Policy, 1914–25* (London: 1952), ch. 1.

11 BS 1/21/25, Treasurer's Private Letter Book, Sir George Anderson to London office, 1 August 1914.

12 4 & 5 George V c.14, repr. in T. E. Gregory (ed.), *Select Statutes, Documents and Reports Relating to British Banking, 1832–1928*, vol. ii, *1847–1928* (Oxford: 1929), pp. 320–2.

Scottish bankers and the Treasury it was agreed (and later confirmed by statutory instrument) that Scottish and Irish banks could issue notes up to 20 per cent above their total deposits. Each bank in this category was given special drawing rights at the Bank of England for its banknotes and for Treasury currency notes.

These fraught days at the beginning of the war were accompanied by bitter arguments between the different parts of the financial community. The London clearing banks were at serious odds with the Bank of England's original suggestions about its charges for the additional note issues. There has been much criticism by later commentators of certain of the emergency measures which were taken, and it has been widely noted that the London clearing banks showed a particular disposition to alarm. By the end of August, however, financial institutions were beginning to adapt to the new situation, although the exchange market recovered only slowly, in line with international developments in both belligerent and non-belligerent countries. The connections between the Scottish aristocracy and the banking world, which went back to the original foundation of Bank of Scotland, once again proved their political importance. When Bonar Law became Chancellor of the Exchequer in 1916, the Scots acquired a powerful supporter: a leader of the Unionist Party, with an industrial background in Glasgow, a skilled debater and an efficient administrator.

The banks and the financial community in Britain naturally assumed that the demands of war finance would be considerable, although very few in Britain in August 1914 anticipated that it would be a long war.[13] In fact, as it was gradually realised that the war would be a protracted and expensive conflict, the Scottish banks, along with the English joint-stock banks, found themselves incorporated into a most effective union of state and finance. The levels of taxation during the first three years of war were certainly too low, and the difference was largely met by government borrowing.[14] Apart from the usual lending to industry, the banks supported government efforts to channel savings to British government securities and placed an increasing part of their ordinary deposits in such stocks. From August to November, funds were raised from the banks and the London money market through the issue of Treasury bills and Ways and Means advances. But these were inadequate, and the Treasury soon realised that they would require to be supplemented by a war loan. In

---

13 This view was not limited to the banking community in Scotland. The majority of the cabinet, for the first few months, believed in the short war: A. J. P. Taylor, *English History 1914–1939* (Oxford: 1965), p. 23.
14 Morgan, *Studies in British Financial Policy*, chs 4 and 10; S. Pollard, *The Development of the British Economy 1914–1967*, 2nd edn (London: 1969), pp. 62–72.

November 1914 the first such was announced, for £350 million. It was to carry interest at 3½ per cent, repayable at par (the face value of the stock) on 1 March 1928, and the government reserved the right to redeem between 1 March 1925 and March 1928.[15] Lloyd George would have preferred to issue at the par price but gave way to City opinion, worried about depreciation should the war last, and it was issued at 95, i.e. £5 per cent below the face value.[16] At a London meeting before the loan was announced, at which the Scottish banks were represented, it was agreed that all the UK banks would subscribe to the extent of one-tenth of their deposits. This was reported to Bank of Scotland directors on 17 November 1914, and the board sanctioned application for £2 million. The considerable drain of deposits in the early months caused some difficulties with intra-bank money flows, but cutbacks in non-essential lending, to stockbrokers for example, enabled these problems to be overcome.[17]

On 21 June 1915, the Bank of England issued the prospectus for the second war loan, drafted by the Treasury, to raise substantial sums for the war, and it was also designed to help banks and other holders of existing government stocks to recoup part of their losses from some previous loans. This new war loan was for an unlimited sum to be raised by 10 July 1915. It was issued without any discount, unlike the first war loan, and trustees could invest 'notwithstanding that the price paid may at the time of investment exceed the redemption value of £100 per cent'.[18] The issue totalled £900 million and carried a gross redemption yield of £4 11s 4d, repayable on 1 December 1945, although the government reserved the right to redeem at any time from 1 December 1935. Special efforts were made to garner funds from small investors, but it was the holders of large volumes of stock who showed especial interest in the new conversion options; for every £100 of new war loan stock purchased, £4 10s fully paid in cash, one of the following options might be taken up:[19]

1. To convert existing holdings of 3½ per cent war loan (1914), 1925–8, to fully-paid stock of the new £4 10s (1915) war loan at the rate of £100 for the £3½ per cent war loan, subject to a payment of £5 per cent, and the holder would then receive £100 of the 4½ per cent war loan.

15 The details of this war loan, and all subsequent war stocks, are taken from Pember and Boyle, *British Government Securities in the Twentieth Century: The First Fifty Years*, 2nd edn (private circulation, London: 1950), pp. 290–1.
16 Sir Bernard Mallet and C. O. George, *British Budgets, 1913–14 to 1920–21*, 2nd series (London: 1929), pp. 42–3, 355; there is a note of this in Morgan, *Studies in British Financial Policy*, p. 108.
17 BS 1/21/25, Treasurer's Private Letter Book, 4 August 1915.
18 'The Second Government Loan', *The Bankers' Magazine*, 100 (July 1915), 21–30, reprints the prospectus of the £4 10s per cent war loan, 1925–45, on pp. 26–9.
19 The figures are taken from Pember and Boyle, *British Government Securities*, pp. 294–5; and see also Morgan, *Studies in British Financial Policy*, p. 109.

2. To convert holdings of £2 10s per cent British government consols to fully-paid stock of the new £4 10s (1915) war loan at the rate of £75 of the consols for £50 of the new £4 10s war loan. There was no cash payment.

3. To convert holdings of £2 15s per cent annuities to fully-paid stock of the new £4 10s (1915) war loan at the rate of £67 of the former for £50 of the new loan.

4. To convert holdings of £2 10s per cent annuities to fully-paid stock of the new £4 10s (1915) war loan at the rate of £78 of the former for £50 of the latter.

These were substantial benefits. It meant that the banks, which held considerable holdings of the stocks, would accept losses on their investments, although most banks, if not all, had already covered these losses by provisions. The actual conversion rates were somewhat higher than market rates. In addition, holders of the new stock were guaranteed that if any further issues of stocks were subsequently made (other than issues made abroad or Exchequer bonds, Treasury bills or other short-dated securities) by the British government for the remainder of the war, this second war loan would be 'accepted at par, plus accrued interest, as the equivalent of cash for the purpose of subscriptions to such issues'.[20] *The Bankers' Magazine* had made previous references to the depreciation of government securities and the effect which this had on bank assets, so it was not surprising that it congratulated the government

> upon having taken so comprehensive a view of the entire financial outlook. The arrangement that has been made with regard to the conversion of the former 3½ per cent war loan is conceived on equitable lines, the treatment, indeed, being almost generous, while it was a bold stroke to carry the conversion principle still further and include consols, the parlous condition of which has been a very real drag on financial progress for a very long time.[21]

Some £611 million was issued for cash and £290 million for conversion of the older stocks.[22] Bank of Scotland converted its entire holding of consols to the war loan stock.[23] The UK banks agreed to subscribe to this second war loan a further 20 per cent of their deposits.

The right to convert existing holdings was written into the issues of £5 and £6 per cent Exchequer bonds in 1915 and 1916, payable in

20 'The Second Government Loan', *The Bankers' Magazine*, 100 (July 1915), 21–30 (p. 28).
21 Ibid., p. 29.
22 Pember and Boyle, *British Government Securities*, p. 294.
23 BS 1/2/3, Lord Balfour, 'Report to the Proprietors', 4 April 1916; the Court authorised application for £1.8 million of the war loan, 'with a view to the conversion into the same stock of Bank's holding of 2½ per cent consols', viz. £1,335,350; BS 1/5, Minutes, 29 June and 13 July 1915.

1919–21, and a substantial conversion was effected when the government issued the 5 per cent war loan, 1929–47, in 1917. Holders of the 4½ per cent war loan, 1915, and the Exchequer bonds, would receive £105 5s 3d of 5 per cent war loan for each £100 of these existing holdings.[24] In 1917, £1,230,764,483 was created for conversion and £836,454,260 for cash. The government also agreed to a scheme whereby the Treasury established a fund for the purchase of this stock when the market price fell below the issue price, and from 1918–22 £156,751,000 was bought up and cancelled.[25] There was no direct contribution from the Scottish banks to the third war loan, but they agreed to make their offices available for subscriptions. Local agents and managers were urged to encourage all possible support and to lend 'reasonable amounts to approved customers for the purpose of assisting them to take up the new war loan'.

The Scottish banks through the years of war experienced the same kind of market situation as in the rest of the UK. Deposits and thus investments increased very rapidly, with a high proportion of the latter represented by government stocks but a somewhat smaller level of industrial lending. The conversion rights, and the sinking fund, were an important recognition of the position which these assets held on bank portfolios. This was also more important north of the Border, where a higher proportion of assets were invested in British government securities.[26] There were changes in the ranking of the banks within Scotland. At the outbreak of war in 1914, and also in 1915, Bank of Scotland occupied first place in the published figure of profits, yet by 1918 it was sixth out of eight and had a poor performance against other banks on profits as a percentage of deposits and paid-up capital, and was in fourth place for total liabilities and seventh for advances.[27] In 1918, the Clydesdale Bank was in first place for liabilities and deposits, but from about the mid-1920s until the Second World War it was the Royal Bank of Scotland which was the strongest performer.

The most important change in the banking structure of England and Wales was the acceleration of the processes of amalgamation of the joint-stock banks. Prior to the First World War, there had been considerable scope for the larger joint-stock banks to increase their branch network, and this was done both by opening new branches and by absorbing smaller banks. In these ways, the major banks extended their coverage in England and Wales.[28] By June 1915, amalgamations had reduced the number of independent joint-stock banks in England and Wales with assets of more

---

24 Pember and Boyle, *British Government Securities*, p. 296.
25 Ibid., p. 297.
26 For a summary view, see *The Economist*, 19 May 1917, p. 862.
27 See Statistical Appendix, Tables A13, A14, A15.
28 A. R. Holmes and E. Green, *Midland: 150 Years of Banking Business* (London: 1986), p. 115.

than £1 million to thirty, including the Bank of England. The larger banks saw continued scope for further acquisitions; by this date there were eight with capital above £4.1 million, and there were some sizeable regional banks as well.[29] By 1920, the five largest banks controlled all but 17 per cent of the total deposits in England and Wales. It was the later years of war that saw the most considerable mergers, and from some quarters this movement was given strong support because, it was argued, amalgamations would better enable the British banks to support the large-scale amalgamation and investment programmes of British industry. Yet this did not go unchallenged. The emergence of the large banks created disquiet in public opinion relating to the possible dangers of less competition and the development of monopolistic practices. The government appointed a Treasury committee on bank amalgamations, commonly known as the Colwyn Committee after its chairman, which reported on 1 May 1918. There were twenty-two members, with a strong preponderance from finance and banking circles. The committee noticed the fall in the ratio of bank capital to deposits and covered a number of other financial matters of concern to commentators. But most interest focused on what it had to say on the appropriate size of banks. The case was presented that the banks should 'grow now to keep pace with the growth in size of business houses generally, and to enable them to deal with the demands of after the war trade'.[30] The alternative view, presented by some industrial interests, the stock exchange and members of the discount market, preferred a wider range of banks to support their particular needs. The discount houses put especial emphasis on the advantages of competition for the success of the bill on London before 1914. In this context, the committee, after listing the range of problems connected with amalgamation and with much genuflection towards the principle of government non-interference, was 'forced to the conclusion that the possible dangers resulting from further large amalgamations are material enough to outweigh the arguments against Government interference, and that, in view of the exceptional extent to which the interests of the whole community depend on banking arrangements, some measure of Government control is essential'.[31]

The committee recommended legislation controlling future amalgamation, and suggested that the Treasury and the Board of Trade should

29 'Proportion of Capital and Reserve to Deposits', The Bankers' Magazine, 99 (June 1915), 859–76 (pp. 872–3); these were London City and Midland Bank (capital, £8.8 million); Lloyds Bank (£8.6m); London County and Westminster Bank (£7.5m); Barclay & Co. (£5.2m); National Provincial Bank of England (£5m); Union of London & Smiths Bank (£4.7m); Parrs Bank (£4.5m); London Joint Stock Bank (£4.1m). Among the larger-sized regional banks were the Manchester & Liverpool District Banking Co.; William Deacon's Bank; Bank of Liverpool; United Counties Bank.

30 Report of the Treasury Committee on Bank Amalgamations, 1918, repr. in T. E. Gregory (ed.), Select Statutes, vol. ii, 1847–1928, p. 327.

31 Ibid. pp. 323–33 (paragraph 8 of the Report).

be required to give their approval. It further recommended a statutory committee of two members, Lord Colwyn and Lord Inchcape, one representing commercial interests and the second financial, and in the event of their disagreement recommended that an arbitrator should be appointed. Certain basic principles were agreed in March 1924, including a ban on any amalgamation among the five largest banks, and with a number of subsidiary clauses which included permission for any of the Scottish banks to amalgamate as they wished except with any of these five in England and Wales. The Colwyn Committee's procedures and conclusions were taken issue with by Joseph Sykes in a volume dealing with the amalgamation movement published in 1926; and, fifty years later, R. S. Sayers in his history of the Bank of England underwrote the comments that Sykes had made.[32] The legislation which the Colwyn Committee had recommended was only half-heartedly put before Parliament, and the discussion on the question rumbled on for several years.

The war years confronted the Scottish banks with a range of central questions relevant to their future. The amalgamation movement south of the Border inevitably provoked thought, and the increasing intervention in trade and industry by the central government, while supported during wartime, prompted a growing concern with developments in the post-war years. There was also a widespread debate about the relationships between the banks and industry, and H. S. Foxwell, the economist, was not alone in underlining what he regarded as the superior merits of the German system.[33] In July 1916, Walter Runciman, President of the Board of Trade, appointed a committee to inquire into the question of the financial facilities for trade, and the Faringdon Report was published in August 1916. Its general conclusions dismissed the idea that British and colonial banks were inadequate in the general provision of finance for domestic trade and for 'large overseas contracts'.[34] The problems identified were in the coordination of the many facilities available through the City and

32 J. Sykes, *The Amalgamation Movement in English Banking 1825–1924* (London: 1926), pp. 160–2; Sayers, *Bank of England*, vol. i, pp. 235–52, especially p. 237, note 3.

33 'If we survey the world generally . . . we shall find that opinion is unanimous except perhaps in this country, that the proper and primary business of a banking system is to finance industry and trade. This was eminently the case with the old Scottish system, which has been praised by experts in all countries and often described as the classical banking system. How comes it then, that there should be any doubt as to the suitability of such work for the English banks today?': H. S. Foxwell, Address to the Royal Institution, April 1917, repr. as 'The Financing of Industry and Trade', *Economic Journal*, 27 (1917), 502–22 (p. 505). Among the other literature from this time is H. S. Foxwell, Address to the Royal Institution, April 1917, repr. as 'The Nature of the Industrial Struggle', *Economic Journal*, 27 (1917), 315–29; H. Mosely, 'The German Method of Banking and How it is Designed to Help Commerce and Industry', *Journal of the Institute of Bankers*, 38 (1917), 335–46. Foxwell's evidence to the committee on bank amalgamations is in the PRO, T 1/12267/50326/18.

34 *Report to the Board of Trade by the Committee Appointed to Investigate the Question of the Financial Facilities for Trade*, Cd 8346, 31 August 1916.

the banks, and in the provision of longer-term finance 'at the inception of undertakings' which British banks, it was claimed, did not provide, but which German banks did; and the committee recommended concerted action by British banks especially in all areas of foreign trade. An initiative was proposed by James Tuke, general manager of the British Linen Bank, and Arthur C. D. Gairdner, general manager of the Union Bank, that the Scottish banks should establish a Scottish Foreign Exchange Bank. It was known that good incomes and connections had been generated for those London joint-stock banks which had formed departments and subsidiary banks to administer foreign business. It was feared that these banks would use their position to poach business. The headquarters for the proposed Scottish bank would be in London and it would have an initial capital of £1 million. James Tuke noted that such a company would be an

> arresting proposition. All agencies including the London branches would contribute exchange transactions of whatsoever kind, the handling of all collections, purchase and sale of foreign and colonial cheques, mail and telegraphic transfers, coupons, dividend warrants, stock cheques, shipping documents, notes and coin, letters of credit, travellers cheques, clean and documentary credits and foreign investments.[35]

In spite of the advantages, and the fact that some of the Scottish banks were already considering closer relationships with the London clearing banks, it proved impossible to secure agreement, even between the general managers. The Royal Bank turned the proposition down, the National Bank preferred to build on its existing relationship with Lloyds Bank, and Bank of Scotland adopted a cautious, neutral attitude which might have become positive had there been a more vigorous response from its fellow bankers. By the end of the war, of the Scottish banks which had no ties with England, only the Union Bank had established its own foreign department. In May 1919, Bank of Scotland announced that customers' overseas business would be negotiated through the London County Westminster & Parr's Bank. With the greater-than-anticipated difficulties of trade after 1921, it was less clear whether an independent, London-based, Scottish trade bank would have been a success.[36]

In 1916, what was soon to become the Midland Bank acquired a site in Glasgow for a post-war branch, an event which much concerned the

35 National Westminster Bank, archives (Ref. 1094), Memoranda on the suggested formation of a Scottish Foreign Exchange Bank, 1916.
36 BS(BL), Uncatalogued, General Manager's Letter Book, R. G. Thomas to F. J. Holden, Barclay's Bank, 14 January 1925; C. A. Malcolm, The History of the British Linen Bank (Edinburgh: 1950), pp. 147–8, for the establishment of a British Linen Bank foreign department in Glasgow utilising expertise from Barclay's Bank.

General Managers Committee. In the following year, the Midland took over the share capital of the Belfast Banking Company in a relationship known as 'affiliation', a new kind of structure that was to serve as a model for the later takeovers of Scottish banks. There were cogent reasons for the English banks to move north. Scotland was a heavily-banked country, and during the war years and immediately afterwards there had been a notable increase in the number of branches. There was also a considerable national and local patriotism which would have resented the complete absorption of the Scottish banks into the English system. Moreover, Scottish banks had a profitable note-issue facility which meant, before the war, that till money did not have to be covered by gold or Bank of England notes, and this helped greatly to keep down the costs of local branches. Straightforward mergers of the type that had built up the English joint-stock banks would lead to the Scottish banks in question forfeiting the right to issue notes. The form adopted, the affiliation, was an ingenious structure which provided all the benefits of mergers without the disadvantages – in the Scottish context – that would have followed.[37] The parent bank took over the greater part or usually the whole of the share capital of the bank that was being absorbed, but the latter remained a separate legal entity. At the board level there were exchanges of directors, but the original name was retained and in practice there was a considerable degree of independence. This was to be the experience of the National Bank, the Clydesdale Bank, the British Linen Bank, and the North of Scotland and Town and County Bank, the four banks taken over in these years.

Amalgamation and growth in size were becoming widely accepted during these war years, and received opinion was a not unimportant factor in persuading some Scottish banks to consider favourably the offers that were to be made from south of the Border. The earliest example of negotiations, which for the time being were regarded as not sufficiently favourable, was those between the Midland Bank and the Clydesdale Bank in 1917. At around this time, negotiations were also held between general managers on the advantages of amalgamations among Scottish banks. James Tuke of the British Linen, for example, discussed this with his opposite numbers at Bank of Scotland and the Royal Bank, yet, as with the form of a foreign-exchange bank, there were disagreements over assets and which would be the lead bank.[38] In July 1918, Lloyds Bank concluded the purchase of the entire capital of the National Bank while leaving the separate board and management structures intact. The National Bank had a successful

37 C. W. Munn, *Clydesdale Bank: The First One Hundred and Fifty Years* (Glasgow: 1988), p. 155ff. for a description of the banking structure known as 'affiliation'.
38 BS 20/21/31, British Linen Bank General Manager's Private Letter Book, J. Tuke to A. Gairdner, 21 June 1917. BS(BL), Uncatalogued, Special Committee of Directors, Minute Book, 1918.

wartime record and profits had risen well, and by 1918 it was one of the stronger banks. With affiliation, a disappointing two decades set in, and its performance by 1935 was similar to the North of Scotland and Town and County Bank.[39] An affiliation between the British Linen and Barclay & Co. was announced on 3 November 1919. Good management ensured a strengthening performance by the British Linen from the mid-1880s: dividends rose to 20 per cent on the paid-up capital of £1.25 million in 1902 and stayed at this level until 1913, when bad debts and the decline in the value of stocks saw a reduction. The satisfactory position of the reserves, at £1.7 million, deteriorated from 1912, and in the six years to 1917 over £600,000 was written off and the dividend was further reduced. Nevertheless, in the course of 1917 the performance very much improved.[40] The unsuccessful negotiations over the Scottish Foreign Exchange Bank, and the failed discussions among the three senior banks, influenced the board in its talks with Barclay & Co. Barclays offered 150 'B' shares of £1 fully paid, or £375 of the 5 per cent national war bonds, for each £100 of British Linen stock.[41] Negotiations were reopened in early November 1919 between the Clydesdale Bank and the Midland Bank, and within two weeks terms had been agreed. The affiliation was based upon an exchange of five paid-up Midland shares of £8 10s per share for one Clydesdale share at £42 10s (the current market price being around £34). Moreover, Clydesdale shareholders would receive their annual dividend of 18 per cent in February 1920, and would then also receive the Midland Bank's dividends starting with the interim due in July, also at 18 per cent per annum, but on this occasion raised with a bonus of 22.5 per cent. At the annual general meeting which followed the acceptance of the affiliation, the shareholders were told that the bank would continue as before with two Midland Bank directors on its board, matched by two Clydesdale directors on the board of the Midland. The Treasury was consulted and found no objections to the proposed affiliation.[42]

The last affiliation in the inter-war years was the North of Scotland and Town and County Bank to the Midland in 1924. There had been long and detailed discussions between the Clydesdale Bank and the North of Scotland Bank. The original suggestion had been for a merger of the two Scottish banks, but the North of Scotland firmly rejected the proposition and became a separate affiliate of the Midland, retaining its name. What is interesting is that the financial terms of this takeover in 1924 were as

39 See Statistical Appendix, Table A13.
40 BS 20/21/31, British Linen Bank General Manager's Private Letter Book, G. McArly to J. Tuke, 19 January 1918. See also Statistical Appendix, Tables A20 and A21.
41 Malcolm, *The British Linen Bank*, pp. 145–7.
42 Details for this are taken from Munn, *Clydesdale Bank*, pp. 157–8.

favourable as in the previous cases, in spite of the sharp decline in the economy after 1921. On this last occasion in 1924, Midland Bank shares were valued at £9 per share, and the North of Scotland shareholders were offered eleven Midland shares for every four North of Scotland, a valuation of £24 15s per share, well above its current market price. Norman Hird, the general manager of the Union Bank, expressed surprise:

> The price paid ... was ridiculous. It works out at £4,034,250. For this the Midland get capital of about £652,000 plus reserves £892,000 = £1,544,000. Even if the North have secret reserves of £1.5 million, which I should think is a full figure, the Midland are paying £1 million for goodwill.[43]

The consequences of affiliation meant the exclusion of the banks concerned from any further entry into the English market, and there was some antipathy from the numerous Scots who supported independent banking companies.[44] There were some moves in the other direction when the Royal Bank of Scotland acquired three English banks.

The years of war encouraged debate and discussion concerning the future of Britain in the post-war world, although among many political and business groups it was assumed that with the victory for Britain the conditions of the pre-war world would be resumed. There were three influential committee reports in 1918: the Committee on Provision of Financial Facilities, chaired by Sir Richard Vassar-Smith of Lloyds Bank; the Treasury Committee on Currency and Foreign Exchanges after the War, known as the Cunliffe Committee; and the Committee on Commercial and Industrial Policy after the War. This last committee made severe criticisms of the backwardness of British industry in a number of key areas.

The first two reports of 1918 were in sympathy with the rapidly-growing hostility towards wartime planning and controls, a sentiment much encouraged by the results of the 'Coupon' general election of December 1918 which returned a large majority for the coalition, especially for the Conservative Party, and no fewer than 179 company directors.[45] The Vassar-Smith report concluded that the existing banking and financial institutions were adequate in terms of what the committee anticipated would be the demands of the post-war years. The report recommended that the banks should increase substantially their paid-up capital, and that there should be more effective methods of company promotion and industrial issues than in pre-war days. In general, the committee emphasised

---

43 BS(U) 1/21/4, Private Letter Book, Norman Hird to Arthur Gairdner, 19 December 1923; see also Holmes and Green, *Midland*, pp. 161–2.
44 Munn, *Clydesdale Bank*, p. 160.
45 C. L. Mowat, *Britain between the Wars 1918–40*, 2nd edn (London: 1956), pp. 2–8.

that the first requisite for the post-war economy was the restoration of financial policy on a sound basis, by which was meant a sharp restriction upon additional credit in order that the pre-war gold standard might be restored as soon as possible. Here, the committee was underlining the more extended conclusions of what was the most important committee of the immediate post-war era, that chaired by Lord Cunliffe.[46]

The first interim report of the Treasury Committee on Currency and Foreign Exchanges after the War was published on 15 August 1918. There had been some argument over the nomination of chairman, but eventually Walter Cunliffe, Governor of the Bank of England, was appointed in December 1917, six weeks after he had been told that from April 1918 he would no longer be Governor. The original terms of reference were 'to consider the various problems which will arise in connection with currency and the foreign exchanges during the period of reconstruction, and report upon the steps required to bring about the restoration of normal conditions in due course', and early in 1918 their reference was extended to cover an inquiry into the Bank Charter Act of 1844 and any changes that might be thought necessary.

The first interim report was the main document published. The war ended soon after it was published, and Cunliffe found it difficult to collect his committee together; only a brief final report appeared in early December 1919, just before Cunliffe's death.[47] The conservative conclusions of the Cunliffe Committee were published in summary form at the end of the report.[48] It was to be of more than historical interest that the committee opened with an idealised view of the working of the currency system and the gold standard before the war, with the 1844 Bank Charter Act as the favoured founding statute. The central assumption throughout was that Britain should, and could, return to the conditions which had existed in the world economy in 1913. The essential basis of those conditions was 'a complete and effective gold standard'. The requirements for the exercise of a workable gold standard had been altered in major ways by government policies during the war years, and in particular by the growth in credit due to government borrowing; and it was urgent and necessary that such borrowing be sharply reduced, if not ended completely. The Bank of England's discount must be restored to its pre-war functions, and the issue of fiduciary notes should once more be limited by law. These were the basic conclusions, and the remainder of the summary provided the detail of policies that were required to achieve the basic objectives.

46 The reports of the Cunliffe Committee are reprinted in full in Gregory, *Select Statutes*, vol. ii, pp. 334–70; for the committee, see Sayers, *Bank of England*, Appendix 7, pp. 57–64.
47 For the personality clashes which involved Cunliffe in 1917, see Sayers, *Bank of England*, pp. 99–109.
48 Gregory, *Select Statutes*, vol. ii, p. 363.

The most important of these policies came to be summarised under the heading of the 'Cunliffe Limit'. This was defined in paragraph 42 of the interim report in terms that would oblige the Bank of England to reduce progressively its fiduciary issue. The committee acknowledged in this same paragraph that it might not be practicable to work to 'any precise rule' and then went on to suggest that, when reductions in the note issue had taken place, 'the actual maximum fiduciary circulation in any year should become the legal maximum for the following year', subject only to the temporary continuance of the Currency and Banknote Act, 1914, s.3.[49] In its final report, the committee urged that the time had come to give effect to this last recommendation; and the Treasury issued a formal minute on 15 December 1919 (Cmd 485) accepting the suggestion that the actual maximum for one year should become the fixed maximum for the following year.[50] Paragraph 7 of the final report referred specifically to the Scottish and Irish banks, and the committee recommended that the pre-war status be restored whereby the notes of Scottish and Irish banks should not be granted the privilege of legal tender; this was accepted by the government in 1920.

The report of the Cunliffe Committee reflected majority opinion in financial circles in Britain and went along with the general agreement in official circles for deregulation and the abolition of wartime controls. There was, furthermore, good reason to be concerned at the rise in prices at the end of the war. Published figures showed that the capital and internal reserves of banks had declined as a percentage of deposits, and a reduction of the note issue would be required as part of a package of measures to correct this problem. Yet there were considerable political pressures against an immediate deflation; especially worrying to government ministers was the widespread agitation for change encouraged by socialist and collectivist ideas. After a slight fall in prices and employment in the months immediately following the Armistice of November 1918, the rise in wholesale prices was rapid and continuous. All the commercial banks benefited from a strong deposit position at the beginning of 1919, and the bank rate remained at 5 per cent until November. R. H. Tawney characterised the general opinion of much of business at this time:

> that the future will necessarily resemble the immediate past; and that trees, if left alone, will grow into the sky; and that upward movement, once started, will continue for ever, seems to be, if not the first article of the practical man's faith, at least a superstition on which, given the opportunity, he is not averse from acting,[51]

49 Ibid., p. 358.
50 Ibid., pp. 369, 371.
51 R. H. Tawney, 'The Abolition of Economic Controls, 1918–1921', *Economic History Review*, 13

adding that 'To these believers in perpetual motion it appeared to be sound sense to buy with borrowed money'. It is clear that with the continued increase in prices and a falling sterling–dollar rate, the Bank of England ought to have moved a good deal earlier than 6 November, when the bank rate was raised to 6 per cent and the Treasury bill rate to 5½ per cent. As it transpired, economic activity reached a peak in the spring of 1920 and continued at a high level throughout the summer, after which there began a precipitous decline. The bank rate, which had moved to 7 per cent on 15 April 1920, remained at this level until April 1921.[52]

The decline in employment and prices was dramatic. There was a 15.8 per cent rise in the cost of living in 1920 and a 9.2 per cent decline the following year. Exports decreased from £1,557,222,600 in 1920 to £810,318,848 in 1921.[53] The numbers covered by unemployment insurance in October 1920 had an unemployment rate of 3.8 per cent; at the close of 1921, the percentage was 15.7. The industries most affected were shipbuilding, iron and steel, engineering and building. The districts which suffered most in this first year of the decline were Northern Ireland (with 25 per cent unemployed), followed by Scotland with 21 per cent. The severity of the collapse from 1921–3, and the sluggish recovery thereafter, took the business community in Scotland by surprise. The difficulties of selling in world markets, the serious problems of labour relations and the uncertain movement of prices dominated analysis in the 1920s, with much emphasis upon wage costs as the centre of the general malaise. This emphasis was common to most of the business and financial associations as well as to the professional economists and commentators; and there was no lack of information about the severity of the crisis.[54] The *Glasgow Herald*'s trade reviews summarised received opinion among the industrialists, and there were detailed surveys three times a year in the *Scottish Bankers Magazine*. What was largely missing from this business literature

(1943), 1–30 (p. 15); see also R. Lowe, 'The Erosion of State Intervention in Britain, 1917–24', *Economic History Review*, 2nd series, 32 (1978), 270–86.

52 Morgan, *Studies in British Financial Policy*, pp. 203–4; D. E. Moggridge, *British Monetary Policy 1924–1931* (Cambridge: 1972), pp. 23–5.

53 Board of Trade, *Statistical Abstract for the United Kingdom for each of the fifteen years 1913 and 1918 to 1931*, 76 (London: 1933), Cmd 4233; Ministry of Labour, *The Labour Gazette*, 28 (1920), 550; 29 (1921), 646.

54 There is a discussion of contemporary views in Campbell, *The Rise and Fall of Scottish Industry*, pp. 155–8. See also idem, 'Costs and Contracts: Lessons from Clyde Shipbuilding between the Wars', in A. Slaven and D. H. Aldcroft (eds), *Business, Banking and Urban History: Essays in Honour of S. G. Checkland* (Edinburgh: 1982), pp. 54–79; for the complicated nature of industrial relations in these post-war years, A. McKinley, 'The Inter-War Depression and the Effort Bargain: Shipyard Riveters and the Workman's Foreman, 1919–1939', *Scottish Economic and Social History Review*, 9 (1989), 55–70; J. Foster, 'Red Clyde, Red Scotland', in I. Donnachie and C. Whatley (eds), *The Manufacture of Scottish History* (Edinburgh: 1992), pp. 106–24; T. Brotherstone, 'Does Red Clydeside Really Matter Any More?', in R. Duncan and A. McIvor (eds), *Militant Workers, Labour and Class Conflict on the Clyde 1900–1950* (Edinburgh: 1992), pp. 52–80.

in the early 1920s was an appreciation of the changed structure of the world market and of what this meant in particular to the export-oriented industries of Scotland.

There were numerous discussions within the Scottish banks which were germane to this fundamental question of trade realignment. The underlying message was to support cost reductions, as a typical comment in the *Scottish Bankers Magazine*, in the course of a survey of shipyards in April 1921, noted: 'only a reduction in costs – which means in effect a substantial reduction in wages – will enable the firms to obtain new contracts'.[55] In January 1919, the Royal Bank issued the first number of its *Financial and Trade Circular*, which was to be widely read in the inter-war years.[56] The general views expressed on the economy, which were always cleared by the general manager, recognised both the changed financial situation facing the country and the difficulties which there would be in expanding the export trade, in particular the strengthened position of Japan, the USA and a number of neutral countries. While this sombre view was shared with other bankers, it was tempered by the optimism in the post-war boom, then only in its early stages, and the tendency to look for ways of expanding production and, mistakenly as it transpired: 'a greater capacity of production' in the traditional industries. In their overall approach to post-war development, the Scottish bankers did not suggest much that was different from the general business community. The publication of the second report from the Cunliffe Committee was widely welcomed.

All Scottish bankers, without exception, welcomed the rise in the value of British government securities which occurred at the close of 1918. There was some deterioration during 1919 and 1920, but an improvement set in with deflation. There was to be much less concern for the rest of the decade about the market value of gilts than there had been prior to 1915. This had an important effect in reassuring the banks over advances on securities, and the frequent discussion on redemption and the decrease in income taxes also helped confidence.[57] This meant that bankers had a direct interest in holding public borrowing down, and they tended to be unsympathetic to schemes of reconstruction, or even to public investment in railways and housing, as not contributing to an increase of productive power.

Inevitably, a return to gold was much discussed, and, while cautionary noises about timing were heard occasionally, the overwhelming view was

55 'Shipbuilding', *Scottish Bankers Magazine*, 13 (1921), 53: Industrial Section, Business Notes.
56 Quotations in this paragraph are from Royal Bank, *Financial and Trade Circular*, 1 (January) and 2 (July), 1919.
57 Pember and Boyle, *British Government Securities*, pp. 35–63.

that a return to gold would benefit the economy, trade, industry and the value of British government securities. There were discordant voices, such as that of Reginald McKenna, chairman of the Midland Bank, who opposed a return to gold, and who in some respects agreed with the views of J. M. Keynes.[58] Another was Norman L. Hird, the general manager of the Union Bank, and his views also deserve recognition. In July 1924, he wrote:

> Any rise in rates is condemned by business, and as for a return to the gold standard at the present time (which I believe not bad as an ultimate goal) I cannot feel that it would be otherwise than disastrous if it occurred suddenly. We should get commodity prices falling, but, on the other hand, it would be difficult to get wages down and the position of trading concerns, already very hardly hit, would be even more difficult.[59]

A few days later, he was blunt about the risks: there was an

> enormous amount of uneconomic business being taken by firms [on the Clyde] in order to keep their staffs together, and to reduce on-cost charges. Some of the rather futile theorists in London have been conducting a campaign to raise the Bank rate in the hope of putting us on a gold basis which, at the present stage, would be simply appalling.[60]

Here was one Glasgow banker who understood shipbuilding. There was, however, no clear or concerted representation to the Treasury from Scottish bankers on this issue, and the *Scottish Bankers Magazine* carried several articles firmly in favour of a return to gold at $4.86.

Several of the Scottish banks had been deeply involved in the post-war industrial boom, especially in the traditional industries of the western region. By 1920, all but one of the steelmakers north of the Border had been acquired by shipbuilding companies. Prices soared for steel products, and it was inevitable that the downturn would bring problems which would present banks and industry with long-term adjustments.[61] The National Bank, to take one example, had £800,000 with Colvilles by the close of the post-war expansion, and it proved impossible to recover this in the next decade.[62] The beginning of mass unemployment and the

---

58 Holmes and Green, *Midland*, p. 176; for a survey of the gold standard, see I. M. Drummond, *The Gold Standard and the International Monetary System 1900–1939* (London: 1987).
59 BS(U) 1/21/24, Private Letter Book of Norman Hird, to London Office, 1 July 1924.
60 BS(U) 1/21/24, Private Letter Book of Norman Hird, to James R. Leisk, chairman, National Bank of South Africa, Pretoria, 10 July 1924.
61 P. L. Payne, 'Rationality and Personality: A Study of Mergers in the Scottish Iron and Steel Industry, 1916–1936', *Business History*, 19 (1977), 162–91 (p. 162), Table 1; Slaven, *Development of the West of Scotland*, p. 193; for prices, Payne, *Colvilles*, p. 148; B. R. Mitchell, *British Historical Statistics* (Cambridge: 1988), p. 764.
62 Payne, *Colvilles*, Table 7.4, 'Credits from National Bank of Scotland, 1921–1930', pp. 185–6; see below, discussion in Chapters 20 and 21.

limited improvement down to 1930 affected business psychology, which became noticeably pessimistic; and the banking community was not exempt from this common disquietude about the future. This underlined the importance of the Agreements and Understandings. The area where the banks could exercise direct influence was over their day-to-day business including interest rates, and the inter-war years saw a strong commitment by the general managers of all eight banks to the Agreements and Understandings. The underlying premise continued to be agreement on everything possible. This gave the Scottish banks a cohesion and undoubtedly strengthened profits. One positive answer which all the Scottish banks made was to increase their outlets for savings by opening new branches. Scotland was already 'over-banked' by comparison with England, but between the wars more than 600 branches were opened, mostly in rural areas and in the new suburbs, the majority opening before 1930.

There was limited competition from other financial institutions. The Trustee Savings banks were able to gather substantial deposits. In particular, the Glasgow Savings Bank was a considerable competitor in the Clyde region; it remained the largest savings bank in the UK in the inter-war years. There was also competition from municipal-owned savings banks, of which there were six in Scotland on the eve of the Second World War. That there were so few owed something to the efforts of the General Managers Committee to frustrate this movement. An early clash arose in May 1924 when the general managers drew attention to the establishment of the Motherwell and Wishaw Municipal Bank Ltd; their resolution read: 'Unanimous agreement that this so-called banking was fraught with danger to the public and [Norman Hird of the Union Bank] undertook to write to Sir Robert Horne MP to suggest that a question might be raised in the House of Commons drawing attention to growth of this feature of municipal enterprise'. Were this done, it was thought the matter might suitably be followed up by articles in *The Scotsman* and *Glasgow Herald*.[63] Hird wrote later in the month to Sir Frederick Williams-Taylor, general manager, Bank of Montreal, in terms which no doubt summarised a widely-held view that 'municipalities and provinces are serious competitors for deposits, and that seems to me to be one of the dangers of the future'.[64]

Emphasis upon the collection of deposits had always been a notable feature of Scottish banking in the nineteenth century, and, while competition for savings had steadily increased, it had been contained before

63 BS, Uncatalogued, General Managers Committee, Minutes, 9 May 1924.
64 BS(U) 1/21/24, Private Letter Book of Norman Hird, 23 May 1924.

1914. The 'deposit receipt' was a peculiarly Scottish financial device which had to be explained to the Macmillan Committee in 1930, but deposit accounts, later to be called savings accounts, were only introduced in 1928 to attract the small savers who found the savings banks very convenient and perhaps more friendly in their approach.[65] The general managers agreed that they would accept very small sums, under the old and unwritten £10 minimum, and monies could be deposited in any branch of a bank, not just the 'home' branch. Each depositor was issued with a 'passbook', and withdrawal was straightforward. The banks also faced competition from the mutual assurance societies, which made considerable efforts in the inter-war years to attract business.

There had long been changes and amendments to the Agreements and Understandings among the banks in Scotland. As time passed and business became more complicated, the number of rules increased, and the general managers would make periodic analyses of the whole text where they could review the overall position. Such an extensive revision was completed in July 1924.[66] A printed copy was made available to the Macmillan Committee, on conditions of secrecy, six years later. The greater part set down the rates to be observed for the discounting of bills, advances, inoperative loans over varying periods of time, loans against warrants for commodities such as iron, copper or tin, and rates on deposits, ending with various administrative arrangements including those for the exchange of note issues of the different banks and the standardisation of business hours.

The instructions regarding interest rates on different kinds of deposits and advances were set down in detail, and the language used was precise and without ambiguity. Thus the paragraph on deposits began: 'The rates of interest shall be advised by the Banks jointly by General Circular. These rates must in every case be strictly adhered to.' The meetings of the general managers were quarterly, on the first Mondays of January, April, July and October; special meetings could be called at the request of any two managers, and during the war and for a few years thereafter they were called together frequently. It should be stressed that their discussions ranged a good deal more widely than the normal banking practices relating to rates of interest and similar matters. In the more difficult conditions of these times, the general managers were quite clear that competition should be limited to quality of service and that costs should, as far as possible, not be added to by such expenses as advertising. They also drew up rotas for

---

65 Macmillan Committee, Minutes of Evidence, vol. i, Q. 2,744ff.; and see M. Gaskin, *The Scottish Banks: A Modern Survey* (London: 1965), p. 60 ff., for a lucid account of the various types of deposit accounts in the Scottish system.
66 BS, Uncatalogued, General Managers Committee, Minutes, 'Agreements and Understandings among the Banks in Scotland', 7 July 1924.

the circulation of public-sector accounts. The usual agreement was that these accounts would be held for two or three years by one bank and then passed on to another bank with a local branch. The only proviso was that the public authority should not be inconvenienced by such moves, but this was rarely a matter of dispute, at least before the general managers. This 1924 revision also confirmed a number of one-off decisions which had been agreed upon by resolution in previous years. On 18 December 1905, for example, the minutes of the general managers recorded that the North of Scotland Bank had opened a branch at Dumfries under the charge of an official who had just resigned from the Commercial Bank. It was agreed that the practice of poaching staff was undesirable and that in future this should not be done without previous communication between the two interested banks. In 1924, while this was embodied as a formal resolution, an additional note agreed that any communication between the interested banks should not be done within twelve months of the official leaving. Among the final resolutions of the 1924 Agreements, it was stated that 'as a general principle the Scottish Banks agree to refrain from utilising the money of their Shareholders for donative purposes' and that each bank should be free to make its own arrangements as to charges for foreign business.

There continued, as before, to be regular amendments to the Agreements in the years that followed. On deposit rates, for example, it was agreed on 17 March 1930 that special (i.e. higher) rates should not be quoted for deposits in London from Scottish customers 'of less than £10,000'; and, in Scotland from 4 July 1938, money from foreign banking correspondents could attract rates left to the discretion of each bank. Among those down to 1939 were several referring to canvassing by branch managers. In January 1938, for example, a resolution was approved:

> With regard to the question of canvassing for such Accounts it was decided to issue a General Circular to the effect that the Managers find it desirable once again to emphasise strongly that Agents must refrain from encouraging either directly or indirectly local agitation or pressure to secure such Accounts at present with other Banks or to prevent the existing rotation of Accounts where they are at present on that footing. Any action of this kind cannot be countenanced by the Managers and meets with their strong disapproval.

In October 1935 and October 1936, it had been agreed that the banks should not increase their present number of advertisements, and this 1938 resolution added that 'it should be left to the discretion of each Bank to deal with local advertisements where the cost does not exceed £5'. The details of the arrangements between the Scottish banks were among the matters examined by the Macmillan Committee, which was especially interested in these, as there was nothing similar south of the Border. The deliberations of the committee provide a most helpful summary of some, but only some, of the working practices of the UK banking system.

The Committee on Finance and Industry, chaired by H. P. Macmillan KC (who was raised to the peerage in 1930), was the most useful of all the monetary inquiries of the inter-war years. It was appointed by the minority Labour government in November 1929. Philip Snowden, Chancellor of the Exchequer, had told the House of Commons soon after the new government came into office on 5 June 1929 that an inquiry into monetary questions was 'under consideration', and the intervening months were taken up with considering whom to appoint to the proposed committee. Macmillan was not the first choice for chairman, but, when approached, he accepted on 28 October 1929. He proved to be highly efficient and competent.[67] The terms of reference were set out in a Treasury minute dated 5 November 1929: 'To enquire into banking, finance and credit, paying regard to the factors both internal and international which govern their operation, and to make recommendations calculated to enable these agencies to promote the development of trade and commerce and the employment of labour'.

The general problems of unemployment in post-war Britain and the relationships between industry, trade, credit and available financial facilities were important matters of contemporary debate. The restoration of the gold standard in 1925 invoked J. M. Keynes's ferocious onslaught in *The Economic Consequences of Mr Churchill*.[68] It advanced the argument that the interests of trade and industry and employees were being sacrificed for the benefit of the financial community, in particular to a high value of the pound sterling – then at the pre-war rate of $4.86. As mentioned before, among the critics was a former Chancellor of the Exchequer, the Rt Hon. Reginald McKenna, chairman of the Midland Bank.[69] Specialist public opinion was divided. For some, the financial institutions were failing in their duties towards industrial reconstruction; this was argued to be especially true of the traditional staple industries, and there were those who continued to believe that 'normality' meant a return to the economic conditions of 1914. The Bank of England and the Treasury did not share these apprehensions, and they were strongly opposed to any inquiry into the detailed workings of the Bank of England or the monetary system in general.[70] They rejected the criticisms that the policies which

67 Sayers, *Bank of England*, vol. i, p. 363, note 3 relates the story of the appointment of Macmillan after several other names had been considered.
68 R. F. Harrod, *The Life of John Maynard Keynes* (London: 1951; repr. New York: 1969), pp. 360–2.
69 McKenna proved one of the outstanding personalities in the committee's discussions. For something of his role, see Holmes and Green, *Midland*, pp. 176–8.
70 There is a useful chapter in Sayers, *Bank of England*, vol. i, ch. 16, which provides the background

they advocated, including the return to gold in 1925 at $4.86 to the pound sterling, could have any damaging effect on British trade and industry in theory or in practice.

The Macmillan Committee opened its public hearings on 28 November 1929, just over a month after the first day of the Wall Street crash when 13 million shares changed hands on 24 October; and the backcloth to the deliberations of the committee was the rapidly worsening economic conditions of the Great Slump. The report of the committee appeared on 13 July 1931 – a day of financial crisis in London – and the minutes of evidence in two volumes were published in November 1931. J. M. Keynes dominated the proceedings and intellectual discussions of the committee, and the other most active personalities included Reginald McKenna, Professor T. E. Gregory, the historian, Ernest Bevin of the Transport Workers Union, and R. H. Brand.[71]

The evidence of the Scottish banking community was presented by George J. Scott, Treasurer of Bank of Scotland, and Sir Alexander K. Wright, general manager and director of the Royal Bank of Scotland. The Scottish bankers had submitted a written statement in answer to a questionnaire which, in the published minutes of evidence, precedes the cross-examination of the two Scottish representatives.[72] The Scottish statement began by explaining that annual accounts of assets and liabilities were made available at the annual general meetings of the individual banks – some banks made half-yearly statements – and that, apart from the monthly totals of note issues which appeared in the *Edinburgh Gazette*, the 'Managers do not think it desirable or expedient to provide further information, and no wish for such has been expressed by either the Shareholders or the public'. The statement then continued with a brief account of the affiliation principle enjoyed by four Scottish banks with English banks, explained briefly the limitations on competition agreed by the meetings of the general managers, stated that the independent Scottish banks were against any amalgamation with the English joint-stock banks, and proceeded to answer a series of questions on banking policies which were to be further discussed in the cross-examination which followed.

The questioning covered much ground as to how advances were made and the conditions which surrounded these, and what might be termed the key matters before the committee were those concerned with the size and

to the appointment of the committee as well as to the attitudes of the Bank of England and the Treasury. The subject of industry and financial institutions was part of the official programme of the Labour Party in the general election of 1929.
71 R. H. Brand, later raised to the peerage, was among the senior management of Lazards and an important part of the City establishment. A member of the economic conference called by the supreme council of the Allies in Genoa in 1922, he was prominent for the rest of the decade.
72 Macmillan Committee, Minutes of Evidence, vol. i, pp. 156–8.

duration of the advances and the relationship between the Scottish banks and their business customers. On several of these matters, differences emerged between the experiences of the English and Scottish banks. The starting point to this discussion was that almost every staple industry in Scotland – iron, steel, coal, shipbuilding, engineering, agriculture, fishing and even whisky – was distressed: 'hardly anything except perhaps linoleum . . . seems to be flourishing'.[73] It was confirmed, although in rather general terms, that the Scottish banks would nurse industries over these harsh times, and that even in normal times the banks would make every effort to help a company in difficulty 'if we saw possibilities of rehabilitation'. Some businesses could not repay advances 'to a certain extent, not by any means to a serious extent; still it is there, and there is a corresponding moderate lock-up'. Yet it proved difficult to persuade companies – shipbuilding and coal were mentioned – to take difficult decisions: 'some [industrialists] are born optimists and go on till the last minute'. Sir Alexander Wright made an interesting observation on the long-established Scottish practice of helping firms in difficulty:

> When an advance is getting into a confirmed condition and becoming large, we may think it necessary to insist upon some measure of reorganisation, just putting it to the people, 'Are your methods all right? What about your Directors? We think we ought to have a representative on the Board.' We have had to do that recently in one or two cases. We have said, 'We must have our man on the board who will carry out our wishes and keep in touch with us'.

While this did not give the full range of bank support for industry, it allowed the committee to inquire whether this was similar to the continental system. But this was a salvage approach: 'we hope to see the business come round if it is properly managed and handled. There is a great deal in the character and competency of the people in charge of a business.' In several answers, George Scott and Sir Alexander Wright tried to convey the idea that medium-sized banks, in the Scottish tradition, had much opportunity for personal contact:

> there really is something, Lord Macmillan, in this question of the personal element. After all, the number of hours in the day is limited, you have no time to see more than a certain number of people, but the mere fact that your business is not too large enables your Manager to take prompt action. In instance, take Glasgow, I am often asked on the telephone, so-and-so would like to see you. Very well. It is a customer, not of head office in Edinburgh, but of Glasgow, or a Glasgow branch, there is no difficulty in him seeing me.

---

73 Ibid., vol. i; quotations which follow are, in order, from questions 2,790, 2,791, 2,792, 2,781, 2,800, 2,802, 2,805, 2,832, 2,796 and 2,768.

Table 19.2 *Classification and comparison of Scottish and English bank advances, 1929–30*[1]

Category	English banks	Scottish banks
Textiles	8.3	4.7
Heavy industries (iron, steel, engineering and shipbuilding)	6.4	7.3
Agriculture and fishing	6.9	7.2
Mining and quarrying	3.0	2.3
Food, drink, tobacco	6.4	5.7
Leather, rubber, chemicals	2.2	1.4
Shipping and transport (including railways)	2.5	3.3
Building trades	4.8	1.5
Miscellaneous trades (incl. retail trades)	14.8	8.6
Local government and public utilities	5.3	6.3
Amusements, clubs, churches, charities etc.	2.7	0.7
Financial (incl. banks and discount houses, stock exchange and building societies)	14.4	23.8
Other advances	22.1	27.1
	99.8	99.9

Note:
1 The figures relate to 'various dates from October 22, 1929, to March 19, 1930'.

Source: Macmillan Report, Appendix 1, Table 8.

Reprinted from M. Gaskin, *The Scottish Banks: A Modern Survey* (London: 1965), p. 156.

The Scots thus dismissed the notion that amalgamations would be advantageous to industry, and in any case, with the larger companies having more than one banker, there was no obstacle to the provision of larger sums if these were required.

The committee raised the provision of advances for smaller-sized businesses, and here the Scottish cash account system (the term was used by Sir Alexander), with its flexible repayments and interest charged only on the outstanding balance, was a considerable benefit to borrowers. Macmillan himself pressed the questioning on the adequacy of overall credit. Yet, the more important question was of seeing a prospect of a loan being advantageous: 'You cannot reasonably expect people to put fresh capital into coal conveyors, coal cutters . . . under present conditions. . . . the same with shipbuilding and other industries'. In spite of the importance of the questions, there was a lack of detail in the probing, which might have offered more extensive insights into how the banks in Scotland worked with business.

The Scots gave some figures of lending by category, and after their session was concluded the committee received from them a breakdown of advances which was then published alongside a similar table for England (see Table 19.2). When George Scott was asked whether most of his bank's customers were engaged in industry or business, he replied that 'all the banks, at the present moment, and for some years past, have made a very substantial amount of their advances against Stock Exchange securities', adding later that advances for investment and on stock-exchange securities were nearly 25 per cent of the total advances.

These matters were central to the remit of the committee, yet several members felt that they were put at a disadvantage, in comparison with the examination of the English banks, over the amount of information which the Scottish banks made available on their activities to the public.[74] These matters were raised at the start of the evidence, which was unfortunate since it immediately became clear that the two Scottish representatives stood by the statement in the written memoranda that they were satisfied with the current position. It also became clear that the members of the committee were equally wholly unconvinced with the Scottish practice, and there followed some hostile questioning. The members of the London clearing house had agreed in January 1921 to begin publishing monthly averages of the details of assets and liabilities, although the more comprehensive recommendations of the Cunliffe Committee had not been adopted.[75] When Professor Gregory asked about the publication of monthly figures on the lines of the English banks, George Scott replied that 'It would serve no purpose', and he expanded his argument in the answer to the following question, making again the point that the general public was not interested.[76] He added that he could see no objection as far as the banks were concerned but that there really was no point to the further information that was being requested. Then J. M. Keynes entered the questioning:

> The information would be wanted for the trained observer rather than for the general public. Monthly figures are available for England, and great importance is attached to them; they are watched very closely. In America, far more detailed information is supplied. If you are to attempt any kind of scientific analysis of the situation you want the data as complete as possible. It is rather hard to wait until the end of the year. I would rather put the point in this way – is any purpose served by concealment?

Scott replied that, of course, there was no concealment, and he then added a new argument, namely that the Scottish banks were not large enough to call for the publication of detailed information from month to month.

---

74 For a succinct discussion of the Scottish banking statistics, see Gaskin, *The Scottish Banks*, pp. 17–20.
75 The Cunliffe Committee produced a proposed monthly statement to be published by the banks in Appendix 1 to their interim report of August 1918, reprinted in Gregory (ed.), *Select Statutes*, vol. ii, p. 365.
76 Quotations which follow are, in order, from questions 2,665, 2,666 and 2,672.

Keynes went on to say that he often analysed the figures put out by the banks, and that he had 'a very crude way of dealing with Scotland; I add ten per cent to the English figures'. The Scottish representatives agreed that compilation of the data being asked for would involve no more work since they were already available inside each bank, but they remained unconvinced. Keynes tried further:

> In the case of the English banks the monthly figures are worth a great deal more than the figures at the end of the year. The end of the year is subject to very disturbing influences, and when one comes to draw conclusions one nearly always prefers to take monthly statements rather than the statement at the end of the year. Experience shows that the statement at the end of the year differs very materially from the monthly statement.

The Macmillan Committee was able to persuade the Scottish bankers to produce monthly averages from 1919 to 1931, and these were printed in Appendix I to its report, although the figures were still aggregated for only six out of the eight Scottish banks. From 1930, the Scottish banks supplied the Bank of England with similar returns; but these, unlike the English figures, were not made public for the rest of the decade.

Yet, even with monthly figures, the committee was aware of the deficiencies. These were calculated from weekly averages, and again the 'make-up' days were not on the same day of the week. Most English banks were concerned to present as favourable an appearance with the Bank of England as possible, and on some occasions – an unknown number – manipulation on the selected 'marking-day' was an acceptable activity. Loans could be called in from the money market and returned the next morning. If the London banks had different days of the week for their 'mark-up', as they did, it could mean that the same liquid resources were serving the banks in turn. The cash ratios shown in the monthly statements, based upon these weekly 'mark-ups', could therefore be interpreted as biased, as they did not reflect the true position.[77]

This was the practice of 'window-dressing' to which the Macmillan Committee devoted considerable attention. It was justified, at least among bankers, where sudden shifts in the cash position of a bank might have offered a misleading impression to the money markets and the public. The Macmillan Committee condemned the practice, and Reginald McKenna provided a statement of the problem as he saw it. He was in discussion with Sir Ernest Harvey, the Deputy Governor of the Bank of England:[78]

> Speaking for myself, I am as opposed to window dressing as you are. My Bank published on 30 June [1930] our cash ratio as 9.7 per cent. Our average for the

---

77 T. Balogh, *Studies in Financial Organisation* (Cambridge: 1947), pp. 45–56.
78 The quotations which follow are, in order, from questions 8,859 and 2,675.

month was over 11 per cent. I have observed that some banks published ratios at the 30th June almost double ours, although their cash ratio throughout the month and throughout the year has been considerably below ours. Why they do it I cannot understand, because nobody would be so foolish as to be taken in by these window-dressing figures. Take our own figures, which are merely a statement of our position on Wednesdays. Those figures form the basis for comparisons which are frequently made between some period of the year and the same period of another year, and yet they may be totally unreliable for that purpose. Our figures vary very much from day to day, and such a comparison might be between the minimum in a week in one year and the maximum in the corresponding week in another year, and there might on the average be in either case as wide a difference as perhaps £10,000,000 between the figure published and the average of the week. If the Committee think it would be of any value, the Bank, I feel sure, would be quite prepared to publish every week their day to day average. I do not say that there would be much variation, but there would be some weeks in which there would be considerable variation, and the average figure would afford a more reliable basis for comparisons.[79]

Reginald McKenna was chairman of the largest joint-stock bank in the world, and no-one would ever doubt its strength; other bankers, including the Scots, felt less confidence when cross-examined over this question. 'Do you understand in Scotland', asked Mr McKenna, 'what is meant by the term "window-dressing"?' 'Very little', replied Scott:

Q. 2,675   (Mr McKenna) The phrase is unknown to you? – We have heard of it as taking place elsewhere.
Q. 2,676   Is it practised in Scotland at all? – One cannot say it is a 'practice' there.
Q. 2,677   Not at all? – I should think, if at all, to a very small extent. (Sir Alexander Wright) It is not a Scottish expression.
Q. 2,678   I wanted to know if you used the expression? – No. It is not in our vocabulary.
Q. 2,679   You understand what I mean by the expression 'window-dressing'? – (Mr Scott) Yes.
Q. 2,680   Are the figures which the Scottish banks publish those which might be the subject of 'window dressing'? – Only I should think in a very mild form.
Q. 2,681   (Mr Keynes) Your average cash, for example, throughout the year, would be nearly the same as you publish in your balance sheet? – Yes.
Q. 2,682   (Mr McKenna) You practically do not 'window-dress' in Scotland? – We practically do not so far as I know.

The members of the committee must have felt this a somewhat dispiriting early stage of the general cross-examination, and it was soon followed in the sequence of questions by a discussion of the degree of competition

79 Macmillan Committee, Minutes of Evidence, vol. ii, p. 277.

within Scottish banking.[80] These matters of balance sheets were clearly regarded as important, yet for the overall conclusions of the committee the relationship of the banks to trade and industry was much more so, and the Scottish interviews might have been handled better. Yet at this time it must be remembered that the banks, in common with most companies and with the government, were still very tightly-knit and concerned that disclosure might have an adverse effect on their public standing. The matter of the internal reserves of the banks was not discussed.

It was unfortunate that the Macmillan Committee received from the Scottish bankers little information which helped its own concerns and considerations. Both the Scottish representatives, it may be surmised, must have found the questions about banking involvement in industrial reconstruction and rationalisation of great interest, but decided to confine their answers to usually more general statements. Towards the end of the session, when Macmillan summed up by saying that their task was to find ways of meeting the current problems of the economy, Sir Alexander Wright replied in terms which reflected the more orthodox position: 'And if I might make a humble suggestion it would be that any such procedure could be quite well handled through the banks themselves'. It was a comment that summed up well enough the difference in view from what the Macmillan Committee was trying to do, and no doubt it has been read in that way by generations of historians. In most but not all regards, it is a correct reading, because Sir Alexander Wright showed himself throughout the examination by the committee to be remarkably orthodox in what he was prepared to say on the role of bankers in an industrial society. Overall, the position of the Scottish banks in this most important of banking inquiries was, at best, marginal. This was perhaps the lowest point in the influence wielded by the Scottish banks on British banking policy for nearly a century.

The internal bank records, and Bank of England papers, however, provide another dimension to the story; all banks had considerable involvement with industries in Scotland, often very long-term. Moreover, at the time of Sir Alexander's interview with the Macmillan Committee, the Royal Bank was involved in highly secret negotiations over Williams Deacon's Bank and the Lancashire Cotton Corporation. The initiative came from the Bank of England, and the Royal Bank only had to obtain the best possible terms for itself; but these negotiations, which in the end were successful, were no doubt in Sir Alexander Wright's mind. Williams Deacon's had its head office in Manchester, was a member of the London

---

80 In the 1920s, as before 1914, there was internal correspondence at both Bank of Scotland and the Union Bank relating to borrowing short-term funds for the balance figures at each year's end.

clearing house and served the north-west of England. Lancashire, its most important county, had important sections of the old staple industries within its region – cotton, iron and steel, coalmining – and Williams Deacon's found itself by the mid-1920s with an increasing volume of bad debts. By the end of 1928, it had made advances to forty cotton-spinning firms which totalled £4 million, much of which was irrecoverable.

There were attempts from 1925 to organise trade associations to meet the problems of the cotton industry, and in 1929 the Lancashire Cotton Corporation was set up in discussion with all the firms on the books of Williams Deacon's. The Bank of England had already established a separate agency, the Securities Management Trust, through which it would channel funds for industrial purposes supported by the bank. Early in 1930, the Bank of England established a second company, the Bankers Industrial Development Company (BIDC). Unlike the Securities Management Trust, which had only nominal capital, BIDC's capital was subscribed by all the clearing banks and most of the large financial institutions which were approached, although most of the capital was not called out but remained as a guarantee fund. The Scottish General Managers Committee agreed on 7 April 1930 to accept participation after Sir Alexander Wright and George Scott had reported on an interview with the Governor of the Bank of England. R. G. Thomas, general manager of the British Linen Bank, surmised that no-one in Scottish banking much 'likes being committed to this company, but it is probably inevitable, if we are to avoid something worse'.[81]

The Governor of the Bank of England had been involved in discussions about a long-term settlement for Williams Deacon's from 1928, and given that the 'big five' London banks were excluded the Royal Bank was approached. It was by then the strongest of the Scottish banks, with a light exposure to bad debts. R. S. Sayers, in his history of the Bank of England, has told the story in detail.[82] Over the next three years, negotiations were complicated and difficult, and the Royal Bank's board was by no means convinced at different points in the negotiation. It was helped by an initial input by the Bank of England of £1.5 million, later increased to a total of £4 million as the true and disastrous position of Williams Deacon's unfolded, and by the sale, on very generous terms, of the business and premises of the Bank of England's branch at Burlington Gardens in the

---

81 BS(BL), Uncatalogued, General Manager's Letter Book, 4 April 1930; and see BS 1/21/22, Treasurer's Private Letter Book, General, 24 March 1930, George Scott to John Rae.
82 Sayers, *Bank of England*, vol. i, pp. 253–9. The official history of the bank, Anon., *Williams Deacon's 1771–1970* (Manchester: 1971), notes an important memorandum from R. T. Hindley, the general manager at the time of the takeover by the Royal Bank, pp. 158–9. There is an important discussion in Sayers about bank–industry relations, ch. 14. For an overview, see M. Collins, *Banks and Industrial Finance in Britain 1800–1939* (London: 1991), ch. 6.

West End of London. The central problem was the necessity to prevent public awareness of the serious financial position in Williams Deacon's in order to avoid what undoubtedly would have been a run on the bank, and probably closure and bankruptcy. The operation in total cost the Bank of England just over £3 million, a sum which must be set against the possible consequences of the failure of an important commercial bank and a much-weakened Lancashire Cotton Corporation. Sayers argues that, in the bleak economic environment of Lancashire in the 1930s, the economy was 'well served'.[83] This was the second English bank acquired by the Royal Bank during the inter-war period. The first was Drummond's Bank, a small private bank at Trafalgar Square which gave the Royal Bank its first West End branch. In 1939 it took over its third English bank – Glyn, Mills & Co. – which like Williams Deacon's retained its own identity along the lines of affiliation.

The issue of notes by Scottish banks has been a theme that runs through banking history in Britain, with a good deal of opposition at most if not all times from south of the Border. On 7 April 1924, the general managers adopted a resolution as follows:

> That this meeting of Scottish Bank Managers having observed a statement by Mr McKenna as chairman of the Midland Bank to the effect that, in his opinion, the right of issuing Bank notes in Scotland should be transferred to the Bank of England, desire unanimously to place on record their determination to oppose such a change by every means competent to them.

This private statement had been preceded by one in public on 1 April, at the annual meeting of Bank of Scotland, by Sir Ralph Anstruther, who presided in place of the Governor and Deputy Governor:

> In passing, I might also refer to the recent suggestion of the Chairman of one of the English Banks, when he favoured the currency note issue being made an issue of the Bank of England, and also the substitution of Bank of England notes for those of Scottish and Irish Banks. I do not propose to discuss the currency note question,[84] but I may say that the proposal so far as the note issue of the Scottish Banks are concerned will be most strenuously opposed. In pre-war days, England had a wasteful currency of gold, and people there had no acquaintance with the £1 note of the Scottish Banks, and a long and honourable record has shown that the confidence of the public was well founded. It is difficult to see on what grounds the change can be advocated, as the protection of the Noteholder is of the most ample nature. The present practice of the Scottish

---

83 Sayers, *Bank of England*, vol. i, p. 259.
84 For an excellent account of the whole question of the Scottish note issue, see Gaskin, *The Scottish Banks*, chs 6 and 7.

Banks having their till-money mainly in their own notes means a considerable saving in the expense of carrying on the widespread Branch system, and the substitution of Bank of England notes would only mean additional charges to the Banks – in other words, a tax upon the Shareholder without any advantage to the public.[85]

There was an interesting exchange about the Scottish banks in the Macmillan Committee's private sessions. These were arranged to allow individual members of the committee to state their own positions, and among them Keynes was prominent. In one such session on 27 November 1930, Keynes made a vigorous critique of the position of the Scottish banks. He argued that the Scottish banks held about £180 million on deposit, against which they held less than £1 million in the Bank of England, 'therefore in that sense [they] are contributing nothing towards the upkeep of the national currency system'; and Keynes thought that it was incumbent on the Scottish banks to keep 7 or 8 per cent at the Bank of England as did the English banks. This was in the middle of a long and involved discussion of fiduciary issues, but nothing related to this particular matter was included in the final report.[86]

The world depression, the abandonment of the gold standard by Britain in 1931, the subsequent fall in the value of the pound sterling against the dollar and other leading currencies, and the imposition of tariffs began a new period in British economic history. There was still much tenaciously-held orthodoxy among businessmen and economists, but there were also the beginnings of new ideas and new thoughts about the workings of the industrial system. Of the two main teaching centres of economics in Britain, the London School of Economics was dominated by the neo-classical theory of Lionel Robbins and the intellectually-allied Austrian School of von Hayek, with Cambridge as the only significant focus for what was to become first the heresy and then the new orthodoxy of Keynesianism. There was little on financial thought in Scotland that was not derivative of these two lines of thought, usually the more orthodox. The Macmillan Report and especially the two volumes of evidence were to exercise a significant influence alongside the simultaneous publication of Keynes's A Treatise on Money on 15 October 1930. The 1930s were to see a concentrated discussion of the economic and social problems of national economies within a global context. The most-publicised episode during the 1930s was Franklin D. Roosevelt's New Deal following his election

85 For criticism of R. McKenna's views, see BS(U) 1/21/4, Private Letter Book, Norman Hird to G. Scott, 31 January 1924, and to H. Jones, Canadian Bank of Commerce, Toronto, 27 May 1924.
86 J. M. Keynes, The Collected Writings of John Maynard Keynes, vol. XX, Activities 1929–1931: Rethinking Employment and Unemployment Policies, ed. D. E. Moggridge (Cambridge: 1981), pp. 202–7 (p. 205).

in the autumn of 1932. In large and small ways, including the coming-to-power of fascism in Germany and its increasingly controlled economy as the most dramatic centre of world politics, new thinking was forced upon the many traditional groups which still looked back to the world of 1914 and its re-establishment as the goal to be worked for.

In Scotland, as everywhere, the new ideas found supporters as well as many opponents, but there were especially difficult problems because of the sluggishness of the economy in the 1920s and the failure to match the upward economic growth in England in the following decade until the very last years, when rearmament encouraged recovery in the great western region of heavy industry and shipbuilding. The Scottish Development Council was founded in 1931, and in April 1936 it set up the Scottish Economic Committee which was strongly backed by important sections of the business community. Two years later, the Earl of Elgin took the chair for another initiative, the Scottish Development Financial Trust, 'to assist in the provision of capital for new and existing enterprises'. The Clydesdale Bank began publishing an annual survey of economic conditions in Scotland – the first issue appeared in February 1934 – and these provided a useful collection of statistics and reports on different sectors of the Scottish economy, tending to take a more industrial view of the Scottish economy than that of the *Financial and Trade Circular* published by the Royal Bank, which remained more orthodox in its attitudes. In the years immediately before the outbreak of the Second World War, the pace of change, in material terms and in ideas, was accelerating, and, while much of the economic improvement was the result of armament expenditures, the problems of the Scottish economy and the need for product and industry diversification were now better appreciated.

Most of the banks in Scotland have cautious histories, but their problems must not be underestimated. It was difficult, as George Scott had indicated to the Macmillan Committee, to find safe industrial investment, and the problems became much worse after 1930. In aggregate, the monetary totals of advances for all the Scottish banks from 1930–9 were for each year below the totals of the second half of the 1920s. But dividend payments throughout the 1930s were consistently higher than in the previous decade.[87] The general conservatism of the banking world was reflected in the decisions of the quarterly meetings of the general managers, although it is difficult, and on occasion impossible, to differentiate the opinions of any one bank or group of banks.

The general managers consistently declined to subsidise commercial, and commercially relevant, educational developments, apart from the

87 S. G. Checkland, *Scottish Banking: A History, 1695–1973* (Glasgow: 1975), p. 745, Table 44; see also Statistical Appendix, Tables A13, A14 and A15.

Institute of Bankers in Edinburgh. In May 1925, they declined to offer £100 per bank to support the Industrial Education Council; in April 1926 the request of the Glasgow and West of Scotland Commercial College for subscriptions was turned down; and the proposal for a Chair of Banking at the University of Edinburgh was refused in April 1929. In the late 1920s, the general managers were greatly concerned with the Agricultural Credits (Scotland) Bill, and they organised a series of meetings with the Secretary of State for Scotland. There was considerable disagreement among the general managers. John Erskine of the Commercial Bank was enthusiastic about the general principles involved, which envisaged government assistance towards the establishment of cooperative marketing societies on the model of some European countries. The discussions went on for a long time. On 7 January 1929, at a meeting of the general managers, Sir Alexander Wright of the Royal Bank expressed the view that while there was still a majority of the banks opposed to the Bill as it was at present drafted, it was highly desirable that the banks should act together. After much negotiation, the Scottish Agricultural Securities Corporation was established in 1933 with the involvement – with much reluctance on the part of three out of the four – of the Commercial Bank, the Royal Bank, the British Linen Bank and the National Bank.

The general managers supported the establishment of the Scottish Development Council in 1931, but they turned down the scheme for the creation of a Scottish finance company to assist Scottish contractors in financing foreign government contracts on the grounds that existing facilities were sufficient. When the Scottish Development Council appealed for subscriptions on behalf of a development board for Glasgow and district, the managers' resolution read, after expressing their general reluctance to depart from their usual non-donative practice:

> Having regard, however, to the very distressed condition of most of the industries of the Country, and that the scheme of the Scottish National Development Council is National in character, it was arranged that each Bank should make a non-recurring contribution of £100 on the footing that it was not to be precedent and that no further application would be made.

The general managers continued to refuse applications throughout the decade. They declined to assist the proposed Dundee Industrial Development Company in 1938, and in the same year they refused to support the Scottish Development Financial Trust in which Sir Steven Bilsland, chairman of the Union Bank, was deeply interested. Their decision, so the minute read, was taken after 'careful consideration'. They had supported in October 1936 the proposed Empire Exhibition, which opened in 1938 at Bellahouston Park – again an initiative of the Scottish Development

Council. Each bank agreed to join in the guarantee fund to the extent of £5,000 on the understanding that the sums from each bank would be aggregated as one total in the list of guarantees. By the time the Second World War began, the Scottish banks, whatever their shortcomings, which were not few, could at least repeat their version of the Abbé Sieyès on the terror years of the French revolution: 'J'ai vécu'; and that may be too harsh a judgement.

CHAPTER 20

CRISIS AND RECOVERY: BANK OF SCOTLAND, 1914–39

ANK OF SCOTLAND was much involved in the discussions which preceded and followed the declaration of war on 4 August 1914. The Governor, Lord Balfour of Burleigh, was one of the two Scottish bankers who explained to the authorities in Whitehall the importance of the note-issuing rights of the Scottish banks; and the Treasurer, Sir George Anderson, had been closely associated with the detailed negotiations initiated by the Bank of England and the Treasury concerning general financial policy in the early days of the war. 'I have had a very anxious and harassing fortnight', he wrote,

> Three visits to London – meaning six nights in the train – long conferences with the Chancellor of the Exchequer and his advisors, meetings with Bankers in London and with the Scotch managers in Edinburgh etc. The concessions and arrangements the Government have agreed for us and other Banks are generous and highly valuable and I am sanguine things will work smoothly and satisfactorily. But of course everything depends on the course of the war.[1]

The attendance record for the war years shows that around twelve directors regularly attended meetings of the main board and the weekly subcommittees.

The internal position of Bank of Scotland was a matter of concern. The value of the holdings of British government securities had fallen by £415,167, measured by current market value, against their cost price, and write-downs on other stocks were now £557,000. The total loss was now £979,995. Of the foreign stocks, an unknown figure, but not below £1.5 million, was 'virtually unsaleable' as no dividends were being received.

1 See above, Chapter 19, quotation from BS 1/21/26, Treasurer's Private Letter Book: Glasgow, Sir George Anderson to John Bisset, BS Glasgow Manager, 14 August 1914.

There were also substantial bad debts on domestic advances, but at this time they were mainly written in the books as good. This was the worst internal position among the eight Scottish banks. Nevertheless, some provision was made: the balance at the fund for losses stood at £1,462,089 and there was £370,000 in the contingent account, with smaller sums at the credit of the profit and loss. The paid-up capital, published reserve funds and dividend balances came to £2,631,910.[2] For the remainder of the war, provisions for losses took between 25 and 30 per cent of annual net profits. In the early months of the war, it is unclear exactly when, the directors agreed to announce to proprietors something of their concern, and their predicament will be appreciated. At a time of national emergency, it would have been irresponsible to announce anything which might have caused panic.

The first annual general meeting after the outbreak of war was held on 6 April 1915, the financial year having closed on 27 February 1915. The report of the Governor, who chaired the meeting, made somewhat mixed reading.[3] Lord Balfour of Burleigh had been Governor since 1904 – and continued as such until his death in 1921 – and noted in this first wartime statement that over the previous years he had reported steadily increasing profits, enlarged reserves and a rise in dividends. On this occasion, he offered the first public glimpse of the situation, caused, he said, 'by diminished receipts for Interest and Commissions from the London Office' as well as by bad debts from the London office. He then adverted to the growing problem over the previous fourteen or fifteen years, not unknown to the public, namely the steady depreciation in value of 'high-class securities', by which he was referring especially to British government securities for (figures on the internal Bank of Scotland position, see Tables 17.10, 17.11 and 20.1).[4] In the 1915 internal accounts, £144,790 of the net profits had already been appropriated to internal funds to cover losses. Lord Balfour now drew the attention of the proprietors to the fact that out of the declared profit, £294,099, the sum of £70,000 had been put to the credit of the investment account to offset this continued depreciation, and that £200,000 had been withdrawn from the reserve fund for the same purpose. He then referred to the published decline in the dividend, first making the point that over the previous dozen years dividends had been raised from 12 to 20 per cent, with income tax paid. Now the rate was

---

2 See Statistical Appendix, Tables A4 and A5, and Tables 17.9 and 17.10.
3 BS 1/2/3–4, Proprietors' Minutes. The reports of the annual meetings were published in a summary form, and there were often reports published in the newspapers.
4 See Statistical Appendix, Table A4. An interesting report, 'Proportion of Capital and Reserve to Deposits', *The Bankers' Magazine*, 99 (June 1915), 859–76, discusses the decrease in the value of British government securities, with an estimate that the total written off by the banks prior to 1914 was as high as '22 or even 23 millions' (p. 861).

Table 20.1 *Build-up of inner reserves, 1913–22*

Year ending 28 February	Balance at fund for losses	Contingent account
1913	854535 [1]	465000
1914	934284 [1]	500000
1915	1462089 [1]	370000
1916	1307100 [1]	370000
1917	2087731 [1]	370000
1918	2106551 [1]	0
1919	2468629	
1920	2734930	
1921	2919360	
1922	2371778	

Note:
1 See Table 17.10, notes 15–20.

Source: BS 1/94, General Ledgers.

being reduced to 16 per cent with a deduction of tax. As he noted, this was by now almost universal practice by banks in the UK.

This was the end of the 'melancholy side', and he suggested that the balance sheet had more attractive figures that could now be looked at. The banknote issue had risen steeply, as had the volume of deposits. The first war loan had been opened for subscription in November 1914 and the Bank had taken up some £2 million, the 10 per cent of its total deposits, as agreed by all the UK banks. General advances were considerably down, and, although he did not mention it, this included a reduction in loans to stockbrokers, again a common feature among all the Scottish banks at this time. The Governor concluded that the considerable amounts of money now available were going to put a great strain upon the directors in their search for 'safe and profitable employment'. In the event, as will be seen, for Bank of Scotland there was to be a long-term and very rapid rise in British government securities as a proportion of all investments.

The financial year 1915–16 showed broadly the same trends that had been set in train during the first six months of the war. Sir George Anderson was only too well aware of the position of the Bank vis-à-vis the other Scottish banks:

we may be very sure that they are not in the unhappy position of Bank of Scotland with millions of its money locked up at the London office from which not a farthing of revenue is coming. It is a fearful burden to have to carry, and I am struggling along with it as best I can amid many discouragements and disappointments. If I could only see progress in any one direction with these big accounts. But no: not one.[5]

5 BS 1/21/25, Treasurer's Private Letter Book, Sir George Anderson to W. Smiles, London office, 19 January 1916.

Profits were again down in the year, and they were to show a further fall in 1916–17 with net profits down to £384,257 and the declared profits also down somewhat. In 1918 there was a slight recovery, to be followed by sharp rises in net profits in 1919 and 1920. The dividend throughout the war years remained at 16 per cent, less tax. Depreciation of the value of investments continued, but there was a notable compensation included in the provisions of the second war loan. This was the remarkably generous introduction of 'conversion' rights. Lord Balfour commented at the 1916 AGM, when deploring the continued depreciation of invested values:

> But in future we will at any rate escape the heavy drain upon us caused by the persistent fall in the price of Consols. We have converted all our holding into the 4½ per cent War Loan Stock which has this three-fold advantage that it is compulsorily redeemable at par at a fixed date, carries a higher rate of interest, and must be accepted at par in payment of subscriptions for any further large loan the Government may issue.

This was a most important guarantee to the banking sector that it would be able to avoid significant losses, consequent on inflation, should the war last and it be required to buy more gilts. Most of the existing provision in the Bank's books against losses on these was now written out as a loss.

As in the previous year, to meet the heavy depreciation on investments and accept the losses associated with British government securities, money was moved out of declared profits – on this occasion the amount was £80,000 – and £150,000 was taken from the reserve fund, in addition to £117,002 from the net profits. Throughout the war, banknote issue continued to grow rapidly – the total in the year to February 1916 was 40 per cent higher than the previous year – and deposits continued to increase. These were trends common to all Scottish banks during the war: the note issue grew at a markedly inflationary rate; deposits increased steadily with fluctuations when the withdrawals for war loans were high; business advances were at a low level; and Bank of Scotland, along with all other banks, accepted defined obligations in connection with exchange operations with the USA, France and Russia. The Bank also responded to the Treasury's requests by disposing of its holdings of American dollar securities either to the Treasury or by selling in the open market. In the aftermath of the 1917 Bolshevik revolution in Russia, the banks, in general, suffered losses.

It was now an urgent matter to replace the Treasurer, Sir George Anderson, who had taken office in early December 1898 after being manager of the North of Scotland Bank at Aberdeen. Through a curious quirk in the history of Bank of Scotland, Anderson acted as Usher of the

White Rod at the coronation of Edward VII and received a knighthood in 1905.[6] It is always difficult to judge the changing abilities of leading managerial figures through their working lives, and no doubt Anderson had attracted the favourable attention of the directors of Bank of Scotland at the time of his appointment. In the years immediately before the First World War, however, and during the early war years, Anderson proved lacking in decision and judgement on the serious situation facing the Bank, as well as failing to impose firmer control from the centre. This latter characteristic was especially marked in his dealings with the London office and the Glasgow chief office, the two most important centres outside Edinburgh.

In the spring of 1916, the board appointed John Rae as assistant Treasurer with the understanding that he would take charge as Treasurer of the Bank in September 1916.[7] Sir George Anderson conveyed the news to William Smiles, the London manager, making the point that he wanted John Rae to find the Bank's affairs in as good order as possible:

There are a number of black spots at the London office, as you and I are too well aware, and some of them are very big spots. I am not very hopeful of much being done to improve the look of these during the next few weeks, but if anything can be accomplished I shall be very glad.[8]

The February 1917 figures were John Rae's first, and they made disappointing reading. In the five months to the balance day, he uncovered a total of 466 separate accounts which were henceforth listed as bad and doubtful debts totalling £2,359,862, against which, in the fund for losses, was £1,076,011.[9] Six months later, after a further review of accounts, John Rae decided that fifteen more had inadequate provision, and three debts, the Madeira–Mamore Railway Co., the Pará Construction Co. Ltd and the Port of Pará, which had been omitted from the February 1917 figures,

---

6 The office of Usher of the White Rod was originally vested in the family of Cockburn of Langton. It was later sold by auction and bought by a proprietor of Bank of Scotland, Sir Patrick Walker of Dalry, and it remained in the family until the death of the last male heir. The Bank then became trustees of the estate, and the Treasurer, after an inquiry by the Committee of Privileges, was permitted to deputise for the deceased baronet: C. A. Malcolm, *The Bank of Scotland, 1695–1945* (Edinburgh: n.d. [1948]), p. 252.
7 John Rae was born in Scotland in 1870. He worked first at the National Bank of Scotland, Dundee, and while there won first prize with honours in the examination of the Scottish Institute of Bankers. In 1891, he moved to Parr's Bank, Warrington. His exceptional talents were soon noticed: in 1902 he was appointed superintendent of branches, in 1911 assistant general manager, and on 1 May 1915 joint general manager. He formally resigned from Parr's Bank on 14 August 1916.
8 BS 1/21/25, January 1916.
9 BS 1/70A/6, Treasurer's Half-Yearly Statements.

now required provision of £396,166. There was further uncertainty over other foreign advances. At this time, almost one year into his tenure, John Rae felt compelled to complain that the position of one Glasgow account, a debt of £57,113, had not been 'truthfully represented'. The position overall, as he later informed the board, was 'unwieldy', and while 160 accounts were now closed, 'time and a considerable measure of good fortune' were required. The task, across much of the Bank's business and covering inquiries at many branches, revealed that local management in several branches, and in Glasgow chief office and in London in particular, had been making decisions with inadequate consideration by head office at the Mound. Rae's report on London in August 1918 explains some of this difficulty:

> As regards administration in London I think we have effected some improvement during the past six months. There has been a regrettable tendency to take unduly optimistic views regarding the safety of accounts and the value of securities held. I have expressed very strong views to the London management in this connection with the result that the following rectifications have been made by them after enquiry insisted on by head office.

	former valuation	present valuation
Denver & Salt Lake RR 1st 5% bonds:	20%	5%
Dominican Brewery Co., shares:	100%	50%
Minnesota & Ontario Power Co., shares:	85%	40%
Sir William Mackenzie's Guarantee:	£36,000	£6,500

> As I write this a letter has come in placing a value of twenty per cent instead of fifty per cent as hitherto on a block of securities with an added suggestion that they be treated for the present as of no value. Fortunately, we have made a provision of £10,000 for the particular debt of £25,000 of Bahia Tramways & Co. Ltd, and a similar provision of £17,500 for an associated account of similar amount – South American Securities Co., but this new opinion will occasion additional provision of say, £10,000, or possibly £25,000. In the bulk of these dormant and irregular accounts at London the Bank occupies a helpless position: but one could wish that London office were more alive to the necessity of keeping themselves in closer touch with conditions and opinions affecting the various commitments which are of a non-banking character.

The most serious problems of the foreign debts remained those owed by companies connected with Latin America. Through brokers in London who also worked for London County Westminster and Parr's Bank, John Rae tried to negotiate a conversion of the Brazil Railway loan into Brazil Government Funding 5% Bonds; 'if' completed, this would have liberated £400,000 of 'dead money as a marketable security'. This was not successful before the close of the war, but underlined the determination shown on the doubtful domestic accounts.

There were, throughout the reports by Lord Balfour, indications to those who followed banking affairs of some of the problems to which the Bank was subject during these years. In 1917, Lord Balfour made the first reference to the Latin American debt, which the conditions of war had greatly exacerbated. He himself was chairman of the São Paulo railway, in which the Bank had considerable investment. He could speak, he said 'in a feeling way of the detrimental incidence of the war'. At the 1917 AGM, the Bank capital was the same, at £1,325,000, the reserve fund was now down to £750,000, and the final dividend was cut, this time to £79,500. Gross trading income was a little above the 1914 figure, but higher interest paid to depositors and increased costs left profits lower. With internal appropriations of £109,500 declared, net profits were also down, to £258,369, the lowest figure since 1907. Two years later, at the annual general meeting in March 1919, Balfour made a long statement which bankers round the country, north and south of the Border, would have read with interest:

> You will have observed from the Report that as the outcome of a very searching scrutiny of the Bank's investments and loans the Directors have, in agreement with the Treasurer decided to take £135,000 for 'Contingencies' and to withdraw £200,000 from the Bank's reserve fund. The transactions which have occasioned this special provision were entered into prior to the war and before the present Treasurer assumed office. They are mainly connected with Mexico and Brazil, and you will easily realise that uncertainty exists in connection with both countries at the present time. It would have been easier and perhaps more pleasant to assume that nominal quotations for some of the securities concerned represent a real value and to have trusted to marketability being possible when conditions, disorganised by the war, had become more normal. What we have done, however, and done under competent advice, is to do our best to consider the intrinsic merits of these particular concerns and to make what we believe to be a very full provision for any eventual loss which we may sustain.

Lord Balfour then announced that Vincent Yorke, a London financier and director of London County Westminster and Parr's Bank, had agreed to join the board of the Bank. He was to remain a board member until 1928.

Two other financial changes of the war years need to be emphasised. The absorption of large subscriptions to war loans during the war meant that the Bank's total resources became heavily weighted towards British government stock. Before 1913, the proportion of government stock in total resources had fluctuated between 5 and 7 per cent, and between 25 and 30 per cent of all investments; from late 1915, gilts rose sharply to 24 per cent of resources by 1917 and to one-third by 1919 (see Figure 17.7 and

Table 20.2 Analysis of employment of Bank's resources,[1] 1909–36

Year	British government stocks	Other investments, debentures, etc.	Total investments	British government stocks as a percentage of total investments	Total resources of Bank of Scotland	British government stocks as a percentage of total resources
1909	1326000	3537000	4863000	27.27	21432000	6.19
1910	1326000	3398000	4724000	28.07	21872000	6.06
1911	1326000	3115000	4441000	29.86	21784000	6.09
1912	1326000	3303000	4629000	28.65	22099000	6.00
1913	1326000	3851000	5177000	25.61	22814000	5.81
1914	1326000	3951000	5277000	25.13	23690000	5.60
1915	1326000	4436000	5762000	23.01	24791000	5.35
1916	5309000	3809000	9118000	58.23	26930000	19.71
1917	6996000	3174000	10170000	68.79	28960000	24.16
1918	6931000	4300000	11231000	61.71	32133000	21.57
1919	12603000	3092000	15695000	80.30	37486000	33.62
1920	15313000	2664000	17977000	85.18	43312000	35.36
1921	13814000	2343000	16157000	85.50	46508000	29.70
1922	15788000	2274000	18062000	87.41	47027000	33.57
1923	19031000	1889000	20920000	90.97	44381000	42.88
1924	16621000	889000	17510000	94.92	40316000	41.23
1925	15236000	603000	15839000	96.19	39092000	38.97
1926	12858000	550000	13408000	95.90	37925000	33.90
1927	11775000	325000	12100000	97.31	37314000	31.56
1928	13345000	240000	13585000	98.23	37297000	35.78
1929	12499000	240000	12739000	98.12	38059000	32.84
1930	11335000	233000	11568000	97.99	38272000	29.62
1931	11325000	219000	11544000	98.10	38717000	29.25
1932	13284000	219000	13503000	98.38	37752000	35.19
1933	17039000	207000	17246000	98.80	40664000	41.90
1934	20721000	259000	20980000	98.77	42520000	48.73
1935	21179000	281000	21460000	98.69	42381000	49.97
1936	23182000	345000	23527000	98.53	43998000	52.69

Note:
1 Figures represent the average amount for the year.

Source: BS 1/70/14, Analysis of the resources of Bank of Scotland.

Table 20.2). The second interesting financial change is the relationship between London and Scotland. With total resources as the benchmark, London had around 26 to 27 per cent immediately before 1914, with Scotland between 45 and 47 per cent. London overtook Scotland in the four years 1917–20 inclusive and then for the rest of the inter-war years there was little between them, with Scotland in most years having a modest lead.

John Rae was a vigorous personality who brought new life into the top management of Bank of Scotland and was responsible for the close scrutiny of the investments and loans over the whole range of the Bank's activities. He expressed himself in very sharp terms to the management in London, which he clearly felt had a much too easy-going attitude towards its accounts and the value of securities held; and it was upon his insistence that Vincent Yorke was brought onto the board of directors. At the AGM of April 1920, it was announced that Rae would shortly retire from the Treasurership to take up a position with the London County Westminster and Parr's Bank but would take a seat on the board of Bank of Scotland; and he remained a director until his death in 1932. His successor was George J. Scott, who had been general manager of the Union Bank of Scotland for just a year, and who was to remain Treasurer until his retirement in 1934.

There was a quite remarkable and frank appreciation of John Rae by Lord Balfour in the report to the 1920 AGM:

> I say on behalf of myself and the Court that Mr. Rae has had a difficult task since he came to Edinburgh. When he came into the service of the Bank he found that as regards the situation of certain of the accounts the position was not as it had been represented to be, and if before coming to Edinburgh all the facts which he elicited had been previously made known to him, he would not, I believe, have accepted the office of Treasurer. In spite of these circumstances he became our Treasurer and continued in the Bank. For this the Proprietors can never be too grateful. It is not too much to say that he has made great sacrifices in remaining with us. He faced the task with great zeal and ability, and the anxiety entailed in the work he accomplished for the Bank of Scotland has told severely on his health.

It is noteworthy that Scott, when approached to succeed John Rae, made the unusual request – which was granted – for access to a number of accounts, including investments, depreciation and provision, the bad and doubtful debts and the irregular accounts in London and Glasgow.

The war years prompted many questions about the nature and character of the banking system, and several of the wartime and post-war inquiries into the financial structures of the UK discussed specifically the problems of the banks in the post-war world. The major banking amalgamations in England were the most obvious structural developments of the war years; and towards the end of the war, secret negotiations began between the Scottish general managers and treasurers on the need to build larger institutions both for increased post-war lending – which was expected – and to provide a stronger platform from which to rebuff English intrusions. These meetings were confined to a few senior officials and directors, and were often unrecorded in the ordinary banking records. There were two main questions that were considered. The Scottish banks could form closer associations between themselves – the possibility of one large bank was at least mentioned – or they should seek closer links with the English banks. James Tuke from the British Linen Bank debated and discussed these matters with his opposite numbers at Bank of Scotland and the Royal Bank, but, as with the discussions for a foreign-exchange bank, they were unsuccessful. The three banks most concerned were sufficiently close in size to encourage a number of what proved to be irreconcilable disagreements. Furthermore, the procedures negotiated by the Colwyn Committee were currently being considered in Whitehall and Threadneedle Street, and this may have hindered specifically Scottish amalgamations. In December 1918, the general manager of the Royal Bank 'unofficially and confidentially' talked the matter over with Lord Inchcape, who happened to be an extraordinary director of the Royal Bank and who advised the government alongside Lord Colwyn on amalgamation policy, and the message received was that further amalgamations 'were not for the present viewed with favour'.[10]

Bank of Scotland did not engage in any amalgamation negotiations in the immediate post-war years. More immediately, it was concerned with the revision of its own constitution. In 1917, the Union Bank of Scotland announced changes in its original 1830 contract of co-partnership – it had already been amended on several occasions – and adopted a constitution which brought that bank within most of the provisions of the Companies Act of 1908. Bank of Scotland had continued to operate within the original Act of 1695, subsequent Acts of the eighteenth century alongside decisions of the Court of Session, and the Bank of Scotland Act, 1873. There had been several amending Acts, mainly related to capital adjustments. The Bank of Scotland Act, 1920 (10 & 11 George V c.31) was a major reconstruction of its powers, and in its legal structure it followed mainly the Union Bank's revisions. In particular, it adopted the articles of association of a limited company, although it had always had the privilege of limitation of liability in the foundation Act of 1695: it was now permitted to open branches and establish managing or consulting

10 BS(BL), Uncatalogued, Special Committee of Directors, Minute Book, 1918. See above, Chapter 19.

committees and local boards anywhere in the UK and in other countries, and it was allowed to act as trustees for those of its customers who wished to avail themselves of its facilities. The Bank could now build roads and infrastructure, and conduct directly the business of any of the Bank's debtors. Obsolete rights and clauses were repealed, and among these was the famous provision which allowed those who invested in the Bank to become naturalised, a right which had been supported by the Court of Session but then, arguably, disallowed by a decision of the House of Lords in 1822. By an oversight, this right was still included in the Act of 1873. A few weeks later, the Royal Bank of Scotland also obtained an Act which revised in considerable measure its own existing constitution; and in 1920, it may be remarked that The Married Women's Property (Scotland) Act was passed which eliminated many of the constraints hitherto imposed upon them in matters of various contractual relationships. This enlarged, at least in the long term, the potential clientele of the Scottish banking community.[11]

The managerial changes introduced by John Rae, the deflation of 1920–1 and the rise in gilts were the prelude to a modest improvement that continued throughout the decade. The industrial and commercial background, as already remarked upon, was not encouraging, with only the late 1920s showing some signs of progress. Lord Balfour died in 1921 and was replaced as Governor by William J. Mure CB, the Deputy Governor, who himself died in 1924 after a long illness. Lord Elphinstone, a director since 1917, Lord Clerk Register of Scotland and Keeper of the Signet, and Deputy Governor from 1921, was created Governor, a post he held for over thirty years until retirement in 1955. New arrangements were now brought in for board committees. There was created a chairman of committees, who was to be available for consultation with the Treasurer at any time, and the first appointment went to William Whitelaw, a member of the Baird family, who was active on the boards of several railway companies. A Treasurer's committee, of four directors and the Governor, was continued. It was also agreed that the Governor and the Deputy Governor would have more limited duties than before, in consequence of the new role for the chairman of the committees. Several appointments at this time strengthened the connection of the Bank with trade and industry: Sir Robert Tuite Boothby, insurance manager, joined in 1922, James Gourlay, chairman of George Outram & Co., publisher of the *Glasgow Herald*, joined in 1926, and John Craig, from Colvilles, joined in 1930. Sir Ralph Anstruther, appointed Deputy Governor in 1924, was already deputy chairman of Nobel Industries.

---

11 See also A. W. Kerr, *History of Banking in Scotland*, 4th edn (London: 1926), especially ch. 31.

The single greatest difficulty facing the Bank for a few years after the war remained the debts from pre-war days. Negotiations continued with the borrowers, and in September 1919 James Dunn (who was to be knighted in 1921) and his associates offered £133,160 to buy the securities covering the debts for the Brazil Railway Co., nominally worth £596,000, held by the Bank against the debt of £410,000. Dunn also offered to buy the securities held for the debts of the Madeira–Mamore Railway Co., the Pará Construction Co. Ltd and the Port of Pará. The debts owed to the Bank on these three accounts were £396,166, the securities a nominal £624,000, and the offer was for £400,000. As acceptance would release funds set aside as provision for losses, the board 'unanimously' resolved in favour.[12] Dunn also offered to buy the Bank's position on the Barcelona Traction, Light & Power Co. Ltd, again for a considerable reduction on the face value of the securities, and other agreements were eventually concluded for pre-war debts. In July 1922, with the worst of the debt overhang removed, the board agreed to sell all foreign government holdings, and within a few years had run down its other foreign stocks.

The Bank was keen to extend advances to trade and industry after the war, and some considerable loans were negotiated. In the case of loans to E. D. Sassoon & Co. (£750,000) and the Burmah Oil Co. (£1,250,000), one of the directors, J. Turnbull Smith, asked that his objections to the size of the advances be minuted, and he was to resign in 1921, although he accepted appointment as an extraordinary director. Apart from these two facilities, the largest single advances in the immediate post-war years were to the Canadian Bank of Commerce (£1.5 million), the Airdrie Savings Bank (£500,000), Wm Younger, the drinks company, (£250,000–£300,000), Barry, Ostlere & Shepherd, linoleum manufacturers, Kirkcaldy (£200,000) and the Glebe Sugar Refining Co., Greenock (£263,000). The largest facility of all was given to the Standard Life Assurance Co. for £4,500,000 on a temporary basis while war bonds were realised. There were numerous facilities for a wide range of business in the £25,000–£100,000 range, many continuing long-standing connections from pre-war days. Advances to customers reached £18.1 million in February 1920 before falling later in the year.[13] As the deflation gathered pace, there were considerable reductions in demand for accommodation, which saw more funds diverted to British government securities. Demand from trade and industry picked up again in 1924 and grew steadily until a peak at the close of the decade. There were numerous

12 BS 1/6/1, Minutes, Weekly board, 30 September 1919, 23 November, 21 and 28 December 1920, 4 January and 1 March 1921.
13 See Statistical Appendix, Tables A5 and A8.

comments by senior managers concerning the reluctance by businessmen to avail themselves of the facilities offered by the Bank, and considerable non-price competition for new business. With the bad-debt position on a more satisfactory basis, the new Treasurer was modestly encouraging in his internal correspondence during his early years. To John Rae, for example, he wrote in March 1923: 'You will be greatly interested in the figures which I hope to show you on Tuesday next. You are aware, however, that we have gone on conservative lines, and you will be able to read between the lines. Our losses have been trifling, and altogether you will be pleased with what you see.' Much of the income generated in the post-war boom was placed to the inner reserves, and this policy was maintained; by 1929 the total reserves, published and unpublished, came to £4,473,696.[14] The decision by the board in 1922, to concentrate investments on British government securities, proved wise. Deflation and tight control of government expenditure helped to underpin the value of gilts, and they performed well for most of the decade, with narrow spreads between high and low prices.[15]

The board made one addition to capital. In December 1925, stock of £262,000 was issued, of which £175,000 was called up. The whole of the premium on the new issue of £332,500 was placed to the reserve fund. The following year, the Bank informed staff that it would finance staff purchases of stock at £4 10s, at the time when the stock was trading at £5 10s 4d. From January 1927, the Bank announced that henceforth all new staff would be required to join a staff assurance scheme to be run by the Scottish Amicable Life Assurance Society and the Scottish Widows Fund and Life Assurance Society. The Bank paid 30 per cent of the net premiums due on the policies. These benefits, together with the regular, secure employment offered by the profession, were most attractive.

It was later in the same year that negotiations began with the North of Scotland Bank concerning a possible amalgamation. It is not clear exactly when serious discussion commenced, but Scott wrote to Harvey H. Smith, the general manager of the North of Scotland at Aberdeen, on 9 November 1923 that he was intending to convey to his own board the discussions that had taken place so far; and he added that he expected they would want to meet for an exchange of views. Scott was very much concerned that, if the North of Scotland wished to seek an amalgamation, 'it should naturally be with the Bank of Scotland, as the oldest bank, provided the arrangements are agreeable to your board. You may take it

14 See Statistical Appendix, Table A7.
15 Pember and Boyle, *British Government Securities in the Twentieth Century: The First Fifty Years*, 2nd edn (private circulation, London: 1950), pp. 49–63. For figures for Bank of Scotland holdings of gilts, see Tables 20.4 and 20.5.

that we would not be prepared to enter into competition with any other institution, in the event of negotiations going so far.'[16]

Scott went on to suggest that the meeting should be in Edinburgh in order that attention should not be as easily aroused as by a deputation from Bank of Scotland going to Aberdeen, and a few days later he suggested a meeting in London in order to prevent any leakage of their negotiations. The directors of Bank of Scotland had established a committee to consider the proposals, and this included John Rae, who had been a member of the Colwyn Committee on Bank Amalgamations in 1918 – a not unhelpful fact, since the minutes of evidence given before the committee were never published and only many years later became available in the Public Record Office.[17] By mid-November, Smith had informed Scott that his directors wanted more time to consider the proposals; and, at the end of the month, having been informed that the North of Scotland Bank was proposing to discuss matters of negotiations with another bank, Scott thereupon ended the matter. The other interested bank was the Clydesdale, already in 'affiliation' with the Midland. The 'affiliation' of the North of Scotland Bank with the Midland was later agreed, but without any merger between it and the Clydesdale Bank.[18]

A more serious set of negotiations began early in 1924 between Bank of Scotland and the Union Bank. The general manager of the latter was Norman L. Hird, who showed himself a man of great vigour and appreciable insight into the problems of the contemporary banking world, being hesitant about the return to gold in 1925. What he proved unable to achieve was a significant improvement in the performance of the Union Bank compared with the other Scottish banks, and just as unfortunate was his manner of working, which created difficulties among his own senior staff as well as in the wider banking community. There were good reasons for negotiations between Bank of Scotland and the Union Bank. Beyond Edinburgh, Glasgow was the most important business centre for Bank of Scotland, and strengthening a banking position in the western region would make very good sense. Moreover, not only in Glasgow but also elsewhere there was a considerable overlap of branches, and a merger would allow for the possibilities of reducing costs. By mid-April 1924, George Scott had arranged a meeting in London with John Rae, Alexander Wallace and Sir Ralph Anstruther (soon to be elected Deputy Governor)

16 BS 1/21/21A, Treasurer's Private Letter Book, George Scott to H. H. Smith, General Manager, North of Scotland Bank, 9, 13 and 17 November 1923.
17 PRO, T 1/12267/50326/18.
18 The story of the amalgamation of the North of Scotland with the Clydesdale is recorded in C. W. Munn, *Clydesdale Bank: The First One Hundred and Fifty Years* (Glasgow: 1988), pp. 158–9; and see above, Chapter 19.

from Bank of Scotland, and Norman Hird and his committee from the Union Bank.[19] Matters looked to be going well, and Scott inquired of Rae what procedures had to be followed to meet the government's regulations concerning amalgamation: 'is it all done in writing?', he asked, 'and how long a time is needed for consideration? Is it a matter that you could carry through for us more expeditiously than we ourselves could do? The difficulty is to keep the thing quiet.' On 22 April 1924, Scott apprised the Governor of the basic terms of their agreement:

> we had no difficulty in adjusting figures on the basis of the assets of each, excluding goodwill in both cases. It is proposed that we give our stock with a cash payment. £112:10/- of our Stock for £100 of theirs with £4 per £100 share in cash in addition. We are all satisfied that these items are quite fair to both. We retain the name, the Head Office here, and the Board will meet here. Details are still to be adjusted.[20]

The Governor was asked to destroy this letter. Within a few days, the issue was raised which in this first round of talks was to bring negotiations to an end. This was the position of the Treasurer, which Bank of Scotland insisted must be one individual at the Mound. By early May 1924, Scott was writing to Rae explaining that 'a full fusion with one head was more than they were at present prepared for', but he added that he expected matters to be reconsidered at some time in the future. Negotiations then faltered for three years.

On 7 June 1927, George Scott wrote to John Rae with the information that the proposal had been raised again from the Union Bank side. The board, he explained, was unanimously in agreement in principle about the proposed merger, subject to two conditions. These were, first, that the known extensive connections of the Union Bank with west-of-Scotland industry were adequately provided for in their inner reserves; and, second, that on no account would Norman Hird be employed in any capacity. Scott wrote on the same day to the Governor, Lord Elphinstone:

> The Directors were all agreed on the principle of amalgamation: the basis would be arrived at after careful analysis of the respective positions. Meantime, the condition our board lay down is that we shall not take over into our service, Mr Hird . . . It is a very stiff qualification but our Board are not prepared to have Mr Hird as Treasurer later or as Assistant now.[21]

Negotiations continued for a few days only, ending with the Union Bank again pulling out. Scott, at least, wanted the proposals to succeed,

19 BS 1/21/21A, Treasurer's Private Letter Book, George Scott to Alexander Wallace, 14 April; to Norman Hird, 15 and 21 April 1924.
20 Ibid., George Scott to Mure, 22 April 1924.
21 Ibid., 7 June 1927.

and he was prepared to compromise over the position of Hird, which might include compensation. Discussions were reopened in December 1927, and in mid-January 1928 George Scott reported to John Rae on a visit from Lord Novar of the Union Bank board, who seemed 'entirely with us' and was afraid that if negotiations failed again there might well be an offer from an English bank; Novar himself was much in favour of a 'national institution' which embraced Edinburgh and Glasgow. There was still being discussed from the Union Bank side the idea of an arrangement similar to the 'affiliation' principle that was used between certain English and Scottish banks, but Bank of Scotland was unanimously against this. Again the proposals came to an end in April 1928, only to be reopened between September and October 1930. Certain of the assumptions held by the Bank board can be explained by the following extracts from a letter written on 21 October 1930 by the Governor, Lord Elphinstone, to the Rt Hon. The Viscount Novar:

> It is, I think, very important that we keep constantly before us the main object sought to be gained by the amalgamation of the two Banks viz. the formation of a large Institution which, both from the size of its resources, and from the widespread network of its branch system would appeal to the Scottish people as in every sense a national Institution. This object will not be attained so long as the two Banks are separate, and none of the advantages of amalgamation will be secured so long as they exist in that state . . . we now suggest to you:
>
> 1. That 'fusion' of the two institutions should take place within one year, or, at the most, within two years.
> 2. That the price to be offered should be on the basis of exchange of the Stocks in proportion to the respective real values of the surplus Assets of the two Banks (excluding Goodwill) to be ascertained by mutually agreed valuation; along with perhaps a moderate cash payment to the Union Bank Shareholders as an inducement to exchange their holdings, always assuming that the earning power of the Union Bank . . . be adequate to provide a margin of profit, after deducting all Charges and Dividends, sufficient to repay this cash payment in a limited number of years.
> 3. That the representatives of the Board of the Bank of Scotland and its Executive should have full information as to the Advances, Investment, and all other business of the Union Bank during the period of affiliation; and, in particular, that all advances for say £5,000 or over should be reported to the Board of the Bank of Scotland by special Return; and that advances of £25,000 or over should be approved by the Bank of Scotland Board or, in case of emergency, by their Treasurer, before being granted . . .[22]

And there the matter rested until 1945.

22 BS 1/21/22, George Scott to the Viscount Novar, 21 November 1930.

All Scottish banks were affected in varying ways by the slump of 1930–2. The relatively poor performance of the Scottish economy compared with the UK overall had already acclimatised the bankers to the exceptional, chronic difficulties facing the traditional industries. Because of the exposure of the banking sector, there were mounting bad and doubtful debts which took several years to run off. There were no exceptions among the banks, although the Commercial Bank weathered these years somewhat more easily.[23] The slump affected Scottish banking profits in absolute terms, and from 1931 there was a sharp fall in profits as a percentage of deposits. Bank of Scotland was the worst-affected: gross trading profits fell by 10 per cent in the year to 1930 and were cut further as many firms connected with the Bank failed to make interest payments or went into liquidation; in 1932, profits were down to just 62 per cent of the 1928 and 1929 figures. The crisis required provision of almost £365,000 in the three years to 1932, although this was well covered by the reserves (see Figure 20.3).

The experience of the slump and the preceding years of economic laggardliness in Scotland confirmed the board in its decisions on inner reserves. The collapse of many companies overseas at this time also underlined the correctness of the withdrawal from investment in foreign stocks. There was now, in 1931, a reiteration that the Bank would invest surplus deposits not required for ordinary lending in British government securities. The Bank's holding of gilts had performed above the cost price after 1922. From 1931 to 1933, the board bought over £9 million (see Tables 20.4 and 20.5). By February 1933, the cost price of the holding, £20.3 million, showed a market-value surplus of £3.4 million, and by 1935 this had grown by another £2 million. This was a very strong position on gilts, which also yielded higher rates of income than prevailing short-term loans on the London money markets. As a percentage of total investments, British government securities stayed just above 98 per cent and hardly altered before 1938–9. As a proportion of total resources, this was just over 35 per cent in 1932, and it remained around this figure for the rest of the decade.[24] There were only three Scottish banks by 1938–9 with significant proportions of non-British government securities as a percentage of their total investment – the Royal Bank, Clydesdale Bank and the Union Bank with proportions of 17.7, 41.5 and 21.2 per cent respectively. Bank of Scotland at the same period, on the last balance sheet before the outbreak of the Second World War, had 3.6 per cent

23 For figures in this paragraph, see Statistical Appendix, Tables A7, A13 and A15.
24 BS 1/70/14, Analysis of the resources of the Bank of Scotland; for an excellent general discussion of the investment ratios of the Scottish banks, see M. Gaskin, *The Scottish Banks: A Modern Survey* (London: 1965), especially chs 9 and 10.

Figure 20.3 Bank of Scotland net business profits per annum[1] as a percentage of total public liabilities compared to all Scottish banks, 1878–1935

All — - — - Bank of Scotland

Note:
1. Net business profits consisted of published net profits less 4 per cent on capital and reserve.

of its total investments in non-British government securities; and the corresponding percentage for the National Bank, the Commercial Bank and the North of Scotland Bank were 5.0, 1.2 and 3.6 respectively.[25]

Bank of Scotland's approach to industrial lending remained similar during and after the slump. Companies were carried through this period in the expectation of improvement, although this was often a slow process. The board decided that more expertise on conditions in the west of Scotland was required, and John Craig's appointment in 1930 was followed by Samuel Crawford Hogarth, a Glasgow shipowner, in 1932 and by Sir Michael Nairn, with his expertise in linoleum, in 1935. By this time, the board thus had excellent connections with the financial sectors in Glasgow and Edinburgh and with railways, steel, chemicals, shipowning and shipbuilding, engineering and publishing.[26]

It is never easy to assess the role of the board of directors compared with that of the Treasurer and Secretary and other leading managers. Indeed, except for certain well-documented periods, decision-making in practice has often been somewhat obscure, involving many individuals and never showing quite clearly where initial ideas originate. It has been much easier to follow the process once agreements on direction have been decided by the board. There were clear changes associated with the time of John Rae, notably a firm control from head office at the Mound over all lending in London, Glasgow and elsewhere through the Inspectors Department. Unannounced visits became more frequent, and managers of branches were allowed less freedom to make choices on how to classify advances and debts. These changes were reinforced under the tenure of George J. Scott. The second change concerned investments: from these years, all decisions on investments, policy and specific purchases were decided by the directors through the Treasurer's committee and the investments committee. There was no role for the London office. These changes marked out an effective line of command and decision-making process which stood the Bank well in the inter-war years. This did mean that some opportunities, which might have been taken up in earlier years, were now lost. One such arose in October 1929 when George Scott proposed to John Rae that they join with interests in Canada to form a new bank there.[27] Angus McLean, a Scot living in New Brunswick, had been granted a charter by

25 The collected data for all the Scottish banks in the financial year prior to the beginning of the Second World War are set out in T. Balogh, *Studies in Financial Organisation* (Cambridge: 1947), p. 117.

26 See J. Scott and M. Hughes, *The Anatomy of Scottish Capital: Scottish Companies and Scottish Capital, 1900–1979* (London: 1980), who noticed that, soon after the war, the main links between Edinburgh investment companies and banking and insurance were via the board of Bank of Scotland and the mutual assurance companies Standard Life, Scottish Widows and Scottish Provident (p. 79).

27 BS 1/21/22, Treasurer's Private Letter Book: General, George Scott to John Rae, 29 and 31 October 1929.

Table 20.4 Bank of Scotland holdings of British government and other stocks, 1915–24

	1915				1916			
	Amount of stock (nominal value)	Price in books [1]	Proceeds at market value	Balance [2]	Amount of stock (nominal value)	Price in books	Proceeds at market value	Balance
War Loan 3.5% Stock 1925–8	1978600	1879670	1879670	0	1980000	1888575	1888575	0
War Loan 4.5% Stock 1925–45					4000000	3965000	3965000	0
War Loan 5%					600000	578085	578085	0
Exchequer 3% Bonds								
Exchequer 5% Bonds								
Exchequer 5.75% Bonds								
Exchequer 6% Bonds								
National War Bonds 5% Redeemable								
National War Bonds 4% Repayable								
Funding Loan 4%								
Victory Bonds 4%								
Treasury Bonds 5.5% Repayable								
Treasury Bonds 4.5%								
Treasury Bonds 5%								
Conversion Loan 3.5%								
India 3% Stock	27700	27423	19598	-7825	27700	27423	19058	-8365
Consols	1335350	1325876	910709	-415167				
All stocks (including British government)		7233734	6253739	-979995		9671552	8964409	-707143

	1917				1918			
	Amount of stock (nominal value)	Price in books [1]	Proceeds at market value	Balance [2]	Amount of stock (nominal value)	Price in books	Proceeds at market value	Balance
War Loan 3.5% Stock 1925–8	1980000	1895833	1877370	-18463	1980000	1781000	1781000	0
War Loan 4.5% Stock 1925–45	2613401	2585000	2585000	0	2750931	2585000	2585000	0
War Loan 5%					2503459	2127812	2495634	367822
Exchequer 3% Bonds	600000	582955	582955	0	600000	582955	582955	0
Exchequer 5% Bonds	1380000	1380000	1380000	0				
Exchequer 5.75% Bonds								
Exchequer 6% Bonds								
National War Bonds 5% Redeemable	1600000	1600000	1600000	0	1600000	1600000	1600000	0
National War Bonds 4% Repayable					2305000	2305000	2305000	0
Funding Loan 4%								
Victory Bonds 4%								
Treasury Bonds 5.5% Repayable								
Treasury Bonds 4.5%					1500000	1509885	1575000	65115
Treasury Bonds 5%					2024400	2048528	2075010	26482
Conversion Loan 3.5%					4380000	2829023	3309637	480614
India 3% Stock					27700	27423	15304	-12119
Consols	27700	27423	14937	-12486				
All stocks (including British government)		11246127	10245949	-1000178		12856400	11874519	-981881 [3]

Table 20.4 continued

	1919				1920			
	Amount of stock (nominal value)	Price in books [1]	Proceeds at market value	Balance [2]	Amount of stock (nominal value)	Price in books	Proceeds at market value	Balance
War Loan 3.5% Stock 1925-8	1980000	1781000	1781000	0	1980000	1781000	1781000	0
War Loan 4.5% Stock 1925-45	2750931	2585000	2585000	0	2750931	2585000	2585000	0
War Loan 5%	3694921	3283598	3674752	391154				
Exchequer 3% Bonds	825000	808401	763558	-44843	825000	808401	755901	-52500
Exchequer 5% Bonds	800000	800000	800000	0	800000	800000	800000	0
Exchequer 5.75% Bonds					800000	800000	800000	0
Exchequer 6% Bonds	3650000	3667911	3667911	0				
National War Bonds 5% Redeemable	4121750	4121750	4121750	0	4132900	4132900	4132900	0
National War Bonds 4% Repayable	250000	253682	253682	0	250000	253300	253300	0
Funding Loan 4%					625000	498337	437500	-60837
Victory Bonds 4%					1310300	1110267	1061343	-48924
Treasury Bonds 5.5% Repayable								
Treasury Bonds 4.5%	979800	984609	963878	-20731				
Treasury Bonds 5%	2024400	2048528	2037052	-11476				
Conversion Loan 3.5%	4380000	2829023	3285000	455977				
India 3% Stock	27700	27423	16862	-10561	27700	27423	13919	-13504
Consols								
All stocks (including British government)		16889862	15986420	-903442 [4]		16233898	15125884	-1108014 [5]

	1921				1922			
	Amount of stock (nominal value)	Price in books [1]	Proceeds at market value	Balance [2]	Amount of stock (nominal value)	Price in books	Proceeds at market value	Balance
War Loan 3.5% Stock 1925–8	1980000	1781000	1743500	–37500	1780000	1608438	1570938	–37500
War Loan 4.5% Stock 1925–45	2750931	2585000	2347690	–237310	3392931	3144784	3144784	0
War Loan 5%								
Exchequer 3% Bonds	250000	250000	197500	–52500	250000	250000	197500	–52500
Exchequer 5% Bonds	800000	800000	792500	–7500				
Exchequer 5.75% Bonds	2400000	2373637	2382000	8363				
Exchequer 6% Bonds								
National War Bonds 5% Redeemable	4132900	4132900	4097600	–35300	6407900	6409020	6373720	–35300
National War Bonds 4% Repayable	250000	252912	250712	–2200	250000	252524	247969	–4555
Funding Loan 4%	625000	498337	441015	–57322	625000	498337	442016	–56321
Victory Bonds 4%	1310300	1110267	1011388	–98879				
Treasury Bonds 5.5% Repayable					4687850	4553354	4553354	0
Treasury Bonds 4.5%								
Treasury Bonds 5%								
Conversion Loan 3.5%								
India 3% Stock								
Consols								
All stocks (including British government)		16105591	14452727	–1652864 [6]		18996685	17755506	–1239179 [7]

Table 20.4 *continued*

	1923				1924			
	Amount of stock (nominal value)	Price in books [1]	Proceeds at market value	Balance [2]	Amount of stock (nominal value)	Price in books	Proceeds at market value	Balance
War Loan 3.5% Stock 1925-8	1780000	1708438	1691000	-17438	1780000	1708438	1697675	-10763
War Loan 4.5% Stock 1925-45								
War Loan 5%	2503459	2127812	2495634	367822	3694921	3283598	3674752	391154
Exchequer 3% Bonds	1000000	1010197	1055625	45428	200000	204095	182250	-21845
Exchequer 5% Bonds								
Exchequer 5.75% Bonds								
Exchequer 6% Bonds								
National War Bonds 5% Redeemable	4046750	4075278	4286160	210882	3346750	3376703	3521175	144472
National War Bonds 4% Repayable	350000	352824	353062	238	350000	352436	353437	1001
Funding Loan 4%	625000	498337	544375	46038	625000	498337	537812	39475
Victory Bonds 4%								
Treasury Bonds 5.5% Repayable	200000	204095	183250	-20845	1500000	1509885	1547812	37927
Treasury Bonds 4.5%	1500000	1509885	1575000	65115	979800	984609	963878	-20731
Treasury Bonds 5%	2024400	2048528	2075010	26482	2024400	2048528	2037052	-11476
Conversion Loan 3.5%	4380000	2829023	3309637	480614	4380000	2829023	3285000	455977
India 3% Stock								
Consols								
All stocks (including British government)		18378276	16727814	-1650462 [8]		17339827	18191684	796857 [9]

Notes:

1 Price in books was price paid when purchased by the Bank.
2 Balance = market value less price in books.
3 Increased to £997651 by net accrued dividends of £15770.
4 Increased to £952196 by net accrued dividends of £48754.
5 Increased to £1199626 by net accrued dividends of £88612.
6 This was reduced to £1239179 by £171239 provision for stocks sold and £280000 appreciation.
7 This was reduced to £900974 by deduction of £438205 provision for stocks already sold, less £100000 sum transferred from 3.5 per cent war loan to reverse entry at 28 February 1918 when that stock was written down from profits.
8 Reduced to £805868 through over-provision/surplus on stocks sold.
9 Reduced to £601109 through over-provision/surplus on stocks sold.

Source: BS, Uncatalogued, Views of Stocks.

Table 20.5 *Bank of Scotland holdings of British government securities and other stocks, 1925–53*

	British government securities				All stocks (including British government)			
	Price in books [1]	Proceeds at market price	Balance sheet figure	Provision made in Fund for losses (i.e. difference between cost and balance sheet figure)	Price in books	Proceeds at market price	Balance sheet figure	Provision made in Fund for losses (i.e. difference between cost and balance sheet figure)
1925	12780881	[2]	12434697	346184	13370020		12774949	595071
1926	11975391	12969691	11645987	329404	12444680	13220463	11873087	571593
1927	11606943	12475040	11277539	329404	11851852	12694633	11471588	380264
1928	13548812	14493574	13220471	328341	13788419	14713584	13409414	379005
1929	10773152	11523224	10580672	192480	11012759	11742330	10769516	243243
1930	11135052	11854944	10998227	136825	11353766	12048135	11168454	185312
1931	13080778	13902263	12917636	163142	13299592	14098215	13087467	212125
1932	13598982	14561871	13398680	200302	13817796	14750351	13566388	251408
1933	20315288	23758106	20126207	189081	20504983	23935468	20272290	232693
1934	20908555	25139322	20677555	231000	21188083	25421254	20915963	272120
1935	22000107	27547552	21735321	264786	22277241	27832845	21969927	307314
1936	23429055	28396838	23109895	319160	24315990	29283226	23934333	381657
1937	24419722	27813618	23986983	432739	25856653	29202037	25334292	522361
1938	24860292	28649631	24427716	432576	26297223	30060179	25775025	522198
1939	24364757	26636765	23971672	393085	25801688	28005077	25333598	468090
1940	25233176	28265660	25103862	129314	26670107	29664790	26497123	172984
1941	27789411	31492818	27744352	45059	29019355	32689936	28939431	79924
1942	31284729	35404387	31245824	38905	32164727	36258534	32095537	69190
1943	35604403	39790886	35584833	19570	36449950	40622222	36413295	36655
1944	39478508	43157052	39407465	71043	40322055	40245008	40245008	77047
1945	44374054	48616563	44352462	21592	45223710	49469250	45196620	27090
1946	47846826	52999729	47827999	18827	48718775	53888315	48699948	18827
1947	53149604	59598138	52864208	285396	54038381	60519952	53752985	285396
1948	51954478	55006630	51378394	576084	53370668	56350240	52720185	650483
1949	53449299	57353518	53075322	373977	57427763	61248610	56911813	515950
1950	53604867	52886108	51267982	2336885	58871257	57693487	56074885	2796372
1951	48251413	48060424	46613390	1638023	53517275	52886649	51436014	2081261
1952	45296075	41718471	[2]	3577604 [3]	50561411	46122920	[2]	4438491 [3]
1953	43603398	41092420	[2]	2510978 [3]	54099661	50948343	[2]	3151318 [3]

Notes:
1 Price in books was price paid when purchased by the Bank.
2 This figure was unavailable from this source due to a change in accounting practice.
3 Difference between cost and market value.

Source: BS, Uncatalogued, Views of Stocks.

the Canadian government for the launch of a bank to fund small business, to be known as the Eastern Bank of Canada, New Brunswick. There was some support from interests in Chicago. Lord Elphinstone had little hesitation in turning the proposal down, and John Rae raised appropriate questions about safeguards and accountability. In common with the other Scottish banks, new branches were opened in the inter-war years: seven in Glasgow, eight in Edinburgh and twenty-two elsewhere in Scotland. Some proved barely profitable and were closed during the Second World War.

By this time, George Scott was heavily involved in the worsening industrial situation. The views of the bank were explained by Sir Ralph Anstruther on 1 April 1930, deputising for Lord Elphinstone who was returning from Ceylon. There were references to the difficulties of trade and industry, and the collapse of the share boom in New York and the high rates of 1929 were much regretted: 'neither good for industry nor for the Banks'. It was now expected that 'trade and industry should materially benefit by cheap credit, although we must not be misled by the idea that this alone will remove our difficulties'.[28] A welcome was given to the attempts to reorganise the cotton and other industries, and the appointment of the Macmillan Committee was noted. In respect of advances, Sir Ralph informed proprietors that Bank of Scotland had advanced to agriculture £1.2 million among 2,170 customers, with a similar sum to the grain and foodstuffs trades. A total of £13 million was lent on various securities to 6,800 customers, and another £3 million to 3,900 on no security, 'the bank relying, in accordance with banking principles in Scotland, upon its knowledge of the character and resources of its customers'. The summary breakdown of the total advances of £16.7 million for 1931 was given, with the note that this showed a decrease of £1.1 million 'which was to be anticipated in view of the depressed state of industry and the resulting diminished demand for credit'. The call for a 'substantial reduction of national expenditure so as to relieve some of the burden of taxation' was a not uncommon call by businessmen in these years. There was a further decline in advances in the following year.

In submitting the directors' report at the annual general meeting on 4 April 1933, Lord Elphinstone also produced an interesting statement which included a listing of the Bank's advances and which can broadly be compared with the earlier classification given to the Macmillan Committee (see Table 20.6). Lord Elphinstone began his report by underlining the depressing state of the world economy and noting that the imposition of tariffs and the Ottawa Agreements, while benefiting Britain in the short run, would encourage the unfortunate practice of economic nationalism throughout the world. International trade could not be expected to be stimulated. When he turned to the Bank's position, he first noted that deposits had shown a substantial increase over the previous year – a common experience for the banking community – and that for Bank of Scotland they now stood at the highest figure since 1922. Liquid assets totalled 80 per cent of all liabilities, with advances inevitably well down on the previous year to a little above £10 million. The experience, common to Bank of Scotland as to most other banks, was the inability of

28 BS 1/2/3–4, Minutes of meetings of Proprietors, 1 April 1930.

Table 20.6 Classification of Bank of Scotland advances: 1930, 1931 and 1933[1]

Category	1930		1931		1933		
	Amount advanced	Amount as percentage	Amount advanced	Amount as percentage	Amount advanced	Amount as percentage	Portion of advances unsecured
Farmers and livestock salesmen	1200000 [2]	7.50	1274000	7.62	1202000	11.55	340000 [7]
Produce importers/grain trade	1000000 [3]	6.25	1100000	6.58	277000	2.66	22000 [8]
Merchants	2000000	12.50	1300000	7.77	3158000	30.34	232000 [9]
Insurance and investment companies and stockbrokers			1100000	6.58			[10]
Timber			90000–1000000	0.54–5.98	168000	1.61	33000 [10]
Fishing			90000–1000000	0.54–5.98			[11]
Iron, coal and steel			90000–1000000	0.54–5.98			
Engineering, gas, electricity, motors			90000–1000000	0.54–5.98	1379000	13.25	287000
Shipping and shipbuilding			90000–1000000	0.54–5.98	574000	5.52	93000
Textile, jute, leather, chemicals			90000–1000000	0.54–5.98	1359000	13.06	230000 [8]
Distillers and brewers			90000–1000000	0.54–5.98	197000	1.89	54000
Public accounts					862000	8.28	264000
Unclassified (a) for general business purposes					1231000	11.83	229000
Unclassified (b) for private purposes							
Miscellaneous			7000000 [5]	41.86			
Total	£16000000 [4]		£16722000 [6]		£10407000		£1784000 [12]

Notes:

1 The figures provided at the annual general meetings of 1930 and 1931 were limited and approximate.

2 The number of customers in this category was 2,170.

3 This is an approximate figure (described in the original source as 'a similar sum' to farmers and livestock salesmen).

4 Distributed among 10,700 customers, of which £13,000,000 was advanced to 6,800 customers on security of a varied nature and £3,000,000 was advanced to 3,900 customers unsecured.

5 The number of customers in this category was 6,000.

6 This total is taken from the published balance sheet as it was not stated in the source, there being only a general statement concerning the number of borrowers: 'Out of 10,600 borrowers 4,300 had overdrafts of £2,100,000 in all without collateral security ... out of a total of 1,900 farmers nearly fifty per cent had unsecured accommodation'.

7 The farming industry ... continues to use its normal figures of over £1,000,000 ... of this amount on a recent date no fewer than 1,316 farmers had unsecured overdrafts for in all £244,273 ...'

8 The classification was changed to 'Merchants, distillers and brewers' in 1933.

9 The classification also included advances on stocks and shares in 1933.

10 The classification was changed to 'Timber and fishing' in 1933.

11 The classification was changed to 'Iron, coal, steel and quarrying' in 1933.

12 The total number of customers with unsecured advances was 5,448.

Source: BS 1/2/3, Proprietors' Minutes, 1908–37.

customers to use the credits at their disposal. In the particular case of the Bank, it was the accounts of those extensively engaged in international trade which showed a dramatic fall in their requirements. The only exception remarked on was the farming industry, 'which continued to use its normal figures of over £1,000,000. It will interest many to know that of this amount on a recent date no fewer than 1,316 farmers had unsecured overdrafts for in all £244,273.' It was a serious attempt by the Governor to explain why the Bank acted as it did, and why general economic conditions militated against a recovery.

He then introduced the figures in Table 20.6 and commented 'that what will surprise some critics of the banks are the number and extent of overdrafts granted without actual security'. Lord Elphinstone concluded the business part of his report with a general comment that offers an insight into some minds of the banking world:

> In view of the criticism which is made from time to time on the dividends paid by the banks, not only by anonymous correspondents to the Press, but by some business men, I should perhaps take the opportunity of saying a word on this subject. Although on our paid-up Capital we pay a dividend of 18 per cent, less Tax, this is by no means what we really pay on the investment of our Stockholders. In a recent volume on Banking and Finance by a distinguished man in the industrial world, amongst other interesting figures he stated that he calculated that in the case of the English Clearing Banks the real Capital, by which he meant the Paid-Up Capital and the outer and inner reserves, is about four times the Paid-Up Capital of the Banks. If his figures are at all near the mark, it means that our Stockholders are really getting not 18 per cent, but 4½ per cent, less Tax, and I venture to say that few would consider such a return excessive. If it be asked why the Banks should accumulate such heavy Reserves, we have only to contrast the experience of this country and the manner in which our Banks passed through the War period and the troubled years which have followed, with recent events in the financial crisis of the United States. I feel sure that in view of my remarks the Public will be satisfied that the real dividends are not without justification, and that the conservative policy of the British Banks has been entirely to the advantage of the country.[29]

This was a most important point that required to be made, to reassure proprietors that the practice on internal reserves was correct, indeed essential.

There are several observations to be made of the classification data, and, while the listing provided for the Macmillan Committee does not fit exactly the headings of the 1933 report, they are close enough for reasonable comparisons to be made. The most notable item in 1933

29 Ibid., 1933.

was the high proportion of all advances in the column which included stockbrokers and advances on stocks and shares. In 1929–30, the figure for six Scottish banks had been 23.8 per cent of all advances against 14.4 per cent for the English clearing banks; by 1933, at the depth of the economic slump, the proportion for Bank of Scotland was just over 30 per cent. On 7 March 1930, when George Scott was giving evidence before the Macmillan Committee, he revealed that the latest figure for these kinds of advances was 'nearly twenty per cent' of the total advanced (Q. 2,769), and he also noted the low proportion under the general heading of industry. As Table 20.6 shows, this was also the situation in 1933, but that was to be expected. The advances to farming were relatively high, as indeed they had always been compared with the English figures. In 1929–30, the Scottish figures for agriculture and fishing were 7.2 per cent of the total advances compared with 6.9 per cent for the English banks, while in Bank of Scotland's listing for 1933 farmers and livestock salesmen took 11.5 per cent of all advances, with a high proportion of the advances being unsecured. Bank of Scotland after its absorption of the Central Bank in 1868 and the Caledonian Bank in 1907 had a particular standing within the Highlands and Islands, although there is no indication concerning the direction of agricultural advances, whether to owner-occupiers or to farming tenants. In the 1950s, something approaching four-fifths of all farming advances were to owner-occupiers.[30] Overall advances were still down at £10 million in 1935. The following year, with £12 million advanced, the Governor could only lament that there was 'no evidence of any substantial increase in the general demand for loans. We would gladly welcome such a demand upon us on the part of those entitled to credit, as we would much rather lend to our customers than be compelled to increase our holdings of Government securities.'

Unfortunately, the impression of the Scottish bankers' evidence to the Macmillan Committee, as well as the decisions of the General Managers Committee discussed in the previous chapter, reinforces the view that the banks were averse to lending. They were quite the opposite, but conditions were such before 1935–6 that businesses made hesitant borrowers, even at the low rates of interest then prevailing. The 1925 issue of new stock brought the paid-up capital to £1,500,000. An extraordinary meeting of the proprietors on 21 December 1937 agreed to a further issue of £150,000 of stock (of which £100,000 was fully paid up), and the resulting paid-up capital of £1,600,000 was later converted into fully-paid stock by the transfer of £800,000 from reserves. The fully paid-up capital of Bank of

30 Gaskin, *The Scottish Banks*, p. 158, quoting G. F. Hendry, 'Bank Advance to Scottish Agriculture', *Scottish Agricultural Economics*, vol. vi (Edinburgh: 1955), p. 41.

Scotland was now £2,400,000, and at that level it was the lowest in subscribed capital of all the Scottish banks save for the British Linen Bank. The new dividend on the fully paid-up stock was reduced to 12 per cent from April 1938, less tax. George Scott had already retired in October 1934, having been Treasurer for nearly fourteen years, and A. W. Morton Beveridge was appointed in his place. In turn, after forty-eight years' service in the Bank, Beveridge retired in October 1938 and J. W. Macfarlane became Treasurer.

The years of war inevitably took many men out of the Bank's service into the armed forces. By November 1915, the Scottish banks estimated that 40 per cent of their men of military age were serving in the armed forces. This was prior to the launch of Lord Derby's recruiting scheme and the introduction of conscription. In his report to the proprietors at the AGM on 4 April 1915, the Governor stated that about 180 of the staff were on military service out of a total of 950, and that to date full salaries had continued to be paid. Bank of Scotland seemed, however, to be reluctant to employ women in the banking service. It was not until May 1916 that the first women were employed in the Edinburgh branches, and by January 1917 there were still only thirty-five women out of a total staff of 804.[31] Bank of Scotland evidently preferred to fill the gaps in its staff with apprentices, who would naturally become eligible for military service in due course. The women employed were on a temporary basis at a weekly wage comparable to that being paid to apprentices, although salaries were increased fairly regularly to meet, at least in part, the rising cost of living. The first women to be recruited in the period from May 1916 to June 1917 started at £1 a week, but by the end of the war salaries for those still engaged would have risen to between £70 and £80 per annum. After June 1917, the Bank began to recruit women at lower rates of pay, some from as little as £39 per annum, although it is not known what their duties were, or whether they were younger or their qualifications were lower and they therefore needed more training. None of the women recruited was married, although one of the women who married and then resigned was readmitted to the Bank's service four months later. Married women may well have been regarded as less satisfactory for a number of reasons. In general, of course, there were at this time a number of occupations where women had to resign on marriage.[32]

Although women were employed during the war years only on temporary contracts, some were retained when peace was declared, and women

---

31 BS(BL) 20/21/16, 1914–1918, Papers re staff of the Scottish banks.
32 For a comment on women in banking, see 'The Future of Women in Banks', *The Bankers' Magazine*, 106 (December 1918), 568–72.

continued to be recruited as clerks. The Bank's accountant wrote a report in October 1919 on what was to be done with the temporary female employees in the accountant's and secretary's department at Head Office. He noted that the pre-war staff figure had been about fifty-seven and that this total had almost been reached, excluding the fourteen temporary clerkesses; and he recommended that the clerkesses should be given notice, which was done.[33] It is possible that the number of women retained after the war had ended was one of the reasons for the tensions between management and staff in the early 1920s. Men returning from military service found their salaries in real terms much reduced and may have thought their prospects less secure as a result of cheaper female labour; and these were some of the fears behind the attempted strike of 1920.[34] Women continued to be employed during the inter-war years, and they were widely distributed throughout Scotland with the growth in numbers of offices and sub-offices. Altogether, between 1914 and 1918, 598 of the staff of Bank of Scotland were on military service, and of this number eighty-two were killed. Their memorial is in the head office at the Mound in Edinburgh.

---

33 BS, Uncatalogued, Miscellaneous papers, Accountant, No. 12, July 1917 to December 1921.
34 S. G. Checkland, Scottish Banking: A History, 1695–1973 (Glasgow: 1975), p. 585 for the reproduction of a leaflet published by the Scottish Bankers Association, 18 June 1920.

CHAPTER 21

THE UNION BANK OF SCOTLAND, 1914–39

THE FIRST HISTORIAN of the Union Bank, Robert Rait, entitled his chapter covering the period 1883–1910 'The Years with Little History'.[1] He highlighted the Baring crisis of 1890 and the continued depreciation of British government securities, but otherwise, he wrote, it was a period of 'singularly little interest in banking history'. Rait thereby confused the particular and the general. At this time, the Union Bank, facing the difficult years of the depression, fell into conservative, even unenterprising, ways at a time when the Clyde region, where the larger part of its lending was conducted, was growing fast. In the middle decades of the nineteenth century it had been the leading bank in Glasgow, but it was already losing ground when Alexander Collie & Co., one of the largest firms in the East India trade, went into bankruptcy in the summer of 1875. The Union Bank was the only Scottish bank to be seriously involved, with losses of £150,000; and, while all the banks suffered serious losses in the depression, it was from these years that the position of the Union Bank in Scottish banking gradually declined.[2] Dividends fell to 12 per cent after the City of Glasgow failure in 1878, decreasing to 11 per cent between 1888 and 1894 and to 10 per cent in 1895–6. Then, in the closing years of the century, an improvement began, and by 1909 the rate was at 13 per cent. All the Scottish banks, except the North of Scotland, saw significant improvements in gross profits by 1896, although it was to prove a struggle for the Union Bank. By the First World War, the Union Bank was towards the bottom end of the table of the eight Scottish banks measured by published net profits, and by net profits as a percentage of paid-up capital, although the performance of net

1 R. S. Rait, *The History of the Union Bank of Scotland* (Glasgow: 1930), ch. 16.
2 N. Tamaki, *The Life Cycle of the Union Bank of Scotland 1830–1954* (Aberdeen: 1983), p. 94ff.

profits as a percentage of liabilities was not markedly different from that of the other Glasgow and Edinburgh banks.[3]

Although the Union Bank had reduced its holdings of British government securities by 1914, to £854,207, the result of their depreciation was still the most serious problem on the asset side of the balance sheet. This reduction required considerable provision before the war, and by April 1915 the directors had transferred £200,000 from the reserve account to cover a depreciation of £199,848. The conversion rights incorporated in the second war loan of 1915 were later taken advantage of, although no specific public mention seems to have been made in the reports to the proprietors.[4] There was some disagreement between the board and the general manager, Arthur C. D. Gairdner, who first wished to take up a smaller part of these rights than that to which the Bank's holding of the second war loan entitled it, but he was persuaded by George J. Scott, at that time the London office manager.[5] As with the other Scottish banks, there was the striking increase in the holdings of government securities. The first war loan brought the total to £2.3 million, while the second and subsequent loans gave the Union Bank a holding of £7.2 million by 1919. The opportunity was taken in 1915 and 1916 to sell holdings of other securities and investments, and in this the Union Bank was in a more favoured position, with readily marketable stocks, than Bank of Scotland.

The Union Bank showed an improvement in its business activities in the five years preceding the declaration of war. Advances through bills, cash accounts and other credits rose from £7.8 million to £11.3 million, and there were increases in the sums placed on the London and Glasgow money markets. In 1910, the dividend was raised to 14 per cent, and it was 15 per cent at the last peacetime annual general meeting in April 1914, at which figure it remained until 1920 when it was raised to 16 per cent. Wartime trends were better than those at Bank of Scotland, conforming broadly to the patterns at the other Scottish banks. Note circulation rose from under £1 million to reach £3.5 million in 1920, although deposits grew less spectacularly than at the other Edinburgh and Glasgow banks, which was to be a problem for the Union Bank throughout the interwar years. There was, in fact, little rise before 1917, but then came a considerable jump in deposits and other accounts, and the growth in deposits continued to an inter-war peak of £35.2 million in 1922. In part, no doubt it was the fierce competition in rural areas, but probably more important was the fact that the Union Bank was in competition,

---

3 See Statistical Appendix, Tables A13, A14 and A16.
4 See above, Chapter 19, for details of the conversion scheme embodied in the terms of the second war loan.
5 BS(U) 1/21/3, Private Letter Book, 25 September 1915.

in the Glasgow conurbation, with the Glasgow Savings Bank, the largest savings bank in the UK. By the mid-1930s, its funds amounted to nearly £34 million and it had over thirty offices in and around Glasgow. The Edinburgh Savings Bank ranked second in the UK with about half the total funds of the Glasgow bank. There was nothing comparable south of the Border, and the two savings banks were obviously important in the financial system of Scotland.[6]

The London and foreign business of the Union Bank had become increasingly important during the thirty years or so before 1914. This was, of course, part of the general increase in the financial activities of London as the centre of the world's capital markets, and a listing of the Union Bank's overseas investments indicated a broad distribution, especially within the countries of the Empire. It was this involvement with overseas investment that no doubt prompted the suggestion by James Tuke, general manager of the British Linen Bank, and Arthur C. D. Gairdner, general manager of the Union Bank, for the establishment of a Scottish Foreign Exchange Bank.[7] The lack of success which greeted the considerable efforts of Tuke and Gairdner led the Union Bank to establish its own foreign department in October 1918 with a former employee of a London merchant bank as its manager. The project, however, for a foreign bank continued to be pursued, and in April 1919 the British Overseas Bank was founded, with seven other banks contributing to the initial subscription of share capital. Arthur Gairdner resigned his position with the Union Bank to become chairman of the new bank in the spring of 1919; indeed, Gairdner was released by the Union Bank's directors because of the 'importance of the prospective relations between the two banks'.[8] The British Overseas Bank came out of the general expectations that the post-war world could expect a recovery in world trade, with more or less a resumption of the general trade conditions of the pre-1914 years; but there was to be disappointment. The British Overseas Bank developed business initially with the Baltic countries, but, although it had a very small business connection with the Bank of England, it was never very successful, and serious problems developed during the depression years. In 1944, it was taken over by Glyn, Mills & Co., the London banking house already taken over by the Royal Bank in 1939.

The administrative changes within the banking staff during the years of the First World War were broadly similar to those of the other Scottish banks. 'Lady clerks' ('clerkesses') were recruited on an initially temporary

---

6 M. Moss and A. Slaven, *From Ledger Book to Laser Beam. A History of the TSB in Scotland from 1810 to 1990* (Edinburgh: n.d. [1992]), ch. 5.
7 See above, Chapter 19.
8 Union Bank of Scotland, *Annual Report* (Glasgow: 1919).

basis; Arthur C. D. Gairdner of the Union Bank was among the first to employ them, and all the Scottish banks followed. The average wage which they received was £50 in the early years of the war, and increased later, although by less than inflation. All members of the bank who were called up as Territorials or who had enlisted – with the agreement of the board – were paid their full salaries until the end of 1914, later extended to 1 April 1915, when the bank continued to pay their salaries less army pay and allowances. All who joined the armed forces were guaranteed, at existing salaries, their reinstatement at the end of the war, and those who were unable to return to work due to wounds came under the Superannuation and Provident Scheme; additional funds were made over for costs of post-war medical treatment. Of the Union Bank's full-time staff, 518 served in the armed forces and eighty-four were killed. Of the 789 employed in the bank at the end of January 1917, 239 were men over military age, 98 were boys and no fewer than 193 were women.[9] Some women came to occupy positions of considerable responsibility. In the subsequent decade, recruitment of women was maintained, but only of those with typing skills. The improved financial position after 1915 allowed the board to pay a bonus of 10 per cent for each of the remaining war years (1916–18) on the salaries of those full-time staff who earned less than £500 a year; but this additional payment only partly met the inflation of wartime. A contributory superannuation scheme had been introduced in 1913, with the pension fund controlled by trustees who were taken from the senior members of the bank. From 1914, an appropriation to the pension funds was made from current profits, ranging from £5,000 in the early years to £25,000 in 1929–30. It is difficult to represent the impact that the war had on the Union Bank, and indeed on all the Scottish banks; the Duke of Atholl's address on the unveiling of the war memorial to the bank's dead was reprinted in R. S. Rait's history.[10]

The Union Bank was the first of the Scottish banks to revise its constitution in the twentieth century.[11] The original contract of co-partnership of 1830, when the bank was known as the Glasgow Union Banking Company, had been amended several times during the nineteenth century – including the important provision of limited liability adopted after the Companies Act, 1879 – but all Scottish banks were now beginning to recognise the gap between their future potentialities, with a wider range of business, and current operating practices under the existing constitutions. The new memorandum of association under the provisions

9   BS(BL) 20/21/16, 1914–1918, Papers re staff of the Scottish banks, 31 January 1917.
10 Rait, *Union Bank*, pp. 351–3.
11 Ibid., pp. 344–5.

of the Companies Acts of 1908 and 1913 was adopted at a special meeting of Union Bank shareholders in Glasgow on 25 April 1917 and confirmed by the Court of Session on 31 October 1917. The most important new feature was the power to establish branches and agencies within 'any part of the United Kingdom, in its colonies and dependencies', and also in foreign countries – a much wider area of operations than had hitherto been granted to companies registered under the Companies Acts and, in particular, a recognition of the foreign-exchange facilities opened the following year. The bank also took stronger powers to act as trustees and executors, and within a few years it was the first Scottish bank to establish a separate department to cover these affairs. Powers were also taken in respect of amalgamations and for the increase or reduction of capital. There were, however, certain important matters which were disallowed by the Court of Session. William Smith, who had been the Reporter to the Court of Session at the time of the submission of the Union Bank's new constitution in 1917, was later to correct A. W. Kerr's account with details of the Court's refusal to sanction certain of the proposed changes:

> Thus: the Bank proposed to take power to use its £4,000,000 of uncalled capital as a fund of credit on which it might borrow; it wished to have its fundamental article as to that uncalled capital in its 'Archives', where it might be altered, instead of in its 'Memorandum', where, without the Court's sanction, it could not; and it proposed to take power to conduct many kinds of independent businesses not merely ancillary to the leading purposes of Banking. All these proposals were disallowed.[12]

Of the minor matters in the new constitution, the procedures for electing the senior officials were altered. Appointments of the chairman and deputy chairman were transferred from the directors to the company in general meeting, while the selection of extraordinary directors remained with the board. The general manager now became one of the ordinary directors, whose numbers were fixed at between nine and fifteen; and the qualification for ordinary directors was 100 shares.

The establishment of the British Overseas Bank and the appointment of Arthur C. D. Gairdner as its first chairman meant that the position of general manager became vacant. George Scott, manager of the London office, became general manager in Glasgow for a year before becoming Treasurer of Bank of Scotland, and on 7 April 1920 he was succeeded by Norman L. Hird, who had also followed him as London office manager in April 1919. Hird was 34 years old: an 'unprecedented age', wrote R. S. Rait. Educated in both England and Scotland, he was first recruited to

12 A. W. Kerr, *History of Banking in Scotland*, 4th edn (London: 1926), p. 337, Appendix J.

the London office in 1903; in 1911 on recognition of his qualities he was despatched to the Inspectors Department in Glasgow, and in March 1914 he was appointed assistant accountant in London. Hird was to remain as general manager until his death in 1945. He was undoubtedly an important personality in the business world of Scotland. He served a term as president of the Institute of Bankers in Scotland, and was a vice-president of the British Bankers Association and of the Glasgow Chamber of Commerce. A reading of the remaining private correspondence suggests that he was indeed a lively and active person who was also hopeful that certain specific perceptions of the pre-war world situation would re-emerge in post-war years. Nevertheless, he showed a considerable appreciation of the difficulties posed for industry and trade by the early return to gold in 1925, and was undoubtedly sympathetic to helping businessmen through these exacting times.

Hird took over as general manager at a time of rapid expansion of business. Deposits had risen by £6.2 million in twelve months; bill discounts were pushed to around £10 million, and other advances to customers were not far short of this figure. Holdings of British government securities were at an all-time high of £9.4 million, and demand for banknotes had reached almost £3.5 million. Profits from the increased activity were also exceptional; even the published profits in 1920 showed the Union Bank with the third largest rise among the Scottish banks, to £311,000. But, for the ensuing seven years, the bank faced a more difficult time, for which the strong connections with the heavy industries of the west of Scotland were largely to blame.

The figures for bad and doubtful debts from 1921 show few years when the annual accounts yielded a surplus, and in several the loss was substantial (see Table 21.1). Total provision from 1921–7, at £473,697, was worse than at Bank of Scotland, and after recoveries it was still £297,823. The majority of the losses occurred at Glasgow chief office and the branches under Glasgow, which took in most of the west of Scotland trade and industry. There were also sizeable losses in some years in London, but Edinburgh and the remaining branches were less seriously affected. It should be noticed that the Union Bank's position on British government securities was strengthened: significant purchases of over £8 million in 1921–2 gave a total of almost £16.2 million, with similar results to the other Scottish banks. Norman Hird inherited a modest internal reserve, at £322,493 for the two leading accounts, and he proceeded to build these to over £800,000 by 1923, with another £100,000 in the income tax reserve account (see Table 21.2).

In the first two years of war, demand for facilities fell below the pre-war figures. There were several occasions when the bank declined a facility where the request did not accord with government guidelines, including the cutbacks in stockbroker funds, but much of the decline was due to an improvement in the cash flow of companies and hence a reduction in overdrafts. By the summer of 1916, demand was rising, although it was concentrated on bill discounts and advances for a few months before payments were received by customers for war contracts. The following year, however, saw an upturn on all advances, especially those associated with cash accounts and overdrafts.[13] Among the largest of these wartime facilities were those for the Tharsis Sulphur & Copper Co. Ltd, £470,000; credit for the Russian banks, £250,000; the Bank of England scheme to improve exchange on the USA; £175,000 for Nobels Explosive Co. Ltd; £10,000 per week for purchases of chemicals in the USA; and £150,000 for the Scottish Co-operative Wholesale Society Ltd, again for foreign purchases. In the war years, there were forty-six new agreements – mostly renewed – for more than £10,000 on the cash account system, and numerous smaller facilities as well.

In the early post-war years, facilities were on average much larger to allow for inflation, and there were more frequent applications. Among facilities granted in 1920 were those for Stewarts & Lloyds, the steelmakers, who took $344,000 for steel imports from the USA in July, £200,000 more in October and another $535,000 in November. John Brown & Co. were granted $120,000 for steel imports, Charles Tennant & Co. borrowed £100,000 against warrants for chemicals, and Arthur C. D. Gairdner of the British Overseas Bank referred part of an issue of notes by the Explosives Trades Ltd to the Union Bank, whose directors agreed to underwrite £300,000 worth, taking £150,000 for the Union Bank. Among the largest grants were £500,000 for the Scottish Co-operative and C$1 million for a new drawing account at the Dominion Bank, Toronto. All the civil engineering companies, including Sir William Arrol & Co. Ltd, took considerable funds in the post-war boom. It is noteworthy that the Union Bank greatly expanded its foreign trade connections under the encouragement of Gairdner and Hird, and a foreign branch was opened in St Vincent Street, Glasgow, in 1922. The bank was soon supporting substantial credits for banks in Belgium, French railway development and a variety of purposes in Poland, Czechoslovakia and the USA, in addition to trade within the Empire. While these operations were not uncommon for British banks, the Union Bank directors clearly saw in them a considerable strengthening of their interest in overseas trade.

By 1922, it was evident that the international business was not expanding at the expected rate and was in decline in some sectors. The

13 These data are given in BS(U) 1/13/3, Minute Book of Large Loans, 1914–19.

Table 21.1 *Union Bank of Scotland provision for loss, 1921–47*

Year ending 2 April	Provision for loss							Recoveries							Net estimated loss/ surplus
	At Glasgow	At Glasgow town branches	At country branches under Glasgow	At Edinburgh	At Edinburgh branches	At London offices	Total provision for loss	At Glasgow	At Glasgow town branches	At country branches under Glasgow	At Edinburgh	At Edinburgh branches	At London offices	Total recoveries	
1921	21367	9086	47687		164	2379	80683	2542	711	5699	3529	9361	3	21844	-58839
1922	53010 [1]	16451	21630	10	110	3023	94233	50	1062	3774	7895	3838	2509	19127	-75106
1923	2178	13737	19726	10	328	742	36720	5236	18790	10372	4390	3250	1089	43128	6407
1924	321	8940	27578	2	22	59181	96043	9103	4487	13197	2530	997	262	30575	-65468
1925	120	7200	3193	15	6017	1000	17545	5699	2076	8383	4716	1309	4063	26245	8700
1926	110006	2118	11334		26	8	123492	1168	7415	5748	155	2976	850	18312	-105179
1927	1256	2725	15985		24	4995	24985	3713	1442	4195	1156	5306	831	16644	-8341
1928	1383	1542	4594		6	3610	11134	1337	1219	755	622	1863	392	6189	-4945
1929	11646	9152	1356	4550	5	69	26779	1000	1264	4230	823	673	99	8089	-18690
1930	3322	5837	3739	118	334	2881	16231	2886	1485	6124	971	143	2352	13961	-2270
1931	15696	12983	22125	10	164	4813	55791	2119	1264	3260	566	153	243	7604	-48187
1932	12296	7335	30895	1	53	20933	72014	22239	1826	7237	1292	69	3050	35714	-36299
1933	17743	11510	7222	132	1038	37315	74959	896	883	2264	500	74	228	4845	-70114 [2]
1934	165	3544	944	1	158	600	5412	5022	3018	7519	1143	898	2482	30082	24671 [2]
1935	3120	622	4869	300	72	4	8988	5363	2297	6563	905	69	2380	17577	8589
1936	82	4185	4092	3	31	6367	14760	11391	4732	4875	7096	1207	77	29378	14618
1937	2	358	904		47	3702	10017	2591	1496	4565	1235	1135	292	11315	1297
1938	0	5771	1822	5003	668	50	8344	346	5852	5374	785	71	2230	14658	6314
1939	1531	2340	5654	33	139	572	13241	57254	3303	2250	156	9115 [3]	1732	73811	60571
1940	28	494	9061	3005	1001	15093	30676	7359	1283	2978	8369 [4]	48	999	21035	-9641
1941	21	1540	6773	5000	859	13163	28365	296	924	5113	171	35	236	6775	-21590
1942	3	4190	2178	6010	934	137	7446	1667	218	3141	6408	128	23	11584	4138
1943	17	2060	513	4	63	1993	5088	1627	4232	3061	512	229	53	9714	4626
1944	22	830	1180	444	62	1104	7202	3811	2134	7815	12721	1431	1406	29319	22117
1945	134	3699	1550	4004	354	172	5914	763	2397	7446	1891	68	10446	23010	17096
1946	4	5633	3377	5	49	17814	26954	12282	1725	5102	1801	3700	11047	35656	8702
1947	85	1456	220	76	350	51	2168	2361	10629	9575	2141	1024	3433	29164	26996

Notes:
1 'With possible modification of £30,000 or so if arrangements carried through by 29th March.'
2 See also BS(U) 1/1/1, UBS Board of Directors Supplementary Minute Book.
3 Includes £692 at Edinburgh Hunter Square placed to Interest account.
4 Includes £7,932 profit on J. Graham Bryon's Life Policies to be placed to guarantee account.

Source: BS(U) 1/13/4–5, Minute Books of Large Loans, 1921–47.

Table 21.2 *Union Bank of Scotland internal reserves, 1902–52*

	Guarantee account	Guarantee investments account	Income tax account
1902	81745		
1903	123745		
1904	169899		
1905	169899		
1906	160006		
1907	184129		
1908	223296		
1909	100054		
1910	99213		
1911	136457		
1912	131854		
1913	59520		
1914	23502		
1915	115408		
1916	127758		
1917	131255		
1918	132197		
1919	163451		
1920	213729	108764	
1921	196955	108764	77287
1922	142793	549831	137952
1923	260742	549831	137952
1924	494152	421230	106453
1925	517913	420156	159453
1926	644076	430044	204453
1927	443751	417009	174596
1928	561923	414203	152818
1929	682543	414127	171350
1930	844263	413634	199384
1931	783385	390734	287095
1932	865553	307885	272019
1933	952772	61439	257208
1934	783130		252757
1935	849882		210312
1936	931231		218997
1937	1076187		200064
1938	1259522		203664
1939	1071103		204106
1940	1240502		200510
1941	1420124		200510
1942	1594470		202309
1943	1642271		199183
1944	1730849		224480
1945	1774675		252546
1946	1843096		293586
1947	1968047		280030
1948	2092321		235119
1949	2262909		193559
1950	2390776		179231
1951	2572907		124063
1952	2692727		127973

Source: BS(U) 1/10/9–13, Quarterly states.

Table 21.3 *Examples of support to customers, 1922–46*

Firm	Range of advances	Time span
Anchor Line (Henderson Bros) Ltd	£50,000–£280,000	1924–35
Blythswood Shipbuilding Co. Ltd	£40,000–£145,000	1924–42
John Brown & Co. Ltd	£200,000	1930–5
Coltness Iron Co.	£25,000–£ 26,000	1923–6
Crawford, Cree & Lawries	£10,000–£ 20,000	1922–9
Lochgelly Iron & Coal Co. Ltd	£50,000–£130,000	1931–7
Malcolm Inglis & Co.	£20,000–£ 50,000	1925–32
Milroy Chemical Co.	£17,000–£ 30,000	1925–30
P. & W. McLellan Ltd	£17,000–£125,000	1922–46
Andrew Ritchie & Son Ltd	£20,000–£ 50,000	1923–43
Simons & Co. Ltd	£10,000–£ 30,000	1923–34
Chas Tennant & Co. Ltd	£14,000–£ 30,000	1928–42
West of Scotland Shipbreaking Co. Ltd	£12,000–£ 40,000	1925–38

Source: BS(U) 1/13/3–5, Minute Books of Large Loans.

Union Bank also faced narrower margins on discount rates for bills for the foreign trades, and was in competition for these bills with Scottish as well as English banks. Within a few years, income from this source was well down, and it remained subdued during the inter-war years. As requests for long-term credit facilities were in decline, the hoped-for expansion of business was now in reverse. Only the investments side of the assets performed well, and capital values rose with the deflation. It should be stressed that the normal pattern of support by the bank for its industrial customers continued: the yearly overview of advances on the cash account system, and careful checking of securities where applicable, usually led to the continuation of the loan. There are numerous examples of how this operated (see Table 21.3)

Some of the larger advances contracted in the early post-war years continued to give the management problems for many years, and seventeen of these were especially difficult from the mid-1920s through into the 1930s. Several factors emerge from a reading of the internal correspondence dealing with these and other accounts. Norman Hird was fully aware of the difficult trading situations in many parts of the world and the tight quotations that many of the Union Bank's customers were forced to make. However, the bank lacked anything approaching an industrial intelligence unit capable of providing information and analysis of particular projects and the marketplace which they faced. Hird, who inevitably was involved with the larger financial accounts that were offering problems, provided his borrowers with a mixture of cajolery, enticement and exhortation together with a great deal of advice based upon the agreed 'common sense' of his times. He was not in any way diffident in offering advice to the businessmen who approached him for advances, and much of his advice was specific. Hird confronted the general question of how close the bank should get to the company asking for loans or overdrafts, and from his early days in office he seems to have decided that it was not advisable for banks to be represented on the boards of individual companies, although he often had very good information on them from branch managers and details of cash flow and investment. From his correspondence, consideration of placing bankers on the boards of companies in difficulty was at least discussed, and in every case, as far as can be ascertained, was to be rejected.

In the 1920s, Hird would appear to have accepted the orthodoxy which conceived a return to 'normality' as a return to the conditions of 1914, and new developments on industrial investment were not encouraged unless they could show clear advantages. Indeed, many of the promising wartime developments in Scotland in vehicles, aero-engines and specialised engineering were among the early casualties of the post-war deflation. Thus, in his dealings with the firm of Mann, MacNeal & Co., whose company activities were coal, oil and shipping, Hird was emphatic that they should concentrate upon their coal and shipping interests. In particular, he wrote: 'I think you should seriously consider cutting out the oil connection'. It may be that this last piece of advice was sensible, given the high-powered ferocity of these involved in the oil business in the 1920s together with the incompetence that Sir Hector MacNeal appears to have displayed in the running of his own businesses.[14] The active partners also included Sir John Mann CA, and the account was held at the London office. The firm had overdraft limits of £150,000 and occasional extra facilities, mainly for bills. From September 1923, the overdraft crept upwards at around £10,000 a month, in part because of investment in the United Anthracite Collieries Co. of Wales, the Channel Fuel Co. and the Forest Shipping Co. United Anthracite was a sound company; its product sold at higher prices than steam coal, and it was intended to float the concern on the stockmarket in October 1923, which would enable the debts to be cleared and raise additional capital for investment. The deterioration in the coal market delayed this into the following year. As the general economic situation was also giving rise for concern, Hird was most concerned that Sir Hector address the scale of the overdraft. The letters which passed on this occasion are familiar to bankers, for whom such correspondence is all too regular, but will serve to indicate how closely Hird followed the many difficult situations which arose. On 2 January 1924, he was writing to John Alexander, manager of the London office:[15]

14 For this, see D. Yergin, *The Prize* (London: 1991), part II.
15 The following two quotes are from BS(U) 1/21/4, Private Letter Book, Norman Hird to John Alexander, London office, 2 January and 21 March 1924; there are many letters on these topics.

> I was rather surprised to see in the weekly return that this firm's indebtedness has increased to such an extent (overdraft £204,000, Discounts £13,000). The last time I saw any figures the amount of the overdraft was about £150,000; the latter sum is *quite full enough*, and I hope the increase is purely temporary. (I see in looking into the matter that, since September, there has been a steady rise of about £10,000 a month.)

In March, he wrote again to London:

> I was glancing at the London Reports today, and I am extremely disappointed to observe that the above Account (Mann, MacNeal and Co Ltd) is still very heavily overdrawn – about £214,000. It is very annoying that the promises have not materialised, and I shall be glad if you will take this matter up . . . As you are aware, I should like the overdraft brought down as rapidly as possible to the £150,000 limit at least, and, of course, I want it ultimately on an even lower basis.

By July, the overdraft stood at £240,000, the industrial relations problems of the industry were worsening, and any rise in wages would have forced the coalowners to raise prices. But 'there are limits to the price that the foreigners will pay for British coal. In the case of anthracite, there are also limits.'[16] By the close of August there was a tone of exasperation, as advances to United Anthracite showed no signs of reduction:

> I cannot quite understand it. MacNeal in his conversations and correspondence *repeatedly* stated that when the Anthracite issue came out [two associates] would put up a very considerable amount of money, which would help to liquidate the Mann, MacNeal advances . . . MacNeal's liabilities, as a whole, are extensive and he is always too much of an optimist. The outlook for the coal trade is not too rosy, although I fancy that the anthracite business is not affected, in the same way as ordinary coal. What about the Company's balance sheet?

In 1926, the Union Bank's board decided to provide for a loss of £250,000 for the Mann, MacNeal & Co. account, placed to a new guarantee account; and this was little reduced thereafter (see Table 21.4), still standing at £216,488 in 1941. This new internal account was designed for long-term debts which would be maintained in the hope that something might come right in the years ahead.

The burgh of Ardrossan, on the Ayrshire coast, had a tradition of shipbuilding in modern times, first in timber and later in iron and steel. In 1898, the Ardrossan Dry Dock and Shipbuilding Co. Ltd assumed responsibility for ongoing ship construction in the main yard of the burgh.[17]

---

16 BS(U) 1/21/4, Private Letter Book, Norman Hird to Sir Hector MacNeal, 29 May 1924.
17 For details of the company, see C. Levy, *Ardrossan Shipyard: Struggle for Survival 1825–1983* (Ardrossan: n.d. [1986]).

Table 21.4 *Union Bank of Scotland Guarantee No. 2 Account*[1]

	Transferred from Contingent account to provide for possible loss	Over-provision transferred	Transferred to write down debt	Transferred to write off debt	Total provided to date [2]
17 Mar 1926	250000				250000 [3]
28 Mar 1928			100000		250000
20 Mar 1929			88466		250000
30 Mar 1932	10000	15005			244995
13 Apr 1932	100000				344995
22 Mar 1933	80000				424995
21 Mar 1934	55000	40000	13017		439995
27 Mar 1935	100000	78906		26094	461089
11 Mar 1936		5000			456089
17 Mar 1937		20000			436089
6 Apr 1938					436089
14 Dec 1938					436089
20 Mar 1940		10000			426089
12 Mar 1941	12000	118512			319577
25 Mar 1942		30000			289577
17 Mar 1943		33810		28190	255767
28 Mar 1945	53925		53925		309692
13 Mar 1946	17703		17703		327395
21 Mar 1951	15000				342395
18 Mar 1953		15000			327395

Notes:

1 On 17 March 1926, it was resolved to open a Guarantee No. 2 Account to which provisions for any probable loss of £10,000 and over on any one account in any one year were to be credited, instead of to the Contingent account as formerly.

2 Where a sum was transferred for the purpose of writing down or writing off a debt, this was still included in the total provision.

3 This was in addition to the provision of £110000 credited to the Contingent account in respect of the three debts of Ardrossan Dry Dock & Shipbuilding Co. Ltd, Mann, Macneal & Co. Ltd and Channel Fuel Co. Ltd.

Source: BS(U) 1/1/1, UBS Board of Directors Supplementary Minute Book.

Most of the work was for merchant vessels, though during the First World War the company secured Admiralty contracts for minesweepers, tugboats and other smaller-sized ships. In 1916, the management commenced construction of a new shipyard covering twenty-two acres. There were 2,300 workers in both yards in 1920, building ships from 500 to 6,600 gross tons. The company was acquired in early 1920 by the Lamport and Holt group, a subsidiary of the Royal Mail Shipping group, as part of that company's extension of its shipbuilding capacity in the post-war building boom. Sir Alfred Read, a director of the Ardrossan Dry Dock, was also chairman and managing director of Coast Lines Ltd, another subsidiary of the Royal Mail consortium. In January 1921, in anticipation of a capital reconstruction and share issue, the Union Bank granted £400,000 for a year, taking a mortgage over the yards and other security including personal guarantees from Sir Hector MacNeal, Sir Alfred Read and other associates.[18] In November, as conditions worsened, the agreement was settled at an overdraft of £250,000 with another £50,000 for occasional use. The Union Bank also agreed to guarantee funds for construction of ships at the yard. In February 1924, it granted the company an extension of its overdraft, bringing it to a maximum of £275,000. The extension was given on condition that the capital arrangements of the shipbuilding company would be arranged more satisfactorily, and Hird argued that the company required £150,000–£200,000 additional capital. The Royal Mail group, led by Lord Kylsant, owned a considerable part of the British merchant fleet, estimated at 15 per cent in 1930, and also owned Harland & Wolff in Belfast and much of the steel production in Scotland through ownership of Colvilles.

Norman Hird tried – but failed – to insist that the company settle the capital question or the bank would reduce or even refuse the advance requested. Lord Kylsant's solutions at this time to the general problems afflicting shipping and shipbuilding were, in the words of the historians of the Royal Mail group, 'to share markets, to build as many modern vessels as possible and to preserve the labour force so that the Group would be poised to take advantage of the predictable improvement in market conditions'. The improvement did not come about, at least for the Royal Mail group, and it was beginning to be in serious trouble by 1926.[19] For the next three years, the group and many of its 140 subsidiaries were reliant upon credit provided by the British banks to manage a satisfactory cash flow. Faced with falling revenues and rising costs, the government was required to intervene in spite of opposition from Lord Kylsant. Extensive inquiries ordered by the creditors and the Treasury led to the creation of a new, more broadly-based board and management structure. Lord Kylsant was removed from an active role in the group's affairs, and in 1931 was prosecuted and convicted on charges that he had issued a false prospectus. He was jailed for a year.

The continued advances to the Ardrossan subsidiary were made on personal security. At an early stage, in 1924, Hird wrote to Sir Alfred Read in the following terms, and he does not seem to have changed his general position in later years:

I need scarcely say that, in the present position of shipbuilding, and with the outlook before us for a number of years, Banks do not look favourably on ship

---

18 BS(U) 1/13/4, Minute Book of Large Loans, 19 January and 23 November 1921.
19 BS(U) 1/21/4, Private Letter Book, February–December 1924; E. Green and M. Moss, *A Business of National Importance: The Royal Mail Shipping Group, 1902–1937* (London: 1982); the quotation in the text is on p. 66. See also A. R. Holmes and E. Green, *Midland: 150 Years of Banking Business* (London: 1986), pp. 184–5.

yards as a satisfactory form of security, and it is purely on personal grounds that the Ardrossan advances have been allowed to continue.[20]

In fact, within a few years there was little choice, and the correspondence suggests that Hird and other bankers with whom he was in touch were unaware of the true position of the Royal Mail group. While the drastic reorganisation of the group proceeded in 1930, the National Shipbuilders Security Ltd was formed. Its task was to negotiate financial compensation for owners of shipyards deemed surplus to industry requirements; there was general support from the banks for the scheme, and from 'most' shipbuilders.[21] Closure of the newer yard at Ardrossan was announced in November. The Union Bank provided for £250,000 of the debts, and the Guarantee No. 2 account stated the amount outstanding against the Ardrossan Dry Dock and Shipbuilding Co. Ltd as £235,000 for 1932, and £201,488 as late as 1941.

The third largest debt of the inter-war years was owed by the Anchor Line, a subsidiary of the Cunard Steamship Co. The Anchor Line specialised in general trade and passenger services and was at the time a household name. During the war, several of its carriers were sunk by enemy action, and, to replace these, eight orders were made during the post-war boom. Under government guarantee, in the form of the Trades Facilities Act, the Union Bank and the Commercial Bank advanced sums which briefly touched £1.6 million. Unfortunately, the difficulties of post-war trade and the reduction in the number of emigrants travelling across the Atlantic, a consequence of us quotas, yielded a much-reduced cash flow; and, while much of the debt was repaid, a reconstruction was required. By 1929, the company owed £850,000 to the Treasury, £300,000 to the Union Bank, £160,000 to Alexander Stephen & Co., shipbuilders, and £145,000 to the Fairfield Shipbuilding Co. Reconstruction was eventually agreed in 1935, and the company was bought from the Cunard Steamship Co. by a consortium led by Bank of Scotland. The debts to the Union Bank were £150,000 by 1934, and these were not finally cleared until the Second World War. Of the seventeen debts covered in the Guarantee No. 2 account, nine were eventually cleared; the maximum exposure was £461,089 in 1934, reduced by 1941 to £255,767. The long-term view of handling large debts took up considerable management time, but was judged to be worthwhile. The slump from 1931 affected the internal reserves, as in all Scottish banks. It was agreed to run down the guarantee investment account, and it was closed in 1934. All reserves fell to a little

20 BS(U) 1/21/4, Private Letter Book, Norman Hird to Sir Henry Read, 10 September 1924.
21 A. Slaven, *The Development of the West of Scotland, 1750–1960* (London: 1975), p. 189.

over £1 million in the worst of the depression, but recovered thereafter, and by 1940 the guarantee account stood at £1,240,502, with smaller sums to the credit of other accounts.

In 1918, the board purchased for £99,000 a corner property at the junction of St Vincent Street and Renfield Street in Glasgow, and it was here that the Union Bank was to build a new head-office building. In the autumn of 1923, Norman Hird went to the USA both to meet the Union's banking correspondents and also to look at American bank buildings and broaden his ideas about how the proposed new building should be designed. His letter books suggest that it was the latter that mostly concerned him, although in a visit to Washington DC he 'had the good fortune to meet practically all the Federal Reserve Board at Washington, and I dined with them and also Mr Andrew W. Mellon'.[22] Hird spent a considerable time in the mid-1920s over the design and plans for the new building, and he saw it as a symbol of the power and importance of the Union Bank. He wrote in February 1924 to a Chicago banker:

> I have mentioned to quite a number of people, including my Board, what a wonderful building you have got, and, although I am not expecting to emulate you so far as that goes, I want to have a new building which will be a striking feature in Glasgow architecture. To a certain extent it means educating the Scottish architect, and, although it is going to mean a considerable amount of work to myself, it will be quite an interesting proposition.[23]

The demolition of the old building began in May 1925. The architect was James Miller, who devised 'a clever British adaptation of some of the good American buildings which I saw when I was in the States last autumn'.[24] The new building took longer than planned after it was discovered that the foundations were of solid rock. The foundation stone was laid by Viscount Novar, who took the opportunity in his speech to extol the virtues of the British banking system and to deny the practicability of any suggestion of nationalisation, a political matter that was still 'in the air' despite the acknowledged conservatism of the first minority Labour government in 1924.[25] The background to Viscount Novar's speech was

22 BS(U) 1/21/4, Private Letter Book, Norman Hird to Harry B. van Sinderen of L. Tennant & Co., New York, 28 December 1923.
23 BS(U) 1/21/4, Private Letter Book, Norman Hird to W. G. Mackintosh, Manager, Foreign Dept, Continental and Commercial National Bank, Chicago, 14 February 1924.
24 BS(U) 1/21/4, Private Letter Book, Norman Hird to Arthur Gairdner, 20 June 1924.
25 For a general account, see R. W. Lyman, *The First Labour Government, 1924* (London: 1957). There is a perceptive comment in BS(U) 1/21/4 in a letter from Norman Hird to H. E. Gordon, Cairo, 31 January 1924. J. Ramsay MacDonald did not form his government until 22 January 1924: 'We are settling down under our own Labour government which, as you will have observed, is of a *most* respectable nature. I doubt whether they will be able to do much, and fortunately, in their Colonial policy, they appear to have adopted the sound principle of continuity.'

the situation in the coal industry that was to lead to the General Strike in May 1926. 'The very success', he said,

> of our Banking system has led some to cast envious eyes in our direction and has suggested the idea that Nationalised Banks would be lucrative to the State. But these optimists forget that the process whereby everything that King Midas touched turned to gold is exactly reversed when the Sovereign State lays a heavy hand on business enterprise. Then the gold disappears and profits turn into deficits; and in no case would this calamitous process be more swift and certain than in the Banking business, which depends so greatly on personal ability, initiative, good management, flexibility in administration, power of quick decision and close intimate touch with the needs of Commerce and Industry.

He ended with an emphasis upon the ways in which the Union Bank 'has resisted the pull of London and maintained its Scots independence', and at this point he was referring to the Union Bank's enlargement of share capital in the previous year and to the increase in the number of shareholders.

Late 1923 had seen the fourth 'affiliation' of a Scottish bank to one of the English clearing banks – that of the North of Scotland Bank to the Midland Bank – and while few could complain about the price paid, many shared the 'mixed feelings' expressed at the time by Norman Hird. The Midland was known to be interested in expanding its branch network, and Hird, together with his board, discussed the various options open to them to keep the Union independent. The directors also considered the post-war movement for wider share and employee ownership. The principle of sharing part of company profits as a bonus among the workforce had been developed in the nineteenth century, and took a number of forms, the most common being cash dividends. In the few years after the First World War, there was considerable discussion in the UK and other countries about the efficiency of such schemes, and the Westminster Bank and Lloyds Bank, for example, both introduced a limited form of profit-sharing.[26] While these ideas were of interest to the Union Bank directors, they decided that their priority was to remove the bank regulation which prescribed ten shares as a minimum holding, and thus open up share-holding to the many who had hitherto felt unable to raise the hundreds of pounds required to reach this threshold. The board used the powers acquired under the 1920 Constitution to alter the denomination of shares. The share capital of £5 million comprised, to this date, 100,000 shares of

26 K. Mackenzie, 'Profit Sharing and Co-Partnership', *Scottish Bankers Magazine*, 16 (1924), 23–30; G. R. Smith, 'Employee Share Schemes in Britain', *Employment Gazette*, 101 (1993), 149–54.

£50 each, with £10 as the paid-up portion. Now, by a Special Resolution of May 1924, the share capital was divided into one million shares of £5 each with £1 as the paid-up portion, with the original resolution being retained, which provided that 'the remaining four-fifths should not be capable of being called up except in the event and for the purpose of the Company being wound up'. In addition, a bonus of 100,000 shares of £1 fully paid from reserves was distributed *pro rata* among the proprietors, who were also offered an additional 100,000 shares of £1, at a price of £3, a substantial reduction on the market price of £4 6s offered as one £1 share with every ten £5 shares now held. These were distinguished as 'B' shares, from the part-paid 'A' shares. This change in share denomination was accompanied by an alteration in the voting powers of the proprietors, and it was now laid down that:

> every Member personally present and entitled to vote shall have one vote on a show of hands, and on a poll every Member present personally or represented by proxy shall have one vote for every share held by him unless the number of shares held by him shall exceed 1,000 in which case he shall have 1,000 votes and no more.[27]

Norman Hird was clear about the board aims on this. The newspapers made favourable comments, including one which he was especially pleased to see from the *Manchester Guardian*.[28]

Like all his contemporaries in banking, Norman Hird, as general manager, was always concerned with the presentation of the annual balance sheet, which in the case of the Union Bank was towards the end of April, with the financial year always closing on 2 April. Due to the perceived weakness in credit, it had to show a strong liquid position with cash and short-term bills. On 18 January 1924, to provide one example, Hird wrote to his London manager about preparations for the annual financial statement:

> The present position of our early April Bills seems to be that on the 1st and 2nd we have £660,000 maturing which should provide us with ample funds for swelling our Bank of England and Glyn Company balances. In addition to that, we have £730,000 maturing from the 3rd to the 12th April, both days inclusive, so that we should be fairly comfortable, and carry through our 'window dressing' on economical terms![29]

27 Rait, *Union Bank*, pp. 344–5.
28 BS(U) 1/21/4, Private Letter Book, Norman Hird to John Alexander, London office, 21 March 1924. To an official at the British Overseas Bank, he wrote: 'Glad you approve of our share-splitting scheme designed to widen interest and increase share-holding now that there are *four* English-owned banks out of eight in Scotland!': ibid., 20 March 1924.
29 BS(U) 1/21/4, Private Letter Book, Norman Hird to London office, 18 January 1924. For the Scottish evidence on window-dressing to the Macmillan Committee, see above, Chapter 19.

The Union Bank had made large advances during the war years and the short-lived boom which followed, but the difficulties thereafter put great pressure on the management. Nevertheless, dividends were maintained at 18 per cent from 1923–39; and although deposits were lower than at Bank of Scotland in the years immediately preceding the Second World War, advances were about the same in the totals for 1938 and 1939. The Union Bank, located to serve the western region which was beginning to benefit substantially from the rearmament programme from 1936, ought to have produced better results. One reason why it did not was the failure to improve its volume of deposits at a faster rate than actually occurred. During Hird's tenure of office between 1920 and 1945, the general increase in deposits of all Scottish banks was 211 per cent (1920 = 100), while the Union Bank's figure was only 179 per cent.[30] The reasons for this lag are not easy to explain. In 1918, the bank had a total of 158 branches, of which twenty-four were in Glasgow and sixteen in Edinburgh. There was little expansion before 1923 when the total was 165, but from then to 1930 the Union opened another ten branches in Glasgow, several of which were in the new suburbs, three in Edinburgh and twenty-seven in other parts of Scotland. This was in addition to the new head office and a second London branch, in Regent Street; Norman Hird had always looked to the West End of London, and envied the purchase by the Royal Bank in 1924 of Drummonds & Co. of Charing Cross. All of this development made sound business sense. By 1939, the Union Bank had 220 branches and sub-branches, a larger number than the British Linen Bank (with 215), the Clydesdale (with 208) or the National Bank of Scotland (with 192). The geographical location of its branches was perhaps less of an explanation for the difficulties with deposits, given the broader spread of branches in the Lothians and other regions beyond Glasgow and the west, which had higher savings rates. The competition of the Glasgow Savings Bank was undoubtedly a factor. Nevertheless, the relative sluggishness of the Union Bank's performance during the inter-war years, compared with its nearest rivals, remained a problem.

The question of provision for retirement, given the increasing longevity of the population, was a matter of growing concern prior to 1914. The Liberal government of 1906 had introduced old age pensions and the social insurance Acts of 1911, and in 1913 Arthur C. D. Gairdner introduced a contributory superannuation scheme. A National Association of Bank Clerks was formed in 1914, and it successfully registered itself as a trade union the following year. The war was mainly responsible for its demise. When peace came, there was a short but more substantial period of trade-

---

30 T. Balogh, *Studies in Financial Organisation* (Cambridge: 1947), p. 117, Table 32.

union activity. The Scottish Bankers Association was formally established in March 1919, and its quite rapid recruitment forced the Scottish banks' attention to problems of wages and the cost of living, the main matters of political concern.[31] There were considerable wage increases across all the Scottish banks. But the Association crucially failed to achieve recognition as a trade union, which meant that it could not press for the establishment of a Whitley council. In 1917, J. H. Whitley's committee had reported in favour of national industrial councils for each industry, to include both employers and trade unionists, and in the event white-collar workers, such as government civil servants, were able to gain their own councils.[32] The Scottish bankers were not, however; and, when the Association held its second AGM in March 1920, a resolution was passed which called for a national strike referendum. The executive agreed to consider strike action if 80 per cent of its membership voted in favour – which they did. The Ministry of Labour now moved in, a number of promises were given which were not adhered to, and by the end of the year the militant mood was passing. The Scottish Bankers Association continued, and its national demands undoubtedly helped to encourage improved conditions, although its own future for the next decade was one of stagnation. Changes in office technology, already present in the USA and Canada since the 1870s, were beginning to affect the skills and duties of the majority of the staff. The first telephone was installed in Bank of Scotland in 1881, in the Glasgow office; in 1895 the Clydesdale Bank's London office began using the first typewriter in Scottish banking, and four years later it acquired the first adding machine. Much of the impetus for technical modernisation came from reports from overseas Scottish bankers, and the activities of the Association undoubtedly encouraged the banks to investigate such changes.[33]

By the mid-1930s, new life was stirring in the bones of the Association, and the best-organised membership was in the Union Bank, for several reasons. Norman Hird was a vigorous and outspoken opponent of trade unionists; he antagonised many of his own staff, and the Union had certain special staff problems. The possibilities, so enticing before the war, of emigration to the Dominions no longer existed on the same scale, and the result was that many within the Union Bank could only look forward to a general absence of promotion. Other banks faced similar problems, but they encouraged early retirement with financial inducements. Not so the Union Bank; and when discontent began to grow once again from

---

31 S. G. Checkland, *Scottish Banking: A History, 1695–1973* (Glasgow: 1975), pp. 582–91.
32 C. L. Mowat, *Britain between the Wars 1918–40*, 2nd edn (London: 1956), pp. 37–8.
33 Checkland, *Scottish Banking*, pp. 510–12.

about 1934, its trade unionists were in the forefront of the agitation. The idea of a strike throughout Scotland was once again discussed; and to make it effective, the Union Bank, as the best-organised, was chosen to lead the attempt. The strike, called for 30 April 1937 and vigorously opposed by all the banks, collapsed almost as soon as it had begun, with its leader being dismissed. This was less of a success for Norman Hird, as it led directly to the loss of the Scottish Co-operative Wholesale Society account. The desired aim of recognition was as far away as ever, although the Association, weakened inevitably by failure, still maintained its existence until the next outbreak of war in September 1939. Its influence upon working conditions, although never decisive, had nonetheless been important in that its standard demands undoubtedly helped to focus the attention of management upon staff matters which otherwise might have been overlooked or disregarded.[34]

34 Ibid., pp. 582-91; and see also BS, Uncatalogued, Memorandum, John Rankin on N. Tamaki's history of the Union Bank. Rankin was assistant secretary to the Union Bank from 1947-53.

CHAPTER 22

THE SECOND WORLD WAR

FOR THE FIRST eight months of the Second World War, the government of Neville Chamberlain was unable to appreciate the scale of the financial resources required for the war effort and the implications thereof for the distribution of the national income. It was also evident that the pre-war ideas held by the banks as to the cost of borrowing for the war would prove a source of conflict. A government loan for £300 million at 3 per cent in March 1940 failed when the banks thought the offer terms too low, and the public authorities were left with two-thirds on their hands.[1] It required the invasion of Denmark and Norway in April and the Benelux countries and France in May 1940, which ended the 'phoney war', to focus attention on the gravity of the financial situation. The administration of Winston Churchill, appointed in May, was much tougher with the City. J. M. Keynes, installed at the Treasury, had a clear vision of how the hostilities should be financed and supported by the Bank of England, and henceforth the government kept a tight rein on money, capital issues and financial institutions throughout the war.[2]

Paying for the mobilisation of fighting forces and the production of munitions was given absolute priority, and to this aim finance was subordinated. The standard rate of income tax rose from 5s 6d to 8s 6d in September 1939 and from the summer of 1940 to 10s; in 1941 this was augmented by a wide range of taxes on goods and by an excess profits tax of up to 100 per cent over a standard pre-war level.[3] A new scheme of

---

1 R. S. Sayers, *The Bank of England 1891–1944* (Cambridge: 1986), vol. 2, ch. 21; idem, *Financial Policy 1939–45* (London: 1956), pp. 159–62. Bank of Scotland took £1.5 million of this loan.

2 Sayers, *Financial Policy*, ch. 2; S. Pollard, *The Development of the British Economy 1914–1967*, 2nd edn (London: 1969), pp. 322–30; J. M. Keynes, 'How to Pay for the War' (1940), in *The Collected Writings of John Maynard Keynes*, vol. ix, *Essays in Persuasion* (London: 1972), pp. 367–439.

3 A. G. McBain, 'Excess Profits Tax', *Scottish Bankers Magazine*, 35 (1943–4), 7–11, 52–6, 92–5, 135–7. A complicated tax, introduced by the Finance (no. 2) Act, 1939, and extended by subsequent

pay-as-you-earn (PAYE) from September 1943, along with frequent re-finements to indirect taxation, sharply reduced personal consumption; and strict rationing procedures on essential foodstuffs and petrol further reduced personal consumption and freed resources for government. After difficulties in the Chamberlain period, borrowing from the public was fixed at 2½ per cent for National War Bonds and 3 per cent for Savings Bonds, and firms could put balances in tax reserve certificates to anticipate future tax demands. Bank rate stayed at 2 per cent from 26 October 1939. Borrowing from financial institutions and the banks was fixed at a rate of 1 per cent for Treasury bills, and wage inflation was eased by subsidies; after a rise in the cost of living of 20 per cent in the winter of 1939–40, it rose by under 10 per cent overall from then to 1945.[4] This was altogether a tighter and far more effective financial regime than that which had been in place during the First World War.

By the spring of 1939, the General Managers Committee of the eight Scottish banks had finalised plans for wartime. Air-raid precautions were undertaken and staff drilled in procedures for fires. Units of the Home Guard were formed, among whose duties were the provision of men to guard the more important bank buildings. Measures were agreed on the duplication of account balances. The banks agreed to open no new offices, to close sub-offices under reciprocal arrangements and to cease 'all ordinary competition between the banks ... entirely'.[5] The supply of silver coin to firms would be suspended, branches of all the banks would lend cash to each other and they would reissue each other's notes. Otherwise, the usual agreements remained in place.[6] Individual banks arranged extra borrowing rights at the Bank of England – £700,000 in the case of Bank of Scotland. Agreement was reached with the English clearing banks over London deposit rates, and the overseas banks and the discount houses were also brought into a general agreement. Further, the GMC agreed that John Crawford, Treasurer of Bank of Scotland, would act as the centre 'for clarification' of all approaches from government departments over the handling of accounts. Thus, when the Ministry of Supply told the Commercial Bank that terms for an account for a government factory in October 1939 must include delivery of new notes and silver to the site, and

Acts, the object was to impose a levy on all profits which exceeded the pre-war standard; exemptions were allowed for firms in certain trades which were classed as depressed in the relevant standard period and were thus of interest to bank managers in the special areas of Scotland which had firms in these classes.

4 Sayers, *Financial Policy*, p. 165.
5 C. W. Munn, *Clydesdale Bank: The First One Hundred and Fifty Years* (Glasgow: 1988), p. 219; BS, Uncatalogued, General Managers Committee, Minutes, 3, 24 July 1939; BS, unpublished, J. F. Wilson, 'Reminiscences of a Lifetime in Scottish Banking, 1939–1984' (1984), pp. 7–8.
6 BS, Uncatalogued, GMC, Minutes, 11 September and 16 October 1939; BS, Uncatalogued, GMC, Miscellaneous papers.

the supply of OHMS cheque forms free of charge, John Crawford instructed the Commercial Bank to refuse.

Inevitably, once war had started and experienced manpower was called up, there was pressure on bank services. Many staff went as soon as war was declared, including men of 'E' Company of the 1st Battalion of the King's Edinburgh Rifles, called up in 1939. By October 1942, 55 per cent of pre-war managerial and clerical staff of the Scottish banks had been called up for war service. Of the 1,261 Bank of Scotland staff on the books in 1939, 657 were called up on active service, and of these forty-eight were subsequently killed in action.[7] Inevitably, cheques were cleared more slowly, and firms were asked to spread the workload that they imposed on the banks. The GMC agreed to remove discretion over the imposition of charges, and the Chief Accountants Committee worked out ways to speed up processing.[8] The pressure on banking staff created by the issue of more banknotes and the circulation of Bank of England notes was reduced somewhat by the issue of each other's notes and reductions in the frequency of exchanges. Section 2 of the Currency (Defence) Act, 1939, made Scottish notes legal tender in Scotland.[9] By an Order in Council of September 1940, all Bank of England notes and cash held by any Scottish bank branch could be counted towards the 'cover' for the fiduciary issue of Scottish notes. By December 1940, the volume of Scottish banknotes with the public had risen 22 per cent over the pre-war figure, from £23.7 million to £30.2 million, and by 1945 to £65.9 million. Bank of Scotland was the largest issuer for virtually the whole of the war, and by 1945 the Union Bank enjoyed the smallest share, behind even the North of Scotland Bank. The demand for notes was due both to the buoyancy of employment and the rise in wages and, apparently, to a strong preference by firms and workmen to hold on to higher than normal cash balances, in spite of requests for the mobilisation of such money for war savings.[10]

The legal framework for lending was similar to that for the English banks. The Courts (Emergency Powers) Act, 1939, prevented the seizure of property and moveables except by due legal process; this was primarily intended to stop seizures of goods by hire-purchase companies, although it also overrode conditions in all bank contracts with customers. Under the

---

7 C. A. Malcolm, *The Bank of Scotland, 1695–1945* (Edinburgh: n.d. [1948]), pp. 152–3, 264.

8 BS, Uncatalogued, GMC, Minutes, 16 November 1942, 1 and 15 March 1943.

9 2 & 3 George VI c.64, 'An Act to amend the law with respect to the application and financing of the Exchange Equalisation Account; to make certain bank notes legal tender', commonly known as the Currency (Defence) Act, 1939. The 'legal tender' authorisation was withdrawn in 1945.

10 The matter of cash holdings by firms was raised by the GMC and at proprietors' meetings; see Bank of Scotland, *Annual Report* (1945), Lord Elphinstone to proprietors, 3 April 1945. The interest rate on deposit accounts was ½–1 per cent, so there was less incentive for firms to return cash than before the war. For Bank of Scotland banknote circulation, see Statistical Appendix, Table A8.

powers of the Defence (Finance) Regulations, the Foreign Transactions Advisory Committee was converted into a new Capital Issues Committee which issued strict guidelines under which capital could be raised. The Treasury dealt with Empire and foreign stock and bill issues, and the Ministry of Health adjudicated on applications from local authorities, a task carried out in Scotland by the Home and Health Department. These regulations and the imposition of direct control on all domestic holdings of dollar securities (around £1 billion) severely restricted the activity of financial houses, stockbrokers and overseas investment trusts. An unaccustomed lull fell on the Scottish bank offices in London. Exchange control on foreign currencies was imposed in August 1939. The clearing banks, acting for the Treasury and the Bank of England, were given the role of arbiter with allowances for normal business, existing contracts, foreign travel in pursuit of business and, occasionally, for legal or personal reasons. The Bank of England appointed the Royal Bank as its agent to deal with applications for exchange allocations from the Scottish banks. The regulations were tightened from March to July 1940 with the aim of detailed control of scarce foreign-exchange resources and the negotiation of bilateral agreements with trading partners.[11]

In wartime, as Norman Hird reminded readers of *The Banker*, the work of banks 'runs on fairly stereotyped lines'.[12] Their primary role was to fund government borrowing, lend to approved borrowers in trade and industry and issue the volume of notes which customers required. To the government, their role in funding debt was crucial. The level of deposits in Scottish banks went up sharply, from £325 million in 1938–9 to £453 million by 1942–3 and at the close of war to £590.3 million. Bank of Scotland deposits rose from £37.8 million to £71.8 million. The distribution of these liabilities into assets showed a divergence from the pattern in England. The GMC was concerned that the pre-war pattern of Scottish bank portfolios should be preserved and that excess funds from deposits should go into medium- and long-dated British government securities (gilts). The ratio of gilts to deposits thus changed little: 56.7 per cent of deposits for all Scottish banks compared with 28.1 per cent for the English clearers in 1938, and 57.8 per cent with 28.6 per cent in England by 1945. In the case of Bank of Scotland, with its even greater holdings in government funds, the figure was 63.3 per cent in 1939 and 61.8 per cent at the end of the war.[13] The prices and yields of gilts remained stable from 1941 to 1945.[14]

11 'The New Finance Regulations', *The Banker*, 52 (1939), 9–28; Sayers, *Financial Policy*, pp. 232–51.
12 N. L. Hird, 'Scottish Banking in 1942/43', *The Banker*, 68 (1943), 73–7.
13 For Bank of Scotland holdings of British government securities, see Table 20.5. See Statistical Appendix, Table A8 for published annual balance-sheet totals.
14 Pember and Boyle, *British Government Securities in the Twentieth Century: The First Fifty Years*,

Prior to the war, the government had raised the bulk of its short-term money requirement from the English clearing banks via the discount market on three-month Treasury bills whose price was governed by bank rate. In 1938, the weekly average fluctuated from £808.6 million to £976 million.[15] The Scottish banks took a collective view from the onset of the cheap money policy in 1932 that the difference in the yield between Treasury bills and longer-dated gilts did not justify the lower yield of the former just to obtain the flexibility that they offered.[16] In 1938, just £8.5 million was laid out in all bill discounts, including Treasury bills – some 2.6 per cent of deposits – whereas the English clearing banks laid out 12.1 per cent of their deposits in this form. From June 1939, the government pushed the demand above £1 billion, although temporary surpluses in tax and exchange accounts slowed down the rise in the demands on the Treasury bill market in the winter and spring of 1940. After the military situation deteriorated in April 1940, the sums outstanding rose by over £100 million per month and had passed £2 billion by November. The contribution from the Scottish banks formed only a minute part of this total: £5.9 million in 1941 (1.4 per cent of deposits) and £7.3 million in 1942 (1.6 per cent).

In July 1940, Treasury Deposit Receipts (TDRs) were devised by the Treasury, after advice from the Bank of England, to supplement the working of the bill market and mop up excess liquidity.[17] This new form of borrowing was arranged between the Treasury and the clearing banks, the Scottish banks and the two central banks in the London market, the Commonwealth Bank of Australia and the National Bank of Egypt. A TDR ran for six months and was non-negotiable, and interest was fixed at 1⅛ per cent and was tied to a gentleman's agreement, sanctioned by the Treasury, that the Bank of England would provide cash for the banks should they need it in an emergency. A TDR thus counted as part of a bank's liquid assets. By December 1940, £312 million had been raised by TDRs, rising to £1 billion by January 1943 and, with fluctuations, above £2 billion by May 1945. However, they were less important than Treasury bills – at their height in 1944 and 1945, they reached a little over 50 per cent of the latter – and, as bankers were keen to return to the

2nd edn (private circulation, London: 1950), pp. 85–95; *Statistical Digest of the War* (London: 1951), p. 197, Table 176, 'Prices and Yields of British Government Securities'; F. W. Forge, 'Scottish Banks Face the Transition', *The Banker*, 80 (1946), 91–4.

15 *Statistical Digest of the War*, p. 196, Table 174, 'Floating Debt'.

16 For the rise in value and income from British government securities after 1932, see above, Chapters 20 and 21; 'Scottish Banks in 1940–41', *The Banker*, 60 (1941), 100–8; 'Scottish Banking and Cheap Money', *The Banker*, 48 (1938), 165–70; M. Gaskin, *The Scottish Banks: A Modern Survey* (London: 1965), p. 121.

17 Sayers, *Financial Policy*, pp. 220–3.

normal bill market, the volume fell away from October 1945. The GMC had little choice but to agree to the scheme, and used it as a reason for reducing deposit interest to 1 per cent.[18] Yet, by the winter of 1941–2, total Scottish holdings of TDRS were £40 million (9.5 per cent of deposits), and at their height in 1945 they had reached £74.5 million or 12.6 per cent of deposits, whereas by 1942 the English clearing banks' ratio of TDRS to deposits was 24.7 per cent, and 35 per cent by 1944.[19] On several occasions, Scottish banks sold TDRS and reinvested in gilts.[20] The reason for the importance of low-priced government stocks, TDRS and Treasury bills was confirmed in 1940. It was agreed that the government should pay directly for national war activity, which would hold down the advance of prices 'besides restricting the holding of stocks of merchandise for home consumption'.[21] It was inevitable that the government would borrow an increased proportion of bank deposits and would wish to minimise the servicing costs.

Lord Elphinstone continued his pre-war support for the strong association of Bank of Scotland with the fortunes of British government medium- and long-dated stocks. 'It is very necessary', he informed proprietors in 1944, 'that a strong liquid position should be maintained, and throughout the year, as always, we have observed orthodox principles with a substantial margin to spare'.[22] Assets in cash, bank balances, cheques in transit, money at call and short notice and bills discounted formed 26 per cent of public liabilities; this was normally regarded as adequate 'narrow' liquidity, but in the war the proportion of deposits placed with the government greatly increased – and Lord Elphinstone referred to all of this wider 'liquidity' as amounting sometimes to as much as 90 per cent of public liabilities. This theme was frequently reiterated, emphasising the value of a 'consistently careful and prudent policy and of strict adherence to those well established principles' upon which Scottish banking had been built and upon which its 'high reputation' rested.[23] These views were shared by the directors of the Union Bank and the British Linen Bank and to a greater or lesser extent by other banks in Scotland.

18 BS, Uncatalogued, GMC, Minutes, 1 July 1940; interest on savings accounts up to £500 was agreed at 1.5 per cent.
19 F. W. Forge, 'Scottish Banking in 1943–44', *The Banker*, 72 (1944), 84–9. Bank of Scotland had a higher ratio of TDRS to deposits – 15 per cent – by 1945, although the ratio fell away after the war.
20 BS 1/6/8, Minutes, 7 March 1944, sale of TDRS and purchase of National War Bonds; also 16 May 1944 and 7 May 1944.
21 BS 1/2/4, Proprietors' Minutes, 1941.
22 BS 1/2/4, Proprietors' Minutes, 1944. Sir Harold Yarrow, chairman of the Clydesdale Bank, was less enthusiastic when he pointed this out to his shareholders: Munn, *Clydesdale Bank*, p. 220.
23 BS 1/2/4, Proprietors' Minutes, 1945. For figures for published annual balance sheets, see Statistical Appendix, Table A8.

The main explanation for the Bank's preference for gilts resulted from the experience of the inter-war slump, especially in the period 1930–6, and its cautious involvement in pre-war industrial expansion. Lord Elphinstone and the board stated their preference at proprietors' meetings in the late 1930s for investment in overseas trade, domestic industry and the shipping industry. The Governor remained ill at ease with domestic public expenditure and rearmament, and persisted in his view that these were 'artificial' stimuli.[24] Domestic industry could only compete with foreigners by assiduous attention to holding down costs, and the banks should be cautious about the degree to which they made advances. This may have underlined the Bank's reluctance to seek out new lending in the engineering and heavy industries of the west of Scotland. In fact, by 1939, under 1 per cent of the advances to the Scottish iron and steel industry were from Bank of Scotland; and although the figures are not ascertainable for engineering, there was no question but that the Clydesdale Bank and the Union Bank were far more important for the finance of west-of-Scotland industry.

Rearmament and war were crucial to the fortunes of the Scottish engineering, shipbuilding, steel and general manufacturing industries, and the rate of increase of the economy as a whole from 1935–6 onwards outstripped that of the rest of the UK. Unemployment fell by 100,000 between January and August 1939 to stand at 186,400. Such was the pressure on the labour market by September 1941 that only 39,900 drew insurance benefit. Employment in the heavy industries (shipbuilding, general and marine engineering, metal goods, vehicles and aircraft) rose from 157,040 in 1939 to 215,640 (27 per cent of the insured workforce) by August 1945.[25] By then twenty, mainly industrial, sectors had benefited from an expansion of employment compared with a contraction of thirty in service and luxury trades, although there were also sharp reductions in the building trades. A number of industrial sectors, including food and drink, timber products, precision instruments and specialised military equipment (such as radios and radar), saw output expand faster than in England, encouraged by persistent activity on the part of the Scottish Home and Health Department. The existence of a clear understanding, before the war, of the deficiencies in the distribution of 'new' industries greatly assisted this work, although a number of the developments directed to Scotland in aircraft, guns and vehicles did not survive long after the end of hostilities. Full employment made a significant difference to the

---

24 BS 1/2/4, Proprietors' Minutes, 1937 and 1939.
25 For a detailed discussion of Scottish industrial trends during the war, see R. Saville (ed.), *The Economic Development of Modern Scotland 1950–1980* (Edinburgh: 1985), p. 31.

overall position of Scottish wage-earners. The Scottish proportion of UK wages rose to 10 per cent by 1943, and, though there was a fall from 1946 to 1947, the figure had recovered to 9.5 per cent by 1949.[26]

The first indication of government restrictions on loans was issued in September 1939 by Sir John Simon, the Chancellor:

> The prohibition of the export of British capital and the restriction on the public issue of new capital for domestic use are measures directed towards conserving the current savings of the country exclusively for government purposes. But these measures would obviously be frustrated if finance were made available by means of banking accommodation in amounts or for purposes which would conflict or compete with this policy and which might result in an unnecessary expansion of credit, contribute to any general rise in prices and cause a diversion of resources towards non-essential needs.[27]

By July 1940, the government had imposed strict controls, and decisions about the extension of plant were made by the Admiralty, the Air Ministry, the War Office and departments of state. Thus the Scottish banks found little room for manoeuvre. Advances fell sharply from 32.4 per cent of non-liquid assets to only 15 per cent by 1945 – a fall from £105.2 million in 1938–9 to £88.7 million by 1945.[28] In the case of Bank of Scotland, advances for trade and industry declined from £10.6 million to £7.84 million.

Most of the work offered to Bank of Scotland in the war was straightforward: each month, managers and directors considered applications from small businesses, retail outlets, solicitors and farmers, requests for temporary advances for trustees to cover death duties, stockbrokers' and other bridging loans, and the occasional, usually unsecured, advance for some person of wealth. Requests for sums under £500 continued to be dealt with by branch managers, usually on the basis of personal knowledge of the circumstances of the customer.[29] Advances fell sharply in this small-loan category and did not equal pre-war figures until 1947 and in real terms not until a year later.[30] Sums from £500 to £2,000 were appraised as

26 A. D. Campbell, 'Changes in Scottish Income, 1924–49', *Economic Journal*, 65 (1955), 225–40 (p. 232, Figure 2); idem, 'Income', in A. K. Cairncross (ed.), *The Scottish Economy* (Cambridge: 1954), pp. 46–64 (p. 52, Table 26).

27 Sir John Simon to Governor of the Bank of England, 26 September 1939. Montagu gave the letter to Crawford, who copied it to GMC members. It was discussed by the GMC on 16 October 1939; the specified exceptions covered armaments, the export trade, coalmining and agriculture.

28 Forge, 'Scottish Banks Face the Transition'; Munn, *Clydesdale Bank*, p. 220.

29 Forge, 'Scottish Banking in 1943–44'; the difference in the legal system which led to the greater emphasis in Scottish banking on 'the character of the borrower and the nature of the use to which [the money] is to be put, and far less on collateral', had its roots in the seventeenth century.

30 Whereas the average of small loans in October 1937, 1938 and 1939 was eighty-three advances totalling £20,282 (average £244), in October 1941 and 1942 only forty-six loans were made totalling £14,410 (average £313).

usual by the executive at the Mound, and applications for greater amounts went forward to the board of directors. Again, as one would expect from the employment figures, the pattern was of contraction for non-essential work and expansion for munitions. Loans for stockbrokers on the three exchanges in Glasgow, Aberdeen and Edinburgh were dutifully curtailed by Bank of Scotland – yet in late 1943 the GMC discovered that the English clearers had partially ignored Treasury rulings on the level of advances to stockbrokers, with the result that members of the London Stock Exchange had attracted extra Scottish business. Some of the work lost by Scottish stockbrokers was not recovered.[31]

The board of Bank of Scotland continued to reconsider all large advances (over £2,000) once a year, and, in the pattern familiar to Scottish practice, rarely urged reduction unless there were problems. Many of these in wartime remained substantial, such as the £1 million (unsecured) support for the Airdrie Savings Bank, the £500,000 (secured) for Canada Life Assurance and the £100,000 (secured) through the London Piccadilly Circus branch for the John Dewar company, whisky distillers. The largest industrial loans made by the Bank went to Barr & Stroud,[32] the demand for whose specialised engineering products such as range-finders had soared. They held two accounts, in Glasgow and Piccadilly Circus, on a secured loan of £200,000. In 1941, with sales of £1,775,604, they had unexecuted orders worth £3.7 million, notwithstanding extensions to their principal factories at Anniesland in Glasgow and the allocation of space in thirty-six others. The 'Company [was] wholly engaged on work of the highest national importance', and in February 1942 the Bank was asked for another £250,000 at Piccadilly Circus and £450,000 at Anniesland, with £50,000 more on a temporary basis. By 1945, the total on loan from the Bank had reached £1 million. The Glasgow managers of the Bank provided other financial support for the company, including temporary overdrafts and cash for wages as requested.

The position of Barr & Stroud was exceptional. The next three large loans (by size and duration) for engineering firms were somewhat smaller.[33] Bulls Metal & Melloid Ltd of Glasgow made aircraft propellers, and in 1939 were granted an unsecured loan of £10,000. It was discovered during the Battle of Britain that cracked wooden propellers were expensive in lives and aircraft, so metal ones were more cost-effective, and Bulls were awarded contracts for bronze and other alloy propellers and shafts. By September 1942, their advance had reached £45,000. Mactaggart, Scott

31 BS, Uncatalogued, GMC, Minutes, 10 January 1944.
32 There is a company history: M. S. Moss and I. Russell, *Range and Vision: The First Hundred Years of Barr & Stroud* (Edinburgh: 1988).
33 BS 1/6/8, Minutes, wartime loans.

& Co., engineers, of Loanhead, held Admiralty contracts from pre-war days. Their secured loan from the Bank was £25,000; in February 1940 this went up to £40,000, and by 1943 to £100,000 (part unsecured). Before the war, the famous nautical instrument-makers Kelvin, Bottomley & Baird of Glasgow had an unsecured loan of £20,000. So important was their work for the navy that the Bank was asked to raise this to £30,000 in 1940 and by degrees to £150,000 by March 1943 (all unsecured). All three firms had to purchase new equipment and to build and renovate factories, and the Bank also found itself involved in various requests over funding for their suppliers.

The range of industrial advances was wide and, as with the above loans to the engineering industry, usually rested on long associations with the borrower. In Dundee, the Buist Spinning Company had received £75,000 by 1943; Sir Alexander Gibb, the consulting engineers, had £86,000 in 1942; and Candles Ltd, the oil and grease merchants, received £100,000 from 1941 until after the war. The Glebe Sugar Refining Co. of Greenock had £100,000 throughout the war; in August 1943, R. S. McColl of Glasgow extended borrowing to £20,000 (unsecured); and Bayne & Duckett, the boot and shoe manufacturers, borrowed £50,000 in Glasgow and London. A number of advances were curtailed under Treasury restrictions, such as that to Falkirk Ice Rink, cut from £15,000 to £10,000 in 1941, although many firms curtailed their borrowing because of better cash flow or as a result of cuts in supplies. There is clear evidence that the Scottish banks benefited in the war from improvement in repayments. Bank of Scotland recorded a surplus of recoveries over new provisions in the bad-debt account, and this was the case in each year of the war. The GMC discussed the apportionment of a number of advances for large-scale projects and developed its own guidelines for marginal cases, although physical controls over materials and labour made it obvious which companies could justify additional loans and cash credits.

The need to grow food at home to save foreign exchange and shipping space ensured that serious attention was paid to the farming community, notably with systems of price support and advances for development and machinery. In pre-war days, the Scottish Agricultural Securities Corporation Ltd had helped cases with a degree of risk attached, but it remained the view of the banks that sufficient funds were available to the farming community. Nonetheless, complaints indicated that hill farmers and tenants in small farms still faced difficulty. War changed this position. In 1940, the Department of Agriculture for Scotland and the GMC agreed to rules for advances to farmers unable to obtain credit in the normal way of banking: these advances would be made by banks on special cash accounts; the borrower would sign an undertaking to repay and as security assign to the bank any subsidies due by the Department; the loans would be on a yearly basis and would be renegotiated after each harvest; and interest would not exceed 5 per cent.[34] Whereas agricultural prices remained flat from 1936 to 1939 (with an index level of 103 by the outbreak of war), they rose to 143 in 1940 and to 196 by 1945.[35] Farmers' incomes in Scotland thus soared: from an average net income of only £202 in 1938–9, they rose to £1,406 by 1941–2. The hill sheep-farmers, whose incomes failed to cover costs in 1938–40, saw a net income of £439 in 1941–2 and £787 by 1944–5. There was more good news for farmers after the war: whereas, at the close of the boom which followed the First World War, farm prices had collapsed, now, by contrast, subsidies saw farm prices in 1950 some 40 per cent above those of 1945.[36] Scotland had 12.5 per cent of the UK income from agriculture in 1948, which reflected the way in which the farm price-support system was skewed towards Scottish outputs.[37] During the war, British agriculture was still in the age of the hand-milking of dairy herds, the potato gangs, hand-binding and stacking at harvest, and dung and lime for fertiliser; there were, for example, 312,710 horse-drawn ploughs in April 1944, twice the number that were tractor-drawn.[38] The commitment to post-war subsidies changed all this.[39] For the next four decades, rural bank branches were given an extra lease of life on the profits culled from farm-support policies.[40]

The underlying position of the Bank deteriorated during the war. Liabilities in 1939 were a little over £50 million, and almost doubled to £96.8 million in 1946; yet the gross trading profits fell from 1939 (£365,134) to 1942 (£272,645) and did not recover the pre-war level until 1945. The board cut dividends from 12 to 11 per cent in 1940 and cut the proportion of gross profits allocated to the declared profits. By these means, inner reserves and the published reserves were strengthened, and stood at £7,351,152 in 1946, a rise of 21 per cent since the outbreak of war.[41] The paid-up capital remained at £2.4 million throughout the war. There were a number of difficulties with the balance sheet, notably over the high level

34 C. J. Shimmins, 'Scottish Banking Notes: Advances to Farmers', *The Banker*, 54 (1940), 180–1.
35 K. A. H. Murray, *Agriculture*, History of the Second World War, United Kingdom civil series (London: 1955), pp. 290, 382–3, Tables XII, XIII: farmers' share of national income increased from 1.2 to 2.4 per cent.
36 Ibid., p. 287; G. F. B. Houston, 'Agriculture', in A. K. Cairncross (ed.), *The Scottish Economy* (Cambridge: 1954), pp. 84–108 (p. 91).
37 Campbell, 'Income', p. 51; it was the system of price support negotiated by the Department of Agriculture for Scotland and not just a reflection of greater regional specialisation in farming.
38 *Statistical Digest of the War*, p. 63, Tables 63, 64.
39 C. J. Shimmins, 'Scottish Trade and Industry', *The Banker*, 76 (1945), 94–6.
40 M. Chase, ' "Nothing Less than a Revolution"?: Labour's Agricultural Policy', in J. Fyrth (ed.), *Labour's High Noon: The Government and the Economy 1945–51* (London: 1993), pp. 78–95.
41 See Statistical Appendix, Table A7.

of investment in medium- and long-dated British government securities, although, at this time, this was not perceived as a potential difficulty but rather as a strength, giving a higher income than shorter-term financial instruments on the London money markets. Although the internal position of the Bank was kept a secret, hints did appear in the press and trade journals.[42] The proprietors' funds, Lord Elphinstone acknowledged in 1948, 'are substantially greater than the nominal amount of capital and published reserves. From time to time over the long lifetime of the Bank large sums have been set aside to cover contingencies and depreciation, and to the extent that they are available the accumulations are used in our day to day business.'[43] At this time, while the published reserves and capital, dividends and the carry-forward of the balance in the profit and loss account came to £5,247,959, the actual total of proprietors' funds was £10,066,619.

42 See Gaskin, *Scottish Banks*, ch. 5 for a discussion of hidden reserves, published at a time when details were still secret; Forge, 'Scottish Banking in 1943–44': 'There is no reason to suppose that the published figures are more representative of real earnings than are those of the clearing banks' (p. 86).
43 Bank of Scotland, *Annual Report* (1948), Lord Elphinstone to proprietors, April 1948.

CHAPTER 23

RECOVERY AND CRISIS, 1945–58

THE END OF the war led to a general election on 5 July 1945 which, much to the surprise of the Labour leadership, resulted in a huge Labour majority. These events meant that the banking community in Scotland was faced with a new set of problems. Aside from the political complexion of the government, most bankers assumed, or feared, that what had happened to the economy after the First World War would happen again. Therefore, they were cautious about long-term advances for older industries which, it was thought, would benefit from a short-lived boom but would then face depression. No-one really appreciated that the industrial world was already on a secular upward growth path. This caution also hindered advances for some newer developments. Further, the experience of the inter-war years in respect of investments had shown that British government securities generated good income and maintained the value of bank funds. This positive feeling about gilts was strengthened by the commitment of Hugh Dalton, the Chancellor of the Exchequer, to hold bank rate at 2 per cent, where it had been since 26 October 1939; and all government stocks rose strongly in 1946.[1] There were also political fears. Among other commitments, the Labour manifesto included an intention to nationalise the Bank of England; it was the first compensation to be arranged, and gave the stockholders a yield slightly above the average of the previous twenty years' 12 per cent dividend. This involved the distribution of £58.2 million in 3 per cent stock redeemable at par after twenty years, and it immediately traded above par. As *The Economist* noted, 'It would take a very nervous heart to register a flutter at what is contained in the bill. Nothing could be more

---

1 Pember and Boyle, *British Government Securities in the Twentieth Century: The First Fifty Years*, 2nd edn (private circulation, London: 1950), pp. 95–7.

moderate.' There was no mention of nationalisation of any other part of the banking system, and it was made clear by the prime minister, Clement Attlee, and his senior finance ministers, that the cabinet was absolutely opposed to such a policy. Nevertheless, fears that the Labour Party would, in fact, proceed with a nationalisation of the clearing banks remained an aspect of political debate.[2]

The views of Bank of Scotland, expressed at the annual general meetings, as to how the Labour government should manage the post-war economy and national finances envisaged less direct involvement and lower spending than the Labour cabinet was prepared to contemplate. The Bank wanted wartime controls to be removed, 'so that the natural forces of supply and demand may be allowed to operate' to restore 'a staple economy' from where Britain could regain its 'pre-eminence as a leader of nations'. 'We must', Lord Elphinstone reiterated, 'get back to fundamentals' – basic economic laws, 'orthodox economics' which laid out urgent, unpalatable facts.[3] By this he meant an overriding concern that inflation should be controlled and that the government should create a 'genuine Budget surplus' and stop wasteful expenditure. Thus the 'ruthless pruning of Government spending should have the highest priority ... swollen department staff could be drastically reduced – with the twofold advantage of releasing manpower for productive industry and easing taxation'.[4] While the board undoubtedly felt that this was a sound way forward for the economy, such a policy would, moreover, tend to support the capital values of gilts. Yet the Bank also welcomed the demise of Dalton's cheap money policy in 1947, and the gradual rise in interest rates thereafter. Shortly before the fall of the Labour government in 1951, the Bank added its weight to the demands for a rise in the Bank of England base rate: 'While there was justification for a cheap money policy during the war and the early post-war period it would seem to be of doubtful advantage now in face of an intensified inflationary threat'.[5]

In the five years to 1950, the Bank's gross trading income rose by more than one-third to £2,157,948 and gross trading profits by 25 per cent to

---

2 The banking journals may have fuelled these fears. The General Managers Committee, in a discussion on nationalisation in January 1949, noted that 'it appeared that all the banks are keeping clearly before them the possibility of legislation being introduced. It was felt it would be undesirable to take any overt steps at present.' In July, the Central Council of Scottish Bank Staffs' Association noted that 'while they were not enamoured of the idea of nationalisation', they wanted a national salary scale 'before this happened': BS, Uncatalogued, GMC, Minutes, 10 January and 4 July 1949. The GMC refused to be drawn into the anti-nationalisation campaigns of 1950 and 1951.
3 When the board, in pre-war days, considered the 250th anniversary of the foundation of Bank of Scotland, the first choice for author of the academic history was Sir Alexander Gray, an orthodox economist.
4 BS 1/2/4, Proprietors' Minutes, 1945, 1946, 1947, 1948.
5 Ibid., 1951.

£501,723.[6] Declared profits rose by only 14 per cent, as the Treasurer and directors increased the total inner allocations; in 1950 these reached £195,000, almost double the figure in 1945. While this strengthened the reserves (both published and inner accounts), which reached £7,748,448 in 1949, as a proportion of liabilities – now £113,574,716 – reserves were still below the level immediately after the war. The Bank's internal figures also showed that during the war the gross trading profits had not maintained their pre-war proportion of gross trading income: in 1939 this ratio was 33.1 per cent, by 1945 only 24.6 per cent, and by 1950 still only 23.3 per cent. The other banking ratios were significantly worse than in pre-war days, although bad debt as a proportion of advances was minimal. As the crucial figure for interest income on advances related closely to the Bank of England minimum discount rate, and earnings in the London money markets bore some relationship to the base rate, it was in the interests of bankers to see a rise in interest charges. Some journals, including *The Economist*, even suggested in 1951 that 4 per cent would be a good position. Yet only a part of the assets of Scottish banks were placed where they would benefit from a rise in income following such a change, and this proportion was generally below the levels found in the English clearing banks.

The board expected the price of the Bank's holdings in gilts to remain stable, and the investments committee continued to make purchases after 1945. By 28 February 1950, these were 45.9 per cent of assets, a little below the 49.4 per cent of 1946.[7] In fact, during the maintenance of cheap money, the price of gilts held by the Bank rose in 1946 and early 1947, yet by the autumn there was a 'serious' decline in gilt values which affected the new issue market.[8] With alarming candour, a correspondent of the *Scottish Bankers Magazine* could write that

> if I were the general manager of a bank I would much rather see my advances increase than my investments. Looking to the fall in the value of Government stocks . . . I should be surprised to learn that any Scottish bank had had to make provision for bad and doubtful debts on anything like the scale for which they have had to provide for depreciation of gilt-edged stocks.[9]

But in the spring and summer of 1948, the response of the investments committee of Bank of Scotland was to increase purchases as the price

6 See Statistical Appendix, Tables A7 and A8.
7 These figures are book values; see Statistical Appendix, Table A8.
8 Pember and Boyle, *British Government Securities*, pp. 97–9; *Monthly Digest of Statistics*, 'Security Prices and Yields: British Government Securities' (1948); 'Market Reports and Business Notes: The Money Market', *Scottish Bankers Magazine*, 39 (1947–8), 180–1.
9 J. Lockie, 'Influences on Banking in 1947', *Scottish Bankers Magazine*, 40 (1948–9), 15–21.

falls made gilts cheaper and boosted the yield. Again, in April 1951, for example, the committee sold £2 million of 3 per cent war loan 1955/59, and 4 per cent consolidated loan payable in 1957 and after, buying £2 million 4 per cent funding loan payable in 1960/90 and £1.5 million 2½ per cent funding loan, 1956/61.[10] There was only a modest purchase of short-dated stock, whose price held up better. While this investments policy was perhaps proper for the needs of the Bank in respect of yield and had proved good for thirty years, it was more difficult to justify when the outlook was for higher interest rates. It was an especially difficult time for the medium- and long-dated securities: those with over five years to run before maturity, and undated stocks, saw sharp falls.[11] By 1949, the fall in gilt prices had had an inevitable impact on the capital value of the Bank holdings, and at the balance day, 28 February 1950, the surplus on stocks account and the investment reserve were both written down to zero. Yet, in the face of the deterioration in market values, the Bank continued to support a flexible interest-rate policy. At the April 1951 AGM, Lord Elphinstone noted that interest rates were still too low. 'Existing rates of interest are somewhat unrealistic and appear actually to aggravate the inflationary trend. In the past bank rate proved its efficiency as a corrective and we believe it could again operate beneficially.'

On 23 February 1950, Labour was returned but with a much-reduced majority. The government was on the defensive until Winston Churchill won the next election on 25 October 1951. Financial policy then changed; bank rate rose on 8 November 1951 to 2½ per cent, the first change for eleven years. On the day of the announcement, the Governor of the Bank of England, C. F. Cobbold, made it clear that the rise in bank base rate should 'be regarded as a definite encouragement to stepping up charges for inessential and marginal borrowing'.[12] It was also made clear that legislation would be introduced to relax taxes on distributed dividends. While equities rose over the next few years, in contrast, British government medium-, long- and undated securities fell.

By 4 December 1951, the deficit on Bank of Scotland gilt holdings, between the purchase price paid for all gilts and their market value, had reached £3,609,611 – almost entirely built up in five weeks since the election. This meant 'the virtual extinction of inner reserves'.[13] Ten days later, J. B. Crawford recalculated the losses: they were now £4,518,000. By 21 December, the gilt portfolio deficit had reached £5,216,318, exceeding

---

10 These stocks lost 12 per cent of their purchase value in the following eleven months.
11 Pember and Boyle, *British Government Securities*, pp. 101–3.
12 J. Fforde, *The Bank of England and Public Policy 1941–1958* (Cambridge: 1992), p. 406.
13 BS 1/6, Minutes, Investments Committee, 4 December 1951; the inner reserves totalled £3,928,521 in February 1951. See Statistical Appendix, Table A7.

total inner reserves. Just before Christmas, in a speech at Cleckheaton, Lord Linlithgow, chairman of the Midland Bank, acknowledged that the prolonged decline in gilts had led to a 'severe retrenchment upon [the] inner reserves' of banks in general,[14] and stockbrokers and the financial press forecast further falls in gilt prices in the new year. Bank of Scotland also possessed a strong published reserve, up from £2.1 million in 1944 to £3 million in 1949, and £2,400,000 of proprietors' stock. The total proprietors' funds – capital, published reserve and inner reserves – on the balance day, 28 February 1951, were £9,328,521, so there was still a comfortable margin before the next balance day, due on 29 February 1952.[15] The deterioration in the value of gilts was a matter for concern, but it was not so severe as to threaten the viability of the Bank in day-to-day business, or the security of customers' funds. Further, the Bank was not alone: all British banks and insurance companies faced losses on their holdings of gilts. There can be no doubt that, if required, the government would have taken appropriate steps to support the banks.

Unfortunately, the Bank's investments and trustee committee – as it was then called – was diverted from the long-term problem of gilts by the related concern to maintain a 'narrow' liquidity ratio of 30 per cent, and directors spent much time debating whether to sell gilts in order to fund this, or whether to delay until nearer the balance date (29 February 1952), rather than addressing the fundamental suitability of gilts as an investment. Further, the Treasurer and Chief Accountant devoted their time to how the balance sheet could be reconstructed in order to *minimise* sales. The auditors, R. A. Manning CA and Graham Usher CA, had to consider carefully the effect of changes in the Bank's accounting policies.[16] Five points emerged: investments would be valued at middle-market price on balance day, not at what the market would pay in the event of a sale; contingency reserves for specific ends would be incorporated in the inner reserve fund; the balance sheet would include a provision for income-tax refunds for the year to 29 February 1952 which would not be payable until June; the investment in the Industrial and Commercial Finance Corporation would be included as a trade investment at cost; and the write-downs of property values from 1945–51 would be reversed, thus boosting the worth of the property accounts.[17] Two days before 29 February, it was realised that the claim for refund of tax on realised losses was 'appreciably less' than the tax paid by deduction from income, and in the circumstances

14 *The Economist*, 29 December 1951.
15 See Statistical Appendix, Table A7.
16 BS 1/7/4, Treasurer's Committee Minutes, 15 February 1952.
17 The reassessment of the true worth of the property portfolio was later accepted as good practice; office and property values rose in the 1950s, so the older policies of depreciation were misleading.

it was decided to sell stock 'until the realised losses closed the margin of tax reclaimable'.[18] In April at the AGM, Elphinstone stated to proprietors that gilts had fallen by ten points and 'the consequential strain upon our resources has been severe. Thanks, however, to the traditionally prudent policy of British Banking which we have followed in the past, we were able to take the strain.' Moreover, he insisted that a policy of dearer money might, with advantage, have been introduced earlier: 'With the bank rate once more exercising its corrective influence and its traditional function as a stabiliser and a deterrent to over-expansion, interest rates are more realistic and the [Bank's] position is now healthier'. This was better interpreted as politics and public relations than as a guide to the effect on the values of British government securities on the Bank's balance sheet. Gilts fell because of dearer money; the expected ending of controls on dividends and unearned income also encouraged institutional and private holders of gilts to shift funds into industrial equities. There was no rethink of investment policy after the AGM, and by 21 May another £734,931 had been wiped from the gilt holdings. Even the Mound head office itself seemed to echo the erosion of gilt-edged valuations. In April, Messrs Carter & Wilson CIE confirmed that severe subsidence had struck the north, east and west retaining walls. The entire structure was unsafe; 'collapse is possible at any time and little warning is likely to be given'.[19]

Could the Treasurer and the investments committee have managed the affairs of the Bank better? Were there alternative policies that they might have adopted? The committee comprised well-connected directors whose expertise ranged widely in trade and industry, the law and accountancy; they had before them the advice of London managers, their own Treasurer, stockbrokers and, it should not be forgotten, some high-ranking politicians. Through their social network, they met men from every part of the establishment in Scotland. Information on Conservative intentions on financial policy was publicly available; hardly a week passed in the winter of 1951–2 without *The Scotsman*, the *Glasgow Herald* and other Scottish newspapers highlighting the weakness of gilts and likely rises in interest rates. In the financial press, much evidence was presented about the long-run decline in the purchasing power of gilt investments, although the conclusions drawn were varied. Moreover, a number of Edinburgh financial institutions had forecast correctly the rise of equities and the fall of gilts. Standard Life, Scottish Widows and Scottish Provident, the mutual assurance societies, moved into industrial investments in 1948 and 1949 and reduced their gilt holdings quite sharply.[20] The *Scottish Bankers*

18 BS 1/7/4, Treasurer's Committee Minutes, 26 February 1952.
19 BS 1/6/9, Minutes, 29 April 1952.
20 L. T. Little, 'Insurance Companies and Industrial Capital', *The Banker*, 95 (1950), 80–7; in 1949,

Magazine printed articles reciting the difficult choices facing holders of gilts.[21]

The Union Bank's position on gilts was similarly difficult, and, in the event, its board was persuaded to approach Bank of Scotland with proposals for amalgamation.[22] Total assets had expanded from £69,381,538 in 1946 to £93,979,829 by 1951. Gilts made up £38,407,567, representing 55.4 per cent of all assets; by 1951 this had become £41,109,719, or 43.7 per cent. To meet any shortfall on investments and bad debts, the paid-up proprietors' stock was £1,200,000 and there was a published reserve of £2 million. Internal funds comprised a guarantee account, an income tax account, a credit at the profit and loss account, and other minor accounts. The guarantee account stood at £1,843,096 in 1946 (see Table 21.2) and by 1951 was £2,572,907, while with other internal accounts the total figure was a little over £3 million. The board did not write down these inner accounts at the balance day in January 1952, but did so six months later, although only by £2.45 million, somewhat below the provision required to cover the losses. This left a credit of £247,588 at the guarantee account. The British Linen Bank also suffered serious losses, and Barclays Bank later funded the deficit.

In the summer of 1952, negotiations were completed in which the Union Bank directors agreed that Bank of Scotland would offer to purchase the stock of the Union Bank.[23] It was an amicable agreement, although the speed with which the negotiations were concluded contributed to difficulties which emerged in later years over seniority of rank, in staffing and over branch closures when a full amalgamation of branch systems began on 1 March 1955.[24] The decision by Lord Bilsland and his board coincided with a slide in the Union share price. After the general election in October 1951, the £5 'A' shares (with £1 paid) rose by around 2s to 89s 9d on the Glasgow exchange, as indeed did Bank of Scotland shares, also up by around 2s to 60s 6d. The change in bank rate on 8 November saw the Union shares fall, and by early December they were down to 83s 9d. By late January 1952, the position was worse: Union Bank shares were at

Standard Life held 46 per cent of funds in industrial capital, while Scottish Widows held 53.8 per cent and Scottish Provident 40.4 per cent.

21 G. Macaulay, 'Investing in Government Securities – I', *Scottish Bankers Magazine*, 42 (1950–1), 89–96; 'The Return of Bank Rate', *Scottish Bankers Magazine*, 43 (1951–2), 201–7; 'Bank Investments', *Scottish Bankers Magazine*, 44 (1952–3), 136–9. See also 'Gilt-edged through Fifty Years', *The Banker*, 95 (1950), 88–96.

22 Figures in this paragraph are from BS(U) 1/10/11–13, Quarterly states. See also Statistical Appendix, Table A22.

23 In one of the uncatalogued files of legal papers, there is a note on past negotiations, which may have referred to those of the 1920s, and there is one suggestion that discussions opened in June 1951.

24 For the views of a contemporary, see BS, unpublished, J. F. Wilson, 'Reminiscences of a Lifetime in Scottish Banking, 1939–1984' (1984), pp. 17–18.

72s 6d, the Bank's at 51s 10d. Of course, the volume of sales was small, and this, coupled with the loyalty of proprietors, protected the price. In the spring and summer, the Bank drifted lower to 47s while the Union remained at 71–73s.

The purchase had the unanimous support of the Union board. The Union share capital was £5.2 million, the dominant part (£5 million) forming the 'A' shares with £1 paid; the £200,000 of 'B' shares were fully paid.[25] The board agreed to create £2.1 million of new Bank of Scotland stock which would be exchanged at the ratio of seven for four Union shares, and 2s 6d cash extra per 'B' share. The effect of this new stock creation and the generous conversion was to raise the value of the Union shares, and they soon traded at around 82s per 'A' share. The formal offer was announced on 9 September, and, by 21 October, 92 per cent of 'A' proprietors and 93 per cent of 'B' proprietors had accepted.

The legal position gave Bank of Scotland ownership of the Union Bank, and four directors from each moved to the other's board; but they remained separate banks. Almost two years of work lay ahead in which the Edinburgh firm of Davidson & Syme ws and the Glasgow firm of McGrigor, Donald & Co. excelled themselves, advised by John Rankin of the Union Bank and Robert McLellan of Bank of Scotland's legal department. The simplest procedure was to follow the method adopted by the Clydesdale and the North of Scotland when they were amalgamated in 1949. Under section 208 of the 1948 Companies Act, 'reconstruction and amalgamation' could be expedited if the two companies were registered under the Companies Acts of 1862 or 1929 or the Consolidation Act of 1908. Bank of Scotland, of course, had not registered and had no intention of so doing. A liquidation of the Union was also ruled out, as such a course was very expensive, would have required separate agreements for each depositor's funds and curtailed the activity of the proposed new bank for months, and might have affected relations with customers. Further, the winding-up 'would involve the disclosure to the public of the size of the inner reserves of the Union at the date of liquidation, which is most undesirable'.[26] This left a petition to the Secretary of State for a provisional order under the Private Legislation Procedure (Scotland) Act, 1936, together with a private Act of Parliament to cover assets in England.

Modifications of the Bank of Scotland Act, 1920, were included in the order placed before the Secretary of State; these included provision to increase the number of ordinary directors to ten, the *de facto* position,

---

25 There was a modest premium for the 'B' shares, as these were fully paid. For an explanation of 'A' and 'B' shares, see above, Chapter 21.
26 BS, Uncatalogued, Davidson & Syme ws, *Memorial for the Bank of Scotland for the Advice of Counsel*, 1953.

and to increase the number of auditors from two to not more than four. The lawyers had to trawl through every aspect of the business of both banks to ensure that no privileges would be lost, the interests of all trusts, depositors and borrowers would be protected and no legal liabilities would be incurred beyond those in existence. Not least of these concerned the banknote issues, so that the new bank would have the full benefit of the fiduciary issue of £851,198, being the issues of the Central Bank of Scotland, the Caledonian Banking Company (taken over by the Bank in 1868 and 1907 respectively), the Aberdeen Banking Company and the Perth Banking Company (taken over by the Union in 1848 and 1858 respectively), as well as the banknotes allowable to Bank of Scotland and the Union Bank by the Act of 1845. After the proprietors had endorsed the terms of the draft provisional order on 27 April 1954, it went forward to Westminster and passed the royal assent in November as the Bank of Scotland Order Confirmation Act, 1954, which duly came into force on 1 March 1955, after the annual balance day of Bank of Scotland. The assets and liabilities of the Union were then legally part of Bank of Scotland.

Amalgamation detracted from the serious problems which faced the two banks over the position of gilts, on which neither board took decisive action. By 22 July 1952, the deficiency on Bank of Scotland gilts had reached £1 million above the deficit of February, but it was six months before the investments committee was persuaded of the need to sell undated stocks. Further, in spite of warnings from London managers and stockbrokers and regular reports in the financial press, the Bank still held over 40 per cent of assets in gilts, usually medium-term, in 1953. The committee was even encouraged by the rise in gilt prices after January 1953 to increase its holdings by £8 million, and by November it held £63 million.[27] As the improvement in prices continued in early 1954, and the recent purchases resulted in gains, the committee agreed that, while advantage 'could be taken from time to time of favourable opportunities to exchange holdings without materially altering the maturity spread, no change in the Bank's investment policy was necessary'.[28] The Bank of England minimum discount rate was reduced from 4 per cent to 3½ per cent on 17 September 1953, and to 3 per cent on 13 May 1954. This helped to support the values of gilts.

The amalgamation of the two investment accounts on 1 March 1955 left the Bank with a huge exposure to gilts of £97.6 million, comprising

27 *Monthly Digest of Statistics*, 'Security Prices and Yields' (1954). From 83.0 in January 1953, medium-dated stock (3 per cent savings bonds) went to 88.6 by December; there were also rises in 2½ per cent consols and 3½ per cent war loan. Pember and Boyle, *British Government Securities in the Twentieth Century: Supplement 1950–1972* (private circulation, London: n.d. [1973]), pp. 26–7.
28 BS 1/7/4, Treasurer's Committee Minutes, 21 May 1954.

undated ($7\frac{1}{2}$ per cent); long-dated, over fifteen years (31 per cent); medium-dated, five to fifteen years (50 per cent); and short-dated, with five years or fewer to maturity ($11\frac{1}{2}$ per cent). On this book price, the deficit was £2.2 million. Unfortunately for Bank of Scotland, the Bank of England rate rose to $3\frac{1}{2}$ per cent on 27 January 1955 and to $4\frac{1}{2}$ per cent on 24 February, and by June 1955 the committee, four from the Bank and three from the Union, had seen a further slide of £3.2 million. As might have been expected, the crisis started a review of the procedure for making such decisions in Bank of Scotland and for considering whether the asset deployment should be altered. J. B. Crawford, the Treasurer, retired in November 1952 and was replaced by William Watson CA, a director since 1943.[29] Watson, who had been on the board of Standard Life since 1941, was a member of the investments committee throughout the period.

The Conservative government was re-elected in 1955, and this was shortly followed by a credit squeeze which involved raising bank rate to $5\frac{1}{2}$ per cent on 16 February 1956; the political crisis of Suez (October 1956) also reduced the prices of British government securities. There was a modest rally from January to April 1957, encouraged by a reduction in bank rate to 5 per cent on 7 February 1957, but the position then worsened. There was a sharp, punitive rise on 19 September, to 7 per cent. In early January 1958, with a book price of £94.3 million, Bank of Scotland's investments committee was faced with a deficit of no less than £12.3 million; 'the deficiency disclosed could not be met from the Bank's inner reserves even allowing for any possible sales made to establish losses for tax purposes'.[30] This position could not continue. Three members of the committee retired from active work around this time, and the Treasurer, William Watson, and the Chief Accountant, James Letham, stepped in. With the full support of the board, they began a long-overdue appraisal of the structure of Bank assets. A similar, detailed appraisal of gilt holdings was supervised at the British Linen Bank by James Gammell.

By 1954, it was apparent that gross trading income at Bank of Scotland was growing strongly, and in the two years after the 1951 election gross trading profits were double those of the last year of the Labour government. Yet, because of the need for sizeable allocations to reserves, declared net profits remained subdued, and even fell a little, to £290,320 in 1952. Thereafter, there was a more encouraging position, although for most years in the decade sizeable sums went to cover the losses on investments. The first three years of the new Bank, 1955–8, showed a

29 William Watson, in 1930 a partner at Baillie, Gifford & Co. handling investment-trust business, became vice-chairman of Standard Life and was knighted in 1963.
30 BS 1/7/4, Treasurer's Committee Minutes, 10 January 1958; the committee agreed to sell such foreign government securities over and above the wiping-out of the inner reserve.

disappointing position on gross trading income, which hovered around an annual average of £5.1 million, and there was a slight decline in gross trading profits; but these figures were much better as a proportion of income, at over 40 per cent, compared with the figures after the war. The other main ratios all showed a striking improvement. This was very much the result of the rise in interest rates which now gave the banks a higher return on their assets than in the era of cheap money. It was unfortunate for the proprietors that so much of the hard work at branch level was diverted to cover the deficit on investments.

In evidence to the Macmillan Committee in 1930, George Scott, Treasurer of Bank of Scotland, had pointed to the inadequate openings for industrial lending north of the Border which were only partially ameliorated by new opportunities in the 1930s. Indeed, as noticed above, total Scottish bank advances in each year before 1939 were below the high point reached from 1928–30. The caution shown towards the initiatives of Sir Steven Bilsland and the Scottish Development Council underlined the point that banks north of the Border had no alternative but to invest a higher proportion of assets in gilts and the money market. Yet opportunities arose in wartime and the period of the Labour government which offered to redress this imbalance, and the unfortunate fate of these initiatives merely confirmed the Bank's connection with gilts.

In October 1942, Thomas Johnston, the Secretary of State for Scotland, asked the General Managers Committee to set up a panel scheme to provide finance for industry in Scotland by long-term credit. The eventual agreement rested on the assumption that there had been difficulties in the provision of finance in the inter-war period, especially for family firms, for the development of new products and for modest extension of existing lines; and further, that recourse to company promoters and a capital issue was not always appropriate in the context of local and family loyalties which were often threatened by a dilution of ownership. Johnston and the GMC agreed on a panel of all eight banks with an observer from the Scottish Home and Health Department.[31] Loans would be authorised up to £10,000 from a fund of £1 million. Applications would be made through the Council of State and its sister the Council of Industry; the borrower would nominate a bank to run the account, interest received over deposit receipt rate would be placed in a 'panel' fund and the profit and loss would be shared between all banks. It was an imaginative scheme, tailor-made for family firms. Unfortunately, the scheme was later abandoned before any business was transacted.[32]

---

31 BS, Uncatalogued, GMC, Minutes, 12 October and 7 December 1942.
32 Earl of Rosebery, 'Scotland's Economic Future', *The Banker*, 64 (1942), 93–6.

The next important initiative was Johnston's scheme for the construction, virtually from scratch, of the hydro-electricity system in the north and north-east of Scotland.[33] This was to be the most ambitious industrial construction scheme in Scotland in the twentieth century. Over fifty dams and dozens of turbine generating stations were built over the twenty years after the passage of the 1943 Hydro-Electric Development (Scotland) Act. It was Johnston's vision to provide the necessary basis by which industry and trade could be expanded in the north-east and the Highlands. He built a coalition of industrialists and politicians to push the bill through Parliament and recruited a strong team of engineers and experts who started work as soon as the statute was in place. They faced enormous obstacles from the vested interests which had opposed such schemes, and it was not until after the war that the position of the Hydro Board was entirely secure.[34] Nevertheless, it was a crucial opportunity for the banks. The GMC decided that the account was to be treated as a local authority account, to rotate around the banks annually 'in the usual order of seniority'; the guarantee of the Treasury would normally be required, although not for the first facility of £100,000 in September 1943, and the rate of interest would be bank rate with a minimum of 2½ per cent and an annual review of the account.[35]

In June 1944, Bank of Scotland directors considered a request for a £3–4 million funding of the Hydro Board for the ensuing three years. They agreed to loans at bank rate renegotiated once a year with the right to raise interest from ½ per cent to 1 per cent above bank rate. The guarantees by the Treasury ensured that such loans were marketable, that they would not lose their original value and that interest rates could be reassessed without arduous negotiation. Unfortunately, there was opposition to the account, which had nothing to do with whether or not the Hydro Board was a sound banking proposition, and the GMC later ruled that a public capital issue was preferable to long-term bank loans, even with a Treasury guarantee. The Scottish banks lost an opportunity to settle all funding through Scottish sources, and the bulk of Hydro Board borrowing was henceforth negotiated in London.

The third important initiative was the formation in 1945 of the Industrial and Commercial Finance Corporation.[36] Its normal limits of

33 P. L. Payne, *The Hydro: A Study of the Development of the Major Hydro-Electric Schemes Undertaken by the North of Scotland Hydro-Electric Board* (Aberdeen: 1988), ch. 4.
34 Ibid., p. 59.
35 BS, Uncatalogued, GMC, Minutes, 6 September 1943, 3 July 1944; BS, Uncatalogued, GMC, Miscellaneous papers.
36 Clydesdale Bank, *Survey of Economic Conditions in Scotland in 1946* (March 1947); 'Finance for Industry: Industrial and Commercial Finance Corporation Limited', *Scottish Bankers Magazine*, 37 (1945–6), 91–3. See the discussion in S. G. Checkland, *Scottish Banking: A History, 1695–1973* (Glasgow: 1975), pp. 598–600.

assistance were from £5,000 to a maximum of £200,000, aimed chiefly at existing firms. At first, the board of Bank of Scotland refused to consider anything but a separate Scottish company under the control of the Scottish banks, and there was a belated attempt to resurrect the 'Panel' proposals of 1942. This discussion faltered; Sir Charles Lidbury from the London clearing banks initially persuaded the GMC to cooperate – '[your] interests will be served by a separate committee with a postal address in Scotland' – but Lord Piercy, the energetic chairman of the ICFC, found it hard work. The GMC procrastinated, and the individual banks were also slow to suggest nominees for the board.[37] By 1949, the Scottish banks had invested £1.8 million in the equity of the ICFC, yet Scotland had received only £792,000 worth of business, to which George Mackenzie, Treasurer of the British Linen, suggested that the ICFC had a laxer standard for loans in England.[38] Similar comments punctuated the next decade, although the Scots increased their support to £3 million.[39] Research carried out at the time by Maxwell Gaskin, the Aberdeen economist, underlined a pessimistic view; in 1959, London firms had 38.5 per cent of ICFC loans, the Midlands 15.3 per cent and the greater Lancashire area 12.1 per cent, yet Scotland received only 6.7 per cent.[40]

The most significant difficulty after the war was the failure to appreciate that, as the public sector was a leading component of capital investment in the Scottish industrial context, this might invite a reappraisal of lending. Instead, the old attitude towards local authority and public-sector accounts, that large issues should go to the public market, remained the stance of the Bank board. Indeed, on a number of occasions when public-sector industries asked for extensive facilities, the Bank took the same view as it had done with the Hydro Board in 1944. This attitude was the dominant one on the GMC, and, in the early post-war years, the eight Scottish banks conducted lengthy discussions over the division of business, in the long-established manner by way of rotation of accounts, based on calculations of the proportion of business held by each bank at the time of nationalisation. J. B. Letham was given the task of representing Bank of Scotland.[41] By the close of the 1950s, under 8 per cent of Scottish

---

37 BS 1/6/8, Minutes, December 1945. The first list was dominated by chartered accountants; W. H. Fraser WS, the chairman of the National Bank and a director of Lloyds and Caledonian Insurance, was the eventual choice.
38 The first ICFC funding consisted of £15 million divided into shares of £1,000 each; the eight Scottish banks took £1,629,000, of which Bank of Scotland took £205,000, the British Linen £165,000 and the Union Bank £162,000.
39 BS, Uncatalogued, GMC, Miscellaneous papers, George Mackenzie to J. B. Crawford, 6 January 1950; BS, Uncatalogued, GMC, Minutes, 17 January 1955, 7 January 1957.
40 M. Gaskin, 'The Supply of Finance in Scotland', unpublished paper (1961), cited in Checkland, *Scottish Banking*, p. 648.
41 BS, Tercentenary Oral History Project, interview by David Antonio of Duncan Ferguson.

bank lending was to the nationalised industries. Had the banks not been hindered by their old attitudes, a more constructive partnership might have evolved. There were a number of specific difficulties. For example, in 1950 the banks advanced £1.5 million to the Gas Council, as the Scottish proportion of its total UK borrowing, at 'a very special rate' of 2 per cent. The Gas Board in Scotland, then wishing to extend its autonomy and investment, asked to be treated as a private industry. This would have meant 4 per cent (£30,000 extra interest income), yet the GMC *opposed* such a change. Loans to local authorities were usually without problems, but the banks faced intermittent criticism; they had opposed the development of municipal banks in the inter-war years; the motivation for controls on savings banks was questioned and they were pilloried by some factions in council chambers. In November 1939, for example, councillors on Glasgow Corporation queried the interest payments on loans of £4.42 million for which the Union Bank (at £800,000) and Bank of Scotland (£700,000) were the largest lenders. Why should the burgh pay 4 per cent for the renegotiation and increase of this loan when bank rate was 2 per cent? The Treasury arranged for the Capital Issues Committee to endorse a public issue at 3 per cent and, in the interim, requested the Scottish banks to provide cover. At first, however, the GMC instructed banks to refuse. Eventually, after a ringing endorsement of the position of the banks by Patrick Dollan, Lord Provost of Glasgow, in which he stated that 'the banks are entitled to a rate equal to the yield on Government securities', £1.65 million was settled at 3 per cent.[42] It was regrettable that relations remained poor with a number of burghs after the war.

It is noteworthy that the banks did try very hard to build a constructive relationship with the South of Scotland Electricity Board (SSEB). The Scottish electricity industry outwith the Hydro Board area at nationalisation was placed under the Central Electricity Authority. As with gas, it had hitherto been largely a municipal enterprise, and in the election of 1951 the Conservative Party promised to form a separate, Scottish, company. This, the SSEB, was granted exceptional terms by the Scottish banks: whereas the Gas Board paid one-third of its borrowing at ½ per cent over bank rate, the SSEB proportion was only 17 per cent, with the remainder at bank rate. Unfortunately, the company proved difficult to negotiate with, and the banks could have been forgiven for thinking that, at times, the SSEB appeared to believe that its role in the atomic power and nuclear technology industries entitled it to a unique position among bank customers. The National Coal Board (NCB) was a more complicated

---

42 BS, Uncatalogued, GMC, Minutes, November 1939, January 1940; the Capital Issues Committee agreed to an issue of £6 million.

problem. For over a decade after the war, coal was sold at prices which failed to cover marginal costs in a market which would have taken more than was produced. This depressed Coal Board incomes and forced schemes for investment to rely on a Treasury sanction for borrowing. All too often, investment was pruned. Had production been sold at marginal cost, then the incomes to the Scottish area of the NCB would have been very much higher. The Scottish banks also suffered through the loss of coal company accounts, and a number of branches were affected when coal mines were closed in the Lanarkshire, Ayrshire and Shotts coalfields in the decade after the war.

The Scottish banks were unwilling to disturb post-war agreements with the English clearers over the division of business for the new boards and nationalised industries. The case of the British Wool Marketing Board is instructive. In 1950 it entrusted virtually all of its banking business to Martins Bank. By 1954, the difficulties encountered with Martins persuaded the board to offer to place 'part or all' of its banking business with a Scottish bank 'provided suitable terms were arranged', the prime question being a reduction in the rate of interest. The English clearers' agreement obliged Martins to charge ½ per cent over the rate applicable to advances covered by Treasury guarantee. British Wool argued that a guarantee was implicit in its public standing and that the Scots could have the business if they cut into this extra ½ per cent. The GMC ruled that it would not interfere because other marketing boards would demand concessions. After a desultory exchange on the lines that British Wool should come to Scotland because of pre-war support for the trade, the matter was dropped.

Much of the competitive framework of Bank of Scotland was decided by the GMC, and, as with pre-war years, on literally dozens of topics, it determined the scope and extent of that competition. It is of crucial importance to appreciate that the GMC proved invaluable in numerous situations where the banks would have been hard pressed. So, the boards continued to take decisions made by the GMC very seriously. It was, for ex-ample, very effective in dealing with the Scottish Co-operative Wholesale Society when it launched a banking department in 1946.[43] Its competition for deposits was countered by higher charges for transactions, and the Co-op was forced to hold larger balances with the Scottish banks. The GMC kept a close watch on the savings banks; when these tried to issue cheques to customers after the war it was first blocked, and later, as a special concession, an issue of two per customer per year was agreed. Nevertheless,

---

43 BS, Uncatalogued, GMC, Minutes, 1 July 1946, 10 January 1949, 14 May 1951, 9 April 1956; BS, Uncatalogued, GMC, Miscellaneous papers, 1956.

the Scottish banks had the support of the Treasury. Legislation to allow customers of savings banks to write cheques without any limit, other than that imposed by the bank concerned, was not passed until 1964.[44] Given the friction over cheques, and other business matters, there were frequent arguments over poaching with the savings banks. Yet times were changing, and in 1956 it was thought fit to bring in the savings banks as a partial member to the Agreements and Understandings. It should be emphasised that the GMC and the Accountants committee were also very important for the sharing of information about fraud, robberies, mishandled accounts, staffing difficulties and political matters. The intelligence system of the Accountants committee was very good; on one occasion it found that a series of Post Office accounts were irregularly conducted on the basis of concealed overdrafts unknown to the Controllers of the Scottish Region of the Post Office. There were several fraudulent operations uncovered on local authority accounts. But probably the greatest advantage of the GMC and the Accountants committee was in their role as an informal club of the senior professional bankers and accountants where matters of mutual interest could be raised. At the level of the everyday work of the banks and in negotiation with larger customers it proved invaluable, which is why it survived.

The GMC was also crucial in masterminding changes in the charging system, which were accelerated during the early stages of the 1952 crisis over British government securities. At this time, interest was expressed in a revision of the charges for current and business accounts and those which involved higher than average costs, such as the provision of cash for wages. The Scottish system levied a charge for the collection of cheques not on the drawer, as in England, but on the payee, although if the relevant accounts were within a local clearing, no charge was made.[45] There were no standing charges, and, with sound management, both personal and business customers could avoid paying for the costs of the banking service. Credit balances could be used to earn income in the short-term markets, but periodic and seasonal fluctuations meant that this income did not cover costs. From time to time, reform was discussed, and representatives of the bank staffs often pressed the case for change. On 15 January 1952, the directors of Bank of Scotland notified the GMC of their wish to introduce English-style charges. The higher incomes of the latter 'enable them to keep a bigger proportion of funds in call money and Treasury bills while the Scottish banks require a higher investment

---

44 M. Moss and A. Slaven, *From Ledger Book to Laser Beam. A History of the TSB in Scotland from 1810 to 1990* (Edinburgh: n.d. [1992]), ch. 7, for the development of the Scottish savings banks in the 1950s.

45 M. Gaskin, *The Scottish Banks: A Modern Survey* (London: 1965), pp. 176–7.

ratio for income purposes. At a time of falling gilt prices this throws an additional strain on the Scottish banks.'[46] In April 1952, through the good offices of Sir Harold Yarrow, chairman of the Clydesdale Bank, a meeting of governors and chairmen together with the senior managers was held to iron out difficulties.[47] Lord Elphinstone and J. B. Crawford represented the Bank, Sir Ernest Wedderburn and J. A. Lang the British Linen, and Lord Bilsland and J. A. Morrison the Union. Lord Bilsland opened the discussion, insisting that they all had to stand together and would all benefit. It was agreed, henceforth, that the banks were free to negotiate individual charges for the more complicated accounts. There would be a charge of 6d per debit entry with a minimum of 10s for each six-month period, with a small credit of 6d for every £100 the account was in credit.[48] Naturally, they were worried about the reaction of the press, and the editors of several Scottish newspapers were called in for lunch before the changes were made public.

The problems of the downward trend in gilt prices led to regular reviews of charges for large customers after 1952. Before nationalisation, much of the collection of electricity and gas accounts had been done by local burghs in collaboration with the banks. On nationalisation, these arrangements ceased, and the North of Scotland Hydro-Electric Board, the Central Electricity Authority, later the SSEB, and the Gas Council asked the banks to provide collection facilities, given the poor distribution of their own outlets. This involved a huge and growing amount of processing work. Amicable arrangements were made with the Gas Board and the Hydro Board, but the Accountants committee regularly reported that those with the SSEB failed to cover costs. Not content with the usual negotiations on these matters, the SSEB made strong claims as to the benefits which the banks derived from the daily balances, claiming they earned money in London, and demanded a breakdown of internal bank costs. In fact, these balances were too erratic to allow much short-term lending in London, and relations with the company remained poor for many years. The GMC acted as the go-between for the banks and the Scottish Co-operative banking department when the latter was informed in 1956 that the turnover charge would be raised from 9d per cent to 1s 3d per cent (the accountants recommended 1s 6d per cent); it was eventually settled at 1s per cent, and the Co-op would lodge a positive balance of £500,000. The first stirring of an argument with the English clearing banks over London deposits broke in 1954; the Scottish practice

46 BS 1/6/9, Minutes, 15 January 1952.
47 BS, Uncatalogued, GMC, Minutes, 23 April and 12 May 1952.
48 Gaskin, *Scottish Banks*, pp. 176–7.

was to pay interest on deposits, in part or whole, on demand after a qualifying period (usually a month) and to continue to pay interest on a daily basis. Complaints from the English clearers, which preferred more stringent conditions, were rejected. In 1955, the Accountants committee, which was perceptibly more important after 1952 than before, was told to make further revisions to the Agreements and Understandings, especially for business accounts. Relations with the English banks were so fraught by 1958 that the majority on the GMC refused to be bound by the credit restrictions requested by the Bank of England in January 1958. The Scottish banks wished to avoid any restriction, and defended their defiance with reference to the state of the Scottish economy. Even so, Sir John Campbell of the Clydesdale Bank announced that he would talk independently to the Governor of the Bank of England.[49] There were other disagreements of varying significance. When the GMC agreed to raise charges to 9d per ledger entry (debits and credits) and the minimum charge rose to 12s 6d per six-month period, Sir John refused to be bound. By the 1960s, it had become more difficult to manage the growth of the subsidiary companies of the Scottish banks through the medium of the GMC, although much valuable work was done before the formal abolition of the Agreements and Understandings in 1968.

In the final year of the war, advances by Bank of Scotland to trade and industry had declined to only 11.9 per cent of assets (£10.7 million) compared with 27.9 per cent (£14.2 million) in 1938–9.[50] With the return of peace, demands from customers grew steadily, although in the last complete year before the purchase of the Union Bank, advances to business only just returned to the pre-war level, with 27 per cent – £30.9 million – of assets so placed. As explained above, it was in the money market, in cash balances with the Bank of England and in British government securities that the board employed most of the Bank's liabilities. The position, as we have seen, was similar at the Union. Indeed, as the Union was more exposed to gilts, the consolidation of the two banks *reduced* advances to business to only 22.1 per cent – £46.7 million. They did not reach 30 per cent until 1959.

Was this disposition of bank funds just the measured intention of the boards, still influenced by pre-war nostrums about how funds should be placed, or was there a genuine problem of a lack of lending opportunities in Scotland? The answer lies somewhere between the two views, and the state of the post-war Scottish economy provides many clues. There is no

---

49 BS, Uncatalogued, GMC, Minutes, 6 January 1958.
50 See Statistical Appendix, Table A8. Advances were divided into those for 'current accounts and other advances' and 'liabilities of banking and other customers for acceptances by the Bank'. The joint figure is given here.

doubt that, as the war came to a close, Scottish institutions, private and public, were convinced of the importance of industrial expansion, but worried lest the immediate post-war boom that everyone predicted should turn into a slump. In fact, peace also resulted in unfortunate closures in the vehicle, aircraft, electrical engineering and precision trades as firms directed to Scotland in war moved south again. Moreover, the recovery of many service and luxury trades and of parts of the textile industry was painfully slow; employment in the building industry also picked up slowly, and outputs of bricks, cement and lime were below pre-war levels as late as 1948. Yet, the post-war expansion showed every sign of continuing, and, in the UK as a whole, the evidence was of opportunity as the policies of demand management, full employment and support by government for reconstruction and capital investment made their mark. As such policies were also pursued in all the leading western economies, the situation was much more lively and dynamic than in the early 1920s. Thus, opinion in Scotland reverted to the older pre-war concern about how Scotland could benefit from this growth.

Lending in Scotland after 1945 grew fast, notably to general and mechanical engineering, farming, extraction industries, brewing and distilling and to a number of 'new' industries. A clear pattern emerged: numerous firms came to Bank of Scotland and the Union Bank, and many of the advances were enlarged year on year. Thus the Ben Nevis Distillers asked for £80,000 in 1948 and a year later £125,000; loans to Scottish industrial companies ranged as high as the £2 million overdraft which the Bank granted to Fairfields in 1950 to finance six ocean-going vessels; there was £200,000 advanced from the Bank to Kelvin, Bottomley & Baird in 1947 and renewed (upwards); and there was the flexible advance of £100,000–£150,000 to Thomson, Shepherd & Co. of Dundee, the jute-spinners and carpet-makers. Where the management was good, the Bank proved exceptionally helpful, as with D. & H. Cohen, the Glasgow clothing manufacturers, who wanted to build a new factory at a cost of £53,000: they received £40,000 as a first instalment on the security of the future plant. Advances were pushed into the new retail trades: S. W. Cohen, the radio dealers, were granted £15,000 for new stock; John Bartholomew, map-makers, received £4,000 for new equipment. Most reminiscences from this time stress that the farming community did well from bank lending. Price support systems provided a benchmark by which to judge the likely cash flow, and farmers took advantage of overdrafts and mortgages 'to the hilt'. As one bank officer put it: 'I used always to think that the farmer felt he had a God-given right to an overdraft'. In some cases where farmers were in difficulty, other farmers would step in: in one case at the end of the war, a Borders cattle dealer who was ill, an

'inveterate gambler' and facing losses of £40,000 was bailed out of his difficulties by other farmers. There were repeated references in banking papers
in the early post-war years to the exceptional contrast in the conditions
faced by agriculture compared with the much more difficult times in pre-
war days.[51] Overall, however, the fact should not go unnoticed that the
majority of advances in most industries and services were for quite small
sums, a few thousand pounds at most, and were not always taken up. By
1950, disquieting evidence had accumulated that, in spite of fast overall
growth, all was not well with a wide tranche of Scottish industry.

The first post-war census of production in 1948 listed net output
per person in Scottish industry with comparable all-British figures; in
fourteen industrial sectors with eighty-six subdivisions, no fewer than
forty-eight had a net output 5 per cent or more below the British average,
and in only twenty-two cases was the Scottish figure 5 per cent or more
above.[52] Many of these firms were long-standing family enterprises which
held steady balances with the banks; they required intermittent advances
but were hesitant about long-term advances and reluctant to go to the
capital market. The pattern of frequent approaches to the banks by the
more dynamic firms obscures this important difficulty. Some of the blame
must be laid at the door of the GMC for its failure to construct the 1942
panel scheme. Johnston was quite precise – he intended it for those
numerous family companies which needed new premises and equipment.
The criticism of the level of investment in Scotland undertaken by the
Industrial and Commercial Finance Corporation may be valid, but it
raises the question as to why the Scottish banks were not more vocal in
encouraging companies to contact the Corporation.

Low productivity and the inefficiencies of British management were
important questions after 1945 and were frequently discussed in the
financial press. The war provided the Board of Trade and spending departments with detailed proof that many sectors of industry lacked sufficient
capital, were slow at innovation and were overstaffed, and that in only a
few sectors was the performance of British firms as good as best practice
elsewhere. While some of the criticisms have exaggerated these failings,
the fact remained that the war effort was hindered by production delays
and inadequate utilisation of resources.[53] It was thus a matter of great
concern that post-war growth of international competition would expose
these deficiencies and that the market position of British companies would
be damaged. In 1948, Lionel Rostas published his pioneering work on

51 BS, Tercentenary Oral History Project, interviews by David Antonio of Duncan Ferguson, George
Craik and Norman Williamson.
52 R. Saville (ed.), *The Economic Development of Modern Scotland 1950–1980* (Edinburgh: 1985),
pp. 38–9; these figures amalgamate returns made by companies.
53 C. Barnett, *The Audit of War: The Illusion and Reality of Britain as a Great Nation* (London: 1986).

pre-war UK–US productivity comparisons.[54] In thirty-one manufacturing industries in 1935–9, the level of output and employment in US firms was over twice the UK level, and this gap grew when allowance was made for the fewer hours put in by the typical US worker. In 1948, Sir Stafford Cripps inaugurated the Anglo–American Council on Productivity, whose object was to convey to British companies the manifest deficiencies of their own organisation compared with good US practice. In 1952, the British Bankers' Association (BBA), the Association of Certified and Corporate Accountants, the Trades Union Congress and the Federation of British Industry all testified before the Royal Commission on the Taxation and Profits of Income that under-capitalisation, poor accounting procedures and lack of attention to product expansion were endemic in industry. Their evidence revealed that manufacturers responded to the sustained growth in demand by employing more labour in old premises, often with outdated machinery, and this continued in spite of the over-whelming testimony of sustained worldwide expansion. The BBA and *The Banker* were greatly concerned about how the industrial situation would affect advances, especially as the English banks had taken action to reduce their exposure to British government securities. *The Banker* and *The Bankers' Magazine* carried articles which highlighted these problems. It was unfortunate that Bank of Scotland and the GMC distanced themselves from this very important discussion. Indeed, of all the Scottish bankers, only Lord Bilsland led new intellectual initiatives.

National income figures and data from the Inland Revenue reinforced a pessimistic view of the transition of the Scottish economy to peacetime compared to the overall British economy. With allowance for the imperfections of both types of data, it was clear that Scotland's national income 'was appreciably smaller, when related to comparative population than that of England' and that the advantages of wartime contracts and wage policies had been insufficient to keep Scotland at the wartime level.[55] Other worrying signs also emerged. From 1931 to 1951, the population had grown by only 5.25 per cent, whereas England and Wales had seen growth of 9.5 per cent; emigration had carried off much of the natural increase – perhaps too many of the better sorts had gone – and there were fewer skilled workers in Scotland as a proportion of the total workforce in 1951. The salaried classes contracted from 8.5 per cent of the UK level in wartime to only 7 per cent by 1948; those in Scotland with incomes above the tax-exemption limit were only 8.6 per cent of the UK total.

54 L. Rostas, *Comparative Productivity in British and American Industry* (Cambridge: 1948); the study was commissioned by the National Institute for Economic and Social Research, the difficulties in drawing comparisons between the two countries being fully explored.
55 Clydesdale and North of Scotland Bank Ltd, *Survey of Economic Conditions in Scotland in 1952* (1953), pp. 1–7.

After this disappointing transition, the guides to Scottish economic performance in the 1950s showed a steadiness in comparison with the UK average; matters did not apparently deteriorate further after 1948 and were assisted by substantial post-war increases in trade, the armaments required for the Korean War and buoyant domestic markets. With the expansion of the heavy and traditional industries of steel, ships, coal and engineering, the Scottish economy more or less held its share of UK gross domestic product down to 1957, in a range from 9.1 to 9.3 per cent.[56] The index of industrial production confirmed that from 1948–54 Scotland almost kept pace with the UK average, but then the growth rate slowed, and from 1957–9 went into reverse. By 1960 a serious gap was apparent, a consequence of the decline in all the traditional trades except for steel.[57] From 1954–63, the rate of growth of Scottish industry was only 2.2 per cent, compared with 2.8 per cent in the UK. The stagnation of the family firm and the failure to invest and diversify now emerged as considerable problems. Unemployment rose to over 160,000 from 1958, and emigration took 83 per cent of the natural increase of the population in the decade to 1961, a poor performance matched only by parts of Ireland and Malta.[58]

The managements of Bank of Scotland and the Union Bank were forced, after 1951, into a much more thorough approach to the incomes which could come from the branch network. It has been stated by more than one source that Norman Hird, before the war, claimed that he could shut all branches and make more money from investments. The war years, for both banks, rather confirmed this approach. Yet there were numerous younger men who wished to see advances pushed much harder, and in some branches by the 1950s a new spirit was growing up. Given the deteriorating investment position, this was fortunate, and confirmed that advances were a profitable route which the senior management of the banks should encourage, especially so with the demise of the cheap money policy.

George Craik's experience as manager at the one-time head office of the Central Bank in Perth is illustrative of how bankers could take advantage of the positive underlying economic trends.[59] Craik started as an apprentice in Forfar in 1923, went to the Inspectors Department as a junior in 1928, and in his years there had a clear view of the bad debts generated by the slump. In 1936, aged 28, he was sent as agent to Lockerbie, a Borders

56 See N. K. Buxton, 'The Scottish Economy, 1945–79: Performance, Structure and Problems', in R. Saville (ed.), *Economic Development*, pp. 47–78, for the issues discussed in this paragraph.
57 P. L. Payne, 'The Decline of the Scottish Heavy Industries, 1945–1983', in ibid., pp. 79–113 (p. 81, table 2).
58 L. Hunter, 'The Scottish Labour Market', in ibid., pp. 163–82 (pp. 165, 173).
59 The information for the next five paragraphs is from BS, Tercentenary Oral History Project, interviews by David Antonio of George Craik, J. H. Collier and Harry Brough.

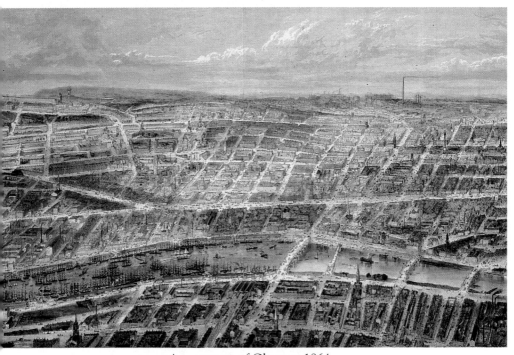

A panorama of Glasgow, 1864.

Laying the keel at J. & G. Thomson's yard, Clydebank, in the 1880s.

Smoking Concert

Bank of Scotland
Constituted 1695

London Office

AT

Andertons' Hotel

Fleet Street, E.C.

Chair to be taken by

Thomas Aitken, Esq.

AT 7-30 P.M.

1st March 1895

Caledonian Bank head office, High Street, Inverness
(now Bank of Scotland's Highland Regional Office and branch).

An Argyll motor car of 1907 with its Aberdeen owners.
(Aberdeen Press and Journal)

The battle-cruiser HMS Indomitable, built at Fairfields, 1908. (UCS records, Strathclyde Regional Archives, reproduced by courtesy of the Principal Archivist and permission of the Keeper of the Records of Scotland)

The corner of Renfield Street and St Vincent Street, Glasgow, pre-1920. (Strathclyde Regional Archives)

The square, Kelso, on market day. (The Trustees of the National Library of Scotland)

The exterior of the Union Bank of Scotland's head office, St Vincent Street, Glasgow, designed by architect James Miller, built 1925-7, and now Bank of Scotland's Glasgow Chief Office.

When he reaches 21

What a start he'll have

with a

UNION BANK
DEPOSIT ACCOUNT

Open it Now

Example of bank advertising in the 1920s and 1930s.

Office of the Peninsular & Oriental Co., originally built for the
Hamburg-Amerika Line, and now Bank of Scotland's London West End office.

Branch staff at the Union Bank of Scotland's office in Ingram Street, Glasgow, in the 1920s.

North Sea oil rig in stormy waters.

town with a large agricultural business, and he stayed until after the war. His next move was to Aberfeldy, and through curling and golf he knew many of the Perth customers before becoming manager in St John Street on a salary of £1,800 plus house. Before moving, he visited the Mound and read the old procedure books, recording all the main correspondence with Perth 'to absorb the history and feel of the branch'. William Watson also told him that 'they were not pleased at the decline in the business, Perth could clearly support a greater volume of lending'. Indeed, it was thought that frequent refusals to lend by his predecessor had 'ruined' the business, and Craik was to meet many former customers. His social round, typical of bank managers, included meeting the competition, and early in his tour of duty the managers of the Commercial and the National Banks greeted him with the thought that they were discussing which account to take off Bank of Scotland next. But pushing lending had its problems, and some time after arrival Craik received a letter from James Taggart, superintendent of branches, noting the generosity of his lending as reported in a full obligation list, which had provoked adverse comment from the directors. Such letters were intimidating, and many men – perhaps most – took the easier course. But not George Craik, who pointed out that he was simply obeying the Treasurer's instructions and added that bad debts were 'piffling' and well covered by a week's interest. Craik later came to the view that managers could 'get by with only a sketchy notion of banking practice provided they have an outgoing personality', essential in the search for new business.

Another example of the advantages of the outgoing view on branch lending came at Glenrothes, under J. H. Collier, who first started as an apprentice at Reform Street, Dundee, in May 1934. The work at that time was 'sheer drudgery', with many legal connections and much form-filling on deposit receipts and jute warrants. His initial impression of the staff was of 'ancient, decrepit, men nearing retirement, disillusioned, discontented and with huge "chips on the shoulder" probably justified, probably men of ability ruined by being forced on routine jobs'. Although the overall business of the office was large, Collier thought that more could have been made of it: 'no-one went out to get business, the officials were content to manage what they had and to wait for new business coming through the door'. It was not until May 1939 that he was moved to Albert Street, Dundee; but this was another underperforming branch, and his main chance came in 1948 when he was appointed to George Street, Perth, under Charles Tennant, who was 'socially marvellous and knew all the country people'. Tennant was the only Union Bank employee who had been educated at Eton, and many of the Perth well-off visited him frequently on their social round. On one occasion, when Charles Tennant returned from a 'prolonged' skiing holiday in Switzerland and inquired about business, he was informed by Collier that there were new advances of £300,000–£400,000 on the books, and promptly announced: 'I think I'll go away again and leave you to it'.[60]

In 1963, Collier had an interview with William Watson regarding 'an appointment' which he mistakenly thought was Crieff, an attractive town on the fringes of the Highlands. It was in fact to be Leslie, 'an unattractive coal bing' in Fife, and the sub-office at Woodside on the edge of the new town of Glenrothes. Just north of Kirkcaldy, Glenrothes new town had been carved out of prime farming land, and was originally intended to house mineworkers working in a new pit nearby. With cutbacks in the Scottish coal industry, this was eventually closed, and it became essential for the Scottish Office and the Glenrothes New Town Development Corporation to bring new jobs and business. In one of these attempts, the Royal Bank lost nearly £400,000 on a farming venture about which Collier, who was brought up on a farm in the Carse of Gowrie, was dismissive. After it collapsed, Brigadier R. S. Doyle, the chief executive of the corporation, asked Collier to help in attracting new business, and together they organised a conference for industrialists on the advantages of locating in Glenrothes. From this time onwards, the excellent relationship between the corporation, business in Glenrothes and the Bank has continued.

Having a role model in the outgoing manager may have been one of the crucial factors in determining the attitudes of younger staff. J. L. Adams, for example, himself trained in the propitious atmosphere of the Union Bank branch in London's Regent Street, was posted as manager to High Street, Dunfermline, in the early post-war years. Described by Harry Brough, a junior at the office, as 'one of the hardest working servants of the Bank', and a 'nightmare' for those who worked under him, Adams went out of his way to seek custom, returning to the office by 5:30 p.m. to commence processing, 'expecting staff to remain with him'. Brough was later posted as accountant to Reform Street, Dundee, where, as thirty years earlier, the line of tellers was still in place, all with their measured existence, who would leave 'at 4:10 p.m. or so, whenever they had balanced their cash, no matter the work remaining elsewhere in the office'. Reform Street had its own, large, securities office and its own nominee company, ruled 'like a major-domo, by the formidable Miss Isles', who had been there 'from time immemorial'. The jute desk was still very specialised. It was difficult to train personnel for it and to hold

---

60 Charles Tennant had some understanding of the problems of the Scottish banks: in 'The Structure of Scottish Banking', *Scottish Bankers Magazine*, 43 (1951–2), 208–13, he suggested that larger banking units 'would be in a better position to resist [the] drift of bank business to the south' (p. 209).

them in reserve once trained. Millions of pounds were involved, 'with the narrowest of margins' and a perpetual haggle with brokers. As documents originated in Calcutta, Dacca and Chittagong, 'the English was often suspect', and 'if the market price happened to be moving the wrong way, any discrepancy was an invitation to wriggle out of a contract'. Reform Street showed, in a particularly sharp focus, the problems of the branch hierarchy, with an exalted place for the tellers, specialised units, clerical and ledger staff doing the same task for years on end. This was a clear under-utilisation of manpower, which together with the lack of leadership over new opportunities often led to tensions among staff.

In Lockerbie, at the outbreak of war, George Craik's staff consisted of one teller, the ledger clerk and an apprentice. In due course they were all called up, and he was left with two girls 'picked with care', who proved to be quick workers and whom Craik decided could handle all the work of the branch, telling included. The volume of paperwork was cut, which included an end to the copying of the state sheets, the sides book and the writing-out of the 'cheques remitted' registers, keeping only a book with amounts and branch numbers of the remitted cheques. This eliminated much of the work done by the ledger clerk. One day, James Letham came down on an inspection and was disappointed not to find the usual books, informing Craik that 'this will never do' – to which Craik, who was capable of speaking his mind, replied that 'as long as the war lasts, I'm not going to run the branch any other way'. When the inspection letter duly arrived, there was only one comment: 'We observe you have stopped using the "Sides book", but we would prefer if this could be continued'. James Letham later recalled that this put 'ideas into my mind', and Craik noticed that when appointed Treasurer, Letham made a serious effort to reduce the amount of paperwork. These interesting stories from Perth, Dundee, Lockerbie and Glenrothes about more go-ahead managers proliferated in the 1950s, but unless there was a clear direction from head office it would have been surprising had more than a few managers adopted more modern views and altered the internal structure for their branch offices. Nevertheless, while these old hierarchies took a long time to shift, there were clearly staff receptive to change, and this forms one of the main themes for branch banking from the 1960s.

The London branches of the Scottish banks continued, after the war, to be very important to the internal money flows of each bank with the demands from discount houses for 'overnight' loans and for other borrowers on bills and to stockbrokers. Again, this was short-term lending, regularly renewed. The London managers, or their assistants, saw the bill brokers each day. Each manager knew the situation of internal funds from head office, and thus how much liquidity was available to be outplaced in these specialist markets. The bill brokers, working for the discount houses, walked round to the banks, stated their view of the market, and offered prices which fitted their assessment. The rates charged, $\frac{1}{8}$ and $\frac{1}{16}$ per cent, were rarely a problem, and 'there was no question of hard bargaining'. Sums for the eight houses which Bank of Scotland dealt with in the 1950s usually came to £500,000 each. The brokers wrote nothing down while in the bank offices, 'but each kept a notebook in his top hat and could be seen jotting down notes once he was outside'. The rise in bank rate in November 1951, and the succession of changes thereafter, meant that the discount houses had to be much smarter in setting rates. They were dealing with short-term bonds and could lose 'a lot of money' on bank rate changes. In fact, it soon became clear that the houses dealing in the gilts markets were in difficulty periodically. But with the secrecy of those days, and the effectiveness of the Bank of England, it was highly unlikely that these positions would become a matter of public discussion.

What were the other lending opportunities in London? Advances to industry, trade and the London money market via the London offices of Scottish banks proved very important in the expansion of business from the 1870s onwards. A number of Scottish companies borrowed heavily in London, and it was here with a diversified marketplace that Bank of Scotland was involved with many contrasting situations, all excellent training for staff. The North British Locomotive Co. built world-class steam engines, but found in a competitive world that some buyers were uncooperative about payment. The Bank was called on to raise the company overdraft, on occasion, to nearly £1 million, and in the end the strain proved too great. Another famous name was Rose's Lime Juice, in almost every larder in post-war Britain. From 1947–52, sales increased from £926,000 to £1.8 million; but, because of keen competition, profit margins were tight. The company needed new premises, and with post-war government controls it had difficulty with extensions. By 1953, the company had an unsecured overdraft of £560,000 at $3\frac{1}{2}$ per cent, and Rose's survived. The long-standing connection of Bank of Scotland with the Scottish-owned oil and petroleum industry made the London office, supported by the executive at the Mound, helpful over requests to fund post-war oil developments. A typical case arose in 1947 over Oil Well Engineering Ltd, jointly owned by two British oil companies and by National Supply Co. of Delaware, one of the large US oil engineering concerns. The company had contracts of £1.5 million to supply oil engineering equipment to the Iraq Petroleum Company and needed funds for manufacture and export. National Supply objected to finance from its two British partners, as 'it would disrupt the proportional interest of the shareholdings' – hence bank loans, and £100,000 from

Bank of Scotland. The structure of the London chief office indicated that the bulk of advances were to the London money market, some £13.6 million out of a total of £20.2 million – with £5,995,073 to industry, services and trade. The Piccadilly branch concentrated on smaller loans, £971,783 in 1952. Later in the decade, William Watson allowed the Piccadilly branch to expand loans to industry and the burgeoning building and service sectors. Nevertheless, in the early 1950s, London managers remained very cautious about advances, and the worry over repeated visits by the Inspectors Department may have hindered the development of links in the London area. To gain business in London, managers had to sell advances. It was a more 'distant' business than was usual in Scotland, and managers seldom saw customers except at annual reviews. Moreover, 'borrowers did not expect to be refused and one got used to having to say yes over the telephone for fairly large amounts'. There was little social interaction, and there were few invitations for senior staff to social events: it was first-name terms in business, but 'no idea regarding the other chap's wife or family, nor indeed where he happened to live'.

There can be no single view of the business behaviour of Bank of Scotland and the Union Bank in the decade after the war. During the war, the banks had had no choice but to lend most of their deposits to government; but thereafter there were choices, and the size of commitment to investment in British government securities did serious damage. The fundamental problems were not properly addressed before amalgamation, and the drift continued for several years. By the late 1950s, the gradual rise in interest rates had ensured that trading income was much improved, so that once the gilts position was dealt with, the overall position of the Bank would be much stronger. Yet this also required a more dynamic management at branch level and in inspection procedures which, while still strict, encouraged advances. In the more buoyant conditions of the postwar years, this was clearly the way forward, and it was a disappointment to the managers who understood the benefits of a positive lending policy that a more energetic position was not adopted earlier. Of course, not all the problems were of the Bank's making. There was a reluctance on the part of many companies in Scotland to borrow. The weakness of regional policy before 1958 and the credit squeezes of 1952 and 1957 weakened interest in expansion. Together, this all meant that Bank of Scotland had considerable unutilised potential in the 1950s. By 1958, William Watson, James Letham and a few members of the board had begun what turned out to be a lengthy but absolutely essential effort to restore the underlying position of the Bank, develop new procedures and launch new products, and this story underpins the subsequent two decades.

CHAPTER 24

BANK OF SCOTLAND: DIFFICULTIES WITH LENDING TO INDUSTRY

T HE FINANCIAL POSITION after the amalgamation with the Union Bank required substantial changes in the management of Bank of Scotland's assets. On the positive side, there had been considerable improvement in the ordinary returns of banking through the branch network, although much of this was due to the rise in interest rates, and profits were required to support the deterioration in gilt values. In the years from 1957, it may be doubted whether the direction taken by the Bank accorded with any particular or well-thought-out plan, and when in doubt the board remained cautious. Yet, as the years passed, the directors were more open-minded in their decision-taking, and a second phase began with negotiations for fusion between the Bank and the British Linen; substantial powers were delegated to the senior executives, and numerous avenues for business development were explored. Further, recruitment from industry brought in ideas of centralised planning and management accounting to control and predict cash flow and profitability; by 1973, these covered virtually every aspect of the Bank.

The changes which broadened the Bank's outlook required more expertise than could be provided by the traditional board of directors and the limited number of effective top managers available in 1957. Moreover, it required a recognition that old structures were inappropriate to changing conditions. This required, in varying ways, the unravelling of the hierarchy of power that ran through the Mound to the branches, enforced by the Inspectors Department. The old inspection system remained proper for the assessment and control of branches but tended, sometimes unconsciously, to block new developments in marketing and corporate lending or in foreign currency dealing. The internal changes developed new ideas in which the edges of corporate, retail, finance-house operations and merchant banking became blurred. It would now be a much more fluid hierarchy than hitherto.

The third main change lay with the politics and regulatory system outside the Bank: whereas Lord Elphinstone and Lord Bilsland could claim, with good reason, to be part of the old system of power within Great Britain, by 1958 this had less relevance for the Bank management. There were few occasions when the government or the Bank of England paid attention to the views of the Scottish bankers; in fact, by the close of the 1950s, a period of isolation had set in. How the Scots handled the situation was significant in relation to modern banking and finance, and it demonstrated that Scotland had immense and enviable professional resources which could be drawn on. This process drew from the intellectual and cultural renaissance among the middle classes in Scotland and the reorganisation of the professions – legal, accounting, banking and academic circles – and the impetus which flowed from the discovery of North Sea oil. This boosted morale and increased executive mobility, which made Scotland a much livelier and more welcoming environment for business, education and the arts than almost anywhere south of the Border. The systematic and homogeneous nature of this recent era in Scottish social history compares favourably with the fragmentation and social difficulties of much of urban and middle-class life in England, and the relative decline of their former regional financial centres including Manchester and Liverpool.

The board of the Bank, in common with the other Scottish banks, had to confront the problem posed for the balance sheet by the holdings in British government securities. In February 1958, the deficit on Bank holdings of medium-term gilts was £7,730,513, and that on long-dated gilts of fifteen years and more was another £4,384,329. Although it was better by £500,000 as compared with October 1957, this deficiency 'could not be met from the Bank's inner reserves even allowing for any possible sales made to establish losses for tax purposes'.[1] The investments committee remained cautious; it agreed to sell foreign government stocks that were unlikely ever to be redeemed. Yet such losses, which were met from internal reserves, were insignificant when considered against the problem of medium-, long-dated and undated British government stocks. In January 1958, the board agreed to sell £2.5 million of 4 per cent Victory bonds to realise tax losses, but then confirmed a commitment to long-dated stocks. This was an inadequate response given the recent trend of interest rates. Medium- and long-dated gilts fell to another historic low in the early months of 1958. Throughout 1959, the range of prices was

1 BS, various committees: Investments Committee, 10 January 1958 and associated papers.

little better than the averages for 1953 and 1954, prices fell again in the summer of 1960 after bank rate went to 6 per cent, and prices continued falling in 1961.[2] In the course of 1958–9, sales of nearly £7 million were made, and the deficit declined with a small fall in interest rates. Little was sold in 1960–1, but in the ensuing two years a determined effort was made to reduce holdings, and by February 1963 the Bank held only £33.2 million, mostly medium- and short-dated.[3] The losses on sales of the long-dated securities were huge but were mitigated by recovery from the tax authorities of almost 50 per cent of the loss. The result was to contain the residual deficit on gilts at under £3 million for the remainder of the decade. By 1965, investments in gilts were down to a much more modest 6 per cent of assets (at £17 million), although inevitably the writing-down of the gilt values throughout the 1960s hindered the profitability of the Bank and hence the dividend, as efforts were made to rebuild the inner reserves. It was an absolutely necessary reorganisation of the asset structure, and with a smaller holding of gilts the Bank was now back to the position enjoyed prior to the First World War. The question of gilts also raised inevitable difficulties for the Bank's trustee department. In trusts where investment guidelines were not laid down, the Trust (Scotland) Acts of 1921 and 1926 restricted the choice of investments to gilts, municipal corporation stocks, colonial stocks and feu duties. Before 1951, this was sufficient to maintain the value of trust funds; but, with the rise in interest rates and the consequent decline of gilt prices, the legislation was seen as restricting the flexibility of trustees. Trustees had to wait for the Investment Act of 1961 for a more general permission to diversify, although some restrictions remained.

In February 1959, the control of borrowing by companies which was exercised by the Capital Issues Committee (CIC) was suspended. One effect of the suspension was that banks could increase their capital; and, in September 1959, resolutions were approved whereby an addition of £1.8 million was required for the capital stock of the Bank – then at £4.5 million – to bring it to £6.3 million.[4] Half of the sum required came from the distribution of £900,000 from the published reserve fund, as a £1 bonus issue of stock for every £5 of existing stock. Further to this

2 Figures for British government securities are from Pember and Boyle, *British Government Securities in the Twentieth Century: The First Fifty Years*, 2nd edn (private circulation, London: 1950); idem, *British Government Securities in the Twentieth Century: Supplement 1950–1972* (private circulation, London: n.d. [1973]).
3 Between 1957 and 1960, there were rapid changes on the board of directors as a result of retirement or death; among those who died were Sir John Maxwell Stirling-Maxwell and Sir John Craig in 1957, and Colonel Hugh Spens in February 1958. Robert McCosh, who succeeded Craig as deputy Governor, died in December 1959, Colonel Norman Kennedy also died in 1959, and A. G. R. Brown died in May 1960.
4 BS 1/6, Minutes, August 1959; 'CIC Suspended', *The Banker*, 109 (1959), 141.

issue, another £900,000 of stock, at £2 10s per £1 stock, was offered to proprietors.[5] This raised £2.25 million, of which £900,000 was added to capital stock and the remainder to the published reserve. With £900,000 from the contingency reserves and £150,000 from the profits for 1958–9, this brought the published reserve to £6 million. Capital and reserves then stood at £16,549,243.[6] The capital of £6.3 million stood until February 1965, when a much-improved position for the Bank allowed £2.1 million of the published reserve to be distributed on the basis of one new £1 stock for every three existing £1 of stock, which duly raised the capital to £8.4 million. A transfer from the contingency account of the inner reserve of £2.1 million then rebuilt the figure for the published reserve, and total reserves and stock stood at £21,918,961.

The move out of British government securities coincided with new pressures on the Bank to extend advances and diversify assets. This was especially important for heavy industry and other industrial sectors in years when owners who lacked sufficient liquid resources were unable to raise the cash to fund expensive investment and overseas operations. Whereas in 1957 advances by Bank of Scotland were only £64 million (27.8 per cent) on assets of £230.1 million, from 1959 advances grew fast and by 1964 had reached £145,141,253, just above 50 per cent of assets of £287 million. The industrial orientation continued to grow thereafter. The spread of advances across industrial sectors confirmed the commitment to industry; by 1963, shipowning, shipbuilding and engineering took 19.2 per cent, with strong representation from other industrial sectors.[7] It should be noted that the figures for industrial advances probably understated the true position of Bank of Scotland. The classification was laid down by the Bank of England and was primarily concerned with the status of the borrower, not what the advance was to be used for, and all the clearing banks were instructed to follow the rules even where common sense might have indicated otherwise.

Without any question, the most challenging problems from the mid-1950s onwards concerned the advances to the traditional industries of Scotland. These were anything but straightforward, and Bank of Scotland after amalgamation with the Union had greater responsibility for these than other Scottish banks. The steel and other metal trades, shipbuilding and the engineering trades remained central to the outlook and wealth of a number of the leading Scottish families with whom the Bank had close connections. Some of these were represented on the board. Further, in

---

5 A new Act was unnecessary, and this was done under section 15 of the Bank of Scotland Confirmation Order Act, 1954.
6 See Statistical Appendix, Table A7.
7 See Statistical Appendix, Tables A8 and A10.

the 1950s and 1960s there were still hundreds of medium-sized and small industrial, service and building firms, and tens of thousands of workmen who relied on subcontracts from these traditional sectors, as well as those employed in numerous legal, accountancy and architectural practices. This ensured that public interest in the welfare of the larger Establishments remained resilient and dominated political life in a way that marked out Scottish politics. All four political parties – the Conservative and Unionist Party, the Labour Party, the Scottish National Party and the Liberal Party – focused on the well-being of these industrial sectors and vied with each other over solutions. It was natural that the Bank, with its two-and-a-half centuries' association with industry and the Establishment of the country, would be actively involved, although the importance of bank advances was overshadowed by government spending and party pronouncements.

From 1951 to 1957, the growth of manufacturing output and GDP in Scotland kept pace with the overall advance in UK levels, although GDP per head remained about 10 per cent below the UK figure. For the rest of the 1950s, there was a decline in both absolute and per capita levels of GDP in Scotland, and, over the decade as a whole, manufacturing output in Scotland increased by only 2.4 per cent per year compared with 3.4 per cent in the UK. By 1960, GDP in Scotland had fallen to 87.5 per cent of the UK average (91.8 per cent in 1951).[8] This poor performance led to lengthy discussions at board level and the GMC as it became evident that the nature of funding for heavy industries would have to change, in particular for the steel and metalworks and the shipbuilding yards. While there was a fall in Scottish shipbuilding output after 1957, world demand from shipowners remained buoyant, and there was every reason to believe that, given a sound structure for raw materials, and containment of labour costs in particular, Scottish output would increase again. An optimistic argument was thus justified for the steel and engineering suppliers.[9]

The first significant development plan for steel in the post-war era came in 1956 from Colvilles, the largest producer of steel and iron products in Scotland. The Colville family had long-standing connections with the Union Bank and with Bank of Scotland.[10] A number of Bank directors

8 N. K. Buxton, 'The Scottish Economy, 1945–79: Performance, Structure and Problems', in R. Saville (ed.), *The Economic Development of Modern Scotland 1950–1980* (Edinburgh: 1985), pp. 47–78 (51–2).
9 P. L. Payne, 'The Decline of the Scottish Heavy Industries, 1945–1983', in ibid., pp. 163–82 (p. 107, table 12).
10 Sir John Craig, the chairman and managing director of Colvilles, was Deputy Governor of the Bank and only stood down from Colvilles in 1957, aged 82. Lord Bilsland was a director of Colvilles from 1936, chairman of the Union Bank and a director of Bank of Scotland from 1955, and Governor when Lord Elphinstone retired in 1957. The first Lord Clydesmuir, Secretary of State 1938–40, was a

also had business, accountancy and legal connections with the company or links with firms which in turn relied on Colvilles' success. In 1957, Colvilles approached the National Bank and Bank of Scotland over an ambitious development programme which involved both new mills and partial reconstruction of existing plant.[11] It would cost £25 million: £6–7 million would come from profits, a similar sum from ordinary shares, £8 million from the National Bank and £4 million from a loan account at the London Chief Office of Bank of Scotland at 1 per cent over bank rate, minimum 3½ per cent, to be repaid over seven to eight years, with interest charged only on the amount outstanding. This plan was considered as part of an intense but optimistic argument over the need for new steelmaking plant capable of manufacturing sheet metal for consumer goods and motor vehicles. A new mill was thought more likely to provide the necessary base to encourage these industries to settle in Scotland. Several senior Conservative and Unionist politicians, among whom were the prime minister, Harold Macmillan, Iain Macleod at the Ministry of Labour and John S. Maclay, Secretary of State for Scotland, were prominent in their support.[12] Unfortunately, there was an inadequate assessment by the government of the probable returns. The Ministry of Power and the Treasury would not entertain the idea of a subsidy. At this point, Colvilles ought to have remained cautious, but the directors were influenced by a desire to remain one of the main producers in the UK and Europe, and they proved susceptible to pressures from political and industrial friends.[13] On 6 November 1958, Macmillan announced that Colvilles would build a steel mill at Ravenscraig, but there would also be another mill in South Wales, a concession to English steel interests. The cost of Ravenscraig was estimated at £50 million, double the earlier proposals, with £45 million from a rights issue and the remainder advanced by the newly-amalgamated National Commercial Bank and Bank of Scotland. Ravenscraig opened in 1963 and proved to be an immense boost to the morale of Scottish business but, unfortunately, a serious financial burden for Colvilles. The Bank was also involved in funding its long-standing client Stewarts & Lloyds, the Scottish firm which had moved to Corby, Northamptonshire, in 1932 and which now required £20 million for refurbishment of its steel mills. The Bank first

director of Colvilles and also sat on the Union board; his son, Ronald John Bilsland Colville, joined the board of Colvilles in 1958 and was Governor of the British Linen to 1971 and Governor of Bank of Scotland from 1972 until 1981.

11 P. L. Payne, *Colvilles and the Scottish Steel Industry* (Oxford: 1979), pp. 363–8; the financial details are from BS 1/7, Treasurer's Committee Minutes, 9 April 1957.

12 The most detailed assessment of the politics involved in the discussion is in J. Foster and C. Woolfson, *The Politics of the UCS Work-In* (London: 1986), p. 102ff.

13 A summary of this situation is in Payne, 'Decline of the Scottish Heavy Industries', p. 94.

offered £12.5 million, which it later increased to £14 million at ½ per cent above bank rate.[14]

The board of Bank of Scotland was kept fully conversant with the changing circumstances of shipbuilding, port facilities and the methods of finance required. From 1951 to 1955, the annual launches on the Clyde averaged 446,000 tons, but from 1956 to 1960 they fell to only 401,000.[15] In 1960, there were twenty-three shipyards left on the Clyde, but only twelve could build larger vessels, and all had problems associated with their physical layout and lack of space. Worse was to come. A brief revival in 1962 was followed by a decline to 258,600 tons in 1963.[16] With falling order books, tight margins and physical constraints, it was inevitable that yards would close; five went in 1963 and 1964. The British shipowning industry was also in difficulties after the war. Heavy losses at sea had not been made good from the government War Risk Insurance scheme, and the monies needed for rebuilding ships thus required running down shipowners' reserves, as well as ploughing back profits and a tight dividend policy. Some relief was accorded by allowances for investment which were not subject to tax. Shipping companies could also claim for depreciation, although there were frequent disputes over what was, or was not, allowable. There were especial difficulties for the smaller shipowners in the tramp-steamer business, who typically owned two or three ships. Apart from using reserves and bank advances, owners had recourse, from 1951, to the underfunded Ship Mortgage Finance Corporation (SMFC), which could provide up to 50 per cent of the costs of ships built in UK yards. Yet much of the lending from the SMFC went to larger shipowning companies because of pressures from the Treasury and the CIC. Further, at the time of the contraction of credit in 1957, there was confusion over government policy. On 22 January 1957, the Economic Secretary to the Treasury announced that the CIC had been instructed to treat shipbuilding as an industry deserving 'a definite urgency under current requirements'.[17] Yet Peter Thorneycroft, the Chancellor of the Exchequer, repudiated this in his Budget speech of 9 April 1957 and instructed the CIC to refuse consent,

---

14 BS 1/6, Minutes, London Chief Office advance, 8 July 1958. The staff at LCO made strenuous efforts on behalf of Stewarts & Lloyds.
15 For a detailed discussion of the Clyde yards at this time, see A. Slaven, *The Development of the West of Scotland, 1750–1960* (London: 1975), pp. 215–20; Payne, 'Decline of the Scottish Heavy Industries', pp. 101–8; Foster and Woolfson, *UCS Work-In*, pp. 108ff.; A. Slaven, 'Growth and Stagnation in British and Scottish Shipbuilding 1913–1977', in J. Kuuse and A. Slaven (eds), *Scottish and Scandinavian Shipbuilding Seminar: Development Problems in Historical Perspective* (Glasgow: 1980), pp. 18–54.
16 Payne, 'Decline of the Scottish Heavy Industries', p. 107, table 12.
17 'Memorandum of Evidence submitted by the General Council of British Shipping', 11 April 1958, in *Principal Memoranda of Evidence submitted to the Committee on the Working of the Monetary System*, vol. ii (HMSO, 1960), pp. 141–3.

however good the purpose of the loan, unless they are satisfied either that there are exceptional features in the case which makes it impossible for the applicant to raise the loan from banking sources, or that the proposed loan is a strictly temporary and short bridging operation pending the completion of funding arrangements.

Foreign owners were treated more favourably:

where the purpose of the proposed loan is to finance exports, and the Export Credit Guarantee Department [ECGD] has already indicated its willingness to issue a guarantee to the bank, refusal of consent would be inconsistent with the general policy of giving such guarantees direct to banks, which was introduced specifically to facilitate loans for the export of major capital goods.

The General Council of British Shipping concluded its evidence to the Committee on the Working of the Monetary System (known as the Radcliffe Committee) by noting that, before 1957, shipowners could obtain funds from banks, discount houses, institutions and occasionally from the SMFC, but the changes of early 1957 had severely restricted advances from the banks, and the long-term facilities offered by other institutions were not suitable. It was extraordinary that government policy on bank lending ensured that foreign owners were better able than their British counterparts to obtain finance in the UK.[18] Faced with lack of interest by the British government, the shipyard owners and the Scottish bankers came up with several important initiatives. In 1959, discussions began between Bank of Scotland and a consortium including Lithgows, Fairfields Shipbuilding and Engineering Co. Ltd and John Brown (Clydebank) to build a graving dock at Greenock on the lower Clyde capable of taking the largest ocean-going tankers. The scheme would enable Scotland to attract more ship-repair work as well as general ship refurbishment. The Bank agreed to advance £700,000 against equity and normal bank overdrafts for the work in progress.[19] The project was slowed down by the insistence of the Treasury that the Industrial and Commercial Finance Corporation (ICFC) should not subscribe the balance of the capital cost, which, they insisted, should come from equity holders. The Firth of Clyde Dry Dock was an excellent initiative although, once operational, it was in competition with a number of subsidised companies abroad.

The second important initiative drew on the Bank's experience in the finance of leased ships: the board agreed to the formation of a company owned by Lithgows and Fairfields to provide finance for the purchase of

18 Ibid., p. 144.
19 BS 1/6, Minutes, 31 July 1958, 19 April 1960.

ships to be built in their yards for foreign-based owners. The difficulties faced by export sales were summed up by Sir John Erskine, chairman of Fairfields and a past general manager of the Commercial Bank, in a memorandum to the board of Bank of Scotland in 1959:

1. It is the prime function of shipbuilders to build ships, not to provide finance to owners for building.
2. Notwithstanding (1), over the years, in times of depression or during periods of temporary difficulty in transferring funds, it has been the practice for builders in the position to do so to provide funds in the form of temporary loans or otherwise for the mutual benefit of (a) building a ship and (b) acquiring it.
3. In recent times increased world competition in building has been the cause of introducing as an inducement to owners to build, deferred terms of a very generous character. These, in the case of certain foreign countries it is thought are made possible by state assistance in one form or another.
4. In the foregoing circumstances it is not possible for the Group to avoid participating, however desirous they may be to concentrate upon building for cash and indeed their effort is directed towards obtaining upon the basis of efficiency and competitive ability, cash business wherever possible.[20]

There was a precedent for Erskine's proposal. In the inter-war years, Lithgows and other yards had built ships 'on spec', before obtaining a firm order, or by loans to approved owners. While this had proved 'comparatively' easy when a vessel of 10,000 deadweight tonnage cost £120,000, it was more of a burden with prices over £1 million, although Lithgows and Fairfields had begun in the 1950s to use their substantial credit balances to offer deferred terms. The time had now come to 'shunt' the borrowing to a finance company which would stand between the shipbuilders and the Bank and which would release capital previously used to assist customers.

Erskine proposed a solely Bank of Scotland scheme, to be known as Kingston Financial Services (Clyde) Ltd (KFS); capital would be £1 million, with £100,000 paid up. The details were to be kept secret. The Fairfields and the Lithgows current balances (then totalling £2,364,000) would be kept with the Bank, and McClelland Moore CA would handle accounts. Only first-class owners would be considered, and could borrow at 1½ per cent over bank rate. Apart from an increase in the nominal capital to £1.5 million, it was agreed in November 1960 that KFS could call on £7.5 million over and above banking services already extended to Lithgows and Fairfields. It was incorporated as a finance

---

20 BS, Board papers, 1959; an initial proposal of 1959 sought a company managed by Hambros which would supply finance alongside Bank of Scotland, the National Commercial and the Westminster. This did not proceed.

company in 1961, with the two shipyards each holding a 50 per cent stake. William Hay, an assistant general manager of the Bank, was made secretary, and in 1964 Sir William Watson (who was knighted that year) replaced Sir John Erskine as chairman.[21] By 1974, KFS had provided loans in connection with fourteen ships, and there were no bad debts. It was then decided that improvements in the management of the London-based ECGD and those responsible for the Home Shipowners scheme had largely negated the usefulness of the company, but it remained in being as a wholly-owned subsidiary of Bank of Scotland in case of changes in government policy.[22] While KFS was aimed at foreign owners, the Bank was keen to persuade the government that an extension of preferential terms was required for British shipowners, and to this the government of Harold Wilson (1964–70) was sympathetic. Under the terms of the Shipbuilding Finance Acts, 1967 and 1969, advances were made to British owners at $5\frac{1}{2}$ per cent. Each loan was agreed with, and guaranteed by, the Ministry of Technology; in 1970, for example, the old clients of the Union Bank, the Blue Star Line, received £13.2 million at this rate for construction of vessels by Swan Hunter.[23]

The Bank also used its financial muscle wherever possible to steer contracts for shipbuilding and engineering to Scottish firms, and on occasion declined facilities for companies which wished to use builders abroad. In July 1961, the board agreed to join a consortium to provide finance of £10 million for British Oil Equipment Credits Ltd for a new refinery in Spain, but only if the contract for the pipeline went to Stewarts & Lloyds.[24] In the same month, a request from a shipbuilding firm in Sweden to borrow £2 million as part-finance to build two 80,000 d.w.t. tankers for Shell Trading was turned down. The board remained enthusiastic over financial arrangements for building in the Clyde yards in addition to contracts arranged through KFS. In February 1962, the Argentine state-owned shipping line Empresa Lineas Maritimas Argentinas (Elma) approached Vickers Cammell Laird Shipbuilders Ltd (VCL), jointly owned by Vickers Armstrong (Shipbuilders), Cammell Laird and Lithgows, for fourteen ships, eleven to be built in the UK and three to be assembled in Argentina. Of the £24.3 million cost, 80 per cent would come from five banks, including Bank of Scotland, to be repaid over ten years and guaranteed by the ECGD.[25] Other contracts followed this pattern, and the expertise of the Bank with its close Clyde connections was called upon by

21 William Hay later became Treasurer-designate, but sadly died before taking up his appointment.
22 The Bank bought the share capital of KFS per 90d share: BS 1/6, Minutes, 22 January 1974.
23 BS 1/6, Minutes, 23 September 1970, Blue Star Line, board papers. Bank of Scotland pressed for a revision of this rate, and from 10 October 1970 it was raised to 7 per cent.
24 BS 1/6, Minutes, finance for Japhet & Co., 4 July 1961.
25 BS 1/6, Minutes, 13 February 1962.

London banks. Some disagreements emerged at the GMC about the terms of these loans, arranged through Bank of Scotland LCO; they were usually at bank rate plus at least ½ per cent, but there were occasions when the Bank offered a slightly lower rate.[26]

Unfortunately, there was an inadequate return on shipbuilding to finance reconstruction of the shipyards. The Bank could offer long-term loans at low interest and was delighted to pioneer every arrangement consistent with eventual repayment. But unless the government was prepared to subsidise shipbuilding and offer grants for rebuilding the shipyards, the fiercely competitive international shipbuilding market remained biased against the Clyde. Further, there was active opposition to the introduction of such supports by a number of multinational companies which had settled in Scotland after the war and which encouraged the government to support a pool of cheap and flexible labour. This view, which condemned as too slow the run-down of the older industries, gained currency from the later 1950s as lack of government interest exacerbated the difficulties which faced the shipyards. At times, the Bank could have been forgiven for feeling that it was alone in the struggle to support John Brown's, Lithgows and Fairfields.

By 1964, Fairfields were in serious difficulty. Yet as late as June 1965, Bank of Scotland was prepared to increase their overdraft to £2.3 million.[27] By October the position was desperate, and the Bank, with the chairman's agreement, appointed a receiver and manager on 19 October 1965. The group employed 5,000 employees, 3,400 at the Govan shipyard; there were 800 creditors, mostly among the small and medium engineering sectors of the west of Scotland. Fairfields owed the Bank £3,894,000, and the board agreed to extend the overdraft limits to pay wages. The receiver ruled that the gap between income and expenditure, estimated at £1 million by 31 March 1966, required government support. Thus, 'unless financial assistance is forthcoming Fairfield must close immediately. Contraction of the UK shipbuilding industry may be inevitable but assistance is required on the ground that until that issue is clarified Fairfields [was] a yard on which several millions has [sic] been spent [and it] should be kept open.'[28] The Bank, too, asked the government for more support for the company.[29]

---

26 BS(BL), Uncatalogued, GMC, Minutes, 23 May 1961; BS 1/6, Minutes, report on LCO advances, 27 June 1961. There was friction on the GMC over credit balances, maximum deposit rates and special agreements (BS(BL), Uncatalogued, GMC, Minutes, 2 October 1962).

27 BS, Minutes, Board papers, 15 June 1965; discussions proceeded with AEI/Hawker Siddeley for a sale of Fairfield-Rowan.

28 BS 1/6, Board papers, A. I. Mackenzie, Receiver and Manager, Report on Fairfields and Fairfield-Rowan, to the board of Bank of Scotland.

29 Foster and Woolfson, UCS Work-In, p. 109; James Lumsden WS, of Maclay, Murray and Spens, who was the legal advisor to UCS and a director of Bank of Scotland, warned the directors of UCS that with

The yard was saved by the intervention of a Labour government criticised for its previous failure to stop closures in the heavy industries. A new company was formed with £500,000 from the Board of Trade, £500,000 from private sources and £1 million on 7 per cent unsecured loan stock 1975, also taken up by the Board of Trade. This provided enough working capital to allow Fairfields to proceed with current building, but not enough for the long-term investment capital which it really needed.[30] The yard was reorganised as a showpiece of social democratic planning in which the management and the unions signed detailed agreements for the modernisation of work practices through ending traditional demarcation between trades. The ease with which all this was achieved caused outrage among the competitor shipbuilders on the Clyde, who had expected the yard to be shut. Bank of Scotland was largely ignored in this settlement, losing a substantial part of its advances; it was small consolation that it retained the current account.

As with other Scottish clearing banks, the Bank acted in innovative ways to help construction projects overseas which involved Scottish firms. Alone, or together with other banks, support was granted to long-standing sugar machinery manufacturers in Paisley with advances for the construction of a cane-sugar refinery in the Sudan. When Imperial Chemical Industries wanted to build a plant in the Soviet Union which required machinery from Scottish companies, the Bank offered its services on similar terms. For all large foreign construction projects, the board insisted that contracts be awarded to Bank customers as a guarantee of participation. Thus the board agreed to join a consortium formed by Exporters Refinance Corporation Ltd in 1970 to finance the construction of the first stage of a hydro-electric power station at Murchiston Falls, Uganda. The Bank committed £5.44 million, being 85 per cent of a subcontract expected to go to Mitchell Construction, Kinnear, Moody Group Ltd.[31] In July 1971, the Bank agreed to join a consortium led by Baring Bros to finance 50 per cent of the UK element of contracts for the construction of a hydro-plant at Marimbondo Falls, Brazil, with Bank finance restricted to its customers.

The board took a similar view of its general remit to support Scottish industry in the case of aluminium. The Bank's first connection with the British Aluminium Company came with the completion of the smelter

such a discrepancy on their balance sheet between liabilities and assets they might find themselves personally liable if the company were not placed into receivership.

30 Those instrumental in the plan were: George Brown, the Minister for Economic Affairs; Derek Palmer, a director of Hill Samuel the London merchant bank; Iain Stewart, the manager of Hall Thermotank; and Roy Thomson, a Canadian businessman and the owner of *The Scotsman*.

31 They were customers of the British Linen: BS 1/6, Minutes, 8 September 1970. Much of this type of lending was guaranteed by the ECGD.

opened in June 1896 on the famous Falls of Foyer, followed by a larger one at Kinlochleven in 1909. A third project, which cost around £5 million, was completed in 1938.[32] It was surprising that the huge demand for aluminium after the Second World War did not result in further plant before construction started of a fourth plant at Invergordon in 1969. The following year, prices reached a temporary peak but then fell, and producers in western Europe responded with a cartel to stockpile ingots.[33] Alufinance and Trade Ltd was launched in the summer of 1971 with a $45 million Eurodollar loan, towards which Bank of Scotland put $2.5 million at ½ per cent over the London inter-bank rate. To keep a watch over proceedings, the board joined with two English banks to appoint a temporary director to British Aluminium. From late 1972, prices rose fast.

Political change proved a major influence on industrial events in Scotland after 1958. For two years before 1960, there promised to be a most constructive partnership between the banks in Scotland, the government and private industry. There was, nevertheless, growing concern at the performance of the Scottish economy compared with the UK as a whole, and this encouraged the government to consider more detailed industrial intervention. Apart from the agreement for the new strip mill at Ravenscraig, there were changes in regional policy with the Distribution of Industry (Industrial Finance) Act of 1958 by which the issue of industrial development certificates was to take into account the needs of designated areas such as central Scotland.[34] Financial assistance was to be made available for new factories in areas of high unemployment. In 1960, a new Employment Act allowed companies concessions but could not direct them northwards. Nevertheless, strenuous efforts were made to entice a car manufacturer to move to Scotland; and, after the intervention of Harold Macmillan, Lord Rootes agreed to locate a new car plant at Linwood. This was all positive. There was a significant relaxation in government fiscal policy in 1958 and 1959 when Macmillan ignored Treasury and Bank of England advice on the maintenance of credit controls. The Scottish banks had complained vociferously in private about Thorneycroft's 1957 policy of high interest rates. The problem was much wider than the effect on gilts, deposits

32 P. L. Payne, *The Hydro: A Study of the Development of the Major Hydro-Electric Schemes Undertaken by the North of Scotland Hydro-Electric Board* (Aberdeen: 1988), pp. 3–15.
33 BS 1/6, Minutes, 1 June 1971. For prices and output, see C. J. Schmitz, *World Non-Ferrous Metal Production and Prices 1700–1976* (London: 1979).
34 G. McCrone, 'The Role of Government', in R. Saville (ed.), *The Economic Development of Modern Scotland 1950–1980* (Edinburgh: 1985), pp. 195–213 (p. 201); a map of the areas covered by the 1958 Act is in D. Sims and M. Wood, *Car Manufacturing at Linwood: The Regional Policy Issues* (Paisley: 1984), p. 19.

and the confidence of customers and business. When in 1957 the GMC was asked to give evidence to the Radcliffe Committee, it was agreed to make these reservations public. The wording was discussed at length by the general managers, and their polished text pointed out the extent of Scottish bankers' disagreements with the Treasury and the Bank of England.[35]

(i) The higher interest rates ruling in the past two years have restricted rather than increased earnings, because additional interest paid on deposits has been greater than the extra income derived from advances and Money Market assets.

(ii) Increases in Bank rate [from 1951] resulted in substantial withdrawals of deposits by customers for investment in Treasury bills.

(iii) These higher interest rates have also resulted in substantial depreciation in the value of investments acquired in the days of cheap money. Confidence in the gilt-edged market has declined to a point at which the banks are obliged to rely mainly on maturities rather than sales of investments for the replenishment of their liquid assets.

(iv) The directives on bank lending have resulted in the loss of goodwill and transfers of business to outside lenders. To implement the request of July, 1955, the banks had to agree to place restrictions on the transfer of accounts from one bank to another. As already indicated, they regard this as workable for a short period only and hold that continuance of such restrictions is extremely undesirable and ultimately, well-nigh impossible to operate.

(v) In the various ways mentioned bank income has been prevented from expanding in proportion to the rise in deposits, but costs have continued to increase.

The GMC proceeded to criticise government policy in respect of industrial advances and the dangers of an unregulated market:

It will be apparent . . . that the direct controls applied to bank lending have been discriminatory in their effects and have prevented the natural expansion and development of banking business. Not only in relation to their own deposits, but in relation also to national income and to the level of capital investment, the total advances of banks have continuously declined. It is not apparent that this restriction has contributed in any marked degree to the restraint of inflation but there is evidence that it has progressively distorted the financial mechanism . . . there has been an increase in lending by institutions whose funds, from the nature of their business, would normally be used for investment. There has also been a growth in lending by finance houses, not only for the hire purchase of consumer goods but also for purposes which, in the

35 'Memorandum of Evidence submitted by the Committee of Scottish Bank General Managers', November 1957, in *Principal Memoranda of Evidence submitted to the Committee on the Working of the Monetary System*, vol. ii (HMSO, 1960), p. 71.

absence of restrictions, would have been financed by the banks. Restrictions on the supply of capital to such finance houses have also brought about a growth in the number of small companies operating in this field, borrowing from the public at high rates of interest but holding little in the way of liquid assets.

The ink was hardly dry before the Chancellor of the Exchequer, Peter Thorneycroft, an exponent of strict monetary policy, was replaced by Derick Heathcoat Amory in January 1958. In his April Budget, Amory announced cuts in indirect taxes and the abolition of restrictions on bank advances, and this was emphasised by further measures in June.[36] The impact of this more open financial environment, together with an upturn in industrial demand in Europe and America, helped UK industrial output to rise by almost 10 per cent and GDP by over 3 per cent in 1959.[37] The board of Bank of Scotland noticed a significant rise in requests for new and enlarged loans throughout 1959; total UK bank advances went to £2,467 million (February 1959), some £250 million above the previous high in August 1955, and at the time *The Banker* estimated that 'more than half' of the expansion was attributed to the relaxation of policy.[38] Amory later admitted that this had gone too far, although it may well have enhanced the support for the government in the election of October 1959, when Macmillan's majority rose from 67 to 107.[39]

Unfortunately, counterpoised to this expansionary policy was the crude view at the Bank of England that inflation demanded higher interest rates, and, if necessary, physical controls on bank advances; and by late 1959 Threadneedle Street was exerting pressure on the government. Macmillan disagreed, not least because of the political effects that restrictions might have in Scotland, where five seats had been lost in the election. He was 'worried – not so much about the boom but the loss of nerve (I sense that the Treasury officials are much more calm)'.[40] He urged the Chancellor to 'consider a stand-still budget', and argued that

36 For the importance of the June 1958 measures, see 'New Guide to the CIC', *The Banker*, 108 (1958), 490–2.
37 S. Pollard, *The Development of the British Economy 1914–1967*, 2nd edn (London: 1969), pp. 475–6. The impact on the hire purchase market is discussed below, Chapter 25.
38 'Advances Gather Speed', *The Banker*, 109 (1959), 205. For the rapid expansion of Scottish banks, see F. S. Taylor, 'Bankers off the Leash', *The Banker*, 109 (1959), 253–8. By February 1960, *The Banker* had pointed out that 1959–60 was the most profitable year since the war, with the huge increase in bank advances 'always the most remunerative of the banks' normal assets': 'The Banks and their Profits', *The Banker*, 110 (1960), 103–6.
39 Harold Macmillan 'was a master of using the Treasury to support electoral aims': A. Horne, *Macmillan: 1957–1986*, vol. ii of the official biography (London: 1989), pp. 141–3. David Alexander, the president of the Scottish Institute of Bankers, recalled in 1960 that he, and by implication others on the GMC, had been unhappy with the complete abandonment of regulation 'in the matter of minimum deposits and the maximum periods for hire purchase transactions and putting the CIC into cold storage might be going too far': David Alexander, 'Presidential Address', *Scottish Bankers Magazine*, 52 (1960–1), 65–71.
40 H. Macmillan, *Pointing the Way 1959–1961* (London: 1972), p. 220, citing his diary, 17 February 1960.

A gentle squeeze may be right; but it cannot be sensible to cheer the economy on vigorously one moment and then push it violently back the next. And there is of course the danger that all this, partly real (e.g the restriction of bank lending) and partly psychological (e.g your desire for a budget surplus) will work too well. What will happen if the motor companies cancel their plans for expansion on Merseyside, etc? What will happen if Pressed Steel decided after all not to set up in the North East? What will happen if our Scottish plans, upon which so much depends, break down? Then I suppose we will have to go back to the stimulant instead of the soporific and the alternation [sic] will become not merely politically impossible but even ridiculous.

Moreover, what is all this based upon? Not the certainty of a loss on the balance of payments; but only upon a very shadowy calculation that our overseas monetary position at the end of the year may be rather less good than it is now. My confidence in the accuracy of figures of this sort is just about as much as I have in Old Moore. The fact is that nobody can make these calculations accurately. You will remember that the shipping figure was £100m or more wrong . . . I have not much confidence in any of these figures and certainly not enough to reverse what seems to me a sound policy of expansion and start again the whole dreary cycle of squeeze and disinflation. It is the policy of Sisyphus and the Governor [of the Bank of England] is well cast for the part.[41]

In spite of this sympathy with regional problems, Macmillan lacked adequate supporting advice to hold his ground, and the Scottish banks were also unable to develop their ideas in a cogent manner. Bank rate went to 5 per cent on 21 January 1960, and in April Macmillan agreed, albeit reluctantly, to tough restrictions on bank advances which failed to distinguish industrial advances from general lending to consumers. There was a further rise on 23 June to 6 per cent. The restrictions of April and June 1960 were resented north of the Border, and, although disagreements were kept confidential, this did not detract from the overwhelming importance of the differences with the City and the Bank of England, which were concerned primarily with the international value of sterling and the earnings of the discount houses. It was felt that there was also a problem with the English banks in that not only did they fail to appreciate the centrality of Scottish banks to industry, but also the Committee of the London Clearing Banks maintained that longer-term lending on Scottish lines was not a suitable activity for banks: 'it was reasonable for the Banks to expect to provide only short-term capital for nationalised industries, [and that companies,] in common with other borrowers, [should] look elsewhere for their "hard-core" borrowing which was of a more permanent nature'.[42] This attitude carried over when the London clearers, under pressure from the Labour government, agreed to create structures to handle

41 Ibid., pp. 221–2 (letter to Heathcoat Amory, 27 February 1960).
42 BS, Uncatalogued, GMC, Minutes, 11 March 1963.

medium-term loans for industry. The Midland Bank's fund was given a ceiling of just £5 million, a figure that *The Banker* ridiculed as derisory. There was an important sequel to this. As the managements of the London institutions looked at business reorganisation in the later 1960s, it seemed that they tended to focus on lending with high profit margins. Long-term lending to industry, which the Scottish banks stayed with, was regarded as less important.

The positions of the Bank of England and the Treasury were strengthened by the publication of the report of the Radcliffe Committee and the evidence taken before it.[43] Radcliffe focused upon the position of the pound sterling, the maintenance of adequate sterling and gold reserves, and on holding down the rate of inflation; but the report paid little attention to the underlying deterioration in the international competitive position of UK industry. Further, Radcliffe had given inadequate attention to the connections between industry and banking. On the positive side, the committee recognised that the traditional definition of money – limited to banknotes, bank deposits and commercial bills – was inadequate due to the growth of new forms of credit. It argued that government policy should recognise that all forms of financial claims, including certain fixed assets, could be used as money, and that such claims did not preserve a constant ratio with bank deposits. It followed that simple controls over banknotes, deposits and bills held by the clearing and Scottish banks could not control the velocity of circulation or innovative forms of credit. This undermined the case for direct physical controls on the narrow, traditional definition of money and on bank liquidity. When the government needed to support sterling or tackle the rate of inflation, the committee argued that it should act on the demand for money by using interest rates in a more aggressive way than hitherto.[44] There was also scope for a relaxation in banks' liquidity ratios. Within eighteen months of publication, as Macmillan's policy collapsed, the government did indeed use interest rates as a means of controlling the demand for advances, but went further and brought in physical controls on the banks as well.

The Deputy Governor of the Bank of England, Sir Cyril Hawker, expressed his lack of sympathy for the difficulties of the Scottish bankers

43 Committee on the Working of the Monetary System (the Radcliffe Committee), *Report*, Cmnd 827 (August 1959); for a discussion of the committee in respect of the Scottish banks, see M. Gaskin, *The Scottish Banks: A Modern Survey* (London: 1965), and S. G. Checkland, *Scottish Banking: A History, 1695–1973* (Glasgow: 1975), pp. 628–30. The *Scottish Bankers Magazine* reported the views of R. S. Sayers, a member of the committee, in his address to the Economic section of the British Association, 1960 ('Notes and Comments: Professor Sayers on Monetary Policy', *Scottish Bankers Magazine*, 52 (1960–1), 127–8).
44 Committee on the Working of the Monetary System, *Report*, Cmnd 827 (August 1959), sections 487–519, and 'Emergency Measures', sections 520–9.

on a visit to Edinburgh in April 1960. The economy was heading for a 'boom condition', he claimed, and 'Although it was not easy to forecast the rate of increase in bank advances there were already signs of strain and over the next few months when a seasonal expansion of credit could be expected it was important that there should be no "large" increase in bank lending'. To underline this, the Bank of England would call for special deposits of 1 per cent of total bank assets in Scotland.[45] But Sir Cyril's real message was to curtail industrial advances, perhaps the worst course that the Bank of England could have taken, 'though apparently less harsh than the call of 2 per cent made upon the English clearing banks'. The Scottish bankers were naturally furious. In his discussion with Macmillan, William Watson (as he then was) had been assured that government financial policy would treat the depressed areas, and Scotland in general, in a more favourable light than England. Indeed, it was on this basis that the Scottish Office and the Board of Trade had proceeded with their negotiations with Rootes, the British Motor Corporation and other companies which were expected to buy sheet steel from Ravenscraig. Against this, the theory behind the Bank of England view was the old story of the supremacy of the interest of the foreign exchanges, which wanted a 'strong pound'. In theory, by the control of industrial lending in the short term, in some vague way, industry would benefit from the restrictions and the accompanying rise in bank rate at a later stage. This theory ignored the regular payments of an expanding economy and was a blow to the solvency of the industrial companies which had invested in new plant and taken on new contracts in the recent expansion.[46] It was also, the GMC argued, blatantly discriminatory. In England from 1955, the rate of growth of personal advances, often to finance consumption and the importing of luxury goods from abroad, had been faster than in Scotland. It was argued that the English banks operated over a more buoyant and varied environment than those in Scotland, and a greater proportion of their overdrafts and advances were for short-run services and personal advances; and therefore the English banks were, on average, better able to provide special deposits by limiting this sort of advance. Scottish industry required stability over the longer term, and cuts in investment and a rise in interest rates could only have had adverse consequences. Walter R. Ballantyne, the general manager of the Royal Bank, suggested that the 'only possible reason for . . . any call on the Scottish banks must be the anticipated reaction of the English banks' and reminded Hawker of the

45 Special deposits were called in May 1960, of £5.8 million; they reached £69.8 million on 15 June, and £142.6 million by August.
46 A rise in interest rates, a stop to industrial advances and restrictions on consumer credit acted to curtail income to industrial firms by lengthening payment times and increasing bad debts, while forcing cutbacks in firms' reserves.

political feeling which the measure would arouse in an already hostile political climate.[47]

> Boom conditions did not exist in Scotland and Scottish industry was in need of every financial encouragement consistent with prudent lending. It was irrational for the Government to try and stimulate Scottish industry if the Bank of England and the Treasury were to work in the opposite direction.[48]

David Alexander, in his presidential address to the Institute of Bankers in Scotland in June 1960, pointed out that frequent and drastic changes in policy shook confidence in customers, 'who are hard put to plan for a future ... without the added problem of credit availability'.[49] It was all hard-hitting. Yet, the Bank of England view 'was that they washed their hands of local industrial conditions, [they] had to take a general picture of the country as a whole ... if certain areas required special treatment that was a matter for the Government'. At best, this showed some misunderstanding of the relationship between the banks and industrial progress. At worst, the Bank of England was perceived as acting solely as the mouthpiece of the London money markets.

This argument went to the core of the new efforts at industrial and commercial development by Bank of Scotland and the other Scottish banks. The special deposit scheme was irksome but was coped with. Proposals for controls over the absolute level of advances or the percentage of advances to deposits were more serious, and it was this type of control that the Bank of England had in mind when requesting the provision by the banks of much more precise statistics, a demand which the GMC strenuously resisted.[50] There was even some mild criticism in public: the Duke of Buccleuch, Governor of the Royal Bank, suggested that special deposits might be abandoned if the level of advances was to be controlled; and Ian Macdonald CA, the general manager of the Commercial Bank, noted that if individual business sectors were to be singled out for restraint, more harm than good might be done.[51] There was little that the Scottish banks could do over interest rates. On 1 August 1960, they were asked by

---

47 Ballantyne pointed to recent criticisms at the Scottish Trades Union Congress that the 'banks were not playing their part in the development of Scottish industry': BS(BL), Uncatalogued, GMC, Minutes, 25 April 1960. The STUC criticised the limited nature of the Linwood development compared to progress in England with new car plants: Sims and Wood, *Car Manufacturing at Linwood*, pp. 29–30.
48 There was no reason why Scotland could not be treated in a different way from England, as Northern Ireland was.
49 David Alexander, 'Presidential Address', *Scottish Bankers Magazine*, 52 (1960–1), 65–71 (p. 66).
50 BS(BL), Uncatalogued, GMC, Minutes, 10 April and 10 October 1961.
51 F. S. Taylor, 'Scots Banks in the New Squeeze', *The Banker*, 112 (1962), 249–50. Total UK bank advances rose to July 1960, fell in August and September and resumed an upward trend later in the year. Scottish bank advances began to fall in the summer of 1960, picked up in the spring of 1961 but were held back in the autumn.

the Bank of England to ensure that advances in mid-December were no higher than in June, although they were supposed to maintain and support exports, a difficult distinction in practice.[52] Within eighteen months, the prime minister was in a much weaker and more isolated position. He later resigned, to be replaced by Alec Douglas-Home, whose foremost task was the political unity of his party.

The arguments over the limited role of ICFC in industrial financing in Scotland continued into the 1960s. The GMC frequently discussed the 'unsatisfactory attitude' of ICFC, 'who in general were not sympathetic towards Scottish undertakings'. The Scots threatened to withdraw capital from ICFC and move it directly to Scottish industry to counter demands from London for special deposits; furthermore, the Scots threatened to announce in public who was to blame for reductions in advances. When the representative of the Scottish banks, W. H. Fraser, retired, Lord Piercy, the chairman, made it clear that the successor would be appointed in London and not by the GMC. In fact, Fraser's replacement was A. I. Mackenzie, a well-known and respected Glasgow chartered accountant and very agreeable to the Scottish bankers. Withdrawal from ICFC was debated, but in view of the proposals for the new Clyde dock a compromise was agreed.[53] In 1962, the ICFC board decided to increase its capital by £5 million but only with a 50 per cent premium, which would give a yield to the subscribing banks of only 4 per cent.[54] William Watson and the board were opposed to further participation. Lord Piercy had made no attempt to discuss the matter independently with the Scots, and 4 per cent was a poor return. Both the board of the Bank and the GMC deprecated the inability of ICFC to increase the proportion of its lending in Scotland; the Royal Bank and the National Commercial agreed, but the Clydesdale and the British Linen supported the subscription, and under the GMC rules it duly went ahead.

There was also a growing realisation that UK export credit facilities were insufficient. Whereas in 1953 the Credit Insurance Association Ltd had been satisfied that available facilities were adequate, by 1957 it was concerned at the growing proportion of contracts for which finance was arranged with difficulty. Indeed, the association pointed to the superiority of the West German system.[55] Worse still, it was clear that the restriction

52 BS 1/6, Minutes, 1 August 1961. The first release of these special deposits was announced on 31 May 1962 when the Bank of England agreed to release ½ per cent of gross deposits.
53 BS(BL), Uncatalogued, GMC, Minutes, 11 July 1960. The restrictions on advances were a factor in the avoidance of a complete rift.
54 BS(BL), Uncatalogued, GMC, Minutes, 29 October 1962.
55 'Memorandum of Evidence submitted by the Credit Insurance Association Ltd', December 1957, in *Principal Memoranda submitted to the Committee on the Working of the Monetary System*, vol. ii (HMSO, 1960), pp. 21–2.

on ECGD cover held up progress on negotiations, and in some cases contracts were lost.[56] It was not until January 1961 that the Bank of England and the English clearers came up with a scheme for medium-term export finance, similar to those pioneered by the Scottish banks. William Watson, skilled in the intricacies of medium- and long-term export agreements, was able to offer useful advice.[57] The Scottish Council of Chambers of Commerce also criticised the ICFC role in Scotland: 'it had to some extent lost sight of its original purpose and . . . become too concerned with producing improved results from its own activities – in opposition to the risk function which it originally assumed'.[58] The ICFC eventually opened an office in Glasgow in 1961 after pressure from the government; the loan book in Scotland was gradually built up, and the earlier criticisms faded.[59]

The Scottish banks faced difficulties from the Scottish Trustee Savings Banks (TSBs).[60] These had little connection with the financing of industrial firms, but wished to issue cheques to their personal customers; such a move threatened to erode the deposits upon which the bulk of industrial advances by the Scottish banks were based. Other concessions were requested by the savings banks, but the right to issue cheques was the main one.[61] The GMC was absolutely opposed; TSBs were to be urged to make fuller use of a revamped credit-transfer scheme. Oblivious to the possible adverse consequences to industry, the Treasury supported the TSBs' case.[62] A. P. Anderson, general manager of the British Linen, accused the Treasury of 'conniving' at an increase in the business of the savings banks, uninvolved in industrial advances, but whose progress affected deposits in the banks. The Bank of England was approached by

56 'Memorandum of Evidence submitted by the Export Group for the Constructional Industries', November 1957, in ibid., pp. 104–8.
57 William Watson raised with the Bank of England the question of the financing under ECGD cover of ships for foreign owners: 'where payment was to be made after the ship was operating . . . if the ship was sunk through act of war, in which the country of the owners was neutral, the ECGD cover would fall and the party who financed the building would only have a personal obligation to fall back on'. For this case, the builder and thus Bank of Scotland would be required to ensure that the vessel was properly insured and would retain a charge over the vessel. This could be difficult where foreign legal jurisdictions were involved.
58 'Memorandum of Evidence submitted by the Council of Scottish Chambers of Commerce', 27 November 1957, in Principal Memoranda of Evidence submitted to the Committee on the Working of the Monetary System, vol. ii (HMSO, 1960), p. 100.
59 'Notes and Comments: ICFC New Glasgow Office', Scottish Bankers Magazine, 53 (1961–2), 74–5.
60 Most TSB customers were lower middle- and working-class, and had little need of cheques. The importance of the introduction of a cheque service to the savings banks is discussed in M. Moss and A. Slaven, From Ledger Book to Laser Beam. A History of the TSB in Scotland from 1810 to 1990 (Edinburgh: n.d. [1992]), pp. 146–8.
61 BS(BL), Uncatalogued, GMC, Minutes, 7 March 1960. The 'savings' banks also asked for immediate credit by the banks for all sums paid into TSB accounts, abolition of the turnover charge and its replacement by a 1½d document charge, and an allowance of 9d per £100 per month on each complete £100 of creditors' balances in TSB accounts. All three requests were refused.
62 Moss and Slaven, From Ledger Book to Laser Beam, p. 148.

William Watson, but prevaricated and let it be known, in private, that, although Anderson might be right, there were political factors involved. The Treasury and the Post Office also wanted a Giro transfer system and thus speedy transfers between all parties including the savings banks. As the English clearers faced weaker competition from the TSBs than the banks in Scotland did, the Bank of England consented, although it was not until April 1964 that final agreement was reached.[63]

63 BS (BL), Uncatalogued, GMC, Minutes, 23 May 1961, 13 April 1964. It should be stressed that in most respects relations between the Scottish banks and the TSBs remained cordial and there was active cooperation on matters of mutual concern. The GMC was prepared to accept a compromise which involved a charge of 11d per TSB cheque.

CHAPTER 25

NORTH WEST SECURITIES AND THE BRITISH LINEN BANK, 1958–70

BANK OF SCOTLAND had long been involved in the provision of finance, either directly or, more usually, by the discounting of bills of exchange on secured 'blocks' of term and hire-purchase agreements.[1] Organised from London Chief Office and the Mound, this trade rapidly expanded in the inter-war years and covered goods as diverse as industrial machinery, railway wagons and electrical plant financed by, typically, renewable three-month bills up to four years.[2] The finance houses had an extensive network of advisors and in-house specialists, and their ability to manage debts and attract deposits turned them into a growing 'secondary' banking sector. They were also very profitable, as total bad debts for the later 1930s were contained at under ½ per cent of the typical loan book. The importance of their contribution to industrial and commercial finance and their detailed industrial expertise was often overlooked in contemporary comment upon consumer hire-purchase agreements.[3]

The Second World War saw a marked reduction in hire-purchase arrangements for household goods. The Courts (Emergency Powers) Act, 1939, and the Liabilities (War Time Adjustment) Act, 1941, modified in 1944, significantly restricted the right to repossess goods, and orders made under the Goods and Services (Purchase Control) Act, 1941, tightened the provision of credit. In January 1943, orders under the

---

1 The block discounting of hire-purchase agreements to a finance house, and on to a London discount house, is discussed in H. Cowen, 'Changes in Hire Purchase Finance', *The Banker*, 85 (1948), 93–9.
2 C. R. Curtis, 'Hire Purchase Finance and Machine Control', *The Banker*, 42 (1937), 118–25.
3 Cowen, 'Changes in Hire Purchase Finance', p. 93; R. Harris, M. Naylor and A. Seldon, *Hire Purchase in a Free Society*, 3rd edn (London: 1961), pp. 26–7.

Defence Regulations prohibited all hire-purchase and credit sales except for industrial machinery, war-damaged goods, renewed contracts and exempt goods which contributed to morale and the efficiency of the user, such as motorcycles, bicycles and wireless apparatus. The result was an inevitable reduction in gross current assets of the eight publicly-quoted finance houses involved in domestic finance from £24.6 million in 1939 to £12.1 million in 1945. Four of the publicly-quoted companies, North Central Wagon (founded in 1861), British Wagon (1869), Bowmaker (1927) and Olds Discount (1926), were able to show some return on their equity capital by focusing on loans for industrial companies. The largest company in 1939, United Dominions Trust (1919), paid no dividend to equity holders throughout the war, although it still controlled one-third of the total assets of all the quoted finance companies in 1945.[4] By 1947, the eight quoted finance houses had almost recovered their pre-war position by rapid expansion of advances to industry. Further, by 1952, 'hundreds' of unquoted companies, with much smaller capitals and often tied to individual retail and industrial firms, were providing funds for hire-purchase and credit arrangements.[5] Under Treasury restrictions on bank advances imposed in 1947, the finance houses, quoted and unquoted, were unable to raise more than £50,000 of new capital in any twelve-month period either by private arrangement or through the market, with a short interlude from August 1954 to February 1955 when the ceiling was lifted. Bank lending was also severely restricted. Although this ceiling of £50,000 hindered the growth of consumer hire purchase, the finance houses were able to raise deposits by offering interest to the general public at rates of 1 per cent and even 1½ per cent above bank rate, whereas deposit rates on offer from the banks were usually 2 per cent below bank rate.[6] Funds were also raised by loans from industrial companies, and in some cases the ceiling of £50,000 was avoided by a subdivision of capital into nominally separate companies, often under identical boards. Sources of funds were diverse: the compensation payments to the previous owners of nationalised industries saw huge financial resources go to numerous family trusts, non-insured pension funds and industrial companies, and some of these monies were deposited with the finance houses. In 1950, almost 200,000 finance-house contracts were recorded, with 224,000 in 1951 and 400,000 by 1953.[7] This represented a significant increase in lending on consumer and industrial goods.

4 Cowen, 'Changes in Hire Purchase Finance', pp. 96–7, Tables 1 and 2.
5 A Special Correspondent, 'Hire Purchase Facilities under Scrutiny', The Banker, 93 (1952), 37–42.
6 J. Marvin, 'How Hire Purchase has Grown', The Banker, 104 (1955), 155–63.
7 'Memorandum of Evidence submitted by the Finance Houses Association Ltd', 11 April 1958, in Principal Memoranda of Evidence submitted to the Committee on the Working of the Monetary System, vol. ii (HMSO, 1960), pp. 25–30. This included a list of all controls on finance houses from 1947 to 1956. See also Harris, Naylor and Seldon, Hire Purchase in a Free Society, p. 295, Appendix I, table.

The first development in the post-war involvement of the Scottish banks with finance houses came in November 1954 when the Commercial Bank bought the entire equity of the Scottish Midland Guarantee Trust (SMGT) and the Second Scottish Midland Guarantee Trust, subsidiaries of the Scottish Motor Traction Co., for £1.75 million. The move was made after the order controlling the terms of hire-purchase credit was temporarily suspended in July 1954. Henceforth the requirement for minimum deposits, then at 33⅓ per cent, was scrapped, and in August the Treasury rules governing the CIC veto on new equity offers by finance houses were relaxed. The Bank of England and the Board of Trade had been concerned for some time about the 'avoidance', as they termed it, of post-war restrictions on the raising of credit by finance houses. But the relaxation was only extant for a short while; the restrictions were re-imposed in February 1955, and they reverted to a 33⅓ per cent minimum deposit rate in July. Nevertheless, the Governor of the Bank of England was privately furious about the Commercial's action and made it clear to the Scottish banks that it was not to be repeated.[8] Profits from SMGT, later renamed Lloyds and Scottish, provided a significant improvement for the Commercial Bank's annual accounts. The move by the Commercial was carefully examined by William Watson, the Treasurer of Bank of Scotland, and the directors.[9] They noticed the high rate of return but were concerned about potential bad debt and a supposed adverse effect on the standing of Bank of Scotland. After the views of the Bank of England were made plain, the matter was shelved.

There was little argument over the attractiveness for the lender of instalment-term finance repaid by fixed sums. Provided that bad debts and costs could be contained, it gave a higher return than that available from cash accounts. *The Banker*, for example, published a table of typical hire-purchase returns in March 1955 to illustrate this. Informal discussions at the GMC continued, and by the summer of 1956 only the opposition from the Governor of the Bank of England held up further acquisitions by the Scottish banks. Yet the tide of opinion was changing even in Threadneedle Street.[10] The CIC and the Bank of England had been concerned about the deposit-taking side of finance houses, mainly because of the support which this gave to increased credit and, less importantly, because many of the hundreds of houses which operated had

---

8 J. Fforde, *The Bank of England and Public Policy 1941–1958* (Cambridge: 1992), pp. 624–5.
9 J. Fforde (ibid., p. 763) states that the Scottish banks were upset by Macdonald's move; whatever the view within the Bank of England of how the Scottish banks viewed this move, there is no record which would support such a statement in the Bank archives for either the British Linen or Bank of Scotland, nor is there any note to this effect in the minutes or miscellaneous papers of the GMC.
10 J. Fforde, *The Bank of England*, pp. 767–9.

inadequate reserves and several were involved in fraudulent practices. The Queen's speech to Parliament on 6 November 1956, at the height of the sterling crisis, included notice that in future such deposit-taking would be controlled, and it was later made clear that this would involve fixed liquidity ratios. After opposition from the Finance Houses Association (FHA) and Conservative backbenchers, the proposal was dropped. Some in the Bank of England favoured informal cooperation with the FHA, but this was impractical.[11] The Bank of England's stance was thus difficult to sustain because of the failure to legislate to halt the mushrooming of the finance industry. The proposed amalgamation of the Commercial Bank with the National Bank meant that Lloyds Bank, through its minority stake in the National, would now have a stake in hire purchase. In June 1958, the theme of the presidential address to the Scottish Institute of Bankers by Walter R. Ballantyne, general manager of the Royal Bank, endorsed hire purchase as 'eminently suitable for the banks'.[12] The Treasury moved in early July when Heathcoat Amory, Chancellor of the Exchequer, announced an end to restrictions on clearing- and merchant-bank involvement in finance-house activities and related lending. Within a few months, British banks had taken a stake in nine of the quoted companies.[13]

On 5 August 1958, a subcommittee of the board of Bank of Scotland, chaired by the Governor, Lord Bilsland, considered two options: a stake in a large, existing, publicly-quoted concern, or the complete acquisition of a smaller company, one of a number available. By 26 August, it had decided to negotiate for the subsidiary company of the Braid motor group, North West Securities Ltd (NWS), whose office was in Chester, Cheshire, and which provided loans over a variable timespan for industrial and commercial plant, motor cars and household goods.

The history of NWS before 1958 was bound up with the distinctive direction and management of Sydney Alfred Jones, who was retained as general manager until his retirement in 1979. It has not been unusual for men to remain in senior positions in banking and finance for several decades, and some reference to Jones's background may facilitate an understanding of how he achieved this for almost his entire career. Jones started in

11 A special correspondent of *The Banker* estimated in 1958 that of around 1,000 small finance houses the vast majority had customers' debts of well under £50,000, and 450 were owed less than £5,000. The thirteen largest provided over 70 per cent of total credit, although as part of their work involved block discounting from smaller houses the total was higher ('The Hire Purchase Structure', *The Banker*, 108 (1958), 598–605). Board of Trade figures listed 1,227 discount houses in 1958.
12 Walter R. Ballantyne, 'Presidential Address: A Banker for Hire Purchase', *The Banker*, 108 (1958), 419–20, quote at p. 420.
13 'The Banks in Hire Purchase', *The Banker*, 108 (1958), 561–80. It did not occur to the government to impose ceilings on the volume of business that the new subsidiaries could run.

the hire-purchase business in 1929 when, aged 15, he was recruited as a clerk by Bowmaker, the Bournemouth-based finance house founded by Percy Butler. Issued with a motorcycle and a satchel, Jones motored up and down the North Wales coast signing up hire-purchase agreements through a string of garages. He was later despatched to Liverpool and Manchester, and for several years worked in Bowmaker's London office. The London car market was a fast-expanding business with a thriving trade in large saloons for businessmen and comparable arrangements for the general public. The outbreak of war found him as assistant manager in Birmingham, and, on call-up, with his managerial expertise, he was placed in charge of supplies for various units of the army. 'This was excellent experience', he recalled later, and he left the army with the rank of major.

The early post-war years were an unfavourable environment for finance houses. On demobilisation, Jones was offered his 1939 salary by Bowmaker, so he moved to Olds Discount Company as Birmingham area manager, where he stayed for three years. His brother, who managed the advertising for the Braid motor group, suggested that he apply for the post of manager of Improved Finance Ltd, its finance subsidiary, one of the hundreds of small in-house companies which proliferated after the war. Formed on 1 February 1945, it was originally owned by a garage in Burton-on-Trent and was acquired by the Braid group for handling hire-purchase agreements. The subsidiary was renamed North West Securities on 3 September 1948, and Jones was brought in to manage the business and to negotiate agreements with other garages and car dealers. Up-to-date methods and accounting procedures were adopted for the credit assessment of potential clients. With these disciplines, the level of bad debts was minimised. In 1954, a branch office was opened in Liverpool, followed in 1957 by one at Preston, while in 1956 the company opened a new head office in Newgate Street, Chester.

By September 1957, NWS had raised funds from four sources. The authorised capital was 5,000,000 one-shilling shares of which 2,500,000 were issued to, and fully paid (£125,000) by, the Braid group. There were small reserves (contingency and general), and a sum of £70,316 was carried forward with the profit and loss account. The company also held deposits of £210,074 at 2 per cent over bank rate (1½ per cent plus a ½ per cent bonus if deposits were left for a minimum period). A further £306,000 was borrowed from Lloyds Bank at 1 per cent over bank rate, and £214,078, also at 1 per cent over bank rate, via bills of exchange secured on hire-purchase agreements. Lloyds Bank was most helpful: it handled up to 1,000 agreements a week by 1957, answered numerous status inquiries, sorted out standing-order payments throughout its branch network and gave advice to NWS on cheques with third-party endorsement before they were cashed. It was an important business connection. From this financial base, NWS had on 30 September 1957 hire-purchase and deferred-payment agreements totalling £985,252 against merchandise invoiced at £2,366,191. A trading profit of £71,993 was made. As the company had to pay interest and other charges of £37,273, the pre-tax profits were £31,887 but after tax only £15,235. From the viewpoint of Bank of Scotland, the important figures were the trading profit, after bad debts, and the net interest margins on bank loans. The growth of the business seemed assured, up by 25 per cent in 1956–7 and with a further advance thereafter.

Why would Robert Braid, the owner, described as a 'hard-headed businessman', consider a sale of NWS to the Bank? The answer lay in the structure of the motor group's profits: predominantly these came from car sales through dealerships and garage servicing. The finance-house subsidiary was an important facilitator for vehicle sales, and that connection Braid was determined to protect. Yet the final profit of NWS was disproportionately small compared to the potential value if it were sold.

Lord Bilsland, Governor of the Bank, sent William Watson, the Treasurer, and James Dowling, one of the directors, to meet Robert Braid, Sydney Jones and David Mitchell, the Braid group chartered accountant, in the Adelphi Hotel, Liverpool. The net worth of the company, should it be closed and the hire-purchase agreements sold on, was around £250,000.[14] This was the figure on which Watson initially focused. Braid wanted £750,000 and refused to yield, and after a lengthy discussion Watson moved up to £500,000. Sydney Jones then persuaded Watson and Dowling to view the monthly accounts, the budgetary controls and the files on bad debts kept in Chester. The following day, Jones, shuttling between the two sides, eventually persuaded Watson to pay £700,000. Braid was assured as to the continued relationship with NWS, and Mitchell and Jones were given seats on the new NWS board. The agreement was signed in the Adelphi, a gain of around £575,000 for the Braid motor group. Although Watson always complained to NWS that the price was too high, he had agreed with Lord Bilsland beforehand that the tax advantages to the Bank of an investment, and other gains cited above, merited a price of up to £900,000, but no more.[15] William Watson was duly congratulated by the board of directors.

The Bank board and the executive had no in-house expertise and finance-house management. Sir Hugh Rose was appointed chairman of

---

14 As of 30 September 1957, net worth comprised a capital of £125,000, reserves, exclusive of the income tax reserve of £52 0s 16d, trade debtors £26,526, cash £20,321, all fixed assets £46,636 less depreciation and any sale costs, and an uncertain sum for hire-purchase agreements sold on.
15 BS 1/6, Minutes, 26 August 1958. The price of £700,000 was noted on 2 September 1958.

NWS, with Alastair Blair, James Dowling and William Marr alongside Watson, Jones and Mitchell as directors. On 4 September, it was agreed that no new deposits would be taken from the public, that interest payable would be reduced to ½ per cent over bank rate and that all the fixed deposits were to be repaid and not renewed. The main account with Lloyds was paid off and the overdraft taken up by London Chief Office of Bank of Scotland, and the ordinary accounts were transferred from Lloyds to the Westminster Bank branch at Chester. The capital was increased to £450,000 which ensured that NWS could join the FHA, and extra facilities were made available by way of overdraft from LCO. It was agreed to expand the NWS branch network, and by the summer of 1963 there were twenty-three offices, six of which lay in Scotland, and, of great significance for future growth, four in the Midlands and six in London and the south-east. With this stronger branch network and the enlarged capital came rapid growth. By 31 January 1959, total assets had reached £1,889,461, and a year later £4,370,316. By January 1961, the assets were £6.8 million.

Initially, a number of errors were made. The Bank board assumed that the business would transfer a substantial part of the operations to Edinburgh, and considered moving the head office from Chester. Premises were converted in George Street, Edinburgh, and Sydney Jones spent much of 1960 there, organising a Scottish staff. He imposed the old format of NWS, with a strong concentration of underwriting authority and little or no leeway given to office managers. A sound system with proper credit-scoring was crucial. This required a quite different attitude to that of the bank manager, for whom personal recommendation and local knowledge remained a cornerstone of lending policy. This clash was highlighted over the appointment of D. J. H. Mackay, a Bank official, as company secretary, and there were prolonged disagreements over attempts to bring NWS closer to the Bank. The arguments festered for two years until Sydney Jones informed Sir Hugh that if the matter of executive control were not resolved, he, and by implication others from his team, might prefer to leave. Sir Hugh then agreed to the functional independence of NWS, with Jones in charge and Ray Hazlehurst and Robert Allen reporting to him. To symbolise the growth of the company, Jones was allowed to proceed with a new headquarters in Chester, a functional brick and concrete structure near the railway station. With this new building, the day-to-day Bank control over NWS was limited to supervision and discussion on the NWS board. It was appreciated at the Mound that the choice of chairman was crucial, and when Sir Hugh retired he was replaced by Sir Alastair Blair (knighted in 1962). It was clear that a directors' committee in Edinburgh, responsible for this very different functional activity and reinforced by visits from the Inspectors Department, was inappropriate. This was also another milestone along the road to rethinking the day-to-day role and authority of the Bank board and the Inspectors Department.

The Bank curtailed loans to other finance companies; in 1959 two organisations' requests were turned down, including one from N. G. Napier for an increase in its cash-account limit from £25,000 to £50,000. The board took the view that publicity about Napier's activities was adverse, and its loan was not renewed at the annual review. Difficulties also arose when the South of Scotland Electricity Board organised its own hire-purchase activities, part of which used Bank advances. It had two tranches of borrowing, one at bank rate, the other at ½ per cent above. In July 1962, the SSEB requested an increase of £1 million on the first tranche, to £6 million, which the GMC correctly surmised was for hire-purchase business and which it therefore refused, as such monies were properly second-tranche.[16] The British Linen Bank was also involved in finance-house development with Barclays Bank, which announced the purchase on 25 July 1958 of 25 per cent (£4 million) of the equity of United Dominions Trust (UDT), of which the British Linen Bank took £100,000 ordinary stock at £4 per £1 stock. Barclays stated that it regarded its stake as an investment and would not seek a closer involvement with UDT than the appointment of a director to the board. It was an unsatisfactory arrangement, with the British Linen Bank too distant from the management to learn how the business operated, and so all matters pertaining to its holding went through Barclays.[17]

Until April 1960, profits from the hire-purchase sector remained good, and the contribution to profits of the banks was excellent. Yet this buoyancy owed much to the lifting of the restrictions on credit and bank advances in 1958, to several cuts in indirect taxes in that year's Budget, and to the expansionary measures announced in the March 1959 Budget, when Heathcoat Amory reduced purchase tax by one-sixth, cut 9d from the standard rate of income tax and encouraged investment by new allowances. As this was an election year, there was also a popular cut in the excise duty on beer; with cuts in other taxes, £300 million in all went into consumers' pockets.[18] Personal expenditure in the year 1959–60 duly soared by 6 per cent.

The boom encouraged every finance company to take on more business in the domestic and motor-car sectors. Total hire-purchase debt grew from £488 million in October 1958 to £937 million in April 1960. Yet the increased availability of hire purchase coupled with the added bank finance served to drag earnings down, as margins were cut and a proportion

16 BS(BL), Uncatalogued, GMC, Minutes, 9 July 1962, 14 January 1963. The SSEB later agreed.
17 BS(BL), Uncatalogued, Directors private letter book, 12 August 1958.
18 S. Pollard, *The Development of the British Economy 1914–1967*, 2nd edn (London: 1969), pp. 475–6.

of the business was unsound and sometimes fraudulent.[19] From the summer of 1960, severe losses were announced.[20] At Lloyds and Scottish, Ian Macdonald claimed that the bad-debt position in 1960 was equal to the 'average' of a typical pre-war year, but in 1961 the figure was far worse. The published losses for all houses from bad debts taken on by 1961 were calculated by *The Banker* at £30 million. The results of the boom surprised the Bank of England, which, reconciled to bank involvement, expected the bankers' care and attention to provide a safer environment for customers and depositors.[21] *The Banker* in January 1961 was blunt:

> the charge against the Government is not that it reimposed controls in 1960 but that it removed them entirely in 1958, with no public murmur of dissent from the industry, thus initiating an orgy of unrestrained competition in lending, the scars of which may remain on the balance sheets for many years to come.[22]

Before the clearing banks had expanded their traditional deposit vehicles, deposit accounts and – in Scotland – deposit receipts, the ownership of NWS enabled the Bank to offer to customers who were seeking higher rates the opportunity to place money on term deposit with NWS. While branch managers were always unhappy about deposits departing from their own books, head office sought to convince them that if the money was going to go, it was better to keep it within the group, as an NWS deposit. To make the operation even easier, it was handled at the Mound, with the receipts signed by NWS's secretary or some other official of the Bank. Thus a useful volume of deposits, which might otherwise have been lost, was kept.

The purchase of NWS encouraged Bank of Scotland to support a second finance-house arrangement, this time with Capital Finance Co. Ltd (CF), of which the full capital of £350,000 was partly owned by the Standard Life Assurance Society of Edinburgh.[23] James Letham, who was the Assistant Treasurer of the Bank, was friendly with a director of CF, who had formulated an innovative idea for personal finance, linking a bank loan (the interest on which was eligible, at that time, for tax relief) with the security of hire-purchase documentation. He called this 'The Capital

---

19 Details of the crisis are given in 'HP's Morning After', *The Banker*, 111 (1961), 15–18.
20 In July 1960, Western Credit, in which Hambros merchant bank and Phoenix Assurance had equity, announced a loss of nearly £500,000. Mercantile Credit and S. J. Claye, a subsidiary of the Charles Roberts engineering group, both reported severe falls in profits, and the National Provincial bank's subsidiary North West Wagon saw profits down £750,000 (50 per cent).
21 The Governor, C. F. Cobbold, in his appraisal at the bankers' dinner on 16 October 1958, noted that 'a more comprehensive organisation is needed within the industry both to maintain safeguards for customers and depositors and also to provide the necessary statistical information'. Both he and his advisors missed the significant danger caused by their deregulation.
22 'HP's Morning After', pp. 17–18. For a discussion of fraud in hire purchase, see 'Hire Purchase: What Went Wrong', *Scottish Bankers Magazine*, 53 (1961–2), 227–31.
23 BS 1/6, Minutes, 4 October 1960.

Plan' and of course needed the cooperation of a bank to operate it, with CF's guarantee against loss. The idea was offered to the Bank and accepted with alacrity, part of the arrangement being that NWS was entitled to operate the same scheme under a different name. In October 1960, the board agreed to provide facilities for Capital Plan loans, to a total of £2.25 million; thus a substantial amount of new business was acquired by the Bank and NWS. Because the loans were technically from the Bank, and indeed constituted by formal cheques, they had to be recorded in the Bank's books; and as the Bank was at that time in the early days of electronic accounting, it was decided to make the record-keeping of these accounts an early specialised application of the new equipment.[24] Unfortunately, in 1964, CF made substantial advances to Rolls Razor Ltd, a company managed by John Bloom, which manufactured washing machines and spin-dryers. In the intensely competitive domestic market, that company failed. There were other losses, and by 29 March 1965 the Bank's overdraft to CF was £3 million. The Bank board agreed with Standard Life that 'public intimation of [losses] would lead to a withdrawal of deposits from the Company with disastrous results'.[25] The chairman of CF was replaced by F. S. Jamieson, assistant general manager of Standard Life. By January 1968, the deficiency of assets had reached £5.4 million. In March 1969, NWS made an agreed offer for CF, taking over the whole of the issued capital for £200,000 and £3 million 7½ per cent unsecured loan stock while retaining a £15.3 million short-term deposit from Standard Life to keep the company afloat. Ultimate losses were sufficient to require payments from Standard Life to cover part of the overdraft at the Bank. A severe retrenchment followed among the staff of CF in Edinburgh, and much of its business was moved to Chester.[26]

Bank of Scotland, in common with other banks, developed schemes for personal loans after 1958. They were offered on similar terms to an NWS loan, but without the stringent controls that Jones and his management team insisted on. Further, they were not conducted through a retailer or car distributor. Thus, there was no certainty that the loans would be used for buying goods, and some cases arose where the money lent was lost on gambling. Agreements were vetted by bank managers, most of whom had limited expertise of unsecured personal loans. The loans were typically sought after by the working classes and those who aspired to middle-class status; bank managers now relearned the hard way all the

24 When UDT announced a copy of this scheme, the Bank and Standard Life agreed that it would be appropriate if they proceeded in cooperation. On this basis, a joint company was formed with 45 per cent owned by UDT, 45 per cent by CF and 10 per cent by NWS. The Bank again granted facilities, this time for £750,000 (BS 1/6, Minutes, 23 July 1963, 10 September 1963).
25 BS 1/6, Minutes, 15 November 1966.
26 Standard Life had 25.1 per cent of the ordinary capital of Capital Finance.

lessons known to NWS. So concerned was the Institute of Bankers at the disastrous repayment experience that it published the experience of one Glasgow bank manager, from the Clydesdale.[27] He suggested that managers' intuition was inadequate for the assessment of risk, and offered guidelines: managers should insist on seeing the rent book and not lend where it was irregular; life policies should be inspected; wives should be at the interview, which should be held several days after an application was made; most references were worthless; and managers should not lend to newly-weds, as 'girls have an unquenchable faith in their ability to reform their fiancés after marriage, but they rarely pull it off'. Dr Charles Munn, the historian of the Clydesdale, recalls that in his time in Glasgow, his manager judged applicants on their general dress and in particular the state of their shoes: 'clean shoes meant a pride in appearance; the manager never lent on dirty shoes'. It took Bank of Scotland some years to catch up with NWS in respect of the subsidiary's expertise with personal loans.

The expertise of the management and the board of directors over industrial and ship finance gave them the extra confidence to react positively to a request by Edinburgh Corporation for advice about its pensions fund. The city had lost money over investments in British government securities and was aware that equities would be a more sensible investment. This became more urgent as its fund acquired additional monies with the increase in council staff. Total funds were already over £5 million, and another £400,000 was available in 1963. The Bank's investment advisory service, supported by a committee from the board, was of considerable assistance in determining overall policy.[28] Requests from other customers followed, and it became clear that the varied advice required by customers warranted a specialist staff in a separate department. Hence, in September 1966, a member of the Inspectors Department, Bruce Pattullo, was seconded to McAnally, Montgomery & Co., the London stockbrokers, and later to Ivory and Sime, the Edinburgh investment managers of British Assets Trust Ltd.[29] The following year, a subsidiary of the Bank, 'Uberior Nominees Ltd', was established for the registration of customers' investments. The new department served three different purposes: a support for the trustee department in that placing of funds in its care, discretionary investment management for private customers and the management of the Bank's investment portfolios which hitherto had been handled by the Chief Accountant's department.

The board had realised by 1967 that it might be advantageous to take an interest in unit trusts. There had been a steady growth in these since

27 G. Macaulay, 'The Personal Loan Interview', *Scottish Bankers Magazine*, 52 (1960–1), 212–20.
28 BS 1/6, Minutes, 12 December 1961, Investment Advisory Service.
29 BS 1/6, Minutes, 6 September 1966.

the 1950s – even when stock-exchange prices were falling – and as time passed they appeared a sound way for the middle classes to combine income with capital growth. Mistakenly, the board decided that the Bank lacked the resources to develop a unit trust on its own. Its view was that a viable size of fund was over £5 million and that it should purchase the stock of an existing company to provide a ready-made organisation without 'teething troubles'. The Bank seriously considered two companies – about one of which reservations were expressed – and settled on Ebor Securities Ltd, which then had 4 per cent of the total UK unit-trust funds. The Bank bought 8,750 shares in Ebor at £25 per £1 share, 10s paid, which represented 35 per cent of the company capital (£218,750). The holding was later diluted, although when sold in 1969 to Save and Prosper it realised £900,000.[30] Save and Prosper had launched the popular Scotbits unit trusts, available over the counter from all Scottish banks. Its chairman, Lord Polwarth, became Deputy Governor of Bank of Scotland in 1960 and Governor in 1966.[31] The British Linen Bank pension fund had long been shareholders in Save and Prosper.

In 1964, a Labour government led by Harold Wilson was elected with a small majority, and in March 1966 it achieved a landslide victory. This encouraged a widespread discussion of the perceived failings of British industry and trade. The Scottish banks were not immune from this, and the Institute of Bankers in Scotland under F. S. Taylor encouraged younger bankers to think more broadly about their work and about how the banks could diversify their activity. Taylor was the right man for the Institute. A fierce defender of the historical legacy of Scottish banking, he had, for example, clashed in print with Professor R. H. Campbell over banking and industrialisation.[32] At the Institute, Taylor modernised the syllabus and encouraged younger bankers to meet and discuss the future. Alan Thomson, then a junior manager at the Bank, recalled regular meetings to assess the chances of change in Scottish banking. In the late 1960s, together with several Bank of Scotland managers, he lunched every Friday at Crawford's in Hanover Street, Edinburgh, to review possibilities for the future. In these years, there was little output from academic circles of relevance to the problems of banking. Neither the articles in the main house journal of Scottish economists, the *Scottish Journal of Political Economy*, nor the other writings of university economists, had much

30 BS 1/6, Minutes, 28 January and 17 June 1969.
31 The GMC played some part in the regulation of the affairs of Save and Prosper: see BS, Uncatalogued, GMC, Minutes, 28 January 1963, request by Lord Polwarth for Scottish banks to display details of Save and Prosper's savings scheme. The request was refused, although the GMC later agreed to advertisements in banks for Scotshares on 29 July 1963.
32 F. S. Taylor, 'Scottish Banks in the Eighteenth Century', *Scottish Journal of Political Economy*, 12 (1965), 110–13; R. H. Campbell, 'A Rejoinder', ibid., 114–15.

practical bearing upon the problems facing the banks, although there was some discussion in the Radcliffe report, which was widely read. The most informative historical perspective was Maxwell Gaskin's *The Scottish Banks: A Modern Survey*, published in 1965, but beyond this bankers had to rely on their internal bank circulars, on the *Scottish Bankers Magazine*, *The Banker* and other insurance and banking journals; and on occasional seminars organised by the Institute and their own circles of officials and managers. Various articles which indicated the scope of internal bank discussions appeared in the *Scottish Bankers Magazine*, including two Institute of Bankers' prize-winning essays in 1966 and 1968 by A. T. Gibson of the Bank's Inspectors Department.[33] These essays addressed the current consensus that the banks should diversify and that, for industrial advances, they could do so in partnership with government agencies. In his 1966 essay, Gibson argued that banks would have to grapple with loss of deposits to new higher-interest-bearing accounts; that they should consider more working-class accounts and lengthen banking hours; that they should move into foreign and commercial fields, credit cards and hire-purchase-type finance; and that they should persevere with computers to reduce costs. In December 1968, the board appointed Gibson as methods planning officer to report directly to the Treasurer, James Letham, who gave him a long list of topics to address.[34] Similar moves were made at the Clydesdale and the Royal Bank. This encouraging development was part of the general ferment of the later 1960s in banking – the spread of computers, marketing initiatives and more rigorous staff training.

In the decade after the acquisition of NWS in 1958, Bank of Scotland made considerable strides. Gross trading income at £10,554,091, in 1967, was slightly above twice the level of 1958; and, as costs had been well controlled, the gross trading profits were in a much stronger position, at 43 per cent of income.[35] These improved figures enabled substantial internal allocations to be made, alongside marked improvements in declared profits. The only dip in the figures occurred in 1963, in the aftermath of the financial difficulties which affected the finance houses. By 1967, the Bank capital stood at £8,400,000, the published reserve at £8 million and the internal reserves at £8,019,456. This was a much-improved position, although it later transpired that inadequate funding had been made for the two pension funds.

---

33 A. T. Gibson, 'The Bank Office of the Future', *Scottish Bankers Magazine*, 58 (1966–7), 66–84; idem, 'All-purpose Banking', *Scottish Bankers Magazine*, 60 (1968–9), 77–95, which was noticed in the Bank minutes. There was an important article by W. P. Brown of the Clydesdale Bank, which criticised the reluctance by many bankers to move into new areas of financial services: 'The Competition for Deposits', *Scottish Bankers Magazine*, 56 (1964–5), 71–91.
34 BS 1/6, Minutes, 17 December 1968, 11 February 1969.
35 See Statistical Appendix, Table A7.

The implications for Scottish banking of the UK's entry into the European Economic Community (EEC) were considered by the Bank from 1965. The board agreed that British interest and participation in Commonwealth markets would diminish whether or not the country left the European Free Trade Association (EFTA), and that in any event trade with the continent would expand. In 1966, the London and Scottish clearing banks were known to be thinking of how their representation in Europe could be strengthened. In February 1967, the board agreed that there was a danger that the Bank might be over-dependent upon English connections; and, as numerous Scottish companies were developing sales links with the EEC, the board felt that the Bank should have an equity stake in European banking. A number of options were considered before the board settled on the French banque d'affaires firm of Banque Worms et Cie, first listed as a publicly-quoted company on 1 January 1967.

The original merchant firm of Worms et Cie was founded in 1848, with a banking department added in 1929. It developed close links with French insurance, motor vehicles, shipping, paper and chemical concerns, usually based on participation in equity capital alongside the provision of medium- and long-term credits. The parent bank controlled a quarter of French shipping tonnage. Its medium- and long-term advances were given as £11 million, and it was the syndicate leader for a further £4 million. The firm's discount limit with the Banque de France was around £7 million, and it had 1,200 private accounts and 2,000 business accounts.

In an ambitious reorganisation of its subsidiary, Worms et Cie envisaged the incorporation into Banque Worms of two small commercial banks and an exchange of shares with Banque de Paris et des Pays-Bas, and a possible similar move with Crédit du Nord, the fourth-largest deposit bank in France, with 350 branches in the industrial north. The Bank of Montreal and the Bank of London and South America (BOLSA) were also to take small stakes. Banque Worms et Cie could assist Bank of Scotland customers who wished to establish business connections in Europe; and, in the reverse direction, it was hoped that opportunities might arise for French concerns to take advantage of labour pools in Scotland. There were also possible hire-purchase connections. After negotiations in April 1967, the Governor, Lord Polwarth, and the Treasurer, Sir William Watson, went to Paris and signed for 75,000 shares at a cost of £1,090,000 sterling, the francs arranged by BOLSA (of which Lord Polwarth was a director) over five years, although the Bank of England later stipulated that official exchange would only be made available after ten years.[36] Eighteen months

---

36 BS 1/6, Minutes, Board papers, 7 February 1967, and Banque Worms et Cie, 19 April 1967. The return was estimated at $4\frac{1}{2}$–5 per cent.

later, Robert Runciman, manager of the London Chief Office, put forward an additional proposal to join with BOLSA and other partners in a second bank deal, this time in Switzerland – Banque Worms et Associés (Genève) SA. Switzerland was a sound place for deposits because of the strength of its currency and the volume of its Eurodollar bond issues. Geneva had good transport links, and several customers of the Bank, ICI and Reuters among them, held funds in Swiss banks, from a well-founded fear of devaluation.[37] In 1970, the Bank combined with BOLSA to take up part of a rights issue to help finance the acquisition by Banque Worms et Cie of some operations of Crédit du Nord. Although BOLSA later withdrew, the Bank decided that the increased volume of transactions across the Channel was sufficient grounds to take up the allotment, giving the Bank a total shareholding in Banque Worms of 14 per cent.[38] In the longer term, there were problems over the retention by Worms et Cie (which meant the Worms family) of 59 per cent of the shareholding and the perceived weak influence of the foreign banks on the board. The hire-purchase connections did not materialise, although there was some benefit to the Bank from joint transactions and a return on capital which rose to over 6 per cent in 1969. After 1981, the French government nationalised a number of banks including Banque Worms et Cie, and Bank of Scotland's shareholding was realised for cash at a profit.

The good relations built up between the Bank and BOLSA led to an agreement in August 1967 to buy each other's shares. The two banks decided on £500,000 of £1 BOLSA shares, then at 40s, and BOLSA would buy a similar value of Bank shares.[39] It was stressed that the mutual interest of the two banks lay in 'having the transaction treated unobtrusively and with the utmost discretion'. In 1965, the board also considered a stake in the small and privately-owned, Glasgow-based British Bank of Commerce, although the Bank of England was unenthusiastic.[40] The question was raised again in November 1967, and again declined. On occasion, foreign banks asked for facilities, and were always carefully vetted. For example, the Mayfair London Bank, a company incorporated in Bermuda, asked for an account in London. The Bank of England, the English clearers and the GMC all refused. There were usually sound reasons for refusal of facilities requested by a number of foreign banks – apart from the ever-present consideration of the difficulty of control and audit.[41]

37 BS 1/6, Minutes, 28 November 1968.
38 BS 1/6, Minutes, 5 May and 14 July 1970. The Bank also doubled its holding of shares in Banque Worms et Associés (Genève) SA later that year.
39 BS 1/6, Minutes, 15 August and 12 September 1967.
40 BS 1/6, Minutes, 16 March 1965, 21 November 1967.
41 The Mayfair London Bank was incorporated in Nassau in December 1964 as a subsidiary of Finance and Mortgage Group (registered in 1958), and was acquired in December 1965 by Grailland

The most important of all the changes in bank relations led to the amalgamation of Bank of Scotland and the British Linen Bank in 1971. One of the central problems identified by the board and the GMC in the later 1960s was the danger associated with the increased financial and political powers of the City of London which, it was thought, could further erode the commercial standing of the Scottish banks. Moreover, under the Wilson government, the Scottish bankers had even less influence than under Harold Macmillan or Sir Alec Douglas-Home. The new government policy encouraged both larger conglomerations and a more competitive framework in banking and finance. These were cornerstones of the reorganisation and modernisation schemes of Harold Wilson and the group of merchant bankers on whom he relied for many of his industrial forays. The Royal Bank and the National Commercial Bank decided that their best defence was provided by amalgamation, and they duly formed the National Commercial Banking Group in 1967. Lord Polwarth raised the matter of amalgamation with the British Linen Bank with Lord Clydesmuir and other bankers in January 1968. The feeling at both the British Linen and Bank of Scotland was that significant business developments could be expected in the UK and that a joint bank would be in a stronger position to develop than two separate banks, particularly if the British Linen was to be subsumed under a bigger, and possibly in future more onerous, London ownership.

There was an undercurrent of concern within the British Linen management that while the bank was highly profitable and its advances were in good order, the Barclays connection hindered the implementation of new ideas, especially on long-term industrial investment and hire purchase. It had invested £400,000 in hire purchase, for instance, but this earned only £45,000 in 1967 and little spin-off business, whereas Bank of Scotland's investment of £700,000 plus capital had given it a whole range of benefits, including extra banking activity at London Chief Office, dividends of 22 per cent, and profits after tax in 1968 of £1,119,000. The board of the British Linen, which was closely connected to other Scottish financial and professional institutions, was also concerned that a proposed merger between Barclays and Martins Bank would weaken its position. However, the Governor of the Bank of England stated that no amalgamation of any UK bank would be allowed before the Monopolies and Mergers Commission had reported on a proposed amalgamation of Barclays and Lloyds, which would also include consideration of the takeover of Martins. There was concern that this would go through

Industrial and Investment Co. for property and investment finance ('Danger Signals for Banking', *The Banker*, 124 (1974), 12–13).

before the British Linen could join with Bank of Scotland.[42] Fears were also expressed about the connection between Barclays and South Africa, which made it difficult to attract student accounts. Fusion with Bank of Scotland would prove a bulwark against attacks from the City, a number of whose financiers were behaving in an increasingly erratic manner. When Lord Polwarth approached the chairman of Barclays, he stressed that a merger would generate greater income than would be possible if the British Linen remained separate. Barclays agreed, though stated that it wished to retain a 'substantial' equity stake and so would have to be granted part of the equity capital of the new bank, rather than accept a cash offer. There was also the question of the internal reserves of the British Linen, which were a liability owed to Barclays. This problem could be avoided in an amalgamation which gave Barclays a stockholding in Bank of Scotland.

To determine the size of this prospective stockholding, Barclays required detailed reports on the Bank and the British Linen. It insisted on the London firm of Peat, Marwick, Mitchell & Co., which established that Bank of Scotland had twice the assets of the British Linen and just over twice the total deposits.[43] When provision for bad and doubtful debts was considered, it was found, in the three years from 1967 to 1969, that Bank of Scotland had *exactly* two-thirds of the profits of the two banks and the British Linen one-third. The comparison of advances indicated the strength of Bank of Scotland in chemicals, metal manufactures and heavy industry compared with a concentration of British Linen advances on services, professional and retail trades and mortgages. Both banks were poorly represented in overseas markets.

The basic financial figures were agreed by early May 1969. The valuation of net tangible assets gave Bank of Scotland £30.1 million (64.9 per cent) and the British Linen £16.2 million (35.1 per cent). There were minor disagreements. The Bank pointed out that the benefits of its new computer systems were not yet fully reflected in profits, that charges to customers had been raised and were expected to bring in another £175,000 to £200,000 per year, and that NWS could be expected to sustain its growth of recent years. There were imponderables over the effects on Barclays' connections.[44] As it was thought that a meeting in central Edinburgh

42 BS 1/6, Minutes, 30 January 1968; *Report of the Monopolies Commission on the Proposed Merger by Barclays Bank Ltd, Lloyds Bank Ltd and Martins Bank* (HMSO, July 1968). The MMC vetoed the main proposal, but allowed the takeover of Martins to proceed because of the poor state of Martins' assets.
43 BS, British Linen merger files, Peat, Marwick, Mitchell & Co., Preliminary Memorandum, 2 April 1969; Memorandum, supplementary to Preliminary Memorandum, 7 May 1969, copy annotated by Lord Clydesmuir.
44 The commitment of Bank of Scotland to heavy industry and employment in the West of Scotland could not be considered in such an exercise as this; the report also made no mention of the damage done to the British Linen Bank's personal account business by the Barclays connection with South Africa.

might be noticed, the agreement was initialled in May 1969 at the house of James Gammell, the British Linen director, who was to play a key role in the new bank. It was agreed, as the gilt funds of the British Linen were in a stronger position than those of the Bank, that the shareholding of Barclays in Bank of Scotland should be 35 per cent of total capital, issued at the rate of £9 of new stock and 4s 8d in cash for every £4 of British Linen stock.[45] The position of Barclays Bank as a stockholder in Bank of Scotland was clearly laid out by an exchange of letters. Lord Polwarth, Governor of Bank of Scotland, wrote on 20 May 1969 to John Thomson, chairman of Barclays:

> With reference to the agreement reached between us, subject to our stockholders' approval, for the purchase of the issued capital of the British Linen Bank, I am writing to confirm the following understandings:- 1. You have given us an assurance that Barclays Bank will not seek to increase or decrease its stockholding in the Bank of Scotland without prior consultation with, and approval of the Bank of Scotland Board, such approval not to be unreasonably withheld. It is expressly agreed, however, that in the event of another party acquiring or attempting to acquire more than ten per cent of the Bank of Scotland capital without your prior approval, you shall be free, after prior consultation with us, to take such action as you consider necessary to protect your interests. 2. You have assured us that it is not your intention to take any action which would prejudice the continued independence of management of the Bank of Scotland. 3. We have assured you that the interests of the staff of the British Linen Bank will be properly safeguarded.[46]

Thomson replied that he confirmed 'our agreement to the understandings as set out in your letter'.

The legal drafting of the amalgamation was a triumph for the flexibility of Scots law.[47] The legal specialists within the two banks, with the advice of the Scottish Office and Parliamentary agents, arranged the Act so that the British Linen Bank was preserved as a separate Scottish company. Under the Act, the remaining capital was reduced to £5,000, and all lands, buildings, investments and assets, heritable and moveable, all other rights whether statutory or otherwise, and all charges, obligations and liabilities were transferred to Bank of Scotland.[48] The right of note issue under the Bank Notes (Scotland) Act, 1845, was transferred, and the Bank

45 Bank of Scotland holdings were then overvalued by £4,269,000 on book prices against only £530,000 for the British Linen. By 1969, 16 per cent of Bank of Scotland profits came from hire purchase.
46 BS, British Linen merger files, 20 and 22 May 1969.
47 Provisional order to provide for the transfer to the Governor and Company of the Bank of Scotland of the business and undertaking of the British Linen bank and for other purposes; 18 & 19 Elizabeth II c.34, 'An Act to confirm a Provisional order under the Private Legislation Procedure (Scotland) Act, 1936, relating to the Bank of Scotland', Local & Personal Act, 23 July 1970.
48 A holding company structure was briefly considered: BS, British Linen merger files, Second Special Steering Committee, 17 October 1969, chairman, Lord Balfour.

was obliged to preserve and retain all papers, documents and bankers' books as laid down in the Bankers Books Evidence Act, 1879. Sir Alastair Blair, in his capacity as a director and lawyer, was able to convince the Privy Council that the new agreement and the presentation of the British Linen Bank in the Act of Parliament were not damaging to the position of the Crown in respect of the royal charter which had founded the British Linen.

The fusion negotiations demanded a detailed knowledge of both banks and considerable tact and diplomacy. The choice fell on Lord Balfour of Burleigh (42), an urbane aristocrat from an old family, who was effective in welding together two groups of directors, some of whom regarded themselves as very important people, as well as two groups of managers and staff concerned about how branch closures would affect their prospects. The details of branch closures were rightly left until after the Act had been passed. The staff side was somewhat eased by the expedient that every pro-motion for five years after fusion was to be decided strictly on origin – one from the Bank, followed by one from the British Linen, and so on in rota, not on merit. When James Letham was unwell and retired as Treasurer of Bank of Scotland in 1970, he was followed by Thomas Wallace Walker from the British Linen. There was general agreement that, henceforth, 70 should be the age of retirement for directors and that twenty board members was a maximum for effective conduct of business. The Duke of Hamilton (Deputy Governor of the British Linen) was appointed an extraordinary director, and Lord Polwarth stayed as Governor; but Lord Clydesmuir took over when Polwarth was appointed to the Scottish Office in 1971.[49] Seven directors resigned, which left the board with sixteen ordinary directors with strong connections with Scottish business. It was agreed that Barclays' shareholding would entitle it to two board positions.

Lord Balfour coordinated a steering committee from both banks which was established in the autumn of 1969 to examine new directions. There was inevitable overlap with the work on organisation and methods carried out within both banks, but it was nonetheless important that directors were conversant with the latest ideas, and at the first meeting they consid-ered the two prize-winning essays by A. T. Gibson. Thus, when detailed plans were laid before the board, they could be seen in a positive context. The central problems were rising costs and the erosion of real profits by inflation. For the older directors who had come through the inter-war years and remained after the war, falling prices formed a strong part of their memory.[50] While all the new board had worked in the 1940s, all directors

49 On his appointment as Governor on 25 July 1971, Lord Clydesmuir announced that he would give three days a week to the Bank.
50 The committee comprised Lord Balfour of Burleigh (aged 42), Lord Polwarth (52), Lord

but one had spent most of their working life against a backcloth of rising prices. This made them more attentive to the way in which costs could erode the net interest earnings between payments to depositors and those received from advances. Yet echoes of the traditional approach remained. James Letham favoured the old-fashioned view that charges should not necessarily aim at a profit, but should be linked in some way to the rate of deposit expansion.[51] There should be a compromise between profitability and service as the latter led to the former. Lord Balfour's view was more modern; surely, he argued, the distinction was that service objectives were motivated by recovery of costs. In general, the board agreed that new high-interest deposit products would need to be introduced if the Bank were to compete effectively. Increases in charges and interest rates were still agreed by the GMC and 'positively adhered to', but all the banks were now thinking along the same lines, and the crises which they were all to face in the following five years further concentrated their efforts.

The question of the use of branches provoked impatience and debate on the steering committee: many staff and managers saw their functions as little more than keeping accounts and processing customers' requests for advances. There were marked disparities, for example, in the business generated for NWS by managers serving similar hinterlands. Indeed, some staff were even thought to be spending too much time on the golf course with existing customers at the cost of developing new business. It was pointed out by James Gammell that, with the advent of modern methods of assessment, many branches – which were the principal fixed assets of the Bank – might be shown to be loss-making when all costs and benefits were considered against alternative use of funds after their market value was realised. Squeezed by merchant banks and hire-purchase companies, the steering committee thought not only about branch rationalisation, inevitable after fusion, but also about the whole idea of what a branch was for. Lord Clydesmuir even suggested that salesmen should be brought in. Sir Hugh Rose pointed to the experience of NWS in the careful selection of business and its ruthless refusal of marginal and uncertain transactions. It was therefore quite clear that the combination of the two banks was bringing together some of the more far-sighted directors in Scottish banking. This, and the undercurrent of activity among the two managements, augured well for the challenges of the next decade.

Clydesmuir (51), James Gammell (49), W. F. Robertson (49), James Lumsden (54) and Sir Hugh Rose (66).
51 James Letham instanced a decision to advance at a 9 per cent return rather than an alternative of 15 per cent on grounds of service and commitment to Scotland.

CHAPTER 26

PROFIT PLANNING
AND NORTH SEA OIL

T HE AMALGAMATION OF the British Linen Bank with Bank of
Scotland brought the issued capital of the new Bank to £12.9
million, with total published capital resources of £42,155,179 and
total liabilities of £516 million. The banknotes in circulation for 1970
reached £49 million and grew steadily thereafter, although at a slower rate
than deposits and overall liabilities. The figures show that the Bank had
advanced £128,769,819 to industry and agriculture, 56.3 per cent of all
advances, the remainder going to a broad mix of services (21.6 per cent)
and miscellaneous finance (11.8 per cent); and at this point personal
finance and mortgages took only a small share. Yet, in spite of considerable
efforts, the end of the 1960s was to show a decline in the percentage of
advances to industry, trade and services, and in some industries, including
shipbuilding, a greater than average fall.[1] The reasons for this lay, very
largely, in the state of the economy. During the 1960s, there were very
considerable changes in the way in which the Bank functioned, and it is
relevant to mention the more important of these, including the adoption
of new methods of financial planning, a continued commitment to a more
outward-looking Bank, and real efforts to shed the old-fashioned image
inherited from earlier times.

A noteworthy achievement of the Inspectors Department in the early
Victorian years, at both the Bank and the British Linen Bank, had been
the development of a systematic reporting system based on standardised
returns recorded on printed sheets which covered the considerable volume
of material on financial data, including costs. This information arrived
in Edinburgh on a weekly basis, and some information came daily, giving
directors and officials some idea of the development of local business

1 See Statistical Appendix, Tables A8 and A11.

685

conditions. The improvements and controls added during the Victorian era had enabled the Scottish bankers to have one of the tightest and most effective reporting mechanisms on the local branches of any banking system at that time, and indeed much of this organisation was adopted by foreign and colonial banks. The reports were the basis for various campaigns on retrenchment of costs, or for example of instructions on past-due bills. As noted above, Treasurers and Inspectors drew up numerous branch comparisons and charted trends, and for a while J. A. Wenley, Treasurer from 1878 to 1898, developed a form of week-by-week profit forecasting. In the post-war era, the Chief Accountant's department still operated a similar system, and produced each week a forecast of the likely total profit for the year. This system depended on the assumption that the funds available to the Bank for the remainder of the year would be the same as in the current week, and so, while the forecast became increasingly reliable as the year progressed, there were often considerable fluctuations in the early weeks. Of course, the well-tried audit and controls developed over the years had led, as has been discussed before, to under-utilisation and misdirection of staff, and had built-in rigidities to the branches which now had to be faced.

By 1968, Sir William Lithgow was able to persuade his colleagues on the board of Bank of Scotland that the real forecasting methods used in the shipbuilding yards might be usefully adapted for banking purposes. For many years, some firms in Scotland had been using yearly forecasting, with monthly monitoring of progress. These methods were an extension of costing work for specific projects. Thus, for a proposed ship, a Clyde yard's management would list all the materials and labour needed and estimate costs over the life of construction, fixing times for completion of the keel, hull and engines using flowcharts and critical paths. It was a very useful aid to management, not least because the financial requirements listed in the budgets demonstrated when Bank borrowing would be required. The arrival of Lord Balfour on the board strengthened this positive view of planning. As fusion with the British Linen Bank was then under discussion, it was also an opportune moment to reduce the funds spent on building and repairs until a thorough review of the resources of both banks had been undertaken as part of the negotiations. The board also commissioned Booz, Allen and Henry to look at the way in which the Bank structures worked; and, from their report, it was agreed to establish an organisation and methods function, out of which grew a new management services unit.

Concern about the rise in charges and branch costs had become a serious topic at board meetings. Wholesale prices, building costs and staff remuneration were matters to be taken seriously, as in some parts of the

Bank the rise in costs by the later 1960s outstripped the Retail Price Index. There was also concern that the progress made on cutting costs as a proportion of income since the amalgamation with the Union Bank might be reversed. The suggestion from Sir William Lithgow and Lord Balfour would permit the forecasting of how costs might rise, given various estimates about inflation. In the autumn of 1968, the board agreed to seek data from branches and bank departments for use in forecasts for a year ahead. This involved managers using the branch data, and their local knowledge of what might happen to business, to draw up a budget and a forecast for the next twelve months.[2] This project required a new manager, and Sir William suggested that the choice should be Alan Jessiman, a young chartered accountant at Fairfields Shipbuilding and Engineering. This produced a mixed response from the executive, 'several of whom were hostile to the idea and resented the use of a man from the Clyde'. The board insisted, however, and in May 1969 Jessiman was placed in the Chief Accountant's department, reporting to its head, John Wilson. That summer, he formed the Management Accountant's section to design a budget and forecasting system which would facilitate profit planning and the control of costs. By the autumn, costing and budget sheets were ready for departments in Glasgow, Edinburgh and London, and within two years all branches were required to participate. The analysis behind the projection included differing assumptions about costs, deposits and interest rates, all of which could be expected to change. North West Securities already had its own controls and forward planning and was not included in this exercise, although its overall forecasts of profits were included in Bank of Scotland group figures. The first compilation of Bank activity and a crude profit-and-loss budget were based on the financial year 1969–70 and projected to 28 February 1971.[3] The results showed a serious potential situation with increased costs and adverse changes in interest rates, which would reduce the current estimated net profit from £7,858,000 to £5,943,000. The basic problems were 'spiralling costs', commitment of funds to unprofitable use and a sluggish growth in deposits. The data provided more accurate and up-to-date comparisons between branches than the older financial reporting systems used by the Treasurer's and Inspectors Departments, although these continued in place. It was perhaps inevitable that there was some resistance to this regular forecasting at branch level from managers who were already feeling the results of an increase in workload. These results led to more discussions by

2 Simply stated, the budget was a forecast of how the component parts of the Bank would spend their income over the next year. At the close of the year, the actual would show how accurate the original forecast was, and appropriate lessons could then be adopted for future forecasts.

3 BS 1/6, Minutes, Board papers, Special Meeting, 17 March 1970, 'Bank of Scotland Profit Plan Year to 28 February 1971'.

the board and executive, both concerned to reduce funds in non-interest-earning areas and to explore the causes of the variance between different uses of funds. This system of monthly financial accounting, although now much changed, has been a permanent part of the work of the Accounting Division ever since.

In March 1970, the board agreed that the five senior executives who attended the board would form the nucleus of a Profit Planning Committee to discuss recommendations on income and costs and place these before the board with a view to determining policy. Many of the questions had been considered already by the GMC, so the ideas were familiar, and in July 1970 the first group of suggestions was put to the directors.[4] These included commitment fees for banking services and realistic charges for standing orders and other services. There were some areas where significant improvements in income could be made, notably by following the fixed-term lending undertaken by NWS; and a review conducted in July 1970 considered similar ideas to the Scotplan 'personal' loans and took a hard look at those overdrafts which were, in practice, long-term loans. The key aspect of term loans was their fixed duration at a flat rate of interest calculated on the initial sum borrowed, which, together with repayments over the timespan of the loan, gave a true interest rate above the nominal level. In July 1971, a new type of personal instalment loan, Scotloan, was launched. It was limited to a maximum of £1,000 and was made available for six to thirty-six months to customers of 'undoubted security'. The flat rate of interest was 7½ per cent per annum calculated on the initial sum borrowed, with a true yield of approximately 13 per cent per annum.[5] The Profit Planning Committee advised on marketing, specialised services, extension of current accounts and the development of the potential in the insurance field. On the costs side, severe controls were imposed on repairs, furnishings and stationery. In anticipation of the upward trend of costs not being halted, the management immediately raised service charges on all current accounts and imposed a common scale of charges for business and personal accounts for both Bank of Scotland and the British Linen Bank; this raised £700,000 in 1970–1, and almost £1 million the following year. An extra ½ per cent was imposed on 'hard-core' overdrafts, designed to raise another £180,000 in a full year.

The next stage for planning was to project the annual budgets over five years.[6] This was not a group profit plan, in the same way as the annual

4 BS 1/6, Minutes, Board papers, 14 July 1970, 'Proposals for Profitability Improvement'.
5 BS 1/6, Minutes, 27 July 1971. In the years that followed, 'Scotloan' almost became a generic term for personal lending in Scotland, so popular did the scheme become.
6 BS 1/6, Minutes, Board papers, 5 January 1971, 'The Bank of Scotland Group, Notes on rough profit projection for the five years ending 29 February 1976', and Appendix I, 'Detailed Assumptions Underlying Five-Year Profit Projection'.

forecasts were, but was looked upon as an attempt to quantify the broad base of the Bank from which planned profit growth, and relevant issues, could then be assessed by management. Since the papers were discussed at length and regularly updated, they deserve some comment, not least because they show the difficulty of planning in an accident-prone world.

The basic method had some similarities to the work on the annual budgets and involved taking current costs and income and extrapolating these on certain assumptions; these included, for instance, a no-change view on innovation, that government regulations on banking would remain the same, as would interest rates, and that there would be uniform rates of growth in subsidiaries. It was not at all surprising, Jessiman argued, that the result showed a decline in the real level of profit: 'almost any company undertaking the same exercise and assuming neither innovation nor expansion would disclose a similar position'. The recognition of this underlying pessimism would give an 'impetus to the possibly radical policies' necessary to alter the trend. Of course, an alert management would always react to adversity, although, as noticed before, a number of the younger, and not-so-young, bankers were aware before these exercises that there had not been enough change in the past. Therefore, while it was doubtful that the projected results would materialise, unless the Bank had known profit objectives and 'knows what additional earnings it must generate to achieve these objectives it is virtually certain that "management reaction" will neither occur early enough nor produce profits high enough'. The board had to assess where profits should be in order to pursue suitable changes and innovations to progress there.

Thus corporate planning quantified the broad effects of existing, largely adverse, future trends, and asked management to provide solutions to maintain real profits while asking questions about how to push these higher. This meant agreement on aims and key tasks and required basic strategies and financial targets for all related factors in computing resources, marketing and staff. When these exercises were complete, the management had to ensure that they were implemented and that the weekly checks of the accruing annual profit would highlight which targets needed modification. Thus stated, corporate planning was a far-reaching discipline which touched all areas of the Bank. It was known that other banks, including Barclays and the National Westminster, had started work on similar lines. It should be remembered that the board and management of Bank of Scotland remained fearful for the future independence of Scottish banking, and corporate planning was seen as one way to improve the overall performance of the Bank. By the close of January 1971, the Profit Planning Committee had been directed to work out how profit objectives, as yet unquantified, for the next five years might be determined; and to assess strategies with a view to raising the profits from existing business; to review the development of new fields of operation; and, lastly, to find out the volume of funds and resources available each year for these innovations.[7]

While this work and the preparation of annual budgets were a necessary part of the reorientation of the Bank and had numerous benefits in prompting staff to think about costs, throughput and a sharper focus to their efforts, there were potential drawbacks. These systems had been in use in a variety of western businesses and industries, private and public, as well as in the Soviet Union and other centrally-planned countries. There was always the chance that targets would be set too high, that scarce managerial talent would be diffused over too many projects, that expertise would be wasted churning over paperwork, and that insufficient thought would be given to schemes with an apparently high return. Innovation sounded sensible but threatened to take the Bank deeper into areas which were less straightforward, such as the trading of foreign currencies at fine margins, or loans on building and property in the south-east of England. In some circumstances, resort would have to be had to consortium lending, where there was always a potential problem of control. The older banking expertise was not something which could be thrown away lightly given the responsibility of the Bank towards industry. There was also a potential staffing difficulty, as central planning of fixed targets put immense strain on senior men already stretched by an increasing workload.[8] Yet it was noticed that the amalgamation gave the Bank a number of enthusiastic younger managers who were at an age when, it was thought, they could appreciate more challenges. As Duncan Ferguson, an assistant general manager in 1972, later recalled, 'I was nearing my fifties and I noticed these chaps of the 28–35 age group – we had a lot of them – beginning to make their mark'.[9] Diversification allowed many to be given charge of new functions, and the Bank saw the rise of the 'almost innumerable' class of assistant general manager, each dealing with a specific aspect of business. While there were many strengths to the long-established directors' committee system, it was agreed that from the autumn of 1971 the trustee committee would now meet only once a year, and the staff committee and the investments committee every three months, which in effect devolved day-to-day decision-making to the executive. Apart from the main board, the east and west boards meeting in Edinburgh and Glasgow respectively, and the London board, the more important

7 BS 1/6, Minutes, Board papers, Management Accounting Committee, 26 January 1971.
8 Scotland had an unenviable record for heart disease, and a number of managers collapsed while at work. Regular medical check-ups were offered to senior staff from 1975. Sir Hugh Rose pointed to the increase in the workload in September 1972.
9 BS, Tercentenary Oral History Project, interview by David Antonio of Duncan Ferguson.

'thinking' functions were devolved to the computer and management accounting committee, chaired by Lord Balfour, and the policy committee, chaired by the Governor, with David Antonio, Secretary, and Thomas Walker, Treasurer, in attendance.[10] In December, the policy committee envisaged its main functions to be the study of individual aspects of the Bank's business and the focus on where diversification might take place. A master plan was required so that proposals for new activities could be seen to fit into this overall framework.[11] For several years, while Alan Jessiman organised the new profit and corporate planning, both these committees retained a prominence, and the range of expertise represented by the directors was an important factor in their success. Nevertheless, as will be seen, the dilution of directors' involvement had both advantages and disadvantages.

With the fusion of the two banks in 1971, the new board issued instructions to the executive to arrange for an appropriate rationalisation of resources, and high on the agenda were branches. First, the overlap in offices could be identified by a straightforward comparison of local business and a decision taken as to which would be closed. Bank of Scotland had numerous main and sub-offices close by similar British Linen branches, and it was inevitable that there would be places where a clear overlap was identified. There was considerable expertise within the banks about how to deal with this; Bank of Scotland, for example, had shut fifty branches from 1954 to 1969 and opened six more in new areas.[12] It was agreed that the head-office administration, scattered in seventeen locations, be reduced to four, collected in Edinburgh at Uberior House, Grassmarket, at the Mound and at the old head office of the British Linen Bank at St Andrews Square, with the computing function at Robertson Avenue. The second exercise was designed to determine the optimum size, nature and distribution of the branch network and the appropriate level of service which should be provided. Launched in October 1972, it grew out of the corporate planning approach. Alan Jessiman identified three broad ways in which this could help. First, it would aid decisions on where branches should be sited, on their rationalisation and on alterations in their type of service, and would help in the assessment of manpower implications. Second, it would be an aid to profit-maximisation by fitting

---

10 The members of the Policy Committee were Lord Polwarth (the Governor) until his resignation when appointed Minister of State at the Scottish Office, 11 April 1972; Lord Clydesmuir, who succeeded as Governor; Lord Balfour, T. R. Craig, James Gammell CA and James Lumsden WS, solicitor with Maclay, Murray and Spens and chairman of Burmah Oil. The Bank was fortunate to have such an effective team.
11 BS 1/6, Minutes, Policy Committee, 10 December 1971.
12 Within three years of its merger with Martins, Barclays had closed 202 branches: 'The Bank Results', *The Banker*, 121 (1971), 254–9.

branches to potential customers. Third, it would set standards by which to judge branches, using a mathematical model to simulate decision-making. Much of this was already done by Jessiman's group, but, because of the sheer volume of work at the senior level, the board agreed to the employment of PA Management Consultants to conduct a preliminary exercise.[13]

The problem for many traditional branches had been summed up by James Gammell: why should a branch be kept open when profits were below what could be achieved by redirection of the capital on sale of the buildings? From the eighteenth century, both banks had been able to work out whether a branch was profitable, yet increased competition had led to a higher ratio of branches to population in Scotland than south of the Border, and many branches were marginal earners. Such a branch had been opened in 1961 by the British Linen in the centre of Drumchapel, a vast new municipal housing estate designed for 60,000 of the overspill from Glasgow.[14] This was an unrewarding environment dominated by the manual working classes. Apart from the Savings Bank of Glasgow, which had expertise with small accounts, no other bank moved in, so at least competition was not a problem. The business ran at a loss, reflecting the expense of a high level of counter activity with only very small residual balances. First and foremost, the board agreed that the Bank owed a responsibility to provide a nationwide service and that its reputation might suffer if it withdrew. Yet the vast amount of cash work for small business and the giro credit brought little return. There might be scope for increasing business, as the second phase of the Drumchapel shopping development would bring a hotel, a supermarket, eighteen more shops and a public house. If closed, the cash business would move to other branches, all the nearest of which were also Bank of Scotland. Reluctantly the board agreed to stay, but with the deterioration of Drumchapel in later years the cost of the full branch could not be justified, and it was eventually merged with Clydebank.

The traditional arguments of coverage, service, personal attention and prospects were clearly inadequate, although branches were retained for all these reasons. Students, for example, were a source of long-term banking connections, and so the profitability of university branches was not the only consideration. The PA report took eighteen months.[15] It claimed to provide a statistically reliable prediction of future business available to a branch and of profit openings related to wider areas than normally

13 BS 1/6, Minutes, Board papers, 3 October 1972. At this time, there were four staff in the Management Accounting department.
14 BS 1/6, Minutes, 27 June 1972.
15 BS 1/6, Minutes, Board papers, 'Branch Location Study', 26 April 1974.

covered by a branch. There were three stages: the total business for all banks in an area was assessed using census and banking data; the share of this trade which Bank of Scotland could reasonably expect to take was worked out together with what would happen to profits if a branch were closed or new ones opened; lastly, where the study indicated closures in an area, a financial appraisal then selected those to be shut. On completion, the study pointed to ten areas where the Bank was unrepresented, three of which were in the north-east, and sixty possible closures, of which twenty-one were in Glasgow and thirteen in Edinburgh. The report was considered at length, but the feeling was that the detailed information within the Bank, such as that for Drumchapel, was a surer guide to closures than that provided by the model. It was also agreed that the expense of the consultants' study should not be incurred again, a view firmly endorsed in later years by Thomas Walker, the Treasurer of the time.[16]

In the years 1971–4, around 130 surplus branches were closed and business transferred to nearby offices, and this process continued for the rest of the decade, although at a more measured pace. This went together with a broader view of how branches could contribute to income, and most were now grouped into sections, each with a district manager whose task was to visit managers and discuss how lending opportunities could be progressed. This took lending officials out of head office and proved successful in encouraging branch officials to aim for specific targets. Reminiscences from this time indicate that officials appreciated the benefit of the new management tier, as the previous system of inspection and direct contact with the Inspectors Department was sometimes seen as overly concerned with audit and control. The Bank remained flexible over its approach to reorganisation. In 1977–8, for instance, when profits were under pressure, there was a determined effort to reduce the number of city-centre branches in Glasgow. Rapid improvements in computerised book-keeping made it possible to telescope branch work, the five district managers were reduced to four – 'not a popular move' – and Hope Street was closed. Of course, not all the innovations were as successful as had been hoped. A new Business Advisory Services section was inaugurated by William Hay, with Harry Brough as assistant general manager, designed to advise branches on matters such as accounting practice and taxation. It was wound up in 1974.

As part of the negotiations between the Bank and the British Linen, there was a fundamental appraisal of the way in which the gilts portfolio

---

16 BS, Tercentenary Oral History Project, interview by David Antonio of Thomas Walker.

was managed. This led to an agreement by the directors to cede day-to-day management. For two years from 1967, periodic recommendations were made to the investments committee from a new Investment Department, run by Bruce Pattullo and Alasdair Macdonald. By June 1970, there was sufficient confidence in this arrangement for the directors to agree to full-scale trading on the basis of an initial realisation of low-yielding issues followed by reinvestment to maximise the overall return, switching gilts thereafter to increase the redemption yield, and a general cutback on long-dated stocks, with an agreement that no stock be purchased with a life above ten years. The responsibility was delegated to the Investment Department and the Chief Accountant working in conjunction with specialist gilt brokers. The combined portfolio of the two banks at September 1970 was £73,843,488 on which there was a deficit of £2.2 million below book value. This was swiftly cut, to £1.2 million by March 1971, with an improvement in yield. The directors then accepted that the executive should be given the right to alter the portfolio in the light of market developments; by June the valuation was almost at par, and by December the surplus had reached £3,624,765.

The thought given to structure and organisation proved crucial to the longer-term well-being of Bank of Scotland. It helped to unite the two managements with a sense of purpose and was important because of the general difficulties of the commercial and political situation which followed any amalgamation. However, the board foresaw conditions in which there might be a threat to the Bank's independence. These threats came from the City of London, where conditions were over-sympathetic to speculation in property and finance, leading to the growth of secondary banking and wholesale markets and to the boom of 1971–3. Mention has been made of the findings of the Radcliffe Committee, with its failure to recognise the specific needs of industry and the harmful restrictions on the banks in 1960–3. Following Radcliffe, the government indeed adopted a more broadly-based view of liquidity in the economy. The traditional definition of the supply of money as limited to banknotes, commercial bills and deposits was widened as Radcliffe argued that with a broader definition of the money supply, about which government operations should be concerned, a greater impact on financial conditions and the 'level of demand' would be achieved. Interest rates remained the main weapon in holding down the growth of the demand for money, with physical controls by special deposits and qualitative guidance on the direction of advances where required. From July 1966, there was another considerable squeeze on bank advances, and further ceilings were imposed in 1968. Therefore, borrowers moved to other sources. As with the growth of finance houses after the war, the secondary banking companies paid higher interest to depositors and therefore proved particularly attractive to local authority and company treasurers looking for higher returns for their balances.[17] Entirely new wholesale and inter-company markets emerged, and the clearing and Scottish banks looked less and less attractive to depositors. From 1963 to 1971, gross deposits in UK clearing banks rose 59.3 per cent but those in the TSBS, building societies, unit-trust and investment companies rose much faster.[18] These deposits were then made available to the new wholesale markets. The banks also noticed that, as company treasurers searched for higher returns, they were less willing to leave large sums in current accounts and on other types of deposit. While the work and expense associated with business accounts increased, the traditional advantages of these accounts decreased.[19]

There were intermittent signs in the late 1960s that the business structure of several secondary deposit-taking banks in London was unsound, with a high proportion of their loan books tied to subsidiaries involved in property and financial speculation and sometimes to directors' personal affairs. In most instances, inadequate liquidity was maintained. This type of unsound banking practice required detailed statutory attention, but in this the government and the Bank of England were content to rely on the inadequate backstop of the Protection of Depositors Act, 1963.[20] Further, in 1968, encouragement was given to expansion of credit when both the Prices and Incomes Board and the Monopolies and Mergers Commission reports on the proposed merger of Barclays Bank with Lloyds Bank and Martins Bank favoured a more competitive environment. The following year, the Labour government adopted the recommendation of the MMC that the true profits and reserves of the clearing and Scottish banks should be published, although the exemption clause in the 1967 Companies Act remained for discount houses, merchant and overseas banks. It was then argued by the general manager of Barclays, as a reason for increasing interest rates under this new, open regime, that banks could no longer rely on internal reserves (belonging to proprietors) to smooth out fluctuations in difficult times.[21] Henceforth, depositors would have to shoulder the

---

17 R. Fry, A Banker's World: The Revival of the City 1957–1970 (London: 1970).

18 'A Survey: All Near-Bankers Now', The Banker, 122 (1972), 636–8. The figures for the rises in UK deposits in institutions other than clearing banks are: 121 per cent for TSBS, 204 per cent in building societies, 437 per cent in unit trusts and 104 per cent in investment trusts.

19 This process was noticed for the English clearers by D. Wood, 'New Deal for Commercial Banking Accounts', The Banker, 121 (1971), 33–40.

20 Six of these unsound companies were wound up under the Protection of Depositors Act, 1963; as The Banker explained, all the signs pointed to serious trouble in the later 1960s. It returned to the theme in May 1971, and pointed out the lessons in 'Danger Signals for Banking', The Banker, 124 (1974), 12–13.

21 D. V. Weyer, 'Clearing Bank Marketing: The Practical Issues Today', The Banker, 120 (1970), 1,061–8.

burden through changes in interest rates. Last but not least, all banks, for various reasons, continued to look for new openings and new ways of doing business. The return of the Conservative Party to power on 16 June 1970 provided an additional impetus.

At first, the new government was cautious in monetary policy. Edward Heath, the prime minister, was determined neither to encourage a wages-led inflation nor to support with public subsidies what John Davies, the Secretary of State for Industry, described as 'lame ducks'. Bank rate was raised to 7 per cent, and in July the Scottish banks were asked to restrict lending. A number of customers of the London and Scottish banks then approached the secondary banking sector for accommodation. In November, government policy was severely tested by a threatened collapse at Rolls-Royce, which had poured immense sums into the RB 211 aero-engine contract and required public support; and, as unemployment rose over the winter in tandem with rising prices and social unrest, a more relaxed regime was adopted. Henceforth, subsidies were more freely available. This all pointed to higher inflation and a growth in the public-sector borrowing requirement. As gilt-edged brokers Pember and Boyle put it, 'Ducks nowadays have but to complain of a slight twinge in the leg and they are immediately revived with copious draughts of brandy'.[22] The framework for the boom was thus established.

In May 1971, the government and the Bank of England announced a new regulatory framework for the clearing and Scottish banks, 'Competition and Credit Control', which owed something to the Radcliffe view on the use of interest rates to ration credit and took further the ideas of those within the Bank of England and the Treasury that physical controls on the banks were inappropriate and that the banks should be allowed to do anything the secondary sector could. The Scottish banks were informed that it was proposed to replace the existing liquidity and lending ceilings by greater reliance on interest rates, occasional calls for special deposits, and replacement of the existing liquidity ratio by a new minimum reserve-assets ratio set at a minimum of $12\frac{1}{2}$ per cent of sterling deposit liabilities. This last caused immediate difficulty. Qualifying assets were: balances with the Bank of England, but not special deposits; London money-market funds at call; Treasury bills and company tax reserve certificates; commercial and local authority bills eligible for re-discount at the Bank of England; and British government securities with a year or under to run. In a slight to the Scots, 'cash', 'other short money' and cheques in course of collection were excluded (as they were in England – but these items were

22 Pember and Boyle, *British Government Securities in the Twentieth Century: Supplement 1950–1972* (private circulation, London: n.d. [1973]), p. ix.

of greater moment in Scotland), as was the cover for Scottish banknotes held by the Bank of England.

The GMC sent Thomas Walker to explain how banknotes supported the branch systems, why cheques in course of clearance should be treated separately from English cheques and why there should be a lower percentage levy on special deposits because of the greater importance of long-term industrial advances in Scotland.[23] The separate treatment of cheques in course of collection was vital to the ability of the Scottish banks to predict short-term liquidity. There was no counterpart in Scotland of the town clearing in London, settlement of whose cheques was made on the day of presentation. Scottish balances with English clearers were settled one day after receipt, and settlement for cheques presented through London clearing agents two or more days later. Thus the Scottish banks had advance knowledge of the main demands on their cash resources and did not require to hold so large a proportion of idle balances. They could borrow, short-term, from the money markets when necessary.[24] These concerns were of little interest in London. In July, after another visit, the GMC reported that the Bank of England 'appeared not to have grasped the points made', or more likely had not wanted to because of its drive for uniformity in the banking system. The English agreed 'that there were differences between the Scots and English economies and the way the two banking systems worked', but it took another month before the Governor of the Bank of England conceded that the proposals involved hardship. A 'limited concession' was offered, but this would not take the form of either a different minimum reserve ratio or a variation in the composition of reserve assets. The Scots could choose an increase in their authorised note issue under the 1845 Currency Act or the end of stamp duty, then worth £640,000 a year. The GMC agreed to the latter but requested that some indulgence should be shown to any Scottish bank which failed on occasion to observe the minimum reserve ratio of $12\frac{1}{2}$ per cent; existing special deposits would be repaid either in cash or gilts; and the Bank of England would be prepared to review the financial position of the Scottish banks if the latter so requested during the period of twelve months from the start of the scheme.[25] The new policy was adopted from 16 September 1971.

As the new policy was intended to force the Scots to hold more short-dated gilts, now allowable as part of the reserve, Bank of Scotland had no choice but to split the gilts portfolio into a 'Liquidity Portfolio' of stocks under one year to run which qualified as reserve assets, and also those

23 BS 1/6, Board paper, 15 June 1971, on meeting with Bank of England, 11 June 1971.
24 The Bank of England may not have seen the explanation in 'New Statistics on Scottish Banking', *Scottish Bankers Magazine*, 52 (1960–1), 129–38.
25 BS 1/6, Minutes, Board papers, 27 July, 12 August, 2 and 7 September 1971.

outwith this category but maturing within two years; and an 'investment portfolio' of stocks over two years. The effect was to reduce the ability to manage the reserve, as the penalty for being forced to sell stocks to correct an illiquid position could now be more severe. The Bank of England's instructions were regarded as unhelpful, and it also announced that it would no longer necessarily respond to requests from the clearing banks to buy British government securities, except where these had one year or under to run. For longer-dated stocks, it reserved the right to purchase 'solely at their discretion and initiative' and would 'be prepared to undertake at prices of their own choosing, exchanges of stock with the market except those which unduly shorten the life' of the gilts portfolio.

The combined effects of the changes in government economic policy and the easing of Bank of England policy towards the structure of assets of clearing banks, together with greater competition for deposits and the provision of new services, created a considerable extension of the business of the secondary deposit-takers. The compound rate of growth per annum of total UK banking-sector assets and advances from October 1971 to December 1973 were 41.4 per cent and 47.8 per cent respectively, far above the long-run average.[26] A range of new products was eagerly taken up by the public; house and office prices rose sharply as money rushed into the property and financial services sectors. The anticipated investment in UK industry proved much more elusive, and the trade deficit grew steadily worse. One of the newer forms of speculation for secondary banks was the forward market in sterling certificates of deposit (SCDs), through which a lender guaranteed to lend at a specified future time at a previously fixed rate. The advantage to the borrower was the certainty of funds at the specified rate and thus control over his interest-rate costs. The borrower often assumed that interest rates would rise, while the lender gambled on a fall. It was a particularly dangerous form of speculation, and the first major casualty of the crisis, the banking department of the Scottish Co-operative Wholesale Society (SCOOP), with a paid-up capital of £2 million, indulged in this type of interest-rate risk on a massive scale. It faced a loss of around £40 million on forward commitments to 1977, and any further rise in rates would worsen the position.[27] At the time, it was not recognised in the City that the SCOOP problem was merely the precursor of a more deeply-seated secondary banking crisis.

The Scottish banks were the lead bankers for SCOOP, although it had often seemed to the GMC a tedious connection kept because the ordinary

26 L. D. Chesher, D. K. Sheppard and J. Whitwell, 'Have British Banks Been Imprudent?', *The Banker*, 125 (1975), 31–9.
27 BS, Uncatalogued, Miscellaneous papers, Scottish Co-operative Wholesale Society banking department, 1973–8.

Co-op accounts were profitable. It was the sort of connection which James Letham doubtless had in mind when he argued that service should be linked to profits. The Bank of England at first took the view that the crisis was the responsibility of the Scots and should not be shared with Threadneedle Street or the London clearers. By May 1973, it had become clear that SCOOP had widespread dealings with London-based banks, and a strict apportionment of losses to lead banks with Bank of England help was the only way forward. The loss was then shared out among the London clearers, the Scots, the Bank of England and the Co-operative Bank, with the Co-op taking over the banking department and managing the run-down of the portfolio of SCDs. Ways in which the costs to the banks could be offset against tax were negotiated with the Inland Revenue. The Bank of England refused to allow the support funds to be regarded as reserve assets, or offset against special deposits, although it had allowed just this in June 1972.[28] It was agreed that £40 million of the loss would be borne as follows:

the first £10 million	by the Co-operative Bank
the second £10 million	by the consortium
the next £5 million	by the Co-operative Bank
any excess over £25 million	shared 50 per cent each side.

Any recoveries were to be set against losses on a 'last in, first out' basis, and the Bank of England fixed its share at 5 per cent of the consortium commitment.

An air of panic enveloped the City of London in the autumn of 1973; while the board of Bank of Scotland was meeting on 13 November 1973, the Chief Cashier of the Bank of England telephoned the news that the trade deficit for October was £298 million and that bank rate would be raised to 13 per cent, with another 2 per cent call for special deposits, bringing these to 6 per cent of sterling assets. The secondary banks were now in dire straits. There was £4,495 million in loans from this sector to the property market and other purely financial schemes.[29] The secondary banks' deposit liabilities had soared: Cedar Holdings, for example, went from £3 million to £67 million in the three years to mid-1973; London and County Securities from £9 million to £88 million in only two years. Some commentators drew an analogy with 1960, but the scale of the deficits was now more serious and, of particular importance, the position of the London clearers more exposed. Many secondary banks had failed to maintain adequate liquidity from their deposits, and, when demands

28 Ibid., Bank of England to Chief Executive Officers from the Disclosure Working Party, October 1973. For a detailed contemporary view from a Bank of Scotland economist, see M. S. MacDougall, 'Control and Supervision of Banking', *Scottish Bankers Magazine*, 67 (1975–6), 277–84.
29 M. Reid, *The Secondary Banking Crisis 1973–75: Its Causes and Course* (London: 1982), p. 61.

were made by depositors, they were unable to meet them. As the London clearers were all involved in wholesale money-market operations, property investment and their own advances to the secondary banks, the scale of the crisis could impinge on their own soundness. As if to confirm this, rumours about the position of the National Westminster resulted in a collapse in its share price, from 200–210p in July to 88p on 29 November.[30] It had bought in huge loans from the wholesale money markets to fund much lending and to pay for the construction of its new skyscraper office in the City. Its chairman was forced to deny that it intended a rights issue or that it had received a 'substantial' amount of support from the Bank of England, and he reiterated that the bank had no exposure to the crisis within the Italian Sidona group. It was well known that the National Westminster was the lead bank for a dozen secondary banking companies, and its exposure was put, in the financial press, at hundreds of millions of pounds. On 19–20 December 1973, the Bank of England coordinated a defence of all concerned with the intent to avoid a collapse of asset values 'should these be sold in a panic'. The solution was a 'lifeboat' for secondary banks, but the Scottish banks were given little choice. Bank of Scotland was allotted 2.6 per cent of all realised losses, the total eventual ceiling on which was agreed at £1.2 billion; thus the Bank was required to assume provision for £31.2 million, in addition to 3.14 per cent of the SCOOP consortium. Early in 1974, the government brought in strict controls on bank lending, which Thomas Walker noted were 'the most severe form of restriction that the banks had ever experienced and the penalties for infringement were savage'.[31] The Bank of England designed a package to contain borrowing on the inter-bank market and to stop competition for funds; but this was a blunt instrument, and it hit industrial customers of the Scottish banks, some of whom wrote in frank language to object about the effect on their business, soon aggravated by the three-day week imposed by the government in its struggle with the National Union of Mineworkers. By February 1974, the in-gathering of bank debts had started to prove more difficult. Further, the Bank of England was ill-prepared to manage the crisis, and only after heated exchanges with the clearing and Scottish banks were 'sound' bankers and accountants sent in to examine the books of the affected secondary banks. The discovery of the true extent of the loss, bad management, property speculation and financial greed, which in some cases involved fraud, was a salutary lesson. Robert Runciman, the manager at London Chief Office, was asked to sit

---

30 *Financial Times*, 30 November 1974; 'Nat West Rumours', *The Banker*, 125 (1975), 8; 'The Story of the City Crisis', *The Banker*, 124 (1974), 87–9; BS, Tercentenary Oral History Project, interview by David Antonio of Robert Runciman.
31 BS 1/6, Minutes, 8 January 1974.

on the Lifeboat committee, sometimes meeting twice a day at the Bank of England during the height of the crisis.

Unlike the London clearers, Bank of Scotland had kept largely clear of the secondary banking companies and had only one, minor, liability to the property crisis apart from the obligations to the scoop consortium and the lifeboat. In all the circumstances, the Bank's position was exceptionally strong. Total advances had grown to £494,137,826 by February 1973, up from £244,243,223 four years earlier;[32] the average loss ratio was a fraction of 1 per cent, and always covered by a prudent allocation to the fund for losses. Indeed, in 1973, this fund was actually in credit. The cumulative balance reserved against advances was £4 million, although in March, because of the exceptional level of new loans, another £1 million was placed to general reserve. This figure again proved generous. Most of the potential Bank losses in these years were for industrial or service firms hit by the rise in interest rates or occasionally by their own bad management, but many accounts were eventually rectified. By February 1975, on outstanding advances of £728,532,000, the Bank had allocated £6,672,000 (0.9158 per cent) to provisions for losses, and in the next year this was increased to £13 million. The crisis also reduced income from consumer advances through the Bank and NWS. The latter's profits rose strongly in 1972, but in the half-year to 30 June 1973 they fell 37 per cent while advances increased 47 per cent. The average cost of money to NWS had risen by 4½ per cent but margins offered by competitors were cut, so this increased cost of deposits could not be passed on. In addition, the increase in money costs was immediate, but income was only recouped over a longer timespan. Sydney Jones's team predicted in August that profits would fall, which they did, but bad debts were few and tightly controlled, and NWS benefited from a restoration of normality in the later 1970s.

In the aftermath of this crisis, it was clear to Scottish bankers that their behaviour had been more prudent than that of some of their London counterparts, and that the Bank of England and the government bore prime responsibility for the disastrous expansion of credit and the consequent property speculation. Yet, far from showing a recognition of the prudent course pursued by the Scots, the Bank of England slapped on an increase in special deposits, which cut £800,000 from interest income over the following year. It also required the banks to deposit with it a percentage of any excess over 8 per cent on the growth of interest-bearing deposits averaged between the quarterly average for October to December 1973 and that for April to June 1974. It might have been thought that the missing components from the 1971 paper on 'Competition and Credit

32 See Statistical Appendix, Table A8.

Control' were proper controls on balance sheets and the composition of the asset split between liquid and illiquid.[33] In the crisis, it appeared that the Bank of England underestimated the liberalising effect of deregulation. A revised version of 'Competition and Credit Control' was announced in 1975.

How did it come about that Bank of Scotland kept out of the London secondary banking market when the Bank's advances grew in the later 1960s? The answer was twofold: the Bank had concentrated on real goods and services, and was in the course of developing expertise in lending to the growing oil and gas industries. The board and the management were undoubtedly helped by the coherence of the underlying philosophy about the uses to which proprietors' money and that of depositors should be put. Both Bank of Scotland and the Union Bank had *always* regarded themselves as long-term industrial and commercial bankers committed to industrial growth and supporting Scottish trade. While the British Linen was thought of as a cautious bank, there was a strong link between all three banks in their reluctance to be involved in property speculation and in their preference for real transactions. All three were reluctant to take a view about what might or might not happen to interest rates, property prices or commodity values. Thus the core of the Bank philosophy in this whole period, before and after amalgamation, was clear: the Bank was prepared to lend long and then nurse companies through bad times, 'so contributing to the process of economic development and the improvement of living standards'. It also requested of politicians the political and legal means to ensure that it had every chance of success.[34] Further, directors were expected to be more active over policy issues, and Thomas Walker supported the moves to involve the board more in the executive and planning side of the Bank. The crisis confirmed that the needs of proprietors and of account holders were best protected by the Bank having the self-confidence to think for itself and not be sucked into the current fashions of the City of London. The crisis also underlined the overriding necessity of good-quality assessments for lending and increasing profits to provide additions to the capital base, 'while paying reasonable dividends to shareholders to justify the attraction of new capital when required'. Long-term development of staff was placed high on the agenda; managers were encouraged to look ahead, participate in forward planning and develop a style of management that looked to controls on costs with a positive approach to marketing and sales. The executive also realised that

---

33 The alternative view, in E. V. Morgan and I. M. Richards, 'A Verdict on Competition and Credit Controls', *The Banker*, 124 (1974), 571–8, appeared naive when the fuller story was available, for which see Chesher, Sheppard and Whitwell, 'Have British Banks Been Imprudent?'
34 BS 1/6, Minutes, Board papers, 11 November 1975.

a key feature would be constructive criticism and innovative thinking at all levels, with an even-handed and not oppressive style from its senior men. All this, and the commitment to permanent employment, was to pay dividends. Last, but not least, the cultural and religious atmosphere of Edinburgh and Glasgow was believed to be an important corrective to the cruder hedonism and diversions of the City of London.

Bank of Scotland was the most adventurous European bank in respect of the North Sea oil industry, both directly and in partnership, and the board took the lead over the establishment of the International Energy Bank in 1973. It should be stressed that, while offshore oil was a new industry, much of the technology, science and engineering which went into it was fully understood in Scotland. Further, oil became a highly-charged political question which required some sensitivity on the part of bankers.

Before 1974, there was little commercial oil exploitation in the UK. It was true that from 1850 to 1962 Scotland was home to production of the lighter grades of oils and paraffins from the immense reserves of shale in the central lowlands, and for many years production reached one to two million tonnes of oils per year.[35] But this was an industry in decline, and apart from analytic chemistry it had little connection with deep-lying oil reservoirs on land or at sea. There was modest onshore oil production in England, but annual production was little more than 100,000 tonnes. Thus most of the UK's oil needs came from imports, and for a variety of reasons the great bulk of primary fuel usage before 1957 was coal. Even ten years later, this source yielded 60 per cent of UK energy needs, while all gas came from coal, and nuclear power remained insignificant.

In August 1959, a Dutch exploration team found natural gas onshore in Groningen and later under the shallow waters offshore. The race to find more gas began in earnest, and by 1967 there were over twenty drilling operations in the southern part of the North Sea. The UK and Norway divided the bulk of the North Sea, with the Netherlands, Germany and Denmark qualifying for smaller slices, a division out of which Norway did particularly well. The UK government, under the UK Continental Shelf Act, 1964, created a new British province and, through the three continental shelf (jurisdiction) orders of 1964, 1965 and 1968, applied Scots law to two-thirds of the UK allocation. All negotiations with oil companies for concessions and all finances were managed in London. But there was no reference to industrial or regional policy in the first round of licences in April 1964 and only a vague mention in two subsequent rounds.[36] Yet the basic premise of exploration was achieved; from 1964

35 J. Butt, 'The Scottish Oil Mania of 1864–6', *Scottish Journal of Political Economy*, 12 (1965), 195–209.
36 Licensing arrangements are reprinted in G. Arnold, *Britain's Oil* (London: 1978), Appendix I; and

to 1973, 266 oil wells were drilled in the UK shelf. The Danes discovered a minor oilfield in 1967 and the Dutch another in 1969, both within the Scottish sector of the North Sea. Thus, by turns, the exploration focused upon oil off Scotland and Norway. While the Norwegians planned comprehensive industrial and social-service policies, it was inevitably a matter of comment that the UK government before 1974 did not follow their lead.

Bank of Scotland was particularly well prepared to finance oil developments. The question of gas production and financing was discussed in the *Scottish Bankers Magazine* in 1966 by Alan Thomson,[37] following meetings of the discussion circle organised by F. S. Taylor. Board members were aware of demands on Scottish engineering through their networks of contacts. Sir William Lithgow, for example, saw the potential for building oil rigs with their high-technology engineering and thousands of tons of steel and alloys, packed with electronic equipment and necessarily built to exacting specifications. Lord Clydesmuir and Sir William were enthusiastic about the possibility of a general boost to the Scottish economy from all parts of the oil business, and through the Scottish Council (Development and Industry) they launched a number of initiatives.

In May 1972, the board agreed that the volume of work required experience in the evaluation of oil reservoirs and recruited David Fleming, formerly managing director of Shell–BP Petroleum Development in Nigeria. There was little difficulty with the engineering specifications from Scottish companies, as the board and management were used to these; but field evaluation was complicated, and the buying-in of proven skills expedited the build-up of knowledge and confidence. The Bank also decided to challenge the London banks on their own ground and sponsored a conference on 'Scottish North Sea Oil' at the Savoy Hotel on 29 June 1972. This excited much interest, and the press started to talk of the 'oil bank'. Bruce Pattullo, who proposed the conference to Thomas Walker, the Treasurer, and who then prepared it, recalled: 'People had already begun to telephone us about this or that oil development and whether Bank of Scotland had taken a decision to participate, and the conference strengthened this standing'. Thus the Bank was approached in 1972 at the start of negotiations for the funding of the Forties field to be operated by British Petroleum, and was the first UK bank to respond positively to the proposal. This was the first major funding in the North Sea oil concessions and was of significance not least because of the way in

see, for the development of the oil business in Scotland, C. Harvie, *Fool's Gold: The Story of North Sea Oil* (London: 1994).
37 A. J. R. Thomson, 'Modern Industries: Natural Gas Exploration', *Scottish Bankers Magazine*, 57 (1965–6), Students' Section, 29–32.

which the burden of risk was shared, with the banks only having a partial recourse to BP and instead having to rely on the value of the oil reservoir in place in the ground.

The total funding for the Forties field was £360 million, with half in sterling and half in US dollars, and was required to finance platforms, a pipeline to Cruden Bay and an onward extension to the BP refinery at Grangemouth. The viability of the project was based on the assumption that oil could be sold at US $4 per barrel. The funding was to be arranged through a separate company, Norex Trading Ltd, 75 per cent owned by BP and 25 per cent by three institutions: Lazard Bros, Morgan Guaranty and the National Westminster. It was proposed that the banks in the consortium would lend forward to Norex, this new company would then buy oil from BP Development, these advance payments would be available to finance the development, and then Norex would sell oil to BP Trading and the funds generated would be used to repay the borrowing. Prior to the commencement of the oil flow, BP Development would reimburse Norex in cash for the loan interest paid out to the banks.[38] British Petroleum was careful to ensure that in the event of disruption or a shortfall in deliveries it would not be liable to repay the loan. But David Fleming confirmed that at 1972 prices there was at least recoverable oil to the value of £1.87 billion (5.2 × £360 million), with a margin of error of 75 per cent built in. The agreement was based on *recoverable* oil, not on the loan funding and interest: if after the close of 1978 the value of the oil fell short of the amount required to service the loan, BP Development would provide Norex with the funds necessary to meet its obligations by the end of 1982 up to an amount equal to the value of oil that was recoverable, less the amount already produced from the field. In determining the amount of oil considered to be recoverable, BP agreed that this should never be less than 44 per cent of the oil originally in place. There was a difficulty over the interest charge. The board of Bank of Scotland thought an interest charge of 1¼ per cent with a ½ per cent commitment fee too fine, but the London clearers and the merchant banks accepted this margin. The board, reassured by David Fleming's comments, accepted the terms proposed, and the Bank was subsequently congratulated on being the first UK clearing bank to commit to the Forties field funding. Fleming was also important in advising Bank customers who wished to move into the oil business but who sometimes lacked knowledge of how the oil companies worked. The Clydesdale Bank, with its long-established connections originating with the North of Scotland Bank, was also very effective in dealing with the new opportunities in the Aberdeen area.

38 BS 1/6, Minutes, Board papers, 13 June 1972.

705

In the summer of 1972, the Bank executive decided that, given the enormous sums required to finance the larger fields and the lack of experience of oilfield financing in the UK, it would be a good move to create a special consortium. William Hay, general manager, spoke to several banks in Europe and Scandinavia. Apart from the Norwegian banks, which could not participate because of political constraints, Hay found a ready response, but the executive decided that something more was required if Bank of Scotland was to raise its profile in the offshore oil industry, in competition, for example, with the large American banks. The idea of the International Energy Bank emerged, and, in the following winter, discussions were held with Banque Worms et Cie and Barclays Bank International. There were difficulties: Barclays insisted that it should have 26 per cent of the equity and that Bank of Scotland should have the same, which would have given the other participants together a minority holding and was liable to cause friction. Further, Barclays insisted that the remit would include finance for nuclear power. It was a member of the recently-formed International Nuclear Credit Corporation which had close connections with the Société Financière Européenne, a consortium run from Luxembourg also interested in nuclear-power programmes, especially those in France. Naturally, there was concern at the Mound that the International Energy Bank might wander from the focus on oil and gas. To counter this, William Hay and the executive approached the Canadian Imperial Bank of Commerce and the Republic National Bank of Dallas, both with recognised track records and contacts in this field. Both these North American banks insisted on a democratic structure for the consortium; and neither was much interested in nuclear power.[39] The discount office at the Bank of England tried to stop the use of 'bank' or 'international' in the title, and 'insisted that the office of the new bank should be situated in the City' and not anywhere else, such as in Edinburgh. The Department of Trade and Industry had no such objections, and made it clear that any name could be used and that the location was also not regulated in any way. However, the office was eventually opened in London.

From the start of the oil boom, the Bank drew a distinction between activities in offshore oilfield development incorporating platforms, drilling and the laying of pipelines, and the separate provision of storage facilities, refining processing and supply services. The board was particularly wary of financing exploration. However, as part of a strategy to project Bank of

39 The shareholding was agreed as: Bank of Scotland 15 per cent, Barclays Bank International 15 per cent, Société Financière Européenne 20 per cent, Banque Worms 10 per cent, Canadian Imperial 20 per cent, Republic National 20 per cent.

Scotland as the oil bank, some equity-type investments were made. The board agreed to holdings in two exploration ventures: Pict Petroleum, established by the Edinburgh merchant bank Noble Grossart, in which the Bank took a 4 per cent (£100,000) stake; and 4.8 per cent of Viking Oil, established by Ivory and Sime. Viking Oil was sold to Sun Oil of California at a substantial profit in 1980. A share of 5 per cent was taken in Viking Equipment, formed in 1972 to build a large pipe-laying barge.[40] This was owned by a Dutch company which needed Scottish banking support, and the Bank was joined by North Sea Assets, which took 20 per cent. However, most of the Bank involvements were more traditional in nature. In the case of Seaforth Maritime, for example, formed to transport supplies to the drilling rigs but which later moved into engineering and land transport, the Bank preferred to offer overdraft and loan facilities. It was another company put together by Iain Noble of Noble Grossart, who brought in two shipping companies, Lyle Shipping and H. Hogarth, both customers of the Bank, and Sidlaw Industries, as shareholders. By 1973, Seaforth operated four supply vessels for oil rigs from its base in Aberdeen.

In June 1976, Standard Oil of California (Chevron) and ICI asked Bank of Scotland to join them in applications for exploration and production licences in the fifth round of oil licensing. The Bank would be in the lead of a group of Scottish companies, but altogether these would have a minority holding. Chevron and ICI wanted a good pedigree 'tartan' of well-known names and were prepared to spend up to £70 million, with the Bank finding perhaps £14 million. The board was concerned that other oil companies might construe this as in conflict with the Bank's growing role as bankers to many of the significant companies in the industry, and the proposal was declined.

It is necessary to underline the gradual but eventually enthusiastic response of Scottish business. Oil-exploration funds came initially from twenty-seven Scottish mutual assurance companies, investment trusts, holding companies and shipping lines, as well as from Bank of Scotland.[41] By 1974, hundreds of industrial and service companies had some connection with the development of North Sea oil, and the Bank found increased demands upon its resources for overdrafts and term loans. A typical scheme of the time was the formation of North Sea Assets, which brought together Noble Grossart, Ivory and Sime, Edward Bates, Stenhouse Holdings, Christian Salvesen and Oil Exploration. It was designed to take

---

40 The connections between the Bank and other Scottish financial institutions interested in oil are discussed in J. Scott and M. Hughes, *The Anatomy of Scottish Capital: Scottish Companies and Scottish Capital, 1900–1979* (London: 1980), pp. 248–56.
41 For the role of Edinburgh's fund managers, see Harvie, *Fool's Gold*, pp. 107–10.

significant minority shareholdings in companies involved in oil services and the subcontractors, mostly in unquoted firms where the London investment institutions were more reluctant to commit themselves. There was special interest in land and property along the north and east coastal areas which might be used to build rigs, refineries or workers' houses. The Bank offered an overdraft of £2.5 million and took £200,000 of the shares in North Sea Assets.[42]

With all this activity in so many areas with good prospects, it should be clear why Bank of Scotland had little sympathy with the secondary banking problems in London and why, by and large, it also kept out of the recycling of the OPEC country surpluses to Latin American borrowers. In April 1975, Lord Clydesmuir confirmed to proprietors that there had been a substantial increase in the proportion of resources directed to manufacturing industry and shipbuilding, much of which was for oil-related work.[43]

From late 1974, Bank of Scotland faced potential problems which detracted from industrial work. The Labour government had announced in March 1974 that it would pursue a purposeful industrial and energy policy, and with the foundation of the British National Oil Corporation it appeared to inaugurate a more interventionist industrial programme than its predecessor. Further, the Chancellor of the Exchequer made it clear to the Bank of England that the secondary crisis was not to provide an excuse for the slowing-down of advances to industry by the clearing banks. Worried by this growing government interest in the economy, the Bank of England explored 'the means by which the private sector could make available funds for productive investment pending a restoration of funds through the capital market' – an alternative to provision of 'similar finance through State agencies'.[44] The Bank of England had in mind extra funding for Finance for Industry Ltd and the Finance Corporation for Industry Ltd, which were merged in 1974. This was hardly a problem for Bank of Scotland, or indeed any of the Scottish banks, and the board felt it inopportune to raise these matters separately with ministers or civil servants. Rather, it accepted that the British Bankers Association and the Bank of England should speak for banking as a whole. While these discussions proceeded, there came a disturbing development. The chairman of Barclays, A. F. Tuke, intimated in December that he intended to end the 'gentlemen's agreement', in existence since 1876, under which

42 BS 1/6, Minutes, 5 September 1972.
43 Bank of Scotland, *Annual Report* (1974–5). Lending to Latin America is discussed below, Chapter 27.
44 BS, Uncatalogued, 'Ad hoc committee on Bank of England proposals for Finance for Industry', 8 November 1974.

the London clearers would not open branches north of the Border and the Scottish banks would not open additional branches in the English provinces; but he assured the Bank that this was neither urgent nor hostile.

On 2 January 1975, the National Westminster, still in the throes of its difficulties with the secondary banks, announced that it was to open an office in Scotland, and the next day Barclays followed suit. While the growth of North Sea oil-related activity had already attracted nearly thirty non-UK banks to open offices in Edinburgh or Glasgow, nevertheless there was extensive media speculation. The worries divided into two parts. First, the English banks were very powerful – 'six to ten times our size' – and could move in, cut margins for corporate borrowers and also offer a range of facilities in England which Bank of Scotland could not match. This was less of a problem at the Royal Bank, which was already widely spread south of the Border through its ownership of Williams and Glyn's, and at the Clydesdale, which was owned by the Midland; but they, too, were both worried. Yet this threat could be met by developing new business south of the Border, and eventually it was. Second, a consensus on the board of Bank of Scotland agreed that the extension of Barclays' activities into corporate banking in Scotland would cut 'sharply across the good relations which had existed between the two banks since the [1971] merger' with the British Linen. The board was unanimous in an expression of regret that the unexpected suddenness of the announcement had given no opportunity for consultation or for agreement on demarcation of functions. And some had darker thoughts, in which it seemed 'like the end of the world'. What were Barclays, or others in the City of London, really planning? When clarification was sought from the Bank of England, the matter was only muddied further. Some managers now thought, rightly or wrongly, that they must be increasingly wary of the predatory intentions of 'their friends' in the City of London.

These dark thoughts were not allayed by events. When Barclays announced its choice of local manager, the Bank board minuted a 'general feeling that the appointment of [this] person . . . would not be in the best interests of either bank owing to the likelihood of a considerable lack of goodwill from certain quarters'. It later transpired that this was a deliberate effort to bring Bank of Scotland into Barclays' corporate strategy. Barclays' view was that its new office in Edinburgh, together with other links, was intended

(1) to provide a liaison between Bank of Scotland and all parts of the Barclays group and to establish a first-class working relationship, (2) To acquire wholesale international business for the Barclays group . . . in competition with the other banks operating in Scotland and to work in close co-operation with the Bank of Scotland in obtaining business which is mutually beneficial. The

main target will be the multinational companies which operate in Scotland and which have ramifications in areas where the Barclays group is already operating, (3) to act as a listening post for Barclays Bank International monitoring competitors' activities, (4) to keep under review the possibilities of development in Scotland.

In the political conditions of the time, an absorption of Bank of Scotland would have been very difficult for Barclays. The Scottish National Party had captured ten seats in 1974, and the government, which was less popular in mid-term than in 1974, was always cautious about Scotland. In February 1976, a senior SNP politician met the Bank to discuss a private member's bill extending legal-tender status to Scottish banknotes. Meetings were held with ministers and civil servants from this time to explain the enormously positive role of the Bank in the oil and shipbuilding industries. Moreover, Barclays was unpopular in many political circles, and there would have been an MMC investigation into its operations had a takeover been attempted. Nevertheless, many at the Mound remained concerned that conditions might change. Less important, but time-consuming, was a clash between the British Bankers Association and the Labour Party over bank nationalisation. From time to time, the Labour Party conference passed resolutions, but no Labour cabinet had ever discussed the matter except to dismiss it, and there was an overwhelming majority against in the cabinet of Harold Wilson. Labour Party leaders were nonetheless concerned about the level of industrial investment and facilities for exports, and on demitting office in 1976 Harold Wilson elected to chair an investigation into finance and the City, which largely exonerated the banks. This committee had the wholehearted backing of the prime minister, James Callaghan.

The remit of the Wilson Committee (as it has usually been called) was to inquire into the role and functioning of UK financial institutions, including the banks, and it considered at some length the provision of funds for trade and industry. The committee called for evidence from the English and Scottish clearers, City of London institutions including the Bank of England, and interested parties.[45] The Scottish banks, through the Committee of Scottish Bank General Managers, agreed to present a single document, as they had done in 1931 to the Macmillan Committee and in 1957 to the Radcliffe Committee. Robert Scott, chief inspector of branches, organised the input from Bank of Scotland, assisted by John Robertson. They found it difficult to attract much interest from the general managers concerned, and, when drafts of the first, second and

45 Committee to Review the Functioning of Financial Institutions (the Wilson Committee), *Report*, Cmnd 7937 (June 1980).

third memoranda were sent to them for comment, they 'might as well have been sent to the moon'. Only John Burke, general manager of the Royal Bank, showed much interest, inviting the representatives of the three banks – Robert Forbes of the Royal Bank, George Young of the Clydesdale, and Robert Scott – to lunch and swapping suggestions as they turned out 'draft after draft'. There was no collaboration with the English or American banks. The Wilson Committee came to Scotland on 20 December 1977, and, after a question-and-answer session held with the general managers, 'Harold Wilson stated that had prizes been given for the quality of presentations, that of the Scottish banks would have received first prize'. Unfortunately, the attitude at the Mound was unenthusiastic, no-one ever said 'thank you' to Scott, there was no contact with the directors, and a year's work was filed away.[46]

It was unwise to dismiss the work of the Wilson Committee. While the circumstances of the appointment were hardly propitious, this was the most important investigation since Radcliffe, and potentially, because of the focus on industry and trade, of great importance to the banks. The committee even published a separate, short, report on the financing of the oil industry which commented favourably on the work of the Edinburgh financial institutions.[47] Indeed, there was little in the avowed philosophy of the Bank with which Wilson disagreed. Had the Scottish banks decided to take the committee more seriously, then they might well have been able to focus the agenda more on their own concerns, foremost among which was the continued independence of the Scottish system. Moreover, the views of the board and the government coincided over the use of the oil revenues, which should not be squandered, as Lord Clydesmuir put it in 1977:

> oil and gas developments have contributed materially to the relative strength of the Scottish economy . . . although it may be that, as a source of new jobs, these developments have passed their peak . . . It is providential that our faltering national economy should have such a stout prop, but it is imperative, if our children's children are not to castigate us as a generation of profligates, that the oil revenues be treated as the seed corn of the future and not dissipated in maintaining an artificially high standard of living.

The challenges of these years encouraged some on the board in their view that the senior management required exceptional encouragement to proceed with internal reform and planning procedures. In 1974, Lord

---

46 Ibid., *Evidence on the Financing of Industry and Trade*, 6 (March 1978), evidence of the Committee of Scottish Clearing Bankers, pp. 122–48.
47 Committee to Review the Functioning of Financial Institutions, *The Financing of North Sea Oil*, Research Report no. 2 (London: 1978).

Balfour organised a thoroughgoing review of the performance since 1970, and this was incorporated into a new corporate plan presented to the board in November 1975. Total funds had grown from £581 million to £1,251 million in five years, while operating profits rose from £5,595,142 in 1971 to £18,806,161 in 1974 but then fell away, in part because of the provisions for bad debts and, more importantly, because of extra funding of the amalgamated pension fund covering all employees from the British Linen and Bank of Scotland, a complicated integration carried through by David Antonio.[48] A comparison of returns on assets for all UK banking groups showed that the Scottish banks all enjoyed relatively high operating margins. The Royal Bank was the strongest because of the activity of Lloyds and Scottish, the finance house, but its group was dragged down by losses at Williams and Glyn's. Bank of Scotland was similarly buoyed up by NWS, with little damage from losses in the secondary sector. Moreover, Bank of Scotland was exceptionally well placed on equity capital/deposits ratios and on free capital. The latter at 4.2 per cent was ahead of every other bank – 4.1 per cent for the Royal Bank, 3.0 per cent for Barclays and 1.8 per cent for the Midland. Bank of Scotland had the only balance sheet without a wholesale subordinated loan capital element. Such borrowing was a cheaper way of expanding the business base than equity, so the Bank was in an exceptionally strong position to increase its industrial advances should it need to. The exercise also showed that the core of the clearing bank's activity – domestic, commercial and industrial accounts and advances in association with a plethora of banking services – was less profitable than activity at NWS.

The board and the executive agreed that it would be foolhardy to diversify into higher-margin operations at the expense of branch banking, yet the growth of staff costs required a determined effort to increase turnover and margins. Unprofitable activities, in estate planning, securities, trustee and tax services, were given a lower profile and specific objectives. A modest diversification was endorsed, and a new International Division under James Young, as general manager, brought together the various activities in foreign exchange and Eurocurrency loans, advances in foreign currencies, and import and export services. It was well equipped to attract oil-related business in the USA, and the first office was opened in Houston, Texas, in 1976. A five-year profit plan was adopted. In 1976, the capital of Bank of Scotland Finance Company Ltd was increased to £8 million, and, using the procedures of the Private Legislation (Scotland) Act, the assets and liabilities were transferred into the dormant shell of the British Linen Bank which, with the consent of the Privy Council, had been preserved

---

48 See Statistical Appendix, Table A12, and footnotes 10 and 11 thereto.

following the merger of the former clearing bank with Bank of Scotland in 1971. However, the quid pro quo was that the bank would now register under Schedule VIII of the Companies Act, and on St Andrew's Day 1977 the finance company re-emerged with the name of British Linen Bank Ltd. By 1979, Bank of Scotland operating profits had reached £25,102,000. Of this figure, NWS contributed £7 million; the exceptional qualities of the management in Chester continued to build a platform for sustained growth.

A group of directors, among whom were Lord Balfour, James Gammell and Thomas Risk, were concerned that some of the senior managers were too influenced by the ideas and aspirations of ordinary branch banking. Moreover, and more worryingly, proposals for large foreign advances were placed before the Bank which followed questionable fashion in the City of London. A number of American and London bankers felt that it was safe to recycle the OPEC surpluses to overseas countries in the belief that a sovereign state could not fail to service its indebtedness. These included various schemes for lending to Latin America and countries in other less-developed regions.[49] In contrast to the short period in which senior managers held office and their perhaps over-long experience in the Inspectors Department and branch offices, the directors had the benefit of decades of experience of various businesses. They tended to be more cautious about advances in politically volatile countries and insisted that industry, oil, NWS and consumer spending should remain the bedrock of Bank of Scotland lending. Within a few years, the correctness of this judgement was confirmed.

In October 1976, Lord Balfour, who succeeded Sir Alistair Blair as chairman of NWS, and Thomas Risk, chairman of the British Linen Bank, were appointed the Deputy Governors, taking office in 1977. They made sure that for the next decade the executive was encouraged by an active and committed board. Together with other directors, they regarded several senior managers as less aggressive and flexible than some junior colleagues who appreciated both the threat from the City of London and the complexity of Scottish politics yet also had a remarkable feel for new business opportunities. This raised a difficult question regarding succession planning. Andrew Russell succeeded Thomas Walker as Treasurer in 1974 and was himself due to demit office at the end of the decade. One of several senior managers was expected to replace Russell. The directors decided that the potential threat of a takeover, and in such circumstances

49 BS 1/6, Minutes, 12 October 1976, request for $13 million Eurocurrency loan and £1 million sterling loan for Brazilian Federal railway system. The Bank analysis was mesmerised by the political regime in Brazil and the rate of growth to 1974. There was also a wish to help GEC and Balfour Beatty because of the potential beneficial effects on Scottish companies.

the possible acquiescence of the Bank of England, required a man of exceptional political sagacity with knowledge of both the strengths and drawbacks of London, combined with a ruthless determination to keep the Bank independent and progress the business. These directors convinced the board, which appointed Bruce Pattullo, then chief executive of the British Linen Bank, aged 41, as deputy Treasurer and chief general manager of Bank of Scotland with effect from 1 November 1979 on the understanding that he would succeed Russell, which duly followed on 4 July 1980. Fortunately for the Bank, the board made the right choice.

First and foremost, the work of Bank of Scotland in the two decades to 1978 indicated an overwhelming commitment to Scottish industry and trade, and to Bank customers in England and Wales. Thus the Bank continued the tradition of nearly three centuries of provision of funds for investment and expansion. The Bank was active in every area of the economy, and its impressive range of expertise was often a key factor in completion of plans for growth. The alacrity with which the Bank supported initiatives on Scottish oil and supported the heavy industries through numerous challenges underlined this. In this modern period, the Bank showed once again that it was prepared to nurse companies through adversity, provided of course that there was a sound possibility of recovery. There were losses in heavy industries, at Fairfields and Upper Clyde Shipbuilders for example; but the history of Scottish banking has been inseparable from industrial difficulties, and Bank of Scotland recognised this challenge and fully intended to continue with the same positive stance in the future.

The introduction of monthly financial accounting and profit and corporate planning, utilising the ideas from other industries, made an important contribution to Bank development in the 1970s and beyond. The skills learnt in these fields and the increasing diversification of the business formed the basis for substantial growth in the group. These changes were among the most important changes since the onset of the Industrial Revolution and the pioneering of the first modern branch networks in the world by Bank of Scotland and the British Linen. The new approach to staff and training allied to the new departments allowed management to flourish; as many officials tended to be younger, the Bank was guaranteed a wide pool of talent which could be drawn on for future developments. It was clear from the record of NWS that it too was building a sound cadre of future managers, and in the later 1970s its profits began a remarkable period of growth.

The history of these years confirmed that Bank of Scotland directors and managers, with their professional advisors, friends and associates, had the resources required to overcome a number of serious problems. They coped well with the strenuous efforts required in the amalgamation process and went on to manage the business in their own way, taking little from experience south of the Border. The 1970s confirmed the importance of directors, from both the Bank and the British Linen, strong enough to demand action from their managements, far-sighted in their horizons and politically astute, able to reach a huge network of business and political contacts. Fortunately for the Bank, this group was absolutely determined to keep the Bank truly independent. These directors built an effective foundation for the intense battles which now followed.

CHAPTER 27

BANK OF SCOTLAND: THREATS TO SCOTTISH BANKING, 1979–81

THE APPOINTMENT OF Bruce Pattullo as Treasurer and chief general manager of Bank of Scotland was the occasion for radical and urgent change. He came to the job with a clear vision of what was needed and with the full support of the board. By 1979, the figures showed that group pre-tax profits had become progressively less dependent on domestic banking. By contrast, North West Securities was showing especially strong returns, and the British Linen Bank and the International Division were also developing well. But for domestic banking – the core operations of Bank of Scotland – there was to be a stringent reappraisal. As one strong supporter of Bruce Pattullo's appointment reflected, 'We had to get this right, and quickly'. Bruce Pattullo knew that he had to find ways to encourage staff in branches to think positively about how they, as individuals and as part of their branch teams, could attract new business and new income. On 20 August 1979, he issued to all senior staff a circular letter in which he explained this new approach, later spoken of internally as 'empowerment'. The policy directly charged each branch manager and departmental head with the responsibility for identifying development opportunities and for building up the business under his or her control. This was only the first of many steps taken at that time to bring about a complete change in the culture of the Bank and in the attitudes of management and staff. Of course, for a time, not all were ready for the changes which the proposals were to bring about. Bruce Pattullo was fully aware of this, and he trod warily, some thought too much so, with some appointments and established procedures. As it transpired, extraordinary events were to occur within eighteen months which would make the timing of his appointment, and of his actions in placing a new, aggressive management team at the head of the Bank with a progressive business strategy, of even more vital importance than had been foreseen.

717

The need for a re-evaluation of domestic banking business was all too apparent, as the 1970s had not been kind. Pre-tax profit was the same in 1978 – £16.7 million – as five years earlier, well down in real terms. This decline reflected the substantial impact of cost and wage inflation. The increase in operating costs was concealed by a combination of high interest rates and wider deposit margins. In fact, the position was reached where, apart from major improvements in the banking price structure, profits could be maintained 'only by dependence on relatively high rates of interest'.[1] A restoration of real profitability would not occur until the growth of new advances 'significantly' exceeded the rate of cost inflation. The point was emphasised by the Governor, Lord Clydesmuir, in 1979: 'although high interest rates produce an immediate benefit in terms of profits, banks would far rather see an upsurge in economic activity accompanied by fuller utilisation of borrowing limits and a spate of new applications for finance'.[2] There was some scope for increasing real income through changes in pricing structures for commissions and fees, but for this there needed to be a measure of cooperation among all banks.

The 1979 profit plan for domestic banking showed that the loss of the Burmah Oil accounts in 1974 had slowed down the rate of growth, and that the long-term trend was not restored thereafter. In respect of operating profitability, Bank margins were consistently below those of the Royal Bank and, on average, slightly below those of the Clydesdale Bank. Both these had achieved better returns on equity, although that of the Clydesdale was accounted for by its lower capital base. The Royal Bank had managed a higher advances:deposits ratio, with a notably higher proportion of its sterling deposits in higher-yield assets. Bank of Scotland was more dependent on relatively low-yield assets. Some deposits were employed at low and even negative margins, which reduced the average return and depressed capital ratios. This last was a familiar predicament in banking history, and as the General Managers Committee had spent years on this problem before 1971 it was worrying to see it recur. Staff costs were also higher per capita than at the Royal Bank or the Clydesdale.

In everyday commercial and retail banking, there was unambiguous information available that it was the Royal Bank which had the largest share of prime banking relationships in Scotland. Further, the Royal Bank did better with all corporate accounts in Scotland; Bank of Scotland's marketing department suggested that out of the 'Scottish top 500' companies the Bank held only 27 per cent of the main accounts (see Table 27.1).[3] The overall figures for advances, sector by sector, showed

1 BS, Board papers, Strategic Plan, 1979–83, p. 5.
2 BS 1/2, Proprietors' Minutes, 283rd Annual General Meeting, 8 May 1979.
3 BS, Board papers, Strategic Plan, 1979–83, p. 12. See also Statistical Appendix, Table A11.

Table 27.1 *Distribution of the prime banking relationships*

	Of the top 112 companies [1] (%)	Of the top 200 companies [2] (%)
Royal Bank of Scotland	41	50
Bank of Scotland	31	24
Clydesdale Bank	23	23
Others	5	3
	100	100

Notes:
1 The top 112 companies in Scotland, defined by *The Banker*.
2 The top 200 companies in Scotland, defined by an ORC survey.

Source: BS 1/6, Board papers, Strategic Plan, 1979–83, p. 12.

an unwelcome decline in manufacturing industry. The competition was fierce in the key sectors of local authority lending and to the professions and services trades, with some competition from the offices of the English and other banks which had arrived since the start of the oil boom. These evaluations must be assessed cautiously because each clearing bank had its own accounting figures which gave clearer measures of true profitability; but, as these were inevitably complicated and commercially sensitive, they were not disclosed, and simpler comparisons, for instance on the return on assets and return on equity, were used to measure performance. On these admittedly inadequate figures, Bank of Scotland was 'rather less profitable' than the Royal Bank or the Clydesdale; but the position compared favourably with the English clearing banks.

Under the 'gentlemen's agreements' which had emerged after the Parliamentary inquiry of 1876, the Scottish banks had agreed not to expand in England beyond London, and, in the case of the Clydesdale, not to extend its north-of-England branch network. Conversely, the English banks would not press for legislation to stop the Scottish banks' right of banknote issue, nor would they open branches in Scotland, although that was not raised as a serious possibility at the time. Events since then had altered perceptions. If the Scottish banks were to have competition in Scotland from the English banks, why should they not compete in England? In the London area, the Bank was 'clearly a small fish'; but the sheer size of the pool offered opportunities in domestic banking. International Division was also well placed for participation in syndicated loans, even if it was unlikely that there would be many opportunities to act as a lead bank, except perhaps in oilfield financings. In 1980, the first move was made when the British Linen Bank opened an office in the City of London with the intention of offering corporate and lending services[4] which could

4 'Scottish Banks: A Story for Hogmanay', *The Banker*, 130 (January 1980), 112–13.

be accommodated 'without significant growth of infrastructure'. There was considerable support from Scots working for foreign and domestic companies. Instructions were also issued to the London management and branches reporting to them to seek out corporate business, and more staff were sent from Scotland.

However, the major challenge and opportunity was seen to be outside London, with an expansion of the Bank's traditional business of lending and deposit-gathering. Competition in London was always fierce. In the wealth-creating regions of England, patronisingly regarded by many in London as 'the provinces', there was much good business to be done which had been left relatively unattended by this concentration of banking head offices in London following the spate of mergers based on the dubious fashion for size. A careful study within the Bank led to the conclusion that the Birmingham area offered the best opportunity for the Bank's first venture into the mainstream of English domestic branch banking. In 1980, a regional office was opened in Birmingham designed to attract business customers.[5] The management at the new Birmingham office also found a strong customer preference for transferring the whole account to the Bank, not just for using it as a secondary relationship. The office was profitable within one year, not the three originally targeted.

The Bank carried out detailed assessments of the personal-account sector within Scotland. As time passed, old-style deposits were considered less important for funding advances, as banks could look to inter-bank borrowing and corporate deposits when they wished to increase their lending portfolio. Nevertheless, the personal market remained a cornerstone of activity in Scotland, not least because the personal loan market, sales of insurance products and some other fee-based earnings gave good returns. In respect of deposits, UK banks had benefited in the decade to 1974 by the fall in the proportion of savings held in National Savings certificates (42.5 to 21.1 per cent), and bank deposits had risen from 34.2 to 40 per cent. But competition from building societies was growing; they had simpler management structures and offered a narrow range of products, mainly mortgages. They offered higher rates of interest and thereby attracted many deposits, so that the proportion of deposits in the societies was close, by 1974, to that held by the banks, up from 21.6 to 38 per cent. By 1979, the societies had pushed well ahead, to 47.1 per cent of total personal-sector deposits, compared to only 31.9 per cent for the banks.[6] There was also evidence that the growth in the proportion of owner-occupied homes tied savers to building societies. Although the competition from building

5 See Appendix 13.
6 D. Vittas and P. Frazer, 'Competition in Retail Banking', *The Banker*, 130 (February 1980), 47–51.

societies was weaker in Scotland, there were lessons to be learnt, and the Royal Bank, for example, launched its own house mortgage scheme. North of the Border, there was also more competition from the Trustee Savings Banks in the personal market.[7]

Bank of Scotland noted all these trends, and senior managers were regularly provided with surveys of personal customer attitudes and the performance of the Bank's products, such as Scotbudget, Scotloan and other new schemes. The main difficulty with the personal sector – familiar to bankers – was to distinguish between groups which would maintain good balances and those which would borrow, also distinguishing those expensive to service and at risk of default. Further, some branches had many low-paid customers who were risky to lend to, located in areas out of which residents who progressed with their jobs were only too keen to move. The Bank's own surveys came down firmly in favour of caution; pensioners, professional people and middle-class housewives tended to maintain high average deposits, while the average balances maintained by manual and clerical workers were the lowest of all groups. Junior professionals, the skilled working class and students also provided good customer bases. There was a gratifying increase of 26.6 per cent in student accounts over the three years to 1979, which, among other explanations, owed something to the weakening association of the British Linen Bank with the Barclays–South Africa connection. There was also a serious problem with product targeting. Advertising, image and implementation were assessed, in the Strategic Plan for 1979–83, as poor compared with the Royal Bank and the Clydesdale Bank. The Scotbudget service, for example, was heavily advertised but had not been taken up in any numbers, 'largely, it would appear, because of resistance from branch managers', who contended that it was time-consuming to monitor and control.

After the somewhat mixed view of the Bank's structure and performance in early 1979, the management accountant and his staff were given the task of trying to assess the environment and outlook in the next four years. Their response involved two quite different approaches. For longer-term planning, they were to think about market conditions and to comment in a general way about likely changes, for example, in international affairs, the regulatory framework and the economy. The second part, the examination of specific targets on profit projection, continued to involve the rigorous methodology of linking profits and income to scenarios on inflation, together with questions on how projected shortfalls in the real value of profits could be met by new business directions. These

---

7 For the Trustee Savings Banks in Scotland, see M. Moss and A. Slaven, *From Ledger Book to Laser Beam. A History of the TSB in Scotland from 1810 to 1990* (Edinburgh: n.d. [1992]), ch. 9.

specific targets were also infused with a knowledge provided by branch reports and an insight into change which provided surprisingly accurate results.[8]

In the aftermath of the 1974 oil-price rise, the oil producers of the Middle East placed considerable sums with western banks, so that international debt formed a rising part of bank portfolios. The problem for the banks was how to find, in turn, suitable lending opportunities where the cash flow from profits or taxation would be sufficient to repay the advance. In normal circumstances, the instinct of the banker would have been to ask some basic questions, such as: what were the ratios of existing debt to the expected flow of income? If relevant, what was the currency-earning capacity? How much debt was long-term? If cash flow declined by, say, 25 per cent or even 50 per cent, what would happen to repayment capacity? And, crucially, in cases of sovereign lending, what was the long-term repayment record of the country concerned? After 1974, the sums arriving on deposit from the oil producers were so huge that some of the basic questions were ignored, or played less of a role in decisions on advances than they would have done in normal times. By 1979, several Latin American states, notably Mexico and Brazil, had built up a ratio of foreign debts to available earnings where default looked possible, should difficulties arise in these countries. Further, many companies operating there were also building up debts at an alarming rate.[9] The City view was that investment in Latin America was safe, and Barclays Bank was pressing International Division. Had this relaxed stance triumphed, then Bank of Scotland would not have had the lowest share of any UK clearing bank in Latin American debts.[10] The Bank avoided the worst excesses because of reservations among the board and management over the assessment of lending to Latin America. As one director put it, these were 'crumbs from other men's tables'. Moreover, within the Bank group, other opportunities for lending funds were being found by the British Linen Bank, North West Securities and, for UK corporate lending, by the Bank itself.

In 1981, François Mitterrand, a socialist, was elected President of France, and his new government announced that it would take control of those private banks and financial institutions remaining in private hands, Banque Worms et Cie included. There were deep-seated historical reasons for this, which went back to the occupation of France in the Second World War. Bank of Scotland took this in its stride and offered detailed advice for the negotiations with the French government, and adequate

8 BS, Board papers, Strategic Plan, 1979–83.
9 For an example of optimism, see M. Blanden, 'The Changing Shape of the Future', *The Banker*, 130 (September 1980), 87–90.
10 See below, Chapter 29.

compensation was forthcoming. The association with Banque Worms et Cie and the good personal relationships which were formed during the period helped the growing internationalism within the Bank, but the outcome reinforced a view that the holding of minority stakes in other banking organisations was not a desirable method of extending the Bank's business.

The discussions within the Bank on the domestic, industrial and commercial picture, from which the Strategic Plan of 1979 was drawn up, proved extremely prescient. It was forecast that as the UK became a net exporter of oil the balance of payments would strengthen and so would sterling, but this would do little for 'low home productivity and uncompetitive exports'. As other countries developed their economic bases, 'current British manufactures may well become unsaleable abroad'. Unemployment was not expected to fall, and the Bank estimated that 500,000 jobs were at risk. Contraction was inevitable in Scotland in the traditional heavy industries, and the problems of the Strathclyde area were likely to worsen. There was also concern about takeovers. It was a common complaint that steady support by the Scottish banks for companies over the years, which meant that they expanded, merely put them into consideration for takeover. In this event, the banks would be denied further opportunities for advances and would often lose the prime banking relationship as well. This was a worrying matter, as takeovers also caused decreases in incomes for other professional clients who had previously supplied services to the company taken over.

The opportunities for Bank of Scotland within the UK as a whole were nevertheless considerable. Banking transaction volumes were expected to continue rising by 7–8 per cent per annum, with growth supported by a shift from weekly to monthly wage payments. Rising personal incomes for the more favoured groups were expected to be a key force in expansion of demand, associated with changes in household expenditures which would favour durable consumer and other expensive household goods. Long-term marketing strategies, focused on new products, were to be developed which would encourage the personal-deposit customers to use additional Bank services. Although the Bank had already introduced improved systems, the growth in transaction volumes might mean more staff. So productivity and the proportion of profitable work had to rise.

With the reassurance of the evidence provided by this well-focused assessment procedure, the management drew up a new domestic banking strategy. For the retail areas, it was agreed to strengthen the marketing effort and to improve advertising. It was known within the Bank that many families had held accounts for generations, and most who opened new accounts expected to keep them. The marketing department was asked to produce clear plans which related to this customer base, such as new insurance products and the ability to issue Barclaycards. By 1983, the Bank offered several new ways of borrowing and of conducting accounts, discussed below, and felt justified in its view that Bank of Scotland was 'A Friend for Life', the new slogan used alongside the Bank's logo.[11] The number of active deposit accounts was to be reduced by persuading customers to switch to the current-account system. The computing and marketing departments were to work together so that customers could be issued with cards for withdrawals at cash dispensers. Problems at the low-profit branches were addressed and closures implemented. The usual targets and profit performance tables for divisions were looked at with renewed energy; after nearly a decade of implementing Alan Jessiman's advice, there were still too many managers unenthusiastic about relating performance to targets, even for simple measures such as sales of insurance products.

With the efforts to pull in new business beginning to show results, the management recognised the need to ensure that the Bank group's long-term capacity should not be constrained by shortage of capital. The Bank itself had an increasing appetite for funds, and it was clear that the growth potential of North West Securities and the British Linen would further raise the group requirement. In the absence of equivalent deposits, which hitherto had come from Scotland, 'market borrowing would also require to increase', and more deposits would need to be garnered from England and overseas. In the next decade, the spread of offices attracted some funds which apparently resulted from the appeal to customers of depositing in a bank almost three centuries old. Further, the needs of the group had to be viewed as a whole to minimise the demands on the market. Expertise with balance-sheet management and the optimisation of taxable capacity was required to support the leasing business of North West Securities and of Capital Leasing, a subsidiary of the British Linen. While the Mound had reservations on how to account for unprovided deferred tax, the Bank of England ruled that this should be regarded as capital. The importance which such matters were beginning to assume, and the need for new skills, became a factor in some senior appointments.

In May 1979, the minority Labour government, which for over two years had governed with the support of the Liberal Party, was defeated at the general election and was replaced by a Conservative administration led by Margaret Thatcher. The incoming government pursued a monetary policy which strengthened the pound sterling. Against the major international currencies index, the pound rose steadily from the spring of

11 See below, Chapter 29.

1979 to reach 96.1 by December 1980 and 105.6 in January 1981. Against the US dollar, the most commonly-quoted comparison, the pound went from $2.07 in May 1979 to $2.39 in December 1980 and a little higher for a month thereafter before it began to weaken. This period of strength had a severe and adverse effect on much domestic manufacturing. There was criticism in the press and, privately, among bankers.[12] Support from public funds for the nationalised industries and private companies alike was curtailed. One overall effect was a reduction in the UK GDP of around 3 per cent in 1980, and industrial production fell by over 10 per cent. In the steel industry, heavy engineering, vehicles and machine tools, the decline was sharper. In Scotland, ship launchings in 1980 were only 53 per cent of the five-year average to 1979. The yards found it difficult to compete with builders supported by governments abroad, and with little sympathy at Westminster capacity reduction was inevitable.[13]

Industrial production in Scotland had moved little from 1975 to 1979 (around 100 on the British government index) but in 1980 fell rapidly, and after a mild recovery in 1982 was down to below 90 the following year. In 1978 and most of 1979, there was little change in employment in the production industries, at around 830,000.[14] In the final quarter of 1979, however, employment dropped sharply and three years later was down to 623,000. In the same time, registered unemployment in Scotland rose from 160,000 to 316,000. As the recession deepened, a succession of long-established companies closed their plants – the Invergordon aluminium smelter, the Bathgate British Leyland plant, Singer's sewing-machine factory in Clydebank, among numerous famous names. Although the largest single accounts were customers via the London offices, by number of bad and doubtful debts it was the Scottish east and west areas of the Bank that suffered most.[15] Bank reports mentioned a variety of difficulties over cash flow, high interest rates and sales in overseas markets, and the ease with which foreign companies, benefiting from the high pound, could sell in the UK.

By 1980, the Mound had noticed an erosion of morale among business-men. Accounts and audited statements would be late in delivery, promises of capital raising and restructuring would not materialise, contracts about to be signed would evaporate and deadlines on payments of interest would pass unmet. There were cases where profitable subsidiaries with strong

12 Central Statistical Office, *Financial Statistics*, 230 (June 1981), Exchange rates.
13 P. L. Payne, 'The Decline of the Scottish Heavy Industries, 1945–1983', in R. Saville (ed.), *The Economic Development of Modern Scotland 1950–1980* (Edinburgh: 1985), pp. 79–113 (p. 107 Table 12).
14 Scottish Office, *Scottish Economic Bulletin*, 28 (1983).
15 Compulsory and creditors' liquidations for industrial companies were 274 in 1978, 238 in 1979, 371 in 1980, 438 in 1981 and 503 in 1982: Scottish Office, *Scottish Economic Bulletin*, 28 (1983).

balance sheets were used in the recession as funding vehicles by their owners. There were a number of cases of outright fraud, and all these problems put senior Bank managers in a difficult position. Many of the companies were long-standing customers – as far back as the eighteenth century in some cases, and many from the later Industrial Revolution. The Bank's ethos, shared with the Royal Bank and the Clydesdale, was to help a management in every way possible. Advice would be given on company doctors, staff would examine businesses directly, connections would be made with other funding agencies, and introductions would be given to those who might be able to facilitate the raising of new capital from the markets or to arrange a capital reconstruction. It was not in the interests of any Scottish bank to see a company close with the resulting loss of jobs, additional provisioning for bad debts, the knock-on effect on other customers, and the great personal distress which always accompanied bankruptcy. This monitoring required the traditional expertise of the branch manager, much to the delight of many who were concerned about the new emphasis on marketing. There was also considerable social pressure from the Kirk, the Scottish Trades Union Congress and the media to support firms in trouble. On occasion, when the prospects for a company looked grim but the businessman was prepared to offer all his personal assets, it was more humane to close it down. The Bank worked closely with the HIDB, the SDA, ICFC and the Scottish Office to try and rescue firms in trouble, but on occasions a closure could not be avoided.

In instances where companies owed the Bank and other creditors substantial sums, the Bank looked long and hard at a variety of routes whereby a smaller, more focused company, after capital restructuring, might trade profitably. This usually involved the Bank in some loss, for example in the conversion of overdraft to preference shares, or partial loan write-offs. But these avenues were often preferable to liquidation. Discussions were especially interesting over general engineering companies, which would typically have a range of projects and outputs and often service contracts at home and abroad. It was rare for all of these to be loss-making. Sometimes the newly-restructured hived-off companies could obtain a wide range of financial support, new capital, leasing facilities and overdrafts, and be secure in the knowledge that Bank of Scotland group would take a long-term view of their requirements.

In summary, the closures and falls in output and profits meant that the specific targets of the 1979 corporate plan had to be revised. In particular, the three years of recession in which activity in Scotland fell further and deeper than in England underlined the continuing urgency of the tasks, and the opportunities, which lay ahead for the group. Fortunately, the Bank itself, North West Securities and the British Linen were ready to develop their businesses and were well attuned to the need for internal change.

Among the more challenging tasks for Scottish bankers over the years has been the conduct of relations with the City of London. The British commercial banking system since the mid-nineteenth century has evinced strong centralising tendencies. By 1979, there were only five large English domestic clearing banks, all with their headquarters in London. Numerous international banks which conducted some domestic UK lending were also represented in London, and many of these derived income and fees from the management of equity portfolios and the support for, or opposition to, takeovers and mergers.

In the political conditions of 1974–9, with a Labour government in power and ten Scottish National Party MPs, a proposal to take over a Scottish bank, hostile or not, would have raised considerable opposition and was described by one authority as 'a political impossibility'. It was this political and nationalist dimension of the few years before 1979 which delayed City of London interest in Scottish banks and quoted companies. Some attention was paid to bank nationalisation, by bankers and on the fringes of the Labour Party, but such a policy had long been ruled out by a majority of the Parliamentary party and leadership. Nevertheless, some bankers spent time worrying about this after 1974, and it is interesting to speculate on whether their discussions encouraged City of London financiers in the view that the Edinburgh banks would have no objection to being part of the City, in the sense of being owned there.

For the bankers at the Mound, continued independence was crucial and, by extension, so was the independence of the Royal Bank and the arm's-length attitude adopted by the Midland Bank to the Clydesdale. This was seen as fundamental to the Scottish system of banking, and was soon to be thoroughly tested. The largest stockholder in Bank of Scotland was Barclays Bank, owning 35 per cent of the stock, which gave a voting entitlement of 24.5 per cent. The position was governed by the agreement between the two banks of May 1969, in respect of the merger with the British Linen Bank, that 'Barclays Bank will not seek to increase or decrease its stockholding in the Bank of Scotland without prior consultation with, and approval of, the Bank of Scotland Board'.[16] If another party acquired 10 per cent or more of Bank of Scotland capital, Barclays would be free after prior consultation with the Bank to take such action as was necessary to protect its interests. This did not arise before 1979, and from the experience of the 1970s Barclays would have been unlikely to take any action which prejudiced independence. Indeed,

16 For the full text, see above, Chapter 25.

relations between the two Barclays directors on the board of the Bank and their fellow directors were described as constructive, and in many respects Barclays showed enthusiasm about the specialised corporate developments inaugurated by the Bank, particularly those on oil. This was, of course, a strengthening of Barclays' investment.

Nevertheless, there were strains. Barclays had the lead position in several loans to Latin American governments and companies, and was keen that Bank of Scotland should participate. The Bank's unwillingness to support this lending to the desired level was a cause for comment. The Barclays corporate plans tended to view the Bank more as a subsidiary, and complementary to itself, rather than as a long-term trade investment. The poor performance of the Scottish personal banking side from 1975 raised further questions. A number of English companies held accounts with branches of Bank of Scotland in Scotland, but the growing number in London was seen as sometimes unwelcome competition. Several Barclays directors were perturbed at the success of North West Securities, set against the rest of the industry and especially the poorer performance of Mercantile Credit, the Barclays finance house. There were complaints about competition from Bank of Scotland International Division and the proposals for establishing more English provincial offices.

The senior managers at the Mound were not surprised when, during a 'diffuse conversation' with their opposite numbers at Barclays on 5 December 1979, these reservations were raised in the context of whether the Barclays stockholding should be extended or diluted.[17] The Polwarth–Thomson agreements of 1969 were no longer 'acceptable to Barclays', although the Barclays side understood the force of these arrangements in banking circles; any disinvestment required a credible explanation, and suitable negotiation would take a long time. A fortnight later, Lord Clydesmuir, together with Thomas Risk (who had been appointed a Deputy Governor in 1979), Bruce Pattullo and Joan Smith, Secretary of the Bank, met Sir Richard Pease and William Birkbeck, the two Barclays directors who sat on Bank of Scotland's board. The preferred position of the Bank was for 'no change whatsoever'. If Barclays felt very strongly, however, the board of Bank of Scotland could be persuaded to accept a reduction to 20–25 per cent, 'provided this was coupled with a renewal of the present undertaking in respect of the residual stockholding'. The board was totally opposed to a reduction below 10 per cent. A number of points were raised by the Bank, of significance to subsequent events:[18]

17 BS, Uncatalogued, Miscellaneous papers, Note of meeting at Barclays, Lombard Street, 5 December 1979.
18 BS, Uncatalogued, Miscellaneous papers, 'Barclays Stockholding in Bank of Scotland', 18 December 1979.

The assurances between our two banks, covered in the correspondence between Lord Polwarth and Sir John Thomson on 20 May 1969 and in a subsequent circular letter to Proprietors, were clear and specific. A reduction to the lower level [of 10 per cent] would not be in keeping with the term or spirit of those assurances.

Moreover,

In UK stock market terms, a continued holding of 20 per cent or more is accepted as significant. A residual holding of 9 per cent would have no such significance [and] would lead to periodic speculation and the need for a significant amount of management time to be devoted to this end.

Mention was made of the effect that a reduction below 20 per cent might have on the currency deposit markets, and there were the recent changes in top management at the Mound to consider (out of the seven most senior posts, four had changed in eighteen months). It was difficult to comprehend the concern within Barclays, at a strategic level, in respect of the real competition which the Bank provided.

Representatives of the two boards later agreed that matters should be left at the status quo, but that 'Barclays desire for some reduction was noted, and that ideally Bank of Scotland, which it was acknowledged needed to reduce its overdependence on the Scottish economy, might identify a strategic development to which a partial disinvestment by Barclays might be conveniently and publicly related'.[19] Both banks were now experiencing the onset of the recession, and the time of senior management was focused more on controlling the growth of bad debts. So the matter rested for the time being.

For many years, the City of London has been confident in thinking of itself as a collection of firms able to operate in a world framework offering all sorts of financial services. The secondary banking crisis was now behind them, and they expected to emerge as the clear leaders of European financial markets. To many in the City, a financial centre in Scotland, although contributing to UK earnings, had little relevance. Bank of Scotland – alongside many other companies – had correctly identified a serious problem with the psychology of the City of London: unsubstantiated rumours about possible takeover targets could persuade company treasurers, unit-trust and pension-fund managers to buy stocks for short-term gains. As J. M. Keynes put it in 1936, the professional investor and the speculator are concerned 'not with what an investment is

19 BS, Uncatalogued, Miscellaneous papers, *Aide-mémoire* for T. H. Bevan from T. N. Risk, for meeting on 31 March 1982.

really worth to a man who buys it 'for keeps', but with what the market will value it at, under the influence of mass psychology, three months or a year hence'.[20] Such behaviour was interested not in long-term forecasts of yields over the life of an investment, but with changes in the value of the stock 'a short time ahead'. Furthermore, stockbrokers and jobbers had no reason to discourage these market rumours which led to increased turnover and generated commission. Thus companies faced threats to their integrity from needs unrelated to those facing them as commercial concerns.

Takeovers of banks were, however, viewed rather differently, and the Bank of England took a clear view of its responsibilities. There were substantive questions; in 1976, when the deputy managing director of Standard Chartered Bank and Sir Michael Herries of the Royal Bank had brief talks on a possible merger, this proposal would have faced considerable political hurdles.[21] The election of 1979 changed this. In that year, Lloyds Bank, with 16.8 per cent of the Royal Bank stock, had brief discussions on similar lines, but these overtures were rejected. On 29 September 1980, Standard Chartered Bank made another secret approach, followed by Lloyds again the next day. After informing the Bank of England, the Royal Bank and Standard Chartered continued their negotiations. There was now every chance of other parties making a bid for the Royal Bank. *The Banker* suggested that what the 'seekers after clean, crisp competition would really like to see is a foreign takeover of a major existing British operation'. The fount of this 'clean, crisp competition', whatever that meant, was guessed as Citibank, a us-based company which was rumoured to be interested in the Royal Bank.[22] Citibank already owned 49 per cent of Grindlays Bank, taken up in the aftermath of the 1974 banking crisis.[23] The Royal Bank shares were well below the net asset value of the group, and it seemed a good buy, made easier by rumours of alleged difficulties between the managements of the Royal Bank and of Williams and Glyn's Bank. On 16 March 1981, the boards of the Royal Bank and Standard Chartered agreed terms: one Standard share and 50p in cash for every five Royal Bank shares (worth £334 million). Lloyds Bank immediately made an offer, announced the following day, for the stock of Lloyds and Scottish, the finance house founded by Ian Macdonald of the Commercial Bank, in which the Royal Bank and Lloyds held 39.3 per cent each. It was

20 J. M. Keynes, *The General Theory of Employment, Interest and Money* (London: 1936; repr. 1970), pp. 154–5.
21 For brief details, see Monopolies and Mergers Commission, *The Hongkong and Shanghai Banking Corporation, Standard Chartered Bank Limited, The Royal Bank of Scotland Group Limited: A Report on the Proposed Mergers*, Cmnd 8472 (London: 1982).
22 T. Hindle, 'Sizing up the Retail Market', *The Banker*, 130 (November 1980), 111–19.
23 In 1979, Grindlays management and Citibank held discussions with Bank of Scotland about a possible purchase by the Bank of the Citibank operation.

highly profitable, and Lloyds swiftly raised its holding above 50 per cent. The loss of this operation was the first Scottish casualty of the Standard Chartered proposal.

Standard Chartered ranked fifty-second in the world bank ratings. It had been formed in 1969 from a merger of the Chartered Bank (founded in 1853) which was strong in the Far East, the Middle East and India, and the Standard Bank (1862) with strong links in Africa. Its overdependence on these markets persuaded the Standard Chartered board to diversify and buy the Hodge Group, a financial holding company, in 1974, and to expand in the UK. In 1979, Standard Chartered enlarged its presence in North America with the purchase of the Union Bank, California, twenty-fourth in size in the USA. These additions gave the group 50,000 staff, in sixty countries, with 1,500 offices. Most of the shares were held in the UK, and the head office was in London. After the announcement, the Hongkong and Shanghai Banking Corporation informed the Bank of England that it, too, wished to purchase the Royal Bank. Registered in Hong Kong, it was larger than Standard Chartered at thirty-third in the world ratings. It had acquired the Mercantile Bank and the British Bank of the Middle East in 1959, and more recently Antony Gibbs, a London merchant bank, and 51 per cent of the Marine Midland Bank of New York. Relations with Peking had varied since 1949, but were improving as more offices were opened in China. Although the Bank of England was opposed to this expression of interest, HSBC went on to offer a much higher price on 7 April – worth £498 million – comprising eight of its shares for every five Royal Bank shares and cash. An enhanced offer followed from Standard Chartered. This was a battle between two colonial banks 'searching for their post-colonial role', and 'at our expense', noted one senior authority at Bank of Scotland. The Office of Fair Trading referred the proposals to the Monopolies and Mergers Commission on 1 May.

The reasons for the interest in the Royal Bank were fully aired before the MMC, and need not be rehearsed. There were, however, conflicting strands in the evidence, especially over the future structure of the Royal Bank group. Both suitors offered the Royal Bank access to their foreign markets: 'a major UK bank, if it is to be fully competitive in modern conditions', had to have 'a strong presence in the major industrial and financial centres of the world [and] assets of sufficient size and quality to handle the largest transactions without unacceptable risk'.[24] Royal Bank customers could be better served through the colonials' networks, which would save the bank the need to build up its own connections. There was little dispute about the bigger role in international financing for the proposed group,

24 Monopolies and Mergers Commission, *Hongkong and Shanghai*, p. 49.

although how the service to existing customers of the Royal Bank could be improved was less clear. Those active overseas usually had relations with several banks, and, once established, conducted business in a variety of ways. The Royal Bank group had a wide network of overseas correspondents; the advantage to domestic customers of a limited number of overseas branches over correspondent services was (and is today) minimal. So this was a largely spurious argument. Further, the sort of larger share in international finance proposed by the colonial banks was typically conducted at very fine margins and did not improve the profitability of the lender; domestic UK advances provided wider margins. Both suitors saw a sterling deposit base as complementary to, and serving, overseas operations within strategies of broadening post-colonial positions. It was less clear how the dual structures of the Royal Bank and Williams and Glyn's domestic banking networks could be continued with the full range of their existing expertise. This concern was applicable to the Royal Bank's Eurocurrency loan portfolio; there would be little point in keeping this. Similar pressures would exist in fund-management functions such as client portfolios and group pension funds. Thus key investment expertise would be lost from Edinburgh. While assurances were, of course, given by the bidders to the MMC about the status quo, these did nothing to dispel fears among Royal Bank managers that the structure would evolve so that their Scottish base would no longer be involved with international trade and foreign operations. There would be, it was bound sooner or later to be suggested, a logic in combining these and other operations either in London or abroad with the existing offices of the colonials. There would be no advantage viewed from London in sharing decision-making about the English retail network with management in Edinburgh. Indeed, the Royal Bank and Williams and Glyn's operated as 'virtually independent banks'. Moreover, the performance of the Williams and Glyn's network in the five years before 1980 was somewhat better. This differing performance and dual structure even led Standard Chartered to suggest that the takeover would lead to the 'creation in Scotland of a major new decision-making unit', with the possibility that an independent Royal Bank group, within which Williams and Glyn's was growing faster than the Royal Bank of Scotland, 'would become increasingly centred on London'.[25] Even the Royal Bank refused to be explicit on the probable location of the headquarters of the proposed UK Domestic Division, although Standard Chartered suggested that it could be in Scotland if this was made a condition of approval. With both proposals, it was difficult to see how 'guarantees' could be regulated and enforced against the argument for centralising UK domestic banking

25 Ibid., p. 55.

at Williams and Glyn's in London, along with everything else. Even the chairman of the Royal Bank was reported as having said that 'assurances of autonomy given now could easily change'.[26]

The use of the term 'merger' to describe what increasingly appeared as a takeover aroused considerable dissent in Scotland. There were urgent discussions among Scottish institutions, including the Scottish Office and the Scottish Council, as to the best way to stop the proposals. After eighteen months of recession, Scottish Conservative politicians were generally united in their opposition. George Younger, Secretary of State for Scotland, 'let it be known in his usual discreet fashion' that he did not look kindly on the Standard Chartered bid, but Alex Fletcher, the industry minister, was 'more vociferous, telling anyone who will listen that in his private view the Royal Bank board is composed of "traitors to Scotland"'.[27] The Scotsman and the Glasgow Herald left little doubt as to business opinion, and the Labour Party, the Scottish National Party and the STUC added their voices. Thus the question became one for Scotland, not just for stockholders. The government, whose popularity had fallen sharply by the spring of 1981 and remained at a low point for another year, was faced with a major political difficulty. The referral to the MMC gave a breathing space.

The board of Bank of Scotland met on 24 March. The position of the Governor, the Treasurer, the directors and line management was clear: the proposals were to be treated as a very serious threat to Scottish business and employment, which, moreover, could easily snowball into a threat against the Bank. The Scottish Council had been quite effective in talking to businessmen, but the detailed consequences were 'not yet appreciated by the public at large'. The board was reminded by those with experience of the City of London 'how unfashionable it had become for a board of directors faced with a bid . . . to have regard to any aspect thereof beyond the short-term purely financial gain to the shareholder'. Emphasis on what was in the public interest thus formed the first, and foremost, plank on which the board rested its opposition. Concern over the attitude of Barclays was also considered as a factor. It was made clear that within the City the reaction would be based purely on the economic and financial case; thus William Birkbeck urged that the board's 'wider view, as seen from Scotland, should be made plain and stated clearly'. Lord Clydesmuir, Thomas Risk and Bruce Pattullo met Sir Anthony Tuke, chairman of Barclays, and other Barclays directors in London on 30 March.

The discussions were, to an extent, reassuring. Sir Anthony made it clear that his board had no intention of making a bid for Bank of Scotland,

26 BS, Uncatalogued, Miscellaneous papers, submission to MMC, Summary of views, p. 5.
27 'Royal Bank: Scottish Syndrome Strikes', The Banker, 131 (June 1981), 22–3.

and neither he nor his successor would wish their bank to make a bid which did not have the support of the Mound. He had no wish to reopen the discussions of December 1979, and even encouraged Bruce Pattullo to utilise Scottish sentiment to the advantage of Bank of Scotland. Nevertheless, Sir Anthony made it clear that the merger between the Royal Bank and Standard Chartered looked to him 'a natural one'. After the disappearance of the Royal Bank as an independent unit, Bank of Scotland might wish to make up its own mind as to what its correct stance might be. Changed circumstances, in other words, might change minds.

Back home, there was no shortage of advice and active lobbying of officials, MPs, civil servants, government ministers and luminaries in the Conservative Party, even members of the European Parliament. It was the only topic for dinner parties among the establishment as it became clearer to wives what their husbands' prospects might be after a takeover. There was also, unsurprisingly, strong opposition within the Royal Bank. Clearly, this was another occasion in Scottish banking history which called for decisive leadership. Thomas Risk, Bruce Pattullo, Alan Jessiman and A. T. Gibson formed a group with the remit to prepare submissions to the MMC, although many others were involved with the supply of facts and figures. There were other tasks, particularly in the political arena, but the case for Scottish banking had to be finely honed on matters of competition and financial development. The key objective for the Bank was to show why banks in Scotland should remain independent, with their head offices in Scotland, in a context where an increased proportion of business was sourced outwith Scotland. Furthermore, it was necessary to remind the outside world that the standards of service offered by the Scottish bankers provided a source of competition for the English clearers. In the final analysis, the MMC had to be persuaded on these grounds. The case on employment was straightforward but was of little value under the new government.

It was of central importance that the MMC should realise that this was no ordinary takeover. If approved, it would be interpreted as an admission that the demise of independent Scottish banking was unimportant, and the loss of Bank of Scotland might swiftly follow. That this was a real possibility was brought home by stockmarket rumours. It was essential, therefore, that the MMC consider the larger issue. It should not conclude that the retention of 'independent Scottish banks was without significance to the economic, social and natural well-being of Scotland'. But a focus on the commercial justification of the status quo was also crucial. The role of the Scottish banks in the development of UK commercial and retail banking had to be made clear. Head offices of six insurance companies, including the largest mutual company in Europe,

The Standard Life Assurance Co., and over thirty investment trusts, fifteen fund managers and seven merchant banks operated from Edinburgh. There were also four insurance companies in Glasgow, two investment trusts in Dundee, one in Aberdeen, and General Accident in Perth.[28] This specialist expertise in Scotland had been of central importance in the financial arrangements for commercial and industrial development, and the MMC was directed to S. G. Checkland's *Scottish Banking: A History, 1695–1973* for the historical background. However useful it would have been to utilise the historical record as evidence, at this time the data for the post-1914 era were not available, except largely in an unsorted archive, although there was very useful information which had been collected for the Wilson Committee, much of which had not been used for that purpose. Nevertheless, it was obvious that there was something special about the business and professional environment in Scotland that enabled local institutions and banks to support the recent investment in North Sea oil, both in traditional forms and in new financing vehicles. Anything which weakened this network, 'and in consequence the structure of professional services which are in measure dependent upon it, either now or in the future, must be supported by strong arguments before it can be considered to be in the public interest'. Takeover of the Royal Bank would remove from Scotland control of the largest bank, 'intimately connected with all important aspects of Scotland's business and commercial life'. In due course, the inevitable erosion of expertise and control would reduce the Royal Bank's acknowledged appetite for innovation and new products that was typically encouraged by an independent existence. The reduction in the flow of business from the centre to locally-based firms which provided professional legal and accounting services would also impact adversely on new products. In these ways, the reduction of the significance of Edinburgh would affect the total of ideas and the spread of thinking in the financial marketplace. Competition would thus suffer.

There was also the question of human capital. It was important to Scottish finance that a 'stratum of high-calibre creative executives' be retained as much for the development of new ideas and products in the financial field as for the view that, by remaining in Scotland, younger executives could reach the top of their profession. The Fraser of Allander Institute suggested in its submission that the loss of the two senior banks would leave other financial institutions 'isolated', with their prospects of development and innovation diminished. There was also a real problem

---

28 Figures are cited in The Fraser of Allander Institute, University of Strathclyde, 'A Memorandum Submitted to the MMC', 1 July 1981. This submission was a close complement to that from Bank of Scotland.

of psychological damage to an already dispirited industrial management. Scotland had seen numerous well-run companies taken over by English and foreign interests, their loss leading to a decline in general managerial confidence. The loss of the two banks would be worse because of the removal of key parts of the system of innovation in finance, with the merchant banks and investment trusts then beholden to the City of London. Their focus on London would exacerbate already admitted problems of recruitment and retention. Both Fraser of Allander and Bank of Scotland were at pains to refer to the 'intangible' links between commercial banks and other financial institutions for a broadly-based market. Aspects of human capital were an important part of the maintenance of true competition in financial services, although for several years this carried little weight with government.

The MMC arrived at its investigation with some inappropriate preconceptions. It asked Bank of Scotland, in the event of a halt to the proposals, whether the Royal Bank would find itself at a disadvantage because of its relatively small size. Only in the UK could such a question be asked. In June 1980, the Royal Bank ranked 125th in the world and Bank of Scotland 192nd. In the USA, there were over 14,000 banks; in that listing, the Royal Bank would rank 20th. In the Federal Republic of Germany, with 250 commercial banks, the Royal Bank would be 17th, in Switzerland 4th out of 31, in Japan 25th out of 75.[29] The top commercial banks of Denmark, Norway, Finland, Sweden and Austria were similar in size to the two senior Scottish banks. All these competitor economies were highly successful, but showed differing models of the relationship of financial services and the banking industry to economic progress. Size did not therefore necessarily mean success. But might the British case be exceptional, where size counted? With five huge English banks, could the Scots indeed be 'at a disadvantage'?

In costs and benefits, neither the Scottish banks nor their customers were placed at any disadvantage. The banks, all three, were not suffering in the usual tests of profitability, mentioned above, or efficiency in the sense that their position would be improved by incorporation into larger groups. There might be some cost savings in commercial lending, but the returns of the English clearers were too volatile to provide proof. In overall costs, the English clearers had nothing to teach the Scots, a point which was, in later years, to be appreciated even in London. The clearing banks could take huge slices of the top corporate loans, but syndication of borrowing among banks typified most large loans anyway. Few of the larger corporations maintained accounts with just one bank, and a number

29 Figures are cited in Fraser of Allander, 'Memorandum', p. 12.

of premier UK companies kept their principal banking relationships with Bank of Scotland, including Scottish and Newcastle Breweries, Arthur Bell & Sons (distillers, of Perth), The Standard Life Assurance Co. and the British National Oil Corporation. The advances to these companies could be huge – £34.5 million to Arthur Bell & Sons, for example, in 1980. From the early nineteenth century, Bank of Scotland had lent widely to English companies – often for long periods – which maintained their main banking relationship elsewhere; what changed over time was the range of facilities. Thus in 1980, among other advances, the Bank lent US $40 million Eurocurrency to British Airways, $60 million Eurocurrency to Shell UK, and $40 million Eurocurrency revolving credit to Guest, Keen and Nettlefolds. Small size did not mean lack of expertise. For instance, the Chief Cashier of the Bank of England asked Bank of Scotland to help teach senior executives of the proposed central board of the Trustee Savings Bank Ltd about syndicated commercial lending, prior to full recognition of their bank. The range of courses offered by the Institute of Bankers in Scotland was a shining example of a soundly-based professional organisation.

It was pointed out to the MMC that most bank advances were to medium-sized and small firms; typical in 1980 from Bank of Scotland were £2.5 million to Don Brothers, Buist & Co., £5.6 million to Seaforth Maritime, £5 million to Timex of Dundee, and £7.6 million to Denholm Line Steamers Ltd under the Home Shipowner scheme over nine years. This size of lending, and thousands of smaller advances and overdraft facilities, would still be the bread and butter of the Royal Bank group after a takeover, with very much smaller sums for the retail trades, house mortgages and advances for cars and household effects that typified local branches of the bank and of Lloyds and Scottish. Big loans with fine margins typified advances overseas, and any commercial bank which concentrated on this business would inevitably be much less profitable than UK banking and finance-house operations which held a broadly-based portfolio.

In contrast to the uncertain advantages of increased size for the English clearers, which were to be severely tested within a few years, the Scottish banks could offer clear benefits. Short lines of internal communication enabled managers to refer requests and receive answers quickly, and to deal effectively with complaints; and corporate customers could obtain access to senior executives. There was also something amiss with the sprawling organisations south of the Border; when Bank of Scotland opened in Birmingham, local companies switched their accounts 'in large numbers'. Williams and Glyn's had long pointed out the advantages of their smaller size. What mattered, the MMC was told, was the quality of management and staff and the way in which the smaller structure facilitated the relationship with customers. In the crucial areas of repeat business, sales of other products and longer-term loans, there was simply no connection between size and results.

Bank of Scotland was prepared to criticise the adverse effect on the Clydesdale and the British Linen of their respective affiliations with English clearers. This may seem surprising, but the Bank could not be certain that the historical record of these two banks would be noticed by the MMC. It was not apparent 'that the acquisition of the Clydesdale Bank by the Midland Bank has contributed anything material to the Scottish or UK public interest'. In recent times, the Clydesdale had made little attempt to expand in foreign fields, and it had no merchant banking subsidiary, finance house or leasing operation. The British Linen before 1971 was 'a very capable domestic bank, but was not noted for innovation outside that sphere'.[30] Affiliation thus had its main adverse effects as reinforcing the conservative tendency in Scottish banking. Here were two cases of 'allocated growth' in hitherto independent organisations now less able to make their way in the world.

Bank of Scotland made a clear statement of the Scottish position on the maintenance of regional centres across the spectrum of industry, commerce and finance, capable of generating new ideas, and argued that this was very much in the interests of the UK. The economic and social consequences of centralisation of headquarters, research and 'thinking' functions in London impeded the ability of regions to promote their own development. Prior to the 1970s, studies had focused on the structure of industry and commerce in peripheral areas, and on the level of demand, which had together caused long-term unemployment and migration.[31] In these post-war years, tremendous efforts had been made to address this by government, banks and local industry. This had mixed results but was a resounding success in respect of raising overall regional incomes and of bringing about a sharp reduction in unemployment compared with the inter-war years and a closer match of skills and age-groups with the English regions. Yet the older regional problem was being overlaid by the emergence of ownership drift which, twenty years on from the war, saw newer forms of disparity in income and class with the Home Counties. It could be measured by rising unemployment, although the indications of firm closures and cutbacks across the regions raised questions 'inevitably connected with increasing centralisation of economic decision-taking', which had results in the loss of research, legal work, accounting and

---

30 BS, Uncatalogued, Miscellaneous papers, 'Memorandum', p. 19; this was not elaborated on.
31 N. K. Buxton, 'The Scottish Economy, 1945–79: Performance, Structure and Problems', in R. Saville (ed.), *The Economic Development of Modern Scotland 1950–1980* (Edinburgh: 1985), pp. 47–78; G. McCrone, 'The Role of Government', in ibid., pp. 195–213.

other professional and white-collar work, and, increasingly as ownership and control settled in London and the Home Counties, in the loss of production processes and manual work.

It will be clear from the history of Scottish banking that the existence of local banks ensured that Scotland was self-sufficient in the financial support of Scottish industry and commerce: 'The indigenous banks are, by the very nature of their history and being, committed to the economic development of Scotland. This is and must be their priority.'[32] Banking facilities were built on close relations with customers, and, although gaps in coverage of foreign conditions were now appreciated, in the UK area the older skills were still a valuable resource, not to be abandoned lightly. The takeover would be unlikely to affect traditional domestic and commercial banking, but would start to impact on development and on intangible connections with the other professions, and in straitened times might lead to conflicts of interest which would then be decided in London. The damage would be more widespread the more functions that were amalgamated and sited in London, or that were run by directors whose focus was international finance and who saw Scotland as a place wherein to shoot grouse. If the MMC recognised the validity of the business orientation, which there was no certainty that it would, 'then it is not sensible to deny its relevance in specific cases and especially in a case of the present importance'. The way in which Bank of Scotland had acted to develop the local role in financing the oil industry was summarised, although the case could also have been advanced for other industries and services.

In the midst of planning the answers to the MMC, events raised the profile of the 'regional' and 'human skills' arguments. From 3–6 July 1981, there were serious riots in Liverpool which culminated in the first large-scale use in Britain of CS gas. By 12 July, riots had occurred in thirty more cities, all in England, including two days of fighting in Manchester, where mobs wrecked police vehicles and tried to ransack Moss Side police station, with serious outbreaks in Birmingham, Leicester, Leeds, Bradford and parts of London. There was no trouble in Scotland. These troubles occurred shortly after Lord Justice Scarman had opened a public inquiry into earlier fighting in Brixton, south London. The view taken in Parliament was that this outbreak was affected by policing arrangements in the area, and by specific cultural questions. But the Liverpool, Manchester and subsequent riots were obviously broader in origin. In a rare consensus, Parliament agreed with the Shadow Home Secretary, Roy Hattersley, that the July riots had happened in 'decaying central areas of old cities

---

32 BS, Uncatalogued, Miscellaneous papers.

where there is intolerably high unemployment, unacceptably low levels of social services and abysmally inadequate housing'.[33] On 27 July, the opposition parties united on a motion that the government's policies were 'spreading mass unemployment, undermining British industry and demoralising the country'. Of course, they lost the vote; but a number of government ministers, among them the Secretary of State for the Environment, Michael Heseltine, forced policy changes in cabinet. An extra £700 million was made available for urban expenditure, and specific initiatives were launched in many areas. Michael Heseltine wrote on 13 August to the clearing and Scottish banks on lines surprisingly close to the arguments put forward by Bank of Scotland, that the financial institutions had retreated from their old industrial beginnings in the provinces and were thus partly to blame for the chaos.

This was too important to ignore. In October, the Bank advised the MMC that 'with hindsight' it was to be regretted that control of Williams Deacon's and the District Bank had been moved from Manchester, and that of Martin's Bank from Liverpool. 'While we are wary of offering simplistic solutions to complex and deep-seated problems we suggest the view that the withdrawal from regional centres such as Manchester or Liverpool (and now Edinburgh) of control of its financial institutions would reduce regional self-sufficiency.' It 'will create a climate less propitious to the generation of and maintenance of industrial life and eventually contribute something to the possibility of social unrest'.[34] The MMC published its findings on 11 January 1982 and found the case for a separate Scottish banking industry sufficiently persuasive to rule against the proposals. Thomas Walker, the retired Treasurer, was in hospital for surgery on the day in question. He greeted his copy of the report with an enthusiastic 'We've won!', and perhaps this hastened his recovery.

---

33 Keesings Contemporary Archives, United Kingdom, Internal Disorders, 18 September 1981.
34 BS, Uncatalogued, Miscellaneous papers, D. B. Pattullo to C. J. M. Hardie, deputy chairman, MMC, 14 October 1981.

CHAPTER 28

NORTH WEST SECURITIES AND NWS BANK plc, 1979–95

FOLLOWING ACQUISITION BY Bank of Scotland, North West Securities' management was faced with a desire by the Bank to move
the headquarters of NWS from Chester to Scotland.[1] Sydney Jones
recognised the difficulties that this would bring, particularly the danger of
losing his senior staff, who would not be willing to relocate to Scotland.
He also believed that Chester was geographically right for the company
to be able to cover all of England, Wales and Scotland. Fortunately for
all, and with the support of Sir Hugh Rose, the chairman from 1958–73,
he succeeded in winning the debate to retain the headquarters at Chester.
The benefit was that NWS was able to develop new areas of business
with a speed and effectiveness which would probably not otherwise have
been possible. Both Sir Hugh Rose and his successor as chairman, Sir
Alastair Blair (1973–8), kept in regular contact with Chester while the
Mound received regular accounting information on the progress being
achieved. Beyond discussions on financial support and broad strategy, it
was the policy of Bank of Scotland to leave NWS alone on operational
and policy matters. The results were impressive. Pre-tax profits rose from
£4,064,000 in 1975 to £7,924,000 in 1978, the latter representing 23 per
cent of Bank of Scotland group profits, with a growth in liabilities from
£117.6 million in 1975 to £273.8 million (see Tables 28.1 and 28.2).
The light but well-informed hand extended by the Bank continued when
Ray Hazlehurst, a long-standing manager and friend of Sydney Jones, was
appointed managing director in January 1980, and also after Harry Bush
was appointed in April 1986. When Sir Alastair Blair stood down in 1978
as chairman, he was succeeded by Lord Balfour of Burleigh, the engineer,
a manager who had experience of similar fast-growing organisations.

1 See above, Chapter 25.

Table 28.1 *North West Securities Ltd results in the context of Bank of Scotland group, 1975–85*

	Pre-tax profits (£000)	Percentage return on capital	Percentage of group profits
1975	4,064	41.1	23.0
1976	6,733	45.6	25.0
1977	7,507	43.4	27.0
1978	7,924	35.1	23.0
1979	7,800	30.8	19.2
1980	6,433	21.4	12.1
1981	12,692	38.5	23.3
1982	10,992	35.8	19.5
1983	15,113	49.4	25.5
1984	17,151	39.3	21.4
1985	18,228	27.5	19.1

Sources: BS, NWS Group board papers, Corporate Plan, 1980–4, p. 3, Table 1; Corporate Plan, 1983–7, p. 2, Table 1; Corporate Plan, 1985–9, p. 2, Table 1.

On my first visit to Chester in 1970, the date of my appointment as director, I was taken around the office by Sydney Jones. Immediately apparent in each department we visited was the vigour and confidence characteristic of a successful organisation, where people moved about clearly feeling that everything they did, or did not do, would have a direct effect on the success of North West. 'Excuse me, Mr Jones' from a supervisor, with a nod of apology to me, and a question put. A helpful suggestion given by Mr Jones, we moved on to meet other department heads.

Lord Balfour recalled that

North-West's success, remarkable and consistent as it has generally been to the present day, was in great part due to the management's ability to retain the confidence and sense of responsibility that was so apparent in the 1970s. The 'Three Musketeers', by which name Sir Hugh Rose referred to Sydney Jones, Ray Hazlehurst and Robert Allen, were responsible for instilling this attitude and for selecting the second generation, Harry Bush and others, who were to follow. It was an extraordinary achievement to be able to maintain this vigour, integrity and directness right through to the present very substantial organisation.

This view was widely held by the leading people associated with Bank of Scotland. W. F. Robertson, for instance, the former Glasgow shipowner and NWS board member, noticed in 1982 that

The Bank and North West Securities are so unlike one another in important ways that the creation of a homogenous whole seems fraught with possibilities of trouble and because of its subsidiary position could so easily lead to the loss of many of the basic advantageous features of North West Securities. I have seen smaller, slimmer organisations taken over by larger ones, and soon

Table 28.2 *North West Securities Ltd summary financial statement, 1975–95*

	Assets						Liabilities					
Year ending 31 December[1]	Instalment credit and other loans	Leasing	Associated companies	Fixed assets	Other	Total assets	Deposits	Deferred tax	Others	Subordinated loan capital	Shareholders' funds	Total liabilities
1975	75.0	38.2	0.5	2.8	1.1	117.6	81.1	18.7	6.4		11.4	117.6
1976	115.8	48.7	0.5	3.1	1.9	170.0	123.4	24.5	7.4		14.7	170.0
1977	130.7	64.8	15.3	3.5	1.9	216.2	150.2	32.3	16.4		17.3	216.2
1978	159.6	86.3	18.7	6.3	2.9	273.8	194.2	41.9	15.2		22.5	273.8
1979	211.9	107.9	26.3	6.6	5.1	357.8	260.7	35.4	18.4		43.3	357.8
1980	244.3	143.5	43.3	6.9	8.5	446.5	329.4	32.8	23.4		60.9	446.5
1981	238.3	178.4	50.8	9.4	15.3	492.2	352.4	31.9	30.3		77.6	492.2
1982	276.3	209.9	59.3	10.3	7.0	562.8	405.0	31.7	39.0		87.1	562.8
1983	321.3	263.0	80.8	10.9	14.0	690.0	492.7	31.6	58.6		107.1	690.0
1984	414.5	331.7	58.7	10.9	13.9	829.7	611.4	49.1	84.0	8.0	77.2	829.7
1985	501.8	499.2	70.1	13.9	25.8	1,110.8	779.3	63.5	171.6	18.0	78.4	1,110.8
1986	668.3	560.7	67.6	18.3	22.9	1,337.8	990.9	63.1	159.4	36.0	88.4	1,337.8
1987	741.5	641.6	150.4	26.5	23.6	1,583.6	1,204.3	59.0	170.0	36.0	114.3	1,583.6
1988	1,020.6	839.5	169.0	35.9	22.0	2,087.0	1,607.8	59.2	218.7	76.0	125.3	2,087.0
1989	1,364.5	1,354.4	155.4	38.9	40.8	2,954.0	2,292.6	103.1	296.2	101.0	161.1	2,954.0
1990	1,670.9	1,874.8	142.5	38.4	34.5	3,761.1	2,936.0	164.5	362.4	121.0	177.2	3,761.1
1991	1,954.0	2,002.8	163.2	39.5	37.1	4,196.6	3,307.0	176.1	395.3	121.0	197.2	4,196.6
1992	2,125.1	1,938.9	176.6	45.9	49.1	4,335.6	3,297.8	176.2	503.2	121.0	237.4	4,335.6
1993	2,386.5	1,788.5	192.3	45.1	37.4	4,449.8	3,581.1	168.4	301.0	121.0	278.3	4,449.8
(Feb 1995)	2,831.9	1,826.8	208.2	54.3	38.0	4,959.2	3,999.7	179.5	364.5	121.0	294.5	4,959.2

Note:
1 The accounting year was restructured in 1994 to conform with the parent company's year-end, so that the figures for 1995 cover a fourteen-month period, from 1 January 1994 to 28 February 1995.

Source: BS, NWS Group board papers, Corporate Plans, 1980–95.

in the process of group development and consolidation adopting the habits of the group, leading to loss of initiative and vitality, of the sense of self-reliant individuality in development, and of that most valuable slimness which on their own they managed to retain.[2]

W. F. Robertson was absolutely correct: the management of NWS ran a tight ship appropriate for fixed-term lending, ranging from a month to five years, and required a huge sales and marketing effort each year to create enough new business just to maintain the size of its portfolio. Diversification within Bank of Scotland also encouraged appreciation of the hard task which the management of NWS faced as a result of overall advances turning over every three years. This understanding was all to the good for intra-group relations, but it remained the case that most of the products and services offered by the Bank were quite different, and it was right to keep the two separate.

When Sydney Jones retired in 1979, the finance-house market was dominated by four companies: Mercantile Credit (a subsidiary of Barclays Bank), Lombard North Central (National Westminster), Lloyds and Scottish (Royal Bank and Lloyds Bank) and Forward Trust (Midland Bank). In the twenty years since its acquisition by Bank of Scotland in 1958, NWS had grown from being only 155th in the rankings of the Finance House Association and was now fifth in size, although there was a considerable gap between it and these four, much larger, houses. United Dominions Trust (a subsidiary of the TSBS) and Chartered Trust were then some way behind. Apart from the enlightened attitude of Bank of Scotland in giving a loose rein to NWS, this extraordinary growth had several causes. In the first fifteen years, many branches were opened, mostly in England, and development of new products for this branch network generated repeat business while it also attracted new customers. Personal links with motor vehicle dealers and retail stores were still very important. Effective sales teams operating from branches, 'cold-calling' potential clients, gradually built up the NWS presence in business and geographical areas hitherto inaccessible. Sydney Jones also put great emphasis on control of bad debt and the pursuit of defaulters, and would often appear in court himself in support of claims by NWS. As the organisation grew, so did the expertise in the effective use of sales staff and branch comparisons.

From the growth of the branch network came the significant development of equipment leasing. This was because branches were dealing with car-fleet buyers, and thus larger sums were involved than was the norm for the average personal customer. The next step was to lease a wider range of equipment, not just vehicles. In 1973, Industrial Bank of

2 BS, Solum, 1A2, Box 3, Miscellaneous excess file, W. F. Robertson to Lord Balfour, 7 December 1982.

Scotland Finance was established, with its head office in Birmingham, managed by John Brown. It specialised in leasing assets to customers, and additionally progressed the development of leasing consortia and a leasing management service. It negotiated with nationalised industries, local authorities and large companies. This proved a sound decision. Equipment leasing was increasingly seen as an economically productive and tax-efficient method of financing the acquisition of assets. The capital costs were borne by IBOS Finance, not by the users (the lessees), repayments came out of revenues being earned by the use of the leased assets, and expert advice on the tax benefits was provided. It was soon agreed that IBOS Finance should participate in larger schemes in which the lead finance would come from elsewhere; this meant 'tramping the streets of the City of London to persuade bankers to look at what IBOS could offer'. As a result of the hard work of John Brown and his team, the subsidiary soon became one of the leading players in the UK asset finance industry, and was to become the core of NWS Corporate Finance, formed in 1988. Over the life of the company, there has been a notable change in the market situation. In the early years, from 1973, life investment allowances were in vogue, tax capacity was short and profit margins were attractive, so 5 or 6 per cent was commonplace. Contrast this with 1995, when tax capacity was in abundance because of the improved profitability of the banks. Yet, investment allowances were low and demand for investment goods weak in the UK. The effect was to drive down profit margins on the leasing business to such an extent that the pricing obtained in the marketplace was, at times, below 50 basis points, a most unattractive position for NWS Bank.

Prior to 1980, North West Securities had acquired equity stakes in three motor dealerships: 25.6 per cent of Henlys, 29.9 per cent of the Braid Group (sold in 1982) and 28.3 per cent of Macrae and Dick, an Inverness company. Whereas the holding of stakes in dealerships was an established route by which to secure income from financing car sales, it was realised that longer-term growth potential lay with joint company operations. Such joint ventures were established with the largest agricultural dealers in Europe, the Burgess Group, and with Caravan International Finance. Two other companies were jointly owned with Renault UK (Renault Loan and Renault Lease). Furthermore, NWS was moving into fields which were closer to commercial banking. The new electronic systems which were appearing at this time enabled the company to make further inroads into ordinary banking business and the new credit card systems which were to play such an important role in consumer expectations in the following decade.

Until 1977, there was steady growth in the NWS share of the commercial and consumer vehicle market. Unfortunately, in the aftermath of the

Table 28.3 NWS group as a percentage of total units registered with Hire Purchase Information (December)

	1975	1976	1977	1978	1979	1980	1981	1982	1983	1984
New cars	4.71	7.97	7.43	6.36	6.37	7.40	6.95	6.84	6.14	7.60
Used cars	3.38	4.46	4.83	4.51	5.01	5.72	5.86	5.93	5.86	6.18
Caravans	4.13	8.21	9.71	8.60	10.57	10.63	11.71	11.94	10.19	10.86
Total consumer	3.41	4.62	5.14	4.86	5.19	6.48	6.47	6.46	6.09	6.96
Tractors	14.90	18.02	19.61	17.78	20.15	15.59	14.51	12.28	8.27	10.65
Farm equipment	32.32	34.82	19.73	30.23	26.07	28.41	23.29	25.22	26.88	31.99
Plant and machinery	7.24	6.02	6.00	5.80	6.31	7.06	9.57	11.23	12.72	14.14
Commercial vehicles	2.87	3.56	3.09	3.00	3.72	3.93	4.31	4.48	4.32	5.63
Total commercial	5.25	5.39	5.24	5.31	6.14	6.50	7.43	8.09	8.02	9.36

Sources: BS, NWS Group board papers, Corporate Plans, 1980–4 and 1985–9, Table 3.

secondary banking crisis of 1974, the clearing banks which owned the four largest houses decided to use their resources to buy market share. The basic tax advantages of leasing assets encouraged the banks to advance resources 'at virtually break-even, to shelter tax'. Lombard North Central and Mercantile Credit were particularly aggressive in this respect. This led the NWS board, by 1978, to the decision to hold margins steady and face a temporary dip in market share of consumer vehicle sales. It was expected that the competition 'would continue to set the pace with the other houses, as a general rule, taking up the role of market followers, not fully in control of product pricing'.[3] The board exempted agricultural equipment sales and leasing from this pricing rigour, as, with these products, NWS could justifiably claim to be the market leader, although competition was fierce; for example, Highland Leasing, a division of the Royal Bank, made especial efforts 'to recruit our staff and quote ridiculously low charges'. The resulting impact to 1984 was varied: there was a dip for several years in the share obtained by NWS from the new car market, although that from used cars and caravans held up better.[4] Margin-cutting by competitors eroded the share of the tractor market and initially that for other farm equipment as well, although these recovered through good marketing. In the more diversified market of plant and machinery, NWS did especially well and increased its share to 14.1 per cent. The overall growth in the commercial market by 1984 was remarkable (see Table 28.3). Apart from the competition in the vehicle and machinery trades, there was also stiffer competition in the personal loan market; the Trustee Savings Bank (unified in 1983), for example, was perceived to be particularly aggressive, especially in Scotland, and several American companies had entered the market in England. There was also some fringe competition from credit unions. Much of the low-margin competition derived from inappropriate pressure placed by parent companies on their finance-house managements, or on those within the clearing banks who carried out similar functions. But there was a fundamental difference between a banking relationship with business and the market for financing consumer durables and commercial leases. In early talks with Ray Hazlehurst after he had succeeded Sydney Jones, Lord Balfour asked him how the competition reacted to the various problems facing the industry. In response,

> he arranged a series of dinners at which I was able to meet the Chairmen and Chief Executives of the finance houses owned by the other major banks and financial organisations who formed our competition. Their collapsing morale at finding themselves unable to resist the determination of their banking parents to bring the control of their finance-house subsidiaries into line by imposing

3 BS, NWS Group board papers, Corporate Plans, 1980–4 and 1985–9, Table 3.
4 BS 1/6, Minutes, 20 August 1985; NWS Corporate Plan, 1985–9.

bankers at the top was only too evident. It resulted in dramatic setbacks for the larger organisations, enabling NWS to surge steadily forward and overtake its rivals.

In the aftermath of the 1974 crisis, inflation had not proved, by itself, an obstacle to business growth. Reducing the proportion of customers' debt to their incomes had a positive effect. By 1978, inflation was down to 8.3 per cent, but it then started to rise and peaked at 18 per cent two years later.[5] What made the situation different, and much worse, was the deterioration in the general economic environment from the second quarter of 1979. This adversely affected the ability of borrowers to effect loan repayments on corporate and personal accounts alike. By December 1979, loss provisioning had reached 2 per cent of debts outstanding, more than double the previous year. It was anticipated by the management of NWS that 1980 would be worse and would include falls in spending by commercial businesses and central and local government. These expectations were confirmed as the recession deepened, with resultant widespread bad debts. By 1980, NWS had negotiated much business with small and medium-sized companies which supplied the larger manufacturers, which in turn had to 'be nursed through their difficulties' by the banks.[6] The reports of the finance houses made grim reading. There were also fears that the government would relax the terms on which finance houses granted credit. Unless all-industry agreements could be reached, this would see further reductions in margins, more imprudent lending and a 'marked increase in defaults and subsequent write-offs'. Moreover, the cost of funds bought in by NWS rose in 1979 and 1980, and this squeezed margins on fixed-interest contracts negotiated in previous years. These rate rises, together with the rise in bad debts, reduced profits in 1980 to £5.2 million, representing only 12.1 per cent of Bank of Scotland group profits, the lowest proportion for almost two decades.

A consensus developed that every effort should be made to restore margins, and NWS set itself the aim, over a five-year span, of achieving gross margins of 7.5 per cent. Traditionally, banks have a high proportion of their lending portfolio earning at variable rates of interest, linked to each bank's own base rate; but NWS had a high proportion of its lending at fixed rates of interest. In the 1970s, looked at in a Bank of Scotland group context, this was not a problem when interest rates rose, overdraft earnings increased and consequently returns rose from current-account credit balances on which interest was not paid. The resultant enhanced profits more than offset the loss of earnings suffered by NWS, which paid

5 P. R. Hughes, *British Economic History, 1945–1987, Broad Historical Narrative*, Queen Mary College, Economic Papers, no. 184 (London: 1988), Statistical Annex.
6 BS, NWS papers, 1980.

more for its money but could not pass the extra cost on to its fixed-rate borrowers. As a result of this policy and the rise in bad debts, NWS's first half-year profits in 1980 were modest. John Mercer, then chief accountant, suggested to Ray Hazlehurst that, because of the high reverse yield on interest rates which moved in favour of funding at long-term rates as providing better value for NWS than continuing with short-term borrowing, NWS should take £100 million of one-year fixed-interest money. The decision proved to be a good one, and profits recovered sufficiently in the second half of 1980. Over the next three years, NWS moved from having a very short-term funding book to having one of a broadly-matched position, with asset and liability cover in preserved margins. This held the company in good stead through the recession of the late 1980s and early 1990s. Many of its competitors' profits collapsed following the rapid increases of Bank of England base rates from 7.5 per cent in May 1988 to 15 per cent in October 1989. In respect of lending in 1980, NWS managers thought that while business opportunities existed at the lower end of the company and personal market, where margins were higher the losses would be much heavier. There were also proportionately higher costs and an adverse effect on 'image' because 'lower grade business, transacted with less credit-worthy people, invariably causes dissatisfaction'. It was also agreed that customers would not pursue connections with products regarded as disreputable by at least part of the general public. Motorcycles and double glazing had a particularly poor image.

Until 1980, NWS had relied heavily on Bank of Scotland for its computer processing and used the Bank's analysts and programmers for product developments. It was agreed by the Bank, because of the growth in the business of NWS and the ever-increasing complexity of its own work, that a team of analysts and programmers should be recruited by NWS in Chester and work remotely, using terminals linked into Bank of Scotland computers. This transition worked well, as it allowed NWS to allocate the perceived correct level of resource and priority to new projects deemed necessary to sustain business growth. In early 1980, NWS purchased its first computer, an IBM System 34. Although small, it led to much bigger things, and within five years Honeywell mainframe computers were installed. These were changed to IBM computers by the end of the decade and were compatible with those at Bank of Scotland's computing centre in Sighthill, Edinburgh. In 1995, the Chester-based Management Services Division employed more than 200 people.

The post-1979 strategy involved an increase in total resources which enabled NWS to expand business and to explore what the strategic plan called the 'contours of diversification'. The proportion of advances for financing vehicles and personal loans were expected to decline, although their absolute level was to be determined by market conditions. New areas agreed on were:

1. Direct sales to consumers and to companies, which gave better margins than indirect sales. A decision was taken to use direct mail within an overall direct marketing initiative as a means of cross-selling personal loan products to the NWS customer base.
2. A move into home mortgages, using a similar strategy to that adopted by Bank of Scotland from 1979.
3. Insurance services which could be cross-sold to existing customers. This was an extension of the creditor insurance products which had been introduced in the mid-1970s as a means of generating additional income for the group and to help safeguard customers' repayments in the event of illness, death or redundancy.
4. Revolving credit schemes using the chequebook-based product 'Paymaster', which had been introduced ahead of its time in 1971 and still formed part of the marketing platform in 1995.
5. In-store credit agreements.
6. Mortgages for yachts and smaller commercial ships, including fishing boats.
7. Closer contact by mail, and personal visits to commercial and agricultural customers. Government subsidies and the family nature of most farms continued to ensure that lending to agricultural customers was soundly based.

The above strategic plan was based on the view that the group commercial and personal customer base remained unduly dependent on the peaks and troughs of the motor trade and that, in this as in the personal loans market, the increase in the number of lenders would provide stiff competition. These new routes, outlined above, would thus help to circumvent the lack of freedom in deciding pricing policy in this traditional business. The personal customer base was important for cross-selling different products and generating repeat sales, and joint ventures with organisations with larger customer bases was a way to address this. It was considered in 1979 that the size of NWS and its standing, as part of Bank of Scotland group, should be utilised to build direct links to third parties for new products and, for instance, to compete with the Visa and Access credit cards. In the 1970s, a variety of in-store credit facilities based on non-electronic plastic cards had been designed in order to improve retail sales and to generate business for NWS. Store cards fostered loyalty, or so it was thought. Several retailers approached NWS, and by 1979 'in-store' credit schemes had been arranged for Marks and Spencer plc and C & A Modes plc. The Marks and Spencer system involved an identification card and chequebook, similar to the 'Paymaster' budget account, whereby the customer agreed to pay a specified sum each month, and, as a multiple of that sum, had an agreed overdraft limit. The organisation of this scheme was divided between Citibank, which took two-thirds, and NWS. For its share, NWS decided whether or not credit should be granted to the applicant and processed the resulting paper-based transactions. It was soon found that the Marks and Spencer facility was regularly used. They sold a wide range of goods including packaged foodstuffs, at prices which tended to discourage poor credit risks from applying for credit. With C & A Modes, which concentrated on retailing clothes, the credit facility was still profitable, but less so because it was less frequently used. Bad-debt problems could also be experienced with in-store cards. Although these types of in-store schemes had a high rejection rate of applicants, the bad-debt levels were also more severe than those experienced by NWS. As one senior manager noted, in regard to one such scheme, this was only 'to be expected given that the target market are young mothers and mothers to be'.[7] It was discovered, as with Visa and Access credit cards, that the rates of interest charged for credit facilities did not deter middle-class consumers. In 1980, option account facilities were opened for Thistle Hotels, which was owned by Scottish and Newcastle Breweries, and for Renault (UK) motor vehicles and Henlys motor dealership. On personal lending, the NWS board decided to discontinue current-account operations at branches. The provision of such branch-based banking services was not cost-effective, generated less profitable business than had been hoped for, and took up a 'totally disproportionate amount of management time', the more so with increased competition and increasing inflation. While the Bank of England encouraged the TSBs in their expansion of retail banking services, it refused banking status to NWS in 1979 irrespective of guarantees offered by Bank of Scotland.

From 1982, the association with Renault UK was strengthened with extra support for Renault Tractor and Truck Finance, designed to work with credit plans for the Dodge and Renault truck dealer network. The market in these years proved harsh. It became public knowledge that Vauxhall, Fiat, Ford and Renault were offering special terms through their respective credit connections. There were arguments among the finance houses on these special relationships with manufacturers, which were not covered by the usual Finance House Association terms. In the case of Renault, it was decided to push sales of the small Renault 5 saloon, which it was hoped would prove as successful as earlier models. The scheme was underwritten by NWS to a high standard, and gross margins were monitored by both parties. It was a symptom of the difficult market situation and confirmed to the finance houses involved, if not to their parent banks, the need for diversification. The recession put particular strain on their relations

7 BS, NWS papers, 27 June 1983.

with the parent banks. In 1982, for example, the Midland Bank decided to enforce 'banking skills' on the staff of Forward Trust; the 'resulting ineffectuality' provided NWS with good opportunities. The TSBs decided to expand their work in the consumer market, but limited the action of UDT in the commercial market. Again, NWS and other houses were quick to spot the sales potential. But the most serious problems arose at Lloyds and Scottish, whose profits plunged to £10.8 million in 1982, only just exceeding the profits of NWS. This was, at first sight, a consequence of bad debts in a range of activities, but industry insiders asked themselves how much of the deterioration was the result of inopportune moves by Lloyds Bank in imposing banking skills, together with the loss of direction at the Royal Bank as a consequence of the takeover struggle.

As NWS faced the depths of the recession, it became clear that the group subsidiary, IBOS Finance, could expect a fast rate of growth in leasing agreements. Its main markets were the top 400 private companies, the nationalised industries and municipal authorities. It took a rising market share of business from the local authorities, with 25 per cent of this market by 1984; typical agreements comprised 75 per cent fixed interest and 25 per cent variable, and a gross yield of around 7 per cent per year. The growth in the municipal market was stimulated by government controls on capital expenditure after 1979. Initially, these controls depressed the market for vehicles and equipment, but Treasury rules allowed authorities to lease equipment by using current year funds, rather than increasing capital expenditure by outright purchase. As a result, leasing business volumes expanded rapidly. There was much repeat business, and NWS developed good relations with authorities, even sponsoring a flat race in the *Local Government Chronicle* meeting at Brighton in September 1988. In addition to the provision of leasing facilities, IBOS Finance endeavoured to overcome the shortfall in tax capacity in Bank of Scotland group, which restricted growth in leasing. This was achieved by means of broking business too large to absorb in-house, arranging for taxable capacity from external companies to be used in leases, and operating back-to-back leases with other lessors. It also moved into the management of leasing portfolios to third parties, and by 1983 had contracts with three major City of London institutions and four from the provinces. A number of profitable cross-selling opportunities were available through leasing; insurance broking, for instance, gave good profits, and there were lower staffing requirements. The work of IBOS Finance and the growing connection with manufacturers and retail stores gradually enlarged the NWS customer list.

The earlier decision to move into the mortgage market had been taken to enhance profits, but was also taken to put some longer-term lending onto the books. The traditional motor and commercial business had an average lifespan of only three years, and NWS had to work very hard to build up the overall loan portfolio, which ran off very quickly unless new business was found to replace it. There was now an opportunity to enter into a much broader market for large leasing transactions. Bank of Scotland had not created specialist teams with knowledge of the leasing market, and NWS saw a way to boost group profits by sharing the risk for large transactions with the Bank. But these would also lengthen the term of the loan portfolio, as some transactions ran for up to twenty years. Another issue to be resolved was the finer margins which normally accompanied such transactions, lower than NWS would normally be prepared to accept. A meeting was held in Edinburgh to discuss these issues, and NWS was given full support by the Bank. It was agreed that finer-margin transactions could be attractive once matching funds were in place, and this opened the door for many large and interesting contracts on aircraft and industrial plant in the years ahead, a number of which were individually in excess of £100 million.

There were regular innovations with store and credit cards in these years. Two may be singled out. On 28 June 1983, NWS, in conjunction with British Rail, launched the British Rail Travel Key system. This was a difficult time for the board of British Rail, as the avowed policy of the government was to provide substantial investment for the road network, which encouraged the long-distance haulage market as well as the personal car market. Investment in railways was not favoured, and the overall subsidy to railway operations dropped steadily to levels lower than were usual for the main European competitors. Rail freight was particularly tightly constrained. Nevertheless, investment in the previous decade had seen improved passenger services on the routes from London to Bristol, Birmingham and other Midlands destinations and daytime services on the east-coast main line to Edinburgh. The introduction of the 125 series of two-engined diesel trains undoubtedly helped. Extra revenues might also be generated with improved marketing. Travel Key was aimed at the business user, and 80,000 brochures were dispatched to potential clients, who were offered 5 per cent discounts on travel and 10 per cent on meals taken on trains and selected hotel rates. IBOS Finance made contact with its own corporate customers, and it was expected that the discounts would encourage a high take-up rate. North West Securities insisted on vetting all applicants for credit, and provision for bad debts was set at 3/4 per cent. Above this bad-debt level, British Rail would be liable. The overall profit target for NWS in the first three years was low, at only £74,000 after costs, but the potential for cross-selling was viewed as significant, and Bank of Scotland earned income from the computer processing of related data.

Following failure to agree satisfactory terms with British Rail in 1986, the contract was not renewed, and twelve months' notice of termination was given, effective from 1 March 1987. Although NWS would have accepted modified terms, these were not forthcoming.

The AA was the largest of the UK's motoring organisations, and, like the Royal Automobile Club, was constituted as a club to which members paid a yearly subscription. For some years, rising inflation and the impact which this had on subscriptions had led the AA to seek other sources of income and new services and benefits for members. The diversification, first into motor insurance and then into other products, had resulted in a substantial shop network. The AA had an existing connection with Mercantile Credit, which offered personal loans to AA members.

The approach by NWS to the AA to promote a branded credit-card product came at an interesting time in the development of credit cards. The use of on-line computer terminals was spreading, and information was available as to how various issuers of the Visa and Access cards intended to enhance their value by linking them to discount packages and by offering a range of premium and gold cards for customers with above-average incomes. There was 'no doubt whatsoever that enhanced value/add ons will become commonplace very soon notwithstanding that it has not happened until now'.[8] Harry Bush pointed out that Barclays was thinking along these lines for Barclaycard, which made significant profits for Barclays Bank, but whose market now faced erosion from Access, American Express, store cards and the various proposals of which the AA branded card was one. Within Bank of Scotland management, there were reservations about the damage which might be done to existing Visa card operations, in particular to Barclaycard and Bank of Scotland's own Visa card, launched in 1982, which was processed by Barclays Bank.[9] Was it 'sensible in relation to the overall interests of the banking and finance industries to invite a non-financial organisation to participate on the basis of sharing the profit and loss'? The AA made it clear that it expected 50 per cent of the profits from any joint venture. Questions were asked concerning how these add-ons might proliferate and distort functions of the credit card, and about possible future loss of the operation 'with the big AA tail wagging the Bank of Scotland Visa dog'.[10] But the consensus was that, if the operation could be sure of long-term and not just transitory

8 BS, NWS papers on Automobile Association, 1984.
9 See below, Chapter 29.
10 BS, Solum, 1A1, Box 3, NWS papers on the AA; J. Wilson, joint general manager, to R. Hazlehurst, 12 September 1983.

Table 28.4 *Automobile Association financial projections: AA Visa card*

£000	1985	1986	1987	1988	1989
Income	6,433	12,514	14,454	15,314	15,995
Cost of funds	2,733	5,536	6,403	6,700	6,959
Gross margin	3,700	6,978	8,051	8,614	9,036
Operating costs	4,148	4,287	4,652	4,925	5,143
Bad debts and specific provisions	320	802	989	1,054	1,100
Total costs/provisions	4,468	5,089	5,641	5,979	6,243
Operating (loss)/profit	–768	1,889	2,410	2,635	2,793
General provision for bad debt	231	140	38	27	24
(Loss)/Profit before tax	–999	1,749	2,372	2,608	2,769
Customer debt (£m)	40	59	64	67	71
Average customer debt (£m)	25	49	62	66	69
Return on average outstandings (%)	–	3.51	3.85	3.95	4.02

AA Budget
Projections for the AA Budget Account indicate a profit of £100,000 in 1985

	£000	£000	£000	£000	£000
Conservative estimates indicate future profits to be:	100	350	550	730	900

Source: BS, NWS Group board papers, NWS Corporate Plan, 1985–9, p. 19, Table 6.

advantage, 'we should go ahead and face any brickbats'. On 7 September 1983, Lord Balfour, Deputy Governor of Bank of Scotland and chairman of NWS, discussed the matter with the Governor, Sir Thomas Risk, who made it clear that, notwithstanding his position as a director of Barclays Bank, he had no objection in principle to the proposal. He later spoke rather positively about it to the board of Bank of Scotland. Bruce Pattullo, the Treasurer, was asked to proceed on the basis of what was commercially advantageous. There was no need to inform Barclays Bank about the proposed AA card as this was a competitive matter, although it was likely that Mercantile Credit would learn of it through its connections. Iain Scott, who was responsible for the Bank's accounting division, and A. T. Gibson, general manager, were asked to check the projections; and a few days later, on 12 September, NWS was told that it could proceed, although certain controlling features 'must remain in our hands', including the level of interest to be charged and the possible future introduction of a fee. The Mound also made it clear that this product would not necessarily be exclusive to the AA. In the financial assessment for projects such as this, focus was placed on four basic figures: the operating costs with their large variable element; the cost of funds; the income; and, of course, bad debts and specific provisions. As shown in Table 28.4, the first year was expected to show a loss and the second year to see a low return. As the return on average cardholder borrowings was very low on the AA credit card, the NWS management insisted on always controlling the assessment procedure for applicants.

The success of the NWS/AA Visa credit card was greater than anticipated. The test mailing of 208,000 AA members in February 1984, on a random sample, gave a response rate of 5.2 per cent, and of these applicants 93.5 per cent were issued with cards. In the first few weeks, applications were processed at the rate of 800 per day, and in the first year 181,500 applications were accepted, although the successful applicant rate later slipped a little to 93 per cent. There was a gross profit return of 13.4 per cent on debts, with an average of £197 outstanding per active account. Of course, Barclays Bank tried hard to retain its share of the overall Visa card market with its Barclaycard, and difficulties arose between NWS and the Barclaycard centre which produced and processed the NWS/AA cards and related transactions. Barclays had been given detailed projections of throughput, but by the close of 1984 delays in its procedures meant that applications were taking eight weeks, and by March 1985 the backlog had reached ten. Yet Barclaycard's own Visa cards were being issued within only three weeks. Although the matter was taken up by Bruce Pattullo with Barclays Bank, the delays confirmed to senior managers at NWS, and to Bank of Scotland, that Visa applications would, sooner rather than later, have to be dealt with by Bank of Scotland group. Profits from the operation were acceptable, although less than the overall targets for use of NWS resources. Other NWS/AA products were launched to help motorists spread the costs of insurance and AA membership.

By April 1983, the NWS group was able to restore the overall gross margin position lost after 1977. In that month, it reached the historically high level of 8.47 per cent, close to the operational strategy target for 1983–7 for fixed gross margins to be 8.5 per cent (see Table 28.5).[11] Nevertheless, in 1983 and 1984 it was evident that the emergence from the recession would be slow and painful for industrial borrowers, whereas consumer and service markets were already seeing strong growth, especially in the south-east and the Midlands. Additionally, long-standing industrial customers were going into bankruptcy, although there was some improvement in defaults and arrears for industrial leasing by 1984. These were also years of pressure on motor distributors. In 1984, over 20 per cent went into liquidation, and it was estimated that 'up to 20% of the remainder faced severe difficulties' as overproduction of cars led to manufacturers fighting over market share with more cut-price offers. Most producers promoted

11 BS, NWS monthly figures; NWS Group Corporate Plan, 1983–7, Table 9.

Table 28.5 *NWS group advances and gross margin objectives, 1983–7*

	Gross margin (%)	Actual (£m) 1982	1983	1984	1985	1986	1987
Motor cars – new	7.50	100.4	125.2	125.8	126.8	122.6	126.9
Motor cars – used	9.00	64.1	73.8	77.0	80.6	80.6	84.6
Total cars	8.00	164.5	199.0	202.8	207.4	203.2	211.5
Commercial vehicles – new	7.00	28.4	26.9	28.0	29.1	30.2	30.8
Commercial vehicles – used	9.50	4.5	3.2	3.3	3.4	3.6	3.7
Total commercials	7.30	32.9	30.1	31.3	32.5	33.8	34.5
Caravans	9.50	6.6	6.7	6.9	7.2	7.4	7.7
Small sailing craft	8.50	3.0	4.8	5.9	6.1	6.3	6.5
Plant and equipment	7.00	100.0	136.5	142.6	147.6	152.8	158.1
Agricultural:							
Tractors	8.00	14.4	13.8	14.3	14.8	15.3	15.9
Machinery	7.50	10.8	11.7	12.3	12.7	13.1	13.6
Livestock	8.50	4.0	4.8	5.5	6.0	6.0	6.0
Total agricultural	8.00	29.2	30.3	32.1	33.5	34.4	35.5
Paymaster	12.25	10.1	11.0	13.0	15.0	18.0	20.0
Store credit	12.50	21.7	25.0	30.0	36.0	40.0	44.0
Personal loans	15.00	24.0	32.6	43.4	55.7	70.1	85.2
First mortgage	1.75		10.0	10.0	5.0		
Marine mortgage	5.00		2.0	2.0	3.0	3.0	3.0
	13.00	55.8	80.5	98.4	114.7	131.1	152.2
	8.50	392.0	488.0	520.0	549.0	569.0	606.0
Percentage increase over previous year			24.6	24.5	6.6	5.6	3.6	6.5
Percentage increase after inflation [1]			21.1	21.0	3.1	2.1	0.1	3.0

Note:
1 Per cent inflation factor = 50 per cent of inflation rate (i.e. 3.5 per cent).

Source: BS, NWS Group board papers, Corporate Plan, 1983–7, p. 22, Table 9.

cut-rate schemes to gain market share, and the result was unpredictable business for dealerships. Throughout these years, NWS maintained a good relationship with Renault, and by 1984 the NWS group's percentage of total units registered with Hire Purchase Information was actually slightly above that of five years before, while of course the total market was rising as the country crawled out of recession. But 1985 was little better than earlier years for dealers, with tighter margins and the effects of the year-long miners' strike of 1984–5, which cut sales and increased debts in the mining areas. It should be added that relations between the finance houses and mineworkers remained cordial. Traditionally, miners had excellent records on repayments, among the best for skilled workers; and, when it was clear that the strike would be prolonged, a variety of agreements to reschedule payments were arrived at to avoid the need for distraint.

There were numerous medium-sized firms, particularly in high technology and services and located in the south-east of England, which found leasing attractive because of its net cost cash value after tax allowances. But there were problems. In the March 1984 Budget, the Chancellor of the Exchequer announced the elimination, by April 1986, of the 100 per cent first-year allowances for capital investment by firms subject to corporation tax, and during the same period stated his intention to reduce the rate of corporation tax from 52 to 35 per cent.[12] Furthermore, first-year tax allowances on leasing would fall to 25 per cent. There was thus concern that larger companies would prefer to finance capital expenditure outright. Yet the leasing market remained buoyant among small and medium-sized companies. There was a somewhat less helpful position in agriculture, where several competitors cut rates sharply, and one of these 'in spite of several years of non-profitability, seem still to be quoting low and unprofitable rates'.[13] Lombard North Central also quoted some leasing rates 'hardly appearing to give a financial return', although its parent would benefit from the tax-shelter utilisation.

With all these difficulties, the management at NWS kept to a 'lightweight' approach for new developments, described as 'not being too far into any specific scheme as to be unable to extricate ourselves quickly', with flexibility in the approach to change. This put pressure on NWS to be good at overall strategy, to encourage new products which could be fitted into group activity and to adapt when competitors' responses affected new group products, which they invariably did. While this encouraged speed in decision-taking, it was vital that the group continued to work well with existing customers to build up long-term relationships and utilise the customer bases for cross-selling insurance and financial products.

From 1984, a new Central Credit Division brought together products which could be administered most efficiently on a centralised basis.[14] In the main, these were the credit cards, but the Credit Division was expected to develop other products and promote them through advertising and direct mail. The management of that Division had to work hard to make a profit: in the five months to 31 May 1986, for example, from over nine separate products, involving huge numbers of customers, there was a pre-tax profit of only £1,635,900. In the thirteen months to this date, four of these products saw negative results, and the overall profit on them was only £797,000. As the competitive situation on in-store retail credit cards grew more intense, NWS managers decided that they had only two to three years to establish the various store cards with clear brand identities and perceived fringe benefits for users. They agreed that their competitors were Visa and Access credit cards but that the in-store cards might be linked to

12 BS 1/6, Minutes, 20 March 1984.
13 BS, NWS Corporate Plan, 1985–9, p. 9.
14 BS, NWS Corporate Plan, 1985–9.

the Electronic Funds Transfer Point of Sale (EFTPOS) system. This point-of-sale system was in the course of development by the Association of Payment and Clearing Services, and close to £100 million had been spent before the UK clearing banks halted further development.[15] The NWS strategy for store cards was to compete not on price but on quality, remaining cost-effective with careful systems evaluation and retention of the vanguard of product and marketing within NWS. The personal loan operation would be developed from the card products, and it was expected that the Credit Division would develop mortgage business through branches, which gave tangible physical assets as security for advances, albeit with lower margins. North West Securities developed successful methods for direct mail and won the Royal Mail Post Office prize for three years in a row from 1982. The development of direct sales to both consumer and commercial markets was important for strategy, as margins were generally above 14 per cent.[16] In 1985, a new Public Services Finance Company was launched to meet the needs of the clerical and executive grades of the Civil Service and local government. Capital Bonds were developed to provide firms with incentives for staff and customers. Club Thomson was launched as a revolving credit plan in the Thomson holiday brochure.

In 1984, the development with the greatest potential in the retail sector came when NWS persuaded Marks and Spencer plc to offer a new credit card, specific to their customers; NWS was to manage the whole of the issue.[17] With this new in-store card, it was considered that Marks and Spencer might increase market share at a substantially lower cost than if they allowed the use of other credit cards, such as Visa and Access, in their stores.[18] Planning proceeded rapidly in early 1984; NWS designed the application system and was to provide the systems and card issue. From June, a test launch was carried out in seventeen Marks and Spencer shops in Scotland. By 13 August 1984, 16,300 applications had been received, of which 14,300 were accepted, a rate of 88.2 per cent. The commercial uncertainty and operational effort were borne entirely by NWS. Only a provisional agreement had been negotiated at this stage for the intended UK operation. Marks and Spencer were 'not obliged to confirm their intention to offer the charge card on a national basis until the early part of 1985 . . . but the Agreement between Marks and Spencer plc and NWS will be entered into in the near future'. It was made plain that the agreement would contain an 'open book accounting' clause to identify the real costs, including computer charges.

15 BS 1/6, Minutes, 21 May 1985.
16 BS, NWS Corporate Plan, 1985–9, p. 11.
17 BS 1/6, Minutes, 13 August 1984.
18 BS, NWS papers, 27 November 1985.

North West Securities thus had to plan on the assumption, but not the certainty, that the project would go forward on a UK-wide basis after the Scottish experiment had been completed. The initial contract, covering only Scotland, was for a five-year period, with either party having a right to terminate at the end of that time, twelve months' notice having been given, and subject to twelve months' notice thereafter. Terms were included for the disposition of the lease on 10,000 square feet of premises utilised by NWS, in Chester, in the autumn of 1984. Recruitment of staff commenced in October. John Mercer, chief accountant of NWS, worked on the budgeted costs and benefits of the arrangements over five years. These budgets included the effect of a risk:asset ratio of 12½ per cent, as seemed likely to be insisted on by the Bank of England.[19] The consequence of this ratio was the likelihood of nil generation of profits for NWS for a number of years. In the projections, clear benefits would not arise before the fifth year. The board of NWS accepted the 'extreme pressure' that the arrangements would involve. Nevertheless, the board considered 'the consequences of proceeding with the development in the light of the possibility of the subsequent termination of the Agreement by Marks and Spencer plc'. But it was felt unlikely that the retailer would 'wish to . . . [the] relationship with Marks and Spencer being excellent'.

Thus, in the summer and early autumn of 1984, NWS pressed ahead on the basis of an assumed five-year agreement. But then came a surprise: a director of Marks and Spencer plc asked for a meeting with senior executives from NWS and with Bruce Pattullo, at which the representatives of NWS were 'disappointed' to learn that the retailer now wished to take full responsibility for the charge-card operation from its inception on a national basis and would wish to proceed with an office development of its own in Chester, but still using the resources and facilities of NWS and Bank of Scotland for a three-year period.[20]

The reaction within NWS can be appreciated. Months of valuable management time had been absorbed, considerable expense incurred and other opportunities turned aside; with NWS acting in good faith, 'one can imagine how the senior staff felt'. In the event, it was agreed that if Marks and Spencer paid the full five-year fees over the shorter three-year span, NWS would continue with the operational work. The agreement included the secondment of John Mercer, who had been newly appointed finance director, with a team of NWS staff to establish what eventually emerged as St Michael Financial Services.

In 1986, Harry Bush, who had been with NWS since 1963, was appointed managing director following the retirement of Ray Hazlehurst, who was

19 For discussion of risk:asset ratios, see below, Chapter 29.
20 BS 1/6, Minutes, December 1984; NWS papers; *aide-mémoire* for Lord Balfour.

invited to take up the position for two years of chief executive of the Finance House Association, later renamed the Finance and Leasing Association. Harry Bush became chief executive at a time when direct telephone marketing methods had proved successful for some company products. His aim was to build up a direct marketing operation in Chester, based on telephone sales, for business as well as personal customers. In the early days of NWS, companies expected sales representatives to call in person when looking for business, but this 'cold-calling' was often very unproductive. Attitudes were changing in the home and at work, and businesses increasingly appreciated a preliminary discussion over the telephone. This change in outlook, together with the use of modern telecommunications equipment, saved time and pushed a great deal of new business towards NWS. The new technology was vital; new systems eliminated the waste of time in direct operator dialling, as calls could now be distributed to individual staff with customer details immediately on screen together with a pre-set pattern of questions. The evolution of such systems and procedures proved to be very effective.

North West Securities was not immune to political difficulties, although these were relatively infrequent. Nevertheless, a potentially serious case arose in April 1987 when several Conservative politicians and London-based newspapers tried to embroil finance houses and the clearing banks in the argument between local authorities and the government over the capping of municipal rates. There was a long-running dispute between the government, which wished to curtail expenditure, and the local authorities, with their statutory obligations for education and services. The authorities found leasing provided by finance houses a constructive way of financing the fulfilment of their duties; and, as highlighted above, IBOS Finance held one of the largest portfolios. The market was complicated, and, inevitably, some of these leasing arrangements were innovative and perhaps appeared perplexing to the uninitiated. Nicholas Ridley, Secretary of State for the Environment, announced that 'The lenders of this money must certainly regard it as high-risk in many cases'.[21] Yet the legal position was clear, and it was reiterated by the Public Works Loan Board, whose supervisory and audit work had long been part of local authority legislation. A categorical written assurance was available that the Loan Board 'would act as lender of last resort' to any local authority as long as it had acted legally and set a rate, irrespective of whether the authority was rate-capped by government. Further, the Loan Board considered 'rates [as being] the primary form of security for advances from the Loan Board'. Thus borrowing by local authorities, however managed,

21 *Accountancy Age*, 16 April 1987; *Sunday Times*, 19 April 1987.

came back to the 'fundamental issue of creditworthiness rather than tangible security'. The lender would look to the cash flow of local authorities and to their observance of the legislation; loans could then be made in accordance with long-running practice. From the point of view of the Loan Board, leasing was just another form of monetary advance. All this was confirmed by the Bank of England, which had no interest in damaging the relations between local authorities and their lenders. Nonetheless, there was concern that maverick elements in the government might seek to impose an arbitrary axe, which could, in certain circumstances, damage existing leasing arrangements. The episode was exceptional, and sharp reminders were delivered to government ministers from the banks and the finance houses about the damage that this might do to the financial standing of the UK. The matter then faded from public view.[22]

Many of the products launched by NWS took time before generating sufficient income to recoup start-up costs and bring in a profit. It was estimated in 1986, for example, that, on average, it took forty-two months for a card operation to generate a profit. Paradoxically, therefore, the more effectively card schemes were sold, the greater the short-term adverse effect on the profits. For this reason, NWS did not actively market Bank of Scotland's Visa card until the AA Visa card was already well established. In the 1985–9 corporate plan, the board agreed to two main routes for new products. Those products with a low-cost launch would be acceptable if they were budgeted to generate net income at £250,000 in the first year, rising to £500,000 by the end of the second year. But the usual high launch overheads made it essential that a minimum of £500,000 income be realised in the first year, with a target of £1.5 million thereafter. Unprofitable services were to be eliminated, except where strong income in other lines might be affected. The primary objective was designed to push profits before tax from £18 million in 1985 to £37 million in 1989, a 15 per cent compound growth rate per annum. There would have to be some widening of margins and a reduction in the 12½ per cent level of the risk:asset ratio insisted on by the Bank of England. The board expected a continued erosion of margins in the traditional business generated by branches, and their contribution to pre-tax profits was expected to steady rather than show dramatic change. Yet Forward Trust and Mercantile Credit were closing branches, in line with their parents' view of operating with large branches covering huge geographical areas. North West Securities' Field Division maintained its wide branch coverage, as this was suited to local businesses,

22 From April 1987, government legislation laid down that municipal capital budgets must henceforth include all leases above one year. There was a possibility that the market would be cut, but new creative leasing, especially off-balance-sheet leasing, provided a solution to this.

which often preferred closer, local contacts. Anyone who bothered to talk to managers of medium-sized and small firms should have been able to work this out. Field Division also brought in a range of new products, revolving credit schemes, flexible leasing arrangements and 'worry-free' insurance.

In general, the Mound left NWS free to develop its business in the way it thought best, and the key representatives of the Bank in the 1980s, among others Lord Balfour, W. F. Robertson and Bruce Pattullo, were adamant that this should endure. But there were occasions when differences appeared. The implications of the free capital ratios for Bank of Scotland group are covered elsewhere.[23] One of the few occasions when the Mound intervened was over a proposed treasury function, whereby NWS would be able to outplace its liquidity and other surpluses into the financial markets by lending to banks and other financial companies. Bank of Scotland's experience of international and domestic treasury functions extended for nearly 300 years, and the Bank was fully aware of the dangers of these markets. They had the real potential to bring down even well-established concerns. In the course of 1985, a new, centralised treasury department was created within Bank of Scotland at the Old Broad Street office, London. It took over the treasury functions of a range of disparate treasury operations in the group, dealing on the financial futures market and in currency, and conducting other financial transactions for the Bank, its subsidiary companies (including NWS) and customers. However, in regard to NWS, in 1989 it was agreed that a new subsidiary, NWS Agencies Ltd, would provide some treasury services. On offer to customers was a secure deposit facility, with no brokers' fees, for deposits over £100,000 for one month to ten years at rates above normal clearing-bank rates.

The allocation of senior management time to cover the expansion of NWS occasioned a thinning in the ranks of the senior executive, aggravated by illness and retirement. Ray Hazlehurst and Harry Bush thought that this would be a temporary problem, noting the 'quality of the people a layer or two below the board'. But for a time this caused difficulty. The launch of the Marks and Spencer card was one demanding matter. As if to illustrate this further, it was discovered in April 1986 that the NWS group had failed to make appropriate claims for tax relief, within the time limits laid down by statute, for the financial years of 1982 and 1983.[24] The potential liability for tax was £15.8 million, and available tax losses lay largely within IBOS Finance. These losses could now only be set against

---

23 See below, Chapter 29.
24 BS, Solum, 1A2, Box 13, Miscellaneous Extra, NWS tax liabilities.

future profits. Thus it would be necessary to fund the resultant immediate payment to the Inland Revenue 'for as long as it took to use up the losses'. The response in this case was clearer and tighter control. There were also problems in the NWS Secretary's Department, with 'significant weaknesses in the organisational structure of the Department'. The staff were very good, but the managerial function, because thinly spread, needed to be strengthened. There were a number of queries from the Mound about the format of the various accounts of the companies in the NWS group and about how bad debts should be properly reported in internal management accounts. These difficulties arose from a shortage of senior posts in the audit and accounting functions. Although W. F. Robertson advised Lord Balfour to be cautious,

> all this comes at a time when the [NWS] atmosphere is one of 'go' and there is a considerable body of fresh activity, some of it of major dimensions, much of it at the formative stages. Harry Bush must surely want a breathing space which would allow him to build up the structure, and let latent talent (which we all believe is there) develop effectively. This is not to say that we should not be on the look-out for fresh useful opportunities, but we seem to be thin on the ground at the top level to take on major new initiatives with our present structure, without running the risks inherent in being stretched too far.

North West Securities was also strong on controlling costs – and sometimes rather too zealous. In 1985, Lord Balfour noticed that alongside the headquarters building in Chester were no fewer than forty-two portable cabins in which staff were located. Eventually, contracts were issued to Norwest Holst for two purpose-built office blocks which were opened in 1988, Capital House and Computer House.

Levels of bad debts have always been a cause for concern within finance houses. The experience of the recession after 1979 was sobering, and the effects continued longer than forecast. Mention has been made of Lloyds and Scottish, but all finance houses suffered; Mercantile Credit, for example, saw serious arrears in 1983–4, with profits down from £42 million to £35 million. Matters deteriorated again in 1985–6 when the economy was doing very much better. Trends seemed to follow North America and Europe. Questions were asked about whether there was something fundamentally wrong with the debt-evaluation systems. Were previously 'sound' people adopting imprudent habits? Should finance houses run regular health checks on their customers? Were the patterns of employment breaking down so that a fringe of sound customers could suddenly be in difficulty through no fault of their own? Or was the reason for bad debts a gradual breaking-down of the old morality that one should try to repay one's debts? Whatever the reason, and the financiers thought there was no simple explanation, the prudent answer was to place more emphasis on credit-scoring systems, look at patterns of geographical linkage and make more use of sociological analysis.

North West Securities decided to extend 'worry-free' insurance cover against accident, sickness, redundancy and death. Over £2 million of insurance was paid out in 1985. This insurance contributed towards the reduction of bad debts and associated recovery costs. Nevertheless, Bank of Scotland was increasingly concerned that the boom which had preceded the 1987 British general election showed no signs of stabilising thereafter. The so-called 'feel-good factor', an impressionistic summary of the national mood conducted by the European Commission and based on whether or not interviewees expected their lives to improve, showed strong positive results in 1987 and 1988. In line with housing mortgages, demand for personal credit and loans for small business continued to rise. In 1986, net write-offs and specific provisions at NWS came to nearly £15 million and in the election year of 1987 to £17.3 million. As a proportion of average total debt, this monetary increase actually represented a fall, from 1.37 to 1.31 per cent. Profits continued to rise. It also became apparent after 1988 that the internally-imposed controls on personal and business credit gave NWS better protection against non-payment of debts by borrowers in the ensuing recession.

In the later 1980s, the extraordinary diversity of the company began to pay off. The financial results were impressive. By 1986, NWS was by far and away the most successful finance house in the UK, measured by profits in relation to advances. While there were temporary difficulties from time to time, it was clear, by the close of the decade, that the changes of the 1980s had been, on the whole, advantageous. In April 1989, North West Securities changed its name to NWS Bank plc, designed to recognise its status as a bank and to indicate to the general public its financial strength. The 1988 report was issued under this new title. In 1989, NWS Bank acquired Equity Bank, a small operation in Dublin. While in the early years progress was made, the management of the company was entering into a number of transactions some of which, with hindsight, should not have been approved; and over the next four years a good deal of management time was expended in putting the situation right. A new chief executive and deputy chief executive were appointed in 1993, the previous incumbents having been dismissed. By 1994, the business was back in profit. Further progress was achieved from then on, and the mistakes made as a result of the acquisition stood NWS Bank in good stead in later acquisitions.

What did NWS Bank look like in 1995? The Field Division, which had been the core of the group's business, had expanded steadily over the years with the addition of new branches from time to time, and by 1995 there were ninety branches covering the UK – far more than any of the other finance houses, which were continuing to centralise their operations. Recognising the benefits of centralisation, but also believing in the value of the strong branch network, the board had decided in the late 1980s to expand the three divisional offices, and new premises were acquired in Edinburgh, Warrington and London. The telemarketing of customers from Edinburgh and Warrington began in 1991, with London handled from Warrington because of the difficulty of finding suitable staff in London at the right cost. The Edinburgh telemarketing function was transferred to Warrington in 1994.

A second phase of the centralisation of Field Division was to set up commercial sales operations in the centres to deal with transactions which were either too complex or too large to be handled by the branches, and the third phase was to set up 'Driveline' units in the divisional offices. These units dealt with business from the larger motor dealers, where a more committed service could be achieved, rather than having several branches cover the same dealer. As John Mercer explained, 'NWS Bank now had the best of both worlds with a three-divisional office structure complementing our extensive branch network'. The final phase of development was to set out to make the branches function as sales units, and to transfer all the routine administration to the divisional offices. This action reduced costs substantially, but, more importantly, led to the provision of a more effective service to the customers of the group.

Central Financial Services started life in 1985 using one of the group's innovative revolving credit products originally conceived in the 1970s. The pro-active contact with its customers by CFS has generated a wide appeal among a host of third-party companies which see customer services and retentions as a priority and the sale of various financial products as a source of additional income. For example, in 1988 a joint company was formed between NWS Bank and the National Farmers Union Mutual Insurance Society to promote a range of agricultural credit packages to the latter's members. The standing of the Insurance Society in the agricultural marketplace, together with a highly-focused and independent sales force, have brought about the development of a very successful business. The later 1980s also saw a further diversification of products continuing with the launch of a mortgage company (The Mortgage Business plc), an innovative, centralised lending operation which rapidly gained credence in an overpopulated marketplace. In 1995, CFS consisted of over fifty separate businesses which have contact with more than 200 different associations and groups through which, using mailing techniques with telephone follow-up, it markets its broad range of facilities. It employs over 1,000 staff who sell personal loans, revolving credit accounts and

Table 28.6 *Major finance companies' pre-tax profit growth (£ million), 1985–94*

	NWS Bank	Lombard North Central	Forward Trust	UDT	Lloyds Bowmaker
1985	18.2	85.6	40.5	12.1	40.8
1986	25.1	83.2	41.4	14.5	60.6
1987	27.1	103.1	52.0	23.4	71.8
1988	32.0	120.1	60.3	43.7	85.3
1989	38.0	86.5	45.3	27.6	84.2
1990	48.1	33.2	31.0	21.2	50.0
1991	55.1	3.2	40.6	25.8	23.8
1992	64.6	92.6	50.2	27.7	16.6
1993	77.1	177.8	61.2	35.5	38.2
1994	98.0	221.1	82.4	54.3	73.2
Percentage growth	438	158	103	349	79

insurance products over the telephone, and is recognised as one of the leading telemarketing companies in Europe.

During the long recession from the late 1980s into the 1990s, when new business was hard to come by, NWS Bank took a decision to concentrate on increasing fee income and insurance commissions, improve profit margins, minimise losses from bad debt, cut out unnecessary tiers of management and reduce staff in non-productive areas. This led to a decrease of 12 per cent of its workforce. Throughout these enormously difficult times, NWS Bank continued to increase profits year on year – unlike its competitors, all of whose profits declined sharply, including the market leader, Lombard North Central. Mercantile Credit, the second largest UK finance house, also found losses mounting, and when these reached over £100 million its owners, Barclays Bank, decided to close the company in 1994, keeping only some of its operations under the Barclays name. It was a remarkable performance by NWS Bank (see Table 28.6).

In April 1994, John Mercer became the fourth managing director in the forty-five years that NWS Bank has been in business, and he and his colleagues set out on further expansion. Over the next twelve months, 700 salespeople were recruited – 400 in Chester on telemarketing and the remainder in positions in branches across the country – taking the total employed by NWS Bank to 3,500. The joint venture with Renault UK, while very successful over a seventeen-year partnership, was also a restriction on opening similar relationships elsewhere. The contract was renegotiated to allow NWS Bank the freedom to approach other vehicle manufacturers and distributors. This policy paid early dividends, and joint ventures with International Motors, MVI group and the South Korean conglomerate Daewoo were secured. New business levels were very strong, and market share increased across the main lending areas of NWS Bank, taking the loan portfolio to £5.6 billion at 30 June 1995.

With the skills which NWS Bank now possessed in telephone sales, motor, commercial and personal lending and in industrial equipment leasing, it was decided to look further afield. In April 1995, KE Financial Services Ltd, a company based in Sydney, Australia, was bought from Kawasaki Steel. This was a company focusing on commercial lending, and a consumer operation was soon established, initially to deal with finance for motor vehicles imported into Australia. The move into the Pacific area complemented other planned developments of Bank of Scotland in Australasia.

The growth of North West Securities, now NWS Bank plc, into the second largest finance house in the UK has been a remarkable achievement. While innumerable factors have contributed to make this a most successful company, several reasons stand out as especially significant. There has been a long-term commitment from Bank of Scotland management to allow NWS to follow its own ideas, while the parent bank offers facilities and finance. The board members, and in particular the chairmen of NWS, have quite properly provided support in negotiations with Bank of Scotland. Undoubtedly, NWS has benefited from a high calibre of staff and flexible internal management, with Sydney Jones ranking as one of the outstanding bankers of the post-war generation. It is quite clear, from the vantage point of 1995, that his successors have been well able to carry out the task of growing the business since 1979, with a fast decision-making process to switch to new developments and close down lines where this is appropriate. The use of new technology, which saves on labour costs, is clearly relevant to the growth of a number of new products. In general, NWS works by implementing radical innovations and by encouraging good teamworking, and the comment by Lord Balfour about the positive atmosphere in Chester remains as accurate for the 1990s as when it was first observed in 1970.

CHAPTER 29

THE SUCCESS OF THE BANK, 1981–95

I T WAS IMPORTANT, and clearly indicative of attitudes within Bank of Scotland, that the directors and the whole management team were united in their reaction to the threat to the Royal Bank. This affair had not only brought into focus a responsibility to speak for the Scottish banking system; it also led to a clearer recognition of the relationship of UK banks to economic progress and provided one explanation for the relative decline in economic activity in the English regions. Within the Bank, it confirmed to everyone that the changes already under way in the Domestic Banking Division should be vigorously progressed. Although the findings of the Monopolies and Mergers Commission vindicated the stand taken by the Bank and were thus reassuring, there could never be room for complacency. As an illustration of this, even while the MMC was compiling its report, new concerns surfaced to test the Bank's resolve to keep its place as an influential and important independent element in the European banking system.

The first of these came from a surprising, non-banking, source. The board had become aware in November 1981 of considerable interest in the Bank's stock, which had risen in a month by 55p to 477p, although this was put down to speculative buying in the City of London which often preceded MMC findings. On 8 December, J. R. Cater, chairman of the Distillers Company Ltd (DCL), telephoned the Governor, Thomas Risk, and asked to come and see him privately. Late the same afternoon, Cater explained that, in view of the matter to be discussed, he would like to bring with him a representative of Robert Fleming & Co. Ltd, a City of London merchant banking house. At 9 a.m. on 9 December, Cater arrived at the Mound alone, heavy snow and ice having delayed the arrival from London of the man from Flemings. Cater revealed that DCL had purchased 4.8 per cent of the Bank's issued capital stock and hoped to obtain the Bank's blessing to acquire the balance. He said that DCL believed that it might be able to buy the Barclays Bank holding of 35.4 per cent and also the Kuwait Investment Office's 8.9 per cent. Apparently, the DCL board and its advisors had thought that the Bank might welcome a bid by another Scottish-based company before publication of the report on the bids for the Royal Bank. The Governor at once made it clear that in his opinion DCL could not have been more mistaken. He sought, and was readily given, an assurance that DCL would take no further action for the time being and, in particular, would not buy any more stock until the Governor had had the opportunity to report to the Bank board and give its response. For his part, the Governor promised to put DCL's ideas before the board and to reply to Cater as soon as possible.

The Governor and the Treasurer cancelled reservations on a flight to the USA scheduled for later that day, retained Morgan Grenfell & Co. as advisors, and arranged an immediate meeting with the directors of that merchant bank that afternoon in London. They were accompanied by Hugh K. Young, deputy chief executive of the British Linen Bank, who later recalled: 'It was all very dramatic. The meeting was held in secret at the Forte Hotel at Heathrow. It was a very serious situation, and Morgan Grenfell were instructed to start work without delay on a suitable defence.' As a matter of courtesy, the Governor called that evening on the Governor of the Bank of England, Gordon Richardson, and told him of the day's developments. It appeared that the Bank of England shared Bank of Scotland's surprise that an industrial company, specialising in alcoholic drinks, should think it appropriate to try to acquire a clearing bank. The following day, Thomas Risk pursued inquiries to establish the seriousness or otherwise of DCL's purpose, and he duly reported the results to a private session of the Bank board on 15 December.[1] To place on record the board's complete unanimity of purpose, the Governor took the, for him, unusually formal step of inviting each director in turn to state whether he had any reservations whatever about the correctness of the decision to justify and fight for the continued independence of Bank of Scotland. All were agreed, and the directors authorised the Governor to tell J. R. Cater that they unanimously rejected his proposal.

It became apparent that DCL and Robert Fleming & Co. intended to proceed despite the rejection of their informal offer. While the Bank believed that the bid would ultimately fail, there was nevertheless some

---

1 BS 1/6, Minutes, private session, 15 December 1981. Present were the Governor, the Deputy Governor, the Treasurer, Lord Clydesmuir, Lord Polwarth, Thomas W. Walker (past Treasurer), Sir William Lithgow and Messrs Pelham Burn, Lumsden, Strachan, MacLeod, Robertson and Birkbeck (also a director of Barclays). John Wilson (general manager) and Dr Joan Smith (Secretary) were the only officials in attendance. Sir Richard Pease confirmed his support to the Governor for the proposed course of action.

apprehension that Fleming's activities in seeking possible sellers of Bank of Scotland stock in order to mount a hostile bid would lead to damaging speculation in the Bank's stock and, should they be successful in buying any significant volume of stock, to another distracting and time-consuming reference to the MMC. These concerns were made known to the Governor of the Bank of England, and considerable time and effort were expended, particularly by Thomas Risk, the Governor, and Bruce Pattullo, the Treasurer, in explaining the Bank's policy and philosophy to senior politicians of all parties, and to civil servants. Their objectives were to ensure that the issues at stake were well understood and that, if the MMC did find against the two bids for the Royal Bank, the cabinet, which would have to approve the MMC's recommendation, would not overturn the report.[2] The Bank also took every opportunity of pointing out to all those responsible for the banking system the serious disadvantages inherent in a major bank becoming a subsidiary of a trading company, however large and apparently secure.

In fact, when in January 1982 the MMC emphatically rejected both bids for the Royal Bank, DCL abandoned its efforts to acquire more Bank of Scotland stock and subsequently sold its holding in 1985. The cabinet had little option but to accept the MMC's conclusions. Yet, as the Lex column in the *Financial Times* suggested, the findings left open the possibility, 'however ludicrous', of a renewed bid by DCL for the Bank, and the board felt it prudent to continue to monitor the situation, although City predators turned now to other targets. Throughout this whole episode, the Scottish press showed its strong support for the continued independence of the Scottish banks. As to the position of the Secretary of State, George Younger, who as mentioned above had steadfastly opposed the bid for the Royal Bank, the *Glasgow Herald* expressed a commonly-held view that it was difficult to see how any Secretary of State for Scotland could have survived a decision to allow a bid for Bank of Scotland which was wholly opposed by the board.[3]

For several years, Bank of Scotland managers believed that their expertise with oil and energy would eventually lead the Bank into more connections with North America, and they planned for that eventuality. The first office was opened in Houston, Texas, in 1976. A limited federal branch was established in New York in 1978, and a representative office in Los Angeles in 1980. All were forbidden, under US regulations, to take deposits or to engage in the range of retail transactions open to ordinary US commercial banks. Some concern was expressed that the 'extremely

---

2 BS 1/6, Minutes, private session, 19 January 1982.
3 R. S. Martin, 'City Comment', *Glasgow Herald*, 17 December 1982.

low margins' earned by the International Division in the US wholesale market would result in an unacceptable lowering of the Bank's return on assets, and there was a view that the Bank should search for higher returns on its overseas operations, especially in the apparently more lucrative US retail trade. Accordingly, it was agreed that the Bank should become an issuer of commercial paper not exceeding US $100 million at any one time; and, as a vehicle for these operations, a wholly-owned subsidiary, Scotland International Finance BV, incorporated in the Netherlands and guaranteed by the Bank, was established. The completion of the issue gave the Bank a healthy free capital ratio of 5.5 per cent. Unfortunately for the Bank, the UK government decided to levy a special tax on banking deposits, which somewhat weakened the position. It was regrettable, noted the Governor in the annual report, that the government 'should have "virtually confiscated" part of our capital base'.[4]

Although ultimate control of the US banking system was in the hands of Congress, which held periodic hearings into finance and legislated extensively, most day-to-day supervision and policy action was implemented at the federal level by three main agencies, each with its own area of banking regulation: the Federal Reserve Board, the Federal Deposit Insurance Corporation and the Comptroller of the Currency. It was an important objective of the legislation, and of the regulators, actively to discourage foreign holdings in US banking companies. These objectives were shared by state legislators; and, together with the federal and state authorities, the three agencies ensured that most US banking continued to operate on a relatively narrow regional basis, with over 14,000 separate banking companies and strict controls on the growth of larger banking groups covering several states. The regulations were in place supposedly to halt a systemic collapse, but the very narrowness of the banking companies almost guaranteed that periodic bank failures would continue to occur. It seemed to some observers that the attitudes of the regulatory bodies were insufficiently flexible and that the strict application of the rules resulted in the loss of what might have been beneficial connections with experienced foreign banks. Perhaps irrational fears based on half-remembered images of the years before the First World War, and the crisis of 1929–31, may have played their part in shaping such attitudes. The plethora of federal and state interests and the mass of consultants and analysts who swarmed over the banking system also seemed to have been completely unable to foresee the Latin American lending crisis. Bank of Scotland's ambitions to develop business in North America came up against the banking regulators and against what seemed to those responsible at the time an

4 Bank of Scotland, *Annual Report* (1981).

American inability to recognise that the structures to which they were accustomed could inhibit the security which they hoped to ensure. For Bank
of Scotland, one such hurdle was the US Bank Holding Act, under which
the Bank was deemed, solely for regulatory purposes, to be a subsidiary of
Barclays Bank so long as Barclays held 25 per cent or more of the Bank's
stock; and as such it was prohibited from acquiring more than 5 per cent of
the equity of any US bank. At that time, Barclays showed no inclination to
reduce its holding below 25 per cent, and the Bank as noted before had no
wish to invite such an action. However, since the Bank wished to explore
the possibility of acquiring an equity holding in a US bank, in June 1981
it approached the Federal Reserve Board in Washington DC to argue that
an injection of Scottish banking experience and practice would benefit US
banking, and that such a development should be facilitated by recognition
of the fact that the special voting structure attached to Bank of Scotland
stock would require only a modest divestment by Barclays (to not much
less than its then 35.4 per cent) to bring its voting power below 25 per
cent. If the Federal Reserve Board would agree that what mattered was the
voting power, not the proportion of shares held, the Bank could be free
to take a controlling interest in any bank in any US state. Unfortunately,
the discouraging response to the latter argument was sufficient to deter the
Bank from its efforts at this time to pursue the acquisition of a US bank.

A second submission to the Federal Reserve Board was later made
through Shearman & Sterling, the Bank's New York attorneys, in cooperation with Barclays' legal advisors, Sullivan and Cromwell.[5] However,
the Federal Reserve again ruled that, under the Act, control referred not
to voting power but to the percentage of stock owned. Furthermore, it
was made clear that, even if the holding were to be reduced below 25 per
cent, the Bank might still be deemed a Barclays subsidiary if a 'substantial
economic interest' remained and that the Federal Reserve would exercise
the right to determine what this meant. The Federal Reserve's lawyers
even contended that, if the Bank were to acquire a controlling interest in a
bank outside New York state, Barclays would have to sell its entire holding
in the Bank, whatever size it might then be, since Barclays would then
have acquired an interest in a bank outside its principal state of banking
operations (New York). This seemed to put an end, for the time being at
least, to Bank of Scotland's thoughts of expansion in the USA.

However, the issues raised in the US context became relevant when
Barclays Bank began to consider its holding in the Bank from a broader
point of view. As a result of informal discussions with Barclays in
December 1979, the Bank had some hint that Barclays might not be

5 BS, papers on Federal Reserve Board, 1982.

opposed to a modest reduction of its holding in the Bank. This view had emerged from earlier discussions in which the Bank had expressed itself as comfortable with the Barclays holding at 35.4 per cent; but the Bank had become reconciled to the fact that sooner or later reduction would become inevitable. The wish to acquire a bank in the USA had thus, from the Bank's own viewpoint, been a useful exploration of Barclays' intentions in light of the Bank's new needs.

A further development on this front was the decision taken by Barclays at a board meeting on 7 January 1982, prior to the MMC report, that 'Subject to the publication of that report and arising from discussions with the Governor of Bank of Scotland, the management felt that whilst the bank would continue to inform Bank of Scotland of its intentions with regard to the shareholding, it was no longer bound by the terms of the agreements' of 1969. Indeed, 'This agreement had been abrogated in recent years'.[6] The minute was ambiguous and was later modified; but the view of Barclays, which had been kept informed of the possibility that the Bank would try to buy a bank in the USA, that it was no longer bound by the 1969 agreements had been revealed, and the security of its shareholding could evidently no longer be relied on by the Bank.

Underlying any thought of a reduction in the Barclays shareholding was the question of its value. Barclays would obviously wish to maximise its return by selling the stock in one block. The Bank, on the other hand, would see no justification for such an approach and would argue that a sale should be at current market price. Such a difference of viewpoint, while entirely natural, held the seeds of possible future disagreement and acrimony which both parties would prefer to avoid. Barclays' directors were conscious of the terms of the MMC report, with its emphasis on maintaining regional interests, and remained persuaded that they should not do anything which was clearly against the wishes or interests of Bank of Scotland, although they 'reserved [their] position that the time might arise when [they] would wish to take action which did not necessarily have the approval of Bank of Scotland'. On this basis, the Governor and Sir Timothy Bevan exchanged private letters, the Governor for his part acknowledging Sir Timothy's helpful reaction to the approach by DCL, while Sir Timothy gave notice that, should a further reduction of Barclays' holding beyond a modest divestment be required, Barclays 'would probably sell out the whole shareholding . . . to whom [we] wished'.

After the general election on 9 June 1983, Margaret Thatcher returned to 10 Downing Street with a majority of 144 over all other parties, although in Scotland the Tories came a poor second to the Labour

6 Barclays Bank, board minutes, 7 January 1982.

Party. A programme of the privatisation of publicly-owned utilities and assets was announced as the cornerstone of government policy. Industrial production was rising in England, and there was greater confidence within government circles than in the previous period of office.[7] It did not appear to matter much in Whitehall that the recovery in Scotland and in several English regions was slower and less sure-footed than in the south of England. The Governor of Bank of Scotland stated in the 1983 annual report that, apart from the oil-related trades and in the wider Aberdeen area, 1982–3 had been a 'difficult and disappointing year for many Scottish businessmen'. As 'the largest share of business for the Domestic Banking Division came from Scotland . . . our prosperity remains closely linked with the fortunes of the Scottish economy'. The reduction in the value of sterling against the US dollar was welcome, but there was clearly room for progress, especially over UK interest rates. Bank of Scotland's average base rate, 13.3 per cent in 1981–2, was still relatively high at 11.4 per cent in the following financial year. Some customers were still in difficulty. However, increasing advances would demonstrate a healthy economy, and lower Bank of England money rates were essential because of their direct relationship with commercial rates. Talk of merger activity in the banking industry had begun to recede, but the Bank shared a widely-held view that Mrs Thatcher's entrenched preferences for unhampered 'market forces', and her dislike of regional policies, meant that in the event of another bid for the Royal Bank she would try to ensure that 'public interest' arguments would carry little weight. 'Competition' in its narrowest sense would, it was suggested, always carry the day. This was an uncomfortable prospect from the Mound, but those in charge there had no intention of allowing the Bank to become vulnerable to such haphazard forces.

An incident occurred about that time which symbolised the difficulties that Scottish bankers experienced when trying to put the regional case to the government of the day. Prime ministers regularly meet business leaders, and in September 1983 Mrs Thatcher attended such a dinner arranged by George Younger at Bute House, the Secretary of State for Scotland's official residence in Charlotte Square, Edinburgh. The Bank Treasurer, Bruce Pattullo, a polite and courteous man, still only 44 but already widely recognised in London and in Edinburgh as one of the outstanding bankers of his generation, queried whether the base rate set by the Bank of England (then at 9.5 per cent) was rather too high compared with inflation (at 4 per cent), and suggested that business activity, as measured by bank

---

7 Among the sources for this period, see P. R. Hughes, *British Economic History, 1945–1987, Broad Historical Narrative*, Queen Mary College, Economic Papers, no. 184, (London: 1988) pp. 31–2; S. Pollard, *The Development of the British Economy 1914–1967*, 2nd edn (London: 1969).

advances, would rise if interest rates were lowered. There ought, one would have thought, to have been a measure of agreement on this basic building-block of economic growth. After all, while speaking to the Queen's speech on 22 June 1983, Thatcher had pointed with pride to 'the lowest level of inflation since 1968'.[8] According to a leaked story in the business section of *The Scotsman*, which is the only published source of what transpired, this straightforward question 'touched a nerve', and after delivering 'two verbal savagings' the prime minister turned to other guests and asked rhetorically: 'What would become of the country if it was run by men like that?' A month later, she wrote to Bruce Pattullo, dissociating herself from the press report: 'Nothing could have been further from my mind than to have disparaged your outstanding professional expertise and achievements, in the way suggested in the press report', adding: 'I count it a great advantage to have been able to learn at first hand from you through our conversation about how professional banks such as yours view the general economic scene which we are concerned to work with in Government'. This somewhat equivocal palliative gave reassuring testimony to the prime minister's political instincts if not to her patience with constructive questions which she did not wish to answer in similar vein.

In the autumn and winter of 1983, the Royal Bank and Bank of Scotland share prices rose sharply, giving rise to speculation in the press; DCL currently held 4.99 per cent of Bank stock, and Lloyds Bank added another 5 per cent of Royal Bank stock to its 16 per cent holding. The reason which Lloyds gave for this action was to protect its position in the finance house Lloyds and Scottish, but the men at the Mound asked themselves 'whether that was the real reason'.[9] Eagle Star Insurance had been bid for by BAT, and also by Allianz, a German insurance company. Did the new appointments in government after the general election, in particular the installation of Nigel Lawson at the Treasury, and the changes in the civil service reflect a change in government attitudes to foreign and hostile bids for companies involved in finance and insurance? Stockbrokers, sensing possible movements, helpfully, and with shrewd self-interest, offered assistance in various ways, and the Bank management continued its policy of keeping in touch with stockholders, civil servants and opinion-formers whose understanding of the real issues would be useful if a contest arose.

One question which had an important bearing on such speculative activities was whether the 1972 guidelines which would rule out an opposed bid for a British clearing bank were still in effect. The fact that this question had to be asked showed that something had changed.

8 M. Thatcher, *The Downing Street Years* (London: 1993), p. 315.
9 BS, papers for meeting with Bank of England, 29 December 1983.

The decision by HSBC to mount an unwelcome bid for the Royal Bank, despite the disapproval of the Governor of the Bank of England, showed that these guidelines' power might have diminished. The Banking Act gave only limited powers of intervention, mainly related to the grant of a banking licence, and the Bank of England had apparently decided not to seek further statutory powers, perhaps in the knowledge that this government would refuse them. So, reliance upon the Bank of England if a bid were made could prove a disappointment. There remained great interest in the banking system on the part of the Office of Fair Trading and of the MMC, which had taken seriously the arguments used in the Royal Bank affairs; but the best way to ensure continued independence was by demonstrating, as the Bank was doing, and as the Royal Bank was beginning to show again that it could do on its own, that the public was best served not by fewer and larger banks but by wider competition spawning a greater variety of service.

Nevertheless, the Bank did not overlook the possibility that the improvement in profitability and market share might be temptations to predators.[10] A paper rehearsing the reasons why regional banks such as the Bank should remain independent was provided to the Bank of England.[11] There was some justification for the Bank's apprehension. By 1983, the thinking of a number of senior politicians and influential London-based civil servants was moving firmly against references to the MMC on 'quality' and regional grounds; in most cases, it was now argued, investigations should focus on competition policy, envisaged rather more narrowly as time passed. These views had been signalled before; for instance, there were arguments in the dissenting comments of the 1982 MMC report on the Royal Bank to the effect that as 'the UK was an economic union of long-standing within which economic resources, including people, were free to move . . . the negative act of banning proposed mergers in the supposed interest of retaining particular responsibilities or levels of decision-making in Scotland could not make enough difference to the otherwise free play of trends and forces to be justified'.[12] There was a feeling in London that market forces moved in irresistible ways and that institutional impediments only led to outcomes which were below the optimum that 'purer' competition would encourage. After the 1983 general election, government took up these ideas and encouraged a rethink of

---

10 See the discussion of Bank of Scotland's performance later in this chapter.

11 BS, *The Case for Ensuring the Continuing Existence of a UK Owned Independent Clearing Bank Group – other than the 'Big Four'*, 16 February 1984.

12 Monopolies and Mergers Commission, *The Hongkong and Shanghai Banking Corporation, Standard Chartered Bank Limited, The Royal Bank of Scotland Group Limited: A Report on the Proposed Mergers*, Cmnd 8472 (London: 1982): Sir A. Neale, note of dissent, pp. 93–4.

merger policy. In early 1984, there was murmuring among some senior Scottish politicians that they were less able to answer the centralising arguments within the admittedly cooler policy process in Whitehall than had prevailed before the election. The problem was to persuade politicians in the fast-changing world of British political life that a long-term focus had to be maintained before the wisdom or otherwise of a merger could be evaluated. The experience after takeovers of Scottish companies was largely negative: 'Nothing, no amount of good will, guidelines, promises or understandings, nothing can stop the decline of the jobs and of the motivation of the people who are left behind simply to do things but to decide less and less'.[13]

In November 1984, the Governor received a telephone call from Sir Timothy Bevan asking him to visit Lombard Street on the evening before the Barclays board meeting. On arrival, he found several senior Barclays men with Sir Timothy, who explained that Barclays had concluded that it must put up its Bank of Scotland holding for sale and that a proposal to this effect would be made at the following day's board meeting. At the board meeting, the Governor, who was also a director of Barclays, was able to convince Barclays' board that it must let the Mound try to find a buyer, the preferred option being a single holder for the 35.4 per cent stake 'if we could identify one whose interest might be in having a link with a successful bank'.[14]

The Scottish mutual assurance societies had substantial holdings of equities, and the idea of very large individual share stakes was not difficult for them. The nature of their liabilities also gave considerable scope and need for long-term holdings, provided that these met strict performance criteria designed to serve the actuarial needs of the assured. While demanding a satisfactory total return, such societies were less concerned with short-term movements in the capital values of their holdings and more anxious to obtain a steady and growing stream of income than were some other types of institutions. The Bank had always had strong connections with the life assurance companies, not least The Standard Life Assurance Company, the largest of them all; and there were many other connections between the Scottish life assurance industry and all three Scottish banks. It was natural, therefore, that the Governor should tell Robert C. Smith, the chairman of Standard Life, on his return to Edinburgh of the possibility that the Barclays stake could be for sale. George Gwilt, chief executive of Standard Life, then discussed the matter with Bruce Pattullo. Bank of

13 Governor to Secretary of State for Scotland, 4 April 1984.
14 Sir Thomas Risk, paper on 'Tercentenary History', 1993. The Governor of the British Linen Bank had sat on the main board of Barclays since affiliation.

Scotland had for years sold many more Standard Life policies than those of any competing company. The Bank had also been the principal banker to Standard Life for 150 years, so there existed a level of knowledge about each other's business from which a constructive dialogue could start. It was an unusually large holding, and Standard Life was especially concerned with long-term growth in earnings. The Bank had to stand back while Standard Life thought hard and then talked directly with Barclays. The announcement of the purchase of Barclays' 35.4 per cent holding for £155 million by Standard Life was made in January 1985 to an unsuspecting market. As the largest mutual life assurance business in Europe, Standard Life's assets were huge: in 1985 they exceeded £8.4 billion, of which £1.34 billion was in property, £2.03 billion in government and local authority securities, and £3.44 billion in equity stocks. In the early 1980s, its actuaries had achieved very good results, and the increased public interest in life assurance saw premium income rise from £525.3 million in 1982 to £866.6 million in 1984, and investment income from £420.1 million to £544.4 million. The excess of income over expenditure in 1984 was £647.5 million.

The question of banknote issue has never been far from the minds of Scottish bankers. Since 1707, it has regularly been pointed out that the Treaty of Union between England and Scotland protected this Scottish right from change unless it could be proved to Parliament that change would be 'to the evident advantage of the subjects of Scotland'. The separate development within the British currency system has been regulated from time to time in conjunction with the Treasury and the Bank of England, most notably in the later eighteenth century and again in 1845, with the understanding that the Scottish banks printed and managed the main currency for Scotland, and that English notes comprised a small part of the circulation. In 1979, the Bank of England intimated that it would replace its £1 sterling banknote by a coin of the same denomination and extend to the rest of its note series in Scotland the right of legal tender, which had hitherto in peacetime attached only to the £1 note. The Committee of Scottish Clearing Bankers and the three Scottish banks supported proposals agreed with the Scottish Office for legislation to extend legal status also to all notes of the three Scottish banks. There was some related debate about where such a move would weigh in future moves towards a single European currency, although the generally-held view in banking and government circles was that Brussels would build in flexibility for continued Scottish note issue. In the event, the government never progressed the matter.

After the election of the Conservative government in 1979, the control exercised by the Bank of England over the issue of foreign exchange was abolished. From 1940, this function had been administered by the Bank of England agency in Glasgow, and some hundreds of jobs were now to go. The agency also maintained links with industry and commerce in Scotland and handled the issue of Bank of England notes to the three Scottish banks and their withdrawal. As the system stood in 1979, the combined circulation of the three Scottish banks averaged £425 million, and they retired £375 million of Bank of England notes. In addition, the four Trustee Savings Banks, other commercial banks, the Post Office and the nationalised industries based in Scotland received notes to the value of £705 million from the Scottish banks. One of the Scottish TSBS and the National Westminster Bank, which had been appointed by the government to supply British Shipbuilders with cash, now asked for Bank of England notes to replace Scottish notes. In the summer of 1980, Threadneedle Street informed the Committee of Scottish Clearing Bankers that it intended to proceed with this substitution, somewhat surprisingly citing the under-use of its Glasgow office as the main reason. Had the Bank of England replaced the whole £705 million, then the Scottish banks would have lost around £1 million in income through lost circulation. In addition, the Scots would have faced significantly increased costs from the receipt and retiral of the hugely increased volume of English notes in circulation. Further, there would be a diminution in the proportion of the Scottish banks' own notes in their till monies, resulting in a further 'substantial' loss of interest. Although impossible to forecast precisely, another £1 million was involved.[15] It was also felt that there was much more to this story than loss of income.

The adverse financial impact would fall especially hard on marginal branches. Many were situated in inner-city areas or in sparsely-populated countryside and provided far less in the form of deposits per head of staff than their counterparts in England. It had to be explained, once again, to the Bank of England that the benefits of the Scottish note issue 'offset to a significant extent' the expense of maintaining this network of marginal offices. Scottish banknotes did not have to be covered by deposits with the Bank of England until they were in circulation, so notes held in tills incurred minimal holding costs.[16] Branches could hold stocks of notes beyond their immediate requirements, with no cost in Bank of England cover, thus reducing considerably the frequency of distribution and associated security costs. All three banks agreed that if the proportion of English notes rose in line with the stated intentions, then the resulting

15 BS, Treasurer Box 1 (5B1), Bank of England note issue in Scotland (Glasgow Cash Centre) papers, 1980–1.
16 M. Gaskin, *The Scottish Banks: A Modern Survey* (London: 1965).

increase in branch holdings, with their associated interest charges, would result in severe pressure on marginal branches.[17] Whether the social effect which closures might have on rural and inner-city life and business would weigh with the government was doubtful, although the Scottish Office was still sympathetic to these arguments. There was a feeling that the Bank of England was once again ignoring genuine concerns. On this occasion, there was a relatively satisfactory ending: the Royal Bank agreed to buy the Bank of England's cash centre as part of its expansion plan agreed after the rejection of the takeover bids.

The lax regime which allowed Latin American governments and companies to increase their debts has been noted. By 1982, the overall position was impossible to recover by normal banking action. Mexican debts ballooned from $20 billion in 1976 to $82 billion by June 1982, with an increase of $18 billion in 1981. Brazilian debts grew by nearly $30 billion in the four years from 1979 to $79 billion. Western banks' total exposure to all Latin American debts had reached $196.5 billion by 30 June 1982, accounting for 12.5 per cent of total external bank assets of $1,570.7 billion. Even at this late stage, after eight years of mounting debts founded in large part on recycled OPEC oil revenues, few bankers, government officials or established commentators could bring themselves to realise that default was a serious possibility. As first Argentina and then Mexico found problems with debt repayments, it became clear that a response from western governments and commercial banks which involved curtailing lines of credit would make it impossible for these two countries, and possibly Brazil as well, to service interest due and perhaps even repay the principal. The result for the banking system in the USA would be unthinkable: a massive reduction of liquidity followed by widespread closures of banks. The Securities and Exchange Commission, another regulator of US banking, announced in November 1982 new guidelines which asked banks to report substantial exposures, and the US newspapers and broadcasting companies performed the role of talking up the crisis. It became clear that the US Interagency Country Exposure Review Committee, established in 1979, was entirely out of its depth because of its narrow focus on a simplistic risk-classification system.

The American public was regaled with another of the laws of banking: US foreclosure on large-scale foreign debts could not just be done without bringing down part of the USA's own banking system. The regulatory bodies in the lending countries, and the International Monetary Fund and the World Bank, were forced to abandon any strict mechanism in respect

17 BS, Treasurer Box 1 (5B1), Bank of England note issue in Scotland (Glasgow Cash Centre), Bank of England notes issued in Scotland, 1980–1.

of the proportions of foreign to domestic lending, as it was agreed that the level of advances to these debtor countries had to be maintained.[18] Some 53 per cent of the $54.541 billion owed to US banks by Mexico, Brazil and Argentina – the three biggest debtors – was due in under one year. Of this sum, 58 per cent was owed in the first instance to just nine US banks. For eight of these, a default would mean writing off their equity base and part of their reserves. The position for some UK banks was also serious. The National Westminster Bank had advanced to Latin America sums equivalent to 86 per cent of its group equity; the Midland Bank at 220 per cent was particularly affected through its ownership of the Crocker Bank. Bank of Scotland was relatively insulated: refusal to grub around under other men's tables, which sometimes annoyed City of London bankers, gave Bank of Scotland a total exposure at this date of $145 million (about £65 million at summer 1982 exchange rates), equivalent to only 29 per cent of group equity, some 0.55 per cent of UK banks' total exposure. This was a strong position to be in. David Jenkins, the then Bank of Scotland economist who made a study of Latin America, suggested that, in the worst-case scenario, default would involve the loss of £90 million in taxable capacity, which would be felt most clearly in the leasing business conducted by Bank of Scotland group.[19] Widespread default in the inter-bank markets might affect liquidity as US banks recalled their loans, but the Bank was well regarded and might be perceived as a safe haven in a crisis. Moreover, the pound sterling would probably appreciate against the dollar in such circumstances.

By January 1983, the total exposure of the Bank's International Division to less-developed countries came to $179.35 million, which included some additional monies extended under rescheduling schemes negotiated by the international agencies. Brazil owed the largest slice; the Bank had $65 million out in loans there and another £17 million guaranteed by the UK Export and Credit Guarantee Department. By 1984, it had become clear that repayment of the principal would be deferred until the 1990s, which was unsatisfactory. The Brazilian economy enjoyed a trade surplus of $13 billion, and with strong protectionist barriers its domestic firms were doing very well; the overall economy in that year grew by 9 per cent. Strong pressure was therefore exerted by western governments and institutions to find other routes for repayment. One outcome was the conversion of debt into equity, with some capital write-off. Bank of Scotland negotiated several such innovative deals in respect of its loans to Chile and Brazil. A successful settlement gave Bank of Scotland, in due course, majority

18 D. Lascelles, 'US Bank Regulation after the Debt "Crisis"', *The Banker*, 133 (January 1983), 21–3.
19 BS, D. Jenkins, 'Consequences of a Latin American Debt Repudiation', p. 3.

ownership of a hotel on Copacabana beach in Rio de Janeiro, a tomato-paste factory in north-east Brazil and a stake in the country's third largest paper producer. There were similar conversions in Chile. In this case, the vehicle company was a conglomerate appropriately called Pathfinder SA, reflecting the fact that this was the first debt-and-equity swap in Chile. In the rarefied world of international banking, commentators came to the not unsurprising conclusion that closer monitoring of the use which borrowers made of external finance might give some protection to lenders.[20] There was even some comment to the effect that the study of previous crises might have avoided the worst of the excesses, although little overt criticism of the social and political structures of the borrowing countries encouraged an inappropriate attitude to international obligations. Some of the New York money centre banks seriously damaged their reputations during this episode. Bank of Scotland emerged virtually unscathed because of management's and directors' reluctance to get caught up in the herd instinct.

In 1984, Bank of Scotland opened a representative office in Chicago, Illinois. However, the board was still looking for a more sizeable opportunity, preferably to purchase a bank with experience of energy finance. The crisis in Latin America did not present a suitable opportunity, but it was considered that the growing oil crisis might. The Organisation of Petroleum Exporting Countries was locked in disagreement over production quotas; and the price of oil (always calculated in US dollars), having earlier multiplied several times, fell sharply from $30 per barrel in 1985 to only $10 by the spring of the following year. This put enormous pressure on producers and inevitably on their suppliers, subcontractors and bankers. Bank of Scotland had excellent information on the position of the industry around the globe, and the eventual opportunity came in Texas.

While the Texan banking system had grown after the oil-price hike in 1974, with huge loans to oil producers and supply trades, the price fall led to great difficulty for many parties. The share prices of local banks fell; many were now below 50 per cent of net asset value, and some very much less. Under Texan law, no bank holding company from outside the state could acquire one of the local banks. But in the aftermath of the Latin American crisis, Congress had passed legislation which would allow, *in extremis*, for the Federal Deposit Insurance Corporation (FDIC) to overrule state legislation. This would be unlikely to happen unless depositors' money was at risk, and would require local political agreement. Nevertheless,

---

20 B. Nowzad, 'Lending and Borrowing Limits: The Futile Search for a Formula', *The Banker*, 133 (February 1983), 25–7; T. E. Krayenbuehl, 'How Country Risk should be Monitored', *The Banker*, 133 (May 1983), 51–3.

the bill was a step in the direction of common sense. Further, the FDIC could agree a safety net which would restrict the liability of a rescuer to specific sums or indeed to none at all.

Why would Bank of Scotland consider an ailing Texas bank exposed to one or more trade losses? The ability of the FDIC to support a rescue in an imaginative way was a clear benefit. The general Texan economy was also a good deal broader than oil. The population stood at 17 million and there were strong industrial sectors, large agricultural and food-processing trades, an extensive building industry, some defence work and, very importantly, large service sectors including medical and health research establishments and a relatively well-off middle class. The city of Houston, already familiar to the Bank, was one of the largest commercial centres on the southern seaboard. An intelligent plan organised on a state-wide basis could transform a problem bank and give the kind of retail and commercial returns sought. In return, it was believed that a Scottish bank was likely to be a very attractive proposition to US bank shareholders in trouble.

The bank in question was the Houston-based First City Bankcorp, a holding company for sixty-four banks, all of which were in Texas except one in South Dakota. Some of these were really very small. First City was involved in the oil industry to the extent of over a quarter of its lending book by the early 1980s, but had compounded this by a $3.5 billion exposure for house- and office-building. This was a classic banking error: over-involvement in a commodity and then another set of advances to the building trades booming because of a rise in the price of that same commodity. There were further, though much smaller, debts in Latin America. By late 1985, the FDIC was aware that First City was in difficulty; the bank's figures indicated almost no profit for the past three years, with advances over $560 million yielding no interest and with $580 million in provisions for bad debt. Matters deteriorated in the first six months of 1986, compounded by the action of Saudi Arabia in increasing its output, which weakened oil prices and spread even more gloom. By the summer, advances yielding no return to the bank had risen to nearly $700 million. In these circumstances, with share prices down to a third of net asset value, the situation justified outsiders exploring a rescue attempt. The management had made its own attempts to cut costs, and had concentrated lending efforts on its domestic middle-class customers in a move away from oil; the latter sector was down to under 20 per cent of assets by the end of 1985, although that was only achieved after a lot of red ink on the loan book.

Bruce Pattullo, as Treasurer, and Peter Burt, as head of International Division, with board approval undertook detailed discussions with the section of the FDIC responsible for 'Failing Banks and Assistance Transactions'. The conclusion reached by Bank of Scotland was that an investment by a Bank-led syndicate to rescue First City should buy between 50 and 60 per cent of equity, amounting to over $350 million. But it was of crucial importance that the FDIC should agree to a clear safety net with tight specifications on the position of every commercial, foreign and retail advance, and cast-iron guarantees about any off-balance-sheet transactions.

On 21 October 1986, the board agreed to initiate discussions with the Bank of England and Standard Life as well as preliminary approaches to potential investors to gauge market reactions. If this went well, then a syndicate could be placed before the FDIC, the Federal Reserve Board and all the other US regulators. Although Bank of Scotland was ultimately not awarded this rescue transaction by the FDIC, the exercise confirmed that in these matters, as in every other, Bank of Scotland was far more attentive to the needs of its own proprietors and to local staff than a number of other non-US banks had been to theirs while pursuing purchases in the USA.

The crisis over the Latin American debts resulted in a welcome interest among bankers in the spread of commercial bank lending across the various types of borrowers and in a new emphasis on raising the proportion of paid-up capital and published free reserves to advances. This debate on such ratios, which became known as capital adequacy, was to permit, at least in theory, reasonably accurate comparisons to be made between banks in different countries, although there were arguments over the accounting for some balance-sheet items, such as deferred taxation and unrealised equity profits. More problematic was the analysis of risk. This was marked by widespread subjectivity and variance between countries and different types of banks, which unfortunately continued to reflect the narrow concerns of some central bankers.

These issues, together with the specific compliance with legislation on the soundness and honesty of all the Bank's dealings, ensured that the position of the Bank Secretary became, for some years, more broadly focused than it had been before the debt crisis. There were certain statutory duties stated in the Bank of Scotland Acts, namely the holding of proprietors' meetings and maintaining the stock registers, keeping required records and generally being able to retrieve information, verifying all legal matters relating to advances, the overview of trustee cases and handling bankruptcies and liquidations. These tasks were onerous and time-consuming, but essential. From 1971–9, the Secretary was David Antonio, originally an employee of the British Linen Bank, whose expertise was on the legal side. Perhaps his most significant, and lengthy, task was to bring together the pension funds of Bank of Scotland, the Union Bank and the British Linen Bank, and to ensure that the resulting single scheme was properly funded. This was a considerable achievement requiring much tenacity. He was succeeded in 1979 by Dr Joan Smith, who had had an early career as a mathematical physicist. She later took a law degree at Aberdeen University and became, in 1950, only the fourth female advocate at the Scottish bar. Dr Smith became company secretary of William Grant & Sons, the distillers; and then, after a period in the law department of Bank of Scotland, she moved to Bank of Scotland Finance Company and oversaw the transfer of its business to the revived British Linen Bank Ltd. After becoming Secretary, she was a founder member of the management board of the Bank before retiring in May 1984.

The aftermath of the crisis over the Royal Bank and the continued concern over the position of Scottish banks persuaded Bruce Pattullo that the post of Secretary now required an understanding of corporate finance matters and the ability to manage the Bank's relationships with its professional advisors. While the legal input was important, such advice was already available both internally and externally. Capital adequacy was now firmly on the agenda along with balance-sheet structures, and was already the subject of discussion within the Bank by 1983. It was fortunate that Hugh Young was available to fill the position; a deputy chief executive and in charge of corporate finance at the British Linen Bank, he had been commissioned in the Royal Scots on National Service, and later became a major in an Edinburgh-based Territorial Army unit. As a young chartered accountant, he had earlier worked in the corporate finance department of Schroders in London.

An assessment in December 1983 of the gearing ratio indicated that Bank of Scotland and the Royal Bank were to all appearances more strongly capitalised than the four English clearers (see Table 29.1). Under pressure to develop a more sophisticated system which took account of the riskiness of assets, the Bank of England categorised assets into different levels of risk and expressed the capital as a percentage of the cumulative products of the assets multiplied by their risk weighting. But the published information was insufficient to allow banks to assess how other competitor banks fared in this assessment, and the Bank of England was not divulging it. Since none could calculate the appropriate figures for others, it was difficult to determine in isolation what ratio any bank should aim at: 'the cynical might suggest that this is one of the reasons that the Bank of England wishes to use this ratio'.[21] The Bank of England

21 BS, I. W. St C. Scott, Manager, Corporate Planning, 'Capital Adequacy'; and BS, Board minutes, 13 September 1983 and 21 February 1984.

Table 29.1 *Bank of Scotland group capital ratios compared to other clearing bank groups (percentage), 1983*

	Barclays	Lloyds	Midland	Nat West	Royal Bank	Bank of Scotland
'Pure equity'	3.67	4.38	2.63	3.46	7.36	5.13
less: Infrastructure	2.93	3.15	2.68	2.41	5.62	3.25
	0.74	1.23	−0.05	1.05	1.74	1.88
Unprovided deferred tax	1.32	1.66	0.85	1.55	1.87	1.95
Minority interests	0.32	0.26	1.02	0.05	—	0.03
General provision	0.39	0.44	0.24	0.33	0.34	0.57
Free equity ratio	2.77	3.59	2.06	2.98	3.95	4.43
Loan capital	1.10	0.90	1.91	1.80	1.23	1.52
Gearing ratio	3.87	4.49	3.97	4.78	5.18	5.95

Source: BS 1/6, Board minutes, 14 December 1983.

advised Bank of Scotland that the ratio should be 9 per cent, and that the unconsolidated accounts of the British Linen Bank should have a 10 per cent ratio and North West Securities 12 per cent. Presumably these figures were worked out because the experts at the Bank of England assumed that the operations of a finance house were riskier than those of a commercial bank! On these figures, Bank of Scotland group appeared to have only around £20 million of 'surplus' capital.

There was little in this that Bank of Scotland regarded as unchallengeable. In published accounts, inter-bank loans under one month were treated as 'money at call and short notice', while all with a month or more to maturity were treated as 'Advances'. All inter-bank advances under one year, irrespective of whether they were to European or US banks, were presumed to involve less risk (weighted at 0.2) than an advance to any corporate customer (weighted at 1.0), regardless of whether the latter was Imperial Chemical Industries, Reuters or a Midlands engineering business, the advance secured or unsecured. To have a loan to a US bank heavily exposed to debts in Latin America weighted as being more secure than one to a blue-chip British customer was at least questionable. The detailed weighting also favoured the balance sheets of the English clearers. Whereas only 7.5 per cent of Bank of Scotland advances were in the inter-bank loan category, 16 per cent of Barclays' were thus, and the corresponding figure for Lloyds Bank was 15 per cent, for the Midland 20 per cent and for the National Westminster 28 per cent. If the Bank of England maintained its stance, it might mean Bank of Scotland having to seek additional capital.

The board and management of Bank of Scotland group had two primary responsibilities: capital ratios had to be 'sufficiently prudent' to satisfy the Bank of England; therefore, given that any broad-brush approach would

Table 29.2 *Distribution of capital through Bank of Scotland group (percentage), 1983*

	Parent bank	BLB Group	NWS Group	Group
'Pure equity'	5.20	3.57	6.05	5.13
less: Infrastructure	3.58	0.86	3.64	3.25
	1.62	2.71	2.41	1.88
Unprovided deferred tax	0.46	3.88	12.04	1.95
Minority interests	—	—	0.34	0.03
General provision	0.49	0.74	0.82	0.57
Free equity ratio	2.57	7.33	15.61	4.43
Loan capital	1.79	—	—	1.52
Gearing ratio	4.36	7.33	15.61	5.95

Source: BS 1/6, Board minutes, 14 December 1983.

have flaws within it, a lengthy disagreement was out of the question. Yet the other responsibility was to ensure that all the capital within the group was utilised to greatest effect, and over the recent past the Bank had 'earned a lower return on average capital than a number of other banking groups'. Since the return on assets was similar, the reason why the return on capital was less must have been because it was supporting a smaller balance sheet and could therefore be deployed more effectively. While the gearing ratio of the group was strong compared with other banking groups, the distribution of that capital was less than optimal. The problem was seen in the gearing ratios within Bank of Scotland group, especially those for the British Linen Bank and NWS; in varying degrees, the respective parent companies of both carried a weaker gearing ratio, due to the fact that most free capital lay within the leasing subsidiaries as unprovided deferred tax so that 'a greater proportion of Bank of Scotland group reserves [lay] within the balance sheets of the leasing subsidiaries'. If no action were taken, this would result in a continuous 'thinning' of the ratios for the unconsolidated accounts of Bank of Scotland, the British Linen Bank and NWS. Barclays Bank had tackled a similar problem by taking a special dividend from Mercantile Credit. Why not Bank of Scotland (see Table 29.2)? It was agreed that the British Linen Bank and NWS would maintain a certain capital level and that the remainder of surplus capital would be transferred to the Bank. The Bank would give an unequivocal undertaking that it would meet any future taxation liabilities which might arise, including the crystallisation of any unprovided deferred tax.

While the issue of deferred taxation was settled in conformity with Bank of England usage, management addressed also the implications for the risk:asset ratio of the perception of the capital base by outsiders. All the clearing banks were looking at their capital positions, and in July 1983 the Midland Bank made a rights issue using Samuel Montagu, its merchant banking subsidiary, as financial advisors. This was not the first time that a clearing bank had used a group company in this way; County Bank had acted thus for the National Westminster. Bank of Scotland directors agreed that there was no reason why the British Linen Bank should not act as advisors to the Bank, if and when a new capitalisation or rights issue was agreed for the Bank. It was now a decade since the two issues of 1973. Unfortunately, the secondary banking crisis of 1974 had then pushed all bank stocks down, and Bank of Scotland stock had temporarily fallen below the issue price, which created bad feeling. This was now in the past. The board thought that an issue of stock to existing proprietors by a capitalisation of part of the reserves would be attractive and would reduce the unit stock price, which had become rather 'heavy'. It was proposed that there would be a capitalisation issue from the reserves, on the basis of £1 of capitalisation stock for every £1 of existing stock held by proprietors (£32,825,459); also, a rights issue fixed at £1 nominal – £16,412,729 – at 260p for every £2 nominal of existing stock held on the record date, 19 April 1984, would raise the sum of £41,573,095 clear of expenses. As part of the aim was to encourage proprietors to take up their rights, it was thought that there was 'an argument for accepting a deeper discount than would normally be necessary'. The expected results would also have to satisfy major stockholders, and an announcement that they would take up their share would enhance the standing of the offer. Timing was important, and, after discussion with the Treasurer, the British Linen Bank recommended an announcement which incorporated the preliminary results for the year ending 28 February 1984, wherein the consolidated profit before taxation had risen by 19.6 per cent over the previous year, with a dividend increase of 16.7 per cent. De Zoete & Bevan and Bell, Lawrie & Co., stockbrokers, recommended no change to the Bank's unique voting structure, although one beneficial aspect of the capitalisation issue would be a larger number of shares in existence, 'a consequence of which the Stock Exchange would approve'. Barclays Bank agreed to take the whole £5,643,225 of Bank stock provisionally allotted to it, and the Kuwait Investment Office took £1,558,000 of stock; each was granted ½ per cent commission for its commitment. The underwriters agreed to accept the remaining £9,211,504 nominal of Bank stock for a 2 per cent commission. The issue was fully subscribed.

An unexpected development was that the 1984 Budget introduced significant changes for lessors, and all the banks now felt compelled to reverse earlier decisions and to provide at a higher level for deferred taxation, with an adverse impact on their capital bases. Encouraged by the success of the previous year's issue, the Bank board unusually decided to proceed with a further rights issue in 1985, again based on good preliminary results; consolidated profits before tax were up 35.6 per cent to £80.4 million, and dividends were up 10.7 per cent. This time, it was intended to issue £41,161,769 of new stock at 200p per £1 nominal on the basis of £1 of new stock for every £2 of existing stock; this would raise £82,323,538 gross. The British Linen Bank advised that, in view of the significant discount to the current market price, underwriting was unnecessary, giving a saving of around £1 million. The offer was indeed generous. The middle market price of 468p translated to a theoretical ex-rights price of 372p. Although it was unusual to have two successive rights issues within a year, the Bank's business was clearly growing. The Bank and De Zoete & Bevan encouraged the directors to proceed if they believed this course to be in the best interests of other proprietors. The Bank had a good story to tell; and, happily, the market accepted the logic of a second issue following the previous year's Budget.[22]

The appraisal by the Bank of England and some other central banks of the varying risks attached to different assets had encouraged the central bankers of the major western nations to draft an internationally acceptable basis for inter-bank comparisons. The Basle Committee on Banking Regulations and Supervisory Practices, whereon sat the central banks and supervisory bodies, took over this work and in July 1988 published suggested guidelines.[23] In October 1988, the Bank of England, appointed by the government as regulator under the UK Banking Act, 1987, issued regulations as to how the agreement would be implemented. A two-tier capital structure was envisaged. Tier 1 would consist, inter alia, of allotted, called-up and fully-paid ordinary stock, non-cumulative irredeemable preference stock and disclosed reserves (excluding revaluation reserves). This tier was deemed by the Basle Committee to be the key element of capital on which emphasis would be placed in any discussion of capital adequacy. Tier 2 capital would consist, inter alia, of hybrid capital instruments and subordinated term debt. Both tiers were eligible for inclusion in a bank's total capital base, but the total of tier 2 was not to exceed that of tier 1.

Initially, there were various weaknesses with the Basle Agreements; the most obvious was the inability to control the quality of assets and the extent of off-balance-sheet items. But they had the advantage of pressing banks, especially foreign ones, to take in more stockholders' funds and did provide some comparison for risk-assessment purposes. Since the Bank would require more capital as advances grew, it occurred to the executive

22 The material here is drawn from BS 1/6, Minutes and papers, from miscellaneous papers and from discussions with Hugh K. Young, general manager and Secretary, 1984–.
23 BS, Basle Committee, 'International Convergence of Capital Measurement and Capital Standards', July 1988: meeting of the central banks of Belgium, the Netherlands, Canada, France, West Germany, Italy, Japan, Sweden, Switzerland, the UK and the USA.

on the Mound that they could take advantage of the Basle agreements, without either calling on proprietors to raise more equity capital or depressing the price of the ordinary stock, by issuing non-cumulative irredeemable preference stock. Again the board decided to accept the British Linen Bank as its advisors, in conjunction with Cazenove & Co. Such an issue of irredeemable preference shares had not been attempted in recent times by any UK banking institution, and initially Hugh Young was told by Cazenove & Co. that a non-cumulative irredeemable issue 'could not be done'. With the uncertainty of inflation in the UK, it was thought that investors would be wary of a fixed return without voting rights and that the non-cumulative nature of the instrument would put off institutional investors.[24] However, after further discussions which included the Bank of England and Cazenove & Co., the various problems were all addressed and solved, and the brokers agreed to procure (as agents for Bank of Scotland) subscribers for the offer, but insisted that Hugh Young accompany them around their client list to help them sell the stock. In due course, this gave the Bank £125,000,000 of 9¼ per cent preference stock, of which £25 million was unissued, and thus increased the total paid-up capital to £329,325,760. This was a trail-blazing issue, and it set the template for other UK banking-sector preference issues. The board announced in the offer document that, in addition to the issue of preference stock, the Bank would increase its capital base in the near future with subordinated long-term borrowing in currencies other than sterling which could qualify as tier 2.

One of the greatest challenges for Scottish bankers and institutions has been the need to adapt to the changing economy and banking climate. The pace of work and innovation became noticeably quicker after 1958 and, it has seemed to staff, has continued to speed up every few years since. The resulting levels of personal stress have made lives more difficult to manage: whereas crises in the nineteenth and eighteenth centuries were serious enough, with a few exceptions they were generally shorter and were usually resolved by a united establishment. Banks hung together, and, in the General Managers Committee and its eighteenth-century precursors, numerous matters were arranged and problems resolved. At a local level, the connections of regular middle-class life with the Kirk and local institutions were invariably strong and reassuring. That this continued long into the twentieth century comes out plainly in the tape recordings of the experiences of Bank senior managers undertaken from

24 BS, 'Proposed creation of £125,000,000 nominal of Preference Stock and division of Ordinary Stock into units of 25p', offer document, p. 9. Voting by the holders was restricted to a resolution for, or in relation to, the winding-up of the company; and a resolution varying, altering or abrogating any of the rights, privileges, limitations or restrictions attached to the preference stock.

1984 by David Antonio, the retired Secretary. These oral records stretch back to reminiscences before the First World War and into the inter-war years, when the bonds of comradeship and shared hardships, from war and illness, and sharper lines of status and authority in which staff knew their place and what they could expect, gave a stable routine. This world faded with the diversification of the Bank. In 1960, William Watson was 'protected' in his Mound office, even from senior staff, by a ritual and a hierarchy stiffer than in the armed forces. The Inspectors Department for the branches and departments was situated directly above him at the Mound, and it mulled over even quite minor Bank transactions. Visits from the Inspectors Department and continuous audit of the Bank books were a notable form of Bank work.

By 1979, with the reforms accompanying and following the amalgamation with the British Linen Bank, this structure was beginning to change. On the appointment of Bruce Pattullo as Treasurer in 1980, the process of structural change accelerated. He saw clearly the benefits to be gained by spreading decision-making and devolving responsibility so as to encourage younger talents to emerge and develop. Improved pay, increased holiday entitlements, the amalgamated pension scheme and above all the feeling that the Bank had a new sense of purpose all helped to encourage unity and dynamism at the senior levels. Yet there remained for some, in addition, a belief that the interaction between senior management and the board of directors could be made more productive. There thus emerged from a radical review of the traditional Bank decision-making processes the concept, entirely new to the Bank, of the management board, a board consisting solely of senior executives of the Bank and chaired by the Treasurer as the Bank's chief executive.

These executives would be required not only to think in terms of their own departments but also to see their wider responsibility for the whole of the Bank: 'to start thinking about where the Bank would be in ten years' time'. The board subcommittee system was abolished, and the board of directors, all non-executive except for the Treasurer, was to meet in future only monthly. It was recognised as essential that, in the discharge of their responsibilities, the directors be kept fully informed not only about decisions being made by the management board but also, as they progressed, about new policies which might eventually require the board's consideration and/or approval. To achieve this, the management board would have more than usually detailed minutes, which would be sent to the directors. On 10 February 1981, the new structure was formally approved by the board, it being agreed 'to delegate to the Management Board the whole banking business of the Bank with full power and authority to exercise the relevant powers so far as is consistent with the provisions of

Bank of Scotland Acts 1695 to 1920'.[25] At the same time, other changes in the operations of the local boards were initiated. Within the tiered structure for approving advances, the east and west boards were to make recommendations to the management board, whose fortnightly meetings commenced on 19 May with authority to approve advances up to £9,999,999. The new arrangements at once demonstrated their value, and the directors could quickly see from the minutes the range of new ideas being discussed and implemented. The dynamism and energy released by this new system of empowerment was, to those who knew what was happening, a vivid demonstration of the potential of the Bank and justification for the belief that it was important, not just for the Bank but also for banking in Scotland and in the rest of the UK, that the Bank fight to maintain its independence.

In July 1982, Bruce Pattullo highlighted the fact that 'the Bank's business is now advances-led', and pointed to the growing need to generate new products on the liabilities side of the balance sheet. This need has not diminished, and its identification has led to increased branch activity with new products and throughput, and to greater emphasis on deposit-collection with new resource-gathering units and a higher profile in the money markets. These years were very active ones at the Mound, and so much could not have been done without the new management structure and firm delegation of tasks and responsibilities which ensured that the senior executives and the board had time to think and plan strategically. The Bank had always been fortunate in having non-executive directors of great distinction and ability. Throughout the 1980s, changes inevitably occurred through death or retirement, but the Bank's reputation for prudence ensured that there was never the slightest difficulty in persuading suitable people carrying heavy responsibilities elsewhere to join the board and to give their time to the affairs of the Bank. Their relevant experience in the running of different businesses was always available to the executive at the Mound.

The crucial financial figures for the Bank remained net interest earnings after deductions of expenses (see Table 29.3). These were dependent on the ability of the Bank to generate deposits at as low a cost as possible, to apply them effectively in order to minimise lower-earning activities, and to contain costs. The inflation of the post-1974 era and its resumption in 1979 had made cost control very difficult, and the recession necessitated higher bad-debt provisions. So there was always pressure on margins. In this situation, it was vital to service as much additional business as possible through the same basic infrastructure, with minimal increase in staff.

25 BS 1/6, Minutes.

Table 29.3 Sources and uses of funds, net interest payments and earnings, 1982–3

Source of funds

Funds £m Actual average	Source of funds	Interest payments Actual £000	Rate % Actual average
38.2	Current accounts – compensating	–	–
455.2	Current accounts – interest-free	–	–
86.8	Current accounts – interest-bearing	9,364	10.79
523.0	Deposit accounts – Scotland	40,183	7.68
40.0	Deposit accounts – London	3,303	8.26
112.9	Deposit receipts	9,981	8.84
47.7	Monthly income accounts	4,500	9.43
572.3	Term deposits	66,580	11.63
1,876.1		133,911	7.14
306.3	Bought-in funds	36,973	12.07
2,182.4		170,884	7.83
0.9	Currency deposit	112	12.45
125.0	Other sources	–	–
210.2	Capital and reserves	–	–
2,518.5	Interest payable – sources	170,996	6.79

Uses of funds

Uses of funds	Funds £m Actual average	Interest earnings Actual £000	Rate % Actual average
Customer advances – compensating	38.2	–	–
Customer advances – interest-bearing	1,515.6	208,394	13.75
Advances – non-matching	72.5	9,250	12.76
Customer bills discounted	3.0	378	12.60
Export and shipping schemes	167.9	22,253	13.25
	1,797.2	240,275	13.37
Market funds	210.2	23,237	11.05
Investments – gilts	159.0	20,569	12.93
Investments – trade	5.3	1,852	34.94
Bank of England cash ratio deposit	8.4	–	–
	2,180.1	285,933	13.12
Non-investible balances	195.5	–	–
Subsidiary and associated companies	19.0	–	–
Fixed assets	123.9	–	–
Interest receivable – uses	2,518.5	285,933	11.35
Other operations			
Sterling – London	118.4	334	0.28
Sterling – back-to-back loans	108.7	44	0.04
Currency	1,262.7	12,354	0.98
Fixed-rate notes (net cost)	–	(257)	–
Net interest – other operations	1,489.8	12,475	0.85
Net interest earnings from operations		127,412	
Dividends from subsidiaries and associates		10,415	
Net interest earnings per trading results		137,827	

Source: BS 1/6, Board minutes.

Commissions and fees had also to rise faster than cost inflation, and any additional work in any department had to be fully charged for and had ideally to make a profit. It may seem unnecessary to reiterate these points, but the strategy of the Bank required personnel to have a clear and perhaps strict view of the difficulties facing retail, low-margin banking.[26]

The Bank placed great reliance on the branches: 'the term bedrock was used some time ago to describe branch operations and this still holds true in respect of profit earned and the broad customer base from which the Bank has been able to diversify and expand'. This meant new products which divided into three groups, the most important being those which repackaged and developed the older cheque and passbook cash account. By 1990, these included the premier investment account, the Money Market chequebook account, Supersavers schemes, Scotloans, mortgages for house purchase and term loans. The most significant new introduction at the retail end was home loans. Bank of Scotland had lent on property and land since the seventeenth century, at first by means of bonds secured over the heritable subjects, and had continued to do so ever since, although this was usually for farming and the top end of the housing market. In 1979, the Bank entered the general residential mortgage market on both sides of the Border, again with the higher-value properties but also with tenement flats and suburban homes.[27] In Scotland, there had been a trend towards building more houses in the private sector allied to growing home ownership. From 1960–70, the proportion of private completions was around 20 per cent of the total build, but this rose by 1979 to 60 per cent, with annual completions of around 12,000–14,000 houses.[28] At the 1981 census, 54.6 per cent of Scottish households still lived in public-sector accommodation, compared with 32 per cent in England and Wales. But the trend from 1970 was for private-sector ownership to grow at a rate close to the UK average. There was a feeling that the growth of home ownership in Scotland might encourage the English building societies to expand their networks, and these might provide more effective competition for the deposit base than the English banks had provided. This also argued for taking the initiative with a move into home loans.

Initially, home-loan rates were agreed at a margin over Bank of Scotland base rate, but in October 1981 the management board recommended a separate Bank Home Loan Rate (HLR), one of whose objectives was to give customers a more stable rate. This also saved on administration. This meant some fluctuation above and below the Bank of England base

26 BS, Managers Conference, 1984: T. Borthwick, 'Financial Performance – The Bank', pp. 2–8.
27 BS, D. B. Pattullo, 'Home Loans', 17 July 1984; BS 1/6, Minutes, 17 July 1984.
28 A. Gibb and D. Maclennan, 'Policy and Process in Scottish Housing, 1950–1980', in R. Saville (ed.), *The Economic Development of Modern Scotland 1950–1980* (Edinburgh: 1985), pp. 270–91 (270–1, 278, 288).

rate, but the average rate charged to July 1984 was +2 per cent, plus initial fees. By then, around 10 per cent of all Bank of Scotland advances were for mortgages. The position was carefully protected by the spread of borrowers, the formal security taken over the heritable subjects, the assignation of an endowment mortgage and the fact that mortgages were usually serviced from regular career incomes rather than revenues from property. For some years, the government continued to favour home-owning, and it was not until 1988 and afterwards that the tax regime was made progressively less favourable.

In addition, branch-based mortgages led to current-account business, initially for repayment purposes, and other regular payments. Central Banking Services sold Bank of Scotland mortgages through brokers and agents, and charged arrangement fees. Total income from fees was over £800,000 in 1984. The Bank formed syndicates to take over part of the portfolio on an assignment basis: participating banks took the entire credit risk and received ¾ per cent to ⅞ per cent over LIBOR (London Inter-bank Offered Rate) in exchange. Bank of Scotland retained all fees and the residual interest earnings; even with the interest margin (the gap) at just over 1 per cent, this was a sound profit for a non-balance-sheet item. Experience from the building societies confirmed that the average length of loans would be seven years, and syndicates were fixed at seven to nine years, with the Bank required to buy back any outstanding loans thereafter. Central Banking Services had developed good relations with no fewer than thirty-eight UK life assurance companies by 1984; these included Standard Life, Scottish Amicable, Equity & Law, Sun Life of Canada, Friends Provident, National Mutual, Scottish Equitable, Scottish Life and Scottish Mutual. The pricing mechanism was always in the hands of Bank of Scotland, and demand could be adjusted by fine-tuning the Bank's HLR. Working through life company agents offered numbers of potential customers far in excess of the capacity of Central Banking Services, so they were 'very discriminating'. Introducers of business were given very fast answers, usually within twenty-four hours, which was just the service they wanted.

There was little bad debt as house prices rose in the UK from the close of the recession, although more slowly in Scotland, to 1989. Arrears in this period would be cleared on sale, and actual losses in the first five years ranged from 0.04 per cent down to only 0.01 per cent. The key was to look at the status of the borrower and not the asset, which encouraged the traditional position of the Bank manager. Further, it should be stated that the Treasurer was fully aware of the dangers of the marketplace; as early as 1984, he warned that 'it is quite conceivable that house prices will stand still or even fall'.

The second group of branch-based products were business and personal financial services, all covered since 1973 by a new Personal Financial Services Department, which became a Division (PFS) in 1988. This brought under one roof the work of the registrar's department, which went back to 1695; the trustee department, which had a continuous history in the Union Bank and Bank of Scotland from the nineteenth century; investment services, started by Bruce Pattullo and Alasdair Macdonald in 1966; tax and estate planning; underwriting of new issues and unit trust trusteeships; and a range of insurance products. To Alasdair Macdonald, working continuously in the area, it was clear that there was enormous scope for new business as middle-class incomes rose and customers found themselves with cash from house and business sales, lump-sum retirement benefits, inheritances and simply the product of their own savings. His team offered a portfolio of services for the corporate and personal customer who sought longer-term growth and asset management rather than day-by-day selling. Tax cases often required complicated negotiations with the Inland Revenue, and PFS developed an expertise with a wide range of customers. With the personal market in mind, the Bank opened an office in Jersey in 1985. The island had been conquered by the Duke of Normandy in AD 933, and from 1066 it has remained a possession of the English Crown with rights of taxation outside the jurisdictions of the English courts or the Inland Revenue. There were considerable tax advantages for non-resident Scots in placing deposits in a Jersey-registered bank. This was a very competitive international market, and, but for the Jersey branch, many such deposits would have gone to overseas competitors. The business grew rapidly, and in retrospect it was clear that the move would have been justified many years earlier.

The third group of products related to technical and electronic payments and transfer systems, and all belonged to the new computer era. North West Securities was keen to develop card-based systems independent of Barclays Bank and the highly successful Barclaycard.[29] The provision of a Visa (or Access) card was becoming an essential part of the services expected by middle-class customers who wished to pay for many types of one-off transaction, such as hotel bills, airline flights and consumer durables, without waiting for the clearance of cheques. In some respects, it was similar to the older-style finance-house cheque account, where a limit was given for total transactions; but the card enabled transactions to proceed without delays apart from a cursory check against the signature and a list of withdrawn cards. Later, security was much enhanced with the introduction of on-line computer terminals

29 See above, Chapter 28.

on retailers' premises. There were high interest charges for overdrawn accounts, but those were mainly cleared monthly and incurred no charges except for cash withdrawals. Cardholders were given a number of benefits including insurance in the event of death or injury occurring while using travel tickets purchased with the card. Here was a product which middle-class people who had hitherto refused to take personal loans, apart from mortgages, were prepared to use. This was an important psychological breakthrough. Nevertheless, the introduction of the card drew criticism from consumer groups, and many customers continued for some time with just a cheque book and cheque guarantee card.

The Bank's enthusiasm and familiarity with computers kept it in the forefront of modern technology, and in 1983 it struck Robin Browning and his team at the newly-formed Management Services Division that outside computer access to the Bank's databanks could be made available to some customers, given the careful use of certain security procedures. Customers provided with a Home and Office Banking Services (HOBS) terminal could then access their accounts on a video screen and move funds between accounts, make interest payments to third parties, and so on. Introduced in early 1985, this soon became, according to David Dunlop, assistant general manager in the marketing department, 'the best vehicle for winning new customers that we've ever had'.[30] At long last, business and personal customers could move their free funds to maximise interest and monitor flows of money through their accounts. The innovation attracted a lot of new customers, both business and personal, and favourable comment, although security requirements made it rather complicated to use, and the manuals were difficult to understand for lay customers with no computer or keyboard experience. Inevitably, there was resistance at some branches to selling the product and using staff time to iron out the initial customer queries. In reality, HOBS was a modern delivery system and not a stand-alone product. With hindsight, it must be seen as a tremendous step in front of the competition, and it was over three years before another system appeared. The introduction of HOBS was well timed, and this pioneering spirit earned much favourable comment for the Bank which in turn helped the managers in their ongoing search for new business. The positive light in which the Bank was viewed also advantageously affected the rating of the Bank's shares on the stockmarket.

The Bank was very careful to ensure that, with all the advantages of computer technology and the introduction of new products in the 1980s, there was no perception of downgrading the importance of the branch network. However, where the sales were conducted by Central Banking

30 BS, Managers Conference, November 1987, p. 88.

Services, customers' payments by Visa card, withdrawals through the automated teller machines and customer-effected transactions via the HOBS connections, it reduced staff requirements as processing was done by central computer systems. More business without extra costs also forced the crucial cost:income ratio downwards. But the management board continued to emphasise repeatedly that products rarely walked off the shelves. They had to be sold by staff who believed that this was now a suitable role for an employee in a Bank branch.

This had to be managed in the traditional context by the branch manager, who had long been required to go out and win ordinary commercial, student and professional accounts, and who was now asked to set realistic targets for sales of Bank products. This would be the only way of expanding the proportion of business done by the Bank in competition against the Royal Bank and the Clydesdale Bank, and in some spheres against the building societies and the Trustee Savings Bank. The opportunities for enthusiastic young managers were regularly pointed out. For example, R. L. Cromar, a general manager based in Glasgow and appointed to the management board in 1982, directed managers to look at the customer portfolio by breaking it down into segments and utilising the information available in the marketing department and within the databases, and to think about the potential income from different groups and their likely needs. Armed with such information, the manager was then to utilise local knowledge:

> I can think for instance of one branch in Glasgow where, following the retiral of a Manager, a 'young blood' was put in his place. The new incumbent looked closely at his portfolio and was very surprised to discover that although the Branch was adjacent to a significant number of tenement properties which were of good quality and structure and which had recently been subject to privatisation from the Local Authority ownership, his analysis showed him home loan figures were very low indeed. He went out of his way to attack, successfully, this segment of his business . . . [and] there was the opportunity of adding on insurance business.[31]

A similar positive attitude would also pay dividends with corporate customers. Bruce Pattullo symbolically disbanded the Business Development Unit on assuming the Treasurer's mantle; he insisted that all managers had to push for corporate business. The turnover in small businesses meant that opportunities were continually occurring in every part of Scotland, and the record of the Bank in looking after corporate customers was a positive one, although this was also true for the Royal Bank and the Clydesdale Bank.

31 BS, Managers Conference, 1984, p. 27.

As Scotland emerged from the recession, there was little excuse for branch managers not pushing new products and scrutinising their local markets. With teamwork and flexibility in the branch, staff time could be better focused on selling – which some staff appeared to prefer to counter work – and the manager could create more time for advising customers and tackling gaps in the market. The senior management and directors sought to provide a framework which supported local initiatives, not just with new products but also with new images and symbolism designed to operate in the longer term on public perception. The message 'A Friend for Life', launched in 1984, was drawn up precisely for this strategic design, alongside more carefully-targeted sponsorship programmes which brought staff as well as customers the feeling that Bank of Scotland was a national institution with additional mundane concerns in sport and general welfare.[32] It also helped to emphasise the greater social cohesion between the higher management and the general staff than existed in English banks. Bank managers had always developed good social relations with farmers and business people, and some staff through their trade union and leisure activities had widespread contacts. But the pressures of the workplace and the spread of television had taken their toll, and many staff were no longer involved with local communities and committees as their predecessors had been.

Bank of Scotland policy was to expand general advances to industry and trade, which was done successfully despite stiffer competition for branch deposits. The Bank, in common with the Royal Bank and the Clydesdale Bank, had little choice but to turn to the wholesale markets. In 1978, no less than 91 per cent of all deposits by value came from the retail branch network, of which 40 per cent were interest-free current accounts; only 9 per cent came from wholesale markets. By 1985, with the growth of the business, the position was quite different: 48 per cent came from branches and 52 per cent from wholesale markets. Of the branch-based deposits, only 16.5 per cent was held in interest-free accounts. This accompanied a gradual squeeze on the overall gap between borrowing and lending rates, from 5.2 per cent in 1979 to 3.8 per cent by 1985. By pushing industrial and commercial advances hard, the gap was inevitably narrower because these assets had to be funded with relatively expensive wholesale deposits.

The development of computers and the 1979 abolition of exchange controls in UK banking meant that banks and companies could move funds as required for any purpose, sound or speculative. The temptation for certain banks and investment houses was to move cash surpluses away from industrial and commercial advances to 'glamorous' international

---

32 BS, Managers Conference, 1984: D. M. Dunlop, 'Marketing Impact – A Friend for Life', pp. 34–40.

dealing operations linked to global futures markets. These attracted huge sums from banks, often traded at tiny margins over very short timespans, as well as longer-term speculation and position-taking on the world stockmarkets. The more traditional markets where firms could purchase a commodity in the future at a price agreed on the spot were rapidly developed into a wide and apparently ever-increasing range of options and swaps in which any speculator could indulge, whether or not he was truly interested in the actual commodity. This was quite different from buying a bill of exchange at a fixed price, as futures involved forecasting which way a market would go. All banks had currency dealing rooms, and all expanded after 1979 with the aid of more effective computer systems. In this situation, some asked why banks should worry about retail offices and retail products when a few traders with computers could make much more money by buying and selling and could thus provide higher returns to shareholders. The answers were similar for all UK banks. They wanted a foot in the door to evaluate the potential profits. But there were not always sufficiently strong controls to limit potential losses, as existed in traditional branch work, where the supervisory system had evolved over long years of experience and lessons had been learnt the hard way. There were to be some serious losses in these markets. In March 1995, the self-destruction of the British merchant bank, Barings, was an extraordinary example. Branches might not appear as glamorous as the dealing rooms in the City of London, but they were good earners with a lot of untapped potential, and were a good deal more useful to local citizens and businesses. In the history of Bank of Scotland, one would have to go back to the early nineteenth century to find examples of branch losses which posed serious threats to the Bank's viability.

How did the performance of Bank of Scotland compare with its two main competitors, the Royal Bank and the Clydesdale Bank, and with the English clearing banks? During the years 1979–82, the damage done by the recession to Bank of Scotland, in common with all UK banks, affected planning arrangements undertaken after the relatively poor performance of the domestic bank in the later 1970s.[33] By 1985 the recession was over, although there remained sizeable pockets in the industrial north of England which provided much less buoyant conditions for bank advances. This was also the penultimate year when direct comparisons within Scotland could be made with the Royal Bank, as it was amalgamating its Scottish retail operations with those of Williams and Glyn's in England. The accounts indicate that Bank of Scotland made sound progress from 1982–3 and that all the domestic Bank operations were making serious

33 For this, see above, Chapter 27.

contributions to profits.[34] Thus the strategy developed by directors and senior management had proved correct. At the Royal Bank there was little improvement in real terms before 1985, and the Clydesdale Bank also struggled to emerge from the recession. As Iain Scott noted in a report to the board of directors in June 1985,

> Obviously we can take some measure of satisfaction from the fact that while in 1979 we produced the lowest profit of the three Scottish Banks, we have for the last two years produced very substantially the largest despite the fact that the Royal [Bank parent] is apparently a slightly larger bank than ours.[35]

In respect of the longer-term health of the Scottish banks, it was not just the level of absolute profit but profitability measured by the return on average equity and the return on average assets. The return on assets again showed an improvement in 1984 and 1985, with the Royal Bank facing the hardest struggle. But even this needs careful qualification. The improvement in the Clydesdale's figure was due to a proportionately small volume of wholesale currency lending, with its relatively fine margins. This business was owned by the Midland Bank. The Midland deliberately restricted the growth of the Clydesdale's asset base because of its own problems, which meant that a greater proportion of its lending book was covered by deposits from the branch system. The position of the Royal Bank reflected its higher component of currency lending, about one-sixth of its loan book going through the inter-bank market. Again Bank of Scotland came out strongly, although the comparison with the other banks is not exact; the Bank's figures benefited from the rise in mortgage business negotiated by CBS, the profits of the new regional offices and the success of the Bank's electronic delivery systems. There were real difficulties for the Clydesdale as the Midland Bank struggled to contain the losses from its Crocker subsidiary in the USA, and this required strict controls over the growth of UK group lending to satisfy the Bank of England over capital adequacy. Some customers of the Clydesdale Bank who had good business propositions decided to move to Bank of Scotland and the Royal Bank, although the Clydesdale's management did its best to protect its position in difficult circumstances.

In the mid-1980s, as the Bank management pursued a 'strategy of product diversification' designed to build upon the expertise acquired in personal and commercial banking, it was combined with a widening of the Bank's geographical horizons. The most interesting of these developments came in 1987 with the purchase of equity in the de-mutualising

---

34 BS, Board papers, Accounting Division, 'Bank of Scotland Group, Divisional Accounting, Year to 28 February 1985', 9 April 1985.
35 BS, Board papers, 18 June 1985: Iain Scott, 'Inter-Bank Performance Comparison Scottish Banks'.

Countrywide Building Society, the second largest society in New Zealand. Discussions had commenced in 1985, after which Iain Scott and Jim Malcolm spent ten days at Countrywide's headquarters in Auckland looking over the loan book. The election of the right-wing Labour government in July 1984, under David Lange, was timely. Reversing the policies of the earlier National Party, Labour proceeded to implement a rolling policy of non-intervention, freer markets, the dismantling of exchange controls and the removal of a whole web of government subsidies, in particular for agriculture. In September 1986, after a further round of discussions with the management of Countrywide, Bank of Scotland announced that it would purchase 40 per cent of the equity, consequent on the passage of legislation enabling the society to de-mutualise and issue shares. In July 1987, the New Zealand Parliament passed the required Act, which was applicable to all building societies and savings banks. The management of Countrywide drew up a plan to allow conversion of the society to a bank, and this was duly endorsed by the society's members.

Once Countrywide had achieved banking status, it was agreed that it would also borrow from the wholesale markets and adopt a diversified lending policy, especially in respect of personal loans. This was a reasonably safe move, as, with average house loans at only 60–65 per cent of house value, there was considerable equity still available in the average house. Countrywide's own criteria also stipulated that monthly repayments (for principal and interest) by its borrowers should not exceed 30 per cent of gross monthly income. There was one significant balance-sheet problem. Under the terms of incorporation for building societies and savings banks, the New Zealand government required a minimum of 25 per cent of society assets to be kept primarily in New Zealand government stocks, which carried a fixed rate of interest. With the new, open financial markets, the commercial rate of interest shot up, reaching 21 per cent in 1985 for retail deposits. The capital value of government stock plummeted, and, had societies and savings banks been forced to realise their portfolios, as Iain Scott noted, 'they would be insolvent as they have insufficient reserves to cover their losses'. Countrywide included its investments at market value, which, in June 1985, was almost NZ $8 million below their nominal value. Bank of Scotland purchased 40 per cent of the total shares, at a cost of NZ $29.7 million, while General Accident, the insurer based in Perth, Scotland, subscribed another 20 per cent. Once this equity was in place, there commenced a considerable increase in overall business. In 1992, it was agreed by Bank of Scotland and General Accident that, as a merger was proposed between Countrywide and United Bank (formerly the largest New Zealand building society), Bank of Scotland would then acquire the whole equity of the newly-formed bank. By 1995, pre-tax profits had risen to NZ $51.7 million, with total assets of NZ $5.2 billion.

In July 1986, negotiations were concluded for the acquisition of 75 per cent of the equity of Commercial Bank of Wales. An exhaustive examination of the books, and those of Forthright Finance Ltd, a finance-house subsidiary specialising in loans on vehicles, was carried out by staff from Bank of Scotland and North West Securities. It was hoped that the company, renamed Bank of Wales after the purchase, would be able to concentrate on support for Welsh trade and industry. There was considerable asset growth – 30 per cent in 1988 – and investment in new infrastructure, an increase in staff and an emphasis on lending to corporate and local authority customers. Once the recession had started, there were difficulties with some corporate accounts, and in May 1991, as a result of an offer to holders of the minority 25 per cent equity, Bank of Wales became a wholly-owned subsidiary. The determination to build a significant Cardiff-based regional bank remained, although, as the recession deepened, it was recognised that this would take longer than anticipated.

In Bank of Scotland's 1990 annual report, the Governor, Sir Thomas Risk, emphasised the regional theme. While the Bank recognised the pre-eminence of London as one of the three leading financial centres of the world, and the maintenance of this position was considered very important, it was also a matter of concern 'that the growing congestion resulting from the unabated centralising pull of government expenditure and patronage is making [London] . . . an increasingly inefficient place to do a day's work'. The argument for regional centres, themselves able to offer a complete range of facilities, was well demonstrated by Bank of Scotland and its subsidiaries. The success of the Bank's corporate offices and the growth in the balance-sheet totals of subsidiaries clearly justified such a view.

After a conversation started over five years earlier, in the summer of 1995 the Bank concluded an agreement to buy the entire equity of an Australian state bank, the Bank of Western Australia, formerly the Rural Industries Bank, based in Perth. As part of the agreement with the state government of Western Australia, the Reserve Bank of Australia and the federal authorities, 49 per cent of the bank, now renamed BankWest, was to be offered to local investors. Hugh Young, the Secretary of Bank of Scotland, was despatched to oversee the 'offer for sale' documentation, and this was successfully completed when the prospectus was formally registered on 20 December 1995. It was a nice coincidence that BankWest was celebrating its centenary in the same year as Bank of Scotland was celebrating its tercentenary and that the purchase was completed on 30 November,

St Andrew's Day, when the final celebratory dinner for Bank customers was being held in Edinburgh.

At the time of the successful defence of the Royal Bank of Scotland, the managers and directors of Bank of Scotland had pointed to the importance of their support for regional developments within the UK. Thereafter, the Bank continued to look for additional investment opportunities, in particular in the corporate business sector. The network of regional offices was extended, to Bristol and Carlisle in 1981, Manchester in 1982, Leicester, Southampton and Newcastle in 1983, Leeds in 1985 and Norwich in 1986. These regional offices offered Bank of Scotland customers cheque and cash services, but the main focus of management was directed to industrial and commercial lending. As in the earlier offices, such as Birmingham, good progress was made quite rapidly.

A key organisational support for regional banking centres was the rapidly-growing number of functions carried out by computers. Bank of Scotland had stayed in the forefront of computer technology and automation ever since the Bank had become, in 1959, the first UK clearing bank to install a computer – an IBM 1401 – to handle accounting information. Around this time, senior managers of all UK clearing banks realised that, as the volume of accounting entries was increasing, however quickly filing and paper-based systems were modified, automation was essential if administrative costs were to be contained. As the Bank was still struggling with the burdens imposed on the balance sheet by the exposure to British government securities, managers had every incentive to adopt cost-cutting measures. The early computers were good at dealing with such matters as ledger entries, printing bank statements and recording transactions from branches at central locations. These developments encouraged a wider focus upon developing new systems to generate further cost savings, not just those designed to emulate traditional methods; and this then became a major part of computer development for the next two decades.

The early computers, by later standards, were low-powered machines requiring considerable manual support and infrastructure: the Bank's IBM 1401, for example, occupied three rooms, and had less power than one laptop PC thirty-five years later. At Bank of Scotland, as in most large organisations, conflicts developed over the best use of these machines. The programmers and systems analysts were working in an environment – Computer Services – which emphasised a computer-oriented culture rather too remote from staff in the Bank's Management Services Department who had a remit to develop new systems and services. While some thought was given to how computers could improve services to the customer, this was not a priority. An example of the difficulty with the old structure came in the late 1970s when the Bank evaluated the early automated teller machines (ATMs), developed in the USA, into which customers inserted a card to withdraw cash, which was debited to their accounts. An internal report looked at these machines from their cost-saving potential and concluded that, at this time, they were not worth the investment. Conversely, a short time later, the Royal Bank of Scotland took the view that these machines would help its customers, and it began a rapid programme of installation. They were an immediate success; 'the senior people at the Mound realised the Royal was on to a winner', and a crash programme was started, eighteen months behind the Royal Bank, which was to lead to the Keycard cash dispensers offering a range of banking services as well as cash withdrawal.

The failure to realise the potential of ATMs 'signalled to the senior people that there might be something wrong'. In 1979, Bruce Pattullo asked Robin Browning, an assistant general manager in the Management Services Department, to set up an automation planning unit on similar lines to the earlier profit planning unit under Alan Jessiman. His remit was to look at the possibilities of the new technologies and to report on how they might support customer services. With only three staff and a secretary, Browning read everything current on computers and customer services, from both British and US experience, looking in particular at the use of plastic chip cards, electronic payments and cash management systems, as well as furthering cost-cutting. It was a difficult remit, in part because of the speed of change in computer technologies, with many competing systems among which only a minority could expect to survive, although there was a clearer appreciation that more and more power could be concentrated in smaller machines, which would be easier to use and cheaper to service.

Robin Browning reported to John Wilson, divisional general manager, that the needs of the Bank for computer services fell into three parts: an automation planning side; systems development, which included programmers and business analysts; and operations, under which came help desks, operators, supervisors and the stationery and printing function. As staff in the two existing departments – 'fiefdoms' would be a not inaccurate description – were becoming restless, with inevitable effects on morale, Wilson accepted the recommendation that the organisations should be merged and functions rationalised. This new organisation was renamed Management Services Division (MSD); Robin Browning was in charge as divisional general manager, with two assistant general managers, responsible for systems and operations respectively, reporting directly to him. The focus required of the new management team was on the redirection of all computer work towards customer services and the rapid provision of computer technologies for Bank departments and branches.

Cost-cutting remained important, but it was thought that this would follow from the provision of efficient customer services. Out of this new MSD came the telecommunications systems of Home and Office Banking Services (HOBS), the inter-bank telephone system (BOSLINK), the computerised and satellite-linked money transmission system for small, regular payments worldwide (TAPS), Keycard and Keycard Plus, and subsequently systems for Visa and Mastercards. This all enabled the Bank to develop its own Switch and CHAPS computer processing centres and the various other card services. Internal information flows were greatly improved. In a number of these areas, the Bank developed new systems and was widely regarded as perhaps the most computer-literate of the UK clearing banks. Moreover, all the new telephone banking services were developed by MSD, although it should be noted that North West Securities was also quick to realise, and to exploit commercially, the possibilities of the new computer technologies.

From the reorganisation, effective from 1980, the use of technology improved 'a very great deal', with good teamworking characteristics and an openness which encouraged the end users, both within and outside the Bank. The process showed that it was possible to convert from a focus upon cost-cutting and automation for its own sake to the development of new products and services. All sorts of new ideas came out of MSD in the 1980s and early 1990s, in a similar process to the rapid innovations then occurring at North West Securities. Mixing people with a background in banking with those who came from data-processing and automation thus proved effective; by 1995, MSD employed nearly 1,000 persons. The friendly competition with the equivalent function in NWS Bank also proved productive for both parties.

In October 1979, the proprietors had authorised the establishment of Inland Revenue-approved profit-sharing stock-ownership and cash schemes under which a percentage of the yearly profits, related to the performance of the Bank and its subsidiaries, was allocated to eligible employees. These schemes were designed to give employees a direct benefit in the profits of Bank of Scotland group, heightening their interest in the group's financial performance and increasing their understanding of, and commitment to, the group's objectives during a time of rapid change. Employees could opt for cash; but, as time passed, more opted for the tax-efficient stock-ownership scheme. Two other 'stock-option' schemes were also introduced later. The first was a savings-related stock-option scheme which aimed to provide a means of contractual saving with the right to take stock in lieu of cash in a tax-efficient way. The second was a more limited executive stock-option scheme allocated at the discretion of the board. As a separate matter, a number of valuable customer benefits were extended in 1988 to those who were also personal stockholders.[36]

In the 1989 annual report, the Governor referred to the effects of the boom engineered by the government, associated in the public mind with Margaret Thatcher and the Chancellor of the Exchequer, Nigel Lawson. Sir Thomas Risk expressed concern over the rising level of prices and the fluctuations in interest and exchange rates. For the Bank, the 'scope and nature of our business nowadays tends to even out the major [adverse] effects', but it was a different matter for business and personal customers. As the Chancellor applied the brakes hard and the UK economy lurched towards what was, in later years, seen as a prolonged recession, the Governor stressed that the Bank would stand by its commitment to 'relationship banking' – the relationship of mutual confidence and trust between the banker and the customer which is at the heart of good banking practice.

The Bank behaved reasonably prudently in numerous ways during the boom of the 1980s. The board refused to support derivatives trading except where instruments could be used to reduce existing interest rates and exchange-rate risks already inherent in the system. In 1987, the Bank had refused to pay the absurd 'but nevertheless fashionable' prices to enter the capital markets business. Continuous close attention was paid to controlling operating expenses; and, by 1990, the cost:income ratio was down to 52.8 per cent, nearly 10 per cent below the level of any other UK clearing bank. The Bank also refused a number of requests for finance from several fast-expanding companies, control of which was thought to be too dependent on a dominant personality. In the discussion of strategic moves, the management board had always been guided by clichéd but common-sense concepts such as 'sticking to the knitting' and 'don't bet the Bank'. Thus, it looked seriously at areas of business such as providing senior debt for structured management buy-outs which required more traditional banking skills, and managed this with considerable success. By the summer of 1990, all parts of the group could see the problems of the UK economy, for both business and personal customers. In his final report as Governor, in February 1991, Sir Thomas Risk blamed the sharp downturn in the UK economy on the need for high interest rates following the wild consumer and property boom. The sudden downturn was aggravated by the war in the Middle East and by the constraints imposed by entry into the European Exchange Rate Mechanism (ERM). The desire to maintain a fixed parity for the pound sterling against the basket of European currencies associated with the ERM was to prove unrealistic. The unanticipated impact on the ERM of the reunification of East and West

36 G. R. Smith, 'Employee Share Schemes in Britain', *Employment Gazette*, 101 (1993), 149–54.

Germany forced the government to keep the bank rate higher than required, a policy which was widely criticised. The effect on all the clearing banks' customers was severe.

On the retirements in 1991 of Sir Thomas Risk as Governor and Lord Balfour as Deputy Governor, it was agreed by the directors that Bruce Pattullo be appointed Governor while continuing as chief executive for the group. This was envisaged as an especially demanding combination in the context of the recession, as it combined the executive function with considerable diplomatic activity and, of course, the responsibility for chairing the board; however, it was thought that Pattullo's exceptional understanding of modern banking would allow him to combine the posts to good effect. It was understood that the Treasurer, Peter Burt, remained responsible for the day-to-day operation of the clearing bank, and other senior executives were expected to retain, and use, their decision-making authority. In the early 1990s, as the recession deepened and the return on assets fell, it was with Peter Burt and the management board that primary responsibility lay for managing the difficult loan situations. Their task was made more difficult with the narrowing of the gap between the interest received from advances and that paid out on deposits. As was pointed out to proprietors, the interest gap of 3.8 per cent in 1985, which remained close to this figure for the next three years, had slipped by 1989 to 3.1 per cent, and in 1992 and 1993 it averaged only 1.75 per cent.[37] The Treasurer made it clear that the underlying situation of the Bank was strong because of the strategy of diversification, and rightly criticised views which failed to distinguish between current short-term results, consequent on high bad-debt provisioning, and the sound prospects for the longer term.

These positive views were to be borne out when the economy emerged from the recession, which also confirmed the wisdom of the Bank's policy of 'staying at the table' and continuing to grow the business through the recession, when many other banks had withdrawn into their shells. From 1986 to 1990, the average rate of growth of Bank assets was 20 per cent per year. There was slower growth during the recession, but still well ahead of inflation. The ratio of costs to income was brought below 50 per cent in 1993, again about 10 per cent better than the other clearing banks. While the recession had proved severe and prolonged, by 1994 the return on the group's total assets from the much-diversified portfolio had again started to improve. In the tercentenary year, the Bank was thus justifiably proud of its sustained success in most of its chosen fields. The group's finance-house subsidiary NWS Bank was now the second largest finance house in the UK, up from 155th in 1958, the Australasian policy

37 Bank of Scotland, *Annual Report* (1994), p. 28.

held great promise and the business in the USA was progressing well. The record of the Bank's core business within the UK was enviable. Bank of Scotland group now had 8 per cent of the gross total of UK sterling lending by the major British banking groups. Total balance-sheet footings were £34 billion, with the management pushing ahead with clearly-thought-out domestic lending policies. It was a remarkable performance of which the proprietors showed their deep appreciation, in their largest-ever turnout, for the 299th annual meeting in the Balmoral Hotel, Edinburgh, in June 1995, one of the highlights of the tercentenary year.

CHAPTER 30

BANK OF SCOTLAND OVER 300 YEARS

Bank of Scotland was founded at an optimistic time in Scottish history. A broad Parliamentary consensus was agreed over the direction that economic policy should take, which, inter alia, encouraged the creation of new business organisations and legislation to support their well-being. This accompanied the ambitious programme of reconstruction of the workings of the more important parts of society. For several years after 1688, notable changes were made in the organisation of the Kirk, of Parliament and the burghs, and of the ways that the legal system supported the rights of landowners; and changes were made in the armed forces so that they buttressed the post-Revolution political settlement. Bank of Scotland was founded for the part that it could play in this national renewal. Parliament thought for several years about the type of bank required; several alternatives were debated and excluded, notably schemes which had a definite lifespan or which came from particular interest groups, and a land-bank scheme was rejected for both these reasons. The most common of the new businesses founded by Parliament were joint-stock companies, a democratic form of business organisation which was thought less susceptible to political interest because it was open to all ranks of society, or more open than private schemes. The Bank took this form, and was created as a public joint-stock company with perpetual succession, endowed with 'sufficient powers and authorities and liberties' and specifically designed to contribute to the broadly-based vision of national economic progress already under way. It was understood by the legislators as an ambitious project. An exceptional flexibility was built into the structures of the Bank in respect of ownership and control: no-one was barred by religion, foreigners could join and receive citizenship by virtue of a subscription, none could demand special privileges because of rank or birth, and proprietors were barred from granting loans to the

Crown or government officers unless repayments were guaranteed by an Act of Parliament. The board of the Bank was carefully divided into the Ordinary and the Extraordinary; and while members of the aristocracy, with their pre-eminent position in politics, always had a number of seats on the extraordinary side, in the ebb and flow of eighteenth- and early nineteenth-century politics this system proved flexible enough to alter the balance between the different parts of the Scottish establishment and to cater for the changing needs of banking. These key parts of the Act, the national perspective for the Bank and the way in which the board could adapt to circumstances ensured that particular interests would not find it easy to sway lending policy in their favour. Indeed, it was evident in practice, as early as 1700, that Bank of Scotland formed an important part of the financial infrastructure of the country, and thus the directors and management had a greater obligation than usual to act in the national interest. This outlook has remained with the Bank ever since and has, from time to time, involved the directors in the high politics of banking and financial legislation. These are perspectives that all large clearing banks have taken in their stride.

The wording of the original Act, and the cautious interpretation of the powers of the Bank by the directors, fitted well with the deeply-held religious convictions of the Scottish lowlanders. In this pattern of faith, two aspects are directly relevant to banking: the belief in the goodness of sustained regular work for individuals, and an understanding that, for society as for families, bad times follow good times, and the correctness of one business scheme or another should thus be judged in the long term, often over generations. The few exceptions when many Scots have taken a shorter-term horizon, notably with the disastrous Darien scheme and the short-lived Ayr bank, underlined this point. The long-term lending commitments of Bank of Scotland, and later of the Royal Bank of Scotland, have proved important, perhaps essential for many families and businesses, in enabling apparently unproductive resources to be utilised for productive ends and in support through crises. These lessons, which are abundant in 300 years of Scottish banking, are still of relevance to the behaviour of the major clearing banks at the end of the twentieth century.

Scottish bankers are sometimes asked whether they have a philosophy of banking. It is not easy to distil the history of the banking system in this way, although there are some pointers which are as relevant today as they were in 1695. As the early directors sifted the applications for bills of exchange and long-term bonds, they rarely neglected that essential checking of the financial status of the borrower, to find out whether the funds for repayment would indeed be available and whether the statements made in the application were truthful. While this was good business practice, it encouraged borrowers to think in terms of repayment and hence of what have been described as early business plans. There was too much sloppy borrowing in Scotland prior to 1688, at high rates of interest, and these bad practices inevitably led to much dispute. The directors frequently reviewed and enforced the rules and regulations, and the first Governor, John Holland, insisted that business would grow best with low rates of interest and long-term connections with customers. Knowing a customer's situation was as relevant then as now, and was an important protection for the Bank and borrower. No bank can benefit when customers are over-extended. Further, it became an axiom of banking that it was immoral to borrow beyond one's means, and bank managers still have a duty to refuse advances, large or small, where there is doubt about the projected cash flow from which a loan will be repaid. Only by appreciating the subtleties of their attitude to lending – which often involved a measure of personal, as well as business, assessment – will the reader begin to understand why the Scottish banks, including Bank of Scotland, have survived.

The history of the Bank has underlined that judicious lending, with the limits of risk carefully worked out, enabled the adverse economic situation in Scotland to be gradually tackled, both in the sense of dealing with hardship and hunger and by the advances made to those, the vast majority, who wished to spend on infrastructure, on plant and equipment, and on the production of goods. This was explained, as a systematic view of economic development, by Thomas Kinnear, a director of Bank of Scotland, in April 1826 in his evidence before the Select Committee on Promissory Notes in Scotland and Ireland, in answer to the question of whether any branch was established which was not expected to be profitable:

> we are in the habit not of looking to that sort of profit to which tradesmen are sometimes apt to look, I mean immediate profit. The directors of Bank of Scotland (and I say that because I can say it as a fact, but I do not mean to assume any praise for them, I think it is the case with every Scotch bank) are in the habit of sitting down and calculating that they will lose by those branches until the improvement they shall effect in the country shall produce a greater accumulation of business that will make them gain; and I consider that is the proper view to take of the interest of the bank.[1]

Thomas Kinnear was expressing a view which drew on the culture and religion of the country to explain the successful nature of Scottish banking.

1 *Report from the Select Committee on the Circulation of Promissory Notes under the Value of £5 in Scotland and Ireland*, 26 May 1826, (402) vol. iii: Thomas Kinnear, Minutes of Evidence, 19 April, p. 132.

It was an attitude of mind which emphasised the mutual obligations of lender and borrower and, in particular, looked to the longer term, where the Bank would establish an affinity with the efforts of people trying to build up business and trade and would also continue an obligation to carry on support, perhaps for many years, before profits were seen from the business to which advances had been made.

Central to the history of Bank of Scotland has been a questioning of business limits, the setting of new horizons and the reorganisation of management. This is a necessary process which can be described in various ways, but central to this is the view that a greater professionalism will result where several bankers are involved in decision-taking, that every layer of bank work requires an audit, and that there should be a strong inspection system. There have also been, in the recent past, occasions when managers of some banks have followed brash ideas which promised an above-average return, such as loans to Latin America and to a rising property market, and have done so without imposing sufficiently strong limits on exposure. In several cases, such changes followed from a lead given by other banks, usually in London, and associated with considerable discussion and promotion in the media. Of course, some of these fashions have worked well, and indeed were essential for the Bank to play its role in the development of Scotland and more recently a larger role in the industrial development of the UK. But it has remained the case that some ideas about where to lend, and to whom, derived from little more than the needs of the City of London, which has induced both a short-term approach to returns on investment and a recklessness in the buying and selling of industrial companies, and for no better end than raising the profits for the City firm involved. Moreover, while the gambling instinct evident in some companies has always coexisted with foreign exchange dealings and the forward buying of commodities, financial wheeling and dealing in its many guises has grown in the past half-century with the reduction in the ability of central banks to cope with very rapid changes in financial services. Some of these new investments, especially in commodity dealing and foreign-exchange transactions, have shown that, where lax controls existed, losses would be inevitable. There has been something quite sinister, though not necessarily criminal, in the way in which long-established and respected banks and industrial companies have been exposed to colossal losses by a process of gambling. A recognition of the strengths of a really tough and effective internal inspection function would have saved, for example, the assets of Barings & Co. in 1995, when a series of bets placed by that company's traders in Singapore on the movements of Japanese stockmarkets proved to be mistaken. There is an important conclusion for bankers from this, and similar episodes, that controls and internal inspection procedures should be part and parcel of all lending and investment decisions.

The reorganisation of Bank of Scotland from time to time has rarely, if ever, lost sight of the advantages of an institutional structure which has enabled change to be thought through slowly and cautiously. This has earned the Bank a deserved reputation, and one columnist on the *Financial Times* labelled the Bank in its tercentenary year the most 'boring' in the UK. This, at a time when other banks were disclosing various disasters, was intended to compliment the Bank on the predictable nature of its profit stream, and is a label which the men on the Mound happily accepted. Moreover, the structure of the Bank, while no longer enjoying an Extraordinary board, has allowed the Ordinary board to take over much of the political functions which the former carried out. The management board, however, is not just an ordinary management board, dealing with advances and supervising the work of banking. In its now fifteen years of operation, it too, as with the main board of directors, has had to cope with questions including financial regulation, European affairs and the strategic direction of the Bank. These wheels may be seen, from outside the Bank, as grinding exceedingly slowly, but inside they are seen as grinding exceedingly fine; and the acquisition of BankWest (formerly the Bank of Western Australia) as part of a developing Australasian policy was only done after five years of building contacts, knowledge and confidence, of which, it may be added, no hint ever leaked to the outside world. This process of care in respect of diversification has also been imposed upon a number of banking matters which are inevitably subject to commercial confidentiality. The Governor of the Bank, Sir Bruce Pattullo, summed up his overview of the modern problem of banking thus:

> The culture in any corporation is important and can help a bank to ride out the [trade] cycle. I would also argue strongly – and my friends in the City of London would be disappointed if I resisted the temptation to make the point – that not having one's headquarters within the Square Mile makes it slightly easier to resist some of the herd instinct and cyclical pressures [to over-extend advances and rashly build up new directions]. . . . Bank of Scotland's tercentenary in 1995 reminds us that our canny forebears must have resisted temptation many times over those 300 years. . . . Mistakes are more likely to occur in corporate life, especially in a bank where one individual is anxious to achieve too much in too short a space of time. There is no substitute for good old-fashioned common sense.[2]

So volatile have movements in trade and industry become, because of repeated crises and recessions, that the long-run rate of profit in British

---

2 D. B. Pattullo, 'Common Sense is the Best Palliative', *Centre for the Study of Financial Innovation*, 10 (November 1994), 9–11 (p. 11).

banking since 1973 has been below a 1 per cent return on total assets; and at times, including the early 1990s, this long-run return fell to 0.5 per cent. Some parts of banking have managed to do much better than the long-run rate, but others, including international lending, have done worse, and in some banking companies have shown a negative rate. The overall experience of banks has varied. While Bank of Scotland emerged from the recessions of both 1979–82 and 1989–92 with only modest bad debts, several other banks encountered exceptional losses in ordinary commercial lending, with problem in foreign lending, inappropriate acquisitions and mismanagement of subsidiaries. Further, while bank managements cannot escape criticism for their difficulties, there have been influences on bank directors, widely aired in the media, which are disturbing. The artificial stimulation of consumer credit, managed so adroitly by Harold Macmillan in 1959, and seen again in the secondary banking crisis of 1971–4, has been a persistent threat to the long-term management of debt. These episodic booms have resulted in a direct increase in bad debts and have also brought in marginal lenders who have, at times, done serious damage to the clearing banks, which the banks have been able to do little about. The results of the boom engineered in the later 1980s are too well known to require repetition, although some of these effects have been exceptionally long-lived by comparison with previous recessions.

Bank of Scotland was founded because of pressing needs within the Scottish economy. Ever since, it has performed an important and at times vital role within Scotland, and now increasingly in the wider British economy. The form of organisation that Parliament chose was the joint stock, and 300 years later this is still the basic form and will probably remain so for the foreseeable future. This, however, says little about the wide range of other important considerations in politics, business behaviour and connections with proprietors, in the way that the directors relate to management, and about the wider Scottish influences upon banking personnel. The mind of the banker continues to be concerned with the individual case history, from the corner shop to the multinational company; and, while the influences upon bankers are often different from those of the eighteenth century, it is not self-evident that these are more difficult or time-consuming now than they were then. Bankers still have to come back to an old-fashioned understanding of human nature, to the weakness of the borrower's appreciation of how difficult economic times may change the business or family circumstances. There has always been an obstinate optimism among borrowers which requires a strong medicinal dose of reality. There are still problems caused by government, or by lack of government understanding, and most Scottish bankers would probably wish for greater cooperation. Furthermore, there have been in recent decades exceptional pressures from the City of London – some positive, some malign – which only government can address and which are difficult to control. This book has offered many of the answers as to why Bank of Scotland has survived all these difficulties, and future historians will undoubtedly identify others; but it will always be clear that the success of the Scottish banking system, and of Bank of Scotland within it, derives from a wide range of advantages not easily replicated, and which have to be worked at to keep them in good order. The maintenance of this competitive system should be regarded as a valuable asset in British banking, and increasingly in the wider world, as we enter the fourth century of Bank of Scotland.

APPENDIX 1

BANK OF SCOTLAND
FOUNDING ACT, 1695

ACT
OF
[the Scottish]
PARLIAMENT
For Erecting a Bank in Scotland
Edinburgh, July 17, 1695

OUR SOVERAIGN LORD Considering how useful a publick Bank may be in this Kingdom, according to the Custom of other Kingdoms and States;[1] and that the same can only be best set up and managed, by persons in Company with a Joynt Stock, sufficiently endowed with these Powers, and Authorities, and Liberties, necessary and usual in such Cases: *Hath therefore Allowed*, and with Advice and Consent of the Estates of Parliament,[2] *Allows* a Joynt Stock amounting to the Sum of *Twelve Hundred Thousand Pounds Money*,[3] to be raised by the Company hereby Established, for the Carrying on and Managing of a publick Bank. *And further Statutes and Ordains* with Advice foresaid, that the persons under-named, *viz.* Mr. *William Areskine* Son to the Lord *Cardross*, Sir *John Swinton* of that Ilk, Sir *Robert Dickson* of *Sornebeg*, Mr. *George Clerk* Junior,

1 This clause allowed the Bank directors to follow the procedures of existing European banks, and the Scottish Court of Session would be expected to allow whatever seemed reasonable practice.
2 The Scottish Parliament was unicameral. There were three estates in 1695: (1) all the nobility; (2) the landed gentry (the lairds), who elected (usually) two of their number from each shire; (3) representatives from the royal burghs. The bishops sat in Parliament to 1690 and were then voted out. In practice, the aristocracy were the dominant group.
3 This was in pounds Scots; the official exchange rate was £1 sterling to £12 Scots, though at the time the Act was passed the actual rate was 1:13. See Appendix 3.

and Mr. *John Watson* Merchants in *Edinburgh*, Mr. *James Fowlis*, Mr. *John Holland*, Mr. *David Nairn*, Mr. *Walter Stuart*, Mr. *Hugh Frazer*, Mr. *Thomas Coutts*, & Mr. *Thomas Deans* Merchants in *London*, or any three of them; and in case of the Decease of any of them, the persons to be chosen by the Survivers, shal have power to appoint a Book for Subscriptions of persons, either Natives or Forraigners, who shall be willing to subscribe and pay in to the said Joynt Stock, which Subscriptions the foresaids persons or their *Quorum*, are hereby Authorized to receive in the foresaid Book, which shall ly open every *Tuesday* or *Friday* from nine to twelve in the Forenoon, and from three to six in the Afternoon, betwixt the first day of *November* next, and the first day of *January* next following, in the publick Hall or Chamber to be appointed in the City of *Edinburgh*, and therein all persons shall have liberty to subscribe for such Sums of Money, as they shall think fit to adventure in the said Joynt Stock, one thousand Pounds *Scots* being the lowest Sum, and twenty thousand Pounds *Scots* the highest, and the two third parts of the saids Stocks; belonging alwise to persons residing in *Scotland*: *Likeas*, each and every person, at the time of his Subscribing, shall pay in to the hands of the forenamed persons, or any three of them, ten of the hundred of the Sums set down in their respective Subscriptions, towards the carrying on the Bank, and all and every the persons Subscribing, and paying to the said Stock as aforesaid, shall be, and are hereby Declared, to be one Body Corporat and Politick, by the name of *the Governour and Company of the Bank of* Scotland, under which name, they shall have perpetual Succession, and shal have a common Seal, and their Successors; by the name foresaid shall be able and capable to Purchase and enjoy, As also, to give, grant, alienate, and dispose of Lands, Tenements, and all other Heretage; As likewise of all Sums of Money, and other Moveable Goods and Gear whatsoever: And further to do and execute all other things, which any other Company or Body Corporat, can or may lawfully do or execute, and that as amply and fully, as if the several matters and things, were particularly set down in this Act.[4] *And* for the better Ordering and Managing of the Affairs of the said Bank: It is hereby further *Statute and Ordained*, that there shal be for ever a Governour, Deputy-Governour, and twenty four Directors, to be Elected and Chosen, as hereafter is appointed, who, or any seven of them, (hereby Declared to be their *Quorum*,) shall have the Management and Direction of the said Bank, which persons, *viz.* Governour, Deputy-Governour, and twenty four Directors, are to be chosen in this manner, *viz.* That within the three Moneths after the foresaid Subscriptions are ended, the persons particularly above-named, or any two of them, shall

4 This clause included distraint on lands on which loans were granted.

appoint a certain day, and make due Intimation of the same, that such and so many of the Adventurers, and none other, as shall each of them have Subscribed for one thousand Pounds Money or upwards in the said Book of the Joynt Stock, may Elect and Choose by Majority of Votes, which are to be given one Vote for every thousand Pounds Share in the Stock, a fit person of the Subscribers, who hath subscribed for himself, at least for eight thousand Pounds, to be Governour of the said Bank, and an other fit person of the Subscribers, who shall have Subscribed for himself, at least for six thousand Pounds, to be Deputy-Governour of the said Bank, and also twenty four others fit persons, who shall have subscribed each of them for himself, at least for three thousand Pounds in the said Joynt Stock, to be Directors of the said Bank,[5] which Governour, Deputy-Governour, and Directors, are to continue in their respective Offices, until the next Election of their Successors, which next Election shall be made within thirty days, after the Expiration of an whole year from the former Election, by the Majority of the Votes of the Members, who are to be Qualified, and their Votes reckoned in manner above-mentioned; and so forth the said Governour, Deputy-Governour, and Directors to be chosen from year to year; and if any of them happen to Decease before the Expiration of his time, then the Members and the Company Qualified as aforesaid, shall elect in manner above-mentioned, an other fit person in the Room and to the Office of the Dec[e]ased, who is to Officiat for the remainder of his time: *And* further, the Governour or his Deputy, and any three of the Directors, or any five of the Directors, without the Governour or his Deputy, may as often as they see Cause, Summon a Meeting of the Adventurers Qualified as said is, at which Meeting by Majority of Votes to be given as said is, the Governour or his Deputy, or any of the Directors for the time, not exceeding two Directors at one Meeting, may be Displaced and Removed for any Miscarriage or Insufficiency in his Office, to which Sentence the person removed is absolutely to Acquiesce without Gain-saying, and an other to be chosen in his Room and Place as aforesaid, to continue till the next General Election, and the Governour, Deputy-Governour, Directors, or any seven of them, their *Quorum* foresaid, may meet together at any convenient place for the Management of the Affairs of the said Bank, and the saids Adventurers at any General Meeting that shall happen to be appointed, shall have power to require the payment of any further part of the Subscriptions, than the ten *per Cent* above-mentioned, at such time as they shall think fit: And in case, any of the

---

5 In the published share lists, all those with sufficient holdings to be eligible for directorships or above were noted. There was nothing in Scots law to preclude women from being elected, though none was. We cannot be certain that none was nominated.

Adventurers shall refuse or neglect to pay in their proportion appointed by the said General Meeting, then he shall Forefeit to the Use and Behove of the said Joynt Stock, whatever he had before payed in to the said Company, and no Governour, Deputy-Governour, or Director, shall be capable of, or continue in their said respective Offices, unless they have the respective Sums above-mentioned in their own Right, and so long as they have the same and no longer, but upon the Diminution of the saids Sums, their Offices are to Determine, and others to be chosen at a General Meeting as aforesaid in their places: And the said Governour, Deputy-Governour, and Directors, are to swear at their Entry to their respective Offices, the Oath following: *I A. B. Do Swear, that the Sum of* *of the Stock of the Governour, and Company of the Bank of* Scotland, *doth at this time, belong to me in my own Right, and not in Trust: And that in the Office of* I will be equal to all *persons, and give my best Advice for the Support of the Bank of* Scotland; *And in the said Office, Honestly Demean my self to the best of my Skill.* And this Oath, the first Governour shall take before the Lord Chancellor, or any other of the Officers of State, and then shall have power to Administrat the same to his Deputy and Directors. And the next Governour and Directors shall swear the same at their Entry as said is, before a General Meeting of the Company, certifying any who shall neglect to swear at his Entry, or within twenty days thereafter, his place shall be void, and an other shall be Elected to it: And the Governour, or Deputy-Governour, with the Directors or their *Quorum*, may choose a Thesaurer, Secretary, and other Officers for the Affairs of the said Company, who are to give their Oaths *de fideli* before the Governour, or his Deputy, or any two of the Directors; and may be removed from the said Offices, at the Pleasure of a General Meeting: *Providing alwise*, that neither the Governour, Deputy-Governour, or any of the Directors, may be chosen to any of the saids Inferior Offices. *And it is further hereby Statute and Ordained*, that it shall be lawful for the said Governour and Company, to Lend upon Real or Personal Security any Sum or Sums, and to receive Annualrent for the same at six *per Cent*, as shall be ordinary for the time: As also, that if the Person borrowing as said is, shall not make payment at the Term[6] agreed upon with the Company; then it shall be lawful for the Governour and Company, to Sell and Dispose of the Security or Pledge, by a Publick Roup for the most that can be got, for payment to them of the Principal Annualrents and Reasonable Charges, and returning the Overplus to the

---

6 The terms referred to were the four customary settlement days in Scotland: Candlemas (2 February), Whitsunday, Lammas (1 August) and Martinmas (11 November).

Person who gave the said Security or Pledge. And it is further hereby *Enacted*, that the foresaid Company and Members thereof, or major part of them assembled at any General Meeting, may make and constitute such By-Laws and Ordinances, as to them shall seem necessary and convenient for the Good of the Company, and under such Penalties as shall be therein-contained; providing that the saids By-Laws and Ordinances, be not contrary to, (but consistent with the Laws of the Kingdom.) And for Ascertaining how the said Joynt Stock and Shares thereof, with all the Lands, Houses, or other Estate thereto belonging, may be Assigned or Transferred: It is hereby *Statute and Ordained*, that there be constantly keeped a Book or Register by the said Governour and Directors, where all the foresaid Assignments shal be Entered & Subscribed by both the Party Assigning, & the Party to whom the Assignment is made in Token of his Acceptance, and that such Assignments so Subscribed, shall make full, Compleat, and Absolute Rights, and no other shall be good, excepting that any Person having Interest in the said Company, may Dispose of the same by Latter Will or Testament, which shall be a Valid and Compleat Transmission in favours of the Person, to whom the Disposition is made, upon the Entering and Recording so much of the said Latter Will, as re-lates to the said Stock in the Books of the said Company, without necessity of Confirmation or further Formality whatsoever. And it is hereby further *Statute*, that no Dividend shall be made, save out of the Interest or Product arising out the Joynt Stock, and by the Consent of the Adventurers in a General Meeting: and for the better Encouragement of the said Company and Adventurers: It is hereby *Statute*, that the Joynt Stock of the said Bank continuing in Money, shall be free from all publick Burden to be imposed upon Money, for the space of twenty one years after the date hereof:[7] And that during this space, it shall not be Leasom to any other persons to enter into, and set up an distinct Company of Bank within this Kingdom, besides these Persons allanarly, in whose Favours this Act is granted.[8] And sicklike, it is hereby *Declared*, that summar Execution by Horning, shal proceed upon Bills or Tickets drawn upon, or granted by, or to, and in Favours of this Bank, and the Managers and Administrators thereof for the time, and Protests thereon in the same manner, as is appointed to pass upon Protests of Forraign Bills, by the 20. *Act, Parl.* 1681. *K. Ch.* 2.[9]

7 By occasional temporary Acts of the Scottish Parliament, persons paying usury (interest) to their creditors were allowed to divert a percentage of their annual payments to the government for payment of taxes due by the borrower. Thus creditors' incomes fell. The clause here excepted debtors of the Bank from all such future enactments. This was put to the test in the Court of Session in June 1697, and judgement was given in favour of the Bank. See above, Chapter 3.

8 The Company of Scotland trading to Africa and the Indies started banking operations and issued banknotes payable to the bearer in June 1696. See Appendix 6.

9 International merchant law, normally accepted by European courts, allowed a summary demand for repayment on a bill of exchange upon all parties obliged to repay. Only in 1681 did the Scottish

And sicklike, that no Suspension pass of any Charge, (for Sums lent by this Bank or to the same,) but upon Discharge or Consignation of the Sums Charged for allanarly. *And further*, for preventing the breaking of the said Joynt Stock and Company, contrary to the Design thereof: It is hereby *Declared*, that the Sums of the foresaid Subscriptions and Shares, may only be Conveyed and Transmitted by the Owners to others, who shall become Partners of the Company in their place in manner above-mentioned, or by Adjudication, or other Legal Conveyance in Favours of one Person allanarly, who in like manner shall succeed to be a Partner in his Predecessors place, so that the foresaids Sums of Subscriptions, may neither be taken out of the Stock, nor parcelled amongst more persons by Legal Diligence in any sort, to the Diminishing or Disturbing the Stock of the said Company and good Order thereof.[10] *And sicklike*, for the greater Security, and more convenient managing of the said Bank or Joynt Stock: It is hereby *Statute and Ordained*, that in case it shall happen any of the Members, Partners, or Subscribers, or other Proprietars of any part of the said Stock to be Registrat at the Horn, or to commit any Crime punishable by Confiscation, or Forefaulture of his said Share and Proportion of the said Joynt Stock and Profit thereof due at the time, then and in that case, it shall be lawful for the Governour, Deputy-Governour, and Directors, or their *Quorum* foresaid, to expose, by publick Roup, such Shares and Profit thereof to any other person, who shall bid the highest Price therefore, after such Legal Intimations to be made for that effect by the said Governour, Deputy-Governour, Directors, or their *Quorum*, as is prescribed by the Act of Parliament for the Sale of Bankrupts Lands, and the Price arising by the said Roup, to be made forthcoming by the said Company to the Creditors, Heirs, or other succeeding in the Right of the Party so Denunced or Forefeit: *Providing alwise*, as it is hereby expresly *Enacted, Provided, and Declared*, that it shall not be lawful nor allowable for the said Company, Governour, Deputy-Governour, Directors or Managers thereof, upon any Ground or Pretence whatsoever, Directly nor Indirectly, to Use, Exerce, or follow any other Commerce, Traffick, or Trade with the Joynt Stock to be imployed in the said Bank, or any part thereof, or Profits arising therefrae, excepting the Trade of Lending and Borrowing Money upon Interest, and Negotiating Bills of Exchange allanarly and no other. *Providing also*, Likeas it is hereby expresly *Provided, Enacted, and*

Parliament bring Scottish legal practice into line; before then, a costly legal process had to be undertaken. The 1681 Act included only foreign bills, however, and not bills drawn between parties within Scotland. The clause in the Bank Act was thus an important step forward which the Bank was able to make good use of. See Appendix 3.

10 This was an attempt to restrict stockjobbing and vexatious lawsuits by holders of subdivisions of shares. Given the state of the London stockmarket before 1720, this was a sensible restriction.

Declared, that in case the Governour, Deputy-Governour, Directors, or other Managers of the said Company, shall at any time happen to Purchase for the Use and Behove of the said Company, any Lands, Rents, or other Heretage belonging to His Majesty, His Heirs, and Successors, or shall Advance or Lend to His Majesty, His Heirs, or Successors, any Sums of Money in Borrowing, or by way of Anticipation upon any part, Branch, or Fond of the Ordinary, Rent, or Casualities of the Crown, or of any Supply, Cess, Excise, Custom, Pole-Tax, or any other Supply or Taxation already granted, or which shall happen to be granted at any time hereafter to his Majesty and his foresaids, any manner of way whatsoever, excepting these Parts, Branches, or Fonds of the saids Rents, Casualities, or Impositions foresaids, upon which a Credit of Loan shall happen to be granted by Act of Parliament allanarly; Then and in that [c]ase, the said Governour, Deputy-Governour, Directors, or other Managers, one or more of the said Company who shal Consent, Agree to, or Approve of the said Purchase, Advance, or Lending to His Majesty and His foresaids, and ilk an of them so Agreeing and Approveing, and being found guilty thereof according to Law, shall be lyable for every such Fault, in the Triple of the Value of the Purchase so made, or the Sums so Lent, whereof a fifth part shall belong to the Informer, and the Remainder to be Disposed of towards such publick Uses, as shall be appointed by Parliament and not otherwise. *And* it is likewise hereby *Provided*, that all Forraigners, who shall joyn as Partners of this Bank, shall thereby be and become Naturalized *Scots-men*, to all Intents and Purposes whatsoever.

Extracted forth of the Records of Parliament, by
TARBAT, *Cl. Registri.*

Edinburgh, Printed by the Heirs and Successors of *Andrew Anderson*, Printer to the Kings Most Excellent Majesty, 1695.

APPENDIX 2

THE ARISTOCRACY
WHO SUBSCRIBED TO
BANK OF SCOTLAND
IN 1695

Among the nobility who subscribed to the Bank were some of the most important politicians of the time. The fortunes of the Cardross–Erskine family were dependent upon the success or otherwise of William of Orange. The record of support for his cause was unambiguous. Henry, third Lord Cardross, married the daughter of Sir James Stewart of Goodtrees, the advocate and author of *Scotland's Grievances* (1671), a pamphlet which condemned the government of Scotland by the Earl of Lauderdale. Cardross himself spent four years in jail from 5 August 1675 and was released only when Lauderdale's power began to wane. The family lands had to be hastily moved to the care of their relative, the Earl of Mar, when Lauderdale tried to assign their estates to his nephew David Maitland. Cardross was involved in trading links with the Americas in the early 1680s and was among the organisers of a scheme to colonise Carolina with Presbyterian Scots. The failure of this was due to underfunding and to the political consequences for the projectors of the discovery in 1683 of the Rye House Plot to assassinate Charles II, which was, in part, laid at the door of Presbyterians.[1] Cardross fled to the Netherlands, and later joined William of Orange. An Act of Parliament was passed in 1689 'anent his damages', and in April of that year he was given permission by the Estates to raise a regiment of 300 dragoons, though these were to be funded from the public purse.[2] Henry was made a Privy Councillor in 1689 because of his business experience, and became in 1691 General of the Mint. He died in 1693 aged only 44. Henry was succeeded in Parliament by his

---

1 For the Rye House Plot, see above, Introduction.
2 Sir Robert Douglas, *The Peerage of Scotland*, ed. J. P. Wood, 9 vols (Edinburgh: 1813), vol. i, pp. 275–7.

son David, the fourth Earl, who went on to organise Scottish support for the Hanoverian succession.[3] Henry's brother, Colonel William Erskine of Torry, was appointed Deputy Governor of Blackness Castle in 1690, and sat in Parliament for Culross. His younger brother John Erskine of Carnock also went to the Netherlands in 1685, returned briefly for the unsuccessful Argyll invasion, and then settled in Utrecht to study law. In 1690 he was appointed Lieutenant Governor of Stirling Castle, and took an active part in Presbyterian affairs.[4] William was named in the Bank Act to sit on the committee to organise the subscription. The brothers initially subscribed £10,000 Scots each, and just before the closure on 31 December raised their holdings to the legal maximum of £20,000 each. From 1696 to 1697, William Erskine was chosen as the Deputy Governor of the Bank. Their close relatives Sir John Erskine of Alva and his son John Erskine added £4,000 between them.

David, third Earl of Leven and second Earl of Melville, whose lands lay mainly in Fife and Forfarshire, subscribed £20,000. He was exiled during the reign of James VII, in the service first of the Protestant Duke of Brandenburg and thereafter of William of Orange. Leven came over in 1688 as a colonel of a foot regiment. As one of the most trusted Scots, he was sworn in as a Privy Councillor, and was appointed colonel of the 25th Regiment of Foot on 19 March 1689. On 4 July, he took over from the Jacobite Duke of Gordon as Governor of Edinburgh Castle.[5] Leven fought at Killiecrankie, and in 1691 married Lady Anne Wemyss, eldest daughter of Margaret, Countess of Wemyss, the head of the successful coalmining family. Leven bought £20,000 of stock, and the Countess bought additional stock in the next decade. For the first two years after the Bank opened for business, Leven, who was resident in the Castle, took an active part in Bank proceedings. In 1697, the adventurers appointed him Governor, and he stayed in the post until his death in 1728, which may have been hastened by the assault on the Bank at that time. His political connections were invaluable, and proved helpful in other ways; thus, when fire broke out on the east side of Parliament Close on 3 February 1700, Leven ordered his soldiers to empty the offices of all Bank papers and cash and stored them in the Castle.[6]

John Hay, the second Earl and first Marquis of Tweeddale (1626–97; subscribed £4,000), spent a short time in jail in 1661 for opposing the

3 Ibid., vol. i, p. 277.
4 Rev. W. Macleod (ed.), *Journal of the Hon. John Erskine of Carnock, 1683–1687*, Scottish History Society Publications, vol. 14 (Edinburgh: 1893).
5 For the details, see W. Ferguson, *Scotland: 1689 to the Present*, The Edinburgh History of Scotland, vol. iv (Edinburgh: 1968), p. 4.
6 Douglas, *The Peerage of Scotland*, vol. ii, p. 117; BS 1/1/1, Lists of Proprietors; C. A. Malcolm, *The Bank of Scotland, 1695–1945* (Edinburgh: n.d. [1948]).

execution of James Guthrie, a cleric who opposed the Restoration of Charles II, although thereafter he rose to be President of the Privy Council. According to Gilbert Burnett (*History of Our Time*) he was the 'ablest and worthiest man of the nobility, only he was too cautious and fearful'. By 1674, he was associated with the opposition and removed from all offices. This was to cost the family dearly, and their ancestral estates were confiscated. Tweeddale was associated with the Duke of Hamilton, and in 1682 was one of the Commissioners who indicted Lord Hatton, the younger brother of the Duke of Lauderdale, over a colossal series of frauds in the Scottish Mint which did immense damage to the coinage.[7] While he kept close links with the exiles after 1685, he was careful not to antagonise James VII. In 1688 he was appointed to the Privy Council, and the Convention Parliament sent him and Leven to persuade the Duke of Gordon to surrender Edinburgh Castle. In December 1689 he was made a Lord of the Treasury, on 5 January 1692 he was appointed Lord Chancellor, and he was created a Marquis on 17 December 1694. During the fourth and fifth sessions of Parliament in 1693 and 1695, he worked hard to ensure the passage of economic and financial legislation, including that for the Bank. His son, John, Lord Yester, who married Lady Anne Maitland, the only child of the Duke of Lauderdale, subscribed a further £3,000 and was appointed a director in 1699.[8] Tweeddale appreciated the need for improved facilities for bills of exchange, and how a Bank might reduce the costs of remittance and perhaps help in the collection of taxation. Unfortunately, at the opening of the fifth session on 9 May 1695, he called for a foreign trading company, and later signed the Act for the Company of Scotland trading to Africa and the Indies. The Tweeddale family retained close links with Bank of Scotland and other Scottish banks at later dates. The crucial importance for the Bank of the Marquis of Tweeddale when Secretary of State, 1742–6, is discussed in Chapter 6.

The actions of the first Marquis in 1695 so annoyed the king that Hay was replaced as Lord Chancellor by Lord Polwarth, Sir Patrick Home of Polwarth, who subscribed £8,000 to the Bank and remained as Lord Chancellor for the rest of the reign.[9] Polwarth had an interesting conspiratorial career. Jailed by Lauderdale in 1675 and 1676, he was implicated in the Rye House Plot and was also associated with the failed Presbyterian scheme for the colonisation of Carolina. Fleeing first to Utrecht, he

---

7 See above, Chapter 4.
8 *Dictionary of National Biography*, ed. L. Stephen and S. Lee (London: 1891), vol. xxv, pp. 268–70; Sir J. B. Paul, *The Scots Peerage, Founded on Wood's Edition of Sir Robert Douglas's Peerage of Scotland* (Edinburgh: 1903), vol. viii, pp. 451–8.
9 H. Doubleday and Lord H. de Walden (eds), *The Complete Peerage* (London: 1945), vol. x, p. 569.

returned with the Earl of Argyll in the failed invasion of Scotland in 1685. He escaped again and his estates were confiscated. In July 1690 the estates were restored, and he was made a Privy Councillor in December 1690, created Lord Polwarth and given a pension of £400 sterling. In 1692 he was made sheriff principal of Berwickshire, and the following year was appointed to the Court of Session. He was appointed as a director of the Bank in 1696; in 1697 he was created Earl of Marchmont, Viscount Blasonberrie and Lord Polwarth of Polwarth, Redbraes and Grienlaw, and was appointed to the Treasury and the Admiralty. It is not surprising that the family remained completely loyal to Crown policy under Anne, and later Hanover.[10]

William Douglas, third Duke of Hamilton (1635–94), was an early associate of Lauderdale, but because of political difficulties they moved apart. By 1673 he was the leader of the opposition in Parliament, though he apparently refused to back proposals to assassinate Lauderdale. In 1685 he was restored to the Privy Council, although he secretly kept in touch with William of Orange, on whose invasion in 1688 Hamilton called a meeting of the Scottish nobility then in London to declare their allegiance.[11] William appointed him President of the Council and his personal Royal Commissioner in the first Scottish Parliament, as well as Lord Admiral for Scotland. Hamilton attracted support because of his position in the peerage, his large family incomes and his personality, which had been sufficiently robust to withstand the intrigues of the Stewart period. However, his 'boisterous temper' made it difficult for other nobles to work with him, and he was probably best as a figurehead rather than as a coordinator of like minds.[12] His wife Anne, Duchess of Hamilton, a strict Presbyterian, was quite outstanding both in the management of her own estates and in Kirk affairs, though she had the misfortune to have as heir James, the later fourth Duke, who for some reason decided to support James VII. James managed to insult William in 1688, and for his own good he was sent to the Tower, probably at the request of his father. James was temporarily barred from the inheritance in 1694, again a sensible precaution at a difficult time in the war with France. When his mother decided he was mature enough, she pleaded on his behalf and he inherited his estates in 1698. He may have been involved with various Jacobite plotters including the ubiquitous Sir James Montgomerie. This (fourth) Duke subscribed £8,000 to the Bank, supported the Darien Company and opposed the Union. Fortunately for the family, he was killed in a duel

10 Sir J. B. Paul, *The Scots Peerage*, vol. vi, pp. 12–16; D. M. Lyon, *History of the Lodge of Edinburgh (Mary's Chapel) no. 1* (London: 1900), p. 97.
11 P. W. J. Riley, *King William and the Scottish Politicians* (Edinburgh: 1979), chs 1 and 2.
12 *DNB*, vol. xv, pp.326–9, 372–3.

on 15 November 1712 and thus missed the 1715 Rebellion. Anne herself subscribed £8,000, as did another of her sons, Lord Basil Hamilton. This last married Mary, heiress to Sir David Dunbar, a cattle laird of Baldoon in Wigtownshire.[13] Lord Basil was appointed a director in 1697, though his brother James was not invited onto the board.

Most of the aristocratic families who subscribed to the Bank benefited from public office. John, second Lord Belhaven (1656–1708), offended James in the 1681 Scottish Parliament with his opposition to the king's policy of toleration for Catholics and Dissenters during the debate on the Test Act. James then jailed him in Edinburgh Castle. Belhaven was one of the Scottish nobles who invited William of Orange to take the Scottish throne in January 1689, and in June he was appointed a Commissioner for executing the office of Lord Clerk Register. The following month, he fought on the government side at Killiecrankie. He was among those who were granted a tack (a lease) of the 1693 poll tax – by which time government fund-raising in Scotland was in serious trouble – and the eighteen months' excise from September 1695. In later years his politics changed, but during William's reign he was a strong loyalist. He subscribed £20,000, and his son, James Hamilton ws, a further £3,000. John, Lord Carmichael (1638–1710), though rather late in welcoming William, was made a commissioner of the office of Lord Privy Seal in 1689, and in January 1690 was granted a pension of £300 sterling. Various ecclesiastical and university appointments followed, and William was sufficiently impressed by his conversation to appoint him Secretary of State for Scotland in 1696, and he continued thereas until the Union. His pension was increased to £1,000 sterling in 1699, and on 25 June 1701 he was created Earl of Hyndford, Viscount of Inglisberry and Nempha, and Lord Carmichael of Carmichael. His family continued to benefit from public office in the next decade, and his son William was appointed a director of the Bank in 1719. David, Lord Ruthven, a talented peer, was appointed to the Privy Council in 1689; he subscribed £8,000 to the Bank and was made a director in 1696, but he was unfortunately drowned in 1701. His family remained loyal to the Hanoverians.[14] The Countess of Rothes, who subscribed £1,000, was the elder daughter of the Rothes who worked with Lauderdale in the Restoration years. She was the mainstay of the family in the 1680s and 1690s, and organised various legal devices and entails to protect the inheritance. Her son, the eighth Earl of Rothes, fought for the government in 1715.[15]

---

13 Douglas, *The Peerage of Scotland*, vol. i, pp. 707–8, citing Anon., *Memoirs of the Life and Family of James, Duke of Hamilton* (1717).
14 Sir J. B. Paul, *The Scots Peerage*, vol. vii, pp. 387–9.
15 Ibid., pp. 302–4.

The case of the family connections of Sir Alexander Bruce of Broomhall, the heir to the Earldom of Kincardine, is most interesting. The family were the direct descendants of Robert the Bruce, whose tremendous victory at Bannockburn in 1314 over the English knights led by Edward II has remained forever ingrained in the heart of the Scottish nation. For various reasons, the family failed to exploit their position as a Royal Family in waiting, and by the close of the seventeenth century still owned relatively modest estates in Fife. These were in areas with extensive limestone and coal measures, and put the family at the forefront of Scottish industrial development from the early seventeenth century. Alexander was the member for Culross in the Restoration Parliaments of 1661–3, 1669–74 and 1678, and for Sanquhar in 1692. He practised as a Writer, was appointed to the Court of Session and was an occasional senior official in the Scottish government under Charles II.[16] By the Revolution, he supported William. As the main organiser of the family coal and lime works, he had considerable business experience, and it may have been this which gained him the post of muster master of the government forces in Scotland in 1690. Yet this was not a lucrative post considering the time and effort which had to be bestowed on it. Potentially more remunerative was his appointment as Receiver General of the Excise from 1693 to 1695, and later revenue posts which he probably owed to his ability to work hard and collect money.[17] His son Thomas Bruce was given the position of muster master in 1692, and he later subscribed £20,000 to the Bank. On 12 June 1702, Alexander was removed from Parliament by the Presbyterian interest after he opposed their imposition of Presbyterian government on the Kirk. The government then investigated his work as tax-gatherer, and Thomas was later accused by a Parliamentary committee in 1706 of owing £140,000 Scots from his time in this position. Parliament granted him freedom from personal liability for the debts of 600,000 merks then on the estates of the Earl of Kincardine.

Apart from the fourth Duke of Hamilton, who had a strong mother to protect the family estate, the exception to the generalisation that the nobility who subscribed to the Bank were loyal to William and Mary was James, fourth Earl of Panmure, and his wife Jean, Countess of Panmure. Their lands lay in Forfarshire and produced linen and wool for export from Montrose. Between them, their subscription came to £11,000. Panmure had been removed from the Privy Council on 10 March 1687 for opposing the abrogation of the penal laws. Yet he refused to acknowledge William

---

16 S. G. Checkland, *The Elgins 1766–1917: A Tale of Aristocrats, Proconsuls and Their Wives* (Aberdeen: 1988), p. 1.
17 Sir J. B. Paul, *The Scots Peerage*, vol. iii, pp. 488–9.

and Mary's right to the throne, and stayed out of Parliament. His position in the Forfarshire area and his business acumen made him an ideal correspondent for the Bank, and he was appointed a director in 1697. Panmure went on to oppose the Union, and in 1715 he supported the Stewarts. His estates were confiscated, and his wife started the long and tedious process of buying them back. Sir George Mackenzie of Tarbat, Viscount of Tarbat, Lord Macleod and Castlehaven, was removed from the Court of Session and the office of Lord Clerk Register in 1689 because of his record of support for James VII. He was labelled a Jacobite after the Revolution, but did nothing to encourage that view. After Killiecrankie, he worked with Breadalbane for a negotiated peace in the Highlands. As he continued loyal he was gradually appointed to high office, his legal and intellectual eminence lending a further aura of respectability to the new regime. Under Anne, Tarbat was Secretary of State in 1703 and 1704, and later Lord Justice General. He supported the Union and the Hanoverian succession. His fourth child, James Mackenzie of Royston, subscribed £6,000 and later rose to the Court of Session, and was appointed to the board of the Bank in 1724.[18]

The contribution of the lairds to the foundation and the subscription has been mentioned, in particular the role of the eventual Deputy Governor, Colonel William Erskine, and the other two Parliamentary appointees to the founding committee, Sir John Swinton of that Ilk and Sir Robert Dickson of Sornbeg. They were originally Quakers and after the Restoration lived and traded in the Netherlands. The forefaulture was lifted and their estates restored in 1690.[19] Swinton distinguished himself as one of the leaders of the gentry in the 1690s concerned with the economic conditions of the country as a whole. Captain Robert Dickson of Sornbeg, of Galston parish, Ayr, was a military officer; he succeeded to his estates in 1690, and in recognition of his loyalty was created a baronet on 28 February 1695. He subsequently bought Inveresk estate, near Edinburgh, and sat in the last Parliament before the Union. His son was later Inspector General of Salt Duties.[20] They both subscribed £10,000 to the Bank. There were other adventurers from among the opposition gentry who had opposed the Stewarts. The father of George Baillie of Jerviswood was executed in 1684 in the aftermath of the Rye House Plot. Baillie later married Grissell, the daughter of Lord Polwarth, whose courage enabled her father to elude his pursuers when the plot was discovered. He subscribed £8,000. Alexander Munro of Bearcrofts, in Stirlingshire, was

18 Ibid., vol. iii, p. 76.
19 *The Acts of the Parliaments of Scotland*, vol. ix, p. 221, c.95, 22 July 1690; the estates were restored by c.41. Malcolm, *Bank of Scotland*, pp. 21–3.
20 G. E. Cockayne, *Complete Baronetage*, ed. H. M. Massingberd (1983), vol. iv, p. 368.

also immersed in the Rye House Plot, was captured and faced torture and execution. He was regarded as sufficiently loyal to be appointed an aide to the Commission of Enquiry into Glencoe of 1695, and was later given a knighthood and pension in recognition of his services. James Elphinstone of Logie was appointed Keeper of the Signet from 1691 to 1696 and given a baronetcy in 1701 'for his pure zeal to King William's Government'.[21] He represented Aberdeenshire in Parliament, and was elected a director in the ballot of 6 August 1696. David Boyle of Kelburn in Ayrshire was an associate of the Duke of Queensberry who led the dominant court faction in the later 1690s. After the Revolution, he was appointed Rector of Glasgow University and at the instigation of Queensberry was appointed to the Privy Council and created Lord Boyle in 1701.[22] Boyle was probably the leading political influence in Scottish university circles, and he regularly attended meetings of the Bank Court of Directors. The subscription of John Stewart of Grandtully in Perthshire is significant, as it came from someone who lacked high office but was successful in estate management; he put in £5,000 on 19 November, followed by another £15,000 a month later. The Stewart family kept a careful record of their credits and debts in the later seventeenth century. They were heavily involved in the flax and linen cloth trade, exporting via Perth; thus they understood the foreign trades and the methods of financing and how improved conditions for the discount of bills of exchange would benefit producers.[23] The sums of money put in by the gentry were around £200,000, the most common holding (twenty-two out of around forty) was £3,000, and the average of £4,700 was thus £2,000 below that of the aristocracy. The main reasons for subscriptions from the gentry were likely to be as an investment and a lever for future borrowing, either on bond or by bill of exchange.

Some may have subscribed because they had developed a long business relationship with a trusted factor in Edinburgh. George Watson may illustrate this point. In 1676, on his return to Edinburgh, he entered the service of Sir James Dick of Prestonhall as book-keeper and cashier, and by the end of the decade he was also trading on his own account.[24] The formal relationship with Sir James's family business lasted for twenty years, which may give an indication of the stability of Watson's personality and perhaps the stress on continuity and dedication in his Presbyterian upbringing. Employment by Sir James probably helped the development

21 Malcolm, *Bank of Scotland*, p. 25.
22 Riley, *King William*, pp. 128, 153.
23 L. A. Ewan, 'Debt and Credit in Early Modern Scotland: The Grandtully Estates, 1650–1765', Ph.D. thesis (University of Edinburgh, 1988), ch. 4.
24 Edinburgh City Archive, Edinburgh Merchant Company MSS, Miscellaneous papers collection, no. 4, George Watson, Ledger and Journal 1679–1683.

of his own private trading: at least as early as 1683, he acted as a factor for Abel Swalle, a London merchant; and, though there were some difficulties with this account, this did not deter Watson from acting as factor for at least five more London merchants by 1694.[25] Watson's account books have partially survived from 1671 to the later 1690s. In the five years before he moved to the Bank, he kept accounts with over twenty London merchants and over eighty correspondents in Scotland, though some of these were only irregular contacts.[26] There were a small number to whom he lent money; fourteen such payments were recorded for 1690–6, with a maximum worth of £533 Scots, and usually the sums were under £400. Several were from the nobility and landed gentry, including the Earl and Countess of Carnwath; and Sir James Hall, the Laird of Dundass, subscribed £6,000 to the Bank. A number of other correspondents were later to subscribe; these included the Countess of Wemyss, Colonel William Erskine, and the Chiesly family.

25 SRO GD 277, Box 8, Bundle 7, London, 3 March 1683 [grant of factory by Abel Swalle]; Box 2, Bundle 1, London, 23 August 1690 [grant of factory by James Chiesly]; Box 8, Bundle 8, London, 14 December 1692 [grant of factory by Joseph Tomlinson, feltmaker, London]; Box 5, Bundle 5, London, 24 August 1693 [grant of factory by William Clopton]; Box 9, Bundle 3, London, 12 May 1694 [grant of factory by Edmund Harris].
26 Edinburgh City Archives, EMC MSS, Miscellaneous papers collection, no. 4, George Watson, Ledger and Journal accounts.

APPENDIX 3

THE REMITTANCE OF MONEY BETWEEN SCOTLAND AND ENGLAND BEFORE 1707: SOME TECHNICAL CONSIDERATIONS

The remittance of money between Scotland and England has been raised briefly in various chapters of this book for the years before 1695, again for the period from the foundation of the Bank to the Union of 1707, and at greater length thereafter, when simpler considerations applied. Remittance is of obvious importance to the business and political relations of Scotland and England, which calls for some additional explanation of technical questions for the years before 1707.

At the core of the question of remittance lies a 'bartering or exchanging of the money of one city or country against that of another'; and, when Alexander Justice wrote this as a general definition, applicable to the monetary relations of all countries, in his study of the exchange published in 1707, he added that this was 'performed by means of an instrument in writing called a bill of exchange'.[1] Generally speaking, the bill was indeed the preferred method of moving money over long distances, and some peculiarities of this, for Scotland, are discussed below. However, as new production of gold and silver continued apace, the movement of coin and bullion remained extremely important, and the sums involved were significant enough to affect the relative prices of gold and silver against other goods, and the rate of exchange between countries. Further, as conditions of production of gold and silver varied, the price ratio of silver to gold bullion rarely remained stable for more than short periods – a few months at most; and this was as true in the seventeenth and eighteenth centuries as it is today.

1 Alexander Justice, *A General Treatise of Monies and Exchanges* (London: 1707), p. 3. Numerous tracts discussing the exchanges were published in the seventeenth and eighteenth centuries; for a clear, modern account, see J. J. McCusker, *Money and Exchange in Europe and America 1600–1775* (London: 1978).

In theory, it should be a straightforward calculation to arrive at the values of one coinage against another. The intrinsic amount of precious metal in coins should decide how much a coin of a particular face value is worth against the face value of a coin in another country. To cite Alexander Justice again, this was called the 'just and certain par' established between monies, according to the real and effective value of each. This was then, to rephrase the matter, a 'par of real monies' assessed by the equality of the intrinsic value of the real species of any country against those of another. The merchants, goldsmiths, exchangers and bankers who were involved in remittance used official edicts which listed the supposed intrinsic values and weights for different coins, although as there were numerous changes in the intrinsic value of coins, and coins in circulation were worn down by use, this required constant attention, both by the use of scales and, less frequently, by goldsmiths and Mints assaying the precious metal content of coins.[2] There were many additional influences determined by market pressures as well as by institutional ones deriving from the actions of Mints.

An appropriate start to the question of the exchange between Scotland and England may be made with the Scottish coinage of 1604 and after, whose details were announced by royal proclamation of James VI and I on 15 November 1604.[3] This was intended as a straightforward and helpful way of arranging the intrinsic values, the types of coinage stated by face value, and the weights of Scottish coins, so that they could be exchanged with English coins without the fuss and uncertainty that had been common before the Union of the Crowns. This plan, had it been successful, would have removed the Scottish–English exchange from the more complicated assessments of the exchanges, as both monies would henceforth have been tied precisely to each other. It was an ambitious plan designed to help the power and majesty of James VI and I over both his kingdoms, reducing the coins of Scotland 'to ane perfyte equalitie' with those of England. This was a monetary conformity, not monetary union, and designed to complement the political work of his government. Gold coin would henceforth be coined only at 22 carats, on both sides of the Border, and silver in Scotland at 11 deniers fine, which was the same as 11 ounces 2 dwt (pennyweight), the English standard. It was enacted that the English pound sterling would henceforth exchange for 12 pounds

2 For an example of such lists, see a report by the Officers of the Mint to Lord Treasurer Sidney Godolphin, 17 July 1702, repr. in W. A. Shaw, *Select Tracts and Documents Illustrative of English Monetary History, 1626–1730* (London: 1896; repr. 1935), pp. 136–43.
3 R. W. Cochran-Patrick, *Records of the Coinage of Scotland*, 2 vols (Edinburgh: 1876), vol. i, pp. 210–15; Sir John Craig, *The Mint: A History of the London Mint from AD287 to 1948* (Cambridge: 1953), pp. 133–5; E. Burns, *The Coinage of Scotland*, 3 vols (Edinburgh: 1887), vol. ii, pp. 414–15.

Scots. Thus, to give some examples, the new Scottish currency pieces of 48s were to be the equivalent of 4s sterling (i.e. the same amount of silver – 11 deniers fine or 11 ounces 2 dwt), and the 30s piece equal in value to a half-crown; and 12 shillings Scots would buy an English shilling, also equivalent in terms of the intrinsic worth of the precious metals in these comparisons. When it came to passing the value of, say, 12 pounds Scots to England, all that the remitter had to do was to send a bill of exchange for one English pound sterling. Of course, the remitter would also allow for other influences, which might include the interest of money (if that was relevant; there was a legal maximum of 10 per cent in 1604); and there was usually a charge for the time that the bill would take to travel to its destination, and a commission for the remitter's time and trouble and his profit. The remitter would also have to allow for the current demand for coin in the two countries: if more coin was asked for in Scotland, then the exchange would move a little below 12:1, to, say, 11¾:1; and if more coin was requested in England, then the exchange would move in favour of the English pound, above 12:1, to, say, 12¼:1. There were also seasonal factors and the influences of war, although it was the state of trade and the price of bullion that exerted the predominant, market-oriented, influences.[4] In later technical jargon, the limits to the use of a 'rate for bills of exchange' by remitters came when it became cheaper to transmit bullion and coin from one country to another, allowing for insurance and freight etc., than to send a bill. These limits were denoted by 'specie' or 'bullion' points, and were liable to variation, drawing closer to the Mint par if the cost of shipping precious metals fell, and vice versa. In troubled times, of which there were many in the seventeenth century, it was safer to send a bill, regardless of how far 'specie' points departed from the Mint parities.

When the new law of 1604 ensured that the coins of Scotland would exchange in the ratio of 12:1 with those of England, the remitter of a bill had only to work out the market-related influences on the value of coins. But in practice, the calculation of value was more complicated. For reasons connected to the operation of the Scottish Mint, located in Edinburgh, Scottish coins slipped a little below the standard compared to their English counterparts. Among the more important of these influences in Scotland was the long-established practice of government officers, in

4 The ratio between the prices of silver and gold, basic to the fluctuations of the coinage, generated a considerable literature. A report of 1702 by the officers of the Tower of London Mint is reprinted in Shaw, *Select Tracts*, pp. 144–7; the production of silver is discussed in I. Blanchard, *Russia's 'Age of Silver': Precious Metal Production and Economic Growth in the Eighteenth Century* (London: 1989), pp. 49–5, 64–70. For an overview of gold and silver, see P. Vilar, *History of Gold and Money 1450–1920* (London: 1976).

need of more money, who often wished to coin more of a given weight of bullion than the Mint par allowed for. There is good evidence that, soon after the royal proclamation of 1604, the Mint officers in Edinburgh indeed began to debase the coinage in this way. During the reign of Charles I, the Mint restarted the production of the Scots mark, or merk (the records give both spellings), representing 13s 4d Scots; and by the civil war it was a common assumption that these merks were below the 12:1 ratio. Indeed, their weight and visage encouraged these to pass for an English shilling. The merk became the most commonly-minted coin in the seventeenth century, and the most frequently-cited in household and merchant accounts. During the civil wars from 1642 to the conquest of Scotland by the English protectorate in 1650–2, most if not all of the coinage struck in Scotland was debased. Some which has survived in the coinage collection of the National Museum of Scotland is little more than base metal covered with a thin film of silver. In 1652, it was officially agreed to devalue the Scottish coinage, giving a legal sanction to the merk of 13s 4d as equal to a shilling.[5] When Cromwell organised his incorporating union of Scotland and England, he introduced a single national currency, the pound sterling, although the Scottish coin continued to circulate.

The remitter had a further problem. The evidence of hoards of coins buried in sixteenth- and seventeenth-century Scotland points to a majority of foreign coins in circulation, both in number and also by value, with English, Dutch and Spanish coins in the majority. Indeed, in some hoards only a few Scottish coins have been found. This evidence of several currencies in the circulating medium of the country is supported by merchant and institutional accounts. Thus, in an entry typical of a household accounts book before 1707, Sir John Foulis of Ravelstone gave to his 'sone Sandie ane old 3 lib peice, three shilling sterling peices, a Leg dollar, a half ducadoon, and half french croun is in all 12: 16: od [Scots]'.[6] The stock of foreign coin delivered to the Bank for recoining in 1707 has been noted in Chapter 5. There was no fundamental change in the use, by the Scots, of foreign currency as the century progressed, for reasons made clear in the early chapters of this book. The remitter's task, given a bag of coin from his client, would be first to evaluate the true worth of each coin and then to record it in the currency concerned and, if there was a foreign-exchange transaction, in the unit of account used by the remitter's payee, as well as in his own unit of account. From 1604,

---

5 Cochran-Patrick, *Records of the Coinage of Scotland*, vol. ii, p. 134.
6 A. W. Cornelius Hallen (ed.), *The Account Book of Sir John Foulis of Ravelston, 1671–1707*, Scottish History Society Publications, vol. 16 (Edinburgh: 1894), p. 182, 17 August 1695.

the preferred denomination with government accounts, also adopted by merchants and remitters, was an accounting unit for the pound Scots with the aforementioned ratio of 12:1, that is to say, with the English pound sterling equal to 12 pounds Scots. Yet, as the century progressed, more Scottish merchants came to use the pound sterling in their accounts, and a combination of sterling and Scots became common, encouraged by the conquest of Scotland by Cromwell. With so much foreign coinage in circulation, there was no necessary reason to record in the pound Scots, although many accounts were kept thus, such as those of Sir John Foulis. It should be noted that the common circulating coinage of merks and copper denominated in the pound Scots was the normal currency for small transactions, and in rural areas the use of the pound Scots continued long into the eighteenth century. It was a degree of convenience which ensured the continued use of the pound Scots in accounts, and the £12 Scots notes continued to be issued by Bank of Scotland for almost three decades after the Union of Parliaments.

This 'unit of account', the pound Scots, was cited frequently in accounts at the 'par of exchange', of 12:1, and with deviations above or below this par. The par before the civil war, and from 1660 to 1686, always and automatically bore this 12:1 ratio in accounts dealing with foreign trans-actions regardless of the true state of the coinage, although these accounts often expressed the amount below the par at which Scottish coins stood. As Alexander Justice put it in his general definition to cover all coinage, the par of exchange was the 'proportion that the imaginary monies of any country bear to those of another'. We may understand this better by noting that, in the ordinary course of business, there was no particular reason to use any Scottish coins before arriving at accounts compiled in the pound Scots or in working out the exchanges between Scotland and England. All that the accountant needed to know was the relationship of each coin to the pound Scots unit of account, or to the pound sterling. When business accounts refer to the exchanges of the Restoration years as so much below the par, they reflect the debasement, and before 1686 they mean against an 'imaginary' par of 12:1, unless otherwise stated in the accounts. But after 1686, before a calculation of the exchanges can be made from merchant accounts, the ratios used in the 'imaginary' par must be ascertained. They were usually 12:1, but historians must be quite certain of this ratio before drawing any conclusions about the state of the exchange.

The abuses of the Earl of Lauderdale, together with his younger brother Charles Hatton, in respect of the restored Scottish coinage after 1660 have been referred to in Chapter 4. There was considerable resentment over their debasement of the silver coinage below 12:1, although the degree to which this was debased against the pound sterling varied, as it did for their debasement of the copper coinage. There were political and military reasons for their actions which need not be repeated at length here; in the main, debasement gave the Crown more cash, and it may have had the beneficial effect of encouraging Scottish exports, although the degree to which this occurred, if it did so, is probably unascertainable.

James VII and II was prepared to support a more stable currency, at least in theory; and, by royal assent given to an Act of 14 June 1686, future manufacture of Scottish coins was to return to the quality-of-silver standard of 1604, but with a reduced weight, specified in the statute.[7] Thus, to give an example, the 60s Scottish coin was to weigh only 427.35 grains troy, as against 465.5 grains troy under the proclamation of 1604 – a reduction of the official Mint par values intrinsic in Scottish coins to 13²/45:1, or, as roughly stated by contemporary pamphleteers, 8.5 per cent from the old par. Indeed, to speak positively about this, the official debasement recognised the existing devaluation of the Scottish coinage below the 1604 standard, and Parliament was aware of the adverse effects on production for export which a revaluation to 12:1 might have. But this was not a recoinage as conducted in 1707, few coins were manufactured in this short reign, and all sorts of coins continued to circulate.

There were two additional complications which deserve special notice. On 14 August 1695, the Scottish Privy Council decided that, as the quality of the silver coinage in England was then so poor, they could safely cry up the Scottish coinage to near the old par of 12:1. But less than a year later, on 2 June 1696, when the English recoinage had initiated the manufacture of good-quality full-weight coins, the Privy Council was forced to decree a return to the value of 1686, of 13²/45:1, where it remained until 1707, when the monetary union was effected and the separate Scottish coinage abolished for the second and final time. A ratio of 13.21:1 was given by Sir Isaac Newton in a report to Sidney Godolphin, the Lord Treasurer, in 1710, following an assay of the 60s Scots piece, which was equivalent to an intrinsic worth of 4s 6½d sterling.[8] The second problem was just this temporary deterioration in the quality of the English coinage, covered in Chapter 3. It has been noted (in Chapter 1) that the nominal capital of Bank of Scotland was £1,200,000 Scots, £100,000 sterling at a rate of conversion of 12:1, and this figure was used in government and Parliamentary affairs (for example, see Table 4.1). John Campbell, the Scottish goldsmith whose exchange shop in the Strand, London, was a

---

7 'Act anent ane humble offer to his Majesty for ane imposition upon certain commodities for defraying the expence of a free coinage and other matters relating to the Mint', 14 June 1686, repr. in Burns, *The Coinage of Scotland*, vol. ii, p. 503.
8 Sir Isaac Newton to Sidney Godolphin, 16 February 1710, repr. in Shaw, *Select Tracts*, p. 150.

forerunner of Coutts & Co., made specific references to the use of 12:1 in accounts; in 1701, for example, in a transaction involving Campbell and Bruce, the Edinburgh merchant house, £146 Scots was listed at the rate of £12 3s 4d sterling, at a time when the usual exchange between the two currencies was 13½:1.[9]

Is it possible to chart the course of the exchange? The answer is that, for some years before 1695, the number of surviving accounts which record remittance and the deviation from the par of exchange was on the increase, although many of the series are intermittent and not sufficiently clear to enable the historian to chart the movements precisely, not least because it is not always clear which 'imaginary par of exchange' – the 12:1 par or that established in 1686 – was being used. One surviving series, of immense value, was used by W. R. Scott for his edition of the records of the New Mills textile company, which spanned the years 1681–1703.[10] The company kept its internal accounts in both pounds Scots and pounds sterling, and used a 12:1 ratio when converting a sum in one currency to another, usually calculating a suitable discount (of pounds Scots against sterling) for remittance to England. For example, on 25 June 1701, the New Mills minute book listed the following payments, in foreign coin, to two Edinburgh advocates:

To Mr Cunninghame	8 dollers [converted in the accounts to]	£23 4 od Scots
to his first man	1 ducatdoune ["]	£ 3 14 od Scots
to his second	1 doller ["]	£ 2 18 od Scots
To Mr Houstone	5 dollers ["]	£14 10 od Scots
To his man	1 doller ["]	£ 2 18 od Scots
	Total ["]	£47 4 od Scots

This sum was then in turn converted to £3 18s 8d sterling, namely a conversion at 12:1.[11]

As W. R. Scott recognised, the nominal value underwritten in law was 'fixed by law or custom somewhat higher than the Mint value', and there would therefore usually be a discount for foreign transactions when using the imaginary par of 12:1.[12] As Scott narrates, with the internal accounts of the New Mills company fixed at 12:1, the New Mills accountant had to work out the deviation from this 'par' of exchange to enable him to

9 Coutts & Co., archives, Letter Book no. 1, 1701. For John Campbell, see E. Healey, *Coutts & Co. 1692–1992: The Portrait of a Private Bank* (London: 1992), chs 1–3.
10 W. R. Scott (ed.), *The Records of a Scottish Cloth Manufactory at New Mills, Haddingtonshire, 1681–1703*, Scottish History Society Publications, vol. 46 (Edinburgh: 1905).
11 Ibid., p. 258.
12 Ibid., p. xxiv; and, for the examples given by Scott, pp. xxiv–xxx.

arrive at 'true' values when remitting sums abroad and to London. An example which Scott gives, of a remittance to Amsterdam via London in November 1701, involved two sets of transactions, one to Amsterdam and one to London. The whole transaction need not be recounted, but the first part, to London, is relevant to the Scottish–English exchange. The company wished to send a bill for payment of £200 sterling to London; to do this, it had to account in its books – as a debit – for £225 10s, which meant an exchange below the 12:1 par of 12¾ per cent. The 'reckoning', in the internal accounts, was made in pounds Scots converted into sterling at 1s 8d for each pound Scots, or 12:1. This discount of 12¾ per cent thus represented a value near to the true par of exchange – very close, it will be recalled, to Sir Isaac Newton's figure of 13.21:1 and the official Mint par of 13²⁄45:1, although this was accidental, as many, and wider, divergences were recorded.

W. R. Scott was one of the finest historians working in Scotland at the end of the Victorian era, and his three-volume study of joint-stock companies (1910–12) is still a important work of reference. Scott approached Lord Balfour of Burleigh, Governor of Bank of Scotland, through whose good offices the chief accountant, James Clark, made calculations of the rates of exchange under which Bank of Scotland had conducted the remittance from 1696 to 1701. Putting the New Mills figures and those of Bank of Scotland together enabled Scott to offer a rough guide to the exchange between London and Edinburgh, based on this imaginary par of 12:1, as this was the basis on which both companies conducted their internal conversion between sterling and the pound Scots when discounting bills on Edinburgh and London. In the period of the overlap in these accounts (1696–1701), the exchange fell from around 12:1 to a discount against the pound Scots of around 15 per cent by March 1697. There were fluctuations thereafter, although always giving a discount in a range between 8 and 17½ per cent. These figures indicate that the Mint par for the exchange on London, of 13²⁄45:1, was indeed met on several occasions, but deteriorated to as much as 14:1 or above – as in May 1700 – at times of particular demand in Scotland for payments in England and abroad. The discount on the exchange seen in the accounts of Bank of Scotland and the New Mills company was thus composed of several aspects, of which one was the use of the unit of account with a conversion of 12:1, which overvalued the pound Scots against sterling, then a calculation of the discount against sterling to be paid in London, in which the seasonal and market influences mentioned above were of greater or lesser importance. The move to monetary union meant that the exchange on London was dependent mostly on these seasonal and market factors, and rarely deviated more than 1 or 2 per cent, except for the crises in the 1760s when the over-issue of paper currency by the Glasgow banks, and an intense demand for coin in England, did have noticeable effects.

As noticed, the movement of monies across borders was conducted both by the physical movement of coin and bullion and by the use of the bill of exchange. Some reference is required to the legal position of the bill of exchange in Scotland as before 1695, which differed from the normal custom of merchants.

The legal system in Scotland, like most other public institutions, was in considerable flux in the seventeenth century. There were three main systems: a Roman Scots law administered by government law officers with the Edinburgh Court of Session at its apex; a feudal law disposed through the heritable jurisdictions of landowners; and a royal prerogative and associated powers which impinged on both, often capriciously and arbitrarily. There was limited progress in securing rights of property under both the feudal and Roman systems after 1603; of particular importance was the listing of all land transactions outside of the royal burghs in the Register of Sasines, set up in 1617. In addition to disputes arising from property and land, contracts and bills of exchange had during the course of the century begun to take up more of the writers' and courts' time, especially so from mid-century onwards. The Cromwellian rule posed a further challenge; the feudal law was abolished, the Court of Session ceased to sit from July 1651, and in May 1652 seven Commissioners for the administration of justice were appointed. They made the common merchant law for obligations, contracts and debts the basis for all disputes over exchange, and streamlined proceedings. As with other legal changes, including a new Admiralty court for shipping cases, rule from London led to a superior administrative system and to an honesty and impartiality which had been absent from the previous tripartite system. No longer could royal favourites, office-holders by right of birth and feudal magnates under the umbrella of their separate system cut across the workings of merchant law. Thus it was during the Commonwealth that paper transactions made their fastest headway to date in Scotland. If the union of the British Isles had lasted, it is doubtful whether Scots law would have survived.

The restoration of Charles II brought back the baggage of the tripartite legal system, and this encouraged uncertainty as to the position of contracts and bills of exchange. Sir James Dalrymple of Stair's *Decisions of the Court of Session 1661–1671* (1683; a second volume published in 1687) and his *Institutions of the Law of Scotland* (1681) stated that, generally speaking, the Edinburgh courts accepted an absolute obligation by the drawer of a bill of exchange to honour the literal wording of the bill, which was another way of stating that the merchant law of Europe would be upheld in Scottish courts.[13] However, in such a complicated period with three legal systems, there was more to the story than this.

The obligations stated on a bill of exchange between one party and one or more others were comprehended by Stair, following European practice, as a loan, or *mutuum*, wherein the subject of the obligation to be repaid (usually money, but it could be wine, grain or even gunpowder) was a thing of a given class, and was thereby said to be *fungible*: thus, 'the delivery of any object [as repayment] which answers to the generic description will satisfy the terms of the obligation'. It did not then have to be the same thing as originally lent.[14] The intention was clear, though, with such as money, wine or fruit: 'the property thereof shall pass to the borrower from the lender and may be by him alienated; and thence is its name for *mutuum est quasi de meo tuum*'.[15] Stair then proceeds, on the basis of his own experience, to state that

the common opinion holds, that the purpose of the contractors is to alienate, because they know without it there can be no use: and if a fungible be not lent to that purpose, but only to be detained, as in some cases it may, as money to make a show with, to appear rich or to make a simulate consignation, there the borrower without injury, could not alienate, neither is there *mutuum* in that case, but *commodatum*; and he who findeth, unwarrantably alieneth his neighbour's money, and may be compelled, not only to render the like in current money, but to render the same species and piece of money. So he who hath the custody of money, if he meddle with it, commits theft by the law. Hence it follows that *in mutuo* the whole peril of the thing lent, after delivery, is the borrower's, *ejus est periculum cujus est dominium*; so that money or any other fungible thing lent, though it were immediately taken away by force, or destroyed by accident, the borrower is obliged to pay it.[16]

Thus the position of Scots law could not be clearer, apparently, on the obligation of the drawer. In the case of the correspondent who would ultimately pay the bill to the creditor or his agent, Stair insisted that the nature and ordinary tenor of bills is that the drawer orders his correspondent to pay the sum as per the instructions in the bill, 'wherein there is implied a mandate to the correspondent, and an obligement upon the

13 Sir James Dalrymple of Stair, *The Institutions of the Law of Scotland*, ed. D. M. Walker (Edinburgh and Glasgow: 1981).

14 J. A. H. Murray, *A New English Dictionary on Historical Principles*, vol. 4, ed. H. Bradley (Oxford: 1901), p. 606, col. 2, which also notes John Erskine's *Institutes of the Law of Scotland*, 'vol. iii, i, s. 18 (1773) I. 418', 'Grain and coin are fungibles, because one guinea, or one bushel or boll of sufficient merchantable wheat, precisely supplies the place of the other'.

15 Dalrymple, *Institutions*, pp. 211–12.

16 Ibid., p. 212, s. 2.

drawer of the bill, to make that mandate effectual'.[17] But Stair then goes on to allow qualifications which meant that the correspondent, and even perhaps the drawer, might impose conditions to the effect that payment would be made 'if provisions come betwixt and the day', or 'if ware or bills in hand do raise the sum'. Moreover, there were limits to the liability of the drawer in certain cases of accident, and for the heir in the case of death.[18]

Scots law was thus less forceful than ordinary European merchant law on the legal rights of the original lender to demand of the drawer or the ultimate acceptor that proper restitution be made. Further, it was unhelpful in that the process of protest was cumbersome and expensive, as before 1681 all bills had to go before a full court hearing. In that year, the Crown proceeded by 'An Act concerning Bills of Exchange' of Charles II, c.86, to a partial recognition of the merchant demand that Scots law conform to European norms. It was laid down that when any foreign bill of exchange was duly protested, in the proper way by a notary, for non-acceptance or for non-payment, this would have 'the authority of the Judges thereof interponed thereto that letters of horning upon a simple charge of six days and other executorials necessary [would] pass thereupon for the whole sums contained in the bill'. The drawer and/or acceptor and the cautioners would also be liable for all exchange costs, interest and other charges.[19] While this was a victory for the merchants, difficulties remained with inland bills, which were excluded from this Act. It was not until the establishment of Bank of Scotland, by an Act passed on 17 July 1695, that summary protest for inland bills was written into the statute book.

This was another defect of the law as laid down by Stair. The definition of quality or intrinsic value of the loan to be repaid was confused. Stair recognised that the chief fungible was money, 'where ordinarily the extrinsic value and common rate is regarded [for repayment] without respect to the matter, and so what is gold may be paid in silver, according to the common rate of the place, unless it be otherwise contracted'. Stair recognised that there were indeed 'difference in kinds of money, silver or gold, and in the intrinsic and extrinsic value; wherein the common opinion is that not only the extrinsic, but intrinsic value is to be respected, that the same weight and species may be repaid. But none make difference

17 Ibid., p. 214, s. 7.
18 Ibid., pp. 214–15, Book 1, Title 11, s. 7; and, for limits to liability, pp. 215–16, Book 1, Title 11, s. x.
19 *The Acts of the Parliaments of Scotland, 1424–1707* (Edinburgh: 1908), p. 141, Charles II, c.86. The protest had to be properly registered within six months of the date of the bill. Those costs of the creditor not specified in the bill could be brought before ordinary process of law. The cautioners would be as liable as the drawer and acceptor for any part of the costs.

of gold and silver, not allayed; and all reject copper or layed money.' The last statute on the intrinsic quality of coin to be used in repayments was a perpetual Act of 1555, from the reign of Mary. Following the tradition of canon law, and two previous Acts of the fifteenth century, all repayments were to be in the same value, weight and fines as the original loan. The wording is quite specific.[20] Stair noted the statute order for repayment by the same intrinsic value, 'but that was well altered by a posterior custom, allowing the current coin for the time, by the extrinsic value to be sufficient, in all redemptions, much more in personal contracts, which is most convenient, seeing money is regarded as the token of exchange, and as fungible, not as a body'.[21]

This led to a potential problem for repayments in cash unless the sum in which the bill was to be paid was tightly specified. Indeed, it became a commonplace to insert the type of coin to be made in payments. Was Stair's view in any way related to his position in the royal government? After 1660, Stair was an ordinary Lord of Session and a loyal supporter of Charles and his Scottish agent, the Earl of Lauderdale. So trusted was he that Lauderdale nominated him to be one of the Scottish Commissioners to negotiate the proposed union in 1670, and Stair remained a Lord through the period of the Covenanter persecutions. His views on the royal prerogative and the coining of money, which were accepted by the Court of Session and laid out in the *Institutions* in 1681, could be interpreted as underpinning the coinage frauds of the government. Stair was one of the outstanding jurists of the Scottish tradition, but not on bills of exchange, the law on which was only brought into line with European practice after the 1689 Revolution.

20 *APS*, vol. 2 (Edinburgh and London: 1814), Acta Parliamentorum Mariae, 1555, c.10, 'anent all reversiounis beirand and contenand gold and silver or ather of the thame of certane speciall valour and price or cuinzie gif sic gold and silver cannot be had nor gotten within the realme he haifaris of thay reversiounis may redeme the landis specifeit thairin be vertew of thair saidis reversiounis geuard gold and silver haifard cours for the time beard of the samin valour, wecht and fynes as the gold and silver specifeit in the saidis reversiounis conforme to the common law'.
21 Dalrymple, *Institutions*, p. 213, s. 5.

What did a bill of exchange look like?

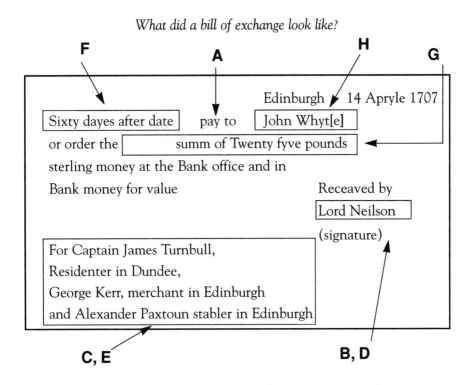

F   **A**   **H**   **G**

Edinburgh 14 Apryle 1707

Sixty dayes after date   pay to   John Whyt[e]
or order the   summ of Twenty fyve pounds
sterling money at the Bank office and in
Bank money for value   Receaved by
     Lord Neilson
     (signature)

For Captain James Turnbull,
Residenter in Dundee,
George Kerr, merchant in Edinburgh
and Alexander Paxtoun stabler in Edinburgh

C, E   **B, D**

Bill reverse

Pay the contents to Mr David Drummond,
Treasurer to the Bank or order
     John Whyt[e]

I

A   An unconditional order in writing
B   addressed by the Drawer(s)
C   to the Drawee(s),
D   signed by the person giving it (the Drawer),
E   requiring the person to whom it is addressed (the Drawee, and, where it is endorsed, the Acceptor)
F   to pay on demand, or at a set time,
G   a fixed sum of money
H   to the person specified in the bill
I   or, if endorsed, to the named bearer.

APPENDIX 4

GENERAL RULES, AND BANK RULES FOR LENDING, APRIL–JUNE 1696

[9 April 1696]

In the house of Patrick Steill, vintner, the overtures and resolutions of the Court of Directors after set down being presented to the general meeting of the Adventurers in the Bank of Scotland. And being diverse times publicly read and spoke to the same were at last unanimously agreed to and approved. And are as follows.

1. That the Committee or Court of Directors in Scotland shall meet once a week at least to consent the affairs of the Bank.
2. That there be a sub-committee of three (and any two to be a quorum) who shall give constant attendance every ordinary day except Saturdays.
3. That there be another sub-committee of three for the Treasury (and any two to be a quorum) to examine and balance the cash with the Treasurer at least once a week. Two of this committee and the Treasurer to have keys of the cash and bills so that the Treasurer may have only in his custody what is necessary for his daily use. The said committee or any two of them are to sign all warrants for the payment of money ordered by the general committee, but that all such warrants shall be first written by the Accountant and certified by him. And also that the Treasurer shall not enter the receipt of any moneys, principal or interest, that shall be paid by the Borrower without a certificate from the Accountant.
4. That in all these committees the Governor and Deputy-Governor shall be supernumerary but no stop to be made 'tho they be absent.
5. That the office be kept open every day of the week except Saturday in the afternoon from the hours of eight in the morning to twelve at noon and from two afternoon till six at night.

6. That the Company may lend money both upon personal and real securities (simple ward lands always secluded). And likewise upon pledge of impoverishable commodities.

7. That in the case of personal security the sum to be lent shall not exceed £500 sterling, nor be under £100 sterling to one person and his cautioners.

8. That any person borrowing on personal security only shall give at least two sufficient cautioners.

9. That personal securities shall be taken payable within six months at furthest.

10. That any person giving real security within burgh shall be obliged to give one sufficient cautioner at least besides the real security on his tenements.

11. That the sum to be lent on real security whither in Burgh or country shall not exceed two-third parts of the unburthened value of the lands with respect always to the rate of the lands out of which the security is offered and the committee being satisfied with the holdings.

12. That the borrower on real security shall be obliged to give in a true accompt of the value of the lands out of which he offers to give the security. And to clear the Committee that his estate is free of all incumbrances such as prior infeftments, apprisings, adjudications, inhibitions and registrat hornings – at least that the estate is free to a third part above the sum he seeks to borrow. And he shall be obliged to condescend upon the incumbrances with this proviso that if the Committee shall after his condescendence find that there be more incumbrances than he has mentioned then no money shall be lent to such a person. And that whatever expences the Company shall be at in searching for incumbrances he who desires to borrow shall be liable to refund the same whither the sum be lent him or not.

13. That real securities shall be conceived thus. The principal sum payable within a year and to continue in the hands of the debitors until any following term. That the Company give thirty days previous advertisement by a lien under the hand of their Secretary or otherwise as the committee shall appoint.

14. That the Company lending money upon pledge, regard is to be had to the rising and falling of the price of the pledge offered and to the quality thereof and the sum to be lent not to exceed two thirds of the value and being payable within six months at furthest.

15. That in the case of all or any of the securities above mentioned, the Company may lend at 6 per cent interest with this proviso that if the borrower pay the interest within thirty days after each term or half year as the same falls due they shall have 2 per cent abatement per

annum thereby reducing the interest to four, with certification that if they do not pay interest punctually as above they are to be liable for 6 per cent, besides payment of the principal sum at any time the Company shall call for it 'tho betwixt terms.

16. That all borrowers on any of the said securities shall have liberty to repay the sums borrowed at any time they please and by what divisions they shall think conversant (the terms of payment notwithstanding) provided the partial payment be not under one hundred pounds sterling nor before elapsing of one month at least after the borrowing and that the debitors clear as well the interest of the whole principal sum for the bygone term as the interest of the partial payment to the very day of the paying thereof.

17. That when any person desires to borrow upon any of the securities aforesaid the Committee shall after debating the matter among themselves put the question, lend or not, which is always to be decided by the billeting box.

18. That for the greater advantage of the Bank a correspondence be settled for circulation of the bills of the Company and negotiating the Exchange to and from the towns of Dundee, Aberdeen and Glasgow, that five shillings sterling on each hundred pounds sterling be the premio for bills delivered to and from Dundee and Glasgow and that six shillings eight pence sterling on each hundred pounds sterling be the premio for bills delivered to and from Aberdeen but that the Committee have power to alter the price of the exchange as they shall see convenient and to settle an office in any other places of the Kingdom that they judge may be for the advantage of the Bank.

19. That there be found out in each of the Towns above mentioned a fit person to be cashier and that each of these cashiers have such a salary off the Company as shall be reasonable and shall be obliged to take the oath, de fideli, and to find sufficient caution.

20. That there be also found out in each of these towns three men of credit and substance to oversee and be cheques to the respective cashiers and that these overseers or any two of them do make up the cash with the cashiers once a week at least. And that the bulk of the cash be at all times in the custody of the said trustees and cashiers. And that two of the Trustees have each a key and the cashier a third key and further that the saids Trustees have some complement or consideration for the pains they shall be at in that Trust which shall be as the Committee shall judge most fit.

21. That all persons transferring any stock in the Bank shall pay one pound Scots upon each thousand pounds Scots, transferred and that the same be paid by the Acceptor.

22. That no officer or servant of the Company shall receive any fee or reward upon pain of forefeiting his place. But that all fees be for the benefit of the Company.

[10 April 1696]

Ordered that the General Committee meet every week on Thursday before 9.00 o'clock in the morning. That whoever is not in the Chamber of meeting before the Town clock hath struck nine shall forfeit seven shillings Scots to the Poors' Box. And that whoever is not in the Chamber before half an hour after nine, he shall forfeit his Court money for that meeting. That the Secretary do set up an half hour glass precisely after the Town Clock hath struck nine.

[13 April 1696]

That any person borrowing shall be allowed eight days free (after his desiring the loan) without interest for preparing his security, but thereafter shall be liable for interest albeit he has not called for or got the money through his own default of which the borrower is to be told the time of his demanding the loan.

[20 April 1696]

1. The committee are of opinion that any person desiring to borrow of the Company shall give in a subscribed note to the Secretary bearing the sum he demands and what security he offers.
2. The committee are of opinion that the Treasurer's Bond of Cautionary be given in to the Secretary.

[21 April 1696]

1. The committee offer to the consideration of the Court of Directors that all moveable bonds for sums lent by the Company be ordered to be writ by the Secretary and that the borrower pay a dollar for the same for the use of the Company.
2. That all Bonds whatsoever shall bear the *annualrent* payable conform to the Act of Parliament constituting the Bank.

[22 April 1696]

The committee considering that during the intervals of the weekly meetings of the Court of Directors several affairs may fall in that require despatch by the sub-committee desires to know how far they may be authorised for acting.

[24 April 1696]

The Court of Directors did unanimously agree that the sub-committee for the time shall exped everything relating to the perfecting and finishing of all business that is, or shall be first agreed upon by the Court of Directors

851

and to correspond by letters and other ways as they shall see cause with the several officers belonging to the Bank and to give instruction to them from time to time.

[4 May 1696]
[Transfers may be done before magistrates of local burgh because of infirmity or other fit reason.]

[7 May 1696]
At the first general meeting of the Adventurers it be offered to their consideration whether the Company (notwithstanding of the general rules already agreed to) may not lend a greater sum than £500 sterling to a burgh or community upon their granting a personal bond for the same, the Court of Directors being always satisfied with the security offered.

[21 May 1696]
When any proposal of borrowing is given in that the Secretary do inquire at the Accountant if any of the persons named be formerly engaged to the Company and for what and that the proposal be marked accordingly.

[22 May 1696]
The committee offer to the Court of Directors that in the case of any persons paying the sum contained in their bond, a general warrant may be enacted allowing the Secretary to deliver up to the Treasurer such bonds as he shall call for upon his granting a receipt for the same to the Secretary in a book to be kept by him for that end. And that the Treasurer upon payment be impowered to retire the bond with a discharge on the back thereof in case it be required by the debitor.

That the Treasurer upon all partial payments of payment of annualrents be allowed to give receipts thereof to the debitor.

It is further offered that the Court may take into consideration the making a general rule how and by whom all discharges and renunciations of heritable right shall be made and upon whose charges whether the Companies or the debitor.

It is also offered that the Court may please to allow of an advertisement to be published intimating that in respect they are now to remove to their own office in the Parliament Close they think it convenient not to receive in any money until Monday 1 June, but in the meantime will pay unto all persons who have their notes or do borrow of them as they have hitherto done at the usual office hours.

[28 May 1696]
When any person desires to borrow upon his giving security on an annualrent or other heritable security belonging to him out of lands

pertaining to a third person, the person desireing to borrow shall be obliged to procure the said common debitors consent to the right otherwise the money not to be lent to him.

In the case of any persons paying the sums due by them upon personal bonds the Secretary do deliver up to the Treasurer such bonds as he shall call for upon his granting a receipt for the same to the Secretary in a book to be kept by him for that end. And that the Treasurer upon payment do retire the bond with a discharge on the back thereof in case it be required by the debitor.

[11 June 1696]
Recommended to the sub-committee for the time being to adjust what shall be paid by each person on whose account the registers are or shall be searched for defraying the charges of the said search according to the general rules relating to the lending of money and that at the time of giving in the proposals for borrowing and that the proposal do bear the persons willingness to pay the said necessary charges.

Source: BS 1/5/1,3, Minutes.

APPENDIX 5

HUGH CHAMBERLAIN'S PROPOSALS FOR A SCOTS LAND BANK, 1693

In June 1693, the Scottish Parliament considered a proposal from Dr Hugh Chamberlain, a London company promoter, for a Scots Land Bank. Chamberlain had unsuccessfully canvassed ideas for land banks in London and was to persist with his schemes, on both sides of the Border, for another decade. The structure of his plan remained the same, although the scope and his fees were more modest in later versions. In spite of the considerable efforts put into lobbying for his schemes and for those of a contemporary, John Briscoe in London, no land-bank company was successfully launched, although two in London came close. They were taken seriously by landowners, but City of London financiers largely ignored them.

On 14 June 1693, the Scottish Parliament referred Hugh Chamberlain's scheme to a special committee comprising the Earls of Linlithgow and Lothian, Viscount Stair, Lord Polwarth, Sir John Lockhart of Castlehill, Sir John Maxwell of Pollok, Sir John Swinton of that Ilk, Duncan Forbes of Culloden, Sir John Hall, Sir Archibald Muir, Sir William Hamilton and James Smollett, plus the officers of state. There may have been other members whose names went unrecorded.

They considered the scheme, reprinted here. It is in two parts: a preamble of five general considerations; and an outline of how the scheme would work. Parliament published a series of comments for and against the plan.

> *First Consideration* Whereas it is most evident that a wise and large estab-lishment and a continued course of considerable trade is a sure way whereby any nation capable of it may attain to honour, wealth and power: because that thereby will arise; first, a great increase of money, which answereth all things; secondly, an increase of people, which is the strength of any kingdom or state and who do always gather to those places where money is in abundance, and,

thirdly, an increase of shipping, which is the strongest rampart of an island and by which merchandise is conveyed to the most profitable mercat. It is therefore the undoubted interest of the people of Scotland, especially those who have the greatest estates, whether of land or money, to imploy themselves to the improvement of trade as universally as is possible. And it is humbly conceived that this proposition needs no other proof or illustration than what plainly arises from the observation of those many and great adventurers derived from trade to the kingdom of England, the states of the United Provinces [of the Netherlands], and all other kingdoms and states that have applied themselves to commerce.

Second Consideration The kingdom of Scotland is as capable of making advantages by trade as any other kingdom or state, being surrounded with good seaports upon all its coasts and having a very great and profitable subject of trade proper to it; the land affording grain, cattle, wool, flax, coal, salt, copper, iron, lead and other native products, besides the fishing of the rivers, loughs, and seas. This kingdom hath likewise great numbers of people, either not employed, or not so fully and profitably as might be. And hath also such a provision of shipping as may serve to begin a trade and may soon be increased if a greater trade be set up. The truth of this consideration will appear by comparing the particulars therein contained to those of the United Provinces where the proper subject of trade comes very far short of that of this kingdom. Which provinces from very small beginnings and under the discouragement of a war with Spain at that time the most potent King of Europe, have yet raised themselves, within a short period of years to that immense wealth, grandeur and power that now they possess. And have acquired it chiefly by their trafficking in those subjects of trade which properly belong to this and other nations.

Third Consideration The people of this Kingdom who have had liberal education are generally in all countries allowed to be of great ingenuity and diligence and so well inclined to virtue and frugality and so averse to luxury that where they are imployed abroad they are outdone by none and the commons being so docile and tractable and likewise robust and vigourous a body and insufficiently inclined to bestow their labour where there is prospect of moderate gain and being hitherto accustomed to small wages. It may justly be concluded that no people in the world are naturally more fitted or better qualified for setting up, manageing and prosecuting a great and considerable trade.

Fourth Consideration It is most certainly true in fact nor can it be unknown to the intelligent of this nation that the greatest tradings in the world are carried on not so much by the species of money which is in stock and cash as by a great credit attained to by means partly of their visible subject of trade partly of their pains in and application to traffick but most of all upon account of the reputation and opinion of the great profits made in the course of a prosperous trade even where the native and proper subject of trade keeps no proportion with the trade carried on, as it is in the United Provinces where credit is the chief instrument of their commerce and that credit raised upon a fund more of opinion or reputation than real. If therefore in this Kingdom the want of a sufficient stock of money for the carrying on a great trade can be made up by a credit grounded upon a more real and substantial fund than the credit of any other nation either at present is or probably can be founded upon then certainly it may most reasonably follow, that this kingdom is rather more capable of carrying on great and national trade than most other kingdoms or states in Europe.

Fifth Consideration The titles and tenures of estates especially land estates in this kingdom being more known sure and stated and with greater ease and certainly examinable by reason of the record here in use [in the Register of Sasines], than in any other country and an evident clear and firm security upon land being the best and most substantial fund of credit. This kingdom is capable in this respect to raise a credit sufficient for improving to the uttermost the great subject of trade that now it unprofitably possesses and this credit as far to exceed that of other nations as a real, solid and permanant fund exceeds those of opinion and reputation for such all those of other nations will be found to be when duly weighed with that hereby proponed for this kingdom.

Upon these considerations which may so justly be presumed to induce the right honourable estates of Parliament to receive and examine a proposal that tenders to this kingdom the certain and effectual means of great wealth and honour.

The said Doctor Hugh Chamberlain humbly offers to the wisdom of this August assembly the following proposal

THE PROPOSAL

That a statute or law of this kingdom may be enacted for nominating certain trustees or commissioners to be appointed now and from time to time by Parliament and accountable thereunto which trustees are to have power to recieve [sic] and examine the titles and estates of all such as are willing to engage their lands for the framing such a secure current credit. Upon finding any such estate clear in title the said trustees to take a conveyance thereof for 150 years upon condition to be void when 100 years payment shall have been made to them of the rent agreed and such rent to be paid, not in money or gold, but only in the bills of credit issued to the granter by the said trustees and the heretor or granter to enjoy the free and undisturbed possession of such estate for the whole term, he duly paying such annualrent. Upon the making over any such estate the trustees thereupon direct their warrant to the master of a proper office therefore to be erected to use 100 years value of such estate in bills of credit of several values the better to accommodate the uses of trade. Which bills of trade are to be thus divided, viz. 40 years value to the proprietor, 30 years value for his use but to be employed in such public trade or trades as the several proprietors shall in a body agree upon, 10 years purchase to the Government in ease of the people in point of taxes and may be appropriated to such uses where the honour of the Crown and interest of the nation may equally meet, and the residue to the use of the said Doctor Chamberlain as master of such office who and his heirs to be perpetually so in reward of this service done the nation. And the master of the office is out of such his part to pay all the charge of the office which will be very great and to answer all contingencies of it and also generous and becoming appointments to those honourable gentlemen to be made trustees by the Parliament to see justice done to the people and the honour, and security of the Bank preserved inviolable. The heritors or proprietors that raise this fund are to be a corporation with perpetual succession and all necessary powers for manageing and carrying on such national trade or trades as they shall agree upon. From 120 to 150 pound sterling per annum is to be made over for the payment of every 100 pound per annum to be engaged for this fund and so in proportion and this to the end that all credit thus to be issued may be supported by a greater value than itself.

That these bills be made current in all payments and as they are paid yearly for rent to the trustees they are by them to be destroyed so that at the end of 100 years they will be all recalled. Bills of credit thus founded upon land and strengthened by the sanction of law and made in a form incapable of forgery will be found an excellent instrument or medium of trade equal in all respects to gold and silver money and superior to them in divers regards. They are more sure than any bills, bonds, or mortgages, or any manner of credit now known in the world. They have a real solid, extrinsic and permanent value, inseparably adhering to them by law. Nor can their value be impaired or their use taken away by any future Parliaments, or by any revolution of state where all mens properties will not also be swallowed up. By this means a considerable part of the rents of the nation may be applied to trade which otherwise could not be done. Thus may all the poor be profitably imployed, all due improvements made in husbandry and all needful arts and manufacturies; the shipping and strength of the nation will be increased by sea and land. Public taxes will become easy to the subjects and all who contribute to this fund will be made richer by it at their very entry into it, besides what their share in the future trade will produce.

No person is forced to be concerned in it, yet all are permitted that shall desire it which renders it truly a free and common good. Although at the end of 100 years all this credit will be called in yet the course of trade managed with it cannot in the meantime but produce gold, silver and other valuable commodities and that to a far greater value than the bills themselves and the trade founded by them will be perpetual. These bills not passing out of the kingdom are an advantage. For all wise laws restrain money from going out and foreign trade ought not to be managed with money but with the native product and manufactures of the kingdom. The banks of Holland and Venice are pregnant instances of the power of credit under wise regulation and yet the credit of both those banks are far inferior to the credit hereby proposed. They take the ready money and imploy it for the Government and give their bills to negotiate in payment, so that in any exigence of state if all their creditors should at once call for their several debts, it may reasonably be doubted if either of these banks should be able to answer their credit so that opinion or reputation is their great support. But the bank hereby proposed touches no mans ready money, makes all men concerned in it presently much richer than before, lays sure foundations of lasting national trades and becomes every year a stronger security than before. For as the term of years lessens, the security becomes more strong. Upon the whole it is humbly conceived to have all the force of demonstration that this kingdom receiving and enacting this proposal cannot fail of a success superior to either of those powerful and opulent states because of the advantages before enumerated that this kingdom possesses over them.

How would Hugh Chamberlain's Scheme have Worked?

1. Hugh Chamberlain would establish a land-bank office, supervised by trustees and commissioners chosen by the Scottish Parliament.
2. A landowner wishing to join the scheme would:
   (a) have the encumbrances on his estate checked in the Register of Sasines;
   (b) agree to convey his estate to the land bank for 150 years;
   (c) agree a rent, fixed for 150 years, to be paid to the land-bank office.
   The clear title to the estate would revert to the landowner after 100 years of these rents. Rentals paid could be greater or lesser than the agreed rental. The difference between 150 years' conveyance and 100 years' rents allowed the landowner to miss payments for up to 50 years for whatever reason, at his discretion.
3. In return for the conveyance, the land-bank office would create a fund of 100 times the agreed annual rent of the said estate to be paid to the office. This would be paid out in paper bills of various denominations. These would be divided as follows: 40 per cent would go to the landowner; 30 per cent to a joint stock managed by the landowners; 10 per cent to the government for taxation; 20 per cent to Hugh Chamberlain.
4. These land-bank bills would be declared legal tender, and the annual rent due from the conveyed estates would be paid over in these bills, which would then be destroyed; thus the total debt attached to a particular estate would decrease.

Criticisms Laid before the Committee

1. The landowner who agreed to pay £100 in rent (for 100 years in 150 years) would receive legal tender worth £4,000. This would be available to pay debts, personal or heritable; thus the creditor would 'be forced to receive his sum in the said tallies'. Yet what use could the creditor 'who lived upon the interest of money' make of this sum, 'seeing in all probability there would be no borrowers on annual rent'? Moreover, the use of the £3,000 for trade, in a corporation run by

landowners, would make it difficult to employ the creditors' tallies 'with any reasonable prospect of advantage'.

2. The natural and artificial product of Scotland was worth £1 million sterling; 'and . . . there are two million of tallies coined, and secured on a real fund, as is proposed'. If one million were spent, what would happen to the other million? 'The person who received them from his debitor must let them lie idle and starve . . . all that is coined above the yearly product of natural and artificial goods must be useless until the product increases.'

3. 'there will be no use nor place for money upon annualrent. In which case, what shall become of the widows and orphans and other persons in the kingdom who are not capable of trade seeing there is neither access to buy land nor lend out the money upon interest?'

4. Forgery would be a great temptation, as some bills would be for £100 or £50 sterling; how would the nation be secured against counterfeit bills?

5. Much of the 'coin' would lie idle unless 'an additional stock in gold and silver' were procured, which would require 'trafficking merchants'; how would these be enticed to Scotland?

6. Those with gold and silver, finding no use for it for loans, would export it to earn annual rent abroad. Thus Scotland would have only the land-bank coin.

7. The land-bank Act might be rescinded at a later date. What would then happen to the statutory coin?

8. 'The proposal being designed for the good of the nation and carrying a manifest and extraordinary advantage to the landed men . . . but seeming rather prejudicial than profitable to the merchants and moneyed men both in respect that the trade of the nation which is now only lodged in their hands comes to be lodged in the lands of the landed men and that the merchants and moneyed men are to be deprived of the security which they formerly had for their money upon the estates of their debitors and of the annualrents whereby many of them lived very plentifully. What method is proper to bring the loss and gain of the landed and moneyed men to a more equal balance? And how the moneyed men shall be secured in the payment of their annualrents at 6 per cent until they be taught the way of trading with their money?'

9. The English Parliament had already rejected the proposal; why should the Scottish Parliament vote for it?

10. 'If money shall be multiplied at the rate of the proposal, all commodities will rise in their prices and workmen will exact greater wages. And it is not to be supposed that people getting their payment in

statutory coin will take the same price as if they were getting payment in gold or silver. And the advantage that masters of manufactories have in this nation, above those in England, is that the wages of the workmen of Scotland is much less than of those in England.'

11. How could the nation ensure that no more coin were made than the precise quantity agreed upon?

All the above points raised serious worries. In particular, the criticisms suggest that this inferior money would drive gold and silver from the realm and that inflation would ensue, with unpredictable consequences. There would be adverse effects, to say the least, for the monied interests and for merchants involved in manufactures (more of these might emigrate), and the benefits of the debasement of Scots coin would be lost. While the scheme might strengthen the landed interest, it might also lead to dominance by one faction or another.

Source: NLS, Advocates MSS, 31.1.7, ff. 30–8, Papers relating to a bank of credit upon land-security proposed to the Parliament of Scotland (printed by the Select Committee of the Scottish Parliament, 1693).

APPENDIX 6

THE BANKING OPERATIONS OF THE COMPANY OF SCOTLAND TRADING TO AFRICA AND THE INDIES, 1696–7

The Act passed in the 1693 session of the Scottish Parliament for a joint-stock trading company and the subsequent Act for the Company of Scotland (26 June 1695) intended the subscription to be used mainly for trading purposes. There was, however, sufficient ambiguity in the later Act for a number of projectors in London to advocate in the summer of 1695 a 'fund of credit' and cross-border banking operations once the Company was established. At what time this intention was taken up as policy is not clear, although William Paterson openly criticised Bank of Scotland in August 1695 when he complained to Sir Robert Chiesly, Lord Provost of Edinburgh, about the Bank Act 'so surreptitiously gained, [which] may be a great prejudice, but is never like to be of any matter of good neither to us nor those that have it'.[1] The intention to use the London subscription for a fund of credit was formally notified at the opening of the London subscription for the Company on 6 November, and this intention was raised in the English Parliament after the books had closed on 22 November 1695.[2] The nominal share issue of the Company of Scotland in London reached £200,000 sterling, from 200 subscribers.[3] By that time, William Paterson was powerful enough to have a clause inserted into the preamble of the London books that he would receive 2 per cent of the capital and 3

---

1 William Paterson, London, to Sir Robert Chiesly, Edinburgh, 15 August 1695, in J. H. Burton (ed.), *The Darien Papers: being a Selection of Original Letters and official Documents relating to the establishment of a colony at Darien by the Company of Scotland trading to Africa and the Indies 1695–1700*, Bannatyne Club, vol. 90 (Edinburgh: 1849), p. 5.
2 *House of Commons Journal*, vol. 9, p. 404, 27 November 1695.
3 For details of the background, see G. P. Insh, *The Company of Scotland Trading to Africa and the Indies* (London: 1932); J. S. Barbour, *A History of William Paterson and the Darien Company* (Edinburgh: 1907).

per cent of profits for twenty-one years, although it was unclear whether this meant from the London subscription, as G. P. Insh has implied, or all of it. There was also some confusion as to whether this was all to go to Paterson; Kincaid and Pitcairn, a firm of London Scottish merchants, thought that this 2 per cent was to be divided among the twelve London directors. Eventually, Paterson agreed to waive the fee.

With the withdrawal of most of the London subscribers in the wake of the decision by the English Parliament to arraign the Company of Scotland directors on charges of treason, the Company was forced back on the Scottish subscriptions, and the book for the Scottish part of the Company of Scotland opened on 28 February 1696. In spite of the difficult agricultural situation, over £300,000 was pledged by 3 April, and a general meeting increased this to £400,000.[4] By the end of May, the tally was £375,000. Thereafter, the pledges came in slowly, and in order to close the subscription at £400,000 on 1 August several subscribers increased their holdings, although this was tied to arrangements to borrow the money back. The first call was for 25 per cent; as the Privy Council devalued the worn parts of the Scots coinage by 12 per cent in May 1696, subscribers were allowed a discount of 12 per cent for payments made before 1 June.[5] The growth of gold and silver held by the Company to the end of May 1697 is shown in the table.

Company of Scotland: the first 25 per cent of subscription

Date 1696	Cash in chest £ sterling	Expenditure	Surplus
1 June	36,062	15,436	20,627
11 July	78,187	25,874	52,313
12 August	88,832	40,918	47,914
22 October	92,495	62,488	30,007
1 December	93,784	67,834	25,950
3 December	93,917	73,319	20,598
1697			
26 February	95,365	82,936	12,429
31 May	98,825	89,854	8,970

Source: NLS, Advocates MSS, 83.5.2, Cash book, 1696–1700.

Sums this large were exceptional for Scotland, and there were demands that it be made available for circulation in the country. Hence a number

4 Royal Bank of Scotland, RBS EQ/9/1, The several Journals of the Court of Directors of the Company of Scotland trading to Africa and the Indies, 1696–8, p. 7, 3 April 1696.
5 Ibid., p. 63, 1 June 1696; Barbour, *William Paterson and the Darien Company*, pp. 20–9.

of agreements were concluded to lend back cash to subscribers as long-term loans. The Edinburgh Merchant Company, for example, subscribed £1,200 but only paid the first 25 per cent on that condition.[6] The directors of the Company of Scotland considered several trading schemes in the spring and summer of 1696, including a new Greenland whale trade, a restart for the old Royal Fishery company, investment in salt refining and a new dry dock for Leith.[7] The immediate issue, as far as Paterson was concerned, was how to utilise this cash base for a bank. In fact, as early as the opening of the subscription, for some in Edinburgh the common name for the Company was simply 'our Africa bank'.[8]

There was some overlap between the boards of directors of Bank of Scotland and the Company of Scotland. Several Bank directors who were involved with the tax-collection system also sat on the board of the Company; of these, Robert Blackwood, George Clerk the elder and Sir Robert Dickson of Sornbeg were to offer their support to Paterson's schemes, as to a lesser extent did Sir John Swinton. The influence of the Bank on the Company of Scotland declined when it became clear that John Holland opposed any agreement between the two. In late March, the Company of Scotland subscribers elected a guiding committee of twenty on which sat no fewer than thirteen Bank adventurers. On 12 May, a new election, this time for twenty-five directors, resulted in only ten who held Bank shares.[9] Sir Robert Dickson then ceased to attend the Bank court, and Robert Blackwood walked out later.

The May election gave William Paterson his chance; on 18 May, the directors ordered him to prepare 'a scheme of his thoughts' for utilising their funds, a signal that they intended to press on with a fully-fledged bank to lend money, discount bills of exchange and issue banknotes.[10] Paterson then set up an office subdivided into a cashier's department and an accountant's office, both supervised by a Treasury subcommittee of the Court of Directors of the Company which included George Baillie of

---

6 Edinburgh City Archive, Edinburgh Merchant Company MSS, vol. 2, Minutes 1694–1704. On 23 March 1696, the EMC agreed to subscribe £1,200 sterling, with the optimistic proviso that half the profits were to go to the poor of the Company. By 10 August 1696, with £180 paid, they were in difficulties with the remaining £120 (to make up the 25 per cent), and they asked the Company of Scotland to lend them the money as part of their banking operation. This was initially refused, although a settlement was reached on a payment of £120 with £100 returned as a loan. When the trading operation ran short of cash in November 1697, the banking side insisted on repayment, and the EMC was forced to borrow.
7 NLS, Advocates MSS, 83.7.1, Minutes of the Committee for Improvements, pp. 1–5; SRO GD 103/2/4, vol. 4/41, Court of Directors, 12 September 1696.
8 Andrew Craick WS, to Earl of Findlater, 28/29 February 1696, in J. Grant (ed.), Seafield Correspondence from 1685 to 1708 (Edinburgh: 1912), pp. 186–7.
9 Royal Bank of Scotland, RBS EQ/9/1, The several Journals, pp. 5 and 32–3, 24 March and 12 May 1696.
10 Ibid., p. 46, 18 May 1696.

Jerviswood, the Receiver General of Taxes for Scotland. Both he and the new chief cashier were Bank of Scotland proprietors but not on the board of directors.

On 26 June 1696, the first Company of Scotland notes were sent out, being £5,000 to Glasgow, £2,000 to Aberdeen, £1,500 to Dundee and £1,000 at the end of July to Dumfries for the cattle trade; and some also went to Montrose.[11] The surviving papers suggest that the note issue reached around £12,000 paid to various subscribers at 4 per cent interest.[12] In Glasgow and Aberdeen, the Company of Scotland pushed most of the Bank of Scotland notes out of circulation and back on the cashiers for coin. By the middle of July, Bank of Scotland directors had 'reason to think that there is a design to surprize us by calling for [Company of Scotland] money all at once'.[13]

The summer was the high point of William Paterson's banking scheme. As the above table indicates, the cash surplus began to diminish by August. The last issue of banknotes was made on 21 September, and a stop to new paper was announced on 2 October followed by sackings of several of the bank staff.[14] The Company of Scotland subcommittees dealing with 'improvements' and 'foreign trade' realised that only a small part of the supplies which they needed could be purchased in Scotland; the Scottish economy was unable to manufacture the cannon and gunpowder which the Company needed, nor much of the ironwork, ropes, sails or the myriad other supplies that were crammed into seventeenth-century ships; in the end, most were imported from the continent. Even the ships themselves had to be built in the Netherlands and at Hamburg, such was the weakness of the Scottish shipbuilding industry. As their mountain of cash deteriorated, the directors gladly accepted William Paterson's suggestion that the cash for the ships should go to London, where bills drawn from the Netherlands and Hamburg could be retired. The advantage, he claimed, in the summer of 1696, was that with the war coming to an end

11 There are differences between the sources about the timing and number of notes issued. According to the Company Journal (NLS, Advocates MSS, 83.3.3, A Journal for the General Trading Ledger, 1696–1701), banknotes were issued as follows: £2,000 to Glasgow on 27 June, £3,000 more to Glasgow on 11 July and £2,000 to Aberdeen; £1,000 to Dumfries on 31 July; £1,000 to Dundee on 14 August; £1,000 in Edinburgh on 19 September and £500 more to Dundee on 21 September; but see also SRO GD 103/2/4, vol. 4/41, Court of Directors, 15 June 1696; Royal Bank of Scotland, RBS EQ/9/1, The several Journals, p. 88, 26 June 1696, order for circulation of notes, and p. 101, 29 July 1696, extension of notes to Dundee and Montrose. See also Burton (ed.), The Darien Papers, preface, p. xxx, and p. 9, abstract of the proceedings of Darien.
12 NLS, Advocates MSS, 83.3.9, Cash ledger for the banking operation; ibid., 83.4.7 (Promissory Notes: Counterfoils and some unissued notes: ?small denominations), for banknote books and stubs; Barbour, William Paterson and the Darien Company, p. 24ff.
13 BS 1/149/1, Letter Book, 18 July 1696.
14 Royal Bank of Scotland, RBS EQ/9/1, The several Journals, p. 146ff., 2 October 1696 and entries for November.

the exchanges would move in London's favour. Paterson was entrusted with £25,000 sterling, from which he paid £21,119 13s 4d to two London merchant houses. James Smyth from Flanders took around £17,000, while the rest went to James Campbell of Campbell and Stewart. Both London houses then bought Bank of England notes as a speculation. In the event (see above, Table 2.1), Bank of England notes continued to fall in value, and when the Dutch bills for the ships fell due they were sold at a loss. Further, Smyth embezzled the £17,000, of which £8,500 was never recovered.[15]

As with most major frauds of this scale, many opposed to the Company either predicted it or had enough sense to keep clear. One of George Watson's correspondents, John Pitcairn of Kincaid and Pitcairn, actually predicted the drift of the fraud as early as June: 'as for your East India Company we call it the slitting fund and everybody believe it will come to nothing, there pretending to drive an exchange trade and there printed shamin paper, of establishing correspondents in sevill parts are tricks to put some of themselves in possession of the Company's cash'.[16] The fraud was later covered up; an investigation avoided censure of anyone in Edinburgh and exonerated Paterson from the charge of collaboration in the theft, though he was refused further paid employment and he went on the first expedition to the Darien coast on his own resources.[17] So ended the Company of Scotland's belief in the expertise of William Paterson.

15 Ibid., p. 74, 22 December 1696: payment to Paterson is given as £26,444, of which £5,226 went to Campbell, and £16,997 to Smyth.
16 SRO GD 277, Box 14, Bundle 8, John Pitcairn to George Watson, 27 June 1696.
17 S. Bannister (ed.), The Writings of William Paterson, Founder of the Bank of England, 2nd edn, 3 vols (London: 1859; repr. New York: 1968), vol. i, pp. xlvii–lv.

APPENDIX 7

THE MANAGEMENT OF BANK OF SCOTLAND AGENCIES: THE CASE OF HADDINGTON, 1801

Bank of Scotland opened an agency in the burgh of Haddington, near Edinburgh, in 1783. It was managed in a similar way to the other provincial agencies – there were twenty-seven by this date – with a resident agent appointed for his local standing and range of contacts, supported by an accountant appointed by head office, and less frequently by a clerical officer. In common with their general policy for agencies, the directors appraised requests for cash accounts and imposed limits on the value of bills of exchange. With the start of the war with France in February 1793, the Bank and the agents received a sharp increase in demands for accommodation by war contractors, expressed in requests for overdrafts on cash account limits, an increase in bill discounts and bill re-discounting. In the autumn of 1793, the extent of re-discounting was regarded by the directors as sufficiently worrying at four agencies – Inverness, Kelso, Stirling and Haddington – for them to replace the agent. On 23 December, a local Haddington writer, Hay Smith ws, took up the agency in the burgh, with instructions to increase the circulation of banknotes by active cash accounts and to reduce the number of past-due bills. Bank of Scotland directors allowed him, in common with other agents, to advance sums to himself and firms with which he was associated on the understanding that these advances were secured to the Bank; the heritable security involved, where applicable, and the cautioners were to be checked in the usual manner. The periodic visits by officials and directors from head office were part of the normal method of inspection. In the conditions of war, agents of all the Scottish banks were pressed for credit as far afield as London and the English provincial centres, which the increase in capital of the Bank enabled the directors and agents to

866

meet. From 1797, Hay Smith entered into partnerships with merchants and manufacturers in a variety of pursuits, including grain distilling, soap boiling and wine imports, and by 1801 his personal connections covered enterprises in Liverpool, Newcastle and London, as well as Leith, Edinburgh, Glasgow and Haddington. For these partnerships, Smith discounted and re-discounted bills using lines of credit at Coutts & Co. under the agreements with Bank of Scotland, and he opened up more lines of credit with other London houses. There was a particular rise in his request for discounts after the crisis of 1797, and thereafter the volume of bills grew steadily. Further, at some point before 1801 (it is unclear when), Smith began to advance exceptional sums, which were to reach over £60,000, for James Sommervail, a Liverpool merchant house. There were many thousands of pounds more for the other companies with which he was involved (see Table 1) in addition to the ordinary business of the agency.

From 1797, Smith provided the Bank with falsified weekly states of the agency and misled officials and directors on their periodic visits. An elaborate credit structure was created which disguised the ultimate recipients of advances. While the Bank thought that the agency had a wide range of debtors who were not directly connected with each other, in fact there were fewer borrowers and the sums involved were larger than was usually allowed except in cases where express permission was granted by the directors.

In May 1801, James Sommervail failed when commodity prices fell and he was unable to provide payment for bills. It was soon apparent to London bankers that, as part of the credit for Sommervail had been provided by Hay Smith ws, the Bank would suffer some loss. The directors at the Mound despatched Robert Forrester, the principal accountant, with instructions to investigate. At this point, the directors believed Smith to have been guilty of no more than poor judgement: 'if you can show clearly to the Directors any plan by which you can be relieved of your present difficulties without prejudice to the Bank there is not the smallest doubt of the willingness of the Directors to harken to it and assist you in it'.[1] But Robert Forrester soon uncovered the deception involved. James Mansfield, the private banker and director of Bank of Scotland, was sent to Liverpool to ascertain the true state of affairs of James Sommervail, and urgent discussions were held with Coutts & Co. and other bankers in London. The abstract of the advances by May 1801 to companies in which Smith was involved is given in Table 2; there was £91,621 owing from these firms to Bank of Scotland and another £4,086

---

1 BS 1/146/1, Private Letter Book, 28 May 1801.

Table 1 *Partnerships and business agreements of Hay Smith* WS

Name of firm	Business	Town	Agreement to advance	Smith to receive	Advance as at 1801 state	Known partners	Date of agreement	Comments
Sommervail, James (i)	merchant	Liverpool	(i) £2,000 interest-free	third of profits	£68,203	Sommervail, J.	Nov. 1797	Advances above £2,000 subject to interest
Sommervail, James (ii)	merchant (flax, rum, seed, brandy)	Leith	(ii) £4,000 interest-free	half of profits	£8,787	Sommervail, J.	May 1798	Advances above £4,000 subject to interest
Allan, William						Allan, William		Allan to purchase goods in the Netherlands and sell in Ireland, mainly
Alston Brydson & Co.	merchants (making linen and worsted types)	Glasgow	£3,000 to capital		£3,000	Alston, William and Brydson, William	1 May 1798	Co-partnery to last seven years, but dissolved May 1800
Brydson, William	starch	Glasgow	£550 capital stock and eight casks of starch	half of profits	£1,200	Brydson, William		Co-partnery to last ten years
Patterson & Co.	soapmakers	Prestonpans			£1,200	Patterson, Thomas		
Sheriff & Bowmaker		London			£6,573			Dissolved – in dispute
Taylor, Andrew	distiller	Linton	£1,700 interest-free	half of profits	£204	Taylor, A.	10 Oct. 1798	Advances above £1,700 subject to interest; partnership to last ten years
Howden, Sanderson & Co.	soap boiling	Dunbar	£300 to capital	fifth of profits	£300		Martinmas 1797	
Dunlop, George & Co.	corn	Edinburgh			£426	Dunlop, G. and Taylor, A.		
Simpson, Walter & Others	herring	Dunbar			£1,057	Craw, John		
Dods, Alexander	sugar	Newmains			£671			
Somervail, Alex & Co.	tallow and kelp	Leith			unknown			
Hay, Charles		Dunbar			unknown			
Laurie, Alex & Craw, John	grain	London			unknown			
Young, William		Ormiston			unknown			
Pringle, James	starch works	Haddington			unknown			
Dods, Hugh	starch works	Haddington			unknown			
Telfer, Robert & Co.	merchants	London			£1,305	Dods, Hugh?		Sequestration awarded
Ross, Alexander & Co.	underwriting concern				£150			
Thomson, Rickyard & Co.	underwriting concern	Hull			£823			

Aitkinson, L. & M.	underwriting concern	Newcastle	£839
Hall, John	underwriting concern	Newcastle	£300
Baird, James	underwriting concern	Edinburgh	£1,274
Craw, John	underwriting concern		£700
	Total known advances to firms in which Smith had an interest:		£97,012

Source: BS 20/18/5, Papers re the debts of Hay Smith, Banker, James Sommervail.

Table 2 *State of the affairs of Hay Smith* WS, *1801*

Funds			£	Value (£)
1 Heritable property			23,850	
minus part of price thereof unpaid			−16,150	
				7,700

2 Sums advanced to stock of the following partnerships or joint concerns

Name of firm	Business	Town	Advance
Sommervail, James	Merchant	Liverpool	68,203
Allan, William	Merchant	Leith	8,787
Alston Brydson & Co.		Glasgow	3,000
Brydson, William		Glasgow	1,200
Patterson & Co.		Prestonpans	1,200
Sheriff & Bowmaker		London	6,573
Taylor, Andrew		Linton	204
Howden, Sanderson & Co.		Dunbar	300
Dunlop, George & Co.	Corn		426
Simson, Walter & Others	Herrings		1,057
Dods, Alexander	Sugar	Newmains	671
			91,621

3 Advances on account of underwriting concerns

Name of firm	Business	Town	Advance
Ross, Alexander & Co.		London	150
Thomson, Rickyard & Co.		Hull	823
Aitkinson, L. & M.		Newcastle	839
Hall, John		Newcastle	300
Baird, James		Edinburgh	1,274
Craw, John			700
			4,086

	£
4 Debts due to Smith	17,333
5 Funds of Robert Telfer & Co.	1,305
6 Interest on Smith's advances – supposed	6,000
7 Personal property	3,397
Total	131,442

Debts	£	
1 Due to Bank of Scotland for monies unaccounted for per state	125,429	
2 Due to sundries	8,017	
Total		133,446
Deficiency to be accounted for		£2,004

Source: BS 20/18/5, Papers re the debts of Hay Smith, Banker, James Sommervail.

for merchant houses which discounted bills. The total was revealed as £133,446.

The Treasurer, James Fraser, felt a deep sense of personal betrayal – they were friends – and made great efforts to persuade Smith to cooperate. A trust deed was made out disponing Smith's estate to a trustee chosen by the directors. The Bank also registered as a creditor on the other bankrupt

Table 3 *State of the debt due by the estate of James Sommervail to Bank of Scotland, 1802*

	Principal (£)	Interest (£)
I Sums advanced to James Sommervail		
1 Bills drawn by Hay Smith upon Treasurer remitted to James Sommervail	2,815	522
2 Bills drawn by Hay Smith upon Coutts & Co., remitted to James Sommervail	11,478	794
3 Bills drawn by Hay Smith upon Treasurer, with the proceeds of which bills on London were purchased and remitted to James Sommervail	14,750	979
4 Cash remitted by Hay Smith to James Sommervail	5,505	955
5 Bills drawn by Hay Smith on Coutts & Co. remitted to Messrs Scott and Landen, by whom the contents were afterwards remitted to James Sommervail	216	18
6 Cash paid for bills on London remitted to James Sommervail	4,060	142
	38,824	3,410
II Sums advanced to Alexander Ross on account of James Sommervail		
1 Bills drawn by Hay Smith upon Coutts & Co., remitted to Ross	6,863	511
2 Bills drawn by Hay Smith upon Treasurer, with the proceeds of which bills on London were purchased and remitted to Mr Ross	4,963	394
3 Cash paid for bills on London remitted to Mr Ross	2,500	83
	14,326	988
III Sums remitted to Coutts & Co. for the purpose of retiring bills granted by Hay Smith for the accommodation of James Sommervail		
Bills drawn by Hay Smith upon Treasurer with proceeds of which bills on London were purchased and remitted to Coutts & Co.	1,134	92
IV Sums remitted to Messrs Robert Freebairn & Co. for the purpose of retiring bills drawn by Hugh Dods etc upon them for the accommodation of James Sommervail		
1 Bills drawn by Hay Smith upon Coutts & Co., remitted to Robert Freebairn & Co.	9,017	117
2 Sums received by Robert Freebairn & Co. from Messrs Wedderburn & Co.	1,439	23
	10,456	140
V Sums paid to sundries on account of James Sommervail	7,218	124
Total debt due	71,958	4,754
Total debt due (principal and interest)		76,712

Source: BS 20/18/5, Papers re the debts of Hay Smith, Banker, James Sommervail.

estates, including that of James Sommervail. As late as 1835, the Bank received a dividend of ½d in the pound from this last (see Table 3 for the extent of the debts on the estate).

The case highlighted the inadequacies of the system of cautioners. Hay Smith ws had four 'bound severally and separately' for £10,000:

David Smith, grazier in Haddington, Adam Watson, merchant in Dunbar, George Rennie of Fantasie, and David Smith, merchant, of Haddington. The four were reminded of their obligations on 1 June 1801, and the £10,000 was called for the following week. Unfortunately, David Smith the merchant collapsed and died a few weeks later. Adam Watson was found to have other debts to the Bank. George Rennie had a guarantor for losses to the Bank up to £2,000, but this turned out to be Andrew Taylor of Linton, a partner of Hay Smith ws in a distillery venture. Difficult negotiations ensued.

So far as the general business of the agency was concerned, Robert Forrester's advice to the directors was to demand payment of all sums on the cash accounts, in part to ascertain the extent of Hay Smith's connections. Letters were written demanding payment of the balances due by Lammas. A few cash accounts were allowed to continue after appeals; the obligants on the 'Kilpallet Burn Road' account and the 'Middle Line Road from Wallyford to White Kirk' account, for example, the former including George, Marquis of Tweeddale and Henry Fletcher of Saltoun, and the latter the Earl of Wemyss. The Marquis of Tweeddale was given leave to delay payment on three accounts in which he was obligant until Martinmas. Each cash account was also examined for its usefulness as well as security to the Bank. In at least two cases, letters were written to the holder explaining that the credit granted on a cash account was not a permanent loan bearing interest, but was intended to be used frequently in order to circulate the Bank's notes. In each case, another year's trial was granted to the holder.[2] Messrs Alexander Fraser & Sons, writers to the signet, Haddington, were appointed as the new agents on 28 July, and were warned that 'the less that is mentioned of this matter in your place the better'.

The size of the fraud and the fact that it had remained undetected forced the directors to consider how such an event could be prevented. On 27 June, almost a month after the Haddington discovery, the directors had written to all the Bank's agents (except Dempster & Son at St Andrews, who were soon to be removed from the agency) to reaffirm an earlier order regarding attestation of the weekly states by branch accountants. This order was extended: at branches where the accountant was absent, the agent was instructed to show the cash to the clerk. The accountants and clerks were to subscribe an attestation on the state, that: 'the Agent's cash has been examined by them and found right as specified in the balance of the State, and that the entries of the Bills and other articles in the State are fair, and in every respect exactly just'.[3]

2 Ibid., pp. 350, 351.
3 Ibid., pp. 190–1.

If this order was not complied with, agents were informed that someone from head office would visit the branch, at the agent's expense, without prior notice, and examine the cash, bills and other aspects of the agency business. Agents were also warned that 'frequent visits will in future be made'. On 13 July 1801, a committee of directors was appointed 'to consider of and bring in such propositions for the consideration of the Directors as appear to be necessary for rectifying some defects at the branches, and for repairing the consequences thereof'.[4]

Just over two weeks later, on 31 July, further instructions were issued to all agents. These were more comprehensive, covering the rules to be followed in bill discounting, the discount limit to be imposed on each customer (not to exceed £5,000 without the permission of the directors), rules on past-due bills, regular and accurate reporting on cash accounts as well as a confirmation of the previous order on weekly states being attested. The principal aim of these instructions was to lessen the risk to the Bank of the most hazardous part of agency business and the one most likely to lead to loss by bad judgement or lax procedure on the part of the agent. There was no office of Bank inspector at this period, but on 15 August 1801 William Brown of the accountant's office at Edinburgh was instructed to proceed to the Bank's branches at Greenock, Kilmarnock and Ayr, and at each of them 'to carefully and accurately examine and compare the Agent's accounts and books with the cash, Bills and other vouchers thereof' before reporting back to the directors.[5] By 23 October 1801, James Marshall of the accountant's office (who had taken over briefly from Robert Forrester at Haddington as interim agent prior to the appointment of Fraser) had reported on the Wigtown and Dumfries branches. Of the five branches inspected by Brown and Marshall, four received unfavourable reports. Only the agent at Ayr, who had been in place for three months, seems to have escaped a reprimand. Most of the complaints stemmed from a lack of accounting in the books, or a failure to keep the required number of books. Thus some, at least, of the failures in accounting at Haddington were not unusual, although there was no suggestion of fraud occurring at the other agencies.

Inevitably, the new limits and instructions raised objections. In response to a letter from Alexander Dunlop at Greenock, the directors explained that the objects of the instructions issued were to

> guard the Bank and the Agents themselves against loss by excessive confidence in any of their Customers, and excessive credit given in consequence thereof;

4 BS 1/18/5, Daily Sheet or Order of Directors, 13 July 1801.
5 BS 1/146/1, Private Letter Book, p. 263.

and to serve the country by a more equal distribution of the credit given to it by the Bank, but which the Directors have reason to know is partially applied by some of the agents to their own particular friends or connexions in trade, or otherwise.[6]

The agent was reminded that any customers requiring credit greater than £5,000 could apply to the directors. When Dunlop finally resigned in April 1802, having accepted the post of manager in the newly-opened Renfrewshire Banking Company, the Treasurer, in a letter seeking assistance from Walter Ritchie of Greenock, alleged that Dunlop had not distributed the Bank's credit impartially, but to a few favourites.[7] Whether this allegation was justified or not, the directors had to come to an agreement with the Rothesay Spinning Co., a customer of the Greenock branch, as a result of the new orders. This company had been accommodated on bills to the extent of £27,000; it was acknowledged that this could not be suddenly reduced to £5,000 without causing great injury, and time was given for gradual reduction.

In reply to William Drysdale, the Kirkcaldy agent who forwarded an 'Address' from the manufacturers of the district, the directors explained that the limitations had not been intended to hurt the manufacturers but rather to check dangerous speculation, and reminded the agent that application could be made for an extension of the maximum 'liberal credit' of £5,000. They did, however, grant two concessions. Bills on London would not be refused for bills due or nearly due, provided that the agent was satisfied that it was not intended thereby to keep up a loan, and bills on Edinburgh or the branches at sight could be taken.[8] In reply to a letter of complaint received by a Kirkcaldy branch customer, J. Melvill & Son of Dysart, the directors reaffirmed their desire to promote industry and encourage manufacturers as long as they carried on their business prudently and did not go beyond the bounds which their own capital could support.[9] William Drysdale was answered thus:

> The situation of things now being materially altered from what they were when the orders for restricting or limiting the extent of discounts at Kirkcaldy and other branches of the Bank were given, the Directors desirous to relieve, as much as the Interest and Safety of the Bank will permit, the friends of the Bank in your place, of the inconvenience they may have felt from that restriction, have resolved not to adhere now strictly to the limitation prescribed to the weekly amount of your discounts; yet they allow you to go no further with

6 Ibid., 4 August 1801, pp. 249–50.
7 Ibid., 6 April 1802, p. 489.
8 Ibid., 31 August 1801, p. 277.
9 Ibid., 17 October 1801, p. 332.

Table 4 *Payments from Bank of Scotland profit and loss account*

Year	Sums paid out of profit and loss account	
1803	£7,955	set aside for Haddington branch
1804	£5,100	set aside for Haddington branch
1805	£5,700	set aside for Haddington branch
1806	£9,400	set aside for Haddington branch
1807	£7,400	loss on account of Hay Smith, late agent at Haddington
1808	£4,000	loss on account of Hay Smith, late agent at Haddington
1809	£2,300	loss on account of Hay Smith, late agent at Haddington
Total	£41,855	

any man than the business he carries on fairly requires, without forcing it by speculation, or than your own safety requires.[10]

A similar letter was sent to the Perth agent on 8 May and to Dunfermline, Dundee and St Andrews during that month. Restrictions on all bill discounts were lifted at all other branches on 28 May 1802.

The claims against the cautioners and the various estates of Hay Smith ws and his partners were insufficient to pay the losses; payments in subsequent years from the Bank profit and loss account are shown in Table 4.

It was the most serious total loss on an agency to date, and, as a result of the changes brought in, the Mound had a much closer grip on the workings of agencies thereafter. Losses occurred from time to time, but not on this scale by fraud, for many years.

10 Ibid., 5 April 1802, p. 487.

APPENDIX 8

BRANCHES AND
SUB-BRANCHES OF
BANK OF SCOTLAND,
1774–1939

Branch		Date opened	Date closed	Summary
Dumfries		1774		
Kelso		1774		
Kilmarnock		1775	1802	
Ayr		1775		
Inverness Union St		1775		
Stirling		1776		
Aberdeen	1	1780		
Dunfermline		1781		
Elgin		1782	1806	
Huntly		1782	1807	
Banff	2	1783	1817	
Haddington		1783		
Montrose		1784	1818	
Perth		1784		
Cupar		1785	1815	
Wigtown		1785	1817	
Kirkcaldy		1785		
Glasgow	3	1787		
Kirkcudbright		1790		
Hawick		1791	1802	
Dundee		1791	1811	
Brechin		1792	1803	
Greenock		1792	1818	
St Andrews		1792		
Thurso		1794	1806	
Forres		1795	1802	
Tain		1795	1814	
Fort William		1825	1830	
Edinburgh Leith		1825		
Stonehaven		1825		
Falkirk		1826		16 BS branches remained open by 1830 (15 closed 1802–30)
Duns		1832		
Dundee	4	1833		
Lauder		1833		

Fraserburgh		1835	
Greenock	5	1835	
Montrose	6	1835	
Airdrie		1836	
Ardrossan		1836	
Paisley		1836	
Banchory		1838	1846
Cumnock		1838	
Kilmarnock	7	1838	
Strathaven		1838	
Whithorn		1838	1846
Blairgowrie		1839	
Castle Douglas		1840	32 BS branches open by 1840
Callander		1842	31 BS branches open by 1850 (two closed 1840–50)
Arbroath		1855	
Coldstream		1855	
Glasgow Laurieston		1855	
Gatehouse		1856	
Auchtermuchty	8	1857	
Barrhead	8	1857	
Galashiels		1857	
Hamilton		1857	
Moffat	8	1857	
Peebles	8	1857	
West Linton	8	1857	
Edinburgh New Town		1860	43 BS branches open by 1860 (including five from Western Bank)
Innerleithen (sub)		1863	
Alyth		1864	1890
Annan		1864	
Beauly		1864	
Edinburgh Clerk St (Southern District)		1864	
Edinburgh Greenside		1864	
Edinburgh Morningside		1864	
Edinburgh Stockbridge		1864	
Glasgow Hutchesontown		1864	
Jedburgh	9	1864	
Motherwell		1864	
Ballachulish		1865	1879
Dysart		1865	
Forfar		1865	
Glasgow Sauchiehall St		1865	
Innerleithen	10	*1865*	
Lossiemouth		1865	
Oban		1865	
Bellshill (sub)		1866	
Broadford, Skye		1866	1869
Helensburgh		1866	
Uddingston (sub)		1866	
Aberfeldy	11	1867	
Glasgow Trongate		1867	
London		1867	
Auchterarder	12	1868	
Blackford	12	1868	
Coupar Angus	12	1868	
Crieff	12	1868	
Dunkeld	12	1868	
Killin	12	1868	
Newburgh		1868	1879
Pitlochry	12	1868	

Branch	Date opened	Date closed	Summary
Uddingston	[10] 1868		
Dunblane	1870		75 BS branches open by 1870 (including seven from Central Bank and one sub; one closed)
Brechin	[13] 1872	1889	
Strathmiglo (sub)	1872		
Glasgow Hillhead	1873		
Bellshill	[10] 1874		
Bonnyrigg	1874	1878	
Buchlyvie	1874		
Carnoustie	1874		
Denny	1874		
Elgin, High St	[14] 1874		
Glasgow Calton	1874		
Glasgow St George's Cross	1874		
Glasgow Whitevale	1874		
Grangemouth	1874		
Johnstone	1874	1882	
Dundee Victoria St	1875		
Fort William	[15] 1875		
Glasgow Miller St	1876		
Kirriemuir	1876		
Wick	1876		
Lockerbie	1877		
Thurso	[16] 1877		
Brodick (sub)	1878		
Dingwall, High St	[17] 1878		
Glasgow Crosshill	[17] 1878		
Kirkwall	1878		
Lamlash	[17] 1878		
Lasswade	1878	1942	
New Cumnock	[17] 1878		
Saltcoats	[17] 1878		
Slamannan	[17] 1878		
Stevenston (sub)	[17] 1878		
Dunbar	1879		
Glasgow Gorbals	1879		
Rothesay	[17] 1879		
Tain	[18] 1879		106 BS branches open by 1880 (including eight from City of Glasgow Bank, three subs; three closed)
Edinburgh West End	1881		
Glasgow East Park (sub)	1881		
Glasgow Anderston	1882		
Glasgow Kinning Park	1883		
Port Glasgow	1883		
Campbeltown	1884		
Edinburgh Newington	1884		
Glasgow Govanhill	1884		
Milngavie	1884		
Perth West End	1884		
Glasgow Dennistoun (sub)	1885		
Glasgow Cathcart (sub)	1887		
Glasgow East Park	[10] 1887		
Aberfoyle (sub)	1889	1894	
Glasgow Hope St	1890		117 BS branches open by 1890 (including six subs; three closed)
Bearsden (sub)	1891		
Glasgow Pollokshields	1891		
Edinburgh South Morningside	1893		

Glasgow Dennistoun	[10]	1893	
Glasgow Sandyford		1894	
Edinburgh Leith Walk		1895	
Eskbank		1896	
Gorebridge (sub)		1896	
Edinburgh Dalry Road		1897	
Edinburgh Corstorphine		1898	
Glasgow Govan		1898	
Glasgow Strathbungo (sub)		1898	
Gullane (sub)		1898	
Aberfoyle (sub)		1899	
Glasgow Partick		1899	
Coatbridge		1900	
Glasgow Springburn		1900	132 BS branches open by 1900 (including nine subs; one sub closed and reopened)
Glasgow Polmadie		1902	1909
Hawick	[19]	1903	
Glasgow Anniesland		1904	
Glasgow Cathcart	[10]	1904	
Glasgow Strathbungo	[10]	1905	
Alexandria		1906	
Dumbarton		1906	
Whiting Bay (sub)		1906	
Glasgow Scotstoun		1907	
Newtonmore (sub)		1907	
Ardgay	[20]	1908	
Avoch	[20]	1908	
Bo'ness		1908	
Bonar Bridge	[20]	1908	
Broadford, Skye	[20]	1908	
Buckie	[20]	1908	
Burghead	[20]	1908	
Cromarty	[20]	1908	
Dingwall, Tulloch St	[20]	1908	
Dornoch	[20]	1908	
Drumnadrochit (Glenurquhart)	[20]	1908	
Elgin, High St II	[20]	1908	
Forres	[21]	1908	
Fort Augustus	[20]	1908	
Fortrose	[20]	1908	
Gairloch	[20]	1908	
Garmouth	[20]	1908	
Glasgow Shawlands		1908	
Grantown-on-Spey	[20]	1908	
Halkirk	[20]	1908	
Hopeman	[20]	1908	1942
Invergarry	[20]	1908	
Inverness, High St	[20]	1908	
Kingussie	[20]	1908	
Kyle of Lochalsh	[20]	1908	
Lairg	[20]	1908	
Lochcarron	[20]	1908	
Lochmaddy	[20]	1908	
Mallaig	[20]	1908	
Muir of Ord	[20]	1908	
Nairn	[20]	1908	
Portree	[20]	1908	
Rothes	[20]	1908	1934

Branch	Date opened	Date closed	Summary
Stornoway	20 1908		173 BS branches open by 1910 (including 32 from Caledonian Bank, nine subs); one closed
Prestwick	1911		174 BS branches open by 1914 (including 32 from Caledonian Bank, nine subs)
Tarbert (sub)	1918		
Bearsden	10 *1919*		
Berwick (sub)	1920		
Edinburgh Gorgie Markets (sub)	1920		
Macduff	1920		
Strathpeffer (sub)	1920		
Tarbert	10 *1920*		179 BS branches open by 1920 (including 11 subs)
Armadale (sub)	1921		
Aviemore (sub)	1921		
Blackwaterfoot (sub)	1921		
Greenock, West End	1921	1943	
Invergarry (sub)	*1921*	*1949*	
Uig (sub)	1921		
Wishaw	1921		
Ayr, Burns Statue Square	1922		
Blackwaterfoot	10 *1922*		
Blyth Bridge (sub)	1922		
Corrie (sub)	1922		
Glasgow Charing Cross	1922		
Grahamston	1922		
Kildonan (sub)	1922		
Lagg (sub)	1922		
Leverburgh (sub)	1922		
Lochranza (sub)	1922		
Muthill (sub)	1922	1928	
Perth Market (sub)	1922		
Pirnmill (sub)	1922		
Shedog (sub)	1922		
Sliddery (sub)	1922		
Aberfoyle	10 *1923*		
Bennan (sub)	1923		
Boat of Garten (sub)	1923		
Bothwell (sub)	1923		
Carr Bridge (sub)	1923		
Edinburgh Ferry Road	1923		
Forfar Market (sub)	1923		
Gullane	10 *1923*		
Invermoriston (sub)	1923		
Inverness Cattle Market (sub)	1923		
Kippen (sub)	1923		
Machrie (sub)	1923		
Nethy Bridge (sub)	1923		
Scalpay (sub)	1923		
Strathmiglo	10 *1923*		
Thornhill (sub)	1923		
Walkerburn (sub)	1923		
Bankfoot (sub)	1924		
Birnam (sub)	1924	1932	
Bonnyrigg	1924		
Braco (sub)	1924		
Bridge of Earn (sub)	1924	1943–6	
Brodick	10 *1924*		

Camelon	1924	
Glasgow Mount Florida (sub)	1924	
Methven (sub)	1924	
Newarthill (sub)	1924	
Stanley (sub)	1924	
Cupar, Fife	[22] 1925	
Glenfarg (sub)	1925	
Leverburgh	[10] *1925*	
Glasgow Mount Florida	[10] *1926*	
Glasgow Renfield St	1926	
Whiting Bay	[10] *1926*	
Bothwell	[10] *1927*	
Gorebridge	[10] *1927*	
Durness (sub)	1928	
Edinburgh Liberton	1928	
Edinburgh Princes St	1928	
Gartmore (sub)	1928	
Scourie (sub)	1928	
Breakish (sub)	1929	
Edinburgh Newhaven	1929	
Elgin Market (sub)	1929	
Kinloch Rannoch (sub)	1929	
Kinlochbervie (sub)	1929	
Kinlochewe (sub)	1929	
Kirkmichael (sub)	1929	1933
London Piccadilly Circus	1929	
Scone	1929	
Kinghorn (sub)	1930	
Edinburgh Drumsheugh	1931	
Edinburgh Marchmont Rd	1931	
Giffnock	1931	
Laurieston (sub)	1931	
Stevenston	[10] *1931*	
Aberdeen West End	1932	
Arisaig (sub)	1932	
Dundee Dock St	1932	1941
Edinburgh Blackhall	1932	
Edinburgh Marchmont Road (sub)	[23] *1932*	
Morar (sub)	1932	
Aultbea (sub)	1933	
Balmacara (sub)	1933	
Edinburgh Mayfield Road	1933	
North Strome (sub)	1933	1940
Poolewe (sub)	1933	
Shieldaig (sub)	1933	
Glasgow Bath St	1934	
Glasgow West George St	1934	
Hillfoot	1934	1943–6
Edinburgh Corstorphine West	1935	
Newton Mearns	1935	
Newtonmore	[10] *1935*	
Hamilton, Quarry St	1936	
Kinghorn	[10] *1936*	
Lanark	1936	
Carradale (sub)	1937	
Glasgow Hillington Road	1937	
Troon	1937	

240 BS branches open by 1930 (including 47 subs); one sub closed

Branch	Date opened	Date closed	Summary
Walkerburn	[10] 1937		
Westerton (sub)	1937	1943–6	
Bishopbriggs	1938		
Leverburgh (sub)	[23] 1939		
North Hillington (sub)	1939		265 BS branches open by 1939 (including 54 subs); three closed (two of which were subs)

Notes:

Those in italics were previously opened as sub-branches or branches.

1 There had been a branch at Aberdeen from 1696–9, 1731–3 and 1764–7.
2 There had been a branch at Banff from 1764–6.
3 There had been a branch at Glasgow from 1696–7 and 1731–3.
4 There had been a branch at Dundee from 1696–8, 1731–3 and 1791–1811.
5 There had been a branch at Greenock from 1792–1818.
6 There had been a branch at Montrose from 1696–9 and 1784–1818.
7 There had been a branch at Kilmarnock from 1775–1802.
8 Former Western Bank branch.
9 In 1865, at Pennyman's Market in Jedburgh (held on 31 May), five banks had tents. The BS agent had as drawings £731, which the directors thought a 'fair beginning' (Malcolm, p. 179).
10 Formerly a sub-branch.
11 Amalgamated with local Central Bank branch in 1868.
12 Former Central Bank branch.
13 There had been a branch at Brechin from 1792–1803.
14 There had been a branch at Elgin from 1782–1806.
15 There had been a branch at Fort William from 1825–30.
16 There had been a branch at Thurso from 1794–1806.
17 Former City of Glasgow Bank branch.
18 There had been a branch at Tain from 1795–1814.
19 There had been a branch at Hawick from 1791–1802.
20 Former Caledonian Bank branch.
21 There had been a branch at Forres from 1795–1802; former Caledonian Bank branch.
22 There had been a branch at Cupar from 1785–1815.
23 Formerly an independent branch.

Sources: Bank of Scotland, *Annual Reports*; C. A. Malcolm, *The Bank of Scotland, 1695–1945* (Edinburgh: n.d. [1948]), p. 175.

APPENDIX 9a

ALEXANDER BLAIR, REPORT TO BOARD OF DIRECTORS, 13 OCTOBER 1857

Circumstances Under Which it is Made

As the prospects of the Country, both foreign and domestic are extremely uncertain, and as our usual prosperous condition is exposed to considerable risk, it seems right to bring under notice the present position and relations of the Bank, in order that the scheme of the business may be considered and amended if necessary.

The political and financial state of France; the Indian Mutiny; the state of credit in America; the unprecedented extension of our commerce; and the great importance of the measures likely to be proposed in the next Session of Parliament are all likely to exercise an important influence on the affairs of the Country. As to the more immediate influences on the Bank, they are, the high rate of interest offered by the Joint Stock Banks on deposits of a permanent character and the departure of most of these Establishments from the ordinary rules under which Banking has hitherto been conducted; the competition for deposits; and the excessive development of the Branch system in Scotland; the frequent fluctuations in the rate of interest, accompanied by corresponding fluctuations in deposits and discounts; the altered state of the Exchequer Bill market, and the increase of those branches of commerce which are accompanied with distant returns. On the other hand must be considered, the manner in which we should be affected by a return to a period of comparative quiet, with a prosperous and extended trade and accumulating Capital, increasing under the influence of the gold discoveries.

Progress of Business

Twenty five years ago the Deposits of the Bank were £3,188,000, the advances in Scotland £1,970,000 and the Reserves in London £2,035,000.

At present the Deposits are £5,327,000, the advances £4,390,000 and the Reserves £1,922,000, by which it appears that while the Reserves are less by £113,000, the deposits have increased £2,139,000 and the Advances £2,355,000. A certain portion of the Reserves however is employed in advances to our Correspondents in Newcastle and Leeds and amounts to £150,000 – two thirds whereof payable at three and one third at six months notice – and another portion is employed in the Discount of bills to the same parties, amounting to £171,000 of which £35,000 are Scottish acceptances.

If these sums be taken into account, the amount of the Reserves will be £2,140,536 and they are invested as follows, vizt.

Bank Stock	£109,000
3 per cent Stock	927,394
Long Annuities	280,518
Annuities 1885	170,595
Exchequer Bills	18,254
Bank of Ireland Stock	12,531
Indian Stock	87,254
Bank of Scotland Stock	192,926
Other Scottish Stocks	20,564
Newcastle advances	321,500
	£2,140,536
Inconvertible	610,000
Convertible	£1,530,536

By a Minute of the 30th November 1840 it was ordered that one third of the liabilities of the Bank should be held in reserve. Accordingly the convertible Reserve should now be £1,800,000.

Transactions of 1857 and Prospective Demand

It appears that during the present year – that is since the 27th January 1857, the deposits have decreased £323,000 and that the discounts and loans have increased £458,000 – causing a draft upon the reserves of £756,000 or about £100,000 per month. The increase on Scottish investments has been made in Glasgow and the sum lent there now amounts to £2,440,475. The whole advances in Scotland have reached the amount of £4,740,000. As regards any further demands for advances in Scotland, it must be kept in view that on the 18th August a sum of £594,775 was still undrawn against the whole credit, given by cash accounts: now altho' the rough estimate of the demand is only £50,000 yet in 1847, this credit was exhausted within £7,031 excluding overdrafts.

Then upon an estimate of the demand for increased discounts at Glasgow, Dundee, Paisley and Greenock, it would appear that £450,000 may be asked for.

These two sums would amount to £1,000,000 and in considering the state of the Bank's business it is impossible to overlook these contingent demands, one half of which arises from the shape which the Cash Account system has assumed; that is an undertaking on the part of the Bank to advance in many cases on large separate credits, ranging from £5,000 to £50,000, a sum of 1,825,286 of which only two thirds is usually required.

The Bank of England's practice is so different that they have refused to admit any operations on our permanent credit with them, unless they suit their convenience at the time they are required.

A general maximum for discounts is fixed for the government of the principal discount Agencies and the Agents are aware of the wishes of the Directors to restrict the present tendency to increased advances.

In consequence of the altered state of the Exchequer Bill market and the absorption of the London loans, an arrangement has been made to obviate the inconvenience of the quarterly closing of the books of the Bank of England, which in the meantime will be useful.

In considering the position of the Bank prospectively, the probability of a draft on the deposits, must not be overlooked. Such a demand might reach £500,000 to £800,000 upon a fall of the Funds, of a temporary character and would arise from the investment of deposits ranging from £3,000 and upwards, of which the amount is £1,500,000.

It therefore appears that if interest continues high and that if our financial and political positions remain much the same, the tendency of our business will be towards an increased demand for money, and that if from any circumstances the adverse probabilities be increased, we may require considerable reserves.

Whether under this view of the subject, it may be proper to call for our advances in England, or to alter our position in other respects, seems to be the question for consideration.

Mode of Meeting Increased Demand, as Respects the Investments in Scotland

It has been already stated that the discount accounts at the Branches are granted under a general limit, vizt.

Glasgow	£1,200,000	£1,188,900
Greenock	140,000	169,000
Dundee	209,000	253,000
Paisley	120,000	132,000
Laurieston	420,000	456,000

If a draft upon the reserve were to arise from the Cash Credits and from a demand for deposits, the course of the Bank's business should be guided by the rule of preserving a due proportion between the different Securities in which the Bank's means are invested. The discounts would therefore be necessarily reduced in the same proportion as the investment in Government Securities and in this way the relative strength of the Bank would be maintained. The advances of a Bank are subject to control, but the only mode of meeting a draft upon the deposits is by maintaining the proper and usual proportion between the Reserve and the Liabilities and this can only be effected by changing the character of a portion of the Assets, which are not immediately convertible.

Supposing then that a limit be placed to the advances on discounts and that under the proposed rule a reduction of discounts should accompany an extraordinary advance upon Cash Accounts or an unusual draft on Deposits, a question immediately arises as to the prudence of granting large Cash Credits which are generally used only at an inconvenient time and so are not only very unprofitable but highly inconvenient. Cash Accounts ranging from £300 to £1,000 were very useful both to the Banks and the Community sixty or seventy years ago, but the character of these advances has now entirely changed and the period seems to have arrived for limiting not only their general extent, but likewise the range of particular credits, which should be restricted to a moderate sum, beyond which, the advance should depend upon the convenience of the Bank.

Overdrafts upon accounts have much increased of late and as a general rule, these should not be allowed except upon Security and for a limited time.

Former Minutes

Upon two former occasions, 30 November 1840 and 18 October 1847, the position of the Bank was carefully considered with reference to the rate of profit; to the high average of the Government Securities and to the proportion between the Liabilities and the Reserve and the principle of one third Reserve was laid down as a rule in the conduct of the Bank's affairs. Since then the average of the Government Securities has been reduced and a power of investment in Short bills and loans (including the Newcastle and Leeds accounts) to the extent of £570,000 has been obtained, but the proposed extended investment in Exchequer Bills has not been continued in consequence of the altered state of the Exchequer Bill market. The present Report is brought before the Board in consequence of the increase of the Scottish investments; the change in their proportionate amount to the investment in Government Securities and the alterations which have taken place in the conduct of the banking business in Scotland.

General Management of the Bank

For many years past, the trading means of the Bank of Scotland have been gradually increased and the London Reserve has shown a tendency to exceed the proportion fixed by the Minute of 30th November 1840.

Under these circumstances in 1840 an arrangement for the employment of money was made with an old Correspondent, the Northumberland & Durham District Banking Company incorporated with Messrs Ridley & Co. and through this connexion and the Leeds Banking Co. we now employ £321,500, as already stated.

For the purpose of a more profitable use of a further portion of the means of the Bank, a second Branch was opened in Glasgow in 1855, which employs about £500,000.

From the tendency towards accumulation of Deposit money and from the expectation of the Gold discoveries leading to increased trade and profit, the measures of the Bank have been taken with the intention of placing an accession of means advantageously.

The trade of the Country has however received such a powerful stimulus by the alteration of the Tariff and the increase of the precious metals as not only to absorb the accumulation of Capital but to press upon the Reserves of the Country to the extent indicated by the high rates of interest.

This result has also been aggravated by the late war, the financial state of France and our existing difficulties in India.

Judging therefore from the facts and experience of the last two years we may expect a comparative scarcity rather than an abundance of available Capital.

In laying down the course of the operations of the Bank under such circumstances, some remarks regarding sections of the business seem to be necessary.

1. As to the use of the Reserves –
The banking principle is that the proportion of the Reserve, that is the available Capital of the Bank, to the other investments, should always be preserved. According to this rule when the Reserve is at or under one third

of the liabilities a reduction of the advances in Scotland should proceed simultaneously with the conversion of Government Securities and it is obvious that much loss and inconvenience must result from a different action. So far however has the practice in Scotland established such a rule that the expectation of the public is directly the reverse. The advances on discount at a period of discredit are expected to be maintained and increased according to the emergency of the day, and the credit on Cash accounts to be fully advanced. Now to realise these expectations in the conduct of the business of the Bank of Scotland would require a sum of £1,000,000 which must be realised by the sale of Stock under very disadvantageous circumstances. If to this be added £1,000,000 as a provision against a draft upon the deposits it follows that £2,000,000 at least yielding only 3 per cent must be set apart for a Reserve.

It appears, however, that if the advances on Cash accounts were not contingent £600,000 of this sum might be otherwise employed and that if upon four months notice a gradual reduction could be effected in the discounts, a further sum of at least £400,000 might be deducted from the Reserve.

Now the actual difference between the return on our Government Securities and the rate of interest on discounts cannot be stated at less than 2 per cent on the average of the last ten years. The difference therefore to the Bank arising from a departure from the correct banking principle is £20,000 per annum. If to this be added the loss arising from paying interest from day to day on sums which cannot be invested from the short term of their deposit, this difference will be much increased, being as it now stands adverse both in the way of convenience and profit to the prosperity of the Bank. The advances to the English Joint Stock Banks are founded on the old connexion and on the discount of Scottish paper to the extent of £35,000 or thereabouts and they are made on terms which include the safety afforded by a deposit of bills and the responsibility of the numerous Shareholders; the same rate of interest as is paid in Scotland; and the power of withdrawing the advances on 3 and 6 months notice respectively. Under this arrangement the advance is a postponed convertible security, whereas the Scottish advances are not only quite inconvertible but at a period of discredit entail the necessity of maintaining large funds to ensure the safety of the Capital already lent. It is evident that in the degree in which this state of things is produced by competition, so does its existence increase competition from the risk and difficulty of realising a fair profit.

It is now proposed that the Directors admit the principle of a simultaneous reduction in the investments of the Bank whether Government Securities or Scottish investments in the manner and on the occasions indicated so far as regards Discounts and that for the future until the order be rescinded no Cash Credit be granted for a larger sum than £10,000 – any further advance being optional to the Bank, whatever the nominal credit may be – or that the money be lent absolutely without option on sufficient security. Also that a general limit be placed to advances of this description. The loss on Cash Accounts is small, but there is no reason why this advantage should not be enjoyed without the present concomitant disadvantage.

Any change in the Bank's practice in the direction of a modification of the terms of existing credits must of course be gradual and put into practice as opportunity occurs. In the meantime the restriction of discounts has been ordered and acted upon, and the limitation of the advance on Cash Accounts rather accords with public feeling in one point as there is a growing disinclination to give Security for an unlimited period. Even as regards the reduction of discounts, it would be merely the revival of former practice, which indeed would become indispensable on the recurrence of such events as occurred in the Market for Capital between 1793 and 1815.

The accounts with the English Joint Stock Banks are satisfactory and profitable. The question therefore arises, as the advances on them really belong to that class of investments called 'London discounts and Loans' whether they should be called up in case of a further demand for money or if Stock should be sold. For the last 25 years the Stock accounts have been so managed as to yield a fair return and still to stand at an average of 97 or thereabouts – a reduction of about 5 per cent on the average of the largest portion of Stock held at the period alluded to.

At present the whole convertible Securities including the Newcastle advances amount to £1,852,036 so that the rule of one third Reserve may be said to be unbroken and in a state to be confirmed or strengthened according to the opinion of the Board.

2. The abundance of Capital and the local causes, adverted to in the beginning of this Report have been thought to stand in the way of much wholesome regulation. It may be that from the great extension of trade and consequent demand for capital and also from national difficulties we may be entering on a new period when dealers in Capital may enjoy an action as independent as they had before 1815, or this state of things may arise from the extension of trade alone. However this may be some check will probably be placed to the abuse of credit, the consequences of which are now appearing in America and will no doubt reach this country and affect those establishments, who have taken excessive risks.

Here it may be right to advert to the action of the other Scotch Banks. But though the position of the Bank of Scotland may not unfairly be compared with that of the Royal Bank and British Linen Co. yet for obvious reasons relating to credit as comparison can be made between the Bank of Scotland and the Joint Stock Banks under unlimited responsibility.

Before closing these remarks it is proper to observe that the Bank's Branch at Laurieston has opened twenty one accounts for discount with English Houses who remit for negotiation and discount their Scottish acceptances and that the Laurieston Agent recommends the discount of the London acceptances of these connexions.

Care is taken to ascertain the stability of these discounters and information regarding the London acceptors can be obtained from our London Correspondents. The cause of such London bills being sent to Scotland is a general difference of the rate of interest between the charge of the English Country Banker or Bill-Broker and of the Scottish Banker in favour of the discounter. This probably arises from London money being more valuable in Scotland than in the English provinces and the difference is increased we apprehend from the practice of the Joint Stock Banks who fill up their London accounts with Bills and we understand re-discount such paper. Of course the Bank of Scotland is obliged to conform to the general wish of the Banks as to the rate of interest on London bills. They may be considered when discounted to our connexions as accessories to the discount of Scottish acceptances and if we do not take the former, we have no reason to expect the latter. Under these circumstances and considering the small effect the rate at which these bills are discounted produces on the Scottish minimum rate, which conforms to the Bank of England rate and also considering the connexion between the Drawer and Scotland and that we have not sought for the business, it is proposed to admit such bills, being bona fide bills and bearing evidence of their connexion with the regular trade of the discounters and being also a subordinate feature of the account.

There is a tendency to interchange transactions between the two countries at present. In some respects this operates against the Scottish Banks by the operations of the English Bill brokers. It does not seem unreasonable therefore to receive business from England, provided it is offered and is not attended with risk or any public inconvenience.

English bills accepted in England elsewhere than London, do not fall within the rules regulating the discounts of the Bank and with regard to the acceptances of Houses in America, the present discredit in the States proves the necessity of excluding all such transactions, including the operations referred to in the letters to the Glasgow Managers of 4th and 10th January 1856 and in the Memorandum of the 10th and Mr M. J. Smith's letter of the 14th January 1856.

The Report is approved.

Source: BS 1/5, Minutes, 13 October 1857.

APPENDIX 9b

REPORT BY THE COMMITTEE OF INVESTIGATION OF THE SHAREHOLDERS OF THE WESTERN BANK OF SCOTLAND, APPOINTED AT A MEETING HELD IN GLASGOW ON 2d DECEMBER 1857

[from *Select Committee on the Bank Acts,1857–8*, Appendix No. 21]

In obedience to the instructions contained in the resolution passed at the above-named meeting, the committee proceeded to make a detailed investigation of the whole of the affairs of the bank, and have now to submit to the shareholders the following report:-

In conducting the examination the committee came to certain resolutions, making a division of the labours necessary to be undertaken by them. They accordingly divided themselves into five sub-committees, among whom were allocated portions of the work to be done, and they assumed as members of committee Mr Finnie, of Kilmarnock, and devolved on him and Mr Raimes, of Edinburgh, an examination of the branches connected with their respective districts.

After a cursory examination of the condition of the company, and after communicating with the manager and directors, and finding the best agencies throughout the country had been transferred with the deposits to other establishments, and that a large amount in value of the depositors had not signified their assent to the proposal for extended time, the committee came to the resolution that a successful resuscitation of the affairs of the bank was at present impossible. The inquiry, therefore, into the value of the assets, as after detailed, proceeded on the principle of the bank winding up its affairs; and being thus confined to a knowledge of mercantile details, the committee did not consider it necessary to take any additional professional assistance. The books which thus necessarily came under their cognisance, and containing the principal evidence of the whole transaction of the company, consisted of:-

1st, *Discount Ledgers* – Showing the detail of all bills discounted and current beyond such as had only a few days to run.

2d, *Deposit Ledgers* – Containing accounts of all parties drawing sums on credit, and operating from day to day.

3d, *Credit Ledgers* – Containing a record of all debts due on securities, either of a partial or of a complete description.

4th, *Books Kept* – For the various branches throughout the country, on the same principle as those stated in the foregoing numbers.

5th, *Ledgers* – Containing abstracts of the foregoing detailed ledgers, and showing the results of the whole business of the company.

In the latter books were kept the accounts bearing on the gains of the company, either upon exchange, upon discounts, upon interest, and an account raised for a guarantee of the bad debts which might from time to time take place in the management of its affairs. In these books were also kept accounts for 'Protested Bills' and for 'Sundry Debtors', the whole of which in the statement exhibited at last meeting was placed under the head of 'Debts in Suspense'.

The yearly result of the transactions on the items in the accounts kept in these books was regularly ascertained, and the whole brought into one focus in an abstracted balance-sheet, certified and signed by the directors of the company for the time being.

In making the investigation into the detail of affairs, it may be proper to premise, that the examination which the committee has gone into does not proceed upon an ascertained book-keeping balance of the affairs of the company; but they have examined into every item of assets, independent of balance-sheets, and endeavoured to find, as far as lay in their power, and by the assistance of information both in the bank and out of it, the accurate and ultimate out-turn of the whole of these assets. In this way, the committee certify that the examination has been as thorough and complete as the limited time for making the investigation would allow.

To each of the five sub-committees was allocated special portions of work:-

Committee No. 1 attended, with the manager and two of the directors, to the general business of the company.

Committee No. 2 investigated the whole accounts in the ledgers, containing the transactions on the letters of the alphabet from A to L.

Committee No. 3 undertook a similar duty in the ledgers for the remaining portion of the alphabet.

Committee No. 4 conducted the examination of the accounts entitled 'Sundry Debtors', and 'Bills Protested', or 'Debts in Suspense', and into the value of the bills held against bankrupt and insolvent estates.

Committee No. 5 took up the state of accounts, and valuations of these, in the whole of the branches throughout Scotland.

Each of these committees had the assistance, when necessary, of one of the directors, and the whole were actively superintended by Mr M'Clelland, as public accountant.

Each committee took up a portion of the work allotted to it, and examined, with as much minuteness as time allowed, the whole accounts in the books committed to their care. The sum at the debit of each was carefully considered, and, where the committee were satisfied, was valued as good, and such portions of the debts as were likely to remain unpaid were assumed as loss.

The losses thus ascertained were classified, for the sake of distinctness and simplicity, under heads corresponding with the items in the vidimus of assets already submitted to the shareholders.

The alterations which have been made on the items contained in the published vidimus will thus be seen at a glance in the abstract vidimus appended to this report, and the result on each head of assets brought out.

It would appear, then, from the investigation, that the amount of the liabilities of the company, including those which are of a nominal character, and which will run off at maturity on the bills payable by other parties, that the total amount of the liabilities on the 9th November last, stand at the sum already reported to the shareholders, viz., 8,911,932*l*, and that the assets for the payment and liquidation of these liabilities, valued and ascertained by the committee, amount to 8,607,240*l*, showing a deficiency of the assets of the company to meet the liabilities of 304,692*l*, and thus making, including the capital and rest reported in last statement at 1,715,892*l*, an estimated loss on the whole transactions of the company of 2,020,584*l*.

In testing the accuracy of the conclusions the committee have come to on the value of each head of assets, considerable labour, inquiry, and pains have been taken; and they are now satisfied, from the mode adopted in the inquiry, that as accurate an approximation has been arrived at on the ultimate value of the assets as can, under present circumstances, be made.

While the committee have thus endeavoured to find out as accurately as they can the loss which may ultimately accrue to the shareholders on the melancholy position of the affairs of this once flourishing company, they cannot disguise from themselves or the shareholders the contingencies which may yet arise from the winding up of so large an establishment. They are at the same time convinced that, by prudent, sagacious, and intelligent management, by parties having a knowledge of the circumstances and condition of the debtors, and who may be acquainted with their standing and character, and by the exercise of a moderate continuance of that reasonable forbearance shown by all classes of creditors, that a large amount of saving on the estimates made the committee may yet accrue to the company; and it may be noticed as a prominent feature favourable to the present and ultimate security of the creditors, that, irrespective of the assets, the aggregate private fortunes of the shareholders are amply able to provide against all contingencies arising from the failure of the assets to meet the debts due to the public. While they have thus arrived, in the discharge of the duty committed to them, at the startling conclusions of the vidimus of affairs now submitted, they have purposely abstained from alluding to the causes which brought these results about; but the committee consider their duty to the shareholders would by no means be completed were allusion to these causes omitted in this report.

It may readily occur to those acquainted with the operations of a banking company, that in the present condition of this bank considerable loss may arise to the company from the position of the share list. According to the return given to the committee, that list stood on the 11th December as follows:-

Stock authorised to be issued by the Company, in shares of 50*l* each, was representing a capital of 1,500,000*l*			30,000
1.	Of these shares there were held in name of the bank	1,388	
2.	In name of others for behoof of bank	283	
3.	In name of the Ayrshire Bank	405	
4.	In name of various bankrupt estates	493	
			2,569
	Leaving in hands of the public		27,431

In this way it will be seen that the shares of the company being now of a valueless description, a large loss will have been sustained by those held in their own hands, or through the insolvency of other parties. The loss under this head cannot be estimated at less than 300,000*l*.

Another present source of loss to the company has arisen from an extensive dealing in policies of insurance effected on the lives of bankrupt debtors. The present value of these policies has been stated in the vidimus at 70,000*l*; but a much larger sum has been disbursed by the bank, although in many cases the debtors undertake the payment of the premiums of insurance.

The assets have also become much deteriorated from the value placed on them being taken as the realisation for winding up, and not as a solvent and going concern.

It appears that from an early period in the history of the company the assets had not been yearly and systematically valued. From time to time, however, deductions were made from profit and loss account before declaring dividends. Under the head of 'Accounts in Suspense', called 'Protested Bills' and 'Sundry Debtors' Account', large sums were carried forward from year to year without the actual loss thereon being ascertained, and placed to the debit of profit and loss. The increasing amount of this account, together with the laxity of lending on insufficient securities, and omitting to make yearly statements, forms another source of loss to the company.

During the latter portion of the management of the deceased manager, however, the affairs appear to have been gradually improving; and had Mr Smith lived and continued in the position he then occupied, the policy he seemed to have been pursuing might have wrought off in a few years a portion at least of the losses standing in the books of the company at the balance of 1852. That gentleman ceased at this period from bad health to take an active part in the management, and thereafter resigned.

In corroboration of the view thus taken of the company's affairs, it may be instructive to make a comparison of the London accounts in the following years:-

In October 1852 the bank were creditors of the London banks in cash and general balance for   378,026

And the practice appears to have ceased at that period of re-discounting bills in London.

In October 1857 the bank were debtors to the London bankers for	303,864
While the discount account at the same period for bills re-discounted had reached the sum of	864,512
Thus, after investing all the deposits, capital, and rest of the company, the bank were indebted to London bankers for	1,168,376

In addition to the precarious character of the business thus pursued in re-discounting, the bank appears to have had a large connection in America not exactly of a banking character; and the capital necessary to support a business of this description at so great a distance has, no doubt, been another cause of helping to cripple the company in its present circumstances.

During the progress of this business, and from the period of Mr Smith ceasing to be manager, the whole conduct of the company seems to have centred in the person of Mr Taylor; and during a large portion of the period of his management, the business, though apparently profitable, was to a great extent of a dangerous and reckless description. He appears to have given credit to many parties who were worthless, to have done so in defiance of remonstrances, and to have pursued a general course of conduct in his management, which when carried out by a man of such character, could not be easily controlled by any Board of directors.

Accordingly, it appears that at the time of his exit from the bank the whole financial condition of the company was in a disorganised state, and the subsequent fall of this once large establishment was hastened by the monetary crisis, which reached its culminating point on the closing of the doors of the bank.

The committee are of opinion, that during the whole of Mr Taylor's career, as well as during a portion of Mr Smith's services, the directors of the bank have been much to blame, in neglecting to perform the ordinary duties incumbent upon them on the acceptance of such a trust. They appear, without sufficient inquiry or examination, to have trusted to the statements of the managers with a simplicity which appears to the committee almost incredible.

While we acquit these gentlemen of any moral blame in their management as directors, and consider that their errors have been those of judgment, and not of intention, we are clearly of opinion that they have failed to perform those ordinary duties in the management of the company which it is well known they all practise with so much fidelity and success in the prosecution of their own private affairs; and their neglect of these duties has been, in part, the means of bringing both pecuniary and mental distress upon hundreds of their fellow-countrymen.

We do not mean these remarks to apply to the present directors alone. They are more or less applicable to all those gentlemen who have been formerly in the management of the company during the period above alluded to; and while they do so, the committee cannot but blame themselves, as well as other shareholders, for relying with too much confidence, for so many years past, on the whole management of the company.

The remarks which have been made in relation to the directors by no means apply to Messrs Alexander Baird and William Logie – two gentlemen who at great personal sacrifice were induced to join the direction on the eve of the bank's difficulties, and have done what in them lay to alleviate the peril of its position.

In conclusion, the committee have much pleasure in stating that they have received from Mr Fleming, as manager, and from every officer of the company, the most unremitting and devoted attention to their wishes, and have been supplied by these gentlemen with a very considerable amount of information in enabling them to value the assets and obtain a knowledge of the present position of the company.

(signed)	Robert Addie	Gavin Miller
	Geo. Baird	James M'Clelland
	Robert Bryson	Jas R. Stewart
	Wm Euing	Robert Wilson

Glasgow, 17 December 1857

APPENDIX 9c

HOW TO MISMANAGE A BANK: A REVIEW OF THE WESTERN BANK OF SCOTLAND

John Gifford (Edinburgh 1859)

In July 1858, the Select Committee of the House of Commons on 'Bank Acts' was issued, containing the details of the crisis of 1857 and of the bankruptcy of the Western Bank of Scotland.

It is not to be wondered at, though it is matter of regret, that with such a mass of conflicting evidence before them the Committee, persuaded 'that no mischief will result from at least a temporary continuance of the present state of things', recommended no practical measure.

The following observations were written some months ago, after a careful perusal of the Report, and are now submitted to those interested in our banking system, in the hope that they may find in them something worthy of their consideration.

Edinburgh, November 1859.

CONTENTS

The Appendix to the Report of the Select Committee of the House of Commons on the workings of the Bank Acts, contains the Annual Accounts of the Western Bank from 1833 to 1857. It is interesting and instructive to look at the account for the last year, issued six months before the Bank closed its doors, and to think that behind these figures, showing an undiminished capital of £1,500,000, a rest of £240,000, and funds to pay a dividend of 9 per cent, there lay hid a loss of nearly THREE MILLIONS!

... How is this enormous discrepancy to be accounted for? How were such losses concealed?

There are various ways in which an account can be falsified so as to conceal loss.

'The Liabilities' may be understated. Accounts which are entered in the balance sheet may be entered erroneously, or liabilities which really lie on the company may be altogether omitted.

Or 'the Assets' may be over-stated. They may contain large sums of money which never can be made good to the Company.

We give the account of June 1857:-

Assets

Credit Accounts	£1,932,024	3	1
Bills Discounted	2,873,293	19	1
Bills with Country Agents	266,272	19	1
Bills Lodged	152,803	6	0
Balances due by London Bankers } Balances due by Sundry Bankers }	108,085	7	2
Balances due by Branches	594,283	12	1
Bills Protested	108,840	16	11
Sundry Debtors	283,661	16	3
Government and other Securities	232,542	7	6
Miller Street Property	49,608	13	9
Bank Note Paper	17,000	0	0
Stamps	856	4	11
Law Expenses	3,000	0	0
Adjusting Account of Interest	14,307	7	7
Balancing of Cash	685,391	10	0
	£7,321,972	3	5

Liabilities

Capital	1,500,000	0	0
Notes Issued	1,627,176	10	0
Deposits	741,119	12	5
Bills for Collection	309,157	18	3
Balances due to London Bankers	—		
Balances due to Sundry Bankers	49,129	4	3
Balances due to Branches	2,715,024	9	5
Sinking Fund	226,777	3	3
Guarantee Fund	20,106	13	10
Dividends	131,062	10	0
Unclaimed Dividends	2,418	2	0
	£7,321,972	3	5

To assist us in pointing out how so many millions were misstated in this account, we have the account of the Committee of Shareholders of the state of affairs in December the same year, where they estimate the loss on the whole operations of the bank at £2,000,000. Future investigations have proved that another million was lost beyond their estimate.[1]

. . . the loss of £2,000,000 was composed of the following items:-

1	On Bills	£437,945
2	On Current Accounts	885,857
3	Foreign Securities held for drafts accepted by the Western	60,000
4	On Past-Due Bills and 'Sundry Debtors' Account'	685,597
5	On 'Other Securities'	22,347

The statement of the Liabilities of the Bank is open to the following remarks:-

1 CAPITAL   £1,500,000

... it is evident that this was not the real capital of the bank. In December 1857, 2,569 shares had been purchased by the bank (equal to about £180,000), and were in hand.

Such shares . . . Mr Taylor [the general manager] seems to have slumped . . . under the title of 'government and other securities', at least so the figures lead us to suspect.

This misinterpretation, though it seems to lessen liability at first, threw the loss on a smaller number of shareholders and cost the shareholders £300,000.

2 NOTES ISSUED

DEPOSITS

BALANCES DUE BY BRANCHES

The misinterpretation these figures contain results from the principle on which the whole balance is framed; and which Mr Fleming, in his evidence before the Parliamentary Committee, thought of sufficient importance to notice to them. It is that the balance is simply that of 'the Head Office transactions', and all that has been done at the branches during the year, is concealed under the Return of 'Balances due to or by Branches'. Much mischief may be concealed under such a return; for instance, a Branch may have £200,000 of deposits and £300,000 of bad debts – all that would appear would be an asset due by such a Branch to Head Office, £100,000! . . .

So with 'the Deposits'. The deposits at Branches are not included. Some £4,000,000 of liabilities unnoticed!

'The Notes issued' included evidently those held by the Bank and its Branches. This is not the real amount of liability to note-holders.

1 The Liquidators' account, submitted on 4 October 1858, estimated the loss at £2,793,356.

The Western had a hundred and one Branches. The effect of such a false principle on the general result must have been very great.

. . .

There is nothing worthy of notice recorded on the side of the liabilities, but there is a question most important to interpose here – *are these all the liabilities of the bank?* The answer to this is found in the account of the Committee of investigation. Under the statement of liabilities there is –

'3 ACCEPTANCES PAST, DUE OR CURRENT'

The three first items of this kind show a responsibility for £920,654, composed chiefly of acceptances, or obligations to accept, foreign correspondents at New York and elsewhere.

. . . The committee reported with their account, that there would be a loss on the securities held at New York, and it is since understood that the loss on these credits amounted to much more than the Committee anticipated.

The objectionable point . . . is the fact of liabilities of £1,000,000 really existing against the Company, and being totally ignored in the account . . .

6 BILLS REDISCOUNTED   £1,073,771

These bills . . . bore the endorsation of the Manager, and till duly retired the recourse against the Bank for repayment of any dishonoured bill was a true and serious liability which it was improper to conceal.

. . . the Liverpool Borough Bank had in London at the time of its failure bills rediscounted to the amount of £3,500,000, and . . . of these . . . £700,000 to £1,000,000 were discounted solely on the credit of the Bank's endorsement . . .

The Northumberland and Durham District Bank when it failed had rediscounted £1,500,000, of which £230,000 came back unpaid, and for which, of course, the company was liable. The Western Bank itself rediscounted during the three years preceding its stoppage about five millions annually. Surely it is a mockery to have such liabilities as these hanging on a company and omit all notice of them . . .

Turning now to the other side of the account, THE ASSETS, let us look at the details . . .

The first entry is:-

CREDIT ACCOUNTS   £1,932,024

This large sum is only what the Head Office advanced . . . There was nearly £1,200,000 advanced by the Branches in October, but . . . this latter sum could not appear.

. . . From the report of the investigation, we find that there were . . . nearly £600,000 of 'over-drafts', that is, advances made to customers on their cheques, without any other security; more than £1,000,000 only partially secured, and about £300,000 on the security of Western Bank Stock!

... The real loss on these accounts is not known; the estimate was ... nearly £1,000,000 ...

'BILLS DISCOUNTED' is the next asset   £2,873,293

This is of course only the discounts of Head Office ...

The loss which accrued to the Western from these discounts was very serious. Almost the whole of the advances to the four bankrupt firms of Macdonald & Co., Monteith & Co., Wallace & Co., and Godfrey Pattison & Co., being in the form of discounts. The sums of their bills were respectively, £417,000; £469,000; £226,000; and £347,000: together, £1,459,000.

A considerable proportion of such bills were 'Accommodation Bills' ...

Passing to the two items of the June Account, 'Protested Bills' and 'Sundry Debtors', their very titles ... prompt the inquiry, 'of what are these accounts composed?' Glancing back through the annual balances, we see in their history a rather suspicious circumstance. 'The Protested Bill Account', up to 1847, ... was £66,000; but in 1848 it rises to £356,000 ... [In 1849] A new account, called 'Sundry Debtors', was raised in the ledger, and £345,000 being transferred to its debit, the protested bill account that year shrunk into the marvellously modest sum of £39,782! From that time to 1857, 'Sundry Debtors' was a remarkably steady asset, appearing in every balance sheet at about £300,000 ... [The committee's valuation of this lot of debts in December 1857] makes a deduction of £685,000 [from the two accounts] leaving only £285,000 ... supposed to be recoverable!

There is one item more must be noticed, that is 'government and other securities'. It has ever been held as a fundamental principle of Scottish Banking, that a reserve, varying from one-third to one-fourth of ... their note circulation and deposits, be held so invested in London, as to be available at all times on the shortest notice. Of course the bulk of such investments must be government stock. ... from 1833 to 1839 [the Western] seem to have held no government stock at all. Up to the balance of 1848, the balance sheet never shows a larger sum invested in government stock and 'other securities' than £53,000, and even till the close of their business, when they had near £6,000,000 of deposits and circulation together, the highest sum stated in that account is £282,000 ...

APPENDIX 10

PROSPECTUS OF THE GLASGOW UNION BANKING COMPANY
Capital, Two million sterling

[reprinted from R. S. Rait, *The History of the Union Bank of Scotland* (Glasgow: 1930), pp. 214–20]

Seventy years have elapsed since a Native Bank was first established in this City, and during the long interval between 1760 and 1829, the population of Glasgow has increased from 25,000 to 200,000 souls; while its Manufactures, Shipping, and General Trade have increased in a much higher ratio. Accordingly, the three local Banking Establishments of this City, (which have in all not more than thirty Partners,) have proved so inadequate to answer the demand for Bank accommodation, that, no fewer than nine Branches of Banks, not indigenous to Glasgow, have been introduced to supply the deficiency, and are now in such active operation, as to engross a very large proportion of her Banking business. Thus have *others* been allowed to reap those profits, which, had her own citizens been more active, and more alive to their own interests, would have been realized by themselves.

Not only, however, are the citizens of Glasgow excluded from participating in the *Banks Profits* created by their own trade, and in a great measure at the mercy of strangers for their bank accommodation, but they have, besides, been for some time back, subjected to great inconvenience, and very many of them to great loss, by the removal of almost all the *Branch Banks*, from the Eastern and Centre to the Western portion of the City. The waste of time thus occasioned to Merchants in the Middle and Eastern Districts, by being compelled to proceed to Virginia Street, Queen Street, or the New Exchange, to transact their Bank business, is a very serious evil, and one universally felt. It is indeed, singular, that along the whole line of the Trongate, there is no Bank farther east than Glassford

903

Street; and yet in that direction lie the *Corn*, the *Fruit*, and *Cattle* Markets; and, generally, a very numerous and opulent body of Capitalists, Manufacturers, and Retail Traders, besides a large body of holders of Heritable Property, all having an obvious interest in the establishment and support of a Bank in that quarter of the City.

The eastern suburban district of Glasgow, too, comes into immediate contact with the great Coal and Agricultural interests of the county, and the proposed Bank would consequently add greatly to the convenience of these parties in transacting their Bank business, whilst the circulation afforded by such a vicinity would materially add to the profits of the Bank. The County Gentlemen, at a Meeting held lately in Hamilton, very strongly expressed their sense of the community of interests which exists between the County and this Town, in their Second Resolution, thus *'That the County has a deep interest in whatever tends to promote the commercial prosperity of the City of Glasgow'*. It can hardly, therefore, be doubted that these Gentlemen will embrace the opportunity now offered to draw the Town and Country interests *still closer together*, by co-operating with their city friends in establishing and supporting the GLASGOW UNION BANKING COMPANY. Such a Bank, placed on a basis at once worthy of the wealthiest and most enterprising County in Scotland, and of the second commercial City in the empire, would form an amalgamation of interests so natural and so necessary, that the undertaking would be no less creditable and advantageous to the parties concerned than beneficial to the public.

It ought not, at same time, to be overlooked, that the community of interests so well expressed in the above resolution as existing between town and country is not confined with respect to Glasgow to the County of Lanark alone; the same may be said of all the neighbouring Counties, especially of the County of Renfrew. Indeed, it may be asked, where is the County in Scotland that is not so connected and so interested? Consequently the advantages to be derived by the establishment of branches in the principal trading towns, by the GLASGOW UNION BANKING COMPANY, will be great and manifold. It will enable merchants and manufacturers who do business with the country, to negotiate their transactions in the shortest possible time, and at the least possible expense. Upon the whole, such a Bank, with its branches under proper management, may be expected to command a large share of the patronage of these merchants and manufacturers who carry on a country trade, as well as of the districts into which such branches may be introduced.

It is thus evident, that a *Local Public Bank*, with a large capital, and numerous proprietors, formed upon liberal principles, is much wanted in Glasgow; and the question, therefore, is, whether such an establishment is likely to be successful? On this point no one at all acquainted with Banks, will have any apprehension.

In England, since the law restricting the number of partners in Banking Companies has been abrogated, so safe and excellent is the Scotch system of Banking considered, that it is fast being adopted into every district of that country. Banks upon such principles, (especially if the proprietors be connected with commercial interests,) cannot fail to insure an extensive business, as the Shareholders will naturally be desirous of securing to themselves, the benefits arising from their own Banking transactions.

The great Banks in Edinburgh of this description have all been eminently successful, as the fortunes acquired by many of their partners, sufficiently attest. The capital stocks of these Banks, in consequence, bear in general a premium of from one to upwards of two hundred per cent.; and the Bank of Scotland, the Royal Bank of Scotland, the British Linen Company, and the Commercial Bank of Scotland, have all found it to be of primary importance to have branches established in Glasgow. Indeed, it is well known, that one of these Banks in particular, owes its success principally to its branch in this City.

It is very remarkable that Glasgow, the greatest commercial and manufacturing town in Scotland, having a constant and active intercourse throughout the kingdom, and an immense foreign trade, should not hitherto have had a Public Local Bank, with a large Capital and numerous Proprietors. *Private Banks* can seldom command sufficient capital to form Establishments upon an extensive scale, with safety either to the public or themselves; nor can they in any thing like the same degree, possess the advantage of such influence and commercial experience, as Banks having numerous proprietors. Neither can *Branch Banks* ever compete with them, as is established by the evidence adduced before the House of Commons, during the late enquiry into the state of the currency. Thus, Mr Kinnear, a most intelligent Edinburgh Banker, when questioned as to the cause why some branches of the Bank of Scotland had given up, states, 'With respect to those that are beyond my memory, I cannot say what was the cause: but those that have been given up within my recollection, in point of fact, *were given up in consequence of the town in which that Branch had originally been established, having accumulated wealth to such a degree, that it could afford a Banking Capital of its own,* and that it had established a Local Bank; then the connection of that Local Bank went so strongly against us, by *fair competition,* that we found we could employ our Capital to better purpose elsewhere, and gave up the Branch'.

Peculiar facilities also, are afforded for the formation of such a Company, by the liberal policy of the Legislature, in conferring by the recent

Act 7, Geo. IV, c. 67, corporate powers upon such associations as the present.

Now is the time, therefore, to institute a Banking Establishment in Glasgow, with a large Capital, and numerous Proprietors. *Such an Establishment*, so greatly wanted, formed upon liberal, yet safe principles, offering local advantages almost unprecedented, cannot fail to meet with the most decided encouragement and success.

To insure the respectability of the Company, and to prevent all jobbing in the stock, it has been resolved –

I   That the name and designation of the Establishment shall be, THE GLASGOW UNION BANKING COMPANY.

II   That the Capital Stock shall be Two Millions sterling, to be increased if necessary, divided into 8,000 shares of £250 each; no individual to subscribe for or hold more than 100 shares, and Partners to be allowed to operate upon their Shares to the extent of one half of their advanced Stock, upon the principle of a cash credit account.

III   That a regular contract of co-partnery, shall be entered into, as soon after the Company has been constituted as possible, containing all such provisions as are required for the security of the Company and the protection of individual Subscribers.

IV   That the first instalment shall not exceed 20 per cent., or £50 per share, the remainder of the Stock, if necessary, to be called up in such a manner and at such periods as shall afterwards be agreed upon.

V   That no transfer of Stock shall be made by any Subscriber until the expiry of one year after the date of the Contract; and in every case of sale the Company to have the first offer.

VI   That the Company shall be considered as formed when the Subscriptions shall amount to 4,000 shares, and the transactions of the Company shall commence and be proceeded in as a Banking Company immediately after Subscribers to the amount of 4,000 shares shall have paid their deposits.

VII   That at all General Meetings, after the contract is approved of, the shareholders shall be entitled to vote after the following ratio:- One share shall be entitled to one vote; three shares to two votes; five shares to three votes; ten shares to four votes; fifteen shares to five votes; twenty shares to six votes; – proxies shall be received, but must be in favour of proprietors, and none shall hold more than one proxy.

VIII That the management shall be vested in a Governor, Deputy-Governor, ten ordinary and ten extraordinary Directors. These Office-Bearers to be elected for the first year, at the first General

Meeting of the Company, and thereafter in terms of the contract of Co-partnery. No person to be eligible as a Director, who does not hold at least, twenty shares of the capital stock.

IX   That in order to extend the business of the Company, Branches shall be established in, and a certain number of shares shall be reserved for, the principal towns in Scotland.

Prospectuses may be had and Subscriptions received at the Office of the interim Secretary, DAVID WILKIE, Esq., Tontine Buildings, Exchange; if by letter, postage free.

Application may also be made in GLASGOW to the following Gentlemen, who act as an Interim Committee, viz:-

David McHaffie, Esq., of Overton, *Chairman*
Robert Stewart, Esq., Merchant in Glasgow
Joseph Bain, Esq., of Morriston
William Dick, Esq., of Wester Lumloch
James W. Robertson, Esq., Merchant in Glasgow
Robert McHaffie, Esq., Merchant in Glasgow
James Stewart, Esq., Merchant in Glasgow
Elias Gibb, Esq., Merchant in Glasgow
James Lockhart Spencer, Esq., Merchant in Glasgow
Walter Ewing, Esq., Merchant in Glasgow
John Miller, Esq., Merchant in Glasgow
Alexr McAslan, Esq., Merchant in Glasgow
John Binnie, Esq., Builder in Glasgow
Alexander Drysdale, Esq., Merchant in Glasgow
William McEwan, Esq., Merchant in Glasgow
George Lewis, Esq., Merchant in Glasgow
Robert Kerr, Esq., Merchant in Glasgow; and
William Mitchell, Esq., Interim Manager.

And In

EDINBURGH, TO Roderick McKenzie, Esq., ws, 5 Forth Street

GREENOCK,	Archibald McKellar, Esq.
STIRLING,	Messrs. Wright & McEwan
PERTH,	John Ballandene, Esq.
AYR,	P. Cowan, Esq.
LANARK,	Thomas Heweit, Esq.
HADDINGTON,	John Stobie, Esq.

DUNBAR,   William Hamilton Ritchie, Esq.
DUNBLANE,   Andrew Malloch, Esq.
PAISLEY,   John Crawford, Esq.
HAMILTON,   Thomas Dykes, Esq.

Glasgow, 1st January 1830.

APPENDIX 11a

GOVERNORS OF BANK OF SCOTLAND, 1695–1995

1696–1697	John Holland
1697–1728	David Melville, third Earl of Leven
1728–1740	Alexander Hume, second Earl of Marchmont, KT
1740–1742	Charles Hope, first Earl of Hopetoun, KT
1742–1762	John Hay, fourth Marquess of Tweeddale
1763–1790	Hugh Hume, third Earl of Marchmont
1790–1811	Henry Dundas, first Viscount Melville
1812–1851	Robert Dundas, second Viscount Melville, KT
1851–1860	James Andrew Broun Ramsay, tenth Earl and first Marquess of Dalhousie, KT
1861–1862	John Campbell, second Marquess of Breadalbane, KT
1863–1870	George Hamilton-Baillie, eleventh Earl of Haddington, KT
1870–1903	Sir John Hamilton Dalrymple, tenth Earl of Stair, KT
1904–1921	Alexander Hugh Bruce, sixth Baron Balfour of Burleigh, KT, GCMG, GCVO
1921–1924	William John Mure, CB
1924–1955	Rt Hon. Sidney Herbert, sixteenth Baron Elphinstone, KT, LLD
1955–1957	Sir John Craig, CBE, DL, LLD
1957–1966	Steven Bilsland, first Baron Bilsland, KT, MC, DL, LLD
1966–1972	Henry Alexander Hepburne-Scott, tenth Lord Polwarth, TD, DL, LLD, DLitt, DUniv, CA
1972–1981	Ronald John Bilsland Colville, second Baron Clydesmuir, KT, CB, MBE, TD, LLD, DSc
1981–1991	Sir Thomas Neilson Risk, BL, LLD, FRSE
1991–	Sir David Bruce Pattullo, CBE, BA, FRSE, FCIBS

APPENDIX 11b

DEPUTY GOVERNORS
OF BANK OF SCOTLAND,
1695–1995

1696–1697	William Erskine
1697–1699	George Clerk, Jr
1699–1702	Robert Blackwood
1702–1704	John Marjoribanks
1704–1706	Robert Watson of Murehouse
1706–1708	James Marjoribanks
1708–1710	John Hay
1710–1712	James Gordon
1712–1714	James Marjoribanks
1714–1716	John Jamieson of Balmure
1716–1718	Thomas Brown
1718–1720	Robert Marjoribanks
1720–1722	John Jamieson of Balmure
1722–1724	James Marjoribanks
1724–1725	John Jamieson
1725–1727	Thomas Brown
1727–1729	Robert Marjoribanks
1729–1731	James Gordon
1731–1733	Andrew Marjoribanks
1733–1735	Alexander Arbuthnot
1735–1737	Andrew Marjoribanks
1737–1739	Alexander Arbuthnot
1739–1742	Andrew Marjoribanks
1742–1745	Alexander Arbuthnot
1745–1748	Andrew Marjoribanks
1748–1750	Thomas Fairholme
1750–1753	Peter Wedderburn, Advocate
1753–1757	John Forrest

1757	David Inglis
1757–1771	John Forrest
1771–1773	David Gavin of Langton
1773–1779	David, Earl of Leven
1779–1789	Henry Dundas
1790–1815	Patrick Miller of Dalswinton
1816–1819	Adam Rolland of Gask, Advocate
1820–1837	Lord Balgray
1837–1843	George, fourth Earl of Glasgow
1843–1848	Sir Alexander Charles Gibson Maitland of Cliftonhall, Bt
1848–1868	Sir George Clerk of Penicuik, Bt
1868–1878	Sir William Stirling-Maxwell, Bt, KT, MP
1878–1883	John William, Lord Ramsay, MP, later Earl of Dalhousie, KT
1884–1904	Lord Balfour of Burleigh, KT
1904–1908	Marquess of Linlithgow, KT, GCMG
1909–1917	Lord Binning, CB, MVO
1917–1921	William John Mure, CB
1921–1924	Lord Elphinstone
1925–1934	Sir Ralph Anstruther of Balcaskie, Bt
1935–1945	Lord Henry Scott
1945–1946	William Whitelaw, LLD
1946–1950	James Gourlay, BSc
1950–1955	Sir John Craig, CBE, DL, LLD
1955–1957	Lord Bilsland, KT, MC, DL, LLD
1957–1960	Robert McCosh, OBE, MC, WS
1960–1966	Lord Polwarth, TD, DL, LLD, CA
1966–1971	James B. Findlay, CBE, DL
1971–1972	Lord Clydesmuir, KT, CB, MBE, TD, LLD, DSc
1972–1977	Thomas R. Craig, CBE, TD, LLD
1977–1981	Thomas N. Risk, BL, LLD, FRSE
1977–1991	Lord Balfour of Burleigh, CEng, FIEE, FRSE
1988–1991	D. Bruce Pattullo, CBE, BA, FRSE, FCIBS
1991–	Thomas O. Hutchison, BSc, FRSE, FRSA
1991–	Sir John Shaw, CBE, KStJ, BL, FRSE, CA, FCMA

APPENDIX 12a

TREASURERS OF BANK OF SCOTLAND, 1695–1995

1696–1699	James Marjoribanks
1699–1700	James Cockburn
1700–1741	David Drummond
1741–1757	David Scott
1757–1767	David Inglis
1767–1790	James Spence
1786–1792	Thomas Steuart
1792–1802	James Fraser
1802–1824	Robert Forrester
1824–1832	William Cadell
1832–1859	Alexander Blair
1859–1863	John Mackenzie
1863–1879	David Davidson
1879–1898	James Adams Wenley
1898–1917	Sir George Anderson
1916–1920	John Rae
1920–1934	George J. Scott
1934–1938	A. W. Morton Beveridge
1938–1942	J. W. Macfarlane
1942–1952	J. B. Crawford
1952–1966	Sir William Watson, CA, FIB(Scot.)
1966–1970	James Letham, DLitt, FIB(Scot.)
1970–1974	Thomas W. Walker, CBE, BL, FIB(Scot.)
1974–1979	Andrew M. Russell, CBE, FIB(Scot.)
1979–1988	D. Bruce Pattullo, CBE, BA, FRSE, FCIBS
1988–	Peter A. Burt, MA, MBA, FCIBS

From 1966, the Treasurer also held the appointment of General Manager, and from 1988 that of Chief General Manager.

APPENDIX 12b

SECRETARIES OF BANK
OF SCOTLAND, 1695–1995

1696–1746	David Spence
1746–1767	James Spence
1767–1786	Thomas Steuart
1786–1792	James Fraser
1792–1796	William Wardrop
1792–1805	George Neilson
1800–1805	William Wardrop
1802–1808	James Fraser
1805–1832	George Sandy
1824–1868	Archibald Bennet
1828–1833	Alexander Brodie
1847–1858	William Simson
1858–1883	George M. Tytler
1883–1892	J. F. Stormonth Darling
1892–1910	Duncan McNeill
1910–1920	Peter Macdonald
1920–1931	A. J. Rose
1931–1937	W. A. Tait, MA
1937–1938	J. W. Macfarlane
1938–1942	J. B. Crawford
1942–1951	A. A. Gunn, MC
1951–1954	John Wilson
1954–1955	James Letham
1955–1971	John B. Rankin, BL, FIB(scot.)
1971–1979	David G. Antonio, FIB(scot.)
1979–1984	Joan Smith, MA, LLB, PhD
1984–	Hugh K. Young, TD, CA, FCIBS

As a result of further research since the publication of Alan Cameron, *Bank of Scotland 1695–1995: A Very Singular Institution* (Edinburgh: 1995), the list of Secretaries from 1696 to 1883 has been revised.

APPENDIX 13

MANAGEMENT BOARD OF BANK OF SCOTLAND, 1981–95

1981–1982	James M. McMillan, TD, FIB(Scot.)
1981–1983	Ivan R. S. Robson, FIB(Scot.)
1981–1984	Joan Smith, MA, LLB, PhD
1981–1984	John F. Wilson, FIB(Scot.)
1981–1985	James M. Young, FIB(Scot.)
1981–1988	D. Bruce Pattullo, BA, FIB(Scot.)
1981–1989	Andrew S. R. Davidson, FIB(Scot.)
1982–1989	Robert L. Cromar, FIB(Scot.)
1983–1992	Archie T. Gibson, FCIBS
1984–1992	Thomas Bennie, FCIBS
1984–	Hugh K. Young, TD, CA, FCIBS
1985–	Peter A. Burt, MA, MBA, FCIBS
1986–	J. Robin Browning, BA, FCIBS
1986–	Gavin G. Masterton, FCIBS
1989–	W. Gordon McQueen, BSc, CA, FCIBS
1989–	Iain W. St C. Scott, CA, FCIBS
1989–1993	Robert J. J. Wickham, FCIBS
1991–1995	Alan J. R. Thomson, FCIBS, MIPM
1992–	Fraser D. Campbell, MA, MSc, FCIBS
1992–	J. Rowland Mitchell, BSc, PhD, FCIBS
1994–	Colin S. McGill, LLB, CA, MCIBS
1994–	Colin Matthew, MBA, FCIBS
1994–	George E. Mitchell, FCIBS

APPENDIX 14

INDEX OF THE FIRST 300 BANK OF SCOTLAND CASH-ACCOUNT HOLDERS, 1729–47

Name	Occupation	Address	Account start
Agnew, Lady Mary			Sep 1739
Allan, Thomas	merchant	Edinburgh	Nov 1736
Anderson, David	writer	Edinburgh	Jul 1734
Anderson, James		Abercairney	Apr 1735
Anderson, James	tenant	Hermistown	May 1736
Anderson, John – see Dunbar, George			
Anderson, Patrick	brewer	Leith	Feb 1739
Anstruther, Charles	advocate		Nov 1739
Arbuthnot & Fairholme, Messrs – see Fairholme & Arbuthnot			
Arbuthnot, Alexander	merchant	Edinburgh	Oct 1731
Arbuthnot, Alexander	merchant	Edinburgh	Jan 1734
Arbuthnot, Alexander (plus Fairholms)	merchant	Edinburgh	Jul 1735
Arbuthnot, Alexander, James Blair and Hay of Montbleiry (trustees)			Jan 1735
Arbuthnot, George	merchant	Edinburgh	Feb 1739
Arrot, Thomas			Oct 1736
Aytoune, William	goldsmith	Edinburgh	Dec 1740
Baillie, Robert	merchant	Edinburgh	Feb 1733
Baillie, Thomas	w.s.		Feb 1740
Baillie, William – see Cuming, William Jr			
Baird, Sir William		Newtylles	Dec 1736
Balcanquell, Henry	writer	Edinburgh	Feb 1741
Balfour, John	merchant	Edinburgh	Jun 1739
Balhaven, Lord John			Sep 1733
Bell, Joseph	writer	Edinburgh	Feb 1734
Belsches, Thomas	sheriff clerk depute	Edinburgh	Aug 1731
Berry, David	merchant	Edinburgh	Aug 1735
Berry, David	merchant	Edinburgh	Nov 1736
Berry, William	merchant	Edinburgh	May 1738
Bissett, James	merchant	Montrose	Jan 1741
Black, William	clerk of regality of Dunfarmling		Jun 1740
Blackwood, Alexander	merchant	Edinburgh	Nov 1729
Blair, Alexander		Balmyle	Nov 1736
Blair, Thomas	merchant	Dundee	May 1734

915

Name	Occupation	Address	Account start
Bogle, George Jr of Daldowie	merchant	Glasgow	Nov 1735
Bogle, John	w.s.	Edinburgh	Mar 1732
Bogle, John	merchant	Glasgow	Jan 1732
Bogle, Matthew	merchant	Glasgow	Jan 1739
Bogle, Robert	merchant	Glasgow	Jan 1730
Bogle, Robert Sr	merchant	Glasgow	Feb 1733
Bonar, Andrew	merchant	Edinburgh	Jul 1740
Borthwick, John		Crookstoun	Feb 1734
Bosewall, George	writer	Edinburgh	Sep 1736
Bosewall, George	writer	Edinburgh	Nov 1742
Brodie, Thomas	w.s.		May 1740
Brown, Thomas	merchant	Edinburgh	Feb 1730
Bruce, David	writer	Edinburgh	Aug 1740
Buchanan, Andrew	merchant	Glasgow	May 1733
Bull, Robert	merchant	Edinburgh	Dec 1735
Burnet, John	merchant	Aberdeen	Dec 1734
Carmichaell, John	merchant	Edinburgh	Jun 1736
Carmichaell, John Jr	merchant	Edinburgh	Jul 1737
Carmichaell, William	advocate	Edinburgh	Dec 1731
Carmichaell, William	advocate	Skirling	Jun 1740
Carnegie, Sir James, Bt		Pillarran	Feb 1741
Carse, William	collector of excise		Dec 1737
Christie, Alexander	writer	Edinburgh	Jan 1734
City of Edinburgh		Edinburgh	Dec 1740
Clarkson, John	baxter	Edinburgh	May 1736
Cleghorn, Thomas	merchant	Edinburgh	Feb 1731
Clerk, Hugh	merchant	Edinburgh	Dec 1729
Cochrane, John	merchant	Edinburgh	Mar 1739
Cochrane, William	Dr of medicine	Roughsoill	May 1739
Cockburn, Archibald	merchant	Edinburgh	Jan 1731
Colvell, James – see Loch, William			
Cormock, Robert	merchant	Leith	Jan 1735
Coult, Oliver	writer	Edinburgh	Dec 1734
Coulter, John	merchant	Glasgow	Mar 1733
Craig, Captain William			Apr 1742
Craigie, John	advocate	Dumbarnie	Mar 1742
Craigie, Patrick	merchant	Edinburgh	Oct 1737
Crawfurd, Hew	w.s.		May 1734
Cree, Patrick	merchant	Perth	Nov 1733
Cuming, William	merchant	Edinburgh	Dec 1735
Cuming, William Jr	merchant	Edinburgh	Mar 1736
Cuming, William Jr for William Baillie	merchant	Edinburgh	Feb 1740
Currie, John	merchant	Edinburgh	Jun 1740
Davidson, John	Clerk to Justiciary		Sep 1733
Dean, James	merchant	Edinburgh	Sep 1736
Dempster, George	merchant	Dundee	Jun 1732
Dempster, George	merchant	Dundee	Nov 1737
Dickson, David	writer	Edinburgh	Dec 1734
Dinwiddie, Laurence	merchant	Glasgow	Nov 1739
Don, John	merchant	Edinburgh	Feb 1732
Donald, Robert	merchant	Greenock	Aug 1731
Donaldson, James Jr	merchant	Edinburgh	Apr 1738
Drummond, George		of Blair Drummond	Nov 1739
Drummond, William		Grange	Mar 1730
Dunbar, George and Anderson, John	merchant	Edinburgh	Mar 1732
Dundas, Robert	merchant	Edinburgh	May 1734
Dundas, Robert of Arniston			Nov 1740

Dundas, Thomas Jr	merchant	Edinburgh	Mar 1740
Dunlop, Robert	merchant	Glasgow	Oct 1735
Eccles, Martin and Spens, David	surgeon	Edinburgh	Jul 1738
Edmonstone, John	writer	Edinburgh	Nov 1736
Eliot, William	writer	Edinburgh	Jun 1734
Eliot, William	writer	Edinburgh	May 1738
Erskine, David of Dun, Esq.	Senator of the College of Justice		Feb 1739
Erskine, Thomas	merchant	Edinburgh	Nov 1740
Ewing, Robert	writer	Edinburgh	Dec 1734
Fairholm, Adam of Greenhill			Jul 1740
Fairholme & Arbuthnot, Messrs			Jan 1741
Fairlie, Ralph	manager, Easter Sugar House (Partner)	Glasgow	Nov 1734
Fairlie, Ralph	manager, Easter Sugar House	Glasgow	Jan 1739
Fairlie, Ralph	manager, Easter Sugar House	Glasgow	Apr 1741
Farquhar, Captain James			May 1738
Farquharson, Charles	w.s.	Edinburgh	Dec 1729
Farquharson, John	writer	Edinburgh	Aug 1734
Fenton, Robert	merchant	Edinburgh	Jul 1736
Forbes, Sir William	advocate		Mar 1739
Forrest, John	merchant	Edinburgh	Sep 1731
Forrest, John & Co.	merchant	Edinburgh	Apr 1740
Fraser, Thomas		Gortulegg	Nov 1740
Fraser, William	w.s.		Sep 1736
Gairden, William	writer	Edinburgh	Aug 1739
Gairles, Lord Alexander – see Garlies, Lord			
Gall, David	writer	Edinburgh	Sep 1740
Galloway, Earl of – see Garlies, Lord			
Gardner, Thomas	merchant	Edinburgh	May 1737
Garlies, Lord Alexander (later Lord Galloway)			Apr 1730
Gibson, Alexander		Pentland	Nov 1732
Gibson, John		Durie	Mar 1734
Gibson, John		Durie	Apr 1743
Gibson, Thomas	Under Clerk of Session	Edinburgh	Jan 1730
Gordon, George Sr of Gordonbank	writer	Edinburgh	Jul 1738
Gordon, Robert	writer		Jan 1739
Graham, William	merchant	Edinburgh	Jul 1731
Granger, William	tenant	Collingtoun	Dec 1741
Grant, Lachlan	writer	Edinburgh	Nov 1739
Grant, William	advocate		Sep 1731
Gray, Captain Charles			May 1738
Greenfield, Andrew	merchant	Dalkeith	Jul 1744
Haigie, George	merchant	Kirkcaldy	Jun 1739
Haliburton, George	merchant	Edinburgh	Mar 1732
Haliburton, John of Muirhouselaw	merchant	Edinburgh	Feb 1736
Halket, Captain Peter			May 1730
Hall, William	one of the principal clerks of session	Whitehall	Jul 1741
Hamilton, Gavin	merchant	Edinburgh	Jul 1737
Hamilton, Hugh	merchant	Edinburgh	Dec 1740
Hamilton, Robert	merchant	Edinburgh	Nov 1732
Hamilton, Robert	merchant	Edinburgh	May 1736
Hamilton, Robert	w.s.		Jan 1740
Hay, Andrew		Mont Blairie	Mar 1743
Hay, James		Tarbet	Oct 1738
Hay, James	w.s.		Dec 1740

Name	Occupation	Address	Account start
Hay, James (factor for execrs of Charles Shirriff)	merchant	Prestonpans	Apr 1741
Hay, John	w.s.		May 1741
Hay, Thomas		Mordingtoun	Mar 1730
Heiggie, George – see Haigie, George			
Henderson, Francis	merchant	Dundee	Jul 1735
Henderson, John Jr		Bredholm	Oct 1735
Hepburn, Robert	w.s.		Dec 1735
Hislop, John	merchant	Dalkeith	Jun 1740
Home, James	w.s.		Jul 1733
Hope, John	merchant	Edinburgh	Sep 1732
Horsburgh, David	Dr of medicine		May 1736
Hunter, William	merchant	Dalkeith (and Edinburgh)	Nov 1736
Hunter, William	merchant	Edinburgh	Jul 1733
Husband, Paul	merchant	Edinburgh	Sep 1747
Hutton, William	merchant	Edinburgh	Dec 1729
Inglis, George	writer	Edinburgh	Jun 1734
Inglis, John	merchant	Edinburgh	Jun 1741
Inglis, Sir John		Cramond	Jul 1737
Jackson, James	merchant	Dalkeith	Apr 1740
Jamieson, Andrew	merchant	Edinburgh	Mar 1733
Jamieson, John	merchant	Leith	Sep 1734
Jamieson, John	Co-partner of the roperie of South Leith	Leith	Nov 1737
Jamieson, John	merchant	Glasgow	Apr 1737
Jamieson, John	merchant	Glasgow	Aug 1740
Jamison, John	merchant	Leith	Mar 1737
Keith, Alexander	Under Clerk of Session	Edinburgh	May 1730
Kinloch, Sir James			Apr 1732
Lauder, John, Esq.		Winepark	Feb 1736
Lesslie, George	merchant	Banff	Sep 1740
Livingston, George	Under Clerk of Session	Edinburgh	Feb 1731
Livingston, George	Under Clerk of Session	Edinburgh	Feb 1735?
Livingston, James	son of George Livingston		Nov 1740
Loch, George	merchant	Edinburgh	Aug 1730
Loch, William	writer	Edinburgh	Feb 1738
Loch, William for Colvell, James	writer	Edinburgh	Feb 1739
Lothian, Edward	jeweller	Edinburgh	Apr 1739
McCulloch & Tod	merchants	Edinburgh	Jun 1740
MacDouall, Patrick	merchant	Edinburgh	Jun 1736
McDougal, William	merchant	Edinburgh	Jul 1731
McDougall, William	merchant	Edinburgh	Nov 1741
McKenzie, Alexander	Principal Clerk of Session	Edinburgh	Mar 1734
McKenzie, John	writer	Edinburgh	Jan 1735
McKenzie, Sir James	Senator of College of Justice	Roystoun	Nov 1731
Mackewan, William	w.s. (eldest son of John Mackewan of Muckley, commissary clerk of Dunkeld)		Apr 1740
McLeod, John	advocate	Muirevenside	Mar 1734
McLeod, John	advocate	Muirevenside	Nov 1738

McLeod, Roderick	w.s.		Feb 1736
McLeod, Roderick	w.s.		Jul 1740
Maitland, Alexander	merchant	Edinburgh	Aug 1731
Malcolm, Robert	merchant	Edinburgh	Jan 1738
Manderston, Pat	merchant	Edinburgh	Jul 1730
Mansfield, James	merchant	Edinburgh	Apr 1737
Marjoribanks, Andrew	merchant	Edinburgh	Jan 1730
Marjoribanks, Andrew	merchant	Edinburgh	Aug 1730
Marjoribanks, Andrew	merchant	Edinburgh	Jun 1734
Marjoribanks, Edward	merchant	Edinburgh	Dec 1734
Marjoribanks, James	merchant	Edinburgh	Aug 1740
Marjoribanks, Robert	merchant	Edinburgh	May 1730
Martin, Arthur		Dunfarmling	Oct 1740
Mason, Alexander – see Meason, Alexander			
Meason, Alexander	merchant	Edinburgh	Apr 1737
Menzies, Robert	writer	Edinburgh	May 1739
Merry, Thomas	merchant	Kirkcudbright	Feb 1730
Miller, George	merchant	Edinburgh	Aug 1730
Miller, George and Spence, David Jr – see Spence, David Jr (cf. Miller, George)			
Miller, William	w.s.		Feb 1737
Milne, James	merchant	Montrose	Feb 1734
Mitchell, David	jeweller	Edinburgh	Jul 1736
Mitchelson, Samuel	w.s.		May 1738
Moffat, William Jr	merchant	Edinburgh	Jun 1738
Montgomerie, Robert	merchant	Edinburgh	Jan 1736
Moubray, Robert Jr	writer	Edinburgh	Dec 1735
Murray, Anthony	merchant	Edinburgh	Jul 1739
Murray, Charles	factor to Robert Lord Blantyre		Apr 1739
Murray, William	Receiver Depute	Edinburgh	Jan 1730
Murray, William	merchant	Edinburgh	Mar 1739
Myln, James		Mylnfield	Jan 1740
Nasmyth, James	writer	Edinburgh	May 1733
Nisbet, John	merchant	Edinburgh	Feb 1737
Nisbet, John	merchant	Edinburgh	Nov 1742
Ogilvie, Thomas	merchant	Dundee	Sep 1731
Ogilvie, Thomas	merchant	Dundee	Oct 1739
Orr, John		Borrowfield	Nov 1734
Oswald, Alexander	merchant	Glasgow	May 1732
Paterson, Thomas	merchant	Dundee	Nov 1739
Patillo, Henry	merchant	Dundee	Feb 1733
Preston, James	w.s.		May 1733
Pringle, Alison	daughter to deceased Rev. Pringle	of Symington (Lanarkshire)	May 1738
Pringle, John	writer	Edinburgh	Jun 1739
Pringle, Robert	advocate		Jun 1735
Pringle, Sir Robert of Stitchill, Bt			May 1740
Pringle, Thomas	w.s.	Edinburgh	Dec 1729
Pringle, Thomas	w.s.		May 1731
Purves, Alexander	merchant	Edinburgh	Sep 1737
Ramsay, Andrew	merchant	Glasgow	Apr 1735
Ramsay, Willoughby	merchant	Edinburgh	Apr 1738
Reid, David	writer	Edinburgh	Aug 1731
Reid, George and Tod, John	merchants	Edinburgh	Sep 1739
Renton, William	tenant	Birsly	Aug 1741
Robertson, Charles	w.s.	Edinburgh	Aug 1730
Robertson, George	w.s.	Edinburgh	Jan 1730
Robertson, James	merchant	Edinburgh	Dec 1740
Robertson, Robert	merchant	Glasgow	Nov 1731
Robertson, William	writer	Edinburgh	Feb 1730

Name	Occupation	Address	Account start
Robertson, William	writer	Edinburgh	Aug 1733
Robertson, William	writer	Edinburgh	Sep 1735
Ross, David of Inverchasley			Jul 1740
Ross, George		Lirkery	Aug 1741
Russell, William	commissar clerk depute	Edinburgh	Mar 1736
Schaw, William	merchant	Edinburgh	Jan 1732
Scott, David	merchant	Edinburgh	Feb 1734
Scott, James		Logie	May 1739
Scott, Sir John		Ancrum	Feb 1737
Seller, William	writer	Edinburgh	May 1730
Seller, William for Westerfedall	merchant	Edinburgh	Nov 1736
Seton, George	tenant	Seton	Sep 1736
Seton, James	merchant	Edinburgh	Jul 1730
Seton, James & Co.	merchant	Edinburgh	May 1734
Seton, James, Treasurer to George Watson's Hospital and merchant co.			Jul 1738
Seton, Robert	writer	Edinburgh	Jun 1738
Shirriff, Alexander	merchant	Leith	Aug 1736
Shirriff, Charles	merchant	Prestonpans	Nov 1734
Shirriff, Charles, executors of – see Hay, James			
Sinclair, Charles	advocate	Hermistoun	Nov 1735
Sinclair, John	writer	Edinburgh	Sep 1740
Skene, George of that Ilk			Mar 1741
Smith, David		Methven	May 1730
Somerville, William	advocate		Jul 1737
Spence, David Jr and Miller, George & Co.	merchants	Edinburgh	Mar 1737
Spence, Henry	writer	Edinburgh	Jun 1739
Spens, David w.s. – see Eccles, Martin			
St Clair, Charles – see Sinclair, Charles			
Stewart, Andrew	merchant	Dundee	Sep 1731
Stewart, Archibald	merchant	Edinburgh	Jan 1731
Stewart, Gilbert	merchant	Edinburgh	May 1733
Stewart, James	merchant	Edinburgh	Dec 1733
Stewart, John	merchant	Edinburgh	Aug 1732
Stewart, John	advocate		May 1734
Stewart, Sir Michael of Blackhall, Bt			May 1738
Stewart, Sir Robert		Tillicoultry	Nov 1732
Stirling, James	merchant	Edinburgh	Dec 1734
Stirling, James	agent for the Scottish Mining Co.		Feb 1741
Swinton, Robert	merchant	North Berwick	Apr 1734
Tod, Archibald	writer	Edinburgh	Apr 1735
Tod, John and Reid, George – see Reid, George			
Tod, Oliver	merchant	Edinburgh	Aug 1740
Tod, William Jr	merchant	Edinburgh	Dec 1736
Traill, John	merchant	Edinburgh	May 1740
Trotter, Thomas	brother to Henry Trotter of Mortonhall		Mar 1737
Turnbull, George	w.s.		Dec 1740
Turnbull, William	merchant	Leith	Nov 1735
Tweeddale, John, Marquis of			Feb 1737
Veitch, William	w.s.	Edinburgh	Jul 1730
Wallace, John & Co.			Apr 1739
Wardrop, John	wright	Edinburgh	Apr 1736
Watson, Alexander	merchant		May 1730
Watson, James	merchant	Stirling	Feb 1730

Watson, James	merchant	Edinburgh	Jul 1737
Watson's, George (Hospital and merchant co.) – see Seton, James			
Wauchope, William	merchant	Edinburgh	Dec 1737
Wedderburn, Peter	advocate	Edinburgh	May 1730
Wedderburn, Robert	merchant	Dunfermline	May 1738
Weir, Alexander	writer	Edinburgh	Mar 1735
Wemyss, George	merchant	Edinburgh	Nov 1739
White, Robert	merchant	Edinburgh	Dec 1729
White, Robert	merchant	Kirkcaldy	Apr 1734
Wight, Alexander	tenant	Ormistoun	Jun 1737
Willison, David	merchant	Dundee	Jul 1740
Wilson, John	merchant	Edinburgh	Mar 1730
Young, Alexander	w.s.	Edinburgh	Dec 1729
Young, John	carpenter	Leith	Feb 1730

Source: BS 1/106/1–6, Cash account progressive ledgers.

APPENDIX 15

INDEX OF BANK OF SCOTLAND CASH-ACCOUNT HOLDERS WHO WERE WOMEN, 1729–63

Name	Address	Account start	Archive reference BS 1/106/
Agnew, Lady Mary		10 Sep 1739	5
Baillie, Dame Grizell		12 Dec 1749	10
Balcarres, Elizabeth, Dowager Countess of		16 Feb 1753	14
Balmerino, Lady Elizabeth		19 Jan 1763	20
Barclay, Mrs B.		10 Jun 1763	20
Beard, Mrs Elizabeth	Huntington	14 Jun 1762	20
Beveridge, Ann	Portsburgh	6 May 1763	20
Binning, Mrs Isobell		27 Sep 1762	20
Blair, Abigail	Kirkbraehead	12 May 1763	20
Bonthorn, Margaret	Elly	16 Jun 1763	20
Boyd, Margaret [1]	Leith Walk	3 May 1763	20
Boyle, Rt Hon. Lady Janet		13 May 1763	20
Boyle, Lady Margaret		1 Jun 1763	20
Brown, Elizabeth and Isobel		11 Oct 1763	20
Brown, Mrs Mary Anne	Edinburgh	29 Oct 1763	20
Buchanan, Marion	Edinburgh	14 Jul 1763	20
Callender, Margaret		13 May 1763	20
Campbell, Helen		2 Mar 1763	20
Carsland, Elizabeth	Edinburgh	19 May 1763	20
Christie, Janet	Edinburgh	16 Dec 1763	20
Cochrane, Catherine		16 Nov 1747	9
Cochrane, Isobel		3 Jan 1763	20
Corbet, Margaret		7 Apr 1763	20
Corser, Janet alias Bell	Dalkeith	17 May 1763	20
Dalrymple, Martha		5 Apr 1763	20
Davidson, Elizabeth	Edinburgh	3 Mar 1763	20
Dickson, Mary		21 Oct 1743	8
Dods, Elizabeth [2]	Edinburgh	23 May 1763	20
Elphinstone, Mary	Grangepans	27 May 1763	20
Fairlie, Margaret		24 Jul 1763	20
Falconer, Mary		4 May 1763	20
Ferguson, Jacobina	Edinburgh	20 Oct 1763	20
Fleming, Agnes		29 Mar 1763	20

Fowler, Marion		20 Jun 1763	20
Gray, Anne [3]		11 Feb 1763	20
Halkett, Lady Emilia		22 Jan 1763	20
Hamilton, Lady Mary of Baldoon		3 Mar 1744	8
Horne, Nelly	Leith	16 May 1763	20
Jaffray, Margaret	Edinburgh	3 Jun 1763	20
Johnston, Jean [4]		16 May 1763	20
Kerr, Barbara		6 Sep 1762	20
Kincardine, Janet, Countess of		22 Jan 1755	13
Lauder, Margaret		17 May 1763	20
Lion, Elizabeth	Edinburgh	10 Dec 1762	20
McAlpine, Elizabeth		31 May 1763	20
McDonald, Margaret	Kingsburgh	10 Jun 1763	20
McGill, Sarah [5]	Kirkcaldy	25 May 1763	20
McKain, Jean [6]	Edinburgh	12 Jan 1763	20
Maitland, Katherine and Ann		10 Feb 1763	20
More, Mary	Caldown	20 May 1763	20
Murray, Margaret	Edinburgh	28 May 1763	20
Nimo, Janet [7]	Bankhead	18 May 1763	20
Nisbet, Ann	Edinburgh	16 May 1763	20
Pringle, Alison		4 May 1738	3
Reid, Margaret		16 May 1763	20
Rhind, Margaret	Edinburgh	18 May 1763	20
Richardson, Euphemia		6 Dec 1762	20
Seton, Dame Barbara		23 Mar 1762	20
Short, Margaret		16 May 1763	20
Skene, Katherine		10 Jan 1763	20
Slater, Lillias	Carcant	18 Dec 1762	20
Sleigh, Mary alias Brodie		22 Feb 1759	16
Smith, Cecilia [8]		6 Dec 1762	20
Smith, Janet [9]		18 Jun 1763	20
Smith, Jannet [10]	Falkirk	28 Jul 1762	20
Spalding, Elizabeth	Edinburgh	18 May 1763	20
St Clair, Margaret		24 Jan 1763	20
Stewart, Katherine [11]	Edinburgh	10 May 1763	20
Strachan, Margaret	Edinburgh	1 Jul 1763	20
Taylor, Margaret	Edinburgh	6 Jun 1763	20
Wade, Ann	Yeaster Park	17 May 1763	20
Walker, Margaret	Eastermains of Ormiston	6 Jul 1763	20
Watson, Margaret [12]	Edinburgh	13 Apr 1763	20
Weemyss, Mrs		16 May 1763	20
Williamson, Janet		11 Mar 1763	20
Williamson, Katherine [13]	Edinburgh	17 May 1763	20
Wilson, Jean	Bridge of Braid	16 Nov 1762	20
Yorstoun, Ann	Cannongate	16 Apr 1763	20

Notes:
1. merchant, Leith Walk.
2. shopkeeper, Edinburgh.
3. servant.
4. attending Lady Buchan.
5. merchant, Kirkcaldy.
6. merchant, Edinburgh.
7. tenant, Bankhead.
8. servant to Commissary Archibald Murray.
9. servant to Mr Congallons, surgeon.
10. merchant, Falkirk.
11. merchant, Edinburgh.
12. schoolmistress, Edinburgh.
13. shopkeeper, Edinburgh.

Source: BS 1/106/1 – 23, Cash account progressive ledgers, 1729–63.

APPENDIX 16

HOW WE BUILT UP THE BRANCH IN BIRMINGHAM

A. A. Whiteford, Manager, Birmingham Region

I do not consider that we in Birmingham do any different a job from that challenging each of the Bank's other Managers, the only factor peculiar to Birmingham is the sheer scope of the business activity, and it was noticeable that proposals were for larger amounts than I had experienced within the Scottish business scene. The English domestic scene is dominated by the major clearers and, to appreciate the environment, one has to recognise that they are highly organised and innovative in their operation. They do, however, suffer from their sheer size, which inhibits their ability to make decisions and, from a customer's point of view, sometimes it makes it extremely difficult for the customer to have a meaningful discussion with senior Officials. When we opened in 1980, the West Midlands were starting the worst recession they have experienced and this worked to our benefit, in that many long established business connections experienced for the first time a downturn and their 'friendly' banker, in some instances, was proving less than helpful. The clearers did, I feel, take an overall view of certain industries, without taking sufficient cognisance of the management running these businesses and this enabled us to obtain several very meaningful connections.

Let me say that the only real way of establishing a business is from dealings with the professional community and the customers, and convincing them that the Bank of Scotland are willing and able to assist them and their clients. One of the major difficulties is in making a meaningful impact on a conurbation as large as the West Midlands, and we did this by a minimum of advertising in the local press, countered by direct approaches to most of the major professional firms of accountants, lawyers, brokers, etc. with, at the same time, a very active input from the members of staff in the local community. I myself identified with the city by buying a house within one mile of the city centre, and during

924

the first 12 months attended as many seminars/functions as possible and while, in many instances, this did not produce business, it did make the business community aware of our presence. At the same time, we perused the Birmingham's *Who's Who* and wrote to all the people therein with a Scottish background, simply advising them of our presence and our willingness to assist them. Initially, it was my experience that we were being offered some very difficult propositions, and some that the clearers were deliberating over for too long a time, and the only way of counteracting this was for us to spend time in doing a thorough assessment and going back to them with an offer as soon as possible. In some instances, in declining proposals you established a good rapport with the clients, in that, at the end of the day, they appreciated that you had been the first financial adviser to give them a decision and this stood you in good stead in future discussions. The other aspect which one must not lose sight of is that it is essential that you quote realistically and competitively and do not thereafter shade your rates materially, as this seriously affects your credibility. In negotiating with clients, I always made the point that we would not expect an offer to be used against us in negotiations with their existing bankers and I found this to be honoured by them in almost every case.

One of my initial anxieties was of our ability to properly service our clients' banking requirements, 300 miles from Edinburgh, and I would just like to pay credit to the various departments within the Bank for their ready co-operation, as it is my experience that we offer, in Birmingham, a service which is cheaper and superior to that enjoyed by clients of the clearing banks and our customers are not slow in letting the business community become aware of this. The lack of a Branch network in the locality did not inhibit our progress, as most of the major connections which we have on our books already used various branches of the clearing banks and their operation was no different when the account was located with us. Our initial reception by the business community was, as one would expect, guarded, as the responsibility really lies with us to prove our expertise which, once established, is your greatest marketing tool.

How did we acquire business? I find this is the most difficult factor to analyse as, like all managers find, the real art is in seeing opportunities and taking advantage of them. Initially, this was extremely difficult, in that one of the biggest single disadvantages is the fact that you do not have an established source of information as to the standing of some of the people that you are dealing with and an assessment of their reputation in the city. The first fact that quickly emerged was that the business community in Birmingham, like most cities, is extremely small and they are fully aware of what business you are discussing and they, for their part, are going to form an assessment of your business acumen by your handling of the situations and the business you take on. When we arrived in Birmingham, I stayed for several weeks in the Thistle Hotel and this gave rise to my meeting the Southern Regional Manager of Scottish and Newcastle Breweries, who very kindly effected several good introductions, which resulted in our obtaining substantial hotel business and, indeed, of our total portfolio of advances, around 20 per cent relates to the hotel and catering industry. On one occasion, we arranged to go for lunch with one of his clients who blithely remarked that he was looking for support to £2 million to enable him to buy his hotel. I was quite amazed when I called upon him to see the scale of his operation and it was interesting that at the end of the day he produced a letter from the TSB offering the £2 million at 1¾ per cent over their base rate, and it was only with the ready assistance of London Administration that we were able to match this at extremely short notice. Another major connection in the hotel industry arose through Central Banking Services forwarding to us a half completed application to Save and Prosper Group for a policy of £1 million which they had received, and it was interesting, when this was followed up, to see that there was a bankable proposition, as it transpired that the proprietor, who was an Asian, had hotel properties with total valuations of £2.7 million, which enabled us to do a Term Loan of £1.1 million and a working capital facility of £250,000. On another occasion, while in the board room at Aston Villa Football Club, I was introduced to a gentleman who announced that he had just purchased a major golf hotel in Scotland for £1.35 million cash, and as a result of this the account was established with ourselves and carried creditor balances of over £100,000 for the first year. Since that time, sums of around £10 million have been expended on the hotel and we are making available facilities of £5 million, against a Charge over the hotel and a covering Guarantee of European Ferries PLC, who are one of the major public companies in the United Kingdom, with a balance sheet surplus of over £250 million.

What became readily apparent in my dealing with potential customers was that many of these customers had borrowings with their own clearing banks of under £1 million, and it was obvious, at that level, that these customers were unable to get access to the local directors of the clearers and they were, for that reason, facing frequent changes of managers and, in some instances, difficulties in getting their request properly placed before the directors, which caused frustration and annoyance and, of our initial portfolio, many connections fell into this category and it is extremely pleasing to see how many of these connections are prospering. In any proposal, the most important ingredient is the management team and in establishing an advances base, it is essential that a flexibility is built into any assessment and I think that this deviation from set criteria, in some instances, more than rewarded us. To illustrate this, I would like to mention a proposal which was put before us by customers in airport safety equipment, purchased against firm orders from major institutions such as British Aviation Authority and Ministry of Defence. They had a conflict with their clearing bank through reluctance to grant a Debenture because of the impact such a registration could have on their customers. The company had made pre-tax profits of over £200,000 in the previous two years, their account fluctuating freely into credit and London Administration were willing to accept the account against Legal Charges over the properties and a cautionary obligation by the two major directors, one of whom, interestingly enough, was attached to the Reagan administration at the White House. The major shareholder was born and bred in Birmingham, having attended King Edward's School, as did his local manager of Lloyds Bank, and it was interesting to have a telephone call from that manager indicating that while he was extremely upset to lose what was his major connection, he was delighted that we were willing to support the customer notwithstanding his own administration's reluctance. In fact, the customers subsequently produced pre-tax profits of over £180,000 and the account has freely fluctuated to over £500,000 at credit. It is a small world, and it was extremely interesting to have a telephone call from Lord Polwarth a matter of a fortnight after we took over the connection to say that while touring in the United States he met the two directors and had been impressed by them.

I remember in another instance being introduced to the chairman of a medium sized building company whose board had decided to put their banking business out to tender. They were dissatisfied with their existing clearing bank and their inability to discuss their future strategy with the local directors, and this resulted in me being interviewed by the board, at which time they placed various scenarios before me as to what I considered our reaction would be to various proposals. At the same time, they asked the National Westminster and Lloyds Bank to quote and it was interesting, at the end of the day, that there was very little variance in the terms quoted and we were successful in acquiring the group business, which has gone on from strength to strength, and is now one of our major connections. The customers, for their part, have expressed the view to various parties that the change of bank was one of the most meaningful business decisions which they have taken.

My considered opinion is that Business Development can be summarised as:

1. establishing a reputation as being the best and most efficient bank
    in town;
2. keeping close to the financial and legal professions, who, as part of
    their remit, want to impress their own clients by good introductions
    to financial institutions;
3. maximising the benefit from your existing customers through being
    knowledgeable about their business and ensuring that you are a party
    to their business expansion;
4. providing a high standard of service and the reputation of being
    willing and able to assist customers;

and latterly, being knowledgeable about the business community in which
you operate and active in pursuing new opportunities.

With regard to the development of the business in Birmingham, from
our initial opening on 1 September 1980 we had obtained in February
1981 advances of some £800,000, with deposits in-house of £500,000,
which by the following year had grown to £15 million and £1.1 million
respectively. The figures for 1983 were £24 million and £2 million, with
the comparative figures for February 1984 being £37 million and £2 million, while at the present moment we have on the books at Birmingham
advances of £44 million and deposits of £2.3 million with, in addition,
unutilised facilities of over £5 million. We have term deposit receipts of
£3.4 million and loans with International Division of £5 million. These
facilities are made available on the usual banking terms and conditions
with the average turn on the lending being marginally over 2 per cent.
With regard to the profit performance, it was interesting that the Branch
had broken even by 28 February 1982, having absorbed the initial five
month loss of £61,700 to February 1981. For the year to date, our projected
profit plan is running at a profit of £600,000, which must be considered
satisfactory bearing in mind that the Branch has only been operating
for four years. The other remit was the establishment of a substantial
corporate business and it is worth recording that over 50 per cent of our
accounts are corporate and included on the books are no fewer than six
public companies. In our last profit plan we projected a growth in advances
of £500,000 per month and it is interesting that this to date has been
achieved, notwithstanding the substantial repayments which are having
to be taken care of within the gross figures.

The operation we have in Birmingham is exactly the same as that of
any branch north of the border, other than the fact that we open every
lunch hour. We cater for our customers in exactly the same way and we
consciously decided to concentrate on the top end of the market which
enables us to provide a high quality personalised service to the business

executives. When we first established, I was amazed at how few people appreciated the fact that we were a major clearing bank, and I would just like to say that I do think that the physical establishment of a branch network in the major English cities does enable the Bank to maximise the return from the various innovative schemes which we have introduced, as there can be no doubt that people like to think, whether it be through the Money Market operation or Central Banking Services, that they are dealing with an institution that is represented locally.

Source: Managers Conference, 1984.

STATISTICAL APPENDIX

Table A1 General account of profit and loss, 1697–1833

Year ending March	Debits					Credits							
	Charges general	To undivided profits	To fund for losses	Misc.	Total debits	Interest account	Inland bills of exchange	Bills discounted	London bills of exchange	Investments	Income from branches	Misc.	Total credits
1697	1518			246 [1]	1764	1025	99					393 [2]	1418 [3]
1698	509			352 [4]	861	934						392 [5]	1425
1699	657	1200 [6]		20 [7]	1877 [8]	710	301					301 [9]	1312
1700	784			1652 [10]	2436	1731	378					330 [11]	2439
1701	679			3460 [12]	4139	2246	526					1367 [13]	4139
1702	616	2000		3480 [14]	6096		513					5583 [15]	6096
1703	988	2000		2711 [16]	5699	2166	436					3097 [17]	5699
1704	574	1800		3211 [16]	5585	2357	503					2725 [18]	5585
1705	651	2000		2885 [16]	5536	1950	362					3225 [19]	5537
1706	537	2600		1118 [20]	4255	1168	159					2928 [21]	4255
1707	535	1000		820 [22]	2355	1139	331					884 [23]	2354
1708	626			2124 [16]	2750	1359	210					1181 [24]	2750
1709	651	1200		2601 [16]	4452	1199	167					3087 [25]	4453
1710	633	2000		1896 [16]	4529	1699	200					2630 [26]	4529
1711	759	3586		207 [27]	4552	2446	209					1898 [28]	4553
1712	650	2000		153	2803 [29]	3378	280					2153 [30]	5811 [29]
1713	690	2828		3784 [31]	7302 [29]	3847	293					153	4293 [29]
1714	808	3143		369 [32]	4320	3875	292					153	4320
1715	799	3065		360 [33]	4224	3834	237					153	4224
1716	807	1008		153	1968	1686	129					153	1968
1717	738	1284		155	2177	1948	76					153	2177
1718	801	1062		885 [34]	2748	2415	178					153	2746
1719	837	1848		197	2882	2568	161					153	2882
1720	805	1925		483	3213	2829	230					153	3212
1721	826	2276		407	3509	2974	133					402	3509
1722	843	2208		412	3463	3061						402	3463
1723	825	2890		435	4150	3500	248					402	4150
1724	941	3340		506 [35]	4787	4087	299					402	4788
1725	1371	3736		550 [36]	5657	4883	372					402	5657
1726	1187	4586		645 [37]	6418	5669	346					402	6417
1727	1055	4577		644 [38]	6276	5560	314					402	6276
1728	1606	4175		532	6313	5785	125					402	6312

1729	1196	1206	402	2402	2375	27				402	2402
1730	1437	2023	402	3862	3295	165				402	3862
1731	1033	2847	526	4282	3719	161				402	4282
1732	1506	1811		3843	3348	93					3843
1733	781	2389	126	3170	3085	85					3170
1734	840	2508	11	3474	3395	78					3473
1735	685	2724		3420	3335	84					3419
1736	742	2733		3475	3332	143					3475
1737	689	2939		3628	3474	154					3628
1738	809	2856		3665	3509	156					3665
1739	746	3243		3989	3728	190					3988
1740	763	2880	71	3714	3565	149				70	3714
1741	751	3055	91	3897	3727	169					3896
1742	1093	3240		4333	4260	73					4333
1743	896	3199		4095	4003	93					4096
1744	1043	3240	58	4341	4085	126				130	4341
1745	981	3289		4270	4144	125					4269
1746	816	2403		3219	3146	72					3218
1747	861	3952		4813	4713	100					4813
1748	840	4425		5265	5178	87					5265
1749	872	4154		5026	4913	113					5026
1750	1171	4579		5750	5588	162					5750
1751	1063	4091		5154	5075	79					5154
1752	915	4870	7	5792	5671	96				25	5792
1753	1260	4591		5851	5754	79				17	5850
1754	1262	4602		5864	5735	107				22	5864
1755	1240	5643		6883	6739	127				17	6883
1756	1786	5366		7152	7027	108				17	7152
1757	1186	5608		6794	6711	67				17	6795
1758	1532	4991		6523	6412	94				17	6523
1759	1984	5080		7064	6968	80				17	7065
1760	1625	5903		7528	7392	120				17	7529
1761	1392	6965		8357	8232	108				17	8357
1762	2806	7644		10450	10366	65				17	10448
1763	6583 [39]	1906		8489	8011	193	221	48		17	8490
1764	2109	6492		8601	8149	93	88	256		17	8603
1765	3668	4900		8568	7587	102	185	302	375 [40]	17	8568
1766	4685	2793	339	7817	6957	73	301	71	375 [40]	39	7816
1767	3680	4022		7702	6817	64	289	141	375 [40]	17	7703

Table A1 continued

Year ending March	Charges general	To undivided profits	To fund for losses	Misc.	Total debits	Interest account	Inland bills of exchange	Bills discounted	London bills of exchange	Investments	Income from branches	Misc.	Total credits
1768	6388	2958			9346	7429	141	1097	488	175 [40]		17	9347
1769	5157	4297		7	9461	7716	117	729	882			17	9461
1770	5198	5061		2	10261	7878	236	1437	693			18	10262
1771	3556	7086			10642	8466	198	1629	333			17	10643
1772	2052	6857		12	8921	5845	68	2267	688			52	8920
1773	2136	5045		26	7207	3626	65	2818	687			12	7208
1774	1969	7550		4	9523	5928		3411	183				9522
1775	3139	9099		378 [41]	12616	8497		2772	206			1141 [42]	12616
1776	2697	14079		581 [43]	17357	12371		2167	469		2338	13	17358
1777	2709	19323		33	22065	15082		1462	507		5014		22065
1778	2529	18688		1925 [44]	23142	16068		964	626		5456	28	23142
1779	3048	16916		123 [45]	20087	15466		495	226		3894	6	20087
1780	2370	17851		61	20282	14871		691	267		4438	14	20281
1781	2773	17350		1234 [46]	21357	15003		530	254	938 [47]	4614	16	21355
1782	2740	17316		1410 [48]	21466	13442		407	368	1576 [49]	5623	51	21467
1783	3063	25642		190	28895	12961		608	1019	7098 [50]	7194	14	28894
1784	3437	24090		663 [51]	28190	10618		472	1810	5450 [52]	9782	58	28190
1785	4179	20376		3725 [53]	28280	10227		519	2035	3860 [54]	11362	277	28280
1786	4309	28991		539 [55]	33839	7777		590	1189	7301 [56]	16949	35	33841
1787	4218	24671		212 [57]	29101	9147		392	780	1499 [58]	17216	66	29100
1788	4348	27673		582 [59]	32603	8602		44	1289	3000 [60]	18960	708	32603
1789	4615	25814		980 [61]	31409	7588		693	1221	2250 [62]	19314	343	31409
1790	4437	24709		3099 [63]	32245	7794		580	1023	4086 [64]	18128	634 [65]	32245
1791	4275	26201		538 [66]	31014	1646		666	1188	7697 [67]	19580	236	31013
1792	7783	26331		2501 [68]	36615			1027	1675	7768 [69]	25064	1081 [70]	36615
1793	11231	26874		1380 [71]	39485			1215	1873	5796 [72]	30563	37	39484
1794	8294	40869		2988 [73]	52151			3537	6133	3345 [74]	38806	330	52151
1795	7701	42732		4869 [75]	55302			2655	5450	6080 [76]	39589	1528	55302
1796	5716	52152		3860 [77]	61728	12976		2548	5726		40180	298	61728
1797	13575	76284		3204 [78]	93063	10436		2742	8181	17599 [79]	53690	415	93063
1798	6458	68196		7651 [80]	82305	14375		3301	7384		57090	154	82304
1799	5878	68304		9083 [81]	83265	19167		2776	6207		55114		83264

Year											
1800	17451	69031		2695 [82]	89177	18620	5780	7222	57556		89178
1801	19342	67087		2878 [83]	89307	5610	7595	7887	68215		89307
1802	18578	67775		2946 [84]	89299	5725	8732	9230	65600	12	89299
1803	6199	68323	6000	19472 [85]	99994	23772	7365	8650	59952	255	99994
1804	4972	72635	3000	11948 [86]	92555	13270	7297	8059	63836	93	92555
1805	6277	72482		15612 [87]	94371	22448	11097	7101	53663	63	94372
1806	9714	75391	5000	18203 [88]	108308	26574	12840	9410	59346	138	108308
1807	13802	72143		13634 [89]	99579	6933	15394	10380	66872		99579
1808	6999	74040		20326 [90]	101365	157	13704	10041	77319	144	101365
1809	12801	74438		14680 [91]	101919	0	14858	8373	78689		101920
1810	15580	75019	5943	12398 [92]	108940	0	14632	9963	83924	420	108939
1811	13597	77782	1861	9064 [93]	102304	15265			87039		102304
1812	20473	78509	1500	13677 [94]	114159	61446			52527	187	114160
1813	19434	79336	2080	13044 [95]	113894	52530			61363		113893
1814	20344	80008	1925	13706 [96]	115983	114717			1015	250	115982
1815	19594	79364	2225	12745 [97]	113928	112769			1159		113928
1816	21619	80214	1929	12724 [98]	116486	115304			1180		116484
1817	18901	88444	384	5184 [99]	112913	112035			863	14	112912
1818	25897	262237		32352 [100]	320486	319877			608		320485
1819	24985	111843		1647 [101]	138475	137722			752		138474
1820	22696	101123		564	124383	123523			859		124382
1821	22920	98156	256	409	121485	120896			589		121485
1822	22716	97134	490	68	120174	119627			547		120174
1823	22193	89156		377	112216	111769			448		112217
1824	21243	81869		502	103614	103013			592	9	103614
1825	23211	242881	539	86	266717	266167			549		266716
1826	27263	81336	24746	364	133709	132934			776		133710
1827	24893	66833	88	163	91977	90451			1527		91978
1828	28185	68627	16000	780	113592	112575			1017		113592
1829	26057	64355	20000	571	110983	110311			671		110982
1830	26270	65668	22000	1356 [102]	115294	114525			770		115295
1831	26708	66974	18000	6237 [103]	117919	117445			474		117919
1832	26669	65324	21453	58	113504	112886			618		113504
1833	27865	67748	12287	2431 [104]	110331	107923				2408	110331

Notes:

1 Includes £163 net loss on English money.
2 Includes £107 by London exchange and £34 by premio bills.
3 Net loss of £347.
4 Includes £347 net loss from previous year.
5 Includes £219 by London exchange, £128 by Rotterdam exchange and £6 by premio bills.

Table A1 *continued*

6 Up to 1713, the dividend was paid directly from the general account of profit and loss. From 1711, a sum was paid into the adventurers' account of profit and loss and a dividend was paid from that account. After 1783, the account was renamed 'undivided profits'.

7 To balance (i.e net profit).

8 Balance over two years.

9 Includes £142 by London exchange and £105 by Rotterdam exchange.

10 Includes £631 loss by fire; £1010 to balance.

11 Includes £192 by London exchange, £92 by Rotterdam exchange and £20 by balance.

12 Includes £56 loss by fire; £3360 to balance.

13 Includes £342 by London exchange; £1010 by balance.

14 Includes £406 to James Foulis, London; £3074 to balance.

15 Includes £2207 by London exchange; £3360 by balance.

16 To balance.

17 Includes £3074 by balance.

18 Includes £2711 by balance.

19 Includes £3211 by balance.

20 Consists of £868 to balance and £250 to adventurers' ledger account (5% on the £5000 called up).

21 Includes £2885 by balance.

22 Consists of £520 to balance and £300 to adventurers' ledger account (6% on the £5000 called up).

23 Includes £868 by balance.

24 Includes £520 by balance and £660 by the commissioners of the Mint.

25 Includes £2124 by balance, £275 on 122 Mint bonds received and £678 by the commissioners of the Mint.

26 Includes £2601 by balance.

27 Includes £54 to John Holland.

28 Includes £1896 by balance.

29 Balance over two years.

30 Includes £2000 by balance.

31 Includes £3225 to balance; £406 to John Holland.

32 Includes £216 to John Holland.

33 Includes £207 to John Holland.

34 Includes £732 net loss on English money.

35 Includes £104 to John Holland.

36 Includes £148 to John Holland.

37 Includes £243 to John Holland.

38 Includes £242 to John Holland.

39 Includes £4238 to 'Andrew St. Clair our Account Current for Charges of £94945 in Specie brought from London' from charges general account.

40 Long annuities 1761.

41 Includes £378 cash paid to James Fraser for loss on light gold belonging to the Bank.

42 Includes £591 from new share subscription.

43 Includes £526 to bad/doubtful debts.

44 Includes £1881 to transferable bonds of Douglas, Heron & Co.

45 Includes £75 cash paid to Douglas, Heron & Co. interest on £600.

46 Includes £50 cash paid for the Treasurers' subscription for building a battery at Leith, £480 to sundry accounts for interest and £662 as half the expense of prosecuting forgeries.

47 By navy and victualling bills.

48 Includes £1000 to bad and doubtful debts, as a part of Robert and Peter Colvile and others' debts of £3800.

49 Includes £1316 by navy and victualling bills and £260 by stock of BS.

50 Includes £5928 by 3% consolidated annuities, £465 by navy and victualling bills and £708 by stock of BS.

51 Includes £388 to Kinloch & Hog.

52 Includes £4700 3% consolidated annuities and £750 stock of BS.

53 Includes £3057 to bad debts; £428 to Kinloch & Hog.

54 Includes £489 3% consolidated annuities, £750 stock of BS and £2621 stock of the Bank of England (BE).

55 Includes £195 to bad/doubtful debts for part of Mercer's bill; £283 to Kinloch & Hog.

56 Includes £950 stock of BE and £6351 proprietors' stock account.

57 Includes £103 to Kinloch & Hog.

58 Includes £1499 stock of BS.

59 Includes £146 to Kinloch & Hog.

60 Includes £1000 stock of BS and £2000 stock of BE.

61 Includes £653 to Kinloch & Hog.

62 Stock of BS.

63 Includes £2230 to John Dickie, late agent at Dunfermline and his cautioners; £444 to Kinloch & Hog.

64 Includes £586 5% annuities and £3500 stock of BS.

65 Includes £204 by general account of stamps.

66 Includes £346 to Kinloch & Hog.

67 Includes £1446 4% annuities, £1701 stock of BS and £4550 stock of BE.

68 Includes £1082 to Kinloch & Hog; £897 to branches.

69 Includes £2391 5% annuities, £827 stock of BS and £4550 stock of BE.

70 Includes £1057 by stamps.
71 Includes £187 to Kinloch & Hog; £417 to branches.
72 Includes £1246 stock of BS and £4550 stock of BE.
73 Includes £881 to Kinloch & Hog; £756 to Coutts & Co.
74 Includes £1000 stock of BS and £2345 stock of BE.
75 Includes £663 to branches; £1733 to Coutts & Co.
76 Includes £1250 stock of BS and £4830 stock of BE.
77 Includes £564 to branches; £1791 to Coutts & Co.
78 Includes £106 to branches.
79 Includes £13090 navy and victualling bills and £4509 proprietors' stock account.
80 Includes £2230 to branches; £2446 to Coutts & Co.
81 Includes £348 to branches; £1721 to Coutts & Co. and £5390 to account of bad and doubtful debts.
82 Includes £472 to branches (of which £368 to Aberdeen branch on account of loss); £2093 to Coutts & Co.
83 Includes £629 to branches; £2449 to Coutts & Co.
84 Includes £455 to branches; £2266 to Coutts & Co.
85 Includes £7955 set aside for Haddington branch, £2686 to Coutts & Co., and £7500 to cost of new building.
86 Includes £5100 set aside for Haddington branch, £4014 to Coutts & Co., and £1515 to cost of new building.
87 Includes £6000 set aside for Dumfries branch, and £3117 to Coutts & Co.
88 Includes £5700 set aside for Haddington branch, £2624 to Coutts & Co., and £1500 to law expenses.

89 Includes £9400 set aside for Haddington branch, £1500 to law expenses, £4016 set aside for property tax and £2500 to cost of new building.
90 Includes £7400 set aside for Haddington branch, £2895 to Coutts & Co., £1000 to law expenses and £6759 set aside for property tax.
91 Includes £4000 set aside for Haddington branch, £6803 set aside for property tax and £4370 to cost of new building.
92 Includes £2300 set aside for Haddington branch and £6843 set aside for property tax.
93 Includes £8010 set aside for property tax.
94 Includes £787 to law expenses, £7236 set aside for property tax and £5654 to general account of salaries.
95 Includes £600 to law expenses, £7078 set aside for property tax and £5116 to general account of salaries.
96 Includes £894 to law expenses, £6965 set aside for property tax and £4847 to general account of salaries.
97 Includes £6693 set aside for property tax and £5682 to general account of salaries.
98 Includes £219 to law expenses, £7070 set aside for property tax and £5228 to general account of salaries.
99 Includes £4776 to general account of salaries.
100 Includes £31784 to bad and doubtful debts.
101 Includes £712 to law expenses and £341 to general account of salaries.
102 Includes £1347 to law expenses.
103 Includes £3500 to India bonds and £2000 to Exchequer bills.
104 Includes £1400 set aside for house alterations, 1832.

Source: BS 1/94/1–44, General Ledgers.

Table A2 *Account of undivided profits (adventurers' account of profit and loss), 1697–1833*

| Year ending March | Credits | | Debits | | | |
	By general account of profit and loss	Misc.	Dividend	Div. 2	Misc.	Reserves
1697						
1698						
1699	1200		1200			
1700						
1701	2000		2000			
1702	2000		2000			
1703	1800		1800			
1704	2000		2000			
1705	2600	250 [1]	2000			
1706	1000	300 [2]	600			
1707			1000			
1708	1200		1200			
1709	2000		2000			
1710	3586		1500			
1711			2000			86
1712	2828		2100			
1713	3143		3000		694 [3]	344
1714	3065		3000			
1715	3000		3000			
1716	1008					1561
1717	1284		2000			
1718	1062		1500			
1719	1848		2000			2254
1720	1925		2000			
1721	2276		2000			
1722	2208		2500		500 [4]	2164
1723	2890		2500			
1724	3340		3000			
1725	3736		4000			4129
1726	4586		4500			
1727	4577		4500			
1728	4175				4000 [5]	4467
1729	1206		1500			
1730	2023		2000			
1731	2847		2500			3042
1732	1811		2000			
1733	2389		2000			
1734	2508		2000			
1735	2724		2000			
1736	2733		2000			
1737	2939		2000			
1738	2856		2000			6501
1739	3243		2000			
1740	2880		2000			
1741	3055		2000			9679
1742	3240		2000			
1743	3199		2000			
1744	3240		2500			
1745	3289		2500		10000 [6]	
1746	2403		2500			
1747	3952		2500			
1748	4425		2500			
1749	4154		2500			
1750	4579		2500			11160

Year ending March	Credits By general account of profit and loss	Misc.	Dividend	Div. 2	Misc.	Reserves
1751	4091		2500			
1752	4870		2500			
1753	4591		3000			17211
1754	4602		4000		10000 [6]	
1755	5643		4000			
1756	5366		4000			11823
1757	5608		4000			
1758	4991		4000			
1759	5080		4000			15503
1760	5903		4000			
1761	6965		5000			
1762	7644		4000			23015
1763	1906		4000			
1764	6492		4000			23414
1765	4900		4000			
1766	2793		4000			23107
1767	4022		4000			
1768	2958		4000			22087
1769	4297		4000			
1770	5061		4500		10000 [6]	
1771	7086		4000	2000		16031
1772	6857		2250	2000	10000 [6]	
1773	5045		2250	2000		7682
1774	7550	1500 [7]	2250	2000	10000 [6]	
1775	9099		3250	6000	3990 [8]	7331
1776	14079		6000	6000		
1777	19323		6000	6000		15494
1778	18688		6000	6000		
1779	16916		6500	6500		
1780	17851		7000	7000		31948
1781	17350		7000	7000		
1782	17316		8000	8000		16530
1783	25642		9000	9000	14084 [9]	42171
1784	24090		9000	9000		
1785	20376		9303	10490	4167 [6]	
1786	28991		12000	12000		47668
1787	24671		12000	12000		
1788	27673		12000	12000		
1789	25814		12000	12000		
1790	24709		12000	12000		
1791	26201		12000	12000		
1792	26331		12000	12000		59068
1793	26874		12000	12000	15824 [10]	
1794	40869		19125	18000		
1795	42732		18000	18723	1383 [6]	
1796	52152		19000	25660	12450 [9]	82639
1797	76284		30000	30000		
1798	68196		30000	30000		
1799	68304		30000	30000	69430 [11]	108883
1800	69031		30000	30000		
1801	67087		30000	30000		
1802	67775		30000	30000		72776
1803	68323		32500	32500		
1804	72635		32500	32500		
1805	72482		32500	32500		

Year ending March	Credits		Debits			
	By general account of profit and loss	Misc.	Dividend	Div. 2	Misc.	Reserves
1806	75391		35000	35000		106606
1807	72143		35000	35000		
1808	74040		35000	35000		
1809	74438		35000	35000		
1810	75019		35000	37500		122246
1811	77782		37500	37500		
1812	78509		37500	37500		
1813	79336		37500	37500		135373
1814	80008		37500	37500		
1815	79364		37500	37500		144745
1816	80214		37500	42500		
1817	88444		42500	47500		158403
1818	262237		47500	47500	200000 [8]	
1819	111843		47500	47500		147482
1820	101123		47500	47500		
1821	98156		47500	47500		156762
1822	97134		47500	47500		
1823	89156		47500	40000		211609
1824	81869		40000	40000		
1825	242881		40000	40000	200000 [8]	536359
1826	81336		40000	40000		
1827	66833		30000	30000		157028
1828	68627		30000	30000		
1829	64355		30000	30000		230009
1830	65668		30000	30000		
1831	66974		30000	30000		182652
1832	65324		30000	30000	30000 [12]	
1833						195724

Notes:

1 From profit and loss account (5% on the £5000 called up).
2 From profit and loss account (6% on the £5000 called up).
3 To house in Pearson's Close.
4 To adventurers' ledger account for 5% interest ordered on last tenth.
5 To general ledger account for 4% profits allowed to the adventurers in payment of another tenth.
6 Adventurers' ledger stock transfer.
7 This sum ordered to be placed to the credit of the account as the valuation of the house and area of the Governor and Company of Bank of Scotland.
8 Dividend.
9 To stock of Bank of Scotland.
10 Consists of dividends of £1352 and £4389 plus £10083 adventurers' ledger stock transfer.
11 Consists of £60000 dividend and £9430 to stock of Bank of Scotland.
12 Transferred to fund for losses.

Source: BS 1/94/1–44, General Ledgers.

Table A3 *Internal position of Bank of Scotland, 1834–64*

Year ending Dec.	Credits (sources of Bank's income)							Gross trading income	Less interest paid [4]	Gross trading profit	Less charges general [5]	Misc.	Net profits
	Bills [1]	Interest received [2]	Interest on bonds	Dividend/interest on investments	Commission	Branches [3]	Misc.						
1834	8738	17208	11734	91092	2219	45686	453 [6]	177130	68176	108954	31376	5550 [7]	72028
1835	7349	22042	10802	94642	2392	50671	1791 [8]	189689	80713	108976	32526		76450
1836	9289	20953	11565	107395	2042	62745	1813 [9]	215802	91249	124553	34456	3636 [10]	86461
1837	11898	29465	13247	101407	2029	89232	1888 [9]	249166	132517	116649	36118	1152 [10]	79379
1838	9723	24928	13211	106847	1555	80229	3194 [11]	239687	116524	123163	38063		85100
1839	12018	17922	12830	88525	1402	114881	2006 [9]	249584	120084	129500	38486	10409 [12]	80605
1840	11955	23137	11764	74152	2150	130971	1758 [9]	255887	138020	117867	37102	1292 [13]	79473
1841	13355	30135	10370	61317	1858	138199	4315 [14]	259549	150978	108571	39504		69067
1842	12905	31305	10425	83799	1565	111074	6914 [15]	257987	145699	112288	39855		72433
1843	9151	31147	5321	84003	1010	88671	4994 [16]	224297	103542	120755	40373	4069 [17]	76313
1844	8870	28407	6810	104277	1181	82939	1845 [9]	234329	104569	129760	39740	4225 [17]	85795
1845	9566	28655	7760	92688	955	91217	1774 [9]	232615	109757	122858	40583	1952 [17]	80323
1846	12212	36574	6600	74758	1264	128865	1804 [9]	262077	144411	117666	40579	1417 [17]	75670
1847	14991	40571	6448	66417	1915	170507	1652 [9]	302501	178152	124349	41500	12800 [18]	70049
1848	12261	35262	5774	68607	1699	152272	1924 [18]	277799	160884	116915	42582		74333
1849	10211	28648	5692	82293	1360	123340	3737 [19]	255281	132947	122334	41444		80890
1850	8514	22883	5123	86600	1526	107442	1671 [20]	233759	103912	129847	41601		88246
1851	9363	19976	5653	80058	1135	109251	2219 [21]	227655	104412	123243	42255		80988
1852	8210	19554	7368	77139	1302	105729	3235 [22]	222537	100991	121546	40869		80677
1853	10562	19076	7943	83665	1481	115964	2857 [23]	241548	112115	129433	42115		87318
1854	14266	22692	7803	70942	2567	160957	3334 [24]	282561	144295	138266	44172		94094
1855	12947	21832	7206	73705	2397	156258	3057 [25]	277402	144093	133309	47985		85324
1856	13675	23674	7084	81082	1903	187031	2437 [26]	316886	176176	140710	48108		92602
1857	17803	27096	6740	67043	1820	247267	2669 [27]	370438	210209	160229	50053		110176
1858	12166	27838	5671	60575	3031	204443	16	313740	138877	174863	57195		117668
1859	3762	14197	6464	85811	515	175834	11	286594	129379	157215	53907		103308
1860	4328	11652	5751	83271	925	209409	7	315343	132582	182761	55703		127058
1861	3584	12705	5077	77010	557	263141	9	362083	162564	199519	55667		143852
1862	2265	7923	2145	93305	653	193666	4	299961	125583	174378	56798	548 [28]	117032
1863	2149	7121	2870	81558	343	219612	4	313657	136752	176905	58761	200 [28]	117944
1864	2688	6545	1982	46276	6846	221379		285716	149023	136693	39008	300 [28]	97385

Table A3 *continued*

Notes:

1 Includes bills discounted at head office only.
2 On cash accounts, deposit accounts and advances to correspondents at head office only.
3 Includes discount on bills, interest received on cash accounts and deposit accounts and commission.
4 Interest paid at head office *and* branches.
5 Charges general figure includes London correspondents' commission, expense of conveyance of notes to and from branches, travelling and other expenses of inspection, salaries at Edinburgh, annuities, allowances to tellers at Edinburgh for losses, allowances to servants, taxes, watching the Bank, notes, cheques, stationery, printing, engraving, banknotes, trades-men's accounts, miscellaneous expenses, and management of branches (agents' salaries and allowances to branch tellers for losses).
6 Interest withdrawn from Alex Anderson's retained salary.
7 Includes £5000 to fund for losses and £500 allowance to Alex Anderson and John McMillan.
8 By rent of Glasgow and Edinburgh heritages.
9 Rent from house property in Glasgow.
10 Re-discount at Edinburgh and branches.
11 Includes £1913 rents from house property in Glasgow and £1281 re-discount.
12 Includes £544 interest (proceeds of new 3½ per cents) and £9865 re-discount at Edinburgh and branches.
13 Re-discount.
14 Includes £1966 rent from house property in Glasgow and £2349 re-discount.
15 Includes £1976 rent from house property in Glasgow and £4938 re-discount.
16 Includes £1921 rent fom house property in Glasgow and £3037 re-discount.
17 Income tax.
18 Fund for losses.
19 Includes £1776 rent from house property in Glasgow, £61 rent from property at St Andrews and £1900 transferred to income tax accounts.
20 Rent from St Andrews property.
21 Rent from St Andrews and Glasgow property.
22 Includes £1607 rent from St Andrews and Glasgow property and £1628 by income tax account.
23 Includes £2257 rent from St Andrews and Glasgow property and £600 transferred from income tax account.
24 Includes £1834 rent from St Andrews and Glasgow property and £1500 transferred from income tax account.
25 Includes £1557 rent from St Andrews and Glasgow property and £1500 transferred from income tax account.
26 Includes £500 transferred from income tax account and £1937 rent from property in Glasgow and St Andrews.
27 Includes £1000 transferred from income tax account and £1699 rent from property in Glasgow and St Andrews.
28 Transferred to income tax account.

Sources: BS, Uncatalogued, Balance Sheets and Income Tax Returns, 1834–49; BS 1/69/4, Annual Records, 1850–55; BS 1/74/1, Annual Records, 1856–64.

Table A4 Internal position of Bank of Scotland, 1865–1920

Year ending February (first year's accounts 14 months)	Credits (sources of Bank's income)							Gross trading income	Less interest paid	Gross trading profit	Less charges general	Net profits	Amount appropriated internally			Declared net profits
	Bills	Interest received	Dividends/interest on investments	Interest on London loans	Commission	Rents	Misc.						To fund for losses	To Misc.	Total appropriated internally	
1866	214634	104326	63389	13897	17853	2845	2043 [1]	418987	226160	192827	65900	126927		-1731 [2]	-1731 [2]	128658
1867	304206	120933	62917	7136	16380	2700	1787 [3]	516059	256670	259389	67745	191644	30000	7216 [4]	37216 [4]	154429
1868	180290	80365	64362	7424	18592	3059	2021 [5]	356113	132372	223741	76674	147067	15000	2346 [6]	17346 [6]	129721
1869	162100	94847	59649	29993	21515	3009	7102 [7]	378215	141383	236832	87917	148915		16499 [8]	16499 [8]	132416
1870	175327	97405	52845	39471	23858	3424	4462 [9]	396792	165692	231100	88623	142477		18699 [10]	18699 [10]	123776
1871	192366	96018	57142	20076	25864	2880	4465 [11]	398811	159073	239738	89398	150340	10000	8000 [12]	18000	132341
1872	200945	95787	38380	41031	34941	994	3881 [13]	415959	166993	248966	92894	156072	8500	10000 [12]	18500	137572
1873	265633	116283	35127	53346	33271	2361	3906 [14]	509927	238224	271703	95188	176515	10000	14570 [15]	24570 [15]	151944
1874	276787	128233	36446	85742	37919	1950	6852 [16]	573929	284814	289115	100893	188222	16000	7000 [12]	23000	165221
1875	235595	137705	41433	77643	36505	2349	3271 [17]	534501	239832	294669	108030	186639		11000 [12]	11000 [12]	175639
1876	231075	152350	40398	60673	37375	2460	2781 [18]	527112	223479	303633	113399	190234	18000		18000	172234
1877	193102	160216	53091	39002	36565	2266	3315 [19]	487557	191453	296104	117751	178353	10000		10000	168353
1878	197075	193896	56896	47121	35312	3012	2501 [20]	535813	213223	322590	119262	203328	20000		20000	183326
1879	225408	235141	45789	52189	39122	4390	7169 [21]	609208	265511	343697	130985	212712	36000		36000	176713
1880	165518	203645	61984	55631	36633	5081	12580 [22]	541072	210699	330373	144740	185633	17000		17000	168633
1881	167227	166433	87998 [23]	110781	40687	4532	10977 [24]	588635	226570	362065	145448	216617		39997 [25]	39997 [25]	176620
1882	194388	182158	75416 [26]	154888	40642	4605	7292 [27]	659389	298509	360880	143379	217501	40000		40000	177501
1883	215653	184353	82887 [28]	147452	42152	4774	3874 [29]	681145	307961	373184	147635	225549	43000		43000	182549
1884	209800	201713	89637	111884	40102	4268	564	657968	271770	386198	148731	237467	50000		50000	187467
1885	185345	206252	86226	104744	36573	4052	670	623862	283609	340253	154998	185255	8000		8000	177254
1886	165389	202505	95777 [30]	82033	35692	3962	814	586172	225006	361166	159024	202142	20000		20000	182142
1887	166525	197303	72954 [31]	103722	34151	3898	1149	579702	232449	347253	158489	188764	14500		14500	174266
1888	171385	190022	73647 [32]	93266	34761	4193	483	567757	223632	344125	158921	185204	16000		16000	169204
1889	162474	192829	87141 [33]	109668	35521	3938	380	591951	239942	352009	156969	195040	33000		33000	162040
1890	175105	186812	119587 [34]	133305	38894	3880	184	657767	284713	373054	159798	213256	48000		48000	165257
1891	208550	191832	116978	153624	41557	4011	415	716967	322116	394851	162749	232102	60000		60000	172102
1892	167614	178227	124689 [35]	104891	39797	3858	359	619435	240293	379142	164314	214828	30000	5000 [36]	35000	179828
1893	128445	173728	113156 [37]	74412	38122	4815	264	532942	184204	348738	164514	184224	14000		14000	170226
1894	142218	192374	107357 [38]	100723	40108	3925	465	587170	210874	376296	166174	210122	17000	20000 [39]	37000	173123
1895	113178	173922	127065 [40]	59011	38175	4574	216	516141	173846	342295	170065	172230	15000		15000	157229
1896	105666	154494	130089 [41]	62237	40056	4909	622	498073	116600	381473	172875	208598	47596		47596	161003
1897	143042	155452	119742 [42]	89114	44298	5845	20133 [43]	577626	168258	409368	173026	236342 [44]	64000 [45]		64000	172342
1898	140748	152848	84454 [46]	97059	42741	9299	67	527216	143767	383449	175233	208216		33000 [47]	33000	175216

Table A4 *continued*

Year ending February (first year's accounts 14 months)	Credits (sources of Bank's income)							Gross trading income	Less interest paid	Gross trading profit	Less charges general	Net profits	Amount appropriated internally			Declared net profits
	Bills	Interest received	Dividends/ interest on investments	Interest on London loans	Commission	Rents	Misc.						To fund for losses	To Misc.	Total appropriated internally	
1899	167908	150866	96101 [48]	111617	40706	8280	55	575533	206295	369238	175070	194168			33001	161167
1900	204653	179234	143185 [49]	114601	42327	9897	41	693938	282321	411617	174208	237409			56000	181409
1901	212763	195748	160132 [50]	139334	44170	10675	140	762962	307210	455752	180691	275061			72641	202420
1902	172260	206104	151326	125994	40613	9807	306	706410	250221	456189	174749	281440			69733	211707
1903	164598	219275	155262 [51]	118122	41308	9960	551	709076	229262	479814	175003	304811			81316	223495
1904	157969	245256	154352 [52]	130630	41113	8895	1103	739318	263016	476302	173750	302552			100499	202053
1905	118189	227423	166498 [53]	122655	40348	9241	491	684845	187576	497269	172756	324513			100700	223813
1906	131980	220821	150200 [54]	126235	57092	7797	224	694349	183268	511081	171971	339110			107011	232099
1907	161537	282216	139473	185894	48348	8225	185	825878	320053	505825	174051	331774			94767	237007
1908	160956	341037	162564 [55]	230198	48407	9241	56	952459	399877	552582	191032	361550			88740	272810
1909	111425	263438	168782 [56]	154990	51739	10076	10	760460	158385	602075	198850	403225			121189	282036
1910	129302	273734	167092 [57]	195513	80700	10068	55	856464	217824	638640	204231	434409			146249	288160
1911	166180	301102	146274	207123	68510	9411	8	898608	288419	610189	206984	403205			110001	293204
1912	147536	279536	161803 [58]	204910	87155	6002	25	886787	244382	642405	208759	433646			127501	306145
1913	147876	301178	182071 [59]	247734	99192	6081	73	984205	318158	666047	213122	452925			134367	318558
1914	155510	356032	188691 [60]	299530	94826	4484	2505	1101578	417513	684065	218450	465615			144790	320825
1915	123683	299298	193471 [61]	241731	71393	6676	17	936269	294450	641819	225720	416099			122000	294099
1916	143305	282187	347063	183180	69366	6486	8	1031595	406104	625491	241234	384257			117002	267255
1917	255360	256193	414411	208909	57074	6116	75	1198138	578652	619486	251617	367869			109500	258369
1918	318522	297244	482690	106772	68072	5444	39	1278783	634340	644443	262811	381632			96124	285508
1919	279716	237754	719123	87121	62715	6916	58	1393403	612194	781209	256882	524327			212000	312327
1920	241234	357401	829974	134309	60647	4646	36736 [62]	1664947	827195	837752	318031	519721			199999	319722

Notes:

1 Interest on bonds.
2 This implies that a transfer was made from inner reserves to declared profits instead of vice versa in 1866.
3 Includes £1547 interest on bonds.
4 £2216 to rented premises account and £5000 to paying a gratuity of 10% on staff salaries.
5 Includes £1282 interest on bonds.
6 Set aside for gratuity to be paid to certain officers.
7 Includes £1076 interest on bonds, £4561 profit on Rupee paper and £1465 from Central Bank suspense account (CBSA).
8 £10000 to Central Bank premium account and £28500 to fund for losses (not clear where the extra funds came from).
9 Includes £664 interest on bonds, £2528 CBSA, £3725 on Bank of Otago £30000 Loan (BOL) and £895 from Glasgow short loans.

10 £40000 to Hardie forgeries and £5000 to Central Bank premium account, less £9230 extra income from sales of property and £17071 by balance of undivided profits applied to Hardie forgeries.
11 Includes £479 interest on bonds, £2102 CBSA, £1500 BOL and £347 on exchange drafts.
12 To Central Bank premium account.
13 Includes £385 interest on bonds, £1987 CBSA and £1500 BOL.
14 Includes £294 interest on bonds, £2410 CBSA and £1197 BOL.
15 £10000 to Central Bank premium account and £4570 to gratuity paid to certain officers.
16 Includes £197 interest on bonds, £3527 CBSA, £72 BOL and £475 on exchange drafts.
17 Includes £3185 CBSA.
18 Includes £2566 CBSA.

19 Includes £2249 CBSA and £1044 on exchange drafts.

20 Includes £2401 CBSA.

21 Includes £2728 CBSA, £2157 on City of Glasgow Bank account (CGBA) and £1812 on Caledonian Bank account (CaBA).

22 Includes £2121 CBSA, £5209 CGBA and £5228 CaBA.

23 Includes surplus on sale of stocks £13697.

24 Includes £624 CBSA, £9382 CGBA and £693 CaBA.

25 Details of internal appropriations not stated.

26 Includes surplus on sale of stocks £4247 and annual interest on New Zealand and Australian Land Co. 4% preference shares held by the Bank.

27 Includes £6718 CGBA and £299 CaBA.

28 Includes annual interest on New Zealand and Australian Land Co. 4% preference shares held by the Bank.

29 Includes £3412 CGBA.

30 Includes surplus on sale of stocks £10443 and annual interest on New Zealand and Australian Land Co. 4% preference shares held by the Bank.

31 Includes dividend at rate of 1.5% only (£1957) instead of 4% on New Zealand and Australian Land Co. 4% preference stock.

32 Includes surplus on sale of stocks £1328 and 2% dividend of £2591 on New Zealand and Australian Land Co. stock.

33 Includes £8539 interest on New Zealand and Australian Land Co. stock.

34 Includes surplus on sale of stocks £8838.

35 Includes surplus on sale of stocks £2013.

36 To write down consols.

37 Includes surplus on sale of stocks £3219.

38 Includes surplus on sale of stocks £2882 and six months' interest in arrears on Atchison, Topeka & Santa Fe Railroad bonds and Philadelphia & Reading Railroad bonds.

39 To a contingent account to provide for possible bonuses during the bicentenary year.

40 Includes surplus on sale of stocks £25308.

41 Includes surplus on sale of stocks £37596.

42 Includes surplus on sale of stocks £33169.

43 Includes £20000 at credit of contingent account transferred to interest account (see note 39).

44 Of which £201342 banking profit, £20000 by contingent account (which was not distributed for the bicentenary) and £15000 profit on sale of consols.

45 £35000 had to be provided for possible loss on account of Gregor, Turnbull & Co. at Glasgow in addition to the £15000 provision which had already been made.

46 Includes surplus on sale of stocks £2962.

47 From 1898 to 1921 no source was available for details of internal appropriations.

48 Includes surplus on sale of stocks £3324.

49 Includes surplus on sale of stocks £10584.

50 Includes surplus on sale of stocks £17259.

51 Includes surplus on sale of stocks £5982.

52 Includes surplus on sale of stocks £6438.

53 Includes surplus on sale of stocks £8679.

54 Includes surplus on sale of stocks £2050.

55 Includes surplus on sale of stocks £647.

56 Includes surplus on sale of stocks £4551.

57 Includes surplus on sale of stocks £7570.

58 Includes surplus on sale of stocks £4058.

59 After deficit on stocks sold £1647.

60 After deficit on stocks sold £5443.

61 Includes surplus on sale of stocks £629.

62 Includes interest on London County Westminster & Parr's Bank accounts £36699.

Sources: BS 1/74/2–8, Annual Records (State of Profits); BS 1/70/4 and 6, Annual Report of the Treasurer, 1866–98.

Table A5 *Bank of Scotland published annual balance sheets, 1865–1920*

| Year ending February | Liabilities to the public | | | | | Liabilities to the proprietors | | | | | | Total liabilities |
	Note circulation	Drafts issued payable within 14 days	Deposits and credit balances[1]	Acceptances, guarantees and other obligations for account of customers	Subtotal	Paid-up capital	Reserve fund	Final dividend payable April	Balance of profits carried forward	Subtotal	Misc.	
1865	553160	225197	6488227	136294	7402878	1000000	250000	50000	6846	1306846		8709724
1866	604437	144394	7014916	198543	7962290	1000000	250000	55000	25504	1330504		9292794
1867	505391	189976	7413022	185643	8294032	1000000	275000	65000	29933	1369933		9663965
1868	447681	184701	7286374	239363	8158119	1000000	300000	65000	9655	1374655		9532774
1869	519644	170603	8384257	748653	9823157	1000000	300000	65000	17071	1382071		11205228
1870	613935	175403	8051637	947424	9788399	1000000	300000	65000	3776	1368776		11157175
1871	651902	224742	8260688	1187355	10324687	1000000	300000	60000	1117	1371117		11695804
1872	697232	149183	8583783	1532232	10962430	1000000	300000	60000	23689	1383689		12346119
1873	849839	265853	9600109	1465680	12181481	1000000	330000	65000	15633	1410633		13592114
1874	628321	261987	10153828	2059930	13104066	1000000	355000	70000	15854	1440854		14544920
1875	626494	179515	10631881	1442775	12880665	1000000	385000	70000	16493	1471493		14352158
1876	601497	187523	10459017	1977086	13225123	1000000	410000	70000	18727	1498727		14723850
1877	639156	195159	10409120	2097162	13340597	1250000	750000	70000	14581	2102081		15442678
1878	603706	245713	10508832	2116823	13475074	1250000	750000	87500	17907	2105407		15580481
1879	704318	201673	11532693	1755814	14194498	1250000	750000	87500	20870	2102120	266475[3]	16563093
1880	736751	253173	12254908	1201951	14446783	1250000	750000	81250	22003	2103253		16550036
1881	697386	123632	12421925	1141065	14384008	1250000	750000	81250	31122	2112372		16496380
1882	725694	221787	12766423	1430581	15144485	1250000	775000	81250	16123	2122373		17266858
1883	744391	241753	12929479	1170592	15086215	1250000	775000	87500	19922	2132422		17218637
1884	761148	193895	13254475	971533	15181051	1250000	775000	87500	22389	2134889		17315940
1885	791946	225901	13826688	1179873	16024408	1250000	775000	87500	19643	2132143		18156551
1886	801314	191770	13312581	936652	15242317	1250000	775000	87500	21785	2134285		17376602
1887	772077	93041	13015471	1038240	14918829	1250000	775000	81250	22302	2128552		17047381
1888	785089	160628	13412069	823639	15181425	1250000	775000	81250	24005	2130255		17311680
1889	801313	132623	13924354	1104229	15962519	1250000	775000	75000	24795	2124795		18087314

Year ending February	Gold and silver coin, notes of other banks	Government securities, cash with London bankers and short loans in London	Bills discounted, cash accounts and other advances	Indian government and other stocks and investments	Liabilities of customers for acceptances by Bank, as per contra	Bank premises and other property [2]	Misc. assets	Total assets
1865	529081	2175919	5488607	390732		125386		8709725
1866	586623	1943872	6316708	314059		131532		9292794
1867	494140	2065477	6657555	303359		143434		9963965
1868	391499	2230143	6420249	339523		151359		9532773
1869	371720	3103894	7359488	199912		170215		11205229
1870	528645	2541968	7667985	232923		185654		11157175
1871	587338	2433727	8270603	215358		188780		11695806
1872	509221	2879272	7057181	174389	1532232	193823		12346118
1873	765524	2898425	8072482	191868	1465680	198136		13592115
1874	346225	3576407	8114756	253961	2059930	193641		14544920
1875	426057	3225865	8765773	296097	1442775	195591		14352158
1876	459337	3091321	8814994	188013	1977086	193099		14723850
1877	514288	3240153	8444571	938749	2097162	207755		15442678
1878	465162	3095430	9227925	458674	2116823	216467		15580481
1879	586938	3063468	10248010	255454	1755814	392395	261014 4	16563093
1880	1127388	3891434	8518184	1061839	1201951	403751	345488 4	16550035
1881	1074208	3730421	8780594	1154230	1141065	410279	205585 4	16496382
1882	1007795	3867216	9379195	1021490	1430581	413827	146755 4	17266859
1883	1168902	3619596	9375836	1477059	1170592	406653		17218638
1884	1204208	3451236	10104167	1179966	971533	404830		17315940
1885	1113059	4743582	9472192	1241648	1179873	166610	239588 4	18156552
1886	1169143	4210009	9678839	973038	936652	408920		17376601
1887	957611	4042055	9348060	1254522	1038240	406893		17047381
1888	1129107	4193050	9628156	1133836	823639	403893		17311681
1889	1075809	5280349	8614281	1612055	1104229	400591		18087314

947

Table A5 *continued*

Year ending February	Liabilities to the public					Liabilities to the proprietors						Total liabilities
	Note circulation	Drafts issued payable within 14 days	Deposits and credit balances [1]	Acceptances, guarantees and other obligations for account of customers	Subtotal	Paid-up capital	Reserve fund	Final dividend payable April	Balance of profits carried forward	Subtotal	Misc.	
1890	871947	153624	14625193	1048992	16699756	1250000	800000	75000	10052	2135052		18834808
1891	937165	223713	15516050	1131560	17808488	1250000	800000	87500	14654	2152154		19960642
1892	933831	118975	15155421	865519	17073746	1250000	800000	87500	21982	2159482		19233228
1893	903149	134828	14726783	1104468	16869228	1250000	800000	87500	24708	2162208		19031436
1894	895150	265433	14759934	973270	16893787	1250000	800000	87500	30331	2167831		19061618
1895	918569	161411	14862095	864276	16806351	1250000	800000	75000	32560	2157560		18963911
1896	1012494	186729	14415554	1147030	16761807	1250000	800000	75000	33563	2158563		18920370
1897	1035781	241401	14478328	1046637	16802147	1250000	825000	75000	15905	2165905		18968052
1898	1040328	166133	14884275	1159265	17250001	1250000	700000	75000	11120	2036120		19286121
1899	1078640	270575	15082739	918847	17350801	1250000	700000	75000	12287	2037287		19388088
1900	1060181	203495	15694411	1685140	18643227	1250000	725000	75000	13696	2063696		20706923
1901	1073920	201198	15887972	1213022	18376112	1250000	775000	75000	11116	2111116		20487228
1902	1092388	253662	16057384	1330340	18733774	1250000	825000	81250	11574	2167824		20901598
1903	1103648	347359	15441406	1302279	18194692	1250000	875000	87500	11319	2223819		20418511
1904	1111531	100839	15237356	1480399	17930125	1250000	900000	87500	13372	2250872		20180997
1905	1095840	176313	15198060	1393173	17863386	1250000	950000	87500	12185	2299685		20163071
1906	1067088	423287	15097363	1509691	18097429	1250000	1000000	93750	13034	2356784		20454213
1907	1099213	273869	16204626	1971630	19549338	1250000	1040000	100000	16291	2406291		21955629
1908	1143613	525256	17655896	1958759	21281524	1325000	1100000	112625	10476	2548101		23829625
1909	1118838	415641	17637831	1650738	20823048	1325000	1150000	112625	12262	2599887		23422935
1910	1193736	204010	19030229	1626823	22054798	1325000	1200000	119250	13547	2657797		24712595
1911	1172060	314625	17648363	1676828	20811876	1325000	1250000	119250	13251	2707501		23519377
1912	1180669	221834	19249180	2849495	23501178	1325000	1300000	132500	12646	2770146		26271324
1913	1296789	311984	20172278	2744799	24523850	1325000	1350000	132500	11204	2818704		27342554
1914	1238666	420989	19639635	2609030	23908320	1325000	1400000	132500	12030	2869530		26777850

	Assets							
Year ending February	Gold and silver coin, notes of other banks	Government securities, cash with London bankers and short loans in London	Bills discounted, cash accounts and other advances	Indian government and other stocks and investments	Liabilities of customers for acceptances by Bank, as per contra	Bank premises and other property 2	Misc. assets	Total assets
1890	1196126	5335014	9128033	1730869	1048992	395774		18834808
1891	1312095	5752669	9433789	1938314	1131560	392215		19960642
1892	1263865	5550820	9247986	1768613	865519	536424		19233227
1893	1274465	5181629	9188030	1721524	1104468	561319		19031435
1894	1296461	4884101	9625086	1719034	973270	563665		19061617
1895	1332848	4796471	10082841	1301301	864276	586176		18963913
1896	1431051	4377843	9957622	1406779	1147030	600045		18920370
1897	1302640	4844130	9908387	1255890	1046637	610368		18968052
1898	1445461	5030133	9382903	1657861	1159265	610500		19286123
1899	1542755	4606407	9108772	2592401	918847	618906		19388088
1900	1428792	4355745	9742665	2875675	1685140	618906		20706923
1901	1610824	5046613	9167175	2830546	1213022	619048		20487228
1902	1598688	4690379	9508494	3154278	1330340	619419		20901598
1903	1626737	4381648	9555703	2932976	1302279	619169		20418512
1904	1357870	4362620	9464061	2897137	1480399	618912		20180999
1905	1562824	4138339	9453182	2996891	1393173	618662		20163071
1906	1535557	4339876	9599374	2851304	1509691	618412		20454214
1907	1669765	4958609	10006940	2730274	1971630	618412		21955630
1908	1607747	4729967	11441108	3394113	1958759	697930		23829624
1909	1547782	5206254	11163664	3161053	1650738	693443		23422934
1910	1448571	5963133	11788551	3196925	1626823	688593		24712596
1911	1773740	5294584	11283951	2802331	1676828	687942		23519376
1912	1763256	5539529	11864891	3570000	2844495	684153		26271324
1913	1876099	6118323	12243448	3682117	2742799	679768		27342554
1914	1808776	5788119	12028203	3855448	2609030	688273		26777849

Table A5 *continued*

Year ending February	Note circulation	Drafts issued payable within 14 days	Deposits and credit balances [1]	Acceptances, guarantees and other obligations for account of customers	Subtotal	Paid-up capital	Reserve fund	Final dividend payable April	Balance of profits carried forward	Subtotal	Misc.	Total liabilities
			Liabilities to the public						Liabilities to the proprietors			
1915	1556979	566184	21103759	2522997	25749919	1325000	1200000	95488	11422	2631910		28381829
1916	2119702	284764	21552004	1052042	25008512	1325000	1050000	87980	12064	2475044		27483556
1917	2492623	248406	26912606	1184764	30838399	1325000	750000	79500	24224	2178724		33017123
1918	3074872	234943	28456735	996397	32762947	1325000	750000	79500	35732	2190232		34953179
1919	4022757	292625	32275869	676162	37267413	1325000	550000	74200	53612	2002812		39270225
1920	4228825	1446699	36943953	673307	43292784	1325000	550000	74200	54934	2004134		45296918

Assets

Year ending February	Gold and silver coin, notes of other banks	Government securities, cash with London bankers and short loans in London	Bills discounted, cash accounts and other advances	Indian government and other stocks and investments	Liabilities of customers for acceptances by Bank, as per contra	Bank premises and other property [2]	Misc. assets	Total assets
1915	2165207	8215566	11309582	3478748	2522997	689730		28381830
1916	3217393	10001524	9981646	2545721	1052042	685230		27483556
1917	3821053	11669149	13424172	2237906	1184764	680080		33017124
1918	4582375	13317966	13254548	2132247	996397	669647		34953180
1919	5863229	17678051	12387339	2003633	676162	661812		39270226
1920	6565604	17856636	18064236	1488607	673307	648528		45296918

Notes:
1 This figure included the Bank's internal reserves.
2 At cost, less amounts written off.
3 Balances at credit of City of Glasgow Bank and Caledonian Bank.
4 Notes and other claims on City of Glasgow Bank and Caledonian Bank.

Source: Bank of Scotland published annual reports, 1865–1920.

Table A6 Bank of Scotland published profit and loss account, 1865–1920

	Debits								Credits						
Year ending February	To half-yearly dividend paid October	To half-yearly dividend to be paid	To reduction of bank premises account	Balance at credit of reserve fund	To reserve fund	Misc.	Balance of undivided profits carried forward	Total	Total	By balance of reserve fund	By balance of undivided profits brought forward	Gross profits [1]	Less expenses of management	Net profits	Total
1865 [2]	90000 [3]	50000	8000	243071	6929		6846	404846	404846	243071				161775	404846
1866	50000	55000	5000	250000			25504	385504	385504	250000	6846			128658	385504
1867	55000	65000	5000	250000	25000		29933	429933	429933	250000	25504			154429	429933
1868	55000	65000	5000	275000	25000		9655	434655	434655	275000	29933			129721	434654
1869	55000	65000	5000	300000			17071	442071	442071	300000	9655			132416	442071
1870	55000	65000		300000			3776 [4]	423776	423776	300000	0 [4]			123776 [5]	423776
1871	60000	60000	5000	300000			11117	436117	436117	300000	3776			132341	436117
1872	60000	60000	5000	300000			23689	448689	448689	300000	11117			137572	448689
1873	60000	65000	5000	300000	30000		15633	475633	475633	300000	23689			151944	475633
1874	65000	70000	5000	330000	25000		15854	510854	510854	330000	15633			165221	510854
1875	70000	70000	5000	355000	30000		16493	546493	546493	355000	15854			175639	546493
1876	70000	70000	5000	385000	25000		18727	573727	573727	385000	16493			172234	573727
1877	70000	87500	5000	410000	340000 [6]	45000 [7]	14581	972081	972081	410000	18727			168353	972080 [8]
1878	87500	87500	5000	750000			17907	947907	947907	750000	14581			183326	947907
1879	87500	81250	5000	750000			20870	944620	944620	750000	17907			176713	944620
1880	81250	81250	5000	750000			22003	939503	939503	750000	20870			168633	939503
1881	81250	81250	5000	750000			31122	948622	948622	750000	22003			176620	948623
1882	81250	81250	5000	750000	25000		16123	958623	958623	750000	31122			177501	958623
1883	81250	87500	10000 [9]	775000			19922	973672	973672	775000	16123			182549	973672
1884	87500	87500	10000 [10]	775000			22389	982389	982389	775000	19922			187467	982389
1885	87500	87500	5000	775000			19643	974643	974643	775000	22389			177254	974643
1886	87500	87500	5000	775000			21785	976785	976785	775000	19643	341165	159024	182142	976785
1887	87500	81250	5000	775000			22302	971052	971052	775000	21785	332755	158489	174266	971051
1888	81250	81250	5000	775000			24005	966505	966505	775000	22302	328125	158921	169204	966506
1889	81250	75000	5000	775000			24795	961045	961045	775000	24005	319008	156969	162040	961045
1890	75000	75000	5000	775000	25000		10052	965052	965052	775000	24795	325055	159798	165257	965052
1891	75000	87500 [11]	5000	800000			14654	982154	982154	800000	10052	334851	162749	172102	982154
1892	75000	87500 [11]	10000 [12]	800000			21982	994482	994482	800000	14654			179828	994482
1893	75000	87500 [11]	5000	800000			24708	992208	992208	800000	21982	334740	164514	170226	992208

Table A6 *continued*

	Debits								Credits					
Year ending February	To half-yearly dividend paid October	To half-yearly dividend to be paid	To reduction of bank premises account	Balance at credit of reserve fund	To reserve fund	Misc.	Balance of undivided profits carried forward	Total	By balance of reserve fund	By balance of undivided profits brought forward	Gross profits [1]	Less expenses of management	Net profits	Total
1894	75000	87500 [11]	5000	800000			30331	997831	800000	24708	339298	166174	173123	997831
1895	75000	75000	5000	800000			32560	987560	800000	30331	327294	170065	157229	987560
1896	75000	75000	10000 [13]	800000			33563	993563	800000	32560	333877	172875	161003	993563
1897	75000	75000	15000	800000	25000		15905	1005905	800000	33563	345368	173026	172342	1005905
1898	75000	75000	5000	700000 [14]		150000 [15]	11120	1016120	825000	15905	350448	175233	175216	1016121
1899	75000	75000	10000	700000			12287	872287	700000 [14]	11120	336237	175070	161167	872287
1900	75000	75000	5000	700000	25000		13696	893696	700000	12287	355616	174208	181409	893696
1901	75000	75000	5000	725000	50000		11116	941116	725000	13696	372751	170331	202420	941116
1902	81250	81250	5000	775000	50000		11574	997824	775000	11116	386456	174749	211707	997823
1903	87500	87500	5000	825000	50000		11319	1060069	825000	11574	398498	175003	223495	1060069
1904	87500	87500	5000	875000	25000		13372	1088372	875000	11319	375803	173750	202053	1088372
1905	87500	87500		875000	50000		12185	1137185	900000	13372	396569	172756	223813	1137185
1906	93750	93750		900000	50000		13034	1194284	950000	12185	404070	171971	232099	1194284
1907	106000	100000		950000	40000		16291	1250041	1000000	13034	411058	174051	237007	1250041
1908	112625	112625		1000000	60000		10476	1329101	1040000	16291	463841	191032	272810	1329101
1909	112625	112625		1040000	50000		12262	1392512	1100000	10476	480886	198850	282036	1392512
1910	119250	119250	5000	1100000	50000		13547	1450422	1150000	12262	492391	204231	288160	1450422
1911	119250	119250	5000	1150000	50000		13251	1506751	1200000	13547	500188	206984	293204	1506751
1912	132500	132500	5000	1200000	50000		12646	1569396	1250000	13251	514904	208759	306145	1569396
1913	132500	132500	5000	1250000	50000		11204	1631204	1300000	12646	531680	213122	318558	1631204
1914	124219	132500	5000	1300000	50000	270000 [17]	12030	1682030	1350000	11204	539275	218450	320825	1682029
1915	93633	95488	5000	1350000	50000	230000 [19]	11422	1706129	1400000	12030	519819	225720	294099	1706129
1916	81708	87980	5000	1200000 [16]		380000 [21]	12064	1478677	1200000	11422	508491	241236	267255	1478677
1917	79500	79500	5000	1050000 [18]		105000 [22]	24224	1320432	1050000	12064			258369	1320433
1918	79500	79500	10000	750000 [20]		335000 [24]	35732	1059732	750000	24224			285508	1059732
1919	75247	74200	10000	750000		160000 [25]	53612	1098059	750000	35732			312327	1098059
1920	74200	74200	10000	550000 [23]			54934	923334	550000	53612			319722	923334

Notes:

1 Gross profits after providing for bad and doubtful debts, interest to be paid and rebate on bills discounted not yet due.

2 The figures for 1865 cover a period of fourteen months, from 1 January 1864 (a change in the Bank's financial year occurred).

3 Two half-yearly dividends of £45000 had been paid (due to the change in the Bank's financial year).

4 All the previous year's balance (£17071) was used to cover the extensive fraud at Leith (forged bills of J. T. Hardie & Co.), for which a total maximum provision of £44000 was required.

5 A portion of the year's gross profits was used to cover the losses at Leith (see note 4), thus reducing the net profits for 1870.

6 Increase in capital used to strengthen reserve fund.

7 To extinguish the balance of the price paid for the business of the Central Bank.

8 Includes £375000 premium received from the new stock.

9 Edinburgh George Street branch required enlargement/rebuilding due to increasing business.

10 £5000 to writing down of property and £5000 to meet improvement and repair costs required.

11 Consisted of dividend of 12% (£75000) plus a 1% bonus (£12500); the bonus had to be dropped in 1895 due to fall in profit derived from investment (as a result of adverse conditions in money market) combined with greater than average provision required for losses from bad and doubtful debts.

12 Cost of new office at Bishopsgate St, London.

13 Towards cost of new London premises (Bishopsgate St).

14 £125000 was removed from reserve fund to provide for contingent loss anticipated in connection with realisation of the property of a firm having estates in the West Indies (value depreciated due to operation of the Continental Sugar Bounties).

15 To provide for contingent loss (see note 14), whereof £25000 from net profits.

16 £200000 was withdrawn from the reserve fund and credited to the investment account.

17 At credit of investment account (whereof £70000 from net profits and £200000 from reserve fund).

18 £150000 was withdrawn from the reserve fund and credited to the investment account.

19 At credit of investment account (whereof £80000 from net profits and £150000 from reserve fund).

20 £300000 was withdrawn to meet the cost of writing down the Bank's investments.

21 To write down investments (£300000), to meet contingencies (£80000).

22 To meet contingencies (£100000), to staff widows' fund (£5000).

23 £200000 was withdrawn from the reserve fund to meet all contingencies following a searching scrutiny of the Bank's investments and loans by the new Treasurer.

24 To meet contingencies (whereof £200000 from reserve fund).

25 To depreciation in investments.

Source: Bank of Scotland published annual reports.

Table A7 The position of the Bank at 28 February, 1921–67

Year ending February	Gross trading income	Less charges	Gross trading profits	Proposed inner allocations						Net profits to be declared	Carried forward from previous year	Total available for distribution
				To reserve fund no. II	To widows' fund	To bank premises	To bad and doubtful debts	Misc. allocations	Total inner allocations			
1921			783453 [1]		5500			468350 [2]	473850 [2]	309603	54933	364536
1922	995413	524025 [4]	471388		5500		125815 [5]	58729 [6]	190044	320242 [7]	76136	396378
1923	1159660	526416 [8]	633244	198375	500	45000		305061 [9]	548936	345177 [10]	72978	418155
1924	1048075	513349	534726	81000	2000	14000		82000 [11]	179000	355726	85200	440926
1925	1052149	552274	499875	50000	2000	10000		72000 [13]	134000	365875	102149	468024
1926	967346	567182	400164		2000	23000		7000 [13]	32000	368164	128824	496988
1927	976055	578936	397119		2000	25000			27000	370119	150347	520466
1928	1025821	593317	432504	25367	2000	32802			60169	372335	153466	525801
1929	1072217	628100	444117		2000	67834 [17]			69834	374283	166801	541084
1930	1023355	619283	404072		2000	29936	6264		38200	365872	170084	535956
1931	1054471	675701 [19]	378770		2000	9900			11900	366870	172456	539326
1932	988915	718735 [21]	270180		2000				2000	268180 [22]	200076	468256
1933	1067780	645074 [25]	422706		2000	6710	33290	67856 [26]	109856	312850	215756	528606
1934	1032176	674333 [29]	357843		500	20000 [30]	14967	15354 [31]	50821	307022	226157	533179
1935	1065601	682479 [32]	383122		500	34000 [33]	6735	31000 [34]	72235	310887	250679	561566
1936	1085079	695488 [36]	389591		500	35000 [37]		38000 [34]	73500	316091	252316	568407
1937	1110568	719856 [41]	390712		500	22500 [42]		50000 [34]	73000	317712	254157	571869
1938	1136166	763913 [44]	372253		500	33500 [45]		25000 [34]	59000	313253	255995	569248
1939	1164663	799529	365134	40000	500	19000 [49]			59500	305634	150084	455718
1940	1139793	837745	302048	10000	500	17000 [51]			27500	274548	151918	426466
1941	1212857	906952	305905	44500	500	7000 [53]			52000	253905	153466	407371
1942	1283019	1010374	272645	32500	500	7000 [53]			40000	232645	155571	388216
1943	1355165	1045797	309368	60000	500	7000 [53]	3744		71244	238124	156217	394341
1944	1418910	1082591	336319	70000	500	17000 [51]			87500	248819	157341	406160
1945	1493902	1126860	367042	100000	500	7000 [53]			107500	259542	159542	418702
1946	1655239	1240109	415130	100000	500	47000 [57]			147500	267630	159703	427333
1947	1826717	1344181	482536	100000	500	57000 [58]	11821	10000 [59]	179321	303215	161133	464348
1948	1938815	1509713	428602	30000	500	22000 [60]	74891		127391	301211	165948	467159
1949	2020222	1577475	442747	137500	500	2000 [61]			140000	302747	168759	471506
1950	2157948	1656225	501723	192500	500	2000 [61]			195000	306723	183106	489829
1951	2249938	1783663	466275	102000	500	2000 [61]	57826		162326	303949	191430	495379
1952	2255529	1300701	954828	212000	500	2000 [61]		452008 [59]	664508	290320	191979	482299

Table header (spanning): **Proposed to be allocated thus (as per published reports)** | **Special recoveries** | **Special losses**

Year ending February	To (published) reserve fund	To reserve for contingencies (no. II)	To dividend	To property	Misc.	Carried forward	Surplus on stocks sold	Fund for losses (bad debts) released	Amount at tax suspense accounts 2 and 3	Misc. special recoveries	Total available special recoveries	Deficits on stocks sold, less tax	Misc.	Total
1953	2342042	1391831	950211 [65]		135560	500				472440 [59]	608500	341711	191099	532810
1954	2675703 [67]	1382809	1292894		245161	500				584632 [59]	830293	462601	185460	648061
1955	2937404 [67]	1426093	1511311		64317	500	19907			938187 [59]	1022911	488400	186311	674711
1956	5160077	2962817	2197260		537614	2450		200 [61]		1013990 [59]	1554254	643006	256055 [70]	899061
1957	5040360	3055544	1984816		314000	3100	13845	200 [61]		1014687 [59]	1345832	638984	256811	895795
1958	5113989	3139094	1974895		334400	3100	93540	200 [61]		906694 [59]	1337934	636961	253545	890506
1959	5532086	3253899	2278187		433000	3100	146420	200 [61]		1006326 [59]	1589046	689141	248256	937397
1960	6314248	3413321	2900927		615000	10525	6753	200 [61]		1378476 [59]	2010954	889973	243397	1133370
1961	6884824	3364258	3230566		610000	13000		200 [61]		1574723 [59]	2197923	1032643	224170	1256813
1962	7523337	3895454	3627883		540000	13000	203518	200 [61]		1780925 [59]	2537643	1090240	220826	1311066
1963	7602997	4222973	3380024		610000	13000		200 [61]		1702905 [59]	2326105	1053919	225079	1278998
1964	7747211	4517308	3229903		520000	13000				1634412 [59]	2167412	1062491	204423	1266915
1965	9049349	4917274	4132075		680000	18250				2206108 [59]	2904358	1227717	192340	1420057
1966	10377736	5454997	4922739		1050000	20000				2012859 [59]	3082859	1839880	184057	2023937
1967	10554091	5935089	4619002		875000	20000				1711161 [59]	2606161	2012841	181737	2194578
1921			148400	20000	120000 [3]	76136								
1922	125000		148400	50000		72978								
1923	125000		157955	50000		85200								
1924	125000		163779	50000		102149	6173	116943		118245 [12]	241361			
1925	125000		164300	50000		128724	45780	18993		4991	69764			
1926	125000		171641	50000		150347	250	49947		5368	55565			
1927	125000		192000	50000		153466	130274	18087			148361		3944	3944
1928	125000		204000	30000		166801	41283	29416		40544 [16]	111243			
1929	125000		216000	30000		170084	199567	74178		134014 [18]	407759			
1930	117500		216000	30000		172456	37551			43472 [18]	81023			
1931	100000		209250	30000		200076	112659				112659		55636 [20]	55636
1932			202500	50000		215756	45664				45664		39283 [23]	39283
1933	60000		202500	40000		226106	17931	37357		115693 [27]	170981			
1934		40000	202500			250679	16487			5857	22344			
1935		50000	209250			252316	194			11848 [35]	12042			
1936	50000		209250	25000 [30]	30000 [38]	254157	284765	128403		179532 [39]	592700			
1937	50000		205875	30000 [30]	30000 [38]	255995	10722	37844		46658 [43]	95224			

Table A7 continued

	Proposed to be allocated thus (as per published reports)						Special recoveries					Special losses		
Year ending February	To (published) reserve fund	To reserve for contingencies (no. II)	To dividend	To property	Misc.	Carried forward	Surplus on stocks sold	Fund for losses (bad debts) released	Amount at tax suspense accounts 2 and 3	Misc. special recoveries	Total available special recoveries	Deficits on stocks sold, less tax	Misc.	Total
1938	50000		204164	25000	30000 [38]	150084 [46]		109732		79373 [47]	189105			
1939		50000	208800		45000 [50]	151918	18279	4511	21161	59	44010			
1940		75000	168000		30000 [38]	153466	6342	718	45222	295811 [52]	348093			
1941		70000	151800		30000 [38]	155571	16055	415	17132	57685 [54]	91287			
1942		70000	132000		30000 [38]	156217	25158	4364		8720	38242			
1943		75000	132000		30000 [38]	157341	14143		132640	33880 [55]	180663			
1944		85000	132000		30000 [38]	159160	142205	8781	107741	725	259452			
1945	75000		144000		40000 [56]	159703	37300	12632	133974		183906			
1946	75000		151200		40000 [56]	161133	64753	8361	130578		203692			
1947	100000		158400		40000 [56]	165948	518989		175501	1213	695703			
1948		110000	158400		30000 [38]	168759	73995		164398	1591	239984			
1949	100000		158400		30000 [38]	183106	61069		328172	150	389391			
1950		100000	158400		40000 [56]	191430	12660	37243	302623	687	353213			
1951		100000	158400		45000 [62]	191979	429836		232796	850	663482			
1952		110000	151200		30000 [38]	191099	59804	204440		100	120720 [63]	457052		457052
1953		100000	217350		30000 [38]	185460	23671	9343		875	8079 [63]	280205		280205
1954		100000	321750		40000 [38]	186311	50706	48523		2630	61297 [63]	113912		113912
1955		100000	346500		40000 [38]	188211	201809			3937	123928 [63]	129578		129578
1956		200000	362250		80000 [38]	256811	36007	179359			114333 [63]	623911		623911
1957		200000	362250		80000 [38]	253545	22104				21987 [63]	175030		175030
1958		200000	362250		80000 [38]	248256	600539				376042 [63]	833291		833291
1959		200000	414000		80000 [38]	243397	741828				397251 [63]	452213		452213
1960	150000	150000	529200 [73]		80000 [38]	224170	19937				19448 [63]	317431		317431
1961	150000	150000	655987		80000 [38]	220826	5415				5415	615409		615409
1962	150000	200000	655987		80000 [38]	225079	3596				3596	359720		359720
1963	150000	150000	694575		80000 [38]	204423	1792				1792	217463	266283 [76]	483746
1964	150000	150000	694575		80000 [38]	192341	10232				10232	42555	137235 [76]	179790
1965	400000	0	756000		80000 [38]	184057						440238	244051 [78]	684289
1966	500000	250000	1012200		80000 [38]	181737						69265	534168 [76]	603433
1967	500000	250000	1428000		80000 [38]	186578	308				308	540	306047 [76]	306587

Position of reserves after allocations from profits and recoveries

Year ending February	Published reserve fund	Profit and loss account carried forward	Reserve fund no. II (inner)	Reserve no. III (capital)	Reserve no. IV (goodwill of subsidiary companies taken over)	Pension fund reserve	Pension fund (former Union Bank)	Investment reserve	Surplus on stocks, less tax	Contingent account for taxes (surplus)	Income tax suspense account	Tax suspense account no. 2	Heritable property sinking fund	Heritable property suspense account	Heritable property suspense account no. 2	London property sinking fund
1921																
1922																
1923	800000	85200	198375			50000		58068	1445782	175000						
1924	925000	102149	370006			50000		181091	1245391	120000						
1925	1050000	128724	434726			50000		221562	1235472	195000						
1926	1507500 [14]	150347	474684			50000		227130	1165877	297000						
1927	1632500	153466	119075 [15]						1030489							
1928	1757500	166801	1305250						1087561							
1929	1882500	170084	1600000						821112							
1930	2000000	172456	1600000						717418							
1931	2100000	200076	1644194						759752							
1932	2100000	215756	1252451 [24]													
1933	2160000	226106	1288294 [28]					33521	2420969		150000		14000	24462		
1934	2200000	250679	1328294					36836	2709107		129091		18000	23962		
1935	2250000	252316	1378294					250000	2912567		131172		22000	40782		
1936	2300000	254157	1307036 [40]					150000	2635310		135155		26000	40703		
1937	2350000	255995	1344880					175000	2561338		149634		18500	41208		
1938	2050000 [48]	150084	1454612					221854	2465282		189245		20500	43813	25000	
1939	2100000	151918	1457719					520876	1768752		214674		22500	45215	50000	
1940	2100000	153466	1581273					587331	1789632		266813		24500	45137	75000	
1941	2100000	155571	1710161					606183	1618845		257076	110000	26500	45098	90000	
1942	2100000	156217	1816491					645436	1389681		254137		28500	45098	105000	
1943	2100000	157341	2077130					672121	1405906		173702		30500	55047	110000	
1944	2100000	159160	2236652					737950	1364885		173595		32500	65047	115000	
1945	2175000	159703	2342652					768064	1273096		195244		34500	64716	120000	
1946	2250000	161133	2446623					772667	1274085		180227		36500	99520	125000	
1947	2600000	165948	2297423					232656	1335924		199440		38500	150696	130000	
1948	2600000	168759	2437423					396503	1396016		235457		40500	162849	135000	
1949	3000000	183106	2337286						1355045		32629		42500	401379	140000	
1950	3000000	191431	2283562								81856		44500	482755	145000	

Table A7 continued

Position of reserves after allocations from profits and recoveries

Year ending February	Published reserve fund	Profit and loss account carried forward	Reserve fund no. II (inner)	Reserve no. III (capital)	Reserve no. IV (goodwill of subsidiary companies taken over)	Pension fund reserve	Pension fund (former Union Bank)	Investment reserve	Surplus on stocks, less tax	Contingent account for taxes (surplus)	Income tax suspense account	Tax suspense account no. 2	Heritable property sinking fund	Heritable property suspense account	Heritable property suspense account no. 2	London property sinking fund
1951	3000000	191979	2582983					367769			87084	217496		481210		
1952	3000000	191099	89301 [64]													
1953	3000000	185460	134859 [64]	29092 [66]												
1954	3000000	186311	3645420 [64]	32111 [68]												
1955	3000000	188211	3059176 [64]	28385 [69]												
1956	4500000	256811	283175 [64]	24883 [69]			500000 [71]								17632	
1957	4500000	253545	2714809 [64]	24883			500000								18197	
1958	4500000	248256	331312 [64]	24883			0 [72]								18776	
1959	4500000	243397	4826308 [64]	21199 [69]											19371	
1960	6000000 [74]	224170	3902021 [64]	8043 [69]											20009	
1961	6150000 [75]	220826	3901428 [64]	8043											20664	
1962	6300000 [75]	225079	4294800 [64]	8043											21336	
1963	6450000 [75]	204423	7849947 [64]	8043	35726										22030 [77]	
1964	6600000 [75]	192340	8383222 [64]	8043	35726											
1965	7000000 [79]	184057	6299178 [64]	0 [80]	35726											0
1966	7500000 [75]	181737	7195589 [64]	0	35726											0
1967	8000000 [75]	186578	7785487 [64]	11665 [81]	35726											0

Notes:

1 Includes (a) recovery from Treasury for five years' o/a notes (£34417) and (b) recovery from other accounts (£407865) (including £386510 on Pará contract) less provision for bad and doubtful debts, almost entirely for debts in the Bank's books for many years (£139471).

2 Consists of income tax suspense account (£75000), investments depreciation account (£363350) and pension fund (£30000).

3 To depreciation in investments.

4 Includes £60000 extra for taxes.

5 'The Treasurer explained that of the sum of £125,815 set aside for Bad and Doubtful Debts £100,000 is being earmarked for the advances of Dr Pearson (deceased) and Sir James H. Dunn and the obligations of Sir Wm. MacKenzie as recommended by the London Committee in January last' (RS 1/6/1).

6 Consists of old life policies provision (£1729), income tax suspense account (£30000) and pension fund (£27000).

7 Includes an extra special addition of £38898 consisting of surplus on stocks sold (£19935), net over-provision for losses on stocks sold (£13477), 'Notes' recovery (£4299) and Provisional Order expenses not required.

8 Includes £82000 extra for taxes.

9 Consists of income tax suspense account (£175000), investments depreciation account (£58061), pension fund (£30000) and pension fund reserve (£42000).

10 Includes an extra special addition of £260869 consisting of net over-provision for bad and doubtful debts (£93375), existing income tax reserve (£75000), existing income tax refund (£30000), surplus on stocks sold (£17729) and net over-provision for losses on stocks sold (£14765).

11 Consists of income tax suspense account (£50000) and pension fund (£32000).

12 Consists of surplus on income tax reserve (£41105) and net over-provision for losses on stocks sold (£114140).

13 To income tax suspense account.

14 i.e. Balance from 1925 (£1050000), transfer from profits (£125000) plus premium on new issue of £262500 stock (£175000 called up) (£332500).

15 Balance c/f from 1926 (£474684) plus surpluses to tax requirements (£127350) and transfer (£588741).

16 Income tax relief on losses on stocks sold (£39973) plus net over-provision for losses (£571).

17 Includes £26750 to heritable property suspense account.

18 Net over-provision for losses on stocks sold.

19 Includes £23000 transferred to capital account on account of building alterations at certain branches.

20 Includes £55140 provision for bad and doubtful debts.

21 Includes £13400 transferred to capital account on account of building alterations at certain branches.

22 There was a delay in deciding how to distribute the declared net profits (perhaps a disagreement?) – see BS 1/6/6.

23 Fresh provision required for depreciation in investments.

24 i.e. Balance c/f from 1931 (£1644194) plus net surpluses on stocks sold (£4786) less transfer (£396529).

25 Includes £5000 transferred to capital account on account of building alterations at certain branches.

26 Consists of income tax suspense account (£43000), investments depreciation account (£18642) and income tax suspense account no. 2 (£6214).

27 Includes £1595 at income tax suspense account, £5000 at tax suspense account no. 2, £79655 at tax suspense account no. 3, and £28138 bonus received in respect of conversion of 5% to 3.5% war loan (applied to reducing cost of holding).

28 i.e. Balance c/f from 1932 (£1252451) plus £142843 transferred from special recoveries, less £107000 transferred to income tax suspense account.

29 Includes £4354 transferred to capital account on account of building alterations at certain branches.

30 To heritable property suspense account.

31 Consists of investments depreciation account (£11177) and suspense account for Investment Mortgage (Philippi) (£4000).

32 Includes £5882 transferred to capital account on account of building alterations at certain branches.

33 Consists of £4000 to heritable property sinking fund and £30000 to heritable property suspense account.

34 To investments depreciation account.

35 Consists of £6656 at income tax suspense account no. 2 not required, £1192 provision released from fund for losses investment account and £4000 at suspense account for investment mortgage (Philippi).

36 Includes £6512 transferred to capital account on account of building alterations at certain branches.

37 Consists of £4000 to heritable property sinking fund and £30000 to heritable property suspense account.

38 To pension fund.

39 Includes £17293 income tax recovered (overpayment), £41828 provision released from fund for losses investment account and £120018 income tax on surpluses.

40 i.e. Balance c/f from 1935 (£1378294) plus £128740 transferred from special recoveries, less £199998 transferred.

41 Includes £4999 transferred to capital account on account of building alterations at certain branches.

42 Consists of £2500 to heritable property sinking fund and £20000 to heritable property suspense account.

Table A7 *continued*

43 Consists of £21531 at income tax suspense account not required, £10000 income tax on surpluses and £15127 transferred from heritable property sinking fund.
44 Includes £3570 transferred to capital account on account of building alterations at certain branches.
45 Consists of £2000 to heritable property sinking fund and £31500 to heritable property suspense account.
46 £110000 was deducted from this sum and transferred to reserve fund in accordance with resolutions passed at a meeting of proprietors on 21 December 1937 in connection with reconstruction of capital.
47 Includes £15127 at income tax suspense account no. 2 not required, £19750 at income tax suspense account no. 3 not required and £43858 income tax on surpluses.
48 i.e. Balance c/f from 1937 (£2350000) plus £110000 transferred from profit and loss, £340000 premium on new issue of stock and £50000 transferred from published profits, less £800000 transferred to capital.
49 Consists of £2000 to London property sinking fund and £17000 to heritable property suspense account.
50 Consists of £30000 to pension fund and £15000 to heritable property accounts.
51 Consists of £2000 to London property sinking fund and £15000 to heritable property suspense account.
52 Includes £295106 provision released from fund for losses investment account.
53 Consists of £2000 to London property sinking fund and £5000 to heritable property suspense account.
54 Provision released from fund for losses investment account.
55 Consists of £32535 provision released from fund for losses investment account.
56 Consists of £30000 to pension fund and £10000 to widows' fund.
57 Consists of £2000 to London property sinking fund and £45000 to heritable property suspense account.
58 Consists of £2000 to London property sinking fund and £55000 to heritable property suspense account.
59 To tax suspense account.
60 Consists of £2000 to London property sinking fund and £20000 to heritable property suspense account.
61 To London property sinking fund.
62 Consists of £30000 to pension fund and £15000 to widows' fund.
63 Less tax.
64 Details of reserve no. II (inner) – see table below.
65 Includes accrued dividend from Union Bank of £75748 from 23 October 1952 to 28 February 1953.
66 i.e. Proportion of dividend payment on Union Bank shares from April to October 1952, less tax (£63380), less expenses of amalgamation (£9288) and payment to UBS 'B' shareholders (12.5p per share – £25000).
67 Includes dividend on UBS shares (gross).
68 i.e. Previous balance plus £3019 (tax difference on proportion of UBS dividend).
69 i.e. Previous balance less expenses of amalgamation.
70 This consisted of £188211 brought forward from the previous year and £67844 brought forward on account of the Union Bank of Scotland Ltd, following fusion on 1 March 1955.
71 i.e. Balance from previous year (£978444) less transfer to reserve no. II (£478444).
72 Balance transferred to trustees of pension fund.
73 i.e. 8% on capital of £4500000 (£220500) and 8% on capital of £6300000 (£308700).
74 i.e. Previous balance less amount capitalised (£900000), plus transfer from reserve no. II (£900000), premium on rights issue (£1350000) and transfer from trading profits (£150000).
75 Previous balance plus transfer from trading profits.
76 To fund for losses, bad and doubtful debts, less tax.
77 Transferred to Bishopsgate property account.

960

78 Consists of £237921 to fund for losses, bad and doubtful debts, less tax and £6130 surpluses on stocks sold, less tax.
79 i.e. Previous balance less amount capitalised (£2100000) plus transfer from reserve no. II (£2100000) and transfer from trading profits (£400000).
80 i.e. Previous balance less part cost of new issue of capital stock.
81 Surplus balance on properties sold.

Note 64: Reserve fund no. II (inner)

Year	Previous balance	By tax suspense accounts	By trading profits	By special recoveries	By sales of property	By investment reserve	By surplus on fund for losses investment account	By cash surpluses	By heritable property suspense account	By heritable property sinking fund	By benevolent fund suspense account	By Union Bank	By pensions and allowances fund	By fund for losses, bad and doubtful debts (provision released)	To special losses	To published reserve	To fund for losses investment account	To fund for losses no. 2 account	To reserve no. IV	To pension fund	To cost of new issue of capital stock	To additional provision required for investments	Special item*	Balance of inner reserve carried forward
1952	2607983	392012	322000	120720	3141	367769			481210	46500	10000				457052		3804982							89301
1953	89301	7747	235560	8078	428	1239000									280205									1299909
1954	1299909	11975	345161	61298			2000000								113912									3604431
1955	3604431	64690	164317	123928											129578									3027788
1956	3027788	96227	737614	114333	25050	2050000		7000							623911		800000							283175
1957	283175	13474	514000	21987	7203							3870629			175030		7450000					2450000		2714809
1958	2714809	9037	534400	376042	17984			5881					478444		833291									331312
1959	331312	6958	633000	397251			3910000								452213					43550				4826308
1960	4826308	8696	765000	19448											317431									3902021
1961	3902021	9523	760000	5415										89878	615409	900000	500000							3901428
1962	3901428	9496	740000	3396											359720		250000							4294800
1963	4294800	2592	760000	1792			3300000	10235							483746				35726					7849947
1964	7849947	32833	670000	10232											179790									8383222
1965	8383222	57308	680000												684289	2100000					4505			6299178
1966	6299178	492	1300000			200000									603433						648		32558	7195589
1967	7195589	21177	875000	308			500000								306587			500000						7785487

*Special item = $\frac{11}{12}$ of special cash payment to staff (£74419), less tax.

Source: BS 1/6/1–12, Record of the Minutes, Weekly Court, 1919–67.

961

Table A8 Bank of Scotland published annual balance sheets, 1921–93

	Liabilities						Capital resources						Assets	
Year ending Feb.	Note circulation	Drafts issued payable within 14 days	Current, deposit and other accounts [1]	Proposed dividend	Subtotal	Acceptances, guarantees and other obligations for account of customers [2]	Issued capital [3]	Reserves	Balance of profit and loss account	Total capital resources [4]	Misc. liabilities	Total liabilities	Cash and balances with the Bank of England [5]	Balances with other banks
1921	4328175	415979	37687358	74200	42505712	841751	1325000	550000	76137	1951137		45298600	4532729	660292
1922	3575429	698000	38624814	74200	42972443	276426	1325000	675000	72978	2072978		45321847	3919555	498208
1923	3338804	563193	34695037	79500	38676534	653019	1325000	800000	85201	2210202		41539755	3878804	755212
1924	3305833	642668	33232600	82150	37263251	460598	1325000	925000	102149	2352149		40075998	3415926	936653
1925	3231858	946829	31429270	82150	35690107	635396	1325000	1050000	128824	2503824		38829328	3402332	579877
1926	3046114	843818	29903512	87362	33880806	768123	1500000	1507500	150348	3157848		37806776	3303302	653070
1927	3015709	269876	31936520	96000	35318105	1045003	1500000	1632500	153466	3285966		39649074	3294556	924188
1928	2874100	784256	30984420	108000	34750776	864578	1500000	1757500	166801	3424301		39039655	3321791	347569
1929	2776147	266951	32068385	108000	35219483	834124	1500000	1882500	170084	3552584		39606191	2989742	449461
1930	3040542	470320	32258308	108000	35877170	802408 [10]	1500000	2000000	172457	3672457		40352035	3124240	251682
1931	2995337	664167	32535468	104625	36299597	622409 [11]	1500000	2100000	200077	3800077		40722083	3020962	344375
1932	3063722	235434	30828263	101250	34228669	500094 [13]	1500000	2100000	215757	3815757		38544520	3023551	363741
1933	3040873	381280	36049096	101250	39572499	831707 [14]	1500000	2160000	226157	3886157		44290363	3204465	379242
1934	2980601	413352	35470014	101250	38965217	625424 [14]	1500000	2200000	250679	3950679		43541320	3040779	455788
1935	3053576	164805	36653815	104625	39976821	535346 [14]	1500000	2250000	252316	4002316		44514483	3212815	344402
1936	3128569	537188	39518484	104625	43288866	1855968 [14]	1500000	2300000	254158	4054158		49198992	3245996	782445
1937	3239247	665602	37635698	102938	41643485	2451194 [15]	1500000	2350000	255995	4105995		48201414	3355208	433593
1938	3363767	388512	39298450	102914	43153643	3712585 [16]	2400000	2050000	150085	4600085		51466313	3552561	694486
1939	3414725	355843	37851691	104400	41729359	4448119 [16]	2400000	2100000	151918	4651918		50829396	3507518	752982
1940	3941242	256190	42137116	90000	46424548	5261274 [17]	2400000	2100000	153467	4653467		56339289	4202371	518720
1941	4834527	706983	47596107	82800	53220417	4858947 [18]	2400000	2100000	155572	4655572		62734936	4560350	575736
1942	5939173	1086590	50593844	72000	57691607	4322846 [20]	2400000	2100000	156217	4656217		66670670	6211471	394265
1943	7415615	608341	60829644	72000	68925600	3470725 [20]	2400000	2100000	157342	4657342		77053667	7774110	379491
1944	8991010	1393939	62235581	72000	72692530	3348591 [20]	2400000	2100000	159161	4659161		80700282	9447122	364733
1945	10043172	993950	71777717	84000	82898839	2820232 [21]	2400000	2175000	159704	4734704		90453775	10527848	372575
1946	10983833	723264	76781160	79200	88567457	3387592 [21]	2400000	2250000	161134	4811134		96766183	11746692	362958
1947	10972730	1992309	87073848	79200	100118087	3574553 [21]	2400000	2600000	165948	5165948		108858588	11515961	968751
1948	9631873		87927503	79200	97638576	2956102 [21]	2400000	2600000	168759	5168759		105764437	10623721	1275545
1949	9887000		94056630	79200	104022830	3968779	2400000	3000000	183107	5583107		113574716	10867427	844159

Year													
1950	9945054	97496902	79200	107521156	3550949	2400000	3000000	191431	5591431		11663536	11068766	904135
1951	10255750	98134108	79200	108469058	5362965	2400000	3000000	191979	5591979		11924002	11658646	885928
1952	11292130	92314908	75600	103682638	5054467	2400000	3000000	191099	5591099		114328204	11767175	1751586
1953	12497834	93483935 [24]	141750	106123519	353873	4500000	3000000	185460	7685460		117162852	13690966	1346798
1954	21859632	170853913	173250	192886795	8851871	4500000	4500000 [27]	251940 [28]	9251940		210990606	23592201	2112425
1955	22948130	176525469	173250	199646849	13116184	4500000	4500000 [27]	256054 [29]	9256054		220190877	25700711	3256210
1956	24448696	171600165	181125	196229986	20703884	4500000	4500000	256811	9256811		226190681	27086502	3673073
1957	26061042	173894731	181125	200136898	20681612	4500000	4500000	253545	9253545		230072055	29144770	353213
1958	27594088	168077105	181125	195852318	22376062	4500000	4500000	248256	9248256		227476636	29581099	3982746
1959	27798670	174049072	232875	202080617	16092348	4500000	4500000	257292	9257292		227430257	30852884	3487610
1960	28185742	183443930	308700	219938372	31160762	6300000	6000000	262792	12562792		255661926	30669593	4101255
1961	28264770	182432173	347287	211044230	33434903	6300000	6150000	268422	12718422		257197555	31528043	
1962	27630851	191975590	347287	219953728	31653468	6300000	6300000	270442	12870442		264477638	30335039	
1963	27067724	196745231	385875	224198830	30140557	6300000	6450000	290277	13040277		267379664	29258808	
1964	29047448	211820676	347287	241215411	32623496	6300000	6600000	306264	13206264		287045171	31949840	
1965	29452417	218477475	370125	248300017	57190528	8400000	7000000	325536	15725536		321216081	32982913	
1966	29766628	236203106	444150 [31]	266413884 [31]	39947214	8400000	7500000	330659	16230659		322591757	33863920	
1967	28479946	248534169	756000	277770115	26953533	8400000	8000000	383101	16783101		321506749	32800100	
1968	29624608	276441484	840000	306906092	39240354	8400000	8500000	498553	17398553		363344999	33533049	
1969	30472891	302458228	808920	333740039	110568838	8400000	9500000	549877	18449877		462758754	33148870	
1970	49209504	419258195 [33]	1290000	469757699		12900000	29255179 [34]		42155179	4110657 [35]	516023535	55138623	
1971	54311286	476731888 [36]	1290000	532333174		12900000	29318092		42218092	6129667 [37]	580680933	63914630	
1972	59353327	578157875 [39]	1419000	638930202		12900000	30305304		43205304	10233815 [40]	692369321	65037081	
1973	63322785	767201023 [41]	1638300	832162108		16125000	53922721		70044721	10274129 [42]	912483958	70627518	
1974	72986000	1006838000 [44]	1225000	1081049000		32250000	52674000		84924000	21163000 [45]	1187136000	79641000	
1975	96402000	1040696000 [47]	1342000	1138440000		32250000	56159000		88409000	23849000 [48]	1250698000	101123000	
1976	110909000	1170517000 [50]	1431000	1282857000		32250000	74532000		106782000	28978000 [51]	1418617000	118221000	
1977	119071000	1399416000 [53]	1575000	1520062000		32250000	83629000		115879000	38653000 [54]	1674594000	129876000	
1978	128478000	1680322000 [57]	1757000	1810557000		32250000	93448000		125698000	43455000 [58]	1979710000	145441000	
1979	148302000	2027740000	1962000	2178004000		32250000	149353000		181603000	33845000 [62]	2393452500	501434000	
1980	163956000	2404293000	2499000	2570748000		32250000	169544000		201794000	43716000 [63]	2816258000	538697000	
1981	171500000	3112900000	3100000	3287500000		32400000	205500000		237900000	42700000 [62]	3568100000	719100000	
1982	167100000	3789700000	3600000	3960400000		32600000	269600000		357000000 [64]	96700000 [64]	4359300000	753400000	
1983	185800000	4638800000	4400000	4874000000		32700000	301900000		408300000 [65]	115500000 [65]	5324100000	938300000	
1984	211300000	5405000000	5400000	5621700000		32800000	289000000		424100000 [66]	199900000 [66]	6143400000	944900000	
1985	241300000	6307000000	7600000	6555900000		82300000	320000000		586800000 [67]	258600000 [67]	7216800000	1317500000	
1986	260000000	6945900000	10500000	7216400000		123800000	390700000		821400000 [68]	394700000 [68]	8125600000	1630400000	
1987	280200000	8104100000	13000000	8397300000		124200000	434400000		861200000 [69]	387200000 [69]	9343100000	1787000000	
1988	254400000	9623400000	15300000	9892700000		124600000	525700000		1036400000 [70]	462500000 [70]	11005500000	2079300000	

Table A8 *continued*

Liabilities / Capital resources / Assets

Year ending Feb.	Note circulation	Drafts issued payable within 14 days	Current, deposit and other accounts [1]	Proposed dividend	Subtotal	Acceptances, guarantees and other obligations for account of customers [2]	Issued capital [3]	Reserves	Balance of profit and loss account	Total capital resources [4]	Misc. liabilities	Total liabilities	Cash and balances with the Bank of England [5]	Balances with other banks
1989	259800000		1244010000	23400000	1272330000		287600000 [71]	538400000		1279200000 [72]	523800000 [72]	1407310000 [72]	264170000	
1990	278100000		1637650000	28000000	1668260000		288600000 [73]	607200000		1538200000 [74]	816100000 [74]	1839450000 [74]	326200000	
1991	280000000		1989920000	32600000	2021180000		390600000 [75]	658400000		1707000000 [76]	834400000 [76]	2209520000 [76]	399400000	
1992	308800000		2206470000	39900000	2241340000		487100000 [77]	773900000		2132200000 [78]	1066700000 [78]	2474110000 [78]	472270000	
1993	345000000		2594650000	41900000	2633340000		489300000 [79]	761500000		2252400000 [80]	1225200000 [80]	2880940000 [80]	560080000	

Fixed assets

Year ending Feb.	Cheques in course of collection	Balances with, and cheques in course of collection on, other banks	Money at call and short notice	Bills discounted [6]	Treasury bills	Special deposit with the Bank of England	Total investments [7]	Advances to customers and other accounts [8]	Amounts advanced on instalment credit and other financial agreements [9]	Trade investments	Property and equipment	Liabilities of customers for acceptances, guarantees etc., as per contra	Misc. assets	Total assets
1921	1380982		2195705	1651467	5005000		14687128	13706357			637189	841751		45298600
1922	1552891		2650000	754993	7158000		18061142	9849492			601142	27426		45321849
1923	1539989		2824731	711316	3660000		16994050	9925374			597261	653019		41539756
1924	1348120		2945971	984025	2820000		17052435	9534617			577652	460598		40075997
1925	1770326		2625000	1170704	2380000		12979177	12726366			560150	635396		38829328
1926	1422527		2525000	752068	2290000		12071936	13484853			535898	768123		37806777
1927	1492005		2815000	1018772	3540000		11665218	13332097			522235	1045003		39649074
1928	1745037		2255000	492075	1610000		13621227	14285379			497000	864578		39039656
1929	1457030		2430000	893638	1920000		10942478	17229718			460000	834124		39606191
1930	1762303		2689000	768731	1335000		11336388	17852283			430000	802408		40352035
1931	1863710		2425000	630195	1410000		13283328	16722003			400000	622409	100 [12]	40722082
1932	1153786		2505000	625129	1115000		13777185	15080934			400000	500094	100 [12]	38544520
1933	1436517		4550000	468109	1785000		20548599	10686623			400000	831707	100 [12]	44490362
1934	1858464		3885000	441772	1230000		21216484	10387509			400000	625424	100 [12]	43541320

Year	A	B	C	D	E	F	G	H	I	J	K	L	M
1935	1360889	3670000	933448	1195000		22274088	10588395			400000	535346	100 [12]	44514483
1936	1352833	4143000	393877	510000		24259950	12254824			400000	1855968	100 [12]	49198993
1937	1534084	3663000	251424	600000		25677132	9799939			435000	2451934	100 [12]	48201414
1938	1380409	4798000	233190	650000		26111694	9868288			465000	3712585	100 [12]	51466313
1939	1647651	4021000	132930	450000		25676699	9727397			465000	4448119	100 [12]	50829396
1940	1837734	4300000	395436	2000000		26841427	10508426			473800	5261274	100 [12]	56339288
1941	2644751	4960000	500280	250000		29289723	9617248			477900	485947	5000000 [19]	62734935
1942	2696667	4800000	242650	525000		32431739	9062132			483900	4322846	5500000 [19]	66670670
1943	5183972	6510000	200697	350000		36765187	8430086			489400	3470725	7500000 [19]	77053668
1944	3921273	5805000	26593	350000		40602928	7840641			493400	3348591	8500000 [19]	80700281
1945	3616485	7400000	162922	500000		45625121	7928592			500000	2802232	1100000 [19]	90453775
1946	3665526	8275000	17776	500000		49097171	9192968			500000	3387592	10020500 [22]	96766183
1947	5581705	9550000	1150958			54159581	11816079			500000	3574553	10041000 [23]	108858588
1948	5476133	9625000	1539092			53158648	13099196			510000	2956102	7500000 [19]	105763437
1949	7589585	8350000	1024021			57418611	14962134			550000	3968779	8000000 [19]	113574716
1950	6224506	12625000	2207065			58193253	17329862			560000	3550949	4000000 [19]	116663536
1951	10997273	8925000	3183525			53310781	21499884			600000	5362965	3000000 [19]	119424002
1952	10325817	9710000	2713604			46528278	25853588			623689	5054467		114328204
1953	12081594	12054000	1704525			48799662	21384827 [25]			646607	353873	2100000 [26]	117162852
1954	17193486	18214000	6286050			95633886	37804619			1302068	8851871		210990606
1955	16661790	17323500	5416024			94889312	44306779			1348577	13116184		222019087
1956	22142423	18814000	4233930			83437657	44695468			1403744	20703884		226190681
1957	27024401	16358000	5674551			84192474	41998283			1459751	20681612		230072055
1958	20683385	21241000	5293596			81995859	40492293			1830596	22376062		227476636
1959	21044817	18860000	3987493			76637173	53112604	1387897		1967431	16092348		227430257
1960	20907985	22270000	4964088			77803166	58479676	3256258		2049143	31160762		255661926
1961	13143939	19700000	3608181		1700000	55816511	74808282	5087691		2134148	33434903	16235857 [30]	257197555
1962	14018143	22995000	5987858		2800000	44557896	86869080	5671355		2481653	31653468	17108146 [30]	264477638
1963	14271188	23833000	4471749			37409965	104936776	5904673		2961469	30140557	1491479 [30]	267379664
1964	14710166	28207000	5946512			37577791	110987741	7276727		2847966	32623496	14917932 [30]	287045171
1965	14313737	22015000	3662677		1100000	23144351	136690042	974934		3123299	57190528	18344600 [30]	321216081
1966	19540103	28932000	5684921		2200000	20166132	139110617	11295220		3291190	39947214	19660440 [30]	322591757
1967	18958979	32297000	9180564		2400000	27271687	127696239	10635763		3525973	26953533	29986911 [30]	321506749
1968	29127806	34877000	8681916		2700000	42512567	124188240	11515828	1652017	5681743	39240354	30134479 [30]	363544999
1969	32791242	35218000	8749776		3700000	53940506	141624370	10345935	1774760	7344587	110568838	3451870 [32]	462758754
1970	47453564	37128219	13002466	3000000		74108778	244243223	21478197	4206420	12564045			516023535
1971	45705194	43675289	15215896	600000	6800000	80916142	270295792	26588045	4516037	17036990		16918 [38]	580680933
1972	37653085	82882482	33015530	0		104332021	312191922	32163015	3552139	21542046			692369321
1973	33745956	132439715	9397138	8000000	16435000	60985520	494137826	42795995	3781738	39571449		568103 [43]	912483958

Table A8 continued

Year ending Feb.	Cheques in course of collection	Balances with, and cheques in course of collection on, other banks	Money at call and short notice	Bills discounted [6]	Treasury bills	Special deposit with the Bank of England	Total investments [7]	Advances to customers and other accounts [8]	Amounts advanced on instalment credit and other financial agreements [9]	Trade investments	Fixed assets Property and equipment	Liabilities of customers for acceptances, etc., as per contra	Misc. assets	Total assets
1974		43957000	165672000	16113000	3080000	30665000	95004000	643714000	51588000	6814000	49746000		1122000 [46]	1187136000
1975		38965000	160186000	24563000	3047000	23105000	52305000	728532000	49315000	6322000	60314000		2921000 [49]	1250698000
1976		52069000	161346000	29899000	39214000	22640000	75547000	756357000	58243000	8841000	49533000		46707000 [52]	1418611000
1977		85585000	196969000	32869000	38299000	21270000	88684000	879195000	82732000 [55]	10267000	50887000		57961000 [56]	1674594000
1978		95812000	216083000	31406000	44598000	29010000	102748000	1058517000 [59]	105530000 [60]	7294000	54010000		89261000 [61]	1979710000
1979	102528000					4865000	109372000	1583060000	16852000	75341000				2393452000
1980	81261000						133536000	1963092000	18931000	80741000				2816258000
1981	100300000						184300000	2455000000	21100000	88300000				3568100000
1982	110100000						193200000	3154700000	23100000	124800000				4359300000
1983	128600000						171700000	3931900000	20200000	133400000				5324100000
1984	107300000						375300000	4564000000	15700000	136200000				6143400000
1985	132100000						339000000	5262600000	12800000	152800000				7216800000
1986	170700000						318000000	5813900000	13900000	178700000				8125600000
1987	131200000						282200000	6928800000	18100000	195800000				9343100000
1988	159000000						239300000	8240900000	31500000	255500000				11005500000
1989	170900000						230400000	10705800000	33700000	290600000				14073100000
1990	163800000						246200000	14364200000	35200000	323100000				18394500000
1991	176800000						230300000	17268900000	38400000	386800000				22095200000
1992	180900000						396500000	18995700000	39300000	406000000				24741100000
1993	203500000						509100000	22006300000	18900000	470800000				28809400000

Notes:
1 From 1921–46 this heading was 'deposits and credit balances', but included internal reserves; the heading changed to 'Deposit, Current and other accounts, including provision for contingencies' in 1947.
2 Headed 'Acceptances to banking and other customers', 1921–46.
3 Between 1949 and 1975 both the authorised and the issued and fully-paid capital were stated.

4 Capital resources included issued capital, reserves, balance of profit and loss account, minority interests in subsidiaries, dated and undated loan capital and subordinated loans.
5 From 1979 the heading was 'Cash and short-term funds'. This changed to 'Cash and balances at central banks' in 1994.
6 Between 1947 and 1963 this figure includes Treasury bills. From 1964–9 it included Treasury bills and refinanceable credits.

7 Investments included quoted British government securities or securities guaranteed by the British government, other quoted investments, and unquoted British Corporation and other stocks.

8 Less provision for bad and doubtful debts (stated from 1947).

9 Less unearned finance charges and provision for all bad and doubtful debts.

10 Including £174562 acceptances to banking customers.

11 Including £179500 acceptances to banking customers.

12 Bankers Industrial Development Co. Ltd, one Ordinary 'A' share of £100000 (£100 paid).

13 Including £53304 acceptances to banking customers.

14 Including £150000 acceptances to banking customers.

15 Including £695000 acceptances to banking customers.

16 Including £650000 acceptances to banking customers.

17 Including £1367248 acceptances to banking customers.

18 Including £530000 acceptances to banking customers.

19 Treasury Deposit Receipts.

20 Including £650000 acceptances to banking customers.

21 Including £500000 acceptances to banking customers.

22 Consists of £10000000 Treasury Deposit Receipts and £20500 Industrial and Commercial Finance Corporation Ltd (205 shares of £1000 – £500 paid).

23 Consists of £10000000 Treasury Deposit Receipts and £41000 Industrial and Commercial Finance Corporation Ltd (205 shares of £1000 – £200 paid).

24 Includes £34071 due to subsidiary bank.

25 Includes £208817 due to subsidiary bank.

26 1000000 'A' shares of £5 each (£1 paid) and 200000 'B' shares of £1 each (fully paid) in subsidiary bank (the Union Bank of Scotland Ltd).

27 i.e. Balance of reserve fund (£5400000), less excess of nominal value of BS stock over nominal value of UBS shares for which the stock was exchanged (£900000).

28 Consists of Bank of Scotland (£186311), subsidiary company (£65629).

29 Consists of Bank of Scotland (£188212), subsidiary company (£67842).

30 Items in transit.

31 Consisted of second interim dividend payable 1 April 1966 (£197400) and final dividend (£246750).

32 Consists of items in transit (£34051870) and shares in subsidiary company whose accounts are not yet consolidated (Bank of Scotland Finance Company Ltd) (£500000).

33 Includes £15238011 of 'other' accounts.

34 i.e. £31755179 reserves, less excess of nominal value of BS stock over capital of BLB in exchange for which it was issued.

35 Provision for retirement benefits net of tax.

36 Includes £26210878 of 'other' accounts.

37 i.e. Provision for retirement benefits (£2861053) and corporation tax (£1249604).

38 Shares in subsidiary company whose accounts are not consolidated (Charlotte Registrars Ltd).

39 Includes £4823541 of 'other' accounts.

40 i.e. Provision for retirement benefits (£7013742), tax (£501623) and deferred tax (£2718450).

41 Includes £2731643 of 'other' accounts.

42 i.e. Provision for retirement benefits (£5957870), tax (£345379) and deferred tax (£3970880).

43 Lapid Developments Ltd Properties.

44 Includes £58835000 of 'other' accounts.

45 i.e. Provision for retirement benefits (£7055000), tax (£2980000) and deferred tax (£11128000).

46 Properties.

47 Includes £49444000 of 'other' accounts.

48 i.e. Provision for retirement benefits (£9085000), tax (£9720000) and deferred tax (£13792000).

49 i.e. Properties (£1395000) and investment in associated company (£1526000).

50 Includes £39875000 of 'other' accounts.

51 i.e. Provision for retirement benefits (£5996000) and deferred tax (£22982000).

52 i.e. Tax recoverable (£1405000), Properties (£1042000), Leased assets (£42175000) and investment in associated company (£2085000).

53 Includes £47596000 of 'other' accounts.

54 i.e. Provision for retirement benefits (£4954000), tax (£393000) and deferred tax (£33306000).

55 Unearned finance charges = £12289000.

56 i.e. Assets leased to customers (£55125000), properties held as trading stocks (£629000), and investments in associated companies (£2207000).

57 Includes £61412000 of 'other' accounts.

58 i.e. Provision for retirement benefits (£29000) and deferred tax (£43426000).

59 Less amounts refinanced by the Exports Credit Guarantee Department and the Department of Industry.

60 Unearned finance charges = £14836000.

61 i.e. Tax recoverable (£29010000), assets leased to customers (£73702000), advances to associated companies (£5270000), properties held as trading stocks (£339000), and investments in associated companies (£7947000).

62 Deferred tax.

967

Table A8 *continued*

63 Consists of tax (£1600000) and deferred tax (£42116000).
64 i.e. Subordinated loan (£54800000 – included in total capital resources) and deferred tax (£4190000).
65 Consists of subordinated loan (£72100000), minority interests in subsidiaries (£1600000) (both included in total capital resources) and deferred tax (£4180000).
66 Consists of loan capital (£100500000), minority interests in subsidiaries (£1800000) (both included in total capital resources) and deferred tax (£9760000).
67 Consists of loan capital (£183000000), minority interests in subsidiaries (£1500000) (both included in total capital resources) and deferred tax (£7410000).
68 Consists of minority interests in subsidiaries (£800000), undated loan capital (£170100000), dated loan capital (£136000000) (included in total capital resources) and deferred tax (£8780000).
69 Consists of minority interests in subsidiaries (£2600000), undated loan capital (£162100000), dated loan capital (£137900000) (included in total capital resources) and deferred tax (£8460000).
70 Consists of minority interests in subsidiaries (£3700000), undated loan capital (£141000000), dated loan capital (£241400000) and deferred tax (£7640000).
71 Consists of preference stock (£100 million) and ordinary stock (£187.6 million).
72 Consists of minority interests in subsidiaries (£4900000), undated loan capital

73 Consists of preference stock (£100 million) and ordinary stock (£188.6 million).
74 Consists of minority interests in subsidiaries (£6200000), undated loan capital (£326800000), dated loan capital (£309400000) (included in total capital resources) tax (£61600000) and deferred tax (£11210000).
75 Consists of preference stock (£200 million) and ordinary stock (£190.6 million).
76 Consists of minority interests in subsidiaries (£7200000), undated loan capital (£286500000), dated loan capital (£364300000) (included in total capital resources), tax (£8700000) and deferred tax (£16770000).
77 Consists of preference stock (£200 million) and ordinary stock (£287.1 million).
78 Consists of minority interests in subsidiaries (£3700000), undated loan capital (£312600000), dated loan capital (£554900000) (included in total capital resources), tax (£700000) and deferred tax (£19480000).
79 Consists of preference stock (£200 million) and ordinary stock (£289.3 million).
80 Consists of minority interests in subsidiaries (£4300000), undated loan capital (£386800000), dated loan capital (£610500000) (included in total capital resources), tax (£3280000) and deferred tax (£19080000).

(£143700000), dated loan capital (£304600000) (included in total capital resources) and deferred tax (£7060000).

Source: Bank of Scotland published annual reports, 1921–94.

968

Table A9 Bank of Scotland published profit and loss account, 1921–69

Year ending February	To half-yearly dividend paid October	To half-yearly dividend to be paid	Balance at credit of reserve fund	To published reserve fund	To reserve for contingencies	To staff pension fund	Misc.	Balance of undivided profits carried forward	Total	By balance of reserve fund	By balance of undivided profits brought forward	Net profits	Misc.	Total
			Debits									Credits		
1921	74200	74200	550000				140000 [1]	76137	914537	550000	54934	309603		914537
1922	74200	74200	550000	125000			50000 [2]	72978	946378	550000	76137	320242		946379
1923	78455	79500	675000	125000			50000 [2]	85202	1093157	675000	72978	345178		1093156
1924	81629	82150	800000	125000			50000 [2]	102149	1240928	800000	85202	355727		1240929
1925	82150	82150	925000	125000			50000 [2]	128824	1393124	925000	102149	365975		1393124
1926	84279	84800	1050000	457500 [3]			52562 [4]	150348	1879489	1050000	128824	368164	332500 [5]	1879488
1927	96000	96000	1507500	125000			50000 [2]	153466	2027966	1507500	150348	370119		2027967
1928	96000	108000	1632500	125000			50000 [2]	166801	2158301	1632500	153466	372335		2158301
1929	108000	108000	1757500	125000			30000 [2]	170084	2298584	1757500	166801	374283		2298584
1930	108000	108000	1882500	117500			30000 [2]	172457	2418457	1882500	170084	365872		2418456
1931	104625	104625	2000000	100000			30000 [2]	200077	2539327	2000000	172457	366870		2539327
1932	101250	101250	2100000				50000 [2]	215757	2568257	2100000	200077	268180		2568257
1933	101250	101250	2100000	60000			40000 [2]	226157	2628657	2100000	215757	312900		2628657
1934	104625	101250	2160000	40000	40000			250679	2693179	2160000	226157	307022		2693179
1935	104625	104625	2200000	50000	50000			252316	2761566	2200000	250679	310887		2761566
1936	104625	104625	2250000	50000		30000	25000 [2]	254158	2818408	2250000	252316	316092		2818408
1937	102938	102938	2300000	50000		30000	30000 [2]	255995	2871871	2300000	254158	317713		2871871
1938	101250	101250	1550000 [6]	500000 [7]		30000	826664 [8]	150085	3259249	2350000	145995 [9]	313254	450000 [10]	3259249
1939	104400	104400	2050000	50000		30000	15000 [2]	151918	2505718	2050000	150085	305634		2505719
1940	78000	90000	2100000		75000	30000		153467	2526467	2100000	151918	274548		2526466
1941	69000	82800	2100000		70000	30000		155572	2507372	2100000	153467	253905		2507372
1942	60000	72000	2100000		70000	30000		156217	2488217	2100000	155572	232645		2488217
1943	60000	72000	2100000		75000	30000		157342	2494342	2100000	156217	238124		2494341
1944	60000	72000	2100000		85000	30000		159161	2506161	2100000	157342	248819		2506161
1945	60000	84000	2100000			30000	10000 [11]	159704	2518704	2100000	159161	259543		2518704
1946	72000	79200	2175000	75000		30000	10000 [11]	161134	2602334	2175000	159704	267630		2602334
1947	79200	79200	2250000	75000		30000	10000 [11]	165948	2964348	2250000	161134	303214	250000 [13]	2964348
1948	79200	79200	2600000	350000 [12]	110000	30000		168759	3067159	2600000	165948	301211		3067159
1949	79200	79200	2600000			30000		183107	3371507	2600000	168759	302748	300000 [15]	3371507
1950	79200	79200	3000000	400000 [14]		30000	10000 [16]	191431	3489831	3000000	183107	306724		3489831
1951	79200	79200	3000000			30000	15000 [16]	191979	3495379	3000000	191431	303948		3495379
1952	75600	75600	3000000		110000	30000		191099	3482299	3000000	191979	290320		3482299

969

Table A9 *continued*

Year ending February	To half-yearly dividend paid October	To half-yearly dividend to be paid	Balance at credit of reserve fund	To published reserve fund	To reserve for contingencies	To staff pension fund	Misc.	Total	Balance of undivided profits carried forward	By balance of reserve fund	By balance of undivided profits brought forward	Net profits	Misc.	Total
								Debits				**Credits**		
1953	75600	141750	3000000		100000	30000		3532810	185460	3000000	191099	341711		3532810
1954	148500	173250	3000000		100000	40000	240000 [17]	3953690	251940	3000000	375103 [18]	578587		3953690
1955	173250	173250	4500000 [19]		100000	40000	140000 [20]	5382554	256054	4500000 [19]	251940	630614		5382554
1956	181125	181125	4500000		200000	80000		5399061	256811	4500000	256054	643007		5399061
1957	181125	181125	4500000		200000	80000		5395795	253545	4500000	256811	638984		5395795
1958	181125	181125	4500000		200000	80000		5390506	248256	4500000	253545	636961		5390506
1959	181125	232875	4500000		200000	80000		5451292	257292	4500000	248256	703036		5451292
1960	220500	308700	4500000	1500000 [21]	150000	80000		7021992	262792	4500000	257292	914700	1350000 [5]	7021992
1961	308700	347287	6000000	150000	150000	80000		7304409	268422	6000000	262792	1041617		7304409
1962	308700	347287	6150000	150000	200000	80000		7506429	270442	6150000	268422	1088007		7506429
1963	308700	385875	6300000	150000	150000	80000		7664852	290277	6300000	270442	1094410		7664852
1964	347288	347287	6450000	150000	150000	80000		7830839	306264	6450000	290277	1090562		7830839
1965	385875	370125	6600000	400000		80000		8161536	325536	6600000	306264	1255272		8161536
1966	394800	197400	7000000	500000	250000	80000	420000 [22]	9172859	330659	7000000	325536	1847323		9172859
1967	672000	756000	7500000	500000		80000		9891101	383101	7500000	330659	2060442		9891101
1968	672000	840000	8000000	500000	100000		7272 [23]	10617825	498553	8000000	383101	2234724		10617825
1969	756000	808920	8500000	1000000		150000	7862 [23]	11772659	549877	8500000	498553	2774106		11772659

Notes:

1 i.e. £120000 to depreciation in investments and £20000 to reduction of bank premises account.

2 To reduction of bank premises account.

3 i.e. £125000 from published profits and £332500 from premium on new issue of stock.

4 i.e. £2562 dividend on new issue of stock and £50000 to reduction of bank premises account.

5 Premium on new issue of stock.

6 £800000 was transferred from reserve fund to capital in accordance with resolutions passed at a meeting of proprietors on 21 December 1937, in connection with reconstruction of capital.

7 i.e. £50000 from published profits, £110000 from balance of undivided profits and £340000 from premium on new issue of stock.

8 i.e. £800000 to increase capital, £1664 dividend on new issue of stock and £25000 to reduction of bank premises account.

9 £110000 was transferred from balance of undivided profits to reserve fund.

10 i.e. £340000 premium on new issue of stock and £110000 by balance of undivided profits (to be transferred to reserve fund).

11 To BS widows' fund (special donation).

12 of which £100000 from published profits and £250000 transfer from reserve for contingencies.

13 By reserve for contingencies.

14 of which £100000 from published profits and £300000 transfer from a contingent reserve no longer required.

15 By contingent reserve no longer required.

16 To BS widows' fund.

17 Amounts appropriated by subsidiary company (£200000 general reserve and £40000 pensions and allowances fund).

18 i.e. £185460 by Bank of Scotland and £189643 by Union Bank of Scotland Ltd.

19 i.e. £3000000 by Bank of Scotland reserve fund and £2400000 by UBS reserves, less £900000 excess of nominal value of BS stock over nominal value of UBS shares for which stock exchanged.

20 Amounts appropriated by subsidiary company (£100000 reserve for contingencies and £40000 pensions and allowances fund).

21 of which £150000 from published profits and £1350000 from premium on new issue of stock.

22 Second interim dividend payable 30 April 1966 (gross).

23 To remuneration of inspectors and of auditors of subsidiary companies.

Source: Bank of Scotland published annual reports.

Table A10 *Classification of advances, 1963–5*

Manufacturing

Year ending mid-Feb.	Food, drinks and tobacco	%	Chemicals	%	Iron, steel and allied trades	%	Non-ferrous metals	%	Engineering etc.	%	Shipping and ship-building	%	Cotton	%	Wool	%	Other textiles	%	Leather and rubber	%	Unclassified industry and trade	%
1963	5130482	5.0	7473150	7.3	611463	0.6	484753	0.5	5092885	5.0	14579489	14.2	87209	0.1	1212518	1.2	1845797	1.8	609630	0.6	4809812	4.7
1964	5418908	5.0	852226	0.8	630916	0.6	1487803	1.4	4583901	4.2	16713129	15.4	65439	0.1	642077	0.6	1671588	1.5	594138	0.6	6024775	5.6
1965	8548279	6.7	2651926	2.1	7575118	5.9	2102118	1.6	5747355	4.5	13266432	10.4	56763	0.0	685679	0.5	2085286	1.6	591411	0.5	6824842	5.3

Other production / **Financial**

Year ending mid-February	Agriculture	%	Fishing	%	Coal mining	%	Quarrying, etc.	%	Builders and contractors	%	Building materials	%	Hire purchase finance companies	%	Other financial	%	Stock-brokers	%	Total	Total (%)
1963	14667255	14.3	273305	0.3	3132	0.0	86727	0.1	5135392	5.0	1256015	1.2	2879025	2.8	9388683	9.2	126780	0.1	102695565	100.0
1964	17620196	16.3	193051	0.2	3700	0.0	256853	0.2	5424275	5.0	1118851	1.0	4443373	4.1	12554315	11.6	74151	0.1	108452751	100.0
1965	20638690	16.1	227323	0.2	3074	0.0	611906	0.5	6445546	5.0	1666448	1.3	7746227	6.1	10991149	8.6	41428	0.0	128116866	100.0

Services

Year ending mid-February	Transport and communications	%	Public utilities (other than transport)	%	Local government authorities	%	Retail trade	%	Churches, charities, hospitals etc.	%	Entertainment	%	Personal and professional	%
1963	588611	0.6	2889582	2.8	1046590	1.0	6489465	6.3	98749	0.1	271582	0.3	15521484	15.1
1964	523206	0.5	1415792	1.3	1107455	1.0	6901740	6.4	77723	0.1	330562	0.3	17722608	16.3
1965	656804	0.5	1039551	0.8	1574777	1.2	7616323	5.9	85414	0.1	351114	0.3	18285883	14.3

Source: BS 1/6/11, Minutes, 1961–1965.

Table A11 *Classification of advances, 1965–79*

Year ending mid-Feb.	Food, drinks and tobacco	%	Chemicals and allied industries	%	Metal manufacturing	%	Electrical engineering	%	Other engineering and metal goods	%	Ship-building	%	Vehicles	%	Textiles, leather and clothing	%	Other manufacturing	%	Total	Total (%)
											Manufacturing										
1965	8548279	6.7	2651926	2.1	9677236	7.6		0.0	5747355	4.5	13266432	10.4		0.0	3419139	2.7	6824842	5.3	50135209	39.3
1966	7391072	5.4	5602306	4.1	10735509	7.9	674521	0.5	3290674	2.4	8182508	6.0	210006	0.2	2415268	1.8	3188434	2.3	41690298	30.6
1967	5917167	4.6	10297160	8.0	4974722	3.9	872054	0.7	3467934	2.7	10302158	8.0	122393	0.1	3337027	2.6	3461974	2.7	42752589	33.3
1968	6240631	5.0	3951294	3.2	5021618	4.0	476963	0.4	2639537	2.1	11742248	9.4	81831	0.1	3045820	2.4	3402806	2.7	36602748	29.3
1969	5355047	4.0	9970813	7.4	5184646	3.8	227170	0.2	5006441	3.7	12417720	9.2	141931	0.1	5017960	3.7	4346892	3.2	47668620	35.3
1970	6909306	5.1	2074814	1.5	4010349	2.9	429781	0.3	7325244	5.4	19908422	14.6	314979	0.2	5092847	3.7	4693013	3.4	50758755	37.1
1971	16587745	7.3	2839506	1.2	5412229	2.4	1690308	0.7	14239584	6.3	28556777	12.5	375159	0.2	7295389	3.2	7903218	3.5	84899915	37.3
1972	14465218	5.6	5417130	2.1	2446982	0.9	1773303	0.7	12320836	4.8	18450326	7.1	667462	0.3	5913479	2.3	7547144	2.9	69001880	26.7
1973	16791000	3.8	12102000	2.8	4810000	1.1	4755000	1.1	14012000	3.2	25814000	5.9	1156000	0.3	5342000	1.2	9656000	2.2	94438000	21.6
1974	34547000	5.8	19454000	3.3	2418000	0.4	10325000	1.7	15396000	2.6	53602000	9.0	1792000	0.3	7759000	1.3	12311000	2.1	157604000	26.5
1975	52717000	7.9	13530000	2.0	4347000	0.7	12568000	1.9	27325000	4.1	67263000	10.1	6348000	1.0	12825000	1.9	13507000	2.0	210430000	31.6
1976	34166000	5.7	8969000	1.5	7778000	1.3	6043000	1.0	19571000	3.3	30903000	5.1	1504000	0.2	14351000	2.4	13236000	2.2	136521000	22.7
1977	35394000	5.1	12094000	1.7	6554000	0.9	3493000	0.5	17416000	2.5	31933000	4.6	1907000	0.2	17333000	2.5	15587000	2.2	141711000	20.2
1978	36483000	4.3	13555000	1.6	5495000	0.6	5944000	0.7	22076000	2.6	34545000	4.1	2054000	0.2	18724000	2.2	17912000	2.1	156788000	18.4
1979	28539000	2.8	23678000	2.3	5594000	0.6	9073000	0.9	23412000	2.3	34112000	3.4	3140000	0.2	15672000	1.5	17702000	1.7	160922000	15.7

| Year ending mid-Feb. | Agriculture and forestry | % | Other production | | | | | | | Total | Total (%) |
			Fishing	%	Mining and quarrying	%	Construction	%		
1965	20638690	16.1	227323	0.2	614980	0.5	8111994	6.3	29592987	23.1
1966	20502166	15.1	180924	0.1	2603375	1.9	8234963	6.1	31521428	23.2
1967	19213335	14.9	194331	0.2	2277639	1.8	6933285	5.4	28618590	22.3
1968	19549266	15.6	322829	0.3	2854802	2.3	6572003	5.2	29298900	23.4
1969	20436849	15.1	188541	0.1	389027	0.3	5915584	4.4	26930001	19.9
1970	20063869	14.7	139375	0.1	177961	0.1	6024781	4.4	26405986	19.3
1971	30471935	13.4	206912	0.1	338974	0.1	12852083	5.6	43869904	19.2
1972	32769476	12.7	321372	0.1	349083	0.1	9219345	3.6	42659276	16.5
1973	40122000	9.1	378000	0.1	210000	0.0	15363000	3.5	56073000	12.7
1974	48971000	8.2	551000	0.1	305000	0.1	21503000	3.6	71330000	12.0
1975	57074000	8.5	758000	0.1	2723000	0.4	23219000	3.5	83774000	12.5
1976	56503000	9.4	917000	0.2	1634000	0.3	24859000	4.1	83913000	14.0
1977	61900000	8.9	1409000	0.2	9813000	1.4	21615000	3.1	94737000	13.6
1978	79471000	9.4	1917000	0.2	25500000	3.0	26987000	3.2	133875000	15.8
1979	103729000	10.2	2922000	0.3	20575000	2.0	28515000	2.8	155741000	15.3

Table A11 *continued*

	Financial																	
Year ending mid-February	Hire purchase finance companies	%	Property companies	%	Insurance enterprises (including pension funds)	%	Unit and quoted investment trusts	%	Stock-brokers and jobbers	%	Building societies	%	UK banks	%	Other financial (including unquoted trusts from 1975)	%	Total	Total (%)
1965	7746227	6.0							41428	0.0					10991149	8.6	18778804	14.6
1966	9580634	7.0	4995025	3.7											5076786	3.7	19933103	14.5
1967	8632079	6.7	5341846	4.2											4062364	3.2	18054100	14.1
1968	8988003	7.2	3976655	3.2											5424709	4.3	18414803	14.7
1969	9064140	6.7	4419874	3.3											4941284	3.6	18526355	13.6
1970	6352208	4.7	4889434	3.6									280658	0.1	4637451	3.4	16106219	11.8
1971	4481625	2.0	6073740	2.7									17811	0.0	15424546	6.8	26691054	11.8
1972	9386443	3.6	8229352	3.2									25436	0.0	16366152	6.3	41756947	16.1
1973	17730000	4.0	11977000	2.7									101057	0.0	54424000	12.4	86194000	19.6
1974	22443000	3.8	21685000	3.6									227126	0.1	86287000	14.5	137985000	23.2
1975	6737000	1.0	16545000	2.5									711143	0.3	79529000	11.9	135198000	20.2
1976	5604000	0.9	23173000	3.9	29971000	5.0	13976000	2.3	397000	0.1			7775000	3.0	8547000	1.4	81668000	13.6
1977	10013000	1.4	19468000	2.8	30284000	4.3	15421000	2.2	226000	0.0	145000	0.0	2063000	0.5	6572000	0.9	82129000	11.6
1978	14104000	1.7	18429000	2.2	14206000	1.7	9391000	1.1	154000	0.0	169000	0.0	7590000	1.3	9966000	1.2	66419000	7.9
1979	4820000	0.5	22043000	2.2	6629000	0.7	19338000	1.9	173000	0.0	230000	0.0	32387000	4.8	12959000	1.3	66192000	6.6

Year ending mid-Feb.	Services														Personal							
	Transport and communications	%	Public utilities/ national govt	%	Local govt services	%	Retail distribution	%	Other distribution	%	Professional, scientific, misc. services	%	Total	%	Bridging finance	%	House purchase	%	Other personal	%	Total	Total (%)
1965	656804	0.5	1039551	0.8	1574777	1.2	7616323	5.9			436528	0.3	11323983	8.7					18285883	14.3	18285883	14.3
1966	5185145	3.8	1130038	0.8	528359	0.4	4730466	3.5	9983560	7.3	5843885	4.3	27401453	20.1			1858383	1.4	12683748	9.3	14542131	10.7
1967	2532067	2.0	1544491	1.2	1815294	1.4	3888348	3.0	9485679	7.4	5958731	4.6	25224610	19.6			2003568	1.6	11122033	8.6	13125601	10.2
1968	3413786	2.7	287493	0.2	3727748	3.0	4142415	3.3	7930352	6.3	7303624	5.8	26805418	21.3			2066628	1.7	11153064	8.9	13219692	10.6
1969	3771109	2.8	758703	0.6	2653617	2.0	4429973	3.3	8380952	6.2	8454612	6.2	28448966	21.1			2394454	1.8	11472171	8.5	13866625	10.3
1970	2538844	1.9	1268989	0.9	3890402	2.9	4380098	3.2	9181439	6.7	8200774	6.0	29460546	21.6			2839779	2.1	9772619	7.2	12612398	9.3
1971	6310395	2.8	4634283	2.0	3424345	1.5	7219871	3.2	10089414	4.4	17549414	7.7	49227722	21.6			6064100	2.7	15937214	7.0	22001314	9.7
1972	5122643	2.0	5649082	2.2	1536495	0.6	10195144	3.9	18537871	7.2	23624346	9.1	64665581	25.0			7302882	2.8	26760216	10.4	34063098	13.2
1973	8316000	1.9	5154000	1.2	18313000	4.2	11761000	2.7	23118000	5.3	51340000	11.7	118002000	27.0			9865000	2.3	64764000	14.8	74629000	17.1
1974	13546000	2.3	1821000	0.3	8817000	1.5	18808000	3.2	20429000	3.4	53467000	9.0	116888000	19.7			14699000	2.5	79060000	13.3	93759000	15.8
1975	19789000	3.0	10083000	1.5	7357000	1.1	20957000	3.1	25118000	3.8	47953000	7.2	131257000	19.7			19565000	2.9	71556000	10.7	91121000	13.6
1976	24631000	4.1	12758000	2.1	13067000	2.2	21458000	3.6	23964000	4.0	54005000	9.0	149983000	25.0	4193000	0.7	18466000	3.0	69234000	11.5	91893000	15.3
1977	29276000	4.2	22787000	3.3	2181000	0.3	27516000	3.9	28328000	4.1	61531000	8.8	171619000	24.6	5655000	0.8	20914000	3.0	75041000	10.8	101610000	14.6
1978	33004000	3.9	25848000	3.0	3704000	0.4	30701000	3.6	33129000	3.9	71973000	8.5	198359000	23.3	7089000	0.8	24602000	2.9	86372000	10.2	118063000	13.9
1979	36082000	3.6	22941000	2.3	3291000	0.3	32841000	3.2	32410000	3.2	84003000	8.3	211568000	20.9	10473000	1.0	28213000	2.8	103103000	10.2	141789000	14.0

Table A11 *continued*

Year ending mid-February	Overseas residents (including banks overseas)	Total %	Total advances	Total (%)
1965	1024488	0.8	128116866	100.0
1966	878415	0.7	136112901	99.9
1967	851422	0.7	128653905	100.2
1968	70466	0.1	125192983	100.0
1969	1153056	0.8	135511033	100.3
1970	904457	0.4	136496960	99.9
1971	6547382	2.5	227594366	100.0
1972	8695000	2.0	258694164	100.0
1973	16556000	2.8	438031000	100.0
1974	16187000	2.4	594122000	100.0
1975	56679000	9.4	667967000	100.0
1976	106017000	15.2	600557000	100.0
1977	174458000	20.6	697823000	99.8
1978	276393000	27.3	847962000	99.9
1979			1012605000	99.8

Source: BS 1/6/12–16, Minutes, 1965–79.

Table A12 Bank's annual balance: trading results, 1968–82

Year ending 28 February	Interest receivable from										Less interest payable	Subtotal
	Current and loan accounts etc.	Market money etc.	Sterling certificates of deposit	Treasury bills	Special deposits with the Bank of England	Currency investment income	Investments (including trade)	Investments (amortisa-tion) [1]	Dividends: subsidiary and associated companies	Subtotal		
1968	9650162	2203136		105482	138901		2038251		500000	14635932	5052421	9583511
1969	10904901	2136024		301662	174984		3068847		550000	17136418	635717	10777701
1970	12739664	1797766		62319	200686		3320975	211622	1042500	19375532	7346098	12029434
1971	13115443	1781853	226255	30565	231312		3292963	364460	1385000	20427851	7138838	13289013
1972	18101169	1617642	211700	14601	219535		1268331	537869	800000	22770847	7003700	20705147
1973	25822358	3217419	169716	129812	191147		4713513	489065	1038000	35771030	11841405	23929625
1974	53020977	9178382	631163	50603	1675019		3825082	482619	280000	69143845	32989346	36154499
1975	72978000	14293000	737000		1629000		4305000	471000	403000	94816000	51336000	43480000
1976	64596000	11707000	1451000	1400000	1811000		5127000	641000	410000	87143000	37038000	50105000
1977	77435000	12171000	165000	2835000	2824000		7813000	1019000	220000	104482000	47304000	57178000
1978	65935000	6408000	481000	1907000	1444000		8652000	728000	2058000	87613000	29836000	57777000
1979	89648000	9924000	855000	3125000	1670000		8567000	67000	2295000	116151000	47021000	69130000
1980	150989000	12250000	1054000	5296000	1070000		10637000	737000	2706000	184739000	96027000	88712000
1981	219011000	17627000	281000	6336000			14906000	1730000	2479000	262370000	156413000	105957000
1982	406084000	17231000		2342000		1869000	20285000	2527000	4391000	454729000	339365000	115364000

Table A12 *continued*

Year ending 28 February	Add:						Less:			
	Commissions	Net income from let property	Net income from occupied property	Income from leasing of machinery etc.	Misc. addition	Subtotal	Expenses	Charge for bad debt provision	Charge for investment realisation suspense account	Misc. deduction
1968	1263377	84899		76644		11008431	6200012			21875 [2]
1969	1793101	88425		60000		12719227	6947712			22500 [2]
1970	2203373	101546		156000	628512 [5]	15118865	8885186	522643	112350	22500 [2]
1971	2925880	126671	705322	186347		17233233	11028782	362136	247173	
1972	4975444	196945	1131151	343700		27352387	18629949	582246	392875	1200000 [7]
1973	6272870	232017	1375482	412397		32222391	19665470	680300	387256	3841200 [9]
1974	8448359	319279	1354248	507864		46784249	21818685	1800533	517670	8493000 [11]
1975	7851000	414000	1425000	498000	218000 [13]	53668000	27883000	4677000	545000	4000000 [14]
1976	9392000	365000	1698000		6000 [16]	61778000	41211000	3520000	317000	1000000 [17]
1977	12699000	415000	1873000		4000 [19]	72171000	47107000	5363000	398000	
1978	14762000	476000	2847000		407000 [22]	75866000	51521000	5041000		22000 [20]
1979	15831000	529000	2956000			88853000	62686000	1030000		35000 [20]
1980	18259000	719000	2922000			110612000	75528000	4237000		1529000 [24]
1981	24053000	770000				130780000	86140000	6510000		281000 [26]
1982	30397000	814000				146575000	99012000	10020000		793000 [31]

Year ending 28 February	Operating profit	Allocation to staff profit-sharing schemes	Taxation	Profit after tax	Extraordinary items	Subtotal	Dividend for year	Retained profit to reserve
1968	4786544		1724633 [3]	3061911	−940000 [4]	2121911	1512000	609911
1969	5749015		1911183	3837832	−1060000 [4]	2777832	1564920	1212912
1970	5576186		2061927	3514259		3514259	2451000	1063259
1971	5595142		1812541	3782601	−201250 [6]	3581351	2451000	1130351
1972	7747317		2637559	5109758		5109758	2580000	2529758
1973	10289365		3780607	6508758	−600000 [8]	5908758	2283300	3625458
1974	18806161		8535163	10270998	−1007020 [10]	9263978	2488894	6775084
1975	12070000		6386000	5684000	−480000 [12]	5204000	2680000	2524000
1976	12730000		6725000	6005000	990000 [15]	6995000	2860000	4135000
1977	18303000		10634000	7669000	141000 [18]	7810000	3146000	4664000
1978	19282000		9656000	9626000	473000 [21]	10099000	3537000	6562000
1979	25102000		12643000	12459000	483000 [23]	12942000	3950000	8992000
1980	29318000		13399000	15919000	494000 [25]	16413000		
1981	37849000	1525000 [27]	17975000	18349000	696000 [28]	19045000	2595000 [29]	16450000 [30]
1982	36750000	1782000	14104000	20864000	−2844000 [32]	18020000	6518000	11502000

Notes:

1 Investments, accrual of discounts, less amortisation premiums.
2 Transfer to widows' fund.
3 Estimate.
4 Internal transfer to reserve no. 2.
5 Excess bad debt provision released.
6 Special provision for bad debts, net of tax relief.
7 Provision for anticipated additional liability for past service pensions.
8 Special provision for bad debts.
9 Consists of provision for additional liability re increase in pensions (£1155000), provision for anticipated additional liability for past service pensions (£2371200), and provision for special losses (Scottish Co-operative Wholesale Society) (£315000).
10 Consists of special provision for bad debts (£500000) and allocation to reserve for retirement benefits in anticipation of new pension scheme (£1500000) less surplus in value of net provision for retirement benefits on account of tax rate change (£992980).
11 Consists of provision for additional liability re increase in pensions (£1483000), provision for anticipated additional liability for past service pensions (£5010000), and special provision for bad debts (£2000000).

Table A12 *continued*

12 Allocation to provision for retirement benefits in anticipation of new pension scheme.
13 Consists of provision released (Seaforth Losses) (£163000) and surplus on sale of plant and machinery (£55000).
14 Consists of provision for additional liability re increase in pensions (£2000000) and special provision for bad debts (£2000000).
15 Consists of net surplus on property sales (£1080000) less trade investments written off (£90000).
16 Surplus on sale of plant and machinery.
17 Provision for additional liability re increase in pensions.
18 Consists of net surplus on property sales (£167000) less trade investments written off (£32000), plus prior year adjustment (£6000).
19 Release from investment realisation suspense account.
20 Loss on sale of plant and machinery.
21 Consists of net surplus on property sales (£731000) less write-down of book value of Lapid Developments Ltd, written off (£70000) less trade investments written off (£188000).
22 Gains in sale of investments.
23 Consists of net surplus on property sales (£517000) less write-down of book value of Lapid Developments Ltd, written off (£37000) less investments written off (£3000).
24 Consists of net transfer to Insurance Services Ltd (£139000), loss on sale of investments (£1360000) and loss on sale of plant and machinery (£30000).
25 Consists of surplus on property sales (£145000) plus increase in value of investment in Lapid Developments Ltd (£308000) plus sundries (£41000).
26 Consists of net transfer to Insurance Services Ltd (£200000), loss on sale of investments (£5000) and loss on sale of plant and machinery (£76000).
27 Estimate.
28 Consists of surplus on property sales (£428000) less decrease in value of trade investments (Pict Petroleum Ltd) (£156000) less investments written off (£3000) plus increase in value of investment in Lapid Developments Ltd (£24000) plus surplus on sale of trade investments (£400000).
29 Interim dividend only.
30 Profit remaining for final dividend and retention.
31 Consists of net transfer to Insurance Services Ltd (£544000), loss on sale of investments (£8000) and loss on sale of plant and machinery (£241000).
32 Consists of surplus on sale of trade investments (£747000), plus surplus on sale of subsidiary company (£553000) plus surplus on sale of property (£3820000) less: decrease in value of trade investments (£11000), decrease in value of subsidiary company (£12000), tax on banking deposits (£7375000), FRN expenses (£566000).

Source: BS 1/6/12–16, Minutes, 1968–82.

Table A15 Scottish banks' published net profits per annum,[1] 1900–35

	Bank of Scotland	Royal Bank of Scotland	British Linen Bank [2]	Commercial Bank	National Bank [3]	Union Bank	Clydesdale Bank [4]	Aberdeen Town & County Bank [5]	North of Scotland Bank [6]	North of Scotland and Town & County Bank [7]	Caledonian Bank [8]	All Scottish banks' total	Bank of Scotland as percentage of total
1900	181000	226000	249000	248000	249000	165000	170000	37000	46000		14000	1585000	11.42
1901	202000	235000	274000	226000	255000	174000	171000	37000	48000		14000	1636000	12.35
1902	212000	245000	277000	246000	258000	180000	181000	38000	48000		15000	1700000	12.47
1903	223000	251000	289000	232000	233000	189000	184000	38000	49000		14000	1702000	13.10
1904	202000	241000	273000	228000	230000	185000	181000	38000	53000		13000	1644000	12.29
1905	224000	240000	299000	244000	221000	188000	172000	38000	60000		15000	1701000	13.17
1906	232000	243000	275000	240000	220000	193000	179000	37000	61000		12000	1692000	13.71
1907	237000	254000	263000	233000	222000	190000	183000	38000	62000			1682000	14.09
1908	273000	240000	265000	240000	231000	193000	192000			76000		1710000	15.96
1909	282000	230000	287000	233000	221000	200000	204000			103000		1760000	16.02
1910	288000	238000	277000	227000	223000	205000	213000			106000		1777000	16.21
1911	293000	247000	269000	230000	228000	201000	217000			107000		1792000	16.35
1912	306000	268000	268000	239000	231000	203000	230000			109000		1854000	16.50
1913	319000	276000	258000	241000	232000	207000	237000			109000		1879000	16.98
1914	321000	266000	266000	250000	237000	209000	251000			116000		1916000	16.75
1915	294000	294000	281000	241000	251000	226000	256000			118000		1961000	14.99
1916	267000	338000	266000	248000	267000	230000	265000			123000		2004000	13.32
1917	258000	304000	296000	283000	298000	250000	286000			127000		2102000	12.27
1918	286000	311000	298000	312000	285000	279000	316000			159000		2246000	12.73
1919	312000	326000	307000	317000	327000	284000	331000			181000		2385000	13.08
1920	320000	375000	340000	302000	295000	311000	337000			153000		2433000	13.15
1921	310000	377000	286000	342000	285000	312000	331000			187000		2430000	12.76
1922	320000	402000	294000	350000	291000	308000	335000			202000		2502000	12.79
1923	345000	426000	310000	347000	296000	326000	331000			206000		2587000	13.34
1924	356000	452000	318000	335000	292000	329000	346000					2428000	14.66
1925	366000	473000	320000	335000	288000	330000	342000					2454000	14.91
1926	368000	477000	318000	327000	285000	316000	334000			268000		2693000	13.67
1927	370000	482000	321000	335000	286000	318000	335000			270000		2717000	13.62
1928	372000	503000	330000	345000	291000	329000	340000			274000		2784000	13.36
1929	374000	505000	327000	368000	281000	336000	332000			277000		2800000	13.36
1930	366000	534000	327000	390000	277000	339000	336000			281000		2850000	12.84
1931	367000	611000	293000	386000	271000	355000	331000			254000		2868000	12.80
1932	268000	605000	292000	377000	265000	330000	310000			251000		2698000	9.93
1933	313000	612000	273000	387000	268000	320000	301000			254000		2728000	11.47
1934	307000	621000	286000	379000	272000	311000	310000			255000		2741000	11.20
1935	311000	629000	290000	397000	270000	313000	312000			260000		2782000	11.18

Notes:
1 All figures rounded to nearest £1000.
2 Became a subsidiary of Barclays in 1919.
3 Became a subsidiary of Lloyds in 1918.
4 Became a subsidiary of Midland in 1919.
5 Merged with North of Scotland Bank in 1907–8.
6 Merged with Aberdeen Town & County Bank in 1907–8.
7 Became a subsidiary of Midland in 1923.
8 Taken over by Bank of Scotland in 1907.

Source: BS 1/70/14, Analysis of the resources of Bank of Scotland (Profit Results).

Table A14 Scottish banks' net business profits per annum[1] as a percentages of paid-up capital, 1878–1935

	Bank of Scotland	Royal Bank of Scotland	British Linen Bank[2]	Commercial Bank	National Bank[3]	Union Bank	Clydesdale Bank[4]	Aberdeen Town & County Bank[5]	North of Scotland Bank[6]	North of Scotland and Town & County Bank[7]	Caledonian Bank[8]	All
1878	8.15	4.33	10.00	8.60	9.50	9.00	6.00	8.73	7.60		9[9]	7.56
1879	7.66	4.40	8.40	5.50	6.80	7.50	4.70	7.14	7.10		9[9]	6.29
1880	7.04	4.45	8.50	9.30	9.10	7.20	6.70	7.54	7.10		9[9]	6.96
1881	7.66	4.55	11.10	8.40	11.40	7.60	7.30	7.54	6.75		1.33	7.66
1882	7.76	5.05	8.30	8.50	10.80	7.90	8.20	7.54	4.50		3.33	7.55
1883	8.07	5.30	8.30	8.90	10.50	9.00	6.20	7.54	6.25		3.33	7.56
1884	8.40	4.30	8.30	8.60	9.10	8.20	5.20	6.35	7.00		4.00	7.01
1885	7.60	3.70	7.60	8.60	8.40	6.30	6.60	6.75	7.00		3.30	6.56
1886	8.00	3.70	8.60	8.40	8.40	7.30	6.60	6.75	7.75		3.33	6.85
1887	7.36	3.70	7.90	8.30	8.20	7.10	5.60	6.75	7.75		2.66	6.51
1888	6.96	3.80	8.10	8.90	8.50	7.70	5.00	7.15	6.25		2.00	6.53
1889	6.40	3.85	8.50	9.50	9.90	7.70	6.20	7.15	4.75		2.66	6.66
1890	6.64	4.00	9.00	10.40	10.40	7.60	7.20	7.54	4.75		4.00	7.15
1891	7.12	4.35	9.90	11.00	9.90	7.10	7.20	7.54	5.00		3.33	7.41
1892	7.76	3.55	10.80	9.90	8.70	7.20	6.50	7.93	4.75		5.33	7.13
1893	6.96	3.80	6.96	11.40	9.60	7.20	6.90	8.33	4.75		5.33	6.97
1894	7.20	-0.15	8.16	9.80	8.10	7.50	5.80	7.54	5.00		4.66	5.88
1895	5.92	2.70	7.51	10.30	8.20	5.60	6.50	8.33	5.25		3.33	6.18
1896	6.24	2.85	13.66	11.90	10.00	7.70	7.40	7.94	5.75		4.00	7.80
1897	7.04	3.30	17.52	12.80	11.40	8.30	8.10	8.33	6.00		2.66	8.90
1898	7.76	3.90	10.80	14.40	21.70	8.40	8.80	8.73	6.25		4.00	9.63
1899	6.64	4.40	12.55	15.80	15.50	9.10	8.90	8.33	6.50		4.66	9.41
1900	8.08	5.60	10.40	16.80	16.10	9.50	10.20	8.33	6.00		3.33	9.88
1901	9.66	6.05	12.32	14.50	16.60	10.30	10.10	8.33	6.50		4.00	10.36
1902	10.32	6.45	12.56	16.30	16.70	10.70	10.90	9.73	6.25		4.66	10.91
1903	11.04	6.75	13.36	14.80	14.20	11.40	11.30	8.73	6.50		4.00	10.86
1904	9.20	6.25	12.00	14.30	13.80	11.00	10.80	8.73	7.25		3.33	10.16
1905	10.88	6.15	14.00	15.90	13.40	11.10	9.70	8.33	9.00		4.66	10.74

Year												
1906	11.28	6.20	12.00	15.50	13.40	11.50	10.30	8.33	9.00			10.56
1907	11.60	6.75	11.28	15.20	14.00	11.10	10.70	8.73	9.25		2.66	10.82
1908	13.28	6.00	11.44	15.80	14.90	11.20	11.40			5.36		10.91
1909	13.81	5.45	13.04	15.10	13.80	11.60	12.40			9.35		11.33
1910	17.74	10.10	16.08	23.30	23.80	19.80	23.70			19.17		18.10
1911	14.26	6.30	11.76	14.90	14.50	11.70	13.30			9.82		11.60
1912	15.17	7.50	12.00	15.80	15.00	11.80	14.50			9.97		12.32
1913	16.00	7.90	11.76	16.40	15.10	12.30	15.10			9.82		12.68
1914	16.00	7.40	12.80	17.70	15.40	12.30	16.40			10.74		13.09
1915	14.49	9.10	14.40	16.80	17.40	14.70	17.20			10.73		13.93
1916	12.98	11.30	13.28	17.80	19.40	15.10	18.20			11.20		14.55
1917	13.10	9.35	15.44	21.30	22.10	17.20	20.00			11.66		15.56
1918	15.25	9.45	15.28	23.50	20.30	19.70	22.30			16.26		16.75
1919	17.74	10.10	16.08	23.30	23.80	19.80	23.70			19.17		18.10
1920	18.34	12.55	18.80	10.80	18.09	22.60	24.30			15.03		17.56
1921	17.50	12.30	14.40	12.80	17.26	22.60	23.70			20.25		17.60
1922	17.89	13.25	15.04	12.17	17.45	22.20	24.00			22.24		16.89
1923	19.40	14.10	15.18	11.77	17.54	23.10	22.80			22.09		17.24
1924	19.78	10.28	15.91	10.91	17.00	23.10	21.73					15.62 [10]
1925	20.08	10.92	15.68	10.80	16.64	22.90	18.24					16.46 [10]
1926	16.13	10.92	15.04	10.23	16.09	21.40	17.36			17.28		15.56
1927	15.93	10.92	14.96	10.56	16.00	21.40	17.44			17.28		14.68
1928	15.66	11.60	15.28	10.97	16.27	21.90	17.60			15.95		14.86
1929	15.47	11.53	14.72	7.20	15.18	22.40	16.08			16.04		13.69
1930	14.60	7.58	14.40	8.09	14.82	22.40	16.23			16.21		12.54
1931	14.33	8.12	11.68	7.82	14.45	18.25	15.85			13.58		11.71
1932	7.67	7.96	11.52	7.42	13.91	16.00	14.23			13.32		10.42
1933	10.53	8.15	9.67	7.82	14.04	15.33	13.54			13.58		10.60
1934	9.93	8.34	10.56	7.55	14.45	14.58	14.23			14.02		10.70
1935	10.07	8.52	10.80	8.05	14.09	14.75	14.23			14.20		10.86

Notes:

1 i.e. Published net profits, less 4% on capital and reserve.
2 Became a subsidiary of Barclays in 1919.
3 Became a subsidiary of Lloyds in 1918.
4 Became a subsidiary of Midland in 1919.
5 Merged with the North of Scotland Bank in 1907–8.
6 Merged with the Aberdeen Town & County Bank in 1907–8.
7 Became a subsidiary of Midland in 1923.
8 Taken over by Bank of Scotland in 1907.
9 Closed for eight months as a result of the City of Glasgow Bank failure.
10 Omitting North of Scotland Bank.

Source: BS 1/70/14, Analysis of the resources of Bank of Scotland.

Table A15 *Scottish banks' net business profits per annum[1] as a percentage of deposits, 1878–1935*

	Bank of Scotland	Royal Bank of Scotland	British Linen Bank [2]	Commercial Bank	National Bank [3]	Union Bank	Clydesdale Bank [4]	Aberdeen Town & County Bank [5]	North of Scotland Bank [6]	North of Scotland and Town & County Bank [7]	Caledonian Bank [8]	All
1878	0.97	0.89	1.34	1.00	0.90	1.00	0.97	1.22	1.18		9	1.01
1879	0.81	0.77	0.96	0.59	0.59	0.88	0.68	0.94	1.02		9	0.76
1880	0.72	0.72	0.93	1.02	0.75	0.75	0.93	1.01	1.05		9	0.82
1881	0.77	0.73	1.21	0.91	0.94	0.75	0.99	0.98	0.95		0.27	0.88
1882	0.75	0.82	0.90	0.91	0.86	0.74	1.08	0.98	0.89		0.62	0.85
1883	0.78	0.85	0.82	0.90	0.82	0.82	0.78	0.96	0.81		0.57	0.83
1884	0.79	0.71	0.82	0.85	0.70	0.76	0.68	0.79	0.93		0.66	0.77
1885	0.69	0.62	0.75	0.85	0.67	0.59	0.85	0.86	0.87		0.57	0.71
1886	0.75	0.64	0.87	0.85	0.66	0.73	0.86	0.86	0.99		0.57	0.77
1887	0.71	0.63	0.77	0.81	0.63	0.72	0.75	0.81	1.01		0.43	0.72
1888	0.65	0.63	0.78	0.86	0.65	0.75	0.63	0.81	0.85		0.32	0.71
1889	0.57	0.61	0.78	0.90	0.72	0.73	0.72	0.80	0.65		0.41	0.71
1890	0.57	0.62	0.78	0.90	0.76	0.69	0.83	0.80	0.60		0.59	0.72
1891	0.57	0.66	0.83	0.94	0.72	0.63	0.81	0.77	0.59		0.48	0.72
1892	0.64	0.55	0.90	0.82	0.64	0.65	0.71	0.81	0.54		0.75	0.69
1893	0.59	0.60	0.73	0.95	0.70	0.66	0.77	0.83	0.55		0.75	0.71
1894	0.61	-0.02	0.85	0.78	0.61	0.70	0.64	0.76	0.56		0.64	0.59
1895	0.50	0.41	0.77	0.77	0.59	0.50	0.70	0.85	0.62		0.47	0.61
1896	0.54	0.44	1.42	0.88	0.69	0.67	0.76	0.79	0.68		0.58	0.76
1897	0.61	0.50	1.78	0.95	0.77	0.73	0.81	0.82	0.71		0.39	0.86
1898	0.65	0.60	1.13	1.07	1.42	0.75	0.86	0.81	0.69		0.57	0.92
1899	0.55	0.66	1.25	1.11	1.00	0.74	0.82	0.74	0.66		0.67	0.86
1900	0.64	0.79	0.97	1.17	1.03	0.75	0.83	0.72	0.61		0.45	0.86
1901	0.76	0.86	1.14	0.99	1.05	0.78	0.86	0.71	0.64		0.52	0.90
1902	0.80	0.92	1.18	1.14	1.04	0.81	0.93	0.72	0.60		0.52	0.95
1903	0.89	0.96	1.30	1.06	0.89	0.84	0.99	0.76	0.64		0.51	0.96
1904	0.75	0.91	1.22	1.03	0.92	0.87	0.97	0.78	0.72		0.42	0.93
1905	0.89	0.90	1.47	1.13	0.95	0.89	0.89	0.73	0.90		0.58	0.99
1906	0.93	0.91	1.22	1.07	0.90	0.89	0.88	0.69	0.88		0.32	0.95

Year											
1907	0.89	0.93	1.08	1.01	0.93	0.84	0.85				0.92
1908	1.00	0.86	1.16	1.08	0.98	0.86	0.95				0.95
1909	1.04	0.79	1.38	1.04	0.91	0.93	1.00				1.00
1910	0.98	0.84	1.27	0.99	0.89	0.94	1.04	0.69		0.48	0.98
1911	1.07	0.87	1.15	1.00	0.88	0.93	1.06		0.83	0.87	0.99
1912	1.04	0.97	1.11	0.98	0.94	0.81	1.01			0.90	0.97
1913	1.05	0.95	1.04	0.91	0.87	0.80	1.01			0.88	0.93
1914	1.08	0.87	1.07	0.93	0.85	0.75	1.02			0.84	0.93
1915	0.91	0.95	1.12	0.88	0.85	0.83	0.95			0.76	0.91
1916	0.80	1.03	0.86	0.78	0.81	0.90	0.80			0.81	0.84
1917	0.65	0.71	0.85	0.80	0.76	1.00	0.76			0.74	0.76
1918	0.71	0.65	0.72	0.77	0.66	0.83	0.75			0.63	0.72
1919	0.73	0.57	0.70	0.65	0.69	0.75	0.68			0.57	0.67
1920	0.66	0.64	0.78	0.46	0.54	0.70	0.63			0.63	0.61
1921	0.62	0.60	0.56	0.51	0.49	0.69	0.63			0.60	0.58
1922	0.61	0.66	0.65	0.53	0.54	0.63	0.70			0.42	0.62
1923	0.74	0.74	0.73	0.58	0.60	0.73	0.73			0.54	0.69
1924	0.79	0.65	0.75	0.55	0.60	0.79	0.77			0.64	0.69 [10]
1925	0.85	0.67	0.72	0.55	0.59	0.83	0.76			0.70	0.70 [10]
1926	0.81	0.67	0.70	0.54	0.57	0.79	0.73			0.92	0.70
1927	0.75	0.62	0.69	0.55	0.57	0.82	0.74			0.92	0.69
1928	0.76	0.65	0.70	0.57	0.57	0.84	0.73			0.83	0.69
1929	0.72	0.62	0.68	0.46	0.52	0.82	0.73			0.86	0.66
1930	0.68	0.51	0.65	0.55	0.51	0.79	0.69			0.89	0.63
1931	0.66	0.62	0.56	0.55	0.55	0.75	0.73			0.79	0.64
1932	0.37	0.54	0.47	0.45	0.45	0.68	0.58			0.69	0.52
1933	0.44	0.52	0.39	0.47	0.45	0.64	0.56			0.64	0.51
1934	0.42	0.54	0.43	0.44	0.45	0.61	0.59			0.65	0.51
1935	0.41	0.50	0.40	0.44	0.44	0.59	0.54			0.56	0.48

Notes:

1 i.e. Published net profits, less 4% on capital and reserve.
2 Became a subsidiary of Barclays in 1919.
3 Became a subsidiary of Lloyds in 1918.
4 Became a subsidiary of Midland in 1919.
5 Merged with the North of Scotland Bank in 1907–8.
6 Merged with the Aberdeen Town & County Bank in 1907–8.
7 Became a subsidiary of Midland in 1923.
8 Taken over by Bank of Scotland in 1907.
9 Closed for eight months as a result of the City of Glasgow Bank failure.
10 Omitting North of Scotland Bank.

Source: BS 1/70/14, Analysis of the resources of Bank of Scotland.

Table A16 Scottish banks' net business profits per annum[1] as a percentage of total public liabilities,[2] 1878–1935

	Bank of Scotland	Royal Bank of Scotland	British Linen Bank [3]	Commercial Bank	National Bank [4]	Union Bank	Clydesdale Bank [5]	Aberdeen Town & County Bank [6]	North of Scotland Bank [7]	North of Scotland and Town & County Bank [8]	Caledonian Bank [9]	All
1878	0.76	0.78	1.17	0.87	0.73	0.89	0.80	1.09	1.03		[10]	0.85
1879	0.66	0.68	0.85	0.52	0.50	0.79	0.55	0.85	0.88		[10]	0.66
1880	0.61	0.66	0.82	0.91	0.64	0.68	0.79	0.91	0.89		[10]	0.72
1881	0.67	0.67	1.07	0.81	0.81	0.69	0.83	0.88	0.82		0.24	0.78
1882	0.63	0.75	0.82	0.81	0.73	0.67	0.89	0.88	0.77		0.53	0.75
1883	0.67	0.77	0.75	0.81	0.71	0.75	0.66	0.87	0.70		0.51	0.73
1884	0.69	0.64	0.75	0.76	0.61	0.70	0.58	0.72	0.79		0.58	0.68
1885	0.59	0.56	0.69	0.77	0.59	0.54	0.73	0.82	0.75		0.51	0.64
1886	0.66	0.58	0.80	0.75	0.59	0.67	0.72	0.79	0.86		0.51	0.68
1887	0.62	0.57	0.71	0.72	0.57	0.66	0.64	0.74	0.87		0.39	0.64
1888	0.57	0.57	0.72	0.77	0.59	0.68	0.54	0.74	0.75		0.28	0.63
1889	0.50	0.55	0.72	0.81	0.64	0.67	0.61	0.73	0.57		0.36	0.63
1890	0.50	0.56	0.71	0.81	0.68	0.62	0.68	0.73	0.53		0.52	0.64
1891	0.50	0.60	0.76	0.85	0.63	0.58	0.66	0.70	0.52		0.42	0.64
1892	0.57	0.49	0.81	0.74	0.57	0.60	0.60	0.74	0.49		0.67	0.62
1893	0.52	0.53	0.67	0.86	0.64	0.60	0.63	0.75	0.49		0.66	0.63
1894	0.53	-0.02	0.77	0.71	0.55	0.63	0.54	0.69	0.50		0.57	0.53
1895	0.44	0.37	0.70	0.70	0.53	0.45	0.59	0.76	0.54		0.41	0.54
1896	0.47	0.39	1.28	0.80	0.61	0.61	0.64	0.72	0.60		0.51	0.67
1897	0.52	0.44	1.58	0.85	0.69	0.67	0.71	0.74	0.62		0.34	0.76
1898	0.56	0.54	0.99	0.97	1.28	0.68	0.76	0.73	0.61		0.49	0.82
1899	0.48	0.57	1.11	1.00	0.89	0.67	0.73	0.67	0.58		0.58	0.76
1900	0.54	0.69	0.86	1.06	0.92	0.68	0.75	0.65	0.53		0.40	0.77
1901	0.66	0.74	1.01	0.90	0.93	0.71	0.77	0.64	0.57		0.45	0.80
1902	0.69	0.80	1.03	1.04	0.94	0.74	0.83	0.66	0.53		0.46	0.84
1903	0.76	0.85	1.15	0.95	0.81	0.77	0.88	0.69	0.57		0.45	0.85
1904	0.64	0.79	1.08	0.94	0.82	0.80	0.88	0.70	0.64		0.37	0.82
1905	0.76	0.79	1.29	1.02	0.85	0.82	0.80	0.66	0.79		0.51	0.88

Year													
1906	0.78	0.78	1.10	0.96	0.81	0.82	0.79	0.63	0.78		0.78	0.28	0.84
1907	0.74	0.80	0.97	0.91	0.84	0.77	0.77	0.63	0.74		0.74		0.82
1908	0.83	0.76	1.01	0.98	0.88	0.80	0.86			0.43			0.84
1909	0.88	0.68	1.23	0.93	0.79	0.85	0.92			0.77			0.88
1910	0.84	0.76	1.15	0.89	0.81	0.86	0.96			0.79			0.88
1911	0.91	0.77	1.06	0.90	0.81	0.86	0.97			0.79			0.88
1912	0.85	0.86	1.03	0.89	0.84	0.74	0.90			0.75			0.86
1913	0.86	0.85	0.96	0.83	0.78	0.71	0.92			0.69			0.83
1914	0.89	0.78	0.93	0.85	0.75	0.67	0.93			0.72			0.82
1915	0.75	0.83	0.98	0.78	0.76	0.76	0.85			0.66			0.80
1916	0.69	0.90	0.74	0.68	0.72	0.79	0.71			0.55			0.73
1917	0.56	0.63	0.73	0.70	0.68	0.85	0.68			0.50			0.67
1918	0.62	0.57	0.62	0.66	0.58	0.74	0.66			0.54			0.62
1919	0.63	0.49	0.60	0.54	0.61	0.65	0.60			0.53			0.58
1920	0.56	0.57	0.66	0.39	0.48	0.61	0.56			0.37			0.53
1921	0.54	0.54	0.50	0.45	0.45	0.62	0.56			0.49			0.52
1922	0.55	0.59	0.58	0.47	0.48	0.58	0.62			0.58			0.55
1923	0.65	0.67	0.65	0.51	0.54	0.66	0.64			0.63			0.62
1924	0.70	0.58	0.65	0.48	0.54	0.71	0.66						0.61 [11]
1925	0.73	0.61	0.64	0.48	0.54	0.74	0.65						0.62 [11]
1926	0.70	0.61	0.61	0.47	0.53	0.70	0.64			0.83			0.63
1927	0.66	0.56	0.61	0.49	0.52	0.73	0.65			0.83			0.61
1928	0.66	0.58	0.61	0.50	0.51	0.75	0.64			0.76			0.61
1929	0.65	0.56	0.60	0.40	0.46	0.72	0.65			0.78			0.59
1930	0.60	0.47	0.58	0.48	0.45	0.70	0.62			0.81			0.57
1931	0.58	0.57	0.50	0.49	0.48	0.68	0.64			0.71			0.58
1932	0.33	0.50	0.42	0.41	0.41	0.62	0.52			0.63			0.47
1933	0.39	0.48	0.35	0.43	0.40	0.59	0.51			0.59			0.46
1934	0.38	0.48	0.39	0.39	0.40	0.56	0.53			0.60			0.46
1935	0.37	0.45	0.36	0.39	0.39	0.54	0.48			0.52			0.43

Notes:

1 i.e. Published net profits, less 4% on capital and reserve.
2 Public liabilities included deposits, note circulation, drafts issued payable withing fourteen days and acceptances.
3 Became a subsidiary of Barclays in 1919.
4 Became a subsidiary of Lloyds in 1918.
5 Became a subsidiary of Midland in 1919.
6 Merged with the North of Scotland Bank in 1907–8.
7 Merged with the Aberdeen Town & County Bank in 1907–8.
8 Became a subsidiary of Midland in 1923.
9 Taken over by Bank of Scotland in 1907.
10 Closed for eight months as a result of the City of Glasgow Bank failure.
11 Omitting North of Scotland Bank.

Source: BS 1/70/14, Analysis of the resources of Bank of Scotland.

Table A17 Inland bills discounted and lending on bonds[1] per month, April 1696 to October 1770[2]

Year	January Bills	January Bonds	February Bills	February Bonds	March Bills	March Bonds	April Bills	April Bonds	May Bills	May Bonds	June Bills	June Bonds
1696								4980 [3]		15350 [4]		4300 [5]
1697												
1698	1123		1147		1464		1705		1228		2029	
1699	1456		1861	4755	690	300	1487	5817 [6]	1833	4289 [7]	2095	2100
1700	2238	1000	3140	1500	3005	600	2555	300	2009	2880	3451	2600 [8]
1701	2947		3755		2856		1798	500	3970	500	3130	
1702	2496	500	3240	500	3481	500	1629		4115	2000	3381	800
1703	2349	1905	2717		3921	800	2181		3060	870	2270	850
1704	2568		2940	1000	3190	650	2880	400	2694		2833	500
1705												
1706	2061	600	3265		1354	1000	2925		2754	1000	2146	800
1707	1658	350	1839	1800	1224		1495		2165		1975	333
1708	810		588		557		560		1030		620	
1709	925		695	1400	1769	1625	985	800	1667	5900	1382	500
1710	1193	2900 [13]	1560	5900	1620	1800	1115		1775	3234 [14]	2436	3650
1711	1747	650	1083	2000	1956	800	1205	1650	2290	2680	4045	1300
1712	2032	1425	2600	1225	1920	550	1525	800	3015	1936	2557	1578
1713	1941	1000	3795	1420	2040	812	2765	962	1585	2368	3100	967
1714	1847	250	2280		2380		2530		2154		2505	
1715	2558		3797		2273		2057		2973		2371	
1716	242		131		454		86		343		539	
1717	2388	200	1210	1400	1694	500	756	100	2611	500	1909	100
1718	1321		1205	1000	886		771	4225	1647	1900	1765	500
1719	2667	200	1508		1281		2269		1996	4450	1969	1300
1720	2490	3450	3427	2400	4213	2500	2358		1386		648	
1721	2460		3344		3755		1556		2325		4704	
1722	2540		3128		3590		3359		2353		3951	5450
1723	1466	2650	3154	2020	3305	2620	1798	1150	3444	1500	2696	500
1724	2241	750	4452	980	3271		2970	2200	4557	3760	3952	3800

Year												
1725	2000	4863	5200	4005	2100	1850	700	3079	2723	5303	200	1956
1726		4421	160	3196	800	2636	270	4014	210	4585	800	1537
1727		1940		1008	350	2521	1000	2958	650	4411	1400	1688
1728		487		934		461		1502		1898		1450
1729	100	2595	590	3881	670	1886	400	1450	250	80		382
1730	1000	2615	900	1867		1930	1200	1417		1487		1326
1731		696		671		1210	2250	1074		2093	500	1633
1732	650	499	500	221	390	710	220	474	620	706	500	696
1733		282	300	1270	200	995	250	1916	1310	1492	300	358
1734		1054		1704	400	877	1006	660	740	771	300	887
1735	500	2097	800	1149	600	837	500	982		1039		1129
1736	600	1392		1392		1049		1286	460	1926	600	1270
1737	150	1986		2380	150	555		2556	420	1704	800	1392
1738		2299		2975		1795	425	918	1800	2067		1623
1739	1260	1543	2000	2425	1500	1472	500	1497		2632	1850	787
1740	400	1810	500	1412	200	630	200	1427	200	1543		545
1741	500	1346	2000	368	550	827		953		2173	850	1689
1742	1000	1150	1940	802		272	440	1336	500	413	550	272
1743	400	2390	900	1563		547	1250	696		1452		1392
1744	300	1200	860	1351		877		1381	400	1427	800	817
1745	2130	948		872	600	1452	2000	1412		1230	300	615
1746	5000	1432	3500	983		373		444		605	3850	303
1747		1326		323	956 15	292		691	400	1432		504
1748	500	494	1270	1129	500	1482		1618	1380	1336		1079
1749		1744		545		1291		1366	300	2556	200	444
1750		1109	200	827		373		1170		998		489
1751	5000	1608	5300	1407	500	650		464		1281		1276
1752	700	484	4000	267	1500	2244		282	500	832		1119
1753		1674	120	897		494	415	494		701		560
1754		711	5000	1775		1457	1850	1124	600	1079	1000	812
1755		413	1200	731		892		892		1492	280	1790
1756		262	1500	1311		857		1472		1649		343
1757	400	630		605	500	731	900	983		282		746
1758		625	2000	776		1772		908	1700	489		565
1759		1687	1700	822		1024		81	500	534		1170

989

Table A17 *continued*

Year	January		February		March		April		May		June	
	Bills	Bonds	Bills	Bonds	Bills	Bonds	Bills	Bonds	Bills	Bonds	Bills	Bonds
1760	660	4650	1860		484		807		923	2500	187	1000
1761	630	700	862		2324		681		403		1981	
1762	605	1000	1644		262		91		3112	3950	2337	4755
1763	1316	10400 [16]	2254	1600	1381		2193	650	766	5000	1775	6000
1764	666		565		353		2753		837		252	
1765	797		363		555		111				464	
1766	252		524		101		444		771		61	
1767	474		590		827		726		3075		726	
1768	1150		3212				232		1966		403	
1769	262		2975		605		625		757		151	
1770	5571		4790		1735		3075		8722		323	

Year	July Bills	July Bonds	August Bills	August Bonds	September Bills	September Bonds	October Bills	October Bonds	November Bills	November Bonds	December Bills	December Bonds
1696												
1697												
1698	1427	1300	1608	600	534	300	1550	2000 [11]	800		729	
1699	2293	5500 [9]	2258	2520 [10]	1773	1000	1957		1451		1359	850
1700	2621	1100	3660	600	4455		3380		1520	3000 [12]	2337	600
1701	4042		2803		4587		3243		4185		3403	300
1702	2844		2905		2688		2972		2613		2526	500
1703	2003	1133	3782	1000	3607	400	2295	500	3092	1400	4170	
1704	2542		5102	500	2374	400	2255		3605	1500	4330	
1705			25	1800	365		740		2750	400	1745	
1706	2364	1045	1923	2100	1245		1587	500	1775	2200	1409	
1707	1932	300	2254	400	926	1500	425	300	1525	1000	2082	
1708	763	1950	1215		1220		1430		410		435	500
1709	1196	1800	1453	2000	1110	1300	1227	800	735	3000	814	300
1710	2092	400	1310	940	2244	200	1480	2700	2003	3000	1595	700
1711	2628	3600	2310	2200	1685	1550	1295	1700	2885	9770	1417	2800
1712	2237	840	3690	850	2986	764	1990		4172	1978	1840	400
1713	2307	1375	4416	1600	2010	900	1517	200	2590	1400	2615	600
1714	1542		2107		1179		1300		3381	1600	2212	
1715	2414		2763		2299				4037		2412	
1716	202		50		121		50		2387		761	
1717	1402	900	3032	100	2097	300	1601	100	4208	1900	1724	300
1718	1523	2300	2334		1215		1533	1000	2551	2300	1064	
1719	2935	1625	1991	1000	1155	600	1311	1600	2841	3000	2409	500
1720	428		211		5874		2400		3600		3218	
1721	3460		4920		2294		1868		3053		3113	
1722	3666	2550	5008	1000	2870	1150	2008	1200	3951	4685	2645	300
1723	3863	3400	4900	5250	3344	1800	1744		3407	4560	3859	500
1724	4578	1180	5044	1000	4732	1000	1684	1400	5555	1050	2995	350
1725	5898	5450	6210	1800	2024		1819		3347	2870	2974	1500
1726	4579	2265	2272		2413	1120	3544	350	4207	1900	3049	750

Table A17 *continued*

Year	July Bills	July Bonds	August Bills	August Bonds	September Bills	September Bonds	October Bills	October Bonds	November Bills	November Bonds	December Bills	December Bonds
1727	928		948		691		565		1054		882	
1728	366		205		131		40		115		221	
1729	2212	100	2899		1341	300	146		534		802	
1730	2213		3435	100	595		439		866	500	1079	
1731	1811		1208	1000	1018	450	1013	135	877		862	300
1732	631		756	400	771		171		2416	1100	1094	500
1733	468		686		680	600	605		423		1935	500
1734	474		792	277	131		383	300	815		1192	850
1735	1659	700	1961	930	1059		1099		1598	1350	1512	
1736	1896	900	1790	800	1190	350	696	500	1805	1500	1992	960
1737	1573	1100	1417		1180		721	500	2228	1450	2113	300
1738	1190		1926	1300	1785		1205		3307		1865	1200
1739	2339	200	625	210	756		2501	350	1941	2500	1734	100
1740	2375	1100	3943		837		1089		2854	300	2244	370
1741	620		1104	230	968		212		625	500	766	
1742	509	400	343		393		766		2228	1300	1523	1650
1743	691	1200	1059	900	862		923	200	2344	200	1250	50
1744	2138		1618	400	691	200	908	5000	2405	1200	958	500
1745	1356	3000	1518	660	20				761		550	
1746	1765	2700	1104		555		998		1724	550	792	
1747	519	280	731		524		277	2560	1195	3700	1427	
1748	1321		580	400	474		751		1336	3500	2234	
1749	776	1400	1654		575		1452	334	4218		766	
1750	590	3110	696		827		605	1000	666	1000	862	
1751	408		1654		1785		792		459		509	
1752	373		464	750	207		413		1255	900	2158	200
1753	1442	500	1220		454		408		1442	300	1997	
1754	2188	800	1684		862		948		918		711	3300
1755	1992	100	847		2284		494		1150		1281	

992

Year												
1756	207		1094		192		1094		575		716	300
1757	1593	300	1432	300	454	900	202		1523	250	1714	450
1758	393		1104	240	504		378	500	2218	2100	353	
1759	484	300	1039	400	590		348		4220		1281	
1760	3368		1356		514		1457		1109	300	686	
1761	131		454		116		61		393	200	988	
1762	1669	4700	5148	9270	676	9750	1437	4000	2022	7700	1785	4500
1763	666	1000	630		630		857	700	363		1855	380
1764	867		892				444		524		1316	
1765	444		378		978		454		4571		948	
1766	434		1170		1664		454		484		30	
1767	2017		333		343		30		948		413	
1768	161		726		827		171		182		1639	
1769	222		3562		1714		1613		4094		1613	
1770	726		2017		3630		2924					

Notes:

All figures are rounded to nearest pound, except where otherwise stated.

1 Lending on personal bond, except where otherwise stated.

2 The figures for bond and bill lending per month cannot be added to give total lending over the year due to their differing forms: the bond was repayable in full when called up by the Bank; the bill was for a fixed term, usually sixty days, with extra interest payable on late bills, and often renewed. The total monthly figure would however represent total new lending agreed by the Bank for that particular month and thus indicate confidence.

3 Includes £2200 lent on heritable bond.

4 Includes £8950 lent on heritable bond.

5 Includes £900 lent on heritable bond.

6 Includes £4167 lent on heritable bond.

7 Includes £1389 lent on heritable bond.

8 Includes £667 lent on heritable bond.

9 Includes £4000 lent on heritable bond.

10 Includes £1060 lent on heritable bond.

11 Includes £1000 lent on heritable bond.

12 Includes £1500 lent on heritable bond.

13 Includes 45000 Merks (1 Merk = $\frac{4}{9}$ £ Scots) (£2500).

14 Includes 20000 Merks (£1111.11).

15 Includes 10000 Merks (£555.56).

16 Consists of five bonds of £4000 (to Essex Duchess of Roxburgh, William Ramsay of Templehall, William Ker of Gateshaw and Henry Balcanqual, writer, Edinburgh), £4000 (to William Elliot, writer in Edinburgh, William Ogilvie of Hartwoodmyres and Cornelius Elliot, WS), £3000 (to Alexander Hay of Drummelzier, Archibald Stirling of Keir and Robert Hay, son to Alexander Hay), £1000 (to John Craigie of Kilgraston, advocate, and Laurence Craigie, WS) and £400 (to George Wilson, mason, Edinburgh and John Wilson, merchant there).

Sources: BS 1/94, General Ledgers (account of inland bills); BS 1/5, Minutes.

Table A18 Monthly states of loans[1] and deposits at Bank of Scotland London office, August 1867 to February 1918

	January		February		March		April		May		June	
	Loans	Deposits	Loans	Deposits	Loans	Deposits	Loans	Deposits	Loans	Deposits	Loans	Deposits
1867												
1868	99310	50974	110898	66743	100273	65459	122796	68703	183624	126882	134745	82906
1869	191550	408174	285045	359118	250325	278591	285302	277426	360034	223792	449700	269062
1870	374343	276296	358678	314620	380209	297316	401993	320767	376919	243655	311358	316486
1871	576710	526387	528539	505633	549034	483452	500291	463517	464329	590414	499732	606605
1872	502288	934533	593566	856729	578600	606231	577662	502606	643810	619003	644239	713169
1873	954724	767009	987467	691493	1107670	589996	995444	617973	830990	422708	703546	519714
1874	941823	697740	684081	600814	584225	618422	569570	550182	690083	585338	831685	666660
1875	922122	995908	988197	894083	936614	681978	748401	568492	813512	604738	932914	658402
1876	956160	753081	887870	627535	972634	643418	1130494	623774	1114298	671503	1149009	627337
1877	957764	703414	1002190	636295	1084800	577756	1108105	628341	1052951	576070	995439	642943
1878	826096	969876	916906	948995	909958	833992	868350	794009	828683	835112	806887	794231
1879	950214	626965	1058116	805977	1139591	657105	1166500	805163	1094341	735036	1279775	715020
1880	1108676	810530	1066248	905949	4396632	896801	4606405	963813	4555065	808426	4571323	928423
1881	4638124	919376	4134148	920552	4528812	819932	4722826	918434	5327312	1038498	5459230	953103
1882	7107769	1052243	4355956	820896	4818896	922785	5085082	963815	5190693	932604	5208422	1034872
1883	4415696	869152	3846452	861981	4343021	1110953	4443591	1162857	4153547	924144	4161748	986988
1884	4336696	910025	3960824	955699	4059351	784158	4258124	852944	4443698	885773	4506986	896815
1885	5055469	858253	4840564	1084636	4989581	1015239	4874139	874176	4451352	834568	4405903	860360
1886	4561784	875528	4523104	1065251	4588154	840205	4754425	992727	4826528	1009234	4835027	1058213
1887	4539104	885740	4388587	974536	4513677	868673	4579152	871369	4998384	1027893	5075654	1041489
1888	5085557	991786	5048281	966352	5153478	784656	5017077	821843	4966575	889264	5094259	923181
1889	5862026	1022089	5556945	821158	5400472	878513	5767074	1030342	5570317	1006469	5153846	958343
1890	5779776	1046506	5716085	1074968	5929563	1167514	6025365	1118340	6196840	1130558	6138833	1156802
1891	6537642	972615	6599189	1059807	6443516	998259	6556050	909104	6434411	890946	6209592	972698
1892	5709440	942229	5817697	966258	6120600	907121	6341295	1005230	6435781	993804	6425241	1070078
1893	6228305	913242	6239930	902172	6258697	818383	6527729	944778	6283616	860114	6577503	970887
1894	5721841	1074992	5509576	979143	5389034	1003260	5828055	1214265	5803740	1048928	6158875	1262091
1895	6002051	1076044	5897254	1005591	5914946	989038	6326327	1147802	6081790	1125620	6257217	1120278

Year												
1896	5641363	1044598	5737531	1170354	5972474	1260453	6183760	1302210	6638992	1264979	6248615	1458282
1897	5833515	997932	6169653	1127228	6569259	1097636	6820505	1485692	6922045	1343427	6603006	1217478
1898	6329695	1223513	6267170	1509303	6140479	1533608	6156834	1331328	6442666	1334955	6054071	1281941
1899	5997654	1325886	5633002	1301743	5704399	1312077	5706897	1487938	5683379	1308570	5384483	1287868
1900	5538335	1577922	5747233	1294328	5946732	1395592	6050226	1318912	6061635	1516315	5972768	1308305
1901	5723442	1319710	5443600	1325485	5328278	1106279	5353077	1286270	5492967	1294939	5328316	1182907
1902	5314840	1120981	5077454	1299335	5119670	1230620	5236535	1363082	4714126	1343259	4915498	1477242
1903	4622150	1215510	4442627	1151660	4766533	1446158	4762115	1287946	4744093	1298102	4650235	1346727
1904	4164140	1346481	4439931	1460945	4432049	1391061	4742362	1588123	4611559	1554635	4181013	1257048
1905	4394241	1516390	4690600	1838673	4720109	1836534	4785177	2043734	4342216	1766575	4584351	1813531
1906	4461962	1489070	4606000	1580833	4794067	1929703	4640808	1798769	4413456	1775175	4592613	1938055
1907	4988130	2002485	5081368	2065826	5183996	2146503	5354483	2273990	5403500	2249830	5217760	2206841
1908	5371842	1992250	5454074	2075933	5320913	2088232	5255856	1951900	5274146	1717483	5291817	1938211
1909	4726671	1715155	5752226	2741635	5412568	2608220	6260815	3393834	6258780	3078933	5781395	2706212
1910	6457634	2995487	7141103	3882956	5726148	2786730	5455896	2612530	5875040	3052947	5507422	2855308
1911	5384607	2184096	5630304	2655657	5203495	2367272	5580103	2577330	5668425	2938976	5442022	2915858
1912	7011676	3602508	7085691	3669347	5591227	2326615	5561370	2249637	5748573	2535111	6048011	3101941
1913	6653507	2694968	7831347	4002671	7269536	3244728	6318212	2383290	6383365	2555796	6010505	2135215
1914	7790804	2508380	7391867	2572928	7424126	2470953	7728080	2545073	7615305	2560789	7870798	2821260
1915	7864532	3155590	8675762	3295220	8253291	3414157	8521842	3325625	8680640	3110667	9625424	3365130
1916	6891902	3348100	6648128	3243566	6747304	2994124	7307492	3255355	7782435	2958588	8512280	3318398
1917	11197396	5511002	8936279	8789626	6931682	3777035	5870130	4389855	6214668	3227660	6648431	3406150
1918	11731002	4344993	10640826	5469260								

Table A18 *continued*

	July		August		September		October		November		December	
	Loans	Deposits	Loans	Deposits	Loans	Deposits	Loans	Deposits	Loans	Deposits	Loans	Deposits
1867			66269	19568	70509	23496	81456	36417	96288	46532	93909	42300
1868	149365	103312	163622	118202	151363	99734	242801	197617	288713	233689	337938	314018
1869	526899	297959	686263	389378	596054	248621	514142	249315	504373	294002	443812	270977
1870	301576	414378	349559	464972	339699	279507	314463	353974	412421	408383	416688	472983
1871	386747	628237	423713	806105	380779	616614	532980	943130	487163	841218	504002	769725
1872	630879	513156	639868	658807	757450	714130	1016656	676087	1035170	636853	881543	657522
1873	685257	540878	863772	604531	1134058	793413	1082027	870615	959387	690004	966180	652752
1874	926784	733574	875780	822919	793012	816367	848499	813719	876521	881630	907085	1071218
1875	921534	782803	1090098	846002	1004019	853547	834060	817454	714379	779850	911965	746463
1876	1132578	800588	1289863	735158	1114265	680186	1091426	795039	996446	797412	955941	799640
1877	1110089	725434	1125632	699323	968063	712421	838809	812037	756018	831893	769718	911658
1878	820932	841028	817198	913639	793233	888393	847602	814321	840529	732542	961960	723090
1879	1348865	738708	1579669	857444	1494395	998871	1667121	977690	1448452	899250	1388128	689276
1880	4705727	883902	5292810	1006231	5217142	1083259	5190313	1103226	5302522	1244150	4982242	1191633
1881	5541816	902630	5449838	852835	5240176	849180	5226221	835250	5151881	854205	4918839	908192
1882	5248882	1157008	5314600	1255031	4973786	1138763	5053882	1322384	4526261	1078094	4391377	1008072
1883	4368350	982502	4476217	1069695	4407425	1018259	4308812	1067616	4487308	1329433	4362203	1070439
1884	4534161	875017	4683378	924568	4911772	894553	4952457	1001929	5436849	1092800	5158720	1019008
1885	4376373	971639	5180562	853970	5030317	812331	5140651	962990	4974639	964577	4464462	876173
1886	4879057	987493	5057132	917495	5007233	1048089	4874167	993931	4644190	979300	4355125	789170
1887	5071199	1030020	5358578	1053899	5094111	1044101	5225415	1036334	5108920	1030258	5157135	1005843
1888	5385425	986895	5346803	881237	5194383	928159	5192294	944330	5794567	945426	5679343	1052983
1889	5502972	980130	5478103	963058	5329295	891660	5368918	849607	5709479	1114160	5692747	1091037
1890	5962544	903515	6217916	934402	6584031	1024845	6641514	934529	6622082	1218549	6244613	966192
1891	6589927	993851	6563899	1053400	6665928	1107793	6328336	1082178	5726619	1030593	5456737	1055650
1892	6680505	954663	6495368	1035221	6656092	1104845	6585633	1097991	6207571	998877	5787829	952987
1893	6528430	1158450	6247875	1071949	6313584	1186466	6301700	1122492	6567393	1272480	5754891	1049337
1894	6058763	1251376	6117328	1312791	6035729	1213500	5957528	1199387	6039121	1215446	6076564	1162756
1895	6547712	1250472	6583074	1300228	6581016	1151430	6668804	1280866	5939777	1100059	5920838	1210637

Year												
1896	6141066	1253381	6299113	1269673	6487476	1250264	5750637	1256204	5673242	1110488	5330896	1032256
1897	6686658	1385626	6744874	1197124	6785511	1312460	6779018	1270257	6204947	1394459	6196952	1232460
1898	6401692	1577301	6153521	1401361	5970766	1210240	6113653	1176593	6099788	1255033	6060603	1296933
1899	5285862	1376337	5347556	1407083	5252418	1315399	5285477	1516229	5357466	1395676	5145679	1593849
1900	6085328	1428779	5628828	1165580	5780973	1206023	6120156	1298811	5654111	1318161	5732125	1255469
1901	5740300	1201086	5848041	1138602	5699818	1096574	5706219	1252317	5933320	1270807	5535691	1180927
1902	4696353	1270755	4639831	1192090	4568031	1251264	4880360	1435648	4867312	1192328	4419228	1101091
1903	4801037	1360561	4598665	1363157	4608082	1381154	4359565	1371794	4067891	1353942	3968030	1205076
1904	4239996	1262408	4365688	1147451	4365069	1276831	4541847	1441251	4348058	1341596	4085416	1282385
1905	4582270	1795236	4528048	1663597	4387905	1692051	3892767	1605367	4321095	1299734	4336690	1460677
1906	4659557	1627316	4798945	1613512	4833509	1848256	4407125	1700878	4595872	1801085	4739186	2031538
1907	5681261	2353698	5441562	2177676	5542841	2290472	5217692	1940841	5053491	1965180	5251152	2149614
1908	5529470	2032788	5797687	1987834	5553188	1874278	5391109	2081048	5169212	1878292	4466202	1736400
1909	5610569	2636624	5722453	2684501	5526336	2632621	5222581	2461923	5740959	2604536	5741621	2574528
1910	5866922	2839330	5650521	2585865	5237548	2231264	5414901	2168814	5691989	2422324	5556340	2453047
1911	5644304	2525592	5850609	2476857	5790755	2506108	6171664	2931887	6066995	2900957	6516822	3829533
1912	5733880	2702395	6199783	2616950	6173535	2714977	5966363	2138336	6278233	2414678	6511681	2926510
1913	6841047	2502887	6791092	2424141	7413133	2664138	7440734	2755576	7232795	2163234	7478886	2669446
1914	7827070	2526259	8264765	2695275	8316862	2817764	8517321	2739397	9142572	2889682	8342953	3105350
1915	8372588	2666256	6986054	2702209	7056077	2739918	6878359	3199124	6551919	3148856	6606071	3124593
1916	9206461	3382474	9615335	3002956	9636870	2915746	9341920	3528780	10013561	4018756	9476053	3736107
1917	8559450	3837302	9509630	4172540	10633823	3921855	11901098	4335691	12269609	4273334	13928449	4855060

Note:
1 Consisted of loans on current accounts, bills discounted, bills past due and short bills. From March 1890, current account loans were broken down between current and loan accounts. The latter formed on average 92% of total loans in this category. From November 1872 the position of the Canadian Bank of Commerce current account was stated separately. This accounted for, on average, 87% of total current account loans between November 1872 and February 1877, and for, on average, 34% of the total between March 1877 and February 1880. Thereafter this account was less important. Special War Loan advances from February 1917–18 were not included in the total lent.

Source: BS 1/71/14–39, State of deposits, loans, investments and circulation.

Table A19 Examples of Glasgow accounts over £2,000 (quarterly states),[1] 1855–65

Company	Anderston Foundry Co.				Robert Barclay & Curle				Coltness Iron Co.				
Month/Year	Bills	Accept-ances[2]	Cash account(s)	Total	Bills	Accept-ances	Cash account(s)	Total	Bills	Accept-ances	Cash account(s)	Misc.[3]	Total
Apr 1855													
Jul 1855													
Oct 1855													
Jan 1856	19015	3900	4955	27870									
Apr 1856	16809	9900	5330	32039									
Jul 1856	15088	16950	190	32228	21425		250	21675					
Oct 1856	12870	13800	2500	29170	19654		349	20003					
Jan 1857	10620	13650	2731	27001	20183		952	21135					
Apr 1857						20002		20002					
Jul 1857	9345	18475		27820	22441		1030	23471	26174[5]			7930	34104
Oct 1857	11977	20725		32702	24563		3175	27738	22400[6]		6240		28640
Jan 1858					21113	533	1961	23607	30406[7]			11245	41651
Apr 1858					23374		590	23964	25253[8]			2630	27883
Jul 1858	11593	18190		29783									
Oct 1858	16756	8700	1400	26856	20499	174		20673					
Jan 1859	22113	8000	7150	37263	19992		1110	21102					
Apr 1859	24433	10400	5900	40733	21637			21637					
Jul 1859	35754	11480		47234	23523		1500	25023					
Oct 1859	20115	7132		27247									
Jan 1860	26796	9855		36651									
Jul 1860	21369	7610		28979									
Jan 1861	28283	4610		32893									
Jul 1861	44888	6280		51168									
Jan 1862	32981	11916		44897									
Jul 1862	25390	9112		34502									
Jan 1863	26911	6127		33038									
Jul 1863	32511	6035		38546									
Jan 1864	17737	4952		22689									

	Bills		Total
Jul 1864	24840	6105	30945
Jan 1865	32741	2825	35566

Company	Monkland Iron & Steel Co. 4					Napier, Robert & Sons, Engineers				Tennant, Charles & Co., St Rollox			
Month/Year	Bills	Accept-ances 2	Cash account(s)	Misc. 3	Total	Bills	Accept-ances	Cash account(s)	Total	Bills	Accept-ances	Cash account(s)	Total
Apr 1855	19620	747	25964	6060	52391	15575	5744	83674	104993	25259		79340	104599
Jul 1855	19355	1386	25964	5754	52459	22837	6024	78583	107444	30705		71780	102485
Oct 1855	12746	1695	25964	3426	43831	33691	5672	72650	112013	29281	74440		103721
Jan 1856	18625	2676	27396	4950	53647	26837	7000	52230	86067	46029		75830	121859
Apr 1856	18624	560	27396	3385	49965	22644	4214	55773	82631	37085		72200	109285
Jul 1856	31249	1100	27396	1495	61240					53769		73550	127319
Oct 1856	28782	4734	24600	7630	65746					48396		75424	123820
Jan 1857	30156	4927	24600	5005	64688					31966		79580	111546
Apr 1857	27713	3902	24600	4560	60775					59931	2462	64660	127053
Jul 1857	32140	5463	24600	8223	70426					22383	5465	74700	102548
Oct 1857	22082	1624	24600	4510	52816					47384	293	81200	128877
Jan 1858	30845		26107	6135	63087					41748		78600	120348
Apr 1858										27596		76230	103826
Jul 1858										19488	950	63900	84338
Oct 1858										19968		67990	87958
Jan 1859	7321	400	25760	7407	40888	40470	1431	56256	98157	9417	100	79000	88517
Apr 1859	8868	748	25760	4490	39866	6250	423	68337	75010	12209	523	78860	91592
Jul 1859	6691	200	24600	7025	38516	3000	1322	90861	95183	11620	2676	76490	90786
Oct 1859	11292		24600	6895	42787	2000		48102	50102	17145	68660		85805
Jan 1860	12319		25848	7328	45495	2000		40236	42236	2139		74900	77039
Jul 1860	12821	550	24600	6909	44880	1500		120310	121810	21243		56680	77923
Jan 1861	14352		25848	6463	46663	3780		136873	140653	28215		74780	102995
Jul 1861		15429	25848	6098	47375	5750	400	187968	194118	17809	6868	71700	96377
Jan 1862	3875		25848	6098	35821	40000	2886	164966	207852	17592	74927		92519
Jul 1862	3677		25848	6098	35623	5950		137376	143326	17489		69263	86752
Jan 1863	3479		25848	6098	35425					8276		74749	83025

Table A19 continued

Company	Monkland Iron & Steel Co. [4]					Napier, Robert & Sons, Engineers				Tennant, Charles & Co., St Rollox			
Month/Year	Bills	Accept-ances [2]	Cash account(s)	Misc. [3]	Total	Bills	Accept-ances	Cash account(s)	Total	Bills	Accept-ances	Cash account(s)	Total
Jul 1863	2892		22516	5339	30747	1101		90995	92096	25201	15053	71676	111930
Jan 1864	2516		22516	4194	29226	169		33828	33997	29945	18179	68761	116885
Jul 1864			22516	3002	25518	6825	1368	28378	36571	29841		65820	95661
Jan 1865			22516	3002	25518	16773		69440	86213	18922		69813	88735

Notes:

1 From January 1860 these are half-yearly rather than quarterly.

2 With the exception of July 1858 all acceptances were to the Coltness Iron Co. (the acceptances to this company in July 1858 were £14550).

3 Overdrawn on deposit account.

4 In October 1857 the company was described as 'highly respectable and their present position believed to be good'. It was reported in January 1859 that the senior partner had died and that the iron trade was depressed. The other quarterly reports of 1859 mentioned the continued depression in the iron trade, while that of July 1860 stated that the iron trade had not been profitable for some time. By January 1863 the company was under trust.

5 Of which £17406 were on the Anderston Foundry Co.

6 Of which £18475 were on the Anderston Foundry Co.

7 Of which £20725 were on the Anderston Foundry Co.

8 Of which £14750 were on the Anderston Foundry Co.

Sources: BS 1/143/10–11 (to January 1861), Averages of Bill Accounts over £2,000; BS 1/155/4 (to January 1865), Customers' Credit Opinion Books.

Table A20 British Linen Bank profit and loss account, 1761–1920

Year ending 30 May/ 15 April/ 15 January [1]	Credits		Total credits	Debits			Total debits	Profit allocation	
	Total gained on interest account [2]	Misc.		Expenses of management	Misc. charges [3]	Interest paid or due to depositors		Net profit	Carried forward from previous year
1761	675	5994 [6]	6670	832	2651 [7]		3482	3187	4351
1762	figures unavailable								
1763	figures unavailable								
1764	4312	772 [8]	5084	642	2440		3082		
1765	3786	634 [10]	4420	596	618		1215		
1766	3627	1094 [11]	4720	687	1320		2007		
1767	2830	309 [12]	3139	649	1553		2202		
1768	2805	100 [13]	2905	673	1650 [14]		2323		
1769	2967	128 [15]	3095	732	1816		2547		
1770	2687	56	2743	675	2165		2840		
1771	2734		2734	755	1298		2053		
1772	3029	69 [16]	3099	771	1009		1780		
1773	2733	45 [16]	2777	750	1025		1776		
1774	3446	121 [16]	3567	781	1275		2056	1511	1002
1775	4494	186 [16]	4680	799	1062		1861		
1776	4653	95 [16]	4748	816	919		1735		
1777	4625	47 [16]	4672	775	651		1426		
1778	4803	80 [16]	4882	832	711		1542		
1779	5011		5011	826	1000		1826	3184	4100
1780	5033		5033	810	1148		1958		
1781	5431		5431	866	1267		2133		
1782	5682		5682	837	1252		2088	3594	4268
1783	5837		5837	910	1415		2325		
1784	5300		5300	836	1286		2122		
1785	7589		7589	1094	1863		2996	4633	4420
1786	5739		5739	1053	372		1425		
1787	5885		5885	1204	129		1333	4553	3000

Table A20 *continued*

Year ending 30 May/ 15 April/ 15 January [1]	Credits		Total credits	Debits				Net profit	Profit allocation	
	Total gained on interest account [2]	Misc.		Expenses of management	Misc. charges [3]	Interest paid or due to depositors	Total debits		Net profit	Carried forward from previous year
1788	6633		6633	1267	189		1455	5178		387
1789	8084		8084	1288	305		1593	6491		3000
1790	7465		7465	1416	191		1607	5858		2000
1791	7695		7695	1546	429		1975	5720		5000
1792	8651		8651	1373	163		1536			
1793	9033		9033	1587	253		1841			
1794	7264		7264	1795	245		2040			
1795	7663		7663	1819	189		2008			
1796	9851		9851	1869	152		2021			
1797	9645		9645	1945	361		2305			
1798	11070		11070	2457	1161 [20]		3617	7453		10000
1799	9811		9811	2259	139		2398			
1800	9876		9876	2330	185		2515			
1801	10946		10946	2471	159		2630	8317		9000
1802	12645		12645	2852	124		2976			
1803	14075		14075	2806	119		2925			
1804	13085		13085	2930	238		3168			
1805	21769		21769	3419	128		3547			
1806	18122		18122	3428	104		3531			
1807	19506		19506	4063	191		4253			
1808	21467		21467	3757	267		4024			
1809	24091		24091	4491	161		4652			
1810	29744		29744	4861	219		5080			
1811	34207		34207	5070	238		5308			
1812	34622		34622	5250	286		5536			
1813	34031		34031	5417	282		5699			
1814	40854	6950 [22]	47804	5421	282		5703			

Year						
1815	54928		54928	5444	369	5813
1816	54490		54490	5225	475	5700
1817	55539		55539	5947	269	6215
1818	59836		59836	6017	386	6403
1819	57945		57945	5843	372	6215
1820	57450		57450	5688	322	6010
1821	51847		51847	5508	287	5795
1822	54275		54275	5542	255	5797
1823	55770		55770	5474	490	5964
1824	52516		52516	5916	371	6287
1825	55022		55022	5640	458	6097
1826	57710		57710	6532	393	6925
1827	33183		33183	7269	433	7702
1828	56491		56491	7254	400	7653
1829	58215		58215	7047	490	7536
1830	63560		63560	6757	579	7335
1831	59833		59833	7024	563	7587
1832	53468		53468	7150	911	8061
1833	54226		54226	6448	630	7077
1834	57107		57107	6813	938	7752
1835	56664		56664	6679	433	7112
1836	59143		59143	6314	220	6533
1837	61024		61024	6572	627	7199
1838	60560		60560	7063	289	7352
1839	64561		64561	6480	714	7194
1840	57272	10000 [25]	67272	7485	221	7706
1841	53800	10000 [25]	63800	7560	607	8167
1842	45185	10000 [25]	55185	7879	531	8410
1843	59172		59172	7390	451	7841
1844	60880		60880	8428	406	8834
1845	58208		58208	7652	442	8094
1846	61288		61288	8598	276	8874
1847	60969		60969	8210	427	8636
1848	63699		63699	8226	878	9104
1849	58972		58972	8000	483	8483

Table A20 *continued*

Year ending 30 May/ 15 April/ 15 January [1]	Credits			Debits				Profit allocation	
	Total gained on interest account [2]	Misc.	Total credits	Expenses of management	Misc. charges [3]	Interest paid or due to depositors	Total debits	Net profit	Carried forward from previous year
1850	65143		65143	8059	620		8679		
1851	107886		107886	9295	572		9867		
1852	111440		111440	8958	251		9209		
1853	104257		104257	10028	166		10194		
1854	113910		113910	10232	321		10553		
1855	120505		120505	9961	298		10258		
1856	125371		125371	10775	291		11065		
1857	136768		136768	10453	153		10605		
1858	118617		118617	10935	264		11200		
1859	116237		116237	11916	174		12090		
1860	116603		116603	11620	498		12118		
1861	117202		117202	11894	208		12102		
1862								108208 [28]	
1863								108490 [28]	
1864								118218 [28]	
1865								151643 [28]	
1866								131432 [28]	
1867								157270 [28]	
1868								137138 [28]	
1869								139307 [28]	
1870								136073 [28]	
1871								137432 [28]	
1872	figures unavailable								
1873	figures unavailable								
1874	figures unavailable								
1875	figures unavailable								21643
1876	figures unavailable								16432

Year									
1877	figures unavailable								
1878	figures unavailable							160000[28]	
1879	figures unavailable							144000[28]	
1880	figures unavailable							146000[28]	
1881								173333[28]	17417
1882								154236[28]	5750
1883								154418[28]	14986
1884								153766[28]	24404
1885	494708		494708	137998		204126	342124	152584[33]	33170
1886	452269		452269	141614		141532	283146	169124[33]	35255
1887	483092		483092	145018		170287	315306	167787[33]	23128
1888	464034		464034	128890	12408	159991	301289	162745[33]	29415
1889	499052		499052	130195	11642	179075	320911	178141[33]	12159
1890	557607		557607	128975	11115	233448	373538	184069[33]	25300
1891	579219		579219	132143	14042	228641	374827	204393[33]	19097
1892	550126		550126	135688	11762	182259	329709	220418[33]	23210
1893	516304		516304	134549	11719	141027	287295	229009[33]	13628
1894	555449		555449	137928	12975	160221	311124	244326[33]	32969
1895	482048		482048	135394	14778	122305	272477	209571[33]	50646
1896	480108	67636[36]	480108	138033	14665	81885	234582	245525[33]	60217
1897	536619	103408[36]	536619	142340	19157	127773	289270	247350[33]	38597
1898	535592		535592	144521	19129	105188	268838	266754[33]	44355
1899	581598	40906[36]	581598	143802	17941	150614	312356	269242[33]	66109
1900	678333		678333	145372	17520	231475	394367	283966[33]	11257
1901	707384		707384	149342	22993	243016	415351	292033[33]	30223
1902	640320	13006[36]	640320	151032	25887	186142	363061	277259[33]	44256
1903	672655		672655	152734	27875	191945	372554	300101[33]	61515
1904	657730	25519[36]	657730	153491	23426	205274	382191	275539[33]	54022
1905	577602	16198[36]	577602	151301	25127	127692	304120	273482[33]	66561
1906	619957		619957	154207	25514	155474	335195	284762[33]	45561
1907[38]	535155		535155	116851	22189	186847	325887	209268[33]	66521
1908	754254	50000[39]	754254	155894	24331	304809	485034	269220[33]	76289
1909	589458	10000[36]	589458	157644	25042	129822	312508	276950[33]	45544
1910	599695	20600[36]	599695	157935	25885	141815	325635	274060[33]	60995
1911	653276		653276	157372	25385	191221	373978	279298[33]	38155

Table A20 *continued*

Year ending 30 May/ 15 April/ 15 January [1]	Credits		Total credits	Debits				Profit allocation	
	Total gained on interest account [2]	Misc.		Expenses of management	Misc. charges [3]	Interest paid or due to depositors	Total debits	Net profit	Carried forward from previous year
1912	625655		625655	158187	24306	170858	353351	272304 [33]	32063
1913		50000 [39]						267917 [28]	47571
1914		100000 [39]						257680 [28]	37545
1915		150000 [39]						266318 [28]	29243
1916		150000 [39]						280585 [28]	62827
1917		100000 [39]						266047 [28]	29509
1918		50000 [39]						296234 [28]	55378
1919								297873 [28]	81612
1920								307216 [28]	67252

Year ending 30 May/ 15 April/ 15 January [1]	Gain to be allocated	Rate of dividend (%)	Dividend (£)	Profit allocation						Capital
				To bad and doubtful debts [4]	To reduction of cost of bank property	To reserve fund	Misc.	To undivided profit [5]	Total allocation	
1761	7538		1876					5663	7539	
1762	figures unavailable									
1763	figures unavailable									
1764	2002							2002	2002	24274 [9]
1765	3205							3206	3206	26276
1766	2714							2714	2714	27411
1767	937							937	937	19893
1768	582							582	582	20829
1769	548							548	548	21412
1770	-97							-97	-97	21959
1771	681							681	681	21863
1772	1318							1318	1318	22544
1773	1002							1002 [17]	0 [17]	1002	23862

1774	2513	4.0	23722	949	1382	322[18]	-140	2513
1775	2819	4.0	24710	989	842		989	2819
1776	3013	5.0	24710	1236	778		1000	3013
1777	3246	5.0	24710	1236	411		1600	3247
1778	3340	5.0	24710	1236	605		1500	3340
1779	7284	5.0	29652	1483		4942[19]	860	7285
1780	3075	5.0	29652	1483			1592	3074
1781	3299	5.0	29652	1483			1816	3299
1782	7862	5.0	34594	1730		4942[19]	1190	7862
1783	3512	5.0	34594	1730			1782	3512
1784	3179	5.0	34594	1730			1449	3179
1785	9053	5.0	39536	1977	1134	4942[19]	1000	9053
1786	4314	5.0	39536	1977	337		2000	4314
1787	7553	5.0	44478	2224		4942[19]	387	7553
1788	5565	5.0	44478	2224	341		3000	5565
1789	9491	5.0	49420	2471	78	4942[19]	2000	9491
1790	7858	5.0	49420	2471	387		5000	7858
1791	10720	5.0	56480	2824	336	7060[19]	500	10720
1792	7116	5.0	80000	4000	616		2500	7116
1793	7193	5.0	80000	4000	1193		2000	7193
1794	5224	5.0	80000	4000	224		1000	5224
1795	5656	5.0	80000	4000	656		1000	5656
1796	7830	5.0	80000	4000	1330		2500	7830
1797	7340	5.0	80000	4000	1340		2000	7340
1798	17453	5.0	90000	4500	452	10000[19]	2500	17452
1799	7414	5.0	90000	4500	414		2500	7414
1800	7361	5.0	90000	4500	361		2500	7361
1801	17317	5.0	100000	5000	316	10000[19]	2000	17316
1802	9669	5.0	100000	5000	669		4000	9669
1803	11150	5.0	100000	5000	2650		3500	11150
1804	9917	5.0	100000	5000	2417		2500	9917
1805	18222	6.0	100000	6000	2903	1319[21]	8000	18222
1806	14591	6.0	100000	6000	2591		6000	14591
1807	15252	6.0	200000	12000	1252		2000	15252
1808	17444	6.0	200000	12000	2444		3000	17444

Table A20 *continued*

Year ending 30 May/ 15 April/ 15 January [1]	Gain to be allocated	Rate of dividend (%)	Capital	Dividend (£)	To bad and doubtful debts [4]	To reduction of cost of bank property	To reserve fund	Misc.	To undivided profit [5]	Total allocation
1809	19439	7.0	200000	14000	2439				3000	19439
1810	24664	7.0	200000	14000	3664				7000	24664
1811	28899	7.5	200000	15000	4899				9000	28899
1812	29086	8.0	200000	16000	5087				8000	29087
1813	28332	8.0	200000	16000	2332				10000	28332
1814	42100	8.0	500000	40000	2101					42101
1815	49115	8.0	500000	40000	4115				5000	49115
1816	48791	8.0	500000	40000	3791				5000	48791
1817	49324	9.5	500000	47500	1824				[23]	49324
1818	53434	10.0	500000	50000	1434				2000	53434
1819	51731	10.0	500000	50000	731				1000	51731
1820	51440	10.0	500000	50000	440				1000	51440
1821	46052	9.0	500000	45000	552				500	46052
1822	48479	9.0	500000	45000	979				2500	48479
1823	49806	9.0	500000	45000	2306				2500	49806
1824	46230	9.0	500000	45000	530				700	46230
1825	48924	9.0	500000	45000	1924				2000	48924
1826	50786	9.0	500000	45000	2785				3000	50785
1827	25481	8.5	500000	42500					[24]	42500 [24]
1828	48838	8.0	500000	40000				8838 [24]	[24]	48838
1829	50679	8.0	500000	40000	2417			8262 [24]	[24]	50679
1830	56225	8.0	500000	40000	6225				10000	56225
1831	52246	8.0	500000	40000	4446				7800	52246
1832	45407	8.0	500000	40000	3407				2000	45407
1833	47148	8.0	500000	40000	5148				2000	47148
1834	49356	8.0	500000	40000	6355				3000	49355
1835	49552	8.0	500000	40000	9552					49552

Year										
1836	52610	8.0	500000	40000	12610					52610
1837	53825	8.0	500000	40000	13825					53825
1838	53208	8.0	500000	40000	13209					53209
1839	57367	8.0	500000	40000	7367			10000 [25]		57367
1840	59566	8.0	500000	40000	9566			10000 [25]		59566
1841	55634	8.0	500000	40000	5634			10000 [25]		55634
1842	46775	8.0	500000	40000	6775					46775
1843	51331	8.0	500000	40000	11332					51332
1844	52046	8.0	500000	40000	12046					52046
1845	50114	8.0	500000	40000	10114					50114
1846	52414	8.0	500000	40000	12414					52414
1847	52333	8.0	500000	40000	12332					52332
1848	54596	8.0	500000	40000	14596					54596
1849	50488	8.0	500000	40000	10488					50488
1850	56464	4.0	500000	20000 [26]	36464					56464
1851	98019	8.0	1000000	80000	3019			15000 [27]		98019
1852	102231	8.0	1000000	80000	7231			15000 [27]		102231
1853	94063	8.0	1000000	80000	14063					94063
1854	103357	8.0	1000000	80000	18357			5000 [27]		103357
1855	110247	8.5	1000000	85000	15247			10000 [27]		110247
1856	114306	9.0	1000000	90000	18306			6000 [27]		114306
1857	126163	9.0	1000000	90000	36163					126163
1858	107418	9.0	1000000	90000	17418					107418
1859	104147	9.0	1000000	90000	14147					104147
1860	104485	9.0	1000000	90000	14485					104485
1861	105100	9.0	1000000	90000	15100					105100
1862	108208	9.5	1000000	93125 [29]					15083 [30]	108208
1863	108490	10.0	1000000	98125 [29]				7134 [31]	3231	108490
1864	118218	10.0	1000000	100000		18218				118218
1865	151643	11.0	1000000	110000		10000		10000 [31]	21643	151643
1866	153075	11.0	1000000	110000		5000		21643 [31]	16432	153075
1867	173702	11.0	1000000	110000		5000		20000 [32]	38702	173702
1868	137138	11.0	1000000	110000		5000	2138	20000 [32]		137138
1869	139307	11.0	1000000	110000		5000	4307	20000 [32]		139307
1870	136073	11.0	1000000	110000		5000	1073	20000 [32]		136073

Table A20 *continued*

Year ending 30 May/ 15 April/ 15 January [1]	Gain to be allocated	Rate of dividend (%)	Capital	Profit allocation						
				Dividend (£)	To bad and doubtful debts [4]	To reduction of cost of bank property	To reserve fund	Misc.	To undivided profit [5]	Total allocation
1871	137432	11.0	1000000	110000		5000	2432	20000 [32]		137432
1872	figures unavailable									
1873	figures unavailable									
1874	figures unavailable									
1875	figures unavailable									
1876	figures unavailable									
1877	figures unavailable									
1878			1000000							
1879			1000000							
1880			1000000						17417	
1881	190750	13.0	1000000	130000		5000	50000		5750	190750
1882	159986	14.0	1000000	140000		5000			14986	159986
1883	169404	14.0	1000000	140000		5000			24404	169404
1884	178170	14.0	1000000	140000		5000			33170	178170
1885	185754	14.0	1000000	140000	5500	5000			35255	185755
1886	204379	14.0	1000000	140000	11250	5000	25000		23128	204378
1887	190915	14.0	1000000	140000	16500	5000			29415	190915
1888	192160	14.0	1000000	140000	10000	5000	25000		12159	192159
1889	190300	14.0	1000000	140000	20000	5000			25300	190300
1890	209369	14.0	1000000	140000	15000	5000	25000	5273 [31]	19097	209370
1891	223490	14.0	1000000	140000	10000	5000	25000	20280 [32]	23210	223490
1892	243628	14.0	1000000	140000	25000	5000	50000	10000 [34]	13628	243628
1893	242637	15.0	1250000	170000	25000	5000		9668 [35]	32969	242637
1894	277295	15.0	1250000	187500	30000	5000		4148 [31]	50646	277294
1895	260217	15.0	1250000	187500	7500	5000			60217	260217
1896	373378	16.0	1250000	200000	20000	5000	100000	9781 [35]	38597	373378
1897	389355	16.0	1250000	200000	15000	5000		125000 [37]	44355	389355

Year										
1898	311109	18.0	1250000	225000	15000	5000	100000		66109	311109
1899	376257	18.0	1250000	225000	35000	5000			11257	376257
1900	295223	18.0	1250000	225000	35000	5000			30224	295224
1901	322256	18.0	1250000	225000	18000	10000			44256	322256
1902	321515	20.0	1250000	250000		10000		25000 [32]	61515	321515
1903	374622	20.0	1250000	250000		10000	50000		54022	374621
1904	329561	20.0	1250000	250000	3000	10000		10599 [35]	66561	329561
1905	365562	20.0	1250000	250000		20000	50000		45561	365561
1906	346521	20.0	1250000	250000	10000	20000			66521	346521
1907 [38]	275789	20.0	1250000	187500	2000	10000			76289	275789
1908	395509	20.0	1250000	250000	6500	10000		83464 [31]	45544	395508
1909	332494	20.0	1250000	250000	11500	10000			60995	332495
1910	355655	20.0	1250000	250000	7500	10000	50000		38155	355655
1911	317453	20.0	1250000	250000	2500	10000		22889 [31]	32063	317452
1912	354367	20.0	1250000	250000	3000	10000		43798 [31]	47571	354368
1913	415487	19.0	1250000	237500		25000		115442 [31]	37545	415487
1914	445224	18.0	1250000	225000		10000		180982 [31]	29243	445224
1915	445560	18.0	1250000	207506 [29]		10000		165227 [31]	62827	445560
1916	443412	16.0	1250000	172980 [29]		10000		230923 [31]	29509	443412
1917	345557	16.0	1250000	154466 [29]		10000		125713 [31]	55378	345557
1918	351612	16.0	1250000	150000 [29]		70000			81612	351612
1919	379485	16.0	1250000	142233 [29]	50000	70000	50000		67252	379485
1920	374468	16.0	1250000	140000 [29]	100000	10000	100000	176086 [31]	48382	374467

Notes:

1 The financial year ended on 30 May for years 1761 to 1849, on 15 April from 1850 to 1906 and on 15 January thereafter.

2 Includes interest on bonds, bill discounts, commission, dividends on stocks and other investments etc.

3 Includes losses, discounts, sundries, legal charges, commission or interest paid, expenses of circulation, specie and charge on notes.

4 Originally referred to as 'insurance account to make good bad and doubtful debts and to pay property tax'.

5 Originally referred to as stock account and added to company's capital.

6 Profits on goods and business.

7 Includes £1123 premio to Mr Tod and £494 premio to Mr McCulloch.

8 Consists of £350 profits on goods and business, £345 gain on London bills and £77 gain on joint concerns.

9 'By Company's Stock at 30 May 1763 declared by the Report of the Directors and a Committee of Proprietors 4 June 1764 to be £46287, from which bad debts of £22013 were deducted'.

10 Consists of £263 profits on goods and business, £288 gain on London bills and £83 gain on joint concerns.

Table A20 *continued*

11 Consists of £722 profits on goods and business and £372 gain on joint concerns.
12 Includes £143 gained on exchange.
13 Includes £96 gained on exchange.
14 Includes £873 commission etc. and £112 buildings or other capital costs.
15 Gained on exchange.
16 Profits on goods and business.
17 'they (the directors) had not added the … gain to the Stock Account in regard there has not been lately a valuation of the doubtfull debts due to the Company and they apprehend when there is, a loss will appear on them. The directors are therefore of the opinion, it is fairer to let the Stock stand as it was at 30 May 1772, than add the gain to it under that apprehension.'
18 To loss on sale of Salton bleachfield.
19 To stock account to increase capital.
20 Included £1000 remitted to Bank of England as the company's subscription to the defence of the country.
21 To credit of account for property of Tweeddale House.
22 Taken from undivided profits to pay dividend on increased capital (leaving £60000 at credit of undivided profits).
23 Increased dividend left nothing to be credited to undivided profits.
24 In 1827 a dividend of 8.5% (amounting to £42500) was paid out of a gain of only £17019. This was to be repaid from future profits, and in 1828 and 1829 sums of £8838 and £8262 respectively were set aside to repay this deficit. Nothing was credited to undivided profits for the years 1827–9 as a result.
25 Carried to interest account to meet contingencies arising from uncertainty as to how profits would be affected by fluctuations in interest/deposit rates. This was brought forward at credit the following year.
26 Half-year's dividend only due to change in financial year from 1850 (see note 1).
27 To credit of new office in St Andrews Square in liquidation of cost thereof.
28 Due to change in accounting method, from 1862 figure represents net profit after fully providing for all bad debts..
29 Less income tax.
30 Bringing credit at reserve accounts, previously hidden, to £296769 (nothing had been publicly credited to undivided profits for the years 1835–61).
31 To provide for depreciation in investments.
32 Special dividend (2% free of tax).
33 This is actual net profit (before deductions for bad and doubtful debts) as opposed to published net profit.
34 To heritable property yielding rent.
35 Bonus to staff.
36 Surplus on sale of investments.
37 Consists of £25000 bonus dividend (2%) plus £100000 to pension reserve fund..
38 Figures for nine months only due to change in financial year (see note 1).
39 Transfer from reserve fund towards depreciation in investments.

Sources: BS(BL) 6/5/1–2, Minutes of the meetings of the proprietors of the British Linen Company, 1746–1871; BS, Uncatalogued, Scotch Banks Annual Reports, 1881–1894; BS(BL) 20/21/10, Abstract profit and loss account, 1886–1912; BS(BL) 6/5/4, Minutes of the meetings of the proprietors of the British Linen Company, 1900–55.

	Liabilities to proprietors					Liabilities to public					
Year ending 15 April/ 15 January [1]	Capital	Reserve	Pension reserve fund	Half-year's dividend payable	Balance of profits carried forward [2]	Deposits	Notes in circulation	Acceptances	Drafts and remittances by advice outstanding payable within 14 days	Total liabilities to public	Total liabilities
1861	1000000	266586			105100	6855145 [5]	479212			7334357	8706043
1862	1000000	281686			108208					7519868	8909762
1863	1000000	296769			108490					7337269	8742528
1864	1000000	300000			118218						
1865	1000000	300000			151643	6886895	442343	276501		7605738	9057381
1866	1000000	300000			131432	7322096	453989	382344		8158428	9589860
1867	1000000	300000			118702	7334702	521067	314527		8170295	9588998
1868	1000000	300000			120840	7123272	571546	452789		8147607	9568447
1869	1000000	340840			84307	7110460	508305	278753	209279	8106798	9531945
1870	1000000	345147			81073	7138095	539884	292763	145098	8115840	9542059
1871	1000000	346220			82433	7032033	472284	277667	167521	7949505	9378157
1872	1000000	348652									
1873	1000000										
1874	1000000	350000			120000	7703000	677000	329000	178000	8887000	10357000
1875	1000000										
1876	1000000	complete figures unavailable									
1877	1000000										
1878	1000000					7456000				8571000	
1879	1000000					8777000				9882000	
1880	1000000	500000				9129000				10369000	11369000
1881	1000000	750000		75000	125750	9263860 [6]	639032	173069	291324	10367285	11993035
1882	1000000	750000		70000	14986	9272454	577821	194498	139602	10184375	12024361
1883	1000000	750000		70000	24404	10082351	606995	178626	139351	11007323	12851727
1884	1000000	750000		70000	33170	10086689	673237	131890	115112	11006928	12860098
1885	1000000	750000		70000	35255	10115010	663743	149369	138896	11067018	12922273
1886	1000000	775000		70000	23128	9831517	651257	107113	114911	10704798	12572926
1887	1000000	775000		70000	29415	10291973	660452	97713	147713	11197851	13072265
1888	1000000	800000		70000	12160	10378206	633752	68834	148172	11228964	13111124

Table A21 *continued*

Year ending 15 April/15 January [1]	Liabilities to proprietors					Liabilities to public					Total liabilities
	Capital	Reserve	Pension reserve fund	Half-year's dividend payable	Balance of profits carried forward [2]	Deposits	Notes in circulation	Acceptances	Drafts and remittances by advice outstanding payable within 14 days	Total liabilities to public	
1889	1000000	800000		70000	25301	10837732	683903	164237	90268	11776140	13671440
1890	1000000	825000		70000	19097	11609223	753274	86723	206666	12655886	14569983
1891	1000000	850000		70000	23210	11903876	775454	127409	164629	12971367	14914577
1892	1000000	900000		70000	13628	12036999	777669	460686	113888	13389241	15372869
1893	1250000	1400000		100000	32969	11843108	741170	283518	179293	13047089	15830058
1894	1250000	1400000		93750	50646	12042608	777652	295200	104065	13219525	16013922
1895	1250000	1400000		93750	60217	12268721	838662	268351	143806	13519539	16323506
1896	1250000	1500000		106250	38598	12036200	850541	278638	144820	13310199	16205047
1897	1250000	1500000	100000	125000 [8]	44355	12338469	873807	472927	137718	13822921	16842276
1898	1250000	1500000	100000	125000	66109	11981277	889109	656229	133678	13660294	16701403
1899	1250000	1600000	100000	112500	11257	12553277	885863	587774	165113	14192026	17265783
1900	1250000	1600000	100000	112500	30224	13415885	918670	59742	160566	15093863	18186586
1901	1250000	1600000	100000	137500	44256	13561931	944756	558693	113917	15179297	18311053
1902	1250000	1600000	100000	137500 [8]	61515	13299671	939568	472798	479989	15192026	18341040
1903	1250000	1650000	100000	125000	54022	12851930	898728	418118	379204	14547981	17727002
1904	1250000	1650000	100000	125000	66561	12295657	890648	514010	235582	13935898	17127458
1905	1250000	1700000	100000	125000	45561	11917010	840105	562434	203186	13522734	16743295
1906	1250000	1700000	100000	125000	66522	12259981	843190	388804	170776	13662751	16904272
1907 [9]	1250000	1700000	100000	62500	76289	12526732	849112	555941	170961	14102745	17291534
1908	1250000	1650000	100000	125000	45544	13107944	805434	370030	257604	14541012	17711556
1909	1250000	1650000	100000	125000	60995	12356946	811116	648433	346325	14162819	17348814
1910	1250000	1700000	100000	125000	38155	11853342	738763	384834	320098	13297037	16510191
1911	1250000	1700000	100000	125000	32063	12118184	737170	339096	221007	13415457	16622520
1912	1250000	1650000	100000	125000	47571	12776504	810145	201007	142125	13929780	17102350
1913	1250000	1550000	100000	112500	37545	13495697	792017	113450	222395	14623558	17673603
1914	1250000	1400000	100000	112500	29243	14108626	796620	193936	231215	15330397	1822214
1915	1250000	1250000	100000	101828	62827	14929671	1048215	661350	488163	17127400	19892055
1916	1250000	1150000	100000	83617	29510	16023675	1441925	419191	505140	18389930	21003056
1917	1250000	1100000	100000	75000	55378	19257797	1889913	866401	293089	22307199	24887578
1918	1250000	1150000	100000	75000	81612	22747305	2334137	545428	924705	26551576	29208188
1919	1250000	1250000	100000	70000	67252	26425026	3182911	391180	876033	30875149	33612401
1920	1250000	1250000	100000	70000	48382	28631068	3399800	593283	673194	33297345	36015727

	Gold and silver coin and money in London at call or short notice [3]	Investments [4]	Bills discounted and advances on cash, credit and current accounts	Loans for short term on stocks and other securities	Securities against acceptances	Bank premises	Misc.	Total assets
1861	1909137	1382975	5181960			231972		8706044
1862	2552810	1280632	4918758			157562		8909762
1863	2289123	1219057	5073905			160443		8742528
1864								
1865	2004277	992163	5926964			133977		9057381
1866	2089752	1010184	6362421			127504		9589860
1867	1884466	901843	6680184			122504		9588998
1868	1834665	816485	6797008			120289		9568446
1869	1742482	707768	6958490			123204		9531944
1870	1980711	650046	6782357			128946		9542060
1871	1815452	625978	6811145			125581		9378156
1872								
1873								
1874	2198000	537000	7493000			129000		10357000
1875								
1876	complete							
1877	figures							
1878	unavailable							
1879								
1880								
1881	1745731	1960423	6296080	1364124	173069	312264		11993035
1882	1830994	1739793	6459030	1377161	194498	322029	141344 [7]	12024361
1883	2082833	1819971	6853326	1582783	178626	334189	100856 [7]	12851728
1884	1741191	1996487	6873156	1785111	131890	332263		12860098
1885	1551466	2525999	6943000	1415446	149369	336994		12922274
1886	1525852	2374835	6556530	1676546	107113	332051		12572927
1887	1945264	2404627	6274671	2018621	97713	331370		13072266
1888	2033774	3017383	5796177	1860912	68834	334045		13111124
1889	2226007	3377538	5504812	2062184	164237	336663		13671440
1890	2345364	3464034	5866387	2465209	86723	342268		14569984
1891	2637980	3656742	5710476	2419943	127409	362029		14914577
1892	1577779	3467099	6782252	2724479	460686	360574		15372869
1893	2580685	3944866	6161425	2491918	283518	367647		15830058
1894	2244121	3932408	6677503	2489529	295200	375160		16013922

Assets

Table A21 *continued*

	Gold and silver coin and money in London at call or short notice [3]	Investments [4]	Bills discounted and advances on cash, credit and current accounts	Loans for short term on stocks and other securities	Securities against acceptances	Bank premises	Misc.	Total assets
							Assets	
1895	2504181	4489458	6251184	2430893	268351	379440		16323506
1896	1613517	4005566	6265705	3653131	278638	388490		16205047
1897	2129608	3838027	6401474	3604631	472927	395611		16842276
1898	1770777	4308617	5781212	3756499	656229	428070		16701403
1899	2029561	3917486	6106280	4149994	587774	474688		17265783
1900	2809669	3963401	6580063	3747126	598742	487587		18186586
1901	3159520	4204165	5935795	3603248	558693	849633		18311052
1902	2224943	4382038	5855909	4516490	472798	888863		18341040
1903	2096020	3829878	6043790	4381760	418118	957437		17727002
1904	2314992	4142321	5817666	3335374	514010	1003095		17127458
1905	1873180	4037149	5469751	3768490	562434	1032292		16743295
1906	2028755	3445345	6232421	3773137	388804	1035811		16904272
1907 [9]	2308592	3673675	6232560	3488313	555941	1032453		17291534
1908	2779005	4376073	6546890	2602630	370030	1036928		17711556
1909	1972151	4726485	5855036	3112347	648433	1034363		17348814
1910	1989014	4097831	5575424	3432139	384834	1030950		16510191
1911	1743056	3910618	5720283	3883158	339096	1026309		16622520
1912	2902964	3744913	5367159	3867270	201007	1019038		17102350
1913	3360140	4195109	5008249	4000632	113450	996025		17673603
1914	3485206	4615591	5270429	3667970	193936	989008		18222139
1915	3773140	5123449	5764439	3584873	661350	984803		19892054
1916	4292842	6902746	6225032	2184721	419191	978525		21003056
1917	5887066	7017585	8211947	1935694	866401	968886		24887578
1918	6589704	6913311	12487595	1773102	545428	899048		29208188
1919	6608777	9578353	14379306	1823188	391180	831598		33612401
1920	6643488	10578908	14863196	2517070	593283	819783		36015727

Notes:

1 The financial year ended on 15 April until 1906 and on 15 January thereafter.
2 Prior to 1882 this figure represented published net profit, less half-year's dividend (but before other deductions in the profit and loss account).
3 Included notes of Bank of England and other banks, cash balances with London bankers, government stocks, Exchequer bills and India bonds.
4 Bank of England and other stocks, bonds, debentures etc.
5 Deposits plus all other public liabilities.

6 Includes £55576 balances due to correspondents.
7 Balances due by City of Glasgow Bank for notes, deposits etc.
8 Including £25000 special dividend.
9 Figures for nine months only due to change in financial year (see note 1).

Sources: BS(BL) 20/21/8, Abstract of general balance sheets, 1861–63, 1887–1911; BS(BL) 6/5/2 and 4, Minutes of meetings of proprietors of the British Linen Bank, 1865–71, 1900–55; UC United 1 and Scotch Bank, Ann. 1 Rep. etc. 1881–94,

Table A22 Union Bank of Scotland annual balance sheets, 1831–1954

Year ending 20 April/ 2 April/ 28 February *	Capital	Capital reserve (share premium account)	Reserve fund	To pay dividend	To other appropriations	Credit of profit and loss account	Deposits	Circulation	Acceptances	Current drafts on London/ Bank of England	Misc.	Total liabilities
1831												748804
1832												908705
1833												1014487
1834	287050										128375 [2]	1132815
1835							717390 [1]					
1836												
1837	300000			18000		19742	888415 [4]	400233			29894 [5]	1656284
1838	349000			20940		46482	882094 [8]	387021			26044 [5]	1711581
1839	399000			27930		55501	1076138 [10]	453634			125490 [5]	2137693
1840	478800			33516		108226	944549 [12]	451887			137650 [5]	2154628
1841	482750			38620		111975	997330 [14]	458513			134841 [5]	2224029
1842	492150			34451		83398	952848 [16]	479728			129875 [5]	2172950
1843	500000			35000		54216	1613900 [1]				1021	2204137
1844	1000000		107624 [18]	75000			5112158 [1]					6294782
1845	1000000		115876	75000			5451636 [1]					6642512
1846	1000000		124942	75000			5495246 [1]					6695188
1847	1000000		133321	80000			5539913 [1]					6753234
1848	1000000		101541	80000			5040121 [1]					6221662
1849	1000000		94067	80000			4888023 [1]					6062090
1850	1000000		97341	80000			6564186 [1]					7741527
1851	1000000		103445	80000			6967177 [1]					8150622
1852	1000000		88851	80000			6746559 [1]					7915410
1853	1000000		99122	80000	20488		7461670 [1]					8661280
1854	1000000		123208	80000	17615		7507365 [1]					8728188
1855	1000000		154963	80000	19153		7035642 [1]					8289758

Table A22 continued

Year ending 20 April/2 April/28 February *	Liabilities to shareholders						Liabilities to public					Total liabilities
	Capital	Capital reserve (share premium account)	Reserve fund	To pay dividend	To other appropriations	Credit of profit and loss account	Deposits	Circulation	Acceptances	Current drafts on London/Bank of England	Misc.	
1856	1000000		160000	90000	35016		6874881 [1]					8159897
1857	1000000		200000	90000	20005		7465527 [1]					8775532
1858	1000000		200000	90000	1292	6932	7529326 [1]					8827550
1859	1000000		200000			104447	7585843 [1]					8890290
1860	1000000		200000			110768	7978899 [1]					9289667
1861	1000000		200000			122999	7773259 [1]					9096258
1862	1000000		200000			102864	7460816					8763680
1863	1000000		67864			95292	7116025	635709				8914890
1864	1000000		78157			118168	7455518	610908	110704			9374455
1865	1000000		109368			143028	7771887	579299	231023			9834605
1866	1000000		172396			131304	8258927	685480	340791		39805 [19]	10628703
1867	1000000		213700			158619	8411240	745250	145980		54217 [19]	10729006
1868	1000000		250000			139103	8055416	734997	162907	90390	40473 [19]	10473286
1869	1000000		270000			143170	8478363	808008	234286	145728	41327 [19]	11120882
1870	1000000		290000			143803	8105956	620539	148257	98487	91517 [19]	10498559
1871	1000000		300000			141166	7899824	692108	142051	40669	141709 [19]	10357527
1872	1000000		307000			149522	8532425	884213	213927	114766	187531 [19]	11389384
1873	1000000		312000			237118	9484342	947262	304622	141329	98075 [19]	12524748
1874	1000000		374000			172701	9404811	887819	223339	60812	136732 [19]	12260214
1875	1000000		380000			173196	9608391	776416	219135	127691	78736 [19]	12363565
1876	1000000		387000			172505	9643801	748687	166943	259651		12378587
1877	1000000		300000			154529	9666687	839317	190182	197322		12348037
1878	1000000		315000			155975	8958567	791072	222294	174677		11617585
1879	1000000		330000			142409	8567259	761013	183007	42552		11026240
1880	1000000		330000			144961	9587492	774508	189785	97043		12123789
1881	1000000		330000			153134	10150931	716663	167915	56852		12575495
1882	1000000		340000			154549	10679642	743717	191914	136735		13246557
1883	1000000		350000			164592	10937157	829112	111858	54783		13447502

Year								
1884	1000000	370000	157254	10774189	795778	70619	154391	13322231
1885	1000000	380000	140849	10764218	777584	85166	67496	13215313
1886	1000000	380000	147951	9939662	772838	57922	59445	12357818
1887	1000000	380000	148011	9904122	709567	97220	39152	12278072
1888	1000000	380000	154741	10275592	783484	93436	107219	12794472
1889	1000000	400000	154227	10601265	796223	79723	74955	13106393
1890	1000000	420000	152581	11085341	858002	120034	131925	13767883
1891	1000000	440000	147185	11237632	820702	60061	52513	13758093
1892	1000000	450000	153193	11066415	820497	27033	41572	13558710
1893	1000000	470000	149837	10962032	830138	65834	47834	13525675
1894	1000000	485000	155335	10734215	887569	83618	108277	13454014
1895	1000000	505000	136408	11263463	914226	95723	68132	13982952
1896	1000000	515000	158623	11443482	949244	74263	94745	14235357
1897	1000000	540000	169632	11298021	965290	134876	62272	14170091
1898	1000000	565000	177005	11239481	946517	87240	136442	14151685
1899	1000000	595000	182591	12238521	1021784	179351	101571	15318818
1900	1000000	625000	188621	12718347	1062979	60842	161862	15817651
1901								
1902	1000000	700000	205330	13242731	1031533	61596	145362	16386552
1903	1000000	785000	161250	13608632	1012339	49180	54576	16670977
1904	1000000	785000	157688	12701679	959889	15373	122677	15742306
1905	1000000	830000	159304	12529573	923981	18008	40968	15501834
1906	1000000	875000	165370	12740020	981811	20463	131324	15913988
1907	1000000	875000	174157	13264345	964797	36366	83854	16398519
1908	1000000	925000	175902	12976988	907274	26087	138855	16150106
1909	1000000	1000000	158909	12477370	876405	151253	118821	15782758
1910	1000000	1000000	174212	12833038	866795	246364	99945	16220354
1911	1000000	1000000	180606	12586538	883747	134587	67616	15853094
1912	1000000	1000000	193393	14573356	912724	320139	71361	18070973
1913	1000000	1000000	185124	15409195	931909	729784	240069	19496081
1914	1000000	1000000	220010	16458022	945432	889972	137020	20650456
1915	1000000	800000	260883	17751946	1217971	401845	97893	21530538

Table A22 *continued*

Year ending 20 April/ 2 April/ 28 February *	Capital	Capital reserve (share premium account)	Reserve fund	To pay dividend	To other appropriations	Credit of profit and loss account	Deposits	Circulation	Acceptances	Current drafts on London/ Bank of England	Misc.	Total liabilities
1916	1000000		800000			261456	16739330	1594494	691890	176934		21264104
1917	1000000		800000			221286	17219195	1895883	955362	219649		22311375
1918	1000000		900000			220452	23648883	2535731	373726	124485		28803277
1919	1000000		1000000			214801	26265016	2987221	418547	666717		32552302
1920	1000000		1000000			205576	32495518	3480280	907566	410847		39499787
1921	1000000		1000000			217708	32702296	3366092	397556	209047		38892699
1922	1000000		1100000			236188	35211965	2840934	273423	138017		40800527
1923	1000000		1200000			257550	31740997	2667304	360186	249538		37475575
1924	1000000		1250000			301198	29334377	2516933	523549	147064		35073121
1925	1000000		1300000			306663	27677789	2554092	589119	45876		33473539
1926	1000000		1350000			297249	27098455	2626224	751024	45284		33168236
1927	1000000		1400000			290000	25619821	2506379	572135	94216		31482551
1928	1000000		1450000			294504	25936327	2556363	685863	22109		31945166
1929	1000000		1500000			305743	27280189	2478485	1221092	17461		33802970
1930	1000000		1550000			340054	28262507	2414224	1071313	41014		34679112
1931	1200000		1800000			389721	29133282	2406820	606995	56380		35593198
1932	1200000		1800000			348632	28305208	2343039	528057	8101		34533037
1933	1200000		1800000			352614	28546761	2339577	485763			34724715
1934	1200000		1800000			352722	28558337	2398015	389973			34699047
1935	1200000		1800000			355184	29944043	2494221	447292			36240740
1936	1200000		1800000			360805	31956544	2536788	1899028			39753165
1937	1200000		1800000			367981	32837084	2640729	1593747			40439541
1938	1200000		1800000			369605	33436818	2662235	1025347			40494005
1939	1200000		1800000			374012	33218668	2648525	1118681			40359886
1940	1200000		1800000			376174	36002367	2933094	1025011			43336646

Year	Bills of exchange	Loans and advances	Liability of customers for bank's acceptances	Consols and other British government securities	Other securities and investments	Money at call and short notice, cash balances due by banking correspondents and cash vouchers in transit	Gold and silver coin, notes of other banks, and cash balances at call in hands of London bankers	Property	Misc.	Total assets
1941	1200000		1850000		383655	36638976	3172479	1175172		44420282
1942	1200000		1900000		387055	41045112	4245194	2959625		51736986
1943	1200000		1950000		392232	46618637	5492169	1339533		56992571
1944	1200000		2000000		394596	51555044	6122038	2514600		63786278
1945	1200000		2050000		402372	54668105	5985860	1397047		65703384
1946	1200000		2100000		413190	58806075	5699466	1162807		69381538
1947	1200000		2150000		416604	66499703	6676169	1656081		78598557
1948	1200000		2150000		417460	69269147	6455908	2090294		81582809
1949	1200000	200000	2000000	118800	165168	69721297	6939232	2096000		82440497
1950	1200000	200000	2000000	118800	172580	70387811	7219592	2858868		84157651
1951	1200000	200000	2000000	113400	184647	77884254	7742849	4654679		93979829
1952	1200000	200000	2000000	113400	188829	71070194	7678391	5049225		87500039
1953	1200000	200000	2000000	113400	189643	74408220	8777342	6095606	174178 [47]	93158389
1954	1200000	200000	2000000	118800	65629	71815827	9067991	5544320	290241 [47]	90302808

Assets

Year	Bills of exchange	Loans and advances	Liability of customers for bank's acceptances	Consols and other British government securities	Other securities and investments	Money at call and short notice, cash balances due by banking correspondents and cash vouchers in transit	Gold and silver coin, notes of other banks, and cash balances at call in hands of London bankers	Property	Misc.	Total assets
1831										748804
1832										908705
1833										1014487
1834		679151						9723	443940 [3]	1132814
1835										
1836										
1837	932722 [6]	339359			49274	78822 [7]	189888	17078	49139	1656282
1838	1039698 [9]	390113			48672	51393 [7]	149081	22119	10505	1711581
1839	1408391 [11]	420970			51935	26446 [7]	200028	25889	4033	2137692
1840	1269040 [13]	490979			33151	112615 [7]	215630	29199	4015	2154629

Table A22 continued

				Assets						
Year ending 20 April/ 2 April/ 28 Feb. *	Bills of exchange	Loans and advances	Liability of customers for bank's acceptances	Consols and other British government securities	Other securities and investments	Money at call and short notice, cash balances due by banking correspondents and cash vouchers in transit	Gold and silver coin, notes of other banks, and cash balances at call in hands of London bankers	Property	Misc.	Total assets
1841	1384547 [15]	426613			30694	165693 [7]	180145	32237	4101	2224030
1842	1141418 [17]	546564			34144	125517 [7]	289228	31576	4504	2172951
1843		1946062					222071	32067	3936	2204136
1844		6209288						85493		6294781
1845		6577437						65075		6642512
1846		6630244						64944		6695188
1847		6684465						68768		6753233
1848		6148425						73237		6221662
1849		5983987						8103		6062090
1850		7650572						90955		7741527
1851		8059235						91387		8150622
1852		7825588						89822		7915410
1853		8570218						91063		8661281
1854		8630660						97527		8728187
1855		8182983						106775		8289758
1856		8049100						110797		8159897
1857		8664634						110899		8775533
1858	3277999	3858501			982548		565686	142817		8827551
1859		6727590			1175300		838717	148683		8890290
1860		7051104			776207		1299616	162741		9289668
1861		6926637			1053303		952008	164309		9096257
1862		6341895			1218861		1039555	163369		8763680
1863		6107951			1570289		1069363	167288		8914891
1864		6771186			1390574		1039334	173361		9374455

Year										
1865		7507748			1311648		842726	172482		9834604
1866		8157504			1412671		893073	165455		10628703
1867		8104085			1406726		1055474	162721		10729006
1868		7648639			2127459		534237	162951		10473286
1869		8176392			2108547		677516	158428		11120883
1870		7765690			2110063		466046	156760		10498559
1871		7326641			2254361		624242	152283		10357527
1872		8198100			2292244		739329	159711		11389384
1873		9029976			2694160		638295	162318		12524749
1874		9026580			2367734		706846	159055		12260215
1875		8645297			2977389		586008	154871		12363565
1876		9057455		2653613			508786	158732		12378586
1877		8133420		3448637			598287	167692		12348036
1878		8143678		2649337			644649	179921	82958 [20]	11617585
1879		7477030		2546454			560602	359195	24970 [20]	11026239
1880	3352350	3810579	189785	1268358	564329	1769886	773745	369788		12123790
1881	3356166	3996262	167915	1295452	836383	1886562	658226	378528		12575494
1882	3153786	4326251	191914	1225633	840277	2394809	737910	375977		13246557
1883	3184599	4663667	111858	1222958	1282874	1690245	919639	371662		13447502
1884	3286874	4593712	70619	1161532	1371588	1633099	835786	369022		13322232
1885	3062132	4472875	85166	1244034	1595054	1591898	796214	367942		13215315
1886	2559676	4725343	57922	1021821	1167307	1593161	862879	369709		12357818
1887	2627129	4699567	97220	1024391	1143287	1633888	689597	362994		12278073
1888	2318545	4660873	93436	1033364	1292225	2191286	844606	360137		12794472
1889	2354788	4834068	79723	1162829	1569326	1992913	755917	356828		13106392
1890	2136697	4266821	120034	1132852	1940750	2973534	843722	353472		13767882
1891	2347874	3926821	60061	1212442	2955934	2075655	814541	364764		13758092
1892	2522742	3618781	27033	1206494	3085953	1920383	815416	361907		13558709
1893	2309632	3601497	65834	1173623	3118585	2050631	840668	365203		13525673
1894	2277117	3884937	83618	1108656	2960576	1825184	946718	367208		13454014
1895	2247796	3965126	95723	1095113	2708514	2547499	961974	361208		13982953
1896	2322352	4448187	74263	1069301	2138282	2762287	1064470	356214		14235356
1897	2368425	4652788	134876	1105769	1543567	2844286	1173352	347027		14170090
1898	2502802	4550817	87240	1100900	1641216	2853994	1072558	342158		14151685

Table A22 continued

						Assets				
Year ending 20 April/ 2 April/ 28 Feb. *	Bills of exchange	Loans and advances	Liability of customers for bank's acceptances	Consols and other British government securities	Other securities and investments	Money at call and short notice, cash balances due by banking correspondents and cash vouchers in transit	Gold and silver coin, notes of other banks, and cash balances at call in hands of London bankers	Property	Misc.	Total assets
1899	2693534	5090601	179351	1118149	1433303	3499835	970833	333211		15318817
1900	2631903	5379751	60842	1116963	1555480	3493137	1249389	330184		15817649
1901										0
1902	2645796	5709605	61596	1351709	1652837	3387926	1254806	322275		16386550
1903	2560590	6176464	49180	1316140	1568101	3425500	1258195	316807		16670977
1904	2532261	5337567	15373	1145641	1512121	3741667	1144865	312811		15742306
1905	2542403	5234651	18008	1140494	1766805	3352357	1129443	317671		15501832
1906	2783421	4995901	20463	1137805	1795609	3755316	1107733	317740		15913988
1907	2945023	5590742	36366	1129092	1782728	3437598	1163326	313643		16398518
1908	2931596	5285018	26087	1160443	2012375	3301643	1119368	313575		16150105
1909	2305522	4935897	151253	1143405	2439740	3277678	1104696	424569		15782760
1910	2596235	4973433	246364	1120180	2276364	3519484	1071190	417104		16220354
1911	2180354	5799947	134587	1031573	2201569	3164915	895589	444561		15853095
1912	2975945	6218044	320139	989173	2078084	3748135	1299978	441475		18070973
1913	2761716	6457008	729784	828613	2277739	4817782	1170499	452941		19496082
1914	3787380	6667542	889972	854207	2763685	4009781	1231406	446483		20650456
1915	3166320	6560531	401845	2330875	2617849	4427429	1570532	455158		21530539
1916	2005749	5293765	691890	5578973	1702165	3780048	1755536	455979		21264105
1917	2071117	7617116	955362	5554477	1000079	2317049	2348179	447997		22311376
1918	9644132	5169037	373726	6028474	679553	3272810	3163005	472540		28803277
1919	10640358	5885432	418547	7219359	655981	3816321	3362649	553656		32552303
1920	9872240	9636515	907566	9378234	569471	4338481	4258644	538636		39499787

Year										
1921	10633333	10560036	397556	8716993	556319	3693093	3796640	538730		38892700
1922	7906565	7204162	273423	16175586	693865	4710250	3297867	538810		40800528
1923	5426132 [21]	7744109	360186	15424496	762970	4174224	3048874	534582		37475573
1924	5685233 [23]	7806919	523549	12318856	845108	4187000	3177030	528528		35073123
1925	3356761 [24]	9550931	589119	11588078	1287134	3548824	3077720	474971		33473538
1926	3259476 [25]	9758086	751024	11346783	1234009	3311830	3004699	502330		33168237
1927	2212976	10529921	572135	10290914	1772496	2753680	2780595	569835		31482552
1928	2680953	11618949	685863	7301131	2904103	3171599	2971363	611206		31945167
1929	3439470	12747588	1221092	6079754	3140448	3628396	2957434	588790		33802972
1930	2752684 [21]	14602249	1071313	6349871	3399501	3111022	2856075	536399	100 [22]	34679114
1931	3941274 [23]	12752204	606995	7798230	3401385	3953403	2622001	517605	100 [22]	35593197
1932	3602151 [24]	12079924	528057	7870031	2765082	4618208	2562629	506855	100 [22]	34533037
1933	3651238 [25]	8852558	485763	11554834	3061856	4164551	2468704	485112	100 [22]	34724716
1934	1514935	8370866	389973	13521050	3805505	4012598	2615269	468749	100 [22]	34699045
1935	1663029	7798510	447292	14547871	4318361	4196340	2817072	452167	100 [22]	36240742
1936	2000544	7744242	1899028	16020011	4039546	4849231	2762298	438116	100 [22]	39753164
1937	1503674	9217449	1593747	16632554	4403930	3611382	3051401	425303	100 [22]	40439540
1938	1416375	10239116	1025347	15970043	3677996	4984881	2769693	410454	100 [22]	40494005
1939	800464	10521897	1118681	15801333	4248022	4717091	2751060	401238	100 [22]	40359886
1940	2481098 [26]	11032985	1025011	15110555	4214829	5627345	3446788	398035		43336646
1941	1494418 [27]	9869407	1175172	16461966	3917109	5939974	3657548	404688	1500000 [28]	44420282
1942	851331 [29]	11129901	2959625	20601938	3606197	5344701	4349155	394138	2500000 [28]	51736986
1943	2150002 [30]	9224170	1339533	23516630	3179499	7668792	5529790	384155	4000000 [28]	56992571
1944	1584444 [31]	8642095	2514600	27850271	3136288	8496828	6177936	383816	5000000 [28]	63786278
1945	1261139 [32]	9001193	1397047	30533312	3117949	7802143	6205160	385441	6000000 [28]	65703384
1946	1611789 [33]	8395314	1162807	33495807	3088340	9514908	6710964	385409	5016200 [34]	69381538
1947	1614544 [35]	10678957	1656081	37372941	3162285	9607450	7563261	410638	6532400 [36]	78598557
1948	1901300 [37]	13512527	2090294	38241712	2605250	10539071	7210443	433612	5048600 [38]	81582809
1949	986472 [39]	14224746	2096000	39023037	2232521	11325652	7518708	468561	4564800 [40]	82440497
1950	710670 [41]	19059536	2858868	37518271	2224686	11774092	7925356	505172	1581000 [42]	84157651
1951	961278 [43]	20878305	4654679	38659302	2702632	11960150	8545901	536582	1081000 [44]	93979829
1952	2069905 [45]	27693635	5049225	29062034	2462356	11677467	8839605	564812	81000 [46]	87500039
1953	3053974 [48]	23370324	6095606	32748543	2483108	14569059	9567415	627275	243085 [49]	93158389
1954	3518285 [50]	20804690	5544320	35952454	2602032	11174701	9824064	632659	249603 [51]	90302808

Table A22 *continued*

Notes:

* The financial year ended on 20 April from 1837 to 1860, on 2 April from 1861 to 1953 and on 28 February 1954.

1 Deposits, circulation and bills for collection – not broken down.
2 Balances due to agents, branches and unclaimed balances.
3 Includes £439270 due by London and country agents, branches and cash.
4 Includes £267548 interest receipts and £142464 due to branches.
5 Other public liabilities.
6 Consisted of bills discounted (£586020), bills of exchange (£213706), branch bills (£124478) and old bills protested (£8518).
7 Balance with other banks.
8 Includes £271553 interest receipts and £146554 due to branches.
9 Consisted of bills discounted (£608140), bills of exchange (£314302), branch bills (£103382) and old bills protested (£13874).
10 Includes £308904 interest receipts and £214497 due to branches.
11 Consisted of bills discounted (£918418), bills of exchange (£308144), branch bills (£177033) and old bills protested (£4796).
12 Includes £308747 interest receipts and £151059 due to branches.
13 Consisted of bills discounted (£755378), bills of exchange (£315027), branch bills (£188979) and old bills protested (£9656).
14 Includes £273942 interest receipts and £315181 due to branches.
15 Consisted of bills discounted (£840826), bills of exchange (£356214), branch bills (£182201) and old bills protested (£5306).
16 Includes £246473 interest receipts and £286015 due to branches.
17 Consisted of bills discounted (£669140), bills of exchange (£337382), branch bills (£109632) and old bills protested (£25264).
18 Following the union with the Glasgow and Ship Bank in November 1843 a reserve fund of £100000 was established.
19 Balances due to banking correspondents etc.
20 Notes of the City of Glasgow Bank.
21 Includes £1090000 British government Treasury bills.

22 Bankers Industrial Development Corporation – one share.
23 Includes £2400000 British government Treasury bills.
24 Includes £2545000 British government Treasury bills.
25 Includes £2825000 British government Treasury bills.
26 Includes £2180000 British government Treasury bills.
27 Including £1325000 British government Treasury bills.
28 British Government Treasury Deposit receipts.
29 Including £510000 British government Treasury bills.
30 Including £1835000 British government Treasury bills.
31 Including £1540000 British government Treasury bills.
32 Including £1035000 British government Treasury bills.
33 Including £1400000 British government Treasury bills.
34 Consists of £5000000 TDRS and £16200 ICFC investment.
35 Including £960000 British government Treasury bills.
36 Consists of £6500000 TDRS and £3240 ICFC investment.
37 Including £1405000 British government Treasury bills.
38 Consists of £5000000 TDRS and £48600 ICFC investment.
39 Including £525000 British government Treasury bills.
40 Consists of £4500000 TDRS and £64800 ICFC investment.
41 Including £500000 British government Treasury bills.
42 Consists of £1500000 TDRS and £81000 ICFC investment.
43 Including £910000 British government Treasury bills.
44 Consists of £1000000 TDRS and £81000 ICFC investment.
45 Including £2000000 British government Treasury bills.
46 ICFC investment.
47 Amount due to holding bank – Bank of Scotland.
48 Including £3000000 British government Treasury bills.
49 Consists of £81000 ICFC investment and £162085 due by holding bank (Bank of Scotland).
50 Including £3500000 British government Treasury bills.
51 Consists of £81000 ICFC investment and £168603 due by holding bank (Bank of Scotland).

Source: BS(U), Uncatalogued, Annual reports of the Union Bank of Scotland, 1831–1955 (boxed).

Table A23 Union Bank of Scotland profit and loss account, 1837–1954

	Income				Appropriations									Balance of reserve fund
Year ending 20 April/2 April/28 Feb.*	Net profit	Carried forward at credit of profit and loss	Total available for appropriation	Capital	Dividend (%)	To dividend (£)	To pay income tax	To write down property	To securities and investments account	To reserve fund	Misc.	Carried forward at credit of profit and loss account[1]	Total appropriations	Balance of reserve fund
1837	31898		37742 [2]	300000	6	18000						19742	37742	37742
1838	37440		67422 [3]	349000	6	20940						46482	67422	67422
1839	36949		83431 [4]	399000	7	27930						55501	83431	83431
1840	39545 [5]		141742 [6]	478800	7	33516						108226	141742	141742
1841	39774	108226	150595 [7]	482750	8	38620						111975	150595	150595
1842	6373 [8]	111975	118348	492150	7	34451						83898	118349	118349
1843	36339	83898	125076 [9]	500000	7	35000	1021				34839 [10]	54216	125076	125076
1844	82624		82624	1000000	7.5	75000				7624			82624	107624 [11]
1845	87851		87851	1000000	7.5	75000				8252			87852	115876
1846	84000		84000	1000000	7.5	75000		4600		9000			84000	124942
1847	88378		88378	1000000	8	80000				8379			88379	133321
1848	48000 [12]		48000 [12]	1000000	8	80000							80000	101541 [12]
1849	84652		84652	1000000	8	80000				4652			84652	94067 [13]
1850	83274 [14]		83274 [14]	1000000	8	80000				3273			83273	97340
1851	86105 [15]		86105 [15]	1000000	8	80000				6105			86105	103445
1852	106000 [16]		106000 [16]	1000000	8	80000					26000 [16]		106000	88851 [16]
1853	110760		110760	1000000	8	80000				10271	20488 [17]		110759	99122
1854	121700		121700	1000000	8	80000				24086	17615 [18]		121701	123208
1855	130909		130909	1000000	8	80000				31756	19153 [19]		130909	154964
1856	130052		130052	1000000	9	90000	2625			5036	35016 [20]		130052	160000
1857	150005		150005	1000000	9	90000	1875			40000	17380 [21]		150005	200000
1858	98224	6349	98224	1000000	9	90000	1875					6349	98224	200000
1859	98098		104447	1000000	9	90000	3750				12572 [22]		104447	200000
1860	110768	12018	110768	1000000	9	90000	3375				5000 [22]	12018	110768	200000
1861	122998	6007	135016	1000000	9	90000					35634 [23]	6007	135016	200000
1862	96857		102864	1000000	9	90000				7864	5000 [22]		102864	67864 [24]
1863	95292		95292	1000000	8	80000				10292	5000 [22]		95292	78156
1864	118168		118168	1000000	8	80000				1212	36956 [22]		118168	109368 [24]

Table A23 continued

	Income				Appropriations									
Year ending 20 April/ 2 April/ 28 Feb. *	Net profit	Carried forward at credit of profit and loss	Total available for appropriation	Capital	Dividend (%)	To dividend (£)	To pay income tax	To write down property	To securities and investments account	To reserve fund	Misc.	Carried forward at credit of profit and loss account [1]	Total appropriations	Balance of reserve fund
1865	148028		148028	1000000	8	80000		5000		63028			148028	172396
1866	136304		136304	1000000	9	90000		5000		41304			136304	213700
1867	163619		163619	1000000	10	100000		5000		36300		22319	163619	250000
1868	121783	22319	144102	1000000	10	100000		5000		20000		19103	144103	270000
1869	129068	19103	148171	1000000	11	110000		5000		20000		13170	148170	290000
1870	135633	13170	148803	1000000	12	120000		5000		10000		13803	148803	300000
1871	132363	13803	146166	1000000	12	120000		5000		7000		14166	146166	307000
1872	140356	14166	154522	1000000	13	130000		5000		5000		14522	154522	312000
1873	160149	14522	237118 [25]	1000000	15	150000		10000		62000		15118	237118	374000 [25]
1874	162583	15118	177701	1000000	15	150000		5000		6000		16701	177701	380000
1875	161494	16701	178195	1000000	15	150000		5000		7000		16196	178196	387000
1876	156309	16196	172505	1000000	13	130000					33000 [26]	9505	172505	300000 [26]
1877	145024	9505	154529	1000000	13	130000				15000		9529	154529	315000
1878	146446	9529	155975	1000000	13	130000				15000		10975	155975	330000
1879	131434	10975	142409	1000000	12	120000		5000				17409	142409	330000
1880	127553	17409	144962	1000000	12	120000		5000				19961	144961	330000
1881	133172	19961	153133	1000000	12	120000		5000				18134	153134	340000
1882	136415	18134	154549	1000000	12	120000	3250	5000		10000		16299	154549	350000
1883	148293	16299	164592	1000000	12	120000	2500	5000		10000		17092	164592	370000
1884	140162	17092	157254	1000000	12	120000	2500	5000		20000		19754	157254	380000
1885	121095	19754	140849	1000000	12	120000	4000					16849	140849	380000
1886	131102	16849	147951	1000000	12	120000	4000	5000				18951	147951	380000
1887	129060	18951	148011	1000000	12	120000	4000	5000				19011	148011	380000
1888	135730	19011	154741	1000000	11	110000	2750	5000		20000		16991	154741	400000
1889	137236	16991	154227	1000000	11	110000	2750	5000		20000		16477	154227	420000
1890	136104	16477	152581	1000000	11	110000	2750	5000		20000		14831	152581	440000
1891	132354	14831	147185	1000000	11	110000	2750	5000		10000		19435	147185	450000
1892	133757	19435	153192	1000000	11	110000	2750	5000		20000		15443	153193	470000
1893	134394	15443	149837	1000000	11	110000	2750	5000		15000		17087	149837	485000

Year														
1894	138249	17087	155336	1000000	11	110000	3200	5000		20000		17135	155335	505000
1895	119273	17135	136408	1000000	10	100000	3333	5000		10000		18075	136408	515000
1896	140548	18075	158623	1000000	10	100000	3333	10000		25000		20289	158622	540000
1897	149343	20289	169632	1000000	11	110000	3667	5000		25000		25965	169632	565000
1898	151039	25965	177004	1000000	11	110000	3667	10000		30000		23338	177005	595000
1899	159253	23338	182591	1000000	12	120000	4000	5000		30000		23591	182591	625000
1900	165030	23591	188621	1000000	12	120000	6000	5000		35000		22621	188621	660000
1901		22621		1000000						40000		25759		700000
1902	179571	25759	205330	1000000	13	130000	7583	5000		40000		22746	205329	740000
1903	188503	22746	211249	1000000	13	130000	8125	5000		45000		23125	211250	785000
1904	184563	23125	207688	1000000	13	130000	5958	5000	45000			21729	207687	785000
1905	187574	21729	209303	1000000	13	130000	6500	5000		45000		22804	209304	830000
1906	192566	22804	215370	1000000	13	130000	6500	5000		45000		28870	215370	875000
1907	190287	28870	219157	1000000	13	130000	6500	5000	40000			37657	219157	875000
1908	193245	37657	230902	1000000	13	130000	6500	5000		50000		39402	230902	925000
1909	199506	39402	238908	1000000	13	130000		5000		75000		28909	238909	1000000
1910	205499	28909	234408	1000000	14	140000		10000	40000		10196 [27]	34212	234408	1000000
1911	201394	34212	235606	1000000	14	140000		15000	40000		10000 [28]	30606	235606	1000000
1912	202786	30606	233392	1000000	15	150000		10000	30000		10000 [28]	33393	233393	1000000
1913	206731	33393	240124	1000000	15	150000		5000	50000			35124	240124	1000000
1914	209887	35124	245011	1000000	15	150000		25000			25000 [28]	45010	245010	1000000
1915	225873	45010	270883	1000000	15	150000		10000			10000 [28]	100883	270883	800000
1916	229507	100883	330390	1000000	15	150000		10000	50000		18935 [30]	101456	330391	800000 [29]
1917	249830	101456	351286	1000000	15	150000		10000	120000		10000 [28]	61286	351286	800000
1918	279167	61286	340453	1000000	15	150000		20000		100000	10000 [28]	60452	340452	900000
1919	284349	60452	344801	1000000	15	150000		30000		100000	10000 [28]	54801	344801	1000000
1920	310775	54801	365576	1000000	16	160000		20000	140000		10000 [28]	35576	365576	1000000
1921	312133	35576	347709	1000000	16	160000		20000	110000		10000 [28]	47708	347708	1000000
1922	308480	47708	356188	1000000	17	170000		20000		100000	15000 [28]	51188	356188	1100000
1923	326362	51188	377550	1000000	18	180000		20000		100000	25000 [28]	52550	377550	1200000

Table A23 continued

Year ending 20 April/ 2 April/ 28 Feb.	Net profit *	Income		Appropriations										Balance of reserve fund
		Carried forward at credit of profit and loss	Total available for appropriation	Capital	Dividend (%)	To dividend (£)	To pay income tax	To write down property	To securities and investments account	To reserve fund	Misc.	Carried forward at credit of profit and loss account [1]	Total appropriations	
1924	328648	52550	381198	1000000	18	180000		30000		50000	25000 [28]	96198	381198	1250000
1925	330464	96198	426662	1000000	18	180000		70000		50000	25000 [28]	101663	426663	1300000
1926	315587	101663	417250	1000000	18	180000		70000		50000	25000 [28]	92249	417249	1350000
1927	317750	92249	409999	1000000	18	180000		70000		50000	25000 [28]	85000	410000	1400000
1928	329505	85000	414505	1000000	18	180000		70000		50000	25000 [28]	89504	414504	1450000
1929	336239	89504	425743	1000000	18	180000		70000		50000	25000 [28]	100743	425743	1500000
1930	339310	100743	440053	1000000	18	180000		50000		50000	25000 [28]	135054	440054	1550000
1931	354668	135054	489722	1200000	18	216000		50000		50000	25000 [28]	148721	489721	1800000 [31]
1932	329911	148721	478632	1200000	18	216000		30000				125000 [32]	107632	478632	1800000
1933	319982	107632	427614	1200000	18	216000		25000			75000 [33]	111614	427614	1800000
1934	311108	111614	422722	1200000	18	216000		20000			75000 [33]	111722	422722	1800000
1935	313463	111722	425185	1200000	18	216000		20000			75000 [33]	114184	425184	1800000
1936	316621	114184	430805	1200000	18	216000		20000			75000 [34]	119805	430805	1800000
1937	318175	119805	437980	1200000	18	216000		20000			75000 [34]	126981	437981	1800000
1938	312625	126981	439606	1200000	18	216000		20000			75000 [33]	128605	439605	1800000
1939	310407	128605	439012	1200000	18	216000		20000			75000 [33]	133012	439012	1800000
1940	303162	133012	436174	1200000	18	216000		15000			75000 [33]	135174	436174	1800000
1941	298481	135174	433655	1200000	18	216000		10000			75000 [33]	142655	433655	1850000
1942	304400	142655	447055	1200000	18	216000				50000	25000 [28]	146055	447055	1900000
1943	306177	146055	452232	1200000	18	216000		10000		50000	25000 [28]	151232	452232	1950000
1944	313364	151232	464596	1200000	18	216000		10000		50000	30000 [28]	148596	464596	2000000
1945	323776	148596	472372	1200000	18	216000		20000		50000	35000 [28]	151372	472372	2050000
1946	331818	151372	483190	1200000	18	216000		20000		50000	40000 [28]	157190	483190	2100000
1947	339414	157190	496604	1200000	18	216000		20000		50000	40000 [28]	160604	496604	2150000
1948	336856	160604	497460	1200000	18	216000		30000			90000 [35]	161460	497460	2150000
1949	242508	161460	403968	1200000	18	216000		30000		50000	40000 [28]	165168	403968	2000000 [36]
1950	246212	165168	411380	1200000	18	118800		30000			120000 [37]	172580	411380	2000000
1951	245467	172580	418047	1200000	18	113400					120000 [37]	184647	418047	2000000
1952	237582	184647	422229	1200000	18	113400					120000 [37]	188829	422229	2000000
1953	234214	188829	423043	1200000	18	113400					120000 [37]	189643	423043	2000000
1954	234786	189643	424429	1200000	18	118800				200000	40000 [28]	65629	424429	2200000

Notes:

* The financial year ended on 20 April from 1837 to 1860, on 2 April from 1861 to 1953 and on 28 February 1954.

1 This sum was referred to as the surplus or the reserved fund prior to 1845.

2 i.e. net profit plus contingent fund (£1185) and premium on stock sold (£4659).

3 i.e. net profit plus contingent fund (£15083) and premium on stock sold (£14899).

4 i.e. net profit plus contingent fund (£31583) and premium on stock sold (£14899).

5 Net profit after setting aside £9646 to meet losses at Glasgow and some of the country branches.

6 i.e. net profit plus contingent fund (£40602) and premium on stock sold (£61595). This was the total available after payments to accounts for the amalgamations with Sir Wm Forbes & Co., the Paisley Union and the Thistle banks.

7 Including premium on stock sold (£2595).

8 Net profit after deduction of losses and charges of business, and placing a sum equal to that of former years to the credit of the accounts connected with the junction with Sir Wm Forbes & Co. and the assumption of the business of the Paisley Union Bank.

9 Including premium on stock sold (£4839).

10 It was decided to liquidate the sums due to the junction account (for acquisition of business of Forbes, Thistle and Paisley Union banks) at one swoop, instead of gradually liquidating this over a number of years out of profits.

11 Following the union with the Glasgow and Ship Bank in November 1843 a reserve fund of £100000 was established.

12 Dividend of 8% could not be paid out of that year's net profit; the deficiency was deducted from reserve.

13 £12125 was deducted from reserve to provide for losses underestimated from the previous financial year.

14 The net profit was £104105, but a further £20831 had to be deducted for losses from the year 1847–8, which had previously been underestimated.

15 The net profit would have been £109000 had it not been for a loss of £23000 at Kirkcaldy branch due to the failure of Alexander Russell & Sons, ironfounders.

16 Although net profit on the business was £106000, the losses at Glasgow were such that the dividend of £80000 could not be met without a deduction of £14596 from reserve. (i.e. Glasgow losses were in the region of £40596).

17 Consists of £7590 to Aberdeen Bank amalgamation account and £12898 to bad debts account.

18 Consists of £2000 to new office, £9615 to Aberdeen Bank amalgamation account and £6000 to bad debts account.

19 Consists of £6000 to new office, £11153 to Aberdeen Bank amalgamation account and £2000 to bad debts account.

20 To Aberdeen Bank amalgamation account.

21 Consists of £11631 to Aberdeen Bank amalgamation account and £5749 to bad debts account.

22 To Perth Bank amalgamation account.

23 Consists of £5000 to Perth Bank amalgamation account and £30634 to a loss on the account of Messrs Blaikie at Aberdeen – an account taken over from the Aberdeen Bank.

24 The failure of the Monkland Iron and Steel Company, which was largely indebted to the Union Bank, in July 1862, prompted an examination of all the accounts by a committee of directors and the appointment of a new Joint General Manager. Accounts causing concern to this committee were investigated by Charles Gairdner (the new manager). These were parties who were nominally solvent, but whose position had become prejudiced by the depreciation of their securities. The possible loss to be provided for on these accounts (including that of the Monkland Iron and Steel Company) was estimated by Gairdner at £140000. It was decided to take this sum from reserve and place it in a Special Guarantee account. £30000 was subsequently transferred back into the reserve fund in 1864 and £62000 in 1873. Although the bank held security over the works and other heritable property of the Monkland Company, which had been competently valued at more than the amount of the loan, the continuing stagnation in the iron trade and the disorganisation arising from the stoppage of the works was so extensive that this security did not protect the bank from heavy loss.

25 On the closing of the old outstanding accounts of 1862, there had been recoveries of £62447, which were now paid back from the Special Guarantee account and available for appropriation. The bulk of the recoveries was added to reserve (see note 24).

26 A new, separate Special Guarantee account of £120000 was set up (with £33000 from net profit and £87000 from reserve) for the purpose of meeting heavy losses caused by the failures in London in June 1875 and aggravated by the fraud of Alexander Collie.

27 Bonus to staff.

28 To pensions and allowances fund.

29 £200000 was transferred from the reserve fund to the Securities and Investments account to meet depreciation in the value of the bank's investments.

30 Consists of £10000 to pensions and allowances fund and £8935 bonus to staff.

31 £200000 from premium on share issue was added to reserve.

32 Consists of £100000 to contingencies and £25000 to pensions and allowances fund.

33 Consists of £50000 to contingencies and £25000 to pensions and allowances fund.

34 Consists of £50000 to contingencies, £25000 to pensions and allowances fund and £25000 to allowances fund for widows.

35 Consists of £50000 to contingencies and £40000 to pensions and allowances fund.

36 By the Companies Act of 1948 a sum of £200000, which was the amount in the reserve fund arising from share premiums, had to be transferred to a separate share premium account.

37 Consists of £80000 to contingencies and £40000 to pensions and allowances fund.

Source: BS(U), Uncatalogued, Annual reports of the Union Bank of Scotland, 1831–1955 (boxed).

BIBLIOGRAPHY

Abbreviations (also used in footnotes)

BS	Bank of Scotland archive
BS(BL)	Bank of Scotland archive, British Linen records
BS(U)	Bank of Scotland archive, Union Bank records
EMC	Edinburgh Merchant Company
GL	Goldsmiths Library, Senate House, University of London
GMC	General Managers Committee
GUBC	Glasgow Union Banking Company
IOL	India Office Library
MSS	Manuscripts
NLS	National Library of Scotland
RBS	Royal Bank of Scotland archive
SRO	Scottish Record Office
UBS	Union Bank of Scotland

Sources consulted for this book are grouped into the following sections. Note that, under 'Parliamentary and Official Documents', items beginning with *First Report*, *Report* or *Second Report* are in date order under *Report*; in other sections, any 'Anon.' books or articles are also in date order. Bank of Scotland papers mentioned in footnotes in Chapters 27–29 remain closed to readers and are not cited in the Bibliography.

> Primary Sources
> Parliamentary and Official Documents
> Works of Reference
> Printed Sources Before 1850
> Printed Sources After 1850: Books
> Articles
> Theses, Dissertations, Reports

PRIMARY SOURCES

Bank of Scotland
BS 1/1/1, Lists of Proprietors.
BS 1/2/1–5, Proprietors' Minutes, 1834–1971.
BS 1/5/1–69, Minutes, 1696–1936.
BS 1/6, Minutes and board papers, 1919 to date.
BS 1/7/1–4, Treasurer's Committee Minutes, 1919–67.
BS 1/18/5, Daily Sheet or Order of Directors.
BS 1/21, Private Letter Books, 1803–1939.
BS 1/30/3, Agents' Letter Book.
BS 1/30/4, Letter Book.
BS 1/31/20, Letter Book to Agents.
BS 1/69/4, Annual Records, 1850–55.
BS 1/70/2, States of the Bank of Scotland.
BS 1/70/3, Private Reports and Statements.
BS 1/70/4–5, Special Reports.
BS 1/70/6, Annual Reports of the Treasurer, 1866–98.
BS 1/70/9, An account of the constitution, objects and practice of the Bank of Scotland (1841).
BS 1/70/11, Figures for annual average of notes in circulation.
BS 1/70/12, Treasurer's (Blair's) Report to the directors on the affairs of Bank of Scotland, 1832–42.
BS 1/70/14, Analysis of the resources of Bank of Scotland.
BS 1/70A/6, Treasurer's Half-Yearly Statements.
BS 1/71, State of deposits, loans, investments and circulation.
BS 1/74, Annual Records.
BS 1/94/1–162, General Ledgers, 1696–1964.
BS 1/106/1–23, Cash account progressive ledgers.
BS 1/143/10–11, Averages of Bill Accounts over £2,000.
BS 1/146/1, Private Letter Book.
BS 1/149/1, Letter Book, 24 April 1696 to 10 October 1711.
BS 1/155/4, Customers' Credit Opinion Books.
BS 1/158/1, Private Letter Book.
BS 1/517/6, Transactions with other Scottish banks (1857 Crisis).
BS 18/1/1, UBS Local Edinburgh Board Minutes, 1830–8.
BS 20/1/1–19 (Miscellaneous papers).
BS 20/2/1, Court of Session information for Archibald Trotter; miscellaneous papers.
BS 20/2/4, Prospectus for the Central Banking Company of Perth, 1833.
BS 20/2/5 (Miscellaneous papers), report on Montrose.
BS 20/2/7, Papers re history of Scottish banks.
BS 20/2/8, Legal opinion on a Branch in London, and on the National Bank branch, 1865.
BS 20/2/10, William Cotton to Alexander Blair, 23 November 1847.
BS 20/2/11, Papers on Banking Topics.
BS 20/2/14 (Miscellaneous papers).

BS 20/2/23, Bank of Scotland correspondence on Barings.

BS 20/3/4, Miscellaneous papers, including: *Address by Sir F. W. Drummond and George Mercer of Gorthy to the proprietors of the Bank of Scotland* (1830); criticism of William Cadell by senior officers, June 1831.

BS 20/3/9, K. Gibson to J. A. Wenley, 19 July 1890.

BS 20/4/1, 'A bill for further increasing the capital stock of the Governor and Company of the Bank of Scotland', 1804.

BS 20/4/7, George Tytler, Secretary, to Proprietors.

BS 20/4/8, Miscellaneous legal papers, 1873.

BS 20/4/12, Treasurer's reports, 'General View of Assets and Liabilities on Deposits, Loans and Cash Accounts', 1863.

BS 20/4/14, Reports and letters re correspondents and other banks.

BS 20/4/17, Scotch Banks: Falling off in the percentage of profits from deposits since 1869.

BS 20/9/1–20 (Miscellaneous papers).

BS 20/10/1–57 (Miscellaneous papers).

BS 20/11/3, Miscellaneous papers on Carron Company.

BS 20/12/1–17 (Miscellaneous papers).

BS 20/13/6 (Miscellaneous papers).

BS 20/18/5, Papers re the debts of Hay Smith, Banker, James Sommervail.

BS 20/18/7, View of bad debts and of the fund applicable thereto, March 1829.

BS 20/18/10 (Miscellaneous papers).

BS 20/18/12, Memo from Glasgow Chief Office, February 1894.

BS 20/20/2–3, British Linen Company papers.

BS 20/21/31, British Linen Bank General Manager's Private Letter Book.

BS 20/26/1, Agreements between the Royal Bank, Bank of Scotland and Sir William Forbes & Co., 1790–1805.

BS 20/29/9, GUBC Edinburgh branch, Bond of secrecy, December 1830.

BS 20/30/9, Miscellaneous papers.

BS 20/30/13, Overend, Gurney & Co., Miscellaneous and legal papers.

BS 20/32/1, Melville Papers, George Home ws, 'Observations on a late conversation'.

BS 20/32/4–202, Melville Papers, 1789–1848.

BS, Board papers, 1959–75.

BS, British Linen merger files, including Second Special Steering Committee, 17 October 1969; Peat, Marwick, Mitchell & Co., Preliminary Memorandum, 2 April 1969; Memorandum, supplementary to Preliminary Memorandum, 7 May 1969.

BS, Minutes and papers from Noble Grossart, 28 December 1971.

BS, Minutes of conferences between the Royal and the Bank, 25 May, 7 and 17 June 1757.

BS, Miscellaneous Committees, Investment Committee Minutes, 1949–77.

BS, Miscellaneous papers, Banque Worms et Cie, 1967.

BS, Tercentenary Oral History Project, interviews carried out by David G. Antonio and Duncan A. Ferguson.

BS, Uncatalogued, 'Ad hoc committee on Bank of England proposals for Finance for Industry', 8 November 1974.

BS, Uncatalogued, Balance Sheets and Income Tax Returns, 1834–49.

BS, Uncatalogued, Branch Letter Book, 1856.

BS, Uncatalogued, Davidson & Syme WS, *Memorial for the Bank of Scotland for the Advice of Counsel*, 1953.

BS, Uncatalogued, General Managers Committee, Minutes [includes the 'Agreements and Understandings among the Banks in Scotland'] and Miscellaneous papers.

BS, Uncatalogued, George Sandy WS, *Observations on the Acts of the Bank of Scotland* (undated).

BS, Uncatalogued, Memorandum, John Rankin on N. Tamaki's history of the Union Bank.

BS, Uncatalogued, Miscellaneous Letter Book (Secretary's), c. 1707–1790s.

BS, Uncatalogued, Miscellaneous papers, Accountant.

BS, Uncatalogued, Miscellaneous papers, SCOOP (papers on Scottish Co-operative Wholesale Society banking department), 1973–8.

BS, Uncatalogued, Views of Stocks.

BS, unpublished, J. F. Wilson, 'Reminiscences of a Lifetime in Scottish Banking, 1939–1984' (1984).

BS(BL) 6/5, Minutes of the meetings of the proprietors of the British Linen Company, 1746–1955.

BS(BL) 6/6, Minutes of meetings of directors, 1806.

BS(BL) 6/8, Minutes of Court of Directors.

BS(BL) 20/21/8, Abstract of general balance sheets, 1861–63, 1887–1911.

BS(BL) 20/21/10, Abstract profit and loss account, 1886–1912.

BS(BL) 20/21/16, 1914–1918, Papers re staff of the Scottish banks.

BS(BL), British Linen Company, Charter, 1806.

BS(BL), Miscellaneous papers, Tables of interest rates.

BS(BL), Stock Ledgers.

BS(BL), Uncatalogued, Directors private letter book, 12 August 1958.

BS(BL), Uncatalogued, General Manager's Letter Books.

BS(BL), Uncatalogued, Special Committee of Directors, Minute Book, 1918.

BS(U) 1/1/1, UBS Board of Directors Supplementary Minute Book.

BS(U) 1/10, Quarterly states.

BS(U) 1/13, Minute Books of Large Loans.

BS(U) 1/21/3–4, Private Letter Books.

BS(U) 1/21/24, Private Letter Book of Norman Hird.

BS(U), Uncatalogued, Annual reports of the Union Bank of Scotland, 1831–1955 (boxed).

BS(U), Uncatalogued, Glasgow Committee minutes, 1843–1955.

BS(U), Uncatalogued, Glasgow Union Banking Company Minutes, 1830–43.

Bank of England

Bank of England, MSS, Court Minutes, vol. E, G4/6.

Bank of England, MSS, Court Minutes, vol. H, G4/11.

Bank of England, MSS, Court Minutes, vol. K, G4/13.

Bank of England, MSS, Court Minutes, G4/21, 2 July 1772.
Bank of England, MSS, Law papers, M5/551.
Bank of England, MSS, Ledger 'B', 1696.

British Library
British Library, 713, Tracts relating to Scottish Life Assurance Offices.
British Library, 1245 (h5) 1–8, 'Information for the Govenor and Company of the Royal Bank of Scotland and William Simpson their Cashier . . .', 13 May 1794.

Coutts & Co.
Coutts & Co., archives, Ledgers, 1850–1860.
Coutts & Co., archives, Letter Books.
Coutts & Co., archives, Special Letter Books.
Coutts & Co., archives, Miscellaneous papers.
Coutts & Co., archives, Miscellaneous papers, 'Memorial of the Governor, deputy-Governor and directors of Bank of Scotland & the Governor, deputy-Governor and directors of the Royal Bank of Scotland. To his Royal Highness the Prince Regent', 1811.
Coutts & Co., Minutes, vol. 16, p. 386, 6 January 1727.
Coutts & Co., MSS, Letter Book of John Campbell, 1692–1694.
Coutts & Co., Secret Letterbook Series, 1858–61.

Edinburgh City Archive
Edinburgh City Archive, Edinburgh Merchant Company MSS, George Watson papers, *Book of solved questions most fit and necessary to know as the ground of . . . Italian book-keeping* (Accession no. 264).
Edinburgh City Archive, EMC MSS, Letter book no. 44, J. Anderson to George Watson [1713].
Edinburgh City Archive, EMC MSS, vol. 1, Minutes 1681–96; vol. 2, Minutes 1696–1704 (Accession no. 264).
Edinburgh City Archive, EMC MSS, Miscellaneous papers collection, no. 4, George Watson, Ledger and Journal 1679–1683.
Edinburgh City Archive, EMC MSS, Miscellaneous papers collection, no. 11, Earl of Argyll, Inveraray, to George Watson, 11 October 1691.

Goldsmiths Library, Senate House, University of London
Goldsmiths, MS 81, 'Report off the state of the Trade of the Nation so farr as can be gathered from the Custom House books, and that from November 1703 to November 1704, taken conforme to order and appointment of the Rt Honourable the Councill of Trade'.
Goldsmiths, MS 579, John Wilkie MSS.

India Office Library
India Office Library, East India Company, Minutes, B/35, 1678–1680.
India Office Library, East India Company, Minutes, B/36, 1680–1682.

India Office Library, East India Company, Minutes, B/37, 1682–1684.
India Office Library, East India Company, Minutes, B/38, 1684–.
India Office Library, East India Company, Minutes, B/39.
India Office Library, East India Company, Minutes, B/40, 1690–1695.
India Office Library, East India Company, Minutes, B/41, 1695.
India Office Library, MSS, L/Accountant general/1/19, Ledger H.

National Library of Scotland

NLS, Advocates MSS, 31.1.7, ff. 30–8, Papers relating to a bank of credit upon land-security proposed to the Parliament of Scotland (printed by the Select Committee of the Scottish Parliament, 1693).

NLS, Advocates MSS, 83.3.3, A Journal for the General Trading Ledger, 1696–1701.

NLS, Advocates MSS, 83.3.9, Cash ledger for the banking operation.

NLS, Advocates MSS, 83.4.7, Promissory Notes: Counterfoils and some unissued notes:?small denominations.

NLS, Advocates MSS, 83.5.2, Cash book, 1696–1700.

NLS, Advocates MSS, 83.7.1, Minutes of the Committee for Improvements.

NLS, MS 1801(ii), List of Scottish Banks, 1695–1848, compiled by John Buchanan, Glasgow, 1862.

NLS, MS 1914, Company of Scotland Letter Book, 1696.

NLS, MS 14422, Yester Papers.

NLS, MS 14427, Yester Papers.

NLS, MS 16538, Fletcher of Saltoun Papers.

NLS, MS 16540, Fletcher of Saltoun Papers.

NLS, MS 17498, Fletcher of Saltoun Papers.

NLS, MS 17591, Fletcher of Saltoun Papers.

NLS, MS 17592, Fletcher of Saltoun Papers.

NLS, MS 17593, Fletcher of Saltoun Papers.

NLS, MS 17698, Fletcher of Saltoun Papers.

NLS, pamphlets 1.349 (11), A Letter to a Member of Parliament, concerning manufacture and trade (1704).

NLS, pamphlets 1.349 (15), Two Overtures Humbly offered to his Grace John, Duke of Argyll. Her Majestie's High Commission and the right Honourable Estates of Parliament (1705).

NLS, pamphlets 1.349 (16), Anon., An Essay for promoting of Trade, and increasing the Coin of the Nation (1705).

National Westminster Bank

National Westminster Bank, archives (Ref. 1094), Memoranda on the suggested formation of a Scottish Foreign Exchange Bank, 1916.

Public Record Office

PRO, Customs, 14, Imports to Scotland.

PRO, T 1/12267/50326/18.

PRO, T 1/223/no. 8.

PRO, T 1/223/no. 17.
PRO, T 1/243/no. 64.
PRO, T 1/248/no. 3.
PRO, T 1/266/no. 7.

Royal Bank of Scotland

RBS CS/13/1, Commercial Bank, Minutes, 1810–14.

RBS EQ/9/1, The several Journals of the Court of Directors of the Company of Scotland trading to Africa and the Indies, 1696–8.

RBS RB/12/1, Minute Book of the Court of Directors, 1727–30.

RBS RB/12/8, Minutes, 1760–3.

RBS RB/12/9, Minutes, 1764–7.

RBS RB/12/10, Minutes, 1767–71.

RBS RB/494, Share Transfer Books, 1777.

RBS, Drummond & Co., General Ledger Books, 1772.

RBS, *Financial and Trade Circular*, 1 (January) and 2 (July), 1919.

RBS, General Journal of the Accounts of the Commissioners of the Equivalent, vol. 3, 1717–21.

RBS, Ledger A, B, C, 1728–31.

St Andrews University, MSS

[Lockhart, George of Carnwath], *Memoirs concerning the Affairs of Scotland from Queen Anne's succession to the throne to the commencement of the Union of the two kingdoms of Scotland and England in May 1707*, St Andrews University archives, MS DA. 805 M2 (old ref. BN. 3.77).

Scottish Record Office

SRO, Privy Council Papers.

SRO, Privy Council Register.

SRO E 7/8, Treasury Registers, 1 March 1693 to 19 March 1700.

SRO E 72/1/18–20, Aberdeen exports and imports, 1 November 1689 to 1 November 1691.

SRO E 72/2/11, Exports, 1 November 1682 to 1 November 1683.

SRO GD 46/II/23–35, Seaforth Muniments, Papers relating to the Muirkirk Iron Company, 1789–1827.

SRO GD 103/2/4, vol. 4/41, Court of Directors, 1696.

SRO GD 103/2/247, Earl of Argyll at Inveraray to Dougall Campbell of Melfort, on prospecting for gold.

SRO GD 277, Box 2, Bundle 1, London, 23 August 1690 [grant of factory by James Chiesly].

SRO GD 277, Box 5, Bundle 5, London, 24 August 1693 [grant of factory by William Clopton].

SRO GD 277, Box 8, Bundle 1, Letters from Michael Kincaid and John Pitcairn as a Company, from London, as to financial dealings, 1695.

SRO GD 277, Box 8, Bundle 7, London, 3 March 1683 [grant of factory by Abel Swalle].

SRO GD 277, Box 8, Bundle 8, London, 14 December 1692 [grant of factory by Joseph Tomlinson, feltmaker, London].

SRO GD 277, Box 9, Bundle 3, London, 12 May 1694 [grant of factory by Edmund Harris].

SRO GD 277, Box 14, Bundle 8, Miscellaneous correspondence to George Watson, 1696, mainly from John Pitcairn and Michael Kincaid, London.

SRO GD 277, Edinburgh Merchant Company, Papers relating to George Watson.

SRO PA 7/17/1, 'Proposal for advancing Trade' (1699).

SRO PC 4/2, Privy Council Minute Book, 2 January 1696 to 28 December 1699.

PARLIAMENTARY AND OFFICIAL DOCUMENTS

The Acts of the Parliaments of Scotland, 12 vols (Edinburgh and London: 1814–75).

The Acts of the Parliaments of Scotland, 1424–1707 (Edinburgh: 1908).

Board of Trade, Board of Trade Labour Gazette, and (after 1917) Ministry of Labour, The Labour Gazette.

Board of Trade, Final Report of the Committee on Commercial and Industrial Policy after the War, Cd 9035, 1918 xiii (London: 1918).

Board of Trade, Statistical Abstract for the United Kingdom for each of the fifteen years 1913 and 1918 to 1931, 78 (London: 1933), Cmd 4233.

Central Statistical Office, Financial Statistics, 230 (June 1981), Exchange rates.

Committee on the Working of the Monetary System (the Radcliffe Committee), Report, Cmnd 827 (August 1959).

Committee to Review the Functioning of Financial Institutions (the Wilson Committee), The Financing of North Sea Oil, Research Report no. 2 (London: 1978); Evidence on the Financing of Industry and Trade, 6 (March 1978); Report, Cmnd 7937 (June 1980).

Further papers relating to the measures taken by HM Government for sustaining credit and facilitating business, Cd 7684, House of Commons 457.

Hansard, T. C., The Parliamentary Debates from the Year 1803 to the Present Time, forming a continuation of the work entitled 'The Parliamentary History of England from the Earliest Period to the Year 1803' (London: various dates) [this becomes Hansard's Parliamentary Debates, 1st, 2nd and 3rd series, etc. (London: various dates)].

House of Commons Journal, vol. 9, p. 404, 27 November 1695.

House of Lords Journal, vol. 19, 7 July 1714.

House of Lords, Library, A bill to amend the laws relating to banking, 1 May 1879.

House of Lords, The trial of Henry, Lord Viscount Melville (London: 1806).

Hume Brown, P. (ed.), The Register of the Privy Council of Scotland, 3rd series, vol. vii, 1681–1682 (Edinburgh: 1915).

Lambert, S. R. (ed.), House of Commons Sessional Papers of the Eighteenth Century, vol. 2, George I, Scotland, 1717–1725.

'Memorandum of Evidence submitted by the Committee of Scottish Bank General Managers', November 1957, in Principal Memoranda of Evidence submitted to the Committee on the Working of the Monetary System, vol. ii (HMSO, 1960).

'Memorandum of Evidence submitted by the Council of Scottish Chambers of Commerce', 27 November 1957, in Principal Memoranda . . ., vol. ii (HMSO, 1960).

'Memorandum of Evidence submitted by the Credit Insurance Association Ltd', December 1957, in Principal Memoranda . . ., vol. ii (HMSO, 1960).

'Memorandum of Evidence submitted by the Export Group for the Constructional Industries', November 1957, in Principal Memoranda . . ., vol. ii (HMSO, 1960).

'Memorandum of Evidence submitted by the Finance Houses Association Ltd', 11 April 1958, in Principal Memoranda . . ., vol. ii (HMSO, 1960).

'Memorandum of Evidence submitted by the General Council of British Shipping', 11 April 1958, in Principal Memoranda . . ., vol. ii (HMSO, 1960).

Ministry of Labour: see Board of Trade.

Monopolies and Mergers Commission, The Hongkong and Shanghai Banking Corporation, Standard Chartered Bank Limited, The Royal Bank of Scotland Group Limited: A Report on the Proposed Mergers, Cmnd 8472 (London: 1982).

Monthly Digest of Statistics, 'Security Prices and Yields: British Government Securities' (1948; 1954).

Morison, William Maxwell (ed.), The Decisions of the Court of Session, vol. xxxviii (Edinburgh: 1801 edn).

Reddington, J. (ed.), Calendar of Treasury Papers, 1720–28 (London: 1889).

First report from the Select Committee appointed to take into Consideration the present state of Commercial credit, 29 April 1793; repr. in S. R. Lambert (ed.), House of Commons Sessional Papers of the Eighteenth Century, vol. 88, George III: Finance and Fees, 1792–93 (Wilmington: 1975).

Report, Together with Minutes of Evidence and Accounts, from the Select Committee on the High Price of Gold Bullion [the 'Bullion report 1810'] (House of Commons, 8 June 1810), repr. in Irish University Press Series of British Parliamentary Papers, vol. i, Monetary Policy General (Dublin: 1969).

Report from the Select Committee on Petitions complaining of Agricultural Distress, 8 July 1820, (255) vol. ii.

Report from the Select Committee on the Circulation of Promissory Notes under the Value of £5 in Scotland and Ireland, 26 May 1826, (402) vol. iii.

Report from the Lords' Committee on the Circulation of Promissory Notes under the Value of £5 in Scotland and Ireland, 6 April 1827, (245) vol. vi.

Report from the Select Committee on Banks of Issue, with the Minutes of Evidence, Appendix and Index, 7 August 1840, (602) vol. iv.

First Report from the Select Committee on Banks of Issue, 4 June 1841, (366) vol. v.

Second Report from Select Committee on Banks of Issue, with the Minutes of Evidence, Appendix and Index, 15 June 1841, (410) vol. v.

Report from the Select Committee on the Bank Acts, together with the Proceedings of the Committee, Minutes of Evidence, Appendix and Index, Part I, Report and Evidence, 30 July 1857, (220) session 2, vol. x: evidence of Weguelin and Sheffield Neave, sections 160, 170, 177, 214, 215.

Report from the Select Committee appointed to inquire into the Operation of the Bank

Act of 1844 and of the Bank Acts for Ireland and Scotland of 1845 . . . together with the Proceedings of the Committee, Minutes of Evidence, Appendix and Index, 1 July 1858, (381) vol. v.

Report from the Select Committee on Banks of Issue, together with the Proceedings of the Committee, Minutes of Evidence, Appendix and Index, 22 July 1875, (351) vol. ix.

Report to the Board of Trade by the Committee Appointed to Investigate the Question of the Financial Facilities for Trade, Cd 8346, 31 August 1916.

Report of the Royal Commission on the Housing of the Industrial Population of Scotland, Urban and Rural, Cd 8731 (1917).

Report of the Committee on Provision of Financial Facilities (chairman: Sir Richard Vassar-Smith, Lloyds Bank and President of the Institute of Bankers), Cd 9227 (1918).

Report of the Monopolies Commission on the Proposed Merger by Barclays Bank Ltd, Lloyds Bank Ltd and Martins Bank (HMSO, July 1968).

Scottish Office, Scottish Economic Bulletin, 28 (1983).

Shaw, W. A. (ed.), Calendar of Treasury Books and Papers, 1729–30 (London: 1897).

Statistical Digest of the War (London: 1951).

Statutes of the Realm (1821), vol. 8, pp. 349–50, 3 & 4 Anne c.6, 'An Act for the effectual securing the Kingdom of England from the apparent dangers that may arise from several Acts lately passed in the Parliament of Scotland'.

Statutes of the Realm (1821), vol. 8, p. 776, 6 Anne c.51, 'An Act for the further directing of the Equivalent money'.

Statutes of the Realm (1821), vol. 9, p. 924, 13 Anne c.12 (1713), 'An Act to discharge and acquit the Commissioners of the Equivalent . . .'.

Statutes of the Realm, 12 Car II c.18, 15 Car II c.7.

WORKS OF REFERENCE

The Annual Register (London: 1855).

Brunton, G. and Haig, D., Account of the Senators of the College of Justice from its Institution in 1532 (London: 1832).

Clydesdale and North of Scotland Bank Ltd, Survey of Economic Conditions in Scotland in 1952 (1953).

Clydesdale Bank, Survey of Economic Conditions in Scotland in 1946 (March 1947).

Cockayne, G. E., Complete Baronetage, ed. H. M. Massingberd (1983).

Dictionary of National Biography, ed. L. Stephen and S. Lee (1885–1901).

Doubleday, H. and Walden, Lord H. de (eds), The Complete Peerage (London: 1945).

Douglas, Sir Robert, The Peerage of Scotland, ed. J. P. Wood, 9 vols (Edinburgh: 1813).

Encyclopaedia of the Laws of Scotland, vol. ii (Edinburgh: 1927).

Jeremy, D. J. (ed.), Dictionary of Business Biography (London: 1984).

Keesings Contemporary Archives, United Kingdom, Internal Disorders, 18 September 1981.

Kennedy, J., Smith, W. A. and Johnson, A. F., *Dictionary of Anonymous and Pseudonymous English Literature*, vol. iv (London: 1928).

Munn, C. W. and Tamaki, N., 'Charles Gairdner', in A. Slaven and S. G. Checkland (eds), *Dictionary of Scottish Business Biography, 1860–1960*, 2 vols, vol. ii, *Processing, Distribution, Services* (Aberdeen: 1990), 403–6.

Murray, J. A. H. (ed.), *A New English Dictionary on Historical Principles*, vol. 2 (Oxford: 1893); vol. 4, ed. H. Bradley (Oxford: 1901).

The New Statistical Account of Scotland, vol. vi, *Lanark* (Edinburgh: 1845).

The New Statistical Account of Scotland, vol. vii, 'Cambusnethan' (Edinburgh: 1845).

Paul, Sir J. B., *The Scots Peerage, Founded on Wood's Edition of Sir Robert Douglas's Peerage of Scotland* (Edinburgh: 1903).

Pember and Boyle [firm], *British Government Securities in the Twentieth Century: The First Fifty Years*, 2nd edn (private circulation, London: 1950).

Pember and Boyle [firm], *British Government Securities in the Twentieth Century: Supplement 1950–1972* (private circulation, London: n.d. [1973]).

Schmitz, C. J., *World Non-Ferrous Metal Production and Prices 1700–1976* (London: 1979).

Sedgwick, R. (ed.), *The House of Commons 1715–1754* (London: 1970), vol. i, *The History of Parliament*, 592–3.

Seligman, E. R. A. (ed.), *Encyclopaedia of the Social Sciences*, 10 vols (New York: 1930–5).

Sinclair, Sir John (ed.), *The First Statistical Account of Scotland*, vol. xii, 'Cambushnethan' (Edinburgh: 1794).

Slaven, A. and Checkland, S. G. (eds), *Dictionary of Scottish Business Biography, 1860–1960*, vol. i (Aberdeen: 1986).

Thomson, G., 'Calderbank', in idem (ed.), *The County of Lanark, The Third Statistical Account of Scotland* (Glasgow: 1960), 222–36.

Thorne, R. G. (ed.), *The History of Parliament: The House of Commons 1790–1820* (London: 1986).

PRINTED SOURCES BEFORE 1850

'Abstract of the Articles of Co-partnery of the Commercial Banking Company of Scotland' [GL 1810].

Anderson, Adam, *An Historical and Chronological Deduction of the Origin of Commerce*, 4 vols (London: 1801; repr. New York: 1867).

Anon., 'Bank Credit or the Usefulness of Security of the Bank of Credit examined in a Dialogue' (London: 1683).

Anon., 'A Letter to a Member of Parliament concerning the Bank of Scotland and the lowering of Interest of Money' (Edinburgh: 1696).

Anon., 'A Letter to a Member of Parliament anent the Application of the £309,885-10sh Equivalent with Consideration of reducing the coin to the value and standard of England' [GL 1706].

Anon., 'A letter from a Gentleman in Glasgow to his friend in Edinburgh concerning bank-notes and paper credit' [GL 1752].

Anon., *Essay on Paper Money, Banking etc.* (London: 1755).

Anon., 'Considerations on the Present Scarcity of Gold and Silver Coin in Scotland' [GL 1763].

Anon, 'Bank Disputes or credit without above, submitted to the considerate observation of stock holders in the Chartered Banks of Scotland' (Edinburgh: 1778) [GL 1778].

Anon., 'A letter to the proprietors of the Bank of Scotland and the Royal Bank' [GL 1778].

Arnot, Hugo, *History of Edinburgh* (Edinburgh: 1777).

Arnot, Hugo, *A Letter to the Lord Advocate of Scotland* (Edinburgh: 18 November 1777).

Blackwell, Captain John, 'A Model for erecting a Bank of Credit with a Discourse in explanation thereof, adapted to the use of any trading country where there is a scarcity of moneys, more especially for His Majesty's Plantations in America' (London: 1688).

Blayney, Frederick, *A Practical Treatise on Life Assurance* (London: 1826).

Burton, J. H. (ed.), *The Darien Papers: being a Selection of Original Letters and official Documents relating to the establishment of a colony at Darien by the Company of Scotland trading to Africa and the Indies 1695–1700*, Bannatyne Club, vol. 90 (Edinburgh: 1849).

Cantillon, Richard, *Essai sur la nature du commerce en général* (London: 1755), ed. H. Higgs (London: 1931).

Dalrymple of Stair, Sir James, *Decisions of the Court of Session 1661–1671*, 2 vols (Edinburgh: 1683–7).

Defoe, Daniel, *The History of the Union between England and Scotland* (n.d.; repr. London: 1786).

Elibank, Lord Patrick, *Thoughts on Money, Circulating & Paper Currency* [written 1753 or 1754, published 1758].

Ferguson, Adam, *An Essay on the History of Civil Society* (Edinburgh: 1767), ed. D. Forbes (Edinburgh: 1966).

Holland, John, *A Short Discourse on the Present Temper of the Nation with respect to the Indian and African Company, and of the Bank of Scotland; also of Mr Paterson's pretended Fund of Credit* (Edinburgh: 1696).

Holland, Richard, *An Historical Account of the Establishment, Progress and State of the Bank of Scotland* ([Edinburgh:] 1728).

Janssen, Sir Stephen Theodore, *A Discourse concerning Banks* (London: 1697) [GL 1742].

Jeffrey, F., *Edinburgh Review*, vol. 3, no. 5 (October 1803), 154–81.

Joplin, Thomas, *On the General Principles and Present Practice of Banking in England and Scotland* (1822).

Justice, Alexander, *A General Treatise of Monies and Exchanges* (London: 1707).

Kinnear, George, *Banks and Exchange Companies* (Glasgow: 1847).

Kinnear, George, *A History of the Rise of Exchange Companies in Scotland, and a Defence of their Proper Business* (Glasgow: 1848).

Law, John, *The Circumstances of Scotland considered with respect to the present scarcity of money, together with some proposals for supplying the defect thereof and rectifying the balance of trade* (Edinburgh: 1705).

Law, John, *Money and Trade Considered, with a proposal for supplying the nation with money* (Glasgow: 1750).

Lawson, W. J., *History of Banking in Scotland* (Edinburgh: 1845).

Mackenzie of Rosehaugh, Sir George, *Memoirs of the Affairs of Scotland* (Edinburgh: 1821).

Macpherson, David, *Annals of Commerce, Manufactures, Fisheries and Navigation*, 4 vols (London: 1805).

Maitland, William, *The History of Edinburgh from its Foundation to the Present Time* (Edinburgh: 1753).

'Memorial for the Governor and Company of the Bank of Scotland' [GL 1727].

Menarty, G., *Life and Letters of Duncan Forbes of Culloden* (London: 1736).

Petty, Sir William, 'A Treatise of Taxes and Contributions', repr. in C. H. Hull (ed.), *The Economic Writings of Sir William Petty*, 2 vols (Cambridge: 1899), vol. i, 1–97.

Petty, Sir William, 'Quantulumcunque concerning money, 1682', repr. in C. H. Hull (ed.), *The Economic Writings of Sir William Petty*, 2 vols (Cambridge: 1899), vol. ii, 466–7.

Philopatris, A. M., *Scotiae Indiculum, or the Present State of Scotland* (London: 1681).

The Precipitation and Fall of Messrs Douglas, Heron & Company, Late bankers in Air with the causes of their distress and ruin investigated and considered by a committee appointed by the Proprietors (Edinburgh: 1778).

'Proceedings in and on the 5 June 1806. Application at the Treasury for an increase of capital by the British Linen Company' (London: 1813).

Scots Magazine, various.

Scott, Sir Walter (Malachi Malagrowther), *Thoughts on the proposed change of currency and other later alterations as they affect, or are intended to affect, the Kingdom of Scotland* (Edinburgh: 1826).

Sinclair, Sir John, *The History of the Public Revenue of the British Empire*, 3rd edn, 3 vols (London: 1803).

Sinclair, Sir John, *Observations on the Report of the Bullion Committee* (10 September 1810).

Smith, Adam, *An Inquiry into the Nature and Causes of the Wealth of Nations* (1776), ed. E. Cannan, 2 vols (London: 1904; repr. 1961).

Steuart, Sir James, *An Inquiry into the Principles of Political Economy being an Essay on the Science of Domestic Policy in Free Nations*, 2 vols (London: 1767), ed. A. Skinner (Edinburgh: 1966).

Stewart, Sir James, of Goodtrees, *An Accompt of Scotland's Grievances by Reason of the Duke of Lauderdale's Ministrie* (1671) [GL 1676].

Sturrock, John, 'An Account of the Trade of the Port of Dundee during the Three Years Ended 31 May 1838', *Journal of the Statistical Society of London*, vol. 1 (London: 1839), 522–9.

Thornton, Henry, MP, *Enquiry into the Nature and Effects of the Paper Credit of Great Britain* (London: 1802).

Tooke, Thomas, *A History of Prices and the State of Circulation from 1793*, 6 vols

(London: 1838–57).

Webster, Alexander, *Account of the Number of People in Scotland* (1755).

PRINTED SOURCES AFTER 1850

Books

Acres, W. M., *The Bank of England from Within: 1694–1900*, 2 vols (London: 1931).

Acworth, A. W., *Financial Reconstruction in England 1815–1822* (London: 1925).

Aldcroft, D. H. and Richardson, H. W., *The British Economy 1870–1939* (London: 1969).

Alford, B. W. E., *Depression and Recovery? British Economic Growth, 1918–1939* (London: 1978).

Anderson, J., *The Story of the Commercial Bank of Scotland Limited during its Hundred Years from 1810 to 1910* (Edinburgh: 1910).

Andreades, A., *History of the Bank of England* (London: 1909).

Anon., *The Western Bank Failure and the Scottish Banking System* (Glasgow: 1858).

Anon., *Williams Deacon's 1771–1970* (Manchester: 1971).

Anon., *A History of the Scottish Amicable Life Assurance Society 1826–1976* (Glasgow: 1976).

Arnold, G., *Britain's Oil* (London: 1978).

Ashton, T. S., *Economic Fluctuations in England and Wales 1700–1800* (Oxford: 1959).

Ashton, T. S. and Philpin, C. H. E. (eds), *The Brenner Debate, Agrarian Class Structure and Economic Development in Pre-Industrial Europe* (Cambridge: 1987).

Bagehot, W., *Lombard Street* (London: 1873).

Balogh, T., *Studies in Financial Organisation* (Cambridge: 1947).

Bank of Scotland, *Annual Reports* (1865 to present day).

Bannister, S. (ed.), *The Writings of William Paterson, Founder of the Bank of England*, 2nd edn, 3 vols (London: 1859; repr. New York: 1968).

Barbour, J. S., *A History of William Paterson and the Darien Company* (Edinburgh: 1907).

Barnett, C., *The Audit of War: The Illusion and Reality of Britain as a Great Nation* (London: 1986).

Barrow, G. L., *The Emergence of the Irish Banking System 1820–45* (Dublin: 1974).

Bhattacharya, S., *Financial Foundations of the British Raj* (Simla: 1971).

Blair, A., *Davidson & Syme, ws : Two Centuries of Law* (private publication, [Edinburgh:] 1980).

Blanchard, I., *Russia's 'Age of Silver': Precious Metal Production and Economic Growth in the Eighteenth Century* (London: 1989).

Boase, C. W., *A Century of Banking in Dundee; being the Annual Balance Sheets of the Dundee Banking Company from 1764 to 1864*, 2nd edn (Edinburgh: 1867).

Bowley, A. L., *Prices and Wages in the United Kingdom 1914–1920*, Carnegie Endowment for International Peace (Oxford: 1921).

Bowley, M., *Housing and the State 1919–1944* (London: 1945).

Burns, E., *The Coinage of Scotland*, 3 vols (Edinburgh: 1887).

Butler, J. R. M., *The Passing of the Great Reform Bill* (London: 1914).

Buxton, N. K., *The Economic Development of the British Coal Industry* (London: 1978).

Cairncross, A. K., *Home and Foreign Investment 1870–1913* (Cambridge: 1953).

Cairncross, A. K. (ed.), *The Scottish Economy* (Cambridge: 1954).

Cameron, A., *Bank of Scotland 1695–1995: A Very Singular Institution* (Edinburgh: 1995).

Campbell, R. H., *Carron Company* (Edinburgh: 1961).

Campbell, R. H. (ed.), *States of the Progress of the Linen Manufacture in Scotland 1727–1754* (Edinburgh: 1973).

Campbell, R. H., *The Rise and Fall of Scottish Industry 1707–1939* (Edinburgh: 1980).

Carswell, C., *The Life of Robert Burns* (London: 1930).

Chalmers, G., *Caledonia or a Historical and Typographical Account of North Britain*, new edn (Paisley: 1889).

Chapman, S. D., *The Rise of Merchant Banking* (London: 1984).

Checkland, S. G., *Scottish Banking: A History, 1695–1973* (Glasgow: 1975).

Checkland, S. G., *The Elgins 1766–1917: A Tale of Aristocrats, Proconsuls and Their Wives* (Aberdeen: 1988).

Church, R. A., *The History of the British Coal Industry*, vol. iii, *1830–1913: Victorian Pre-eminence* (Oxford: 1986).

Clapham, J. H., *The Bank of England. A History*, 2 vols (Cambridge: 1944).

Clapham, J. H., *An Economic History of Modern Britain: The Early Railway Age, 1820–1850* (Cambridge: 1967).

Clapham, J. H., *An Economic History of Modern Britain* [vol. ii]: *Free Trade and Steel, 1850–1886* (Cambridge: 1932).

Clapham, J. H., Appendix 3: 'Sir John Clapham's Account of the Financial Crisis in August 1914', in R. S. Sayers, *The Bank of England 1891–1944*, vol. iii (Cambridge: 1976), 31–45.

Clark, D. M., *The Rise of the British Treasury: Colonial Administration in the Eighteenth Century* (New Haven: 1960).

Clark, V., *The Port of Aberdeen: A History of its Trade and Shipping from the 12th Century to the Present Day* (Aberdeen: 1921).

Cleere, H. and Crossley, D., *The Iron Industry of the Weald* (Leicester: 1985).

Clow, A. and Clow, N. L., *The Chemical Revolution* (Oxford: 1952).

Cobden, R., *The Political Writings of Richard Cobden* (notes by F. W. Chesson), 4th edn (London: 1903).

Cochran-Patrick, R. W., *Records of the Coinage of Scotland*, 2 vols (Edinburgh: 1876).

Cockburn, H., *Memorials of His Time* (Edinburgh: 1856), new edn (Edinburgh: 1910).

Cockburn, H., *Examination of the Trials for Sedition in Scotland which have hitherto Occurred in Scotland*, 2 vols (Edinburgh: 1888; repr. in 1 vol., New York: 1970).

Collins, B. and Robbins, K. (eds), *British Culture and Economic Decline*

(London: 1990).

Collins, M., *Banks and Industrial Finance in Britain 1800–1939* (London: 1991).

Cornelius Hallen, A. W. (ed.), *The Account Book of Sir John Foulis of Ravelston, 1671–1707*, Scottish History Society Publications, vol. 16 (Edinburgh: 1894).

Cottrell, P. L., *Industrial Finance, 1830–1914: The Finance and Organisation of English Manufacturing Industry* (London: 1980).

Craig, Sir John, *The Mint: A History of the London Mint from AD 287 to 1948* (Cambridge: 1953).

Crick, W. F. and Wadsworth, J. E., *A Hundred Years of Joint Stock Banking* (London: 1936).

Crossley, D. and Saville, R., *The Fuller Letters 1728–1755: Guns, Slaves and Finance* (Lewes: 1991).

Crouzet, F. (ed.), *Capital Formation in the Industrial Revolution* (London: 1972).

Dalrymple of Stair, Sir James, *The Institutions of the Law of Scotland*, ed. D. M. Walker (Edinburgh and Glasgow: 1981).

Davis, A. M., *Colonial Currency Reprints 1682–1751* (Boston, MA: 1910; repr. New York: 1964).

Davis, R., *The Industrial Revolution and British Overseas Trade* (Leicester: 1979).

Deane, P., *The Evolution of Economic Ideas* (Cambridge: 1978).

Deane, P. and Cole, W. A., *British Economic Growth 1688–1959* (Cambridge: 1962).

Devine, T. M., *The Tobacco Lords: A Study of the Tobacco Merchants of Glasgow and their Trading Activities c. 1740–1790* (Edinburgh: 1990).

Dickson, A. (ed.), *Scottish Capitalism, Class, State, and Nation from before the Union to the Present* (London: 1980).

Dickson, P., *Red John of the Battles* (London: 1973).

Dickson, P. G. M., *The Financial Revolution in England: A Study in the Development of Public Credit, 1688–1756* (London: 1967).

Dingwall, H. M., *Late Seventeenth-century Edinburgh: A Demographic Study* (Aldershot: 1994).

Donaldson, G., *Scotland, James V to James VII*, The Edinburgh History of Scotland, vol. iii (Edinburgh: 1965).

Donaldson, G. (ed.), *Scottish Historical Documents* (Edinburgh: 1970).

Donovan, A. L., *Philosophical Chemistry in the Scottish Enlightenment: The Doctrines and Discoveries of William Cullen and Joseph Black* (Edinburgh: 1975).

Drummond, I. M., *The Gold Standard and the International Monetary System 1900–1939* (London: 1987).

Drury, A. C., *Finance Houses: Their Development and Role in the Modern Financial Sector* (London: 1982).

Duckham, Baron Frederick, *A History of the Scottish Coal Industry*, vol. i, 1700–1815 (Newton Abbot: 1970).

Durie, A., *The Scottish Linen Industry in the Eighteenth Century* (Edinburgh: 1979).

Dutt, R., *The Economic History of India in the Victorian Age*, 2nd edn (London: 1906).

Edelstein, M., *Overseas Investment in the Age of High Imperialism: The United*

Kingdom, 1850–1914 (London: 1982).

Ensor, R. C. K., *England 1870–1914* (Oxford: 1936).

Feavearyear, Sir Albert, *The Pound Sterling: A History of English Money*, 2nd edn, revised by E. V. Morgan (Oxford: 1963).

Ferguson, W., *Scotland: 1689 to the Present*, The Edinburgh History of Scotland, vol. iv (Edinburgh: 1968).

Ferguson, W., *Scotland's Relations with England: A Survey to 1707* (Edinburgh: 1977).

Fetter, F. W., *The Irish Pound* (London: 1955).

Fetter, F. W., *The Development of British Monetary Orthodoxy 1797–1875* (Cambridge, MA: 1965).

Fforde, J., *The Bank of England and Public Policy 1941–1958* (Cambridge: 1992).

Fleming, J. S., *Scottish Banking: A Historical Sketch with Notes and an Appendix*, 3rd edn (Edinburgh: 1877).

Flinn, M. W. (ed.), *Scottish Population History from the Seventeenth Century to the 1930s* (Cambridge: 1977).

Forbes, Sir William, *Memoirs of a Banking House* (Edinburgh: 1860).

Forsyth, D. J. C., *US Investment in Scotland* (New York: 1972).

Fossen, A. B., *Jørgen Thormøhlen, Forretningsmann, Storreder, Finansgeni* (Bergen: 1978).

Foster, J. and Woolfson, C., *The Politics of the UCS Work-In* (London: 1986).

Fry, R., *A Banker's World: The Revival of the City 1957–1970* (London: 1970).

Furber, H., *Henry Dundas, First Viscount Melville 1742–1811* (Oxford: 1931).

Gairdner, C. D., *Autobiography* (Kilmarnock: 1902).

Gash, N., *Mr Secretary Peel: The Life of Sir Robert Peel to 1830* (London: 1961).

Gaskin, M., *The Scottish Banks: A Modern Survey* (London: 1965).

Gauldie, E. (ed.), *The Dundee Textile Industry 1790–1885, From the Papers of Peter Carmichael of Arthurstone*, Scottish History Society, 4th series, vol. 6 (Edinburgh: 1969).

Gayer, A. D., Rostow, W. W. and Schwartz, A. J., with the assistance of I. Frank, *The Growth and Fluctuation of the British Economy 1790–1850*, 2 vols (Oxford: 1953).

Gerschenkron, A., *Economic Backwardness in Historical Perspective* (London: 1965).

Gibb, A., *Glasgow: The Making of a City* (London: 1983).

Gibson, A. J. S. and Smout, T. C., *Prices, Food and Wages in Scotland 1550–1780* (Cambridge: 1995).

Gilbart, J. W., *The History, Principles and Practice of Banking*, 2 vols (1911).

Gill, C., *The Rise of the Irish Linen Industry* (Oxford: 1925).

Goodhart, C. A. E., *The Business of Banking 1880–1914* (London: 1972).

Graham, W., *The One Pound Note in the Rise and Progress of Banking in Scotland* (Edinburgh: 1886).

Grant, J. (ed.), *Seafield Correspondence from 1685 to 1708* (Edinburgh: 1912).

Green, E. and Moss, M., *A Business of National Importance: The Royal Mail Shipping Group, 1902–1937* (London: 1982).

Gregory, T. E. (ed.), *Select Statutes, Documents and Reports Relating to British*

Banking, 1832–1928, 2 vols (Oxford: 1929).

Gregory, T. E., *The Westminster Bank Through a Century*, 2 vols (London: 1936).

Gurley, J. G. and Shaw, E. S., *Money in a Theory of Finance* (Washington, DC: 1960).

Haldane, R. B. S., *The Drove Roads of Scotland*, 2nd edn (Edinburgh: 1973).

Hall, A. R. (ed.), *The Export of Capital from Britain, 1870–1914* (London: 1968).

Hall, F. G., *The Bank of Ireland* (Dublin: 1949).

Hamilton, H., *The Industrial Revolution in Scotland* (Edinburgh: 1932).

Hamilton, H., *An Economic History of Scotland in the Eighteenth Century* (Oxford: 1963).

Harris, R., Naylor, M. and Seldon, A., *Hire Purchase in a Free Society*, 3rd edn (London: 1961).

Harrod, R. F., *The Life of John Maynard Keynes* (London: 1951; repr. New York: 1969).

Harvie, C., *Fool's Gold: The Story of North Sea Oil* (London: 1994).

Hawke, G. R., *Railways and Economic Growth in England and Wales 1840–1870* (Oxford: 1990).

Hawtrey, R. G., *A Century of Bank Rate* (London: 1938).

Healey, E., *Coutts & Co. 1692–1992: The Portrait of a Private Bank* (London: 1992).

Henderson, T., *The Savings Bank of Glasgow: One Hundred Years of Thrift* (Glasgow: 1936).

Hewins, W. A. S., *The Whitefoord Papers* (Oxford: 1898).

Hirst, F. W. and Allen, J. E., *British War Budgets* (Oxford: 1926).

Holmes, A. R. and Green, E., *Midland: 150 Years of Banking Business* (London: 1986).

Hopkins, P., *Glencoe and the End of the Highland War* (Edinburgh: 1986).

Hoppit, J., *Risk and Failure in English Business, 1700–1800* (Cambridge: 1987).

Horne, A., *Macmillan: 1957–1986*, 2 vols, vol. ii of the official biography (London: 1989).

Horne, H. O., *A History of Savings Banks* (Oxford: 1947).

Horsefield, J. K., *British Monetary Experiments, 1650–1710* (London: 1960).

Houston, R. A., *Scottish Literacy and the Scottish Identity: Illiteracy and Society in Scotland and Northern England 1600–1800* (Cambridge: 1985).

Hughes, P. R., *British Economic History, 1945–1987, Broad Historical Narrative*, Queen Mary College, Economic Papers, no. 184 (London: 1988).

Hume, J. and Moss, M., *Beardmore: The History of a Scottish Industrial Giant* (London: 1979).

Hutchinson, I. G. C., *A Political History of Scotland, 1832–1924* (Edinburgh: 1986).

Hutton, G., *We Too Can Prosper: The Promise of Productivity* (London: 1953).

Hutton, R., *Charles the Second King of England, Scotland, and Ireland* (Oxford: 1989).

Ingham, G., *Capitalism Divided? The City and Industry in British Social Development* (London: 1984).

Insh, G. P., *Scottish Colonial Schemes, 1620–1686* (Glasgow: 1922).

Insh, G. P., *The Company of Scotland Trading to Africa and the Indies* (London: 1932).

Jackson, G., with K. Kinnear, *The Trade and Shipping of Dundee 1780–1850*, Abertay Historical Society, no. 31 (Dundee: 1991).

Jackson, W. T., *The Enterprising Scot: Investors in the American West after 1873* (Edinburgh: 1968).

Jenks, L. H., *The Migration of British Capital to 1875* (London: 1927).

Johnston, T. L., Buxton, N. K. and Mair, D., *Structure and Growth of the Scottish Economy* (London: 1971).

Jones, D. W., *War and Economy in the Age of William III and Marlborough* (Oxford: 1988).

Keith, A., *The North of Scotland Bank* (Aberdeen: 1936).

Keith, T., *Commercial Relations of England and Scotland 1603–1707* (Cambridge: 1910).

Kenwood, A. G. and Lougheed, A. L., *The Growth of the International Economy 1820–1990: An Introductory Text*, 3rd edn (London: 1992).

Kerr, A. W., *History of Banking in Scotland* (1st edn, 1884; 2nd edn, 1902; 3rd edn, 1908), 4th edn (London: 1926).

Keynes, J. M., *The General Theory of Employment, Interest and Money* (London: 1936; repr. 1970).

Keynes, J. M., *A Treatise on Money*, 2 vols (1930), in *The Collected Writings of John Maynard Keynes*, vols v–vi (London: 1971).

Keynes, J. M., *How to Pay for the War* (1940), in *The Collected Writings of John Maynard Keynes*, vol. ix, *Essays in Persuasion* (London: 1972), 367–439.

Keynes, J. M., *The Collected Writings of John Maynard Keynes*, vol. xvi, *Activities 1914–1919: The Treasury and Versailles*, ed. Elizabeth Johnson (London: 1971).

Keynes, J. M., *The Collected Writings of John Maynard Keynes*, vol. xx, *Activities 1929–1931: Rethinking Employment and Unemployment Policies*, ed. D. E. Moggridge (Cambridge: 1981).

King, W. T. C., *History of the London Discount Market* (London: 1936).

Kumar, D. and Raychaudhuri, T. (eds), with the assistance of M. Desai, *The Cambridge Economic History of India*, vol. ii, *c. 1757 to c. 1970* (Cambridge: 1983).

Kyd, J. G. (ed.), *Scottish Population Statistics: including Webster's Analysis of Population, 1755*, Scottish History Society, 3rd series, vol. 43 (Edinburgh: 1952).

Kynaston, D., *The City of London*, vol. i, *A World of Its Own, 1815–1890* (London: 1994).

Landes, D. S., *The Unbound Prometheus: Technological Change and Industrial Development in Western Europe from 1750 to the Present* (Cambridge: 1970).

Lang, A., *Life, Letters and Diaries of Sir Stafford Northcote, First Earl of Iddesleigh*, 2nd edn (Edinburgh: 1891).

Lang, A., *A History of Scotland from the Roman Occupation*, 2nd edn, 4 vols (Edinburgh: 1909).

Lardner, D., *The Electric Telegraph Popularised* (London: 1855).

League of Nations, *The Network of World Trade: A Companion Volume to 'Europe's*

Trade' (Geneva: 1942).

Lee, C. H., *British Regional Employment Statistics 1841–1971* (Cambridge: 1979).

Lenman, B. P., *From Esk to Tweed: Harbours, Ships and Men of the East Coast of Scotland* (Glasgow: 1975).

Lenman, B. P., *An Economic History of Modern Scotland 1660–1976* (London: 1977).

Lenman, B. P., *Integration, Enlightenment and Industrialisation, Scotland, 1746–1832* (London: 1981).

Lenman, B. P., *The Jacobite Risings in Britain 1689–1746* (London: 1984).

Lenman, B. P., Lythe, C. and Gauldie, E., *Dundee and its Textile Industry, 1850–1914*, Abertay Historical Society, no. 14 (Dundee: 1969).

Levi, L., *History of British Commerce* (London: 1872).

Levy, C., *Ardrossan Shipyard: Struggle for Survival 1825–1983* (Ardrossan: n.d. [1986]).

Lewis, J. P., *Building Cycles and Britain's Growth* (London: 1965).

Lloyd George, D., *War Memoirs*, vol. i (London: 1938).

Lyman, R. W., *The First Labour Government, 1924* (London: 1957).

Lyon, D. M., *History of the Lodge of Edinburgh (Mary's Chapel) no. 1* (London: 1900).

McCann, T. J., *The Correspondence of the Dukes of Richmond and Newcastle 1724–1750*, Sussex Record Society, vol. 73 (1982–3).

McCulloch, J. R., *A Treatise on Metallic and Paper Money and Banks* (Edinburgh: 1858).

McCusker, J. J., *Money and Exchange in Europe and America 1600–1775* (London: 1978).

Mackinnon, J., *The Union of England and Scotland: A Study of International History* (London: 1896).

Macleod, Rev. W. (ed.), *Journal of the Hon. John Erskine of Carnock, 1683–1687*, Scottish History Society Publications, vol. 14 (Edinburgh: 1893).

Macmillan, H., *Pointing the Way 1959–1961* (London: 1972).

Malcolm, C. A., *The Bank of Scotland, 1695–1945* (Edinburgh: n.d. [1948]).

Malcolm, C. A., *The History of the British Linen Bank* (Edinburgh: 1950).

Mallet, Sir Bernard and George, C. O., *British Budgets, 1913–14 to 1920–21*, 2nd series (London: 1929).

Marder, A., *British Naval Policy 1880–1905* (London: 1940).

Marion, M., *Histoire financière de la France depuis 1715*, vol. v, 1819–1875 (Paris: 1928).

Marshall, G., *Presbyteries and Profits: Calvinism and the Development of Capitalism in Scotland, 1560–1707* (Oxford: 1980).

Marwick, J. D. (ed.), *Extracts from the Records of the Convention of the Royal Burghs of Scotland 1677–1711* (Edinburgh: 1880).

Marx, K. and Engels, F., *Correspondence, 1846–1895. A Selection with Commentary and Notes* (London: 1934).

Matheson, C., *The Life of Henry Dundas, First Viscount Melville* (London: 1933).

Mathias, P., *The First Industrial Nation*, 2nd edn (London: 1983).

Mathieson, W. L., *Scotland and the Union: A History of Scotland from 1695 to 1747* (Glasgow: 1905).

Maxwell, H., *Annals of the Scottish Widows Fund Life Assurance Society 1815–1914* (Edinburgh: 1914).

Meikle, H., *Scotland and the French Revolution* (Glasgow: 1912).

Menarty, G., *Life and Letters of Duncan Forbes of Culloden* (London: 1936).

Michie, R. C., *Money, Mania and Markets. Investment, Company Formation and the Stock Exchange in Nineteenth-Century Scotland* (Edinburgh: 1981).

Mitchell, B. R., *British Historical Statistics* (Cambridge: 1988).

Mitchell, B. R. and Deane, P., *Abstract of British Historical Statistics* (Cambridge: 1962).

Mitchison, R., *Agricultural Sir John: The Life of Sir John Sinclair of Ulbster 1754–1835* (London: 1962).

Mitchison, R., *A History of Scotland* (London: 1970).

Mitchison, R., *Lordship to Patronage, Scotland 1603–1745* (Edinburgh: 1983).

Moggridge, D. E., *The Return to Gold 1925* (Cambridge: 1969).

Moggridge, D. E., *British Monetary Policy 1924–1931* (Cambridge: 1972).

Morgan, E. V., *Studies in British Financial Policy, 1914–25* (London: 1952).

Morley, J., *The Life of William Ewart Gladstone*, 3 vols, vol. ii (London: 1903).

Moss, M. and Russell, I., *Range and Vision: The First Hundred Years of Barr & Stroud* (Edinburgh: 1988).

Moss, M. and Slaven, A., *From Ledger Book to Laser Beam. A History of the TSB in Scotland from 1810 to 1990* (Edinburgh: n.d. [1992]).

Mossner, E. C. and Ross, I. S., *The Correspondence of Adam Smith* (Oxford: 1977).

Mowat, C. L., *Britain between the Wars 1918–40*, 2nd edn (London: 1956).

Munn, C. W., *The Scottish Provincial Banking Companies, 1747–1864* (Edinburgh: 1981).

Munn, C. W., *Clydesdale Bank: The First One Hundred and Fifty Years* (Glasgow: 1988).

Munro, N., *The History of the Royal Bank of Scotland 1727–1927* (Edinburgh: 1928).

Mure, W. (ed.), *Selections from the Family Papers Preserved at Caldwell*, 2 vols, Part 1, *1733–1764*; Part 2, *1765–1821*, Proceedings of the Maitland Club, 71 (Glasgow: 1854).

Murray, K. A. H., *Agriculture*, History of the Second World War, United Kingdom civil series (London: 1955).

O'Brien, P. and Quinault, R. (eds), *The Industrial Revolution and British Society* (Cambridge: 1993).

Ollerenshaw, P., *Banking in Nineteenth Century Ireland: The Belfast Banks, 1825–1914* (Manchester: 1987).

Payne, P. L. (ed.), *Studies in Scottish Business History* (London: 1967).

Payne, P. L., *Colvilles and the Scottish Steel Industry* (Oxford: 1979).

Payne, P. L., *The Hydro: A Study of the Development of the Major Hydro-Electric Schemes Undertaken by the North of Scotland Hydro-Electric Board* (Aberdeen: 1988).

Payne, P. L., *Growth & Contraction Scottish Industry c. 1860–1990* (Glasgow: 1992).

Peden, G. C., *Keynes, the Treasury and British Economic Policy* (London: 1988).

1053

Peebles, H. B., *Warshipbuilding on the Clyde: Naval Orders and the Prosperity of the Clyde Shipbuilding Industry, 1889–1939* (Edinburgh: 1987).

Phillipson, N. T., *David Hume* (London: 1989).

Phillipson, N. T. and Mitchison, R. (eds), *Scotland in the Age of Improvement* (Edinburgh: 1970).

Plumb, J. H., *Sir Robert Walpole: The King's Minister* (London: 1960).

Plumb, J. H., *The Growth of Political Stability in England 1675–1725* (London: 1967).

Pollard, S., *The Genesis of Modern Management* (London: 1967).

Pollard, S., *The Development of the British Economy 1914–1967*, 2nd edn (London: 1969).

Pollard, S. (ed.), *The Gold Standard and Employment Policies between the Wars* (London: 1970).

Popplewell, L., *A Gazetteer of the Railway Contractors and Engineers of Scotland 1831–1914*, 2 vols, vol. i, *1831–1870* (Bournemouth: 1989).

Porter, B., *The Lion's Share. A Short History of British Imperialism 1850–1883*, 2nd edn (London: 1984).

Powell, E. T., *The Evolution of the Money Market* (London: 1915).

Prebble, J., *The Darien Disaster* (London: 1968).

Pressnell, L. S., *Country Banking in the Industrial Revolution* (Oxford: 1956).

Rae, G., *The Country Banker* (London: 1917 edn).

Rait, R. S., *The Parliaments of Scotland* (Glasgow: 1924).

Rait, R. S., *The History of the Union Bank of Scotland* (Glasgow: 1930).

Reed, M. C. (ed.), *Railways in the Victorian Economy* (Newton Abbot: 1969).

Reid, J. M., *The History of the Clydesdale Bank, 1838–1938* (Glasgow: 1938).

Reid, M., *The Secondary Banking Crisis 1973–75: Its Causes and Course* (London: 1982).

Renwick, R. (ed.), *Extracts from the Records of the Burgh of Glasgow*, Scottish Burgh Records Society, vol. xi, *1823–1833* (Glasgow: 1916).

Riley, P. W. J., *The English Ministers and Scotland 1707–1727*, Institute of Historical Research Publications, no. 15 (London: 1964).

Riley, P. W. J., *The Union of England and Scotland* (Manchester: 1978).

Riley, P. W. J., *King William and the Scottish Politicians* (Edinburgh: 1979).

Rimmer, W. G., *Marshalls of Leeds, Flax Spinners, 1788–1886* (London: 1960).

Roberts, R., *Schroders: Merchants and Bankers* (London: 1992).

Roseveare, H., *The Treasury: The Evolution of a British Institution* (London: 1969).

Roseveare, H., *The Treasury: 1660–1870* (London: 1973).

Rostas, L., *Comparative Productivity in British and American Industry* (Cambridge: 1948).

Saville, R. (ed.), *The Economic Development of Modern Scotland 1950–1980* (Edinburgh: 1985).

Sayers, R. S., *Financial Policy 1939–45* (London: 1956).

Sayers, R. S., *Central Banking after Bagehot* (Oxford: 1957).

Sayers, R. S., *Modern Banking*, 3rd edn (Oxford: 1967).

Sayers, R. S., *The Bank of England 1891–1944* (Cambridge: 1986).

Scott, J. and Hughes, M., *The Anatomy of Scottish Capital: Scottish Companies and*

Scottish Capital, 1900–1979 (London: 1980).

Scott, W. R. (ed.), *The Records of a Scottish Cloth Manufactory at New Mills, Haddingtonshire, 1681–1703*, Scottish History Society Publications, vol. 46 (Edinburgh: 1905).

Scott, W. R., *The Constitution and Finance of English, Scottish and Irish Joint-Stock Companies to 1720*, 3 vols (Cambridge: 1910–12).

Scott, W. R. and Cunnison, J., *The Industries of the Clyde Valley during the War* (Oxford: 1924).

Shaw, J. S., *The Management of Scottish Society 1707–1764* (Edinburgh: 1983).

Shaw, W. A., *Select Tracts and Documents Illustrative of English Monetary History, 1626–1730* (London: 1896; repr. 1935).

Sheppard, D. K., *The Growth and Role of UK Financial Institutions 1880–1962* (London: 1971).

Simpson, J., *Scottish Banking: A Historical Sketch* (Edinburgh: 1877).

Sims, D. and Wood, M., *Car Manufacturing at Linwood: The Regional Policy Issues* (Paisley: 1984).

Slaven, A., *The Development of the West of Scotland, 1750–1960* (London: 1975).

Smout, T. C., *Scottish Trade on the Eve of Union 1660–1707* (Edinburgh: 1963).

Smout, T. C., *A History of the Scottish People 1560–1830* (London: 1969).

Smout, T. C., *A Century of the Scottish People 1830–1950* (London: 1986).

Stamp, J., *Taxation during the War*, Carnegie Endowment for International Peace (Oxford: 1932).

Steuart, J., *An Inquiry into the Principles of Political Economy*, ed. A. Skinner (Edinburgh: 1966).

Summerson, Sir John, *Georgian London* (London: 1945).

Supple, B., *The Royal Exchange Assurance: A History of British Insurance, 1720–1970* (Cambridge: 1970).

Sykes, J., *The Amalgamation Movement in English Banking 1825–1924* (London: 1926).

Symon, J. A., *Scottish Farming Past and Present* (Edinburgh: 1959).

Szechi, D., *Jacobitism and Tory Politics 1710–14* (Edinburgh: 1984).

Tamaki, N., *The Life Cycle of the Union Bank of Scotland 1830–1954* (Aberdeen: 1983).

Tayler, A. and Tayler, H., *Jacobites of Aberdeenshire and Banffshire in the Rising of 1715* (Edinburgh: 1934).

Taylor, A. J. P., *English History 1914–1939* (Oxford: 1965).

Taylor, F. S., *Banking in Scotland*, Scottish Banking Practice, no. 1 (Edinburgh: 1949).

Thatcher, M., *The Downing Street Years* (London: 1993).

Thomas, W. A., *The Finance of British Industry, 1918–1976* (London: 1978).

Thomson, W. T., *The Present Position of the Life Assurance Interests of Great Britain* (Edinburgh: 1852).

Timperley, L. R. (ed.), *A Directory of Landownership in Scotland c. 1770*, Scottish Record Office, new series, no. 5 (Edinburgh: 1976).

Tolliday, S., *Business, Banking and Politics: The Case of British Steel, 1918–1939* (Cambridge, MA: 1987).

Union Bank of Scotland, *Annual Reports* (Glasgow: 1858–1954).

Vilar, P., *History of Gold and Money 1450–1920* (London: 1976).

Warden, A. J., *The Linen Trade Ancient and Modern* (London: 1864).

Watson, J. S., *The Reign of George III 1760–1815* (Oxford: 1960).

Whetstone, A. E., *Scottish County Government in the Eighteenth and Nineteenth Centuries* (Edinburgh: 1981).

Wolowski, L. F., *La Banque d'Angleterre et les banques d'Ecosse* (Paris: 1867).

Woodward, L., *The Age of Reform, 1815–1870* (Oxford: 1962).

Yamey, B. S., Edey, H. C. and Thomson, H. W., *Accounting in England and Scotland: 1543–1800* (London: 1963; repr. New York: 1982).

Yergin, D., *The Prize* (London: 1991).

Yogev, G., *Diamonds and Coral: Anglo-Dutch and Eighteenth-Century Trade* (Leicester: 1978).

Youngson, A. J., *The Making of Classical Edinburgh 1750–1840* (Edinburgh: 1966).

Youngson, A. J., *After the Forty-Five: The Economic Impact on the Scottish Highlands* (Edinburgh: 1973).

Ziegler, D., *Central Banking, Peripheral Industry: The Bank of England in the Provinces 1826–1913* (Leicester: 1990).

Articles

Adie, D. K., 'English Bank Deposits before 1844', *Economic History Review*, 2nd series, 23 (1970), 285–97.

'Advances Gather Speed', *The Banker*, 109 (1959), 205.

Aitken, J., 'Official Regulation of British Overseas Investment, 1914–1931', *Economic History Review*, 2nd series, 23 (1970), 324–35.

Anderson, B. L., 'Money and the Structure of Credit in the Eighteenth Century', *Business History*, 12 (1970), 85–101.

Anderson, M., 'Population and Family Life', in A. Dickson and J. H. Treble (eds), *People and Society in Scotland*, vol. iii, *1914–1990* (Edinburgh: 1992), 12–47.

Antonio, D. G., 'Thomas Corrie', *Scottish Bankers Magazine*, 47 (1955), 38–43.

Ashton, T. S., 'The Bill of Exchange and Private Banks in Lancashire 1790–1830', in R. S. Sayers (ed.), *Papers in English Monetary History* (Oxford: 1953), 37–49.

Atherton, C., 'The Development of the Middle Class Suburb: The West End of Glasgow', *Scottish Economic and Social History Review*, 11 (1991), 19–35.

Bailey, J. D., 'Australian Borrowing in Scotland in the Nineteenth Century', *Economic History Review*, 2nd series, 12 (1959–60), 268–79.

Ballantyne, W. R., 'Presidential Address: A Banker for Hire Purchase', *The Banker*, 108 (1958), 419–20.

'Bank Investments', *Scottish Bankers Magazine*, 44 (1952–3), 136–9.

'The Bank of England – Agent of the Royal Bank of Scotland', *The Three Banks Review*, 39 (September 1958), 33–49.

'The Bank Results', *The Banker*, 121 (1971), 254–9.

'Banking and Hire Purchase', *Scottish Bankers Magazine*, 46 (1954–5), 204–8.

'The Banks and their Profits', *The Banker*, 110 (1960), 103–6.

'The Banks in Hire Purchase', *The Banker*, 108 (1958), 561–80.

Best, M. H. and Humphries, J., 'The City and Industrial Decline', in B. Elbaum and W. Lazonick (eds), *The Decline of the British Economy* (Oxford: 1986), 223–39.

Beveridge, Sir William, 'The Trade Cycle in Britain before 1850', *Oxford Economic Papers* (1940), 74–109.

Blanden, M., 'The Changing Shape of the Future', *The Banker*, 130 (September 1980), 87–90.

Bloomfield, G. T., 'New Integrated Motor Works in Scotland 1899–1914', *Industrial Archaeology Review*, 5 (1981), 127–41.

'Board of Agriculture for Scotland. Proposed Credit to Farmers against Government Guarantee', *Scottish Bankers Magazine*, 9 (1917), 275.

Brady, F., 'So Fast to Ruin: The Ayr Bank Crash', *Collections of the Ayrshire Archaeological and Natural History Society*, 11 (1973), 27–44.

Brotherstone, T., 'Does Red Clydeside Really Matter Any More?', in R. Duncan and A. McIvor (eds), *Militant Workers, Labour and Class Conflict on the Clyde 1900–1950* (Edinburgh: 1992), 52–80.

Brown, W. P., 'The Competition for Deposits', *Scottish Bankers Magazine*, 56 (1964–5), 71–91.

Butt, J., 'The Scottish Oil Mania of 1864–6', *Scottish Journal of Political Economy*, 12 (1965), 195–209.

Butt, J., 'The Scottish Cotton Industry during the Industrial Revolution 1780–1840', in L. M. Cullen and T. C. Smout (eds), *Comparative Aspects of Scottish and Irish Economic History 1600–1900* (Edinburgh: 1977), 116–28.

Buxton, N. K., 'Economic Growth in Scotland between the Wars: The Role of Production, Structure and Rationalisation', *Economic History Review*, 2nd series, 33 (1980), 538–55.

Buxton, N. K., 'The Scottish Economy, 1945–79: Performance, Structure and Problems', in R. Saville (ed.), *The Economic Development of Modern Scotland 1950–1980* (Edinburgh: 1985), 47–78.

Cairncross, A. K., 'Investment in Canada, 1900–1913', in A. R. Hall (ed.), *The Export of Capital from Britain, 1870–1914* (London: 1968), 153–86.

Cairncross, A. K. and Hunter, J. B. K., 'The Early Growth of Messrs J. & P. Coats, 1830–83', *Business History*, 29 (1987), 157–77.

Cairncross, A. K. and Weber, B., 'Fluctuations in Building in Great Britain 1785–1849', *Economic History Review*, 2nd series, 9 (1956–7), 282–97.

Campbell, A. D., 'Income', in A. K. Cairncross (ed.), *The Scottish Economy* (Cambridge: 1954), 46–64.

Campbell, A. D., 'Changes in Scottish Income, 1924–49', *Economic Journal*, 65 (1955), 225–40.

Campbell, R. H., 'Investment in the Scottish Pig Iron Trade 1830–43', *Scottish Journal of Economic History* (1954), 233–49.

Campbell, R. H., 'Edinburgh Bankers and the Western Bank of Scotland', *Scottish Journal of Political Economy*, 2 (1955), 133–48.

Campbell, R. H., 'The Financing of Carron Company', *Business History*, 1 (1958), 21–34.

Campbell, R. H., 'Early Malleable Iron Production in Scotland', *Business History*,

4 (1961), 22–33.

Campbell, R. H., 'The Anglo-Scottish Union of 1707, II: The Economic Consequences', *Economic History Review*, 2nd series, 16 (1963–4), 468–77.

Campbell, R. H., 'A Rejoinder' to F. S. Taylor on Scottish Banks in the Eighteenth Century, *Scottish Journal of Political Economy*, 12 (1965), 114–15.

Campbell, R. H., 'Costs and Contracts: Lessons from Clyde Shipbuilding between the Wars', in A. Slaven and D. H. Aldcroft (eds), *Business, Banking and Urban History: Essays in Honour of S. G. Checkland* (Edinburgh: 1982), 54–79.

Campbell, R. H. and Devine, T. M., 'The Rural Experience', in W. H. Fraser and R. J. Morris (eds), *People and Society in Scotland*, vol. ii, 1830–1914 (Edinburgh: 1990), 46–72.

Cassis, Y., 'Bankers in English Society in the Late Nineteenth Century', *Economic History Review*, 2nd series, 38 (1985), 210–29.

Cassis, Y., 'Management and Strategy in the English Joint-Stock Bank, 1890–1914', *Business History*, 27 (1985), 301–15.

'The Chairman of the Clydesdale Bank on the Problems of the War Crisis', *Scottish Bankers Magazine*, 8 (1916), 30–4.

Chase, M., '"Nothing Less than a Revolution"?: Labour's Agricultural Policy', in J. Fyrth (ed.), *Labour's High Noon: The Government and the Economy 1945–51* (London: 1993), 78–95.

Checkland, S. G., 'Two Scottish West India Liquidations after 1793', *Scottish Journal of Political Economy*, 4 (1957), 127–43.

Checkland, S. G., 'Adam Smith and the Bankers', in A. Skinner and T. Wilson (eds), *Essays on Adam Smith* (Oxford: 1975), 504–23.

Chesher, L. D., Sheppard, D. K. and Whitwell, J., 'Have British Banks Been Imprudent?', *The Banker*, 125 (1975), 31–9.

'CIC Suspended', *The Banker*, 109 (1959), 141.

Clarke, T. and Dickson, T., 'Class and Class Consciousness in Early Industrial Capitalism, Paisley 1770–1850', in T. Dickson (ed.), *Capital and Class in Scotland* (Edinburgh: 1982), 8–60.

Clarke, T. and Dickson, T., 'Social Concern and Social Control in Nineteenth Century Scotland: Paisley 1841–1843', *Scottish Historical Review*, 65 (1986), 48–60.

Collins, M., 'The Banking Crisis of 1878', *Economic History Review*, 2nd series, 42 (1989), 504–27.

Collins, M. and Hudson, P., 'Provincial Bank Lending: Yorkshire and Merseyside 1826–1860', *Bulletin of Economic Research*, 31 (1979), 69–79.

Cowen, H., 'Changes in Hire Purchase Finance', *The Banker*, 85 (1948), 93–9.

Crouzet, F., 'Capital Formation in Great Britain during the Industrial Revolution', in idem (ed.), *Capital Formation in the Industrial Revolution* (London: 1972), 162–222.

Curtis, C. R., 'Hire Purchase Finance and Machine Control', *The Banker*, 42 (1937), 118–25.

'Danger Signals for Banking', *The Banker*, 124 (1974), 12–13.

Devine, T. M., 'Sources of Finance for the Glasgow Tobacco Trade c. 1740–1780',

Business History, 16 (1974), 113–29.

Devine, T. M., 'Colonial Commerce and the Scottish Economy, c. 1730–1815', in L. M. Cullen and T. C. Smout (eds), *Comparative Aspects of Scottish and Irish Economic History 1600–1900* (Edinburgh: 1977), 177–90.

Devine, T. M., 'The Merchant Class of the Larger Scottish Towns in the Later Seventeenth and Early Eighteenth Centuries', in G. Gordon and B. Dicks (eds), *Scottish Urban History* (Aberdeen: 1983), 92–111.

Devine, T. M., 'The Union of 1707 and Scottish Development', *Scottish Economic and Social History Review*, 5 (1985), 23–40.

Devine, T. M., 'Urbanisation', in T. M. Devine and R. Mitchison (eds), *People and Society in Scotland*, vol. i, 1760–1830 (Edinburgh: 1988), 27–52.

Dillen, J. G. van, 'The Bank of Amsterdam', in idem (ed.), *History of the Principal Public Banks accompanied by Extensive Bibliographies of the History of Banking and Credit in Eleven European Countries* (The Hague: 1934), 79–124.

Dodgshon, R. A., 'Agricultural Change and its Social Consequences in the Southern Uplands of Scotland 1600–1780', in T. M. Devine and D. Dickson (eds), *Ireland and Scotland, 1600–1850: Parallels and Contrasts in Economic and Social Development* (Edinburgh: 1983), 46–59.

Donnachie, I. L. and Butt, J., 'The Wilsons of Wilsontown Ironworks (1779–1813): A Study in Entrepreneurial Failure', *Explorations in Entrepreneurial History*, 4 (1967), 150–68.

Drummond, I., 'Britain and the World Economy, 1900–45', in R. Floud and D. McCloskey (eds), *The Economic History of Britain since 1700*, vol. ii, 1860 to the 1970s (Cambridge: 1981), 286–307.

Dwyer, J. and Murdoch, A., 'Paradigms and Politics: Manners, Morals and the Rise of Henry Dundas, 1770–1784', in J. Dwyer, R. Mason and A. Murdoch (eds), *New Perspectives on the Politics and Culture of Early Modern Scotland* (Edinburgh: 1981), 210–48.

Dyer, M., '"Mere Detail and Machinery": The Great Reform Act and the Effects of Redistribution on Scottish Representation, 1832–1868', *Scottish Historical Review*, 62 (1983), 17–34.

'Early Scottish Railways', *The Three Banks Review*, 74 (June 1967), 29–39.

Fairlie, S., 'Dyestuffs in the Eighteenth Century', *Economic History Review*, 2nd series, 17 (1965), 488–510.

Ferguson, W., 'The Making of the Treaty of Union of 1707', *Scottish Historical Review*, 43 (1964), 89–110.

Ferguson, W., 'The Reform Act (Scotland) of 1832: Intention and Effect', *Scottish Historical Review*, 45 (1966), 105–14.

'Finance for Industry: Industrial and Commercial Finance Corporation Limited', *Scottish Bankers Magazine*, 37 (1945–6), 91–3.

Fleming, J. S., 'On the Theory and Practice of Banking in Scotland', *Journal of the Institute of Bankers* (1883), 129–58.

Forge, F. W., 'Scottish Banking in 1943–44', *The Banker*, 72 (1944), 84–9.

Forge, F. W., 'Scottish Banks Face the Transition', *The Banker*, 80 (1946), 91–4.

Foster, J., 'Red Clyde, Red Scotland', in I. Donnachie and C. Whatley (eds), *The Manufacture of Scottish History* (Edinburgh: 1992), 106–24.

Foster, W., 'The East India Company, 1600–1740', in H. H. Dodwell (ed.), *The Cambridge History of India*, vol. v, *British India 1497–1858* (Cambridge: 1929), 97–8.

Foxwell, H. S., Address to the Royal Institution, April 1917, repr. as 'The Nature of the Industrial Struggle', *Economic Journal*, 27 (1917), 315–29.

Foxwell, H. S., Address to the Royal Institution, April 1917, repr. as 'The Financing of Industry and Trade', *Economic Journal*, 27 (1917), 502–22.

Freebairn, C. F., 'An Old Banking Institution: The Paisley Union Bank', *Scottish Bankers Magazine*, 16 (1924), 110–20.

'The Future of Women in Banks', *The Bankers' Magazine*, 106 (December 1918), 568–72.

Gaskin, M., 'The Note Issue in Modern Scottish Banking', *Scottish Journal of Political Economy*, 1 (1954), 154–73.

Gaskin, M., 'The Profitability of the Scottish Note Issues', *Scottish Journal of Political Economy*, 3 (1956), 188–204.

Gaskin, M., 'Anglo-Scottish Banking Conflicts, 1874–1881', *Economic History Review*, 2nd series, 12 (1960), 445–55.

Gaskin, M., 'Radcliffe on the Scottish Banks', *Scottish Journal of Political Economy*, 7 (1960), 65–8.

Gaskin, M., 'The Supply of Finance in Scotland', unpublished paper (1961).

Gibb, A. and Maclennan, D., 'Policy and Process in Scottish Housing 1950–1980', in R. Saville (ed.), *The Economic Development of Modern Scotland 1950–1980* (Edinburgh: 1985), 270–91.

Gibson, A. T., 'The Bank Office of the Future', *Scottish Bankers Magazine*, 58 (1966–7), 66–84.

Gibson, A. T., 'All-purpose Banking', *Scottish Bankers Magazine*, 60 (1968–9), 77–95.

'Gilt-edged through Fifty Years', *The Banker*, 95 (1950), 88–96.

Gourvish, T. R., 'Bank of Scotland, 1830–45', *Scottish Journal of Political Economy*, 16 (1969), 288–305.

Gourvish, T. R., and Reed, M. C., 'The Financing of Scottish Railways before 1860 – A Comment', *Scottish Journal of Political Economy*, 18 (1971), 209–20.

Gray, M., 'The Kelp Industry in the Highlands and Islands', *Economic History Review*, 2nd series, 4 (1951–2), 197–209.

Green, R., 'Real Bills Doctrine', in J. Eatwell, M. Milgate and P. Newman (eds), *The New Palgrave* (London: 1989), 310–13.

Gurley, J. G. and Shaw, E. S., 'Financial Aspects of Economic Development', *American Economic Review*, 45 (1955), 515–38.

Hamilton, H., 'The Founding of Carron Ironworks', *Scottish Historical Review*, 25 (1928), 185–93.

Hamilton, H., 'Scotland's Balance of Payments Problem in 1762', *Economic History Review*, 2nd series, 5 (1953), 344–57.

Hamilton, H., 'The Failure of the Ayr Bank, 1772', *Economic History Review*, 2nd series, 8 (1956), 405–17.

Harley, C. K. and McCloskey, D., 'Foreign Trade: Competition and the Expanding International Economy', in R. Floud and D. McCloskey (eds), *The*

Economic History of Britain since 1700, vol. ii, *1860 to the 1970s* (Cambridge: 1981), 50–69.

Harsin, P., 'La Banque et le système de law', in J. G. van Dillen (ed.), *History of the Principal Public Banks accompanied by Extensive Bibliographies of the History of Banking and Credit in Eleven European Countries* (The Hague: 1934), 273–300.

Hawke, G. R. and Reed, M. C., 'Railway Capital in the United Kingdom in the Nineteenth Century', *Economic History Review*, 2nd series, 22 (1969), 269–86.

Heckscher, E. F., 'The Bank of Sweden in its Connection with the Bank of Amsterdam', in J. G. van Dillen (ed.), *History of the Principal Public Banks accompanied by Extensive Bibliographies of the History of Banking and Credit in Eleven European Countries* (The Hague: 1934), 161–99.

Hendry, G. F., 'Bank Advance to Scottish Agriculture', *Scottish Agricultural Economics*, vol. vi (Edinburgh: 1955), 41.

Hindle, T., 'Sizing up the Retail Market', *The Banker*, 130 (November 1980), 111–19.

Hird, N. L., 'Scottish Banking in 1942/43', *The Banker*, 68 (1943), 73–7.

'The Hire Purchase Structure', *The Banker*, 108 (1958), 598–605.

'Hire Purchase: What Went Wrong', *Scottish Bankers Magazine*, 53 (1961–2), 227–31.

Hobsbawm, E., 'Capitalisme et agriculture: les réformateurs écossais au XVIII siècle', *Annales: économies, sociétés, civilisations*, 33:3 (May–June 1978), 580–601.

Holmes, G., 'The Hamilton Affair of 1711–1712: A Crisis in Anglo-Scottish Relations', in C. Jones and D. L. Jones (eds), *Peers, Politics and Power: The House of Lords, 1603–1911* (London: 1986), 151–76.

Horsefield, J. K., 'The Duties of a Banker, I: The Eighteenth Century View', in T. S. Ashton and R. S. Sayers (eds), *Papers in English Monetary History* (Oxford: 1953), 1–15.

Horsefield, J. K., 'The "Stop of the Exchequer" Revisited', *Economic History Review*, 2nd series, 35 (1982), 511–28.

Houston, G. F. B., 'Agriculture', in A. K. Cairncross (ed.), *The Scottish Economy* (Cambridge: 1954), 84–108.

'HP's Morning After', *The Banker*, 111 (1961), 15–18.

Hueckel, G., 'Agriculture during Industrialisation', in R. Floud and D. McCloskey (eds), *The Economic History of Britain since 1700*, 2 vols, vol. i, *1700–1860* (Cambridge: 1981), 182–203.

Hume, D., 'Of Money', 'Of Interest' and 'Of the Balance of Trade', in E. Rotwein (ed.), *David Hume: Writings on Economics* (Edinburgh: 1955), 33–46, 47–59, 60–77.

Hunter, L., 'The Scottish Labour Market', in R. Saville (ed.), *The Economic Development of Modern Scotland 1950–1980* (Edinburgh: 1985), 163–82.

Hutton, G. M., 'Stair's Public Career', in D. M. Walker (ed.), *Stair Tercentenary Studies*, Stair Society Publications, 33 (Edinburgh: 1981), 1–68.

Imlah, A. H., 'British Balance of Payments and Exports of Capital, 1816–1913',

Economic History Review, 2nd series, 5 (1952–3), 208–39.

Irving, R. J., 'The Profitability and Performance of British Railways, 1870–1914', *Economic History Review*, 2nd series, 31 (1978), 46–66.

Jones, P., 'The Scottish Professoriate and the Polite Academy, 1720–46', in I. Hont and M. Ignatieff (eds), *Wealth and Virtue: The Shaping of Political Economy in the Scottish Enlightenment* (Cambridge: 1985), 89–117.

Joslin, D. M., 'London Bankers in Wartime 1739–84', in L. S. Pressnell (ed.), *Studies in the Industrial Revolution* (London: 1960), 156–77.

Krayenbuehl, T. E., 'How Country Risk should be Monitored', *The Banker*, 133 (May 1983), 51–3.

Lascelles, D., 'US Bank Regulation after the Debt "Crisis"', *The Banker*, 133 (January 1983), 21–3.

Lehmann, W. C., 'John Millar, Historical Sociologist: Some Remarkable Anticipations of Modern Sociology', *British Journal of Sociology*, 3:1 (March 1952), 30–46.

Lenman, B. P. and Donaldson, K., 'Partners' Incomes, Investment and Diversification in the Scottish Linen Area, 1850–1921', *Business History*, 13 (1971), 1–18.

Lenman, B. P. and Gauldie, E. E., 'The Industrial History of the Dundee Region from the Eighteenth to the Early Twentieth Century', in S. J. Jones (ed.), *Dundee and District* (Dundee: 1968), 162–73.

'Letters from a Young Lady' [Miss Marianne Thornton to Mrs Hannah More], *The Three Banks Review*, 6 (June 1950), 29–46.

Little, L. T., 'Insurance Companies and Industrial Capital', *The Banker*, 95 (1950), 80–7.

Lockie, J., 'Influences on Banking in 1947', *Scottish Bankers Magazine*, 40 (1948–9), 15–21.

Logan, J. C., 'Electricity Supply, Electrical Engineering and the Scottish Economy in the Inter-war Years', in A. J. G. Cummings and T. M. Devine (eds), *Industry, Business and Society in Scotland since 1700: Essays presented to Professor John Butt* (Edinburgh: 1994), 101–24.

Lowe, R., 'The Erosion of State Intervention in Britain, 1917–24', *Economic History Review*, 2nd series, 32 (1978), 270–86.

Luard, C. E., 'The Indian States 1818–57', in H. H. Dodwell (ed.), *The Cambridge History of India*, vol. v, *British India 1497–1858* (Cambridge: 1929), 570–88.

Macaulay, G., 'Investing in Government Securities – I', *Scottish Bankers Magazine*, 42 (1950–1), 89–96.

Macaulay, G., 'The Personal Loan Interview', *Scottish Bankers Magazine*, 52 (1960–1), 212–20.

McBain, A. G., 'Excess Profits Tax', *Scottish Bankers Magazine*, 35 (1943–4), 7–11, 52–6, 92–5, 135–7.

McCrone, G., 'The Role of Government', in R. Saville (ed.), *The Economic Development of Modern Scotland 1950–1980* (Edinburgh: 1985), 195–213.

MacDougall, M. S., 'Control and Supervision of Banking', *Scottish Bankers Magazine*, 67 (1975–6), 277–84.

McEwan, A., 'The Securities Department during the War: A Brief Sketch',

Scottish Bankers Magazine, 12 (1920), 20–7.

Mackenzie, K., 'Profit Sharing and Co-Partnership', *Scottish Bankers Magazine*, 16 (1924), 23–30.

McKinley, A., 'The Inter-War Depression and the Effort Bargain: Shipyard Riveters and the Workman's Foreman, 1919–1939', *Scottish Economic and Social History Review*, 9 (1989), 55–70.

McKinstry, S., 'The Albion Motor Car Company: Growth and Specialisation, 1899–1918', *Scottish Economic and Social History Review*, 11 (1991), 36–51.

Macpherson, W. J., 'Investment in Indian Railways, 1845–1875', *Economic History Review*, 2nd series, 8 (1955–6), 177–86.

McRae, H., 'London's Shifting Money Markets', *The Banker*, 120 (1970), 33–40.

'Market Reports and Business Notes: The Money Market', *Scottish Bankers Magazine*, 39 (1947–8), 180–1.

Martin, R. S., 'City Comment', *Glasgow Herald*, 17 December 1982.

Marvin, J., 'How Hire Purchase has Grown', *The Banker*, 104 (1955), 155–63.

Marwick, J. D. (ed.), 'Register containing the State and Condition of every Burgh within the Kingdom of Scotland in the Year 1692', *Miscellany of the Scottish Burgh Records Society* (1881).

Marwick, W. H., 'The Cotton Industry and the Industrial Revolution in Scotland', *Scottish Historical Review*, 21 (1924), 207–18.

Mason, W. E., 'Ricardo's Transfer-Mechanism Theory', *Quarterly Journal of Economics*, 71 (1957), 107–15.

Mitchison, R., 'The Movements of Scottish Corn Prices in the Seventeenth and Eighteenth Centuries', *Economic History Review*, 2nd series, 18 (1965), 278–91.

Mitchison, R., 'Scotland 1750–1850', in F. M. L. Thompson (ed.), *The Cambridge Social History of Britain 1750–1950*, 2 vols (Cambridge: 1990), vol. i, *Regions and Communities*, 155–207.

Montgomery, F. A., 'Glasgow and the Movement for Corn Law Repeal', *History*, 64 (1979), 363–79.

Montgomery, F. A., 'Glasgow and the Struggle for Parliamentary Reform, 1830–1832', *Scottish Historical Review*, 61 (1982), 130–45.

Morgan, E. V. and Richards, I. M., 'A Verdict on Competition and Credit Controls', *The Banker*, 124 (1974), 571–8.

Morgan, N. and Trainor, R., 'The Dominant Classes', in W. H. Fraser and R. J. Morris (eds), *People and Society in Scotland*, vol. ii, *1830–1914* (Edinburgh: 1990), 103–37.

Morris, R. J., 'Urbanisation and Scotland', in W. H. Fraser and R. J. Morris (eds), *People and Society in Scotland*, vol. ii, *1830–1914* (Edinburgh: 1990), 73–102.

Mosely, H., 'The German Method of Banking and How it is Designed to Help Commerce and Industry', *Journal of the Institute of Bankers*, 38 (1917), 335–46.

Moss, M. S., 'William Todd Lithgow – Founder of a Fortune', *Scottish Historical Review*, 62 (1983), 47–72.

Munn, C. W., 'Aspects of Bank Finance for Industry: Scotland 1845–1914', in R. Mitchison and P. Roebuck (eds), *Economy and Society in Scotland and Ireland*

1500–1939 (Edinburgh: 1988), 233–41.

Murdoch, A. and Sher, R. B., 'Literacy and Learned Culture', in T. M. Devine and R. Mitchison (eds), *People and Society in Scotland*, vol. i, *1760–1830* (Edinburgh: 1988), 127–42.

'Nat West Rumours', *The Banker*, 125 (1975), 8.

Nenadic, S., 'The Rise of the Urban Middle Class', in T. M. Devine and R. Mitchison (eds), *People and Society in Scotland*, vol. i, *1760–1830* (Edinburgh: 1988), 109–26.

Nenadic, S., 'The Small Family Firm in Victorian Britain', *Business History*, 35 (1993), 86–114.

'The New Finance Regulations', *The Banker*, 52 (1939), 9–28.

'New Guide to the CIC', *The Banker*, 108 (1958), 490–2.

'New Statistics on Scottish Banking', *Scottish Bankers Magazine*, 52 (1960–1), 129–38.

Nielson, A., 'De authoriserde pengsedler i det nordenfjeldske norge 1695–1696', *Bergens historiske Foreningsskrifter*, 33 (1927), 41–91.

'Notes and Comments: ICFC New Glasgow Office', *Scottish Bankers Magazine*, 53 (1961–2), 74–5.

'Notes and Comments: Professor Sayers on Monetary Policy', *Scottish Bankers Magazine*, 52 (1960–1), 127–8.

Nowzad, B., 'Lending and Borrowing Limits: The Futile Search for a Formula', *The Banker*, 133 (February 1983), 25–7.

Ogilvie, F. W., 'Who Promoted the Bank of Scotland in 1695?', *Scottish Historical Review*, 23 (1926), 234–5.

Pascal, R., 'Property and Society: The Scottish Historical School of the Eighteenth Century', *The Modern Quarterly*, 1:2 (March 1938), 167–79.

Pattullo, D. B., 'Common Sense is the Best Palliative', *Centre for the Study of Financial Innovation*, 10 (November 1994), 9–11.

Payne, P. L., 'Rationality and Personality: A Study of Mergers in the Scottish Iron and Steel Industry, 1916–1936', *Business History*, 19 (1977), 162–91.

Payne, P. L., 'The Decline of Scottish Heavy Industries 1945–1983', in R. Saville (ed.), *The Economic Development of Modern Scotland 1950–1980* (Edinburgh: 1985), 79–113.

Phillipson, N. T., 'Lawyers, Landowners and the Civic Leadership of Post Union Scotland: An Essay on the Social Role of the Faculty of Advocates 1661–1830 in 18th Century Scottish Society', *Juridical Review*, 21 (1976), 97–120.

Phillipson, N. T., 'The Scottish Enlightenment', in R. Porter and M. Teich (eds), *The Enlightenment in National Context* (Cambridge: 1981), 19–40.

Phillipson, N. T., 'Politics, Politeness and the Anglicisation of Early Eighteenth-century Scottish Culture', in R. A. Mason (ed.), *Scotland and England 1286–1815* (Edinburgh: 1987), 226–46.

Pollard, S., 'The Decline of Shipbuilding on the Thames', *Economic History Review*, 2nd series, 3 (1950–1), 72–89.

Pollard, S., 'A New Estimate of British Coal Production 1750–1850', *Economic History Review*, 2nd series, 33 (1980), 212–35.

'Presidential Address', *Scottish Bankers Magazine*, 52 (1960–1), 65–71.

Pressnell, L. S., 'The Rate of Interest in the Eighteenth Century', in idem (ed.), *Studies in the Industrial Revolution* (London: 1960), 178–214.

Price, J. M., 'The Rise of Glasgow in the Chesapeake Tobacco Trade, 1707–1775', *William and Mary Quarterly*, 3rd series, 11 (April 1954), 179–99.

'Proportion of Capital and Reserve to Deposits', *The Bankers' Magazine*, 99 (June 1915), 859–76.

Ramesar, M. D., 'Indentured Labour in Trinidad 1880–1917', in K. Saunders (ed.), *Indentured Labour in the British Empire, 1834–1920* (London: 1984), 57–77.

'The Return of Bank Rate', *Scottish Bankers Magazine*, 43 (1951–2), 201–7.

Ricardo, D., 'The High Price of Bullion, a Proof of the Depreciation of Bank Notes', repr. and ed. P. Sraffa and M. H. Dobb, *The Works and Correspondence of David Ricardo*, 11 vols, vol. iii, *Pamphlets and Papers 1809–1811* (Cambridge: 1951), 47–99, and 'Appendix', 99–127.

Robertson, D. J., 'Population Growth and Movement', in A. K. Cairncross (ed.), *The Scottish Economy* (Cambridge: 1954), 9–20.

Rodger, R., 'Concentration and Fragmentation: Capital, Labour, and the Structure of the Mid-Victorian Scottish Economy', *Journal of Urban History*, 14 (1988), 178–213.

Rosebery, Earl of, 'Scotland's Economic Future', *The Banker*, 64 (1942), 93–6.

'The Royal Bank and the London–Edinburgh Exchange Rate in the Eighteenth Century', *The Three Banks Review*, 38 (June 1958), 27–36.

'Royal Bank: Scottish Syndrome Strikes', *The Banker*, 131 (June 1981), 22–3.

Saville, J., 'Sleeping Partnership and Limited Liability, 1850–1856', *Economic History Review*, 2nd series, 8 (1954), 418–33.

Saville, J., 'Some Retarding Factors in the British Economy before 1914', *Yorkshire Bulletin of Economic and Social Researh*, 13 (1961), 51–60.

Sayers, R. S., 'Ricardo's Views of Monetary Questions', *Quarterly Journal of Economics*, 67 (1953), 30–49.

Scott, G., 'The London Money Market', *Scottish Bankers Magazine*, 12 (1921), 254–68.

'Scottish Banking and Cheap Money', *The Banker*, 48 (1938), 165–70.

'Scottish Banks: A Story for Hogmanay', *The Banker*, 130 (January 1980), 112–13.

'Scottish Banks in 1940–41', *The Banker*, 60 (1941), 100–8.

'The Second Government Loan', *The Bankers' Magazine*, 100 (July 1915), 21–30.

Shannon, H. A., 'The Coming of General Limited Liability', *Economic History*, 2 (1931), 267–91.

Sheridan, R. B., 'Planter and Historian: The Career of William Beckford of Jamaica and England, 1744–1799', *Jamaican Historical Review*, 4 (1964), 36–58.

Shimmins, C. J., 'Scottish Banking Notes: Advances to Farmers', *The Banker*, 54 (1940), 180–1.

Shimmins, C. J., 'Scottish Trade and Industry', *The Banker*, 76 (1945), 94–6.

'Shipbuilding', *Scottish Bankers Magazine*, 13 (1921), 53: Industrial Section, Business Notes.

Sieveking, H., 'Die Hamburger Bank', in J. G. van Dillen (ed.), *History of the Principal Public Banks accompanied by Extensive Bibliographies of the History of Banking and Credit in Eleven European Countries* (The Hague: 1934), 125–60.

Slaven, A., 'Growth and Stagnation in British and Scottish Shipbuilding 1913–1977', in J. Kuuse and A. Slaven (eds), *Scottish and Scandinavian Shipbuilding Seminar: Development Problems in Historical Perspective* (Glasgow: 1980), 18–54.

Smith, G. R., 'Employee Share Schemes in Britain', *Employment Gazette*, 101 (1993), 149–54.

Smout, T. C., 'The Anglo-Scottish Union of 1707, I: The Economic Background', *Economic History Review*, 2nd series, 16 (1963–4), 455–67.

Smout, T. C., 'The Landowner and the Planned Village in Scotland, 1730–1830', in N. T. Phillipson and R. Mitchison (eds), *Scotland in the Age of Improvement* (Edinburgh: 1970), 73–102.

Smout, T. C., 'The Strange Case of Edward Twistleton: Paisley in Depression, 1841–3', in idem (ed.), *The Search for Wealth and Stability: Essays in Economic and Social History presented to M. W. Flinn* (London: 1979), 218–42.

Smout, T. C., 'Where Had the Scottish Economy Got to by the Third Quarter of the Eighteenth Century?', in I. Hont and M. Ignatieff (eds), *Wealth and Virtue: The Shaping of Political Economy in the Scottish Enlightenment* (Cambridge: 1985), 45–72.

Smout, T. C. and Fenton, A., 'Scottish Agriculture before the Improvers – An Exploration', *Agricultural History Review*, 12 (1964), 73–93.

Soltow, L., 'Inequality of Wealth in Land in Scotland in the Eighteenth Century', *Scottish Economic and Social History*, 10 (1990), 38–60.

A Special Correspondent, 'Hire Purchase Facilities under Scrutiny', *The Banker*, 93 (1952), 37–42.

'The Story of the City Crisis', *The Banker*, 124 (1974), 87–9.

'A Survey: All Near-bankers Now', *The Banker*, 122 (1972), 636–8.

Sutherland, L. S., 'Samson Gideon and the Reduction of Interest, 1749–50', *Economic History Review*, 1st series, 16 (1946), 15–29.

Sutherland, L. S., 'Samson Gideon: Eighteenth Century Jewish Financier', *Transactions of the Jewish Historical Society of England*, 17 (1951–2), 79–90.

Tawney, R. H., 'The Abolition of Economic Controls, 1918–1921', *Economic History Review*, 13 (1943), 1–30.

Taylor, F. S., 'Bankers off the Leash', *The Banker*, 109 (1959), 253–8.

Taylor, F. S., 'Scots Banks in the New Squeeze', *The Banker*, 112 (1962), 249–50.

Taylor, F. S., 'Scottish Banks in the Eighteenth Century', *Scottish Journal of Political Economy*, 12 (1965), 110–13.

Tennant, C., 'The Structure of Scottish Banking', *Scottish Bankers Magazine*, 43 (1951–2), 208–13.

Thomson, A. J. R., 'Modern Industries: Natural Gas Exploration', *Scottish Bankers Magazine*, 57 (1965–6), Students' Section, 29–32.

Thomson, G., 'The Iron Industry of the Monklands: The Individual Ironworks', *Scottish Industrial History*, 6 (1983), 10–29.

Timperley, L. R., 'The Pattern of Landholding in Eighteenth Century Scotland', in M. L. Parry and T. R. Slater (eds), *The Making of the Scottish Countryside* (London: 1980), 137–54.

Tranter, N. L., 'The Demographic Impact of Economic Growth and Decline: Portpatrick 1820–1891', *Scottish Historical Review*, 57 (1978), 87–105.

Treble, J. H., 'The Performance of the Standard Life Assurance Company in the Ordinary Market for Life Assurance 1825–50', *Scottish Economic and Social History Review*, 5 (1985), 57–77.

Treble, J. H., 'The Occupied Male Labour Force', in W. H. Fraser and R. J. Morris (eds), *People and Society in Scotland*, vol. ii, *1830–1914* (Edinburgh: 1990), 167–93.

Tyson, R. E., 'Scottish Investment in American Railways: The Case of the City of Glasgow Bank *1856–1881*', in P. L. Payne (ed.), *Studies in Scottish Business History* (London: 1967), 387–416.

Tyson, R. E., 'The Failure of the City of Glasgow Bank and the Rise of Independent Auditing', *The Accountant's Magazine*, 78 (April 1974), 126–31.

Vamplew, W., 'The Railways and the Iron Industry: A Study of their Relationship in Scotland', in M. C. Reed (ed.), *Railways in the Victorian Economy* (Newton Abbot: 1969), 33–75.

Vamplew, W., 'Sources of Scottish Railway Share Capital before 1860', *Scottish Journal of Political Economy*, 17 (1970), 425–40.

Vittas, D. and Frazer, P., 'Competition in Retail Banking', *The Banker*, 130 (February 1980), 47–51.

Ward, W. R., 'The Land Tax in Scotland, 1707–98', *Bulletin of the John Rylands Library* (1953–4), 288–308.

Weyer, D. V., 'Clearing Bank Marketing: The Practical Issues Today', *The Banker*, 120 (1970), 1,061–8.

Withrington, D. J., 'Education and Society in the Eighteenth Century', in N. T. Phillipson and R. Mitchison (eds), *Scotland in the Age of Improvement* (Edinburgh: 1970), 169–99.

Withrington, D. J., 'Schooling, Literacy and Society', in T. M. Devine and R. Mitchison (eds), *People and Society in Scotland*, vol. i, *1760–1830* (Edinburgh: 1988), 163–87.

Wood, D., 'New Deal for Commercial Banking Accounts', *The Banker*, 121 (1971), 33–40.

Wright, L. C., 'Monetary Policy in Theory', *Scottish Bankers Magazine*, 52 (1960–1), 186–92.

THESES, DISSERTATIONS, REPORTS

Dingwall, H. M., 'The Social and Economic Structure of Edinburgh in the Late Seventeenth Century', Ph.D. thesis (University of Edinburgh, 1989).

Durie, A. J., 'The Scottish Linen Industry, 1707–45, with Special Reference to the British Linen Company', Ph.D. thesis (University of Edinburgh, 1972).

Ewan, L. A., 'Debt and Credit in Early Modern Scotland: The Grandtully Estates, 1650–1765', Ph.D. thesis (University of Edinburgh, 1988).

Fraser of Allander Institute, University of Strathclyde, 'A Memorandum Submitted to the MMC', 1 July 1981.

Gibson, I. F., 'The Economic History of the Scottish Iron and Steel Industry, 1830–1880', Ph.D. thesis (University of London, 1955).

Schmitz, C. J., 'Patterns of Scottish Portfolio Foreign Investment 1860–1914', unpublished report (St Andrews: 1991).

Teviotdale, D. A., 'Glasgow Parliamentary Constituencies 1832–1846', B.Litt. dissertation (University of Glasgow, 1963).

Thomson, A., 'The Scottish Timber Trade, 1680 to 1800', Ph.D. thesis (University of St Andrews, 1991).

Timperley, L. R., 'Landownership in Scotland in the Eighteenth Century', Ph.D. thesis (University of Edinburgh, 1977).

INDEX